The Key to All Joyo Kanji

-A Study Guide Using Common Shapes and Character Histories

共通形と字源による常用漢字の学習ガイド

Noriko Kurosawa Williams

Title: The Key to All Joyo Kanji – A Study Guide Using Common Shapes and Character Histories – 共通形と字源による常用漢字の学習ガイド

Some typos corrected. May 2025

Editors: Jonathan Hinton, Linda Stringer

Cover design: Mark S. L. Williams

Preparation: Masako Swihart, Kazumi Wilson

PREFACE

A somewhat overly generalized statement about the composition of kanji came to my mind fifteen years ago when I finished writing a reference book for the first half of the Joyo kanji (*The Key to Kanji - A Visual History of 1100 Characters* 漢字絵解き) – "Wherever the same shape appears in any kanji, its meaning (and often sound) is also the same." It occurred to me that if I grouped multiple kanji that contain the same component shape and explained the relationship they share, it could make for a useful study guide that would facilitate the acquisition of a large number of kanji. I also noticed that the reason why the same shapes have the same meaning across multiple kanji is that they share the same origin. From these realizations, two concepts — identifying the common shapes in kanji, and linking them to their etymological origins — became the guiding principles for this kanji study guide.

In assembling this guide, I imagined that anyone who would take on the ambitious task of learning all of the Joyo kanji would likely be an adult with a certain degree of life experience, who values the opportunity to make their own judgment based on facts. It followed that sharing with the reader the images of ancient character lineages, which are the basis of my accounts of the development of each component shape, would be beneficial to their understanding of kanji (and perhaps even fun, by giving each reader a try at being their own "kanji detective"). I consulted various references by Japanese kanji scholars with rich heritages of scholarship, whose accounts I then re-interpreted to adapt for the needs of an English-speaking kanji learner in a non-kanji cultural environment. Once I had completed an etymological survey of each kanji and identified the commonly appearing shapes, assigning each kanji to the appropriate common shape group became a relatively simple matter of determining its most prominent component.

I am grateful to all the readers of the blog I started in 2013, which formed the first steps in the years-long process of compiling and completing this project. I deeply appreciate their interest, encouragement, and comments (both in private communication and via the site), and their patience in waiting for me to complete and make available my accounts of the entirety of the Joyo kanji. I would also like to express my deep gratitude to Yasuyo Tokuhiro for so generously allowing me to use the frequency-of-use data from her research. Much gratitude is also due to the two English-language editors, Jonathan Hinton and Linda Springer. The final version of the English accounts benefited from Jonathan's exceptionally thoughtful edits, which he approached with the eyes and mind of a discerning reader and long-time learner of Japanese. Needless to say, responsibility for the content of this guide lies with me.

CONTENTS

Introduction

1. Introduction

1-1 The two foundations of this book

This study guide/reference book of the 2,136 Joyo kanji (常用漢字—the commonly used Chinese characters in Japanese) has been developed on two foundations—the individual histories of ancient Chinese characters, and the common shapes in present-day kanji in Japanese. First, when we look at ancient characters used in various inscriptions found on historical artifacts in China, we see that in each ancient character there was a discernable, often pictorial connection between the shape of a character and its meaning and/or sound. Furthermore, those relationships continue to be reflected in the makeup of present-day kanji.

Secondly, when looking at present-day kanji, we see that many shapes reappear in multiple kanji with the original bond between their shape and their meaning and/or sound undisturbed. Grouping multiple kanji that share the same shape highlights not only their commonality but also the differences among the member kanji. Cultivating a view that extends over multiple kanji—rather than focusing on individual kanji—can be helpful to a reader who wishes to learn a large number of Joyo kanji efficiently. This book has been devised to take the reader on a journey, starting with an exploration of the fascinating world of ancient Chinese characters, and ending with a practical knowledge of present-day Japanese kanji.

1-2. Ancient characters and the birth of kanji

As civilization developed, an increasing number of new characters were needed to express more complex ideas. To meet that demand, the creators of new characters combined existing characters or their components into new forms. When ancient China was unified (221 BCE) and power was centralized, communication using characters of the ancient style became too time-consuming, inconvenient, and impractical for administrative officials, and a dire need arose to create a more efficient, standardized writing system. A drastic renovation was undertaken to simplify the ancient characters through the process of straightening, shortening, merging, or omitting lines, and standardizing their orientations—and this was the birth of 漢字, or kanji (*hanzi* in Chinese, "the writing of the Han people," i.e. the Han Dynasty of 202/206 BCE – 9 CE, 25 – 220 CE). In kanji, the visually recognizable close relationship between the shape, meaning, and sound of the ancient forms was significantly diminished. As a result, kanji has the appearance of a complex amalgam of lines, like an inorganic entity. In this book, by tracing each kanji's lineage, we attempt to restore a connection to the elements of everyday life once represented by their ancient precursors.

2. Recreation of Ancient Characters

2-1. Recreation of 4,500 ancient kanji precursors

For the exploration of ancient precursors of kanji, over 4,500 ancient forms were redrawn by hand from photo compilations (Akai 1985, 2010, and others). These compilations include photos of different types of inscriptions: inscriptions chiseled by knife on tortoise plastrons or pieces of animal bone and used in divination (and therefore called oracle bone–style characters, 甲骨文 *kookotsubun* or 甲骨文字 *kookotsu-moji*); ink rubbing copies of inscriptions cast into the surface of bronzeware (bronzeware-style characters, 金文 *kinbun*); and inscriptions on stone steles, official seals and other surfaces (seal-style characters, 篆文 *tenbun*). For this book, 755 oracle bone–style precursors to 541 kanji, 1,472 bronzeware-style precursors to 948 kanji, and 2,305 seal-style precursors to1991 kanji were recreated. In these ancient characters, it was possible to discern what object each shape originally represented. This characteristic was mostly lost with the development of kanji, which marked the end of the ancient character era. Orthographic-style kanji (an unsimplified style used in the Kangxi Dictionary, published in 1716 in China) and kyuji (old-style kanji predating the Toyo kanji designation of 1946 in Japan) are provided where ancient precursors are unavailable. Each precursor form is labeled in Japanese with its corresponding writing style, above succinct English accounts of the historical development of each kanji.

2-2. Four formulation methods of ancient characters and kanji

Ancient characters were traditionally classified into six types (六書 *rikusho*), as described in *Setsumon Kaiji* (説文解字 Shuowen Jiezi), the first comprehensive analytical kanji dictionary, compiled by Kyoshin (許慎 Xu Shen) during the Late Han in 100 CE. Of the six types of characters, two types were made up of existing characters, either borrowed for their sound (仮借文字 *kashamoji*, borrowed characters), or assigned a new meaning derived from a previous meaning (転注文字 *tenchuumoji*, derivative characters). The remaining four types were defined by how a character was formulated in the first place. Three of these types were defined by a shape-meaning relationship: (a) indicative characters (指事文字 *shijimoji*), used for abstract notions such as number or location, indicated by a line relative to another reference point; (b) pictographic characters (象形文字 *shookeemoji*), in which meaning was represented by a single pictorial image; and (c) semantic composite characters (会意文字 *kaiimoji*), in which two or more existing characters or their components were selected for their shape-and-meaning relationship and combined to create a new composite shape with a new meaning, and their original sounds were discarded. (The sound came instead from the word to which the new character was assigned.) Because each ancient shape represented a meaning, and many of them originated from pictorial images, in these first three types of character formulation there was a visually discernable connection between a shape and its meaning.

On the other hand, the fourth type, (d) semantic-phonetic composite characters (形声文字 *keeseemoji*), differs in that while one component was taken for its meaning, the other component was taken for its sound, and its meaning was discarded. This method of using an existing shape solely for the relationship between its shape and sound, discarding its meaning, gave kanji creators enormous latitude to create new characters even if they might have lacked their predecessors' ingenious artistic talent or skill for creating new shapes. This type of formulation was seen only in very small numbers in oracle bone–style, but it came to be aggressively used later, resulting in an enormous number of characters. It should be noted that in the term 形声文字, 形 "shape" was used to mean "meaning," revealing one of the guiding principles of character formulation used by these ancient creators—that the shape of a character was to be a visible representation of its meaning.

2-3. Relevance of formulation types to our kanji study

This principle that a shape can represent either a meaning or a sound remains undisturbed in kanji, and in kanji that originated from indicative, pictographic and semantic composite types, the meaning in many of these shapes may still be visually perceived. This fact can be very helpful when trying to grasp the makeup of individual kanji of one of these types, since the key to deciphering them lies in their shape. In contrast, studying a semantic-phonetic composite kanji is more cumbersome, since deciphering its phonetic component requires knowledge of the sound of the source component or character. According to one study, six out of ten Joyo kanji belong to this type (Shirakawa 2004), while many other studies treat a much larger portion of Joyo kanji as belonging to this type. As the reader of this study guide progresses and advances through each of the four kanji study levels, the complexity of the kanji increases, along with an increase in relative volume of semantic-phonetic kanji (36% of Level **A** kanji, gradually increasing to 77% of Level **D** kanji).

Additionally, we should remain aware of the important but often-overlooked fact that when the creator of a kanji first selected a phonetic component out of many other candidates with the same sound, they often adopted one whose original meaning was close to the new meaning. A remarkably large number of semantic-phonetic composite characters were composed in this way. Some scholars even treat kanji containing components that were primarily used for their sound, but also for their meaning, as belonging to a separate type of formulation (or a sub-type of the semantic-phonetic composite formulation), which they call 会意兼形声文字 *kaii-ken-keisee-moji*, "semantic composite-cum-semantic-phonetic composite character" (Todo, et. al. 2011). Put simply, even though a large number of Joyo kanji contain a component that is used primarily for its sound (called a "phonetic feature"), its shape may bear an additional, visually-perceivable meaning. This study guide takes advantage of this fact in the English accounts of each kanji's formulation.

2-4. English-language accounts

This guide provides a brief English-language account of each kanji's historical development, closely following the lineage of its ancient precursors. Views regarding the origin of specific kanji sometimes differ between the various reference sources, due to a lack of consensus among scholars as to which of three aspects of a character (shape, sound, or meaning/use) made the most crucial contribution to its creation. Readers of this guide may also differ in their estimation of whether a particular etymological account is believable, convincing, or useful. We have made every effort to present actual ancient forms, along with English explanations, so that the reader themselves can retrace the history that led to the present-day form and meaning and/or sound of each kanji, and thereby gain invaluable insight. One of the reasons we have compiled this study guide is to provide readers an opportunity to personally verify these etymological accounts. However, while this guide utilizes such historical information, please keep in mind that our goal is not that the reader attain knowledge of kanji etymology per se, but rather that they develop their own skills to discern the exact makeup of each kanji through examination of the discrete units of shape-meaning-sound that existed in their ancient precursors.

3. COMMON SHAPES IN KANJI

3-1. Identification of 432 common shapes in kanji

The fact that most kanji are a composite of two or more components leads us to our next point: studying related kanji in groups enables one to study multiple kanji simultaneously. Four hundred thirty-two common shapes are identified in this book. Fewer than one-third of kanji align with traditional bushu designations (which are mostly semantic features), while the remaining common shapes are components or fragments of kanji that have their own meaning and/or sound.

The order in which this book introduces these 432 common shapes is somewhat unusual. Because the approach taken in this guide uses historical evidence from ancient characters, we have categorized the common shapes based on their sources. The 14 categories used are as follows:

- I. Parts of the Body (62 common shapes), such as the eye, mouth, ear, nose, hand, and footprint
- II. Postures (55 shapes), such as standing, crouching, and walking
- III. Plants (34 shapes), such as trees, grass, grain, and gourds
- IV. Animals (53 shapes), including parts of animals
- V. Nature (32 shapes), such as the sun, moon, and mountains
- VI. Habitats (31 shapes), such as houses, agricultural fields, and roads
- VII. Sharp Objects and Weapons (53 shapes), such as needles, knives, axes, halberds, and arrows
- VIII. Threads and Clothing (18 shapes)

IX. Valuables (7 shapes), such as cowries, bronze vessels, and jewels
X. Religious Matters (10 shapes), such as altars and brooms used in sanctification rituals
XI. Food and Eating (17 shapes), such as bowls of rice and cooking implements
XII. Table, Tool, and Vessel (41 shapes), such as tables, carpentry and agricultural tools, and containers
XIII. Tied or Bundled (10 shapes)
XIV. Other Shapes (9 shapes)

By seeing how "life" in ancient times was depicted in these shapes, the reader may find themselves drawn into an affinity with the otherwise dry, inorganic appearance of kanji.

3-2. Table of The Kanji Common Shapes, Their Origins and Meanings, and Kanji Levels

A partial sample from the table of The Kanji Common Shapes – Origins, Meanings and Sounds, Kanji (with Study Guide numbers), and Their Levels, and Page Numbers – is shown here. For the full table, please see pages 7-14.

THE KANJI COMMON SHAPES – ORIGINS, MEANINGS AND SOUNDS, KANJI AND THEIR LEVELS, AND PAGES

漢字共通形・字源の形・意味と音・
漢字と SG 番号と学習レベル・ページ数

Common Shapes 共通形	Origins 字源	Meanings and Sounds 意味と音	Study Guide Numbers, Kanji, Study Levels 学習書の順番・漢字・学習レベル	Page ページ
I PARTS OF THE BODY				
1 Eye				
1a 目		eye; to see	SG-0001 目A省A看C	15
1b 相		facing each other; mutual; *soo*	SG-0004 相A想A箱B	16
1c 直		straight, direct; *choku/shoku/chi*	SG-0007 直A置A値A植B徳B殖D	16
1d 𥃭		eye with an eyebrow	SG-0013 夢A蔑D眉D	17
1e (冃)		eyes covered, headgear; *boo/mee*	SG-0016 冒C帽C冥D	18
1f 曼		boundless; *man*	SG-0019 慢C漫D	19
1g 民		people; *min*	SG-0021 民A眠C	19
1h 臣		watchful eye, loyal retiner	SG-0023 臣B臨B	19
1i 監		to examine carefully, monitor; *kan/ran*	SG-0025 監B覧C鑑C艦C濫D藍D	20
2 Mouth				
2a 口		mouth, goods, area, hole; a box of prayers; to speak, eat; **bushu *kuchihen***	SG-0031 口A品A告A号A器A造A呼A甘B唱C舌C叫C喪C吐C叱D	21
2b 可		possible, good; *ka*	SG-0045 可A何A河B荷B苛D	24
3 Ear				
3a 耳		ear; to hear, listen	SG-0050 耳A聞A聖B聴B恥C摂D	25
3b 取		to take, grab	SG-0056 取A最A撮C	26
4 Nose				
4 自		nose,face, oneself	SG-0059 自A面A息B鼻C臭C嗅D憩D	27
5 Head and neck				
5a 首		head, chief, neck	SG-0066 首A道A導B	28
5b 亢		straight; *koo*	SG-0069 航B抗B坑D	29
6 Hand				
6a 手		hand	SG-0072 手A失A尺C	29
6f 叔		small, good; *toku/jaku/shuku,* etc.	SG-0097 督C寂C叔D淑D戚D	34
6g 乂		a variation of "a right hand"	SG-0102 右A父A事A史A使A丈C吏D	35
6h 左		left hand; to help	SG-0109 左A佐A尋C	36
7 A hand holding something				
7a 寸		hand	SG-0112 寸A守A村A対A討B	37
7b 付		to hand out, attach; *hu*	SG-0117 付A府A符C附D	38
7c 尉		to smooth out; *i*	SG-0121 慰C尉D	39
7d 采		to pick by hand; *sai*	SG-0123 採B菜B彩C采D	39
7e 孚		to take care of a child	SG-0127 浮B乳B	40
7f 争		to fight; *soo/joo*	SG-0129 争B浄C	40
7g 受		to receive; *ju*	SG-0131 受A授B	41
7h 爰		*en/dan/kan*	SG-0133 援B暖C緩C媛D	41
8 Two or more hands raising something				
8a 共		both; reverential; *kyoo/ koo*	SG-0137 共A供B恭D洪D	42
8b 業		servant; to strike; *boku*	SG-0141 僕B撲D	43
8c 廾		two hands holding up something	SG-0143 弁B弄D	43
8d 夫		to dedicate something	SG-0145 奏C泰C	[illegible]
8e 朕		to raise reverentially	SG-0147 勝A謄D朕D	44
8f		a reverential act by many people	SG-0150 与A興B承B挙B誉C	45
9 A hand with a tool				
9a 君		to control, rule; *kun/gun*	SG-0155 君A群B郡B	46
9b 殳		to strike, hit; **bushu *hokozukuri/rumata***	SG-0158 役A設A投A段A殺B殻D穀D鍛D毀D	47
9c 攵 攴		to cause an action; **bushu *bokuzukuri/ nobun***	SG-0167 改A数A教A修B敬B警B散B激B枚B厳B悠D敢D赦D傲D	48
9d 支		to branch out, support; *shi/ki;* **bushu *shinyoo/ edanyoo***	SG-0181 支A技A枝B岐C肢D伎D	51
10 Heart				
10a 心		heart, mind, emotion	SG-0187 心A忠B患C串C隠C穏C寧D忌D芯D	52
10b 忄		heart, emotion; **bushu *risshinben***	SG-0196 快C怪C悟C惧D	54
11 Forward-facing footprint				
11a 止		to stop; a forward step	SG-0200 止A企A歩A歳A渉B渋B頻D捗D	55
11b 正		just; to conquer; *see/shoo*	SG-0208 正A政A証B征C	56

When we organize the kanji common shapes and their ancient forms and meanings into a table, it is easy to see that the original units of shape and meaning have survived in identifiable forms (albeit with a little imagination in some cases). We may add that it also demonstrates that in kanji, commonality in shape ensures commonality in meaning or sound. Some common shapes were used for their meaning (a semantic feature), some for their sound (a phonetic feature, shown above in italics), and some for both meaning and sound (a dual feature). The table also shows the four levels of study designation for the member kanji in each common shape group, as detailed in **4-1**.

4. COMPILATION OF THIS STUDY GUIDE

4-1. Kanji study in four rounds

To guide the reader on the long journey of studying such a large number of kanji, this book divides the 2,136 Joyo kanji into four groups (**A**, **B**, **C**, and **D**) according to their complexity and frequency of appearance in Japanese publications (denoted by their F-number, as described by Tokuhiro [2014]). This four-level designation guides the reader to learn kanji in a cyclic fashion.

In the first round of study, the reader studies or reviews only the Level-**A** kanji (566 kanji), familiarizing themselves with the approach behind this guide, learning to analyze kanji by common shapes (267 common shapes for Level **A**), and skipping the Level **B**, **C**, and **D** kanji. Some kanji that appear with less frequency (i.e., with higher F-numbers), but are key components in other kanji, are also included in the Level **A** group. Many features that are useful for kanji study are provided for each kanji (as described in 4-2). The sample words do not necessarily match the study level designation, but they demonstrate the breadth of sounds, meaning, and usage for each kanji.

In the second, **B**-level round of study, the reader first does a quick review of the **A**-level kanji, focusing on shapes they share with **B**-level kanji. The reader may then examine the unfamiliar components of the new **B**-level kanji, learning to distinguish between related kanji. Because the common shapes are already familiar, the reader can focus on dissimilar components and learn to differentiate related kanji, while remaining aware of the common threads connecting them. By the end of the second cycle, the reader has been introduced to 525 new kanji (for a total of 1,091 kanji), and 116 new common shapes (for a total of 383 shapes). A cyclic learning style such as this allows the reader to make progress without encountering more complex kanji, which there is no pressing need to learn at that particular point in their study, while at the same time reinforcing their knowledge of previously learned kanji.

The third cycle (Level **C**) introduces 520 new kanji with 44 new common shapes (for a total of 1,611 kanji and 427 common shapes), and the fourth cycle (Level **D**) introduces 525 new kanji with 5 new common shapes (for a total of 2,136 kanji and 433 common shapes).

4-2. The features of the kanji table

The following items of information are provided for each kanji:

7g 受 "to receive/(give)" [from a hand handing a vessel down to another hand]; *ju* 受授 

<table>
<tr><td rowspan="2">SG-0131 受</td><td>Meanings</td><td>Kun and On</td><td>Romaji</td><td>Bushu</td><td>Stroke Order and Number</td></tr>
<tr><td>to receive, take, accept</td><td>う-ける
ジュ</td><td>u-keru
ju</td><td>又</td><td>一 ⺈ ⺤ 爫 𤓯 受 8</td></tr>
<tr><td>受
A
F-0142</td><td colspan="4">甲骨文1 1, 甲骨文2 2, 金文 3, 説文 4, 受
1,2,3, and 4 all comprised three components: "a hand reaching down from above," "a vessel containing a valuable thing," and "a hand reaching up from below." Together, they signified "a hand handing down something valuable, and another hand receiving it," and the character originally meant both "to receive" and "to bestow." Later the original two meanings were divided into two separate kanji, 受 and 授 SG-0132, and the kanji 受 is used for the act of receiving only. The kanji 受 means "to receive, take, accept." <⺤冖又></td><td>受ける to receive [うけ˥る]; 受付 reception [うけつけ]; 引き受ける to undertake [ひきうけ˥る]; 受け取る to receive [うけとる]; 受験する to sit for an exam [じゅけんする]; 受信 signal reception, receipt of message [じゅしん]; 受信料 (TV) license fee [じゅし˥んりょう]</td></tr>
</table>

Above the kanji table: The common shape

Kanji Table: Top Row

1. **SG number and kanji** ① **SG- serial number** for this book (**SG** stands for **S**tudy **G**uide); and ② the kanji in **kyokasho-style** (handwritten style)
2. **Meanings** English meanings of the kanji
3. ***Kun* & *On* readings** *Kun* readings (訓読み) in hiragana, and *on* readings (音読み) in katakana. A *kun* reading is how the kanji is read when used in a word of Japanese origin. An *on* reading is the character's reading that is derived from its Chinese pronunciation.
4. **Readings in romaji** Romanized *kun* reading in normal font and italicized *on* reading. This book uses a modified *kunrei-shiki* system of romanization.
5. **Bushu** Bushu (部首; kanji radical, dictionary index, or section header), as used in traditional kanji dictionaries.
6. **Stroke order** Handwritten stroke order
7. **Total stroke number**, for looking up an unfamiliar kanji.

Kanji Table: Bottom Row

8. **Kanji level designation** ① **Kanji in Mincho style**, the font type typically used in printed and web publications. ② The letter **A**, **B**, **C**, or **D**, designating four progressive levels of kanji study.

   ③ **F-0000 number** (**F** for **f**requency ranking): This ranking denotes the frequency of the kanji's appearance in many Japanese publications, such as newspapers, etc., as compiled by Tokuhiro (2014). The lower the number, the more frequently the kanji appears.
9. **English account with ancient character forms** ① **Historical Forms**: Each ancient form is labeled with its style 骨文 oracle bone–style form, 金文 bronzeware-style form, 説文 seal-style form from 説文解字, or 篆文 additional seal-style form), and numbered for cross-referencing with the English account of the character's historical development. 旧字 (old-style kanji based on the Kangxi Dictionary 康熙字典) are also provided. ② **English account of the character's historical development**, focusing on components that contributed to present-day kanji. ③ **Breakdown of the kanji** by its present-day components (inside angle brackets < >).
10. ***Kun* and *on* reading sample words** ① Several sample words are provided with English glosses to show the breadth of the kanji's meaning in actual use. Words featuring *kun* or *on* readings that are not on the Joyo kanji list but are commonly used may be included after a pair of forward slashes //. ② **Word accent** The pronunciation in hiragana is marked by an angled downward arrow (˥) to indicate where an accentual tonal fall occurs in standard Japanese, and by a middle dot (・) to indicate a new tonal phrase.

5. APPENDICES

Four types of indices are provided at the end of the book for cross-referencing purposes:

Index 1 The Order of Kanji (by SG number) 本書の導入順漢字表(SG 番号順)

Index 2 Kanji by *On* and *Kun* Reading in Japanese Syllabary Order 音訓読みによる漢字表（五十音順）

Index 3 Kanji by Total Stroke Number 総画数による漢字表

Index 4 Kanji by Bushu 部首による漢字表

The Kanji Common Shapes

– Origins, Meanings and Sounds, Kanji and their Levels, and Pages

漢字共通形•字源の形•意味と音•
漢字と SG 番号と学習レベル•ページ数

Common Shapes	Origins	Meanings and Sounds	Study Guide Numbers, Kanji, Study Levels	Page
共通形	字源	意味と音	学習書の順番・漢字・学習レベル	ページ
I Parts of the Body				
1 Eye				
1a 目		eye; to see	**SG-0001** 目**A**省**A**看**C**	*15*
1b 相		facing each other; mutual; *soo*	**SG-0004** 相**A**想**A**箱**B**	*16*
1c 直		straight, direct; *choku/shoku/chi*	**SG-0007** 直**A**置**A**値**A**植**B**徳**B**殖**D**	*16*
1d 苗		eye with an eyebrow	**SG-0013** 夢**A**蔑**D**眉**D**	*17*
1e (冃)		eyes covered, headgear; *boo/mee*	**SG-0016** 冒**C**帽**C**冥**D**	*18*
1f 曼		boundless; *man*	**SG-0019** 慢**C**漫**D**	*19*
1g 民		people; *min*	**SG-0021** 民**A**眠**C**	*19*
1h 臣		watchful eye, loyal retiner	**SG-0023** 臣**B**臨**B**	*19*
1i 監		to examine carefully, monitor; *kan/ran*	**SG-0025** 監**B**覧**C**鑑**C**艦**C**濫**D**藍**D**	*20*
2 Mouth				
2a 口		mouth, goods, area, hole; a box of prayers; to speak, eat; **bushu *kuchihen***	**SG-0031** 口**A**品**A**告**A**号**A**器**A**造**A**呼**A**甘**B**唱**C**舌**C**叫**C**喪**C**吐**C**叱**D**	*21*
2b 可		possible, good; *ka*	**SG-0045** 可**A**何**A**河**B**荷**B**苛**D**	*24*
3 Ear				
3a 耳		ear; to hear, listen	**SG-0050** 耳**A**聞**A**聖**B**聴**B**恥**C**摂**D**	*25*
3b 取		to take, grab	**SG-0056** 取**A**最**A**撮**C**	*26*
4 Nose				
4 自		nose,face, oneself	**SG-0059** 自**A**面**A**息**B**鼻**C**臭**C**嗅**D**憩**D**	*27*
5 Head and neck				
5a 首		head, chief, neck	**SG-0066** 首**A**道**A**導**B**	*28*
5b 亢		straight; *koo*	**SG-0069** 航**B**抗**B**坑**D**	*29*
6 Hand				
6a 手		hand	**SG-0072** 手**A**失**A**尺**C**	*29*
6b 扌		an act done by hand; **bushu *tehen***	**SG-0075** 押**B**捜**C**拝**C**揺**C**把**D**挿**D**拐**D**挨**D**拶**D**	*30*
6c 又		hand	**SG-0084** 又**A**友**A**収**A**	*31*
6d 反		to push back, turn back; *han/hen*	**SG-0087** 反**A**返**A**坂**B**阪**B**板**B**仮**B**販**B**	*32*
6e 臤		hard; to tighten; *kin/ken*	**SG-0094** 緊**B**賢**C**堅**C**	*33*
6f 叔		small, good; *toku/jaku/shuku,* etc.	**SG-0097** 督**C**寂**C**叔**D**淑**D**戚**D**	*34*
6g 乂		a variation of "a right hand"	**SG-0102** 右**A**父**A**事**A**史**A**使**A**丈**C**吏**D**	*35*
6h 左		left hand; to help	**SG-0109** 左**A**佐**A**尋**C**	*36*
7 A hand holding something				
7a 寸		hand	**SG-0112** 寸**A**守**A**村**A**対**A**討**B**	*37*
7b 付		to hand out, attach; *hu*	**SG-0117** 付**A**府**A**符**C**附**D**	*38*
7c 尉		to smooth out; *i*	**SG-0121** 慰**C**尉**D**	*39*
7d 采		to pick by hand; *sai*	**SG-0123** 採**B**菜**B**彩**C**采**D**	*39*
7e 孚		to take care of a child	**SG-0127** 浮**B**乳**B**	*40*
7f 争		to fight; *soo/joo*	**SG-0129** 争**B**浄**C**	*40*
7g 受		to receive; *ju*	**SG-0131** 受**A**授**B**	*41*
7h 爰		*en/dan/kan*	**SG-0133** 援**B**暖**C**緩**C**媛**D**	*41*
8 Two or more hands raising something				
8a 共		both; reverential; *kyoo/ koo*	**SG-0137** 共**A**供**B**恭**D**洪**D**	*42*
8b 業		servant; to strike; *boku*	**SG-0141** 僕**B**撲**D**	*43*
8c 廾		two hands holding up something	**SG-0143** 弁**B**弄**D**	*43*
8d 奏		to dedicate something	**SG-0145** 奏**C**泰**C**	*44*
8e 朕		to raise reverentially	**SG-0147** 勝**A**謄**D**朕**D**	*44*
8f		a reverential act by many people	**SG-0150** 与**A**興**B**承**B**挙**B**誉**C**	*45*
9 A hand with a tool				
9a 君		to control, rule; *kun/gun*	**SG-0155** 君**A**群**B**郡**B**	*46*
9b 殳		to strike, hit; **bushu *hokozukuri/rumata***	**SG-0158** 役**A**設**A**投**A**段**A**殺**B**殻**D**穀**D**鍛**D**毀**D**	*47*
9c 攵 攴		to cause an action; **bushu *bokuzukuri/ nobun***	**SG-0167** 改**A**数**A**教**A**修**B**敬**B**警**B**散**B**激**B**枚**B**厳**B**悠**D**敢**D**赦**D**傲**D**	*48*
9d 支		to branch out, support; *shi/ki*; **bushu *shinyoo/ edanyoo***	**SG-0181** 支**A**技**A**枝**B**岐**C**肢**D**伎**D**	*51*
10 Heart				
10a 心		heart, mind, emotion	**SG-0187** 心**A**忠**B**患**C**串**C**隠**C**穏**C**寧**D**忌**D**芯**D**	*52*
10b 忄		heart, emotion; **bushu *risshinben***	**SG-0196** 快**C**怪**C**悟**C**惧**D**	*54*
11 Forward-facing footprint				
11a 止		to stop; a forward step	**SG-0200** 止**A**企**A**歩**A**歳**A**渉**B**渋**B**頻**D**捗**D**	*55*
11b 正		just; to conquer; *see/shoo*	**SG-0208** 正**A**政**A**証**B**征**C**	*56*
11c 之		to go; *shi*	**SG-0212** 市**A**志**B**誌**B**芝**B**乏**C**	*57*
11d 出		to go out	**SG-0217** 出**A**拙**D**	*58*
11e 寺		to hold, sustain; *ji/too/toku*	**SG-0219** 寺**A**時**A**持**A**待**A**等**A**特**A**詩**B**侍**C**	*59*
11f 足 𧾷		leg; **bushu *ashihen***	**SG-0227** 足**A**促**B**跡**C**踏**C**践**D**捉**D**踪**D**	*60*
11g 定		to determine; *joo/tee*	**SG-0234** 定**A**錠**D**綻**D**	*61*

12 Footprints				
12a 夂		to retreat, come down; **bushu** ***suinyoo/ chinyoo***	**SG-0237** 後**A**夏**A**愛**A**優**A**慶**C**憂**C**曖**D**	*62*
12b 各		*kaku/raku/ro*	**SG-0244** 各**A**客**A**格**A**落**A**路**B**絡**C**露**C**酪**D**賂**D**	*63*
12c 韋		to patrol; different; *i*	**SG-0253** 違**B**囲**B**衛**B**偉**C**緯**D**	*65*
12d 舛		two feet off the ground; downward feet	**SG-0258** 無**A**舞**B**降**B**隣**B**瞬**C**傑**D**	*66*
12e 乗		to ride; *joo*	**SG-0264** 乗**A**剰**D**	*67*
12f 癶		to start; **bushu** ***hatsugashira***	**SG-0266** 発**A**登**B**廃**B**灯**C**澄**D**	*68*
Bone joints				
13a 咼		to pass through; round, smooth; *ka*	**SG-0271** 過**A**骨**B**滑**C**渦**D**鍋**D**禍**D**	*69*
13b 歹		a dead body, skeleton; **bushu** ***kabanehen*** • 列 row, line; *retsu*	**SG-0277** 死**A**•例**A**列**B**葬**C**烈**C**裂**C**殉**D**	*70*
14 Brains				
14 (囟)		brains	**SG-0284** 思**A**細**B**脳**B**悩**C**	*71*
15 Animal meat/flesh				
15 月		parts of the human body; **bushu** ***nikuzuki***	**SG-0288** 筋**B**肩**B**胸**B**胃**C**肺**C**腕**C**肌**C**腸**C**肯**C**腎**D**股**D**膝**D**肘**D**脊**D**	*72*
16 Teeth				
16 歯		teeth	**SG-0302** 歯**B**齢**B**	*74*

II POSTURES

17 Person				
17a 亻		person, an act that a person does; **bushu** ***ninben***	**SG-0304** 人**A**千**A**休**A**体**A**仁**B**極**B**俺**C**囚**D**	*75*
17b 介		to help; in-between; *kai*	**SG-0312** 介**A**界**A**	*76*
17c 大		person; large	**SG-0314** 大**A**天**A**夫**A**太**A**文**A**添**C**汰**D**扶**D**爽**D**	*77*
17d 因		to depend; conventional; *in/on*	**SG-0323** 因**B**恩**C**姻**D**咽**D**	*78*
17e 奇		to lean over; lopsided; *ki*	**SG-0327** 奇**B**寄**B**崎**B**埼**C**椅**D**	*79*
17f 央		center; *oo/ee*	**SG-0332** 央**A**英**A**映**B**	*80*
17g 夾		sandwiched, narrow; *kyoo*	**SG-0335** 狭**C**峡**D**挟**D**	*80*
17h 冘		to hold one's head down	**SG-0338** 沈**C**枕**D**	*81*
17i 夭		supple, young and pliable; *yoo*	**SG-0340** 笑**B**咲**C**妖**D**沃**D**	*81*
17j 呉		swaying and talking; *go*	**SG-0344** 呉**C**誤**C**娯**D**	*82*
17k 若		young; *jaku/daku/toku*	**SG-0347** 若**A**諾**D**匿**D**	*82*
17l 鬼		demon, ghost・田 fearsome	**SG-0350** 鬼**C**魅**C**魔**C**魂**C**塊**D**•異**B**畏**D**	*83*
17m 司		to administer; *shi*	**SG-0357** 司**B**詞**C**飼**C**后**D**嗣**D**伺**D**	*84*
18 Multiple persons				
18a 立		to stand; *ritsu/ryuu*	**SG-0363** 立**A**位**A**泣**B**粒**C**拉**D**	*85*
18b 並		to form a line, rank with	**SG-0368** 並**B**普**B**替**B**譜**D**	*86*
18c 従		to follow; *juu*	**SG-0372** 従**B**衆**B**縦**C**	*87*
18d 并		two people united; *hee*	**SG-0375** 併**C**瓶**D**餅**D**塀**D**	*88*
18e 㑒		to carefully examine goods; *ken*	**SG-0379** 検**A**験**B**険**B**剣**C**倹**D**	*88*
18f 坐		to sit; *za*	**SG-0384** 座**B**挫**D**	*89*
18g 匕		a dead body, person, spoon; **bushu** ***saji***	**SG-0386** 化**A**花**A**北**A**背**B**	*90*
18h 比皆		people in a row, compare・皆 everyone; all; *kai*	**SG-0390** 比**A**批**B**陛**D**・皆**B**階**B**諧**D**楷**D**	*90*
18i 艮		to retreat, remain; *kon*; **bushu** ***konzukuri***	**SG-0397** 限**A**根**A**銀**A**退**B**眼**B**恨**D**痕**D**	*92*
18j 疑		in doubt; *gi/gyoo*	**SG-0404** 疑**B**凝**D**擬**D**	*93*
19 Person in a crouched posture				
19a 令 卩卬㔾 己巴包		a person in a crouched posture, etc.	**SG-0407** 令**A**命**A**鈴**B**•印**B**迎**B**節**B**抑**C**仰**C**•危**B**宛**D**怨**D**厄**D**•丸**A**•己**A**選**A**港**B**•色**A**肥**C**•包**B**抱**B**砲**C**胞**C**泡**C**飽**D**	*94*
19b 欠		to lack, become chipped; in want of	**SG-0431** 欠**A**次**A**歌**A**資**A**姿**B**飲**B**吹**B**炊**D**款**D**諮**D**恣**D**	*98*
19c 儿		person (with the knees bent); **bushu** ***ninnyoo***	**SG-0442** 光**A**先**A**元**A**完**A**院**A**児**B**洗**B**冠**C**玩**D**	*100*
19d 兄		elder male person (praying)	**SG-0451** 兄**B**祝**B**競**B**況**B**呪**D**	*102*
19e 兑		to let go of	**SG-0456** 説**A**税**A**脱**B**悦**D**	*103*
19f 見		to see	**SG-0460** 見**A**現**A**親**A**覚**B**	*104*
19g 夋		*san/shun/sa*	**SG-0464** 酸**B**俊**C**唆**D**	*105*
19h 尸		a slumped person, dead body, buttock, roof; **bushu** ***shikabane***	**SG-0467** 局**A**展**B**居**B**届**B**殿**C**尻**C**泥**C**尿**C**据**C**尼**D**・久**A**	*105*
20 Use of legs				
20a 交		to cross; *koo*	**SG-0478** 交**A**校**A**効**B**郊**C**絞**C**	*107*
20b 走		to run; walk in a hurry; **bushu** ***soonyoo***	**SG-0483** 走**A**起**A**超**A**越**B**徒**B**趣**C**赴**D**奔**D**	*108*
20c 王		straight, to put out; *tee*	**SG-0491** 望**A**程**B**呈**D**	*109*
21 Person with a headdress				
21 頁		head, person; **bushu** ***oogai***	**SG-0494** 頭**A**顔**A**額**A**領**B**類**B**項**B**須**C**頃**C**傾**C**頑**C**顕**D**煩**D**寡**D**頒**D**頻**D**顎**D**	*110*
22 Child; infant				
22a 子		child	**SG-0510** 子**A**学**A**字**A**保**A**孔**D**	*113*
22b 𠫓		a newborn baby	**SG-0515** 充**A**流**A**統**A**育**A**棄**C**硫**D**	*114*
23 Woman				
23a 女		woman, female; feminine; **bushu** ***onnahen***	**SG-0521** 女**A**安**A**案**A**好**A**妻**B**接**B**努**B**姉**B**娘**B**怒**B**妙**C**姫**C**宴**C**妥**C**如**C**奴**C**妃**C**婿**D**妬**D**	*115*
23b 毋 每		mother; every; busy	**SG-0540** 母**A**毎**A**海**A**毒**B**梅**B**敏**C**悔**C**侮**D**	*119*
23c 身		body	**SG-0548** 身**A**	*120*
23d 免		barely; *men/ben/ban*	**SG-0549** 免**B**勉**B**晩**C**逸**D**	*121*

23e 奐		to change, exchange; *kan*	SG-0553 換B喚D	*121*
23f 覀		important, essential	SG-0555 要A腰C遷D	*122*
23g 票		ballot; floating; *hyoo*	SG-0558 票B標B漂D	*122*

24 Long hair, soft hair

24a 耂		old; a long time; *koo/roo*; **bushu *oigashira***	SG-0561 考A老B孝B寿B拷D	*123*
24b 長 微		長 long; *choo* 微 small; 徴 sign	SG-0566 長A張B帳C・微C徴C懲D	*124*
24c 而		soft, gentle	SG-0572 需C耐C端C儒D	*125*

25 A hand doing something

25a 及		to reach; *kyuu*	SG-0576 及A急A級B扱B吸B	*126*
25b 巩		to strike with an instrument	SG-0581 恐B築B	*127*
25c 埶		to care	SG-0583 芸A勢A熱B	*127*
25d 幸		good luck; to invert	SG-0586 幸A報A執C摯D	*128*
25e 孰		ripe; to mature; *juku*	SG-0590 塾C熟C	*129*

26 A person behind a screen

26 亡		to disappear, not exist; *boo/koo/moo*	SG-0592 亡B忘B荒C忙C盲C慌D妄D	*129*

27 A person upside down

27a 真		truth; *shin/chin/ten*	SG-0599 真A慎C鎮C塡D	*130*
27b 屰		to reverse	SG-0603 逆B訴B斥D遡D塑D	*131*

III Plants

28 Tree

28a 木		tree	SG-0608 木A林A森A	*133*
28b 本 末未制 朱		木 with an extra stroke	SG-0611 本A鉢D・末A抹D・未A味A妹B昧D・制A製A・株A朱C殊C珠C	*133*
28c 木		tree, wood, tree name; **bushu *kihen***	SG-0625 楽A薬A査A業A松A条B桜B困B床B染B枠B柳C巣C梨C桃C桑C棚C栃C柿C朴D朽D楼D椎D鬱D慄D	*136*
28d 喿		busy; *soo*	SG-0650 繰C操C藻D燥D	*140*
28e 果		a tree with fruits/nuts/berries; *ka*	SG-0654 果A課A菓C裸C彙D	*141*
28f 某		*bai/ boo*	SG-0659 謀C某D媒D	*142*
28g 片		a piece; *hen/han*	SG-0662 片B版B	*142*
28h 奉		to offer reverentially; *hoo*	SG-0664 奉C棒C俸D	*143*
28i 夆		a mountain ridge; *hoo*	SG-0667 峰C縫D蜂D	*143*

29 Plants growing

29a 世		new plant growth	SG-0670 世A葉A	*144*
29b 艹		plant, vegetation; **bushu *kusakanmuri***	SG-0672 草B茶B藤B華B茂C菊C菌C茨D芋D	*144*
29c 莫		hidden, dark, vast; nothing; *bo/mo/baku/maku*	SG-0681 模B暮B幕C募C墓C膜D漠D慕D	*146*
29d 生		fresh; life; *see*	SG-0689 生A性A産A星A姓C	*147*
29e 青		blue, fresh; *see*	SG-0694 青A情A清A静B精B晴B請B	*148*
29f 垂		to dangle; *sui*	SG-0701 郵B垂D睡D唾D	*150*
29g 乇		*taku*	SG-0705 宅B託C	*150*
29h 平		level, flat; *hyoo/hee*	SG-0707 平A評B坪C	*151*

30 Grain plants

30a 禾		rice plant with crop, harvest; **bushu *nogihen***	SG-0710 年A私A和A利A秋A差A香A委A秒B移B季B秀B誘B稲B透C穂C秩C稿C稚D愁D萎D	*151*
30b 厤		to chronicle; *reki*	SG-0731 歴B暦C	*155*
30c 兼		two things at the same time; *ken*	SG-0733 兼B嫌C謙C鎌C廉D	*156*
30d 米		rice grain; **bushu *komehen***	SG-0738 米A迷B粋C粘D謎D粧D	*156*
30e 朮		a method to stick to; to follow; *jutsu*	SG-0744 術A述B	*157*
30f 麦		(barley)	SG-0746 来A麦C麺D	*158*
30g 甫		to protect, spread; *ho*	SG-0749 補B捕B浦B舗D哺D	*158*
30h 尃		to spread; broaden; *haku/bo*	SG-0754 博B薄B敷C簿C縛D	*159*

31 Bamboo

31 竹		bamboo; **bushu *takekanmuri***	SG-0759 竹A算A箸D	*160*

32 A flower calyx, thorns, gourd, acorns

32a 不		not; *hu/hi/hai*	SG-0762 不A否B杯C	*161*
32b 咅		to double, split; *bu/bai/boo*	SG-0765 部A倍B培D賠D陪D剖D	*161*
32c 朿		a thorny stick with a sharp end; *saku/shi*	SG-0771 策A刺C	*162*
32d 責		debt; *seki*	SG-0773 責B積B債B績C漬D	*163*
32e 麻		hemp, linen; *ma*	SG-0778 麻B摩C磨D	*164*
32f 由		coming out; to originate from; *yuu*	SG-0781 由A油A抽C笛D	*164*
32g 瓜		*ko*	SG-0785 孤C弧D	*165*
32h 白		white; *haku*	SG-0787 白A百A迫B泊C拍C伯C	*165*

IV Animals

33 Animal meat

33a 肉		meat	SG-0793 肉A腐C	*167*
33b 月		a piece of animal meat	SG-0795 有A多A賄D	*167*
33c 肖		to resemble; *shoo*	SG-0798 消A削B肖D硝D	*168*
33d 隋		*zui/da*	SG-0802 随C髄D堕D惰D	*169*
33e 且		many; to pile up; *so*	SG-0806 組A助A祖C狙C畳C粗C阻D宜D租D且D	*169*

34 Ox, cow

34a 牛		ox, cow	SG-0816 牛A物A件A牧C牲D	*171*
34b 半		half; *han*	SG-0821 半A判A伴B畔D	*172*

35 Sheep

35a 羊		sheep; goodness, desirability; *yoo*	SG-0825 羊A美A様A達A洋A養B詳C窯D羨D羞D	*173*

Shape	Seal	Meaning	Kanji	Page
35b 善		goodness; *zen*	SG-0835 善 B 繕 D 膳 D	175
35c 義		just; morality; *gi*	SG-0838 義 A 議 A 儀 C 犠 C	176
36 Pig, hog, boar				
36a 豕		pig, hog, boar; **bushu *inoko***	SG-0842 家 A 塚 B 嫁 C 豚 C 稼 C 逐 D	176
36b 㒸		to fall down; *tai/tsui/sui*	SG-0848 隊 B 遂 C 墜 D	178
36c 亥		*gai/kaku*	SG-0851 刻 B 核 B 該 D 骸 D 劾 D	178
36d 豸		beast, boar; **bushu *mujinahen***	SG-0856 懇 C 墾 D 貌 D	179
37 Other animals				
37a 犬		dog	SG-0859 犬 B 献 C 伏 C 獣 D	180
37b 犭		dog, beast; **bushu *kemonohen***	SG-0863 犯 B 狂 C 猛 C 狩 C 獄 C 猿 C 猟 D	180
37c 馬		horse	SG-0870 馬 A 駅 A 駐 B 驚 C 騒 C 駆 C 駒 C 駄 D 騎 D 騰 D 篤 D 罵 D	182
37d 虍		tiger, a tiger headdress	SG-0882 劇 B 虎 C 慮 C 虚 C 虐 D 戯 D 虜 D 膚 D 逓 D 虞 D	184
37e 象		elephant, image; *zoo/shoo*	SG-0892 象 B 像 B	186
37f 為		to do; *i/gi*	SG-0894 為 B 偽 C	186
37g 鹿		deer	SG-0896 鹿 B 薦 C 麗 D 麓 D	186
37h 屈		to submit, give in; *kutsu*	SG-0900 屈 C 堀 C 掘 C 窟 D	187
37i 属		to join, belong to	SG-0904 属 B 嘱 D	188
38 Parts of an animal				
38a 皮		skin; *hi/ha*	SG-0906 皮 A 彼 A 波 A 破 B 被 B 披 D 婆 D	188
38b 革		leather, hide	SG-0913 革 B 靴 C 覇 C	189
38c 毛		hair	SG-0916 毛 B 尾 B 耗 D	190
38d 犮		plucking hair; *hatsu*	SG-0919 抜 B 髪 C	191
38e 角		horn, antler	SG-0921 角 A 解 A 触 B	191
38f 牙		fang, tusk, fingernail, claw; *ga*	SG-0924 芽 C 邪 C 牙 D・爪 D	192
38g 隶		to catch, follow	SG-0928 逮 C 隷 D	192
38h 求		to seek, demand; *kyuu*	SG-0930 求 A 球 A 救 B	193
39 Marine creatures				
39a 魚		fish	SG-0933 魚 B 鮮 B 漁 C 鯨 D	193
39b 辰		to tremble, shake; *shin*; agricultural; *noo*	SG-0937 農 B 振 B 震 B 濃 C 唇 D 辱 D 娠 D	194
40 Bird				
40a 鳥		bird	SG-0944 鳥 B 鳴 C 鶏 D	195
40b 隹		bird; **bushu *hurutori***	SG-0947 進 A 集 B 準 B 旧 B 雄 B 離 B 推 B 雑 B 双 B 催 B 雇 C 維 C 雅 C 携 C 顧 C 奪 C 焦 C 誰 C 唯 C 奮 C 擁 D 隻 D 准 D 礁 D 雌 D	196
40c 蒦		to grab firmly; *kaku*	SG-0972 護 B 獲 C 穫 D	200
40d 雚		*kan/ken*	SG-0975 権 A 観 A 勧 B 歓 C	201
40e 隺		*kaku*	SG-0979 確 A 鶴 C	202
40f 飞		to fly	SG-0981 飛 B 迅 D	202
40g 羽		wings	SG-0983 羽 B 習 B 翌 B 翼 B 扇 D 翁 D	202
40h 翟		to leap, flap; *yoku/yoo*	SG-0989 曜 B 躍 C 濯 D	203
40i 非		against; not; *hi/hai*	SG-0992 非 A 悲 B 輩 C 俳 C 排 C 扉 C	204
41 Insect, animal paw, carcass				
41a 虫		insect, worm	SG-0998 虫 B 独 B 虹 C 蛇 D 蛍 D 濁 D 蚊 D 蚕 D	205
41b 昆		*kon* ・ rope	SG-1006 混 B 昆 D・縄 B	206
41c 也		a flat area; *ta*	SG-1009 他 A 地 A 池 B・万 A	206
41d 禺		*guu*	SG-1013 遇 C 隅 C 偶 C 愚 D	207
41e 釆		to take a step forward; **bushu *nogome***	SG-1017 番 A 審 B 奥 B 翻 D 藩 D	208
41f 尺		*taku/yaku/shaku*	SG-1022 沢 A 訳 B 択 C 釈 C	209
41g 龹		rolled up; *ken*	SG-1026 券 A 巻 B 圏 C 拳 D	210
41h 暴		to expose; *boo/baku*	SG-1030 暴 B 爆 B	211
42 Mystical animals, and others				
42a 竜		dragon	SG-1032 竜 C 滝 C 襲 C 籠 D	211
42b 能		able	SG-1036 能 A 態 B 熊 C 罷 D	212
42c		(other animals)	SG-1040 風 A 易 B 甲 B 卯 B 亀 C	213
V NATURE				
43 The sun				
43a 日		the sun, day; bright	SG-1045 日 A 早 A 春 A 昼 B 暇 C 晶 C 暁 D	214
43b 朝		morning; *choo*	SG-1052 朝 A 潮 C 嘲 D	215
43c 昔		to repeat, place over top of; *jaku/shaku, etc.*	SG-1055 昔 B 借 B 籍 C 措 C 惜 C 錯 D	216
43d 旦		dawn; *tan*	SG-1061 (1) 恒 C 旦 D 但 D・(2) 担 B 胆 D	217
43e 昜		to rise, heighten; *joo/yoo/too/shoo*	SG-1066 場 A 陽 B 傷 B 湯 B 揚 C 瘍 D	218
44 A moon				
44a 夕		early evening	SG-1072 夕 A 名 A 夜 A 液 C 銘 C	219
44b 月		moon, evening	SG-1077 月 A 明 A 盟 B 宵 D	220
45 Water and ice				
45a 氵		flowing water; **bushu *sanzui***	SG-1081 水 A 決 A 浜 A 満 A 汚 B 沿 C 没 C 汁 C 淡 C 潟 C 潜 C 湿 C 渓 D 漆 D 淫 D 氾 D	221
45b 冫		ice; freezing; **bushu *nisui***	SG-1097 冬 A 終 A 冷 A 寒 B 氷 B 凍 C 凄 D	223
46 River, fountain				
46a 川		river	SG-1104 川 A 州 A 順 B 訓 B 巡 C・回 A	225
46b 永		a long time; *ee*	SG-1110 永 B 泳 C 詠 D	226

Shape		Meaning	Kanji	Page
46c 𠂢		faction, vein, derivation	**SG-1113** 派**A**脈**C**	*227*
46d 才		to exist, accumulate; *zai/zon*	**SG-1115** 才**A**在**A**存**A**財**A**材**B**	*227*
46e 泉		fountain, spring; *sen/gen*	**SG-1120** 泉**A**原**A**線**A**源**B**願**B**腺**D**	*228*
47 Dirt, soil				
47a 土		dirt, soil, ground	**SG-1126** 土**A**圧**B**陸**B**埋**C**垣**C**壇**D**睦**D**堆**D**	*229*
47b 圭		fief, tall pile of dirt	**SG-1134** 封**C**掛**C**佳**C**涯**C**崖**D**	*231*
48 Mountains, rocks, valleys				
48a 山		mountain	**SG-1139** 山**A**島**A**仙**B**嵐**C**崩**C**峠**D**岬**D**	*232*
48b 丘		hill	**SG-1146** 丘**B**岳**C**	*233*
48c 石		rock, stone	**SG-1148** 石**A**岩**B**拓**C**礎**C**砕**D**	*233*
48d 小 少		small; a little; *shoo*	**SG-1153** 小**A**少**A**砂**B**沙**D**抄**D**	*234*
48e 谷		valley and others; *koku/yoku/zoku*	**SG-1158** 谷**A**欲**B**浴**C**俗**C**	*235*
48f 容		to receive, contain; *yoo*	**SG-1162** 容**A**溶**C**	*236*
49 Fire				
49a 火		fire	**SG-1164** 火**A**炎**B**災**B**焼**B**炭**B**灰**C**煙**C**	*236*
49b 赤		red	**SG-1171** 赤**A**嚇**D**	*237*
49c 灬		fire; **bushu *renga/rekka***	**SG-1173** 黒**A**然**B**燃**C**黙**C**蒸**C**勲**C**墨**C**庶**D**薫**D**遮**D**	*238*
49d 𭕄		rigorous activity; thriving	**SG-1183** 労**A**営**A**栄**B**	*240*
49e 尞		dormitory; *ryoo*	**SG-1186** 療**B**僚**C**寮**C**瞭**D**	*240*
49f 菫 𦰩		菫 scarce; *kin*, 𦰩 difficulty; *nan/kan, etc.*	**SG-1190** 勤**B**謹**D**僅**D**・難**B**漢**C**嘆**C**	*241*
50 Metal nuggets in the ground				
50 金		metal, mineral; **bushu *kanehen***	**SG-1196** 金**A**鉄**B**針**B**銃**C**錦**C**鋭**C**鉛**C**釜**D**鋳**D**	*242*
51 Metrological phenomena				
51a 雨		rain, atmospheric; **bushu *amekanmuri***	**SG-1205** 雨**A**雪**B**雲**B**霊**C**霧**C**零**C**漏**D**曇**D**霜**D**	*244*
51b 申		lightning; divine; *shin*	**SG-1214** 申**A**神**A**電**A**伸**B**雷**C**紳**D**	*245*
51c 气		air, steam; *ki*	**SG-1220** 気**A**汽**C**乞**D**	*247*
VI HABITATS				
52 House				
52a 宀 冖		a house, large roof, cover; ***ukanmuri/ wakanmuri***	**SG-1223** 宇**B**宙**B**宣**B**宿**B**縮**B**寛**C**塞**D**賓**D**・写**A**冗**D**	*248*
52b 广		eaves, canopy; **bushu *madare***	**SG-1233** 度**A**席**A**応**A**庁**A**渡**A**	*250*
52c 内		inside	**SG-1238** 入**A**内**A**納**B**	*251*
53 Door				
53a 戸		a single door	**SG-1241** 戸**A**所**A**涙**B**戻**B**房**B**啓**C**炉**C**	*251*
53b 扁		one side; lopsided; bound tablets behind a door; *hen*	**SG-1248** 編**B**偏**C**遍**D**	*253*
53c 門		closed double doors; unknown; **bushu *mongamae***	**SG-1251** 門**A**間**A**開**A**問**A**関**A**閉**B**閣**B**闘**C**簡**C**潤**D**欄**D**閥**D**閑**D**閲**D**	*254*
54 Rooms, an opening in a house				
54a 呂		many rooms connected	**SG-1265** 宮**A**呂**D**侶**D**	*256*
54b 尚		high; *shoo/too;* 尚 facing	**SG-1268** 尚**A**当**A**党**A**常**A**賞**A**堂**B**償**C**掌**D**・向**A**	*257*
55 Tall structure				
55a 高		tall; tower	**SG-1277** 高**A**厚**B**豪**C**	*259*
55b 喬		high with a bent top; *kyoo*	**SG-1280** 橋**A**矯**D**	*260*
55c 京		capital	**SG-1282** 京**A**景**A**影**A**就**B**涼**C**蹴**D**憬**D**	*260*
55d 享		to enjoy; watchtower	**SG-1289** 享**D**郭**D**	*261*
55e 亭		pavilion; *tee*	**SG-1291** 停**B**亭**C**	*262*
56 Various (dwellings)				
56a 亜		secondary; suppressed	**SG-1293** 悪**A**亜**C**	*262*
56b 井		well, roof slate	**SG-1295** 井**A**丹**C**耕**C**丼**D**・瓦**D**	*262*
57 Rice field				
57a 田		rice paddies	**SG-1300** 田**A**男**A**町**A**画**A**留**B**略**B**畑**B**塁**C**畝**D**	*263*
57b 苗		rice plant seedling; *byoo*	**SG-1309** 描**B**猫**C**苗**D**	*265*
57c 里		neatly lined; village; *ri*	**SG-1312** 里**A**野**A**理**A**厘**D**	*266*
58 Town, area				
58a 阝		town, village; **bushu *oozato***	**SG-1316** 都**A**郷**B**邦**B**那**C**	*266*
58b 囗		an enclosure, boundary; **bushu *kunigamae***	**SG-1320** 図**A**	*267*
58c 公		public	**SG-1321** 公**A**	*268*
59 Cave, hole				
59 穴		cave, hole, emptiness; **bushu *anakanmuri***	**SG-1322** 穴**A**空**A**深**A**究**A**突**B**探**B**窓**B**控**C**	*268*
60 Crossroads				
60a 行		to go; one's conduct; **bushu *yukigamae***	**SG-1330** 行**A**街**B**衡**C**桁**D**	*270*
60b 廴		to extend; **bushu *ennyoo***	**SG-1334** 延**B**誕**C**	*271*
60c 廷		royal court; *tee*	**SG-1336** 庭**B**廷**C**艇**D**	*271*
60d 建		to build; *ken*	**SG-1339** 建**A**健**A**鍵**D**	*272*
60e 辶 (辶)		to move forward; **bushu *shinnyuu/ shinnyoo***	**SG-1342** 送**A**辺**A**込**B**遅**B**迭**D**	*272*
61 Hills, mountains				
61 阝 (阜)		hills, boundary, obstruction, ladder; **bushu *kozatohen***	**SG-1347** 隆**C**陥**C**陵**D**阜**D**隙**D**	*273*

62 Wooden stakes				
62a 弋		*dai/tai*	SG-1352 代A貸B袋B	274
62b 弟		order	SG-1355 弟A第A	275
62c 用		to utilize; *yoo*	SG-1357 用A庸D	276

VII SHARP OBJECTS AND WEAPONS

63 Tattooing needles				
63a 辛		hard; word	SG-1359 辛B辞B	277
63b 章		emblem; *shoo*	SG-1361 章B障B彰C	277
63c 言		word, language; to say; **bushu *gonben***	SG-1364 言A話A記A信A計A語A談A読A誇C訟C謡D	278
63d 音		sound; unclear, indistinct; *on/in*	SG-1375 音A暗B響B闇D韻D	280
63e 意		thought, meaning, intention; *i/oku*	SG-1380 意A・億A憶C臆D	281
63f 竟		ending; *kyoo*	SG-1384 境B鏡C	282
64 A surgical knife with a handle				
64a 余		remain, excess; *yo/jo/to*	SG-1386 余B除B途B徐C塗C叙D	282
64b 舍		house; to let go; *sha*	SG-1392 舎B捨C	284
65 Knife, sword				
65a 刀		knife, sword; to cut	SG-1394 刀A切A窃D	284
65b 分		to divide into two; *hun*	SG-1397 分A粉C貧C紛C雰D	285
65c 刂		knife; to cut; **bushu *rittoo***	SG-1402 別A前A創B刷C刈C煎D利D剥D	286
65d 契		Contract, pledge; *kee/ketsu/kitsu*	SG-1410 契B潔C喫C	287
65e 召		to call for; *shoo*	SG-1413 召A昭A照B招B沼B紹C詔D	288
65f 刃		blade	SG-1420 認A刃C忍C	289
66 Surgical knife				
66a 俞兪		to cure; move to somewhere else; *yu*	SG-1423 輸B諭C愉D癒D喩D	290
66b 宰		to take charge	SG-1428 宰D	291
66c 辟		*heki*	SG-1429 壁B避C癖D璧D	291
67 Small knife				
67a 氏		clan; *shi/kon*	SG-1433 氏A紙A婚B	292
67b 旨		(1) tasty; *shi* (2) to make a bow; *kee*	SG-1436 (1)指A旨C脂C・(2)詣D稽D	292
67c 氐		low; bottom; *tee*	SG-1441 低A底B邸C抵C	293
67d 舌		*katsu*	SG-1445 活A括C	294
68 Ax				
68a 王		king; *oo*	SG-1447 王A皇B往C旺D	294
68b 士		warrior, man; *shi*	SG-1451 士A仕A	295
68c 斤		a hand ax	SG-1453 斤A近A新A兵A質B断B析B哲B祈C折C誓C匠D逝D薪D斬D暫D漸D	296
69 Halberd				
69a 戈		halberd	SG-1470 戒C械C伐D	299
69b 武		military, warrior; *bu*	SG-1473 武A賦D弐D	299
69c 成		to complete, accomplish; *see*	SG-1476 成A城B誠B	300
69d 幾		a small amount; *ki*	SG-1479 幾A機A畿D	300
69e 𢦏		to cut, begin; *sai/tai*	SG-1482 裁B載C栽C戴D繊D	301
69f 藏		to store; hideaway; *zoo*	SG-1487 蔵B臓C	302
69g 戠		signal, knowledge; to discern; *shoku*	SG-1489 職A識B織B	303
69h 或		protected area	SG-1492 我B・国A域B惑C	303
69i 咸		to protect; seal; *kan*	SG-1496 感A減A威C滅C憾D	304
69j 戋		thin objects in layers; *zan/sen*	SG-1501 残A浅B銭C桟D箋D	305
69k 矛		lance, pike with a long shaft	SG-1506 務A柔B矛D	306
70 A bow and an arrow				
70a 弓		bow	SG-1509 弓A強A引A弱B弥C弦C溺D	307
70b 射		to shoot; *sha*	SG-1516 射B謝C窮D	308
70c 黄		yellow, spacious; *koo*	SG-1519 黄A広A横A拡B鉱C	309
70d 矢		arrow	SG-1524 矢A知A医A短A候B侯D喉D	310
70e 至		an end	SG-1531 至A室A屋A到B倒B致B握C窒D緻D	311
70f		pertaining to an arrow	SG-1540 演B備B弔D	313
71 Shield, other weapons				
71a 干		*kan*	SG-1543 岸B干C刊C汗C肝C	314
71b 単		*tan*	SG-1548 単A戦A弾B	315
71c 盾		shield	SG-1551 盾C循D	315
71d 周		to go around: full; *shuu/choo*	SG-1553 周A調A週A彫C	316
71e 古		old; *ko*	SG-1557 古A故B苦B枯D	316
71f 固		solid; *ko*	SG-1561 固A個A湖C箇D錮D	317
72 Banner				
72a 㫃		travelling	SG-1566 旅A族A遊B施B旗C旋D	318
72b 倝		raised high; *kan*	SG-1572 幹B韓B乾C	319
72c 中		middle, center; *chuu*	SG-1575 中A仲B沖B	320
73 Military				
73a 車		vehicle	SG-1578 車A連A庫B撃B陣B範C軸C軒C軟C軌C較D	321
73b 軍		military	SG-1589 軍A運A揮C輝C	323
73c 官		official; *kan*	SG-1593 官A追A管B師B館B遣C棺D	323

VIII Threads and Clothing

74 Skein of threads

74a 糸		thread; continuous; **bushu *itohen***	**SG-1600** 糸**A**約**A**総**A**給**B**絵**B**紀**B**絶**B**継**B**紅**B**縁**B**網**C**綿**C**絹**C**紋**C**紺**D**紡**D**糾**D**繭**D**・素**B**紫**C**繁**C**索**C**累**D**	*326*
74b 亦		phonetic use	**SG-1623** 変**A**恋**B**湾**B**蛮**D**	*330*
74c 系		lineage, system; *kee*	**SG-1627** 系**A**係**A**孫**C**遜**D**	*331*
74d 県		*ken*	**SG-1631** 県**A**懸**C**	*332*

75 Short threads

75a 幺		short threads; young	**SG-1633** 幼**B**率**B**	*332*
75b 茲		to flourish; ji	**SG-1635** 滋**C**磁**C**慈**D**幽**D**	*333*
75c 玄		dark	**SG-1639** 玄**C**畜**C**蓄**C**	*333*
75d 屯		camp; to gather; *ton*	**SG-1642** 純**B**鈍**C**屯**D**頓**D**・了**B**	*334*

76 Warps on a weaver; braided

76a 圣		to go through; straight; *kee*	**SG-1647** 経**A**軽**B**径**C**茎**D**	*335*
76b 冉 冓		configuration, structure; *koo*	**SG-1651** 再**A**構**A**講**B**購**C**溝**C**・称**C**	*336*

77 Clothing

77a 衣		clothing	**SG-1657** 衣**A**表**A**裏**B**依**B**哀**C**衰**C**俵**D**衷**D**褒**D**	*337*
77b 衤		clothing; **bushu *koromohen***	**SG-1666** 初**A**裕**B**袖**D**襟**D**裾**D**・卒**B**	*339*
77c 袁		distant; *en*	**SG-1672** 遠**B**園**B**	*340*
77d 褱		chest; *kai*	**SG-1674** 壊**C**懐**C**	*341*
77e 睘		round, circle; to return; *kan*	**SG-1676** 環**B**還**C**	*341*
77f 襄		*joo*	**SG-1678** 譲**C**嬢**D**醸**D**壌**D**	*342*

78 Cloth

78a 巾		cloth	**SG-1682** 巾**B**布**B**帯**B**希**B**飾**C**怖**C**滞**C**帥**D**	*342*
78b 敝		to tire, become torn; *hee/shoo*	**SG-1690** 幣**D**弊**D**蔽**D**	*344*

IX Valuables

79 Cowrie, bronze vessel

79a 貝		shell, monetary value; valuable	**SG-1693** 貝**A**実**A**売**A**続**A**得**A**価**A**買**A**負**A**貴**B**敗**B**貨**B**遺**B**賛**B**賃**B**貯**C**貿**C**貫**C**慣**C**貢**C**鎖**C**唄**C**賜**D**賭**D**潰**D**	*345*
79b 員		(bronze) vessel, the valuables	**SG-1717** 員**A**円**A**具**B**損**B**賊**D**	*350*
79c 則		rule	**SG-1722** 側**A**則**B**測**B**	*351*
79d 貞		faithful; *tee*	**SG-1725** 貞**C**偵**D**	*351*
79e 賁		to gush out, burst out; *hun*	**SG-1727** 噴**C**墳**D**憤**D**	*352*
79f 玉		crown jewel, ball shape	**SG-1730** 玉**A**宝**B**瑠**D**璃**D**璽**D**	*352*
79g 珏		divided into small groups	**SG-1735** 班**C**斑**D**	*353*

X Religious Matters

80 Religious rites

80a 示		religious matter; to manifest	**SG-1737** 示**A**禁**B**奈**B**宗**B**崇**D**	*354*
80b 祭		celebration of a deity	**SG-1742** 祭**A**際**A**察**B**擦**C**	*355*
80c 礻		religious matter; **bushu *shimesuhen***	**SG-1746** 社**A**視**B**礼**B**祉**C**祥**C**禅**D**	*355*
80d 斉		in good order; *see/sai*	**SG-1752** 済**A**剤**B**斉**C**斎**C**	*357*

81 Imperial

81a 帝		imperial; *tee*	**SG-1756** 帝**B**締**B**諦**D**	*357*
81b 商		legitimate, proper; *teki/chaku*	**SG-1759** 適**B**敵**C**摘**C**滴**D**嫡**D**	*358*

82 Divination

82a 卜		divination	**SG-1764** 外**A**点**A**店**A**占**B**貼**D**訃**D**	*359*
82b 兆		divination, sign; *choo/too*	**SG-1770** 兆**B**逃**B**挑**C**跳**D**眺**D**	*360*

83 Cleansing

83a 帚		broom; to sweep, cleanse	**SG-1775** 帰**A**婦**B**掃**C**	*361*
83b 㑴		*shin*	**SG-1778** 寝**B**侵**C**浸**C**	*362*

XI Food and Eating

84 Food

84a 食		food; eating; **bushu *shokuhen***	**SG-1781** 食**A**飯**B**飢**D**餓**D**餌**D**	*363*
84b 既		immediately, already	**SG-1786** 即**B**・既**C**概**C**慨**D**	*364*
84c 曽		many layers; to add; *soo*	**SG-1790** 会**A**増**A**層**B**贈**B**曽**C**僧**C**憎**D**	*365*
84d 甚		exceedingly, very	**SG-1797** 勘**C**甚**D**堪**D**	*366*
84e 鬲		grain storage	**SG-1800** 融**B**徹**C**撤**C**隔**C**	*367*
84f 午		pestle	**SG-1804** 午**A**許**B**康**B**御**B**唐**C**糖**C**卸**C**・臼**D**	*367*

85 Fermentation

85a 酉		alcohol beverage, cask, wine; **bushu *sakezukuri***	**SG-1812** 酒**A**配**A**酔**C**酷**D**酵**D**酬**D**醜**D**酎**D**酌**D**醒**D**	*369*
85b 酋		revered	**SG-1822** 尊**B**猶**D**爵**D**遵**D**	*371*

86 Scales and Utensils

86a 良		good, excellent; *ryoo/roo*	**SG-1826** 良**A**郎**B**朗**C**浪**C**廊**D**	*372*
86b 斗		measured amount	**SG-1831** 料**A**科**A**斜**C**斗**D**	*372*
86c 升		to lift, rise; *shoo*	**SG-1835** 昇**B**升**D**	*373*
86d 复		to repeat, return; *huku*	**SG-1837** 復**B**複**B**腹**B**履**C**覆**C**・両**A**	*374*
86e 皿		shallow vessel, bowl, tray	**SG-1843** 皿**A**血**A**温**B**盛**B**塩**B**益**B**盗**C**尽**C**盆**C**蓋**D**	*375*
86f 是		this; right; *ze/dai/tee*	**SG-1853** 是**A**題**A**提**B**堤**C**	*377*
86g 卓		to stand out	**SG-1857** 卓**C**悼**D**	*378*
86h 卑		lowly, crude, abject; *hi*	**SG-1859** 卑**D**碑**D**	*378*
86i 勺		to scoop up	**SG-1861** 的**A**釣**C**	*378*

XII Table, Tool, and Vessel

87 Table, bed

Shape	Form	Meaning	Kanji	Page
87a 几		(low) table, stool	SG-1863 机B処B拠C	379
87b 其		that; *ki*	SG-1866 基A期A欺D棋D碁D	379
87c 丙		*hee*	SG-1871 商A柄B丙D	380
87d 更		furthermore; *koo*	SG-1874 更B便B硬C梗D	381
87e 丬		(long) table, bed; **bushu *shoohen***	SG-1878 状A将B装B荘C壮C奨D	382
87f 疒		illness; **bushu *yamaidare***	SG-1884 病A痛B症B疲C疫D疾D痴D痢D痩D痘D嫉D	383

88 Tools and containers

Shape	Form	Meaning	Kanji	Page
88a 工		craft, a skilled person; *koo*	SG-1895 工A江A攻B功B巧C	385
88b 式		a set way of doing; **bushu *shikigamae***	SG-1900 式A試B拭D	386
88c 壬		thick in the middle; *nin*	SG-1903 任A妊C	386
88d 乍		to create, make; *saku/sa*	SG-1905 作A昨A酢D詐D搾D	387
88e 巨		huge, giant; *kyo*	SG-1910 巨B拒C距C・規B	388
88f 丁		a square block; *choo/tee, etc.*	SG-1914 丁A打A頂C訂C・克C	389
88g 専		to turn, rotate, roll	SG-1919 専A伝A転A団A恵B	390
88h 予		in advance	SG-1924 予A預A幻C序C・互B	391
88i 录		*roku/ryoku*	SG-1929 緑B録B	392

89 Agricultural tools

Shape	Form	Meaning	Kanji	Page
89a 方		square, four directions; *hoo/boo*	SG-1931 方A放A防A訪B芳C坊C妨C傍D肪D倣D	392
89b 以		by means of	SG-1941 以A似B	394
89c 台		to begin	SG-1943 台A治A始A怠D胎D冶D	394
89d 力		power, strength	SG-1949 力A加A協A賀B励C脇C劣C脅C架C勃D	396

90 Nets

Shape	Form	Meaning	Kanji	Page
90a 罒		a dragnet; to capture	SG-1959 罪B署B罰C羅D	397
90b 害		to harm, damage; *katsu*	SG-1963 害A割A憲B轄D	398

91 Molds and frames

Shape	Form	Meaning	Kanji	Page
91a 岡		hill, strong; *koo*	SG-1967 岡A綱C鋼C剛C	399
91b 开		a square shape; *kee*	SG-1971 形A型A研A刑B	400

92 Vessel

Shape	Form	Meaning	Kanji	Page
92a 豆		*too*	SG-1975 豆A豊A壱D艶D	401
92b 畐		wealth; *huku*	SG-1979 福A副A富A幅B	402
92c 甬		to pass through; *tsuu/yoo/yuu*	SG-1983 通A勇B踊C湧D	402
92d	-	borrowing	SG-1987 西A曲B	403

93 A lid, cover

Shape	Form	Meaning	Kanji	Page
93a 合		to fit well; *goo/too*	SG-1989 合A答A拾C塔C搭D	404
93b 今		to put a lid over	SG-1994 今A含B念B倉B陰C吟D貪D捻D	405
93c 全		to gather all; *zen/sen*	SG-2002 全A栓D詮D・傘C	406
93d 吉		good luck; *kitsu/ ketsu*	SG-2006 吉A結A詰C	407
93e 缶		can, tin	SG-2009 缶C陶D	407
93f 去		to leave; *kyo/kyaku*	SG-2011 去A法A却C脚C	408

94 A vessel for transporting

Shape	Form	Meaning	Kanji	Page
94a 舟		boat, tray	SG-2015 舟A船A舶D舷D	409
94b 般		to transport; general; *han*	SG-2019 般B盤B搬D・服B	409
94c 凡		all; *bon/hon*	SG-2023 凡C帆D汎D	410

95 Writing brush, etc.

Shape	Form	Meaning	Kanji	Page
95a 聿		upright	SG-2026 書A津B律C筆C粛D	411
95b 冊		fence, book	SG-2031 典B冊B柵D	412
95c 侖		things in good order; *ron/rin*	SG-2034 論A輪B倫C	412
95d 主		staying in one place; *shu/chuu*	SG-2037 主A住A注A柱B	413

96 Musical instruments

Shape	Form	Meaning	Kanji	Page
96 鼓		musical instruments	SG-2041 声A南A琴C・喜B樹B膨D鼓D	414

XIII Tied or Bundled

97 Tied, bundled

Shape	Form	Meaning	Kanji	Page
97a 東		*too*	SG-2048 東A棟C陳C	416
97b 柬柬		to refine, knead; *ren*	SG-2051 練B錬D	416
97c 曹		low-level officer; *soo*	SG-2053 曹D遭D槽D	417
97d 量		mass, amount; *ryoo*	SG-2056 量A糧C	417
97e 重		heavy; *juu/hoo/doo*	SG-2058 重A動A種A働B衝C腫D	418
97f 童		young child; *doo/too*	SG-2064 童C瞳C鐘D憧D	419
97g 束		bundle	SG-2068 束A速A整A頼B瀬B疎D勅D辣D	420
97h 必		fastened tightly; *hi/mi*	SG-2076 必A密B秘B蜜D泌D	421
97i 弗		to disperse; *hi/hutsu*	SG-2081 費A払B仏B沸D	422
97j 者		*sha/cho*	SG-2085 者A着A諸B緒B著B暑C煮C	423

XIV Other Shapes

98 Shapes

Shape	Form	Meaning	Kanji	Page
98a 彡		pretty shape; *san;* **bushu *sanzukuri***	SG-2092 参A杉B診C珍C惨D	425
98b 同		a tubelike shape, cylindrical; *doo*	SG-2097 同A銅C筒C洞D胴D	426
98c 乙		to straighten	SG-2102 乱B札B乙C	427
98d 凵		receptacle	SG-2105 凶C凸D凹D	427
98e 匸		a hiding place	SG-2108 区A欧B匹C殴D枢D	428
98f 勹		wrapping around	SG-2113 均B旬B句C拘D匂D勾D	429
98g 曷		*katsu*	SG-2119 掲C葛D喝D渇D褐D謁D	430
98h		Numerals	SG-2125 一A二A三A四A五A六A七A八A九A十A	431
98i		Location	SG-2135 上A下A	432

Study Guide of the 2,136 Joyo Kanji

甲骨文 oracle bone-style form; 金文 bronzeware-style form; 説文 seal-style form in 説文解字; 篆文 seal-style form; 正字 orthographic-style kanji; 旧字 (kyuji) old-style kanji; and 新字 (shinji) present-day kanji

I Parts of the Body

1 Eye

1a 目 "eye; to see" [from an eye] 目省看

SG-0001 目	Meanings	*Kun* and *On*	Romaji	Bushu	Stroke Order and Number
	to see, experience, estimate; important; an eye, marking, unit	め・ま モク・ボク	me, ma *moku, boku*	目	丨冂冃月目 5
目 **A** F-0038	甲骨文1 (1) 甲骨文2 (2) 金文 (3) 説文 (4) 目 1, 2, and 3 were the outline of an eye, showing the pupil and the whites of the eye. They meant "eye, seeing." In 4, the shape was given a 90-degree turn and became a vertical shape. Different functions of the eye gave rise to various meanings, including "important" (from keeping eyes on something); "to experience" (from encountering); "marking" or "target"; "estimation" (from eyeballing something); and "unit of classification." The kanji 目 means "to see, experience, estimate; important; an eye, marking, unit." <目>		目の前 in front of, within one's reach [めのま↓え]; ~に目がない to like very much without reservation [~に・め↓が・な↓い]; 目方 weight [めかた]; 四人目 fourth person [よにんめ↓]; 目の当たりにする to see with one's own eyes [まのあ↓たりにする]; 注目する to pay attention to [ちゅうもくする]; 目的 purpose [もくてき]; 面目をつぶす to be disgraced, lose face [めんぼくをつぶす]		

SG-0002 省	Meanings	*Kun* and *On*	Romaji	Bushu	Stroke Order and Number
	to look carefully, reflect, omit; government ministry	かえり-みる・はぶ-く セイ・ショウ	kaeri-miru, habu-ku *see, shoo*	目	丨小小少省省 9
省 **A** F-0258	甲骨文 (1) 金文1 (2) 金文2 (3) 説文古文 (4) 説文 (5) 省 1 through 5 all comprised "an eye" and "a plant sprouting" above the eye, which was used for the sounds *see/shoo* to mean "a little." Together they signified squinting in an effort to look carefully, and thus the character meant "to examine carefully, reflect on." 省 also meant "to inspect the land and properties under one's control." It also became used for other derived meanings such as "to abbreviate" (from blocked vision, or 少 "little" in 4) and "government ministry." The kanji 省 means "to look carefully, reflect, leave off; government ministry." <少目>		省みる to reflect [かえりみ↓る]; 省く to omit, leave off [はぶ↓く]; 反省する to reflect [はんせいする]; 自省 self-reflection [じせい]; 省略する to leave out, shorten [しょうりゃくする]; 経済産業省(経産省) Ministry of Economy, Trade and Industry (METI) [けいざいさんぎょ↓うしょう, けいさ↓んしょう]; 省力化 labor-saving, elimination or reduction of labor [しょうりょくか]		

SG-0003 看	Meanings	*Kun* and *On*	Romaji	Bushu	Stroke Order and Number
	to watch attentively	カン	*kan*	目	一三手看看 9
看 **C** F-1101	説文或体 (1) 説文 (2) 看 1 comprised 倝 "a streamer fluttering high," used for the sound *kan*, and 目 **SG-0001** "an eye," together signifying "to look afar." 2 comprised "a hand with five fingers showing" (龵, a variation of 手 **SG-0072**) and "an eye." Together they signified a hand shading the eyes in the bright sun to help one to see farther. 2 became the kanji 看 and means "to watch attentively." <龵 目>		看護する to care for the sick [か↓んごする]; 看護士 nurse [かんご↓し]; 看板 signboard, the public face of an organization [かんばん]; 看過する to turn a blind eye to, fail to notice [か↓んかする]; 看病 tending to a sick person, nursing [か↓んびょう]; 看守 prison guard, warden [かんしゅ]		

1b 相 "facing each other; mutual" [from an eye and a tree facing each other]; *soo* 相想箱 

SG-0004 相	Meanings	*Kun* and *On*	Romaji	Bushu	Stroke Order and Number
	to face each other; mutual; phase, aspect, government minister	あい ソウ・ショウ	ai *soo, shoo*	目	一十才札相 9

相 **A** F-0107

甲骨文 1 金文1 2 金文2 3 説文 4 相

1, 2, 3, and 4 comprised "a tree" (木 **SG-0608**) and "an eye" (目). A person and a tree facing each other signified "to face each other; mutual." More specifically, the character meant "looking at a phase or an aspect" of a matter. It also came to mean "government minister," in the sense of someone who keeps a close eye on changing situations. The kanji 相 means "to face each other; mutual; phase, aspect, minister." <木目>

相手 partner, opponent [あいて]; 相談する to talk over, consult [そうだんする]; 相思相愛 two people in love with each other [そうし・そうあい]; 血相を変える to change facial color, become angry [けっそうを・かえる]; 人相 facial features, physiognomy [にんそう]; 円相場 the yen exchange rate [えんそうば]; 首相 prime minister [しゅしょう]

SG-0005 想	Meanings	*Kun* and *On*	Romaji	Bushu	Stroke Order and Number
	idea; to imagine, recall, visualize	ソウ・ソ	*soo, so*	心	木 札 相 想 想 13

想 **A** F-0398

説文 想

The seal-style form comprised 相, "facing each other" (used for the sound *soo*), and 心 **SG-0187** "heart/mind." When one squarely faces one's thoughts and ideas, they also recall and visualize them in their mind. The kanji 想 means "idea, to imagine, recall, visualize." <相 心>

想像する to imagine, visualize [そうぞうする]; 感想 impression, reactions, feelings [かんそう]; 空想 idle fancy, imagination [くうそう]; 予想 expectation, surmise [よそう]; 連想 association of ideas [れんそう]; 想定 projection, supposition [そうてい]; 回想 retrospection, recollection [かいそう]; 愛想のいい friendly, affable [あいその・いい]

SG-0006 箱	Meanings	*Kun* and *On*	Romaji	Bushu	Stroke Order and Number
	box	はこ	hako	竹	⺮ 笁 箱 箱 15

箱 **B** F-1063

説文 箱

The seal-style form comprised 竹 **SG-0759** "bamboo" and 相 **SG-0004** "facing each other," used for the sound *soo*. Pliable materials such as bamboo sheathe were used to make lightweight baskets. When traveling, two bamboo baskets were hung facing each other on either side of a horse. The kanji 箱 means "box." <⺮相>

箱 box [はこ]; 箱入り in a box, boxed, precious [はこいり]; 薬箱 medicine box [くすりばこ]; 重箱 nest of boxes (for food) [じゅうばこ]

1c 直 "straight, direct" [from an eye looking straight]; *choku/shoku/chi* 直置値植徳殖

SG-0007 直	Meanings	*Kun* and *On*	Romaji	Bushu	Stroke Order and Number
	to straighten, do over; direct, immediate, straight	ただ-ちに・なお-す チョク・ジキ	tada-chini, nao-su *choku, jiki*	目	一十冇直直 8

直 **A** F-0160

甲骨文 1 侯馬盟書 2 説文 3 直

1 was "an eye" (目) with "a straight line" above it. An eye looking straight at something meant "straight." In 2, a small dot on the straight line above the eye emphasized "straight," and a curved line signified "to straighten" and "to do over" (⊾). A straight way was a direct, immediate way, and thus the character also meant "direct; at once." The kanji 直 means "to straighten, do over; direct, immediate, straight." <直 ⊾>

直ちに straightaway [ただちに]; やり直す to start afresh, redo [やりなおす]; 一直線 a straight line [いっちょくせん]; 直行する to go without stopping [ちょっこうする]; 直前 immediately before [ちょくぜん]; 日直 day duty [にっちょく]; 正直 honest, earnest [しょうじき]; 直々に in person, personally [じきじきに] // 直ぐ at once, immediately [すぐ]

SG-0008 置	Meanings	*Kun* and *On*	Romaji	Bushu	Stroke Order and Number
	to place, leave, lay	お-く チ	o-ku *chi*	网	罒 罒 罜 置 置 置 13

置 **A** F-0373

説文 置

The seal-style form comprised "a net (网, 罒) to catch birds," and 直 "straight, direct," used for the sound *chi,* together signifying a net placed straight up to catch birds. The kanji 置 means "to place, leave, lay." <罒直>

置く to place, lay something [おく]; 一日置き every other day [いちにちおき・いちにちおき]; 置物 a decorative object [おきもの]; 物置 storeroom, shed [ものおき, ものおき]; 位置 position [いち]; 放置する to leave as it is [ほうちする, ほうちする]; 処置する to dispose of, treat [しょちする]

	Meanings	Kun and On	Romaji	Bushu	Stroke Order and Number
SG-0009 値	value, approximation, pricing	ね・あたい チ	ne, atai *chi*	人	亻亻什佑値値 10

値 **A** F-0515

説文

The seal-style form comprised “a person” (亻, bushu *ninben* “an act that a person does”), and 直 “straight, direct,” used for the sound *chi*. It signified a person looking directly at something to assess its value. The kanji 値 means “value, approximation, pricing.” <亻直>

値 price [ね]; value, worth [あたい]; 値下げ lowering of price [ねさげ]; 値段 price [ねだん]; 値打ち value, worth [ねうち]; 価値 value [かち]; 数値 numerical value [すうち]

	Meanings	Kun and On	Romaji	Bushu	Stroke Order and Number
SG-0010 植	to plant; plant, vegetation	う-える ショク	u-eru *shoku*	木	一十木⁺朩植植 12

植 **B** F-0822

説文 1, 説文或体 2

In 1 and 2, 木 **SG-0608** “tree” was combined with 直 **SG-0007** “straight” in 1, and 置 **SG-0008** “to place” in 2. Both right-side components were used for the sound *shoku.* When planting a tree, one placed the tree straight up. The kanji 植 means “to plant; plant, vegetation.” <木直>

植える to plant [うえる]; 植木 garden tree [うえき]; 田植え planting out rice seedlings [たうえ]; 植物 plant [しょくぶつ]; 植民地 colony [しょくみんち]; 植樹祭 tree planting ceremony [しょくじゅさい]

	Meanings	Kun and On	Romaji	Bushu	Stroke Order and Number
SG-0011 徳	goodness, virtue, merit, good act	トク	*toku*	彳	彳行徳徳徳徳 14

徳 **B** F-0909

甲骨文1 1, 甲骨文2 2, 金文1 3, 金文2 4, 金文3 5, 説文 6, 旧字 7

1, 2, and 3 comprised “an eye with a straight line above it” (𢛳) and “a crossroads, conduct” (彳), signifying “conducting oneself in an upright manner.” In 4 and 5, “a heart” (心 **SG-0187**) was added for “morality.” The line (from ㇄ in 直) above 心 in 6 and 7 disappeared in the shinji. From the sense of being moral and properly conducting oneself, the kanji 徳 means “goodness, virtue, merit, good act.” <彳𢛳心>

道徳 morality, morals [どうとく]; 人徳 one’s natural goodness [じんとく]; 悪徳業者 crooked businessman [あくとくぎょうしゃ]; 背徳行為 immoral conduct [はいとくこうい] // 徳利 sake serving bottle [とっくり] (phonetic substitute kanji)

	Meanings	Kun and On	Romaji	Bushu	Stroke Order and Number
SG-0012 殖	to increase, multiply (money/investment)	ふ-える ショク	hu-eru *shoku*	歹	一ア歹歹⁺歼殖殖 12

殖 **D** F-1627

説文

The seal-style form comprised “skeletal remains” (歹), and 直, used for the sound *shoku* (from the kanji 植 **SG-0010** “to plant”). Decayed animal bones make good fertilizer for plants to grow strong and multiply. The kanji 殖 means “to increase, multiply (money/investment).” <歹直>

(Note: For a group of kanji that contains 歹 bushu *kabane/gatsuhen*, please see **SG-0277** through **SG-0283**.)

殖える to increase [ふえる]; 増殖 multiplication, increase [ぞうしょく]; 生殖 reproduction, generation [せいしょく]; 繁殖 breeding, propagation [はんしょく]

1d “eye with an eyebrow” 夢蔑眉

	Meanings	Kun and On	Romaji	Bushu	Stroke Order and Number
SG-0013 夢	dream	ゆめ ム	yume *mu*	夕	一艹苎萝萝夢夢 13

夢 **A** F-0505

甲骨文1 1, 甲骨文2 2, 説文 3

1 and 2 comprised “a bed placed vertically” and “a person lying on a bed with their eyes open wide.” The person was “seeing a dream.” 3 comprised “eyes with big eyebrows” (𦭝) and “a moon (夕)” that was covered, signifying “darkness or night,” or “the body,” from its relation to 月, bushu *nikuzuki*. What one saw at night while asleep was a dream. The kanji 夢 means “dream.” <𦭝冖夕>

夢 dream [ゆめ]; 夢見る to dream [ゆめみる, ゆめみる]; 夢物語 fantastic story, empty story [ゆめものがたり]; 夢中になる to become preoccupied [むちゅうになる]; 悪夢 nightmare [あくむ]

	Meanings	Kun and On	Romaji	Bushu	Stroke Order and Number
SG-0014 蔑	to disdain, scorn; contempt	さげす-む ベツ	sagesu-mu *betsu*	艸	艹苎苎苗茂蔑蔑 14

蔑 **D** F-2359

甲骨文 1 　甲骨文 2 　金文 3 　説文 4

The etymology of this character is obscure. One view explains that 1 through 4 depicted a person with inflamed eyes (indicated by inverted eyelashes, 苜) caught by a halberd (戍), who thus could not see, and that not looking at something was a show of "disdain." Another view explains that the character depicted a spiritual medium (with "large eyes and eyebrows"), who had cast a curse on enemy soldiers, and had been struck and killed from behind by an enemy's halberd. Breaking a curse and regaining one's agency or power gave the meaning "to belittle; contemptuous." The kanji 蔑 means "to scorn; contempt." <苜戍丶>

蔑む to despise, scorn [さげすむ]; 蔑視 slight, disdain [べっし, べっし]; 軽蔑する to belittle, scorn [けいべつする]

	Meanings	Kun and On	Romaji	Bushu	Stroke Order and Number
SG-0015 眉	eyebrow	まゆ ビ・ミ	mayu *bi, mi*	目	フコア尸尸眉眉 9

眉 **D** F-1946

甲骨文 1 　甲骨文 2 　説文 3

1 was "an eye with an eyebrow," while 2 depicted an entire person with their eyes and eyebrows emphasized. They meant "eyebrow." Another view explains that in oracle-bone style times, 眉 was used to mean "to inspect." The kanji 眉 means "eyebrow." <尸目>

眉・眉毛 eyebrows [まゆ, まゆげ]; 愁眉 knitted brow, a worried look [しゅうび]; 眉間 the middle of the forehead, the brow [みけん]

1e 冃 "eyes covered, headgear"; *boo/mee* 冒帽冥

	Meanings	Kun and On	Romaji	Bushu	Stroke Order and Number
SG-0016 冒	to cover, venture out; beginning	おか-す ボウ	oka-su *boo*	冂	冂冃冃冒 9

冒 **C** F-1393

金文 1 　説文古文 2 　説文 3

1 comprised "an eye" (目 SG-0001) and "a cover," which became 冃 (曰, later) "a head or eye cover, helmet" in 3. Wearing protective headgear enabled one to take bolder action. The character meant "adventurous; to take a risk," and "to begin" such an adventure. With 曰 and 目 together, the kanji 冒 means "to cover, venture out; beginning." <曰目>

危険を冒す to venture out into danger [きけんをおかす]; 冒険 adventure [ぼうけん]; 感冒 common cold (head cold) [かんぼう]; 冒頭に at the beginning, at the onset [ぼうとうに]

	Meanings	Kun and On	Romaji	Bushu	Stroke Order and Number
SG-0017 帽	hat, head cover	ボウ	*boo*	巾	ｌ冂巾巾巾巾帽帽 12

帽 **C** F-1636

No ancient form. For the kanji 帽, 巾 SG-1682 "cloth, scarf" was added to 冒 "headgear," used for the sound *boo*. A head covering made of cloth meant "hat, head cover." The kanji 帽 means "hat, head cover." <巾冒>

帽子 hat [ぼうし]; 学帽 school cap [がくぼう]; 脱帽する to take off one's hat, admire greatly [だつぼうする]; 野球帽 baseball cap [やきゅうぼう]; 制帽 regulation cap, school cap [せいぼう]

	Meanings	Kun and On	Romaji	Bushu	Stroke Order and Number
SG-0018 冥	darkness, afterlife, invisible divine favor	メイ・ミョウ	*mee, myoo*	冖	冖冖冝冝冥冥 10

冥 **D** F-2273

説文

The seal-style form depicted "a cloth (冖) covering the eyes of the deceased (日) with the knotted string" (六), and had the sound *mee*. Taken together, these components signified "darkness, the world of the dead, the invisible realm." The character also means "invisible divine favor or protection." The kanji 冥 means "darkness, afterlife, invisible divine favor." <冖日六>

冥想 (瞑想) meditation, contemplation [めいそう]; 冥土 Hades, the shadowy kingdom of the dead (Buddhism) [めいど]; 冥福を祈る to pray a soul may rest in peace [めいふくをいのる]; 冥利 providence, advantage [みょうり]

1f 曼 "boundless" [from the boundless beauty of a hooded woman's flirtatious sideways-glance]; *man* 慢漫

	Meanings	*Kun and On*	Romaji	Bushu	Stroke Order and Number
SG-0019 慢	lazy, slow, haughty; to neglect	マン	*man*	心	14

慢 **C** F-1593

説文

The seal-style script comprised "a heart" (忄, bushu *risshinben*), and 曼 "boundless," used for the sound *man*. When one's heart or self-pride swelled beyond the bounds of moderation, they would become "neglectful or haughty." The kanji 慢 means "lazy, haughty; to disregard, neglect." <忄日罒又>

自慢する to boast about, brag about [じまんする]; 自慢げに braggingly, proudly [じまんげに]; 我慢する to endure, put up with [がまんする]; 腕自慢 pride in one's skill [うでじまん]; 高慢ちきな arrogant, haughty [こうまんちきな]; 慢心する to be puffed up, swell with pride [まんしんする]

	Meanings	*Kun and On*	Romaji	Bushu	Stroke Order and Number
SG-0020 漫	random; to ramble, wander	マン	*man*	水	14

漫 **D** F-1699

No ancient form. The kanji 漫 comprises 氵 bushu *sanzui* "flowing water," and 曼 "long, boundless," used for the sound *man*. Together, they signified water spreading in no particular direction. The kanji 漫 means "something random; to ramble, wander." <氵曼>

漫画 comics, *manga* [まんが]; 注意力散漫な distracted, inattentive [ちゅういりょく・さんまんな]; 冗漫な wordy, lengthy [じょうまんな]; 世界漫遊 a tour around the world, globe-trotting [せかい・まんゆう]

1g 民 "people" [from people blinded by a needle through the eye]; *min* 民眠

	Meanings	*Kun and On*	Romaji	Bushu	Stroke Order and Number
SG-0021 民	the people, the masses; non-governmental	たみ ミン	tami *min*	氏	5

民 **A** F-0105

金文1 1, 金文2 2, 金文3 3, 説文 4

1, 2, 3, and 4 comprised "an eye" and "a needle piercing the eye to make a person blind." In ancient times, captives of war were sometimes made slaves. The character represented people who would blindly follow the orders of their master or leader, and originally referred to people under government rule. The kanji 民 means "the people, the masses, non-governmental." <民>

民 the people, subjects [たみ]; 国民 people, citizens, national [こくみん]; 市民 citizen, resident of a city [しみん]; 民主主義 democracy [みんしゅしゅぎ]; 民間の non-governmental [みんかんの]; 民主化 democratization [みんしゅか]; 移民 emigrant, emigration, immigration [いみん]; 民芸品 object of folk art [みんげいひん]

	Meanings	*Kun and On*	Romaji	Bushu	Stroke Order and Number
SG-0022 眠	to sleep; slumber; sleepy	ねむ-る ミン	nemu-ru *min*	目	10

眠 **C** F-1108

篆文 1, 呉熙載 2

1 was the same as the non-Joyo kanji 瞑 "to close the eyes" (which comprised 目 and 冥 **SG-0018**, and signified "eyes covered"). For the same meaning, the present-day kanji uses 目 **SG-0001** "eye," and 民 **SG-0021** in its sense of a blinded eye (i.e., "not seeing"), and for its pronunciation *min*. The kanji 眠 means "to sleep; slumber; sleepy." <目民>

眠る to sleep, slumber [ねむる]; 眠い・眠たい sleepy, drowsy [ねむい, ねむたい]; 居眠り doze [いねむり]; 睡眠 sleep [すいみん]; 仮眠を取る to take a nap [かみんをとる]

1h 臣 "watchful eye, loyal retainer" [from a wide-open eye] 臣臨

	Meanings	*Kun and On*	Romaji	Bushu	Stroke Order and Number
SG-0023 臣	loyal subject, government minister	シン・ジン	*shin, jin*	臣	7

臣 **B** F-1088

甲骨文 1, 金文1 2, 金文2 3, 説文 4

1, 2, 3, and 4 depicted a large, wide-open eye viewed from the side. Someone who kept a watchful eye was a "loyal subject or retainer." A person who kept a close eye on matters of governance was a "government minister." The kanji 臣 means "loyal subject, government minister." <臣>

臣下 subject [しんか]; 大臣 government minister [だいじん]; 外務大臣 minster of foreign affairs [がいむだいじん]; 総理大臣 prime minister, the premier [そうりだいじん]

SG-0024 臨	Meanings	Kun and On	Romaji	Bushu	Stroke Order and Number
	to look out on, deal with, be present at; provisional	のぞ-む リン	nozo-mu *rin*	臣	18

臨 **B** F-0923	金文1 1 · 金文2 2 · 説文 3 · 臨 — 1 and 2 comprised "a watchful eye" (臣) connected to "boxes," alongside "a standing person." Together, they signified a person who watched over goods or matters. In 3, the person became taller and looked down over the goods (品 **SG-0032**). Watching over things meant being "ready to deal with the matter at hand" or "provisional." The kanji 臨 means "to look out on, deal with, be present at; provisional." <臣𠂉品>	臨む to face, attend [のぞむ]; 試合に臨む to face a match (sports) [しあいにのぞむ]; ご臨席 attendance by a dignitary (honorific) [ごりんせき]; 臨時電車 special unscheduled trains [りんじでんしゃ]; 臨海公園 ocean-side park [りんかいこうえん]; 臨床実験 clinical trial [りんしょうじっけん]; 臨終 one's dying hour [りんじゅう]

1i 監 "to examine carefully, monitor" [from a person looking down at their reflection in a vessel of water]; *kan/ran* 監覧鑑艦濫藍

SG-0025 監	Meanings	Kun and On	Romaji	Bushu	Stroke Order and Number
	to watch attentively, supervise, monitor	カン	*kan*	皿	15

監 **B** F-0851	甲骨文 1 · 金文 2 · 説文 3 · 監 — 1 depicted "a stooped person looking down into a vessel," signifying "a person examining something carefully." In 2 and 3, a short line above the vessel indicated that there was water inside, serving as a water mirror. The person was examining their reflection in the water. In the kanji, all the components—a watchful eye, a person, a vessel with water inside—are present. The kanji 監 means "to watch attentively, supervise, monitor." <臣𠂉皿>	監督 manager, supervision [かんとく]; 監視カメラ surveillance camera [かんしカメラ]; 監修者 supervising editor [かんしゅうしゃ]; 監獄 prison [かんごく]; 監査 inspection [かんさ]; 会計監査 accounting audit [かいけいかんさ]

SG-0026 覧	Meanings	Kun and On	Romaji	Bushu	Stroke Order and Number
	to view (from a high place), have a whole view	ラン	*ran*	見	17

覧 **C** F- 1353	説文 1 · 旧字 2 · 覧 — 1 comprised 臣 "a watchful eye," "a person looking down," "water in a vessel," and 見 **SG-0460** "to look at." Looking something over carefully from a higher position meant "to look out over a wide area, command a bird's-eye view." The kyuji 覽 (2) reflected 1, but in the shinji 覧, the "vessel" was dropped, while keeping the three references to "viewing." The kanji 覧 means "to view (from a high place), have a whole view." <臣𠂉見>	一覧表 table, list [いちらんひょう]; ご覧になる to look honorific) [ごらんになる]; 展覧会exhibition [てんらんかい]; 閲覧室 viewing room, reading room [えつらんしつ]; 遊覧バス sightseeing bus [ゆうらんバス]

SG-0027 鑑	Meanings	Kun and On	Romaji	Bushu	Stroke Order and Number
	paragon; to heed	かんが-みる カン	kanga-miru *kan*	金	23

鑑 **C** F-1572	金文1 1 · 金文2 2 · 説文 3 · 鑑 — 1 was the same as 2 for 監 **SG-0025**, pronounced *kan*, whereas in 2 and 3 "bronze, metal" (金 **SG-1196**) was added to mean that the water mirror had become a bronze mirror. Something used as a standard for reflecting on one's own deeds was a "paragon, model." The kanji 鑑 means "paragon; to heed." <金監>	鑑みる to take into consideration [かんがみる]; 鑑別する to discriminate, differentiate [かんべつする]; 鑑定 expert judgment, appraisal [かんてい]; 年鑑 yearbook, almanac [ねんかん]; 図鑑 illustrated reference book [ずかん]; 鑑賞する to admire, appreciate [かんしょうする]

SG-0028 艦	Meanings	Kun and On	Romaji	Bushu	Stroke Order and Number
	warship	カン	*kan*	舟	21

艦 **C** F-1475	No ancient form. The kanji comprises 舟 **SG-2015** "boat," and 監, used here for its sound *kan* (from non-Joyo kanji 檻 "a cage for an animal," or for the meaning of "surveillance"). A military ship with a protected area on the deck was a "warship." The kanji 艦 means "warship." <舟監>	軍艦 warship [ぐんかん]; 母艦 mother ship [ぼかん]; 航空母艦 aircraft carrier [こうくうぼかん]; 旗艦店 flagship store [きかんてん]

	Meanings	Kun and On	Romaji	Bushu	Stroke Order and Number
SG-0029 濫	to flood, overdo, misappropriate; beyond moderation	ラン	*ran*	水	氵氵氵氵濫濫 18

濫 **D** F-2454

説文

濫 The seal-style form comprised "flowing water" (氵), and 監 **SG-0025**, used here for the sound *ran* to mean "flooding, excessive." When something goes beyond moderation, it becomes an abuse of power. The kanji 濫 means "to flood, overdo, misappropriate; beyond moderation." <氵監>
(Note: Before the Joyo kanji revision in 2010, the kanji 乱 **SG-2102** was often substituted for 濫 in words such as 乱用 or 乱発.)

氾濫 flood [はんらん]; 濫用 abuse, extravagant use [らんよう]; 濫発 excessive issue, over-issue [らんぱつ]

	Meanings	Kun and On	Romaji	Bushu	Stroke Order and Number
SG-0030 藍	indigo, indigo blue	あい ラン	ai *ran*	艸	艹 芦 萨 藍 18

藍 **D** F-2046

説文

藍 The seal-style form comprised "plant" (艸,艹) and 監, used for the sound *ran*. A plant called *ran* was "indigo." The kanji 藍 means "indigo, indigo blue." <艹監>

藍色 indigo blue [あいいろ]; 藍染 indigo dyeing [あいぞめ]; 出藍の誉れ surpassing one's master [しゅつらんのほまれ]

2 Mouth

2a 口 "mouth, goods, area, hole, a box of prayers; to speak, eat"; bushu *kuchihen* 口品告号器造呼甘唱舌叫喪吐叱

	Meanings	Kun and On	Romaji	Bushu	Stroke Order and Number
SG-0031 口	mouth, opening, hole, population; speak	くち コウ・ク	kuchi *koo, ku*	口	丨 冂 口 3

口 **A** F-0133

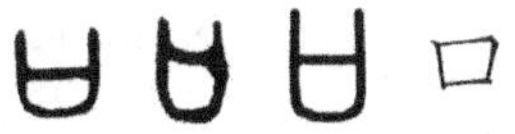
甲骨文 1 金文 2 説文 3

口 The shape 口 appears in a large number of kanji. Since the compilation of *Setsumon Kaiji* (説文解字 Shuowen Jiezi, referred to as *Setsumon* in this book), the origin of 口 has traditionally been considered to be "a mouth," and thought to pertain to speaking or eating. A drastically different proposed view is that it depicted a box of prayers and benedictions (Shirakawa 2003, 2004). In this book we shall adopt both views when the shape is used as a component or bushu *kuchi* or *kuchihen*. The kanji 口 means "mouth, opening, hole, population; to speak." <口>

口 mouth [くち]; 一口 bite-size, share [ひとくち]; 口コミ by word of mouth [くちこみ]; 出口 exit [でぐち]; 人口 population [じんこう]; 口頭の oral, verbal, spoken [こうとうの]; 開口一番 the first thing one says [かいこういちばん]; 口調 manner of talking [くちょう]

	Meanings	Kun and On	Romaji	Bushu	Stroke Order and Number
SG-0032 品	goods, quality, class	しな ヒン	shina *hin*	口	丨 口 口 口 口 口 品 9

品 **A** F-0131

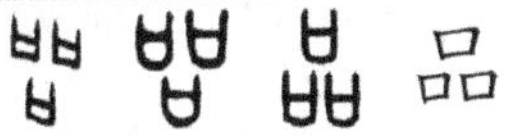
甲骨文 1 金文 2 説文 3

品 In 1, 2, and 3, the three 口 signified "many names of many goods." Goods have different levels of quality, and thus the character also meant "quality, class." The kanji 品 means "goods, quality, class." <口口口>

品 goods, item [しな]; 品物 goods [しなもの]; 手品 magic, conjuring trick [てじな]; 品のいい/-ない having natural beauty/vulgar [ひんのいい, -ない]; 上品な refined, stylish [じょうひんな]; 作品 (creative) work [さくひん]; 品行 (moral) conduct, behavior [ひんこう]

	Meanings	Kun and On	Romaji	Bushu	Stroke Order and Number
SG-0033 告	to tell, inform, announce	つ-げる コク	tsu-geru *koku*	口	ノ 𠂉 牛 生 告 告 告 7

告 **A** F-0325

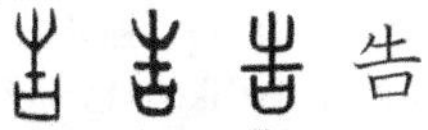
甲骨文 1 金文 2 説文 3

告 One view explains that 1 and 2 comprised "to emerge" (生 **SG-0689**), and "a mouth" (口). Words coming out of a mouth signified "to proclaim, inform." Another view explains that the character depicted a prayer box hung from the branch of a tree, signifying "to tell a deity." The kanji 告 means "to tell, inform, announce." <⺧口>

告げる to announce, tell [つげる]; お告げ oracle, divine message [おつげ]; 告げ口 spreading rumors [つげぐち]; 広告 advertisement [こうこく]; 告白 confession [こくはく]; 通告 notification, warning [つうこく]

	Meanings	Kun and On	Romaji	Bushu	Stroke Order and Number
SG-0034 号	to call out in a loud voice; name, number	ゴウ	*goo*	虍	 5

号 **A** F-0369

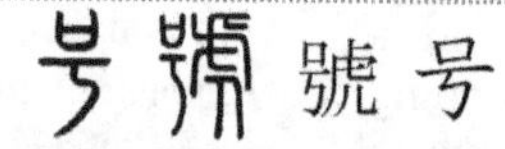

号-説文 1 號-説文 2 旧字 3

1 comprised 口 "mouth" and 丂 "a bent shape (of a throat)," used for the sound *goo*. One consciously uses the throat to make the voice loud, and the character meant "to call out." In 2 and 3, "a tiger" (虎 **SG-0883**), an animal that roared loudly, was added, but was dropped in the shinji. Calling out a name or a number in a loud voice gave the character the meaning "name, number." The kanji 号 means "to call out in a loud voice; name, number." <口丂>

番号 number [ばんごꜜう]; 五号 No. 5 [ごꜜごう]; 屋号 store name [やꜜごう]; 記号 symbol, sign, mark [きごう]; 信号 signal [しんごう]; 号泣 wailing [ごうきゅう]; 号外 extra issue [ごうがい]; 号令をかける to give or shout an order [ごうれいをかけꜜる]

	Meanings	Kun and On	Romaji	Bushu	Stroke Order and Number
SG-0035 器	container, receptacle, vessel, caliber, talent	うつわ キ	utsuwa *ki*	口	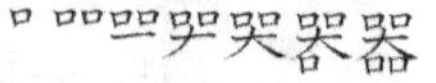 15

器 **A** F-0382

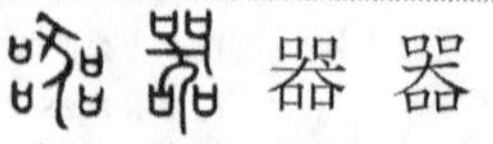

金文 1 説文 2 旧字 3

One view explains that 1 and 2 comprised four 口 "vessels, goods," and "a dog" (犬 **SG-0859**) that was guarding them. Another view holds that this character was a borrowed character (that is, with no relevance to the original meaning). The meaning "vessel, container" was also used to mean a person's capacity or talent. The kanji 器 means "container, receptacle, vessel, caliber, talent." <口口大口口>

(Note: 犬 used as a component in kyuji often became 大 in shinji.)

器 vessel, container, bowl, ability [うつわ]; 楽器 musical instrument [がっき]; 食器 dishes, tableware [しょっき]; 石器時代 Stone Age [せっきじꜜだい]; 受話器 telephone receiver [じゅわꜜき]; 器具 equipment [きꜜぐ]; 器用な skillful, dexterous [きꜜような]; 大器晩成 Great talents are slow to mature (proverb) [たꜜいき・ばんせい]

	Meanings	Kun and On	Romaji	Bushu	Stroke Order and Number
SG-0036 造	to make, create	つく-る ゾウ	tsuku-ru *zoo*	辵	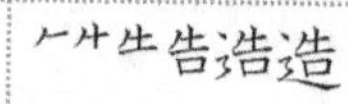 10

造 **A** F-0485

金文1 1 金文2 2 金文3 3 説文 4

1, 2, and 3 comprised "a growing plant," "a box or mouth," and "a crossroads (with a footprint)," with "a vessel" in the top-left of 1, or "a house" over the top of 2. What these components added up to is obscure. One view explains it as "building a shrine," giving the meaning "to create." Another view takes it as borrowing. In 4, "a crossroads" and "a footprint" became 辵, which further became ⻌, bushu *shinnyuu/shinnyoo* in kanji. The right side 告 was used for the sound *zoo*. The kanji 造 means "to make, create."<告⻌>

造る to make [つくꜜる]; 創造 creation [そうぞう]; 造作なく easily [ぞうさなꜜく]; 造詣の深い to have profound knowledge [ぞうけいのふかꜜい]; 人造湖 man-made lake [じんぞꜜうこ]; 造花 artificial flower [ぞうか]

	Meanings	Kun and On	Romaji	Bushu	Stroke Order and Number
SG-0037 呼	to call out to someone, exhale	よ-ぶ コ	yo-bu *ko*	口	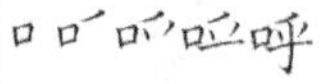 8

呼 **A** F-0518

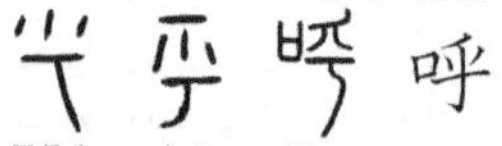

甲骨文 1 金文 2 説文 3

One view takes 1 and 2 to depict a breath going upward and dispersing in a 八 shape, signifying "exhaling," while another view takes them to depict "a clapperboard used for calling out (to a deity)," pronounced *ko*. "The sound of a master calling a subject" signified "to call out." In 3, "a mouth" was added to 乎. The kanji 呼 means "to call out to someone, exhale." <口乎>

呼ぶ to call out [よぶ]; 呼び名 name one is called, nickname [よびな]; 呼び捨て saying someone's name without an honorific suffix [よびすて]; 呼び出す to summon, send for [よびだꜜす]; 呼吸 breathing, respiration [こきゅう]; 点呼 roll call [てꜜんこ]

	Meanings	Kun and On	Romaji	Bushu	Stroke Order and Number
SG-0038 甘	sweet	あま-い カン	ama-i *kan*	甘	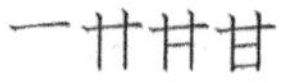 5

甘 **B** F-1049

甲骨文 1 金文 2 説文 3

1, 2, and 3 depicted "a mouth with something inside." Something pleasant to put in one's mouth was something sweet. The kanji 甘 means "sweet." <廿一>

甘い sweet [あまい]; 甘口 sweet (as opposed to dry or spicy) [あまくち]; 甘える to behave like a spoiled child, avail oneself of someone's kindness [あまえる]; 甘やかす to pamper, spoil [あまやかꜜす, あまやかす]; 甘党 someone who likes sweets [あまとう]; 甘味料 sweetener [かんみꜜりょう]

	Meanings	*Kun* and *On*	Romaji	Bushu	Stroke Order and Number
SG-0039 唱	to sing, chant, advocate	とな-える ショウ	tona-eru *shoo*	口	口 口口 口日 唱 唱 11

唱 **C** F-1144 — 説文

The right side of the seal-style form comprised 日 **SG-1045** "bright as the sun," and ⺜ "a lively voice coming out of a mouth" (non-Joyo kanji), used for the sound *shoo*. With the addition of 口, the character meant "to sing, recite." The kanji 唱 means "to sing, chant, advocate." <口日⺜>

唱える to chant, advocate [となえる]; 合唱 choral singing [がっしょう]; 唱歌 children's songs [しょうか]; 二重唱 duet singing [にじゅうしょう]; 提唱する to advocate [ていしょうする]

	Meanings	*Kun* and *On*	Romaji	Bushu	Stroke Order and Number
SG-0040 舌	tongue	した ゼツ	shita *zetsu*	舌	ノ 二 千 舌 舌 6

舌 **C** F-1329 — 甲骨文 1, 説文 2

1 depicted a forked shape at the tip of a tongue, which signified a tongue moving about. Moving the tongue inside the mouth meant articulating sounds in speaking, or chewing food. 2 retained the forked shape, but it became a single short stroke in the kanji. The kanji 舌 means "tongue." <千口>

舌 tongue [した]; 巻き舌 rolling one's tongue, trill [まきじた]; 舌打ちする tut-tut [したうちする]; 舌足らず garbled speech, poor explanation [したたらず]; 舌を巻く to be astonished [したをまく]; 二枚舌 double-dealing [にまいじた]; 毒舌家 a person with a sharp tongue [どくぜつか]; 饒舌な talkative [じょうぜつな]

	Meanings	*Kun* and *On*	Romaji	Bushu	Stroke Order and Number
SG-0041 叫	to shout, yell, scream	さけ-ぶ キョウ	sake-bu *kyoo*	口	口 叫 叫 叫 6

叫 **C** F-1386 — 篆文

The seal-style form comprised 口 "mouth," and 丩 "twisted ropes," used for the sound *kyuu* to mean "a shrieking noise," together signifying "to shout." The kanji 叫 means "to shout, yell, scream." <口丩>

叫ぶ to shout, yell [さけぶ]; 叫び声 scream [さけびごえ]; 絶叫 scream [ぜっきょう]

	Meanings	*Kun* and *On*	Romaji	Bushu	Stroke Order and Number
SG-0042 喪	to mourn; loss	も ソウ	mo *soo*	口	一 十 亠 亠 亠 亟 亟 喪 12

喪 **C** F-1394 — 甲骨文 1 1, 甲骨文 2 2, 金文 3, 説文 4

1 and 2 comprised "a mulberry tree" (桑 **SG-0640**), used for the sound *soo*, and "a few prayer vessels or speaking mouths," signifying "a ritual." 4 had the addition of 亡 **SG-0592** "to disappear, not exist" (or, euphemistically, "to die"). Many people crying loudly at a funeral rite over the death of a person meant "to mourn, loss." The kanji 喪 means "to mourn; loss." <十口口𧘇>

喪主 the chief mourner [もしゅ]; 喪に服す to be in a mourning period [もにふくす]; 喪服 mourning clothes [もふく]; 喪失する to lose, be deprived of [そうしつする]; 喪失感 a sense of loss [そうしつかん]

	Meanings	*Kun* and *On*	Romaji	Bushu	Stroke Order and Number
SG-0043 吐	to vomit, spit out, exhale, confess	は-く ト	ha-ku *to*	口	口 口一 口十 吐 6

吐 **C** F-1622 — 説文

The seal-style form comprised 口 **SG-0031** "mouth," and 土 **SG-1126** "ground, dirt," used for the sound *to*, signifying "spitting on the ground." The kanji 吐 means "to vomit, spit out, exhale, confess." <口土>

吐く to vomit, spit out [はく]; 吐き捨てる to spit out [はきすてる]; 吐血する to cough up blood [とけつする]; 嘔吐 vomiting [おうと]; 真情を吐露する to express one's true sentiments [しんじょうをとろする]

	Meanings	*Kun* and *On*	Romaji	Bushu	Stroke Order and Number
SG-0044 叱	to scold, rebuke	しか-る シツ	shika-ru *shitsu*	口	口 口ノ 叱 5

叱 **D** F-2026 — 篆文

The right side of the seal-style form was used for the sound *shitsu*, which indicated a noise made when clicking the tongue in disgust or disapproval (like "tut" in English). With 口 "mouth" added, the character signified "to disapprove, scold." The kanji 叱 means "to scold, rebuke." <口匕>

叱る to scold [しかる]; 叱られる to be told off, be scolded [しかられる]; 叱咤激励 rigorous encouragement [しった・げきれい]; 叱責する to reproach, reprimand [しっせきする]

2b 可 "possible, good" [from a twig and a mouth, or a hoarse voice forced out of the throat]; *ka* 可

可何河荷苛

SG-0045 可	Meanings	Kun and On	Romaji	Bushu	Stroke Order and Number
	to enable; possible; permission	カ	*ka*	口	一 丁 𠁣 𠮛 可 5

可 **A** F-0200

甲骨文1 甲骨文2 金文 説文
1 2 3 4

The bent shape in 1 and 2 depicted "a bent twig," and it was used together with 口 **SG-0031** "mouth" for the sound *ka*, to mean "permission, good." Another view says the character represented a hoarse voice forced out of the throat, signifying "giving permission reluctantly, enabling." The kanji 可 means "to enable; possible; permission." <一口亅>

可否 right and wrong, for and against [か]ひ]; 不可欠な indispensable, vital [ふか]けつな]; 生半可な immature [なまはんかな]; 可決 approval, passage [かけつ]; 可能な possible [かのうな]; 不可解な incomprehensible, inexplicable [ふか]かいな]; 可視化 visualization [かしか]

SG-0046 何	Meanings	Kun and On	Romaji	Bushu	Stroke Order and Number
	what, interrogative	なに・なん カ	nani, nan *ka*	人	亻 仁 仃 何 何 7

何 **A** F-0216

甲骨文 金文1 金文2 説文
1 2 3 4

1 depicted "a person carrying a halberd over their shoulder." 2 and 3 meant "a person carrying a load over the shoulder or on the back," and was pronounced *ka*. The character's use as the interrogative "who" was a borrowing. The kanji 何 means "what, interrogative." <亻可>

何 what [な]に]; 何人 person of what nationality [なに]じん], how many people [な]んにん]; 何で why, for what reason [な]んで]; 何はともあれ at any rate, at least [な]には・と]もあれ]; 何事も everything [なにごとも]; 何時 what time [な]んじ]; 何日 what day [な]んにち]; 幾何学 geometry [きか]がく]

SG-0047 河	Meanings	Kun and On	Romaji	Bushu	Stroke Order and Number
	river	かわ カ	kawa *ka*	水	氵 汀 沔 河 河 8

河 **B** F-0652

甲骨文 金文 説文
1 2 3

In 1, a pair of bent twigs was used for the sound *ka*. 2 and 3 comprised "flowing water," and 可, replacing the bent twigs for the sound *ka*. The character was originally used in the name of a specific river (黄河). The kanji 河 means "river." <氵可>

河 river [かわ]]; 河口 river mouth, estuary [かこう]; 大河 great river [た]いが]; 河川 river, watercourse [か]せん]; 運河 canal, waterway [う]んが]; 河岸 riverbank [かがん]

SG-0048 荷	Meanings	Kun and On	Romaji	Bushu	Stroke Order and Number
	load, burden, luggage	に カ	ni *ka*	艸	艹 芢 茾 荷 荷 10

荷 **B** F-1025

説文

The seal-style form comprised "plants" (艸, 艹 bushu *kusakanmuri*), and 何 **SG-0046**, used for the sound *ka*, and originally signified "a lotus leaf." A large lotus leaf rested on the water's surface. After 何 had lost its original meaning of "to carry over the shoulder," a new character was appropriated to fill the void—荷. The kanji 荷 means "load, burden, luggage." <艹亻可>

荷 load, burden, freight [に]]; 荷造りする to pack up [にづ]くりする]; 重荷 heavy burden [おもに]; 荷物 baggage, load, shipment [に]もつ]; 手荷物 carry-on baggage, hand luggage [てに]もつ]; 積み荷 cargo, freight, load [つみに]; 出荷する to ship out merchandise [しゅっかする]; 負荷 burden, load [ふ]か]

SG-0049 苛	Meanings	Kun and On	Romaji	Bushu	Stroke Order and Number
	caustic, hard, cruel, irritating	カ	*ka*	艸	艹 芀 苦 苛 8

苛 **D** F-2433

金文 説文
1 2

1 and 2 comprised short grass or plants (艸, 艹), used to mean "rampantly growing, crude," and 可 **SG-0045** for the sound *ka* to mean "crude, hard; friction." The kanji 苛 means "caustic, hard, cruel, irritating." <艹可>

苛酷な extremely hard, severe [かこくな]; 苛烈な relentless, severe [かれつな]; 苛性ソーダ caustic soda, sodium hydroxide [かせいソ]ーダ]

3 Ear

3a 耳 "ear; to hear, listen" [from an ear] 耳聞聖聴恥摂

	Meanings	Kun and On	Romaji	Bushu	Stroke Order and Number
SG-0050 耳	ear, hearing	みみ ジ	mimi *ji*	耳	一丅F耳 · 丅丌丌月耳耳 6

耳 **A** F-0617

甲骨文 1 金文 1 2 金文 2 3 説文 4 耳

1, 2, 3, and 4 was an image of a person's ear, signifying "ear" and "hearing." The kanji 耳 means "ear, hearing." <耳>

耳 ear [みみ]; 耳学問 learning by listening [みみがくもん]; 耳鳴り ringing in the ears [みみなり]; 耳にする to hear information or rumors [みみにする]; 耳を疑う cannot believe what one heard [みみをうたがう]; 中耳炎 middle-ear inflammation [ちゅうじえん]; 耳鼻科 ear and nose doctor [じびか]

	Meanings	Kun and On	Romaji	Bushu	Stroke Order and Number
SG-0051 聞	to listen to, inquire, hear	き-く ブン・モン	ki-ku *bun, mon*	耳	丨 門 門 門 門 門 聞 聞 14

聞 **A** F-0263

甲骨文 1 1 甲骨文 2 2 金文 3 説文 4 聞

1 and 2 depicted "a person on their knees listening intently with their oversized ears to the words of a deity, and speaking back." The character was pronounced *mon/bun*, and signified "to listen, inquire." 3 had the same elements. 4, however, had a very different construction—"closed double doors" (門 **SG-1251**), signifying "something unknown behind closed doors," and "an ear" (耳 **SG-0050**), with no speaking element. It meant "to listen to what was being said and ask questions." The kanji 聞 means "to listen to, inquire, hear." <門耳>

(Note: Other kanji which contain 門, bushu *mongamae*, are discussed from **SG-1251** through **SG-1264**.)

聞く to hear, listen, ask [きく]; 聞き耳を立てる to strain one's ear [ききみみをたてる]; 聞き流す to brush aside, dismiss [ききながす]; 聞き捨てならない not to be excused, unpardonable [ききずてならない]; 新聞 newspaper [しんぶん]; 見聞 experience, observation [けんぶん]; 風聞 talk, hearsay [ふうぶん]; 前代未聞 unprecedented, unparalleled [ぜんだい・みもん]

	Meanings	Kun and On	Romaji	Bushu	Stroke Order and Number
SG-0052 聖	sage, saint, sacred	セイ	*see*	耳	耳 耳口 聖 聖 聖 聖 13

聖 **B** F-0720

甲骨文 1 金文 2 説文 3 聖

1 comprised "a standing person with an oversized ear listening attentively" (耳 **SG-0050**), and "a mouth, speaking" (口 **SG-0031**) behind them. 2 had the same elements, except that the person's leg had a short line to indicate that they were standing (壬, 王 in kanji) on their toes to catch the words of a faraway deity. Someone who could hear a deity's words and give advice to people was "a revered sage or saint." In 3, the ear got separated from the body. The kanji 聖 means "sage, saint, sacred." <耳口王>

聖人 saint [せいじん, せいじん]; 神聖な sacred [しんせいな]; 聖域 consecrated ground [せいいき]; 聖職 priesthood [せいしょく]; 聖書 the Bible [せいしょ]; 聖典 sacred book [せいてん]; 大聖堂 cathedral [だいせいどう]; 聖火リレー the Olympic Torch Relay [せいかリレー] // 聖徳太子 Prince Shotoku [しょうとくたいし]

	Meanings	Kun and On	Romaji	Bushu	Stroke Order and Number
SG-0053 聴	to listen carefully	き-く チョウ	ki-ku *choo*	耳	丅 F 耳 耳 聴 聴 聴 17

聴 **B** F-0882

甲骨文 1 金文 1 2 金文 2 3 説文 4 旧字 5 聽 聴

1 and 2 comprised a very large ear and one or two vessels or mouths. They meant "to listen to what is said." In 3 and 4, "a standing person" (indicated by the mark on the shin) was added, and in 4, 直 **SG-0007** "straight eyes" and 心 **SG-0187** "a heart" were added on the right side. Taking these components together, a person with a heart and an extraordinary ability for listening (to a deity's) words signified "straining one's ears to listen carefully." The kanji 聴 means "to listen carefully." <耳 𢖻 心>

聴く to listen to [きく]; 聴衆 audience, listeners [ちょうしゅう]; 傾聴する to listen attentively [けいちょうする]; 聴覚 auditory sense [ちょうかく]; 聴力 hearing ability [ちょうりょく]; 視聴者 TV program viewer [しちょうしゃ]; 聴解 listening comprehension [ちょうかい]; ご静聴ありがとうございました Thank you for listening [ごせいちょう・ありがとうございました]

	Meanings	Kun and On	Romaji	Bushu	Stroke Order and Number
SG-0054 恥	to be embarrassed; shame	はじ・は-ずかしい チ	haji, ha-zukashii *chi*	心	10

恥 **C** F-1448

説文

The seal-style form comprised "an ear" (耳 **SG-0050**) and "a heart" (心 **SG-0187**). When embarrassed, one's ears become red and give away their feelings. The kanji 恥 means "to be embarrassed; shame." <耳心>

恥 shame [はじ˥]; 恥をかく to embarrass oneself, disgrace oneself [はじ˥をかく]; 恥ずかしい to feel embarrassed, be ashamed [はずかし˥い]; 羞恥心 sense of shame [しゅうち˥しん]; 破廉恥な shameless, disgraceful [はれ˥んちな]

	Meanings	Kun and On	Romaji	Bushu	Stroke Order and Number
SG-0055 摂	to take charge; proxy, regency	セツ	*setsu*	手	13

摂 **D** F-1738

説文 1 旧字 2

1 comprised "an act done by hand" (扌), and "three ears" (耳 **SG-0050**), used for the sound *setsu* to mean "to collect and manage," together signifying "to take charge." A person who took charge of someone's business was a "proxy or regent." With two of the ears reduced to ⺍, the kanji 摂 means "to take charge; proxy, regency." <扌耳⺍>

摂生する to carefully mind one's health [せっせいする]; 不摂生な careless about one's health [ふせ˥っせいな]; 摂取する to take in, ingest [せ˥っしゅする, せっしゅする]; 摂政 regency, regent [せ˥っしょう]; 摂理 Providence [せ˥つり]

3b 取 "to take, grab" [from a hand grabbing a person by the ear] 取最撮

	Meanings	Kun and On	Romaji	Bushu	Stroke Order and Number
SG-0056 取	to take, grab	と-る シュ	to-ru *shu*	又	8

取 **A** F-0109

甲骨文 1 金文1 2 金文2 3 説文 4

1, 2, 3, and 4 comprised "an ear" 耳 **SG-0050** and "a hand" 又 **SG-0084**. One view explains that grabbing a person or an animal by the ear would give one a better grip, hence the meaning "to grab." Another view says that in battle, an enemy's ear was cut off as proof of one's feat and was placed on an altar in a victory ceremony. The kanji 取 means "to grab, take." <耳又>

取る to take, grab [と˥る]; 取り上げる to pick up, confiscate [とりあげる]; 取り下げる to withdraw, discontinue [とりさげる]; 聞き取りテスト listening comprehension test [ききとりテ˥スト]; 取引 transaction [とり˥ひき]; 先取りする to take in advance, preempt, anticipate [さきどりする]; 取り止める to cancel, call off, withdraw [とりやめる, とりやめ˥る]; 取得する to obtain, acquire [しゅとくする]

	Meanings	Kun and On	Romaji	Bushu	Stroke Order and Number
SG-0057 最	the most, utmost	もっと-も サイ	motto-mo *sai*	曰	12

最 **A** F-0115

説文

The seal-style form comprised "a warrior's helmet" (冃, 曰), signifying "to attack," and "a hand grabbing an ear" (取). Taking the ear of an enemy in battle was a great feat, which gave the meaning "the most, utmost." Another view takes it to be a borrowing. The kanji 最 means "the most, utmost." <曰取>

最も the most [もっと˥も]; 最終 final, the last [さいしゅう]; 最近 of late, recently, these days [さいきん]; 最たるもの the prime example, the most conspicuous item [さ˥いたるもの]; 最優先 top priority [さいゆ˥うせん]; 最盛期 the height of prosperity, the best of times [さいせ˥いき] // 最寄りの the nearest, nearby [もよりの]

	Meanings	Kun and On	Romaji	Bushu	Stroke Order and Number
SG-0058 撮	to take (a photo), pluck	と-る サツ	to-ru *satsu*	手	15

撮 **C** F-1198

説文

The seal-style form comprised "an act done by hand" (扌), and 最 **SG-0057**, used for the sound *satsu* to mean "attack, grab." Together they originally signified "to pluck something by hand," and in modern times this meaning has become used to describe the action of taking a photo. The kanji 撮 means "to take (a photo), pluck." <扌最>

写真を撮る to take a photo [しゃしんをと˥る]; 撮影 shooting, filming [さつえい]; 盗撮 taking a photo without the subject knowing [とうさつ]

4 Nose

4 自 "nose, face, oneself" [from a nose on a face] 自面息鼻臭嗅憩

	Meanings	Kun and On	Romaji	Bushu	Stroke Order and Number
SG-0059 自	oneself; starting from, of itself	みずか-ら ジ・シ	mizuka-ra *ji, shi*	自	丨冂冃自 6

自 **A** F-0048

甲骨文 1 金文 2 説文 3

1, 2, and 3 depicted "a nose on a person's face," viewed from the front. The nose is the center of one's face, and the character meant "oneself." A newborn baby's life starts from breathing through the nose, whence "starting from." Breathing is instinctive, whence "of itself." The kanji 自 means "oneself; starting from, of itself." <自>

自ら oneself, personally [み↴ずから]; 自分 oneself [じぶん]; 自由 liberty, freedom [じゆ↴う]; 自立 independence, self-supportive [じりつ]; 自他ともに to everyone's eyes, apparently [じ↴た・ともに]; 自決する to determine for oneself, commit suicide [じけつする]; 自発的 spontaneous, voluntary [じはつてき]; 自然 nature [しぜん] // 自ずと spontaneously, by itself [おのずと]

	Meanings	Kun and On	Romaji	Bushu	Stroke Order and Number
SG-0060 面	face, mask, phase, side	おも・おもて・つら メン	omo, omote, tsura *men*	面	一丆丙而而面 9

面 **A** F-0208

甲骨文 1 説文 2

1 depicted "an eye" with an outline all around it, signifying "a face." 2 depicted a face with a nose in the middle, framed in a square shape. A mask is something that one puts over the face, so that all that is shown is "a phase or side of something." The kanji 面 means "face, mask, phase, side." <一囗自>

面白い interesting [おもしろ↴い]; 面 face [おもて↴]; mask, aspect, side [めん]; 面当て out of spite [つらあて]; 上っ面 exterior, surface [うわっつら]; 仮面 mask [かめん]; 面食らう to be bewildered, be taken aback [めんくら↴う]; 面倒な troublesome, tiresome [めんど↴うな]; 面会 interview, meeting [めんかい]; 面談 interview [めんだん]

	Meanings	Kun and On	Romaji	Bushu	Stroke Order and Number
SG-0061 息	breath, living, son; to multiply	いき ソク	iki *soku*	心	丿白自息息 10

息 **B** F-0669

説文

The seal-style form comprised 自 **SG-0059** "a nose," and 心 **SG-0187** "a heart." One's heartbeat is linked with breathing through the nose, whence the meaning "breath." Breathing sustains a living creature, whence "living." A living animal proliferates, whence "to increase or multiply," including in the sense of one's "son." The kanji 息 means "breath, living, son; multiply." <自心>

息をする to breathe [い↴きをする]; ため息をつく to sigh [ためい↴きを・つ↴く]; 消息 news about a person, whereabouts [しょうそく]; 休息する to rest, take a break [きゅうそくする]; 利息 interest [りそく]; 子息 someone's son (honorific) [し↴そく] // 息子 son [むすこ]; 息吹 breath, vitality [い↴ぶき]

	Meanings	Kun and On	Romaji	Bushu	Stroke Order and Number
SG-0062 鼻	nose	はな ビ	hana *bi*	鼻	白自畠畠畠鼻鼻 14

鼻 **C** F-1177

説文

The seal-style form comprised 自 **SG-0059** "a nose," and 畀, used for the sound *bi* to mean "something protruding." The feature of a face that protrudes is "a nose." The kanji 鼻 means "nose." <自田廾>

鼻 nose [はな]; 鼻が高い to be proud; long-nosed [はながたか↴い]; 出鼻を挫かれる to be baffled at the onset [でばなをくじかれ↴る]; 鼻をつまむ to hold one's nose [はなをつまむ]; 鼻をかむ blow one's nose [はなをかむ]; 鼻炎 rhinitis [びえん]

	Meanings	Kun and On	Romaji	Bushu	Stroke Order and Number
SG-0063 臭	an unpleasant smell; to stink; suspicious	くさ-い・にお-う シュウ	kusa-i, nio-u *shuu*	自	白自皀臭臭 9

臭 **C** F-1520

甲骨文 1 1 甲骨文 2 2 説文 3 旧字 4

1, 2, and 3 comprised "a nose" and "a dog." A dog has a sharp sense of smell, whence the meaning "smell." The meaning of ill-smelling also gave rise to "suspicious." 犬 was replaced by 大. The kanji 臭 means "an unpleasant smell; to stink; suspicious." <自大>

臭い smell, odor [くさ↴い]; 生臭い fishy, smell of blood [なまぐさ↴い]; 臭う to stink [にお↴う]; 臭気 odor [しゅ↴うき]; 異臭を放つ to give off a stench [いしゅうをはな↴つ]; 口臭 foul breath, mouth odor [こうしゅう]; 消臭剤 air freshener, deodorant [しょうしゅ↴うざい]; 面倒臭い extremely tiresome [めんどうくさ↴い]

	Meanings	Kun and On	Romaji	Bushu	Stroke Order and Number
SG-0064 嗅	to smell, sniff	か-ぐ キュウ	ka-gu *kyuu*	口	口 口 口自 口自 口臯 嗅 嗅 13

嗅 **D** F-2724

嗅 篆文

The seal-style form comprised 鼻 "nose" and 臭 "smell." In the shinji 嗅, 鼻 was replaced by 口. Unlike 臭 **SG-0063**, the kanji 嗅 retains 犬. The kanji 嗅 is used for the verb "to smell, sniff." <口自犬>

臭いを嗅ぐ to smell [におꜜいを・かぐ]; 嗅ぎ出す to sniff out [かぎだꜜす]; 嗅ぎ回る to nose about, snoop around [かぎまわꜜる]; 嗅覚 the sense of smell [きゅꜜうかく]

	Meanings	Kun and On	Romaji	Bushu	Stroke Order and Number
SG-0065 憩	to repose, rest	いこ-い ケイ	iko-i *kee*	心	ノ 二 千 舌 舌' 舌自 憩 16

憩 **D** F-1800

愒 憩
篆文 1 正字 2

The origin of the kanji 憩 is obscure. 1 and 2 comprised "a heart," and 曷, used for the sound *kee* to mean "to relax." 2 in orthographic style was replaced by 憩 in the kanji, which comprised 舌 **SG-0040** "a tongue," 自 **SG-0059** "a nose," and 心 **SG-0187** "a heart." Activities connected to these components, such as "eating food," "taking deep breaths," and "feeling rested," led to the meaning "to rest." The kanji 憩 means "to repose, rest." <舌自心>

憩う to rest, repose [いこꜜう]; 憩い quiet relaxation [いこい]; 休憩 rest, break, time off [きゅうけい]; 休憩室 lounge, tearoom [きゅうけꜜいしつ]

5 Head and neck

5a 首 "head, chief, neck" [from a face with hair] 首道導

	Meanings	Kun and On	Romaji	Bushu	Stroke Order and Number
SG-0066 首	head, chief, neck	くび シュ	kubi *shu*	首	` `` 䒑 𦣻 首 9

首 **A** F-0128

首
甲骨文 1 金文1 2 金文2 3 金文3 4 説文 5

1, 2, and 3 depicted "an outline of a face with an eye and hair," whereas 4 and 5 had a face with a nose and hair. (A face was represented by an eye or a nose in many characters.) The character meant "head" and came to be used to mean "the head of an organization," and "the neck" as a part of the head. The kanji 首 means "head, chief, neck." <䒑自>

首 neck [くび]; 首輪 necklace, collar [くびわ]; 首になる to get fired, get sacked [くびになꜜる]; 首都 capital, metropolis [しゅꜜと]; 自首する to surrender oneself to the police [じしゅする]; 首都高速 the Tokyo Metropolitan Expressway [しゅとこꜜうそく]; 党首 head of a political party [とꜜうしゅ]

	Meanings	Kun and On	Romaji	Bushu	Stroke Order and Number
SG-0067 道	road, way	みち ドウ・トウ	michi *doo, too*	辵	䒑 𦣻 首 `首 ⺡首 道 12

道 **A** F-0079

道
金文1 1 金文2 2 侯馬盟書 3 説文 4

1, 2, and 3 comprised "a head" (首) inside "a crossroads" (彳 or 行), with "a footprint" (止) in 1 and 3, or "a hand" (又), showing "the way to go," in 2. Taken together, these components meant "a way, road." In 4, 彳 and 止 were aligned vertically and became 辵, which then became ⻌, bushu *shinnyuu* "to move forward," in the kanji. The kanji 道 means "road, way." <首⻌>

道 road, way [みち]; 近道 shortcut [ちかꜜみち]; 道草を食う to loiter on the way, waste time [みちくさをくꜜう]; 道路 road [どꜜうろ]; 歩道 pedestrian walkway, sidewalk [ほどう]; 道理で it is no wonder, indeed [どうりꜜで]; 書道 calligraphy, the art of writing with brush and ink [しょꜜどう]; 東海道 the Tokaido Highway [とうかꜜいどう]; 神道 Shinto [しꜜんとう]

	Meanings	Kun and On	Romaji	Bushu	Stroke Order and Number
SG-0068 導	to lead the way, guide	みちび-く ドウ	michibi-ku *doo*	寸	䒑 𦣻 首 ⺡首 道 導 導 15

導 **B** F-0563

導
金文 1 説文 2

1 comprised the same components as 2 for 道 **SG-0067** ("a crossroads, a head, and a hand"), and had the sound *doo*. In 2, a footprint was added to form 辵 (⻌). "A hand" (寸) at the bottom signified "to guide." Together, these components meant "a hand guiding the way forward" (導). The kanji 導 means "to lead the way, guide." <首⻌寸>
(Note: When two kanji shared the same early forms, such as 道 and 導, the earlier one generally had a broader meaning, with other components added later to avoid ambiguity.)

導く to lead the way [みちびꜜく]; 指導する to guide, teach someone [しどうする]; 指導者 leader [しどꜜうしゃ]; 導入する to introduce or bring in something new [どうにゅうする]; 先導的な leading [せんどうてきな]; 半導体 semiconductor [はんどうたい]

5b 亢 "straight" [from a straight line of one's long neck]; *koo* 航抗坑 

	Meanings	*Kun* and *On*	Romaji	Bushu	Stroke Order and Number
SG-0069 航	to navigate, sail	コウ	*koo*	舟	丿 介 舟 舟' 舟' 航 10

航 **B** F-0916

 航

篆文

The seal-style form comprised 方 **SG-1931**, one meaning of which was "a boat, vessel," and 亢 "straight," used for the sound *koo*. Together they depicted a ship moving in a straight line, thus signifying "navigation, to sail." In the kanji, 方 was replaced by 舟 **SG-2015** "boat, ship." In modern times, this character is also used to mean air navigation. The kanji 航 means "to navigate, sail." <舟亢>

航空会社 airline company [こうくうがいしゃ]; 航空便 airmail, air freight [こうくうびん]; 航海 voyage, journey by sea [こうかい]; 航路 sea route, flying route [こうろ]; 欠航 cancellation of a ferry or plane service [けっこう]; 航空写真 aerial photograph [こうくうしゃしん]

	Meanings	*Kun* and *On*	Romaji	Bushu	Stroke Order and Number
SG-0070 抗	to resist, struggle, defy	コウ	*koo*	手	一 寸 扌 扩 抗 7

抗 **B** F-1011

 抗

說文 1 說文或体 2

The left side in 1 was "a hand" (扌, bushu *tehen*), whereas in 2 it was 木 **SG-0608** "wood." The right side was 亢 "straight," used for the sound *koo*. In protesting or resisting, one puts out a hand and elongates the neck. The kanji 抗 means "to resist, struggle, defy." <扌亢> (Note: 2 became the non-Joyo kanji 杭 "stake" *kui*.)

抵抗する to resist, hold out against [ていこうする]; 抗体 antibody [こうたい]; 抗議 protest [こうぎ]; 対抗する to confront, rival, antagonize [たいこうする]; 抗菌グッズ antibacterial products [こうきんグッズ]; 反抗期 rebellious phase [はんこうき]; 拮抗 evenly matched rivalry [きっこう] // 抗う to resist, protest [あらがう]

	Meanings	*Kun* and *On*	Romaji	Bushu	Stroke Order and Number
SG-0071 坑	mine, pit	コウ	*koo*	土	一 十 土' 圹 坑 7

坑 **D** F-2015

 坑

篆文

The seal-style form comprised "tall hills, mountains," and 亢 "straight down," used for the sound *koo*. Dropping straight down from a high place gave the meaning "pit, hole, mine." In the kanji, 土 bushu *tsuchihen* "dirt, soil, ground," replaced the left side. The kanji 坑 means "mine, pit." <土亢>

炭坑 coal pit [たんこう]; 坑道 gallery, underground tunnel [こうどう]; 廃坑 disused mine, abandoned mine [はいこう]

6 Hand

6a 手 "hand" [from an open palm with five fingers showing] 手失尺 

	Meanings	*Kun* and *On*	Romaji	Bushu	Stroke Order and Number
SG-0072 手	hand, person with a skill; to work, obtain	て・た シュ	te, ta *shu*	手	一 二 三 手 4

手 **A** F-0029

 手

金文 1 說文 2

Both 1 and 2 depicted five fingers, an open palm, and a wrist. The kanji 手 means "hand, person with a skill; to work, obtain." When a hand appears on the left side of a kanji, it becomes 扌, bushu *tehen,* to mean "an act done by hand." <手>

手 hand [て]; やり手 an enterprising man [やりて]; 手に入れる to obtain [てにいれる]; 大手 leading company [おおて]; 手間 working time, effort [てま]; 手繰る to haul in, trace [たぐる]; 下手な unskillful [へたな]; 手法 method [しゅほう]; 運転手 driver [うんてんしゅ]; 選手 participating athlete, player [せんしゅ] // 上手な skillful [じょうずな]

	Meanings	*Kun* and *On*	Romaji	Bushu	Stroke Order and Number
SG-0073 失	to lose; loss	うしな-う シツ	ushina-u *shitsu*	大	ノ ㇒ 二 牛 失 5

失 **A** F-0417

 失

說文

The seal-style form was "a hand," with a contour line at the bottom right to signify that something was slipping out of the hand. The kanji 失 means "to lose; loss." <𠂉人>

失う to lose [うしなう]; 見失う to lose sight of, miss [みうしなう]; 失敗 failure [しっぱい]; 失明 loss of eyesight [しつめい]; 失望 disappointment [しつぼう]; 損失 loss [そんしつ]; 失神する to faint, lose consciousness [しっしんする]; 過失 mistake, blunder, negligence [かしつ]

	Meanings	Kun and On	Romaji	Bushu	Stroke Order and Number
SG-0074 尺	*shaku*, (old unit of measurement approximately 30 cm in length)	シャク	*shaku*	尸	フコ尸尺 4

尺 **C** F-1539 説文

The seal-style form has been explained as a thumb and a middle finger being stretched into a 又-like shape to measure a handbreadth. A handbreadth was used to measure short lengths. In Japan, 尺 was an old unit of length, equivalent to approximately 30 cm, one foot, or ten *sun* (寸 **SG-0112**). <尸㇏>

尺 *shaku* [しゃく]; 尺度 measure, scale [しゃくど]; 巻尺 tape measure [まきじゃく]; 尺貫法 old system of measuring length and weight [しゃっかんほう]; 縮尺 reduced scale [しゅくしゃく]

6b 扌 "an act done by hand"; bushu *tehen* 押捜拝揺把揷拐挨撈

	Meanings	Kun and On	Romaji	Bushu	Stroke Order and Number
SG-0075 押	to push, press, force; seal/insignia	お-す オウ	o-su *oo*	手	一十扌扣扣押押 8

押 **B** F-0820

No ancient form. The kanji 押 comprises 扌 "an act done by hand," and 甲 **SG-1042**, used for the sound *oo* to mean "to press," together signifying "pressing something firmly." The kanji 押 means "to push, press, force; seal/insignia." <扌甲>

押す to push [おす]; 押さえる to hold down [おさえる]; 手押し hand-driven, pushed by hand [ておし]; 押し入る to force one's way into, burglarize [おしいる]; 押し付ける to press against, force on [おしつける]; 押入れ deep cupboard built into the wall inside a Japanese house [おしいれ]; 押収 confiscation [おうしゅう]; 押印 affixing one's seal [おういん]

	Meanings	Kun and On	Romaji	Bushu	Stroke Order and Number
SG-0076 捜	to search, look for	さが-す ソウ	saga-su *soo*	手	一十扌扣押押捜 10

捜 **C** F-1109 説文 1 旧字 2

1 comprised 扌 "an act done by hand" on the left side, and "a house" (宀), "a fire" (火), and "a hand" (又), for the sound *soo*, on the right side. Together they signified searching for a fire or a light inside a house. In the kyuji 搜 (2), 叟 alone contained three hands ("a pair of hands" holding something between them, and an additional hand 又), so altogether the character depicted as many as four hands. The kanji 捜 means "to search, look for." <扌由又>

捜す to search for, look for [さがす]; 探し出す to find out, track down [さがしだす]; 捜索 manhunt, search [そうさく]; 捜査 criminal investigation [そうさ]; 科学捜査 scientific crime detection [かがくそうさ]

	Meanings	Kun and On	Romaji	Bushu	Stroke Order and Number
SG-0077 拝	to worship, revere; affix for humble forms	おが-む ハイ	oga-mu *hai*	手	一十扌扌扌拝拝 8

拝 **C** F-1241 金文 1 説文 2 説文或体 3 旧字 4

1, 2, and 3 depicted "a plant with many flowers on many branches," used for its sound *hai*, and "a hand." When picking flowers, one bent the body as if bowing, meaning "to worship, revere." In the kanji, the shape was reduced to 拝. The kanji 拝 also appears often as an affix in humble verb forms . The kanji 拝 means "to worship, revere; affix for humble forms." <扌一丰>

拝む to press the hands together, worship, beg for [おがむ]; 拝み倒す to persuade by pleading [おがみたおす]; 礼拝 church service [れいはい]; 拝見する to look at (humble) [はいけんする]; 拝読する to read (humble) [はいどくする]; 拝借する to borrow (humble) [はいしゃくする]

	Meanings	Kun and On	Romaji	Bushu	Stroke Order and Number
SG-0078 揺	to sway, jolt, agitate	ゆ-れる ヨウ	yu-reru *yoo*	手	一十扌扌揺揺揺 12

揺 **C** F-1228 説文 1 旧字 2

1 comprised 扌 bushu *tehen* "an act done by hand," and 䍃, used for the sound *yoo* to mean "to move far away," together signifying "to sway something by hand." The kanji replaced 月 in 䍃 with "fingers from above" (爫). The kanji 揺 means "to sway, jolt, agitate." <扌爫缶>

揺れる to shake, sway [ゆれる]; 揺さぶる to shake, jolt [ゆさぶる]; 横揺れ roll, shake horizontally [よこゆれ]; 動揺する to tremble, stir, feel agitated [どうようする]

	Meanings	Kun and On	Romaji	Bushu	Stroke Order and Number
SG-0079 把	to grip, hold on; handful of	ハ	*ha*	手	一 十 扌 扌 把 把 把 7

把 **D** F-1666

説文

The seal-style form comprised 扌 "an act done by hand," and "a handle with a handgrip," used for the sound *ha*. A hand holding a handgrip meant "to grip, grasp." It was also used as a counter for bundled things, and meant "a handful." The kanji 把 means "to grip, hold on, a handful of." <扌巴>

把握する to grasp, really understand [はあくする]; 大雑把に roughly, loosely [おおざっぱに]

	Meanings	Kun and On	Romaji	Bushu	Stroke Order and Number
SG-0080 挿	to insert, stick something into	さ-す ソウ	sa-su *soo*	手	一 十 扌 扌 挿 挿 挿 10

挿 **D** F-1936

篆文 1 旧字 2

1 comprised bushu *tehen* (扌), and "a pestle in a mortar," used for the sound *soo* to mean "to insert, put in," together signifying "two hands inserting something." When the kyuji 插 (2) became the shinji 挿, the center line became longer. The kanji 挿 means "to insert, stick in." <扌二申>

挿す to insert [さす]; 挿絵 cut, illustration [さしえ]; 一輪挿し vase for a single flower [いちりんざし]; 挿入 insertion, interposition [そうにゅう]

	Meanings	Kun and On	Romaji	Bushu	Stroke Order and Number
SG-0081 拐	to deceive, kidnap	カイ	*kai*	手	一 十 扌 扌 拐 拐 8

拐 **D** F-2005

No ancient form. The kanji 拐 comprises 扌 bushu *tehen*, and 另 on the right side, used for the sound *kai* to mean "to catch, hitch on." Hitching something by hand gave the kanji 拐 the meaning "to deceive, kidnap." <扌口刀>

誘拐 abduction [ゆうかい]

	Meanings	Kun and On	Romaji	Bushu	Stroke Order and Number
SG-0082 挨	(to push)	アイ	*ai*	手	一 十 扌 挨 挨 10

挨 **D** F-2473

篆文

The right side of the seal-style form was used for the sound *ai* to mean "to strike someone from behind." With 扌 bushu *tehen* "an act done by hand," it may originally have meant "to push." This character is only used in the word 挨拶, "greeting." <扌ム矢>

挨拶 greeting [あいさつ]

	Meanings	Kun and On	Romaji	Bushu	Stroke Order and Number
SG-0083 拶	to bow	サツ	*satsu*	手	一 十 扌 拶 拶 9

拶 **D** F-2309

No ancient form. The origin of the kanji 拶 is unclear. The right side appears to have come from "a skull with hair attached." Together with 扌 bushu *tehen*, it meant "to pick up something." This kanji also meant "to push from behind," perhaps to make something bow. In Japanese, it is only used with 挨 in 挨拶, "greeting." <扌巛夕>

挨拶 greeting [あいさつ]

6c 又 "hand" [from a hand viewed from the side] 又友収

	Meanings	Kun and On	Romaji	Bushu	Stroke Order and Number
SG-0084 又	also, or, again	また	mata	又	フ 又 2

又 **A** F-1336

甲骨文 1 金文 2 説文 3

1, 2, and 3 depicted "a right hand with fingers showing." (In 2, "a thumb" was recognizable.) The character originally meant "a right hand" but came to mean "also, in addition to." For the original meaning of "right hand," the new kanji 右 **SG-0102** was created. The kanji 又 means "also, or, again." <又>

又 also, in addition to, again [また]; 又貸し sublease [またがし]; 又は or, alternatively [または]; 又聞き hearsay, secondhand information [またぎき]; 又の名 another name, alias [またのな]; 又従兄弟 second cousin [またいとこ]; 又しても yet again [またしても]; 又とない unique, matchless [またとない]

	Meanings	Kun and On	Romaji	Bushu	Stroke Order and Number
SG-0085 友	friend	とも ユウ	tomo *yuu*	又	一ナ方友 4

友 **A** F-0247

甲骨文 1　金文 1 2　金文 2 3　金文盟書 1 4　金文盟書 2 5　説文 6

1, 2, 3, 4, 5, and 6 all depicted "two right hands side by side," signifying two people giving each other a helping hand. In 4 and 5, 曰 "to say" signified a pledge of mutual help. The kanji 友 means "friend." <ナ又>
(Note: The two kanji 曰 and 日 are not to be confused: the non-Joyo kanji 曰 "to say" (as in the word *iwaku*) is wider in appearance than 日 "sun.")

友達 friend [ともだち]; 親友 close friend, best friend [しんゆう]; 友好国 ally country [ゆうこうこく]; 旧友 old friend [きゅうゆう]; 友情 friendship [ゆうじょう]; 友愛 friendship, fraternity [ゆうあい]

	Meanings	Kun and On	Romaji	Bushu	Stroke Order and Number
SG-0086 収	to collect, obtain, assemble, accept	おさ-める シュウ	osa-meru *shuu*	攴	丨丩屮収 4

収 **A** F-0413

説文 1　旧字 2

1 comprised "two strings twisted and pulled," and 攴 "a hand holding a stick or tool," for the meaning of "to cause something to happen." Pulling things together into one meant "to collect in one place, obtain, store." In the kyuji 收 (2) the left side became 丩, and "a hand holding a stick" (攴) coalesced into 攵, which later reverted to just a hand (又) in the shinji. The kanji 収 means "to collect, obtain, assemble, accept." <丩又>

収める to obtain (results), assemble [おさめる]; 収入 income [しゅうにゅう]; 領収書 receipt [りょうしゅうしょ]; 収集 collection [しゅうしゅう]; 回収 recovery, retrieval [かいしゅう]; 月収 monthly income [げっしゅう]; 国際収支 balance of international payments [こくさいしゅうし]; 収容する to accommodate, admit, detain, intern [しゅうようする]

6d 反 "to push back, turn back"; *han/hen* 反返坂阪板仮販

	Meanings	Kun and On	Romaji	Bushu	Stroke Order and Number
SG-0087 反	to turn back, push back, warp	そ-る ハン・ホン・タン	so-ru *han, hon, tan*	又	一厂万反 4

反 **A** F-0205

甲骨文 1　金文 1 2　金文 2 3　説文 4

For 1, 2, 3, and 4, there are various accounts of the combined meaning of 厂 and 又: (a) a piece of hanging cloth being pushed back by a hand; (b) a cliff which someone is trying to climb up; and (c) a thin, warped wooden board being pushed back by hand. The kanji 反 means "to turn back, push back, warp." <厂又>

反る to bend, warp [そる]; 反り返る to curl up [そりかえる]; 反対 opposition [はんたい]; 造反 rebellion [ぞうはん]; 反語 irony, rhetorical question [はんご]; 反動 reaction [はんどう]; 反感 antipathy, ill feeling [はんかん]; 謀反を起こす to rebel [むほんを・おこす]; 反物 fabric for making kimono [たんもの]

	Meanings	Kun and On	Romaji	Bushu	Stroke Order and Number
SG-0088 返	to reverse, turn back, return, flip back	かえ-す ヘン	kae-su *hen*	辵	一厂反反汳返 7

返 **A** F-0375

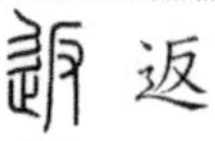

説文

The seal-style form comprised "a crossroads" and "a footprint," forming 辵 (辶,bushu *shinnyuu/shinnyoo* "to move forward"); and 反 **SG-0087** "to return," used for the sound *hen*. Taken together, these components signified "going and coming back" and "to flip back." The kanji 返 means "to reverse, turn back, return, flip back."<反辶>

返す to return [かえす]; 繰り返す to repeat [くりかえす, くりかえす]; 取り返しのつかない there is no mending, can't be undone [とりかえしのつかない]; 見返りがある there is a reward/collateral [みかえりがある]; 仕返し an eye for an eye, retaliation in kind [しかえし]; 返事 response [へんじ]; 返金 repay, reimbursement [へんきん]; 返品 returned goods [へんぴん]

	Meanings	Kun and On	Romaji	Bushu	Stroke Order and Number
SG-0089 坂	slope, incline	さか ハン	saka *han*	土	一十圡圲坂坂 7

坂 **B** F-0712

金文

The bronzeware-style form represented "someone trying to climb steeply inclined ground using their hands." "Dirt" (土) at the bottom, an emphatic bulge on the slope, and 反 **SG-0087** used for the sound *han* together meant "to push back." The kanji 坂 means "slope, incline." <土反>

坂 slope, incline [さか]; 下り坂 downhill, decline [くだりざか]; 急な坂 [きゅうなさか] steep hill, 登坂車線 [とうはん, とはんしゃせん] climbing lane

SG-0090 阪	Meanings	Kun and On	Romaji	Bushu	Stroke Order and Number
	slope (used in names)	ハン	*han*	阜	７ ３ 阝 阝 阞 阪 阪 7

阪 **B** F-0647

金文 1 説文 2 阪

1 comprised "hills, mountains" (阝, bushu *kozatohen*), and 反, used for the sound *han* to mean "to push back," together signifying "a dirt slope." In Japanese, the kanji 坂, rather than 阪, is used to mean "slope, incline," and 阪 is only used in names, such as 大阪 and the surrounding region. <阝反>

阪神地方 the Osaka and Kobe area [はんしんちほう] // 大阪 Osaka [おおさか]

SG-0091 板	Meanings	Kun and On	Romaji	Bushu	Stroke Order and Number
	board, plate	いた ハン・バン	ita *han, ban*	木	十 木 木 朾 杤 板 8

板 **B** F-0741

甲骨文 1 金文 2 板

No direct reference to 1 or 2 is found in our reference sources, but the character is generally viewed as comprising a thin piece of wood (from 木 "wood") that has a tendency to warp (反). The kanji 板 means "board, plate." <木反>

板 board [いた]; トタン板 galvanized iron sheet [トタンいた]; 板ガラス sheet glass [いたガラス]; 立て板に水 having flowing eloquence [たていたにみず]; 合板 plywood [ごうはん]; 甲板 deck [かんぱん]; 血小板 blood platelet [けっしょうばん]; 回覧板 circular bulletin [かいらんばん]

SG-0092 仮	Meanings	Kun and On	Romaji	Bushu	Stroke Order and Number
	false, temporary	かり カ・ケ	kari *ka, ke*	人	亻 仮 仮 仮 6

仮 **B** F-0793

金文 1 説文 2 旧字 3 假 仮

In 1, "two hands" were "trying to uncover precious metal from a rock" (one view), or "removing a mask from the face" (another view). A mask hides one's true identity, whence "false." In 2, 亻 bushu *ninben* "an act that a person does" was added to 叚, used for the sound *ka*, which was replaced by 反 in the shinji. The kanji 仮 means "false, temporary." <亻反>

仮 temporary [かり]; 仮に as a makeshift, if [かりに]; 仮にも even a little, even for an instant [かりにも]; 仮説 hypothesis,supposition [かせつ]; 仮定する to suppose, assume, postulate [かていする]; 仮病 feigned illness, phony sickness [けびょう] // 仮名 Japanese phonetic letter (*hiragana* and *katakana*) [かな]; 振り仮名 phonetic guide for kanji [ふりがな]

SG-0093 販	Meanings	Kun and On	Romaji	Bushu	Stroke Order and Number
	to sell, trade	ハン	*han*	貝	冂 目 貝 貝 販 販 11

販 **B** F-0860

説文 販

The seal-style form comprised 貝 **SG-1693** "a cowrie, valuable," and 反 "to turn back," used for the sound *han*. Cowries were sometimes used as money. Together, these components meant selling goods in exchange for money. The kanji 販 means "to sell, trade." <貝反>

(Note: A large number of kanji that contain 貝 "cowrie, valuable" are discussed from 貝 **SG-1693** through 潰 **SG-1716**.)

販売 sale [はんばい]; 販売員 salesperson [はんばいいん]; 量販店 mass retailer [りょうはんてん]; 市販品 goods on the market [しはんひん]; 自販機・自動販売機 vending machine [じはんき, じどうはんばいき]; 再販制 resale system [さいはんせい]

6e 臤 "hard; to tighten"; *kin/ken* 緊賢堅

SG-0094 緊	Meanings	Kun and On	Romaji	Bushu	Stroke Order and Number
	to tighten, fasten; imminent	キン	*kin*	糸	丨 厂 戶 戶 臣 臤 竪 竪 緊 15

緊 **B** F-1008

説文 緊

The seal-style form comprised 臤 "hard," used for the sound *kin*, and 糸 **SG-1600** "a skein of threads." Pulling hard on a skein of threads or a rope to bring it closer signified "to tighten; imminent." The kanji 緊 means "to tighten, fasten; imminent." <臣又糸>

緊急の extremely urgent [きんきゅうの]; 緊張する to feel nervous and tense, be keyed up [きんちょうする]; 緊縮財政 reduced budget [きんしゅくざいせい]; 緊迫する to grow strained, become acute [きんぱくする]

SG-0095 賢	Meanings	Kun and On	Romaji	Bushu	Stroke Order and Number
	wise, sharp, shrewd	かしこ-い ケン	kashiko-i *ken*	貝	丨 厂 戶 臣 臤 臤 賢 賢 賢 16

賢 **C** F-1289

金文 1 説文 2 賢

1 and 2 comprised 臤 "hard," used for the sound *ken*, and 貝 **SG-1693** "a cowrie; valuable." A hard cowrie was good quality. Someone who owned valuable things such as solid cowries had good fortune and a sharp mind for business. The kanji 賢 means "wise, sharp, shrewd." <臤貝>

賢い wise, clever, smart [かしこい]; 悪賢い cunning, crafty [わるがしこい]; 賢明な wise, intelligent [けんめいな]; 賢者 wise man [けんじゃ]

	Meanings	Kun and On	Romaji	Bushu	Stroke Order and Number
SG-0096 堅	hard, firm, solid	かた-い ケン	kata-i *ken*	土	堅 12

堅 **C** F-1275

説文

The seal-style form of the kanji 堅 comprised 臤 "hard," used for the sound *ken*, and 土 **SG-1126** "dirt, ground." Taken together, "hard-packed soil" meant something solid and firm. The kanji 堅 means "hard, firm, solid." <臤土>

堅い solid, hard [かたい]; 堅苦しい stiff-mannered, formal [かたくるしい]; 堅物 straight-laced person [かたぶつ]; 堅実に steadfastly [けんじつに]; 中堅社員 reliable mid-level employee [ちゅうけんしゃいん]; 堅固な strong, solid [けんごな]

6f 叔 "little, small, good"; *toku/jaku/shuku/seki* 督寂叔淑戚

	Meanings	Kun and On	Romaji	Bushu	Stroke Order and Number
SG-0097 督	to supervise, keep guard, be in command of	トク	*toku*	目	督 13

督 **C** F-1207

説文

The seal-style form comprised 叔 **SG-0099**, used for the sound *toku* (from *shuku*) to mean "to attach," and 目 **SG-0001** "an eye," together signifying "to keep eyes on, guard, supervise." The kanji 督 means "to supervise, keep guard, be in command of." <尗又目>

監督 director, manager, supervision [かんとく]; 総督 governor-general [そうとく]; 督促状 demand notice, dunning letter [とくそくじょう]; 家督 being the head of a family [かとく, かっとく]

	Meanings	Kun and On	Romaji	Bushu	Stroke Order and Number
SG-0098 寂	still, silent, forlorn, desolate	さび-しい・さみ- しい ジャク・セキ	sabi-shii, sami-shii *jaku, seki*	宀	寂 11

寂 **C** F-1585

説文 1 説文或体 2

In 1, 尗, inside a family mausoleum (宀, bushu *ukanmuri* "house"), was used for the sound *jaku* to mean "small, little." In 2, 言 "word, language; to speak" was added. In a mausoleum or a house where very little was spoken, it was "still, silent." In the kanji, 宀 and 叔 **SG-0099**, for the sounds *jaku/seki*, were used. The kanji 寂 means "still, silent, forlorn, desolate." <宀叔>

寂しい lonesome [さびしい, さみしい]; 寂れる to become desolate [さびれる]; 物寂しい lonely, dreary [ものさびしい, ものさびしい]; 寂しがる to feel lonely, miss [さびしがる, さみしがる]; 静寂な still, hushed [せいじゃくな]; 寂寞たる lonesome, desolate [せきばくたる]

	Meanings	Kun and On	Romaji	Bushu	Stroke Order and Number
SG-0099 叔	uncle, younger brother of one's parent	シュク	*shuku*	又	叔 8

叔 **D** F-1915

金文1 1 金文2 2 説文 3 説文或体 4

1, 2, 3, and 4 comprised "a vine bearing small beans" on the left side, which signified "small" and had the sound *shuku*, and "a hand" on the right side. Together they depicted small beans picked up by hand, signifying "small, young." Another view takes the left side to be "the sharp blade of a hand ax (top component) gleaming white (denoted by the three short lines "shining" from the bottom)," used for the sound *shuku*. Due to its similarity to the sound to *shoo* "little" (少), the character became used for "younger sibling of one's parents," and also, more loosely, for an aunt or uncle. The kanji 叔 means "(younger) sibling of one's parent, uncle, aunt."<尗又>

叔父 uncle [おじ]; 叔母 aunt [おば]; 大叔母 great aunt [おおおば]

	Meanings	Kun and On	Romaji	Bushu	Stroke Order and Number
SG-0100 淑	graceful, ladylike; to revere	シュク	*shuku*	水	淑 11

淑 **D** F-1893

金文1 1 金文2 2 金文3 3 説文 4

Setsumon explains 淑 (4) to mean "pure and clear water," comprised of 氵 "flowing water," and 叔, used for the sound *shuku* to mean "good." Another view explains that the top of the bronzeware forms 1, 2, and 3 was borrowed from "an arrow with a net attached to catch and retrieve a shot bird 弔 **SG-1542**, also for the sound *shuku* to mean "good." The bottom component was a vessel of water. 4 became "water" and 叔, which formed the meaning "pure and placid quality of water." The kanji 淑 is used to describe a woman with a graceful, ladylike manner. It is also used to mean "to revere someone in one's heart" (possibly a figurative reading of the reflection in the "vessel of water" as a paragon for one's own deeds). The kanji 淑 means "graceful, ladylike; to look up to someone as a role model." <氵叔 >

淑女 lady [しゅくじょ]; 私淑する to revere someone in one's heart [ししゅくする]; 貞淑な chaste, virtuous [ていしゅくな]

	Meanings	Kun and On	Romaji	Bushu	Stroke Order and Number
SG-0101 戚	relative; (small, close)	セキ	*seki*	戈	丿厂厈戚戚戚 11

戚 **D** F-2340

金文1 1 金文2 2 金文3 3 説文 4

1, 2, and 3 comprised 戊 "a broad-bladed ax," and 尗, for the sound *seki* (from *shuku*) to mean "small," together signifying "a small ax." The original meaning is rarely used, and the character is generally used to mean "one's close blood relations." The kanji 戚 means "relative; (small, close)." <戊 尗>

親戚 relatives, relations [しんせき]; 外戚 maternal relation [がいせき]; 姻戚関係 marital relations [いんせきかꜜんけい]

6g A variation of "a right hand" 右父事史使丈吏 𠂇

	Meanings	Kun and On	Romaji	Bushu	Stroke Order and Number
SG-0102 右	right side	みぎ ウ・ユウ	migi *u, yuu*	口	ノナオ右右 5

右 **A** F-0210

甲骨文 1 金文1 2 金文2 3 説文 4

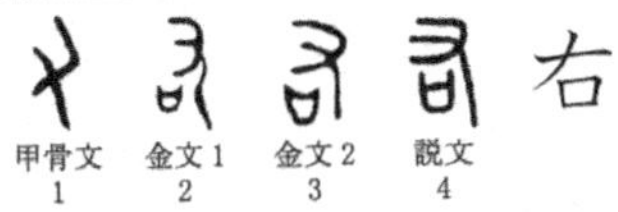

1 depicted "a right hand," the same as 1 for 又 **SG-0084**. When 又 came to be used to mean "also," the new form with 口 was created, as in 2, 3, and 4, to carry the meaning "right hand." Another view holds that the character comprised a hand and helping words (口), and that 右 originally meant "to help." The kanji 右 means "right side." <ナ口>

右の方 the right side [みぎのほꜜう]; 右手 a right hand [みぎて]; 右寄り to the right, slightly rightist [みぎより]; 右回り around to the right, clockwise [みぎまꜜわり]; 回れ右 About face!, Right face! [まわれ・みぎ]; 右折禁止 no right turn [うせつきんし]; 右派 conservative faction of a political party [うꜜは]; 右傾化 rightward shift, conservative trend [うけいか]; 左右 both sides, right and left [さꜜゆう]

	Meanings	Kun and On	Romaji	Bushu	Stroke Order and Number
SG-0103 父	father; paternal	ちち フ	chichi *hu*	父	′′ハグ父 4

父 **A** F-0272

甲骨文 1 金文 2 説文 3

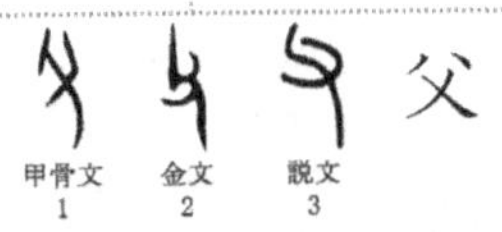

1, 2, and 3 depicted "a hand holding a rock (or the blade of an ax)." The ability to defend a clan was essential to leading it, and so a hand ax symbolized the father or the paternal head of the clan. The kanji 父 means "father; paternal." <ハ乂>
(Note: The kanji 王 **SG-1447** "king," 士 **SG-1451** "warrior," and 父 "father" all originated from a drawing of an ax.)

父 father [ちちꜜ, ちꜜち]; 実父 one's father by blood [じっぷ]; 義父 father-in-law [ぎふ]; 養父 adoptive father, foster father [よꜜうふ]; 父兄 parents, guardians [ふꜜけい] // お父さん father [おとꜜうさん]; 小父さん a man [おじさん]

	Meanings	Kun and On	Romaji	Bushu	Stroke Order and Number
SG-0104 事	work, business, matter, situation	こと ジ・ズ	koto *ji, zu*	亅	一㇆写亊亊事 8

事 **A** F-0034

甲骨文 1 金文1 2 金文2 3 金文3 4 説文 5

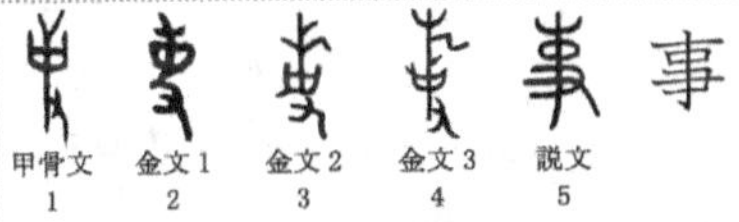

1, 2, 3, and 4 depicted "a hand holding a pole, with a box or vessel with a flag or streamer on top." A streamer marked a government office where administrative matters were dealt with. The character meant "work, matter, or situation." In 5, the hand gripped the pole firmly from the side (⺕). The kanji 事 means "work, business, matter, situation." <亖⺕亅>

事 matter, business [ことꜜ]; 事がら (事柄) affair, matter [ことがら, ことがꜜら]; 事欠く lack, want [ことꜜかく]; 事なかれ主義 a fear of rocking the boat [ことなかれしゅꜜぎ]; 用事 errand [ようじ]; 事件 incidence [じꜜけん]; 事情 circumstances, the situation [じじょう]; 無事な in safety, without a hitch [ぶじな]; 大事な a great task, a matter of great concern [だいじな]

	Meanings	Kun and On	Romaji	Bushu	Stroke Order and Number
SG-0105 史	history; to chronicle	シ	*shi*	口	㇆口中史 5

史 **A** F-0470

甲骨文 1 金文1 2 金文2 3 説文 4

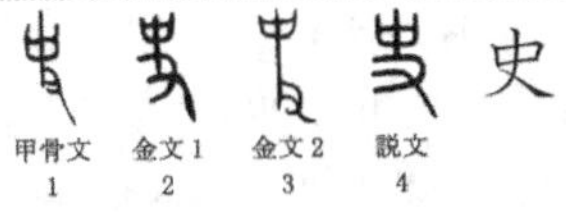

1, 2, 3, and 4 were the same as 1, 2, 3, and 4 for 事, except they did not have a flag or streamer at the top. One view explains that the box at the top of the pole contained tallies for keeping track of celestial movements, thus signifying "keeping chronological records." The kanji 史 means "history; to chronicle." <口乂>

歴史 history [れきし]; 世界史 world history [せかいし]; 史実 historical fact/evidence [しꜜじつ, しじつ]; 女史 Madame: Miss [じょꜜし]; 史上 in history [しじょう]; 日本史 History of Japan [にほんし]; 西洋史 European history [せいよꜜうし]; 歴史家 historian [れきしか]

SG-0106 使	Meanings	Kun and On	Romaji	Bushu	Stroke Order and Number
	to use, make someone do, send a person as a proxy; envoy	つか-う シ	tsuka-u *shi*	人	イ 仁 佢 佢 使 8

使 **A** F-0151

甲骨文 1 金文 2 説文 3

1 and 2 were the same as 1 and 2 for 事, originally an image of a government official working under a flag. By 3, the character had become 吏 **SG-0108** "government official," here used for the sound *shi*, and イ bushu *ninben*, "an act that one does," was added. Together they signified "to make someone work," or "to send a person as a proxy." The kanji 使 means "to use, make a person work, serve; envoy, proxy." <イ 吏>

使う use [つかう]; お使いに行く to go on an errand (for someone else) [おつかいにいく]; 人使いが荒い to be a hard master; work one's staff hard [ひとづかいが・あらい]; 使い古し worn-out, used [つかいふるし]; 使い分け using different things for different purposes [つかいわけ]; 天使 angel [てんし]; 使命 mission, duty [しめい]; 使用人 servant, personal employee [しようにん]; 大使 ambassador [たいし]

SG-0107 丈	Meanings	Kun and On	Romaji	Bushu	Stroke Order and Number
	sturdy, healthy; length	たけ ジョウ	take *joo*	一	一 ナ 丈 3

丈 **C** F-1193

説文

The seal-style form depicted "a hand holding a cane." It was used to mean a unit of measurement approximately 3 meters long (equivalent to ten *shaku* 尺 **SG-0074**). In Japanese 丈 also means "sturdy, healthy." The kanji 丈 means "sturdy, healthy; length." <一乂>
(Note: The kanji for the original meaning "cane" is the non-Joyo kanji 杖 *tsue*.)

丈 length, all [たけ]; 背丈 stature, height [せたけ]; 有りっ丈 all that there is [ありったけ]; 思いの丈 one's whole heart [おもいのたけ]; 丈夫な strong and healthy, durable [じょうぶな]; 頑丈にする to strengthen [がんじょうにする]

SG-0108 吏	Meanings	Kun and On	Romaji	Bushu	Stroke Order and Number
	government worker, official	リ	*ri*	口	一 㔾 吏 吏 6

吏 **D** F-2137

甲骨文 1 金文1 2 金文2 3 説文 4

1, 2, 3, and 4 were the same as 1 and 2 for 使 **SG-0106**. One view explains that the character was an abbreviated form of 事 **SG-0104**, whose meaning split into 事 for "work" and 吏 for "an official who does the work." The kanji 吏 means "government worker, official." <一史>

官吏 public servant [かんり]; 能吏 capable official [のうり]

6h 左 "left hand; to help" 左佐尋 𠂇

SG-0109 左	Meanings	Kun and On	Romaji	Bushu	Stroke Order and Number
	left side; left	ひだり サ	hidari *sa*	工	一 ナ 𠂇 左 左 5

左 **A** F-0223

甲骨文 1 金文1 2 金文2 3 説文 4

1 and 2 were the mirror image of 1 for 右 **SG-0102** "right (hand)," and meant "left hand." In 3, 工 **SG-1895** "craft, work table" was added. In making a craft, the left hand held down the thing being worked on, assisting the right hand doing the work, but the original meaning of "to assist, help" was lost in the kanji. The kanji 左 means "left side; left." <ナ工>

左側 left side [ひだりがわ]; 左手 left hand [ひだりて]; 左利き left-handed [ひだりきき]; 左右する to have control of, affect [さゆうする]; 左官 plasterer [さかん]

SG-0110 佐	Meanings	Kun and On	Romaji	Bushu	Stroke Order and Number
	to assist; aid	サ	*sa*	人	イ 仁 仕 佐 佐 7

佐 **A** F-0388

甲骨文 1 金文 2

1 and 2 were the same ancient forms of 左 **SG-0109**. By adding イ bushu *ninben*, "an act that a person does," to 左 (for the sound *sa*) the original meaning of 左 "to assist, help" was restored. The kanji 佐 means "to assist; aid." <イ 左>

補佐 aid, assistant [ほさ]; 大佐 colonel, captain [たいさ]

SG-0111 尋	Meanings	*Kun* and *On*	Romaji	Bushu	Stroke Order and Number
	to inquire, seek for	たず-ねる ジン	tazu-neru *jin*	寸	⁊ヨ ⺕ 㝷 㝷 尋 尋 12
尋 **C** F-1596	説文 尋 The seal-style form comprised “a left hand” 左 (top left), “a right hand” 右 (top right), and another “hand” 寸 (bottom). Right and left, one looked all around for a deity, a person, or some other thing, and thus it meant “to make an inquiry for, seek for.” The kanji 尋 means “to inquire, seek for.” <ヨエロ寸>			尋ねる to inquire, ask [たずねꜜる]; 尋ね人 missing person [たずねꜜびと]; お尋ね者 wanted man [おたずねもの]; 尋問 questioning, inquest [じんもん]; 尋常な ordinary [じんじょうな]	

7 A hand holding something

7a 寸 “hand” [from a hand holding something] 寸守村対討

SG-0112 寸	Meanings	*Kun* and *On*	Romaji	Bushu	Stroke Order and Number
	a little; measurement; old unit of length approximately 3 cm	スン	*sun*	寸	一 十 寸 3
寸 **A** F-1388	説文 寸 The seal-style form comprised “a right hand,” and “a short line” below it. The role of this short line is obscure, but one view holds that it was a finger of another hand pointing to the place a little below the wrist where the pulse was taken. The length between the wrist and this point was small, and 寸 meant “a little.” It was an old unit of length (about 3 cm). The kanji 寸 means “measurement; a little.” <寸> (Note: When used as a component in kanji, 寸 retains the meaning “something in hand.”)			寸法 measurements, plan [すんぽう]; 原寸 original dimensions, full size [げんすん]; 寸志 a little token of one’s gratitude [すꜜんし]; 採寸 taking measurements [さいすん]; 寸分の差 slight difference [すんぶんのさ]; 寸前 immediately before [すんぜん]; 寸詰まり a little short, too small [すんづまり]; 一寸先 the immediate future [いっすꜜんさき]	

SG-0113 守	Meanings	*Kun* and *On*	Romaji	Bushu	Stroke Order and Number
	to keep, preserve, protect	まも-る・も-り シュ・ス	mamo-ru, mo-ri *shu*, *su*	宀	' 宀 宀 守 守 6
守 **A** F-0345	金文1 1 金文2 2 説文 3 守 1, 2, and 3 comprised “a hand” or “a hand holding something” (又 in 1 and 寸 in 2), “under a covering or in a house (宀, bushu *ukanmuri*).” They signified “a hand engaged in work or protecting something in a house.” The kanji 守 means “to keep, preserve, protect.” <宀寸>			守る to protect [まもꜜる]; 見守る to watch over [みまもる]; お守り good luck charm, amulet [おまもり]; 守衛 watch guard [しゅえい]; 保守的な conservative [ほしゅてきな]; 留守 away from home [るꜜす]; 居留守を使う to pretend not to be home [いるすをつかう]	

SG-0114 村	Meanings	*Kun* and *On*	Romaji	Bushu	Stroke Order and Number
	village	むら ソン	mura *son*	木	一 十 木 木 村 村 7
村 **A** F-0140	篆文 1 魏晋墓碑 2 正字 3 村 1 comprised 屯 “growing grass,” for the sound *ton/son*, and 邑 “an area where many people live, a town.” A grassy area where people lived meant “a village.” The orthographic form (3) reflected 1. Another view is that 2 comprised 木 “tree,” and 寸, used for the sound *son*, and that 村 originally was the name of a tree. In Japanese, 村 is used to mean “village,” and is the smallest category of local jurisdiction—smaller than 町. <木寸>			村 village [むらꜜ]; 選手村 athletes’ camp, Olympic Village [せんしゅむら]; 農村 farming village [のうそん]; 漁村 fishing village [ぎょそん]; 市町村 cities, towns and villages [しちょꜜうそん]; 村落 village, hamlet [そꜜんらく]	

SG-0115 対	Meanings	Kun and On	Romaji	Bushu	Stroke Order and Number
	a pair of; facing against; to confront	タイ・ツイ	*tai, tsui*	寸	' 亠 ナ 文 対 対 7

対 **A** F-0083

甲骨文 1 金文1 2 金文2 3 説文 4 説文或体 5 旧字 6 對 対

1 through 6 all had "a hand" (又 or 寸) on the right side. Accounts for the left side differ. One view takes it to be "a notched stand on the ground where musical instruments hang." Two such stands facing each other gave the meaning "a pair; to face." Another view explains that it depicted dirt or gravel between two boards being pounded down by hand to make a firm foundation. From two boards that faced each other, it meant "a pair" or "facing each other." The shinji 対 looks much closer to the oracle bone-style form (1). The kanji 対 means "a pair of; facing against; to confront." <亠メ寸>

反対する to oppose [はんたいする]; 対立 opposition, antagonism [たいりつ]; 対象 target, aim [たいしょう]; 絶対に absolutely [ぜったいに]; 対応する to correspond to, be equivalent to [たいおうする]; 対人関係 personal relations, interpersonal relationships [たいじんかんけい]; 対になっている to be in a pair [ついになっている]; 一対 one pair [いっつい]

SG-0116 討	Meanings	Kun and On	Romaji	Bushu	Stroke Order and Number
	to inquire thoroughly, attack, accuse	う-つ トウ	u-tsu *too*	言	亠 言 言 言 討 討 10

討 **B** F-0776

説文 討

The seal-style form comprised 言, bushu *gonben* "words; to say," and 寸, which shared the same sound *chuu* with another kanji that meant "to accuse." Together, they signified "to inquire thoroughly." Inquiring thoroughly to find the guilty party also meant "to accuse, attack." The kanji 討 meant "to inquire thoroughly, attack, accuse." <言寸>

討つ to attack, defeat [うつ]; 討論する to debate, discuss [とうろんする]; 検討する to investigate, examine thoroughly [けんとうする]; 討議 discussion, deliberation [とうぎ]; 討伐する to subjugate, put down [とうばつする]

7b 付 "to hand out, attach" [from a hand handing out something to another person]; *hu* 付府符附

SG-0117 付	Meanings	Kun and On	Romaji	Bushu	Stroke Order and Number
	to issue, hand out, submit, stick to, attach	つ-ける フ	tsu-keru *hu*	人	亻 仁 付 付 5

付 **A** F-0157

金文1 1 金文2 2 金文3 3 説文 4 付

1, 2, 3, and 4 comprised "a person" (亻), and "a hand" (寸) behind them. Together they signified the hand of an official giving out or granting something to another person. The proximity between the two people (such as in 2) also gave the meaning "to attach." The kanji 付 means "to issue, hand out, submit, adhere, attach." <亻寸>

付ける to attach [つける]; 付く to attach itself to, adhere, touch [つく]; 受け付ける to accept (an application) [うけつける]; 交付する to issue, to grant [こうふする]; 送付する to send [そうふする]; 付与する to grant, bestow [ふよする]; 付近 the neighborhood, vicinity [ふきん]; 添付ファイル attached file [てんぷふぁいる]

SG-0118 府	Meanings	Kun and On	Romaji	Bushu	Stroke Order and Number
	government office, prefecture	フ	*hu*	广	' 亠 广 庁 庁 府 府 8

府 **A** F-0227

金文1 1 金文2 2 説文 3 府

1 and 2 comprised "the eaves of a house" (广, bushu *madare*), 付 "to grant, issue," used for the sound *hu*, and 貝 **SG-1693** "cowrie; valuable." Together, they meant "a place where important government documents or money were kept." In 3 the cowrie was dropped. The kanji 府 means "government office, prefecture." Among prefectures in Japan, Osaka and Kyoto are called 府 *hu,* due to their historical importance, while the remaining 43 prefectures are called 県 **SG-1631** *ken.* <广付>

大阪府 Osaka prefecture [おおさかふ]; 京都府 Kyoto prefecture [きょうとふ]; 政府 government [せいふ]; 幕府 military government (historical) [ばくふ]

SG-0119 符	Meanings	Kun and On	Romaji	Bushu	Stroke Order and Number
	sign, mark, tag	フ	*hu*	竹	⺮ 竹 符 11

符 **C** F-1484 説文

The seal-style form comprised 竹 **SG-0759** "bamboo," and 付 **SG-0117** "to issue," used for the sound *hu*. One of bamboo's many uses was for making "tallies." A notched tally was used to seal and validate an agreement. The kanji 符 means "sign, tally, tag." <⺮付>

符号 sign, mark [ふごう]; 割り符 tally [わりふ]; 切符 ticket [きっぷ]; 音符 musical note [おんぷ]

SG-0120 附	Meanings	Kun and On	Romaji	Bushu	Stroke Order and Number
	to attach, be affiliated with	フ	*hu*	阜	阝 附 8

附 **D** F-2024 金文 1 説文 2

1 comprised "mounds of dirt" (阝), and two sets of "a hand holding something" (寸), together signifying "making mounds of soil by adding more dirt by hand." In 2 "a person" (亻) was added to a single 寸, forming 付 for the sound *hu,* and meaning "to attach." Another view takes 附 as a borrowing to mean "to attach; attachment." The kanji 附 means "to attach, be affiliated with." <阝付>. (Note: Before the Joyo kanji revision, the kanji 付 often stood in for 附 in words such as 附則, 附属 and 寄附.)

附随 incidental, accompanying [ふずい]; 附設 annex [ふせつ]; 附属 affiliated [ふぞく]; 寄附金 donation, contribution [きふきん]; 附則 additional clause, bylaw [ふそく]

7c 尉 "to smooth out" [from a hand smoothing out creases with heat]; *i* 慰尉

SG-0121 慰	Meanings	Kun and On	Romaji	Bushu	Stroke Order and Number
	to comfort, console	なぐさ-める イ	nagusa-meru *i*	心	尸 尉 慰 15

慰 **C** F-1611 説文

The seal-style form comprised "a heart" (心 **SG-0187**) inside 尉 **SG-0122**, used for the sound *i*, which originally meant "a hand smoothing creases out of cloth using heat," together signifying "soothing someone's heart; to comfort." The kanji 慰 means "to comfort, console." <尉心>

慰める to comfort, console [なぐさめる]; 慰問 a visit to express concern [いもん]; 慰安 relaxation, recreation [いあん]; 慰労会 party given in appreciation of someone's services [いろうかい]

SG-0122 尉	Meanings	Kun and On	Romaji	Bushu	Stroke Order and Number
	military officer	イ	*i*	寸	尸 尉 11

尉 **D** F-2082 説文

The seal-style form comprised "a draping cloth," "a hand," and "a fire" (火 **SG-1164**), signifying "a hand smoothing out creases in a piece of cloth using heat, like ironing." The meaning applied to people, and meant someone such as a military or prison officer who would straighten out the conduct of a soldier or convict. The kanji 尉 means "military officer." <尸示寸>

大尉 captain (army), lieutenant (navy) [たいい]

7d 采 "to pick by hand" [from ⺤ "fingers picking berries" on 木 "a tree"]; *sai* 採菜彩采

SG-0123 採	Meanings	Kun and On	Romaji	Bushu	Stroke Order and Number
	to pick by hand, adopt	と-る サイ	to-ru *sai*	手	扌 採 11

採 **B** F-0771

No ancient form. The kanji 採 comprises 扌 bushu *tehen*, and 采 **SG-0126** "a hand picking fruits and berries" (⺤ and 木), used for the sound *sai*, together signifying "to pick by hand." The kanji 採 means "to pick by hand, adopt." <扌⺤木>
(Note: 采 *sai* (8 strokes) is distinct from 釆 bushu *nogome* (7 strokes). For 釆, please see the common shape 41e 釆—番 **SG-1017** through 藩 **SG-1021**.)

採る to pick [とる]; 採用する to hire, adopt [さいようする]; 採光 lighting [さいこう]; 採算の取れる profitable [さいさんのとれる]; 採集 [さいしゅう]; 採血 drawing blood [さいけつ]; 採掘する to mine [さいくつする]; 採取する to pick, gather, collect [さいしゅする]

SG-0124 菜	Meanings	Kun and On	Romaji	Bushu	Stroke Order and Number
	vegetable, household dish, side dish	な サイ	na *sai*	艸	艹 菜 11

菜 **B** F-0942 説文

The seal-style form comprised "plants, vegetation" (艸, 艹 bushu *kusakanmuri*), and 采 **SG-0126** "to pick," used for the sound *sai,* together signifying "a hand picking greens or vegetables." The character is also used to mean

菜っ葉 leafy vegetable [なっぱ]; 青菜 greens [あおな, あおっな]; 野菜 vegetable [やさい]; 白菜 *hakusai*, Chinese cabbage [はくさい, はくさい]; 惣菜 daily dish,

	"side dish, household dish." The kanji 菜 means "vegetable, household dish, side dish." <⺾ 采 >	household dish [そうざい]; 前菜appetizer [ぜんさい];菜食主義者vegetarian [さいしょくしゅぎしゃ]

	Meanings	Kun and On	Romaji	Bushu	Stroke Order and Number
SG-0125 彩	colorful; color scheme, embellishment, garnish	いろど-る サイ	irodo-ru *sai*	彡	一 ⺍ 平 采 彩 11
彩 **C** F-1103	説文	The seal-style form comprised 采 **SG-0126** for the sound *sai*, and 彡 bushu *sai* "pretty pattern, coloring," signifying "colorful; coloring." The kanji 彩 means "colorful; color scheme, embellishment, garnish." <采彡>	彩り color scheme, decorative touch [いろどり]; 色彩 color scheme, coloring [しきさい]; 水彩画 water color painting [すいさいが]; 多彩な colorful, many-sided [たさいな]; 無彩色 achromatic color [むさいしょく]; 精彩を欠く lackluster, lifeless [せいさいをかく]		

	Meanings	Kun and On	Romaji	Bushu	Stroke Order and Number
SG-0126 采	to pick, manage; coloring, appearance	サイ	*sai*	采	⺈ ⺍ ⺤ 平 采 8
采 **D** F-2590	甲骨文 1 金文 2 説文 3	1, 2, and 3 depicted "fingers picking berries or nuts (⺤) from a tree." Fingers reaching from above signified "to manage." Berries are "colorful," and the character pertains to "appearances, state, condition." The kanji 采 means "to pick, manage; coloring, appearances." <⺤ 木>	采配を振るう to take command, manage in person [さいはいをふるう]; 風采の上がらない unattractive in appearance, unkempt [ふうさいのあがらない]; 拍手喝采 acclaim, roaring applause [はくしゅ・かっさい]		

7e 孚 "to take care of a child" [from a hand pulling up a child] 浮乳

	Meanings	Kun and On	Romaji	Bushu	Stroke Order and Number
SG-0127 浮	to float, wander; groundless	う-く フ	u-ku *hu*	水	氵 氵 泙 浮 浮 浮 10
浮 **B** F-0856	金文 1 説文 2	1 and 2 comprised "flowing water" (氵, bushu *sanzui)* and 孚, used for the sound *hu* to mean "a hand lifting a child." Lifting a child from the water by hand or keeping it afloat meant "to float." Being afloat also meant "groundless; to wander." The kanji 浮 means "to float, wander; groundless." <氵 ⺤ 子>	浮かぶ・浮く to float, be groundless [うかぶ, うく]; 浮き世 transitory world, fleeting life [うきよ, うきよ]; 浮世絵 style of Edo-period woodblock prints [うきよえ]; 浮き沈み rising and falling [うきしずみ, うきしずみ]; 浮かれる to be cheerful, be happily excited [うかれる]; 浮遊物 floating object [ふゆうぶつ] // 浮気 unfaithful love, flirtation [うわき]; 浮つく to become frivolous [うわつく]		

	Meanings	Kun and On	Romaji	Bushu	Stroke Order and Number
SG-0128 乳	milk, milking, breast	ちち・ち ニュウ	chichi, chi *nyuu*	乙	⺤ 孚 孚 孚 乳 8
乳 **B** F-1038	甲骨文 1 説文 2	In 1, a woman on her knees is nursing or holding a child in her arms. It meant "to nurse; breast, milk." 2 comprised ⺤ "a hand from above," over 子 "a child." The right side (乚) has various interpretations, including "a hand caring for a baby," "a swallow which brings a baby" (similar to a stork in Western folktales), and "supporting an infant." The kanji 乳 means "milk, milking, breast." <⺤ 子 乚>	乳 milk, breast [ちち]; 乳飲み子 infant [ちのみご]; 牛乳 cow's milk [ぎゅうにゅう]; 母乳 mother's milk [ぼにゅう]; 豆乳 soy milk [とうにゅう]; 乳製品 dairy products [にゅうせいひん]; 乳化する to emulsify [にゅうかする] // 乳母 wet nurse, nanny [うば]		

7f 争 "to fight" [from a hand trying to take a stick held by another hand]; *soo/joo* 争浄

For the kanji 静, please see 静 SG-0697.

	Meanings	Kun and On	Romaji	Bushu	Stroke Order and Number
SG-0129 争	to fight; dispute, conflict	あらそ-う ソウ	araso-u *soo*	爪	⺈ ⺈ 乌 刍 争 6
争 **B** F-0658	説文 1 旧字 2	1 comprised "a hand or fingers reaching down from above," and "a stick firmly held by another hand," signifying a person trying to take what another person has, and further signifying "two parties fighting over control," or "to fight; conflict." The top (⺤) of the kyuji 爭 (2) was replaced by ⺈ in the shinji. The kanji 争 means "to fight; dispute, conflict." <⺈ ⺕ 亅>	争う to fight [あらそう]; 争い dispute, fight [あらそい]; 言い争い quarrel, argument [いいあらそい]; 争議 fight, dispute [そうぎ]; 抗争 struggle, antagonism [こうそう]; 論争 dispute, contention [ろんそう]; 政争 political strife [せいそう]		

	Meanings	Kun and On	Romaji	Bushu	Stroke Order and Number
SG-0130 浄	clean, pure	ジョウ	*joo*	水	浄 9

浄 **C** F-1498

説文 1 旧字 2

1 comprised "flowing water" (氵), and 爭 (the kyuji for 争 **SG-0129**), used for the sound *joo* to mean "clean." It was the name of a specific lake. The kanji 浄 was borrowed to mean "clean, pure," as well as "the Pure Land of the afterlife" in Buddhist theology. <氵争>

浄水池 clean water reservoir [じょうすꜜいち]; 洗浄する to wash, rinse out [せんじょうする]; 浄化槽 septic tank, purifying chamber [じょうかꜜそう]; 極楽浄土 Pure Land, Paradise (Buddhism) [ごくらくじょꜜうど]

7g 受 "to receive" [from a hand handing a vessel down to another hand]; *ju* 受授

	Meanings	Kun and On	Romaji	Bushu	Stroke Order and Number
SG-0131 受	to receive, take, accept	う-ける ジュ	u-keru *ju*	又	受 8

受 **A** F-0142

甲骨文 1 1, 甲骨文 2 2, 金文 3, 説文 4

1, 2, 3, and 4 all comprised three components: "a hand reaching down from above," "a vessel containing a valuable thing," and "a hand reaching up from below." Together, they signified "a hand handing down something valuable, and another hand receiving it," and the character originally meant both "to receive" and "to bestow." Later the original two meanings were divided into two separate kanji, 受 and 授 **SG-0132**, and the kanji 受 is used for the act of receiving only. The kanji 受 means "to receive, take, accept." <爫冖又>

受ける to receive [うけꜜる]; 受付 reception [うけつけ]; 引き受ける to undertake [ひきうけꜜる]; 受け取る to receive [うけとる]; 受験する to sit for an exam [じゅけんする]; 受信 signal reception, receipt of message [じゅしん]; 受信料 (TV) license fee [じゅしꜜんりょう]

	Meanings	Kun and On	Romaji	Bushu	Stroke Order and Number
SG-0132 授	to bestow, grant	さず-ける ジュ	sazu-keru *ju*	手	授 11

授 **B** F-0664

説文

The kanji 授 was created by adding an additional hand (扌 "an act done by hand") to 受 (**SG-0131**), used for the sound *ju*, to distinguish between the two meanings "to receive" (受) and "to give" (授). The new character represented an act of giving by someone in a higher position, and thus meant "to bestow." The kanji 授 means "to bestow, grant." <扌受>

授ける to bestow, grant, confer [さずけꜜる]; 才能を授かる to be gifted [さいのうをさずかꜜる]; 授業 class instruction [じゅꜜぎょう]; 教授 professor [きょうじゅ]; 授受 giving and receiving, transfer [じゅꜜじゅ]; 授与式 awarding ceremony, investiture [じゅよꜜしき]

7h 爰(爰) [from a person pulling something with both hands]; *en/dan/kan* 援暖緩媛

	Meanings	Kun and On	Romaji	Bushu	Stroke Order and Number
SG-0133 援	to assist, help, pull	エン	*en*	手	援 12

援 **B** F-0659

説文

In the seal-style form, 爰 (爰) depicted "a person pulling something with both hands," and had the sound *en*. Another hand (扌) was added to give it the meaning "to assist." The kanji 援 means "to assist, help, pull." <扌爰(爫友)>

応援する to support, assist, cheer (a team) [おうえんする]; 援助 aid, help [えꜜんじょ]; 支援 support [しꜜえん]; 後援会 supporters' association [こうえꜜんかい]; 義援金 contribution (of money), donation [ぎえんきん]

	Meanings	Kun and On	Romaji	Bushu	Stroke Order and Number
SG-0134 暖	warm; to warm up	あたた-かい ダン	atata-kai *dan*	日	暖 13

暖 **C** F-1230

説文 1 2

1 comprised 火 "fire," and 爰, used for the sound *dan*, together signifying "warm." The earlier kanji 煖 in 2 reflected 1, but in the current kanji 暖, the left side uses 日 "sun" instead of 火. The kanji 暖 means "warm; to warm up."<日爰>

暖かい warm [あたたかꜜい]; 暖める to warm up [あたためꜜる]; 暖房 (room) heating [だんぼう]; 温暖な warm and mild (weather) [おんだんな]; 地球温暖化 global warming [ちきゅꜜう・おんだんか, ちきゅうおんだんか]; 寒暖の差 temperature differential [かんだんのさ]

	Meanings	Kun and On	Romaji	Bushu	Stroke Order and Number
SG-0135 緩	loose, slow, gentle	ゆる-い カン	yuru-i *kan*	糸	幺糸紀緩綏緩 15

緩 **C** F-1247

説文 1 説文或体 2

The left-side component of 1 was 素 **SG-1618** "natural," which originally depicted "the top of a bundle of threads yet to be dyed," while 2 had 糸 **SG-1600**, "a skein of threads." 爰 was used for the sound *kan* to mean "to pull by hand." Pulling a skein of threads by two hands would loosen the bundle, giving the meaning "loose." The kanji 緩 means "loose, slow, gentle." <糸爰>

緩い lax, loose [ゆるい]; 緩やかに gently, slowly [ゆるやかに]; 緩める to loosen [ゆるめる]; 緩急 speed fluctuation [かんきゅう]; 弛緩する to slacken, lax [しかんする]

	Meanings	Kun and On	Romaji	Bushu	Stroke Order and Number
SG-0136 媛	refined woman	エン	*en*	女	く女女ˊ娐媛 12

媛 **D** F-1742

説文

The seal-style form comprised 女 **SG-0521** "woman," and 爰, used for the sound *en* to mean "pulling, drawing." A graceful or beautiful woman attracted people's attention. The kanji 媛 means "beautiful woman, refined woman." <女爰>

才媛 accomplished woman [さいえん] // 愛媛県 Ehime prefecture [えひめけん]

8 Two or more hands raising something

8a 共 "both; reverential" [from a person holding up something with both hands]; *kyoo/koo* 共供恭洪

	Meanings	Kun and On	Romaji	Bushu	Stroke Order and Number
SG-0137 共	both; together	とも キョウ	tomo *kyoo*	八	一十廾共共 6

共 **A** F-0206

甲骨文 1 金文1 2 金文2 3 説文 4

1, 2, 3, and 4 depicted two hands holding or raising a vessel. Using both hands signified "both; together" (when used as kanji) as well as a reverential or polite act (when used as a component in other characters). The kanji 共 means "both; together." <廾八>

〜と共に together with X [〜とともに]; 共倒れ failing together, mutual downfall [ともだおれ]; 共有する to share, own jointly [きょうゆうする]; 共著 co-authoring [きょうちょ, きょうちょ]; 共演者 co-stars [きょうえんしゃ]; 共同 sharing, partnership, community [きょうどう]; 共学 coeducational [きょうがく]; 共産主義 communism [きょうさんしゅぎ]; 反共 anticommunism [はんきょう]

	Meanings	Kun and On	Romaji	Bushu	Stroke Order and Number
SG-0138 供	to give offering, present, accompany	そな-える・とも キョウ・ク	sona-eru, tomo *kyoo, ku*	人	亻仁仳供供 8

供 **B** F-0559

金文 1 説文 2

1 was similar to 3 for 共 **SG-0137**, "two hands holding up a box." In 2, 亻 "an act that one does" was added to 共, used for the sound *kyoo*. Taken together, they meant "a person presenting or offering something reverentially with both hands." In Japanese, the character also means "to accompany another person." The kanji 供 means "to give an offering, present, accompany." <亻共>

お供え an offering placed on an altar [おそなえ]; お供する to accompany a person (humble) [おともする]; 子供 child [こども]; 提供する to sponsor [ていきょうする]; 供給 supply [きょうきゅう]; 自供 confession [じきょう]; 供養 memorial service [くよう]; 供物 offering at the altar [くもつ]

	Meanings	Kun and On	Romaji	Bushu	Stroke Order and Number
SG-0139 恭	reverential, deferential	うやうや-しい キョウ	uyauya-shii *kyoo*	心	一艹共恭恭恭恭 10

恭 **D** F-1634

説文

The seal-style form comprised 共 **SG-0137**, used for the sound *kyoo* to mean "a reverential act using both hands," with "a heart" (⺗ , bushu *shitagokoro*) underneath. The kanji 恭 means "reverential, deferential." <共⺗>

恭しく respectfully, reverentially [うやうやしく]; 恭順 dutiful submission to an order [きょうじゅん]; 恭賀新年 Best Wishes for a Happy New Year (in writing) [きょうがしんねん]

SG-0140 洪	Meanings	Kun and On	Romaji	Bushu	Stroke Order and Number
	flood; vastly	コウ	*koo*	水	氵氵氵汁泄洪洪 9

洪 **D** F-1660

説文

洪 The seal-style form comprised "flowing water" (氵), and 共, used for the sound *koo* to mean "together," signifying "water coming together; flood." A flood covers a vast area, whence "vastly." The kanji 洪 means "flood; vastly." <氵共>

洪水 flood [こうずい]; 洪水注意報 heavy flood advisory [こうずいちゅういꜜほう]

8b 菐 "servant; to strike" [from two origins involving two hands]; *boku* 僕撲

SG-0141 僕	Meanings	Kun and On	Romaji	Bushu	Stroke Order and Number
	servant; I, me (in male speech)	ボク	*boku*	人	亻亻亻亻亻僕僕僕 14

僕 **B** F-0963

甲骨文 1 金文 1 2 金文 2 3 金文 3 4 説文 5

僕 In 1, "a man with a tattooing needle or a crown on their head" was "holding a basket of offerings with both hands." It signified "a person serving the deity," or later just "a servant." 2 comprised 亻 "an act that a person does," and "a person with a tattooing needle" carrying "a basket" on their head, used for the sound *boku*. In 3 and 4, "two upward-reaching hands" were added at the bottom to mean "serving with hands." 5 in seal style, however, appeared to have a different origin—"a board with a notched top (業 **SG-0628**) and "two hands," which became 菐 for the sound *boku* in kanji. Taken together they meant "a servant." The character also came to mean "I," used by a male speaker when humbling himself. The kanji 僕 means "servant; I/my/me (in male speech)." <亻菐(业䒑夫)>

僕 I (in male speech) [ぼꜜく, ぼく], servant [しもべꜜ]; 公僕 public servant [こうぼく]; 下僕 manservant [げぼく]

SG-0142 撲	Meanings	Kun and On	Romaji	Bushu	Stroke Order and Number
	to beat, stroke	ボク	*boku*	手	扌扌扌扌扌撲撲 15

撲 **D** F-1690

金文1 1 金文2 2 説文 3

撲 1 comprised "two hands holding a board with a notched top" (菐), used for the sound *boku*, and "a halberd," together signifying "to beat hard." In 2, the two sides were swapped. In 3, "an act done by hand" (扌) replaced the halberd. The kanji 撲 means "to beat, stroke." <扌菐>

打撲傷 bruise, contusion [だぼくしょう]; 撲滅 eradication [ぼくめつ] // 相撲 sumo wrestling [すもう]; 相撲取り sumo wrestler [すもꜜうとり]

8c 廾 "two hands holding up something" 弁弄

SG-0143 弁	Meanings	Kun and On	Romaji	Bushu	Stroke Order and Number
	to argue, make a final decision; flower petal, valve	ベン	*ben*	辛瓜	㇜ム厶弁弁 5

弁 **B** F-0623

金文 1 説文籀文 2 説文 1 3 説文 2 4

弁 In 1, 2, and 4, two hands are holding up an official's hat or headdress. This shape 弁, used for the sound *ben*, is now used in place of three different kyuji, (a) 辨, (b) 辯, and (c) 瓣, each with their own meaning and history as below:

(a) 辨: 1 and 2 depicted two people, a plaintiff and a defendant, pleading their cases, and a knife in the middle signified the final judgment. The kanji 辨 meant "to divide; final decision."

(a) 金文 1 説文 2 辨 旧字 3 弁

(b) 辯: 1 had 言 "words" in the middle, and meant "to argue, make a logical argument."

(b) 説文 1 辯 旧字 2 弁

(c) 瓣: The kyuji had 瓜 in the middle and meant "flower petal, valve."

(c) 瓣 旧字 弁

The kanji 弁 means "to argue, make a final decision; flower petal, valve." <ム廾>

弁 valve [べꜜん]; 花弁 flower petal [かべん]; 弁が立つ to speak eloquently [べꜜんが・たꜜつ]; 答弁 answer, account [とꜜうべん]; 弁護士 legal attorney [べんごꜜし]; 関西弁 Kansai dialect [かんさいべん]; 弁当 boxed lunch [べんとꜜう]; 弁解する to defend (oneself), justify (oneself) [べんかいする]; 詭弁 sophism, logic-chopping [きべん]

SG-0144 弄	Meanings	Kun and On	Romaji	Bushu	Stroke Order and Number
	to take pleasure in, toy with	もてあそ-ぶ ロウ	moteaso-bu *roo*	廾	一丅王王弄弄 7

弄 **D** F-2521 — 金文 1, 說文 2 弄

1 comprised "jewels strung together (王, from 玉 **SG-1730**)" and "two hands (廾)," signifying "enjoying fiddling with jewels with both hands." The kanji 弄 means "to take pleasure in, toy with." <王廾>

弄ぶ to take pleasure in, toy with [もてあそぶ, もてあそꜜぶ]; 翻弄する to toss about, trifle with [ほんろうする]; 愚弄する to make sport of, ridicule [ぐろうする]

8d 夫 "to dedicate something" [from two hands offering up something] 奏泰

SG-0145 奏	Meanings	Kun and On	Romaji	Bushu	Stroke Order and Number
	to report to a ruler, play music	かな-でる ソウ	kana-deru *soo*	大	三夫夫奏奏奏 9

奏 **C** F-1148 — 說文 奏

The seal-style form depicted "two hands making a ritual offering of a sacrificial animal that was cut open or some other thing for a rite," signifying "to dedicate, present." The two upward-reaching hands became 夫. Music was played during a ceremony for a ruler, whence "to play music." The kanji 奏 means "to report to a ruler, play music." <夫夭>

奏でる to play music [かなでꜜる]; 演奏 musical performance [えんそう]; 伴奏 musical accompaniment [ばんそう]; 上奏 report to the throne [じょうそう]

SG-0146 泰	Meanings	Kun and On	Romaji	Bushu	Stroke Order and Number
	calm, restful, peaceful	タイ	*tai*	水	三夫泰泰泰 10

泰 **C** F-1351 — 說文古文 1, 說文 2 泰

1 comprised "a person," with an abbreviation of "water" underneath. 2 comprised "a person" (大) and "two hands over the water," signifying "two hands rescuing someone from drowning." Being rescued made one feel secure and peaceful. The kanji 泰 means "calm, restful, peaceful." <夫氺>

安泰 peace, security [あんたい]; 泰然たる composed, collected [たいぜんたꜜる]; 天下泰平 state of universal peace [てꜜんか・たいへい]

8e 朕 "to raise reverentially" [from a vessel transporting an important object] 勝謄朕

SG-0147 勝	Meanings	Kun and On	Romaji	Bushu	Stroke Order and Number
	to gain, win, exceed; victory	か-つ・まさ-る ショウ	ka-tsu, masa-ru *shoo*	力	月 月` 月䒑 朕 勝 勝 12

勝 **A** F-0193 — 說文 勝

The seal-style form comprised "a shallow vessel" (月); "two hands holding up an important object" (关), used for the sound *shoo*; and "a plow" (力) for "strenuous work"; together signifying "raising something important with might." By doing so, one would eventually win or achieve their desired result. The kanji 勝 means "to gain, win, exceed; victory." <月关力>

勝つ to win [かꜜつ]; 勝ち目のない having no chance to win [かちめのなꜜい]; 勝手に without permission [かってに]; 身勝手な selfish, self-centered [みがꜜってな]; 勝る to surpass, exceed [まさꜜる]; 男勝り spirited (woman), heroic (woman) [おとこまꜜさり]; 勝利 victory [しょꜜうり]; 決勝戦 a final, a championship match [けっしょうせん, けっしょꜜうせん]

SG-0148 謄	Meanings	Kun and On	Romaji	Bushu	Stroke Order and Number
	to make a copy, duplicate	トウ	*too*	言	月 月` 月䒑 朕 謄 謄 17

謄 **D** F-2427 — 篆文 謄

The seal-style form comprised "a shallow vessel or a boat for transport" (月), and "two hands holding up an important object" (关), forming 朕 **SG-0149,** and used for the sound *too*; and "word, language" (言). In order to pass along important documents to another party, a duplicate had to be made. The kanji 謄 means "to make a copy, duplicate." <月关言>

謄本 certified copy, transcript [とうほん]; 謄写版 mimeograph [とうしゃばん]; 戸籍謄本 certified copy of one's family domiciliary register [こせきとꜜうほん]

SG-0149 朕	Meanings	Kun and On	Romaji	Bushu	Stroke Order and Number
	I (imperial we)	チン	*chin*	月	月 月` 月䒑 朕 朕 10

朕 **D** F-2596 — 甲骨文1 1, 甲骨文2 2, 金文1 3, 金文2 4, 說文 5 朕

1, 2, 3, and 4 comprised "a shallow vessel or a tray; to transport" (舟, 月), and "two hands holding up a precious object," together signifying "to carry an important thing in a vessel and present it reverentially

朕 I, imperial we (old) [ちꜜん]

	with both hands." The character was used by the emperor as the formal-style first-person pronoun "imperial we." In 5, the thing being presented became the shape 火 (no relevance to "fire"). In the kanji 朕, the two elements coalesced and became 关. The kanji 朕 means "I (imperial we)." <月关>	朕 I, imperial we (old) [ちꜜん]

8f "a reverential act involving many people" [from many hands raising a thing or person] 与興承挙誉

SG-0150 与	Meanings: to bestow, participate, be involved	Kun and On: あた-える ヨ	Romaji: ata-eru *yo*	Bushu: 臼	Stroke Order and Number: 一与与 3
与 **A** F-0330	金文1 1, 金文2 2, 説文古文 3, 説文 4, 旧字 5 — 1 and 2 comprised "two pairs of hands," "an interlocking shape" in the center, and "a vessel of prayers" or "a mouth." The interlocking shape in the center was an ivory object signifying "precious; importance." Many people's hands carrying something important together meant "to be involved, participate." It was also used to mean "to bestow." In the shinji 与, only the shape of the ivory object has remained. The kanji 与 means "to bestow, share, participate, be involved." <与>				与える to bestow [あたえる]; 給与 salary, wage [きゅꜜうよ]; 関与する to have a part, get involved [かꜜんよする]; 与党 party in power [よꜜとう]; 貸与する to grant some the use, loan [たꜜいよする]; 参与 senior counselor [さꜜんよ]

SG-0151 興	Meanings: to raise, start, arouse	Kun and On: おこ-す コウ・キョウ	Romaji: oko-su *koo, kyoo*	Bushu: 臼	Stroke Order and Number: 〡𠂉 𦥑 𦥑冂 𦥑同 𦥯 興 16
興 **B** F-0896	甲骨文 1, 金文 2, 説文 3 — 1 and 2 comprised "two pairs of hands" carrying or raising something between them. The character meant "to raise (as a group), start something together." In 3, the top component became 同, held from the sides by two hands (𦥑), and in the kanji 興, the two hands on the bottom were simplified to 六. The kanji 興 means "to raise, start, arouse." <同𦥑六>				興す to start something new, revive [おこꜜす]; 町興し revitalization of a locality [まちおꜜこし]; 新興の newly risen [しんこうの]; 興行 show, public entertainment [こうぎょう]; 興味 interest [きょꜜうみ]; 即興で extemporaneously [そっきょうで]; 興醒め loss of interest or enthusiasm [きょうざめ]

SG-0152 承	Meanings: to obey, follow, accept humbly	Kun and On: うけたまわ-る ショウ	Romaji: uketamawa-ru *shoo*	Bushu: 手	Stroke Order and Number: 了了手手承承 8
承 **B** F-0974	金文1 1, 金文2 2, 説文 3 — 1 and 2 comprised "a master kneeling" and "the hands of his servant lifting him," together signifying "to follow, obey." In 3, another "hand" raising the person was added in the center. In the kanji 承, the shape was considerably simplified and means "to obey, follow, accept humbly." <氶 三>				承る to hear, receive, accept [うけたまわる, うけたまわꜜる]; 承知する to consent to, assent to [しょうちする]; 口承文学 oral literature, folklore [こうしょうぶꜜんがく]; 伝承 transmission, handing down [でんしょう]; 継承 succession, accession [けいしょう]; 承服しかねる cannot accept [しょうふくしかねꜜる]; 不承不承 reluctantly [ふしょうぶꜜしょう]; 起承転結 a literary process of introduction, development, denouement, and conclusion [きしょうてんけつ, きしょꜜう・てんけつ]

SG-0153 挙	Meanings: to raise, carry out	Kun and On: あ-げる キョ	Romaji: a-geru *kyo*	Bushu: 手	Stroke Order and Number: 丶丷 丷 兴 兴 挙 10
挙 **B** F-0693	説文 1, 旧字 2 — 1 had all the elements that made up the precursors of the kanji 與 (the kyuji for 与 **SG-0150**), with an additional hand (手). Altogether there were five hands, signifying many people working together to raise something high. In the shinji 挙, the top component was simplified to ⺍. Hands carried out tasks, whence the meaning "to conduct, carry out." The kanji 挙 means "to raise (a hand), carry out."< 兴 手>				式を挙げる to conduct a ceremony [しきꜜを・あげる]; 一挙に at a stroke [いꜜっきょに]; 挙手 raising a hand [きょꜜしゅ]; 快挙 outstanding achievement [かꜜいきょ]; 挙行 performance of a rite [きょこう]; 検挙 arrest, roundup [けꜜんきょ]; 選挙権 suffrage, the right to vote [せんきょꜜけん]

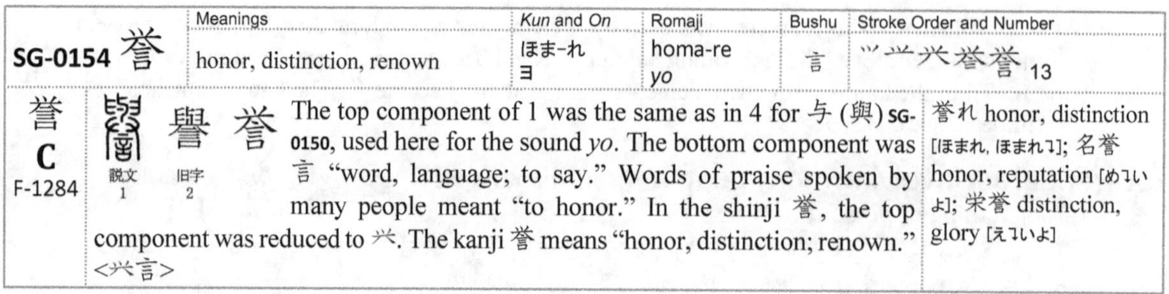

	Meanings	*Kun* and *On*	Romaji	Bushu	Stroke Order and Number
SG-0154 誉	honor, distinction, renown	ほま-れ ヨ	homa-re *yo*	言	⺍ ⺌ 兴 誉 誉 13

誉 **C** F-1284	説文 1 旧字 2 The top component of 1 was the same as in 4 for 与 (與) **SG-0150**, used here for the sound *yo*. The bottom component was 言 "word, language; to say." Words of praise spoken by many people meant "to honor." In the shinji 誉, the top component was reduced to 兴. The kanji 誉 means "honor, distinction; renown." <兴言>	誉れ honor, distinction [ほまれ, ほまれ˥]; 名誉 honor, reputation [め˥いよ]; 栄誉 distinction, glory [え˥いよ]

9 A hand with a tool

9a 君 "to control, rule" [from a hand holding a stick and a mouth]; *kun/gun* 君群郡

	Meanings	*Kun* and *On*	Romaji	Bushu	Stroke Order and Number
SG-0155 君	sovereign, lord; you (in male speech)	きみ クン	kimi *kun*	口	フ ヨ ヨ 尹 君 7

君 **A** F-0498	甲骨文 1 金文1 2 金文2 3 説文 4 1, 2, 3, and 4 all comprised "a hand holding a stick to perform a task" (尹), and "a mouth" (口) for speaking, together originally signifying "an official." The character later came to be used to mean "sovereign, lord." It is also used as a form of address toward one's male peers or juniors (primarily in male speech). <尹口>	君 you (addressing someone junior in male speech) [きみ]; 君が代 the national anthem of Japan [きみがよ]; 君主 monarch [く˥んしゅ]; 主君 one's liege lord, one's master [しゅ˥くん]; 明君 enlightened monarch [め˥いくん]; 君子 man of noble character [く˥んしゅ]; 君付けで呼ぶ to call someone by *kun* [くんづけでよぶ]

	Meanings	*Kun* and *On*	Romaji	Bushu	Stroke Order and Number
SG-0156 群	group, throng, herd, flock	む-れる・むら-がる グン	mu-reru, mura-garu *gun*	羊	ヨ 尹 君 君' 君䒑 群 13

群 **B** F-0914	金文1 1 金文2 2 説文 3 1 and 2 comprised 君 **SG-0155**, used for the sound *gun* to mean "to command, lead," and "sheep" (羊 **SG-0825**). Sheep stayed together in a flock, herded by a shepherd. In the kanji, the two components were placed side by side. The kanji 群 means "group, throng, herd, flock." <君羊>	群れ flock, herd, group [むれ˥]; 群がる to crowd together, swarm, throng [むらが˥る]; 群衆 crowd, throng [ぐんしゅう]; 大群 a large crown/heard/swarm [たいぐん]; 一群 a group of people/animals [いちぐん]; 群島 archipelago [ぐんとう]

	Meanings	*Kun* and *On*	Romaji	Bushu	Stroke Order and Number
SG-0157 郡	county, subprefecture	グン	*gun*	邑	ヨ ヨ 尹 君 君' 君ᄀ 郡 10

郡 **B** F-0733	説文 The left side of the seal-style form was 君, used for the sound *gun* to mean "official, local lord." The right side comprised "an area" (口) with "a person/people" (巴), together forming the meaning "a town." This component coalesced to 阝, bushu *oozato*, in the kanji. The character meant "a town or an area (阝) where a local lord (君) governs." The kanji 郡 means "county, subprefecture." In Japan, 郡 constitutes a grouping of 町 "towns" and 村 "villages" within 県 "a prefecture." <君阝>	郡 county [ぐ˥ん]; 郡部 rural district, county [ぐ˥んぶ]

9b 殳 "to strike, hit" [from a hand holding a spear-like weapon or tool]; bushu *hokozukuri*/ *rumata* [from ル and 又 *mata*, or *hoko* "pike"] 役設投段殺殻穀鍛毀

SG-0158 役	Meanings	Kun and On	Romaji	Bushu	Stroke Order and Number
	battle, military service, part, role	ヤク・エキ	*yaku, eki*	彳	彳 彳 彸 役 役 7

役 **A** F-0235

甲骨文 1 · 甲骨文 2 · 説文古文 3 · 説文 4 · 役

1 and 2 comprised "a person standing or on their knees," and "a hand holding a spear-like weapon behind them," together signifying "a person being conscripted to fight in a war." In 3, the top-right component depicted the decorative cover of a spear, and together with 又 "hand," it formed 殳, bushu *hokozukuri/rumata* "to strike, hit." In 4, 彳 "a crossroads" was added to suggest "going to battle." The sense of "military service" gave the meaning "a role to carry out." The kanji 役 means "battle, military service, part, role." <彳殳>

役員 officer of an organization [やくꜜいん]; 役人 government official [やくにん]; 主役 leading role (in a play) [しゅやく]; 役に立つ to be useful, beneficial [やくꜜにたつ]; 役目 role, obligation [やくめꜜ]; 役者 actor [やくしゃ]; 兵役 military service [へいえき]; 服役 to do time in prison [ふくえき]; 賦役 labor in lieu of taxes [ふえき]

SG-0159 設	Meanings	Kun and On	Romaji	Bushu	Stroke Order and Number
	to set up, provide, establish	もう-ける セツ	moo-keru *setsu*	言	言 言 訁 設 設 11

設 **A** F-0298

甲骨文 1 · 説文 2 · 設

1 comprised "a wedge" and "a hand holding a tool," signifying "to set up." In 2, the wedge was misconstrued to be a tattooing needle, the origin of 言 **SG-1364** "word; to speak." The kanji 設 means "to set up, provide, establish." <言殳>

設ける to prepare, establish, enact [もうけꜜる]; 設立する to establish [せつりつする]; 開設 inauguration, opening [かいせつ]; 設置する to install [せっちする]; 仮設 temporary installation [かせつ]

SG-0160 投	Meanings	Kun and On	Romaji	Bushu	Stroke Order and Number
	to throw, hurl, toss, give up, cast off	な-げる トウ	na-geru *too*	手	一 十 扌 抆 投 7

投 **A** F-0353

説文 · 投

The seal-style form comprised 扌 "an act done by hand," and 殳 "a hand holding a lance," together signifying "to throw, hurl." The character is also used to mean "to cast off or give up" more generally. The kanji 投 means "to throw, hurl, toss, give up, cast off." <扌殳>

投げる to throw [なげꜜる]; 投げつける to fling, hurl, pepper [なげつける, なげつけꜜる]; 放り投げる to toss [ほうりなげꜜる]; 投げやりな slovenly, irresponsible [なげやりな]; 投手 pitcher (baseball) [とꜜうしゅ]; 投資 investment [とうし]; 投薬する to dispense medicine [とうやくする] // 投網 casting a net [とあみ]

SG-0161 段	Meanings	Kun and On	Romaji	Bushu	Stroke Order and Number
	step, flight of stairs, grade, paragraph	ダン	*dan*	殳	亻 𠂤 𠂤 𣪊 段 段 9

段 **A** F-0509

金文 1 · 説文 2 · 段

One view explains that 1 comprised "a hearth with metal pieces" and "a hand holding a pounding tool," together signifying "forging thin metals." Layers of forged thin metals gave the meaning "stratum." Another view explains that 2 comprised 𠂤 to mean "to separate," used for the sound *tan*, and "to hit" (殳), together signifying "to separate things by hitting; a stratum." The kanji 段 means "step, flight of stairs, grade, paragraph." <𠂤殳>

段階的な incremental, gradual [だんかいてきな]; 石段 stone steps [いしだん]; 段取り course of action, arrangement [だんどꜜり, だんどり]; 別段 especially, particularly [べつだん]; 段々 stairs, steps [だんだꜜん], gradually, little by little [だんだん]; 段落 paragraph [だんらく]; 手段 a means, method, step [しゅꜜだん]

SG-0162 殺	Meanings	Kun and On	Romaji	Bushu	Stroke Order and Number
	to kill, reduce	ころ-す サツ・サイ・セツ	koro-su *satsu, sai, setsu*	殳	ノ メ 㐅 杀 剎 殺 10

殺 **B** F-0556

甲骨文 1 · 金文 2 · 説文古文 3 · 説文 4 · 旧字 5 · 殺

1 and 2 depicted "a wild boar" (豕). 3 and 4 comprised "a wild boar" and 殳 "to hit with a stick," together originally signifying "to kill a boar." In the kyuji 殺, 5, the animal was simplified to 朩 with a dot, and then 朩 alone in the shinji. The kanji 殺 means "to kill, reduce." <メ木殳>

殺す to kill [ころす]; 見殺しにする to leave in the lurch [みごろしにする]; 殺し文句 clincher, killing words [ころしもꜜんく]; 殺人 murder, homicide [さつじん]; 殺害する to kill, murder, commit a homicide [さつがいする]; 殺風景 desolate, bleak [さっぷꜜうけい]; 相殺する to offset each other, cancel out [そうさいする]; 殺生 killing (in Buddhism) [せꜜっしょう]

	Meanings	Kun and On	Romaji	Bushu	Stroke Order and Number
SG-0163 殻	hull, husk, empty shell	から カク	kara *kaku*	殳	一士声壳壳売殼殻 11

殻 **D** F-1824

甲骨文1 1 甲骨文2 2 説文 3 旧字 4

1 and 2 comprised "a hand holding a tool" and "an empty shell" or "an empty rice husk." What was left after threshing rice was the "hull." In 3 and 4, the two components swapped positions, placing 壳, for the sound *kaku*, on the left, and 殳 "to strike with a tool" on the right. The kanji 殻 means "hull, husk, empty shell." <士冗殳>

殻 hull, husk [から⌝]; 卵の殻 egg shell [たま⌝ごの・から]; 貝殻 shell [かいが⌝ら, かいがら]; 煙草の吸い殻 cigarette butts [たばこのすいがら]; 地殻 earth's crust [ちかく]; 地殻変動 crustal activity [ちかくへ⌝んどう]

	Meanings	Kun and On	Romaji	Bushu	Stroke Order and Number
SG-0164 穀	grain, rice	コク	*koku*	禾	士声壴幸穀穀穀 14

穀 **D** F-1664

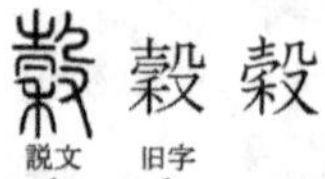

説文 1 旧字 2

The previous kanji, 殻 **SG-0163** "empty hull," was modified by replacing "empty rice husk" with 禾 "unhulled rice crop," which was used for the sound *koku*. Together with the right side, 殳 "hitting with a tool," the character signified "threshing unhulled rice," and more specifically the unhulled state of the "grain." The kanji 穀 means "grain, rice." <士冖禾殳>

穀物 grain, cereal [こく⌝もつ]; 脱穀 threshing, thrashing [だっこく]; 穀倉地帯 granary, farm belt [こくそうち⌝たい]

	Meanings	Kun and On	Romaji	Bushu	Stroke Order and Number
SG-0165 鍛	smithy; to forge, harden, train, drill, discipline	きた-える タン	kita-eru *tan*	金	𠆢午金釘釿鍜鍛 17

鍛 **D** F-1886

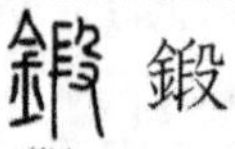

篆文

The seal-style form comprised 金 **SG-1196** "metal," and 段 **SG-0161**, used for the sound *tan* to mean "blacksmith's hearth," together signifying the work of a blacksmith. The meaning can also apply to one's mind, skills, or body, in the sense of "to train, drill, discipline." The kanji 鍛 means "smithy; to forge, harden, train, drill." <釒段>

鍛える forge, drill [きたえ⌝る]; 鍛錬 tempering, annealing [た⌝んれん] // 鍛冶屋 blacksmith [かじや]

	Meanings	Kun and On	Romaji	Bushu	Stroke Order and Number
SG-0166 毀	to break, destroy, damage	キ	*ki*	殳	𠂉白臼㿟毀毀 13

毀 **D** F-3257

説文古文 1 説文 2

1 and 2 comprised "a standing child so young that their skull has yet to close" (signifying "fragile"), and 殳 "hitting with a weapon." A fragile thing hit by a tool breaks easily. The kanji 毀 means "to break, destroy, damage." <臼土殳>
(Note: A line on the child's shin signified that it was standing and became 土 in the kanji. For the shape 臼, please refer to the kanji 児 **SG-0447**.)

毀損 damage, injury [きそん]; 名誉毀損 defamation of character, slander [めいよきそ⌝ん, め⌝いよ・きそん]; 廃仏毀釈 anti-Buddhist movement in the Meiji era [はいぶつき⌝しゃく]

9c 攵 (攴) "to cause an action" [from a hand using a stick or tool]; bushu *bokuzukuri/nobun* 攴

改数教修敬警散激枚厳悠敢赦傲

	Meanings	Kun and On	Romaji	Bushu	Stroke Order and Number
SG-0167 改	to renew, force, change	あらた-める カイ	arata-meru *kai*	攴	ᄀ コ 己 己 改 改 7

改 **A** F-0234

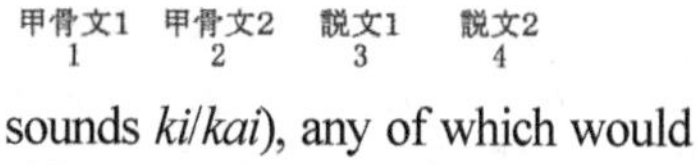

甲骨文1 1 甲骨文2 2 説文1 3 説文2 4

The origin of the kanji 改 is unclear. It has been suggested that the left side depicted "a crooked string," "a person on the verge of getting up" or "a snake" (己, used for the sounds *ki/kai*), any of which would have signified "a sudden change." The right side was "a hand holding a stick," signifying "to cause an action," and became 攴 in 3 and 4. The moment of something being caused to change meant "sudden or drastic change." 攴 further coalesced to 攵, bushu *bokuzukuri/nobun* in the shinji 改. The kanji 改 means "to renew, force, change." <己 攵>

改める to renew, change [あらため⌝る]; 改正 revision [かいせい]; 改良する to improve [かいりょうする]; 改札口 ticket gate [かいさつ⌝ぐち]; 改善する to improve [かいぜんする]; 改心する to reform oneself, turn over a new leaf [か⌝いしんする]

	Meanings	Kun and On	Romaji	Bushu	Stroke Order and Number
SG-0168 数	number; to count, quantify; a few, many	かず・かぞ-える スウ・ス	kazu, kazo-eru *suu, su*	攴	丶 丷 半 米 娄 数 数 13

数 **A** F-0108

説文 1 旧字 2

Views regarding the left-hand component vary. One view explains that the left side (婁) depicted female inmates or slaves (女) joined together in a row (毌), signifying "to link many things in a row," and was used for the sound *roo* to mean "to count using calculation rods." Taken together with the right side 攴 (攵) "to cause an action," the character meant "to count numbers." The kanji 数 means "number; to count/ quantify; a few, many." <米女攵>

数 number [かず]; 数知れない countless, innumerable [かずしれない]; 数える to count [かぞえる]; 字数 number of letters or characters [じすう]; 数学 mathematics [すうがく]; 少数 small number, a few [しょうすう]; 少数点 decimal point [しょうすうてん]; 数十人 tens of people [すうじゅうにん]; 英数字 English alphabet and numeric characters [えいすうじ]; 数量化 quantification [すうりょうか]; 数寄屋 tea ceremony hut [すきや]

	Meanings	Kun and On	Romaji	Bushu	Stroke Order and Number
SG-0169 教	to teach, learn; lesson	おし-える・おそ-わる キョウ	oshi-eru, oso-waru *kyoo*	攴	十 土 耂 考 孝 教 教 11

教 **A** F-0154

甲骨文 1 金文 2 説文 3 旧字 4

1 and 2 comprised 爻 "to mingle," and 攴 "to cause an action." In 3, 子 "child" was added to signify the mingling of pupils and a teacher, i.e., teaching and learning. The shinji 教 became comprised of 孝 **SG-0563** and 攵. The kanji 教 means "to teach, learn; lesson." <孝 攵>

教える to teach [おしえる]; 教え teaching, lesson [おしえ]; 教え子 one's former pupil/student [おしえご]; 教わる to be taught, learn [おそわる]; 教育 education [きょういく]; 教師 teacher, schoolteacher [きょうし]; キリスト教 Christianity [キリストきょう]; 宗教 religion [しゅうきょう]; 教会 church [きょうかい]

	Meanings	Kun and On	Romaji	Bushu	Stroke Order and Number
SG-0170 修	to pursue, master skills or knowledge, correct	おさ-める シュウ・シュ	osa-meru *shuu, shu*	人	亻 亻 伫 攸 修 修 10

修 **B** F-0531

説文

The seal-style form of the kanji 修 comprised "a person" (亻) with cleansing water trickling down (丨) on their back, 攴 (攵) "an action," and 彡 "beautiful shape," for the meaning "to tidy up." Taken together, they meant "one training very hard to experience the ablution of their soul and actions, and becoming more virtuous." The kanji 修 means "to pursue, master skills or knowledge, correct." <攸(亻丨攵)彡>

修める to pursue, complete [おさめる]; 研修会 training session [けんしゅうかい]; 修学旅行 school excursion [しゅうがくりょこう]; 修士号 master's degree [しゅうしごう]; 修道院 monastery, nunnery [しゅうどういん]; 修正する to amend [しゅうせいする]; 修行 ascetic practices [しゅぎょう]

	Meanings	Kun and On	Romaji	Bushu	Stroke Order and Number
SG-0171 敬	to respect, revere	うやま-う ケイ	uyama-u *kee*	攴	一 艹 芍 苟 苟 敬 敬 12

敬 **B** F-0910

甲骨文 1 金文 1 2 金文 2 3 説文 4

1 and 2 were "a person kneeling while wearing a sheep headdress." A sheep was often used as a sacrificial animal, and was associated with worship. 苟, used for the sound *kee* to mean "to admonish," and 攴 (攵 bushu *bokuzukuri*) "to cause," together meant "to make a bending posture to show respect." The kanji 敬 means "to respect, revere." <艹句攵>

敬う to respect, revere [うやまう]; 尊敬する to respect [そんけいする]; 敬礼する to salute [けいれいする]; 失敬な impudent, impolite [しっけいな]; 失敬する to steal, pilfer [しっけいする]; 敬意 respect [けいい]; 敬語 polite language, honorific [けいご]

	Meanings	Kun and On	Romaji	Bushu	Stroke Order and Number
SG-0172 警	to warn; alarm, guard	ケイ	*kee*	言	一 艹 芍 苟 敬 警 警 19

警 **B** F-0694

説文

The seal-style form comprised 敬, used for the sound *kee* to mean "to admonish," and 言 "word, language; to say," together signifying "to warn with words." The kanji 警 means "to warn; alarm, guard." <敬 言>

警告 admonition, warning [けいこく]; 警察官 policeman, police officer [けいさつかん, けいさつかん]; 警報 alarm [けいほう]; 警護. protection, guard [けいご]; 警世の書 book that rebukes society [けいせいのしょ]; 警句 witty remarks [けいく, けいく]

	Meanings	Kun and On	Romaji	Bushu	Stroke Order and Number
SG-0173 散	to disperse, scatter; useless	ち-る サン	chi-ru *san*	攴	一 艹 廾 昔 昔 散 散 12

散 **B** F-0843

金文 1 説文 2

1 comprised "bamboo," "a piece of meat" (月), and "a hand holding a stick or tool" (攴,攵) to mean "pounding." In 2, "hemp plants" replaced "bamboo" as the top-left component. One might pound a piece of tough meat to tenderize it, or hemp plants to extract fibers. Pounding caused some plants or flesh to be "torn or scattered," which led to the additional meaning of "useless." The kanji 散 means "to disperse, scatter; useless." <艹月攵>

花が散る flower petals fall [はなˀが·ちる]; 散らかす to scatter, leave in chaos [ちらかす]; 散り散りになる to disperse, break up [ちりじりになˀる]; 散々 severely, unsparingly [さんざん, さんざˀん]; 散散な目に遭う to have a terrible experience [さんざˀんなめに·あˀう]; 解散 breakup, split-up [かいさん]; 散在する to be found here and there [さんざいする]; 散文 prose [さんぶん]; 一目散に to run for one's life, run at full speed [いちもˀくさんに]

	Meanings	Kun and On	Romaji	Bushu	Stroke Order and Number
SG-0174 激	intense, violent; to agitate	はげ-しい ゲキ	hage-shii *geki*	水	氵 泊 浡 滂 滂 激 激 16

激 **B** F-0846

説文

The seal-style form comprised 氵 "flowing water"; and 敫, used for the sound *geki*, made up of 白 **SG-0787** "white," 方 **SG-1931** "all directions," and 攴 "to cause an action." Together, they described water gushing out, hitting rocks, and creating white water hurling in all directions. The kanji 激 means "intense, violent; to agitate." <氵白方攵>

激しい violent, intense [はげしˀい]; 過激な extreme, excessive [かげきな]; 感激 deep emotion, enthusiasm [かんげき]; 激流 torrent [げきりゅう]; 激化する to intensify [げきかする]; 激論 heated argument [げきろん]; 激戦地 closely contested election district [げきせんˀち]; 激増 drastic increase [げきぞう]

	Meanings	Kun and On	Romaji	Bushu	Stroke Order and Number
SG-0175 枚	counter for thin flat objects	マイ	*mai*	木	一 十 朩 朸 枚 8

枚 **B** F-0855

金文 1 説文 2

1 and 2 comprised "a tree" (木), signifying "a piece of wood," and 攴 (攵), "to cause an action." Using a tool (such as an ax), one obtained thinner and smaller pieces of wood. The kanji 枚 is used as the counter for thin, flat objects, such as those made of paper or cloth. <木攵>

(紙)何枚 how many sheets of paper [(かみ)なˀんまい]; 切符三枚 three tickets [きっぷにˀまい]; 枚数 number of sheets/flat objects [まいすˀう]

	Meanings	Kun and On	Romaji	Bushu	Stroke Order and Number
SG-0176 厳	solemn, strict	おごそ-か·きび-しい ゲン·ゴン	ogoso-ka, kibi-shii *gen, gon*	口	𭕄 产 产 产 嚴 厳 17

厳 **B** F-0929

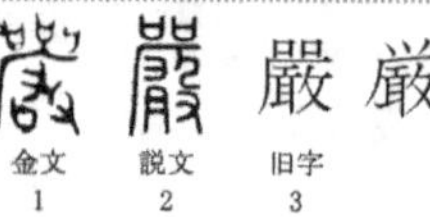

金文 1 説文 2 旧字 3

One view explains that 1 comprised three 口 **SG-0031** "mouths or prayer boxes" over "a cliff or canopy," and "a pitcher for sanctifying spirits," used for the sound *gen*. Together, these components meant "to sanctify an area." In the kyuji 嚴 (3), the inside became 敢 **SG-0178**, and in the shinji 厳, the two 口 were reduced to the ⺍ shape. From the solemn ceremony of sanctifying an area, the kanji 厳 takes the meaning "solemn, strict." <𭕄厂耳攵>

厳かな solemn, dignified [おごˀそかな]; 厳しい severe, strict [きびしˀい]; 手厳しい harsh, unsparing [てきびしˀい]; 厳格な stern, strict [げんかくな]; 厳禁 strictly prohibited [げんきん]; 厳密な precise, scrupulous [げんみつな]; 厳正中立 observe strict neutrality [げんせいちゅうりつ]; 荘厳な solemn, stately [そうごんな]

	Meanings	Kun and On	Romaji	Bushu	Stroke Order and Number
SG-0177 悠	calm, long-lasting, composed	ユウ	*yuu*	心	亻 亻 仆 攸 悠 悠 11

悠 **D** F-1697

説文

The left side and the upper part of the right side of the seal-style form contained 攸 "long-lasting" (from "trickling water cleansing a person's back"), and was used for the sound *yuu*. Inside it was 心 **SG-0187** "a heart." After cleansing the soul, one feels calm, gentle, and composed. The kanji 悠 means "calm, long-lasting, composed." <攸心>

(Note: The kanji 悠 **SG-0177**, 修 **SG-0170**, and 条 **SG-0630** share the same origin.)

悠久 eternity [ゆうきゅˀう]; 悠然と calmly, in a grand manner [ゆうぜんと]; 悠々と quietly, slowly [ゆうゆうと]; 悠長な leisurely, slow [ゆˀうちょうな]; 悠々自適 living free from worldly cares [ゆうゆうじてき]

SG-0178 敢	Meanings	Kun and On	Romaji	Bushu	Stroke Order and Number
	to dare, venture to	カン	*kan*	攴	⁻ エ 耳 耴 敢 敢 12

敢
D
F-2010

金文1 1 金文2 2 金文3 3 説文籀文 4 説文 5

Ancient forms for the kanji 敢 appeared in many places, but how their odd, irregular figures were to be construed is unclear. One view explains that 1, 2, and 3 comprised 口 **SG-0031** "mouth, box," "a ladle or pitcher for spirits," and "a hand," together depicting a hand scooping spirits with a ladle in a sanctification rite. In this rite, an awestricken supplicant would venture out to speak to an ancestral deity, saying, "if I may be permitted to talk to you." From that came the meaning "to dare, venture to." Another view holds that the character depicts two hands (in the middle and on the right side) trying to grab something that was used for the sound *ran/kan* on the left side. The manner of daring to grab something gave the meaning "to dare, venture to." The kanji 敢 means "to dare, venture to." <頁 攵>

果敢な resolute, daring [かꜜかんな]; 勇敢な brave, valiant [ゆうかんな]; 敢然と fearlessly, undauntedly [かんぜんと] // 敢えて言うと if I may venture to say [あꜜえていうと]

SG-0179 赦	Meanings	Kun and On	Romaji	Bushu	Stroke Order and Number
	to forgive	シャ	*sha*	赤	土 ナ 方 赤 赤ˊ 赦 11

赦
D
F-2181

金文 1 説文 2 説文或体 3

1 and 3 comprised 尗, used for the sound *sha* to mean "to abandon," and 攴 "to hit, cause." Taken together, they meant "to abandon hitting a person for punishment." The kanji reflected 2, which uses 赤 (not related to "red"). The kanji 赦 means "to forgive." <赤攵>

恩赦 government pardon, amnesty [おꜜんしゃ]; 容赦無く mercilessly [よꜜうしゃなく]; ご容赦ください Please forgive us for the inconvenience (formal) [ごよꜜうしゃください]; 赦免 pardon, absolution [しゃめん]; 大赦 amnesty, general pardon [たꜜいしゃ]

SG-0180 傲	Meanings	Kun and On	Romaji	Bushu	Stroke Order Number
	arrogant, boastful	ゴウ	*goo*	人	亻 仹 傍 傍 傲ˊ 傲 13

傲
D
F-2623

中山王器 1 説文 2

The origin of the kanji 傲 is obscure. One view explains that 2 comprised 亻 "an act one does," and 敖 (出 "to go out," 方 **SG-1931** "to disperse in all directions," and 攴 "action"), used for the sound *goo*. The character originally signified "to be free to go, do things freely." Being excessively free meant "arrogant." The kanji 傲 means "arrogant, boastful." <亻土方攵>

傲慢な arrogant, haughty [ごうまんな]

9d 支 "to branch out, support" [from a hand holding a bamboo twig with hanging leaves]; *shi/ki*; bushu *shinyoo/edanyoo* 支技枝岐肢伎

SG-0181 支	Meanings	Kun and On	Romaji	Bushu	Stroke Order and Number
	branch; to support, hold, hinder	ささ-える シ	sasa-eru *shi*	支	一 十 方 支 4

支
A
F-0318

説文古文 1 説文 2

In 1 and 2, a hand is holding a bamboo twig in the middle (1) or from below (2) to support it. The kanji 支 means "branch; to support, hold, hinder." <十又>

支える to support [ささえる]; 支持する to support [しꜜじする]; 支店 branch store [してん]; 支配する to rule over, control [しꜜはいする]; 支出 expenditure [ししゅつ]; 支度する to arrange, prepare [したくする]; 支流 tributary, fork [しりゅう] // 差し支えない may, can, be all right [さしつかえなꜜい]

SG-0182 技	Meanings	Kun and On	Romaji	Bushu	Stroke Order and Number
	(manual) skill, technique	わざ ギ	waza *gi*	手	亅 扌 扌ˊ 抆 技 7

技
A
F-0405

説文

The seal-style form comprised "a hand/an act done by hand" (扌, bushu *tehen*), and 支 **SG-0181**, used for the sound *gi*, together signifying "a skill that requires the hand." The kanji 技 means "(manual) skill, technique." <扌支>

技 technique, move (in sports) [わざꜜ]; 技術 technology, skill [ぎꜜじゅつ]; 技能 skills [ぎꜜのう]; 特技 special talent [とꜜくぎ]; 演技 acting, performance [えꜜんぎ]; 技巧的な technically accomplished [ぎこうてきな]

	Meanings	Kun and On	Romaji	Bushu	Stroke Order and Number
SG-0183 枝	branch, bough; to branch out	えだ シ	eda *shi*	木	十 木 木 杉 枝 8
枝 **B** F-1009	枝 (説文) 枝 The seal-style form comprised 木 **SG-0608** "tree," and 支 **SG-0181** "branch," used for the sound *shi*, together signifying "a branch of a tree." The kanji 枝 means "branch, bough; to branch out." <木支>			枝 tree branch [えだ1]; 枝分かれ branching out [えだわかれ]; 小枝 twig [こえだ]; 枯れ枝 withered branch [かれえだ]; 枝葉末節 unimportant details [しつよう・まっせつ]	

	Meanings	Kun and On	Romaji	Bushu	Stroke Order and Number
SG-0184 岐	fork in a path, byway	キ	*ki*	山	丨 山 山 山 岐 岐 7
岐 **C** F-1592	(説文古文 1) (説文 2) 岐 1 comprised 木 "tree," 支 **SG-0181** "branch" (used for the sound *ki*), and 山 **SG-1139** "mountain," together signifying "a fork in a mountain path." In 2, 木 was dropped, and 山 moved to the left. The kanji 岐 means "fork in a path, byway." <山支>			分岐点 junction, node [ぶんき1てん]; 岐路 forked road, crossroads, turning point [き1ろ]; 岐路に立たされる to be at a crossroads [き1ろに・たたされ1る]; 多岐にわたる encompassing many topics [た1きにわたる]	

	Meanings	Kun and On	Romaji	Bushu	Stroke Order and Number
SG-0185 肢	hands and feet, the limbs, alternative	シ	*shi*	肉	月 月 月 肢 8
肢 **D** F-1830	(説文 1) (説文或体 2) 肢 1 and 2 contained 月, bushu *nikuzuki* "part of the body." The right side of 1 is of unclear origin, while 2 had 支 "a branch; to support," used for the sound *shi*. These precursors meant "the limbs of one's body," which were the arms and legs. The sense of something that branched out from the main body also gave the meaning "alternative." The kanji 肢 means "hands and feet, the limbs, alternative." <月支>			四肢 the limbs, the legs and arms [し1し]; 肢体 the limbs, the body and the limbs [したい]; 下肢 the legs [か1し]; 肢体不自由 physical disability [したいふじ1ゆう]; 選択肢 (to choose between) alternatives, options, choices [せんたく1し]	

	Meanings	Kun and On	Romaji	Bushu	Stroke Order and Number
SG-0186 伎	skills, skilled artisan, entertainer	キ	*ki*	人	亻 什 仗 伎 6
伎 **D** F-2021	(説文) 伎 The seal-style form of the kanji 伎 comprised 亻, bushu *ninben* "an act that one does," and 支, used for the sound *gi* to mean "manual skills," signifying "a person with manual or artistic skills." The kanji 伎 meant "skills, skilled artisan, entertainer." <亻支>			歌舞伎 kabuki play [かぶき]; 伎能 (技能) technical skills, ability [ぎ1のう]	

10 Heart

10a 心 "heart, mind, emotion" [from the anatomical shape of a heart]

心忠患串隠穏寧忌芯

	Meanings	Kun and On	Romaji	Bushu	Stroke Order and Number
SG-0187 心	heart, mind, emotion, core	こころ シン	kokoro *shin*	心	丶 心 心 心 4
心 **A** F-0050	(金文1 1) (金文2 2) (説文 3) 心 1, 2, and 3 were an anatomical depiction of the chambers of a heart, with an artery added in 3. From being situated in the center of the chest, it also meant "core." The character meant "heart, mind, emotion, core." <心> (Note: "A heart" has two other bushu shapes — 忄 (the common shape 10b, bushu *risshinben*, when used on the left side of a kanji; and 㣺, bushu *shitagokoro*, as in 恭 **SG-0139**, 添 **SG-0319**, and 慕 **SG-0688**.)			心 heart, mind; [こころ]; 心がける to be mindful of [こころがけ1る]; 気心の知れた trusted [きごころのしれた]; 真心 sincerity; a true heart [まごころ]; 心配する to be worried [しんぱいする]; 心臓 heart [しんぞう]; 安心する to feel relieved [あんしんする]; 中心 central, middle, center [ちゅうしん]; 心中 double suicide [しんじゅう] // 心地よい to feel good, pleasant [ここちよ1い]	

	Meanings	Kun and On	Romaji	Bushu	Stroke Order and Number
SG-0188 忠	faithful to one's master, sincere	チュウ	*chuu*	心	8

忠 **B** F-0872

中山王器 1　説文 2

1 comprised 中 "center," used for the sound *chuu*, and 心 **SG-0187** "heart." A heart that stayed unwaveringly centered meant "loyal." The kanji 忠 means "faithful to one's master, sincere." <中 心>

忠告 advice [ちゅうこく]; 忠実に faithfully [ちゅうじつに]; 忠義 loyalty, fidelity, devotion [ちゅうぎ]; 忠孝 loyalty and filial piety [ちゅうこう]; 忠義者 loyal person [ちゅうぎもの]

	Meanings	Kun and On	Romaji	Bushu	Stroke Order and Number
SG-0189 患	to suffer; ill, afflicted with	わずら-う カン	wazura-u *kan*	心	11

患 **C** F-1126

説文古文1 1　説文古文2 2　説文 3

1 comprised 門 "closed double doors," signifying "something hidden inside," and "a heart pierced through." On the other hand, 2 and 3 comprised "cowries pierced through" (串 **SG-0190**), used for the sound *kan*, and "a heart" (心 **SG-0187**). Piercing through one's heart meant "painful; suffering." The kanji 患 means "to suffer; ill, afflicted with." <串 心>

患う to be sick, suffer from [わずらう]; 長患い protracted illness, lingering disease [ながわずらい]; 患者 patient [かんじゃ]; 急患 urgent patient [きゅうかん]; 患部 diseased part, wound [かんぶ]; 疾患 malady, ailment, disease [しっかん]

	Meanings	Kun and On	Romaji	Bushu	Stroke Order and Number
SG-0190 串	skewer, spit	くし	kushi	丨	7

串 **C** F-1813

No ancient form. The shape 串 came from two cowries pierced through, and was pronounced *kan*. (It is similar to 毌 "cowries strung through," except that in 串 they are vertically arranged.) The kanji 串 means "skewer, spit." <串>

串 skewer [くし]; 金串 metal skewer [かなぐし]; 串揚げ deep-fried delicacies on skewers [くしあげ]; 玉串 a sprig of *sakaki* in a Shinto ceremony [たまぐし]; 串団子 sweet rice dumplings on a skewer [くしだんご]

	Meanings	Kun and On	Romaji	Bushu	Stroke Order and Number
SG-0191 隠	hidden; to hide	かく-す イン	kaku-su *in*	阜	14

隠 **C** F-1237

説文 1　旧字 2

1 had "tall hills, mountains" (阝, bushu *kozatohen*) on the left side." The right side, used for the sound *in*, comprised "two hands" ("a hand reaching down" and "a sideways hand") hiding something between them, and "a heart" (心 **SG-0187**). Taken together, they meant emotions such as grief or mourning that were suppressed or hidden, and the character meant "hidden." In the shinji 隠, 工 was dropped. The kanji 隠 means "hidden; to hide." <阝爫 彐 心>

隠れる to hide [かくれる]; 隠し芸 display hidden talent [かくしげい]; 隠し事 secret [かくしごと]; 隠居 a retired person [いんきょ]; 隠語 jargon, slang, secret language [いんご]; 目隠し blindfold [めかくし]

	Meanings	Kun and On	Romaji	Bushu	Stroke Order and Number
SG-0192 穏	calm, tranquil, placid	おだ-やか オン	oda-yaka *on*	禾	16

穏 **C** F-1523

説文 1　旧字 2

The right side of the kanji 穏 had the same components as that of 隠 **SG-0191**, "hiding emotions," and was used for the sound *on*. With 禾 "rice plant with crop" added, the character signified "storing harvested rice out of view." Having a good harvest stored gave one peace of mind. The kanji 穏 means "calm, tranquil, placid." <禾 爫 彐 心>

穏やかな calm, placid, tranquil [おだやかな]; 穏健派 moderate faction [おんけんは]; 穏便に amicable, in a private way [おんびんに]; 不穏な disquieting, alarming [ふおんな] // 安穏な peaceful [あんのんな]

	Meanings	Kun and On	Romaji	Bushu	Stroke Order and Number
SG-0193 寧	peace of mind, tranquility, quietness	ネイ	*nee*	宀	14

寧 **D** F-1842

甲骨文 1　金文1 2　金文2 3　説文1 4　説文2 5

1 through 5 comprised "a mausoleum roof," and "a heart of a sacrificial animal in a shallow vessel placed on an altar table," together signifying "praying for peace and tranquility." The kanji 寧 comprises 宀, 心, 罒 (for 皿) and 丁, and means "peace of mind, tranquility, quietness." <宀心罒丁>

丁寧な courteous, careful [ていねいな]; 安寧 national tranquility [あんねい]; 馬鹿丁寧に excessively polite [ばかていねいに]; 丁寧語 polite language [ていねいご]

	Meanings	Kun and On	Romaji	Bushu	Stroke Order and Number
SG-0194 忌	to shun, have an aversion to; mourning, the anniversary of a death	い-む キ	i-mu *ki*	心	フコ己己忌忌忌 7

忌
D
F-1782

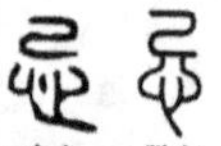

金文 1　説文 2

1 and 2 comprised 己, used for the sound *ki* to mean "to avoid," and 心 "heart," together signifying "to have an aversion to, avoid." Death was something to be avoided or shunned. The kanji 忌 means "to shun, have an aversion to; mourning, anniversary of a death." < 己 心 >

忌まわしい disgusting, unpleasant [いまわしꜜい]; 忌み嫌う to detest, loathe [いꜜみきらう]; 忌中 in mourning [きちゅう]; 三回忌 third anniversary of death [さんかꜜいき]; 一周忌 first anniversary of death [いっしゅꜜうき]

	Meanings	Kun and On	Romaji	Bushu	Stroke Order and Number
SG-0195 芯	center, wick, core, interfacing (of a garment)	シン	*shin*	艸	一艹艹芯芯 7

芯
D
F-1961

No ancient form. The kanji comprises 艹 (bushu *kusakanmuri* "plants)," and 心 **SG-0187**, used for the sound *shin* to mean "center." A particular type of bulrush was used to make the inner material of a lamp, i.e., the wick. The character is also used for refills for a mechanical pencil. The kanji 芯 means "center, wick, core, interfacing (of a garment)." < 艹 心 >

芯 core, center, wick [しꜜん]; 芯地 interfacing, padding (in garments) [しんじ]; 芯の強い having inner strength [しꜜんの・つよꜜい]; シャーペンの芯 leads for mechanical pencil [シャーペンのしꜜん]

10b 忄 "heart, mind, emotion"; **bushu *risshinben*** 快怪悟惧

	Meanings	Kun and On	Romaji	Bushu	Stroke Order and Number
SG-0196 快	pleasant, cheerful, rapid	こころよ-い カイ	kokoroyo-i *kai*	心	忄忄忄快快 7

快
C
F-1079

説文

The seal-style form comprised "a heart" (忄, bushu *risshinben*) and "a knife with a sharp blade" held by "a hand" (coalesced to 夬 in kanji), used for the sound *kai* to mean "decisively removing blockage." When something troubling the heart was removed, one became "cheerful, pleasant." Having no obstacles in the way also gave the meaning "rapid." The kanji 快 means "pleasant, cheerful, rapid." < 忄 夬>

快い pleasant [こころよꜜい]; 快適な comfortable, pleasant [かいてきな]; 快速電車 rapid train [かいそくでꜜんしゃ]; 快方に向かう to get better, be recovering [かいほうにむかう]; 全快 complete recovery (of health) [ぜんかい]

	Meanings	Kun and On	Romaji	Bushu	Stroke Order and Number
SG-0197 怪	mystic, suspicious, dubious	あや-しい カイ	aya-shii *kai*	心	忄忄怪怪怪怪 8

怪
C
F-1554

説文

The seal-style form comprised 忄 "a heart," and 又 "a hand" with 土 "pile of soil" for the sound *kai*. The development of 圣 above right) shows that it originally depicted two hands presenting a ball of dirt, to appease an earth spirit. Together, these components meant "the extraordinary spirits of the soil, mystic," which further lead to the meaning "suspicious, dubious.' The kanji 怪 means "mystic, suspicious, dubious." < 忄 圣>

怪しい strange, mysterious [あやしい]; 怪しむ to doubt, suspect [あやしꜜむ]; 怪人 mysterious figure [かいじん]; 怪物 apparition, monster [かいぶつ]; 妖怪 ghost, apparition, monster [ようかい]; 奇怪な mysterious, weird, [きかいな] // 怪我 injury, wound [けがꜜ]; 物の怪 ghost, supernatural being [もののけ]

	Meanings	Kun and On	Romaji	Bushu	Stroke Order and Number
SG-0198 悟	to become aware, become enlightened	さと-る ゴ	sato-ru *go*	心	忄忄忄悟悟悟 10

悟
C
F-1515

説文古文 1　説文 2

1 comprised two sets of crossed lines separated by three horizontal lines (used for the sound *go* to mean "clear"), and "a heart" below them, together signifying "to perceive, comprehend." In 2, the heart became 忄 bushu *risshinben*. The kanji 悟 means "to become aware, become enlightened." < 忄 吾>

悟る to perceive, be spiritually enlightened [さとꜜる]; 覚悟 readiness, resignation [かꜜくご]

SG-0199 惧	Meanings	Kun and On	Romaji	Bushu	Stroke Order and Number
	to fear	グ	*gu*	心	丷 忄冂 忄目 忄且 惧 11

惧
D
F-2685

No ancient form. One view takes the kanji to be the informal style of the non-Joyo kanji 懼 (comprising 忄, bushu *risshinben* "a heart," and 瞿 "a bird with two restless eyes," together meaning "to fear, feel scared"). The kanji 惧 comprises 忄 "a heart," and 具 for the sound *gu*, with the side lines of the 目 component touching the horizontal line below. The kanji 惧 means "to fear." <忄具>
(Note: When written by hand, it is acceptable to write the right side as 具 **SG-1719**.)

危惧する to feel apprehensive [きぐする]; 絶滅危惧種 endangered species [ぜつめつきぐしゅ]

11 Forward-facing footprint

11a 止 "to stop; a forward step" [from a forward-facing footprint] 止企歩歳渉渋頻捗 𣥂

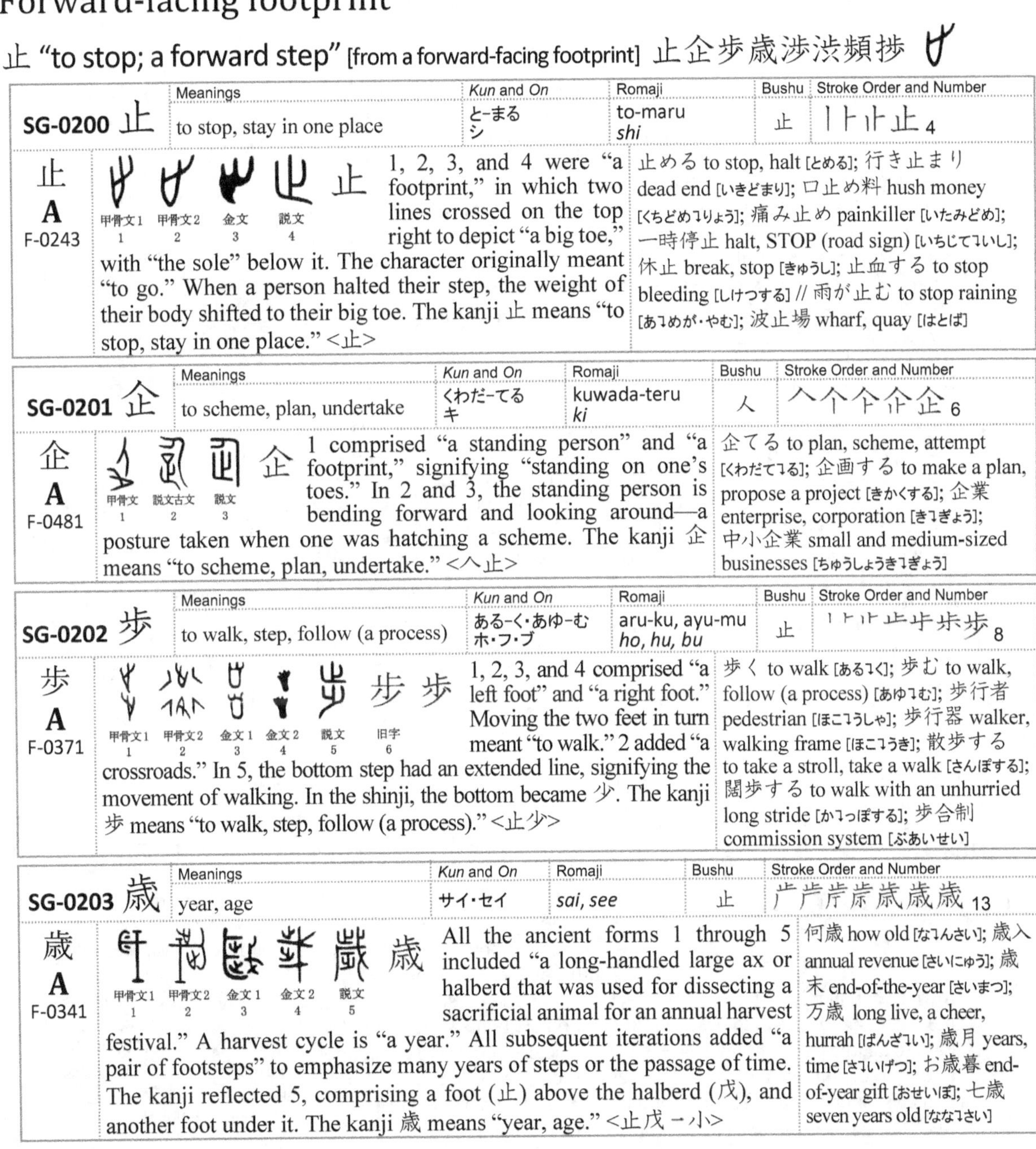

SG-0200 止	Meanings	Kun and On	Romaji	Bushu	Stroke Order and Number
	to stop, stay in one place	と-まる シ	to-maru *shi*	止	丨 ト 𣥂 止 4

止
A
F-0243

甲骨文1 (1), 甲骨文2 (2), 金文 (3), 説文 (4)

1, 2, 3, and 4 were "a footprint," in which two lines crossed on the top right to depict "a big toe," with "the sole" below it. The character originally meant "to go." When a person halted their step, the weight of their body shifted to their big toe. The kanji 止 means "to stop, stay in one place." <止>

止める to stop, halt [とめる]; 行き止まり dead end [いきどまり]; 口止め料 hush money [くちどめりょう]; 痛み止め painkiller [いたみどめ]; 一時停止 halt, STOP (road sign) [いちじていし]; 休止 break, stop [きゅうし]; 止血する to stop bleeding [しけつする] // 雨が止む to stop raining [あめがやむ]; 波止場 wharf, quay [はとば]

SG-0201 企	Meanings	Kun and On	Romaji	Bushu	Stroke Order and Number
	to scheme, plan, undertake	くわだ-てる キ	kuwada-teru *ki*	人	𠆢 个 仐 仚 企 6

企
A
F-0481

甲骨文 (1), 説文古文 (2), 説文 (3)

1 comprised "a standing person" and "a footprint," signifying "standing on one's toes." In 2 and 3, the standing person is bending forward and looking around—a posture taken when one was hatching a scheme. The kanji 企 means "to scheme, plan, undertake." <𠆢止>

企てる to plan, scheme, attempt [くわだてる]; 企画する to make a plan, propose a project [きかくする]; 企業 enterprise, corporation [きぎょう]; 中小企業 small and medium-sized businesses [ちゅうしょうきぎょう]

SG-0202 歩	Meanings	Kun and On	Romaji	Bushu	Stroke Order and Number
	to walk, step, follow (a process)	ある-く・あゆ-む ホ・フ・ブ	aru-ku, ayu-mu *ho, hu, bu*	止	丨 ト 𣥂 止 𣥂 歨 歩 8

歩
A
F-0371

甲骨文1 (1), 甲骨文2 (2), 金文1 (3), 金文2 (4), 説文 (5), 旧字 (6)

1, 2, 3, and 4 comprised "a left foot" and "a right foot." Moving the two feet in turn meant "to walk." 2 added "a crossroads." In 5, the bottom step had an extended line, signifying the movement of walking. In the shinji, the bottom became 少. The kanji 歩 means "to walk, step, follow (a process)." <止少>

歩く to walk [あるく]; 歩む to walk, follow (a process) [あゆむ]; 歩行者 pedestrian [ほこうしゃ]; 歩行器 walker, walking frame [ほこうき]; 散歩する to take a stroll, take a walk [さんぽする]; 闊歩する to walk with an unhurried long stride [かっぽする]; 歩合制 commission system [ぶあいせい]

SG-0203 歳	Meanings	Kun and On	Romaji	Bushu	Stroke Order and Number
	year, age	サイ・セイ	*sai, see*	止	广 产 岸 崇 歳 歳 歳 13

歳
A
F-0341

甲骨文1 (1), 甲骨文2 (2), 金文1 (3), 金文2 (4), 説文 (5)

All the ancient forms 1 through 5 included "a long-handled large ax or halberd that was used for dissecting a sacrificial animal for an annual harvest festival." A harvest cycle is "a year." All subsequent iterations added "a pair of footsteps" to emphasize many years of steps or the passage of time. The kanji reflected 5, comprising a foot (止) above the halberd (戊), and another foot under it. The kanji 歳 means "year, age." <止戊一小>

何歳 how old [なんさい]; 歳入 annual revenue [さいにゅう]; 歳末 end-of-the-year [さいまつ]; 万歳 long live, a cheer, hurrah [ばんざい]; 歳月 years, time [さいげつ]; お歳暮 end-of-year gift [おせいぼ]; 七歳 seven years old [ななさい]

	Meanings	Kun and On	Romaji	Bushu	Stroke Order and Number
SG-0204 渉	to cross water, traverse, pass over	ショウ	*shoo*	水	氵氵氵氵涉涉渉 11

渉 **B** F-1000

甲骨文 1 1, 甲骨文 2 2, 金文 3, 説文籀文 4, 説文 5, 旧字 6

1 and 2 comprised "a left foot" and "a right foot" on either side of "flowing water," marked by a contour. In 3, "water" was moved over to the left side, and the right side became two feet separated by a line. Together, these components meant "a person trying to wade across a river." In the kanji, the water became 氵, bushu *sanzui.* The kanji 渉 means "to cross water, traverse, pass over." <氵止少>

交渉 negotiation [こうしょう]; 渉外 liaison, external relations [しょうがい]; 干渉する to interfere, meddle [かんしょうする]; 内政不干渉 non-intervention in internal affairs [ないせいふかんしょう]; 労使交渉 labor-management negotiations [ろうしこうしょう]

	Meanings	Kun and On	Romaji	Bushu	Stroke Order and Number
SG-0205 渋	gridlock, astringent juice; reluctant, hesitant, subtly tasteful	しぶ-い ジュウ	shibu-i *juu*	水	氵氵氵氵氵渋渋 11

渋 **B** F-1021

篆文 1, 正字 2, 旧字 3

1 comprised "a pair of forward-facing footprints" (bottom) and a second pair of inverted footprints (top), facing each other vertically. Neither of the two opposing pairs of footprints could move forward—"gridlock." In 2 and 3, "flowing water" (氵) was added to signify "to stagnate." The right side of 澀 also gave the meaning "unwilling or hesitant to move." In Japanese, the character is also used for *shibu,* the astringent juice of a persimmon. From that, it also has the meanings "tart, sober, quiet and simple." The two 止 were reduced to ⺀ in the kanji. The kanji 渋 means "gridlock; astringent juice; reluctant, hesitant, subtly tasteful." <氵止⺀>

渋い astringent, unobtrusively elegant [しぶい]; 渋る to hang back, be reluctant [しぶる]; 買い渋る reluctant to buy [かいしぶる]; 渋々 grudgingly [しぶしぶ]; 茶渋 tea staining [ちゃしぶ]; 苦渋 predicament; distress [くじゅう]; 車の渋滞 traffic jam, traffic gridlock [くるまのじゅうたい]

	Meanings	Kun and On	Romaji	Bushu	Stroke Order and Number
SG-0206 頻	often; frequent	ヒン	*hin*	頁	⺊止步歩頻頻頻 17

頻 **D** F-1880

説文 1, 正字 2, 旧字 3

1 had "two footsteps" with "water" between them, signifying "feet in front of water." The right side was 頁 "person or head." Taken together, these components originally meant "a person halting their steps and wincing at the water." The character came to be used to mean "often." 2 (瀕) comprised 渉 and 頁, and in the shinji 頻, "water" was dropped. The kanji 頻 means "often; frequent." <歩頁>

頻度 frequency [ひんど]; 頻出語 word that occurs frequently [ひんしゅつご] // 頻りに frequently, incessantly [しきりに]

	Meanings	Kun and On	Romaji	Bushu	Stroke Order and Number
SG-0207 捗	to make progress, be well under way	チョク	*choku*	手	扌扌抄抄捗捗 10

捗 **D** F-3034

No ancient form. The kanji 捗 comprised 扌 bushu *tehen* and 歩 "walking, steps; to follow progress," used for the sound *choku*. In Japanese, the kanji 捗 means "to make progress, be well under way." <扌歩>

進捗 progress [しんちょく] // 捗る to make good progress [はかどる]

11b 正 "just; to conquer" [from soldiers' feet advancing on a town]; *see/shoo* 正政証征

	Meanings	Kun and On	Romaji	Bushu	Stroke Order and Number
SG-0208 正	just, right, correct, authentic	ただ-しい・まさ セイ・ショウ	tada-shii, masa *see, shoo*	止	一丅下正正 5

正 **A** F-0065

甲骨文 1 1, 甲骨文 2 2, 金文 1 3, 金文 2 4, 説文 5

1 and 2 comprised "a wall surrounding a town," and "soldiers' footsteps," together signifying "soldiers walking into a town to conquer it." This was a just act for a conqueror, so the character meant "just." We need to bear in mind that oracle bone–style characters (and to a large extent bronzeware–style characters, too) were created for a ruler to communicate with a deity, and so they are often defined from a ruler's point of view. The top component in 3, 4, and 5 became a single line. The kanji 正 means "just, right, correct, authentic." <一止>

正しい correct, right, just [ただしい]; 正す to rectify, straighten [ただす]; 正しく just, precisely [まさしく]; 正式 formal [せいしき]; 正常な normal [せいじょうな]; 不正 injustice, dishonest, corrupt [ふせい]; 正月 New Year's Holidays [しょうがつ]; 正気 consciousness, sanity [しょうき]; 大正 Taisho era (1912-1926) [たいしょう]

	Meanings	Kun and On	Romaji	Bushu	Stroke Order and Number
SG-0209 政	to govern; administrative, political	まつりごと セイ・ショウ	matsurigoto *see, shoo*	攴	丅 下 正 正' 政 政 9

政 **A** F-0179

甲骨文 1 金文 2 説文 3 政

1, 2, and 3 comprised "a town wall" with "a footstep," signifying "conquering, just act" (正, for the sound *see*); and "a hand holding a stick," signifying "to cause an action" (攴, 攵). Taken together, these components originally meant "a just way of governing." The kanji 政 means "to govern; administrative, political." <正攵>

政 government, rule [まつりごと]; 政治 politics [せいじ]; 国政 national government [こくせい]; 行政 administration, governance [ぎょうせい]; 政情 political situation [せいじょう]; 政界 political circles [せいかい]; 圧政 oppressive regime [あっせい]

	Meanings	Kun and On	Romaji	Bushu	Stroke Order and Number
SG-0210 証	to certify; proof, certificate	ショウ	*shoo*	言	言 訂 訂 訴 証 12

証 **B** F-0528

説文 1 旧字 2 証

1 comprised 言, bushu *gonben* "word, language; to say," and 登 **SG-0267** "to climb," used for the sounds *too/shoo* to mean "to make proof," together signifying "to make a statement while presenting verification or obtaining certification." The kyuji (2) was replaced by an unrelated kanji, 証 (with 正 used for the sound *shoo*). The kanji 証 means "to certify; proof, certificate." <言正>

証人 witness [しょうにん]; 証言 testimony [しょうげん]; 保証 guarantee [ほしょう]; 証書 deed, documents [しょうしょ]; 公証人 notary public [こうしょうにん]; 証券 bill, security [しょうけん, しょꜜうけん]; 実証する to corroborate, prove [じっしょうする]; 証明 proof [しょうめい]

	Meanings	Kun and On	Romaji	Bushu	Stroke Order and Number
SG-0211 征	to advance to subjugate, travel afar	セイ	*see*	彳	彳 彳 行 征 征 8

征 **C** F-1556

甲骨文 1 金文1 2 金文2 3 説文 4 説文或体 5 征

1 was similar to 2 for 正 **SG-0208** "just act," used for the sound *see*, while in 2 and 3, 彳 bushu *gyooninben* "a crossroads" was added to signify "to advance." Taken together, these components signified "to advance and conquer." The kanji 征 means "to move to subjugate, travel afar." <彳正>

遠征 expedition, tour [えんせい]; 征服 conquer [せいふく]; 出征兵士 a soldier leaving for the front [しゅっせいへꜜいし]; 征伐 subjugation, punitive expedition [せꜜいばつ]

11c 之 "to go" [from a footprint going beyond a line]; *shi* 市志誌芝乏 㞢 㞢

	Meanings	Kun and On	Romaji	Bushu	Stroke Order and Number
SG-0212 市	market, city, municipality	いち シ	ichi *shi*	巾	亠 亡 市 市 5

市 **A** F-0026

金文 1 説文 2 市

1 comprised 之 "to go," from a footprint going beyond a line, and 丁 **SG-1914** "signpost, block." Together they meant "a market with a sign where people go." The character also meant "municipality, city." In the kanji the shape changed to 亠 and 巾 **SG-1682**. The kanji 市 means "market, city, municipality." <亠巾>

市 city, municipal [しꜜ], market [いꜜち]; 蚤の市 flea market [のみのꜜいち]; 市場 marketplace [しじょう, いꜜちば]; 市民 citizen [しꜜみん]; 市政 city administration [しせい]; 都市 city, town [とꜜし]

	Meanings	Kun and On	Romaji	Bushu	Stroke Order and Number
SG-0213 志	one's will, aspiration	こころざ-す・こころざし シ	kokoroza-su, kokorozashi *shi*	心	一 十 士 志 志 7

志 **B** F-0696

説文 志

The seal-style form comprised "a footstep above a line," signifying "to go (to a goal)," used for the sound *shi*; and 心 **SG-0187** "a heart." Together they signified "where one's heart desires to go; one's will." In the kanji, the top was replaced with the phonetically identical 士. The kanji 志 means "one's will, aspiration." <士心>

志 aspiration [こころざし]; 志す to aspire, aim, shoot for [こころざꜜす]; 志望者 applicant [しぼꜜうしゃ]; 同志 comrade, each other [どꜜうし]; 有志 volunteer [ゆꜜうし]; 立志伝 story of a self-made man [りっしꜜでん]; 志向 inclination, orientation [しこう]

	Meanings	*Kun* and *On*	Romaji	Bushu	Stroke Order and Number
SG-0214 誌	journal	シ	*shi*	言	言訁計誌誌 14

誌 **B** F-0863 — 說文

The seal-style form comprised 言 **SG-1364** "word, language; to say," and 志 **SG-0213** "one's desire, aspiration," for the sound *shi*. A journal was where one wrote down their thoughts to preserve memories. The kanji 誌 means "journal." <言士心>

雑誌 magazine [ざっし]; 誌面 page space [しめん]; 会誌 journal of an association [かいし]; 月刊誌 monthly magazine [げっかんし]; 日誌 journal [にっし]; 同人誌 magazine published by a group of like-minded people [どうじんし]

	Meanings	*Kun* and *On*	Romaji	Bushu	Stroke Order and Number
SG-0215 芝	grass, turf	しば	shiba	艸	一艹艹芝芝 6

芝 **B** F-0976 — 說文

The seal-style form comprised "plants" (艸, 艹, bushu *kusakanmuri*) and 之 "to go," used for the sound *shi*. Together, they originally meant "a fast-growing mushroom or herb" that was believed to help longevity. In Japanese, the kanji 芝 is used to mean "grass, turf." <艹之>

芝 lawn grass, turf [しば]; 芝刈り mowing the lawn [しばかり]; 芝居 theatrical play [しばい]; 紙芝居 storytelling with pictures [かみしばい] // 芝生 lawn, grass, turf [しばふ]

	Meanings	*Kun* and *On*	Romaji	Bushu	Stroke Order and Number
SG-0216 乏	scanty, meager, destitute	とぼ-しい ボウ	tobo-shii *boo*	ノ	一ィ乏乏 4

乏 **C** F-1507 — 金文 1, 中山王器 2, 說文 3

The origin of the kanji 乏 is obscure. One view explains that it was a flipped image of the kanji 正 **SG-0208**—in 1 and 3, the short hook shape was on the left, while in 正 "just, right," it was on the right. Things that were "wrong or not correct" did not develop well, resulting in their being "scanty or destitute." The kanji 乏 means "scanty, meager, destitute." <一之>

乏しい scanty, meager [とぼしい]; 欠乏 insufficiency, deficiency [けつぼう]; 貧乏人 poor person, pauper [びんぼうにん]; 貧乏性 a parsimonious spirit, tendency to be frugal [びんぼうしょう]; 器用貧乏 jack-of-all-trades and master of none, "Versatility never pays" [きようびんぼう]

11d 出 "to go out, come out" [from a footprint leaving behind the outline of a heel] 出拙

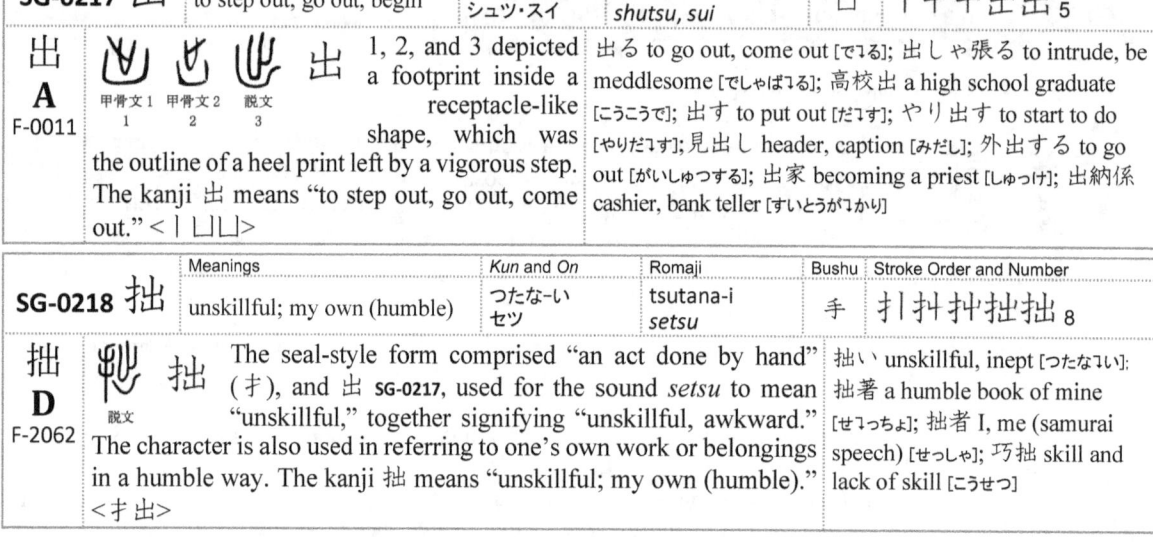

	Meanings	*Kun* and *On*	Romaji	Bushu	Stroke Order and Number
SG-0217 出	to step out, go out, begin	で-る・だ-す シュツ・スイ	de-ru, da-su *shutsu, sui*	凵	丨十中出出 5

出 **A** F-0011 — 甲骨文1 1, 甲骨文2 2, 說文 3

1, 2, and 3 depicted a footprint inside a receptacle-like shape, which was the outline of a heel print left by a vigorous step. The kanji 出 means "to step out, go out, come out." <丨凵凵>

出る to go out, come out [でる]; 出しゃ張る to intrude, be meddlesome [でしゃばる]; 高校出 a high school graduate [こうこうで]; 出す to put out [だす]; やり出す to start to do [やりだす]; 見出し header, caption [みだし]; 外出する to go out [がいしゅつする]; 出家 becoming a priest [しゅっけ]; 出納係 cashier, bank teller [すいとうがかり]

	Meanings	*Kun* and *On*	Romaji	Bushu	Stroke Order and Number
SG-0218 拙	unskillful; my own (humble)	つたな-い セツ	tsutana-i *setsu*	手	扌扌扌拙拙 8

拙 **D** F-2062 — 說文

The seal-style form comprised "an act done by hand" (扌), and 出 **SG-0217**, used for the sound *setsu* to mean "unskillful," together signifying "unskillful, awkward." The character is also used in referring to one's own work or belongings in a humble way. The kanji 拙 means "unskillful; my own (humble)." <扌出>

拙い unskillful, inept [つたない]; 拙著 a humble book of mine [せっちょ]; 拙者 I, me (samurai speech) [せっしゃ]; 巧拙 skill and lack of skill [こうせつ]

11e 寺 "to hold, sustain" [from 之 or 止, and 寸]; *ji/too/toku* 寺時持待等特詩侍

	Meanings	Kun and On	Romaji	Bushu	Stroke Order and Number
SG-0219 寺	temple	てら ジ	tera *ji*	寸	一十土圭寺寺 6

寺 **A** F-0580

金文1 1, 金文2 2, 金文3 3, 説文 4

1 through 4 all comprised 之 "to go" (from a footprint above a line), used for the sound *ji*, and 寸, "a hand (holding something in 3 and 4)." One view explains that this was the original form of 持 **SG-0221** "to hold in hand, have," and that it changed to mean "government office." Another view explains that 寺 represented officials working using their "hands" (寸), and "feet moving about" (之), and thus meant "a government office." Later the building was understood to be occupied by Buddhist monks, and the meaning changed to "temple." In the kanji, 之 became 土. The kanji 寺 means "temple." <土 寸>

寺 temple [てらꜛ]; 寺子屋 private elementary school in the Edo period [てらこや]; 寺院 large temple [じꜛいん]; 東大寺 Todaiji Temple [とうだいじ]; 菩提寺 ancestral temple [ぼだいじ]

	Meanings	Kun and On	Romaji	Bushu	Stroke Order and Number
SG-0220 時	time, hour, era, opportunity; o'clock	とき ジ	toki *ji*	日	日 日一 日十 日土 日圭 時 10

時 **A** F-0019

甲骨文1 1, 甲骨文2 2, 甲骨文3 3, 石鼓文 4, 中山王器 5, 説文 6

1, 2, 3, and 5 comprised "a footprint above a line; to go" (from 之), and "the sun" (日 **SG-1045**) or "a hand" (寸), signifying "the sun moving." 4 and 6 became the combination of "the sun" and 寺, used for the sound *ji*. The sun moving means "time." The kanji 時 means "time, hour, era, opportunity; o'clock." <日 寺>

その時 at that time, then [そのときꜛ]; 時々 sometimes [ときどき]; 潮時 good timing [しおどき]; 時には at times [ときꜛには]; 時間 time, duration of time [じかん]; 何時 what time [なꜛんじ]; 時代 era, period [じだい]; 時世 times, day and age [じせい]; 五時 five o'clock [ごꜛじ] // 時計 clock, (wrist) watch [とけい]

	Meanings	Kun and On	Romaji	Bushu	Stroke Order and Number
SG-0221 持	to hold in hand, possess, sustain	も-つ ジ	mo-tsu *ji*	手	扌 扌 扌十 扌土 扌圭 持 持 9

持 **A** F-0194

金文 1, 金文2 2, 説文 3

1 and 2 were the same as 1 and 3 for 寺 **SG-0219**, and were pronounced *ji*. One view explains that 寺 (*ji*) had the meaning "to hold, sustain," and another hand (扌, bushu *tehen*, "an act that one does by hand") was added to distinguish it from other characters that contained 寺. Taken together, these components signified "to hold something in hand." The kanji 持 means "to hold in hand, possess, sustain." <扌 寺>

持つ to own, have, hold in hand [もꜛつ]; 持っている to own, have [もꜛっている]; 持ってくる to bring [もってくꜛる]; 持ち物 belonging [もちꜛもの]; 持続する to last a long time [じぞくする]; 持参する to bring (with one) [じさんする]; 持病 chronic illness [じびょう]; 所持する to possess, have on one's person [しょꜛじする]

	Meanings	Kun and On	Romaji	Bushu	Stroke Order and Number
SG-0222 待	to wait, be hospitable to, attend upon, serve	ま-つ タイ	ma-tsu *tai*	彳	彳 彳十 彳土 彳圭 待 9

待 **A** F-0479

金文 1, 説文 2

1 comprised 彳, bushu *gyooninben* "a crossroads," and 寺, used for the sound *ji* to mean "to hold, sustain." Holding back one's steps at a crossroads signified "waiting." Anticipating and being prepared for someone's arrival also gave the meaning "hospitable." The kanji 待 means "to wait, be hospitable to, attend upon, serve." <彳 寺>

待つ to wait [まꜛつ]; 待ち合わせる to meet up [まちあわせる, まちあわせꜛる]; キャンセル待ち on a waitlist [キャンセルまち]; 招待する to invite [しょうꜛたいする]; 待望の eagerly expected [たいぼうの]; 期待する to hope for [きたいする]; 接待 (corporate) entertainment [せꜛったい]; 待機する to stand by on alert, be on call [たꜛいきする]

	Meanings	Kun and On	Romaji	Bushu	Stroke Order and Number
SG-0223 等	equal, equivalent; such things as, etc.	ひと-しい トウ	hito-shii *too*	竹	⺮ 笁 笙 等 等 12

等 **A** F-0430

説文

1 comprised 竹 "bamboo," and 寺, used for the sound *too*. Bamboo writing tablets were cut to equal lengths to be bound into a rolled book. The character is also used to mean "such things as, et al." to include things that are similar or have equal qualities. The kanji 等 means "equal, equivalent; such things as, etc." <⺮ 寺>

等しい equal [ひとしꜛい]; ～等 such things as X, etc. (noun suffix) [～とꜛう]; 等分する to divide equally [とうぶんする]; 高等な advanced [こうとうな]; 三親等 kinsman of the third degree (of consanguinity) [さんしꜛんとう]; 平等 equality [びょうどう] // ～等 such things as X, etc. [～なꜛど]; 我等 we all [わꜛれら]

	Meanings	*Kun* and *On*	Romaji	Bushu	Stroke Order and Number
SG-0224 特	to stand out; special, especially superior, particular	トク	*toku*	牛	丿 牛 牛+ 特 特 特 10

特 **A** F-0204 — 説文 — The seal-style form comprised 牛 "an ox or cow," and 寺, used for the sound *toku* to mean "to stay in one place." A large bull standing still among other oxen stood out. The kanji 特 means "to stand out; special, especially superior, particular." <牛寺>

特に especially [とくに]; 特別な special [とくべつな]; 特売 special sale [とくばい]; 特価 specially priced [とっか]; 特上 finest, choicest [とくじょう]; 特定する to specify, designate as [とくていする]; 不特定 unspecified [ふとくてい]; 特質 characteristic, property [とくしつ]

	Meanings	*Kun* and *On*	Romaji	Bushu	Stroke Order and Number
SG-0225 詩	poetry	シ	*shi*	言	言 言+ 計 詩 詩 詩 13

詩 **B** F-0937 — 説文 — The seal-style form comprised 言 "word, language," and 寺, used for the sound *shi* (from 志 **SG-0213**) to mean "one's wish." Words that expressed one's own thoughts or ideas, or writing down what was held in the heart, meant "poetry." The kanji 詩 means "poetry." <言寺>

詩 poetry [し]; 詩人 poet [しじん]; 抒情詩 lyric poem, lyrical verse [じょじょうし]; 叙事詩 epic poetry [じょじし]; 風物詩 charms of a season [ふうぶつし・ふうぶつし] // 詩歌 poetry [しいか]

	Meanings	*Kun* and *On*	Romaji	Bushu	Stroke Order and Number
SG-0226 侍	*samurai*; to wait upon	さむらい ジ	samurai *ji*	人	亻 什 仕 侍 侍 8

侍 **C** F-1607 — 説文 — The seal-style form comprised 亻 "an act that a person does," and 寺 **SG-0219**, used for the sound *ji* to mean "to hold, sustain," together signifying "to closely attend upon a nobleman." In Japan, the character is also used to mean "*samurai* (warrior)." The kanji 侍 means "*samurai*; to wait upon." <亻寺>

侍 *samurai* [さむらい]; 侍従 chamberlain, gentleman in waiting [じじゅう]; 侍医 court physician [じい] // 侍る to wait upon (nobleman) [はべる]

11f 足 𧾷 "leg" [from a foot and a knee]; bushu *ashihen* 足促跡踏践捉踪

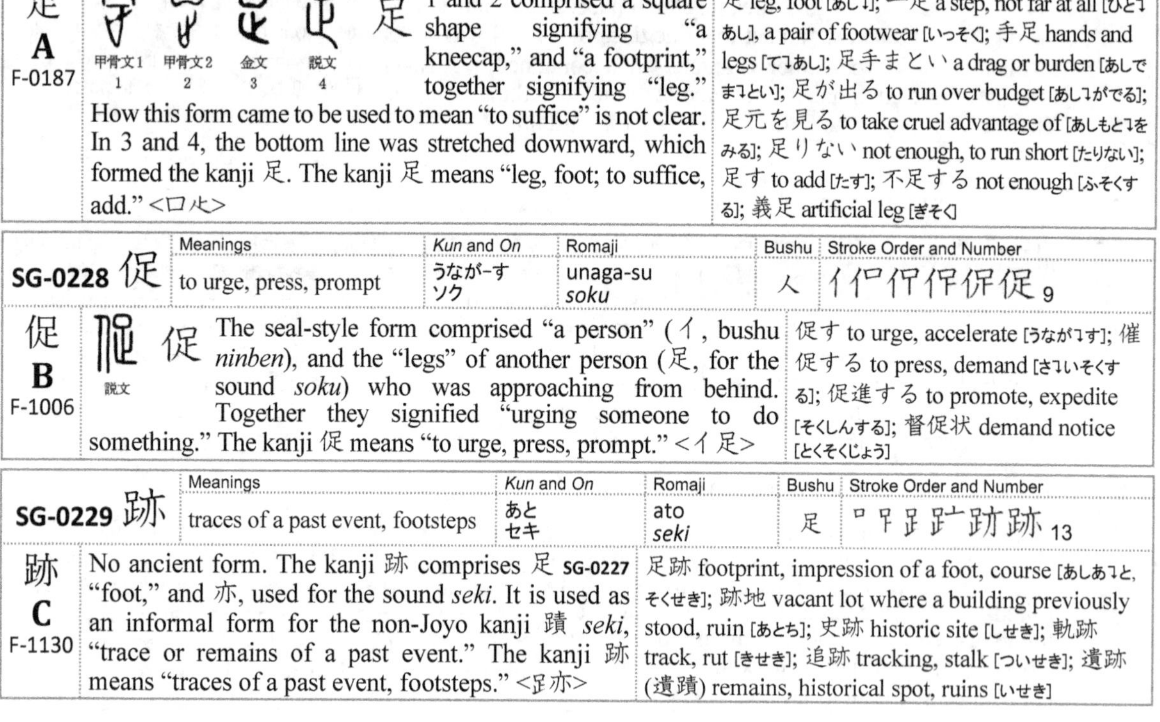

	Meanings	*Kun* and *On*	Romaji	Bushu	Stroke Order and Number
SG-0227 足	leg, foot; to suffice, add	あし・た-りる ソク	ashi, ta-riru *soku*	足	口 早 足 足 7

足 **A** F-0187 — 甲骨文1 1, 甲骨文2 2, 金文 3, 説文 4 — 1 and 2 comprised a square shape signifying "a kneecap," and "a footprint," together signifying "leg." How this form came to be used to mean "to suffice" is not clear. In 3 and 4, the bottom line was stretched downward, which formed the kanji 足. The kanji 足 means "leg, foot; to suffice, add." <口𤴓>

足 leg, foot [あし]; 一足 a step, not far at all [ひとあし], a pair of footwear [いっそく]; 手足 hands and legs [てあし]; 足手まとい a drag or burden [あしでまとい]; 足が出る to run over budget [あしがでる]; 足元を見る to take cruel advantage of [あしもとをみる]; 足りない not enough, to run short [たりない]; 足す to add [たす]; 不足する not enough [ふそくする]; 義足 artificial leg [ぎそく]

	Meanings	*Kun* and *On*	Romaji	Bushu	Stroke Order and Number
SG-0228 促	to urge, press, prompt	うなが-す ソク	unaga-su *soku*	人	亻 𠆢 伊 伻 促 促 9

促 **B** F-1006 — 説文 — The seal-style form comprised "a person" (亻, bushu *ninben*), and the "legs" of another person (足, for the sound *soku*) who was approaching from behind. Together they signified "urging someone to do something." The kanji 促 means "to urge, press, prompt." <亻足>

促す to urge, accelerate [うながす]; 催促する to press, demand [さいそくする]; 促進する to promote, expedite [そくしんする]; 督促状 demand notice [とくそくじょう]

	Meanings	*Kun* and *On*	Romaji	Bushu	Stroke Order and Number
SG-0229 跡	traces of a past event, footsteps	あと セキ	ato *seki*	足	口 早 𧾷 跅 跡 跡 13

跡 **C** F-1130 — No ancient form. The kanji 跡 comprises 足 **SG-0227** "foot," and 亦, used for the sound *seki*. It is used as an informal form for the non-Joyo kanji 蹟 *seki*, "trace or remains of a past event." The kanji 跡 means "traces of a past event, footsteps." <𧾷亦>

足跡 footprint, impression of a foot, course [あしあと, そくせき]; 跡地 vacant lot where a building previously stood, ruin [あとち]; 史跡 historic site [しせき]; 軌跡 track, rut [きせき]; 追跡 tracking, stalk [ついせき]; 遺跡 (遺蹟) remains, historical spot, ruins [いせき]

SG-0230 踏	Meanings	Kun and On	Romaji	Bushu	Stroke Order and Number
	to tread on, step on, experience	ふ-む トウ	hu-mu *too*	足	𧾷 𧾷' 𧾷ʼ 𧾷ʼ 𧾷水 踏 15

踏 **C** F-1189	篆文 踏 The seal-style form comprised 足 "leg," and "a bird flapping its wings forcefully," for the sound *too*, together signifying "to stomp one's feet like a bird flapping its wings." Another view holds that 沓 in the kanji was used for the sound *too* and meant "to repeat." Together with 𧾷, the character signified "to walk in place." The kanji 踏 means "to tread on, step on, experience." <𧾷 水 日>	踏む to step on, tread on [ふむ]; 足踏みする to stamp one's feet in place [あしぶ1みする, あしぶみする]; 踏まえる to be based on [ふまえ1る]; 踏切 railway crossing [ふみきり]; 踏み台 step stool [ふみだい]; 踏み倒す to kick down, leave a bill unpaid [ふみたおす]; 雑踏 hustle and bustle, a throng [ざっとう]; 高踏的な transcendent, high-toned [こうとうてきな]

SG-0231 践	Meanings	Kun and On	Romaji	Bushu	Stroke Order and Number
	to put into practice, carry out, execute	セン	*sen*	足	𧾷 𧾷 𧾷 践 践 践 13

践 **D** F-1916	説文 1 旧字 2 践 1 and 2 comprised 足 **SG-0227** "leg," and 戔, used for the sound *sen* to mean "layers." Tracing or following the steps of a plan meant "to carry out, execute." In the shinji 践, 戔 was reduced to 戋. The kanji 践 means "to put into practice, carry out, execute." <𧾷 戋>	実践する to put a theory into practice [じっせんする]; 実践的な practical, pragmatic [じっせんてきな]

SG-0232 捉	Meanings	Kun and On	Romaji	Bushu	Stroke Order and Number
	to grab, catch, grasp	とら-える ソク	tora-eru *soku*	手	扌 扌 扌 扌 扌 捉 10

捉 **D** F-1995	説文 捉 The seal-style form comprised "an act done by hand" (扌), and "leg" (足), used for the sound *soku*. A hand grabbing someone's leg meant "to grab." The kanji 捉 means "to grab, catch, grasp." <扌足>	捉える to capture, grasp, understand [とらえ1る]; 捉え処のない hard to figure out, vague [とらえどころのな1い]

SG-0233 踪	Meanings	Kun and On	Romaji	Bushu	Stroke Order and Number
	trace, whereabouts	ソウ	*soo*	足	𧾷 𧾷 𧾷 𧾷 𧾷 踪 15

踪 **D** F-2708	No ancient form. The kanji 踪 comprises 𧾷 bushu *ashihen* "leg, walking," and 宗, used for the sound *soo* to mean "something that lasts for a long time." Footprints that remained visible meant "a trace of someone's whereabouts." The kanji 踪 means "trace, whereabouts." <𧾷宗>	失踪する to disappear, go missing [しっそうする]

11g 定 "determine" [from a fixed point in a house]; *joo/tee* 定錠綻

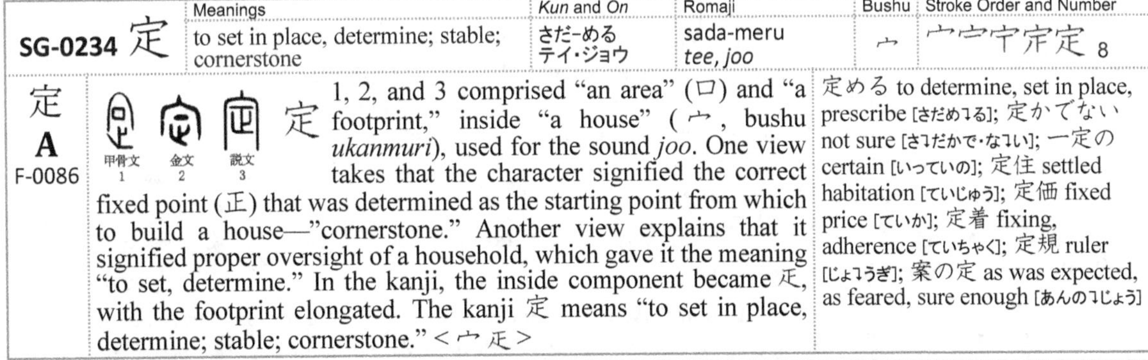

SG-0234 定	Meanings	Kun and On	Romaji	Bushu	Stroke Order and Number
	to set in place, determine; stable; cornerstone	さだ-める テイ・ジョウ	sada-meru *tee, joo*	宀	宀 宀 宀 宇 定 定 8

定 **A** F-0086	甲骨文 1 金文 2 説文 3 定 1, 2, and 3 comprised "an area" (口) and "a footprint," inside "a house" (宀, bushu *ukanmuri*), used for the sound *joo*. One view takes that the character signified the correct fixed point (正) that was determined as the starting point from which to build a house—"cornerstone." Another view explains that it signified proper oversight of a household, which gave it the meaning "to set, determine." In the kanji, the inside component became 疋, with the footprint elongated. The kanji 定 means "to set in place, determine; stable; cornerstone." <宀 疋>	定める to determine, set in place, prescribe [さだめ1る]; 定かでない not sure [さ1だかで・な1い]; 一定の certain [いっていの]; 定住 settled habitation [ていじゅう]; 定価 fixed price [ていか]; 定着 fixing, adherence [ていちゃく]; 定規 ruler [じょ1うぎ]; 案の定 as was expected, as feared, sure enough [あんの1じょう]

SG-0235 錠	Meanings	Kun and On	Romaji	Bushu	Stroke Order and Number
	to lock; medicinal tablet, pill	ジョウ	*joo*	金	𠆢 全 金 錠 錠 錠 錠 16

錠 **D** F-1929	篆文 錠 The seal-style form comprised 金 **SG-1196** "metal," and 定 **SG-0234** "to set in place," used for the sound *joo*. In the sense of a lump of metal that holds something in place, it signified "to lock." From "a lump of metal," it was also used to mean	錠 lock, padlock, latch [じょう]; 錠前 lock, bolt [じょうまえ]; 解錠する to unlock [かいじょうする]; 錠剤 pill, tablet [じょうざい]; 二錠服用

	medicine in a small round shape—"medicinal tablet." The kanji 錠 means "to lock; medicinal tablet, pill." <金 定>	taking two tablets [にꜜじょう・ふくよう]

	Meanings	Kun and On	Romaji	Bushu	Stroke Order and Number
SG-0236 綻	to unravel	ほころ-びる タン	hokoro-biru *tan*	糸	幺 糸 綻 綻 綻 綻 14
綻 **D** F-2261	No ancient form. The kanji 綻 comprises 糸 "a skein of threads," and 定 **SG-0234**, used for the sound *tan*, signifying "unsewn; to unravel." The kanji 綻 means "to unravel." <糸 定>				綻びる to unravel, become unsewn [ほころびꜜる]; 破綻する to fail, collapse [はたんする]

12 Footprints

12a 夂 "to retreat, come down" [from a backward or downward footprint]; bushu *suinyoo/chinyoo* 後夏愛優慶憂曖

In this study guide/reference book, 夊 "a dragging foot" and 夂 "a downward foot" are not treated separately.

	Meanings	Kun and On	Romaji	Bushu	Stroke Order and Number
SG-0237 後	to fall behind, be late; behind; back	のち・うし-ろ・あと・おく-れる ゴ・コウ	nochi, ushi-ro, ato, oku-reru *go, koo*	彳	彳 彳 彸 後 後 9
後 **A** F-0040	金文1 金文2 説文 (1 2 3) 1 comprised "a crossroads" (彳); "a forward-facing footprint" (止), signifying "moving;" "a skein of short threads" (幺); and "a dragging foot" (夂); together signifying "small steps, slow walk." Small, dragging steps cause one to fall behind, hence "behind, late." In 2 and 3, "forward footstep" was dropped. The kanji 後 means "to fall behind, be late; behind; back." <彳 幺夂>				後ほど sometime later [のちほど]; 後 later, at a later time [あꜜと・のちꜜ];後ろ behind, the back [うしろ]; 後ろ前 backwards [うしろꜜまえ]; 後ろめたい feel guilty [うしろめたꜜい]; 後ずさりする to move backward, back out [あとずꜜさりする]; 後々 the (distant) future [あとあと]; 後れる to fall behind, be tardy [おくれる]; 手後れになる to be too late, be beyond medical aid [ておꜜくれになる];食後 post-meal [しょくご]; 十年後 ten years later [じゅうねんご]; 後半 second half [こうはん]; 後部 the rear, back [こꜜうぶ]

	Meanings	Kun and On	Romaji	Bushu	Stroke Order and Number
SG-0238 夏	summer	なつ カ・ゲ	natsu *ka, ge*	夂	一 百 百 夏 夏 10
夏 **A** F-0302	金文 説文 (1 2) 1 and 2 comprised "a head with a mask on," "two hands putting on the mask," "a body," and "a backward footprint, foot in the air" (夂). The character depicted a masked dancer showing off their skill. Even though the meaning of "summer" is believed in some views to be a borrowing, the components make sense as a depiction of "a masked person dancing in a summer festival for a deity." The kanji uses the top of 頁 bushu *oogai* "head," and 夂. The kanji 夏 means "summer." <一 自 夂>				夏 summer [なつꜜ]; 真夏 midsummer [まなつ]; 真夏日 summer day hotter than 30°C [まなつꜜび]; 夏場 during summer [なつば]; 夏ばて summer fatigue [なつばて]; 夏季 summer season [かꜜき]; 夏至 summer solstice [げし]

	Meanings	Kun and On	Romaji	Bushu	Stroke Order and Number
SG-0239 愛	to cherish; love, one's favorite	アイ	*ai*	心	爫 𤓰 悉 愛 愛 13
愛 **A** F-0217	中山王器1 中山王器2 説文 (1 2 3) 1 and 2 comprised "a person" (facing backward in 1 and facing forward in 2), and "a heart" (心 **SG-0187**). In 3, 夂 "a dragging foot" was added. A person with a heart so full of emotion that they had difficulty moving was feeling "love." In the kanji, "a caring hand reaching down" (爫) was added at the top to signify "to cherish; one's favorite." The kanji 愛 means "to cherish; love, one's favorite." <爫 冖 心 夂>				愛情 affection, love [あいじょう]; 恋愛 love, romance [れんあい]; 愛用する to use habitually, cherish [あいようする]; 愛車 one's own car [あいしゃ] // 愛しい dear, beloved [いとしꜜい]; 愛娘 someone's loving daughter [まなむꜜすめ]; 愛弟子 one's favorite disciple or student [まなでし]

	Meanings	*Kun* and *On*	Romaji	Bushu	Stroke Order and Number
SG-0240 優	graceful, excellent; actor	やさ-しい・すぐ-れる ユウ	yasa-shii, sugu-reru *yuu*	人	亻亻亻亻優優 17

優 **A** F-0278

説文

The right-side component of the seal-style form is 憂 **SG-0242**, which comprised "a person wearing a mask," "a heart," and 夂 "dragging feet" (to mean "gracefully moving footwork"), and was used for the sound *yuu*. Together with 亻, bushu *ninben* "an act that a person does," it formed the meaning of "an actor"—someone with a mask who performed intricate footwork and skillfully portrayed emotions. The kanji 優 means "graceful; excellence, actor." <亻 憂 (𦣻心夂)>

優しい gentle-hearted [やさしい]; 優れる to excel [すぐれ⌝る]; 優先する to prioritize [ゆうせんする]; 優秀な excellence [ゆうしゅうな]; 俳優 actor [はいゆう]; 声優 voice actor [せいゆう]; 女優 actress[じょゆう]

	Meanings	*Kun* and *On*	Romaji	Bushu	Stroke Order and Number
SG-0241 慶	to rejoice; auspicious	ケイ	*kee*	心	亠广户庐廌慶慶 15

慶 **C** F-1085

金文1 1 金文2 2 説文 3

1 and 2 are difficult to decipher, but by inferring from 3 we can conjecture that the top component was "the head of a deer with antlers," the middle "a heart," and the bottom "its legs." *Setsumon* explains that a deer skin was given as a gift of congratulations on auspicious occasions. The kanji 慶 means "to rejoice; auspicious." <声一心夂>

慶弔金 monetary gift to express congratulations or condolences [けいちょうきん]; 慶事 auspicious event [け⌝いじ]

	Meanings	*Kun* and *On*	Romaji	Bushu	Stroke Order and Number
SG-0242 憂	to feel anxious, be worried; melancholy	うれ-える・う-い ユウ	ure-eru, u-i *yuu*	心	一丆百𦣻惪憂憂 15

憂 **C** F-1527

金文1 1 金文2 2 金文3 3 説文 4

1 and 2 depicted a mourning person with a veil over their head, with a hand holding their feet in place. 2 added another "hand" in front, as if pushing the person back. The character meant "the immobilizing sorrow one feels when mourning." In 4, it comprised 頁 "a person, head" with "a heart" (心) inside their chest. In the kanji 憂, 夂 "a dragging foot" was added. The kanji 憂 means "to feel anxious about, be worried about; melancholy." <𦣻心夂>

憂い anxiety, worry, distress [うれ⌝い, うれい]; 憂い顔 sorrowful face [うれいがお]; 物憂い languorous, melancholy [ものう⌝い]; 憂慮する to fear, dread, be apprehensive about [ゆ⌝うりょする]; 杞憂に終わる to be proven unfounded [きゆうにおわる]; 一喜一憂 glad and sad by turns [いっ⌝き・いちゆう]

	Meanings	*Kun* and *On*	Romaji	Bushu	Stroke Order and Number
SG-0243 曖	unclear, obscure, ambiguous	アイ	*ai*	日	日日'日"日愛曖曖 17

曖 **D** F-2461

No ancient form. The kanji 曖 comprises 日 "the sun," and 愛 **SG-0239**, used for the sound *ai* to mean "shadow." The sun hidden by a cloud signified "not clearly visible." The kanji 曖 means "unclear, obscure, ambiguous." <日愛>

曖昧な ambiguous, obscure [あいまいな]; 曖昧模糊 vague, shadowy [あいまいも⌝こ]

12b 各 phonetic use [from a downward-footprint 夂 and an area 口]; *kaku/raku/ro*

各客格落路絡露酪賂

	Meanings	*Kun* and *On*	Romaji	Bushu	Stroke Order and Number
SG-0244 各	individual, each	おのおの カク	onoono *kaku*	口	ノク夂各各 6

各 **A** F-0178

甲骨文1 1 甲骨文2 2 金文 3 説文 4

1 and 2 were mirror images of each other, comprising 夂 "a downward footprint," and 口 "a place" The character originally signified "to come down from a high place," and had the sound *kaku*. Later it came to be used to mean "individual, each." The kanji 各 means "individual, each." <夂 口>

各, 各々 each [おの⌝おの]; 各人 each person [か⌝くじん]; 各界 every field of life, various circles [かくかい]; 各階 each floor (of a building) [か⌝くかい]; 各地 every location, various parts of the country [か⌝くち]; 各自 each one [か⌝くじ]; 各種学校 vocational school [かくしゅが⌝っこう]

	Meanings	Kun and On	Romaji	Bushu	Stroke Order and Number
SG-0245 客	guest, traveler, visitor; away from home	キャク・カク	*kyaku, kaku*	宀	宀 ... 客 9

客 **A** F-0360 金文 1 說文 2 客

In 1 and 2, 各 was placed inside "a house" (宀), and was used for the sounds *kaku/kyaku* to mean "to arrive, reach a destination." Someone who had traveled to arrive at a house was "a guest, visitor" The kanji 客 means "guest, traveler, visitor; away from home." <宀各>

客 guest [きゃく]; 観客 spectator [かんきゃく]; 客車 passenger car of a train [きゃくしゃ]; 客室 guest room [きゃくしつ]; 客観的な objective [きゃかんてきな]; 集客 drawing customers [しゅうきゃく]; 過客 traveler [かっかく] (poetic); 客死 death while on a journey [かくし]

	Meanings	Kun and On	Romaji	Bushu	Stroke Order and Number
SG-0246 格	standard, class, lattice	カク・コウ	*kaku, koo*	木	一 十 ... 格 10

格 **A** F-0377 金文 1 說文 2 格

1 and 2 comprised 木 **SG-0608** "a tree, wood," and 各, used for the sounds *kaku* and *koo* to mean "tall, high, square," together signifying "a tall straight tree, square lumber." A straight piece of lumber was used to measure other long objects, which gave the meaning of "standard." Uniform wooden pieces were used in latticework. The kanji 格 means "standard, class, lattice." <木各>

格 standing, status, rank [かく]; 同格 same status, equal footing [どうかく]; 失格 disqualified [しっかく]; 品格 grace, class, style [ひんかく]; 格付けする to grade, rate [かくづけする]; 合格する to pass, come up to standard [ごうかくする]; 格子戸 latticed door [こうしっど]

	Meanings	Kun and On	Romaji	Bushu	Stroke Order and Number
SG-0247 落	to fall, drop, settle, fall on hard times	お-ちる ラク	o-chiru *raku*	艸	一 ... 落 12

落 **A** F-0512 說文 落

The seal-style form comprised "plants, vegetation" (艸, bushu *kusakanmuri*), and 洛, used for the sound *raku* to mean "the sound of falling water." It signified leaves falling from a tree. The kanji 落 means "to fall, drop, settle, fall on hard times." <艹氵各>

落ちる to fall, drop [おちる]; 落とす to drop, lose [おとす]; 見落とす to overlook, lose sight of [みおとす, みおとす]; 手落ち slip-up, careless mistake [ておち]; 引き落とし (automatic) deduction from a bank account [ひきおとし]; 下落 drop in price [げらく]; 落書き graffiti, scribbling [らくがき]; 落下する to fall, come down [らっかする]; 落語 traditional comic storytelling [らくご]

	Meanings	Kun and On	Romaji	Bushu	Stroke Order and Number
SG-0248 路	road, way	じ ロ	ji *ro*	足	... 路 13

路 **B** F-0529 金文 1 說文 2 路

1 and 2 comprised "a leg" (足 **SG-0227**), and 各 **SG-0244**, used for the sound *ro* to mean "to be connected." A heavily-used connecting pass became a road. The kanji 路 means "road, way." <𧾷各>

家路 the way home [いえじ]; 路地 road, street [ろじ]; 十字路 crossroads [じゅうじろ]; 路面 road surface [ろめん]; 一路 en route to, directly [いちろ]; 三叉路 three-forked road [さんさろ]; 末路 last days, fate [まつろ]; 通路 passageway [つうろ]; 水路 waterway, aqueduct, fairway [すいろ]

	Meanings	Kun and On	Romaji	Bushu	Stroke Order and Number
SG-0249 絡	to tangle, entwine, connect	から-む ラク	kara-mu *raku*	糸	... 絡 12

絡 **C** F-1280 說文 絡

The seal-style form comprised 糸 **SG-1600** "a skein of threads," and 各 **SG-0244**, used for the sound *raku* to mean "to get tangled easily," together signifying "tangled threads." Tangled threads are connected. The kanji 絡 means "to tangle, entwine, connect." <糸各>

絡む to become entwined, get involved [からむ]; 一絡げ bundle, lump [ひとからげ]; 連絡 contact [れんらく]; 連絡船 ferryboat, ferry steamer [れんらくせん]; 短絡的な simplistic [たんらくてきな]

	Meanings	Kun and On	Romaji	Bushu	Stroke Order and Number
SG-0250 露	dew; to expose, reveal	つゆ ロ・ロウ	tsuyu *ro, roo*	雨	... 露 21

露 **C** F-1347 說文 露

The seal-style form comprised 雨 **SG-1205** "rain, precipitation," and 路 **SG-0248**, used for the sound *ro.* When moisture in the air becomes dew, it covers everything outside. Being exposed to the elements gave the meaning "to reveal." The kanji 露 means "dew; to expose, reveal." <雨 路>

露 dew [つゆ]; 夜露 night dew [よつゆ]; 雨露 rain and dew, weather, the elements [あめつゆ]; 露見する to come to light [ろけんする]; 露出 exposure [ろしゅつ]; 暴露する to intentionally reveal or expose a secret [ばくろする]

SG-0251 酪	Meanings	Kun and On	Romaji	Bushu	Stroke Order and Number
	dairy	ラク	*raku*	酉	冂 西 酉 酉 酪 酪 13

酪 **D** F-2071 — 説文

The seal-style form comprised 酉 "cask for fermented liquid," and 各 **SG-0244**, used for the sound *raku* to mean "to curdle," together signifying "dairy products made of fermented milk." The kanji 酪 means "dairy." <酉 各>

酪農 dairy farming [らくのう]; 酪農製品 dairy products [らくのうせいひん]

SG-0252 賂	Meanings	Kun and On	Romaji	Bushu	Stroke Order and Number
	bribe, payoff	ロ	*ro*	貝	冂 目 貝 賂 賂 13

賂 **D** F-2689 — 篆文

The seal-style form comprised 貝 **SG-1693** "a cowrie, valuable," and 各, used for the sound *ro*, together signifying "to give a present." The original meaning of "an apology gift" eventually evolved to mean "a bribe." The kanji 賂 means "bribe, payoff." <貝 各>

賄賂 bribe, payoff [わいろ]

12c 韋 "to patrol; different" [from two sideways feet facing opposite directions and walking around an area]; *i* 違囲衛偉緯

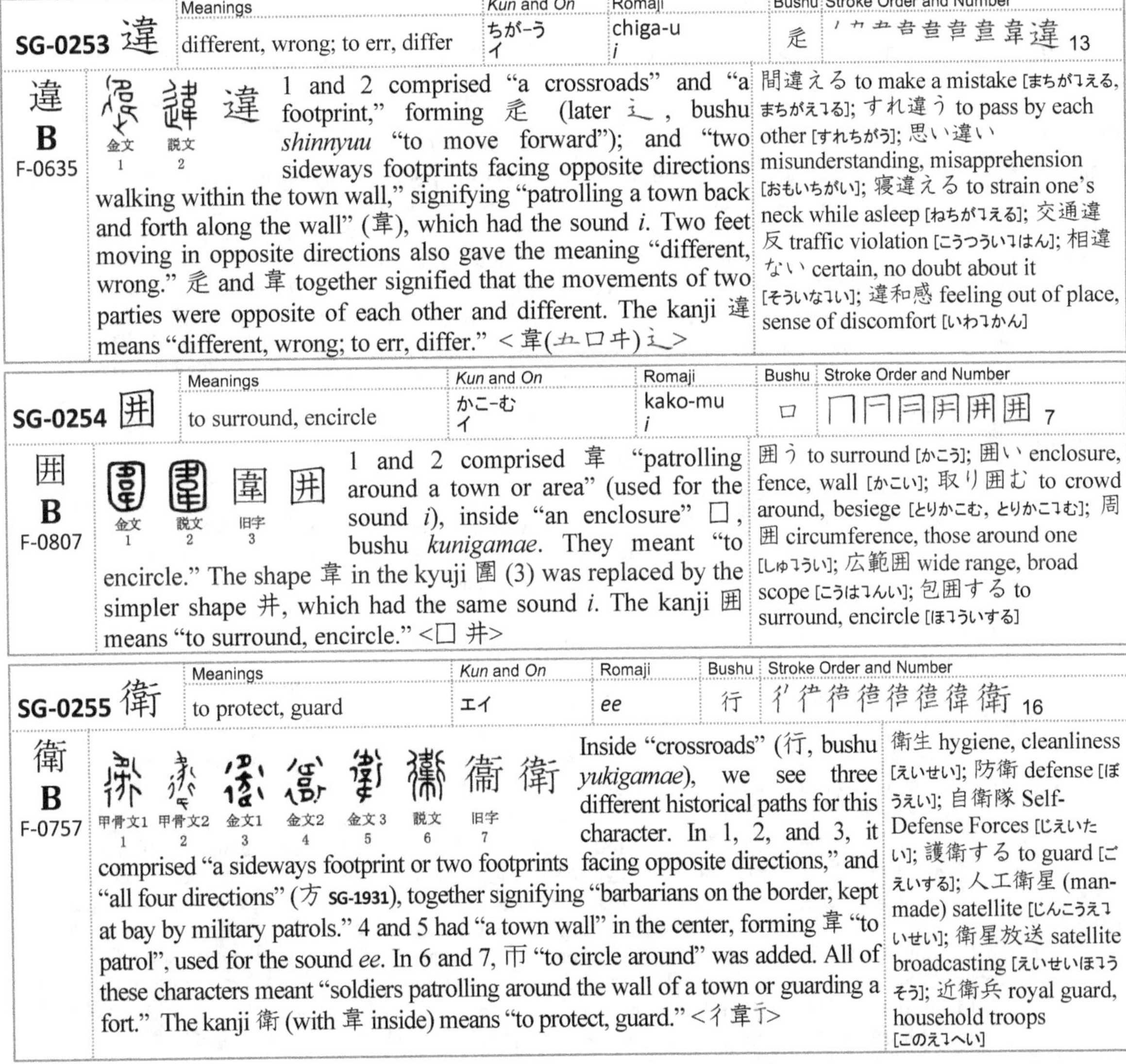

SG-0253 違	Meanings	Kun and On	Romaji	Bushu	Stroke Order and Number
	different, wrong; to err, differ	ちが-う イ	chiga-u *i*	辶	ノ ㄘ 丑 吾 吾 吾 韋 韋 違 13

違 **B** F-0635 — 金文 1, 説文 2

1 and 2 comprised "a crossroads" and "a footprint," forming 辵 (later 辶, bushu *shinnyuu* "to move forward"); and "two sideways footprints facing opposite directions walking within the town wall," signifying "patrolling a town back and forth along the wall" (韋), which had the sound *i*. Two feet moving in opposite directions also gave the meaning "different, wrong." 辵 and 韋 together signified that the movements of two parties were opposite of each other and different. The kanji 違 means "different, wrong; to err, differ." <韋(⻌口⽜)辶>

間違える to make a mistake [まちがえる, まちがえる]; すれ違う to pass by each other [すれちがう]; 思い違い misunderstanding, misapprehension [おもいちがい]; 寝違える to strain one's neck while asleep [ねちがえる]; 交通違反 traffic violation [こうつういはん]; 相違ない certain, no doubt about it [そういない]; 違和感 feeling out of place, sense of discomfort [いわかん]

SG-0254 囲	Meanings	Kun and On	Romaji	Bushu	Stroke Order and Number
	to surround, encircle	かこ-む イ	kako-mu *i*	口	冂 冂 冃 冄 冊 囲 7

囲 **B** F-0807 — 金文 1, 説文 2, 旧字 3

1 and 2 comprised 韋 "patrolling around a town or area" (used for the sound *i*), inside "an enclosure" 囗, bushu *kunigamae*. They meant "to encircle." The shape 韋 in the kyuji 圍 (3) was replaced by the simpler shape 井, which had the same sound *i*. The kanji 囲 means "to surround, encircle." <囗 井>

囲う to surround [かこう]; 囲い enclosure, fence, wall [かこい]; 取り囲む to crowd around, besiege [とりかこむ, とりかこむ]; 周囲 circumference, those around one [しゅうい]; 広範囲 wide range, broad scope [こうはんい]; 包囲する to surround, encircle [ほういする]

SG-0255 衛	Meanings	Kun and On	Romaji	Bushu	Stroke Order and Number
	to protect, guard	エイ	*ee*	行	彳 㣔 衎 徫 徫 徫 衛 衛 16

衛 **B** F-0757 — 甲骨文1 1, 甲骨文2 2, 金文1 3, 金文2 4, 金文3 5, 説文 6, 旧字 7

Inside "crossroads" (行, bushu *yukigamae*), we see three different historical paths for this character. In 1, 2, and 3, it comprised "a sideways footprint or two footprints facing opposite directions," and "all four directions" (方 **SG-1931**), together signifying "barbarians on the border, kept at bay by military patrols." 4 and 5 had "a town wall" in the center, forming 韋 "to patrol", used for the sound *ee*. In 6 and 7, 帀 "to circle around" was added. All of these characters meant "soldiers patrolling around the wall of a town or guarding a fort." The kanji 衛 (with 韋 inside) means "to protect, guard." <彳 韋 亍>

衛生 hygiene, cleanliness [えいせい]; 防衛 defense [ぼうえい]; 自衛隊 Self-Defense Forces [じえいたい]; 護衛する to guard [ごえいする]; 人工衛星 (man-made) satellite [じんこうえいせい]; 衛星放送 satellite broadcasting [えいせいほうそう]; 近衛兵 royal guard, household troops [このえへい]

SG-0256 偉	Meanings	Kun and On	Romaji	Bushu	Stroke Order and Number
	grand, eminent, illustrious	えら-い イ	era-i *i*	人	… 偉 12

偉 **C** F-1561

説文

The seal-style form comprised 亻 "a person," and 韋, used for the sound *i* to mean "different" (from "two people patrolling along a town wall in opposite directions"). Someone different who stood out from the crowd might be someone with extraordinary qualities. The kanji 偉 means "great, eminent, illustrious." <亻 韋>

偉い great, eminent, Good job! [えらい]; 偉そうに with a grand air [えらそうに]; 偉ぶる to put on airs, swagger [えらぶる]; 偉大な illustrious [いだいな]; 偉人伝 biography of a great figure [いじんでん]; 偉業 great achievement, enterprise [いぎょう]

SG-0257 緯	Meanings	Kun and On	Romaji	Bushu	Stroke Order and Number
	weft, latitude	イ	*i*	糸	… 緯 16

緯 **D** F-1761

説文

The seal-style form comprised 糸 **SG-1600** "a skein of threads," and 韋, "patrolling back and forth," used for the sound *i*, together signifying "weft (horizontal threads in weaving)." The shuttling motion of the weft in weaving was similar to the back-and-forth movement of a patrol. The character is also used to mean "geographic latitude." The kanji 緯 means "weft, latitude." <糸 韋>

緯度 latitude [いど]; 経緯 details, longitude and latitude, [けいい]; 北緯 north latitude [ほくい]

12d 舛 "two feet off the ground; downward feet" [夕夂 and 㐄] 無舞降隣瞬傑

SG-0258 無	Meanings	Kun and On	Romaji	Bushu	Stroke Order and Number
	nothing; not; without	な-い ム・ブ	na-i *mu, bu*	火	… 無 12

無 **A** F-0182

甲骨文 1 金文1 2 金文2 3 説文 4

1, 2, and 3 depicted "a person performing a votive dance with elaborate adornments on their sleeves," in front of a deity in a rite or festival. The character was borrowed for the word "nothing," due to having the same sounds *mu/bu*. In 4, 亡 "to disappear, not exist" was added. In the kanji 無, the bottom became 灬 (bushu *rekka* "fire"). The kanji 無 means "nothing; not; witho無." < 灬>

無い not exist [ない]; 無理な unreasonable [むりな]; 無味乾燥な dry, uninteresting [むみ・かんそうな]; 皆無 absolutely none [かいむ]; 無効 invalid [むこう]; 無人の unattended, automated [むじんの]; 無難な safe, flawless [ぶなんな]; 無愛想な unsociable [ぶあいそうな]

SG-0259 舞	Meanings	Kun and On	Romaji	Bushu	Stroke Order and Number
	to dance	ま-う ブ	ma-u *bu*	舛	… 舞 15

舞 **B** F-0561

甲骨文 1 金文1 2 金文2 3 説文古文 4 説文 5

The kanji 舞 was created because the original character for "dancing," 無 **SG-0258**, had been borrowed to mean "nothing." 1 and 2 were originally forms of 無, but in 3 and 5, 舛 "a pair of downward-facing feet raised from the ground in dancing" was added. Two wings were added in 4, describing the manner of dancing. The kanji 舞 means "to dance." <無 舛(夕 㐄)>

舞いを舞う to gracefully perform a choreographed dance, dance a dance [まいをまう]; 見舞う to inquire after one's health [みまう, みまう]; 見舞われる be struck by, suffer [みまわれる]; きりきり舞い moving about busily engaged in work [きりきりまい]; 舞台 stage [ぶたい]; 歌舞伎 kabuki performance [かぶき]; 舞踊 dancing [ぶよう]

SG-0260 降	Meanings	Kun and On	Romaji	Bushu	Stroke Order and Number
	to come down, get out of (a vehicle), fall, surrender	お-りる・ふ-る コウ	o-riru, hu-ru *koo*	阜	… 降 10

降 **B** F-0902

甲骨文 1 金文1 2 金文2 3 説文 4

1, 2, 3, and 4 comprised 阝, bushu *kozatohen* "mountains or tall hills," and "a pair of downward-facing feet" (to mean "a deity or a person descending"), together signifying "coming down from a high place." The character also means "to fall from the sky." The kanji 降 means "to come down, get out of (a vehicle), fall from the sky, surrender." <阝夂㐄>

乗り降り getting on and off (a train, etc.) [のりおり]; 降りる to get off, get down [おりる]; 飛び降りる to leap down, jump off [とびおりる]; 雨が降る it rains [あめがふる]; 土砂降り pouring rain, downpour [どしゃぶり]; 下降する to descend [かこうする]; それ以降 since then [それいこう]; 降雨量 amount of rainfall [こううりょう]

	Meanings	Kun and On	Romaji	Bushu	Stroke Order and Number
SG-0261 隣	neighbor; next to	となり リン	tonari *rin*	阜	16

隣 **B** F-1036

金文1 1, 金文2 2, 中山王器 3, 説文 4

1 comprised "a person with a will-o'-the-wisp" (鬼火 *onibi*) around them," and "a pair of raised feet." In 2, "a ladder, hills" and "an area" were added to the flickering lights, signifying a row of houses. The character meant "neighborhood." 4 comprised two fires over a pair of raised feet, used for the sound *rin*, and 邑 (阝) "an area where people live." In the kanji, 阝 moved back to the left side of 粦. The kanji 隣 means "neighbor; next to." <阝 粦 (米舛)>
(Note: The kanji 鄰 with 邑 (阝, bushu *oozato*) still exists but is not used in Japanese.)

隣 next door [となり]; 隣り合う to adjoin, be next door to each other [となりあう]; 隣付き合い neighborly relations [となりづきあい]; 向こう隣 neighbors across the street [むこうどなり]; 隣人愛 neighborly love [りんじんあい]; 近隣 nearby in one's neighborhood [きんりん]

	Meanings	Kun and On	Romaji	Bushu	Stroke Order and Number
SG-0262 瞬	in the blink of an eye, in a flash; to blink	またた-く シュン	matata-ku *shun*	目	18

瞬 **C** F-1298

正字1 1, 正字2 2

No ancient form. Of the two orthographic-style kanji, 1 comprised "an eye" and "an arrow," whereas 2 had "an eye" and 寅 "straightening an arrow with both hands," used for the sound *shun*. Both meant "fast as the blink of an eye like an arrow." In the present-day kanji 瞬, the right-hand component became 舜, which had the same sound *shun*, and was used to mean "flash, blink." The kanji 瞬 means "in the blink of an eye, in a flash; to blink." <目 舜 (爫冖舛)>

瞬く間に in a twinkling, in no time [またたくまに]; 瞬間 moment, a second [しゅんかん]; 瞬時 a second, a moment, an instant [しゅんじ]; 一瞬にして in a flash, instantaneously [いっしゅんにして]; 瞬発的に in the blink of an eye [しゅんぱつてきに]

	Meanings	Kun and On	Romaji	Bushu	Stroke Order and Number
SG-0263 傑	to stand out, surpass	ケツ	*ketsu*	人	13

傑 **D** F-1874

説文

The seal-style form comprised 亻 "a person," and 舛 "a pair of raised feet" on top of 木 "a tree," which was used for the sound *ketsu*. A person who stood on top of a tree would stand out. The kanji 傑 means "to stand out, surpass." <亻 舛木>

傑作 masterpiece [けっさく]; 豪傑 strong man, bold man [ごうけつ]; 傑出した outstanding [けっしゅつした]

12e 乗 "to ride" [from a person with both feet on a tree]; *joo* 乗剰

	Meanings	Kun and On	Romaji	Bushu	Stroke Order and Number
SG-0264 乗	to climb, board, mount, add, multiply	の-る ジョウ	no *joo*	丿	9

乗 **A** F-0365

甲骨文 1, 金文 2, 説文 3, 旧字 4

1 depicted "a person standing on top of a tree," signifying "to climb to the top of a tree." In 2 and 3, the pair of feet (not touching the ground) were made more visible. The character meant "a person mounting something." The kyuji 乘 (4) reflected 3. The kanji 乗 means "to climb, board, mount, add, multiply." <乗>

乗る to ride [のる]; 乗り物 vehicle, public transportation [のりもの]; 乗り気 eagerness, enthusiasm [のりき]; 上乗せする to add on, sweeten (offer) [うわのせする]; 乗車 getting into a car [じょうしゃ]; 乗客 passenger [じょうきゃく]; 便乗する to take advantage of [びんじょうする]; 二乗 square, multiply by itself [じじょう]

	Meanings	Kun and On	Romaji	Bushu	Stroke Order and Number
SG-0265 剰	surplus; besides	ジョウ	*joo*	刀	11

剰 **D** F-1757

篆文 1, 旧字 2

The kanji 剰 did not share an origin with the kanji 乗 **SG-0264.** 1 comprised "a flat vessel" on the left side; and 朕 **SG-0149** "to transport an important thing in a vessel" and 貝 "a cowrie; valuable" on the right side. Having an abundance of precious items in a vessel gave the meaning "surplus." In the kyuji 剩 (2), 乘 was used for the sound *joo*, and 刂 "knife" signified what was cut off due to being surplus. The kanji 剰 means "surplus; besides."<乗 刂>

余剰米 surplus rice [よじょうまい]; 過剰な excessive [かじょうな]; 自信過剰 overconfidence [じしんかじょう]; 剰余金 surplus funds, balance in hand [じょうよきん]

12f 癶 "to start" [from a pair of forward-facing feet]; **bushu *hatsugashira***
発登廃灯澄

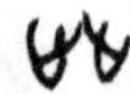

	Meanings	Kun and On	Romaji	Bushu	Stroke Order and Number
SG-0266 発	to start (suddenly), depart, reveal, emerge; occurence	ハツ・ホツ	*hatsu, hotsu*	癶	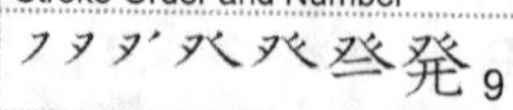 フヲヲ゛癶癶発発発 9

発 **A** F-0102

甲骨文 1 説文 2 旧字 3 (發 発)

1, 2, and 3 comprised "a bow" (弓 **SG-1509**), "a pair of feet lined up ready to depart" and 殳, bushu *hokozukuri* "to strike; action." An arrow on the verge of being shot out gave the meaning "to start suddenly, depart; occurrence." Something coming out into view also meant "to reveal, emerge." In the shinji, the component under 癶 was simplified to 癶. The kanji 発 means "to start (suddenly), depart, reveal; occurrence." <癶死>

発する to release, emit, issue, originate from [はっする]; 出発 departure [しゅっぱつ]; 発見 discovery [はっけん]; 発売日 first day on sale [はつばいび]; 発生 occurrence, outbreak [はっせい]; 発車 departure [はっしゃ]; 先発する to start first [せんぱつする]; 自発的 spontaneous, voluntarily [じはつてき]; 発作 attack, fit, seizure [ほっさ]

	Meanings	Kun and On	Romaji	Bushu	Stroke Order and Number
SG-0267 登	to climb, go upward, register	のぼ-る トウ・ト	nobo-ru *too, to*	癶	 フヲヲ゛癶癶癶登登登 12

登 **B** F-0595

甲骨文 1 金文 2 説文 3 (登)

1 and 2 comprised "two feet lined up ready to go" (癶), and "a bowl raised in both hands" (豆 **SG-1975**), used for the sound *too* to mean "to climb, raise," together signifying "to climb up to the top." The two hands were dropped in 3. Offering up one's name to a government office meant "to register." The kanji 登 meant "to climb, go upward, register." <癶豆>

登る to climb [のぼる]; 山登り mountain climbing [やまのぼり]; 登記 registration (for real estate, etc.) [とうき]; 登用する to appoint, promote [とうようする]; 登録する to register [とうろくする]; 登山 climbing a mountain [とざん, とざん]

	Meanings	Kun and On	Romaji	Bushu	Stroke Order and Number
SG-0268 廃	obsolete; to fall out of use	すた-れる ハイ	suta-reru *hai*	广	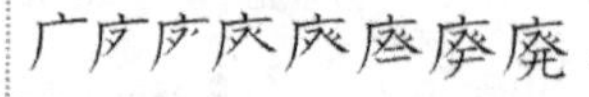 广户庐庐庐廃廃廃 12

廃 **B** F-1033

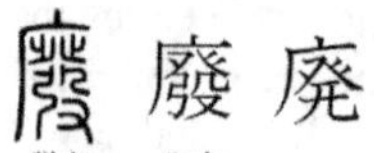

説文 1 旧字 2 (廢 廃)

1 and 2 comprised "eaves of a house" (广, bushu *madare*), and 發 (発 **SG-0266**), used for the sound *hai* to mean "to collapse, fall apart," together signifying "an abandoned house." The kanji 廃 means "obsolete; to fall out of use." <广発>

廃れる to go out of vogue, decline in prosperity [すたれる]; 廃校 closing of a school [はいこう]; 撤廃する to abolish, repeal [てっぱいする]; 廃液 waste fluid [はいえき]; 廃物利用 utilization of waste material [はいぶつりよう]; 退廃的な decadent, degenerate [たいはいてきな]; 老廃物 waste matter [ろうはいぶつ]

	Meanings	Kun and On	Romaji	Bushu	Stroke Order and Number
SG-00269 灯	light, torch	ひ トウ	hi *too*	火	 丶丷少火灯灯 6

灯 **C** F-1333

篆文 1 旧字 2 (鐙 燈 灯)

1 comprised 金 **SG-1196** "metal," and 登 **SG-0267**, used for the sound *too*, signifying "light, torch." In the kyuji 燈 (2), 金 was replaced by 火 **SG-1164** "fire, light." For the shinji, the unrelated kanji 灯, originally "a fiercely burning fire," is used. The kanji 灯 means "light, torch." <火丁>

灯 light [ひ]; 灯火 light [ともしび, ともしび]; 灯台 lighthouse [とうだい]; 灯台下暗し "It is harder to see what is right under your nose." [とうだいもとくらし]; 灯篭 hanging lantern [とうろう]; 石灯籠 stone lantern [いしどうろう] // 行灯 paper-shade lamp [あんどん]

	Meanings	Kun and On	Romaji	Bushu	Stroke Order and Number
SG-0270 澄	clear water	す-む チョウ	su-mu *choo*	水	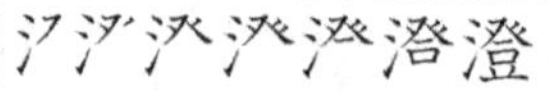 氵氵氵氵澄澄澄 15

澄 **D** F-1655

篆文1 1 篆文2 2 (澄)

Of the two seal-style forms, 1 (澂) was pronounced *choo*, and meant "clean water." The current kanji 澄 reflects 2, which was a variant of 1. The kanji 澄 means "clear water." <氵登>

澄む to become transparent [すむ]; 澄み切った crystal clear, lucid [すみきった]; お澄まし a prim girl [おすまし]; 上澄み supernatant liquid [うわずみ]; 清澄な clear, serene [せいちょうな]

13 Bone joints

13a 咼円 "to pass through; round, smooth" [from a bone fitted into a circular joint moving smoothly]; *ka* 過骨滑渦鍋禍

SG-0271 過	Meanings	*Kun* and *On*	Romaji	Bushu	Stroke Order and Number
	to pass through; excessive; mistake	す-ぎる・あやま-ち カ	su-giru, ayama-chi *ka*	辵	冂 冎 冎 円 咼 渦 過 12

過 **A** F-0427

金文 1 説文 2

1 and 2 comprised "a crossroads" with "a footprint" (辵, 辶, bushu *shinnyuu*), signifying "to move forward," and "a skeletal joint" (咼), used for the sound *ka* and lending the meaning of "smooth passing." Together they signified "passing through easily." Something that passes too easily could end up being "excessive" or even "a mistake." The kanji 過 means "to pass through; excessive; mistake." <冎口辶>

過ぎる to pass through [すぎ˺る]; 食べ過ぎる to overeat [たべすぎる, たべすぎ˺る]; 過ごす to spend time [すご˺す]; 過ち mistake, error [あやま˺ち, あやまち]; 過日 some days ago, recently [か˺じつ]; 過分な unmerited, undeserved [かぶんな]; 過度に excessively [か˺どに]

SG-0272 骨	Meanings	*Kun* and *On*	Romaji	Bushu	Stroke Order and Number
	bone	ほね コツ	hone *kotsu*	骨	冂 冎 冎 骨 骨 10

骨 **B** F-0702

説文

The seal-style form comprised "skeletal joint," signifying "smooth movement," and 月, bushu *nikuzuki* "flesh," together signifying "a bone with flesh attached" (on a living body). The kanji 骨 means "bone." <冎月>

骨 bone [ほね˺]; 骨休め relaxation, rest [ほねや˺すめ]; 魚の小骨 small fish bones [さかなのこぼね]; 骨格 frame, build [こっかく]; 骨太な sturdy [ほねぶとな]; 骨組み framework, skeletal structure [ほねぐみ]; 接骨 bone-setting [せっこつ]; 骸骨 skeleton [が˺いこつ]; 無骨な(武骨な) rustic, boorish [ぶこつな]

SG-0273 滑	Meanings	*Kun* and *On*	Romaji	Bushu	Stroke Order and Number
	to slide; smooth	すべ-る・なめ-らか カツ・コツ	sube-ru, name-raka *katsu, kotsu*	水	氵 氵冂 氵冎 氵冎 滑 滑 13

滑 **C** F-1262

説文

The seal-style form comprised "flowing water" (氵), and 骨 **SG-0272**, used for the sound *katsu* to mean "smooth passing." Water runs smoothly. The kanji 滑 means "to slide; smooth." <氵骨>

滑る to slip [すべ˺る]; 滑り台 slide [すべり˺だい]; 地滑り landslide [じす˺べり]; 滑らかな smooth [なめ˺らかな]; 円滑な smooth, uninterrupted [えんかつな]; 滑走 gliding [かっそう]; 滑走路 runway, airstrip [かっそ˺うろ]; 滑稽な humorous, funny [こっけいな]

SG-0274 渦	Meanings	*Kun* and *On*	Romaji	Bushu	Stroke Order and Number
	whirlpool, swirl, vortex	うず カ	uzu *ka*	水	氵 氵冂 氵冎 氵冎 渦 渦 12

渦 **D** F-1846

No ancient form. The kanji 渦 comprises 氵, bushu *sanzui* "flowing water," and 咼, used for the sound *ka* to mean "a circular hole." Water flowing in a circle created a "whirlpool." The kanji 渦 means "whirlpool, swirl, vortex." <氵咼>

渦 vortex [う˺ず]; 渦巻き vortex, coiled [うず˺まき]; 渦中の人 person in turmoil [か˺ちゅうのひと]

SG-0275 鍋	Meanings	*Kun* and *On*	Romaji	Bushu	Stroke Order and Number
	cooking pot	なべ	nabe	金	𠆢 午 金 釒冂 釒冎 鍋 鍋 17

鍋 **D** F-1683

No ancient form. The kanji 鍋 comprises 金 **SG-1196** "metal," and 咼, used for the sound *ka* to mean "a circular hole." A round metal item with an opening was "a cooking pot." The kanji 鍋 means "cooking pot." <金咼>

鍋 pot [な˺べ]; 鍋物 dish cooked in a pot at the table [なべもの]; 土鍋 earthenware pot [どなべ]; 鍋うどん hot *udon* noodle in an individual pot [なべう˺どん]; 鍋つかみ potholder [なべつ˺かみ]

SG-0276 禍	Meanings	Kun and On	Romaji	Bushu	Stroke Order and Number
	curse, misfortune, disaster, calamity	カ	*ka*	示	ラ ネ ネ冂 ネ冋 ネ咼 禍 13

禍 **D** F-2011

中山王器 1　説文 2　旧字 3

1, 2, and 3 comprised "an altar with an offering laid on it" (示, ネ, bushu *shimesuhen*), and 咼 for the sound *ka* to mean "to shout, rebuke." Together they signified "harm or calamity brought by the wrath of a deity." The kanji 禍 means "curse, misfortune, disaster, calamity." <ネ咼>

戦禍 the turmoil of war, wartime chaos [せんか]; 舌禍 unfortunate slip of the tongue [ぜつか, ぜっか]

13b 歹 "a dead body, skeleton" [from human skeletal remains]; **bushu *gatsuhen*/ *kabanehen*,** and 列 "a row, a line" [from bodies or animal bones in display]; *retsu*

死例列葬烈裂殉

SG-0277 死	Meanings	Kun and On	Romaji	Bushu	Stroke Order and Number
	to die; death; obsolete	し-ぬ シ	shi-nu *shi*	歹	一 丆 歹 歹 歹' 死 6

死 **A** F-0197

甲骨文 1　甲骨文 2　金文 1 3　金文 2 4　説文 5

The scene in 1 and 2 was a poignant one—"a person in mourning looking down at skeletal remains." In 3, 4, and 5, "the remains" 歹 (bushu *gatsuhen/kabanehen*) and "a mourner" were placed side by side. In the kanji, the top of the remains extended over "the person" ヒ. The kanji 死 meant "to die; death; obsolete." <歹ヒ>

死ぬ to die [しぬ]; 死亡 death [しぼう]; 死去 death [しきょ]; 死相 shadow of death [しそう]; 死者 fatality, a dead person [ししゃ]; 死語 dead language, obsolete word [しご]; 決死の risking death, desperate courage [けっしの, けっしの]; 過労死 death from overwork [かろうし]

SG-0278 例	Meanings	Kun and On	Romaji	Bushu	Stroke Order and Number
	example; for instance; customary	たと-える レイ	tato-eru *ree*	人	亻 亻一 亻万 亻歹 亻歹丨 例 8

例 **A** F-0331

説文

The seal-style form comprised 亻, bushu *ninben* "an act that a person does," and 列 SG-0279, used for the sound *ree* to mean "to line up." Together, they meant "a person displaying things" which served as "examples." The kanji 例 means "example; for instance; customary." <亻歹刂>

例えば for example [たとえば]; 例 example, customary [れい]; 例の話 the previously discussed story [れいのはなし]; 実例 actual example [じつれい]; 事例 precedent, case [じれい]; 例年 ordinary year, annually [れいねん]; 判例 judicial precedent, prior case [はんれい]; 一例として by way of illustration, as an example [いちれいとして]

SG-0279 列	Meanings	Kun and On	Romaji	Bushu	Stroke Order and Number
	row, line; to line up in a row	レツ	*retsu*	刀	丆 歹 歹 列 6

列 **B** F-0731

説文

The seal-style form depicted "a severed head (of an enemy) with the hair still attached" (歹), cut off with "a knife, sword" (刂, bushu *rittoo*). 歹 had the sound *retsu*. This character originally signified severed heads laid in a row as a show of victory, and later came to mean simply "a row." Another view explains that it represented cut-up animal bones laid in a row. The kanji 列 means "row, line; to line up in a row." <歹刂>

列 row, line, column [れつ]; 行列 a line, queue, procession, parade [ぎょうれつ]; 列挙する to enumerate, list [れっきょする]; 列強 the world powers [れっきょう]; 整列乗車 lining up for the train [せいれつじょうしゃ]; 列国 all countries, the nations of the world [れっこく]; 時系列 chronological order [じけいれつ]

SG-0280 葬	Meanings	Kun and On	Romaji	Bushu	Stroke Order and Number
	to bury, inter, hush up	ほうむ-る ソウ	hoomu-ru *soo*	艸	一 艹 芀 苑 葬 葬 12

葬 **C** F-1314

説文

The seal-style form comprised "plant, vegetation" (艸, 艹 bushu *kusakanmuri*), "a person mourning over skeletal remains" (死 SG-0277), and "hands holding up the remains" (廾). Together they signified "people carrying the remains of the deceased in preparation for burial." Another view takes the bottom to be "grass," suggesting that the body was left on the ground, exposed to the elements until only the bones remained for a later burial. The kanji 葬 meant "to bury, inter, hush up." <艹死廾>

葬る to bury, inter, hush up [ほうむる]; 葬式 funeral [そうしき]; 埋葬 burial [まいそう]; 葬儀 funeral rite [そうぎ]

SG-0281 烈	Meanings	Kun and On	Romaji	Bushu	Stroke Order and Number
	fierce, boisterous, intensely cruel	レツ	*retsu*	火	ア歹列列列列列烈 10

烈 **C** F-1435 — 金文 1, 説文 2, 烈

1 comprised the non-Joyo kanji 剌 "to spring back, bounce" (used for the sounds *ratsu/retsu*), and "a knife." 2 comprised "a severed head with hair attached" and "a knife" (forming 列 **SG-0279**), and 火 "fire" (灬, bushu *rekka*). A severed head being burnt meant "intense, fierce." The kanji 烈 means "fierce, boisterous, intensely cruel." <列灬>

烈火 blazing fire, furious flames [れっか]; 強烈な intense, strong, severe [きょうれつな]; 熱烈な ardent, passionate [ねつれつな]; 烈風 heavy wind, gale [れっぷう]; 熾烈な fierce [しれつな]; 鮮烈な striking, glaringly vivid [せんれつな]

SG-0282 裂	Meanings	Kun and On	Romaji	Bushu	Stroke Order and Number
	to tear, split up	さ-けつ レツ	sa-keru *retsu*	衣	ア歹列列裂裂裂 12

裂 **C** F-1451 — 説文, 裂

The seal-style form comprised 列, used for the sound *retsu* to mean "to cut bones," and 衣 **SG-1657** "clothes," signifying cutting clothes or cloth in a violent manner. The kanji 裂 means "to tear, split cloth." <列 衣>

裂く to tear, split up, drive apart [さく]; 裂ける to split, tear, rip [さける]; 裂け目 rift, crack, crevasse [さけめ]; 八裂きにする to tear apart [やつざきにする]; 決裂する to break down, collapse [けつれつする]; 破裂 explosion, rupture [はれつ]; 炸裂音 the sound of a violent explosion [さくれつおん]

SG-0283 殉	Meanings	Kun and On	Romaji	Bushu	Stroke Order and Number
	to die dutifully; death in the line of duty	ジュン	*jun*	歹	ア歹歹歹殉殉 10

殉 **D** F-2091

No ancient form. The kanji 殉 comprises 歹 "death," and 旬 **SG-2114** (from the non-Joyo kanji 徇 "to follow a master"), used for the sound *jun* to mean "to follow, obey." The kanji 殉 means "to die dutifully; death in the line of duty." <歹勹日>

殉じる to sacrifice oneself, die for the cause [じゅんじる]; 殉死 self-immolation on the death of one's lord [じゅんし]; 殉職 death in the line of duty [じゅんしょく]

14 Brains

14 (囟) "brains" [from brains in a skull] 思細脳悩

SG-0284 思	Meanings	Kun and On	Romaji	Bushu	Stroke Order and Number
	to think; thought	おも-う シ	omo-u *shi*	心	冂冊田田思思 9

思 **A** F-0104 — 説文, 思

The seal-style form comprised 囟 "a baby's head with fontanels," signifying "brains" and used for the sound *shi*; and 心 **SG-0187** "a heart," signifying "to think." In the kanji, 囟 became 田. The kanji 思 means "to think; thought." <田 心>

思う to think [おもう]; 思い出す to recall, remember, recollect [おもいだす]; 思い出 memory [おもいで]; 思いがけず unexpectedly [おもいがけず]; 思想 thought, ideology [しそう]; 意思 one's will, intent [いし]; 不思議な wonderful, strange, mysterious, incredible [ふしぎな]

SG-0285 細	Meanings	Kun and On	Romaji	Bushu	Stroke Order and Number
	long and thin, very small	ほそ-い・こま-かい サイ	hoso-i, koma-kai *sai*	糸	幺糸糸細細細細 11

細 **B** F-0569 — 説文, 細

The seal-style form comprised "a skein of threads" (糸 **SG-1600**) for "something long and thin," and 囟 (田), used for the sound *sai*. The kanji 細 means "long and thin, very small." <糸 田>

細い thin [ほそい]; 細字ペン a pen for fine writing [ほそじペン]; 細かい・細かな small, detailed [こまかい, こまかな]; 細部 details [さいぶ]; 細断 shredding [さいだん]; 細心の attentive to the finest details, scrupulous [さいしんの]; 子細 reasons, circumstances [しさい]

SG-0286 脳	Meanings	Kun and On	Romaji	Bushu	Stroke Order and Number
	brain	ノウ	*noo*	肉	月肜肜脳脳脳 11

脳 **B** F-0584 — 説文 1, 旧字 2, 腦 脳

1 (㛴) comprised "a standing person," "hair," and "a skull with brains inside," together signifying "(a person's) brains." In the kyuji 腦 (2), "person" was replaced by 月, bushu *nikuzuki* "part of the body." In the shinji 脳, the right-hand component became ⺍, and メ for the brains inside 凵. The kanji 脳 means "brain." <月㐫 (⺍凶)>

脳 brain, brains [のう]; 頭脳 brains [ずのう]; 大脳 the cerebrum [だいのう, だいのう]; 小脳 cerebellum [しょうのう, しょうのう]; 脳みそ brain tissue, brain [のうみそ]; 脳卒中 stroke, cerebral apoplexy [のうそっちゅう]; 脳震盪(脳しんとう) cerebral concussion [のうしんとう]; 脳死移植 transplant from brain-dead donor [のうしいしょく]

	Meanings	Kun and On	Romaji	Bushu	Stroke Order and Number
SG-0287 悩	to suffer torment or distress, be perturbed; worry	なや-む ノウ	naya-mu *noo*	心	丶 忄 忄⺍ ... 悩 10

悩 **C** F-1194

説文 1 旧字 2

The right side of the kanji 悩 shares its history with that of 脳 **SG-0286**. 1 contained 女 **SG-0521** "woman," signifying the appearance of a woman in distress. The kyuji 惱 (2) comprised 忄 bushu *risshinben* "a heart," and 𡿺 for the sound *noo*. A heart and brains together signified "to worry." The kanji 悩 means "to suffer torment or distress, be perturbed; worry." <忄𡿺>

悩む to suffer torment, be troubled [なやˀむ]; 悩ましい disturbing, perturbing [なやましˀい]; 伸び悩み sluggish growth [のびなやみ]; 頭を悩ます to puzzle over, worry oneself [あたまˀを・なやまˀす]; 苦悩する to agonize, suffer anguish [くのうする]; 悩殺する to fascinate, captivate [のうさつする]

15 Animal meat/flesh

15 月 "parts of the human body" [from a piece of animal meat with streaks of tendon or muscle showing]; bushu *nikuzuki* 筋肩胸胃肺腕肌腸肯腎股膝肘脊

	Meanings	Kun and On	Romaji	Bushu	Stroke Order and Number
SG-0288 筋	muscle, tendon, string, reason, storyline	すじ キン	suji *kin*	竹	⺈ ⺮ ... 筋 12

筋 **B** F-0815

説文

The seal-style form comprised "bamboo" (竹 **SG-0759**), whose straight, fibrous lines signified "streak"; "part of the body" (月, bushu *nikuzuki*); and "muscle of a strong arm" (力 **SG-1949**). A part of the body that was fibrous signified "tendon, muscle." In Japanese, "fibrous lines all the way through" also gave the meaning "reason, storyline." The kanji 筋 means "muscle, tendon, string, reason, storyline." <⺮月力>

筋 muscle, tendon, story [すˀじ]; 道筋 route, reasoning [みちすじ]; 筋の通らない unreasonable [すˀじの・とおらˀない]; 血筋 blood, lineage [ちすじ]; 筋書きどおりに as planned, as scheduled [すじがきどˀおりに]; 背筋を伸ばす to straighten one's spine [せすじをのばˀす]; 筋金入り hard-core [すじがねいり]; 筋肉 muscle [きˀんにく]; 鉄筋コンクリート steel-reinforced concrete [てっきんコンクリˀート]

	Meanings	Kun and On	Romaji	Bushu	Stroke Order and Number
SG-0289 肩	shoulder	かた ケン	kata *ken*	肉	一 ⺕ 戸 戸 肩 肩 8

肩 **B** F-0913

説文 1 説文俗体 2

1 and 2 comprised "a shoulder blade" and "part of the body" (月), together signifying "shoulder joint." The kanji 肩 means "shoulder." <戸月>

肩 shoulder [かˀた]; 肩書き professional title [かたがき]; 右肩上がり growing in value over time [みぎかたあˀがり]; 肩叩き pounding the shoulder to relieve stiffness, pressuring someone into early retirement [かたたˀたき]; 肩甲骨 shoulder blade [けんこˀうこつ]; 肩身の狭い to feel inhibited, feel ashamed [かたみのせまˀい]; 肩の荷 burden, load [かˀたのに]

	Meanings	Kun and On	Romaji	Bushu	Stroke Order and Number
SG-0290 胸	chest, bosom, heart, mind	むね・むな キョウ	mune, muna *kyoo*	肉	月 肑 肑 ... 胸 胸 10

胸 **B** F-0999

金文 1 説文 2

1 comprised "a body part between the limbs (凶), used for the sound *kyoo*, and "flesh, part of the body" (月), together signifying "a chest." In 2, 凶 was placed inside the shape 勹 "a body bending over," without 月. In the kanji, 月 returned on the left side as bushu *nikuzuki*. The kanji 胸 means "chest, bosom, heart, mind <月勹凶>

胸 the breast, the lungs, one's heart [むねˀ]; 胸を張る to be puffed up with pride [むˀねをはる]; 胸が塞がる full of deep emotion [むねˀが・ふさがる]; 胸元 the bosom [むなもと]; 胸算用 anticipation, calculation [むなざˀんよう]; 胸囲 one's chest measurement [きょˀうい]; 度胸 boldness, daring [どˀきょう]; 胸筋を開く to be frank, have a hear-to-heart talk [きょうきんをひらˀく]

	Meanings	Kun and On	Romaji	Bushu	Stroke Order and Number
SG-0291 胃	stomach	イ	*i*	肉	丨 冂 冊 田 ... 胃 胃 9

胃 **C** F-1186

金文 1 説文 2

1 and 2 comprised "a stomach containing food particles" (indicated by the dots), and 月 "flesh, part of the body," together signifying "stomach." The stomach component was simplified to 田. The kanji 胃 means "stomach." <田月>

胃腸 stomach and intestines [いちょう]; 胃弱 weak digestion [いじゃく]; 胃炎 inflammation of the stomach, gastritis [いえん]; 胃薬 indigestion medicine, antiacid [いぐˀすり]

SG-0292 肺	Meanings	Kun and On	Romaji	Bushu	Stroke Order and Number
	lung	ハイ	*hai*	肉	刀 月 月' 肀 肻 肺 肺 9

肺 **C** F-1283 説文

The seal-style form comprised 月 "part of the body," and "a plant branch with full leaves," used for the sound *hai* to mean "to open up." The part of the body that opened up to take in air was "the lung." In the shinji 肺, the right-side component became 市. The kanji 肺 means "lung." <月 市>

肺 the lungs [はい]; 片肺 single lung [かたはい]; 肺炎 pneumonia [はいえん]; 肺活量 lung capacity [はいかつりょう]; 肺癌 lung cancer [はいがん]; 肺病 lung disease [はいびょう]; 心肺停止 cardiopulmonary arrest [しんぱい・ていし]

SG-0293 腕	Meanings	Kun and On	Romaji	Bushu	Stroke Order and Number
	arm	うで ワン	ude *wan*	肉	刀 肸 肸 胺 腕 腕 12

腕 **C** F-1165

No ancient form. The kanji 腕 comprised 月 "flesh," and 宛 **SG-0416**, used for the sound *wan* to mean "to bend." 宛 derived from 夕, "plump flesh" of one's thighs when "kneeling" (㔾). A plump, bending part of the body was an arm. The kanji 腕 means "arm." <月 宀 夗>

腕 arm, ability, prowess [うで]; 両腕 both arms [りょううで]; 右腕 right arm [みぎうで]; 腕競べ a trial of skill [うでくらべ]; 腕利き a person of ability, master-hand [うできき]; 腕組みをする to fold one's arms [うでぐみをする]; 腕前 ability, skill [うでまえ]; 腕力 brute strength, muscle [わんりょく]; 手腕 ability, savvy [しゅわん]

SG-0294 肌	Meanings	Kun and On	Romaji	Bushu	Stroke Order and Number
	skin, characteristic, disposition	はだ	hada	肉	刀 肌 肌 6

肌 **C** F-1279 説文

The seal-style form comprised 月 "flesh," and 几, used for the sound *ki*, together signifying "skin." In Japanese, 肌 also means "characteristic, disposition." The kanji 肌 means "skin, characteristic, disposition." <月 几>

肌 skin [はだ]; 肌着 underwear, lingerie [はだぎ, はだぎ]; 肌触り how something feels to the touch [はだざわり]; 親分肌 bossiness [おやぶんはだ]; 素肌 bare skin, without makeup [すはだ]; 一肌脱ぐ to pitch in and help [ひとはだ・ぬぐ]; 肌が合わない not get along well [はだが・あわない]; 肌がけ布団 lighter-than-normal *futon* [はだがけぶとん]

SG-0295 腸	Meanings	Kun and On	Romaji	Bushu	Stroke Order and Number
	intestine, gut	チョウ	*choo*	肉	刀 肑 胆 胆 腸 腸 腸 13

腸 **C** F-1522 説文

The seal-style form comprised "part of the body" (月), and 昜, used for the sound *choo* to mean "long." The part of the body that was long was "the intestine." The kanji 腸 means "intestine, gut." <月 昜(日一勿)>

腸 intestine, gut [ちょう]; 大腸 the large intestine [だいちょう]; 小腸 the small intestine [しょうちょう]; 盲腸 the appendix [もうちょう]; 腸詰め sausage [ちょうづめ]

SG-0296 肯	Meanings	Kun and On	Romaji	Bushu	Stroke Order and Number
	to agree, consent	コウ	*koo*	肉	丨 卜 止 肯 肯 肯 8

肯 **C** F-1575 金文 1 説文古文 2 説文 3

1 comprised "bones" and 月 "flesh." In 2 and 3, the flesh was placed inside 冂 "bone" (from 冎), signifying "flesh and bone bonded together." The character was borrowed to mean "to agree, consent." In the kanji, 止 replaced "bone" at the top. The kanji 肯 means "to agree, consent." <止 月>

肯定 affirmation [こうてい]; 肯定する to confirm, acknowledge [こうていする]

SG-0297 腎	Meanings	Kun and On	Romaji	Bushu	Stroke Order and Number
	kidney; important	ジン	*jin*	肉	丨 𠂆 戸 臣 臤 臤 腎 腎 13

腎 **D** F-1770 説文

The seal-style form comprised 臣 **SG-0023**, used for the sound *jin* to mean "important," 又 **SG-0084** "a hand," and 月 "part of the body." Together they meant an important organ—"the kidney"—and "important" in general. The kanji 腎 means "kidney; important." <臤月>

腎臓 kidney [じんぞう]; 肝腎な (or 肝心な) important, essential, vital [かんじんな]; 副腎 adrenal gland [ふくじん]

SG-0298 股	Meanings	Kun and On	Romaji	Bushu	Stroke Order and Number
	crotch; between the legs; forked; to have it both ways	また コ	mata *ko*	肉	月 肌 肌 股 股 8

股 **D** F-1905 説文

The seal-style form comprised "flesh, part of the body" (月), and 殳, used for the sound *ko*, together signifying "crotch; between the legs; forked shape." The character also means "to have it both ways." The kanji 股 means "crotch; between the legs; forked; to have it both ways." <月 殳>

股 crotch, fork [また]; 内股 inner thigh [うちまた]; 大股 long stride [おおまた]; 二股をかける to play it both ways, sit on the fence [ふたまたをかける]; 股関節 hip joint [こかんせつ]

SG-0299 膝	Meanings	Kun and On	Romaji	Bushu	Stroke Order and Number
	knee	ひざ	hiza	肉	月 胩 脎 膝 膝 膝 15

膝 **D** F-2256	篆文 1 正字 2 膝 1 and 2 comprised 桼, used for the sound *shitsu*, and 卩 "a kneeling person," for the meaning of "knees." In 3, 月, bushu *nikuzuki* "part of the body," was added to 桼. The kanji 膝 means "knee." <月桼(木𠆢氺)>	膝 knee [ひざ]; 立膝する to sit with one knee drawn up [たてひざする]; お膝元 home territory of an influential figure [おひざもと]; 膝小僧 knee joint [ひざこぞう]; 膝掛け lap robe [ひざかけ, ひざかけ]

SG-0300 肘	Meanings	Kun and On	Romaji	Bushu	Stroke Order and Number
	elbow	ひじ	hiji	肉	月 月 肘 肘 7

肘 **D** F-2451	説文 肘 The seal-style form comprised "flesh" (月), and "a hand" (寸), used for the sound *chuu*. The original kanji for "elbow" (丑) came to be used in the Chinese celestial calendar, so the meaning of "elbow" was applied to the homophonous kanji 肘 instead. The kanji 肘 means "elbow." <月寸>	肘 elbow [ひじ]; 肘鉄砲を食らう to be rebuffed [ひじてっぽうをくらう]; 肘掛 arm rest, elbow rest [ひじかけ]; 肘掛け椅子 armchair [ひじかけいす]

SG-0301 脊	Meanings	Kun and On	Romaji	Bushu	Stroke Order and Number
	spine, backbone, vertebra	セキ	*seki*	肉	= = 夫 脊 10

脊 **D** F-2568	説文 脊 The seal-style form comprised "backbone, spine," and 月 "flesh," signifying "the backbone of the body." The kanji 脊 means "spine, backbone, vertebra." <脊(==人月)>	脊髄 spinal cord [せきずい]; 脊椎 the vertebrae, the spine [せきつい]

16 Teeth

16 歯 "teeth" 歯齢

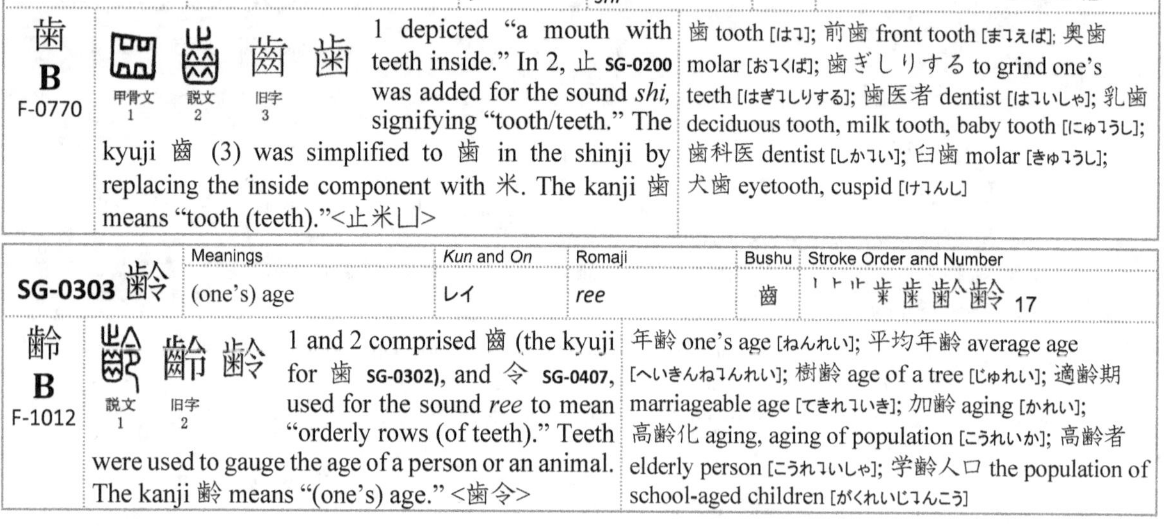

SG-0302 歯	Meanings	Kun and On	Romaji	Bushu	Stroke Order and Number
	tooth (teeth)	は シ	ha *shi*	齒	丨 ⺊ 止 歩 歯 歯 歯 12

歯 **B** F-0770	甲骨文 1 説文 2 旧字 3 1 depicted "a mouth with teeth inside." In 2, 止 **SG-0200** was added for the sound *shi,* signifying "tooth/teeth." The kyuji 齒 (3) was simplified to 歯 in the shinji by replacing the inside component with 米. The kanji 歯 means "tooth (teeth)."<止米凵>	歯 tooth [は]; 前歯 front tooth [まえば]; 奥歯 molar [おくば]; 歯ぎしりする to grind one's teeth [はぎしりする]; 歯医者 dentist [はいしゃ]; 乳歯 deciduous tooth, milk tooth, baby tooth [にゅうし]; 歯科医 dentist [しかい]; 臼歯 molar [きゅうし]; 犬歯 eyetooth, cuspid [けんし]

SG-0303 齢	Meanings	Kun and On	Romaji	Bushu	Stroke Order and Number
	(one's) age	レイ	*ree*	齒	丨 ⺊ 止 歩 歯 歯 齢 17

齢 **B** F-1012	説文 1 旧字 2 齢 1 and 2 comprised 齒 (the kyuji for 歯 **SG-0302**), and 令 **SG-0407**, used for the sound *ree* to mean "orderly rows (of teeth)." Teeth were used to gauge the age of a person or an animal. The kanji 齢 means "(one's) age." <歯令>	年齢 one's age [ねんれい]; 平均年齢 average age [へいきんねんれい]; 樹齢 age of a tree [じゅれい]; 適齢期 marriageable age [てきれいき]; 加齢 aging [かれい]; 高齢化 aging, aging of population [こうれいか]; 高齢者 elderly person [こうれいしゃ]; 学齢人口 the population of school-aged children [がくれいじんこう]

II Postures

17 Person

17a 人 "person" [from a standing person viewed from the side]; 亻 "an act that a person does"; bushu *ninben* 人千休体仁極俺囚

SG-0304 人	Meanings	*Kun* and *On*	Romaji	Bushu	Stroke Order and Number
	person, people, human, others	ひと ジン・ニン	*hito* *jin, nin*	人	ノ 人 2

人
A
F-0006

甲骨文 1　金文 1 2　金文 2 3　篆文 4　説文 5

1, 2, 3, 4, and 5 depicted "a standing person viewed from the side." Their hands were in front of them, and their knees were slightly bent. In the kanji, the head and the hands became the first stroke, and the torso and the legs the second stroke. When used as bushu, it became a vertical narrow shape 亻, called *ninben,* and it usually means "an act that a person does." The kanji 人 means "person, people, others, human." <人>

人のいい good-natured [ひとのいꜜい]; 人々 people, everybody [ひꜜとびと]; 人のことを言う to speak of others [ひとのことꜜを・いう]; 人手不足 manpower shortage [ひとでぶꜜそく]; 外国人 foreigner, foreign national [がいこくꜜじん]; 人格 character, personality [じんかく]; 人間 human being, man [にんげん]; 三人 three people [さんにꜜん] // 一人 one person [ひとꜜり]; 二人 two people [ふたり]

SG-0305 千	Meanings	*Kun* and *On*	Romaji	Bushu	Stroke Order and Number
	thousand; numerous	ち セン	chi *sen*	十	ノ 二 千 3

千
A
F-0119

甲骨文 1 1　甲骨文 2 2　説文 3

1, 2, and 3 comprised "a standing person" (亻) with a short line (一) on their shin, and indicated "a group of one thousand (soldiers)." A thousand is a large number, which gave the more general meaning of "numerous." The kanji 千 means "thousand; numerous." <ノ 十>
(Note: In oracle bone style, two lines denoted two thousand, and three lines denoted three thousand, as shown at right.)

千代 a thousand generations [ちꜜよ]; 千 a thousand [せꜜん]; 海千山千 crafty old hand, seasoned campaigner [うみせんやません]; 笑止千万 highly ridiculous, quite absurd [しょうꜜし・せんばん]; 千客万来 thronged with customers [せんきゃくばんらい]; 千円札 thousand-yen note [せんえꜜんさつ]; 一日千秋の思い waiting impatiently for [いちにちせんしゅうのおもꜜい]; 一刻千金 every moment is precious [いっこくせんきん]

SG-0306 休	Meanings	*Kun* and *On*	Romaji	Bushu	Stroke Order and Number
	to rest; holiday, break, a day off; closed	やす-む キュウ	yasu-mu *kyuu*	人	亻 仁 什 休 休 6

休
A
F-0391

甲骨文 1 1　甲骨文 2 2　金文 3　説文 4

1 through 4 depicted "a standing person (亻) with their back against a tree (木)." A traveler resting against a tree meant "to rest." A day on which a person rests is a day off, or the day that a business's doors are closed. The kanji 休 means "to rest; holiday, break, a day off; closed." <亻 木>

休む to rest, be absent from work or school [やすꜜむ]; 昼休み lunch break [ひるやꜜすみ]; 一休み short break [ひとꜜやすみ]; 夏休み summer vacation [なつやꜜすみ]; 気休め a temporarily soothing word or action [きやすめ]; 休息 relaxation, respite [きゅうそく]; 運休 suspension of transportation service [うんきゅう]; 定休日 regular day off [ていきゅꜜうび]

SG-0307 体	Meanings	*Kun* and *On*	Romaji	Bushu	Stroke Order and Number
	body, style, entity, substance, appearance	からだ タイ・テイ	karada *tai, tee*	骨	亻 什 什 休 体 7

体
A
F-0045

説文 1　旧字 2

1 and 2 comprised 骨 **SG-0272** "bone," and 豊 **SG-1976** "full; abundance," together meaning the entire body of a person. In the shinji, the entirely different shape 体 was used. When used to mean "outward appearance," it is usually pronounced as *tee*. The kanji 体 means "body, style, entity, substance, appearance"<亻 本>

体 body [からだ]; 体重 one's body weight [たいじゅう]; 本体 main body, true form [ほꜜんたい]; 一体化 unification, combining into a single unit [いったいか]; 一体何故 why on earth [いったいなꜜぜ]; 自治体 local government [じちたい]; 体裁が悪い not fit to be seen, in bad shape [ていさいがわるꜜい]; 有り体に言うと to put it bluntly [ありていにいうと]; 体のいい nice-sounding [ていのいꜜい]

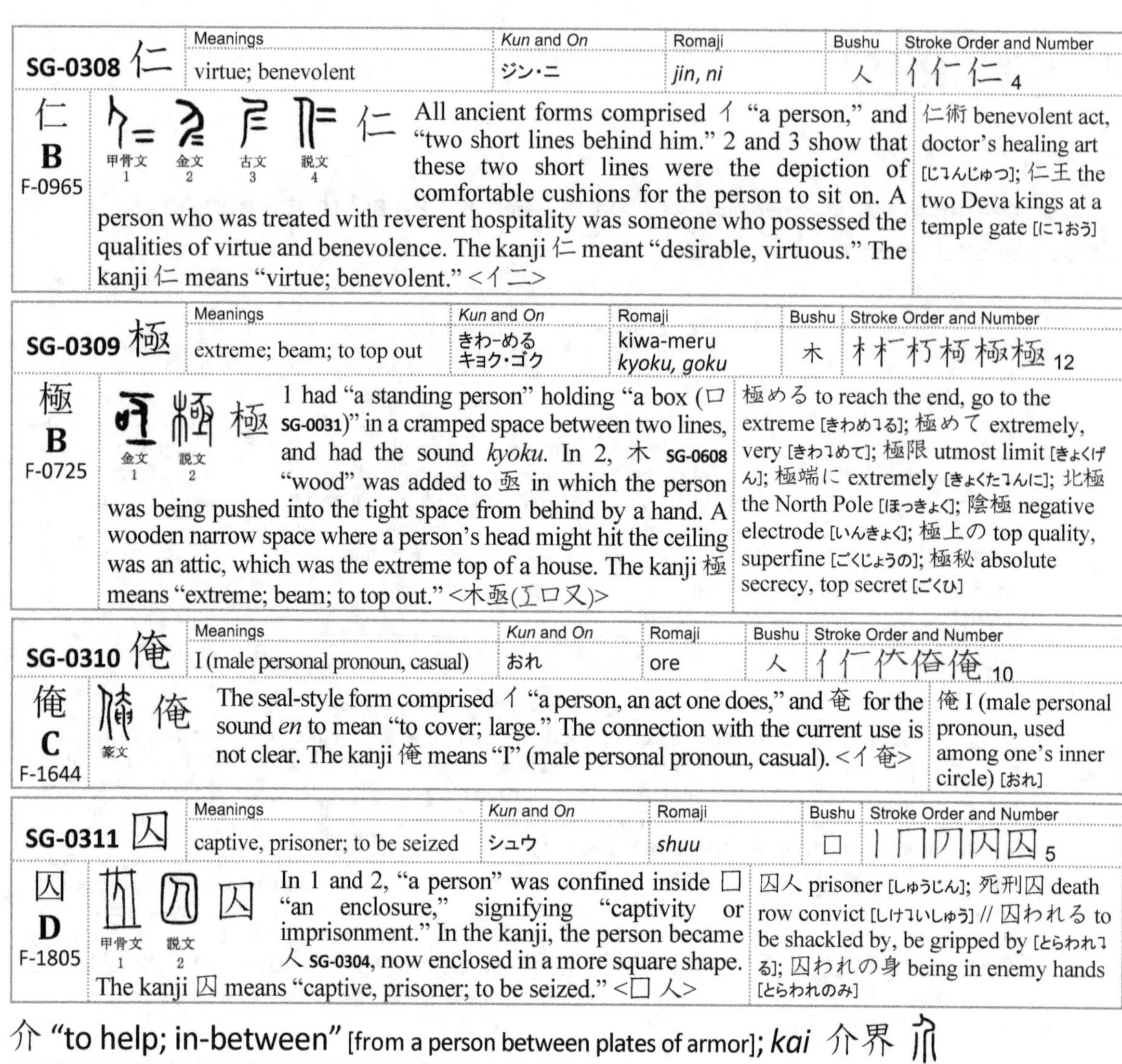

SG-0308 仁	Meanings	Kun and On	Romaji	Bushu	Stroke Order and Number
	virtue; benevolent	ジン・ニ	*jin, ni*	人	亻 仁 仁 4

仁 **B** F-0965 — 甲骨文 1, 金文 2, 古文 3, 説文 4, 仁

All ancient forms comprised 亻 "a person," and "two short lines behind him." 2 and 3 show that these two short lines were the depiction of comfortable cushions for the person to sit on. A person who was treated with reverent hospitality was someone who possessed the qualities of virtue and benevolence. The kanji 仁 meant "desirable, virtuous." The kanji 仁 means "virtue; benevolent." <亻二>

仁術 benevolent act, doctor's healing art [じ˥んじゅつ]; 仁王 the two Deva kings at a temple gate [に˥おう]

SG-0309 極	Meanings	Kun and On	Romaji	Bushu	Stroke Order and Number
	extreme; beam; to top out	きわ-める キョク・ゴク	kiwa-meru *kyoku, goku*	木	木 朾 朽 柯 極 極 12

極 **B** F-0725 — 金文 1, 説文 2, 極

1 had "a standing person" holding "a box (口 **SG-0031**)" in a cramped space between two lines, and had the sound *kyoku*. In 2, 木 **SG-0608** "wood" was added to 亟 in which the person was being pushed into the tight space from behind by a hand. A wooden narrow space where a person's head might hit the ceiling was an attic, which was the extreme top of a house. The kanji 極 means "extreme; beam; to top out." <木亟(工口又)>

極める to reach the end, go to the extreme [きわめ˥る]; 極めて extremely, very [きわ˥めて]; 極限 utmost limit [きょくげん]; 極端に extremely [きょくた˥んに]; 北極 the North Pole [ほっきょく]; 陰極 negative electrode [いんきょく]; 極上の top quality, superfine [ごくじょうの]; 極秘 absolute secrecy, top secret [ごくひ]

SG-0310 俺	Meanings	Kun and On	Romaji	Bushu	Stroke Order and Number
	I (male personal pronoun, casual)	おれ	ore	人	亻 仁 佧 俺 俺 10

俺 **C** F-1644 — 篆文, 俺

The seal-style form comprised 亻 "a person, an act one does," and 奄 for the sound *en* to mean "to cover; large." The connection with the current use is not clear. The kanji 俺 means "I" (male personal pronoun, casual). <亻奄>

俺 I (male personal pronoun, used among one's inner circle) [おれ]

SG-0311 囚	Meanings	Kun and On	Romaji	Bushu	Stroke Order and Number
	captive, prisoner; to be seized	シュウ	*shuu*	囗	丨 冂 闪 囚 囚 5

囚 **D** F-1805 — 甲骨文 1, 説文 2, 囚

In 1 and 2, "a person" was confined inside 囗 "an enclosure," signifying "captivity or imprisonment." In the kanji, the person became 人 **SG-0304**, now enclosed in a more square shape. The kanji 囚 means "captive, prisoner; to be seized." <囗 人>

囚人 prisoner [しゅうじん]; 死刑囚 death row convict [しけ˥いしゅう] // 囚われる to be shackled by, be gripped by [とらわれ˥る]; 囚われの身 being in enemy hands [とらわれのみ]

17b 介 "to help; in-between" [from a person between plates of armor]; *kai* 介界 𠆢

SG-0312 介	Meanings	Kun and On	Romaji	Bushu	Stroke Order and Number
	to mediate, help; go-between	カイ	*kai*	人	ノ 人 介 介 4

介 **A** F-0754 — 甲骨文 1, 説文 2, 介

1 and 2 comprised "a standing person," with something both in front of and behind them. They depicted a soldier encased on both sides by a suit of armor. A suit of armor protected the soldier wearing it and helped him to survive, whence "to help." A person in between two things also gave the meaning "to mediate; go-between." The kanji 介 means "to mediate, help; go-between." < 介 >

魚介類 fish and shellfish [ぎょか˥いるい]; 仲介 mediation [ちゅうかい]; 介護 nursing care, caregiving [か˥いご]; 介添え helper, assistant [かいぞえ]; 介助 help, aid [か˥いじょ]; お節介 meddlesomeness, busybody [おせ˥っかい]

SG-0313 界	Meanings	Kun and On	Romaji	Bushu	Stroke Order and Number
	world, area	カイ	*kai*	田	口 田 田 甲 界 界 9

界 **A** F-0336 — 説文 1, 正字 2, 界

The seal-style form comprised 田 **SG-1300** "rice paddies with levees dividing the fields," and 介 **SG-0312**, used for the sound *kai* to mean "in-between," together signifying "an area within boundaries." 田 and 介 in 2 畍 were rearranged in the shinji. The kanji 界 means "an area divided by boundaries, world."<田介>

世界 world [せ˥かい]; 限界 limit [げんかい]; 境界 boundary [きょうかい]; 財界 financial world, business circle [ざいかい]; 他界する to die [たかいする]; 界隈 neighborhood [か˥いわい]; 視界 range of vision [しかい]; 芸能界 the entertainment business [げいのˉうかい]

17c 大 "person; large" [from a person with their arms and legs spread wide]

大天夫太文添汰扶爽

	Meanings	Kun and On	Romaji	Bushu	Stroke Order and Number
SG-0314 大	large, grand	おお-きい ダイ・タイ	oo-kii *dai, tai*	大	一ナ大 3

大 **A** F-0003

甲骨文 1 金文 1 2 金文 2 3 説文 4

1, 2, 3, and 4 all had a simple shape in common—"a standing person facing forward with their arms spread slightly downward and their legs open wide." Spreading the arms and legs made a person look large. The kanji 大 meant "large, grand." When 大 was used as a component, it retained its original meaning of "person, human." <一人>

大きい large, grand [おおきꜜい]; 大げさな exaggerated [おおげさな]; 大いなる great [おꜜおいなる]; 莫大な huge, enormous [ばくだいな]; 大学 university, college [だいがく]; 大作 monumental work [たいさく]; 大河ドラマ a TV saga that runs for many episodes [たいがドꜜラマ] // 大人 adult, grown-up [おとな]

	Meanings	Kun and On	Romaji	Bushu	Stroke Order and Number
SG-0315 天	the sky, heaven, the top; by nature	あめ・あま テン	ame, ama *ten*	大	一二チ天 4

天 **A** F-0185

甲骨文 1 金文 1 2 金文 2 3 説文 4

In 1 and 2, the small circle at the top represented the person's head. In 3 and 4, the top component became a line to signify what was above one's head—the sky. The kanji 天 means "the sky, heaven, the top." <一大>

天地の heaven and earth [あꜜめつちの] (literary); 天下り government official landing an industry job [あまくだり]; 天下 world, ruling power [てꜜんか]; 天火 oven [てꜜんぴ]; 天日干し sun-drying [てんぴぼし]; 天気 weather [てꜜんき]; 天引き withholding, deduction [てんびき]; 先天性の congenital [せんてんせいの]

	Meanings	Kun and On	Romaji	Bushu	Stroke Order and Number
SG-0316 夫	man, husband	おっと フ・フウ	otto *hu, huu*	大	一二チ夫 4

夫 **A** F-0253

甲骨文 1 金文 2 説文 3

1, 2, and 3 depicted "a man wearing an ornamental hairpin." A bridegroom or a young man in a coming-of-age rite wore a hairpin on his chignon as part of his formal attire. The kanji 夫 means "man, husband." <一大>

夫 husband [おっと]; 丈夫な strong, robust, durable [じょうぶな]; 夫妻 married couple [ふꜜさい]; 夫人 wife of, Mrs. [ふじん]; 前夫 one's former husband [ぜꜜんぷ]; 水夫 sailor [すꜜいふ]; 人夫 laborer [にꜜんぷ]; 工夫する to devise [くふうする]

	Meanings	Kun and On	Romaji	Bushu	Stroke Order and Number
SG-0317 太	peaceful, thick, fat, big; very	ふと-い タイ・タ	huto-i *tai, ta*	大	一ナ大太 4

太 **A** F-0271

金文 1 説文古文 2 説文 3

1 was the same as 大, whereas 2 and 3 were the same as the kanji 泰 **SG-0146**, and used for the sounds *tai* or *ta*. The two short lines inside 2 were a simplification of "flowing water," 氵. 3 depicted "a person saved from the water by two hands," and signified "safe, peaceful." The inside component of 3 was drastically reduced to a single short stroke in the kanji. The character was also used as an intensifier—"very." The kanji 太 means "peaceful, thick, fat, big; very." <大丶>

太い thick [ふとꜜい]; 太る to gain weight, become fat [ふとꜜる]; 図太い bold, impudent [ずぶとꜜい]; 太字 thick writing, boldface [ふとじ]; 太平洋 the Pacific Ocean [たいへꜜいよう]; 太古 ancient times, remote past [たꜜいこ]; 丸太 log [まるた]; 太刀 long sword [たꜜち]

	Meanings	Kun and On	Romaji	Bushu	Stroke Order and Number
SG-0318 文	writing, literary work, fine arts, culture, civilization, scholarship, humanities; civil	ふみ ブン・モン	humi *bun, mon*	文	' 亠ナ文 4

文 **A** F-0093

甲骨文 1 金文 1 2 金文 2 3 金文 3 4 説文 5

1, 2, 3, and 4 were "a person with an ornate body painting of a heart on the chest." An elaborate shape was used to mean a character and further encompassed a broader range of the things human civilization had created. In 5, the inside shape was dropped. The kanji 文 means "writing, literary work, fine arts, culture, civilization, scholarship, humanities," and "civil" in contrast with "military might" (武 **SG-1473**). <文>

文 letter (archaic) [ふꜜみ], writing, sentence [ぶꜜん]; 文化 culture [ぶꜜんか]; 文明 civilization [ぶんめい]; 文系 humanities, liberal arts [ぶんけい]; 文通 exchange of letters [ぶんつう]; 文字 writing, character, letter [もꜜじ]; 一文無し penniless [いちもꜜんなし]; 古文 classics [こꜜぶん]; 古文書 historical documents [こぶꜜんしょ, こもꜜんじょ]

SG-0319 添	Meanings	Kun and On	Romaji	Bushu	Stroke Order and Number
	to add, accompany	そ-える テン	so-eru *ten*	水	氵氵𣲾添添添 11

添 **C** F-1357

No ancient form. For the kanji 添, 氵 "water," signifying "plenty of water for soaking," was added to 忝, which was used for the sound *ten* to mean "add, attach." In Japanese, the character also means "to marry." The kanji 添 means "to add, accompany, marry." <氵忝(天⺗)>

忝-説文

添える to add, garnish [そえる]; 添い遂げる to live together in happy union until parted by death [そいとげꜜる]; 後添い one's second wife [のちぞい]; 添付する to attach, append [てんぷする]; 別添 attachment, accompanying (letter) [べってん]; 添加物 additive [てんかꜜぶつ]

SG-0320 汰	Meanings	Kun and On	Romaji	Bushu	Stroke Order and Number
	plentifully, amply; to sort out	タ	*ta*	水	氵氵汁汰汰 7

汰 **D** F-2110

No ancient form. The kanji 汰 comprises 氵, bushu *sanzui* "flowing water," and 太, used for the sound *ta* to mean "a lot, a large amount." Taken together, they meant "a great gush of water separating good from bad." The kanji 汰 means "plentifully; to sort out." <氵太>

淘汰 selection, weeding out [とꜜうた]; 手持ち無沙汰 being at a loose end, bored [てもちぶꜜさた]; 気違い沙汰 insane behavior [きちがいざた]; 沙汰 verdict, communication, affair [さたꜜ, さꜜた]

SG-0321 扶	Meanings	Kun and On	Romaji	Bushu	Stroke Order and Number
	to support, help	フ	*hu*	手	一寸扌扌扶扶扶 7

扶 **D** F-1901

金文 1 説文古文 2 説文 3

1 and 2 comprised 夫 **SG-0316** "man," used for the sound *hu* to mean "to help"; and "a hand holding a stick; to cause," signifying "a person giving a helping hand." 3 comprised 扌, bushu *tehen* "an act done by hand," and 夫. The kanji 扶 means "to support, help." <扌夫>

扶養家族 dependent, a mouth to feed [ふようかꜜぞく]; 相互扶助 mutual assistance [そうごふꜜじょ]; 扶助金 grant, relief fund [ふじょきん]; 扶持米 rice ration [ふちまい] (historical)

SG-0322 爽	Meanings	Kun and On	Romaji	Bushu	Stroke Order and Number
	refreshing, invigorating	さわ-やか ソウ	sawa-yaka *soo*	爻	一㐅ㄨ㸚爽爽 11

爽 **D** F-2498

金文 1 説文 2

1 comprised 大 **SG-0314** "a person" in the center, in this case a deceased woman with "red tattooed patterns decorating her breasts." The beauty of vivid red tattoos gave the meaning "vivid." 2 became the kanji 爽. The kanji 爽 means "refreshing, invigorating." <大メメメメ>

爽やか fresh, invigorating, clear [さわꜜやか]; 爽快な refreshing, exhilarating [そうかいな]; 颯爽として dashingly [さっそうとして]

17d 因 "to depend; conventional"; *in/on* 因恩姻咽

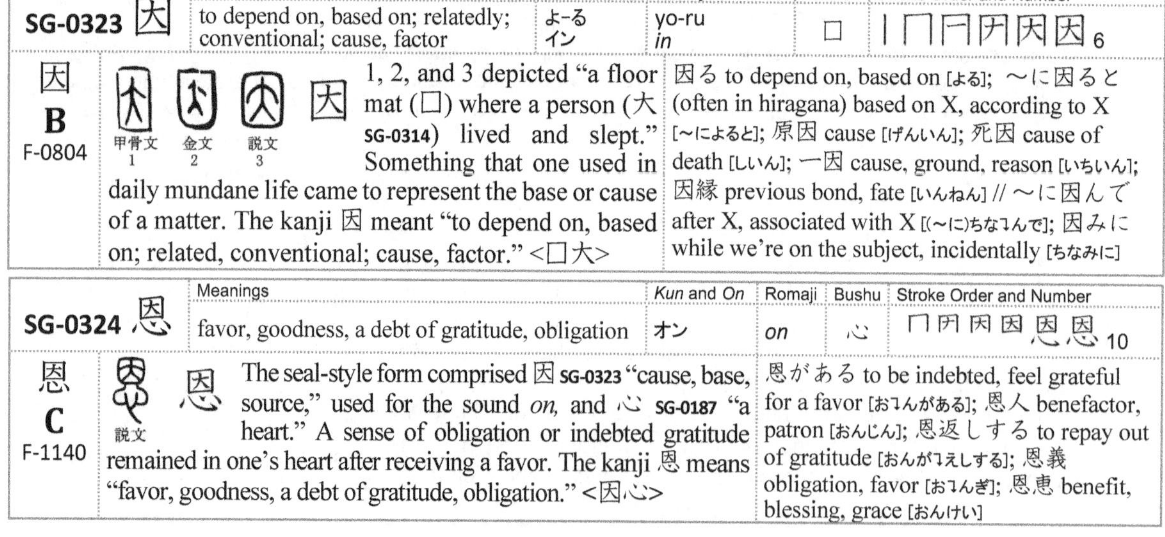

SG-0323 因	Meanings	Kun and On	Romaji	Bushu	Stroke Order and Number
	to depend on, based on; relatedly; conventional; cause, factor	よ-る イン	yo-ru *in*	囗	丨冂冃冈因因 6

因 **B** F-0804

甲骨文 1 金文 2 説文 3

1, 2, and 3 depicted "a floor mat (囗) where a person (大 **SG-0314**) lived and slept." Something that one used in daily mundane life came to represent the base or cause of a matter. The kanji 因 meant "to depend on, based on; related, conventional; cause, factor." <囗大>

因る to depend on, based on [よる]; ～に因ると (often in hiragana) based on X, according to X [～によると]; 原因 cause [げんいん]; 死因 cause of death [しいん]; 一因 cause, ground, reason [いちいん]; 因縁 previous bond, fate [いんねん] // ～に因んで after X, associated with X [(～に)ちなꜜんで]; 因みに while we're on the subject, incidentally [ちなみに]

SG-0324 恩	Meanings	Kun and On	Romaji	Bushu	Stroke Order and Number
	favor, goodness, a debt of gratitude, obligation	オン	*on*	心	冂冃冈因恩恩 10

恩 **C** F-1140

説文

The seal-style form comprised 因 **SG-0323** "cause, base, source," used for the sound *on,* and 心 **SG-0187** "a heart." A sense of obligation or indebted gratitude remained in one's heart after receiving a favor. The kanji 恩 means "favor, goodness, a debt of gratitude, obligation." <因心>

恩がある to be indebted, feel grateful for a favor [おꜜんがある]; 恩人 benefactor, patron [おんじん]; 恩返しする to repay out of gratitude [おんがꜜえしする]; 恩義 obligation, favor [おꜜんぎ]; 恩恵 benefit, blessing, grace [おんけい]

SG-0325 姻	Meanings	Kun and On	Romaji	Bushu	Stroke Order and Number
	marriage	イン	*in*	女	姻 9

姻 **D** F-2116 説文

The seal-style form comprised 女 **SG-0521** "woman; female," and 因 **SG-0323**, used for the sound *in* to mean "to depend on, be based on." When a woman married, the family she was married into became the basis of her life. The kanji 姻 means "marriage." <女因>

婚姻 marriage [こんいん]; 姻戚関係 related by marriage [いんせきかんけい]

SG-0326 咽	Meanings	Kun and On	Romaji	Bushu	Stroke Order and Number
	throat; to be stifled, be choked	イン	*in*	口	咽 9

咽 **D** F-2435 説文

The seal-style form comprised 口 "mouth," and 因, used for the sounds *in* or *etsu* to mean "to be stifled." When the passage of air is blocked in the throat, one chokes. The kanji 咽 means "throat; to be choked." <口因>

咽喉 the throat, pharynx and larynx [いんこう]; 咽頭炎 pharyngitis [いんとうえん] // 嗚咽する to sob [おえつする]; 咽る to be choked, be smothered [むせる]

17e 奇 "to lean over; lopsided"; *ki* 奇寄崎埼椅

SG-0327 奇	Meanings	Kun and On	Romaji	Bushu	Stroke Order and Number
	odd, lopsided, peculiar	キ	*ki*	大	奇 8

奇 **B** F-1269 説文

The seal-style form comprised 大 **SG-0314** "person," and 可 **SG-0045**, used for the sound *ki* to mean "a bent or crooked shape." (Another view is 口, and 㐫 for *ki.*) A person with a crooked leg standing lopsided gave the meaning "unusual, peculiar, odd, lopsided." The kanji 奇 meant "odd, lopsided, peculiar, unusual." <大可>

奇怪な mysterious, weird [きかいな]; 奇異な queer, singular, odd [きいな]; 奇行 eccentric behavior [きこう]; 奇抜な extremely unusual, wild [きばつな]; 奇妙奇天烈な extremely odd [きみょう・きてれつな]; 奇術師 conjurer, magician [きじゅつし]

SG-0328 寄	Meanings	Kun and On	Romaji	Bushu	Stroke Order and Number
	to be inclined to, to drop by	よ-る キ	yo-ru *ki*	宀	寄 11

寄 **B** F-0666 説文

The seal-style form had "a house" (宀), inside of which was 奇 "a lopsided person," for the sound *ki*. Together they signified "to be inclined to, to stop by someone's house." The kanji 寄 means "to be inclined to, to drop by." <宀奇>

寄る approach, lean, gather on one side, drop by [よる]; 寄せる to draw near [よせる]; 寄せ書き message card written by a few people [よせがき]; 年寄り old person [としより]; 身寄り close relative [みより]; 寄り道 to drop by along the way, make a stop [よりみちする]; 車寄せ covered driveway, carriage porch [くるまよせ]; 寄宿舎 boarding house (for students) [きしゅくしゃ]

SG-0329 崎	Meanings	Kun and On	Romaji	Bushu	Stroke Order and Number
	cape; steep	さき	saki	山	崎 11

崎 **B** F-0532

No ancient form. The kanji 崎 comprises 山 "mountain," and 奇, used for the sound *ki* to mean "uneven; to be unbalanced," together signifying "a steep area on a mountain." In Japanese, the character came to mean "cape." The kanji 崎 means "cape; steep." <山奇>

三崎 Misaki (place name and surname) [みさき]

SG-0330 埼	Meanings	Kun and On	Romaji	Bushu	Stroke Order and Number
	cape	さい	sai	土	埼 11

埼 **C** F-1242

No ancient form. The kanji 埼 comprised 土 **SG-1136** "dirt, ground," and 奇 **SG-0327**, used for the sound *ki* to mean "uneven," together signifying "a rugged landscape." The kanji 埼 is a variation of 崎, and is used only in names such as 埼玉県 "Saitama prefecture." <扌奇>

埼玉・埼玉県 Saitama prefecture [さいたま,さいたまけん]

SG-0331 椅	Meanings	Kun and On	Romaji	Bushu	Stroke Order and Number
	chair	イ	*i*	木	椅 12

椅 **D** F-2164 説文

The seal-style form comprised 木 **SG-0608** "wood," and 奇 **SG-0327**, used for the sound *i*. The kanji 椅 was originally the name of a tree, but came to mean "chair." The kanji 椅 means "chair." <木奇>

椅子 chair [いす]; 長椅子 sofa, couch, pew, bench [ながいす]; 車椅子 wheelchair [くるまいす]; 座椅子 legless chair used in a tatami room [ざいす]

17f 央 "center" [from a person with a yoke around the neck indicating the center of their body]; *oo/ee* 央英映

SG-0332 央	Meanings	Kun and On	Romaji	Bushu	Stroke Order and Number
	center; central	オウ	*oo*	大	丨 冂 口 央 央 5

央 **A** F-0579 — 甲骨文 1, 金文 2, 説文 3, 央

1, 2, and 3 originally signified fastening a yoke around someone's neck as punishment, with an extended meaning of "calamity." For 央, the meaning of "calamity, bad fortune" was dropped, and the character came to mean "center." The kanji 央 now means "center; central." <冂大>

中央 center, central [ちゅうおう, ちゅうおう]; 中央出口 central exit [ちゅうおうでぐち]; 震央 epicenter (of an earthquake) [しんおう]

SG-0333 英	Meanings	Kun and On	Romaji	Bushu	Stroke Order and Number
	beautiful, bright; excellence, England, English language	エイ	*ee*	艸	一 艹 艹 苎 英 英 8

英 **A** F-0266 — 説文, 英

The seal-style form comprised "plants, grass" (艸, 艹 bushu *kusakanmuri*), and 央 "center," used for the sound *ee* to mean "prosperous; to flourish." Flourishing plants and flowers are "beautiful." When applied to a person, it meant "excellent, smart." The kanji 英 is also used to mean England/English, from the phonetic similarity of the first syllable in Chinese, *ying*. The kanji 英 means "beautiful, bright; excellence, England, the English language." <艹央>

英国 England, The United Kingdom [えいこく]; 英語 the English language [えいご]; 英訳 English translation [えいやく]; 英和辞典 English-Japanese dictionary [えいわじてん]; 英雄 hero [えいゆう]; 英気を養う to store up one's energy [えいきを・やしなう]; 英会話 English conversation [えいかいわ]; 英断 excellent decision, bold decision [えいだん]

SG-0334 映	Meanings	Kun and On	Romaji	Bushu	Stroke Order and Number
	to shine, reflect, be projected on a screen	うつ-る・は-える エイ	utsu-ru, ha-eru *ee*	日	日 日 日 日 映 映 9

映 **B** F-0578 — 説文, 映

The seal-style form comprised 日 **SG-1045** "the sun," and 央, used for the sound *ee* to mean "flourishing, shining," together signifying "the sun shining." A shining light also reflects on objects. The kanji 映 means "to shine, reflect, be projected on a screen." <日央>

映る to reflect, to be imaged [うつる]; 映える to glow, shine, look better [はえる]; 映画 movie [えいが]; 反映する to reflect [はんえいする]; 上映される to be shown/ screened [じょうえいされる]; 放映 televising, telecasting [ほうえい]; 映像 screen image, video image [えいぞう]

17g 夹 (夾) "sandwiched, narrow" [from a person between two people]; *kyoo* 狭峡挟

SG-0335 狭	Meanings	Kun and On	Romaji	Bushu	Stroke Order and Number
	narrow	せま-い キョウ	sema-i *kyoo*	犬	ノ 了 犭 犭 犭 狭 狭 9

狭 **C** F-1476 — 西狭 1, 旧字 2, 狭

1 was taken from an inscription on a stone stele written in *rei*-style, the oldest kanji style. 2 comprised 犭, bushu *kemonohen* "beast," and 夾, used for the sound *kyoo* to mean "a narrow path between two sides." A trail made by animals was very narrow, and the character meant "narrow." In the shinji 狭, 夾 was simplified to 夹. The kanji 狭 means "narrow." <犭夹>

狭い narrow, cramped [せまい]; 手狭な cramped, undersized (work space) [てぜまな]; 所狭しと crowdedly [ところせましと]; 狭量な small-minded, intolerant [きょうりょうな]; 狭義 narrow meaning [きょうぎ] // 狭まる to become narrow, contract [せばまる]

SG-0336 峡	Meanings	Kun and On	Romaji	Bushu	Stroke Order and Number
	ravine, gorge	キョウ	*kyoo*	山	丨 山 山 山 峡 峡 9

峡 **D** F-1750 — 旧字, 峡

The kyuji 峽 comprised 山 **SG-1139** "mountain," and 夾 (夹), used for the sound *kyoo* to mean "something squeezed between two things," together signifying "a ravine or gorge." The kanji 峡 means "ravine, gorge." <山夹>

海峡 strait, channel [かいきょう]; 峡谷 ravine, gorge[きょうこく]

SG-0337 挟	Meanings	Kun and On	Romaji	Bushu	Stroke Order and Number
	to insert, interject, put in between	はさ-む キョウ	hasa-mu *kyoo*	手	扌 扌 扌 挟 挟 9

挟 **D** F-2067 — 説文 1, 旧字 2, 挟

1 comprised "an act done by hand" (扌), and 夾, used for the sound *kyoo* to mean "to put in between, insert." The kanji 挟 means "to insert, interject, put in between." <扌夹>

挟む to hold between, insert [はさむ]; 挟まれる to be jammed [はさまれる]; 口を挟む to cut in, interrupt [くちをはさむ]; 言葉を挟む to interpose, put in [ことばを・はさむ]; 洗濯挟み clothes peg, clothespin [せんたくばさみ]

17h 冘 "to hold one's head down" 沈枕

	Meanings	Kun and On	Romaji	Bushu	Stroke Order and Number
SG-0338 沈	to sink, submerge	しず-む チン	shizu-mu *chin*	水	氵氵沪沈 7

沈 **C** F-1258

甲骨文1 1, 甲骨文2 2, 金文 3, 説文 4 沈

1 and 2 depicted a sacrificial cow, put into a river in a rite to appease a river deity. The character meant "to sink, drop down." In 3, the "flowing water" moved out to the left, and eventually became 氵, bushu *sanzui.* On the right side, "a person with a bar across their neck" 冘 was used for the sound *chin* to mean "to submerge." The kanji 沈 means "to sink, submerge." <氵冘>

沈む to sink [しずむ]; 地盤沈下 ground sinking, subsiding [じばんちんか]; 沈殿 sedimentation [ちんでん]; 沈黙 silence [ちんもく]; 意気消沈する greatly discouraged [いきしょうちんする]

	Meanings	Kun and On	Romaji	Bushu	Stroke Order and Number
SG-0339 枕	pillow	まくら	makura	木	一十木朩枕 8

枕 **D** F-1763

説文 枕

The seal-style form comprised 木 **SG-0608** "wooden," and 冘, used for the sound *chin* to mean "to hold one's head down," together signifying a person resting his head on a wooden pillow to sleep. The kanji 枕 means "pillow." <木冘>

枕 pillow, lead-in talk [まくら]; 枕詞 set epithet in classical Japanese poetry [まくらことば]; 腕枕する to use one's arm as a pillow [うでまくらする]; 枕木 railway tie [まくらぎ]

17i 夭 "supple, young and pliable" [from a dancing person with their head tilted and their arms moving about]; *yoo* 笑咲妖沃

	Meanings	Kun and On	Romaji	Bushu	Stroke Order and Number
SG-0340 笑	to smile, laugh	わら-う・え-む ショウ	wara-u, e-mu *shoo*	竹	⺈⺮笁竺笑笑 10

笑 **B** F-0546

説文 笑

The seal-style form comprised "bamboo twigs" (竹 **SG-0759**), signifying "swaying easily," and "a person dancing by swaying their head and moving their hands up and down" (夭), signifying "supple, pliable." Someone so flexible could easily broaden their mouth into a smile. Another view explains that 笑 was the name of a plant that was pronounced *shoo*, and it was borrowed to mean "to smile." The kanji 笑 means "to smile, laugh." <⺮夭>

笑う to smile, laugh [わらう]; 笑い声 laughter [わらいごえ]; 笑い話 funny story [わらいばなし]; 苦笑い a wry smile [にがわらい]; 笑い顔を見せる to break into a smile [わらいがおをみせる]; ほほ笑む to smile [ほほえむ]; 笑顔 smiling face [えがお]; 苦笑する to smile wryly [くしょうする]; 冷笑する to sneer at, mock [れいしょうする]

	Meanings	Kun and On	Romaji	Bushu	Stroke Order and Number
SG-0341 咲	to bloom	さ-く	sa-ku	口	ロ ロ' 口¨ 咩 咲 9

咲 **C** F-1181

篆文 咲

The seal-style form was the same as that of the kanji 笑 **SG-0340** "to smile." The kanji has "a mouth" (口) on the left side, and the right side (关) is a reduction of 笑. An open-mouthed smile was likened to a flower in Japanese, and the kanji 咲 means "to bloom." <口关> (Note: 关 in 送 **SG-1342** has a different origin from the right side of 咲.)

咲く to bloom [さく]; 返り咲く to be reinstated, come back [かえりざく]; 狂い咲き unseasonable flowering [くるいざき]; 咲き乱れるto bloom in profusion [さきみだれる]; 早咲き early blooming [はやざき]

	Meanings	Kun and On	Romaji	Bushu	Stroke Order and Number
SG-0342 妖	fascinating, captivating, bewitching	あや-しい ヨウ	aya-shii *yoo*	女	女 女' 女ᐟ 妖 妖 7

妖 **D** F-1944

篆文 妖

The seal-style form comprised 艸 "plant," 女 **SG-0521** "a woman," and 夭 "a person with a supple body," used for the sound *yoo*. In the kanji, "plant" was dropped. "A seductively dancing woman" meant "captivating." The kanji 妖 means "fascinating, captivating, bewitching." <女夭>

妖しい mysterious, alluring, dubious [あやしい]; 妖艶な sensual charm [ようえんな]; 妖怪 ghost, apparition [ようかい]; 妖気 ghostly air [ようき]

	Meanings	Kun and On	Romaji	Bushu	Stroke Order and Number
SG-0343 沃	fertile; rich soil	ヨク	*yoku*	水	氵氵氵' 汙 沃 7

沃 **D** F-2597

説文 沃

The seal-style form comprised 艸 "plant or vegetation," 氵 "flowing water," and 夭, used for the sound *yoku* to mean "fertile." Irrigation made farmland fertile. 艸 was dropped, and the kanji 沃 means "fertile; rich soil." <氵夭>

肥沃な fertile [ひよくな]; 沃土 fertile soil [よくど]

17j 呉 "swaying and talking" [from a person with a tilted head enjoying himself]; *go* 呉誤娯 

	Meanings	*Kun* and *On*	Romaji	Bushu	Stroke Order and Number
SG-0344 呉	the Wu state; Japanese-style clothes	ゴ	*go*	口	口吕吕呉 7

呉 **C** F-1621

呉 1 and 2 are mirror images comprised of 口 **SG-0031** "a mouth," and 夭 "a supple body with a tilted head," that originally signified "a person enjoying themselves and laughing heartily." There are a few different uses for the kanji 呉: (a) the name of Wu, a warring state in ancient China; (b) fabric made by a weaving method introduced to Japan from the state of Wu, and the Japanese attire made using such fabric (呉服 *gohuku*); (c) the earlier pronunciation of kanji brought to Japan before *kan-on* pronunciation (呉音 *go-on*); and (d) the verb 呉れる *kureru* "to give (to a giver's inferior/junior)" (non-Joyo kanji use). <呉>

呉音 the earlier Chinese sound of kanji in Japanese [ごおん]; 呉服 Japanese attire, kimono [ごふく]; 呉服屋 kimono fabric store [ごふくや] // 呉れる to give (to me) [くれる]

	Meanings	*Kun* and *On*	Romaji	Bushu	Stroke Order and Number
SG-0345 誤	to make a mistake, err; error	あやま-る ゴ	ayama-ru *go*	言	言 訁 訁口 誤 誤 誤 14

誤 **C** F-1117

(説文) 誤 The seal-style form comprised 言, bushu *gonben* "word, language," and 呉, used for the sound *go*. In 呉, a mouth next to a tilted head signified that the speaker had not said what he had intended to say. The kanji 誤 means "to make a mistake, err; error." <言呉>

誤る to make a mistake [あやまﾌる]; 誤り mistake, error [あやまり]; 誤解 misunderstanding [ごかい]; 誤字 wrong letter [ごじ, ごﾌじ]; 誤差 error [ごﾌさ]; 正誤表 errata [せいごひょう]; 誤算 miscalculation [ごさん]; 誤訳 mistranslation [ごやく]

	Meanings	*Kun* and *On*	Romaji	Bushu	Stroke Order and Number
SG-0346 娯	to enjoy; talking and laughing	ゴ	*go*	女	𡿨 女 如 娯 娯 娯 10

娯 **D** F-1781

(説文) 娯 When the kanji 呉 **SG-0344**, originally "enjoying conversation," was re-appropriated for the name of the warring state of Wu, a new kanji was created for the original meaning by adding 女 "woman." The kanji 娯 means "to enjoy; talking and laughing." <女呉>

娯楽 enjoyment, entertainment [ごらく]

17k 若 "young" [from the pliant posture of a young woman dancing]; *jaku/daku/toku* 若諾匿

	Meanings	*Kun* and *On*	Romaji	Bushu	Stroke Order and Number
SG-0347 若	young; a few; if	わか-い・も-しくは ジャク・ニャク	waka-i, mo-shikuwa *jaku, nyaku*	艸	一 艹 ㄗ 芓 若 8

若 **A** F-0311

若 1, 2, and 3 were "a long-haired maiden or spiritual medium performing a votive dance." The pliant and supple movements of her body and hands signified "young." 4 comprised her long hair (艸), and a hand over a prayer box or a mouth (右). Later, the character acquired a number of different meanings, including "a few" and "if." The kanji 若 means "young; a few; if." <艹右>

若い young [わかﾌい]; 若返る to feel young again, to be rejuvenated [わかがﾌえる]; 若々しい young and fresh [わかわかしﾌい]; 若しくは or, either [もﾌしくは]; 若年層 younger generation [じゃくねﾌんそう]; 若干 a little, a few [じゃっかん]; 若輩 young and immature [じゃくはい]; 老若 young and old [ろうにゃく] // 若人 young man, youth, the young [わこﾌうど]

	Meanings	*Kun* and *On*	Romaji	Bushu	Stroke Order and Number
SG-0348 諾	to consent, agree	ダク	*daku*	言	言 訁 訁艹 訁芓 諾 諾 15

諾 **D** F-1878

諾 1 and 2 were similar to or the same as 1 and 2 for 若 **SG-0347**, with 口 included in 1, but not in 2. The character was used for the sound *jaku* to mean "to agree; yes." In 3, 言 **SG-1364** "word; to say" was added, and it meant "words of agreement." The kanji 諾 means "to consent, agree." <言若>

承諾する to comply, give one's consent [しょうだくする]; 快諾する to readily give consent [かいだくする]; 内諾 informal consent [ないだく]

SG-0349 匿	Meanings	*Kun* and *On*	Romaji	Bushu	Stroke Order and Number
	to conceal, hide	トク	*toku*	匚	一二开井若匿 10

匿 **D** F-1908

金文 1 説文 2 匿

In 1, "a young maiden dancing" (若 **SG-0347**), used for the sound *toku*, was enclosed inside 匚 "to hide something." It represented "a young woman or spiritual medium doing a votive dance in secret." Another view takes it to depict "hiding young mulberry leaves" (桑 **SG-0640**), which were precious feed for silkworms. The kanji 匿 meant "to conceal, hide." <匚若>

匿名 anonymity, incognito [とくめい]; 隠匿する to conceal, shelter, harbor [いんとくする]

17I 鬼 "demon, ghost" [from the startlingly ugly face of a corpse] 鬼魅魔魂塊・異畏

SG-0350 鬼	Meanings	*Kun* and *On*	Romaji	Bushu	Stroke Order and Number
	ogre, demon, ghost, pitiless person; "it" (in children's games); after death	おに キ	oni *ki*	鬼	' 一 由 申 鬼 鬼 10

鬼 **C** F-1182

甲骨文 1 金文 2 説文古文 3 説文 4 鬼

1 and 2 depicted "a person with an extraordinary face or mask, kneeling or bending their back." The startlingly ugly face signified "a spirit of the dead." In 3 an altar table with an offering was added, but disappeared in 4. 3 and 4 had the hook shape (ム), for a floating spirit. The kanji 鬼 means "ogre, demon, ghost, pitiless person, fanatic; "it" (in children's games); after death." <由儿ム>

鬼 ogre, devil [おに]; 鬼退治 slaying the ogre [おにたいじ]; 鬼ごっこ a game of tag [おにごっこ]; 仕事の鬼 demon for work, workhorse [しごとのおに]; 鬼才 genius, a person of extraordinary talent [きさい]; 鬼門 weak point, area to be avoided [きもん]; 鬼籍に入る to join the death register, die [きせきに(or きせきに)はいる]

SG-0351 魅	Meanings	*Kun* and *On*	Romaji	Bushu	Stroke Order and Number
	to bewitch, be fascinated; charm	ミ	*mi*	鬼	巾 鬼 鬼 鬽 魅 魅 15

魅 **C** F-1350

籀文 1 古文 2 篆文 1 3 篆文 2 4 魅

1 and 2 comprised "an extraordinary face or mask," and "a beast," signifying "a beast-like ghost." In 3, 彡 "a pretty shape" was added, whereas in 4, 未 **SG-0615** was added for the sound *mi*. Together, the left- and right-side components signified "being bewitched by a spirit." The kanji 魅 means "to bewitch, be fascinated; charm." <鬼未>

魅せられる to be fascinated, be captivated [みせられる]; 魅了する to attract, fascinate [みりょうする]; 魅力 attraction, charm [みりょく]

SG-0352 魔	Meanings	*Kun* and *On*	Romaji	Bushu	Stroke Order and Number
	demon, devil, evil influence	マ	*ma*	鬼	广 麻 麻 磨 魔 魔 21

魔 **C** F-1413

説文 魔

The seal-style form comprised 麻 **SG-0778**, used for the sound *ma*, and 鬼 **SG-0350** "spirit, ghost." The kanji 魔 means "demon, devil." <麻鬼>

悪魔 devil, demon, evil spirit [あくま]; 魔物 demon, evil spirit [まもの]; 魔術 magic [まじゅつ]; 邪魔 hindrance, obstruction [じゃま]; 睡魔 sleepiness, drowsiness [すいま]; 魔女 witch, sorceress [まじょ]; 通り魔 random street attacker/killer [とおりま]; 魔が差す to fall into temptation by impulse [まがさす]

SG-0353 魂	Meanings	*Kun* and *On*	Romaji	Bushu	Stroke Order and Number
	soul, spirit	たましい コン	tamashii *kon*	鬼	云 云' 云由 魂 魂 14

魂 **C** F-1437

説文 魂

The seal-style form comprised 云 "rising cloud" for "something floating," and 鬼 **SG-0350** "the spirit of the dead." From the belief that the spirit of the dead floated like a cloud, the kanji 魂 means "soul, spirit." <云鬼>

魂 soul [たましい]; 大和魂 the Japanese spirit [やまとだましい]; 商魂 salesmanship, commercial spirit [しょうこん]; 鎮魂歌 requiem [ちんこんか]; 入魂の作 work made with one's whole soul poured into it [にゅうこんのさく]

SG-0354 塊	Meanings	*Kun* and *On*	Romaji	Bushu	Stroke Order and Number
	lump, mass, chunk	かたまり カイ	katamari *kai*	土	一 十 坤 塊 塊 13

塊 **D** F-1859

説文 1 説文或体 2 塊

1 contained "dirt" (土 **SG-1126**) inside "a box or a hole" (凵), and had the sound *kai* to mean "lump of dirt." In 2, the box was replaced by 鬼 **SG-0350**, a totally different shape but was used for the sound. 土 and 鬼 together signified "lump of dirt." The kanji 塊 means "lump, mass, chunk." <扌鬼>

塊 lump, mass, chunk [かたまり]; 金塊 nugget of gold, gold ingot [きんかい]; 団塊の世代 baby-boomer generation [だんかいのせだい]

田 "fearsome face" [from an extraordinary mask in a votive play] 異畏

	Meanings	*Kun* and *On*	Romaji	Bushu	Stroke Order and Number
SG-0355 異	different, dissimilar, extraordinary	こと イ	koto *i*	田	冂 田 甲 畀 異 異 11

異 **B** F-0613

甲骨文 1 金文1 2 金文2 3 説文 4

1, 2, and 3 depicted "a person putting on a mask of a fearsome face for a votive play." Putting on a mask of such an extraordinary face changed the wearer into another person, and thus the character meant "different." In 4, a stage was added at the bottom. The kanji 異 means "different, dissimilar, extraordinary." <田共>

異なる・異にする to be different, differ from~ [ことなる, ことにする]; 異説 conflicting view [いせつ]; 人事異動 personnel reshuffling [じんじいどう]; 異文化 different culture [いぶんか]; 異変 strange event, emergency [いへん]; 変異 mutation [へんい]; 異物 foreign matter [いぶつ]; 異様な strange, bizarre [いような]

	Meanings	*Kun* and *On*	Romaji	Bushu	Stroke Order and Number
SG-0356 畏	to fear, revere, obey respectfully, be in awe of	おそ-れる イ	oso-reru *i*	田	冂 田 甼 畏 畏 9

畏 **D** F-2416

甲骨文 1 金文1 2 金文2 3 金文3 4 説文古文 5 説文 6

1, 2, and 3 depicted "a person wearing an extraordinary mask" or "an evil entity holding a stick in its hand." 4 had the component "to cause to happen" (攴) added. A devil with a stick made people afraid or in awe, and people in awe obeyed respectfully. The kanji 畏 means "to fear, revere, obey respectfully, be in awe of." <田𧘇>

畏れる to revere, be in awe of [おそれる]; 畏友 respected friend [いゆう]; 畏敬の念 reverence, awe [いけいのねん]; 畏怖の念 fearful, with awe [いふのねん] // 畏まる to obey respectfully, humble oneself [かしこまる]; 畏まりました Certainly, I understand (humble) [かしこまりました]

17m 司 "to administer"; *shi* 司詞飼后嗣伺

	Meanings	*Kun* and *On*	Romaji	Bushu	Stroke Order and Number
SG-0357 司	to administer, take charge of; official	シ	*shi*	口	𠃍 ㇆ 司 5

司 **B** F-0582

甲骨文 1 金文1 2 金文2 3 説文 4

The origin of the kanji 司 is obscure. One view explains that 1 and 2 comprised 口 **SG-0031** "a box of prayers," and "a person with his hands forward." Together they signified "to inquire about a deity's will." Other views are that they signified a person who was looking through a hole to inquire about a deity's wish (that is, "a minister"), or a person who was managing matters that pertained to speaking (口). In 3, "untangling threads with both hands" was added to signify "bringing order" in a more general sense. Someone in control of a matter was an official or an administrator. The kanji 司 means "to administer, take charge of; official." <司>

司会 master of ceremony [しかい]; 司法 the judiciary [しほう, しほう]; 司法試験 bar exam [しほうしけん]; 司書 librarian [ししょ]; 司令官 commander, commanding officer [しれいかん]; 行司 sumo referee [ぎょうじ, ぎょうじ]; 宮司 Shinto priest [ぐうじ] // 司る to take charge of, preside over [つかさどる]

	Meanings	*Kun* and *On*	Romaji	Bushu	Stroke Order and Number
SG-0358 詞	phrase, lyrics, part of speech	シ	*shi*	言	言 訂 訶 詞 12

詞 **C** F-1319

説文

The seal-style form comprised 言, bushu *gonben* "word, language; to speak," and 司 **SG-0357**, used for the sound *shi*, from 嗣 **SG-0361**, which meant "to continue." From words that were connected or continued, the kanji 詞 means "phrase, lyrics, part of speech." <言司>

名詞 noun [めいし]; 動詞 verb [どうし]; 形容動詞 adjectival noun, -*na* adjective [けいようどうし]; 歌詞 lyrics [かし]; 作詞者 lyricist [さくししゃ] // 祝詞 Shinto prayer [のりと]

	Meanings	*Kun* and *On*	Romaji	Bushu	Stroke Order and Number
SG-0359 飼	to feed (an animal), keep (an animal)	か-う シ	ka-u *shi*	食	𠆢 刍 飠 飣 飼 13

飼 **C** F-1439

No ancient form. The kanji comprises 飠, bushu *shokuhen*, from 食 **SG-1781** "food"; and 司, used for the sound *shi* to mean "to administer, take charge of." The kanji 飼 means "to feed (an animal), keep (an animal)." <食司>

飼う to keep (an animal) [かう]; 飼い主 owner of an animal [かいぬし]; 放し飼い pasturage, grazing [はなしがい]; 羊飼い shepherd [ひつじかい]; 飼育する to raise an animal [しいくする]; 飼料 feed [しりょう]

SG-0360 后	Meanings	Kun and On	Romaji	Bushu	Stroke Order and Number
	empress consort	コウ (ゴウ)	*koo (goo)*	口	厂斤斤后后后 6

后 **D** F-1767

甲骨文 1 金文 2 説文 3

The kanji 后 has an odd etymology. Many scholars agree that 1 was also the oracle-bone style form for the non-Joyo kanji 毓 "to foster, rear, multiply." One view explains that it showed the moment of childbirth (an empress consort giving birth to a baby whose head was facing downward with amniotic fluid), which ensured posterity, and thus it signified "later time; behind." Another view takes 2 and 3 to be the mirror image of 司 **SG-0357** ("to administer"), and explains that the reversed meaning of 司 meant "taking charge of a later matter, looking behind." In the present-day usage, the kanji 后 means "empress consort." <厂 一 口>

皇后 empress, empress consort [こうごう]; 皇太后 emperor dowager [こうたいごう]

SG-0361 嗣	Meanings	Kun and On	Romaji	Bushu	Stroke Order and Number
	to succeed (to a throne); heir	シ	*shi*	口	口月刷刷嗣嗣 13

嗣 **D** F-2106

金文1 1 金文2 2 説文古文 3 説文 4

1 and 2 showed "a person and a prayer box" (司 **SG-0357**) over "writing tablets tied together" (冊 **SG-2037**). Writing tablets tied together were important records that were handed down, and new writing tablets could be continuously added. 3 had 子 "child," signifying "an heir," under 司, and 4 became the kanji. The kanji 嗣 means "to succeed (to a throne); heir." <口 冊 司>

継嗣 successor, inheritor [けいし]; 皇嗣 imperial heir/heiress [こうし]

SG-0362 伺	Meanings	Kun and On	Romaji	Bushu	Stroke Order and Number
	to inquire, pay a visit (humble)	うかが-う シ	ukaga-u *shi*	人	亻门伺伺伺 7

伺 **D** F-2162

説文

The seal-style form comprised 亻 "a person, an act that one does," and 司, used for the sound *shi* to mean "to inquire." Together they signified "a person visiting someone superior to ask for their opinion." The kanji 伺 means "to inquire, pay a visit" in humble speech. <亻 司>

伺う to ask, visit (humble) [うかがう]; 進退伺 preliminary letter of resignation [しんたいうかがい]; ご機嫌伺い courtesy visit [ごきげんうかがい]

18 Multiple persons

18a 立 "to stand" [from a person standing on the ground]; *ritsu/ryuu* 立位泣粒拉

SG-0363 立	Meanings	Kun and On	Romaji	Bushu	Stroke Order and Number
	to stand, rise up, become, found, build	た-つ リツ・リュウ	ta-tsu *ritsu, ryuu*	立	' 亠 亣 立 立 5

立 **A** F-0073

甲骨文 1 金文1 2 金文2 3 説文 4

1, 2, 3, and 4 each depicted "a person standing on the ground or at a fixed place facing forward" (2 might be a side view), and thus they signified "to stand." The kanji 立 means "to stand, rise up, become, found, build." <立>

立つ to stand [たつ]; 立ち上がる to rise up [たちあがる, たちあがる]; 目立つ to stand out [めだつ]; 立場 standpoint, situation [たちば]; 成立する to come into existence, become effective [せいりつする]; 直立の upright [ちょくりつの]; 立法 legislation, lawmaking [りっぽう]; 立派な praiseworthy, impressive [りっぱな]; 建立 erection of a temple or shrine [こんりゅう]

SG-0364 位	Meanings	Kun and On	Romaji	Bushu	Stroke Order and Number
	rank, social standing, digit, approximate amount	くらい イ	kurai *i*	人	亻亻'亻亠亻立位 7

位 **A** F-0230

甲骨文 1 金文 2 説文 3

1 and 2 were the same as 1 and 3 for 立. In 3, 亻 "a person, an act that a person does" was added. In the royal court, subjects stood according to their ranks, and thus the character meant "rank, position, a digit in a number." In Japanese, it also means "approximate amount." The kanji 位 means "rank, social standing, digit, approximate amount." <亻 立>

位 position, status, digit [くらい]; 百の位の数 in the hundreds [ひゃくのくらいの・かず]; 二ヶ月位 approximately two months [にかげつぐらい]; 各位 Dear all (in correspondence) [かくい]; 地位 position, status [ちい]; 位置 location [いち]; 第三位 third place [だいさんい]; 王位 the throne, the crown [おうい]

G-0365 泣	Meanings	Kun and On	Romaji	Bushu	Stroke Order and Number
	to cry, weep	なーく キュウ	na-ku *kyuu*	水	氵 氵 汁 汁 泣 8

泣 **B** F-1013 — 説文

The seal-style form comprised "flowing water" (氵), and 立 **SG-0363**, used for the sound *ryuu* to mean "granule." A standing person with drops of water signified "to weep." The kanji 泣 means "to cry, weep." <氵立>

泣く to cry [なく]; 泣きつく to implore [なきつく]; 泣きじゃくる to sob [なきじゃくる]; 泣き言を言う to complain, whine [なきごとをいう]; 泣く泣く reluctantly [なくなく]; 号泣する to cry loudly [ごうきゅうする]

SG-0366 粒	Meanings	Kun and On	Romaji	Bushu	Stroke Order and Number
	grain, granule, particle	つぶ リュウ	tsubu *ryuu*	米	丷 半 米 粒 粒 11

粒 **C** F-1545 — 古文 1, 篆文 2

1 comprised 立 **SG-0363**, used for the sound *ryuu* to mean "granules, pieces," and "a covered bowl of food" (an earlier form of 食 **SG-1781**). 2 had 米 **SG-0738** "rice," for "granular," and 立, now on the right side. The kanji 粒 means "grain, granule, particle." <米立>

粒 granule [つぶ]; 粒よりの handpicked, select [つぶよりの]; 一粒の a single grain of [ひとつぶの]; 粒子 particle [りゅうし]; 顆粒状 granular [かりゅうじょう]

SG-0367 拉	Meanings	Kun and On	Romaji	Bushu	Stroke Order and Number
	to crush in the hand, pull by hand	ラ	*ra*	手	一 扌 扌 拉 拉 8

拉 **D** F-2349 — 篆文

The seal-style form comprised 扌, bushu *tehen* "an act done by hand," and 立 **SG-0363**, used for the sound *ra*. The kanji 拉 means "to crush in the hand, pull by hand." <扌立>

拉致 abduction, kidnapping [らち]

18b 並 (竝) "to form a line, rank with" [from two or more people standing side by side]

並普替譜

SG-0368 並	Meanings	Kun and On	Romaji	Bushu	Stroke Order and Number
	to stand in line, match; equal, ordinary	ならーべる・なみ ヘイ	nara-beru, nami *hee*	立	丷 䒑 并 並 並 8

並 **B** F-0588 — 甲骨文 1, 金文 2, 説文 3, 旧字 4

In 1 and 2, two people stood side by side, signifying "to stand in a row." Two people on par with each other also meant "to match; equal," as well as "ordinary." In 3, the form was elongated and had uniform straight lines. The kyuji 竝 (4) comprised two 立 **SG-0353**, but in the shinji it was simplified to 並. The kanji 並 means "to stand in line, match; equal, ordinary." <並(䒑业)>

並べる to queue, line up [ならべる]; 並みの ordinary [なみの]; 人並みの生活 a decent life like other people's [ひとなみのせいかつ]; 並々ならぬ uncommon, extraordinary [なみなみならぬ]; 並木道 tree-lined street [なみきみち]; 平年並み same as in an average year [へいねんなみ]; 並列 parallel [へいれつ]

SG-0369 普	Meanings	Kun and On	Romaji	Bushu	Stroke Order and Number
	universal, ordinary, not special	フ	*hu*	日	丷 䒑 并 並 並 普 普 12

普 **B** F-0827 — 説文

The seal-style form comprised two people standing side by side (竝), signifying "spreading sideways," and 日 **SG-1045** "the sun." The sun's light spreads over everything. People lining up also gave the meaning "ordinary." The kanji 普 means "universal, ordinary, not special." <並日>

普通 ordinary [ふつう]; 普遍的な universal [ふへんてきな]; 普及する to spread, permeate [ふきゅうする]; 普段 every day, habitual [ふだん] // 普く universal, everywhere [あまねく]

SG-0370 替	Meanings	Kun and On	Romaji	Bushu	Stroke Order and Number
	to replace, substitute; stand-in	かーえる タイ	ka-eru *tai*	曰	二 夫 夫夫 替 替 12

替 **B** F-0859 — 金文 1, 説文 2, 説文或体 3

1 showed two people standing on the ground in perspective. Perspective indicated passage of time, with one thing coming first, and another coming later to replace the earlier one. It meant "to replace." 2 comprised 竝, and 曰 (*etsu*), "a voice coming out; to speak." According to some views, it signified two people standing in court, taking turns arguing. In the kanji 替, the top was simplified to two 夫 ("man"), and the bottom was 曰. The kanji 替 means "to replace, substitute; stand-in." <夫夫曰>

替える to replace with a new one [かえる]; 振替送金 transfer remittance [ふりかえそうきん]; 替え玉 stand-in, extra helping of noodles [かえだま]; 立て替え payment on someone's behalf [たてかえ]; 交替 change, replacement, substitute [こうたい]; 代替 substitution [だいたい] //

	(Note regarding 日 and 曰: In some typefaces, it is not easy to differentiate 日 *nichi/jitsu* "sun" from 曰 *etsu* "to speak; to rise." In practical writing by pen, they are rarely written differently. Among the Joyo kanji that originally had 曰 are 替曲更曹曽漫慢最, and the several kanji that contain 曷.)	外国為替 foreign exchange [がいこくかわせ]

	Meanings	Kun and On	Romaji	Bushu	Stroke Order and Number
SG-0371 譜	genealogy, musical score, record, table	フ	*hu*	言	19

譜 **D** F-1707	説文. The seal-style form had 言, bushu *gonben* "word, language; to say," next to 普 **SG-0369**, used for the sound *hu* to mean "to spread (sideways)." Together they meant something that continued in a sequence, such as written records, a family genealogy, or a musical score. The kanji 譜 means "genealogy, musical score, record, table." <言普>	年譜 annuals [ねんぷ]; 楽譜 musical score [がくふ]; 譜面台 music stand [ふめんだい]; 暗譜で弾く to play by ear, play from memory [あんぷでひく]; 譜代 hereditary vassalage [ふだい]

18c 従 (从) "to follow" [from a person following another viewed from the side]; *juu* 従衆縦

	Meanings	Kun and On	Romaji	Bushu	Stroke Order and Number
SG-0372 従	to follow, obey	したが-う ジュウ・ショウ・ジュ	shitaga-u *juu, shoo, ju*	彳	10

従 **B** F-0715	甲骨文1 1, 甲骨文2 2, 金文1 3, 金文2 4, 説文 5, 旧字 6. 1 comprised "a crossroads," and "two people, one following the other," whereas 2 did not have a crossroads. In 3, "a footprint" (indicating a movement) was added, and 4 was the mirror image of 3 without a crossroads. Two people following one another in the same direction meant "to follow." In 5, "a crossroads" and "footprint" became 辵, but contrary to the usual development that would become bushu *shinnyuu*, in 6 the footprint moved back to the right side under two small 人. In the shinji, the two people 从, used for the sound *juu*, were further simplified to ソ. The kanji 従 means "to follow, obey." <彳ソ龰>	従う to follow, obey [したがう]; 従える to be attended, conquer [したがえる]; 従事する to engage in, practice [じゅうじする]; 主従 master and servant [しゅじゅう]; 従業員 employee, worker [じゅうぎょういん]; 従軍記者 war correspondent, embedded reporter [じゅうぐんきしゃ]; 合従 alliance (of states against a powerful enemy) [がっしょう] // 従兄弟 male (first) cousin [いとこ]

	Meanings	Kun and On	Romaji	Bushu	Stroke Order and Number
SG-0373 衆	a lot of people, mass	シュウ・シュ	*shuu, shu*	血	12

衆 **B** F-0787	甲骨文1 1, 甲骨文2 2, 金文 3, 説文 4. 1, 2, 3, and 4 had three standing people, signifying "many people." Views about what the top component signified differ: "the sun"; "an area with a dot indicating that it is not empty"; and "an eye watching over one's workers (㐺)." In the kanji 衆, the top became 血 (probably not related to its meaning). The kanji 衆 means "a lot of people, mass." <血㐺>	大衆文化 popular culture [たいしゅうぶんか]; 群衆 crowd, throng [ぐんしゅう]; 会衆 those in attendance [かいしゅう]; 観衆 spectator, audience [かんしゅう]; 聴衆 audience, attendance [ちょうしゅう]; 民衆 mass of the people, the people [みんしゅう]; 衆生 living things, sentient beings (in Buddhism) [しゅじょう]

	Meanings	Kun and On	Romaji	Bushu	Stroke Order and Number
SG-0374 縦	continuous, vertical; as one pleases	たて ジュウ	tate *juu*	糸	16

縦 **C** F-1250	説文 1, 旧字 2. 1 comprised 糸 **SG-1600** "thread" (for "continuity"), and 従 **SG-0372** "to follow," which was used for the sound *juu*. A continuous line to follow led to the meaning "vertical." A thread could continue extending, and from that came "something without restraint," or "as one pleases, at will." The kanji 縦 means "continuous, vertical; as one pleases." <糸従>	縦 vertical, length [たて]; 縦糸 the warp [たていと]; 縦書き vertical writing [たてがき]; 縦横に in all directions [じゅうおうに, じゅうおうに]; 縦断する to travel through, divide vertically [じゅうだんする]; 操縦する to navigate, control [そうじゅうする]

18d 幷 "two people united" [from two people tied together at the feet]; *hee* 併瓶餅塀

	Meanings	Kun and On	Romaji	Bushu	Stroke Order and Number
SG-0375 併	to unite, merge, consolidate	あわ-せる ヘイ	awa-seru *hee*	人	亻亻' 亻'' 佯 併 8

併 **C** F-1227

篆文 1 説文 2 旧字 3

In 1 and 2, the right side (幷 in the kyuji), used for the sound *hee*, has two different interpretations: (a) two people standing with two lines crossing them signified that the two people were "united", and (b) two sticks of equal length signified "equal." Taken together, the two interpretations meant two people united on equal terms, or "to merge." The kanji 併 means "to unite, merge, consolidate." <亻 幷>

併せる to combine, merge [あわせ1る]; 合併 union, merger [がっぺい]; 併記する to record both [へ1いきする]; 併合 annexation, amalgamation [へいごう]; 併用 parallel use [へいよう]; 合併症 complication (illness) [がっぺいしょう]

	Meanings	Kun and On	Romaji	Bushu	Stroke Order and Number
SG-0376 瓶	Glass bottle, jug	ビン	*bin*	瓦	丷 并 瓩 瓶 瓶 瓶 11

瓶 **D** F-1809

金文 1 篆文1 2 篆文2 3 旧字 4

1, 2, and 3 comprised "two people standing connected," which was used for the sound *hee*, and "a well bucket" or "a water jug." The component for two people (幷) became 并 in the shinji. The kanji 瓶 means "glass bottle, jug." <并瓦>

瓶 glass bottle, decanter [び1ん]; 小瓶 flask, small bottle [こびん]; 花瓶 flower vase [かびん]; 瓶詰め bottled [びんづめ]; 空き瓶 empty bottle [あきびん]; 魔法瓶 vacuum bottle, thermos [まほ1うびん]; ビール瓶 beer bottle [ビール1びん]

	Meanings	Kun and On	Romaji	Bushu	Stroke Order and Number
SG-0377 餅	rice cake	もち ヘイ	mochi *hee*	食	𠆢 今 飠 飦 餅 15

餅 **D** F-1970

旧字

The kyuji 餠 comprised 飠(食), bushu *shokuhen* "food," and 幷(并), which was used for the sound *hee* to mean "flat." Together they signified "steamed sweet rice that was made into in a flat shape"—that is, "a rice cake." The kanji 餅 means "rice cake." <飠 并>

餅 rice cake [もち]; 焼き餅 toasted rice cake, jealousy, envy [やきも1ち]; 供え餅 rice cake offered at Shinto altar table [そなえ1もち]; 煎餅 rice cracker [せ1んべい]; 尻餅をつく to fall heavily on one's buttocks [しりも1ちをつく]

	Meanings	Kun and On	Romaji	Bushu	Stroke Order and Number
SG-0378 塀	fence, wall	ヘイ	*hee*	土	土 圷 坪 堀 塀 12

塀 **D** F-1980

説文 1 旧字 2

1 had 尸 "roof, cover," over 幷, used for the sound *hee* to mean "to block," together forming 屏 to mean "screen." In the kyuji 塀 (2), 土 "dirt, soil" was added to signify that the barrier was made of dirt. The kanji 塀 means "fence, wall." <土 尸 并> (Note: The non-Joyo kanji 屏 "screen" and 風 "draft, wind" form the word 屏風 *byoobu*, "folding screen."

塀 fence [へい]; 土塀 earthen fence [どべい]; 石塀 stone fence [いしべい]

18e 㑒 (僉) "to carefully examine goods" [from people evaluating things under a roof]; *ken* 検験険剣倹

	Meanings	Kun and On	Romaji	Bushu	Stroke Order and Number
SG-0379 検	to examine, inspect	ケン	*ken*	木	木 朴 桧 検 検 12

検 **A** F-0454

説文 1 旧字 2

1 comprised 木 "tree, wood," and 僉 "many people gathering under one roof and examining goods," which was used for the sound *ken*. Together they signified "officials checking the wood tallies used to keep records of goods." In the shinji, 僉 was simplified to 㑒. The kanji 検 means "to examine, inspect." <木 㑒>

検査 inspection, testing [け1んさ]; 検疫官 quarantine officer [けんえきか1ん]; 検温する to take one's temperature [けんおんする]; 検事 public prosecutor [け1んじ]; 検証する to verify, identify [けんしょうする]; 首実検 identification of a suspect [くびじ1っけん]; 車検 car inspection [しゃけん]; 検体 specimen, sample [けんたい]

	Meanings	Kun and On	Romaji	Bushu	Stroke Order and Number
SG-0380 験	to examine, test; sign, proof of	ケン・ゲン	*ken, gen*	馬	「 『 馬 馬 馬 馬 騎 験 験 18

験 **B** F-0678

験 験 験 (説文 1, 旧字 2)

1 comprised 馬 **SG-0870** "horse," and 㑒 "people gathering under a roof to evaluate goods," used for the sound *ken*. Together they signified "to examine horses that were gathered in one place." The meaning of "horse" was dropped. The kanji 験 means "to examine, test; sign, proof of." <馬㑒>

実験 experiment [じっけん]; 体験 experience [たいけん]; 被験者 subject of an experiment [ひけんじゃ]; 検定試験 certification exam [けんていしけん]; 験担ぎ being superstitious [げんかつぎ]; 治験 clinical trial [ちけん]

	Meanings	Kun and On	Romaji	Bushu	Stroke Order and Number
SG-0381 険	danger; steep, harsh	けわ-しい ケン	kewa-shii *ken*	阜	⁷ 阝 阝 阾 险 険 11

険 **B** F-0801

険 險 険 (説文 1, 旧字 2)

1 comprised "tall hills, mountains," and 㑒, used for the sound *ken* to mean "danger, difficulty." Together they signified "danger on a steep mountain." In 2, the left side became 阝, bushu *kozatohen*. The kanji 険 means "danger; steep, harsh." <阝㑒>

険しい steep, challenging, grim [けわしい]; 危険な dangerous [きけんな]; 保険 insurance [ほけん]; 陰険な sly, double-dealing [いんけんな]

	Meanings	Kun and On	Romaji	Bushu	Stroke Order and Number
SG-0382 剣	sword, dagger	つるぎ ケン	tsurugi *ken*	刀	ノ 人 合 佥 㑒 剣 10

剣 **C** F-1118

劒 劒 劍 剣 (金文 1, 説文 2, 旧字 3)

1 comprised "metal" (金), and 㑒, used for the sound *ken*. 2 had 㑒 and 刃 **SG-1413** "blade," together signifying "a double-edged sword worn at the side, dagger." In 3, the blade changed to 刂, bushu *rittoo*. The kanji 剣 means "sword, dagger." <㑒刂>

剣 sword, blade [つるぎ, けん]; 短剣 dagger [たんけん]; 剣客 swordsman [けんかく・けんきゃく]; 剣術 swordsmanship, swordplay [けんじゅつ]; 刀剣類 swords [とうけんるい]; 真剣勝負 a game played in earnest [しんけんしょうぶ]

	Meanings	Kun and On	Romaji	Bushu	Stroke Order and Number
SG-0383 倹	frugal, thrifty	ケン	*ken*	人	イ 仒 佮 俭 倹 10

倹 **D** F-2199

儉 儉 倹 (説文 1, 旧字 2)

1 comprised イ "an act that one does," and 㑒, used for the sound *ken* to mean "to live a frugal life by carefully minding one's spending." The kanji 倹 means "frugal, thrifty." <イ㑒>

倹約 frugality, thrifty [けんやく]; 節約 economy, saving, thrift [せつやく]; 倹約家 thrifty person, economizer [けんやくか]

18f 坐 "to sit" [from two people sitting on the ground facing each other]; *za* 座 挫 坐

	Meanings	Kun and On	Romaji	Bushu	Stroke Order and Number
SG-0384 座	to sit; seat, troupe, company	すわ-る ザ	suwa-ru *za*	广	广 庅 庇 座 座 10

座 **B** F-0596

No ancient form. The kanji comprised 广, bushu *madare* "eaves of a house," and 坐 for the sound *za*. The non-Joyo kanji 坐 "to sit, be" shown on the right means "a group of people sitting on the ground (土) facing each other." From people sitting and doing something together under the eaves, the character also came to mean "troupe" or "company." The kanji 座 means "to sit; seat, troupe, company." <广坐(人人土)>

坐 坐 坐 (説文古文 1, 説文 2, 漢字坐 3)

座る to sit [すわる]; 居座る to stay on for a long time [いすわる]; 正座する to sit on one's heels, sit up straight [せいざする]; 土下座する to kneel down on the ground (begging for forgiveness) [どげざする]; 一座 troupe [いちざ]; 座が白ける "A pall falls over the room" [ざがしらける]; 座右の銘 one's favorite motto [ざゆうのめい]

	Meanings	Kun and On	Romaji	Bushu	Stroke Order and Number
SG-0385 挫	to dispirit, depress, sprain	ザ	*za*	手	一 扌 扖 拟 挫 挫 10

挫 **D** F-2078

挫 挫 (説文)

The seal-style form comprised 扌, bushu *tehen*, and 坐 for the sound *za* to mean "a plaintiff and the accused sitting in court facing each other." A person being defeated by another in court, losing the judgment, and being punished came to mean "to dispirit, sprain." The kanji 挫 means "to dispirit, depress, sprain a joint." <扌坐>

挫折 setback, breakdown [ざせつ]; 捻挫する to sprain (one's ankle) [ねんざする]; 頓挫する to come to a standstill [とんざする] // 挫く to sprain, dishearten [くじく]

18g 匕 Different meanings: (1) a dead body, (2) person, (3) spoon; 化花北背 匕

	Meanings	Kun and On	Romaji	Bushu	Stroke Order and Number
SG-0386 化	to change, change shape, turn into, become	ば-ける カ・ケ	ba-keru *ka, ke*	匕	ノイイ'化 4

化 **A** F-0100

甲骨文 1 金文 2 説文 3 化

In 1 and 2, the left side was "a standing person facing left" (亻), and the right side, 匕, was used for the sound *ka*. One view takes the character to depict a 180-degree turn of 亻, and thus a person who is upside down (i.e., "a dead person"), signifying a change in a person's state from living to dead. Another view holds that the right side depicted "a person sitting," and that the change of posture from standing to sitting gave the meaning "to change." In either view, the change occurred in a single person. The kanji 化 means "to change, change shape, turn into, become." <亻匕>

化ける to change into [ばける]; お化け ghost [おばけ]; 文字化け garbled text (on a computer screen), character corruption [もじばけ]; 化学 chemistry [かがく]; 文化 culture [ぶんか]; 近代化 modernization [きんだいか]; 風化する weathering, weakening over time [ふうかする]; 化身 incarnation, personification [けしん]

	Meanings	Kun and On	Romaji	Bushu	Stroke Order and Number
SG-0387 花	flower	はな カ	hana *ka*	艸	一艹ナ花花 7

花 **A** F-0347

説文 1 旧字 2 華 花

1 comprised "plants" (艸, 艹, bushu *kusakanmuri*), and 化, used for the sound *ka* to mean "to change." A flower changes shape many times from bud to blossom, and eventually to seeds. The kanji 花 means "flower." <艹化> (Note: The kyuji 華 (2) is used for the Joyo kanji 華 **SG-0675**, meaning "gorgeous, showy.")

花 flower [はな]; 花盛り flowers at their best, flowering [はなざかり]; 生け花 *ikebana,* art of flower arrangement [いけばな]; 花火 firework [はなび]; 火花 spark [ひばな]; 開花する to bloom [かいかする]

	Meanings	Kun and On	Romaji	Bushu	Stroke Order and Number
SG-0388 北	north; to be defeated	きた ホク	kita *hoku*	匕	一十扌北北 5

北 **A** F-0077

甲骨文 1 金文 2 説文 3 北

1, 2, and 3 depicted two people standing back to back, and originally meant "to turn one's back on another." Another view holds that if one lived in a house built facing south, one had his back to the north, and thus the character meant "north." To turn away from an enemy also meant "to be defeated." The kanji 北 means "north; to be defeated." <扌匕>

北向き facing north [きたむき]; 北側 north side [きたがわ]; 東北地方 northeast region [とうほくちほう]; 北米 North America [ほくべい]; 敗北 defeat [はいぼく]; 北海道 Hokkaido Island [ほっかいどう]

	Meanings	Kun and On	Romaji	Bushu	Stroke Order and Number
SG-0389 背	one's back; to disobey, revolt, abandon	せ・せい・そむ-く ハイ	se, see, somu-ku *hai*	肉	一十扌北北背背 9

背 **B** F-0657

説文 背

The seal-style form comprised 北 **SG-0388**, "two people standing back to back," used for the sound *hai* (from *hoku*); and 月 "part of the body." Because the original writing for "back" (北) came to mean "north; to be defeated," a new kanji was created using 月. Doing something behind someone's back was "a breach of trust; to revolt." The kanji 背 means "one's back; to disobey, revolt, abandon." <北月>

背中 one's back [せなか]; 背伸びする to stretch upward, attempt beyond one's ability [せのびする]; 背が高い tall in stature [せ(い)が・たかい]; 背く to revolt, violate [そむく]; 背景 background [はいけい]; 背信 betrayal [はいしん]

18h 比 "people in a row, compare" [from people standing still in a row]; *hi* 比批陛, and 皆 "everyone, all"; *kai* 皆階諧楷

	Meanings	Kun and On	Romaji	Bushu	Stroke Order and Number
SG-0390 比	to compare	くら-べる ヒ	kura-beru *hi*	比	一ヒヒ'比 4

比 **A** F-0326

甲骨文 1 金文1 2 金文2 3 説文 4 比

1, 2, 3, and 4 depicted two people standing still and facing right. In ancient forms, a person facing right often had a connotation of "not moving." It is easier to compare two people standing still. The kanji 比 means "to compare." <ヒ匕>

比べる to compare [くらべる]; 比較する to compare [ひかくする]; 比例して proportionately [ひれいして]; 前年比 compared to the previous year [ぜんねんひ]

SG-0391 批	Meanings	Kun and On	Romaji	Bushu	Stroke Order and Number
	to disparage, criticize	ヒ	*hi*	手	扌扌扌批批批 7

批 **B** F-1031 篆文

The origin of the kanji 批 is not clear. One view explains that the right side, containing 比 **SG-0390**, was used for the sound *hi* to mean "a hand slapping back." With 扌, bushu *tehen* "an act done by hand" added, the seal-style form signified "to hit hard by hand." In the kanji, the right side became just 比. The kanji 批 means "to disparage, criticize." <扌比>

批評 critique, review [ひひょう]; 批判 criticism, attack, fault-finding [ひはん]

SG-0392 陛	Meanings	Kun and On	Romaji	Bushu	Stroke Order and Number
	His/Her/Your Majesty	ヘイ	*hee*	阜	阝阝阝阝阝陛 10

陛 **D** F-1718 説文

The seal-style form comprised 阝 "tall hills, stairs," and 比 **SG-0390** "people standing in a row" on the ground (土 **SG-1126**), used for the sound *hee*. Together they signified the stairs that led to the emperor, with his subjects standing in line on the ground below. The kanji 陛 means "His/Her/Your Majesty." <阝比土>

陛下 His, Her, or Your Majesty [へいか]; 両陛下 Their Majesties, the emperor and empress [りょうへいか]

皆 "everyone, all"; *kai* 皆階諧楷

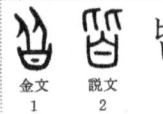

SG-0393 皆	Meanings	Kun and On	Romaji	Bushu	Stroke Order and Number
	everyone, all	みな カイ	mina *kai*	白	ヒヒ比比皆皆皆 9

皆 **B** F-1097 金文 1 説文 2

1 and 2 comprised "two people standing in a row" (比, **SG-0390**), and "to talk"(曰 *etsu*), together signifying "many people talking." Another view of 2 takes the bottom to be a person's nose (自 **SG-0059** "self"), which later became 白. The kanji 皆 means "everyone, all." <比白>

皆・皆んな everybody, all [みな、みんな]; 皆さん everyone, you all [みなさん]; 皆目分からない to have no clue, have not the faintest idea [かいもくわからない]; 皆無 nonexistence, complete absence [かいむ]; 皆勤 without absence, perfect attendance [かいきん]

SG-0394 階	Meanings	Kun and On	Romaji	Bushu	Stroke Order and Number
	stairs, floor, class, gradation	カイ	*kai*	阜	阝阝阝阝階 12

階 **B** F-0576 説文

The seal-style form comprised 阝, bushu *kozatohen* "hills, stairs," and 皆, which was used for the sound *kai* to mean "many things neatly lined up." The kanji 階 means "stairs, floor, class, gradation." <阝皆>

階段 stairs, stairways [かいだん]; 二階 second floor, upstairs [にかい]; 階下 downstairs, lower floor [かいか]; 階級 class, caste [かいきゅう]; 音階 musical scale [おんかい]; 中二階 mezzanine floor [ちゅうにかい]; 中産階級 middle class [ちゅうさんかいきゅう]

SG-0395 諧	Meanings	Kun and On	Romaji	Bushu	Stroke Order and Number
	playful talking	カイ	*kai*	言	言訁訁訁諧 16

諧 **D** F-2531 篆文

The seal-style form comprised 言, bushu *gonben* "word, language; to speak," and 皆 **SG-0393** for the sound *kai* to mean "harmoniously arranged." From words that are spoken in a good, relaxed mood, the kanji 諧 means "playful talking." <言皆>

諧謔 jest, joke, good-humored banter [かいぎゃく]; 俳諧 playful linked verse, *haiku* poetry [はいかい]

SG-0396 楷	Meanings	Kun and On	Romaji	Bushu	Stroke Order and Number
	neat, well-formed; kai-style standard writing	カイ	*kai*	木	木朴朴朴楷 13

楷 **D** F-2795 説文

The seal-style form comprised 木 "tree, wood," and 皆 for the sound *kai* to mean "neatly lined up." Together, they signified a type of well-shaped tree. From the meaning of a neat, well-formed tree, the kanji 楷 is used for *kaisho* (楷書), a standard noncursive style of (brush) writing.<木皆>

楷書 non-cursive standard style of blush writing [かいしょ]

18i 艮 "to retreat, remain" [from a person unable to move forward or looking back]; *kon* 
bushu *konzukuri* 限根銀退眼恨痕

	Meanings	Kun and On	Romaji	Bushu	Stroke Order and Number
SG-0397 限	boundary; to restrict, limit	かぎ-る ゲン	kagi-ru *gen*	阜	了阝阝ヨ阝艮阝艮限 9

限 **A** F-0483

金文 1 1 金文 2 2 説文 3 限

1 and 2 comprised "a high earthen wall, mountains," and "a person turning back to see a big glaring eye." An awestruck person unable to move forward signified "facing a boundary." 3 comprised 阝, bushu *kozatohen* "mountains, hills," and 艮, containing "an eye" and "a backward-facing person." The kanji 限 means "boundary; to restrict, limit." <阝艮>

限る to limit [かぎ]る]; 見限る to abandon, turn one's back on [みかぎる]; 限りない endless, best [かぎりな]い]; 最大限 maximum [さいだ]いげん]; 制限 restriction [せいげ]ん]; 上限 upper limit, cap [じょうげん]; 期限 time limit [き]げん]

	Meanings	Kun and On	Romaji	Bushu	Stroke Order and Number
SG-0398 根	root, origin, perseverance, stamina, root (in mathematics); fundamental	ね コン	ne *kon*	木	木朩ヨ朩艮根根根 10

根 **A** F-0357

説文 根

The seal-style form comprised 木 **SG-0608** "tree," and 艮, used for the sound *kon* to mean "unable to move, remain." The part of a tree that cannot move is the root. A root is where a tree originates, and thus it meant "origin; fundamental." When applied on person, it meant "perseverance; stamina." The kanji 根 means "root, origin, perseverance, stamina, root (in mathematics); fundamental." <木艮>

根 root [ね]]; 根も葉もない groundless [ね]も・はもな]い]; 根っから from the start, by nature [ね]っから]; 根本的な fundamental [こんぽんてきな]; 根気よく perseveringly [こんきよ]く]; 根負けする to have one's patience exhausted, give in [こんまけする]; 根比べ test of endurance [こんく]らべ]; 平方根 square root [へいほ]うこん]

	Meanings	Kun and On	Romaji	Bushu	Stroke Order and Number
SG-0399 銀	silver	ギン	*gin*	金	仐金金ヨ金艮金艮銀 14

銀 **A** F-0332

説文 銀

The seal-style form comprised 金 **SG-1196** "metal, precious nuggets concealed underground," and 艮, used for the sound *gin* (from *kon*) to mean "white." Together they signified "white metal" in the ground—that is, "silver." The kanji 銀 means "silver." <金艮>

銀 silver [ぎ]ん]; 銀行 bank [ぎんこう]; 水銀 mercury [すいぎん]; 金銀 gold and silver [き]んぎん]; 銀賞 silver prize, second-place prize [ぎんしょう]; 燻し銀 oxidized silver, somber silver color [いぶしぎん]

	Meanings	Kun and On	Romaji	Bushu	Stroke Order and Number
SG-0400 退	to retreat, move backward, withdraw, retire	しりぞ-く タイ	shirizo-ku *tai*	辵	ヨ日艮艮`艮退退 9

退 **B** F-0530

甲骨文 1 1 甲骨文 2 2 金文 3 中山王器 4 説文古文 5 説文 6 説文或体 7 退

1 and 2 signified "walking (from 'a footprint') toward the entrance of a house." 3, 4, 5, and 6 comprised "a crossroads" and "a forward-facing footprint," forming 辵(辶) "to move forward"; and "sun" (日) with "a backward-facing footprint" (夂), forming 艮 "to retreat." One view explains that the sun going down and disappearing meant "to regress, retreat." Another view explains that the two footprints in opposing directions (止 and 夂 in 4 and 5) signified "walking forward with an offering to an altar table and then coming back." 7 reflected the essence of 1 and 2. The kanji 退 means "to retreat, move backward, withdraw, retire." <艮辶>

退く to retreat, move backward [しりぞ]く]; to move aside, retire [の]く]; 後退 retreat, regress [こうたい]; 退職 resignation or retirement from a job [たいしょく]; 退屈な boring, tedious, dull [たいくつな]; 退院する to be discharged from the hospital [たいいんする]; 引退 retirement from public life [いんたい] // 立ち退く to get out, vacate [たちのく, たちの]く]

	Meanings	Kun and On	Romaji	Bushu	Stroke Order and Number
SG-0401 眼	pupil, eyeball, eye	まなこ ガン・ゲン	manako *gan, gen*	目	目目ˉ目ヨ目艮目艮眼 11

眼 **B** F-1010

説文 眼

The seal-style form comprised 目 **SG-0001** "eye," and 艮, used for the sound *gan* or *gen* to mean "an eyeball." The kanji 眼 means "pupil, eyeball, eye." <目艮>

眼 eye [ま]なこ]; 近眼 near-sightedness, myopia [きんがん]; 遠眼鏡 long-distance spectacles [えんがんきょう]; 肉眼 naked eye, unaided eye [にくがん]; 眼中にない outside of consideration, think nothing of [が]んちゅうに・な]い]; 千里眼 clairvoyance [せんりがん]; 眼科医 eye doctor, ophthalmologist [がんか]い]; 開眼 a Buddhist "eye-opening" ceremony for consecrating a newly made image of the Buddha [かいがん, かいげん] // 眼 eye [め]]; 眼鏡 eye glasses [め]がね]

SG-0402 恨	Meanings	Kun and On	Romaji	Bushu	Stroke Order and Number
	grudge, ill feeling, malice	うら-む コン	ura-mu *kon*	心	9

恨 **D** F-1746 (説文) The seal-style form comprised "heart" (忄), and 艮 "something that remains," used for the sound *kon*. What one held in one's heart that would not go away was "a grudge." The kanji 恨 means "grudge, ill feeling, malice." <忄艮>

恨む to bear a grudge against, blame [うらむ]; 恨めしい hateful, deplorable [うらめしい]; 逆恨みする to unjustly resent [さかうらみする]; 悔恨 remorse, regret [かいこん]; 怨恨 grudge [えんこん]

SG-0403 痕	Meanings	Kun and On	Romaji	Bushu	Stroke Order and Number
	scar, marking	あと コン	ato *kon*	疒	11

痕 **D** F-2016 (金文 1, 説文 2) 1 had "a vertically-placed bed" with a sick person lying on it, forming 疒, bushu *yamaidare* "illness," and 艮 "to remain," used for the sound *kon*. A mark left by illness or injury was a scar. The kanji 痕 means "scar, marking." <疒艮>

傷跡 scar, old wound [きずあと]; 血痕 bloodstain [けっこん]; 痕跡 trace, sign from the past [こんせき]

18j 疑 "in doubt" [from a person standing still, unable to decide their next move]; *gi* 疑凝擬

SG-0404 疑	Meanings	Kun and On	Romaji	Bushu	Stroke Order and Number
	to doubt; doubtful	うたが-う ギ	utaga-u *gi*	疋	14

疑 **B** F-0630 (甲骨文1 1, 甲骨文2 2, 金文 3, 説文 4) Components of the kanji 疑 varied throughout history. 1 had "a person with their head facing forward," while 2 had "a person with their head facing backward." In both 1 and 2, the person carried a stick, and in 1 they stood at a crossroads. The person was not sure which way to go, whence the meaning "in doubt." 3 contained "an ox" on the top left, whereas 4 showed "an arrow," and "a footprint" was added to both. The kanji 疑 means "to doubt; doubtful." <疑(匕矢マ疋)>

疑う to doubt [うたがう]; 疑い suspicion, doubt [うたがい]; 疑問 question, concern [ぎもん]; 疑念 a feeling of doubt, misgivings [ぎねん]; 半信半疑 uncertain as to the veracity of someone's story [はんしんはんぎ]; 容疑者 suspect [ようぎしゃ]

SG-0405 凝	Meanings	Kun and On	Romaji	Bushu	Stroke Order and Number
	to solidify, become engrossed, elaborate	こ-る ギョウ	ko-ru *gyoo*	冫	16

凝 **D** F-1759 (説文) The seal-style form comprised "ice" (冫), and 疑 **SG-0404**, used for the sound *gi*. Together they signified a change to a fixed, immovable state, like water becoming ice. The kanji 凝 means "to solidify, become engrossed, elaborate." <冫疑>

凝る to get stiff, become totally engrossed, develop a passion for [こる]; 肩凝り stiff shoulders [かたこり]; 肩が凝る to get stiff shoulders [かたがこる]; 凝った elaborate, ornate [こった]; 凝り性 a tendency to become totally immersed [こりしょう, こりしょう]; 凝固 solidification, condensation, clotting [ぎょうこ]; 凝視する to stare fixedly at, watch something intently [ぎょうしする]

SG-0406 擬	Meanings	Kun and On	Romaji	Bushu	Stroke Order and Number
	to imitate, liken, mmodel after	ギ	*gi*	手	17

擬 **D** F-1903 (説文) The seal-style form comprised 扌 "an act done by hand," and 疑 **SG-0404** "doubtful," used for the sound *gi*. Together they signified a person imitating someone or something else. The kanji 擬 means "to imitate, liken, model after." <扌疑>

擬人化する personification [ぎじんかする]; 模擬試験 mock examination [もぎしけん]

19 Person in a crouched posture

19a-1 令 "a person kneeling humbly under a roof"; *ree* 令命鈴

	Meanings	*Kun* and *On*	Romaji	Bushu	Stroke Order and Number
SG-0407 令	command, order, law, proclamation; pure and beautiful; honorific affix	レイ	*ree*	人	ノ 𠆢 今 令・ノ 𠆢 今 令 5

令 **A** F-0680

甲骨文 1 (1), 甲骨文 2 (2), 金文 1 (3), 金文 2 (4), 金文 3 (5), 説文 (6)

1 and 2 were mirror images of each other. 1 through 6 depicted "a person kneeling down with his head lowered under a roof." The top component 亼 signified "to gather many things under a roof." A ruler gathered people and gave them commands. His command became "orders, law." Another view explains that the different forms depicted "a priest wearing a ceremonial headdress, listening to a deity's words on his knees." The meaning of "pure and beautiful," from the goodness of serving a deity, came to be used as an honorific affix in referring to another's family members. The kanji 令 means "command, order, law, proclamation, pure and beautiful; honorific affix." <令 (亼 卩) or 令 (亼マ)>

命令 order, decree, directive [めいれい]; 法令 laws and ordinances [ほうれい]; 辞令 written notice of an appointment [じれい]; 政令 government ordinance, cabinet order [せいれい]; 令状 warrant [れいじょう]; 令嬢 daughter, young lady [れいじょう]; 発令する to announce officially, issue regulations [はつれいする]; 令和 Reiwa era (May 2019 – present) [れ]いわ, れいわ]

	Meanings	*Kun* and *On*	Romaji	Bushu	Stroke Order and Number
SG-0408 命	order, life	いのち メイ・ミョウ	inochi *mee, myoo*	口	ノ 𠆢 合 合 命 8

命 **A** F-0196

甲骨文 1 (1), 甲骨文 2 (2), 金文 1 (3), 金文 2 (4), 説文 (5)

1 and 2 shared their form with 1 and 2 for 令 **SG-0407**. In 3, 4, and 5, 口 "mouth, speaking" was added to 令, originally to mean "words of a deity or ruler, order." One view explains that one's life arises from the will of a deity, whence the meaning "life." The kanji 命 means "order, life." <令口>

命 life, most important thing, order [いのち]; 命がけで desperate, risking one's life [いのちがけで]; 命拾い narrow escape from death [いのちびろい]; 命日 anniversary of a death [めいにち]; 使命 mission [しめい]; 一生懸命 with all one's might, very hard [いっしょうけんめい]; 運命 lot, fate [うんめい]; 命 one's lifespan [じゅみょう]

	Meanings	*Kun* and *On*	Romaji	Bushu	Stroke Order and Number
SG-0409 鈴	bell, chime	すず レイ・リン	suzu *ree; rin*	金	亼 金 鈊 鈴 鈴 鈴 3

鈴 **B** F-0755

金文 1 (1), 金文 2 (2), 説文 (3)

1 and 2 comprised 金 **SG-1196** "metal," and 令 **SG-0407**, used for the sound *ree*, together signifying an onomatopoeic word for the ringing of a bell. The kanji 鈴 means "bell, chime." <金令>

鈴 small bell [すず]; 予鈴 first bell, warning bell [よれい]; 風鈴 wind chime [ふうりん]; 呼び鈴 call bell, doorbell [よびりん]

19a-2 卩 "a kneeling person"; 印 "to welcome; one pressing down the other" 印迎節・抑仰

	Meanings	*Kun* and *On*	Romaji	Bushu	Stroke Order and Number
SG-0410 印	sign, seal, symbol, emblem, stamp, mark	しるし イン	shirushi *in*	卩	ſ E E7 印 6

印 **B** F-0586

甲骨文 1 (1), 甲骨文 2 (2), 金文 1 (3), 金文 2 (4), 説文 (5)

1, 2, 3, 4, and 5 comprised "a hand from above" and "a person kneeling," together signifying that someone's hand (⺕) was "pushing down" on another person to make them kneel (卩). The act of pushing down was analogous to firmly pressing down on a seal. The kanji 印 meant "to press a seal; a seal." In the kanji 印, the two components were placed side by side, with the person taking the reduced shape 卩. The kanji 印 means "sign, seal, symbol, emblem, stamp, mark." <⺕ 卩>

印 mark, sign [しるし]; 目印 mark, sign, landmark [めじるし]; 印刷 printing [いんさつ]; 印鑑 stamp, seal[いんかん]; 印字 printing, printed letter [いんじ]; 消印 canceled stamp [けしいん];印税 royalty (on a book) [いんぜい]

	Meanings	*Kun* and *On*	Romaji	Bushu	Stroke Order and Number
SG-0411 迎	to welcome, greet	むか-える ゲイ	muka-eru *gee*	辵	𠂆 卬 印 卭 迎 7

迎 **B** F-0773 — 説文

The seal-style form comprised 辵 "to move forward," and 卬, used for the sound *gee* to mean "a standing person and a kneeling person." Together they signified that a kneeling person was welcoming a standing person who had just arrived. The kanji 迎 means "to welcome, greet." <卬辶>
(Note: The shape 卬 carries two related, but different, meanings: One is "to welcome humbly," as in 迎 **SG-0411** and 仰 **SG-0414**; and another is "to press down" as in 印 **SG-0410** and 抑 **SG-0413**.)

迎える to receive someone [むかえる]; 迎えに行く to go to pick up someone [むかえ⁀にいく]; 出迎える to go out to meet [でむかえる, でむかえ⁀る]; 歓迎 welcome [かんげい]; 送迎バス courtesy bus [そうげいバ⁀ス]; 迎合する to go along with someone's view without having one's own opinion [げいごうする]

	Meanings	*Kun* and *On*	Romaji	Bushu	Stroke Order and Number
SG-0412 節	joint, section, moderation, holiday, occasion, tune (of a song), delegate, paragraph	ふし セツ・セチ	hushi *setsu, sechi*	竹	𥫗 笃 笸 筫 節 節 13

節 **B** F-0943 — 金文 1, 説文 2, 旧字 3

1 and 2 comprised "bamboo" (竹 **SG-0759**), and 即 **SG-1786**, used for the sound *setsu* to mean "to cut." A long stalk of bamboo has "joints or sections." Being punctuated at a regular interval like the nodes on a bamboo stalk prevents something from becoming excessive, and thus the character meant "moderation." A foreign envoy to the imperial court had a bamboo tally that proved he was a genuine envoy, whence the meanings "mission, delegate." One's life or year was punctuated by special occasions, whence the meanings "occasion, holiday." The kanji 節 means "joint, section, moderation, holiday, occasion, tune (of a song), delegate, paragraph." <𥫗艮卩>

節 section, tune, occasion, paragraph [ふし⁀]; 節目 turning point [ふしめ⁀]; 節々 joints [ふし⁀ぶし]; 節度を持つ to have restrained good behavior [せ⁀つどを・もつ]; 関節 joint [かんせつ]; 節電 energy conservation [せつでん]; 使節 mission, envoy, delegate [し⁀せつ]; 一節 paragraph, passage [いっせつ⁀]

	Meanings	*Kun* and *On*	Romaji	Bushu	Stroke Order and Number
SG-0413 抑	to press down, restrain	おさ-える ヨク	osa-eru *yoku*	手	扌 扌 扩 抑 抑 7

抑 **C** F-1086 — 説文 1 (1), 説文 2 (2)

Aside from "a hand" in 1, 1 and 2 shared the same components: "a person kneeling" and "a hand (fingers) from above." While the same two components formed the kanji 印 **SG-0410**, with the inclusion of 扌, bushu *tehen*, this character emphasized that the hand was pressing down on another person, and thus meant "to restrain someone." The kanji 抑 means "to press down, restrain." <扌卬>

抑える to press down, restrain an action [おさえ⁀る]; 抑圧的な oppressive [よくあつ⁀てきな]; 抑制する to restrain [よくせいする]; 抑揚 inflection, modulation [よくよう]; 抑止力 deterrent force (of a weapon) [よくし⁀りょく]

	Meanings	*Kun* and *On*	Romaji	Bushu	Stroke Order and Number
SG-0414 仰	to look up, respect	あお-ぐ・おお-せ ギョウ・コウ	ao-gu, oo-se *gyoo, koo*	人	亻 亻 𠆢 仰 仰 6

仰 **C** F-1546 — 説文

The seal-style form comprised three shapes of a person: 亻 "a person, an act that one does," "a standing person facing right," and "a person kneeling down" (卬 *koo/gyoo*). Together they meant that "a kneeling person was looking up to a standing person to show a respect." The kanji 仰 means "to look up, respect." <亻卬>

師と仰ぐ to look up to as a mentor [し⁀と・あお⁀ぐ]; 天を仰ぐ to look up in the sky [て⁀んを・あお⁀ぐ]; 仰ぎ見る to look upward, revere [あおぎみ⁀る]; 仰向け facing upward [あおむけ]; 仰せになる to say (honorific) [おおせにな⁀る]; 仰天する to be astounded [ぎょうてんする]; 大仰に with exaggeration [おおぎょうに]; 信仰 belief, faith [しんこう] // 仰る to say (honorific) [おっしゃ⁀る]

19a-3 㔾 "a person curled up" 危宛怨厄・丸

	Meanings	*Kun* and *On*	Romaji	Bushu	Stroke Order and Number
SG-0415 危	danger; perilous	あぶ-ない・あや-うい キ	abu-nai, aya-ui *ki*	卩	⺈ ⺈ 产 角 危 6

危 **B** F-0651 — 説文

The seal-style form depicted a person stooping perilously on top of a cliff (厂, bushu *gandare*), which meant "danger" and had the sound *ki*. Under the cliff, another person coiled up or crouched in fear of danger. The kanji 危 means "danger; perilous." <⺈厂㔾>

危ない dangerous, risky [あぶない]; 危うくする to endanger, imperil, jeopardize [あやうくする]; 危険 danger [きけん]; 危機 crisis, pinch [き⁀き]; 危機的な critical [ききてきな]; 危害を加える to endanger, expose someone to serious harm [き⁀がいを・くわえる]

	Meanings	*Kun* and *On*	Romaji	Bushu	Stroke Order and Number
SG-0416 宛	addressed to (in correspondence)	あ-てる, (-あて)	a-teru, (-ate)	宀	宀 宊 𡧋 宛 8

宛 **D** F-2221 — 説文1 1, 説文或体 2

1 and 2 had 宀 "house," and 夗 ("a crouched person," from 夕 "flesh" and 㔾 "crouched"), used for the sound *en*, and "a heart" in 2 to signify humility. The original meaning, "to stoop over; humble posture," is no longer used. In Japanese, 宛 means "addressed to" in correspondence. <宀夗>

宛名 address of a letter [あてな]; ～宛の手紙 a letter addressed to X [～あてのてがみ]

	Meanings	*Kun* and *On*	Romaji	Bushu	Stroke Order and Number
SG-0417 怨	grudge	エン・オン	*en, on*	心	ク タ タ㇆ 夗 怨 怨 9

怨 **D** F-2216 — 説文古文 1, 説文 2

In 1, under "a cover" (亼) were "a heart" (心 **SG-0187**) and "a crouching person" (㔾). 2 comprised 夗 (夕 "flesh" and 㔾), used for the sound *en*, and 心. Together, these components signified "an emotion that one suppressed, grudge." The kanji 怨 means "grudge." <夗心>

怨恨 grudge, enmity [えんこん]; 怨念 deep-seated grudge [おんねん] // 怨み a bitter or spiteful feeling [うらみꜜ]

	Meanings	*Kun* and *On*	Romaji	Bushu	Stroke Order and Number
SG-0418 厄	misfortune, calamity, ill luck	ヤク	*yaku*	厂	一 厂 厂㇆ 厄 4

厄 **D** F-1991 — 金文 1, 説文 2

Views on the origin of the kanji 厄 vary. One view explains that, based on the shape of the kanji 厄 (and also on form 2), it derives from "a curled up person (㔾) facing a cliff and in trouble," and thus it signified "misfortune." Another view explains that 1 was "a horse carriage yoke," and took on the meaning "misfortune" as a borrowing. The kanji 厄 means "misfortune, calamity, ill luck." <厂㔾>

厄介な troublesome, burdensome [やꜜっかいな]; 厄払い an exorcism ceremony [やくばꜜらい]; 厄年 unlucky year [やくꜜどし]

丸 "round; whole"

	Meanings	*Kun* and *On*	Romaji	Bushu	Stroke Order and Number
SG-0419 丸	round; whole, entirety, bullet	まる ガン	maru *gan*	丶	ノ 九 丸 3

丸 **A** F-0416 — 甲骨文 1, 金文 2, 説文 3

1 depicted "a bow with a rock on the string, slingshot," and meant "a round rock or bullet." Another view takes 2 and 3 to depict "a person with his back bent, facing a cliff," and holds that from a coiled-up body under a cliff, it meant "round." In Japanese, a round shape also meant "whole, entirety." The kanji 丸 means "round; whole, entirety, bullet." <九丶>

丸い round [まるい]; 丸焼き roasting whole [まるやき]; 丸ごと whole, altogether [まるごと]; 丸つぶれ complete destruction, utter failure [まるつぶれ]; 日の丸 Japanese flag [ひのまる]; 丸暗記 rote memorization [まるあꜜんき]; 丸薬 medicinal pellet [がんやく]

19a-4 己 "self, person" 己選港

	Meanings	*Kun* and *On*	Romaji	Bushu	Stroke Order and Number
SG-0420 己	self, I	おのれ コ・キ	onore *ko, ki*	己	㇆ コ 己 3

己 **A** F-0982 — 甲骨文1 1, 甲骨文2 2, 金文 3, 説文 4

Scholars' views on the origin of the kanji 己 differ widely: (a) "a rectangle tool for carpentry"; (b) "a part of a pattern imprinted on pottery"; (c) "a piece of bent string"; and (d) "a snake on the verge of striking." It was borrowed to mean "self." The kanji 己 means "self, I." <己>

己 self [おのれ]; 自己 oneself [じꜜこ]; 知己 a close friend, acquaintance [ちꜜき]; 克己心 self-denying spirit [こっきꜜしん]; 利己的 selfish [りこてき]

	Meanings	*Kun* and *On*	Romaji	Bushu	Stroke Order and Number
SG-0421 選	to choose, select	えら-ぶ セン	era-bu *sen*	辶	㇆ 己 己己 巺 巽 ⻌巽 選 15

選 **A** F-0221 — 金文 1, 説文 2

1 comprised "two people bending their backs," "a footstep," and "a crossroads" (which became 辵, 辶), signifying "two people doing a votive dance." In 2, a stage to perform on was added and became 巽 to mean "select votive dancers participating on a stage," which was used for the sound *sen*. Together, these components meant "to send out select people." The kanji 選 means "to choose, select." <己己共辶>

選ぶ to choose, select [えらꜜぶ]; 選挙 election [せꜜんきょ]; 再選 reelection [さいせん]; 選定する to select, make a choice [せんていする]; 選任する to select and appoint [せんにんする]; 予選 preliminary match [よせん]; 落選する to be defeated in an election [らくせんする] // 選りすぐる to choose out of many good candidates [えりすぐꜜる]

SG-0422 港	Meanings: port	Kun and On: みなと コウ	Romaji: minato *koo*	Bushu: 水	Stroke Order and Number: 氵汁洪洪港港 12

港 **B** F-0543	篆文 港 The seal-style form comprised "flowing water," and 巷 "road, passage, place where people gather," used for the sound *koo*. Together they signified "waterway." The development of 巷 ("street," from "roads to a place where many people gather") is shown at right. At an estuary where a waterway ended, there was a landing stage for boats—that is, a port. The kanji 港 means "port." <氵共己> (説文1, 説文2, 旧字3: 巷 巷)	港 port [みなと]; 空港 airport [くうこう]; 漁港 fishing port [ぎょこう]

19a-5 巴 "a person crouching" 色肥

SG-0423 色	Meanings: color, characteristics; amorous	Kun and On: いろ ショク・シキ	Romaji: iro *shoku, shiki*	Bushu: 色	Stroke Order and Number: ク 勺 刍 刍 色 6

色 **A** F-0350	説文 色 The seal-style form depicted "a person" above "a crouched person," together signifying "intimacy, sex; amorous." The meaning of "color" came from the redness of a face impassioned with emotion, for example, anger. The character also came to mean "characteristics." The kanji 色 means "color, characteristics; amorous." <ク巴>	色 color [いろ]; 色々 various [いろいろ]; 色違い different colors [いろちがい]; 色付けする to color [いろづけする]; 色気のある sexually attractive [いろけのある]; 色目を使う to cast a flirtatious glance [いろめをつかう]; 好色 sensual, amorous, dirty [こうしょく]; 難色を示す to frown upon [なんしょくをしめす]; 物色する to look for, select [ぶっしょくする]; 気色ばむ to become indignant [けしきばむ]

SG-0424 肥	Meanings: fat, corpulent, rich, fertile; to enrich	Kun and On: こ-やす ヒ	Romaji: ko-yasu *hi*	Bushu: 肉	Stroke Order and Number: 月 月 月 月 肥 8

肥 **C** F-1421	説文 肥 The seal-style form comprised 月 "part of the body, flesh," and 巴 "a crouching person." When one knelt, their thighs showed more, signifying "much flesh." The character meant "fat, corpulent." It also meant "rich, fertile; to enrich." The kanji 肥 means "fat, corpulent, rich, fertile; to enrich." <月巴>	肥える to get fat, put on weight [こえる]; 肥やす to fertilize, enrich, fatten up [こやす]; 肥やし manure, fertilizer [こやし]; 堆肥 compost, organic fertilizer [たいひ]; 肥大する to enlarge, swell [ひだいする];肥満症 obesity [ひまんしょう]

19a-6 包 "to wrap, envelop" [from baby in a fetal position in its mother's womb]; *hoo*

包抱砲胞泡飽

SG-0425 包	Meanings: to wrap, envelop	Kun and On: つつ-む ホウ	Romaji: tsutsu-mu *hoo*	Bushu: 勹	Stroke Order and Number: ノ 勹 勺 匀 包 5

包 **B** F-0927	説文 包 The seal-style form was "a baby in a fetal position wrapped in its mother's womb." From the way the mother's womb wrapped around the baby, the kanji 包 means "to wrap, envelop." <勹己>	包む to wrap [つつむ]; 包み紙 wrapping paper [つつみがみ]; 梱包 packing [こんぽう]; 包装紙 wrapping paper [ほうそうし]

SG-0426 抱	Meanings: to embrace, hold in one's arms, hug	Kun and On: だ-く・いだ-く・かか-える ホウ	Romaji: da-ku, ida-ku, kaka-eru *hoo*	Bushu: 手	Stroke Order and Number: 寸 扌 扚 拘 抱 8

抱 **B** F-0991	説文1 説文或体2 抱 Inside of the wide-open collar in 1 was "a fetus in the womb; to wrap around" (包 **SG-0425**), used for the sound *hoo*. The character meant "to embrace." In 2, 扌 "an act done by hand" was added to 包. Together they meant "arms embracing someone or holding something," and also "to take on responsibility." The kanji 抱 means "to embrace, hold in one's arms, hug, take on." <扌包>	抱く to embrace [だく], to harbor, cherish [いだく]; 抱える to hold in one's arms, employ [かかえる]; 抱擁 embrace, hug [ほうよう]; 辛抱する to bear, be patient [しんぼうする]

SG-0427 砲	Meanings: cannon, gun	Kun and On: ホウ	Romaji: *Hoo*	Bushu: 石	Stroke Order and Number: 厂 石 矽 砲 砲 10

砲 **C** F-1474	No ancient form. The kanji comprises 石 **SG-1148** "rock, stone," and 包 **SG-0425** "to wrap, envelop," used for the sound *hoo*. A weapon in which a stone was enveloped in gunpowder and discharged was a cannon. The kanji 砲 means "cannon, gun." <石包>	大砲 cannon, gun [たいほう]; 鉄砲 gun, firearms [てっぽう];空砲 blank shot [くうほう]; 祝砲 gun salute [しゅくほう]

	Meanings	Kun and On	Romaji	Bushu	Stroke Order and Number
SG-0428 胞	placenta, cell, fellow countrymen	ホウ	*hoo*	肉	月 月' 肑 胸 胞 9

胞 **C** F-1576

篆文

The seal-style form comprised 月, bushu *nikuzuki* "part of the body," and 包 **SG-0425** "to wrap, envelop," used for the sound *hoo*. The part of the body that (partially) enveloped a fetus was the "placenta." A cell wall enveloped a cell. The character was also used to mean people from the same home country. The kanji 胞 means "placenta, cell, fellow countrymen." <月包>

細胞 cell [さいぼう]; 幹細胞 stem cell [かんさいぼう]; 同胞 fellow countrymen [どうほう]; 胞子 spore [ほうし]

	Meanings	Kun and On	Romaji	Bushu	Stroke Order and Number
SG-0429 泡	bubble, foam	あわ ホウ	awa *hoo*	水	氵 氵' 沟 泃 泡 8

泡 **C** F-1604

説文

The seal-style form comprised "flowing water" (氵, bushu *sanzui*), and "to wrap, envelop" (包 **SG-0425**), used for the sound *hoo*. Air that was enveloped in water was "a bubble." The kanji 泡 means "bubble, foam." <氵包>

泡 bubble [あわ]; 泡立つ to bubble, lather [あわだつ]; 泡立て器 eggbeater, whisk [あわだてき]; 水泡 bubble, foam [すいほう]; 発泡酒 low-malt beer [はっぽうしゅ]; 発泡スチロール Styrofoam, styrene foam [はっぽうスチロール]

	Meanings	Kun and On	Romaji	Bushu	Stroke Order and Number
SG-0430 飽	full, weary of; to become tired of	あ-きる ホウ	a-kiru *hoo*	食	𠆢 今 食 飣 飽 飽 13

飽 **D** F-1726

説文古文 1 1 · 説文古文 2 2 · 説文 3

1 comprised "covered food in a raised bowl" (飠 bushu *shokuhen*), and "a hand above a baby," together signifying "feeding a baby to fill the baby's stomach." 2, with "two doors to an altar," signified "to offer food to satisfy a deity." In 3, 飠 and 包 **SG-0425** (for the sound *hoo* to mean "full") signified that after eating much food, one's stomach became full, and that too much of something made a person become weary. The kanji 飽 means "full, weary of; to become tired of." <飠包>

飽きる to grow weary of, become tired of [あきる]; 飽きが来る to grow tired of [あきがくる]; 飽き足りない unsatisfying [あきたりない]; 聞き飽きた got tired of hearing it [ききあきた]; 飽きっぽい to get easily bored, lose interest easily [あきっぽい]; 飽くまで to the bitter end, to the last, stubbornly [あくまで, あくまで]; 飽和 saturation [ほうわ]

19b 欠 "to lack, become chipped; in want of" [from a person with their mouth open]

欠次歌資姿飲吹炊款諮恣

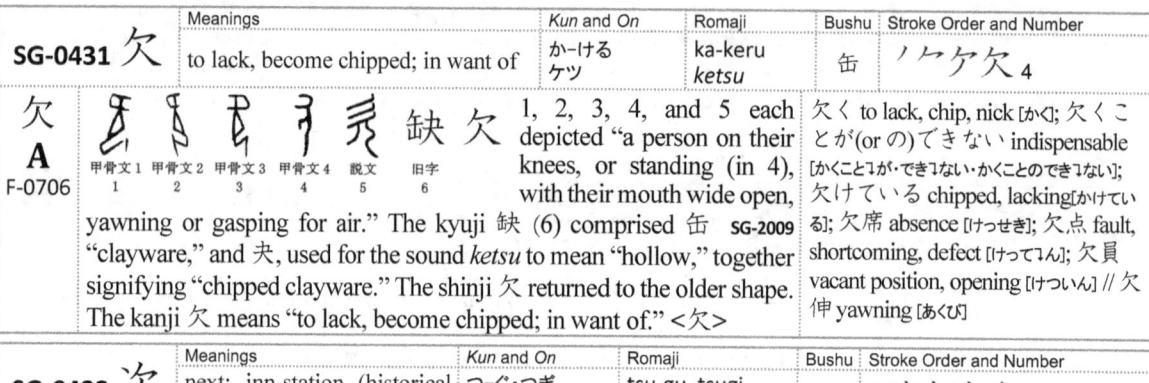

	Meanings	Kun and On	Romaji	Bushu	Stroke Order and Number
SG-0431 欠	to lack, become chipped; in want of	か-ける ケツ	ka-keru *ketsu*	缶	ノ 𠂊 ケ 欠 4

欠 **A** F-0706

甲骨文 1 1 · 甲骨文 2 2 · 甲骨文 3 3 · 甲骨文 4 4 · 説文 5 · 旧字 6

缺 欠

1, 2, 3, 4, and 5 each depicted "a person on their knees, or standing (in 4), with their mouth wide open, yawning or gasping for air." The kyuji 缺 (6) comprised 缶 **SG-2009** "clayware," and 夬, used for the sound *ketsu* to mean "hollow," together signifying "chipped clayware." The shinji 欠 returned to the older shape. The kanji 欠 means "to lack, become chipped; in want of." <欠>

欠く to lack, chip, nick [かく]; 欠くことが(or の)できない indispensable [かくことができない・かくことのできない]; 欠けている chipped, lacking[かけている]; 欠席 absence [けっせき]; 欠点 fault, shortcoming, defect [けってん]; 欠員 vacant position, opening [けついん] // 欠伸 yawning [あくび]

	Meanings	Kun and On	Romaji	Bushu	Stroke Order and Number
SG-0432 次	next; inn-station (historical use)	つ-ぐ・つぎ ジ	tsu-gu, tsugi *ji*	欠	冫 冫' 次 次 次 6

次 **A** F-0198

甲骨文 1 · 金文 2 · 説文 3

1, 2, and 3 depicted "a person kneeling down or standing with their mouth open to breathe deeply" (欠). The two lines (冫, 二) gave the sound *ji*, and also meant "to stop briefly (from the same sound as 止 "stop") before the next move." The kanji 次 means "next; inn-station" (historical use). <冫欠>

次 next, following [つぎ]; 次に next, after this [つぎに]; 相次いで one after another [あいついで]; 次々に one after another [つぎつぎに]; 次回 next time [じかい]; 目次 table of contents [もくじ]; 次点 runner-up [じてん]; 次期 next term [じき]; 東海道五十三次 the fifty-three inn-stations on the old Tokaido highway (historical) [とうかいどう・ごじゅうさんつぎ]

	Meanings	*Kun* and *On*	Romaji	Bushu	Stroke Order and Number
SG-0433 歌	to sing; song	うた カ	uta *ka*	欠	可 可 哥 哥 哥 歌 14

歌
A
F-0320

1 and 2 comprised 言 "words, language; to speak," and 可 **SG-0045**, used for the sound *ka* to mean "coarse voice." Together, thesse components signified "song; to sing." 2 and 3 contained two 可, with either 欠 "someone with his mouth open wide" (in 2) or 言 "word" (in 3). The kanji 歌 means "to sing; song." <可可欠>

歌う to sing [うたう]; 歌 song [うたꜜ]; 歌手 singer [かꜜしゅ]; 国歌 national anthem [こꜜっか]; 演歌 *enka* song [えꜜんか]; 歌謡曲 popular song [かようꜜきょく]; 歌曲 song (usually classical) [かꜜきょく]; 和歌 Japanese poetry [わꜜか]; 短歌 a short Japanese poem of 31 syllables, arranged in the lines of 5-7-5-7-7 syllables [たꜜんか]

	Meanings	*Kun* and *On*	Romaji	Bushu	Stroke Order and Number
SG-0434 資	resource, capital, innate talent; to assist financially	シ	*shi*	貝	冫 冫 次 次 洛 資 資 13

資
A
F-0390

The seal-style form comprised 次 **SG-0432**, for the sound *shi* and the meaning "ready for what's next/what's yet to come," and 貝 **SG-1693** "cowrie, money; valuable." Taken together, money and valuables for future use meant "resource, capital." An innate talent is a valuable resource for one's future. The kanji 資 means "resource, capital, innate talent; to assist financially." <次貝>

資本 capital [しꜜほん]; 資格 qualification, license [しかく]; 資料 data, material [しꜜりょう]; 資産 property, wealth [しꜜさん]; 外資系 foreign-owned firms [がいしけい]; 投資 investment [とうし]; 資源 resources [しꜜげん]

	Meanings	*Kun* and *On*	Romaji	Bushu	Stroke Order and Number
SG-0435 姿	appearance, figure, guise, state	すがた シ	sugata *shi*	女	冫 次 次 姿 姿 9

姿
B
F-0568

The seal-style form comprised 次 **SG-0432** "next, upcoming" used for the sound *shi*, and 女 **SG-0521** "woman." It signified "a woman dressing herself in preparation for an upcoming event." The kanji 姿 means "appearance, figure, guise, state." <次女>

姿 figure, form [すꜜがた]; 晴れ姿 appearance in one's shining moment [はれすꜜがた]; 後ろ姿 appearance from behind [うしろすꜜがた]; 姿を消す to disappear [すꜜがたを・けす]; 姿勢 attitude, posture [しせい]; 容姿 appearance [よꜜうし]

	Meanings	*Kun* and *On*	Romaji	Bushu	Stroke Order and Number
SG-0436 飲	to drink, swallow	の-む イン	no-mu *in*	食	今 含 食 飲 飲 飲 12

飲
B
F-0719

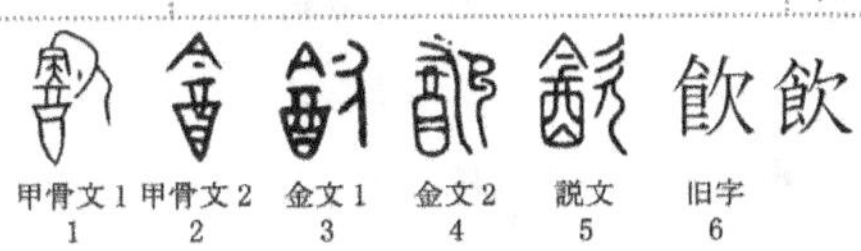

1 depicted "a person trying to drink wine from a large cask." The person's tongue had a forked shape for licking (as seen in the origin of the kanji 舌 **SG-0040** "tongue"). It meant "to drink." 2 was "a large wine cask (酉) with a stopper (亼)," which also appeared in 3, 4, and 5, next to the person trying to drink or opening their mouth wide. In the kyuji 飮 (6), however, the cask was replaced by bushu *shokuhen* "to eat; food." The kanji 飲 means "to drink, swallow." <食欠>
(Note: The bushu *sakezukuri* 酉 "wine cask" is discussed in kanji 酒 **SG-1812** through 醒 **SG-1821**.)

飲む to drink, swallow [のꜜむ]; 飲み込む to swallow, understand [のみこꜜむ]; 飲み込みがいい quick to comprehend [のみこみがいꜜい]; 飲食店 restaurant [いんしょくꜜてん]; 飲料水 drinking water [いんりょꜜうすい]; 誤飲 drinking or swallowing by mistake [ごいん]

	Meanings	*Kun* and *On*	Romaji	Bushu	Stroke Order and Number
SG-0437 吹	to breath out, exhale, blow, puff	ふ-く スイ	hu-ku *sui*	口	口 吖 吹 吹 7

吹
B
F-1027

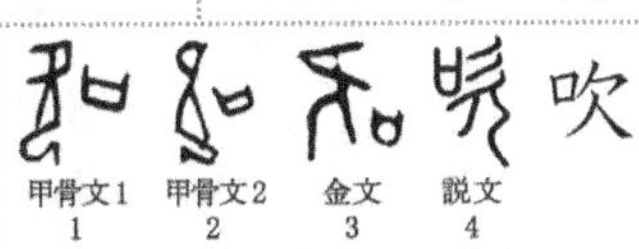

1, 2, and 3 each had "a person with their mouth open" (欠 **SG-0431**), with 口 **SG-0031** "mouth" in front of or behind them. The form was a sideways view of a person breathing out. It meant "to breathe out, blow air." In 4, the two components swapped positions. The kanji 吹 means "to breathe out, exhale, blow, puff." <口欠>

吹く to blow [ふꜜく]; 風が吹く the wind blows [かぜがふꜜく]; 口笛を吹く to whistle [くちぶえをふꜜく]; 吹き出す to spout, puff, burst into laughter [ふきだꜜす]; ほら吹き empty boaster, braggart [ほらꜜふき]; 吹奏楽 wind instrument music [すいそꜜうがく]; 鼓吹する to instill courage in, inspire [こすいする] // 吹雪 snowstorm, blizzard [ふꜜぶき]

	Meanings	*Kun* and *On*	Romaji	Bushu	Stroke Order and Number
SG-0438 炊	to boil, cook	た-く スイ	ta-ku *sui*	火	丷 ナ 炉 炒 炊 8

炊 **D** F-1682

説文

The seal-style form comprised 火 **SG-1164** "fire," and 欠 **SG-0431** "to breathe out." Blowing air into a fire in a stove would keep the fire going, and the character signified "to cook." The kanji 炊 means "to boil, cook (over heat)." <火欠>

炊く to cook rice, boil [た˥く]; 御飯を炊く to cook rice [ご˥はんを・た˥く]; 炊き込み御飯 rice cooked with vegetables or meat [たきこみご˥はん]; 炊事 cooking, kitchen work [すい˥じ]; 電気炊飯器 electric rice cooker [でんきすいは˥んき]; 自炊する to cook for oneself [じすいする]

	Meanings	*Kun* and *On*	Romaji	Bushu	Stroke Order and Number
SG-0439 款	clause, hospitality (archaic); to engrave	カン	*kan*	欠	一 十 士 寺 款 款 款 12

款 **D** F-1963

説文 1 説文或体 2

The origin of this character is obscure. One view explains that the left side comprised a plant or a tree with an altar table, and the right side was 欠 to indicate "a hollow." Together they meant "carving a sincere promise on a wooden board in front of an altar." A carved message meant "article, clause; to be engraved." In older times, the character was also used to mean "to be rejoiceful; hospitality," but for that meaning it has been replaced by another kanji (歓 **SG-0978**). The kanji 款 means "clause, hospitality (archaic); to engrave." <士示欠>

定款 articles of incorporation [ていかん]; 借款 loan (between countries, institutions, or corporations) [しゃっかん]; 落款 a painter's sign or seal [らっかん] // 款待 (now written as 歓待) cordial reception [かんたい]

	Meanings	*Kun* and *On*	Romaji	Bushu	Stroke Order and Number
SG-0440 諮	to consult, confer	はか-る シ	haka-ru *shi*	言	言 言 訁 諮 諮 16

諮 **D** F-2153

No ancient form. The kanji 諮 comprised 言, bushu *gonben* "word, language; to speak," and 咨, used for the sound *shi* to mean "to consult." The kanji 諮 means "to consult, confer." <言欠口>

諮る to consult with, deliberate [はか˥る]; 諮問 question, submit to for deliberation [しもん]; 諮問委員会 advisory committee [しもんいい˥んかい]

	Meanings	*Kun* and *On*	Romaji	Bushu	Stroke Order and Number
SG-0441 恣	self-indulgent; to have one's own way	シ	*shi*	心	冫 次 次 恣 恣 10

恣 **D** F-2612

説文

The seal-style form comprised 次 **SG-0432** for the sound *shi*, and 心 **SG-0187** "heart." A person taking a deep breath and giving their heart a good rest led to the meaning "to indulge oneself." The kanji 恣 means "self-indulgent; to have one's own way." <次心>

恣意的な arbitrary [しいてきな]

19c 儿 "person" [from kneeling with one's hands in front]; **bushu *ninnyoo***

光先元完院児洗冠玩

	Meanings	*Kun* and *On*	Romaji	Bushu	Stroke Order and Number
SG-0442 光	light, ray; bright; to shine	ひか-る・ひかり コウ	hika-ru, hikari *koo*	儿	丨 ⺌ 业 屮 光 6

光 **A** F-0155

甲骨文1 1 甲骨文2 2 金文1 3 金文2 4 説文 5

1, 2, 3, and 4 depicted a person on their knees in a solemn posture with their hands in front of them, carrying fire on their head. A fire gives "light." Keeping or carrying a light in a religious rite was an important job. In the kanji 光, the person on their knees was reduced to 儿, bushu *ninnyoo*. The kanji 光 means "light, ray; bright; to shine." <⺌儿>

光 light [ひかり]; 稲光 flash of lightning [いなび˥かり]; 親の七光り capitalizing on having a famous parent [おやのななひ˥かり]; 日光 sunlight [に˥っこう]; 月光 moonlight [げっこう]; 光沢のある glossy, sheeny [こうたくのあ˥る]; 脚光を浴びる to step into the limelight [きゃっこうをあびる]

	Meanings	*Kun* and *On*	Romaji	Bushu	Stroke Order and Number
SG-0443 先	to precede; ahead, past, previous	さき セン	saki *sen*	儿	ノ 𠂉 牛 生 先 6

先 **A** F-0101

甲骨文 1 金文 2 説文 3

1, 2, and 3 comprised "a footprint" on top of "a person." Like the kanji 光, what was above the person signified what they were doing. In this case, "a footprint" signified walking. When one was walking,

先にやる do first [さきにやる]; 先程 a while ago [さきほど]; 先生 teacher, form of address for a doctor, lawyer, or politician

	one's foot always went before the body, and thus was "ahead." What went ahead became "past, previous." In the kanji 先, a short, slanted stroke was added for emphasis. The kanji 先 means "to precede; ahead; past, previous." <⺧儿> (Note: A short slanted stroke added to the top left for emphasis is seen in several kanji, including 制 **SG-0619**, 朱 **SG-0622**, 生 **SG-0689**, 牛 **SG-0816**, and 矢 **SG-1524**.)	[せんせつい];先人 predecessor, pioneer [せんじん]; 先方 the other party [せんぽう]; 先日 some days ago [せんじつ]; 先頭 the forefront, the lead [せんとう] // 先ず first of all [まつず]

	Meanings	*Kun* and *On*	Romaji	Bushu	Stroke Order and Number
SG-0444 元	head, origin, source; former	もと ゲン・ガン	moto *gen, gan*	儿	4

元 **A** F-0175

甲骨文1 1 甲骨文2 2 金文1 3 金文2 4 説文 5

1, 2, 3, 4, and 5 all depicted a standing person with an enlarged head, a shoulder line, a hand, and a torso, with the leg bent. The head is where one's thoughts and ideas originate, and thus the character meant "source, origin." The kanji 元 means "head, origin, source; former." <元(二儿)>

根元 the part near the root, base [ねもとつ]; 元社長 former company president [もつとしゃちょう]; 手元 one's grip, close to oneself [てもとつ]; 親元 (親許) one's parental roof [おやもと]; 元気 spirited, peppy, in good health [げつんき]; 元首 head of a country [げつんしゅ]; 元旦 the first day of a year [がんたん]; 元来 originally [がつんらい]

	Meanings	*Kun* and *On*	Romaji	Bushu	Stroke Order and Number
SG-0445 完	complete, perfect	カン	*kan*	宀	7

完 **A** F-0465

説文

The seal-style form comprised "a house" (宀) whose walls reached the ground completely, and 元 **SG-0444** "a person with the head emphasized." The walls of a house completely surrounding a person gave the meaning "complete." The kanji 完 means "complete, perfect." <宀元>

完全 perfect, complete [かんぜん]; 完了 completely finished [かんりょう]; 完備する to furnish fully [かつんびする]; 完結する to conclude, terminate [かんけつする]; 未完の incomplete, unfinished [みかんの]; 不完全な imperfect, defective [ふかつんぜんな]; 完売 sold out [かんばい]

	Meanings	*Kun* and *On*	Romaji	Bushu	Stroke Order and Number
SG-0446 院	institution, large public building	イン	*In*	阜	10

院 **A** F-0289

説文

The seal-style form comprised "a high dirt wall" (阝, bushu *kozatohen*), and 完 **SG-0445** "a house with a person inside" for the sound *kan*, which later became *in*. Together they signified "a house surrounded by a high wall." The kanji 院 means "a large public building, institution." <阝完>

病院 hospital [びょういん]; 入院する to become hospitalized [にゅういんする]; 医院 physician's private practice office [いついん]; 上院 the Upper House, the Senate [じょういん]; 下院 the Lower House, the House of Representatives [かいん]; 大学院 graduate school [だいがくついん]

	Meanings	*Kun* and *On*	Romaji	Bushu	Stroke Order and Number
SG-0447 児	young child	ジ・ニ	*ji, ni*	儿	7

児 **B** F-0611

甲骨文 1 金文 2 説文 3 旧字 4

1, 2, and 3 all showed a semi-circle of broken lines at the top, which has been explained as "a baby's fontanel that had yet to close." The character signified "a young child." Another view explains that it showed "two tufts of a young girl's hair on either side of her head," also signifying "a young child." In the shinji, 臼 at the top became 旧. The kanji 児 means "a young child." <旧儿>

児童 elementary school pupil [じつどう]; 乳児 infant [にゅつうじ]; 乳幼児 baby, infant [にゅうようつじ]; 問題児 problem child [もんだついじ]; 私生児 illegitimate child [しせついじ]; 異端児 nonconformist [いたつんじ]; 小児科医 pediatrician [しょうにかつい]

	Meanings	*Kun* and *On*	Romaji	Bushu	Stroke Order and Number
SG-0448 洗	to wash, cleanse	あら-う セン	ara-u *sen*	水	9

洗 **B** F-0893

説文

In the seal-style form, "flowing water" (氵) was added to 先 **SG-0443**, used for the sound *sen* and originally depicting "a footprint" and "a person." Travel made one's feet dirty, and washing the feet meant "to wash, cleanse." The kanji 洗 means "to wash, cleanse." <氵先>

洗う to wash [あらう]; (お)手洗い washroom, toilet, bathroom [てあつらい, おてあつらい]; 洗いたて freshly washed [あらいたて]; すすぎ洗い rinsing [すすぎあつらい]; 水洗便所 flush toilet [すいせんべつんじょ]; 洗車 car washing [せんしゃ]; 洗礼 baptism [せんれい]; 洗面所 lavatory, toilet, washroom [せんめんじょ]

SG-0449 冠	Meanings	Kun and On	Romaji	Bushu	Stroke Order and Number
	crown; to put on one's head	かんむり カン	kanmuri *kan*	冖	冖 冠 冠 冠 冠 9

冠 **C** F-1440

説文

The seal-style form comprised 冂 "a cover or a house," 元 **SG-0444** "a person with the head emphasized," and 寸 **SG-0112** "a hand" positioned behind the person. Together they meant "a person receiving a headdress from behind during a ceremony," and thus "crown." The kanji 冠 means "crown; to put on one's head." <冖元寸>

冠 crown [かんむり]; 戴冠式 coronation ceremony [たいかんしき]

SG-0450 玩	Meanings	Kun and On	Romaji	Bushu	Stroke Order and Number
	to take pleasure in, fiddle, toy with	ガン	*gan*	玉	丁 Ŧ 玗 玩 玩 8

玩 **D** F-2065

説文古文 1　説文 2

Next to "a person" (元 **SG-0444**), used for the sound *gan*, was "a cowrie, something precious" (貝 **SG-1693**) in 1, and "a jewel, gem" (王 **SG-1447**) in 2. Together they meant "a person enjoying handling a precious item such as a cowrie or jewel," and further meant "to take pleasure in." The kanji 玩 means "to take pleasure in, fiddle, toy with." <王元>

玩具 toy [がんぐ]; 愛玩動物 pet animal [あいがんどうぶつ]

19d 兄 "an elder male person (praying)" 兄祝競況呪

SG-0451 兄	Meanings	Kun and On	Romaji	Bushu	Stroke Order and Number
	elder male person, elder brother	あに ケイ・キョウ	ani *kee, kyoo*	儿	口 口 兄 兄 5

兄 **B** F-0642

甲骨文 1 1　甲骨文 2 2　金文 3　説文 4

1, 2, 3, and 4 depicted a person with a large head, signifying the eldest of male siblings. Another view explains that the top component was "a prayer box," and the character depicted "a person engaged in prayer." In 2, the person was kneeling, while in 3, he was performing a votive dance with adornments on his sleeves. A person who carried out a religious rite was an eldest sibling or an elder in the family, and thus the character meant "elder brother, elder male person." The kanji 兄 means "elder male person, elder brother." <口儿>

兄 older brother [あに]; 兄貴 (my) older brother (in male speech) [あにき]; 兄嫁 older brother's wife [あによめ]; 諸兄 you gentlemen [しょけい]; 長兄 oldest brother [ちょうけい]; 兄弟 brother(s) [きょうだい] // お兄さん older brother [おにいさん]

SG-0452 祝	Meanings	Kun and On	Romaji	Bushu	Stroke Order and Number
	to celebrate; blessing	いわ-う シュク・シュウ	iwa-u *shuku, shuu*	示	ラ ネ 祀 祀 祝 9

祝 **B** F-0960

甲骨文 1　金文 2　説文 3　旧字 4

1, 2, and 3 comprised "an altar table with offerings on it" (示 **SG-1737**), and "elder brother, elder person" (兄), together signifying "an elder person worshipping and celebrating the ancestral deity at an altar" in order to receive a "blessing." The kanji 祝 means "to celebrate; blessing." <ネ兄>

祝う to celebrate [いわう]; お祝い返し return gift for a wedding or other celebratory event [おいわいがえし]; 祝い酒 celebration drink [いわいざけ]; 祝賀会 celebratory party [しゅくがかい]; 祝辞 congratulatory address [しゅくじ]; 祝言 marriage ceremony [しゅうげん]; 祝儀 gratuity paid on a celebratory occasion [しゅうぎ] // 祝詞 Shinto prayer [のりと]

SG-0453 競	Meanings	Kun and On	Romaji	Bushu	Stroke Order and Number
	to compete, make a bid	きそ-う・せ-る キョウ・ケイ	kiso-u, se-ru *kyoo, kee*	立	立 音 竟 竸 競 競 20

競 **B** F-0862

甲骨文 1　金文1 2　金文2 3　説文 4

1 depicted two people topped with heads or mouths, standing side by side with a single line above them. In 2, 3, and 4, both sides had become a tattooing needle with a mouth (signifying 言 "to say") on top of a person (儿). Explanations vary: (a) two people ardently saying prayers, giving the appearance that they were "competing"; (b) two noblemen wearing special headdresses, participating in an ancient ritual; or (c) two people arguing. In the kanji 競, the top components became two 音 (for 言), and the bottom became two 儿, "persons." The kanji 競 means "to compete, make a bid." <音儿音儿>

競う to compete, strive with a rival [きそう]; 競り auction [せり]; 競争 competition [きょうそう]; 競売 public uction [きょうばい]; 競技 game, sporting event [きょうぎ]; 競馬 horse race [けいば]

	Meanings	Kun and On	Romaji	Bushu	Stroke Order and Number
SG-0454 況	increasingly, still more; situation	キョウ	*kyoo*	水	氵沪沪況 8

況 **B** F-0878

甲骨文 1 説文 2

The origin of this character is unclear. 1 and 2 may have depicted a person watching a thing changing state, which was represented by "flowing water" (氵), thus giving the meaning "situation." 兄 contributed the sound *kyoo*. Some hold the view that this character is a borrowing. The kanji 況 means "increasingly, still more; situation." <氵兄>

状況 state of affairs, circumstance [じょうきょう]; 現況 the present state [げんきょう]; 不況 depression, slump, weak market [ふきょう]; 盛況 prosperity, boom [せいきょう]; 実況放送 live broadcast [じっきょうほうそう]; 活況 liveliness, sparkle, gusto [かっきょう] // 況んや still more, let alone [いわんや]

	Meanings	Kun and On	Romaji	Bushu	Stroke Order and Number
SG-0455 呪	to put a curse on; spell	のろ-う ジュ	noro-u *ju*	口	口叩呪呪 8

呪 **D** F-1922

No ancient form. The kanji 呪 comprises 口 **SG-0031** "mouth, speaking," and 兄 **SG-0451** "an elder male person," who was conducting a rite. Together they signified praying for a calamity to befall someone—that is, "a curse"—in contrast to the kanji 祝 **SG-0452**, "celebration of deity to receive a blessing." Another view holds that the character signified chanting to avoid misfortune. The kanji 呪 means "to put a curse on; spell." <口兄>

呪う to curse, put someone under a spell [のろう]; 呪文を唱える to cast a spell, chant [じゅもんをとなえる]; 呪術 incantation, enchantment [じゅじゅつ]; 呪縛 a spell [じゅばく]

19e 兑 (兌) "to let go of" [from ハ "to release" and 兄 "a senior male person"] 説税脱悦

	Meanings	Kun and On	Romaji	Bushu	Stroke Order and Number
SG-0456 説	to explain, preach, persuade; view, theory	と-く セツ・ゼイ	to-ku *setsu, zee*	言	言訁訁訁説説 14

説 **A** F-0280

説文 1 旧字 2

1 and 2 comprised 言 "word, language; to speak," and 兌, used for the sounds *zee/setsu* to mean "to release, let go of," together signifying "a matter being elucidated in words." 兌 in the kyuji (2) changed to 兑 in the shinji. The kanji 説 means "to explain, preach, persuade; view, theory." <言兑>

説く to explain, preach [とく]; 口説く to persuade, seduce [くどく]; 説明 explanation [せつめい]; 解説 commentary [かいせつ]; 説教する to preach [せっきょうする, せっきょうする]; 説得する to persuade, prevail on [せっとくする]; 学説 theory, doctrine [がくせつ]; 逆説 paradox [ぎゃくせつ]; 遊説 canvassing [ゆうぜい]

	Meanings	Kun and On	Romaji	Bushu	Stroke Order and Number
SG-0457 税	tax, levy	ゼイ	*zee*	禾	二千禾禾税税 12

税 **A** F-0317

説文 1 旧字 2

1 and 2 comprised 禾 "rice crops, harvest," and 兌/兑, used for the sound *zee* to mean "to let go of; get released." Part of a harvested crop was taken away as "a levy." The kanji 税 means "tax, levy." <禾兑>

税金 tax [ぜいきん]; 所得税 income tax [しょとくぜい]; 納税 payment of tax [のうぜい]; 関税 tariff [かんぜい]; 税務署 taxation office [ぜいむしょ]; 税率 rate of taxation [ぜいりつ]; 消費税 consumption tax, sales tax [しょうひぜい]

	Meanings	Kun and On	Romaji	Bushu	Stroke Order and Number
SG-0458 脱	to take off, slip off, free oneself from	ぬ-ぐ ダツ	nu-gu *datsu*	肉	月月'月'脱 11

脱 **B** F-0829

説文

The seal-style form comprised 月, bushu *nikuzuki* "flesh, part of the body," and 兌/兑, used for the sound *datsu* to mean "to let go of; something getting released." Something leaving the body meant "to take off, rid." The kanji 脱 means "to take off, slip off, free oneself from." <月兑>

脱ぐ to take off clothes [ぬぐ]; 脱げる clothes slip off [ぬげる]; 脱する to escape from, free oneself from [だっする]; 脱力感 feeling lethargic [だつりょくかん]; 脱出する to escape [だっしゅつする]; 脱税 tax evasion [だつぜい]; 脱皮 molting [だっぴ]

	Meanings	Kun and On	Romaji	Bushu	Stroke Order and Number
SG-0459 悦	to be delighted; happy	エツ	*etsu*	心	八忄'忄'悦 10

悦 **D** F-1739

No ancient form exists. The kanji 悦 comprised 忄, bushu *risshinben* "a heart," and 兌/兑, used for the sound *etsu* to mean "something getting released." When lingering feelings and worries are let go of, one feels happy. The kanji 悦 means "to be delighted; happy." <忄兑>

満悦 great delight [まんえつ]; 悦に入る to chuckle to oneself [えつにいる]

19f 見 "to see" [from a person with big eyes] 見現親覚

SG-0460 見	Meanings	Kun and On	Romaji	Bushu	Stroke Order and Number
	to see, look at, show; visible	みーる ケン	mi-ru *ken*	見	冂目月見 7

見
A
F-0022

甲骨文 1 甲骨文 2 金文 説文
1 2 3 4

1, 2, and 3 depicted "a person standing or kneeling with an enlarged eye to look closely." The character meant "to look (closely), see, gaze at." In 4, the oversized eye became a vertical shape, 目. The kanji 見 means "to see, look at, show; visible." <目儿>

見る to see, look at [みる]; 見える to be visible [みえる]; 見せる to show [みせる]; 見方 how one looks at something [みかた、みかた]; 見所 a point worthy of note, sign of promise [みどころ]; 見合い marriage prospect meeting [みあい]; 見た目 appearance [みため]; 見す見す before one's very eyes [みすみす]; 一見して casting a glance at [いっけんして]; 見地 standpoint, angle [けんち]; 会見 interview [かいけん]

SG-0461 現	Meanings	Kun and On	Romaji	Bushu	Stroke Order and Number
	to appear; visible, present	あらわ-れる ゲン	arawa-reru *gen*	玉	丁王王l 王l冂 珇現 11

現
A
F-0125

鄧石如

No ancient form. The kanji 現 comprised 王 **SG-1730** "jewels strung together," and 見, used for the sound *gen* to mean "to see." Grinding and polishing a precious stone would reveal a shine that was not visible before, and thus the character signified "to become visible." What is seen is "present." The kanji 現 means "to appear; visible, present." <王見>

現れる to become visible, appear [あらわれる]; 現金 cash [げんきん]; 現在 presently, now [げんざい]; 実現する to become realized, materialize [じつげんする]; 現実 actuality, a hard fact [げんじつ]; 現存する to be in existence [げんそんする]; 現地 the actual locale, the spot [げんち]; 現場 the actual spot, the scene of, job site [げんば]

SG-0462 親	Meanings	Kun and On	Romaji	Bushu	Stroke Order and Number
	parent; intimate, close	おや・したーしい シン	oya, shita-shii *shin*	見	立辛亲親親 16

親
A
F-0255

金文 1 金文 2 詛楚文 説文
1 2 3 4

1 and 2 comprised "a sharp tattooing needle with an ink reservoir," and "a person with an enlarged eye." In 2, they are inside a house. Together they signified "a person inside a house looking closely like a sharp needle (辛 **SG-1359**)." 3 and 4 comprised 亲, from 辛 and 木, used for the sound *shin,* and 見 "a person watching." Proximity (signified by the sharpness of a needle) while looking at a tree being cut gave the meaning "intimate." Someone who keeps a close eye is a parent. The kanji 親 means "parent; intimate, close." <亲(立木)見>

(Note: The kanji 親 shares the same component 亲 and the phonetic feature *shin* with 新 **SG-1455** and 薪 **SG-1466**.)

親 parent [おや]; 親子 parent and child [おやこ]; 里親 foster parent [さとおや]; 親知らず wisdom tooth [おやしらず]; 親しい familiar, close, intimate [したしい]; 両親 parents [りょうしん]; 親近感 feeling of intimacy, familiarity [しんきんかん]; 近親者 close relative [きんしんしゃ]

SG-0463 覚	Meanings	Kun and On	Romaji	Bushu	Stroke Order and Number
	to become aware, remember, memorize; awareness	おぼーえる・さーめる カク	obo-eru, sa-meru *kaku*	見	丶丷⺍𭕄覚 12

覚
B
F-0728

説文 旧字
1 2

The top (𦥯) of 1 comprised "two caring hands (𦥑)," "two crosses" for "mingling" (爻), and "a house" (冖), which was the origin of the kanji 学 **SG-0511** "to study" and also was used for the sound *kaku*, meaning "to be awake." Together with 見 **SG-0460** "to look," these components signified "to become aware; consciousness, awareness." In Japanese, another meaning, "to remember, memorize," was added. In the shinji 覚, the top was replaced by ⺍. The kanji 覚 means "to become aware, remember, memorize; awareness." <⺍見>

覚える to memorize [おぼえる]; 覚えている to remember, recall [おぼえている]; 覚書 memorandum [おぼえがき]; 目が覚める to awake [めがさめる]; 目覚まし時計 alarm clock [めざましどけい]; 自覚する to be conscious of [じかくする]; 感覚 the senses, feeling, sensation [かんかく]

19g 夋 *san/shun/sa* 酸俊唆

	Meanings	Kun and On	Romaji	Bushu	Stroke Order and Number
SG-0464 酸	acidic, sour	す-い サン	su-i *san*	酉	14

酸 **B** F-1040 — 説文 — The seal-style form of the kanji 酸 comprised 酉 "a wine cask," and 夋, used for the sound *san* (from *shun*) to mean "sour." When wine goes bad, it becomes sour. The kanji 酸 means "acidic, sour." <酉夋>

酸っぱい sour [すっぱꜜい]; 甘酸っぱい sweet and sour [あまずっぱꜜい]; 酸素 oxygen [さꜜんそ]; 酸性 acidity [さんせい]; 塩酸 hydrochloric acid [えんさん]; 酸化する to oxidize [さんかする]; 炭酸飲料水 carbonated drink [たんさんいんりょꜜうすい]; 乳酸菌 lactic acid bacteria [にゅうさんきん]

	Meanings	Kun and On	Romaji	Bushu	Stroke Order and Number
SG-0465 俊	excellence, brilliance	シュン	*shun*	人	9

俊 **C** F-1160 — 説文 — The seal-style form of the kanji 俊 comprised 亻 "an act that a person does," and 夋, used for the sound *shun* to mean "something grand." Together they signified a person who has the quality of excellence or brilliance. The kanji 俊 means "excellence, brilliance." <亻夋>

俊敏な agile, alert [しゅんびんな]

	Meanings	Kun and On	Romaji	Bushu	Stroke Order and Number
SG-0466 唆	to incite, allure, entice	そそのか-す サ	sosonoka-su *sa*	口	10

唆 **D** F-2050 — No ancient form. The kanji 唆 comprised 口 "mouth," and 夋, used for the sound *sa*. The kanji 唆 means "to incite, allure, entice." <口夋>

唆す to tempt, allure, seduce, instigate [そそのかꜜす]; 示唆 suggestion [しꜜさ]; 教唆 instigation [きょꜜうさ]

19h 尸 "a slumped person, dead body, buttock, roof"; **bushu *shikabane***
局展居届殿尻泥尿据尼・久

	Meanings	Kun and On	Romaji	Bushu	Stroke Order and Number
SG-0467 局	circumstance, phase, section, government agency	キョク	*kyoku*	尸	7

局 **A** F-0281 — 説文 — Views regarding the seal-style form vary: (a) a body bent for burial with a prayer box"; (b) folding one's body into a small shape, signifying "a small section, limit"; and (c) two intersecting hooks forming "a section." A section is to a larger thing as a circumstance or phase is to a larger matter. The government had divisions and sections, which led to the meaning "government agency." The kanji 局 means "circumstance, phase, section, government agency." <尸コ口>

破局 collapse, catastrophe [はきょく]; 医局 doctor's office in a hospital [いきょく]; 郵便局員 post office clerk [ゆうびんきょꜜくいん]; 当局 the authorities [とꜜうきょく]; 局地的な localized, isolated [きょくちてきな]; 時局 state of affairs [じきょく]; 大局的 broad perspective [たいきょくてき]

	Meanings	Kun and On	Romaji	Bushu	Stroke Order and Number
SG-0468 展	to extend, display	テン	*ten*	尸	10

展 **B** F-0606 — 説文 — The seal-style form comprised 尸, bushu *shikabane* "a person sitting on something, applying his weight"; "layers of bricks," used for the sound *ten* to mean both "to extend," and "a weight"; and "clothing." Clothes that were spread or pressed flat gave the meaning "to extend, display." The kanji 展 means "to extend, display." <尸㠭>

展開する to unfold, spread [てんかいする]; 展覧会 exhibition [てんらꜜんかい]; 個展 one-artist exhibition [こてん]; 親展 confidential (letter), "for your eyes only" [しんてん]; 発展 development, spread [はってん]; 展望台 observatory, a spot with a panoramic view [てんぼうだい]

	Meanings	Kun and On	Romaji	Bushu	Stroke Order and Number
SG-0469 居	to be, exist, stay in place	い-る キョ	i-ru *kyo*	尸	8

居 **B** F-0708 — 金文 1, 金文 2, 説文 3 — 1 and 2 comprised 尸 "a person sitting with his two hands thrust out," and 古 **SG-0559**, used for the sounds *ko* and *kyo* to mean "to fix in place." Together they signified "a person staying in one place." The kanji 居 means "to be, exist, stay in place." <尸古>

居る to exist [いる]; 居直る to become high-handed, sit upright [いなおꜜる]; 居心地のいい comfortable to live in [いごこちのいꜜい]; 長居する to stay for a long time [ながꜜいする]; 住居 housing [じゅꜜうきょ]; 居住地 one's dwelling place [きょじゅꜜうち]; 新居 new residence [しꜜんきょ]; // 一言居士 ready critic [いちげんこꜜじ]

	Meanings	Kun and On	Romaji	Bushu	Stroke Order and Number
SG-0470 届	to reach, register, be delivered	とど-く	todo-ku	尸	8

届 **B** F-0898

説文 1 旧字 2

1 comprised 尸 "a person in a slumped position, a body," and "dirt" (土) in "a hole" (凵), originally signifying "burying a body or other thing deep in the ground." The kyuji (2) also had "dirt" inside the hole, but in the shinji 届, it was replaced by 由. In Japanese, the kanji 届 is used to mean "to reach, deliver, register." The kanji 届 means "to reach, register, be delivered." <尸由>

届く to reach, arrive at, be delivered [とどく]; 届ける to deliver, register [とどける]; 届け物 home delivery, gift [とどけもの]; 見届ける to ascertain, verify [みとどける]; 届出 notification [とどけで]

	Meanings	Kun and On	Romaji	Bushu	Stroke Order and Number
SG-0471 殿	palace, lord, form of address in a letter	との・どの デン・テン	tono, dono *den, ten*	殳	13

殿 **C** F-1201

説文

The seal-style form comprised "a person sitting" (尸) on "a chair" (共), to mean "buttock," and "a hand holding a weapon or stick" (殳), for the meaning "to strike." Together they originally signified a hand slapping someone on the buttock, and thus "buttocks." However, this character took on the meaning "an impressive structure that spreads wide," such as a palace, and also became a form of addressing royalty who lived in such a palace. The kanji 殿 means "palace, lord, form of address in a formal or official letter." <尸共殳>

(Note: The original meaning of "buttock" became the non-Joyo kanji 臀, that is, 殿 with 月, bushu *nikuzuki* "part of a body," underneath.)

殿 form of address for one's feudal lord, My Lord [との]; 鈴木一郎殿 to: Mr. Ichiro Suzuki (in correspondence) [すずきいちろうどの]; 本殿 main palace [ほんでん]; 宮殿 palace [きゅうでん]; 殿下 His/Her/Your Highness [でんか]

	Meanings	Kun and On	Romaji	Bushu	Stroke Order and Number
SG-0472 尻	buttocks, bottom, the rear, the last	しり	shiri	尸	5

尻 **C** F-1232

説文

The origin of the kanji 尻 is not clear. The seal-style form comprised 尸 (bushu *shikabane* "a man sitting"), and 九 **SG-2133**, used for the sound *koo*, together signifying "buttock." The kanji 尻 means "buttocks, bottom, the rear, the last." <尸九>

尻 the buttocks, the back [しり]; 尻込みする to flinch from, shy away [しりごみする, しりごみする]; 尻切れとんぼ half-done [しりきれとんぼ]; 帳尻を合わせる to balance a budget [ちょうじりをあわせる]; 尻拭いをする to clean up someone's mess [しりぬぐいをする]; 目尻 corner of the eye [めじり] // 尻尾 tail, tail end [しっぽ]

	Meanings	Kun and On	Romaji	Bushu	Stroke Order and Number
SG-0473 泥	mud; to be particular, adhere to	どろ デイ	doro *dee*	水	8

泥 **C** F-1455

説文

The seal-style form comprised "water flowing" (氵), and 尼 **SG-0476**, used for the sound *dee*. Originally taken from the name of a muddy river, it meant "mud." Mud sticks to a thing or the hand, and thus it also meant "to adhere to, be obsessive about." The kanji 泥 means "mud; to be particular, adhere to." <氵尸匕>

泥 dirt, mud [どろ]; 泥縄 measure taken in haste [どろなわ]; 泥仕合 mud-slinging [どろじあい]; 泥棒 thief [どろぼう]; こそ泥 sneaky thief [こそどろ]; 拘泥する to worry too much about, be a stickler for [こうでいする]

	Meanings	Kun and On	Romaji	Bushu	Stroke Order and Number
SG-0474 尿	urine	ニョウ	*nyoo*	尸	7

尿 **C** F-1635

甲骨文 1 甲骨文 2 篆文 3

1 and 2 showed "a standing person urinating," and meant "to urinate; urine." 3 had water underneath an animal tail, signifying an animal urinating. The kanji 尿 means "urine." <尸水>

尿 urine [にょう]; 排尿する to pass water, urinate [はいにょうする]; 糞尿 human excrement [ふんにょう]; 尿意 desire to urinate [にょうい]; 夜尿症 bed-wetting [やにょうしょう]

	Meanings	Kun and On	Romaji	Bushu	Stroke Order and Number
SG-0475 据	to place, install	す-える	su-eru	手	11

据 **C** F-1646

説文

The seal-style form comprised 扌, bushu *tehen* "an act done by hand," and 居 **SG-0469**, used for the sound *kyo* to mean "to stay." In Japanese, this character is used to mean "placing something at a fixed location." The kanji 据 means "to place, install." <扌居>

据える to place, fix [すえる]; 上げ膳据え膳 no need to do anything [あげぜん・すえぜん]; 据付ける to fasten, install [すえつける]; 据え置き leaving unchanged [すえおき]

SG-0476 尼	Meanings	Kun and On	Romaji	Bushu	Stroke Order and Number
	nun	あま ニ	ama *ni*	尸	⺂コ尸尼 5

尼 **D** F-1773

説文

The seal-style form comprised "a slumped person" (尸, bushu *shikabane*), and "another person (匕) with their back leaning against the slumped person," originally signifying people who were close to each other. Later, for the sound *ji/ni*, it came to mean "nun." The kanji 尼 means "nun." <尸匕>

尼 nun [あ↓ま]; 尼さん nun [あまさん]; 尼僧 sister, priestess [にそう, に↓そう]; 尼寺 nunnery [あま↓でら]

久 "long time"

SG-0477 久	Meanings	Kun and On	Romaji	Bushu	Stroke Order and Number
	long time; lasting	ひさ-しい キュウ・ク	hisa-shii *kyuu, ku*	丿	ノク久 3

久 **A** F-0438

説文

The seal-style form depicted "the body of a deceased person propped up by a long stick." Another view explains that it depicted a person who was being pulled from behind so that they would stay longer. The kanji 久 means "long time; lasting." <久(ク㇏)>

久しい long, continued [ひさし↓い]; 久しぶり・久方ぶり after a long interval or absence [ひさしぶり．ひさかたぶり]; 永久 eternal [えいきゅう]; 半永久的 semi-permanent [は↓ん・えいきゅうてき]; 久遠 eternity [くおん]

20 Use of legs

20a 交 "to cross" [from a person with their legs crossed]; *koo* 交校効郊絞

SG-0478 交	Meanings	Kun and On	Romaji	Bushu	Stroke Order and Number
	to cross, intersect, intermingle, exchange	まじ-わる・か-わす コウ	maji-waru, ka-wasu *koo*	亠	亠六六亣交 6

交 **A** F-0153

甲骨文 1　金文1 2　金文2 3　説文 4

1, 2, 3, and 4 depicted "a person with their legs crossed," and meant "to cross, mix." In the kanji, it took the form of a cross, below 六 to represent the upper body with arms. The kanji 交 means "to cross, intersect, intermingle, exchange." <亠父>

交わる to intersect, keep company with [まじわ↓る]; (言葉)を交わす to exchange (words) [(ことば↓を)かわす]; 交通 traffic [こうつう]; 交換する to exchange [こうかんする]; 交互に alternately [こ↓うごに]; 交代する to take turns [こうたいする]; 交流する to interchange, mingle [こうりゅうする]

SG-0479 校	Meanings	Kun and On	Romaji	Bushu	Stroke Order and Number
	to check; school, military officer, cross shape	コウ	*koo*	木	木朩朩朩校校 10

校 **A** F-0399

説文

The seal-style form comprised 木 **SG-0608** "tree, wood," and 交 **SG-0478** "to cross, mix," used for the sound *koo*, together signifying "a pair of wooden shackles on a prisoner's ankles." "Crossing" gave the meaning "to check, compare." A school was where knowledge was exchanged between a teacher and students, and 校 also meant "school." Piling logs in an interlocking manner made a crossed-log wall or fence in a military installation, and thus it also meant "military officer." The kanji 校 means "to check; school, military officer, cross shape." <木交>

学校 school [がっこう]; 校舎 school building [こ↓うしゃ]; 校正 proofreading [こうせい]; 将校 commissioned officer [しょ↓うこう]; 登校する to attend school [とうこうする]; 転校生 transfer student [てんこ↓うせい] // 校倉造り crossed-log structure [あぜくらづ↓くり]

SG-0480 効	Meanings	Kun and On	Romaji	Bushu	Stroke Order and Number
	to have effect; effect; valid	き-く コウ	ki-ku *koo*	力	亠六亣交効効 8

効 **B** F-0656

甲骨文1 1　甲骨文2 2　金文 3　篆文 4　旧字 5

The kanji 効 went through many changes throughout its history. 1, 2, and 3 comprised "an arrow" and "a hand holding a stick" (攴), together originally signifying "to straighten an arrow." In 4, "arrow" was misconstrued as "a person with their legs crossed" (交 **SG-0478**) for the sound *koo*, and it became the kyuji 效 (5). In the shinji 効, 攵 (from 攴) was further replaced by 力 **SG-1949** "power." The kanji 効 means "to have effect; effect; valid." <交力>

効く to be effective, act [きく]; 効き目 efficacy, effect [ききめ]; 効力 effect, healing potency [こ↓うりょく]; 効果 effect, effectiveness, result [こ↓うか]; 効能書き written statement of the effects of a drug [こうのうがき]; 発効 coming into effect [はっこう]; 有効 valid, good [ゆうこう]; 時効 statute of limitations, expiry of a right [じこう]

SG-0481 郊	Meanings	Kun and On	Romaji	Bushu	Stroke Order and Number
	suburbs	コウ	*koo*	邑	亠六交交交郊郊 9

郊 **C** F-1342 説文

The seal-style form comprised 交 **SG-0478**, used for the sound *koo* to mean "to mix, intermingle," and 邑 "a town," from "an area where many people were located" (阝, bushu *oozato*). Together they meant an area adjacent to a town—"the suburbs." The kanji 郊 means "suburbs." <交 阝>

郊外 suburbs [こうがい]; 近郊 outskirts, area close to town [きんこう]

SG-0482 絞	Meanings	Kun and On	Romaji	Bushu	Stroke Order and Number
	to wring, squeeze, press out	しぼ-る・し-める コウ	shibo-ru, shi-meru *koo*	糸	幺糸紵紵紵絞 12

絞 **C** F-1450 説文

The seal-style form comprised 糸 **SG-1600** "skein of threads," and 交 **SG-0478** "to intersect, mix" for the sound *koo*. Together they signified "to strangle, wring." In Japanese, the kanji 絞 means "to wring, squeeze, press out." <糸交>

絞る to wring, squeeze [しぼる]; 絞り染 tie-dying [しぼりぞめ]; 絞り出す to force out, squeeze out [しぼりだす]; 絞める to choke, strangle [しめる]; 絞首刑 execution by hanging [こうしゅけい]; 絞殺 strangulation [こうさつ]

20b 走 "to run, walk in a hurry" [from a person with a long stride and moving arms]; bushu *soonyoo* 走起超越徒趣赴奔

SG-0483 走	Meanings	Kun and On	Romaji	Bushu	Stroke Order and Number
	to run, walk hurriedly	はし-る ソウ	hashi-ru *soo*	走	一十土キ卡走 7

走 **A** F-0376 金文1 1 金文2 2 説文 3

1 and 2 comprised "a person with a long stride and, arms up and down" and "a footprint," emphasizing the use of the feet. Together these components signified "to run, walk fast." In 3, the footprint (止) became extended (疋), and the running person (大) changed to 土. The kanji 走 means "to run, walk hurriedly." <土 疋>

走って来る to run up to [はしってくる]; 走り書き hasty writing, scribble [はしりがき]; 小走りに scurrying [こばしりに]; 一っ走りする to go for a run [ひとっぱしりする]; 先走りする to proceed rashly, act on impulse [さきばしりする]; 脱走する to escape, run away, desert [だっそうする]; 百メートル走 the 100-meter dash [ひゃくメートルそう]

SG-0484 起	Meanings	Kun and On	Romaji	Bushu	Stroke Order and Number
	to get up, arise, happen, occur	お-きる キ	o-kiru *ki*	走	土キ走起起起 10

起 **A** F-0256 説文古文 1 説文 2

1 comprised "a crossroads," 巳 "a serpent" (used for the sound *ki*), and "a footprint." A quick move like a serpent straightening itself signified "to get up, arise." 2 comprised "a person running" (走) and "a half-coiled serpent." In the shinji 起, 巳 became 己, and 走, whose last stroke elongated to the right, became bushu *soonyoo*. The kanji 起 means "to get up, arise, happen, occur." <走 己>. (Note: 巳 as a component in kyuji all changed to 己 in shinji.)

起きる to get up, occur [おきる]; 起こす to wake a person, raise, start [おこす]; 起き抜けに as soon as one gets up [おきぬけに]; 起立する to rise from one's seat [きりつする]; 起因する to originate from [きいんする]; 起業家 entrepreneur [きぎょうか]; 一念発起 firmly resolve to accomplish [いちねんほっき]

SG-0485 超	Meanings	Kun and On	Romaji	Bushu	Stroke Order and Number
	to exceed, go over	こ-える チョウ	ko-eru *choo*	走	土キ走起超超 12

超 **A** F-0519 説文

The seal-style form comprised 走 "to run, walk fast," and 召 **SG-1405**, used for the sound *choo* to mean "to jump over." The kanji 超 means "to exceed, go over." <走召>

超える to exceed [こえる]; 超過する to exceed [ちょうかする]; 超過料金 excessive charges [ちょうかりょうきん]; 超越する to rise above, transcend [ちょうえつする]; 超然として detachedly, aloofly [ちょうぜんとして]

SG-0486 越	Meanings	Kun and On	Romaji	Bushu	Stroke Order and Number
	to go across, go beyond, cross over, pass through	こ-える エツ	ko *etsu*	走	土キ走走赱赵越越 12

越 **B** F-0753 金文 1 説文 2

1 comprised "a person on the ground," and 戉 ("a broad-edged halberd"), used for the sound *etsu* to mean "to cross over." In 2, the left side became the shape for 走 "walk hurriedly." Together with the sound *etsu*, the character meant "to cross over on foot." The kanji 越 means "to go across, go beyond, cross over, pass through." <走戉>

越える to cross over [こえる]; 引っ越す to move [ひっこす]; 繰り越し transfer, carryover [くりこし]; 年越しそば buckwheat noodles eaten on New Year's Eve (for continued long life) [としこしそば]; 越冬 wintering [えっとう]

	Meanings	Kun and On	Romaji	Bushu	Stroke Order and Number
SG-0487 徒	follower; on foot, in vain	ト	*to*	彳	彳往徒 10

徒 **B** F-0781

金文1 1 金文2 2 説文 3

Even though the kanji 徒 contains 走, its origin differs from other kanji containing 走. 1 and 2 in the bronzeware form comprised "a crossroads" (彳), "a mound of soil" (土, for the sound *to*), and "a footprint," together signifying "walking on dirt." However, in the seal-style form (3), the footprint appeared under a crossroads, forming 辵 "to move forward," leaving 土 on the right side. An accompanying servant would follow on foot, and the character meant "follower." A foot soldier did not have heavy gear and thus was not very effective, hence which gave the additional meaning "without purpose, in vain." In the kanji 徒, the footprint moved back to the right side. The kanji 徒 means "follower; on foot, in vain." <彳走>

生徒 student [せ1いと]; 信徒 follower, believer [しんと]; 徒労 vain effort, waste of labor [とろう]; 徒歩 walking, going on foot [とほ]; 清教徒 Puritan [せいきょ1うと]; 徒長 spindly growth due to lack of light [とちょう] // 徒らに in vain, for nothing, aimlessly [いたずらに]

	Meanings	Kun and On	Romaji	Bushu	Stroke Order and Number
SG-0488 趣	tendency, taste, preference, scheme	おもむき シュ	omomuki *shu*	走	走赴趄趣趣 15

趣 **C** F-1335

金文 1 説文 2

The left side of 1 and 2 comprised "a person" and "a footprint," forming 走 **SG-0483**. On the right side, "a large ear" with "a hand" signified "to grab" (取 **SG-0056**), used for the sound *shu*. Together they meant "to run to grab something that one wants; preference." A preference could be "a tendency" or "one's hobby." The kanji 趣 means "tendency, taste, preference, scheme." <走取>

趣のある elegant, in cultivated taste [おもむきのあ1る]; 趣味 hobby [しゅ1み]; 趣向 plan, idea, contrivance, design [しゅこう]; 悪趣味な bad taste [あくしゅ1みな]; 少女趣味 girlish taste [しょうじょしゅ1み]

	Meanings	Kun and On	Romaji	Bushu	Stroke Order and Number
SG-0489 赴	to go (promptly) to one's assigned place	おもむ-く フ	omomu-ku *hu*	走	キ走赴赴 9

赴 **D** F-1849

説文

The seal-style form comprised 走 **SG-0483** "to run, walk hurriedly," and 卜, used for the sound *hu* to mean "to hurry, go," signifying "to go promptly." The kanji 赴 means "to go (promptly) to one's assigned place." <走卜>
(Note: The kanji 赴 was closely related to the non-Joyo kanji 訃 **SG-1769** "news of a death.")

赴く to proceed, head for a destination [おもむ1く]; 赴任する to go to start a new post [ふにんする]; 単身赴任 unaccompanied assignment, working away from one's family [たんしんふ1にん]

	Meanings	Kun and On	Romaji	Bushu	Stroke Order and Number
SG-0490 奔	to work busily, bustle	ホン	*hon*	大	夲本奆奔奔 8

奔 **D** F-2083

金文1 1 金文2 2 説文 3

The kanji 奔 shared a closely related origin with 走. 1 comprised "a person running energetically" with "three footsteps" at the bottom, together signifying "to run about quickly, be busily working." In 2, the bottom was miscopied as "three hands," which remained in 3, and was reduced to the shape 廾, bushu *nijuuashi,* in the kanji. The kanji 奔 means "to work busily, bustle." <大十廾>

奔走する to bustle about, busy oneself [ほんそうする]; 自由奔放 unrestrained, uninhibited [じゆ1う・ほんぽう]; 出奔する to vanish, run away [しゅっぽんする]

20c 王 (壬)"straight, to put out" [From a person standing upright on the ground]; *tee*

望程呈

	Meanings	Kun and On	Romaji	Bushu	Stroke Order and Number
SG-0491 望	to hope, look far, wish	のぞ-む ボウ・モウ	nozo-mu *boo, moo*	月	亠亡切望望望 11

望 **A** F-0374

甲骨文1 1 甲骨文2 2 金文1 3 金文2 4 金文3(亡) 5 篆文 6 説文(亡) 7

The kanji 望 had two different lines of history, one including 臣 **SG-0023** and, and another including 亡 **SG-0592.** 1, 2, 3, and 4 depicted a person with a big eye (臣 **SG-0023**)

望む to look in the distance, hope for, wish [のぞむ, のぞ1む]; 望み hope [のぞみ1]; 待ち望む to anticipate, look for [まちのぞ1む]; 望遠レンズ telephoto lens [ぼうえんレ1ンズ];

	standing on a mound of soil or on tiptoe (𡈼) to look into the distance, and meant "to look at the distance." In 3, "a moon" (月 **SG-1077**) was added to represent an object in the distance, and this form was the basis of 6. In 5, however, the big eye was replaced by 亡, used for the sound *boo* to mean "distance." A person looking afar gave the meaning "to wish, want, desire." 5 was reflected in 7, and the "standing person" (𡈼) became 王 in the kanji. The kanji 望 means "to hope, look far, wish." <亡月王>	展望 outlook, prospect [てんぼう]; 望郷の念 home-sickness [ぼうきょうのねん]; 本望 one's long-cherished desire [ほんもう]; 所望する to wish for [しょもうする]

	Meanings	*Kun* and *On*	Romaji	Bushu	Stroke Order and Number
SG-0492 程	degree, extent, bounds, amount	ほど テイ	hodo *tee*	禾	⼆禾和秬程 12

程 **B** F-0626

程 程 (説文)

The seal-style form comprised "rice crops, harvest" (禾), and 呈 **SG-0493**, used for the sound *tee* to mean "to present or submit in a straightforward manner." A rice crop was offered in neat piles, giving the meaning "certain length or size, extent, amount." The kanji 程 means "degree, extent, amount." <禾呈(口王)>

どれ程 how much, how many [どれほど, どれほど]; 程よい good, temperate [ほどよい]; 程々にする to do things in moderation [ほどほどにする]; すればする程 the more you do… [すれば・するほど]; 余程 to a considerable degree, absolutely [よほど]; 程度 degree, extent [ていど]; 日程 the order of the day, itinerary [にってい]

	Meanings	*Kun* and *On*	Romaji	Bushu	Stroke Order and Number
SG-0493 呈	to present, offer, put out	テイ	*tee*	口	⼂口早呈 7

呈 **D** F-1769

呈 呈 (説文)

The seal-style form comprised 口 "prayer box, mouth," and 𡈼 "a person with his shin marked," signifying a person standing straight on the ground" (𡈼,王) and used for the sound *tee.* Together they meant "to present documents in a straightforward manner," or "to present something" in general. The kanji 呈 means "to present, offer, put out." <呈(口王)>

贈呈 presentation, awarding [ぞうてい]; 呈示する to present [ていじする]; 進呈する to give [しんていする]; 進呈本 complimentary copy [しんていぼん]; 謹呈 respectful presentation [きんてい]

21 Person wearing a headdress

21 頁 "head, person" [from a person wearing a formal headdress]; bushu *oogai* 頭顔額領類項須頃傾頑頴煩寡頒頻顎

	Meanings	*Kun* and *On*	Romaji	Bushu	Stroke Order and Number
SG-0494 頭	head, beginning, chief, counter for large animals	あたま・かしら トウ・ズ・ト	atama, kashira *too, zu, to*	頁	豆豆頭頭頭 16

頭 **A** F-0276

頭 頭 (説文)

The seal-style form comprised 豆 **SG-1975**, used for the sound *too* to mean "head," and 頁 "a person wearing a ceremonial headdress," signifying "a head." It was also used as a counter for large animals. The kanji 頭 means "head, beginning, chief, counter for large animals." <豆頁>

頭 head, chief [あたま]; ringleader, master [かしら]; 頭がいい having a good mind, smart [あたまがいい]; 頭ごなしに without giving a chance to explain [あたまごなしに]; 頭でっかち top-heavy, overly theoretical [あたまでっかち]; 頭文字 capital letter, initial [かしらもじ]; 頭角を現す to distinguish oneself, stand out [とうかくをあらわす]; 馬二頭 two horses [うま・にとう]; 頭痛 headache [ずつう]

	Meanings	*Kun* and *On*	Romaji	Bushu	Stroke Order and Number
SG-0495 顔	face	かお ガン	kao *gan*	頁	立产彦彦顔 18

顔 **A** F-0435

顔 顔 顔 顔 顔 (金文 1, 説文籀文 2, 説文 3, 旧字 4)

The left side of 1, 2, and 3 comprised "pretty tattoo or facial painting" (文 **SG-0318**), "a well-defined forehead" (厂), and "pretty; neat pattern" (彡), forming 彦, "a man with a well-defined face," which was used for the sound *gan.* Together with "head" (頁, bushu *oogai)*, they meant "face." The kanji 顔 means "face." <彦頁>

顔 face [かお]; 顔色 facial color [かおいろ]; 顔が利く to have a lot of influence [かおがきく]; 顔を出す to put in an appearance [かおをだす]; 顔合わせ preliminary meeting [かおあわせ]; 洗顔 washing the face [せんがん]; 顔料 pigment [がんりょう]

SG-0496 額	Meanings	Kun and On	Romaji	Bushu	Stroke Order and Number
	forehead, plaque, framed artwork, sum of money	ひたい ガク	hitai *gaku*	頁	宀 穷 客 客頁 額 18

額 **A** F-0469 — 篆文

The seal-style form comprised 各 **SG-0244**, used for the sound *gaku* to mean "a wide area," and 頁 "head," signifying the wide area on the head, which is "the forehead." Something wide that was hung at the top of an entrance or room (over a person's head) was "a framed picture or calligraphy, plaque." The character also meant "an amount of money," from "the face value written on a currency note." With 各 replaced by 客, the kanji 額 means "forehead, plaque, framed artwork, sum of money." <客頁>

額 forehead [ひたい]; 額面 face value, par value [がくめん]; 定額 fixed amount [ていがく]; 半額 half sum, half the price [はんがく]; 巨額 colossal sum [きょがく]; 高額 large sum of money [こうがく]; 少額 small amount of money [しょうがく]; 額縁 picture frame [がくぶち]

SG-0497 領	Meanings	Kun and On	Romaji	Bushu	Stroke Order and Number
	territory, dominion, head	リョウ	*ryoo*	頁	亼 令 令丆 令百 領 14

領 **B** F-0661 — 説文

The seal-style form comprised 令 **SG-0407**, used for the sound *ryoo* to mean "neck," and 頁 "head." The neck and head, which were vital parts of the body, signified someone who controlled things. A land controlled by such a person is "a territory or dominion." The kanji 領 means "territory, dominion, head." <令頁>

領主 the lord of the manor [りょꜜうしゅ]; 領土 territory, domain [りょꜜうど]; 英領 British territory [えいりょう]; 領事館 consulate [りょうじꜜかん]; 占領軍 occupation forces [せんりょꜜうぐん]; 受領 receipt, acceptance [じゅりょう]; 要領 the main point, the gist [ようりょꜜう]; 要領を得ない be off the point, be elusive [ようりょꜜうを・えꜜない]

SG-0498 類	Meanings	Kun and On	Romaji	Bushu	Stroke Order and Number
	kind, sort, variety	たぐ-い ルイ	tagu-i *rui*	頁	丷 米 类 类丆 类百 類 18

類 **B** F-0624 — 説文 1, 旧字 2

1 comprised "scattered rice grains" (米 **SG-0738**), representing grain and food in general; "a dog" (犬 **SG-0859**), representing sacrificial animals; and "a person wearing a formal headdress" (頁). The various offerings that a person in formal attire gave in a rite signified "kind, variety." 犬 in the kyuji became 大 **SG-0314** in the shinji 類. The kanji 類 means "kind, sort, variety." <米大頁>

類い type, sort, analog [たぐい, たぐꜜい]; 類いない unique [たぐいなꜜい]; 衣類 clothing, apparel [いꜜるい]; 人類 humankind, homo sapiens [じꜜんるい]; 書類 document [しょるい]; 分類する to classify, group, sort [ぶんるいする]; 親類 relative, relation [しんるい]; 類推 analogical inference [るいすい]

SG-0499 項	Meanings	Kun and On	Romaji	Bushu	Stroke Order and Number
	item, clause, nape	コウ	*koo*	頁	丅 工 工丆 工百 項 12

項 **B** F-1041 — 説文

The seal-style form comprised "a pole supporting two boards" (工 **SG-1895**), used for the sound *koo*, and 頁 "a head," together signifying "the upright part of a neck, the nape." A nape leads to the head, so the character came to mean "an important matter." It also meant "an individual item." The kanji 項 means "item, clause, nape." <工頁>

項 clause, a paragraph [こꜜう]; 事項 matters, facts, articles, items [じꜜこう]; 項目 item, category, clause [こうもく]; 要項 essential points [ようこう]

SG-0500 須	Meanings	Kun and On	Romaji	Bushu	Stroke Order and Number
	essential	ス	*su*	頁	彡 彡丆 彡百 須 12

須 **C** F-1141 — 金文1 1, 金文2 2, 説文 3

1 depicted "a man's head with a long, hanging beard." 2 also showed "a shallow vessel of water" for the man to groom himself. In 3, the beard became separated as 彡 "pretty, neat." A beard was important to a man's appearance, whence "essential." The kanji 須 means "essential." <彡頁>

必須 essential [ひっす]; 急須 small teapot for green tea [きゅうす]

SG-0501 頃	Meanings	Kun and On	Romaji	Bushu	Stroke Order and Number
	short period of time	ころ	koro	頁	一 匕 匕丆 匕百 頃 11

頃 **C** F-1543 — 説文

The seal-style form comprised 匕 "a person in a kneeling position," and 頁 "a head, an official in a formal attire." One view explains that the person was "tilting their head, bowing." Bowing takes just a moment of time. From that the kanji 頃 means "a short period of time." <匕頁>

その頃 about that time [そのこꜜろ]; この頃 these days, lately [このごろ]; 見頃 best time to see (flowers) [みごろ]; 近頃 these days, of late [ちかꜜごろ]; 年頃 marriageable time [としごろ]; 日頃 usually, at normal times [ひごろ]; 手頃な handy, suitable [てごろな]; 頃合い suitable time, moderateness [ころあい]

	Meanings	Kun and On	Romaji	Bushu	Stroke Order and Number
SG-0502 傾	to tilt, incline, tip, decline	かたむ-く ケイ	katamu-ku *kee*	人	亻亻化価傾傾 13

傾
C
F-1187

説文

傾 The kanji 傾 was created by adding "a person, an act one does" (亻) to the kanji 頃, which originally meant "to tilt one's head," and also was used for the sound *kee*. Tilting is the beginning of "declining." The kanji 傾 means "to tilt, incline, tip, decline." <亻ヒ頁>

傾ける to incline, tilt, devote oneself [かたむけ]る]; 傾斜 inclination, pitch [けいしゃ]; 右傾化 rightward (conservative) shift [うけいか]; 傾向 tendency [けいこう]; 傾倒する to devote oneself to, admire [けいとうする]

	Meanings	Kun and On	Romaji	Bushu	Stroke Order and Number
SG-0503 頑	stubborn, obstinate, stout, robust	ガン	*gan*	頁	二元元´頑頑頑 13

頑
C
F-1483

説文

頑 The seal-style form comprised 元 **SG-0444**, used for the sound *gan* to mean "hard or stiff" like an uncut log, and 頁 "a head." Together they signified "stubborn, hard-headed." Another view holds that the sound *gan* was the same as 丸 **SG-0419** "round," and that with 頁 added, the character meant "a round-shaped head." The kanji 頑 means "stubborn, obstinate, stout, robust." <元頁>

頑固 obstinate, bullheaded [がんこ]; 頑丈な solid, tough [がんじょうな]; 頑張る to be tenacious, keep at it [がんばる]; 頑強な stubborn, sturdy [がんきょうな]; 頑として determinedly, resolutely, stoutly [がんとして] // 頑なに obstinately [かたくなに]

	Meanings	Kun and On	Romaji	Bushu	Stroke Order and Number
SG-0504 顕	to become visible, manifest	ケン	*ken*	頁	日目且显顕顕 18

顕
D
F-1702

金文1 金文2 説文 旧字
1 2 3 4

顯 顕 1, 2, and 3 depicted "a standing person wearing a formal headdress (on the right side), who was examining "two strands of silk threads under the sun" (on the left side). The sun enables one to see details, such as threads, clearly. The character meant "clearly visible; to manifest." In the shinji, the two skeins of threads were reduced (业). The kanji 顕 means "to become visible, manifest." <日业頁>

顕著な conspicuous, marked, salient [けんちょな]; 顕在化 manifestation [けんざいか] // 顕れる to turn up, show itself [あらわれ]る]

	Meanings	Kun and On	Romaji	Bushu	Stroke Order and Number
SG-0505 煩	to trouble, be distressed about	わずら-う ハン・ボン	wazura-u *han, bon*	火	''ﾉ炉煩煩煩 13

煩
D
F-2135

説文

煩 The seal-style form of the kanji 煩 comprised "a fire" (火) and "a head" (頁, bushu *oogai*). *Setsumon* explained it to depict "a headache caused by fever." When inflicted by a headache, one felt ill and weighed down. The kanji 煩 means "to worry a lot about, be distressed about." <火頁>

煩わせる to trouble, cause inconvenience to someone [わずらわせ]る]; 煩わしい bothersome, annoying [わずらわし]い]; 思い煩う to worry a lot [おもいわずら]う]; 煩雑な complicated, bothersome [はんざつな]; 煩悩 earthly desires [ぼんのう]; 子煩悩 doting on one's children [こぼんのう]

	Meanings	Kun and On	Romaji	Bushu	Stroke Order and Number
SG-0506 寡	widow; little, few	カ	*ka*	宀	宀宀宜宣寡寡 14

寡
D
F-2160

金文1 金文2 説文
1 2 3

寡 1 and 2 depicted "a woman with a head scarf inside a mausoleum or a house (宀)," signifying "a widow in mourning praying alone." In 3, 分 **SG-1389** "to divide" was added, possibly to mean "separated from the rest of the family." A widow had few family members—whence the meaning "few." The kanji 寡 meant "widow; little, few." <宀直分>

寡黙な reticent, uncommunicative [かもくな]; 寡婦 widow [かふ, やもめ]; 寡占 oligopoly, control of a market [かせん]

	Meanings	Kun and On	Romaji	Bushu	Stroke Order and Number
SG-0507 頒	to divide, distribute	ハン	*han*	頁	ハ分分´頒頒頒 13

頒
D
F-2583

篆文

頒 The seal-style form comprised 分 **SG-1389**, used for the sound *han* to mean "to divide," and 頁 "head, person." The origin of the character is not clear, but it was used to mean "to divide things and give them to people." The kanji 頒 means "to divide, distribute." <分頁>

頒布 distribution, circulation [はんぷ]

SG-0508 頬	Meanings	Kun and On	Romaji	Bushu	Stroke Order and Number
	cheek	ほお・ほほ	hoo, hoho	頁	16

頬 D F-2877

説文 1, 2

The seal-style form (1) comprised 夾 "a person with two people on either side," which signified "having something on each side," and was used for the sound *kyoo*; and 頁 "a head, face," (containing 自, originally from a depiction of a nose). On both sides of a person's nose were the cheeks. The kanji 頬 (頰) means "cheek." <夹頁> (Note: The kanji 頬 (2) is used in printed and web publications, while the kanji 頬 (3) is used in handwritten text.)

頬 cheek [ほお, ほほ]; 頬紅 cheek rouge, blusher [ほおべに]; 頬張る to take a big mouthful of [ほおばる]

SG-0509 顎	Meanings	Kun and On	Romaji	Bushu	Stroke Order and Number
	jaw	あご ガク	ago *gaku*	頁	18

顎 D F-2856

No ancient form. The kanji 顎 comprised 咢, used for the sound *gaku* to mean "rugged," and 頁 "head, face." *Setsumon* explained that it signified an imposing face with high cheek bones. In Japanese, this kanji is used to mean "jaw." <咢頁>

顎紐 chin strap [あごひも]; 上顎 upper jaw [うわあご]

22 Child, infant

22a 子 "child"[from an infant wiggling its hands] 子学字保孔

SG-0510 子	Meanings	Kun and On	Romaji	Bushu	Stroke Order and Number
	child, man, offspring, minuscule matter	こ シ・ス	ko *shi, su*	子	3

子 A F-0018

甲骨文1 1, 甲骨文2 2, 金文1 3, 金文2 4, 説文 5

1 through 5 depicted "a baby with its hands wiggling," and meant "a child." A child signified something "small or minuscule." The character was also used to mean "a son" or "a man." The kanji 子 means "child, man, offspring, minuscule matter." <子>

子供 child [こども]; どこの子 whose child; [どこのこ]; 男の子 boy, male child [おとこのこ]; 女子girls, young women [じょし]; 弟子入りする to apprentice oneself to [でしいりする]; 利子 financial interest [りし]; 子音 consonant [しいん, しおん]; 遺伝子 gene [いでんし]

SG-0511 学	Meanings	Kun and On	Romaji	Bushu	Stroke Order and Number
	to learn, study; scholarship, education	まな-ぶ ガク	mana-bu *gaku*	子	8

学 A F-0049

甲骨文 1, 金文 2, 説文 3, 旧字 4

The top (𦥯) of 1, 2, and 3 showed "two caring adult hands" (𦥑), "a cross shape" (爻) (to mean "mingling"), and "a house" (冖). In 2 and 3, "a child" (子) was added. Together they signified children being taught in a house under the caring guidance of adults. The kyuji 學 (4) reflected all the elements of 3, but in the shinji 学, the top (𦥯) was reduced to ⺍. The kanji 学 means "to learn, study; scholarship, education." <⺍子>

学ぶ to learn, study [まなぶ]; 学び舎 place of learning [まなびや]; 小学校 elementary school [しょうがっこう]; 学生 student [がくせい]; 通学する to commute to school, attend school [つうがくする]; 学習 learning, study [がくしゅう]; 語学力 language skills [ごがくりょく]; 大学 university [だいがく]; 学士号 bachelor's degree [がくしごう]

SG-0512 字	Meanings	Kun and On	Romaji	Bushu	Stroke Order and Number
	writing, letter, character, nickname	あざ ジ	aza *ji*	子	6

字 A F-0284

金文1 1, 金文2 2, 説文 3

1, 2, and 3 comprised "a child" (子) inside "a house" (宀). Children were born in a house one after another. Analogously, writing involved producing characters one after another. The kanji 字 means "writing, letter, character, nickname." <宀子>

字名 a called name or nickname [あざな]; 文字 writing, letter, character [もじ]; 数字 figure, numeral [すうじ]; 字引 dictionary [じびき]; 字幕 subtitle, superimposed dialogue [じまく]; 字体 typeface, print, font [じたい]; 字余り poem with an extra syllable [じあまり]; 十文字 crossed right angles [じゅうもんじ]

	Meanings	Kun and On	Romaji	Bushu	Stroke Order and Number
SG-0513 保	to keep, maintain, protect	たも-つ ホ	tamo-tsu *ho*	人	亻伃伻保保 9

保 **A** F-0126

甲骨文 1 金文 2 三体石経 3 説文 4

1 and 2 depicted "an adult holding an infant in their arms." 3 had 亻 "an act one does" and "an infant with a caring hand or a diaper," and signified "to take good care of a baby." 4 showed "a baby wearing diapers," which became 呆. A person caring for a baby gave the meaning "to protect, keep." The kanji 保 means "to keep, maintain, protect." <亻口木>

保つ to keep, maintain [たもつ]; 保母 nursery school teacher [ほぼ]; 保存する to preserve [ほぞんする]; 保育園 day nursery, nursery school [ほいくえん]; 保温性 heat retention [ほおんせい]; 保身術 the art of self-protection [ほしんじゅつ]; 保養地 health resort [ほようち]

	Meanings	Kun and On	Romaji	Bushu	Stroke Order and Number
SG-0514 孔	hole, cavity	コウ	*koo*	子	了孑孔 4

孔 **D** F-1913

金文1 1 金文2 2 説文 3

1, 2, and 3 showed "an infant," with something else on the top right or on the right, but what these components signified is obscure. The character had been used to mean "hole." The kanji 孔 means "a hole, cavity." <子乚>

空気孔 air vent [くうきこう]; 孔子 Kongzi, Confucius [こうし]

22b 𠫓 "a newborn baby" [from a baby at childbirth] 充流統育棄硫

	Meanings	Kun and On	Romaji	Bushu	Stroke Order and Number
SG-0515 充	to fill, fulfill, satiate; full	あ-てる ジュウ	a-teru *juu*	儿	亠𠫓充 6

充 **A** F-0934

説文

One view holds that the top of the seal-style form was "a baby with his head facing down" (𠫓) as he was born. The bottom (儿) was "a person." From the time of birth to the time of adulthood, a baby's body fills out, and thus the character meant "to fill; full." Another view takes the seal-style form as a single shape of a person with a fat belly in the middle, meaning "to fill; full." The kanji 充 means "to fill, fulfill, satiate; full." <充(𠫓儿)>

充てる to appropriate, set aside [あてる]; 充分な plenty, ample [じゅうぶんな]; 補充する to replenish [ほじゅうする]; 充満 fullness, permeation [じゅうまん]; 充実した substantial, full, complete [じゅうじつした]; 不充分な insufficient, unsatisfactory [ふじゅうぶんな]

	Meanings	Kun and On	Romaji	Bushu	Stroke Order and Number
SG-0516 流	to flow, wash out, cancel, broadcast; a flow, stream	なが-れる リュウ・ル	naga-reru *ryuu, ru*	水	氵氵汁浐浐流 10

流 **A** F-0295

説文篆文 1 説文 2

1 and 2 comprised 氵 "flowing water," and 㐬 "a child or person upside down with their hair dangling." 2 included an additional "flowing water" on the right side. A person in flowing water signified "a body in water during a flood." Another view explains that the character depicted a baby being born with amniotic fluid. The kanji 流 means "to flow, wash out, cancel, broadcast; a flow, stream." <氵𠫓儿>

流れる to flow, run, drain [ながれる]; 流す to drain, wash down, broadcast [ながす]; 流し台 kitchen sink [ながしだい]; 清流 clear stream [せいりゅう]; 一流の first-rate [いちりゅうの]; 逆流する to flow backward or upstream [ぎゃくりゅうする]; 交流 alternating current, exchange [こうりゅう]; 中流階級 the middle class [ちゅうりゅうかいきゅう]; 流転 perpetual motion, transmigration [るてん]

	Meanings	Kun and On	Romaji	Bushu	Stroke Order and Number
SG-0517 統	to unify, bring together; leader	す-べる トウ	su-beru *too*	糸	幺糸糸' 紡統 12

統 **A** F-0415

説文

The seal-style form comprised 糸 **SG-1600** "a skein of threads" and 充 **SG-0515** "to fill, full," used for the sound *too* from *juu*. Together they signified "to weave many threads into one." A person who unified people was "a head of state." The kanji 統 means "to unify, bring together; leader." <糸充>

統べる to unify [すべる]; 統一する to unify [とういつする]; 系統 line, system, lineage [けいとう]; 統計 numerical statistics [とうけい]; 正統な legitimate, orthodox [せいとうな]; 大統領 the president of a country [だいとうりょう]; 血統 line of descent, lineage [けっとう]; 統合する to integrate, consolidate [とうごうする]

SG-0518 育	Meanings	Kun and On	Romaji	Bushu	Stroke Order and Number
	to bring up, raise a child, grow	そだ-つ・はぐく-む イク	soda-tsu, haguku-mu *iku*	肉	' 亠 𠫓 育 育 8

育 A F-0453

甲骨文1 1 · 甲骨文2 2 · 金文1 3 · 金文2 4 · 説文 5 · 説文或体 6

The history of the kanji 育 is complex. 1 and 2 comprised "a woman" and "a newborn baby with his head downward," signifying "giving birth to a child." In 3 and 4, under the upside-down baby was amniotic fluid from childbirth or, according to some views, long hair (which seems less likely on a baby's head). In 5, with 月 "flesh," it signified a newborn baby putting on flesh as it grew. 6 became the non-Joyo kanji 毓 "to raise, proliferate." The shinji 育 reflects 5, comprising 𠫓 and 月. The kanji 育 means "to bring up, raise a child, grow." <𠫓月>

育つ to grow [そだつ]; 育てる to raise [そだてる]; 育む to nurture, foster [はぐくむ]; 教育 education [きょういく]; 育児 child-rearing [いくじ]; 体育 physical education [たいいく]; 育ちのいい having a good upbringing [そだちのいい]; 人材育成 bringing on new recruit, human resources development [じんざいいくせい]

SG-0519 棄	Meanings	Kun and On	Romaji	Bushu	Stroke Order and Number
	to abandon, discard	キ	*ki*	木	𠫓 𠫔 奋 奋 𠁁 㚔 棄 13

棄 C F-1417

甲骨文 1 · 金文 2 · 説文古文 3 · 説文 4

1 and 2 comprised "an infant" (in 2, upside down) "a basket," and "two hands holding the basket." The character originally meant "to throw away or abandon a baby." In ancient times, there was a superstitious custom that involved abandoning a newborn once but then getting it back. In 3, the basket disappeared, leaving "two hands throwing away a newborn." In 4, the basket reappeared. The kanji 棄 means "to abandon, discard." <𠫓世木>

棄権 abstention from voting [きけん]; 廃棄物 waste, trash [はいきぶつ]; 破棄する to destroy, annul [はきする] // 棄てる to throw away, dispose of, dump [すてる]

SG-0520 硫	Meanings	Kun and On	Romaji	Bushu	Stroke Order and Number
	sulfur	リュウ	*ryuu*	石	石 石' 砬 砬 硫 12

硫 D F-1935

No ancient form. The kanji 硫 comprises 石 **SG-1148** "rock," and 㐬 "to flow," used for the sound *ryuu*. During a volcanic eruption, rocks flowed out and sulfur spread. The kanji 硫 means "sulfur." <石𠫓儿>

硫酸 sulfuric acid [りゅうさん] // 硫黄 sulfur, brimstone [いおう]

23 Woman

23a 女 "woman, female; feminine" [from a woman kneeling in a pliant posture]; **bushu *onnahen*** 女安案好妻接努姉娘怒妙姫宴妥如奴妃婿妬

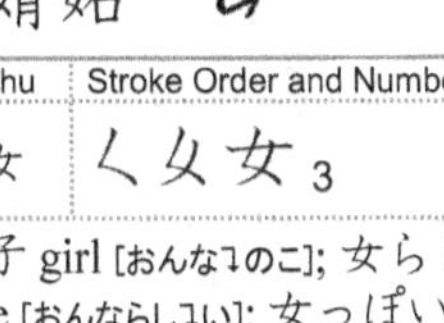

SG-0521 女	Meanings	Kun and On	Romaji	Bushu	Stroke Order and Number
	woman, female; feminine	おんな・め ジョ・ニョ・ニョウ	onna, me *jo, nyo, nyoo*	女	く 女 女 3

女 A F-0054

甲骨文1 1 · 甲骨文2 2 · 金文1 3 · 金文2 4 · 金文3 5 · 説文 6

1 through 6 each depicted a woman sitting with her knees bent and arms crossed in front. Her pliant, gentle posture signified "woman." The kanji 女 means "woman, female; feminine." <く丿一>

女 woman [おんな]; 女の子 girl [おんなのこ]; 女らしい woman-like, feminine [おんならしい]; 女っぽい feminine with sex appeal [おんなっぽい]; 女々しい effeminate, unmanly [めめしい]; 女性 woman [じょせい]; 長女 first-born daughter [ちょうじょ]; 男女 both sexes, a man and a woman [だんじょ]; 女人禁制 Women Not Admitted [にょにんきんせい]

SG-0522 安	Meanings	Kun and On	Romaji	Bushu	Stroke Order and Number
	safe, secure, peaceful, inexpensive, cheap	やす-い アン	yasu-i *an*	宀	' 宀 宀 安 安 6

安 A F-0088

甲骨文 1 · 金文 2 · 説文 3

1, 2, and 3 comprised 女 "a woman on her knees" in 宀 "a house," signifying "tranquility; peaceful, safe." In Japanese, the character also means "inexpensive, cheap," from the fact an inexpensive thing requires less effort to obtain. The kanji 安 means "safe, secure, peaceful, inexpensive, cheap." <宀女>

安らかな peaceful [やすらかな]; 安い inexpensive [やすい]; 安上がり inexpensive, lower cost [やすあがり]; 安値 low price [やすね, やすね]; 目安 rule of thumb, rough estimate [めやす]; 安心 security, ease [あんしん]; 一安心する to stop worrying (for the time being) [ひとあんしんする]; 不安な anxious, restless [ふあんな]

SG-0523 案	Meanings	Kun and On	Romaji	Bushu	Stroke Order and Number
	plan, proposal; to be anxious, worry	アン	*an*	木	宀安安安案案 10

案 **A** F-0383

説文

The seal-style form comprised 安 **SG-0522**, used for the sound *an*, and 木 **SG-0608** "wood," signifying "a wooden table with legs, or a desk." At a desk, one thought about matters to present or proposals to make. The kanji 案 means "plan, proposal, idea; to be anxious, worry." <安木>

案を練る to work out a plan [あ˥んを・ね˥る]; 立案する to make a proposal [りつあんする]; 案内 guiding, showing around a place [あんな˥い]; 不案内な unfamiliar with [ふあ˥んないな]; 案ずる to be anxious, worry [あんずる]; 案外 not as expected, surprisingly [あ˥んがい]; 名案 splendid plan, well-devised scheme [めいあん]; 思案する to ponder, contemplate [し˥あんする]

SG-0524 好	Meanings	Kun and On	Romaji	Bushu	Stroke Order and Number
	to like, be fond of; good, desirable	す-く・この-む コウ	suku, kono-mu *koo*	女	𡿨女女好好好 6

好 **A** F-0294

甲骨文1 1 甲骨文2 2 金文1 3 金文2 4 説文 5

1 through 5 depicted a small child (子 **SG-0510**) on the knees of or next to a woman (女 **SG-0521**), signifying the tender way that a woman cared for a child. The positions of the two components were swapped in 5. From the tender way that a woman cares for a child, the kanji 好 means "to like, be fond of," and also "good, desirable." <女子>

好きな being fond of; to like [すき˥な]; 子供好きな being fond of a child [こどもずきな]; 好きずきな a matter of individual taste or preference [すき˥ずきな]; 好む to favor, like [この˥む]; お好みの (your) favorite, of your choice [おこのみの]; 好青年 nice young man, congenial youth [こうせ˥いねん]; 好物 favorite food [こ˥うぶつ]

SG-0525 妻	Meanings	Kun and On	Romaji	Bushu	Stroke Order and Number
	wife	つま サイ	tsuma *sai*	女	彐彐事妻妻 8

妻 **B** F-0552

説文古文 1 説文 2

1 and 2 comprised "a woman" (女 **SG-0521**), and "an elaborate hair accessory," as would be worn on the head of a bride. In 2, "a hand" added in the middle might depict the woman's hand as she put the hair accessory on her head, or it could show a groom taking the woman to be his bride. The kanji 妻 means "wife." <一彐丨女>
(Note: The man depicted in the kanji 夫 **SG-0316** "husband, man" also had a hair accessory on his head, and the character originally meant "bridegroom.")

妻 wife [つ˥ま]; 人妻 (another man's) wife [ひとづま]; 稲妻 flash of lightning [いなづま]; 夫妻 married couple, husband and wife [ふ˥さい]; 妻子 wife and child [さ˥いし]; 悪妻 bad wife [あくさい]; 亡妻 deceased wife, late wife [ぼうさい]; 後妻 second wife [ごさい]

SG-0526 接	Meanings	Kun and On	Romaji	Bushu	Stroke Order and Number
	close; to contact, touch	つ-ぐ セツ	tsu-gu *setsu*	手	一扌扌接接 11

接 **B** F-0572

説文

The right side (妾) of the seal-style form was used for the sound *setsu* to mean "being nearby." A hand (扌, bushu *tehen*) pulling the nearby person closer formed the meaning "to contact, touch." The kanji 接 means "close; to contact, touch." <扌立女>

接ぐ to join, piece together, splice [つぐ]; 接する to come in contact, adjoin, look after [せっする]; 接近 to approach, move in close [せっきん]; 応接室 reception room, parlor [おうせつ˥しつ]; 直接 directly [ちょくせつ]; 間接的な indirect [かんせつてきな]; 接待 (company) entertainment [せ˥ったい]

SG-0527 努	Meanings	Kun and On	Romaji	Bushu	Stroke Order and Number
	to try hard; endeavor, labor	つと-める ド	tsuto-meru *do*	力	𡿨女奴努努 7

努 **B** F-0727

No ancient form. The kanji 努 comprised 奴 **SG-0536**, used for the sound *do*, and 力 **SG-1949** "might," from "a plow, hard fieldwork." Hard, strenuous work in a field came to signify "trying hard" in general. The kanji 努 means "to try hard, endeavor, labor." <女又力>

努める to strive, force oneself to do [つとめ˥る]; 努力 an endeavor, labor, effort [ど˥りょく]

SG-0528 姉	Meanings	Kun and On	Romaji	Bushu	Stroke Order and Number
	older sister	あね シ	ane *shi*	女	𡿨女女'女亠姉姉 8

姉 **B** F-0767

金文 1 説文 2 正字 3

1 and 2 comprised "a woman" (女 **SG-0521**), and the right-side component, which lent the sound *shi*. In the orthographic-style kanji 姊 (3), the right side depicted "a stake with a vine wrapping around it, with the top emphasized." The character signified the eldest of female siblings, "older sister." In

姉 older sister [あね]; 姉妹 sisters [し˥まい]; 姉御肌 big-sisterly disposition [あねご˥はだ]

	the shinji 姉, the kanji 市 was used on the right side for its sound *shi*. The kanji 姉 means "older sister." <女市> (Note: In a similar way, the kanji 弟 **SG-1355** "younger brother" came from a stake wrapped in a vine that was emphasized at the bottom.)	// お姉さん older sister [おねえさん]

	Meanings	Kun and On	Romaji	Bushu	Stroke Order and Number
SG-0529 娘	daughter, young woman	むすめ	musume	女	10

娘 **B** F-0823

説文1 説文2 正字 (1 2 3)

1 comprised "a device for selecting good grain" (良 **SG-1826**), and "female" (女). A good woman or beautiful woman meant "a daughter" or "a beautiful young woman" (in honorific speech). 2 was the basis for the orthographic-style 孃 (3), with the right-side component 襄 used for the sound *joo*. This became the kanji 嬢 **SG-1679** "a young lady (of a good family)." The shinji 娘 reverted to the original two components from 1, 女 and 良. The kanji 娘 means "daughter, young woman." <女良>

娘 daughter, young woman [むすめ]; 一人娘 one's only daughter [ひとりむすめ]; 愛娘 one's beloved daughter [まなむすめ]; 生娘 naive young woman [きむすめ]; 小娘 untutored young girl [こむすめ]; 看板娘 a pretty girl who attracts customers [かんばんむすめ]

	Meanings	Kun and On	Romaji	Bushu	Stroke Order and Number
SG-0530 怒	anger, wrath; to have words, reprimand	いか-り・おこ-る ド	ika-ri, oko-ru *do*	心	9

怒 **B** F-1070

説文

The seal-style form comprised 奴, used for the sound *do* to mean "intensity," and 心 "heart," together signifying an agitated state of mind, such as anger. It also described the act of reprimanding someone in a state of agitated emotion. The kanji 怒 means "anger, wrath; to have words, reprimand." <奴心>

怒る to get angry, rebuke, reprimand [おこる]; 怒りっぽい cross, grumpy, touchy [おこりっぽい]; 怒り wrath, rage, indignation [いかり]; 怒り肩 square shoulders [いかりがた]; 激怒 rage, fury [げきど]; 怒号 roar, outcry [どごう]

	Meanings	Kun and On	Romaji	Bushu	Stroke Order and Number
SG-0531 妙	beautiful, exquisite, strange	ミョウ	*myoo*	女	7

妙 **C** F-1166

説文

The seal-style form comprised 糸 "a skein of threads," and 少 **SG-1154** "small, minuscule," used for the sound *myoo*. Together they signified "minuscule, delicate." The kanji 妙 has 女 **SG-0521** "a woman" instead of a skein of thread. The delicate beauty of a woman gave the meaning "exquisite, charming," as well as "unexplainable, strange." The kanji 妙 means "beautiful, exquisite, strange." <女少>

妙に mysteriously, queerly [みょうに]; 神妙に meekly [しんみょうに]; 微妙な delicate, subtle [びみょうな]; 妙薬 miracle medicine [みょうやく]; 絶妙な exquisite, superb [ぜつみょうな]; 奇妙な curious, peculiar [きみょうな]; 軽妙な light-hearted [けいみょうな] // 白妙 white, white silk cloth [しらたえ]

	Meanings	Kun and On	Romaji	Bushu	Stroke Order and Number
SG-0532 姫	princess; small	ひめ	hime	女	10

姫 **C** F-1244

甲骨文 金文1 金文2 説文 (1 2 3 4)

1, 2, and 3 comprised "two breasts" and "a woman wearing hair accessories," originally signifying "a mature woman." Another view holds that the character was the name of a noble family, and it meant "noble woman, princess." In 4, the right side became 臣 "retainer," possibly breasts miscopied. A woman (女) with a retainer is a noble person or princess. A dainty princess also gave the meaning "small." The kanji 姫 means "princess; small." <女臣>

姫 princess, a young lady of noble birth [ひめ]; 姫君 princess [ひめぎみ]; 歌姫 songstress [うたひめ]; 一姫二太郎 first a daughter, then a son [いちひめ・にたろう]

	Meanings	Kun and On	Romaji	Bushu	Stroke Order and Number
SG-0533 宴	banquet, party	エン	*en*	宀	10

宴 **C** F-1481

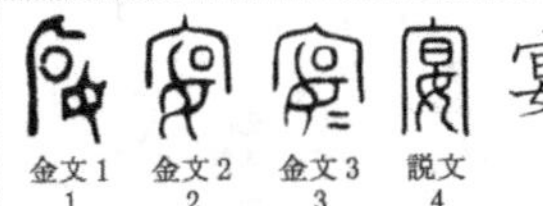

金文1 金文2 金文3 説文 (1 2 3 4)

The origin of this character is not clear. 1, 2, and 3 showed "a jewel" and "a woman" (女), under a hidden place in a house (宀). 4 had 日 instead of a jewel. One view holds that it was a reconfiguring of 晏, used for the sound *an*, with the meaning "peacefully resting (安) after a sunset (日)," signifying "relaxing, unwinding." From that, it meant "relaxing, merrymaking." Another view holds that the original meaning of "a woman (女) with a gem in a rite in a hidden sacred area (匚 in 1) of an ancestral mausoleum" (1 through 4) lost its religious sense, and was used to mean "banquet, party." The kanji 宴 means "banquet, party." <宀日女>

宴 banquet, party [うたげ]; 宴会 banquet, party [えんかい]; 披露宴 wedding reception [ひろうえん]

SG-0534 妥	Meanings	Kun and On	Romaji	Bushu	Stroke Order and Number
	settled, peaceful, conciliatory	ダ	*da*	女	一 ⺤ 妥 7

妥 **C** F-1566

甲骨文 1 金文 2 説文 3

1, 2, and 3 showed "a hand reaching down to a woman," signifying "someone calming a woman by placing a hand on her." It also gave the meaning "conciliatory." The hand reaching down from above became the shape ⺤. The kanji 妥 means "settled, peaceful, conciliatory." <⺤女>

妥協 compromise, concession [だꜜきょう]; 妥結する to reach an agreement, make a compromise agreement [だけつする]; 妥当な appropriate, suitable [だとうな]

SG-0535 如	Meanings	Kun and On	Romaji	Bushu	Stroke Order and Number
	equal, similar; as if	ジョ・ニョ	*jo, nyo*	女	く 女 女 如 如 6

如 **C** F-1608

甲骨文1 1 甲骨文2 2 金文 3 説文 4

1, 2, 3, and 4 comprised "a mouth, a prayer box" and "a woman." The pliant posture of the woman 女 with 口 signified "to follow what is said." Another view takes it to depict "a (female) medium praying for instruction from a deity." The character was also used to mean "similar; as if." The kanji 如 means "equal, similar; as if." <女口>

突如に suddenly [とꜜつじょに]; 欠如する to miss, be lacking [けꜜつじょする]; 如才ない shrewd, adroit, sociable [じょさいなꜜい]; 如実に truly, vividly [にょじつに]; 不如意な going contrary to one's wishes, hard up for money [ふにょꜜいな] // 例の如く as usual [れꜜいのごとく]; 如何 in what way, how, how about [いかꜜが]

SG-0536 奴	Meanings	Kun and On	Romaji	Bushu	Stroke Order and Number
	servant, enslaved person, bloke, chap	ド	*do*	女	く 女 女 奴 5

奴 **C** F-1626

金文 1 説文古文 2 説文 3

1, 2, and 3 comprised "a woman" (女) or "a person," and "a hand" (又 **SG-0084**), signifying "a woman who did manual work." Another view holds that a woman (or a person in 2) grabbed by a hand would have been "an enslaved person or low-level servant." The kanji 奴 means "servant, enslaved person, bloke, chap." <女 又> (Note: The kanji 奴 is not used to refer to women, despite the bushu *onnahen*.)

奴隷 enslaved person [どれい]; 売国奴 traitor to one's country [ばいこꜜくど]; 守銭奴 miser, scrooge [しゅせꜜんど] // 奴 fellow, chap, bloke [やꜜつ]; 奴さん that guy [やっこさん]; 冷や奴 tofu served cold [ひややꜜっこ]

SG-0537 妃	Meanings	Kun and On	Romaji	Bushu	Stroke Order and Number
	princess, queen	ヒ	*hi*	女	く 女 女 妃 妃 妃 6

妃 **C** F-1645

甲骨文 1 金文 2 説文 3

The origin of 妃 is obscure. One view explains that 1, 2, and 3 comprised 己, used for the sound *hi* to mean "religious matter" (from 祀 "to worship"), and "woman, female" (女 **SG-0521**). A woman from a noble family served a deity, and the character meant "princess, imperial consort." Another view explains that "a female spouse" (配 **SG-1813** in 配偶者 "spouse") meant "a queen." The kanji 妃 means "princess, queen." <女己>

王妃 queen, empress [おꜜうひ]; 皇太子妃 the crown princess [こうたいしꜜひ]; 妃殿下 Her Imperial Highness [ひでꜜんか]

SG-0538 婿	Meanings	Kun and On	Romaji	Bushu	Stroke Order and Number
	son-in-law, bridegroom	むこ セイ	muko *see*	女	女 女 女 婿 婿 12

婿 **D** F-2155

篆文1 1 篆文2 2

The left side of 1 was "dirt, ground," whereas in 2 it was "a woman." On the right side, both 1 and 2 had 足 (⺪) "a leg," and 月, which was used for the sound *see* to mean "a pair." A woman was "a pair" with her husband. To her parents, he was a son-in-law. The kanji 婿 is used to mean "son-in-law, bridegroom." <女⺪月>

婿 bridegroom, son-in-law [むꜜこ]; 娘婿 son-in-law [むすめむꜜこ]; 花婿 bridegroom [はなむꜜこ,はなꜜむこ]; 入り婿 a man who is adopted by his wife's family [いりむこ]

SG-0539 妬	Meanings	Kun and On	Romaji	Bushu	Stroke Order and Number
	jealous; to envy	ねた-む ト	neta-mu *to*	女	く 女 女 妬 妬 妬 8

妬 **D** F-2368

篆文

The seal-style form comprised 女 "woman, female," and 戸 "door." In the kanji, the right side changed from 戸 to 石 **SG-1148**, which was used for the sound *to*. One view explains that the old sound of 石 was the same as "to become red." A jealous woman became excited and turned red. The kanji 妬 means "jealous; to envy." <女石>

妬む to envy, feel jealous [ねたꜜむ]; 嫉妬 jealousy [しっと]

23b 母 "mother" [from a nursing woman with breasts]; 毎 "every; busy" [from a woman with hair accessories] 母毎海毒梅敏悔侮

毎 in kyuji changed to 毎 in shinji.

SG-0540 母	Meanings	Kun and On	Romaji	Bushu	Stroke Order and Number
	mother; maternal	はは ボ	haha *bo*	毋	母 5

母 **A** F-0285

甲骨文 1 金文1 2 金文2 3 説文 4

Even though the shapes of the two kanji 女 SG-0521 and 母 show little mutual resemblance, the ancient forms tell us that they shared the same origins. Each of the ancient forms of 母 (1, 2, 3, and 4) depicted a woman kneeling down in a pliant posture with her hands crossed in front, as did the ancient forms of 女. The difference was that 母 included two dots on the woman's chest that signified breasts for nursing. A woman who nursed was a mother. The kanji 母 means "mother; maternal." <母>

母 mother [はꜜは]; 母方の maternal side of one's family [はははかたの]; 父と母 father and mother; parents [ちꜜちと・はꜜは]; 父母 parents [ふꜜぼ]; 母校 one's alma mater [ぼꜜこう]; 分母 denominator [ぶꜜんぼ]; 母音 vowel [ぼいん, ぼおん]; 実母 one's mother by blood, birth mother [じつぼ, じꜜつぼ] // お母さん mother [おかꜜあさん]; 母屋 main house [おꜜもや]

SG-0541 毎	Meanings	Kun and On	Romaji	Bushu	Stroke Order and Number
	every	マイ	*mai*	毋	毎 6

毎 **A** F-0551

甲骨文 1 金文1 2 金文2 3 説文 4 旧字 5

1, 2, 3, and 4 showed "a mother," and a straight or wiggly line above her that signified "hair accessories." The character represented a woman wearing hair accessories, busily working at a shrine, and thus the character meant "busy; every." Another view takes the top of 4 to be "a growing plant," which was meant to liken a rigorously growing plant to a mother giving a birth to one child after another; hence, the character meant "to increase one after another," and, by extension, "every," from the idea of repeated occurrences. The kyuji 毎 (5) kept two dots that signified breasts, but in the shinji they merged into a slightly slanted single line. The kanji 毎 means "every." <𠂉母>

毎日 every day [まいにち]; 毎月 every month [まいつき] // ～する毎に every time one does X [～するごꜜとに]; 一週間毎 every week, by the week [いっしゅうかんごꜜと]; 日毎に day by day [ひごꜜとに, ひごとに]; 夜毎に night after night, nightly [よごとに]

SG-0542 海	Meanings	Kun and On	Romaji	Bushu	Stroke Order and Number
	ocean, sea	うみ カイ	umi *kai*	水	海 9

海 **A** F-0112

金文1 1 金文2 2 説文 3 旧字 4

1, 2, and 3 comprised "water" (氵), and 毎, used for the sound *kai* to mean "dark, unknown." Vast, dark, unknown water signified "an ocean." The kanji 海 means "ocean, sea." <氵毎>

海 ocean, sea [うꜜみ]; 日本海 Japan Sea [にほꜜんかい]; 海水 sea water [かいすい]; 大海 an ocean, the sea [たいかい]; 海流 ocean current [かいりゅう] // 海苔 *nori*, dried seaweed [のりꜜ]; 海原 an ocean, the open sea [うなばら]; 海女・海人 woman diver, male diver [あꜜま]

SG-0543 毒	Meanings	Kun and On	Romaji	Bushu	Stroke Order and Number
	poison; venomous, gaudy	ドク	*doku*	毋	毒 8

毒 **B** F-0966

説文古文 1 説文 2

Two different precursors contributed to the current usage of the kanji 毒. 1 comprised "plants" (艸), and 畐 with 刀, for the sound *doku* to mean "poison," together signifying "poisonous plants." In 2, the three lines at the top were "elaborate hair accessories in a woman's hair." Too many hair accessories made the woman appear gaudy or venomous. The kanji 毒 means "poison; venomous, gaudy." <龶 母>

毒 poison [どくꜜ]; 毒々しい gaudy, excessively showy [どくどくしꜜい]; 無毒 not harmful [むꜜどく]; (お)毒味 tasting before serving (for poison) [どくみ, おどくみ]; 消毒 disinfection, sterilization [しょうどく]; 中毒 poisoning, addiction [ちゅꜜうどく]; 毒物 toxic substance [どくꜜぶつ]; 解毒剤 antidote for poison [げどくざい, げどくꜜざい]

SG-0544 梅	Meanings	Kun and On	Romaji	Bushu	Stroke Order and Number
	ume plum, Japanese apricot	うめ バイ	ume *bai*	木	十 朩 杧 杬 梅 梅 10

梅
B
F-1028

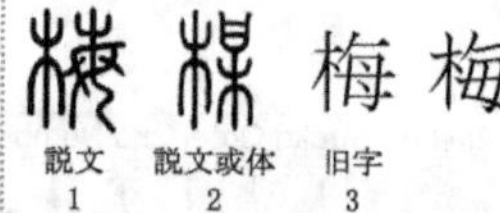 梅 梅

説文 1 説文或体 2 旧字 3

Next to the left-side component 木 **SG-0608** "tree," 毎 (毎 **SG-0541**) was used in 1 for the sound *mai* to mean "proliferation," whereas 某 **SG-0660** was used in 2 for the sound *boo* to mean "sour fruit." (The sounds *mai, bai,* and *boo* were related.) They meant "*ume* plum." An *ume* fruit is distinctively pungent and very tart. In Japan, green *ume* are pickled to make 梅干し *umeboshi,* which are tart, salty *ume* pickles. Green *ume* fruits are harvested during the month-long rainy season, and the word for "rainy season" is written as 梅雨, read *tsuyu* or *baiu*. The kanji 梅 means "*ume* plum." <木毎>

梅干し pickled *ume*/plum [うめぼし]; 梅酒 *ume* liquor [うめしゅ]; 梅雨 rainy season [つゆ, ばいう]; 塩梅 seasoning, taste, physical condition [あんばい]; 梅雨時 rainy season [つゆどき]

SG-0545 敏	Meanings	Kun and On	Romaji	Bushu	Stroke Order and Number
	swift, quick, alert	ビン	*bin*	攵	ノ 𠂉 𠂋 句 毎 毎 敏 敏 10

敏
C
F-1164

敏 敏

甲骨文1 1 甲骨文2 2 金文 3 説文 4 旧字 5

1, 2, 3, and 4 comprised "a woman wearing hair accessories," and "the hand of another person arranging the woman's hair." In 4 and 5, the right side became 攴 or 攵, bushu *bokuzukuri* "to cause an action." One view holds that the character meant "a woman working swiftly during a rite." Another view holds that 毎 (毎 **SG-0541**) "one after another," and 攴 "to cause an action," were combined to signify "a person handling many tasks swiftly." The kanji 敏 means "swift, quick, alert." <毎攵>

敏感な sensitive, impressionable [びんかんな]; 過敏な oversensitive, hyper-acute [かびんな]; 機敏な smart, shrewd, prompt [きびんな]; 敏捷性 nimbleness, agility [びんしょうせい] // 目敏い sharp-eyed, easily awakened [めざとい]

SG-0546 悔	Meanings	Kun and On	Romaji	Bushu	Stroke Order and Number
	to regret, repent; vexing	く-いる・くや-しい カイ	ku-iru, kuya-shii *kai*	心	丶 忄 忙 悔 悔 悔 9

悔
C
F-1501

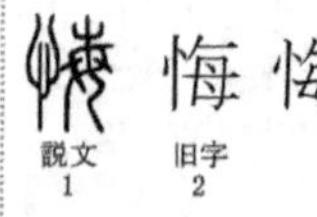

説文 1 旧字 2

1 and 2 comprised "a heart" (忄, bushu *risshinben*), and 毎, used for the sound *kai* to mean "dark; to regret." Together they signified "to regret, vex." The kanji 悔 means "to regret, repent; vexing." <忄毎>

悔いる to repent, regret [くいる]; 悔やむ to regret [くやむ]; 悔しい vexing, regretful [くやしい]; お悔やみ my condolences [おくやみ]; 後悔する to regret [こうかいする]

SG-0547 侮	Meanings	Kun and On	Romaji	Bushu	Stroke Order and Number
	to disdain, scorn, slight	あなど-る ブ	anado-ru *bu*	人	亻 仁 仛 侮 侮 侮 8

侮
D
F-2094

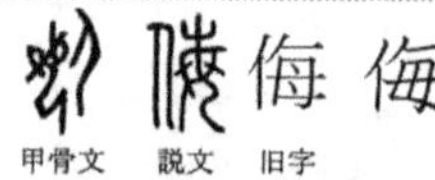 侮

甲骨文 1 説文 2 旧字 3

1 comprised 毎 (毎) "woman wearing hair accessories," used for the sound *bu* to mean "dark; not seeing," and 亻 "a standing person looking down at the woman." Together they signified "to slight (by not looking at)" and "to look down on." In 2, the positions of the two components were reversed. The kanji 侮 means "to disdain, scorn, slight." <亻毎>

侮る to despise, disdain [あなどる]; 侮辱 an insult, a slight [ぶじょく]; 侮蔑 contempt, slighting [ぶべつ]

23c 身 "body" [from a pregnant woman] 身 ⻎

SG-0548 身	Meanings	Kun and On	Romaji	Bushu	Stroke Order and Number
	body, flesh, person	み シン	mi *shin*	身	ノ 冂 自 身 身 7

身
A
F-0202

金文 1 説文 2

1 was "a pregnant woman with a large belly" viewed from the side, signifying "being pregnant." By extension, it was used to mean "one's body." The kanji 身 means "body, flesh, person." <身>
(Note: The bulged stomach shape in 身 was misconstrued for "a bow and an arrow" in the kanji 射 **SG-1516**, 謝 **SG-1517**, and 窮 **SG-1518**.)

身 body, person, one's life [み]; 身内 relatives, family [みうち]; 身軽な agile [みがるな]; 身の上話 one's life story [みのうえばなし]; 身分 one's social standing, status [みぶん]; 身重 pregnant [みおも]; 自身 self, oneself [じしん]; 出身地 one's hometown [しゅっしんち]; 身体 the body, the person [しんたい], 心身 mind and body, body and soul [しんしん]

23d 免 "barely" [from childbirth]; *men/ben/ban* 免勉晩逸

SG-0549 免	Meanings	Kun and On	Romaji	Bushu	Stroke Order and Number
	to miss, escape from, become exempted, avoid, be allowed to	まぬか-れる メン	manuka-reru *men*	儿	8

免 **B** F-0993

金文 1 説文 2 旧字 3

One view holds that 1 depicted "a soldier being allowed to take off his armor" at camp in a battle, giving the meaning "to be exempted from, be allowed to." 2 depicted "a woman straining during childbirth." A baby coming through a narrow passage gave the meaning "barely." Barely managing to escape also came to mean "being exempted from." Even though the two origins were distinctly different, they were both used for the same meaning. Another view holds that form 2 was the sole origin of the character. The kanji 免 means "to miss, escape from, become exempted, avoid; be allowed to." <ケロ儿>

免れる to escape [まぬかれる]; 運転免許証 driver's license [うんてんめんきょしょう]; 免疫 immunity [めんえき]; ご免なさい I am sorry [ごめんなさい]; ご免下さい Hello! (called out at the door of someone else's home) [ごめんくださ い] (when entering), [ごめんください] (when leaving); 放免 release, acquittal [ほうめん]; 仮免・仮免許 temporary license [かりめん, かりめんきょ]; ~に免じて out of consideration for X [~にめんじて]

SG-0550 勉	Meanings	Kun and On	Romaji	Bushu	Stroke Order and Number
	to exert oneself, try hard	ベン	*ben*	力	10

勉 **B** F-0740

説文 1 旧字 2

1 comprised 免 "doing a strenuous act," used for the sound *ben*, and 力 **SG-1949** "hard work using a plow." Together they signified "working strenuously." The kanji 勉 means "to exert oneself, try hard." <免力>

勉強する to study, reduce the price [べんきょうする]; 勤勉な diligent, assiduous [きんべんな]; 勉学 study, pursuit of knowledge [べんがく]; 猛勉強 hard study [もうべんきょう]; ガリ勉 studying hard, a grind [がりべん]; 不勉強 lack of diligence, slackness [ふべんきょう]

SG-0551 晩	Meanings	Kun and On	Romaji	Bushu	Stroke Order and Number
	evening, night; late	バン	*ban*	日	12

晩 **C** F-1128

説文 1 旧字 2

1 comprised "the sun" (日), and "barely" (免 **SG-0549**), used for the sound *ban*. A time when the sun was barely seen was the "evening." The character was also used to mean "late." The kanji 晩 means "evening, night; late." <日免>

晩 evening, early in the night [ばん]; 今晩 this evening [こんばん]; 昨晩 yesterday evening (formal) [さくばん]; 晩年 one's last years [ばんねん]; 晩春 late spring [ばんしゅん]

SG-0552 逸	Meanings	Kun and On	Romaji	Bushu	Stroke Order and Number
	to escape, slip away, go astray	イツ	*itsu*	辵	11

逸 **D** F-1662

金文1 1 金文2 2 金文3 3 説文 4 旧字 5

1, 2, 3, and 4 comprised "a crossroads" with "a footprint" for "to move forward" (辵, 辶, bushu *shinnyuu*), and "a rabbit." A rabbit ran quickly and slipped away easily, giving the meaning "fast, quick; to slip away." The kyuji 逸 (5) contained the non-Joyo kanji 兔 (兎) "rabbit," which changed to 免 in the shinji. The kanji 逸 means "to escape, slip away)," go astray." <免辶>

逸材 a person of exceptional talent [いつざい]; 安逸な idle, leisured [あんいつな]; 逸脱する to deviate from, overstep [いつだつする]; 秀逸な superexcellent, supremely excellent [しゅういつな]

23e 奐 "to change, exchange" [from two hands delivering a baby]; *kan* 換喚

SG-0553 換	Meanings	Kun and On	Romaji	Bushu	Stroke Order and Number
	to change, exchange	か-える カン	ka-eru *kan*	手	12

換 **B** F-0838

説文

Thee seal-style form comprised 扌 "an act done by hand," and 奐 "two hands carefully delivering a newborn baby," which had the sound *kan*. Together they signified "to take out, exchange." The kanji 換 means "to change, exchange." <扌奐>

換える to change, substitute [かえる]; 置き換える to replace [おきかえる]; 引き換え exchange, conversion [ひきかえ]; 乗り換え changing trains, buses; etc. [のりかえ]; 換金 conversion of goods into money, cash (a check) [かんきん]; 転換 conversion, diversion, switch [てんかん]; 交換台 switchboard [こうかんだい]; 換算する to convert [かんさんする]

SG-0554 喚	Meanings	Kun and On	Romaji	Bushu	Stroke Order and Number
	to shout	カン	*kan*	口	口口′叱吶喚喚喚 12

喚 **D** F-1671

篆文

The right side (奐) was used for the sound *kan* to mean "to shout." Together with 口 "mouth," the kanji 喚 means "to shout." <口奐>

喚起する to awaken, evoke (interest) [かんきする]; 喚問する to issue a summons [かんもんする]; 召喚 summon, call, citation [しょうかん]

23f 襾 "important, essential" [from a woman's waist] 要腰遷

SG-0555 要	Meanings	Kun and On	Romaji	Bushu	Stroke Order and Number
	vital, essential, important; to require, need	かなめ・い-る ヨウ	kaname, i-ru *yoo*	襾	一襾襾覀要要要 9

要 **A** F-0132

甲骨文 1 説文古文 2 説文 3

1 showed "two hands placed on the waist (hipbones or spine)," and originally meant "waist, hip." A woman's hips are especially prominent, and so in 2, 女 "a woman" was added for emphasis. In 3, the spine at the center of the body had come to mean something that was "vital, essential," and a "necessity." The kanji 要 means "vital, essential, important; to require, need." <襾女>

要 pivot, main vital point [かなめ]; 要る to need, require [いる]; 要因 primary factor, cause [よういん]; 重要な important, essential, vital, primary [じゅうような]; 要する to require [ようする]; 所要時間 the time required [しょようじかん]; 要人 very important person, VIP [ようじん]

SG-0556 腰	Meanings	Kun and On	Romaji	Bushu	Stroke Order and Number
	waist, hip	こし ヨウ	koshi *yoo*	肉	月肝腰腰腰腰 13

腰 **C** F-1077

説文古文 1 説文 2

The kanji 腰 was created because the original kanji for "waist, hip" (要 SG-0555), which had the sound *yoo*, had come instead to mean "important, essential." For the original meaning, 月, bushu *nikuzuki* "part of the body," was added. The kanji 腰 means "waist, hip." <月要>

腰 lower back, waist, hips [こし]; 丸腰 without carrying a weapon, unarmed [まるごし]; 及び腰 a bent posture, timidity [およびごし]; 物腰の柔らかい gentle-mannered [ものごしのやわらかい]; 腰掛け seat, stepping-stone (job) [こしかけ, こしかけ]; 腰痛 lower-back pain [ようつう]

SG-0557 遷	Meanings	Kun and On	Romaji	Bushu	Stroke Order and Number
	to move, change location	セン	*sen*	辵	一襾覀覀䙴䙴遷 15

遷 **D** F-1972

金文 1 古文1 2 古文2 3 説文 4

1 showed four hands holding something essential (襾), and "a town" (邑), signifying people moving something important, such as a capital, to another location. (2 and 3, given as pre-seal style forms, were thought to be informal variants.) In 4, 辵 "to move forward" was added to 䙴, used for the sound *sen* to mean "people holding something essential" (襾). The kanji 遷 means "to move, change location." <䙴 (襾大己)辶>

変遷 changes, transition [へんせん]; 左遷 relegation, demotion [させん]; 遷都 relocation of a capital [せんと]

23g 票 "ballot; floating" (襾 and 示); *hyoo* 票標漂

SG-0558 票	Meanings	Kun and On	Romaji	Bushu	Stroke Order and Number
	small piece of paper, ballot	ヒョウ	*hyoo*	示	一襾襾覀覀票票 11

票 **B** F-0847

説文

The seal-style form comprised 囟 "vertebrae" between two hands (𦥑), and "a fire." When a body was burned, the force of the flames sent thin pieces of ash floating into the air, much like small pieces of paper. In the kanji, the top became 襾, and the bottom became 示 SG-1737. The kanji 票 means "small piece of paper, ballot." < 襾 示 >

票 vote [ひょう]; 投票 voting, balloting [とうひょう]; 白票 blank ballot [はくひょう]; 伝票 slip, ticket [でんぴょう]; 住民票 certificate of residence [じゅうみんひょう]

SG-0559 標	Meanings	Kun and On	Romaji	Bushu	Stroke Order and Number
	signpost, marking, target; to post high	ヒョウ	*hyoo*	木	十朾標標標標 15

標 **B** F-0711

説文

The seal-style form comprised 木 SG-0608 "wood," and 票 "small thin pieces that float in the air," used for the sound *hyoo*. Together they signified a piece of wood that stayed lifted above the ground—that is, "a wooden signpost." The kanji 標 means "signpost, marking, target; to post high." <木票>

標本 specimen, sample [ひょうほん]; 標的 target, mark [ひょうてき]; 指標 indicator, barometer [しひょう]; 座標 coordinates [ざひょう]; 商標 trademark, brand [しょうひょう]; 音標文字 phonogram [おんぴょうもじ]; 標準 standard, criterion [ひょうじゅん]

SG-0560 漂	Meanings	*Kun* and *On*	Romaji	Bushu	Stroke Order and Number
	to float, drift	ただよ-う ヒョウ	tadayo-u *hyoo*	水	氵 沪 洒 漂 漂 漂 14

漂 **D** F-1754

説文

The seal-style form comprised 氵 "flowing water," and 票 **SG-0558**, used for the sound *hyoo* to mean "something floating or wafting." Together they signified "to drift about in the water." The kanji 漂 means "to float, drift." <氵 票>

漂う to drift about, float [ただよ↑う]; 漂着する to cast ashore, drift ashore [ひょうちゃくする]; 漂白 bleaching, decolorization [ひょうはく]; 漂流 to drift on the tide, be adrift [ひょうりゅう]; 漂白剤 bleach [ひょうはく↑ざい, ひょうはくざい]

24 Long hair, soft hair

24a 耂 "old; a long time" [from a long-haired old man stooping over a walking stick]; *koo/roo*; bushu *oigashira* 考老孝寿拷

SG-0561 考	Meanings	*Kun* and *On*	Romaji	Bushu	Stroke Order and Number
	to think over, consider, ponder	かんが-える コウ	kanga-eru *koo*	老	一 十 土 耂 耂 考 6

考 **A** F-0244

金文1 1, 金文2 2, 説文 3

1, 2, and 3 comprised "a stooping, long-haired old man," and a bent shape (丂), used for the sound *koo*, at the bottom. The character originally meant "one's late father." The bent shape signified the meandering nature of thoughts, and referred to the way that an elderly person took time to think things over. Thus, the character came to mean "to think over, ponder." The kanji 考 means "to think over, consider, ponder." <耂 丂>

考える to think [かんが↑える]; 考え thought, idea [かんが↑え]; 思考 thinking [しこう]; 参考になる to provide one with useful information [さんこうにな↑る]; 参考書 reference book (for study) [さんこうしょ]; 考慮する to consider, mull over [こ↑うりょする]; 熟考する to think seriously about, give careful thought [じゅっこうする]

SG-0562 老	Meanings	*Kun* and *On*	Romaji	Bushu	Stroke Order and Number
	to become old; aged, old	お-いる・ふ-ける ロウ	o-iru, hu-keru *roo*	老	十 土 耂 耂 老 6

老 **B** F-0615

甲骨 1, 金文1 2, 金文2 3, 金文 4, 説文 5

1 depicted "a long-haired old man with a cane." In 2, 3, 4, and 5, under the long-haired man (耂) was a fallen or dead person (匕). Together they signified "a person who was getting close to death," that is, "old." The kanji 老 means "to become old; aged, old." <耂 匕>

老いる to become old, age [おい↑る]; 老ける to grow old [ふけ↑る]; 老人 old person [ろうじん]; 老化 aging [ろうか]; 老後 one's old age [ろうご]; 元老 senior member, grand old man [げんろう]; 敬老 respect for the aged [けいろう]; 家老 principal retainer of a feudal lord [か↑ろう] // 老若男女 people of all ages and both genders [ろうにゃくな↑んにょ]

SG-0563 孝	Meanings	*Kun* and *On*	Romaji	Bushu	Stroke Order and Number
	filial responsibility; filial	コウ	*koo*	子	十 土 耂 耂 孝 孝 7

孝 **B** F-0981

甲骨文 1, 金文1 2, 金文2 3, 説文 4

1 had "long hair," signifying "an old person," and "a child." In 2, 3, and 4, a long-haired person stooped over a child. A child (子) propping up an old person (耂) gave the meaning "filial." The kanji 孝 means "filial responsibility; filial." <耂 子>

親孝行 filial duty, kind to one's parents [おやこ↑うこう]; 忠孝 loyalty and filial responsibility [ちゅ↑うこう]; 親不孝者 undutiful or unthankful son or daughter [おやふこうもの]

SG-0564 寿	Meanings	*Kun* and *On*	Romaji	Bushu	Stroke Order and Number
	auspicious; long life	ことぶき ジュ	kotobuki *ju*	士・寸	三 丰 寿 寿 寿 7

寿 **B** F-0987

金文1 1, 金文2 2, 説文 3, 旧字 4

1, 2, and 3 had "a long-haired old man" at the top. Below it were "boxes of benedictions placed along continuous levies in a rice field," which signified praying for an abundant harvest and had the sound *chuu*. The old person and continuous levies together signified longevity, which was "auspicious." The kyuji 壽 (4) was simplified to 寿. The kanji 寿 means "auspicious; long life." <三 丿 寸>

寿 congratulations, cause for celebration [ことぶき]; 長寿 longevity, long life [ちょ↑うじゅ]; 寿命 one's natural term of existence, life [じゅみょう]; 喜寿 one's 77th birthday [き↑じゅ]; 白寿 one's 99th birthday [は↑くじゅ]; 米寿 one's 88th birthday [べ↑いじゅ]

SG-0565 拷	Meanings	*Kun* and *On*	Romaji	Bushu	Stroke Order and Number
	to torture, hit hard	ゴウ	*goo*	手	一 丨 扌 拷 拷 拷 拷 9

拷 **D** F-2159	No ancient form. The kanji 拷 comprises 扌, bushu *tehen* "an act done by hand," and 考, which was used for the sound *goo* to mean "to hit hard, pound," together signifying "to hit hard, torture." The kanji 拷 means "to torture, hit hard." <扌考>	拷問 torture [ごうもん]

24b 長 (镸) "long" [from the long hair of an old person]; *choo* 長張帳, and 微 "small" and 徴懲 "sign"

SG-0566 長	Meanings	*Kun* and *On*	Romaji	Bushu	Stroke Order and Number
	chief; long, older	なが-い チョウ	naga-i *choo*	長	丨 F 長 長 長 8

甲骨文 1 金文 1 2 金文 2 3 説文 4

長 **A** F-0013	1 and 2 had an old man with or without a walking stick, whose hair grew very long," depicting a chief or an elder of a clan. It signified "long" (from hair) and "old" (from a walking stick) and "chief." 3 and 4 enveloped "a fallen person (匕)," adding the meaning of aging. The elder's very long life with many life experiences was also used in parallel to the general concept that time leads to growth, development, and good or superior quality. The kanji 長 means "long, older; chief, good quality." <镸匕>	長い long [なが↑い]; 身長 one's height [しんちょう]; 長男 firstborn male child [ちょ↑うなん, ちょうな↑ん]; 市長 mayor [し↑ちょう]; 長幼の序 order of senior and junior [ちょうようのじょ↑]; 最年長 the oldest [さいね↑んちょう]; 成長 growth [せいちょう]; 長短 [ちょ↑うたん] relative length, merits and demerits; 長所 strong point [ちょ↑うしょ]

SG-0567 張	Meanings	*Kun* and *On*	Romaji	Bushu	Stroke Order and Number
	to stretch, tense up, strain, paste	は-る チョウ	ha-ru *choo*	弓	㇇ 弓 引 弫 张 張 張 11

中山王器 1 説文 2

張 **B** F-0557	1 comprised "a skein of thread" to mean "long and continuous," and 長 for the meaning "long" and the sound *choo*. 2 added 弓 "bow" to mean "to stretch." The character meant "to pull something long, stretch, strain." The kanji 張 also was used as a substitute for the kanji 貼 **SG-1768** to mean "to paste, post" before the Joyo kanji revision. The kanji 張 means "to stretch, tense up, strain, paste." <弓長>	張る to tense up, stretch [はる]; 見張り watch, lookout [みはり]; 我を張る to assert oneself [がをはる]; 突っ張る to cramp up, tighten [つっぱ↑る]; 出張 business trip [しゅっちょう]; 主張する to insist, assert, claim [しゅちょうする]; 張力 tension, tensile force [ちょ↑うりょく]; 張本人 ringleader, main culprit [ちょうほ↑んにん]

SG-0568 帳	Meanings	*Kun* and *On*	Romaji	Bushu	Stroke Order and Number
	drapery, booklet, ledger	チョウ	*choo*	巾	丨 口 巾 帄 帳 帳 帳 11

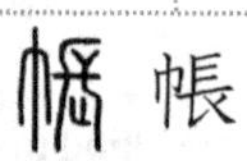

説文

帳 **C** F-1169	The seal-style form comprised 巾 "a piece of long cloth, draped or folded," and 長, which was used for the sound *choo* to mean "long." Together they signified "a drapery." Something that was long and folded or bound together was "a booklet, ledger." The kanji 帳 meant "drapery, booklet, ledger." <巾長>	手帳 pocketbook [てちょう]; 帳面 notebook [ちょうめ↑ん]; 几帳面 exact, methodical [きちょうめ↑ん]; 帳簿 account book [ちょうぼ]; 帳消し writing off a debt, balancing the books [ちょうけし]

微 "small" [from the small step of a long-haired old man]

SG-0569 微	Meanings	*Kun* and *On*	Romaji	Bushu	Stroke Order and Number
	tiny, obscure	ビ	*bi*	彳	彳 彳 彳 徉 徉 微 微 13

甲骨文 1 金文 2 説文 3

微 **C** F-1156	1 and 2 comprised "a long-haired old man," and "a hand holding a stick" (攴, signifying "to cause an action), and had the sound *bi* to mean "tiny." In 3, the addition of 彳 "a crossroads" signified that the long-haired old person was taking small steps forward, giving the meaning "minute, faint." The kanji 微 means "tiny, obscure." <彳𢼸攵>	顕微鏡 microscope [けんびきょう]; 微生物 microorganism, germ [びせ↑いぶつ]; 微々たる of small value, negligible [び↑びたる]; 機微 fine points, subtleties [き↑び]; 微動だにしない not budge an inch [びどうだ↑にしない]; 微笑 faint smile [びしょう]

徴 "sign" 徴懲

SG-0570 徴	Meanings	Kun and On	Romaji	Bushu	Stroke Order and Number
	to levy, summon; sign, indication	チョウ	*choo*	彳	彳 彳' 徃 𢓊 徴 徴 徴 14

徴 **C** F-1178

金文1 1 · 金文2 2 · 説文古文 3 · 説文 4 · 旧字 5

1 comprised "a long-haired elder of a clan," "a crossroads" (彳), and "a footprint." At the crossroads in 2, 3, and 4, a standing elder (𡈼), used for the sound *choo*, was forced to do something (from "a hand and a tool," 攴 and 攵). The scene depicted an official either demanding that an elder of the clan pay a levy—hence "to impose"; or looking for a sign of hidden valuables—hence, "sign, indication." The kanji 徴 means "to levy, summon; sign, indication." <彳𡈼攵>

象徴 symbol [しょうちょう]; 特徴 characteristic, peculiarity [とくちょう]; 課徴金 surcharge [かちょうきん]; 徴収する to collect, impose [ちょうしゅうする]; 徴兵制度 conscription system [ちょうへいせいど]

SG-0571 懲	Meanings	Kun and On	Romaji	Bushu	Stroke Order and Number
	to chastise, punish; discipline	こ-りる チョウ	ko-riru *choo*	心	彳 𢓜 徨 徴 懲 18

懲 **D** F-1737

旧字

No ancient form. The top of the kanji 徴 was used for the sound *choo* to mean "a sign," and the bottom was 心 "heart." Someone who has done something wrong should show signs of remorse. The kanji 懲 means "to chastise, punish; discipline." <徴心>

懲りる to learn the hard way [こりる]; 懲らしめる to chastise, punish, discipline [こらしめる]; 懲罰 disciplinary measure, castigation [ちょうばつ]; 勧善懲悪 rewarding good and punishing evil [かんぜんちょうあく]; 懲戒処分 disciplinary action [ちょうかいしょぶん]; 懲役 imprisonment with forced labor, penal servitude [ちょうえき]

24c 而 "soft, gentle" [from a person with a chignon-less head] 需耐端儒

SG-0572 需	Meanings	Kun and On	Romaji	Bushu	Stroke Order and Number
	to demand, ask for, seek, count on	ジュ	*ju*	雨	一 雨 需 需 需 需 14

需 **C** F-1372

金文1 1 · 金文2 2 · 説文 3

1 and 2 comprised "rain" (雨 **SG-1205**), and "a person with a chignon-less head," such as a priest. The character signified a priest who performed a "rainmaking rite," and was used to mean "to seek, demand." The kanji 需 means "to demand, ask for, seek, count on." <雨而> (Note: When 氵, bushu *sanzui* "water," is added to 需, they form the non-Joyo kanji 濡れる *nureru* "to get wet.")

需要 demand [じゅよう]; 需要と供給 supply and demand [じゅようときゅうきょう]; 必需品 necessities [ひつじゅひん]; 軍需産業 military industry [ぐんじゅさんぎょう]

SG-0573 耐	Meanings	Kun and On	Romaji	Bushu	Stroke Order and Number
	to endure, bear	た-える タイ	ta-eru *tai*	而	一 丆 而 而 耐 耐 9

耐 **C** F-1316

説文 1 · 説文或体 2

1 comprised "a man without a chignon on his head" (而), and 彡 "a neat shape," together signifying shaving off a beard as a light punishment. In 2, 寸 **SG-0112** "a hand" was used in place of 彡. "A light punishment" was "bearable." The kanji 耐 means "to endure, bear." <而寸>

耐える to endure, withstand, hold up [たえる]; 忍耐 patience, perseverance [にんたい]; 耐火 fire resistance [たいか]; 耐久性 durability [たいきゅうせい]; 耐震 earthquake-proof [たいしん]; 耐熱ガラス heat-resistant glass [たいねつガラス]; 耐性菌 resistant bacteria [たいせいきん]

SG-0574 端	Meanings	Kun and On	Romaji	Bushu	Stroke Order and Number
	upright, orderly; edge, beginning	はし・は・はた タン	hashi, ha, hata *tan*	立	立 立' 䇂 竮 端 端 14

端 **C** F-1120

説文

The seal-style form comprised "a person standing straight" (立 **SG-0363**), and 耑 "neatly cut hair," used for the sound *tan*. Together they meant "orderly, decent, upright." The edge of neatly cut hair also gave the meaning "edge, beginning." The kanji 端 means "upright, orderly; edge, beginning." <立山而>

端 end, tip, extremity, edge [はた, はし]; 右端 right edge [みぎはし]; 片っ端から absolutely every little bit, thoroughly [かたっぱしから]; 井戸端会議 housewives' gossiping [いどばたかいぎ]; 半端 odds and ends [はんぱ]; 異端 heresy [いたん]; 準備万端 everything is ready [じゅんび・ばんたん]; 発端 the origin, the genesis, the outset [ほったん]; 端的に forthrightly, flatly [たんてきに]

SG-0575 儒	Meanings	Kun and On	Romaji	Bushu	Stroke Order and Number
	Confucianism; Confucian	ジュ	*ju*	人	㐌 伓 倕 偄 儒 儒 16

儒 **D** F-2142	説文 儒 The seal-style form comprised 亻 "an act that one does," and 需 **SG-0572** "a priest who conducts a rainmaking rite," which had the sound *ju*. Rainmaking rites were said to have been conducted by Confucians. The kanji 儒 means "Confucianism; Confucian." <亻需>	儒教 Confucianism [じゅうきょう]; 儒家 Confucian scholar [じゅうか]; 儒者 Confucianist [じゅうしゃ]

25 A hand doing something

25a 及 "to reach" [from a person chased from behind by another person's hand]; *kyuu*

及急級扱吸

SG-0576 及	Meanings	Kun and On	Romaji	Bushu	Stroke Order and Number
	to reach over, touch on, affect; also	およーぶ キュウ	oyo-bu *kyuu*	又	ノ 乃 及 3

及 **A** F-0685	甲骨文1 (1) 甲骨文2 (2) 金文1 (3) 金文2 (4) 説文 (5) 及 1 and 2 depicted "a standing person with the hand of another person reaching for them from behind." In 4 and 5, the hand from behind caught up to the standing person, giving the meanings "inclusive; also." Eventually the two elements coalesced into one. The kanji 及 means "to reach over, touch on, affect; also." <ノ又>	及ぶ to reach, extend, stretch [およぶ]; 及び and, in addition to [および]; 追及する to investigate, accuse [ついきゅうする]; 波及する to infect, extend [はきゅうする]

SG-0577 急	Meanings	Kun and On	Romaji	Bushu	Stroke Order and Number
	to rush; in a hurry; haste	いそーぐ キュウ	iso-gu *kyuu*	心	ク ⺈ 刍 急 急 9

急 **A** F-0268	説文 急 The seal-style form comprised 及 (as in 5 for **SG-0576**), used for the sound *kyuu*, and "a heart" (心 **SG-0187**). A person's heart being reached from behind by the hand of another person signified "a feeling of being chased or rushed." The kanji 急 means "to rush; in a hurry; haste." <⺈ヨ心>	急ぐ to hurry, rush [いそぐ]; 急行 express [きゅうこう]; 急速に rapidly [きゅうそくに]; 救急車 ambulance [きゅうきゅうしゃ]; 急場しのぎ stopgap, quick fix [きゅうばしのぎ] // 急かす to rush someone [せかす]; 気が急く to feel rushed [きがせく]

SG-0578 級	Meanings	Kun and On	Romaji	Bushu	Stroke Order and Number
	order, grade, class, level	キュウ	*kyuu*	糸	幺 糸 紉 級 級 9

級 **B** F-0577	説文 級 The seal-style form comprised 糸 **SG-1600** "threads," and 及 **SG-0576**, used for the sound *kyuu* to mean "to draw out." The threads on a loom were laid in a set order, giving the meaning "order" and "class." The kanji 級 means "order, grade, class, level."<糸及>	等級 rank, grade [とうきゅう]; 一級品 first-rate goods [いっきゅうひん]; 級友 classmate [きゅうゆう]; 上級生 upper-class student [じょうきゅうせい]; 同級生 classmate [どうきゅうせい]; 進級 promotion to next level [しんきゅう]; 高級な high rank, high grade [こうきゅうな]

SG-0579 扱	Meanings	Kun and On	Romaji	Bushu	Stroke Order and Number
	to handle, treat	あつかーう	atsuka-u	手	一 十 扌 扨 扱 6

扱 **B** F-0957	篆文 扱 The seal-style form comprised "a hand or an act done by hand" (扌), and 及 **SG-0576**, used for the sound *kyuu* to mean "to reach," together originally signifying "to take in." In Japanese, the kanji 扱 means "to handle, treat." <扌及>	扱う to handle [あつかう]; 取り扱い注意 handle with care [とりあつかいちゅうい]; 取扱い書 manual, instructions [とりあつかいしょ]; 特別扱い preferential treatment [とくべつあつかい]

SG-0580 吸	Meanings	Kun and On	Romaji	Bushu	Stroke Order and Number
	to inhale, breathe in	すーう キュウ	su-u *kyuu*	口	口 叩 吸 吸 6

吸 **B** F-1019	説文 吸 The seal-style form comprised 口 **SG-0031** "mouth," and 及 **SG-0576**, used for the sound *kyuu* to mean "to breathe in." The kanji 吸 means "to inhale, breathe in." <口及>	吸う to suck, absorb, inhale [すう]; 吸い取る to suck up water, siphon off [すいとる]; (お)吸い物 broth, soup [(お)すいもの]; 吸収 absorption [きゅうしゅう]; 吸入器 inhaler [きゅうにゅうき]; 吸引力 suction power [きゅういんりょく]; 吸水 water-absorbent [きゅうすい]; 吸音材 acoustic-absorbing materials [きゅうおんざい]

25b 巩 "to strike with an instrument" [from hands holding a striking implement] 恐築 巩

	Meanings	Kun and On	Romaji	Bushu	Stroke Order and Number
SG-0581 恐	to fear; fearful; awe	おそ-れる キョウ	oso-reru *kyoo*	心	10

恐 **B** F-1017

金文 1 中山王器 2 說文古文 3 說文 4

1 showed "a person holding a tool in both hands," used here for the sound *kyoo* to mean "to fear." In 2 and 3 the two hands were replaced with 心 "a heart." Together they meant "to fear." In 4, "hands doing something" returned, which became the shape 凡. The kanji 恐 means "to fear; fearful; awe." <工凡心>

恐れる to fear [おそれる]; 恐ろしい frightful, horrifying, horrible [おそろしい]; 恐る恐る fearfully, in trepidation [おそるおそる]; 恐れ入りますが I am terribly sorry to bother you, but… [おそれいりますが]; 恐慌 financial crisis [きょうこう]; 恐縮する to be obliged, be grateful, deeply appreciate [きょうしゅくする]

	Meanings	Kun and On	Romaji	Bushu	Stroke Order and Number
SG-0582 築	to build, construct, put up	きず-く チク	kizu-ku *chiku*	竹	16

築 **B** F-0873

金文 1 說文 2

1 comprised 竹 **SG-0759** "bamboo," 工 "craft work," 木 "wood," and "a person using both hands." 竹, 工, and 木 all pertained to construction, and the character meant "a person engaged in building using wooden boards and bamboo sticks." The top component 筑 had the sound *chiku*. The kanji 築 means "to build, construct, put up." <⺮工凡木>

築く to construct, build [きずく]; 建築 architecture [けんちく]; 建築家 architect [けんちくか]; 新築家屋 newly built house [しんちくかおく]; 改築する to remodel, make an alternation [かいちくする]; 構築する to build [こうちくする] // 築山 man-made hill in a pond [つきやま]

25c 埶 "to care" [from hands tending a plant in soil] 芸勢熱 埶

	Meanings	Kun and On	Romaji	Bushu	Stroke Order and Number
SG-0583 芸	skill, art	ゲイ	*gee*	艸	7

芸 **A** F-0510

甲骨文1 1 甲骨文2 2 金文 3 說文 4 旧字 5

1 and 2 depicted a person holding a plant carefully with both hands. 3 comprised "a plant in soil" on the left side, and "two hands" and "a woman" on the right. Together they signified "a woman taking care of a plant carefully with both hands," and gave the general meaning "manual skills, art." In 4, "woman" was dropped. The kyuji 藝 (5) comprised 艹 "plants," 埶 "to care for plants," and 云 "clouds rising" to mean "growing upward." In the shinji 芸, however, all of the original elements of "an art of tending plants by hand" were dropped, and the character became 芸, an empty shape conveying little of its origins. The kanji 芸 means "skill, art." <艹云>

芸 skill, art [げい]; 芸術 art, fine arts [げいじゅつ]; 工芸品 craft products [こうげいひん]; 手芸 needlecraft [しゅげい]; 園芸 gardening [えんげい]; 芸当 feat, trick [げいとう]; 芸者 *geisha*, a hostess in a kimono who entertains patrons with dance and song [げいしゃ]

	Meanings	Kun and On	Romaji	Bushu	Stroke Order and Number
SG-0584 勢	vigor, momentum, impetus, group of	いきお-い セイ	ikio-i *see*	力	13

勢 **A** F-0486

說文

The seal-style form comprised 埶 "hands tending plants in soil" (the same component of 4 for 芸), and "plow" (力 **SG-1949**). Together they signified "a plow thoroughly tilling the soil to help plants grow vigorously." The kanji 勢 means "vigor, momentum, impetus, group of." <坴丸力>

勢いのいい vigorous, having good momentum [いきおいのいい]; 勢力 power, force [せいりょく]; 加勢する to support, back up [かせいする]; 気勢をそぐ to discourage [きせいをそぐ]; 大勢 many people [おおぜい]; 政治情勢 political situations [せいじじょうせい]; 威勢のいい spirited, animated [いせいのいい]; 形勢 the situation, developments [けいせい]; 日本勢 Japanese team (in sports) [にほんぜい]

	Meanings	Kun and On	Romaji	Bushu	Stroke Order and Number
SG-0585 熱	heat, temperature, fervor, enthusiasm	あつ-い ネツ	atsu-i *netsu*	火	15

熱 **B** F-0540

說文

The seal-style form comprised 埶 "two hands carefully tending a plant in soil," and 火 **SG-1164** "fire," together signifying "heat, warmth," and referring to the fact that plants grow better in a warm environment. The character also meant "zeal, enthusiasm." In kanji, the fire became 灬, bushu *renga/rekka*. The kanji 熱 means "heat, temperature, fervor, enthusiasm." <坴丸灬>

熱い hot [あつい]; 熱 heat [ねつ]; 熱がある to have a fever [ねつがある]; 熱っぽく intently, enthusiastically [ねつっぽく]; 熱気 enthusiasm [ねっき]; 熱狂的な exuberant, enthusiastic [ねっきょうてきな]; 熱演する to give an impassioned performance [ねつえんする]

25d 幸 "good luck; to invert" 幸報執摯

	Meanings	Kun and On	Romaji	Bushu	Stroke Order and Number
SG-0586 幸	luck, happiness	さいわ-い・さち・しあわ-せ コウ	saiwa-i, sachi, shiawa-se *koo*	干	一十土去击幸 8

幸 **A** F-0424

甲骨文1 1 甲骨文2 2 篆文 3

1 and 2 each comprised a symmetrical shape that depicted "a pair of handcuffs with locks in the middle." One view holds that a punishment of getting handcuffed was luckier than more severe punishment, and thus signified "good luck," while another view holds that the character signified *avoiding* getting handcuffed (unlike 1 and 2 for the kanji 執 **SG-0588**), and thus "good luck." 3, another shape used for the same meaning, comprised 夭 "a person being struck on the head," and 屰 "to reverse" (as in the kanji 逆 **SG-0603**). A reversal of the misfortune of being struck on the head meant "good luck." The kanji 幸 means "luck, happiness." <幸>

幸いに fortunately [さいわいに]; 幸あれ good luck!, all the best! [さちあれ]; 幸せな happy [しあわせな]; 幸福 happiness, bliss, joy [こうふく]; 不幸 misfortune, adversity, unhappiness [ふこう]; 幸か不幸か fortunately or not [こうか・ふこうか] // 幸先の良い it augurs well, is a good beginning [さいさきのよい]

	Meanings	Kun and On	Romaji	Bushu	Stroke Order and Number
SG-0587 報	to reward; retribution, report	むく-いる ホウ	muku-iru *hoo*	土	土击幸幸⁷郣郣報 12

報 **A** F-0275

甲骨文 1 金文 2 説文 3

1 comprised "a pair of handcuffs" (幸), and "a hand holding a stick; to cause an action" (攴). On the right side of 2 and 3, "a person" was being pushed down by a hand from behind (𠬝). The two sides 幸 **SG-0586** and 𠬝 together depicted a scene in which a criminal was caught and handcuffed, and thus the character meant "retribution." With the reversing power of 幸 that changed calamity to fortune, 報 also meant "reward for a good deed." A reward was reported at the ancestral altar, whence "to report." The kanji 報 means "to reward; retribution, report." <幸𠬝>

報いる to return, reward, avenge oneself [むくいる]; 報告 report [ほうこく]; 一報する to let someone know [いっぽうする]; 誤報 incorrect report, misreport [ごほう]; 報酬 remuneration, honorarium [ほうしゅう]; 果報者 a very lucky person, the most fortunate of men [かほうもの]; 社内報 company's in-house magazine [しゃないほう]; 速報 prompt report, news flash [そくほう]

	Meanings	Kun and On	Romaji	Bushu	Stroke Order and Number
SG-0588 執	to assume power, take up, grab; persistent	と-る シツ・シュウ	to-ru *shitsu, shuu*	土	土击幸幸丿執執 11

執 **C** F-1142

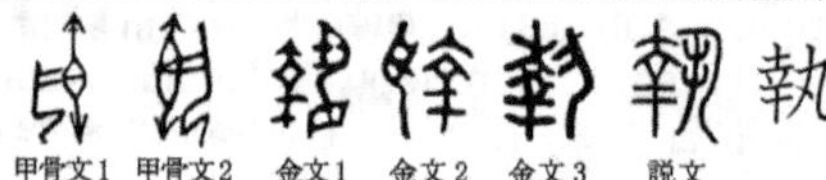

甲骨文1 1 甲骨文2 2 金文1 3 金文2 4 金文3 5 説文 6

1 through 6 all depicted "a person in a submissive posture putting their hands out to be shackled (幸 **SG-0586**)." In 3, the person also wore a shackle on their ankle. The scene envisions an official (not appearing here) restraining a criminal with handcuffs, and thus it meant "to retain, take up, grab firmly." Being grabbed firmly gave the meaning "persistent, obstinate." The connotation of an act by authority remains in the kanji. The kanji 執 means "to assume power, take up, grab; persistent." <幸丸>

執る to assume power [とる]; 固執する to adhere to, hold fast to [こしつする]; 執務中 at work, during work [しつむちゅう]; 執権 regent (historical) [しっけん]; 刑の執行 execution of punishment [けいの・しっこう]; 執刀 surgical operation [しっとう]; 執念深い vengeful, spiteful [しゅうねんぶかい]; 執着する to be deeply attached [しゅうちゃくする]

	Meanings	Kun and On	Romaji	Bushu	Stroke Order and Number
SG-0589 摯	sincere, earnest	シ	*shi*	手	土击幸丿幸九執埶摯摯 15

摯 **D** F-2551

甲骨文1 1 甲骨文2 2 説文 3

1 and 2 comprised "a person on their knees with their hands out to be handcuffed," forming 執 for the sound *shitsu,* and "the hand of an authority grabbing the person firmly" from behind on the top right. In 3, the official's hand (手 **SG-0072**) was placed at the bottom, signifying "having a firm handle on something and working seriously." The connotation of "criminal" was later dropped, and the kanji 摯 means "sincere, earnest." <幸丸手>

真摯な very earnest, very sincere [しんしな]

25e 孰 "ripe; to mature" [from a person with his hands over a cooking stove]; *juku* 塾熟

SG-0590 塾	Meanings	Kun and On	Romaji	Bushu	Stroke Order and Number
	private tutoring classes; *juku* (cram school)	ジュク	*juku*	土	亠 亨 享 孰 孰 塾 塾 14

塾 C F-1161

篆文

The top component of the seal-style form comprised "a cooking stove with a lid," "sheep, tasty meat" (羊 **SG-0825**), and "a person with two caring hands," together forming 孰 for the sound *juku*. The bottom component was "the ground" (土). Thoroughly cooked mutton signified "maturing, ripening." In the kanji, 羊 was replaced by "a child" (子 **SG-0510**), and the character meant "a place where caring hands helped children to mature in their knowledge," or a school for private education. The kanji 塾 mean "school for private education; *juku* (cram school)." <享(亠口子)丸土>

塾 [じゅ7く]; 私塾 private class or school [し7じゅく, しじゅく]; 学習塾 tutoring school [がくしゅ7うじゅく]; 政治塾 private political seminar [せいじ7じゅく]

SG-0591 熟	Meanings	Kun and On	Romaji	Bushu	Stroke Order and Number
	to mature, ripen; thoroughly	う-れる ジュク	u-reru *juku*	火	亠 亨 享 孰 孰 孰 熟 15

熟 C F-1345

No ancient form. The kanji 熟 comprised "a cooking stove," "a child" (享), and "caring hands" (丸) (together forming 孰 for the sound *juku*), and "a fire" (灬, bushu *rekka*). Putting food on a stove over a fire meant cooking it thoroughly. The kanji 熟 meant "to mature, ripen; thoroughly." <享丸灬>

熟れる to ripen [うれ7る]; 熟する to ripen [じゅくす7る]; 機が熟する ripe opportunity [き7が・じゅくす7る]; 完熟トマト ripe tomato [かんじゅくト7マト]; 未熟な immature [みじゅくな]; 早熟な子供 precocious child [そうじゅくなこども]; 熟年層 mature people, middle-aged and older [じゅくね7んそう]; 熟慮の末 after thorough deliberation [じゅ7くりょのすえ]

26 A person behind a screen

26 亡 "to disappear, not exist"; *boo/koo/moo* 亡忘荒忙盲慌妄

SG-0592 亡	Meanings	Kun and On	Romaji	Bushu	Stroke Order and Number
	to die [euphemistic], disappear	な-くなる ボウ・モウ	na-kunaru *boo, moo*	亠	' 亠 亡 3

亡 B F-0946

甲骨文1 1 甲骨文2 2 甲骨文3 3 金文1 4 金文2 5 金文3 6 説文 7

1, 2, 4 and 5 each depicted the body of a deceased person with the arms and legs folded. The character meant "to die, disappear, pass away." Another view takes 3, 6 and 7 to be "a person (人) hiding behind a screen." A person disappearing also meant "to die" euphemistically. The kanji 亡 means "to die, disappear." <亡>

亡くなる to pass away, die [なくなる]; 亡き人 departed person, deceased [な7きひと]; 存亡 life or death, existence, fate [そんぼう]; 亡命 flight from one's own country, exile [ぼうめい]; 亡霊 departed spirit, ghost [ぼうれい]; 未亡人 widow [みぼ7うじん]; 亡者 the dead, the deceased [も7うじゃ]

SG-0593 忘	Meanings	Kun and On	Romaji	Bushu	Stroke Order and Number
	to forget	わす-れる ボウ	wasu-reru *boo*	心	' 亠 亡 忘 忘 7

忘 B F-0931

金文1 1 金文2 2

1 and 2 comprised 亡 **SG-0592**, used for the sound *boo* to mean "to disappear," and 心 **SG-0187** "a heart." To have something disappear from one's heart or mind was "to forget." The kanji 忘 means "to forget." <亡心>

忘れる to forget [わすれる]; 忘れ物 leaving something behind inadvertently, lost article [わすれもの]; 物忘れ slip of memory [ものわ7すれ]; 忘年会 end-of-the-year party [ぼうねん7かい]; 健忘症 forgetfulness, amnesia [けんぼうしょう]; 備忘録 memorandum, written reminder [びぼ7うろく]

SG-0594 荒	Meanings	Kun and On	Romaji	Bushu	Stroke Order and Number
	rough, dreary, violent	あら-い・あ-れる コウ	ara-i, a-reru *koo*	艸	一 艹 芒 芒 芒 荒 9

荒 C F-1096

中山王器 1 説文 2

1 and 2 comprised "vegetation, plants" (艸, 艹), and 㐬, used for the sound *koo* to mean "random, wild." Together they signified "a desolate scene." Another view explains that 㐬 depicts a skeleton to which hair was still attached, and the character signified a bleak area where bones were abandoned. The kanji 荒 means "rough, dreary, violent." <艹亡儿>

荒い rough, violent [あらい]; 手荒な harsh, rough [てあらな]; 荒っぽい rough, crude, careless [あらっぽ7い]; 荒涼たる dreary, desolate, bleak [こうりょうた7る]; 荒廃した disused and abandoned [こうはいした]; 荒唐無稽な nonsensical, absurd [こうとうむけいな]; 荒れ果てる to fall to utter ruin, become seriously dilapidated [あれはて7る]

SG-0595 忙	Meanings	Kun and On	Romaji	Bushu	Stroke Order and Number
	busy, hectic	いそが-しい ボウ	isoga-shii *boo*	心	忙 6

忙 **C** F-1458

No ancient form. It comprised 忄 "a heart," and 亡 **SG-0592**, used for the sound *boo* to mean "to be lost, disappear." Originally, the character signified "to be dazed, become stupefied." When busy, one would lose one's concentration, and so it came to be used to mean "busy." The kanji 忙 means "busy, hectic." <忄亡>

忙しい busy [いそがしꜜい]; ご多忙中のところ Excuse me for taking so much of your valuable time [ごたぼうちゅうのところ]; 忙殺される to be very busily occupied, be inundated with work [ぼうさつされる]

SG-0596 盲	Meanings	Kun and On	Romaji	Bushu	Stroke Order and Number
	blind	モウ	*moo*	目	盲 8

盲 **C** F-1642

説文

The seal-style form comprised 亡 "to disappear," used for the sound *moo*, and 目 **SG-0001** "eye, sight." Eyes that could not see were "blind." The kanji 盲 means "blind." <亡目>

盲目 blind [もうもく]; 盲目的に blindly [もうもくてきに]; 文盲 illiterate person [もんもう]; 盲従する to follow blindly, follow like sheep [もうじゅうする]; 盲点 blind spot [もꜜうてん]; 盲滅法に recklessly [めくらめꜜっぽうに]

SG-0597 慌	Meanings	Kun and On	Romaji	Bushu	Stroke Order and Number
	to be flustered, become disconcerted, panic	あわ-てる コウ	awa-teru *koo*	心	慌 12

慌 **D** F-1976

No ancient form. The kanji 慌 comprised 忄, bushu *risshinben* "heart," and 荒 **SG-0594**, used for the sound *koo* to mean "unclear, dreary," together signifying "losing one's state of mind." The kanji 慌 means "to be flustered, become disconcerted, panic." <忄荒>

慌てる to be flustered [あわてる]; 大慌てで in a frantic haste, in a mad rush [おおあꜜわてで]; 慌て者 careless person, rash person [あわてもの]; 慌ただしく hurriedly [あわただꜜしく]; 恐慌 panic [きょうこう]; 金融恐慌 financial panic [きんゆうきょꜜうこう]

SG-0598 妄	Meanings	Kun and On	Romaji	Bushu	Stroke Order and Number
	without due cause, at random, recklessly	モウ	*moo*	女	妄 6

妄 **D** F-2192

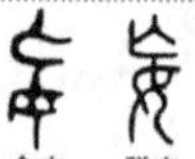

金文 1 説文 2

1 and 2 comprised 亡, used for the sound *moo* to mean "not to exist, lose," and 女 "woman." Together they signified "a man bewildered by a woman losing her senses." The kanji 妄 means "without due cause, recklessly." <亡女>

妄想 fancy, foolish imaginings [もうそう]; 誇大妄想 delusions of grandeur [こだいもꜜうそう]; 被害妄想 paranoia, persecution mania [ひがいもꜜうそう]

27 A person upside down

27a 真 "truth" [from an upside-down image of a deceased person]; *shin/chin/ten* 真慎鎮填 眞

SG-0599 真	Meanings	Kun and On	Romaji	Bushu	Stroke Order and Number
	truth; genuine	ま シン	ma *shin*	目	真 10

真 **A** F-0136

石鼓文 1 古文 2 説文 3 旧字 4

One view explains that 1, 2, and 3 comprised "the body of a deceased person lying down," and "a head upside down with the hair dangling," together signifying "a dead person who met an unnatural death." A deceased person can no longer undergo any change, and thus, death is the ultimate, eternal truth. Another view explains that 1 and 2 comprised "a spoon" (匕) and "a tripod to cook food," and that filling a pot with food by using a spoon signified "fullness," which further meant "true." 匕 in the kyuji (4) was replaced by a truncated 十 in the shinji. The kanji 真 means "truth; genuine." < 直亓>

真面目な serious, earnest [まじめな]; 真っ先に first, at the very beginning [まっさꜜきに]; 真似 imitation, mimicry [まね]; 真っ向に対立する to have completely the opposite opinion [まっこꜜうに・たいりつする]; 真ん中 center [まんなか]; 写真 photograph [しゃしん]; 真実 truth [しꜜんじつ];真剣に in all seriousness [しんけんに]

SG-0600 慎	Meanings	Kun and On	Romaji	Bushu	Stroke Order and Number
	to refrain from, abstain from; discreet	つつし-む シン	tsutsushi-mu *shin*	心	慎 13

慎 **C** F-1208

金文 1 説文古文 2 説文 3 旧字 4

1 and 2 (in *Setsumon)* meant "discreet, prudent." 3 and 4 comprised 忄, a bushu *risshinben* "a heart, emotions," and 眞 for the sound *shin,* together signifying "to treat with courtesy and consideration." The right side 眞 was replaced by 真 **SG-0599** in the shinji. The kanji 慎 means "to refrain from, abstain from; discreet" <忄真>

慎む to be discreet, abstain from [つつしꜜむ]; 謹慎する to restrain one's own behavior [きんしんする]; 慎重に prudently, deliberately [しんちょうに]

	Meanings	Kun and On	Romaji	Bushu	Stroke Order and Number
SG-0601 鎮	to suppress, quieten, tranquilize, weigh down	しず-める チン	shizu-meru *chin*	金	𠆢 午 余 金 金⁻ 鈩 鎮 鎮 18

鎮 **C** F-1568

鎮 鎮 鎮 (説文 1, 旧字 2)

One view holds that 1 comprised 金 **SG-1196** "metal," and 眞 (which originally meant "a person who met an unnatural or untimely death"), used for the sound *chin*, and that it signified a special ceremony for the repose of the deceased's soul. Another view holds that the sound *chin* on the right side meant "to fill" (as in 填 **SG-0602**), and that together with 金 it meant "a heavy metal weight." By analogy of a metal weight pressing down, the character also meant "to suppress, calm, tranquilize." The kanji 鎮 means "to suppress, quieten, tranquilize, weigh down." <金真>

鎮める to appease [しずめ↴る]; 鎮圧する to suppress, subjugate [ちんあつ]; 鎮痛剤 pain killer [ちんつうざい]; 鎮火 quenching of a fire [ちんか]; 鎮魂歌 requiem song [ちんこ↴んか]; 文鎮 paper weight [ぶんちん]; 重鎮 prominent figure, authority [じゅうちん]

	Meanings	Kun and On	Romaji	Bushu	Stroke Order and Number
SG-0602 填	to fill until full, seal, cover	テン	*ten*	土	一 十 扌 ... 填 13

填 **D** F-3227

填 填 填 (説文 1, 2, 3)

The seal-style form comprised 土 **SG-1126** "soil, ground," and 眞 (真 **SG-0599**), which was used for the sound *ten*. One view explains that it showed a deceased body that was sealed underground for the repose of the person's soul, and thus had the meanings "to seal; cover," and also "to fill." Another view explains that it meant "filling a vessel," and thus "to fill." The kanji 填 means "to fill until full, seal, cover." <扌真> (Note: The kanji 塡 [2] is used in printed or web media, and the kanji 填 [3] is used in handwritten text.)

充填する to fill in, replenish [じゅうてんする]; 補填する to fill, supply a deficiency, compensate for, filling [ほてんする]

27b 屰 "to reverse" [from a person upside down] 逆訴斥遡塑

	Meanings	Kun and On	Romaji	Bushu	Stroke Order and Number
SG-0603 逆	to reverse; wrong way; backward, contrary	さか-らう ギャク	saka-rau *gyaku*	辶	丷 屰 屰 屰 逆 逆 9

逆 **B** F-0775

逆 (甲骨文 1, 金文 2, 説文 3)

1, 2, and 3 comprised "a person upside down" (屰), which has the sound *gyaku*, and "a footprint" and "a crossroads," together signifying "to go backward." Another view explains that the upside-down person signified "someone coming," who was being welcomed by another person represented by the forward-facing footprint, and that the meaning "reverse" derived from its original meaning. The kanji 逆 means "to reverse; wrong way; backward, contrary." <屰 辶>

逆さ upside down, backward [さかさ]; 逆らう to resist, fly in the face of, oppose [さから↴う]; 逆に conversely, vice versa [ぎゃくに]; 反逆 revolt [はんぎゃく]; 逆算 calculating backward [ぎゃくさん]; 逆上する to explode, go wild with rage [ぎゃくじょうする]; 逆光 light from behind, backlight [ぎゃっこう]; 逆行する to move backward [ぎゃっこうする]

	Meanings	Kun and On	Romaji	Bushu	Stroke Order and Number
SG-0604 訴	to sue, appeal, take legal action	うった-える ソ	utta-eru *so*	言	言 訂 訢 訴 12

訴 **B** F-0947

訴 (説文 1, 説文或体1 2, 説文或体2 3)

1 comprised "word, language; to say" (言), and "inversion" (屰) under "eaves," used for the sound *so*. Together these components signified "to sue," which could be described as a request for a change of the present state. To verbally request the reversal of a decision is "to appeal." 2 and 3 comprised 月 "a moon," signifying "returning to the beginning of a month," and 屰, doubling the meaning of "reversal." In the kanji 訴, 斥 **SG-0605** "to reverse" is used. The kanji 訴 means "to sue, appeal, take legal action." <言斥>

訴える to appeal, sue, take legal action [うったえ↴る]; 訴訟事件 lawsuit case [そしょうじ↴けん]; 告訴 accuse, charge [こ↴くそ]; 訴状 written complaint in a lawsuit [そじょう]; 起訴 prosecution, indictment [き↴そ]; 民事訴訟 civil litigation [みんじそ↴しょう]; 刑事訴訟 criminal action [けいじそ↴しょう]

	Meanings	Kun and On	Romaji	Bushu	Stroke Order and Number
SG-0605 斥	to send away, refuse, defeat	セキ	*seki*	斤	一 厂 斤 斤 斥 5

斥 **D** F-2165

斥 (篆文)

The seal-style form comprised 广 "eaves," and 屰 "contrary; the reverse," used for the sound *seki*. Ejecting someone from a house or office meant "to refuse, defeat." Another view explains that it depicted an ax splitting a piece of wood, signifying "to push something away." The kanji became 斥 and means "to send away, refuse, defeat." <斤丶>

排斥する to repel, reject [はいせきする]; 斥候 scout [せっこう]; 斥ける to send away, defeat, turn down [しりぞけ↴る]

SG-0606 遡	Meanings	*Kun* and *On*	Romaji	Bushu	Stroke Order and Number
	to retroact, be backdated, go upstream	さかのぼ-る ソ	sakanobo-ru *so*	辵	丷 䒑 屰 朔 `朔 溯 遡 14
遡 **D** F-2745	篆文 遡 The seal-style form comprised "to move forward" (辵), "an upside-down person" (屰) for "reversal," and "(a cycle of) a moon" (月 **SG-1077**). Going back to the beginning of a month signified "a passage of time inverted." The kanji 遡 means "to retroact, be backdated, go upstream." <屰 月 辶>				遡る to date back, retroact, go upstream [さかのぼる]; 遡及的に retroactively, retrospectively [そきゅうてきに]

SG-0607 塑	Meanings	*Kun* and *On*	Romaji	Bushu	Stroke Order and Number
	figurine; to plasticize	ソ	*so*	土	丷 䒑 屰 朔 塑 塑 塑 13
塑 **D** F-2478	No ancient form. The kanji 塑 comprises "the first day of a month (from 屰 and 月) for the sound *saku* or *so*, and 土 **SG-1126** "soil, dirt, clay," signifying "making a clay image or a figurine; to plasticize." The kanji 塑 means "figurine; to plasticize." <朔 土>				可塑性 plasticity [かそせい]; 塑像 clay figure [そぞう]; 塑性 plasticity [そせい]

III Plants

28 Tree

28a 木 "tree" [from one or many standing trees] 木林森

SG-0608 木	Meanings	Kun and On	Romaji	Bushu	Stroke Order and Number
	tree, wood, timber, Thursday; wooden	き・こ ボク・モク	ki, ko *boku, moku*	木	一十才木 4

木 **A** F-0097	甲骨文1 (1), 甲骨文2 (2), 金文1 (3), 金文2 (4), 説文 (5), 木
	[A single tree] 1 through 5 depicted "a single standing tree with large limbs growing upwards and downwards." Another view takes the downward lines to be the roots of the tree. The character meant "tree." A tree that was felled was made into "timber or wood." In Japanese it is also used to mean "Thursday." The kanji 木 means "tree, wood, timber, Thursday; wooden." <木>
	木 tree [きꜜ]; 植木 garden tree [うえき]; 木立 a cluster of trees, grove [こꜜだち]; 木の葉 leaves on a tree [こꜜのは, きꜜのは]; 木洩れ日 a ray of sunlight shining through the branches of trees [こもれび]; 大木 big tree [たいぼく]; 木工品 woodwork [もっこうひん]; 木曜日 Thursday [もくようꜜうび]

SG-0609 林	Meanings	Kun and On	Romaji	Bushu	Stroke Order and Number
	woods, grove	はやし リン	hayashi *rin*	木	一十木村林 8

林 **A** F-0270	甲骨文 (1), 金文 (2), 説文 (3), 林
	[Two trees] All of the ancient forms comprised two standing trees side by side. The kanji 林 means "woods, grove." <木木>
	林 wooded area, grove [はやし]; 松林 pine grove, pinery [まつばꜜやし]; 雑木林 thickly wooded area, thicket [ぞうきばꜜやし]; 林業 forestry [りんぎょう]; 林立する to stand close together [りんりつする]; 林間学校 school camp in summer in the woods [りんかんがꜜっこう]

SG-0610 森	Meanings	Kun and On	Romaji	Bushu	Stroke Order and Number
	forest; solemn, mystic	もり シン	mori *shin*	木	一十木森森 12

森 **A** F-0264	甲骨文1 (1), 甲骨文2 (2), 説文 (3), 森
	[Three trees] "Three trees" were placed in a triangular shape (1, 3), or in a row (2). Many standing trees meant "forest." Deep in a forest it was "solemn." The kanji reflected the layout in 1 and 3. The kanji 森 means "forest; solemn, mystic." <木木木>
	森 forest [もꜜり]; 森林 forest [しんりん]; 森羅万象 all things in nature [しꜜんら・ばんしょう]

28b 木 with an extra stroke

本 "source, base" [from a bulge in a tree trunk] 本鉢

SG-0611 本	Meanings	Kun and On	Romaji	Bushu	Stroke Order and Number
	origin, base, book; true, authentic, serious; counter for long objects	もと ホン	moto *hon*	木	一十才木本 5

本 **A** F-0009	金文 (1), 説文 (2), 本
	In 1 and 2, a small bulge or line was added at the lower end of a tree trunk to mean its "root" and "the root or origin of a matter." The root of a matter also signifies "true nature." In ancient times, wooden writing tablets were bound together into "a book." The kanji 本 means "origin, base, book; true, serious." It is also used as a counter for long, slender objects. <木一>
	本 base, origin [もとꜜ, もと], book [ほꜜん]; 見本 sample, model [みほん]; 本人 the person himself, the person in question [ほꜜんにん]; 本気 seriousness [ほんき]; 本社 headquarters, head office [ほꜜんしゃ]; 一本道 single path [いっぽꜜんみち]; 一本化する to unify, centralize [いっぽんかする]; 本物 genuine article [ほんもの]

SG-0612 鉢	Meanings	Kun and On	Romaji	Bushu	Stroke Order and Number
	bowl, pot, vessel, head	ハチ・ハツ	*hachi, hatsu*	金	⺈ 乍 金 針 鉢 鉢 13
鉢 **D** F-1797	篆文 鉢 The seal-style form comprised 犮, used for the sounds *hatsu/hachi*, and 皿 SG-1843 "a shallow vessel." It originally signified a Buddhist monk's meal bowl, called a *hatara* (from [patra] in Sanskrit), and more generally "bowl, pot, vessel." Its round rim also represented the circumference of "a head." The kanji 鉢 means "bowl, pot, vessel, head." <釒本>				鉢合わせする to bump against each other, head-on [はちあわせする]; 火鉢 indoor charcoal brazier for heating [ひばち]; 小鉢 small bowl [こばち]; 植木鉢 planter [うえきばち]; 金魚鉢 fish bowl [きんぎょばち]; 托鉢する to go about asking for alms (as a friar) [たくはつする]

末 "end" [from a line marking a tree top]; *matsu* 末抹

SG-0613 末	Meanings	Kun and On	Romaji	Bushu	Stroke Order and Number
	end; last	すえ マツ・バツ	sue *matsu, batsu*	木	一 二 キ 才 末 5
末 **A** F-0392	金文 1, 説文 2 末 1 and 2 had a dot or a line at the tip of a tree, marking the "end." The kanji 末 means "end; last." <一木>				末 end [すえ]; 末永く everlastingly, forever [すえながく]; 末広がり increasing prosperity as time goes on [すえひろがり, すえひろがり]; 末っ子 youngest child [すえっこ]; 月末 end of a month [げつまつ]; 始末する to deal with, put in order [しまつする]; 結末 conclusion, result [けつまつ]; 端末機 terminal [たんまつき]

SG-0614 抹	Meanings	Kun and On	Romaji	Bushu	Stroke Order and Number
	to erase, rub, reduce to powder	マツ	*matsu*	手	一 扌 扌 抹 抹 8
抹 **D** F-2127	No ancient form. The kanji 抹 comprised 扌, bushu *tehen* "an act done by hand," and 末 for the sound *matsu* to mean "powder." Painting over with wetted powder erased what had been written or drawn before. The kanji 抹 means "to erase, rub, reduce to powder." <扌末>				抹茶 high-quality powdered green tea [まっちゃ]; 抹消する to erase, cross out [まっしょうする]; 一抹の不安 a tinge of worry [いちまつのふあん]; 抹香臭い smelling of incense, overly pious [まっこうくさい]

未 "not yet, still" [from a line on top of a tree to indicate continuing growth]; *mi/mai* 未味妹昧

SG-0615 未	Meanings	Kun and On	Romaji	Bushu	Stroke Order and Number
	not yet, still	ミ	*mi*	木	二 キ 才 未 5
未 **A** F-0502	甲骨文1 1, 甲骨文2 2, 金文 3, 説文 4 未 1 through 4 depicted "a tree with its top limbs growing upward," signifying that the limbs were still growing. Something that was not yet complete meant "not yet, still." Another view takes this to be a borrowing. The kanji 未 means "not yet, still." <一木>				未来 future [みらい]; 未明 the hour before dawn [みめい]; 未然に防ぐ to prevent, nip in the bud [みぜんにふせぐ]; ~未満 less than X [~みまん]; 未知の unknown, strange [みちの]; 未成年 minor, underage [みせいねん] // 未だに still, even now [いまだに]

SG-0616 味	Meanings	Kun and On	Romaji	Bushu	Stroke Order and Number
	flavor; to taste	あじ ミ	aji *mi*	口	口 口二 吽 味 味 8
味 **A** F-0367	説文 味 The seal-style form comprised 口 SG-0031 "a mouth," and 未 "still, not yet," used for the sound *mi*. It described the process of tasting something, in which one has not yet determined the flavor of something in the mouth. The kanji 味 means "flavor; to taste." <口 未>				味 taste [あじ]; 味見する to try/taste something [あじみする]; 塩味 salty taste [しおあじ]; 後味の悪い having an unpleasant aftertaste [あとあじのわるい; あとあじの・わるい]; 味覚 sense of taste [みかく]; 賞味期限 best-before date, food expiration date [しょうみきげん]; 味方する to take someone's side [みかたする]; 嫌味を言う to make sarcastic remarks [いやみをいう]

SG-0617 妹	Meanings	Kun and On	Romaji	Bushu	Stroke Order and Number
	younger sister	いもうと マイ	imooto *mai*	女	く 女 女 妘 妹 妹 8
妹 **B** F-0828	甲骨文1 1, 甲骨文2 2, 金文 3, 説文 4 妹 1, 2, and 3 comprised 未 SG-0615 "a short tree that has yet to grow" (used for the sound *mi* or *mai*), and 女 SG-0521 "a female person." Taken together, a female member of a family who was still growing meant "a younger sister." The two components swapped positions in 4. The kanji 妹 means "younger sister." <女 未>				妹 younger sister [いもうと]; 姉妹 sisters [しまい]; 姉妹校 sister school [しまいこう]; 義妹 sister-in-law [ぎまい] // 従姉妹 female (first) cousin [いとこ]

	Meanings	Kun and On	Romaji	Bushu	Stroke Order and Number
SG-0618 昧	dark, vague; self-absorption	マイ	*mai*	日	冂 日二 日干 日未 昧 9

昧
D
F-2573

金文 1 1 金文 2 2 説文 3 昧

1 comprised "a tree that has yet to grow" 未, used for the sound *mai,* and "the sun" 日 **SG-1045**, together signifying "the darkness before the sun has risen." In 2, "a heart/mind" overshadowed by a tree signified "a mind in a vague, dark state." It also described a state of mind in which one was absorbed in a thought or a task. In 3, the sun and 未 were placed side by side. The kanji 昧 means "dark, vague; self-absorption." <日未>

曖昧な ambiguous, vague [あいまいな]; 読書三昧 indulgence in reading books [どくしょざんまい]; 釣り三昧 self-indulgence in fishing [つりざんまい]; 贅沢三昧 indulgence in luxury and extravagance [ぜいたくざんまい]; 曖昧模糊 undefined, obscure, vague [あいまいもこ]

制 "to control" [from overgrown limbs being pruned with a knife]; *see* 制製

	Meanings	Kun and On	Romaji	Bushu	Stroke Order and Number
SG-0619 制	to put in order, control, regulate; system	セイ	*see*	刀	ノ 𠂉 午 𠂔 制 8

制
A
F-0231

説文 制

The seal-style form comprised "a luxuriantly growing tree" (未 **SG-0615**), and "knife, cutting tool" (刂). Pruning an overgrown tree with a pair of shears meant "to put in order, neaten." The slanted short stroke (ノ) in the kanji indicates the tips of branches that have been pruned, or a general sense of "control, regulating." The kanji 制 means "to put in order, control, regulate; system." <𠂔 刂>

制する to have the upper hand over, control [せいする]; 制度 system, institution, regime [せいど]; 体制 regime, system [たいせい]; 学区制 school district system [がっくせい]; 強制的に by compulsion or enforcement [きょうせいてきに]; 官僚制 bureaucracy [かんりょうせい]; 共和制 republicanism [きょうわせい]; 反体制派 dissidents, dissident groups [はんたいせいは]

	Meanings	Kun and On	Romaji	Bushu	Stroke Order and Number
SG-0620 製	to manufacture; product; made in	セイ	*see*	衣	𠂉 午 𠂔 制 制 製 製 製 14

製
A
F-0433

説文 製

The seal-style form comprised 制 "to put in order," used for the sound *see*, and 衣 **SG-1657** "clothing," together signifying manufacturing well-made clothing or "manufactured products" in general. The kanji 製 means "to manufacture; product; made in." <制 衣>

既製服 ready-made clothes, off-the-rack clothing [きせいふく]; 製図 drafting, drawing [せいず]; 製本 bookbinding [せいほん]; 自家製 homemade [じかせい]; 冷製 served cold [れいせい]; 木製 wooden [もくせい]; 和製英語 Japanese English [わせいえいご]

朱 "red" [from the color of the center of a tree trunk]; *shu* 株朱殊珠

	Meanings	Kun and On	Romaji	Bushu	Stroke Order and Number
SG-0621 株	tree stump, stub, share, stock	かぶ	kabu	木	木 木' 杵 株 株 10

株
A
F-0472

説文 株

The seal-style form comprised 木 "tree," and 朱 **SG-0622** "red," used for the sound *shu*, and signifying "a tree stump, stub." The character is also used for "share or stock" in a corporation. The kanji 株 means "a tree stump, stub, share, stock." <木 朱(𠂉木)>

株 stock, share, stump [かぶ]; 切り株 tree stump, stubble [きりかぶ, きりかぶ]; 株式会社 corporation, Ltd., Inc. [かぶしきがいしゃ]; 株主 shareholder [かぶぬし]; お株を取られる to be outdone by another person with the same talent [おかぶをとられる]; 古株 old stump, old-timer [ふるかぶ]; 株安 a period of weak stock prices [かぶやす]

	Meanings	Kun and On	Romaji	Bushu	Stroke Order and Number
SG-0622 朱	red, vermillion	シュ	*shu*	木	ノ 𠂉 牛 牛 朱 6

朱
C
F-1525

甲骨文 1 1 甲骨文 2 2 金文 1 3 金文 2 4 説文 5 朱

1 through 5 depicted a tree with a line or a bulge going through in the center of the trunk, indicating a place on the trunk where a cut was made. A freshly cut trunk was reddish in color, and from that the character signified "red." The kanji 朱 means "red, vermillion." <朱 (𠂉木)>

朱色 vermillion [しゅいろ]; 朱肉 vermilion inkpad [しゅにく]; 朱に交われば赤くなる "Bad company corrupts good character." [しゅにまじわれば・あかくなる]

	Meanings	Kun and On	Romaji	Bushu	Stroke Order and Number
SG-0623 殊	distinctive; especially, above all, most importantly	こと シュ	koto *shu*	歹	一ア万歹歺歼殊 10

殊 **C** F-1548 説文	The seal-style form comprised 歹, bushu *gatsuhen/ kabanehen* "a dead body," and 朱 for the sound *shu.* 朱 originally depicted a tree trunk cut in the middle, and it gave the meaning "to decapitate." From the extremity of such punishment it came to mean "special." The kanji 殊 means "distinctive; especially, above all, most importantly." <歹朱>	殊に especially, above all things [こ↑とに]; 殊更に intentionally, deliberately, in particular [ことさらに]; 殊の外 exceedingly, uncommonly [ことのほか]; 殊勝な laudable, commendable [しゅしょうな]; 特殊な special, distinctive, peculiar [とくしゅな]; 殊勲賞 Outstanding Performance Award [しゅく↑んしょう]

	Meanings	Kun and On	Romaji	Bushu	Stroke Order and Number
SG-0624 珠	jewel, pearl, a round object; beautiful	シュ	*shu*	玉	丁王'王'' 玝 珠 10

珠 **C** F-1606 説文	The seal-style form comprised 王 **SG-1447** "string of gems," and 朱, used for the sound *shu* to mean "round." "A round gem" meant "pearl." The kanji 珠 means "jewel, pearl, a round object; beautiful." <王 朱>	珠玉の bejeweled [しゅぎょくの]; 珠算 calculating on an abacus [しゅざん]; 真珠 pearl [しんじゅ] // 数珠 Buddhist rosary [じゅず]

28c 木 "tree, wood; tree name" [木 in combination with another shape]; **bushu *kihen***

楽薬査業松条桜困床染枠柳巣梨桃桑棚枥柿朴朽楼椎鬱慄

	Meanings	Kun and On	Romaji	Bushu	Stroke Order and Number
SG-0625 楽	music; pleasant, enjoyable, comfortable	たの-しい ガク・ラク	tano-shii *gaku, raku*	木	白白'白'泊' 泊' 泊楽 13

楽 **A** F-0201 甲骨文 1, 金文 2, 説文 3, 旧字 4	Views regarding the origin of the kanji 楽 vary, and many of them pertain to musical instruments: (a) a pellet drum with its cords, hung on a wooden stand; (b) bells with ornamental threads on both sides of their handles; (c) a stringed instrument, from a fingernail (白 **SG-0787**) plucking two threads (幺); and (d) acorns on a *kunugi* oak tree, used for the sounds *raku/gaku* to mean "fun; merrily; to enjoy." A musical instrument making pleasant rhythmic sounds meant "music; pleasant, comfortable." The kanji 楽 means "music; pleasant, enjoyable, comfortable." <白 ⺀ 木>	楽しい enjoyable [たのし↑い]; 楽しみにする to look forward to [たのし↑みにする]; 音楽 music [お↑んがく]; 楽屋 dressing room, backstage [がくや]; 気楽な carefree, easygoing [きらくな]; 楽々と with great ease [らくら↑くと]; 楽勝 easy victory, landslide victory, a breeze (colloquial) [らくしょう] // 神楽 sacred Shinto music and dancing [か↑ぐら]

	Meanings	Kun and On	Romaji	Bushu	Stroke Order and Number
SG-0626 薬	medicine, chemicals; pharmaceutical	くすり ヤク	kusuri *yaku*	艸	艹 甘 苜 苜 薬 薬 16

薬 **A** F-0496 金文 1, 説文 2, 旧字 3	1 and 2 comprised 艸 "plants" (艹, bushu *kusakanmuri*) and 樂 (for 楽) "enjoyable," used for the sound *yaku.* The character meant "herbs that soothed pain; medicinal," and also referred in general to any chemical substance that causes a reaction. The kanji 薬 means "medicine, chemicals; pharmaceutical." <艹楽>	薬 medicine, pill [くすり]; 薬屋 pharmacy [くすりや]; 飲み薬 internal medicine[のみぐ↑すり]; 目薬 eye drop [めぐ↑すり]; 薬品 medicine, chemicals [やくひん]; 薬局 pharmacy [やっきょく]; 漢方薬 Chinese herbal medicine [かんぽ↑うやく]; 薬物 medicines, drugs [やく↑ぶつ]; 火薬 gunpowder, explosive [かやく]

	Meanings	Kun and On	Romaji	Bushu	Stroke Order and Number
SG-0627 査	to examine closely, inspect	サ	*sa*	木	一十木 杏 杳 査 9

査 **A** F-0495	No ancient form. The kanji 査 comprises 木 "wood," and 且 **SG-0815** used for the sound *sa* to mean "to combine," originally signifying "tying many logs together to make a raft." Later on, from logs lined up together it came to be used to mean "to examine closely, inspect." The kanji 査 means "to examine closely, inspect." <木 且>	検査 inspection [け↑んさ]; 調査 survey, investigation [ちょ↑うさ]; 査証 visa [さしょう]; 巡査 police officer, constable [じゅ↑んさ, じゅんさ]; 審査員 judge, examiner [しんさ↑いん]; 査定額 assessed amount/value [さて↑いがく]

	Meanings	Kun and On	Romaji	Bushu	Stroke Order and Number
SG-0628 業	skill, work, one's deeds, act, karma	わざ ギョウ・ゴウ	waza *gyoo, goo*	木	業 13

業 **A** F-0134

金文1 1, 金文2 2, 説文 3

One view explains that 1 and 2 depicted a wooden stand with notches for hanging musical instruments. Playing musical instruments required skill, and the character signified "skills, work." Another view explains that it depicted wooden frames used in construction for compacting dirt to stabilize the foundation or walls of a building, and it meant "work." In Buddhist teaching it was used for "karma," from a Sanskrit word that meant "one's deeds or acts." The kanji 業 means "skill, work, one's deeds, act, karma." < 業(业ㄓ未)>

業 work, skill [わざꜜ]; 仕業 one's doing, act [しわざ]; 授業 class, lecture [じゅꜜぎょう]; 工業 manufacturing industry [こꜜうぎょう]; 産業 industry [さんぎょう]; 業 karma, inevitable retribution [ごう]; 因業な hardhearted, cruel [いんごうな]; 自業自得 natural consequence of one's own foolish deed [じꜜごう・じとく, じごうじꜜとく]

	Meanings	Kun and On	Romaji	Bushu	Stroke Order and Number
SG-0629 松	pine tree	まつ ショウ	matsu *shoo*	木	松 8

松 **A** F-0315

説文 1, 説文或体 2

1 comprised 木 "tree," and 公 **SG-1321**, used for the sound *shoo*. The role of 容 **SG-1162** in 2 is unclear, other than for the use of its sound (*yoo*). The kanji 松 means "pine tree." Because they are robust and evergreen, pine trees are also regarded as auspicious symbols. And since pine resin can be burned to produce bright light, it has traditionally been used in torches. The kanji 松 means "a pine tree." < 木ハム >

松 pine tree [まꜜつ]; 松茸 *matsutake* mushroom [まつたꜜけ]; 門松 *kadomatsu*, a New Year decoration pair of pine and bamboo placed on a front gate [かどꜜまつ]; 松竹梅 pine-bamboo-plum (auspicious grouping) [しょうちくꜜばい] // 松明 torch [たꜜいまつ]

	Meanings	Kun and On	Romaji	Bushu	Stroke Order and Number
SG-0630 条	line, streak, clause	ジョウ	*joo*	木	条 7

条 **B** F-0533

説文 1, 旧字 2

1 comprised "a person" (亻), "water trickling down" (丨), and "a hand holding a stick" (攴, 攵), forming 攸 for the sound *yuu* (later *joo*); and "a tree" (木), together signifying "a hand shaking twigs under trickling water." It depicted a person undergoing a rite of ablution. From water dripping down it became used for "lines" in documents, and "a section or article of a law." In the shinji 条 the left half was dropped, and 攵 became 夂. The kanji 条 means "line, streak, clause." < 夂木 > (Note: The kyuji 條 and the kanji 悠 **SG-0177** share the same origin.)

条件 condition [じょうけꜜん, じょうけん]; 条約 treaty [じょうやく]; 条例 ordinance, regulations [じょうれい]; 一条の光 a ray of light [いちꜜじょうの・ひかり]; 憲法九条 Article 9 of the Constitution [けꜜんぽう・きゅꜜうじょう]; 金科玉条 golden rule [きꜜんか・ぎょくじょう]; 別条ない without any problem [べつじょうなꜜい]

	Meanings	Kun and On	Romaji	Bushu	Stroke Order and Number
SG-0631 桜	cherry tree, cherry blossom	さくら オウ	sakura *oo*	木	桜 10

桜 **B** F-0665

説文 1, 旧字 2

1 comprised "a tree" (木), and "a necklace made from shells strung together" (貝 **SG-1693**) that "a woman" (女 **SG-0521**) wore. 嬰 was used for the sound *oo*. The character originally meant "fruit tree," but in Japanese it specifically means a cherry tree, most popular for flower viewing. The kanji 桜 means "cherry tree, cherry blossom." <木ツ女>

桜 cherry tree, cherry blossom [さくら]; 夜桜 cherry blossoms viewed in the evening [よざꜜくら]; 葉桜 a cherry tree with sprouting leaves [はざꜜくら] // 桜桃 cherry [おうとう, (さくらんぼ)]

	Meanings	Kun and On	Romaji	Bushu	Stroke Order and Number
SG-0632 困	to be in trouble, be inconvenienced; perplexed	こま-る コン	koma-ru *kon*	口	困 7

困 **B** F-0900

甲骨文 1, 説文古文 2, 説文 3

In 1 and 3, the tree 木 inside 囗, bushu *kunigamae* "an enclosure," cannot move freely, thus signifying "to be in trouble." Another view holds that 1 depicted a block of wood in a wooden latch and signified "shutting a gate," and that 2 with 止 "to stop" and 木 together signified "a wooden latch that stopped a person from coming in." By extension it meant "to be in trouble." The kanji 困 means "to be in trouble, be inconvenienced; perplexed." < 囗木 >

困る to be troubled, be inconvenienced [こまꜜる]; 困り物 a thorny problem, bother [こまりもの]; 困難な hard, arduous, trying [こꜜんなんな]; 困惑する to become confused, be at a loss [こんわくする]; 貧困 poverty [ひんこん]; 疲労困憊 exhaustion [ひろうこんぱい]

SG-0633 床	Meanings	Kun and On	Romaji	Bushu	Stroke Order and Number
	(wooden) floor, base, bed	ゆか・とこ ショウ	yuka, toko *shoo*	广	丶亠广户床床 7

床 **B** F-0996

牀 床 旧字

The kyuji 牀 comprised 爿 "a wooden plank with legs," for the sound *shoo*, and 木 "wood," signifying "wooden floor, base, bed." The informal style 床 has become the shinji. The kanji 床 means "(wooden) floor, base, bed." <广木>

床 floor [ゆか]; 床下 underfloor [ゆかした]; 床屋 barber shop [とこや]; 床を取る to lay out a *futon* to sleep [とこをとる]; 床の間 alcove for hanging scroll [とこのま]; 寝床 sleeping bed, berth [ねどこ]; 温床 hotbed [おんしょう]; 起床時間 the hour of rising, the time one gets up [きしょうじかん]

SG-0634 染	Meanings	Kun and On	Romaji	Bushu	Stroke Order and Number
	to dye, permeate	そ-める・し-みる セン	so-meru, shi-miru *sen*	木	氵氿氿汍染染 9

染 **B** F-1024

說文 染

The seal-style form comprised "water, liquid" (氵), "wilted leaves" (九), and "tree" (木), signifying "soaking fabric in tree extract to dye." The kanji 染 means "to dye, permeate." <氵九木>

染める to dye [そめる]; 染みる to soak, permeate [しみる]; 心に染みる to sink into one's heart [こころに (or こころに)・しみる]; 染色 dyeing [せんしょく]; 染料 dye [せんりょう]; 感染 infection [かんせん]; 感染者 carrier, infected person [かんせんしゃ]; 汚染 contamination, pollution [おせん]

SG-0635 枠	Meanings	Kun and On	Romaji	Bushu	Stroke Order and Number
	framework, quota, restriction	わく	waku	木	一十木朾枠枠 8

枠 **B** F-1054

The kanji 枠 is a 国字 (*kokuji*), or kanji created in Japan, and thus has no ancient form. It comprises 木 "tree, wood" and 卆 "spool, reel of thread, beam in a weaving apparatus," together signifying a wooden framework. The kanji 枠 means "framework, quota, restriction."<木卆(九十)>

別枠 separate quota, particular case [べつわく]; 黒枠 black border, mourning border [くろわく]; 大枠 general framework [おおわく]; 枠組み frame, scheme [わくぐみ]

SG-0636 柳	Meanings	Kun and On	Romaji	Bushu	Stroke Order and Number
	willow tree	やなぎ リュウ	yanagi *ryuu*	木	木杉杉枊枊柳 9

柳 **C** F-1139

甲骨文 1, 金文 2, 說文 3, 柳

1, 2, and 3 comprised 木 "tree," and 卯, used for the sound *ryuu*, together signifying a tree with long, supple branches swaying freely—"a willow tree." The kanji 柳 means "willow tree." <木 卯>

柳 willow tree [やなぎ]; 川柳 *senryu* verse, a 5-7-5 syllable form of comic verse [せんりゅう]

SG-0637 巣	Meanings	Kun and On	Romaji	Bushu	Stroke Order and Number
	nest	す ソウ	su *soo*	巛	丶丷⺍当単巣 11

巣 **C** F-1248

甲骨文 1, 金文 2, 說文 3, 旧字 4 巢, 巣

1, 2, and 3 depicted "a bird's nest at the top of a tree," signifying "nest." The top of the kyuji, 巢, retained the little heads of three chicks sticking out of the nest (甾), which became ⺍ in the shinji. The kanji 巣 means "nest." <⺍田木>

巣箱 bird box, birdhouse [すばこ, すばこ]; 巣立つ to leave the nest, become independent [すだつ]; 空き巣 burglary of a house while residents are away [あきす]; 巣篭もり nesting [すごもり]; 古巣 one's former haunts [ふるす]; 病巣 focus of disease, lesion [びょうそう]; 帰巣本能 homing instinct [きそうほんのう]

SG-0638 梨	Meanings	Kun and On	Romaji	Bushu	Stroke Order and Number
	pear	なし	nashi	木	二禾利利梨梨 11

梨 **C** F-1286

說文 梨

The top of the seal-style form (棃) had the sound *ri* and meant "the crisp sound of a knife cutting." It was later replaced by 利 **SG-0713** for the same sound. A crisp fruit on a tree (木) is "a pear." The kanji 梨 means "pear." <利木>

梨 pear [なし, なし]// 梨園 the world of Kabuki [りえん]

SG-0639 桃	Meanings	Kun and On	Romaji	Bushu	Stroke Order and Number
	peach	もも トウ	momo *too*	木	木杉杉桃桃 10

桃 **C** F-1360

說文 桃

The seal-style form comprised 木, and 兆 **SG-1770**, a shape split down the middle and pronounced *too*. A peach splits easily into two. The kanji 桃 means "peach." <木 兆>

桃 peach [もも]; 桃色 pink [ももいろ]; 白桃 white peach [はくとう]

	Meanings	Kun and On	Romaji	Bushu	Stroke Order and Number
SG-0640 桑	mulberry tree	くわ ソウ	kuwa *soo*	木	フヌ叒叒桑桑桑 10

桑 **C** F-1454 — 甲骨文 1, 説文 2, 桑

1 depicted "a mulberry tree." The top of 2 depicted many large leaves on the mulberry tree. Another view explains that it depicted many hands busily feeding mulberry leaves to hungry, growing silkworms. In the kanji, the "leaves or hands" became three 又 **SG-0084**. The kanji 桑 means "mulberry tree." <又又又木>

桑 mulberry tree [くヿわ]; 桑畑 mulberry field [くわばヿたけ]

	Meanings	Kun and On	Romaji	Bushu	Stroke Order and Number
SG-0641 棚	shelf	たな	tana	木	木 杊 桕 棚 棚 12

棚 **C** F-1497 — 篆文, 棚

The seal-style form comprised 木 "wood," and 朋 "boards bridged over each other in layers," used for the sound *hoo* to mean "to arrange, put in order." Together they signified "a shelf." The kanji 棚 means "shelf." <木月月>

棚 shelf [たな]; 本棚 bookshelves [ほヿんだな]; 戸棚 cupboard [とだな]; 吊り棚 hanging shelf [つりだな]; 大陸棚 continental shelf [たいりくだな]; 棚上げにする to shelve (a problem), put on hold [たなあげにする]

	Meanings	Kun and On	Romaji	Bushu	Stroke Order and Number
SG-0642 栃	*tochi* tree (horse-chestnut)	とち	tochi	木	木 杉 枦 枥 栃 9

栃 **C** F-1530

The kanji 栃 was created in Japan, for the name of a tree called a *tochi-no-ki*. The character has its origin in word play—Multiplying *too* (十, ten) by "*chi*" (千, thousand) made 10,000 (一万). The kanji 栃 comprises 木 "tree", 厂, and 万 "ten thousand," and is pronounced *tochi*. It is also used in the name of Tochigi Prefecture (栃木県). <木 厂 万>

栃木県 Tochigi prefecture [とちぎヿけん]; 栃の木 Japanese horse-chestnut [とヿちのき]

	Meanings	Kun and On	Romaji	Bushu	Stroke Order and Number
SG-0643 柿	persimmon	かき	kaki	木	木 木' 木 柿 柿 9

柿 **C** F-1560 — 篆文 1, 正字 2, 柿

The right side of 1 was used for the sound *shi*. In orthographic style it became 柹 (2). The kanji 柿 means "persimmon." <木市>

柿 persimmon [かき]; 渋柿 sour persimmon [しぶヿがき]; 干し柿 dried persimmon [ほしヿがき]

	Meanings	Kun and On	Romaji	Bushu	Stroke Order and Number
SG-0644 朴	simple, ingenuous, naïve	ボク	*boku*	木	木 朴 朴 6

朴 **D** F-1796 — 説文, 朴

The seal-style form comprised 木, and 卜 used for the sound *boku* to mean "to peel," together signifying "to peel tree bark." From the sense of "something with no exterior" it meant "simple and ingenuous." The kanji 朴 means "simple, ingenuous, naïve." <木 卜>

素朴な simple, ingenuous, artless [そぼくな]; 朴訥さ rugged honesty, simplicity and modesty [ぼくとつさ]

	Meanings	Kun and On	Romaji	Bushu	Stroke Order and Number
SG-0645 朽	to rot, decay, crumble into decay	く-ちる キュウ	ku-chiru *kyuu*	木	木 木 朽 6

朽 **D** F-1882 — 説文 1, 説文或体 2, 朽

1 and 2 had 丂 "a bent or curved shape" as their right-hand component, used for the sound *kyuu*. The left side of 1 was "skeletal remains," whereas 2 had 木 "wood." Both of these are things that decay and rot. The kanji 朽 means "to rot, decay, crumble into decay." < 木 丂 >

朽ちる to rot, molder, crumble [くちる]; 老朽化 deterioration [ろうきゅうか]; 不朽の immortal, everlasting [ふきゅうの]

	Meanings	Kun and On	Romaji	Bushu	Stroke Order and Number
SG-0646 楼	many-storied building, tower	ロウ	*roo*	木	木 杧 栄 梾 楼 楼 13

楼 **D** F-1850 — 説文 1, 旧字 2, 楼

1 comprised 木 "wood, tree," and 婁, used for the sound *roo* to mean "*layers*," signifying "a wooden structure that had many levels." With 婁 simplified to its present form, the kanji 楼 means "many-storied building, tower." < 木 米 女>

楼閣 many-storied building, high tower [ろうかく]; 蜃気楼 mirage [しんきヿろう]

SG-0647 椎	Meanings	Kun and On	Romaji	Bushu	Stroke Order and Number
	chinquapin tree, mallet, vertebra	ツイ	*tsui*	木	木 朾 柎 柎 桁 椎 12

椎 **D** F-2009 — 説文

The seal-style form comprised 木 "tree," and 隹 for the sound *tsui*, together signifying "a hard tree," such as a chinquapin tree, from which tools such as mallets could be made. A vertebra is round and mallet-shaped, whence the meaning "spine, vertebra." The kanji 椎 means "chinquapin tree, mallet, vertebra." <木 隹 >

脊椎 the vertebrae, the spine [せきつい]; 椎間板 an intervertebral disk [ついかんばん] // 椎(の)木 chinquapin tree [しいのき]; 椎茸 *shiitake* mushroom [しいたけ]; 干し椎茸 dried shiitake mushroom [ほししいたけ]

SG-0648 鬱	Meanings	Kun and On	Romaji	Bushu	Stroke Order and Number
	melancholy, low-spirited, depressed, dense, thick; to be boxed in, block	ウツ	*utsu*	鬯	木 木木 林 楙 楙 欝 鬱 鬱 29

鬱 **D** F-2628 — 金文 1, 説文 2, 常用漢字 3, 略字 4

1 depicted "a person in the midst of luxuriant woods," signifying "luxuriant growth" or the state of "being boxed in." The extremely complex 2 and 3 comprised 缶 SG-2009 "a clay container" inside 林 "a forest"; 冖 "a cover"; 鬯 "fragrant herbs in a container to flavor the spirits"; and 彡 "shape." Together, they signified fragrances confined in a container, or trapped air unable to escape, and thus "to be boxed in." It is also used to describe stagnant emotions, such as "melancholy, low-spirited, depressed." The kanji 鬱 (3) means "melancholy, low-spirited." This 29-stroke kanji is sometimes written as 欝 (4). <木缶木冖凶匕彡>

憂鬱な gloomy, depressed, melancholy [ゆううつな]; 鬱病 depression, depressive psychosis [うつびょう]; 陰鬱な melancholic, dismal, sullen [いんうつな]; 鬱血する to be congested with blood [うっけつ]; 鬱積 buildup (of grievances) [うっせき]; 鬱蒼とした thick (growth) [うっそうとした]

SG-0649 慄	Meanings	Kun and On	Romaji	Bushu	Stroke Order and Number
	to shudder, to quiver	リツ	*ritsu*	心	忄 忄 忄 慄 慄 慄 13

慄 **D** F-2695

No ancient form. The kanji 慄 comprises 忄 "heart," and 栗 "a chestnut," which had spiky burrs, and was used for the sound *ritsu*. Together, they signified "a heart that quivers as if hit continuously by spiky burrs." The kanji 慄 means "to shudder, quiver." <忄栗(西木)>

戦慄 shivering, shuddering [せんりつ]; 慄然とする to be horror-stricken, shiver with fear [りつぜんとする]

28d 喿 "busy" [from mouths of many birds chirping noisily in a tree]; *soo* 繰操藻燥 喿

SG-0650 繰	Meanings	Kun and On	Romaji	Bushu	Stroke Order and Number
	to manipulate, push or pull one after another; repeatedly	く-る	ku-ru	糸	幺 糸 紀 紀 縕 繰 19

繰 **C** F-1127 — 説文

The seal-style form comprised 糸 SG-1600 "skein of threads," and 喿, used for the sound *soo* to mean "spinning busily," together signifying "to busily reel thread, push one after another; continuously." The kanji 繰 means "to manipulate, push/pull one after another; repeatedly." <糸 喿 (品木)>

繰り言 the same story told over and over again, grumble [くりごと]; 繰り延べ postponement, deferment [くりのべ]; 繰り上げる to move up the date of an event [くりあげる]; 繰り返す to repeat [くりかえす, くりかえす]; 資金繰り cashflow management [しきんぐり]; 繰り広げる to roll out, unfold [くりひろげる]

SG-0651 操	Meanings	Kun and On	Romaji	Bushu	Stroke Order and Number
	to operate; integrity, fidelity	みさお・あやつ-る ソウ	misao, ayatsu-ru *soo*	手	扌 扌 扣 挹 操 16

操 **C** F-1146 — 説文

The seal-style form comprised 扌 "an act done by hand," and 喿, used for the sound *soo* to mean "to busily conduct." "A hand busily ruffling threads" gave the meaning "to operate." Good self-conduct meant "integrity, fidelity." The kanji 操 means "to operate; integrity, fidelity." <扌喿>

操 fidelity, chastity [みさお]; 操る to manipulate, handle [あやつる]; 操作 operation, manipulation [そうさ]; 体操 gymnastics, physical exercises [たいそう]; 操業休止 shutdown of operations [そうぎょうきゅうし]; 操縦士 pilot of an aircraft [そうじゅうし]; 節操がない having no principles [せっそうがない]

	Meanings	Kun and On	Romaji	Bushu	Stroke Order and Number
SG-0652 藻	algae, seaweed, beautiful writing (historical)	も ソウ	mo *soo*	艸	艹 萍 萍 藻 藻 藻 19

藻 **D** F-1992

説文 1 説文或体 2

1 comprised “plants” (艸, 艹), “flowing water” (氵), and 巢, used for the sound *soo*, together signifying “algae, seaweed.” Seaweed floating in water created pretty patterns, and in classical literature it was used to mean “beautiful writing, literary work.” In 2, 巢 was replaced by 喿, which has the same sound. The kanji 藻 means “algae, seaweed, beautiful writing (historical).” <氵喿>

藻 algae, seaweed [も]; 川藻 river algae [かわも]; 海藻 seaweed, marine plants [かいそう]

	Meanings	Kun and On	Romaji	Bushu	Stroke Order and Number
SG-0653 燥	to dry; restless	ソウ	*soo*	火	丷 炉 炉 燥 燥 17

燥 **D** F-2191

説文

The seal-style form comprised 火 **SG-1164** “fire,” and 喿 “busy, restless,” used for the sound *soo*, together signifying “to dry; restless.” The kanji 燥 means “to dry; restless.” <火喿>

乾燥する to dry, become dry [かんそうする]; 焦燥感 irritability, feeling of impatience [しょうそうかん]; 衣類乾燥機 clothes dryer [いるい·かんそうき]

28e 果 “a tree with fruit/nuts/berries”; *ka* 果課菓裸彙

	Meanings	Kun and On	Romaji	Bushu	Stroke Order and Number
SG-0654 果	fruit, result; to perish, end, carry out	は-たす カ	ha-tasu *ka*	木	丨 口 旦 甲 果 8

果 **A** F-0401

金文1 1 金文2 2 説文 3

1 and 2 depicted fruit, nuts or berries on a tree. In 3 the dots were dropped. Fruit, nuts, and berries were the end result of flowering, and thus the character meant “result; to carry out to the end.” Fruits and berries perish quickly, and in Japanese this kanji also means “to perish.” The kanji 果 means “fruit, result; to perish, end, carry out.” <果(曰木)>

果たす “to carry out, accomplish” [はたす]; 果て end [はて]; 果てる to perish, die [はてる]; 果実 fruit, fruition [かじつ]; 結果 result [けっか]; 因果 cause and effect, retribution, karma [いんが] // 果物 fruit [くだもの]

	Meanings	Kun and On	Romaji	Bushu	Stroke Order and Number
SG-0655 課	section of study, lesson; to charge, impose	カ	*ka*	言	言 訂 諢 課 課 15

課 **A** F-0458

説文

The seal-style form comprised 言 “word; to say,” and 果, used for the sound *ka* to mean “to use” or “to try.” Originally, the character meant the materials that an applicant studied before taking a test. The kanji 課 means “section of study, lesson; to charge, impose.” <言果>

課する to levy, impose, assess [かする]; 課目 subject of study [かもく]; 第三課 Lesson 3, Third section [だいさんか]; 課題 assignment, question, problem [かだい]; 課税 taxation [かぜい]; 課長 section manager [かちょう]

	Meanings	Kun and On	Romaji	Bushu	Stroke Order and Number
SG-0656 菓	sweets, snacks	カ	*ka*	艸	一 艹 节 茸 菓 11

菓 **C** F-1419

No ancient form. In ancient times, fruits (果 **SG-0654**) were eaten for their sweet flavor, or as a dessert. The kanji for “sweets” was created by adding 艹 “plant” to 果, used for the sound *ka*. In Japan it originally meant “fruit processed with sugar,” and later referred to sweets made with bean or rice powder and sugar, and snacks in general. The kanji 菓 means “sweets, snacks.” <艹果>

お菓子 snacks, sweets [おかし]; 和菓子 Japanese-style sweets [わがし]; 洋菓子 Western-style sweets [ようがし]; 生菓子 Japanese (unbaked) sweets [なまがし]; 菓子折り a box of confectionaries as a thank-you gift [かしおり, かしおり]

	Meanings	Kun and On	Romaji	Bushu	Stroke Order and Number
SG-0657 裸	bare, naked	はだか ラ	hadaka *ra*	衣	ネ ネ ネ 初 裎 裸 13

裸 **C** F-1487

説文

In the seal-style form, 果 (used as an abbreviated form for the non-Joyo kanji 羸 “naked” and its sound *ra*) was placed inside “clothes” (衣) that were wide open, signifying “naked.” Another view holds that the character was meant to draw a connection between the smooth skin of a fruit and that of a human body. In the kanji, 衣 **SG-1657** became 衤, bushu *koromohen*. The kanji 裸 means “bare, naked.” <衤果>

裸 naked, bare [はだか]; 裸ん坊 bare-naked [はだかんぼう]; 真っ裸 completely nude [まっぱだか]; 赤裸々な unvarnished, frank [せきらら な]; 裸体 bare body [らたい]; 全裸 completely naked [ぜんら]

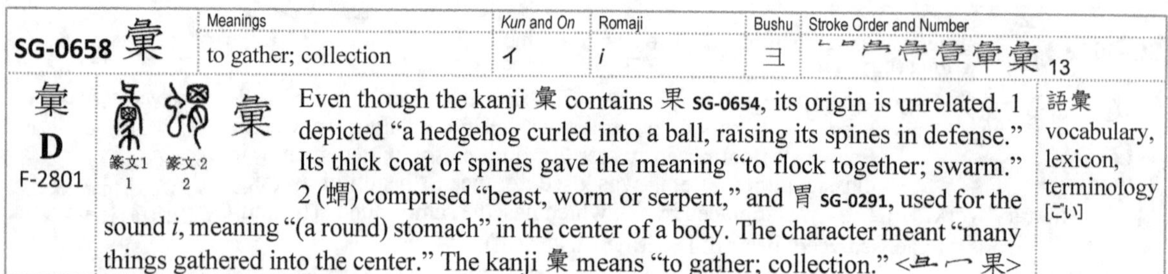

SG-0658 彙	Meanings	Kun and On	Romaji	Bushu	Stroke Order and Number
	to gather; collection	イ	*i*	ヨ	彙 13

彙 **D** F-2801

篆文1 1 篆文2 2

Even though the kanji 彙 contains 果 **SG-0654**, its origin is unrelated. 1 depicted "a hedgehog curled into a ball, raising its spines in defense." Its thick coat of spines gave the meaning "to flock together; swarm." 2 (蝟) comprised "beast, worm or serpent," and 胃 **SG-0291**, used for the sound *i*, meaning "(a round) stomach" in the center of a body. The character meant "many things gathered into the center." The kanji 彙 means "to gather; collection." <彑冖果>

語彙 vocabulary, lexicon, terminology [ごい]

28f 某 *bai/boo* 謀某媒

SG-0659 謀	Meanings	Kun and On	Romaji	Bushu	Stroke Order and Number
	to consult, plan, betray, deceive, plot	はか-る ボウ・ム	haka-ru *boo, mu*	言	謀 16

謀 **C** F-1643

說文古文1 1 說文古文2 2 說文 3

1 and 2 were early forms of 咨, "to consult with, ask the opinion of." 3 comprised 言 "word; to say," and 某 **SG-0660**, used for the sound *boo* and the meaning "unspecified," together signifying "to consult about an unknown matter." The sense of "unspecified/unknown matter" also gave the meaning "to do something behind someone's back, to plot, betray." The kanji 謀 means "to consult, plan, betray, deceive, plot." <言某(甘木)>

謀る to consult with, refer to [はかる]; 共謀 conspiracy, collusion [きょうぼう]; 参謀 staff officer, advisor [さんぼう]; 陰謀 plot, dark design [いんぼう]; 無謀な impudent, reckless [むぼうな]; 謀叛 (謀反) rebellion, treason [むほん]

SG-0660 某	Meanings	Kun and On	Romaji	Bushu	Stroke Order and Number
	a certain (person), some (amount); unspecified	ボウ	*boo*	木	某 9

某 **D** F-1899

金文 1 說文古文 2 說文 3

One view treats the kanji 某 as having been taken from the non-Joyo kanji 楳 *boo* "plum," and borrowed for the meaning "certain; some." (In Japanese the kanji 梅 **SG-0544** is used for "plum.") Another view takes 1 and 3 to depict "a prayer box on a tree bough," signifying "to ask a deity's will," or to inquire in general. From that the character came to mean "unspecified/unknown." The kanji 某 means "a certain (person), some (amount); unspecified." <某(甘木)>

某氏 a certain person, a person who shall remain nameless [ぼうし]; 某紙 a certain newspaper [ぼうし] // 何某•某 a certain person, Mr. So-and-So, some (amount) [なにがし]

SG-0661 媒	Meanings	Kun and On	Romaji	Bushu	Stroke Order and Number
	matchmaking, medium	バイ	*bai*	女	媒 12

媒 **D** F-1933

說文

The seal-style form comprised 女 **SG-0521** "woman," and 某, used for the sound *bai*, together signifying "to consult about marriage; matchmaking." The kanji is also used to mean something that promotes an action, such as a "catalyzer." The kanji 媒 means "matchmaking, medium." <女某>

触媒 catalyzer [しょくばい]; 媒酌人 matchmaker, go-between [ばいしゃくにん]; 媒介する to mediate, serve as a medium [ばいかいする]; 広告媒体 advertising media [こうこくばいたい]

28g 片 "a piece" [from the right half of a tree] 片版

SG-0662 片	Meanings	Kun and On	Romaji	Bushu	Stroke Order and Number
	piece, chip; far from the center	かた ヘン	kata *hen*	片	片 4

片 **B** F-0867

甲骨文 1 說文 2

1 and 2 depicted "the right half of a tree" or "a piece of wood." The kanji 片 means "a piece (of something), a chip." In Japanese it also means "piece, chip; far from the center, distant." <片>

片方 one side, one party [かたほう]; 片言 imperfect speech, baby talk [かたこと]; 片手落ち partiality, one-sidedness [かたておち]; 片時も～ない to not even for a moment [かたときも～ない]; 片手間 spare time [かたてま, かたでま]; 片田舎 remote country place, backwoods [かたいなか]; 断片的 fragmental [だんぺんてき]; 一片の piece of, scrap of [いっぺんの]

SG-0663 版	Meanings	Kun and On	Romaji	Bushu	Stroke Order and Number
	printing block, edition	ハン	*han*	片	丿丿'片片'片片'版版 8

版 **B** F-0777 (説文) The seal-style form comprised 片 "a piece of wood," and 反 **SG-0087** "to warp," used for the sound *han*. A thin piece of wood tended to warp, and the character signified a wooden printing block which was shaved clean in preparation for printing a new publication or edition. The kanji 版 means "wooden printing block, edition." <片反>

版画 woodblock print [はんが]; 出版 publication, publishing [しゅっぱん]; 決定版 definitive version [けっていばん]; 改版 revised edition [かいはん]; 海賊版 pirated edition [かいぞくばん]; 活版印刷 type printing, typography [かっぱんいんさつ]; 現代版 modern version [げんだいばん]

28h 奉 "to offer reverentially" [from two hands raising a consecrated bough]; *hoo* 奉棒俸

SG-0664 奉	Meanings	Kun and On	Romaji	Bushu	Stroke Order and Number
	to offer up, present respectfully	たてまつ-る ホウ・ブ	tatematsu-ru *hoo, bu*	大	三夫夫叁奉 8

奉 **C** F-1610 (金文 1, 説文 2) 1 comprised 丰 "a tree branch that is offered to a deity," and "two hands presenting," together signifying "to offer up, present reverentially." In 2 another hand was added to reinforce the idea of "a reverential act." The kanji 奉 means "to offer up, present respectfully." <𡗗丰>

奉る to present respectfully [たてまつる]; 奉納 dedication, offering [ほうのう]; 信奉する to believe in, adhere to [しんぽうする]; 奉行 magistrate historical) [ぶぎょう]

SG-0665 棒	Meanings	Kun and On	Romaji	Bushu	Stroke Order and Number
	pole, stick, partner	ボウ	*boo*	木	十村栚桂棒 12

棒 **C** F-1403 (篆文) The seal-style form of 棒 comprised 木 **SG-0608** "wood," and 咅, used for the sound *boo* to mean "a stick," together signifying "a long pole." In the kanji, 咅 was replaced by 奉 for the same sound. The kanji 棒 means "pole, stick, partner." <木奉>

棒 pole, stick [ぼう]; 相棒 partner [あいぼう, あいぼう]; 泥棒 thief [どろぼう]; 棒立ちになる to stand petrified, stand bolt upright [ぼうだちになる]; 金の延べ棒 gold bar [きんの・のべぼう]; 棒に振る to waste [ぼうにふる]; 鬼に金棒 having a decisive advantage [おにに・かなぼう]

SG-0666 俸	Meanings	Kun and On	Romaji	Bushu	Stroke Order and Number
	stipend, salary, pay	ホウ	*hoo*	人	亻仨侠倴俸 10

俸 **D** F-2151 No ancient form. The kanji comprised 亻 "an act that one does," and 奉 **SG-0664**, used for the sound *hoo*, and originally meant "monetary offering." In the sense of monetary offerings paid to people for their service, it came to mean "stipend or payment." The kanji 俸 means "stipend, salary, pay." <亻奉>

減俸 pay cut, salary cut [げんぽう]; 年俸 annual salary [ねんぽう]

28i 夆 "a mountain ridge" [from a mountain peak from which a deity descended]; *hoo* 峰縫蜂

SG-0667 峰	Meanings	Kun and On	Romaji	Bushu	Stroke Order and Number
	mountain ridge	みね ホウ	mine *hoo*	山	丨山山'山夂峰峰峰 10

峰 **C** F-1404 (説文) The seal-style form comprised 山 **SG-1139** "a mountain"; 夂 "a foot coming down"; and 丰 "a tree branch for offering," used for the sound *hoo*. Together they signified "a mountain peak from which a deity descended." In the kanji, 山 moved to the left side of 夆. The kanji 峰 means "mountain ridge." <山夆(夂丰)>

峰 peak, summit [みね]; 名峰 celebrated mountain [めいほう]; 最高峰 the highest peak, the supreme authority, the culmination [さいこうほう]

SG-0668 縫	Meanings	Kun and On	Romaji	Bushu	Stroke Order and Number
	to sew	ぬ-う ホウ	nu-u *hoo*	糸	糸糸'糸夂糸夆緳縫 16

縫 **D** F-1771 (説文) The seal-style form comprised 糸 **SG-1600** "threads," and 逢, used for the sound *hoo* to mean "to meet." Putting two pieces of cloth together using thread was "sewing." The kanji 縫 means "to sew." <糸夆辶>

縫う to sew [ぬう]; 縫い針 sewing needle [ぬいばり]; 縫い代 seam allowance [ぬいしろ]; 縫い目 seam, stitch [ぬいめ]; 仮縫い fitting (in sewing), basting [かりぬい]; 裁縫 sewing [さいほう]; 縫製 sewing (by machine), sewing pieces together [ほうせい]

	Meanings	Kun and On	Romaji	Bushu	Stroke Order and Number
SG-0669 蜂	bee	はち ホウ	hachi *hoo*	虫	口中虫虫夂蚉蜂 13

蜂 **D** F-1947

蜂 (説文)

The top of the seal-style form comprised 辵 "to move forward," and 夆, used for the sound *hoo*; the bottom was a pair of "insects" (虫 **SG-0998**). Together, these components signified insects that swarm in large numbers—bees. In the kanji 蜂, 辵 and one 虫 were dropped. The kanji 蜂 means "bee." <虫夆>

蜂 bee [はち]; 蜂の巣 beehive [はちのす]; 蜂蜜 honey [はちみつ]; 蜂起する to rise up in revolt [ほ˥うきする]

29 Plants growing

29a 世 "new plant growth" 世葉

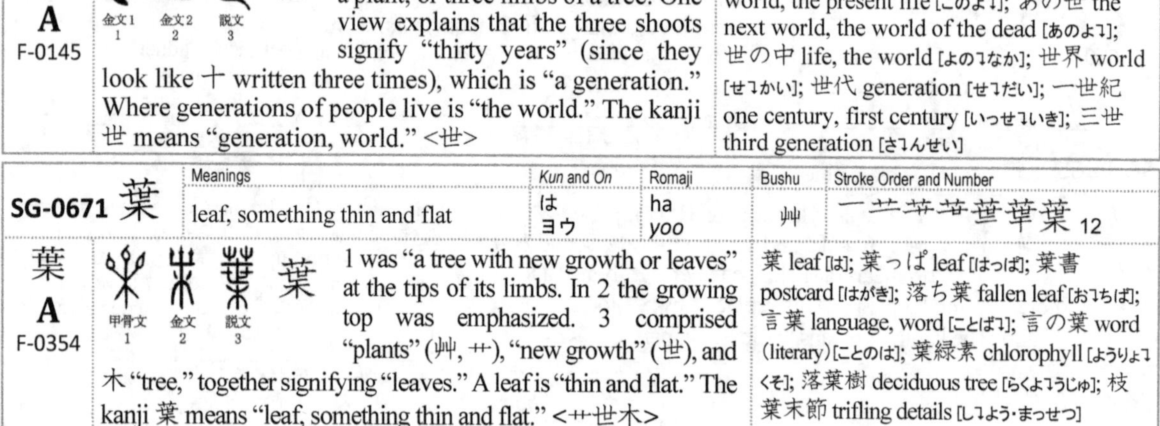

	Meanings	Kun and On	Romaji	Bushu	Stroke Order and Number
SG-0670 世	generation, world	よ セ・セイ	yo *se, see*	一	一十廿世 5

世 **A** F-0145

金文1 (1), 金文2 (2), 説文 (3), 世

1, 2, and 3 depicted new shoots on a plant, or three limbs of a tree. One view explains that the three shoots signify "thirty years" (since they look like 十 written three times), which is "a generation." Where generations of people live is "the world." The kanji 世 means "generation, world." <世>

世 world, public, era, reign [よ˥]; この世 this world, the present life [このよ˥]; あの世 the next world, the world of the dead [あのよ˥]; 世の中 life, the world [よの˥なか]; 世界 world [せ˥かい]; 世代 generation [せ˥だい]; 一世紀 one century, first century [いっせ˥いき]; 三世 third generation [さ˥んせい]

	Meanings	Kun and On	Romaji	Bushu	Stroke Order and Number
SG-0671 葉	leaf, something thin and flat	は ヨウ	ha *yoo*	艸	一艹䒑苹華華葉 12

葉 **A** F-0354

甲骨文 (1), 金文 (2), 説文 (3), 葉

1 was "a tree with new growth or leaves" at the tips of its limbs. In 2 the growing top was emphasized. 3 comprised "plants" (艸, 艹), "new growth" (世), and 木 "tree," together signifying "leaves." A leaf is "thin and flat." The kanji 葉 means "leaf, something thin and flat." <艹世木>

葉 leaf [は]; 葉っぱ leaf [はっぱ]; 葉書 postcard [はがき]; 落ち葉 fallen leaf [おち˥ば]; 言葉 language, word [ことば˥]; 言の葉 word (literary) [ことのは]; 葉緑素 chlorophyll [ようりょ˥くそ]; 落葉樹 deciduous tree [らくよ˥うじゅ]; 枝葉末節 trifling details [し˥よう・まっせつ]

29b 艹 (艸, ++) "plant, vegetation" [from plants growing]; bushu *kusakanmuri*

草茶藤華茂菊菌茨芋

In traditional kanji dictionaries, bushu *kusakanmuri* is listed as a six-stroke bushu (艸), or as a four-stroke bushu (++) made of two 十.

	Meanings	Kun and On	Romaji	Bushu	Stroke Order and Number
SG-0672 草	grass, weed, plant; informal	くさ ソウ	kusa *soo*	艸	一艹节�草 9

草 **B** F-0600

石鼓文 (1), 説文 (2), 草

1 comprised "an acorn" (早 **SG-1046**, used for the sound *soo*), surrounded at each corner by "overgrown plants." It meant "grass or plant." Grass and weeds grow fast, which suggested a quickly-written informal draft. In 2, the two plants at the bottom were dropped. In the kanji the two remaining plants 艸 became 艹, bushu *kusakanmuri*. The kanji 草 means "grass, weed, plant; informal." <艹早>

草 grass, weeds [くさ]; 枯れ草 withered grass, dried grass [かれくさ]; 雑草 weed [ざっそう]; 草案 draft [そうあん]; 起草する to draw up a proposal [きそうする]; 草稿 draft, manuscripts [そうこう]; 薬草 medicinal herb [やくそう]; 草書体 cursive- or grass-style character [そうしょたい]

	Meanings	Kun and On	Romaji	Bushu	Stroke Order and Number
SG-0673 茶	tea	チャ・サ	*cha, sa*	艸	一艹苁苶茶 9

茶 **B** F-0732

茶-説文 (1), 茶 (2), 茶

The original kanji was 荼 (2), which was identical to the seal-style form (1). It included 余, which meant "bitter" and was used for the sound *cha*. The kanji 茶

お茶 tea [おちゃ]; 新茶 first-crop mild tea [しんちゃ]; 緑茶 green tea [りょくちゃ]; 番茶 tea of inferior quality [ばんちゃ]; 焙じ茶 roasted tea [ほうじ˥ちゃ]; 茶番劇 farce [ちゃば˥んげき]; 日常茶飯事 daily

	means "a short shrub whose leaves make a bitter drink," otherwise known as "tea." <艹ヘホ>	occurrence, a matter of no importance [にちじょうさはꜜんじ]; 茶道 Japanese art of tea ceremony [さꜜどう]

	Meanings	*Kun* and *On*	Romaji	Bushu	Stroke Order and Number
SG-0674 藤	rattan, wisteria	ふじ トウ	huji *too*	艸	18

藤 **B** F-0364	No ancient form. The kanji comprises 艹 "plant," and 滕, used for the sound *too* and meaning "to climb." Together they signified "a climbing plant or vine," such as wisteria. The kanji 藤 means "rattan, wisteria." <艹月关>	藤 wisteria [ふじ], rattan [とꜜう]; 藤棚 wisteria trellis [ふじだな]; 藤色 light purple, lilac, lavender [ふじいろ]; 籐椅子 rattan chair [とういす]; 葛藤 being torn between conflicting emotions [かっとう]

	Meanings	*Kun* and *On*	Romaji	Bushu	Stroke Order and Number
SG-0675 華	gorgeous, showy, Chinese	はな-やか カ・ケ	hana-yaka *ka, ke*	艸	10

華 **B** F-0747	金文1 1 金文2 2 説文1 3 説文2 4 華 1 and 2 depicted "a plant with flowers and leaves," signifying "flower." 3 and 4 had wavy lines to represent full flowers or leaves hanging down, with 3 also including 艸 on top, which was kept as 艹, bushu *kusakanmuri*, in the kanji 華. Later the new kanji 花 **SG-0387** was created to mean "flower," and the kanji 華 came to mean "gorgeous, showy." It is also used for the sound *ka* to mean "Chinese." <艹𠂹十>	華やかな gorgeous [はなꜜやかな]; 華麗な magnificent, ornate, exuberant [かれいな]; 中華街 Chinatown [ちゅうかꜜがい]; 華氏 Fahrenheit [かꜜし]; 旧華族 former peerage [きゅꜜう・かꜜぞく]; 繁華街 busy shopping streets, amusement area [はんかꜜがい]; 華僑 Chinese living overseas [かꜜきょう]

	Meanings	*Kun* and *On*	Romaji	Bushu	Stroke Order and Number
SG-0676 茂	to grow densely; thicket	しげ-る モ	shige-ru *mo*	艸	8

茂 **C** F-1206	説文 茂 The seal-style form comprised 艸 (艹, bushu *kusakanmuri*) "plants, vegetation," and 戊 "halberd, battle-axe," used for the sound *mo* and meaning "to cover." Together they signified "a densely-growing thicket." The kanji 茂 means "to grow densely; thicket." <艹戊>	茂る to grow thick [しげꜜる]; 茂み thicket [しげみ]; 繁茂 thick growth [はꜜんも]

	Meanings	*Kun* and *On*	Romaji	Bushu	Stroke Order and Number
SG-0677 菊	chrysanthemum	キク	*kiku*	艸	11

菊 **C** F-1212	説文 菊 The seal-style form comprised "plants" (艸, 艹), and 匊, which depicted the round bloom of a dianthus or chrysanthemum and was used for the sound *kiku*. The kanji 菊 means "chrysanthemum." <艹勹米>	菊 chrysanthemum [きくꜜ]; 除虫菊 Dalmatian pyrethrum (used as insecticide) [じょちゅꜜうぎく]; 菊人形 a figure covered with chrysanthemum flowers [きくにꜜんぎょう]

	Meanings	*Kun* and *On*	Romaji	Bushu	Stroke Order and Number
SG-0678 菌	fungus, germ, bacterium	キン	*kin*	艸	11

菌 **C** F-1509	説文 菌 The seal-style comprised "plants" (艸, 艹), and 囷, used for the sound *kin* to mean "crowding, crowd." Plants that grew in a crowded condition were "fungi or bacteria." The kanji 菌 means "fungus, germ, bacterium." <艹囗禾>	細菌 bacterium, microbe [さいきん]; ばい菌(黴菌) germ, bacterium [ばいきん]; 殺菌 disinfection, sterilization [さっきん]; 抗菌 antimicrobial [こうきん]; 無菌状態 germ-free condition, aseptic condition [むきんじょꜜうたい]; 菌糸 hypha [きꜜんし]; 保菌者 germ or disease carrier [ほきꜜんしゃ]

	Meanings	*Kun* and *On*	Romaji	Bushu	Stroke Order and Number
SG-0679 茨	thorn bush	いばら	*ibara*	艸	9

茨 **D** F-1704	説文 茨 The origin of the kanji 茨 is not clear. The seal-style form comprised "plants" (艸, 艹), and 次 **SG-0432**, used for the sound *shi*. The kanji 茨 meant "thorny bush," and is part of the name of Ibaraki Prefecture, 茨城県 *Ibaraki-ken*. <艹次>	茨城県 Ibaraki Prefecture [いばらきꜜけん]; 茨の道 thorny path, a road beset with many hardships [いばらのみち]

SG-0680 芋	Meanings	Kun and On	Romaji	Bushu	Stroke Order and Number
	taro, yam, potato	いも	*imo*	艸	艹 芏 芋 6

芋 **D** F-1845 — 説文

The seal-style form comprised 艸 (艹) "plants," and 于 "a large bent or round shape," used for the sound *u*. A large, round-shaped plant meant "taro or coco-yam." Later the meaning came to include "potato." The kanji 芋 means "taro, yam, potato." <艹于>

芋 potato [いもꜜ]; 里芋 taro root [さといも]; 長芋 Chinese yam [ながいも]

29c 莫 "hidden, dark, vast; nothing" [from the sun setting behind tall grass]; *bo/mo/baku/maku* 模暮幕募墓膜漠慕

SG-0681 模	Meanings	Kun and On	Romaji	Bushu	Stroke Order and Number
	model, prescribed form; to copy	モ・ボ	*mo, bo*	木	一 木 朩 栉 棤 模 14

模 **B** F-0845 — 説文

The seal-style form comprised 木 "tree," and 莫, used for the sound *mo*, together signifying "a wooden mold." From "a wooden mold," the kanji 模 means "model, prescribed form; to copy." <木莫(艹日大)>

模型 model, dummy [もけい]; 模様 pattern, design [もよう]; 模造品 imitation [もぞうひん]; 模写 copy, reproduction, replica [もしゃ, もꜜしゃ]; 規模 scale, magnitude [きꜜぼ]

SG-0682 暮	Meanings	Kun and On	Romaji	Bushu	Stroke Order and Number
	dusk, sundown, twilight, end of a year; to live life	くれ・く-らす ボ	*kure, ku-rasu bo*	日	一 艹 苗 莫 暮 暮 14

暮 **B** F-1057 — 莫-甲骨 1, 金文1 2, 金文2 3, 金文3 4, 説文 5

1 through 5 comprised "the sun" surrounded on all sides by "grass." The character depicted the time when the sun went down behind tall grass and disappeared, in other words "sundown or twilight." The kanji comprised 艹 "plants, grass," 日 **SG-1045** "the sun," 一 and 八, and an additional "sun" 日. The seemingly redundant use of two suns was necessary to differentiate 暮 from the non-Joyo kanji 莫 *baku*, which meant "nothing," from its sense of "hidden completely." The meaning of "dusk" was also used metaphorically to mean "the end of a year." In Japanese 暮 also means "to live." The kanji 暮 means "dusk, sundown, twilight, end of a year; to live life." <莫日>

暮 end of a day or year [くれ]; 日暮れ dusk [ひぐれ]; 夕暮れ evening twilight [ゆうぐれ]; 暮らす to live a life [くらす]; 一人暮らし living alone [ひとりぐꜜらし]; 日暮らし all day long [ひぐらし]; 野暮な unsophisticated, witless [やꜜぼな]

SG-0683 幕	Meanings	Kun and On	Romaji	Bushu	Stroke Order and Number
	drapery, curtain, tent, military government (*bakufu*)	マク・バク	*maku, baku*	巾	艹 苗 草 莫 幕 幕 13

幕 **C** F-1113 — 説文

The seal-style form comprised 莫 "to hide, invisible," used for the sound *baku*, and 巾 **SG-1682** "draping cloth." A long piece of cloth was "drapery, a curtain for concealing something." A military headquarters in a battlefield had a drapery around it, and so this character came to represent the military government, called 幕府 "*bakufu*." The kanji 幕 means "drapery, curtain, tent, military government (*bakufu*)." <莫巾>

幕 theater curtain, act in a play [まくꜜ]; 幕開け beginning [まくあけ]; 幕内力士 senior-grade sumo wrestler [まくうちりꜜきし]; 幕の内弁当 box lunch packed with different small pieces of food [まくのうちべꜜんとう]; 幕末 final years of the Tokugawa era [ばくまつ]; 幕僚 military staff, strategic adviser [ばくりょう]

SG-0684 募	Meanings	Kun and On	Romaji	Bushu	Stroke Order and Number
	to recruit, raise funds	つの-る ボ	*tsuno-ru bo*	力	艹 苗 草 莫 募 募 12

募 **C** F-1188 — 説文

The seal-style form comprised 莫, used for the sound *bo* to mean "an unspecified wide area," and 力 **SG-1949** "strength, power," together signifying "to search widely for help, recruit people, raise money." The kanji 募 means "to recruit, raise funds." <莫力>

募る to raise money, recruit personnel [つのꜜる]; 募らせる to increase in intensity [つのらせꜜる]; 募集 recruiting, taking applications [ぼしゅう]; 応募する to apply for a job [おうぼする]; 公募する to invite contributions or applications from the public [こꜜうぼする, こうぼする]; 募金 raising money [ぼきん]

		Meanings	Kun and On	Romaji	Bushu	Stroke Order and Number
SG-0685	墓	tomb, grave	はか ボ	haka *bo*	土	艹 苜 荁 莫 莫 墓 墓 13

墓 **C** F-1409

説文

墓 The seal-style form comprised 莫 "to hide, invisible," used for the sound *bo*, and 土 "soil, ground." A buried corpse was hidden in the ground, and thus could not be seen. The kanji 墓 means "tomb, grave." <莫土>

墓・お墓 tomb, grave [はか↑, おはか]; 墓参り visit to a grave [はかまいり]; 墓地 cemetery [ぼち]; 墓碑 tombstone [ぼひ]; 墓石 tombstone [はかいし, ぼせき]; 自ら墓穴を掘る to bring about one's own ruin ("dig one's own grave") [みずから・ぼけつをほる]; 墓場 graveyard [はかば]

		Meanings	Kun and On	Romaji	Bushu	Stroke Order and Number
SG-0686	膜	membrane, thin film	マク	*maku*	肉	月 肝 胪 胪 膜 膜 14

膜 **D** F-1719

篆文

膜 The seal-style form comprised 月, bushu *nikuzuki* "flesh, part of the body," and 莫 "to cover; drapery," used for the sound *maku*. What covers an organ of the body is a "membrane or thin film." The kanji 膜 means "membrane, thin film." <月莫>

膜 thin film [まく]; 鼓膜 eardrum [こまく]; 粘膜 membrane [ねんまく]; 網膜 retina [もうまく]; 結膜炎 conjunctivitis [けつまくえん]

		Meanings	Kun and On	Romaji	Bushu	Stroke Order and Number
SG-0687	漠	vast; desert	バク	*baku*	水	氵 氵 浐 浐 漠 漠 13

漠 **D** F-1835

説文

漠 The seal-style form comprised "water" (氵), and 莫 "vast," used for the sound *baku,* signifying "a vast area of drifting sand." Another possible explanation is that 莫 was used for the meaning "nothing," and the character meant "a place that has no water," which was "a desert." The kanji 漠 means "vast; a desert." <氵 莫>

砂漠 desert [さばく]; 漠然と vaguely, obscurely, hazily [ばくぜんと]; 漠とした vague, unarticulated [ばくとした]

		Meanings	Kun and On	Romaji	Bushu	Stroke Order and Number
SG-0688	慕	to yearn for, adore	した-う ボ	shita-u *bo*	心	艹 苎 苩 莫 莫 慕 慕 14

慕 **D** F-1934

金文1 金文2 説文
1 2 3

慕 1 and 2 had "a heart," under 莫 "not visible," used for the sound *bo*. The character signified something hidden in the heart, such as an intense feeling of longing or "yearning." In the kanji, "heart" became ⺗, bushu *shitagokoro.* The kanji 慕 means "to yearn for, adore." <莫⺗>

慕う to yearn for, make an idol of someone [したう, したう]; 慕情 yearning, longing [ぼじょう]; 恋慕 tender emotion, love [れんぼ]

29d 生 "fresh; life" [from a newly sprouted plant on the ground]; *see* 生性産星姓 

		Meanings	Kun and On	Romaji	Bushu	Stroke Order and Number
SG-0689	生	life, person (who is learning); raw; pure; to grow, be born, live	い-きる・う-まれる・お-う・き・なま・は-える・ふ セイ・ショウ	i-kiru, u-mareru, o-u, ki, nama, ha-eru, hu *see, shoo*	生	ノ 𠂉 牛 生 5

生 **A** F-0024

甲骨文1 甲骨文2 金文1 金文2 説文
1 2 3 4 5

生 1 and 2 depicted "a plant sprouting from the soil." In 3 and 4, the small dot under the emerging leaves indicated the soil (土 **SG-1126**) or an emphasis on the growth. A plant sprouting from the ground meant "to emerge, grow; life." In the kanji, a slanted short stroke was added on the top left to indicate the emergence of life or the upward growth. The kanji 生 means "life, person (who is learning); raw; pure; to grow, be born, live." <𠂉 土>

生きる to live life, sustain a life [いきる]; 生まれる to be born [うまれる]; 生い茂る to grow profusely, be overgrown [おいしげる]; 生える to shoot, sprout, spring up [はえる]; 生一本な straightforward, honest [きいっぽんな]; 生 raw [なま]; 生々しい vivid, graphic [なまなましい]; 生徒 pupil [せいと]; 発生する to occur, break out [はっせいする]; 生年月日 date of birth [せいねんがっぴ]; 平生 ordinarily, usually [へいぜい]; 一生 one's entire life [いっしょう]; 出生地 one's birthplace [しゅっしょうち (legal), しゅっせいち]

	Meanings	Kun and On	Romaji	Bushu	Stroke Order and Number
SG-0690 性	natural character, innate nature, gender, sex, property of matter	セイ・ショウ	*see, shoo*	心	丶 忄 忄 忤 性 性 8

性
A
F-0158

説文

The seal-style form comprised 忄 "heart" (bushu *risshinben*), and 生 "to be born; life," also used for the sound *see*, together signifying "the heart that one was born with," "innate nature," and "gender, sex." It is also used to mean characteristics/property of a thing. The kanji 性 means "natural character, innate nature, gender, sex, property of matter." <忄生>

性 innate nature, gender, sex [せい]; 性質 one's disposition, character [せいしつ]; 性急な impatient, hasty [せいきゅうな]; 異性 opposite sex [いせい]; 性欲 sexual desire [せいよく]; 性分 temperament [しょうぶん, しょうぶん]; 本性 true nature [ほんしょう]; 根性 guts, grit, push [こんじょう]; 安全性 safety [あんぜんせい] // 性 one's nature, fate [さが]

	Meanings	Kun and On	Romaji	Bushu	Stroke Order and Number
SG-0691 産	to give birth, manufacture; product	う-む・うぶ サン	u-mu, ubu *san*	生	丶 亠 立 产 産 産 11

産
A
F-0190

金文 1 説文 2

1 and 2 comprised 文 **SG-0318** "design, pattern," 厂 "a well-defined forehead," and 生 "emerging life," together signifying "a pattern painted on the forehead of a newborn child in a rite; the birth of a beautiful child." From that, it also means "to produce goods; products." The kanji 産 means "to give birth, manufacture; product." <立丿生>

産む to produce, give birth [うむ]; 産声 first cry of a newborn baby [うぶごえ, うぶごえ]; お産 childbirth [おさん]; 出産 childbirth [しゅっさん]; 国産 domestic product [こくさん]; 産業革命 the Industrial Revolution [さんぎょうかくめい]; 石油産出国 oil producing country [せきゆさんしゅつこく]; 国民総生産 (GNP) gross national product [こくみんそうせいさん];

	Meanings	Kun and On	Romaji	Bushu	Stroke Order and Number
SG-0692 星	star	ほし セイ・ショウ	hoshi *see, shoo*	日	口 日 旦 早 星 9

星
A
F-0339

甲骨文1 1 甲骨文2 2 金文 3 説文 4 説文或体 5

1 and 2 comprised "emerging life, fresh and new" (生), used for the sound *see*, and small circles or squares signifying "glistening stars." Stars reappear each night as if born anew. In 3, 4, and 5, the stars became 日 "sparkling, shining," and were placed on top of the emerging plant. The kanji 星 means "star." <日生>

星 celestial star [ほし]; 流れ星 shooting star [ながれぼし]; 白星 win, success [しろぼし]; 黒星 loss, failure [くろぼし]; 図星 bullseye [ずぼし]; 星座 constellation [せいざ]; 明星 Venus [みょうじょう]

	Meanings	Kun and On	Romaji	Bushu	Stroke Order and Number
SG-0693 姓	family name, surname	セイ・ショウ	*see, shoo*	女	𡿨 𡚨 女 女' 女ᐩ 姓 姓 8

姓
C
F-1427

甲骨文 1 金文1 2 金文2 3 説文 4

1 and 4 depicted "a woman kneeling" (女 **SG-0521**), watching over "an emerging plant or life" (生 **SG-0689**), used for the sound *see*. New life given by a woman signified "female lineage." 2 had 生 only, and 3 had 亻 "a person." The kanji 姓 means "family name, surname." <女生>

姓名 full name [せいめい]; 旧姓 maiden name, one's original family name [きゅうせい]; 同姓同名 having the same surname and given name [どうせいどうめい]; 夫婦別姓 separate surnames for a married couple [ふうふ・べっせい]; 百姓・お百姓 farmer, peasant [ひゃくしょう, おひゃくしょう]

29e 青(靑) "blue, fresh" [from 生 "fresh, new life" and "clean water in a well"]; *see* 青情清静精晴請

	Meanings	Kun and On	Romaji	Bushu	Stroke Order and Number
SG-0694 青	blue, young, fresh, inexperienced, green	あお セイ・ショウ	ao *see, shoo*	青	一 十 丰 青 青 青 8

青
A
F-0282

金文 1 説文 2 旧字 3

The top of 1 and 2, used for the sounds *see/shoo*, was 生 **SG-0689** "a plant sprouting from the soil," here signifying "fresh, young" (later becoming 丰 in the kanji). On the bottom was "a clean water well" with a line inside to mean "a mineral pigment," such as vermillion (丹, 円), or perhaps just a reflection in clean blue water. Together, these components signified "fresh, young, blue, clean." "Being young" also lent the meaning "not experienced." The color of fresh

青い blue, inexperienced [あおい]; 青々とした very fresh [あおあおとした]; 青臭い smelling like freshly cut grass, inexperienced [あおくさい]; 青信号 green traffic signal [あおしんごう]; 青二才 green youth [あおにさい]; 青年 youth, young man [せいねん]; 青少年 young people, the youth [せいしょうねん]; 青春 the bloom of

	plants is "green." In Japanese, historically, the word *ao* ("blue") was inclusive of the color green, while *midori* (緑 **SG-1929**) meant "(the color) green" more specifically. The kanji 青 means "blue, young, fresh, inexperienced, green." <青(丰月)>	or youth [せいしゅん]; 青果店 greengrocer [せいかてん]; 群青色 lapis, ultramarine [ぐんじょういろ] // 真っ青な very blue, deathly pale [まっさおな]

SG-0695 情	Meanings	Kun and On	Romaji	Bushu	Stroke Order and Number
	feeling, emotion, circumstances	なさ-け ジョウ・セイ	nasa-ke *joo, see*	心	丶 忄 忄 忄 情 情 11

情 **A** F-0287

説文

The seal-style form comprised 忄 "a heart," and 青 (靑) "fresh, pure," used for the sounds *see/joo*. Together they signified untainted, pure emotion that one was born with. The character also applied to circumstances that evoked an emotional response. The kanji 情 means "feeling, emotion, circumstances." <忄青>

情け pity, sympathy, clemency [なさけ]; 情けない regrettable, pitiful [なさけない]; 情深い good-hearted, compassionate [なさけぶかい]; 愛情 love [あいじょう]; 情熱 passion [じょうねつ]; 同情 sympathy [どうじょう]; 事情 circumstances [じじょう]; 風情のある to have refined tastes, suggestive of [ふぜいのある]

SG-0696 清	Meanings	Kun and On	Romaji	Bushu	Stroke Order and Number
	pure, perfectly clear	きよ-い セイ・ショウ	kiyo-i *see, shoo*	水	氵 汁 清 清 清 11

清 **A** F-0335

説文 1 旧字 2

1 comprised 氵 "flowing water," and 青 (靑) "clear, blue," used for the sound *see*, together signifying "pure, clear." The kanji 清 means "pure, perfectly clear." <氵青>

清い pure [きよい]; 清らかな pure [きよらかな]; 清める to purify, cleanse [きよめる]; 清潔な clean, sanitary [せいけつな]; 清算する to settle an account [せいさんする]; 清掃する to clean [せいそうする]; 清楚な tidy, trim [せいそな] // 清々しい refreshing, invigorating [すがすがしい]; 清水 spring water, clear fresh water [しみず]

SG-0697 静	Meanings	Kun and On	Romaji	Bushu	Stroke Order and Number
	quiet, still, serene	しず-か セイ・ジョウ	shizu-ka *see, joo*	青	一 十 丰 青 青 静 静 静 14

静 **B** F-0591

金文1 1 金文2 2 説文 3 旧字 4

1 and 2 comprised "newly sprouted plants," "a clean well" to mean "tranquility," and "a hand driving a plow." Together they signified "tranquility after a good harvest." The composition of 3 was very different, and it has been explained as "tranquility (of well water, from 青 **SG-0694**, used for the sound *see*) after a battle (爭, 争 **SG-0129**)." The kanji 静 means "quiet, still, serene." <青争>

静かな quiet, serene [しずかな]; 静まる to become quiet, subside, die down [しずまる]; 動静 developments, trend [どうせい]; 鎮静する to quiet down, stabilize, be restored to [ちんせいする]; 静観する to wait and see [せいかんする]; 平静な calm, tranquil [へいせいな]; 静脈 vein [じょうみゃく]

SG-0698 精	Meanings	Kun and On	Romaji	Bushu	Stroke Order and Number
	pure, detailed; essence, spirit, mind, soul	セイ・ショウ	*see, shoo*	米	丷 半 米 米 粁 精 精 14

精 **B** F-0660

説文 1 旧字 2

1 comprised 米 **SG-0738** "rice, grain," and 青 (靑), used for the sound *see* to mean "pure, clear," together signifying "to select pure rice or quality grains of all kinds." "Grains" also gave the meaning "details." The sense of purity eventually became applied to the mind and soul. The kanji 精 means "pure, detailed; essence, spirit, mind, soul." <米青>

精米 rice milling [せいまい]; 精神 spirit, mind, soul [せいしん]; 精鋭の elite, select [せいえいの]; 精根尽きる to exhaust one's energies [せいこん・つきる]; 精力的に energetically, vigorously [せいりょくてきに]; 精子 sperm [せいし]; 精通している familiar with, knowledgeable about [せいつうしている]; 精進料理 Buddhist vegetarian cooking [しょうじんりょうり]

SG-0699 晴	Meanings	Kun and On	Romaji	Bushu	Stroke Order and Number
	clear sky, sunny weather; to become clear	は-れる セイ	ha-reru *see*	日	冂 日 日一 日十 日丰 晴 晴 12

晴 **B** F-0713

説文 1 旧字 2

1 comprised 夕 "moon, night," and 生, used for the sound *see* to mean "new life, fresh," together signifying "a clear night sky after a rain." In the kyuji 晴 (2), the previous components were replaced by 日 "the sun" and 青 "blue" to signify "a clear day with a blue sky." The kanji 晴 means "clear sky, sunny weather; to become clear." <日青>

晴れ clear weather [はれ]; 晴れる to clear up [はれる]; 疑いを晴らす to remove suspicion [うたがいをはらす]; 気が晴れ晴れとしない to be in low spirits, feel depressed [きが・はればれと・しない]; 秋晴れ crisp fine autumn day [あきばれ]; 晴天 fine weather [せいてん]; 快晴 bright and clear weather [かいせい]

SG-0700 請	Meanings	Kun and On	Romaji	Bushu	Stroke Order and Number
	to request, undertake; request	こ-う・う-ける セイ・シン	ko-u, u-keru *see, shin*	言	言 言一 計 請 請 請 15

請 **B** F-0871

請 説文 請 The seal-style form comprised 言 "word or language," and 青 (靑), used for the sound *see* to mean "to have an audience with," together signifying "to request an audience, request guidance." The kanji 請 means "to request, undertake; request." <言青>

請う to request, appeal, beg [こう]; 請けおう to undertake, take on [うけおう]; 請け負 undertaking, contract [うけおい]; 請願書 written petition [せいがんしょ]; 請求書 bill, charges [せいきゅうしょ]; 要請 demand, request [ようせい]; 申請書類 application documents [しんせいしょるい]; 安普請 cheaply built [やすぶしん]

29f 垂 "to dangle, hang down" [from a plant with dangling leaves that reach the ground]; *sui* 郵垂睡唾

SG-0701 郵	Meanings	Kun and On	Romaji	Bushu	Stroke Order and Number
	the post, postal service	ユウ	*yuu*	邑	一 二 千 乒 垂 垂 郵 郵 11

郵 **B** F-0736

郵 説文 郵 The seal-style form comprised 垂 **SG-0702** and 邑 "town" (阝, bushu *oozato*). The end of the earth was believed to hang over a cliff like a low-hanging plant, so 垂 here meant "frontier, peripheral area." With "town" added, 郵 meant a messenger or carrier of government documents who traveled even to frontier towns. This came to mean "postal service." The kanji 郵 means "the post, postal service." <垂阝>

郵便 postal service, the post, mail [ゆうびん]; 郵送する to send by postal service [ゆうそうする]; 郵便局 post office [ゆうびんきょく]; 郵便番号 postal code [ゆうびんばんごう]; 郵便受け mail box [ゆうびんうけ]

SG-0702 垂	Meanings	Kun and On	Romaji	Bushu	Stroke Order and Number
	to hang down, dangle; vertical	た-れる スイ	ta-reru *sui*	土	一 二 千 乒 垂 垂 8

垂 **D** F-1696

垂 説文 垂 The seal-style form depicted "a plant growing in soil with its leaves hanging low enough to reach the ground," and it had the sound *sui*. Hanging down to the ground signified "vertical." The kanji 垂 means "to hang down, dangle; vertical." <垂>

垂れる to hang down, droop [たれる]; 垂れ幕 hanging banner [たれまく]; 雨垂れ rain dripping from eaves [あまだれ]; 垂直 vertical, at a right angle [すいちょく]; 胃下垂 gastric ptosis [いかすい]

SG-0703 睡	Meanings	Kun and On	Romaji	Bushu	Stroke Order and Number
	to sleep	スイ	*sui*	目	目 𥄉 䀿 睡 睡 睡 13

睡 **D** F-1814

睡 説文 睡 The seal-style form comprised 目 "eye," and 垂 **SG-0702** "to hang down," used for the sound *sui*. Eyelids hanging down to close the eyes signified "to sleep." The kanji 睡 means "to sleep." <目垂>

睡眠 sleep [すいみん]; 熟睡する to sleep soundly, fall into a deep sleep [じゅくすいする]; 睡魔におそわれる to be overcome by drowsiness [すいまに・おそわれる]; 睡眠薬 sleeping pills [すいみんやく]

SG-0704 唾	Meanings	Kun and On	Romaji	Bushu	Stroke Order and Number
	spit, saliva	つば ダ	tsuba *da*	口	目 𥄉 䀿 睡 睡 睡 11

唾 **D** F-2369

唾 説文 唾 The seal-style form comprised 口 "mouth," and 垂 "to hang down," used for the sound *sui*. Something that dripped down from the mouth was "saliva, spit." The kanji 唾 means "spit, saliva." <口垂>

唾 spit, saliva [つば]; 生唾 saliva in one's mouth [なまつば, なまつば]; 唾液 saliva [だえき] // 固唾をのむ to await anxiously [かたずをのむ]

29g 乇 [from a leaning or deeply-rooted plant]; *taku* 宅託

SG-0705 宅	Meanings	Kun and On	Romaji	Bushu	Stroke Order and Number
	house, home	タク	*taku*	宀	' 宀 宀 宅 宅 6

宅 **B** F-0554

甲骨文 1, 金文 2, 説文古文 3, 説文 4 宅 1, 2, 3, and 4 comprised "a house" (宀), and 乇, used for the sound *taku* to mean "to entrust," together signifying a place where one relaxes—"one's home." Another view explains that 乇 was "a deeply-rooted plant," likened to a person at home. The kanji 宅 means "house, home." <宀乇>

自宅 one's home [じたく]; お宅 your home [おたく]; 帰宅する to return home [きたくする]; 在宅 staying home [ざいたく]; 私宅 private residence [したく]; 社宅 company-owned house/apartment [しゃたく]; 別宅 another house, second house [べったく]; 宅配便 home delivery [たくはいびん]

	Meanings	Kun and On	Romaji	Bushu	Stroke Order and Number
SG-0706 託	to entrust, consign	タク	*taku*	言	言 言 訁 託 10

託 **C** F-1163

説文

The seal-style form comprised 言 "word, language; to say," and 乇, used for the sound *taku* to mean "to entrust." The kanji 託 means "to entrust, consign." <言乇>

託す to entrust, leave in someone's care [たくす]; 受託研究 commissioned research [じゅたくけんきゅう]; 信託 trust [しんたく]; 託児所 public day nursery, day care center for children [たくじしょ]; 委託する to entrust, deposit, leave [いたくする]; 結託する to conspire with, be in collusion with [けったくする]

29h 平 "level, flat"; *hee/hyoo* 平評坪

	Meanings	Kun and On	Romaji	Bushu	Stroke Order and Number
SG-0707 平	flat, level, even; peace	たい-ら・ひら ヘイ・ビョウ	tai-ra, hira *hee, byoo*	干	一 ㇒ 亠 平 5

平 **A** F-0137

金文1 1 金文2 2 説文 3

1, 2, and 3 were "a water plant floating flat on the surface of water," signifying "flat, level." Another view explains that the character depicted "a hand axe chipping a piece of wood to make it flat," in which ハ was sawdust. "Evenness" also signified "without turbulence; peace." The kanji 平 means "flat, level, even; peace." <㇒十>

平らな flat [たいらな]; 平たい flat, level [ひらたい]; 水平な horizontal, level, even [すいへいな]; 平穏に peacefully [へいおんに]; 不平 discontent, grievance, complaint [ふへい]; 地平線 horizontal line [ちへいせん]; 平成 Heisei era (1989-2019 年) [へいせい]; 男女平等 equality for men and women [だんじょ・びょうどう]

	Meanings	Kun and On	Romaji	Bushu	Stroke Order and Number
SG-0708 評	to discuss fairly; evaluation, critique	ヒョウ	*hyoo*	言	言 言 訂 評 評 12

評 **B** F-0547

No ancient form. The kanji 評 comprised 言, bushu *gonben* "word; to say," and 平 SG-0707, used for the sound *hyoo* to mean "even, level." Together, they signified "to discuss fairly; fair judgment." The kanji 評 means "to discuss fairly; evaluation; critique." <言平>

悪評 bad reputation, unfavorable criticism [あくひょう]; 好評な well-thought-of, popular [こうひょうな]; 評判 reputation [ひょうばん]; 評論 critique, review [ひょうろん]; 評価額 appraisal price, evaluation [ひょうかがく]; 風評 rumor, hearsay, talk [ふうひょう]

	Meanings	Kun and On	Romaji	Bushu	Stroke Order and Number
SG-0709 坪	unit of area (one *tsubo*, 3.3 m^2)	つぼ	tsubo	土	一 十 扌 圷 坧 坪 8

坪 **C** F-1558

金文 1 説文 2

1 and 2 comprised 平 SG-0707 "level," and 土 SG-1126 "ground, soil." In Japanese, 坪, *tsubo*, is used as a unit of measurement for area or land, and one *tsubo* is 3.3 m^2, or roughly the area of two *tatami* mats. With the adoption of the metric system 平米 *heebee* "square meters" became the official unit of measurement for area. <扌平>

坪 *tsubo*, 3.3 m^2 [つぼ]; 建坪 building area [たてつぼ]; 延べ坪 total area [のべつぼ]; 坪数 number of *tsubo*, acreage [つぼすう]; 坪当たり per *tsubo* [つぼあたり]

30 Grain plants

30a 禾 "rice plant with crop, harvest" [from a rice plant drooping with full crop]; bushu *nogihen* 年私和利秋差香委秒移季秀誘稲透穂秩稿稚愁萎

	Meanings	Kun and On	Romaji	Bushu	Stroke Order and Number
SG-0710 年	year, age; annual	とし ネン	toshi *nen*	干	ノ 𠂉 仁 仨 年 6

年 **A** F-0004

甲骨文1 1 甲骨文2 2 金文1 3 金文2 4 説文 5

1 through 5 depicted "a standing person" with "a rice plant" on his head. One view explains that it was a person with a headdress of rice plants, dancing in a harvest festival. The cycle of harvesting a rice crop was one year. The kanji 年 means "year, age; annual." <年(𠂉㐄)>

年 year, one's age [とし]; 年寄り old person [としより]; 年甲斐もなく unbecoming of one's age [としがいもなく]; 去年 last year [きょねん]; 来年 next year [らいねん]; 年代 era, decade [ねんだい]; 年末 end of year [ねんまつ]; 年々 every year, year after year [ねんねん]

SG-0711 私	Meanings	Kun and On	Romaji	Bushu	Stroke Order and Number
	I; private, personal	わたくし・わたし シ	watakushi, watashi *shi*	禾	二千禾私私 7

私
A
F-0091

説文

The seal-style form comprised "a rice plant with crop" (禾) and "a hoe" (ム) of a tenant farmer on private land owned by a landowner, together signifying "private." The meaning was extended to mean the personal pronoun "I." Another view takes ム to be a person bending his arm to claim crops that belonged to him, thus "mine." The kanji 私 means "I; private, personal." <禾ム>

私 I [わたくし・(わたし)]; 私的な private [してきな]; 私物 private property, personal belongings [しぶつ]; 公私の別 distinction between public and private [こうしのべつ]; 私立 private, nongovernmental [しりつ]; 私用 personal errand [しよう]; 私服 street clothes, not in uniform [しふく]

SG-0712 和	Meanings	Kun and On	Romaji	Bushu	Stroke Order and Number
	peace, harmony; tranquil, Japanese	やわ-らぐ・なご-む ワ・オ	yawa-ragu, nago-mu *wa, o*	口	二千禾禾和和 8

和
A
F-0082

金文1 金文2 中山王器 説文
1 2 3 4

1 and 2 comprised 木 "a wooden sign on the gate of a military installation" with 口 "a document box," together signifying "a military peace agreement." Another view takes 3 and 4 to comprise 口, to mean "speaking," and 禾, for the sound *ka* to mean "to add," together signifying "people talking harmoniously, harmony." 和 had the same sound as the old name for Japan 倭, *wa,* and so became used to mean "Japanese; Japan." The kanji 和 means "peace, harmony; tranquil, Japanese." <禾口>

和らぐ to become mild, soften [やわらぐ]; 痛みが和らぐ pain is eased [いたみが・やわらぐ]; 和やかな calm, peaceful, congenial [なごやかな]; 平和 peace [へいわ]; 和服 Japanese-style clothing [わふく]; 和気あいあいと friendly, congenially [わき・あいあいと]; 和風 Japanese-style [わふう]; 和尚 Buddhist priest [おしょう] //大和 old name of Japan [やまと]; 日和見 weather vane [ひよりみ]

SG-0713 利	Meanings	Kun and On	Romaji	Bushu	Stroke Order and Number
	sharp, useful, advantageous; (monetary) interest	き-く リ	ki-ku *ri*	刀	二千禾利利 7

利
A
F-0219

甲骨文1 甲骨文2 金文1 金文2 説文
1 2 3 4 5

1, 2, 3, and 4 comprised "a rice plant with crop" and "a plow spattered with soil." A sharp, pointed plow that could dig up the soil effectively was "useful and advantageous." In 5 "a knife" replaced the plow. The kanji comprises 禾 "rice crop" (bushu *nogihen)* and 刂 "knife" (bushu *rittoo*), and means "sharp, useful, advantageous; (monetary) interest." <禾刂>

顔利き influential person, a big wheel [かおきき]; 利口な clever, bright, shrewd [りこうな]; 利用する to make good use of [りようする]; 利害 one's concern, interest [りがい]; 利下げ lowering of interest rate [りさげ]; 有利な advantageous [ゆうりな]

SG-0714 秋	Meanings	Kun and On	Romaji	Bushu	Stroke Order and Number
	autumn, fall	あき シュウ	aki *shuu*	禾	二千和秒秋 9

秋
A
F-0304

甲骨文1 甲骨文2 甲骨文3 説文
1 2 3 4

1 and 2 depicted "a bug that eats rice or other grain." 3 had "a fire" at the bottom, signifying "burning bugs that eat grain" or "heating a crop to dry it." The season for harvesting and drying crops was "autumn." In 4, 火 **SG-1164** "fire" and 禾 "rice plant with crop" swapped positions. The kanji 秋 means "autumn, fall." <禾火>

秋 autumn, fall [あき]; 立秋 the first day of autumn by the lunar calendar [りっしゅう]; 秋分の日 Automnal Equinox Day [しゅうぶんのひ]; 春秋に富む many years to live, young [しゅんじゅうにとむ]; 一日千秋の思い a long wait that feels like an eternity [いちにちせんしゅうのおもい]

SG-0715 差	Meanings	Kun and On	Romaji	Bushu	Stroke Order and Number
	difference; (emphatic prefix)	さ-す サ	sa-su *sa*	工	丷䒑䒑羊差差 10

差
A
F-0370

金文 説文
1 2

1 and 2 depicted "a rice plant" over 左, used for the sound *sa* to mean "unevenness." Rice plants drooping unevenly meant "different." The kanji 差 means "difference." <𦍌工>

差し出す to hold out in front of someone, present, offer [さしだす]; 差出人 sender, addresser [さしだしにん]; 指差す to point with a finger [ゆびさす]; 差し止める to prohibit, ban [さしとめる, さしとめる]; 日差し sunlight, sunray [ひざし]; 差 difference [さ]; 差額 balance [さがく]; 格差 difference in quality, gap [かくさ]

SG-0716 香	Meanings	Kun and On	Romaji	Bushu	Stroke Order and Number
	pleasant smell, fragrance	か・かお-り コウ・キョウ	ka, kao-ri *koo, kyoo*	香	二千禾禾香香 9

香 **A** F-0407	甲骨文1 1 · 甲骨文2 2 · 説文 3 · 香 — 1 and 2 depicted "cooked millet in a raised bowl." 3 comprised 禾 "millet plant" and 曰 "a mouth with tasty, fragrant millet inside it," originally signifying the taste of fragrant millet in one's mouth. The kanji 香 means "pleasant smell, fragrance." <禾曰>	移り香 lingering scent [うつりꜜが]; 香り fragrance [かおり]; 香水 perfume [こうすい]; 香料 fragrance [こꜜうりょう, こうりょꜜう]; 線香 incense stick [せꜜんこう]; 香を焚く to light incense [こうをたく]; 香典 monetary funeral offering [こうでん]

SG-0717 委	Meanings	Kun and On	Romaji	Bushu	Stroke Order and Number
	to comply easily, entrust	ゆだ-ねる イ	yuda-neru *i*	女	二千禾委委委 8

委 **A** F-0480	甲骨文 1 · 説文 2 · 委 — 1 and 2 comprised "a rice plant drooping with crop" (禾) and "a woman" (女 **SG-0521**). The woman's pliant posture and the drooping top of the rice plant heavy with crop both signified "to comply easily, to entrust." The kanji 委 means "to comply easily, entrust." <禾女>	委ねる to entrust [ゆだねꜜる]; 委任する to put someone in charge of a matter, authorize [いにんする]; 委任状 proxy [いにんじょう]; 委員会 committee [いいꜜんかい]; 委細 details [いꜜさい]

SG-0718 秒	Meanings	Kun and On	Romaji	Bushu	Stroke Order and Number
	a little; second (unit of time)	ビョウ	*byoo*	禾	二千禾利秒秒 9

秒 **B** F-0539	篆文 · 秒 — The seal-style form comprised 禾 "rice plant heavy with crop" and 少 **SG-1154** "a little," together signifying "an awn," one of the tiny bristles on the tips of a rice plant. This led to the character being used as a very small unit of time—"one second." The kanji 秒 means "a little; second (unit of time)." <禾少>	毎秒 every second [まいびょう]; 秒針 second hand (of a clock) [びょうしん]; 秒速 speed per second [びょうそく]

SG-0719 移	Meanings	Kun and On	Romaji	Bushu	Stroke Order and Number
	to move, transfer	うつ-る イ	utsu-ru *i*	禾	二千禾秒移移 11

移 **B** F-0598	説文 · 移 — The seal-style form comprised 禾 "rice plant heavy with crop," and 多 **SG-0796**, used for the sound *i* to mean "to move." Rice plants swaying in unison in the wind signified "to move, transfer." The kanji 移 means "to move, transfer." <禾多>	移る to move, transfer [うつꜜる]; 移り気な capricious, fickle [うつりぎな]; 移ろい changing, fading [うつろい]; 移り変わる to change, shift [うつりかわꜜる]; 移動 movement, transfer, shifting [いどう]; 移転 relocation, moving (house) [いてん]; 移住 emigration [いじゅう]

SG-0720 季	Meanings	Kun and On	Romaji	Bushu	Stroke Order and Number
	season; quarterly	キ	*ki*	禾・子	一二禾季季季 8

季 **B** F-0634	甲骨文 1 · 金文 2 · 説文 3 · 季 — 1, 2, and 3 comprised "a rice plant drooping with crop" (禾) over the head of "a child" (子 **SG-0510**), used to mean "small." Another view explains that the character represented a child dancing at an annual harvest festival (in line with the etymology of the kanji 年 **SG-0710**). Later it came to mean agricultural cycles or "seasons" (three months). The kanji 季 means "season; quarterly." <禾子>	季節 season [きꜜせつ]; 四季 the four seasons [しꜜき]; 季語 season word in *haiku* poem [きꜜご]; 冬季オリンピック Winter Olympics [とꜜうき・オリンピꜜック]; 雨季 rainy season, the monsoons [うꜜき]; 季節風 seasonal wind, monsoon [きせつふう]; 年季の入った seasoned, experienced [ねんきのはꜜいった]

SG-0721 秀	Meanings	Kun and On	Romaji	Bushu	Stroke Order and Number
	to excel, exceed, outmatch	ひい-でる シュウ	hii-deru *shuu*	禾	二千禾秀秀 7

秀 **B** F-0786	石鼓文 1 · 説文 2 · 秀 — 1 and 2 comprised "rice plant drooping with crop" (禾) and "a plant grown long." A rice plant that had grown strong and tall stood out from the rest, which gave the meaning "to surpass, outstrip." The kanji 秀 means "to excel, exceed, outmatch." <禾乃>	秀でる to excel, excellent [ひいでꜜる]; 秀才 genius [しゅうさい]; 優秀な superior, excellent [ゆうしゅうな]

	Meanings	Kun and On	Romaji	Bushu	Stroke Order and Number
SG-0722 誘	to invite, induce	さそ-う ユウ	saso-u *yuu*	言	誘 14

誘
B
F-0970

説文 1 説文或体 2

Many scholars view 1, listed in *Setsumon*, to be an incorrect form of 誘. 2 comprised 言, bushu *gonben* "word; to say," and 秀, used for the sound *yuu* to mean "to take the lead and surpass others." From taking the lead to extend an invitation, the kanji 誘 means "to invite, induce." <言秀>

誘う to invite, induce [さそう]; 勧誘 persuasion, urging [かんゆう]; 誘導 guidance, induction, encouragement [ゆうどう]; 誘惑 temptation [ゆうわく]; 誘致する to lure, enticement, invite [ゆうちする]; 誘発する to induce, bring about [ゆうはつする]

	Meanings	Kun and On	Romaji	Bushu	Stroke Order and Number
SG-0723 稲	rice plant	いね・いな トウ	ine, ina *too*	禾	稲 14

稲
B
F-1034

金文 1 1 金文 2 2 説文 3 旧字 4

1 comprised "a rice plant," "a hand," and "scooping rice grain in a mortar," used for the sound *too*. 2 comprised many elements—"rice plant" (禾), "fingers picking something up" (爫), "flowing water," "rice grain," and "a mortar" (臼 **SG-1811**). Quite an assembly! It depicted how rice seedlings were grown in paddies immersed in water. 3 and 4 comprised "a rice plant" and "a hand handling rice in a mortar." The kanji 稲 means "rice plant." <禾爫旧>

稲 rice plant [いね]; 稲刈り rice reaping, rice harvesting [いねかり]; 稲妻 bolt of lightning [いなずま]; 稲作農家 rice-farming family [いなさくのうか]; 稲荷 the god of harvests [いなり]; 水稲 rice grown in rice paddies [すいとう]

	Meanings	Kun and On	Romaji	Bushu	Stroke Order and Number
SG-0724 透	to pass through; transparent, clear	す-ける トウ	su-keru *too*	辵	透 10

透
C
F-1195

篆文

The seal-style form comprised 辵 (辶) "to go forward," and 秀 **SG-0721**, used for the sound *too* to mean "to slip out of, pass." The kanji 透 means "to pass through; transparent, clear." <秀辶>

透ける to pass through [すける]; 透し彫り openwork carving [すかしぼり]; 見透かす to see through [みすかす, みすかす]; 透明な transparent [とうめいな]; 透視 clairvoyance, perspective [とうし]; 浸透する to permeate, penetrate [しんとうする]; 半透明 translucent, opaque [はんとうめい]

	Meanings	Kun and On	Romaji	Bushu	Stroke Order and Number
SG-0725 穂	ear (of rice)	ほ スイ	ho *sui*	禾	穂 15

穂
C
F-1334

篆文 1 1 篆文 2 2 旧字 3

1 comprised 禾 "rice plant," and 惠, used for the sound *sui* to mean "hanging, drooping." 2 depicted "fingers picking grains from a rice plant," signifying "an ear of rice." The right side of 3 (惠) was simplified to 恵 **SG-1923** in the shinji. The kanji 穂 means "ear (of rice)." <禾由心>

稲穂 ear of rice [いなほ]; 穂先 tip of an ear, ear of wheat [ほさき]

	Meanings	Kun and On	Romaji	Bushu	Stroke Order and Number
SG-0726 秩	order; neatly	チツ	*chitsu*	禾	秩 10

秩
C
F-1531

説文

The seal-style form comprised 禾 "rice plant with crop," and 失 **SG-0073**, used for the sound *chitsu* to mean "to pile up neatly; neatly arranged." Neatly piling up harvested rice plants signified "order; neatly." It also meant a "rice stipend" that officials historically received according to their positions. The kanji 秩 means "order; neatly." <禾失>

秩序 public order, discipline [ちつじょ]; 無秩序 disorder, chaos [むちつじょ]; 秩序立った orderly [ちつじょだった]

	Meanings	Kun and On	Romaji	Bushu	Stroke Order and Number
SG-0727 稿	manuscript, draft	コウ	*koo*	禾	稿 15

稿
C
F-1638

説文

The seal-style form comprised 高 **SG-1277**, used for the sound *koo* to mean "dry," and 禾 "rice plants," together signifying "dry rice plants" or "straw." Scattered dry straw was likened to the scattered scribbles or notes of a manuscript. The kanji 稿 means "manuscript, draft." <禾高>

原稿 manuscript [げんこう]; 原稿用紙 lined paper for writing, manuscript paper with squares for individual kana or kanji [げんこうようし]; 投稿する to submit an article [とうこうする]; 草稿 (rough) draft [そうこう]

SG-0728 稚	Meanings	Kun and On	Romaji	Bushu	Stroke Order and Number
	infantile, naïve, very young	チ	*chi*	禾	二千利利' 秆秆稚 13

稚 **D** F-1688

篆文 稚

The seal-style form (穉) comprised 禾 "rice plant" on the left, with the right-side component used for the sound *chi* to mean "late" (as in the kanji 遲 **SG-1345** "late"). Late-ripening rice plants gave the meaning "very young, infantile." The right-side component was replaced by 隹 "bird." The kanji 稚 means "infantile, naïve, very young." <禾隹>

稚魚 fry, juvenile fish [ちぎょ]; 幼稚園 kindergarten [ようちえん]; 幼稚な childish, immature, primitive [ようちな]; 丁稚奉公 apprenticeship [でっちぼうこう]

SG-0729 愁	Meanings	Kun and On	Romaji	Bushu	Stroke Order and Number
	to grieve, be distressed; melancholy	うれ-える シュウ	ure-eru *shuu*	心	禾 秈 秋 秋 秋 愁 愁 13

愁 **D** F-2054

說文 愁

The seal-style form comprised 火, 禾 used for the sound *shuu* to mean "to shrink, contract," and 心 **SG-0187** "a heart." Together they signified an emotion where the heart felt contracted from distress or grief. The kanji 愁 means "to grieve, be distressed; melancholy." < 禾火心>

愁い grief, distress, concern [うれい, うれい]; 愁い顔 sad worried look [うれいがお]; 旅愁 loneliness on a journey [りょしゅう]; ご愁傷様 my condolences [ごしゅうしょうさま]

SG-0730 萎	Meanings	Kun and On	Romaji	Bushu	Stroke Order and Number
	to wilt, lose strength, droop, be paralyzed	な-える イ	na-eru *i*	艸	艹 艹 苿 苿 萎 萎 11

萎 **D** F-2610

篆文 萎

The seal-style form comprised 艸 (艹) "plants," and 委 **SG-0717** "pliant," used for the sound *i*. Together they meant "plant withering away." When applied to a person, the character means "to lose strength, be paralyzed." The kanji 萎 means "to wilt, lose strength, droop, be paralyzed." <艹委>

萎える to wither, droop, weaken [なえる]; 萎縮する to wither, shrivel, droop, become atrophied [いしゅくする] // 萎れる to droop, wilt [しおれる]

30b 厤 "to chronicle" [from trees or rice plants arranged at intervals]; *reki* 歴暦 厤厤厤

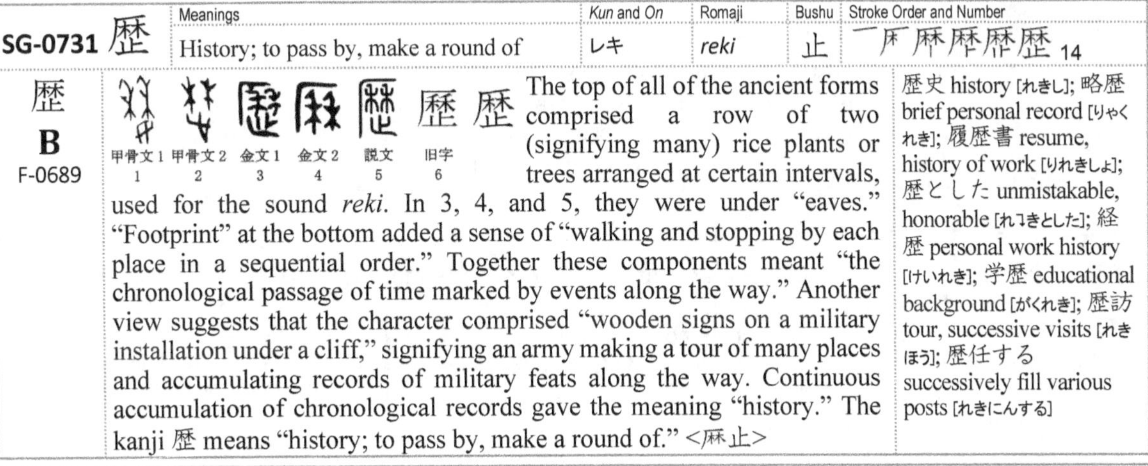

SG-0731 歴	Meanings	Kun and On	Romaji	Bushu	Stroke Order and Number
	History; to pass by, make a round of	レキ	*reki*	止	一 厂 厤 厯 厯 歴 14

歴 **B** F-0689

甲骨文1 (1), 甲骨文2 (2), 金文1 (3), 金文2 (4), 說文 (5), 旧字 (6) 歴

The top of all of the ancient forms comprised a row of two (signifying many) rice plants or trees arranged at certain intervals, used for the sound *reki*. In 3, 4, and 5, they were under "eaves." "Footprint" at the bottom added a sense of "walking and stopping by each place in a sequential order." Together these components meant "the chronological passage of time marked by events along the way." Another view suggests that the character comprised "wooden signs on a military installation under a cliff," signifying an army making a tour of many places and accumulating records of military feats along the way. Continuous accumulation of chronological records gave the meaning "history." The kanji 歴 means "history; to pass by, make a round of." <厤止>

歴史 history [れきし]; 略歴 brief personal record [りゃくれき]; 履歴書 resume, history of work [りれきしょ]; 歴とした unmistakable, honorable [れっきとした]; 経歴 personal work history [けいれき]; 学歴 educational background [がくれき]; 歴訪 tour, successive visits [れきほう]; 歴任する successively fill various posts [れきにんする]

SG-0732 暦	Meanings	Kun and On	Romaji	Bushu	Stroke Order and Number
	calendar, almanac	こよみ レキ	koyomi *reki*	日	一 厂 厤 暦 暦 14

暦 **C** F-1577

金文 (1), 說文 (2), 旧字 (3) 暦

The top of 1 and 2 (厤) was "many trees or rice plants arranged in good order under some eaves," signifying "many things in a linear order," and was used for the sound *reki*. Together with 日 **SG-1045** "the sun," they signified the regular movement of the sun, which was recorded in an "almanac, calendar." Another view takes the character to depict "a military gate under a cliff" with 曰 "a box of documents," together signifying a recognition ceremony for distinguished service in war. In this view, 曰 was mistakenly interpreted as the sun 日, and the character came to be used to mean "calendar." The kanji 暦 means "calendar, almanac." <厤日>

暦 calendar [こよみ]; 太陽暦 solar calendar [たいようれき]; 西暦 Christian era, A.D. [せいれき]; 旧暦 old lunar calendar [きゅうれき]; 還暦 one's sixtieth birthday [かんれき]

30c 兼 "two things at the same time" [from two rice plants held in a hand]; *ken*

兼嫌謙鎌廉

SG-0733 兼	Meanings	Kun and On	Romaji	Bushu	Stroke Order and Number
	to serve two at the same time, double as	か-ねる ケン	ka-neru *ken*	八	丷 兰 当 兯 兼 兼 10
兼 **B** F-0940	金文 1, 説文 2, 兼 1 and 2 depicted "two rice plants" (禾) held by "a hand from the side" (彐), signifying "to have two things at the same time." The kanji 兼 means "to serve two at the same time, double as." <兼(丷彐⺢)>	兼ねる to combine two things, possess both, serve both [かね1る]; し兼ねる to hesitate to do, be reluctant to do [しかね1る]; 兼任 hold two offices [けんにん]; 兼用 serving two purposes [けんよう]			

SG-0734 嫌	Meanings	Kun and On	Romaji	Bushu	Stroke Order and Number
	to dislike, detest, not want	きら-う・いや ケン・ゲン	kira-u, iya *ken, gen*	女	女 妒 姘 姘 嫌 嫌 13
嫌 **C** F-1089	説文, 嫌 The seal-style form comprised 女 **SG-0521** "woman, female," and 兼 **SG-0733**, used for the sound *ken* to mean "unsatisfying." Together they signified "not satisfied; to dislike." The kanji 兼 means "to dislike, detest, not want." <女兼>	嫌う to dislike [きらう]; 嫌だ to not want, be reluctant to do [いや1だ]; 嫌がる to refuse, avoid, dislike [いやが1る]; 嫌気がさす to grow tired of [いやけがさ1す]; 嫌悪する to hate, abhor [け1んおする]; 嫌疑 suspicion, charge [け1んぎ]; 機嫌がいい in good humor [きげんがい1い]; 不機嫌な displeased, ill-humored [ふき1げんな]			

SG-0735 謙	Meanings	Kun and On	Romaji	Bushu	Stroke Order and Number
	to humble oneself; modest	ケン	*ken*	言	言 訁 訁 謙 謙 謙 17
謙 **C** F-1385	説文, 謙 The seal-style form comprised 言 **SG-1364** "word; to say," and 兼, used for the sound *ken* to mean "to cave in, lower oneself." A bow is a way of humbling oneself to show respect. The kanji 謙 means "to humble oneself; modest." <言兼>	謙虚に in a humble manner, modestly [け1んきょに]; 謙譲語 deferential language, self-effacing words [けんじょうご]			

SG-0736 鎌	Meanings	Kun and On	Romaji	Bushu	Stroke Order and Number
	sickle	かま	kama	金	𠆢 金 釒 鎌 鎌 鎌 鎌 18
鎌 **C** F-1537	説文, 鎌 The seal-style form comprised 金 **SG-1196** "metal," and 兼 "two rice plants held in the hand," used for the sound *ken*, together signifying "a metal tool that cuts rice plants," that is, "a sickle." The kanji 鎌 means "sickle." <金兼>	鎌 sickle [か1ま]; いざ鎌倉 in the event of an emergency [い1ざ・かまくら]; 鎌をかける to ask a trick question [か1まをかけ1る]			

SG-0737 廉	Meanings	Kun and On	Romaji	Bushu	Stroke Order and Number
	upright, reliable, honest, inexpensive	レン	*ren*	广	亠 广 产 庐 廉 廉 廉 13
廉 **D** F-2103	説文, 廉 The seal-style form comprised 兼 **SG-0733**, used for the sound *ren* to mean "one-sided, side," and 广, bushu *madare*, "corner or nook (of a house)." It was later borrowed for its sound *ren* to mean "upright, reliable, honest." It also meant "inexpensive, low-priced." The kanji 廉 means "upright, reliable, honest, inexpensive." <广兼>	清廉潔白な of spotless integrity [せいれんけっぱくな]; 破廉恥な shameless, disgraceful [はれ1んちな]; 大廉売 big bargain sale [だいれ1んばい]; 廉価 low price [れ1んか]			

30d 米 "rice grain" [from grains on a rice plant]; **bushu *komehen*** 米迷粋粘謎粧

SG-0738 米	Meanings	Kun and On	Romaji	Bushu	Stroke Order and Number
	rice; America	こめ ベイ・マイ	kome *bee, mai*	米	丶 丷 䒑 半 米 米 6
米 **A** F-0044	甲骨文1 1, 甲骨文2 2, 説文 3, 米 1, 2, and 3 depicted a stalk of grain, such as millet or rice, to which small grains were still attached, either diagonally or scattered in four directions. The meaning of "millet" was lost, and the kanji 米 means "rice." The kanji 米 is also used to mean "America," from its use as the sound in the stressed syllable *me* in the old way of writing "America," 亜米利加. <丷木>	米 rice [こめ1]; 米作り rice farming [こめづ1くり]; 糯米 sweet glutinous rice [もちごめ]; 日米関係 Japan-U. S. relations [にちべいか1んけい]; 米国 The United States of Ameria [べいこく]; 親米派 pro-U.S. group or person [しんべいは]; 反米的 anti-American [はんべいてき]; 新米 first rice crop of the year, newcomer [しんまい]			

	Meanings	Kun and On	Romaji	Bushu	Stroke Order and Number
SG-0739 迷	to be perplexed, get lost	まよ-う メイ	mayo-u *mee*	辵	丷半米迷迷 9

迷 **B** F-1007

金文 1 中山王器 2 説文 3

1 comprised "a crossroads," "scattered grain" (for the sound *mee*), and "a footprint." 2 comprised 米 **SG-0738**, used for *mee* to mean "unclear," and "a person," together signifying "a person perplexed about which way to go." 3 comprised 辵 (辶) "to move forward," and 米. The kanji 迷 means "to be perplexed, get lost." <米辶>

迷う to lose one's way, hesitate, waver [まよꜜう]; 血迷う to lose control of oneself, go wild [ちまよꜜう]; 混迷 turmoil [こんめい]; 低迷する hang low [ていめいする]; 迷宮入り unsolved [めいきゅういり] // 迷子 stray child, missing child [まꜜいご. まよいꜜご]

	Meanings	Kun and On	Romaji	Bushu	Stroke Order and Number
SG-0740 粋	pure, chic, refined, sophisticated	いき スイ	iki *sui*	米	丷半米米粋粋 10

粋 **C** F-1580

説文 1 旧字 2

1 comprised 米 **SG-0738**, and 卒 **SG-1671**, used for the sound *sui*, together signifying "grains not mixed; pure." In the shinji, 卒 changed to 卆. In Japanese the character also took the meaning of "smartness; chic, refined." The kanji 粋 means "pure, chic, refined, sophisticated." <米卆>

粋な chic, sophisticated, high-spirited [いきな]; 粋な計らい smart move [いきなはからい]; 純粋な pure [じゅんすいな]; 抜粋 excerpts [ばっすい]; 無粋な (or 不粋な) lacking in polish, unromantic [ぶすいな]

	Meanings	Kun and On	Romaji	Bushu	Stroke Order and Number
SG-0741 粘	sticky, glutinous; to persevere	ねば-る ネン	neba-ru *nen*	米	丷丷半米米米粘 11

粘 **D** F-1654

篆文

The seal-style form (黏) comprised 黍 "millet," and 占 **SG-1767**, used for the sound *nen* to mean "to stick to." Together they signified the glutinous characteristic of millet. Being glutinous and sticky also gave the meaning "to persevere." In the kanji, 米 **SG-0738** replaced "millet." The kanji 粘 means "sticky, glutinous; to persevere." <米占>

粘る sticky, glutinous, to persevere [ねばꜜる]; 粘り気 stickiness [ねばりけ]; 粘り強い tenacious, persistent [ねばりづよꜜい]; 粘土 clay [ねꜜんど]; 粘着性 adhesion, stickiness [ねんちゃくせい]; 粘膜 mucus membrane [ねꜜんまく]

	Meanings	Kun and On	Romaji	Bushu	Stroke Order and Number
SG-0742 謎	a game of riddles, mystery	なぞ	nazo	言	言言丷詳詸謎謎 17

謎 **D** F-1721

篆文

The seal-style form comprised 言, bushu *gonben* "word; to say," and 迷 **SG-0739** "to be perplexed," used for the sound *mee*. Together they signified "jargon, secret words." In Japanese the character means "riddle, mystery." The kanji 謎 means "a game of riddles, mystery." <言米辶>

謎 riddle [なぞ]; 謎々 game of riddles [なぞなぞ]; 謎解き solving a mystery [なぞとき]

	Meanings	Kun and On	Romaji	Bushu	Stroke Order and Number
SG-0743 粧	to tidy oneself	ショウ	*shoo*	米	丷半米粁粧粧 12

粧 **D** F-1717

甲骨文 1 金文 2 篆文 3

1, 2, and 3 comprised "a vertically placed table" (爿), used for the sound *shoo*, and "woman" (女 **SG-0521**), together signifying "a woman dressing herself at a table." The kanji 粧 comprises 米 **SG-0738** "rice grain," from which white facial powder was made, and 庄, used for the sound *shoo*, together signifying "to brush up." The kanji 粧 means "to tidy oneself." <米庄>

化粧する to put on makeup [けしょꜜうする]; 化粧室 powder room, makeup room [けしょꜜうしつ]; 厚化粧 heavy makeup [あつげꜜしょう]

30e 朮 "a method to stick to; to follow" [from millet grains sticking to a hand]; *jutsu* 術述

	Meanings	Kun and On	Romaji	Bushu	Stroke Order and Number
SG-0744 術	method, means, art	ジュツ	*jutsu*	行	彳往彳朮術術術 11

術 **A** F-0441

説文

The seal-style form comprised the full shape of "a crossroads" (行, bushu *yukigamae* "to conduct, carry out"), with "a hand with sticky millet grains" (which became 朮) inside. People adhered to certain ways of doing things, and the character means "means, skills, art, magic." The kanji 術 means "method, means, art." <彳朮亍>

芸術 fine arts [げいじゅつ]; 手術 surgical operation [しゅꜜじゅつ]; 戦術 strategy, tactics [せんじゅつ]; 美術館 fine art museum [びじゅつꜜかん]; 話術 the art of narration [わꜜじゅつ]; 学術書 academic book [がくじゅつしょ]; 術後 postoperative, post-op [じゅつご]

	Meanings	Kun and On	Romaji	Bushu	Stroke Order and Number
SG-0745 述	to say, state, iterate	のーべる ジュツ	no-beru *jutsu*	辵	一十木朮朮述述 8

述 **B** F-0619 — 金文 1, 説文 2, 述

1 and 2 comprised 朮, used for the sound *jutsu* to mean "to follow," and "a crossroads" with "a footprint," forming 辵 (⻌) "to go forward." From following or repeating what someone else had said, the character meant "to iterate, state." The kanji 述 means "to say, state, iterate." <朮⻌>

述べる to state, say [のべる]; 述語 predicate [じゅつご]; 記述する to describe, write down [きじゅつする]; 前述の aforementioned [ぜんじゅつの]; 口述筆記 writing down at someone's dictation [こうじゅつひっき]

30f 麦 (麥) [from a barley or wheat plant] 来麦麺

	Meanings	Kun and On	Romaji	Bushu	Stroke Order and Number
SG-0746 来	to come; next, upcoming; from	く-る・きた-る・き-て・こ-ない ライ	ku-ru, kita-ru, ki-te, ko-nai *rai*	人 木	一丆丒平来来 7

来 **A** F-0110 — 甲骨文 1, 金文1 2, 金文2 3, 説文 4, 旧字 5 (來), 来

1, 2, 3, and 4 depicted "a barley or wheat plant." The character was borrowed to mean "to come." The kyuji 來 (5) was reduced to 来 in the shinji. The kanji 来 means "to come; next, forthcoming, upcoming; from." <来(丆木)>

来る to come [くる], upcoming [きたる]; 出来る can do, capable of [できる]; 出来高 yield, output, turnover [できだか]; 来ない not coming [こない]; 従来の existing, current [じゅうらいの]; 本来 originally, essentially [ほんらい]; 来月 next month [らいげつ]; 先日来 since a few days ago, recently [せんじつらい]

	Meanings	Kun and On	Romaji	Bushu	Stroke Order and Number
SG-0747 麦	barley, wheat plant	むぎ バク	mugi *baku*	麥	一十キ丰声麦麦 7

麦 **C** F-1251 — 甲骨文 1, 金文 2, 説文 3, 旧字 4 (麥), 麦

1, 2, and 3 comprised "a barley or wheat plant" and "a backward- or downward-facing footprint" (夊). In early spring, a farmer treaded back and forth over new wheat plants to control their growth. Another view explains that the downward footprint signified "coming toward (you)," and that it meant a grain plant brought from far away. Many views hold that 来 originally meant "wheat," and 麦 "to come," but their uses got reversed. The kanji 麦 means "barley, wheat plant." <主夂>

麦 barley, wheat plant [むぎ]; 小麦粉 wheat flour [こむぎこ]; 麦茶 roasted barley tea [むぎちゃ]; 麦飯 rice and barley cooked together [むぎめし]; 麦芽 malt [ばくが] // 蕎麦 buckwheat noodle [そば]

	Meanings	Kun and On	Romaji	Bushu	Stroke Order and Number
SG-0748 麺	noodle	メン	*men*	麥	一十キ麦麺麺麺麺 16

麺 **D** F-2226 — 篆文 1, 旧字 2 (麵), 麺

1 comprised 麥 "barley," and 丏, used for the sound *men* (for 面 **SG-0060** "flat surface," as in 2). 麪 or 麵 signified wheat or barley flour that was kneaded flat, that is, "noodles." The kanji 麺 means "noodle." <麦面>

麺 noodle [めん]; 素麺 *somen* noodle [そうめん]; 麺類 noodle, pasta [めんるい]; 麺棒 rolling pin [めんぼう]

30g 甫 "to protect, spread" [from a young plant whose roots were wrapped or protection]; *ho* 補捕浦舗哺

	Meanings	Kun and On	Romaji	Bushu	Stroke Order and Number
SG-0749 補	to fill a gap, supplement, compensate	おぎな-う ホ	ogina-u *ho*	衣	礻衤衤衦裥補補 12

補 **B** F-0759 — 説文, 補

The seal-style form comprised 衣 **SG-1657** "clothing," and 甫 "a protectively wrapped young plant," used for the sound *ho*, together signifying "mending a hole in clothes." The meaning was extended for more general use. In the kanji, 衣 became 衤, bushu *koromohen.* The kanji 補 means "to fill a gap, supplement, compensate." <衤甫>

補う to compensate for, supplement [おぎなう]; 補修工事 repair work, maintenance work [ほしゅうこうじ]; 補助 assistance, support [ほじょ]; 補償する to indemnify, make up for [ほしょうする]; 立候補 announcing one's candidacy [りっこうほ]

	Meanings	Kun and On	Romaji	Bushu	Stroke Order and Number
SG-0750 捕	to catch, seize	と-らえる・つか-まえる ホ	to-raeru, tsuka-maeru *ho*	手	一 十 扌 打 扪 捎 捕 捕 10

捕 **B** F-0858 — 說文 — The seal-style form comprised 扌, bushu *tehen* "an act done by hand," and 甫 "protected young plant," used for the sound *ho* to mean "to grab, catch." Together, they signified "grabbing something firmly in the hand." The kanji 捕 means "to catch, seize." <扌甫>

捕らえる to catch [とらえる]; 分捕る to plunder, loot [ぶんどる]; 生け捕る to capture alive [いけどる]; 捕まえる to capture, seize [つかまえる]; 逮捕する to arrest, apprehend [たいほする]; 捕鯨 whaling [ほげい]; 捕獲枠 fishing or hunting quota [ほかくわく]

	Meanings	Kun and On	Romaji	Bushu	Stroke Order and Number
SG-0751 浦	creek, inlet, seashore	うら	ura	水	氵 汀 浿 浦 浦 10

浦 **B** F-0994 — 說文 — The seal-style form comprised "flowing water" (氵), and 甫 "to spread," used for the sound *ho*, together signifying "a wide area along water." The kanji 浦 means "creek, inlet, seashore." <氵甫>

津々浦々 from coast to coast, all over the country [つつ・うらうら]

	Meanings	Kun and On	Romaji	Bushu	Stroke Order and Number
SG-0752 舗	a shop; to lay, pave	ホ	*ho*	舌	亼 今 舎 舗 舗 舗 15

舗 **D** F-1705 — 篆文 1, 旧字 2 — 1 comprised 金 **SG-1196** "metal," and 甫, used for the sound *ho*, together signifying "a metal piece used in a door lock or handle." 甫 also had the meaning "to spread, lay" (from planting young seedling one by one), whence the meaning "to pave a road." With 金 replaced by 舍 "hut" (舎 **SG-1392**), it came to mean "a shop." The kanji 舗 means "a shop; to lay, pave." <舎甫>

舗装道路 paved street [ほそうどうろ]; 店舗 storefront [てんぽ]; 舗道 paved street [ほどう] // 老舗 a long-established store [しにせ]

	Meanings	Kun and On	Romaji	Bushu	Stroke Order and Number
SG-0753 哺	to catch in the mouth	ホ	*ho*	口	口 口 叮 听 哨 哺 哺 10

哺 **D** F-2673 — 說文 — The seal-style form comprised 口 "mouth," and 甫, used for the sound *ho*, together signifying "a bird putting food into its chick's mouth," or "to chew." The kanji 哺 means "to catch in the mouth." <口甫>

哺乳類 Mammalia [ほにゅうるい]; 哺乳瓶 baby's bottle [ほにゅうびん]

30h 尃 (尃) "to spread, broaden" [from a hand carefully planting seedlings to gradually cover an area]; *haku/bo* 博薄敷簿縛

	Meanings	Kun and On	Romaji	Bushu	Stroke Order and Number
SG-0754 博	breadth of knowledge, gambling; spreading, wide	ハク・バク	*haku, baku*	十	一 𠂇 忄 博 博 博 博 博 12

博 **B** F-0698 — 金文1 1, 金文2 2, 說文 3 — 1, 2, and 3 comprised 尃 (尃) "young seedlings with the roots protected by a hand" (used for the sound *haku*), and 十 "full," together signifying "planting young seedlings to cover a wide area," or more generally "spreading; to broaden." Later, the kanji 博 came to mean "breadth of knowledge." The sounds *haku/baku* also had the meanings "to hit; gamble." The kanji 博 means "breadth of knowledge, gambling; spreading, wide." <十甫寸>

博覧会 exhibition, exposition [はくらんかい]; 万博 world fair, international exposition [ばんぱく]; 博識 extensive knowledge, encyclopedic knowledge [はくしき]; 博士 doctor [はくし]; expert [はかせ]; 賭博 gambling [とばく]; 博打 gambling, speculation [ばくち]

	Meanings	Kun and On	Romaji	Bushu	Stroke Order and Number
SG-0755 薄	thin, pale	うす-い ハク	usu-i *haku*	艸	艹 艹 洋 浦 薄 薄 薄 16

薄 **B** F-1060 — 說文 — The seal-style form comprised "plants" (艸, 艹), "flowing water" (氵), and 尃 (尃) "wide; to cover broadly," used for the sound *haku*. It signified planting bundles of seedlings one by one over a wide area like a thin covering of water. The kanji 薄 means "thin, pale." <艹氵尃>

薄い thin, weak, watery, pale [うすい]; 薄める to dilute, weaken [うすめる]; 薄暗い gloomy, dusky, dim [うすぐらい, うすぐらい]; 品薄 scarcity of goods [しなうす]; 軽薄な indiscreet, frivolous [けいはくな]; 薄情な heartless, coldhearted [はくじょうな]; 肉薄する to close in on an enemy, close in on [にくはくする]

	Meanings	Kun and On	Romaji	Bushu	Stroke Order and Number
SG-0756 敷	to spread out, stretch	し-く フ	shi-ku *hu*	攴	亩甫重専専敷敷敷 15

敷 **C** F-1301

金文 1 説文 2

1 depicted "a young seedling with its roots (甫)" protected by "a hand" (寸), and had the sound *hu*. In 2, "causing an action" (攴, 攵) was added, and together these components signified "to plant seedlings in the ground by hand and level the ground" or "to lay, spread." In the kanji, 方 **SG-1931** "square, four directions" replaced 寸. The kanji 敷 means "to spread out, stretch." <甫方攵>

敷く to spread, pave, lay out [しく]; 敷地 building site, lot, the ground [しきち]; 屋敷 estate, mansion, residence [やしき]; 座敷 Japanese-style tatami room, drawing room [ざしき]; 敷き布団 sleeping mat [しきぶとん]; 敷居 doorsill, threshold [しきい]; 敷設する to construct, build [ふせつする]

	Meanings	Kun and On	Romaji	Bushu	Stroke Order and Number
SG-0757 簿	register, bookkeeping record	ボ	*bo*	竹	𥫗氵簿簿簿簿簿簿 19

簿 **C** F-1406

No ancient form. The kanji comprises ⺮, bushu *kurakanmuri* "bamboo," and 薄 **SG-0755** "thin," used for the sound *bo*. Thin wood or bamboo tablets with writing on them were bound together for record keeping. The kanji 簿 means "register, bookkeeping record." <⺮氵尃>

名簿 roll, name list [めいぼ]; 帳簿 an account book, ledger [ちょうぼ]; 簿記 bookkeeping, register [ぼき, ぼき]; 戸籍簿 a *koseki* record, official family register [こせきぼ]; 家計簿 book of housekeeping accounts [かけいぼ]

	Meanings	Kun and On	Romaji	Bushu	Stroke Order and Number
SG-0758 縛	to bind, restrain	しば-る バク	shiba-ru *baku*	糸	糸紆絧縛縛縛縛 16

縛 **D** F-1865

説文

The seal-style form comprised 糸 "skein of threads," and 尃 "a young seedling held in a hand," used for the sound *baku*. Something held tightly in the hand and bound with strings gave the meaning "to bind, restrain." The kanji 縛 means "to bind, restrain." <糸尃>

縛る to bind [しばる]; 歯を食い縛る to brave, endure [はをくいしばる]; 金縛りにあう to be paralyzed, be petrified [かなしばりにあう]; 束縛 restraint, shackles [そくばく]

31 Bamboo

31 竹 "bamboo"; ⺮ **bushu *takekanmuri*** 竹算箸 竹

	Meanings	Kun and On	Romaji	Bushu	Stroke Order and Number
SG-0759 竹	bamboo	たけ チク	take *chiku*	竹	ノ𠂉ケ竹竹竹 6

竹 **A** F-0343

中山王器 1 説文 2

1 and 2 depicted two bamboo stalks with drooping, narrow, pointed leaves. The character meant "bamboo." A bamboo stalk had many uses due to its sturdiness, ready availability, and pliancy. Before paper was invented, bamboo was cut into tablets to write on. When used at the top of kanji, it becomes ⺮ bushu *takekanmuri*. The kanji 竹 means "bamboo." <竹>

竹 bamboo [たけ]; 竹細工 bamboo craft [たけざいく]; 竹藪 bamboo thicket [たけやぶ]; 竹を割ったような straightforward, open-hearted [たけをわったような]; 破竹の勢い forceful initial thrust [はちくのいきおい]; 竹馬の友 childhood friend [ちくばの・とも]; 竹簡 bamboo strips or tablets used in ancient times for writing [ちくかん]

	Meanings	Kun and On	Romaji	Bushu	Stroke Order and Number
SG-0760 算	to calculate, count, compute; arithmetic	サン	*san*	竹	⺮⺮笇笪笪算 14

算 **A** F-0329

説文

The seal-style form comprised "bamboo" (⺮) and "two hands holding bamboo tallies or an abacus." The kanji 算 means "to calculate, count, compute; arithmetic." <⺮目廾>

計算 calculation [けいさん]; 算数 arithmetic [さんすう]; 予算 budget [よさん]; 打算的 calculating, prudent [ださんてき]; 概算 rough estimate [がいさん]; 足し算 addition [たしざん]; 引き算 subtraction [ひきざん]; 掛け算 multiplication [かけざん]; 割り算 division [わりざん]; 暗算 mental calculation, working out sums in one's head [あんざん]

	Meanings	Kun and On	Romaji	Bushu	Stroke Order and Number
SG-0761 箸	chopsticks	はし	hashi	竹	15

箸 **D** F-2373

説文

The seal-style form 箸 comprised "bamboo," and 者 **SG-2085**, used for the sound *cho* to mean "to gather in one place." A pair of bamboo sticks used to gather and pick up food were chopsticks. The kanji 箸 means "chopsticks." <⺮者>

箸 chopsticks [はし]; 割り箸 half-split disposable chopsticks [わりばし, わりばし]; 箸置き chopstick rest [はしおき, はしおき]; 取り箸 serving chopsticks [とりばし, とりばし]

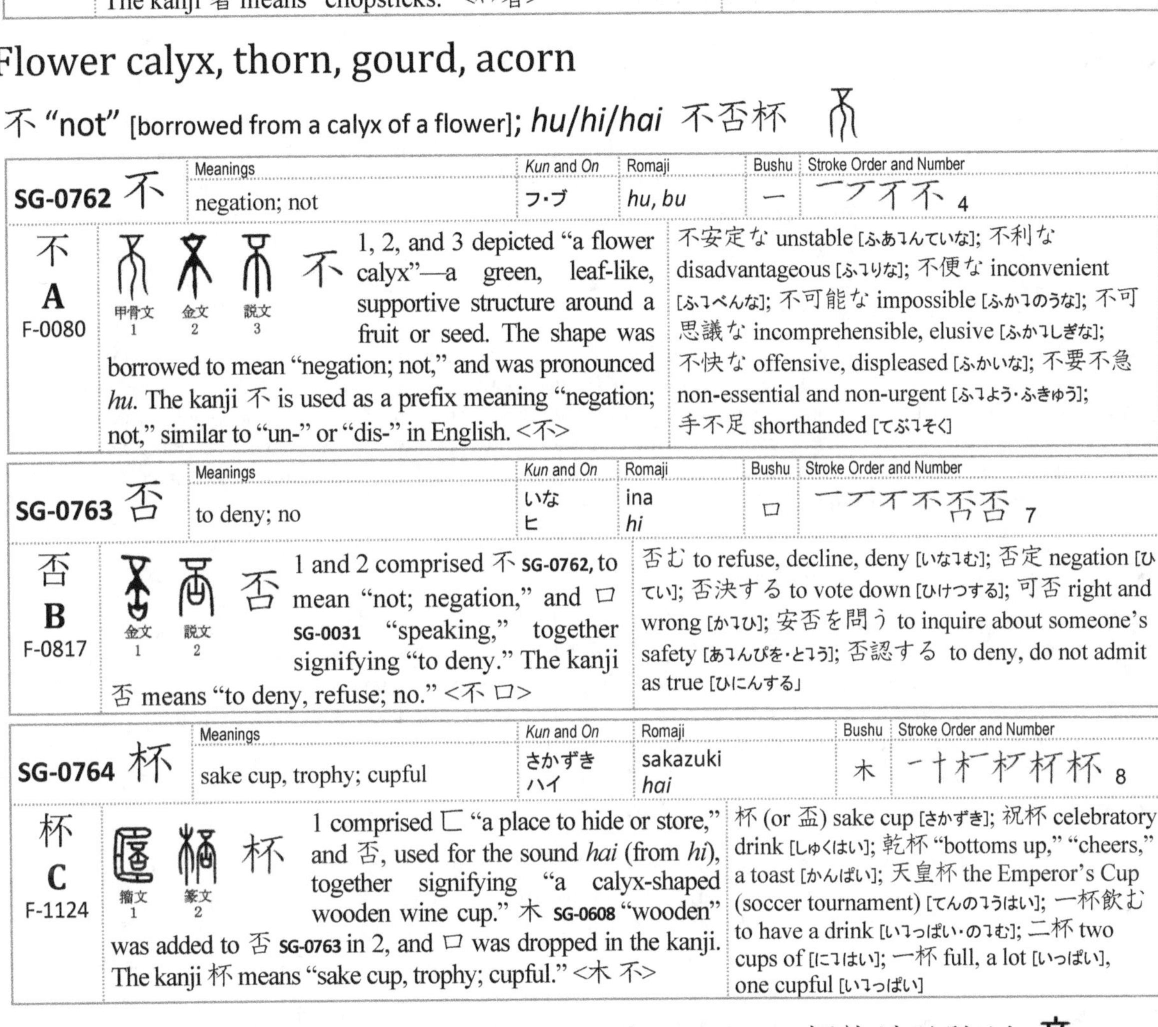

32 Flower calyx, thorn, gourd, acorn

32a 不 "not" [borrowed from a calyx of a flower]; *hu/hi/hai* 不否杯

	Meanings	Kun and On	Romaji	Bushu	Stroke Order and Number
SG-0762 不	negation; not	フ・ブ	*hu, bu*	一	一ア不不 4

不 **A** F-0080

甲骨文 1 金文 2 説文 3

1, 2, and 3 depicted "a flower calyx"—a green, leaf-like, supportive structure around a fruit or seed. The shape was borrowed to mean "negation; not," and was pronounced *hu*. The kanji 不 is used as a prefix meaning "negation; not," similar to "un-" or "dis-" in English. <不>

不安定な unstable [ふあんていな]; 不利な disadvantageous [ふりな]; 不便な inconvenient [ふべんな]; 不可能な impossible [ふかのうな]; 不可思議な incomprehensible, elusive [ふかしぎな]; 不快な offensive, displeased [ふかいな]; 不要不急 non-essential and non-urgent [ふよう・ふきゅう]; 手不足 shorthanded [てぶそく]

	Meanings	Kun and On	Romaji	Bushu	Stroke Order and Number
SG-0763 否	to deny; no	いな ヒ	ina *hi*	口	一ア不不否否 7

否 **B** F-0817

金文 1 説文 2

1 and 2 comprised 不 **SG-0762**, to mean "not; negation," and 口 **SG-0031** "speaking," together signifying "to deny." The kanji 否 means "to deny, refuse; no." <不 口>

否む to refuse, decline, deny [いなむ]; 否定 negation [ひてい]; 否決する to vote down [ひけつする]; 可否 right and wrong [かひ]; 安否を問う to inquire about someone's safety [あんぴを・とう]; 否認する to deny, do not admit as true [ひにんする]

	Meanings	Kun and On	Romaji	Bushu	Stroke Order and Number
SG-0764 杯	sake cup, trophy; cupful	さかずき ハイ	sakazuki *hai*	木	一十木杠杯杯 8

杯 **C** F-1124

籀文 1 篆文 2

1 comprised 匸 "a place to hide or store," and 否, used for the sound *hai* (from *hi*), together signifying "a calyx-shaped wooden wine cup." 木 **SG-0608** "wooden" was added to 否 **SG-0763** in 2, and 口 was dropped in the kanji. The kanji 杯 means "sake cup, trophy; cupful." <木 不>

杯 (or 盃) sake cup [さかずき]; 祝杯 celebratory drink [しゅくはい]; 乾杯 "bottoms up," "cheers," a toast [かんぱい]; 天皇杯 the Emperor's Cup (soccer tournament) [てんのうはい]; 一杯飲む to have a drink [いっぱい・のむ]; 二杯 two cups of [にはい]; 一杯 full, a lot [いっぱい], one cupful [いっぱい]

32b 咅 "to double, split" [from a ripe fruit about to split]; *bu/bai/boo* 部倍培賠陪剖

	Meanings	Kun and On	Romaji	Bushu	Stroke Order and Number
SG-0765 部	part, department, section, counter for copies of a document	へ ブ	he *bu*	邑	11

部 **A** F-0047

説文

The seal-style form comprised 咅, used for the sound *bu* to mean "to split, divide; doubled," and 邑 "town," together signifying "to divide a town into sections." It meant "part, portion of a whole, section of an organization." In the kanji, 邑 was reduced to 阝, bushu *oozato* "town." The kanji 部 means "part, department, section," and is used as a counter for copies of a document. <咅 阝>

部屋 room [へや]; 全部 all [ぜんぶ]; 部分 part, portion [ぶぶん]; 本部 headquarters [ほんぶ]; 学部 academic department [がくぶ]; 部首 section header, radical, *bushu* (in a kanji dictionary) [ぶしゅ]; 部数 number of copies [ぶすう]

SG-0766 倍	Meanings	Kun and On	Romaji	Bushu	Stroke Order and Number
	to become doubled; double	バイ	*bai*	人	亻 亻 亻 位 倍 倍 10

倍 **B** F-0560 説文

The seal-style form comprised 亻 "an act that one does," and 咅 "a ripe fruit about to split," used for the sound *bai* to mean "to divide." Together they signified splitting something, resulting in a double quantity. The kanji 倍 means "to become doubled; double." <亻咅>

二倍 double [にばい]; 倍率 magnification, magnifying power [ばいりつ]; 倍増 doubling [ばいぞう]; 人一倍 (work) twice as hard as other people [ひといちばい]

SG-0767 培	Meanings	Kun and On	Romaji	Bushu	Stroke Order and Number
	to cultivate, grow	つちか-う バイ	tsuchika-u *bai*	土	一 十 士 圵 垃 培 11

培 **D** F-1677 説文

The seal-style form comprised 土 **SG-1126** "soil, dirt," and 咅 "doubled," used for the sound *bai*, together signifying "ground where more soil is added to grow plants" or "ground where plants are multiplying." The kanji 培 means "to cultivate, grow." <土咅>

培う to cultivate, nurture [つちかう]; 栽培する to grow [さいばいする]; 培養する to culture, cultivate [ばいよう]; 培養菌 cultured cell [ばいようきん]

SG-0768 賠	Meanings	Kun and On	Romaji	Bushu	Stroke Order and Number
	to compensate, pay reparation	バイ	*bai*	貝	冂 目 貝 貝 貯 賠 賠 15

賠 **D** F-1687

No ancient form. The kanji 賠 comprised 貝 **SG-1693** "cowrie; monetary value," and 咅, used for the sound *bai* (from 倍 "to double"). One view suggests that the character may originally have meant "to pay double the monetary value of damages." The character is now used to mean "to compensate with equal value." The kanji 賠 means "to compensate, pay reparation." <貝咅>

賠償 compensation, indemnity [ばいしょう]; 損害賠償 compensation for damage, indemnity from damage [そんがいばいしょう]; 賠償責任 liability, responsibility for damages [ばいしょうせきにん]

SG-0769 陪	Meanings	Kun and On	Romaji	Bushu	Stroke Order and Number
	to attend, accompany (a superior)	バイ	*bai*	阜	⁷ 了 阝 阝 阝 陪 陪 11

陪 **D** F-1945 説文

The seal-style form comprised 阝, bushu *kozatohen,* signifying "adding one on top of another" (from "a pile of dirt"), and 咅, used for the sound *bai.* "Adding more people" gave the meaning of "an entourage" sitting close to a superior person. The kanji 陪 means "to attend, accompany (someone superior)." <阝咅>

陪審員 juror [ばいしんいん]; 陪食する to dine with a superior [ばいしょくする]; 陪席する to sit with (one's superior) [ばいせきする]

SG-0770 剖	Meanings	Kun and On	Romaji	Bushu	Stroke Order and Number
	to divide, cut, dissect	ボウ	*boo*	刀	丶 亠 立 咅 剖 剖 10

剖 **D** F-1954 説文

The seal-style form comprised 咅 "to split in two" (used for the sound *boo*), and 刂 "knife; to cut," together signifying "to divide or dissect using a knife." The kanji 剖 means "to divide, cut, dissect." <咅刂>

解剖する to dissect [かいぼうする]; 病理解剖 pathological dissection [びょうりかいぼう]; 解剖図 anatomical chart [かいぼうず]

32c 朿 "a thorny stick with a sharp end"; *saku/shi* 策刺

SG-0771 策	Meanings	Kun and On	Romaji	Bushu	Stroke Order and Number
	plan, measure, scheme, strategy	サク	*saku*	竹	⺮ 竺 笁 笨 策 策 12

策 **A** F-0513 中山王器 1 説文 2

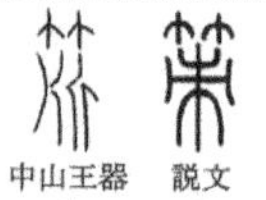

1 and 2 comprised ⺮, bushu *takekanmuri* "bamboo," and 朿 "a long, thorny stick," used for the sound *saku* (from *shi*), together signifying "a horsewhip." A bundle of long bamboo sticks looked similar to bamboo writing tablets tied together, on which measures and plans were written. The kanji 策 means "plan, measure, scheme, strategy." <⺮朿>

対策 measure, counterplan [たいさく]; 政策 policy [せいさく]; 解決策 solution strategy [かいけつさく]; 策略 scheme, strategy [さくりゃく]; 策士 strategist, hustler [さくし]; 方策 plan, policy, means [ほうさく]; 失策 blunder, bungle [しっさく]

	Meanings	Kun and On	Romaji	Bushu	Stroke Order and Number
SG-0772 刺	to sting, pierce, stab, embroider	さ-す シ	sa-su *shi*	刀	一𠃍市朿朿刺 8

刺 **C** F-1102

説文

The seal-style form comprised 朿 "a thorny twig with a sharp tip" (used for the sound *shi*), and "a knife" (刂, bushu *rittoo*) that could inflict pain, together signifying "to sting, stab with a pointed knife or needle." A needle piercing fabric was "embroidering." The kanji 刺 means "to sting, pierce, stab, embroider." <朿 刂>

(Note: Two 朿 make up the non-Joyo kanji 棘 *toge*, "thorn, splinter.")

刺す to stab, sting [さす]; 虫刺され bug bite [むしさされ]; 刺身 sashimi, slices of raw fish [さしみ]; 刺激 stimulus, impetus [しげき]; 刺繍 embroidery [ししゅう]; 名刺 business card [めいし]

32d 責 "debt" [from a thorny twig with a sharp tip, 朿, and a cowrie, 貝]; *seki* 責積債績漬

	Meanings	Kun and On	Romaji	Bushu	Stroke Order and Number
SG-0773 責	to torment, blame, reprimand; liability	せ-める セキ	se-meru *seki*	貝	一十主青青責 11

責 **B** F-0646

甲骨文 1 金文1 2 金文2 3 説文 4

1 through 4 comprised "a thorny twig" (朿, later becoming 主), used for the meaning "to stab or pierce" and the sound *seki*, and "cowrie, monetary value" (貝 **SG-1693**). An official taunting a person to submit tax payment gave the meaning "to blame; liability." The kanji 責 means "to torment, blame, reprimand; liability." <主 貝>

責める to blame, condemn, torture [せめる]; 引責辞任 resignation assuming responsibility [いんせきじにん]; 自責の念 self-reproof, self-reproach [じせきのねん]; 責任 responsibility [せきにん]; 無責任な irresponsible [むせきにんな]; 文責 responsibility for the wording of an article [ぶんせき]

	Meanings	Kun and On	Romaji	Bushu	Stroke Order and Number
SG-0774 積	to pile; mathematical product, intention, preparation	つ-む セキ	tsu-mu *seki*	禾	二千禾禾⁺秸積積 16

積 **B** F-0677

金文 1 説文 2

1 and 2 comprised 禾 "rice crop," and 責 "tax, levy," used for the sound *seki*, originally signifying tribute or tax paid in piles of crops. In Japanese the character also means "preparation, intention." The kanji 積 means "to pile; mathematical product, intention, preparation." <禾責>

積む to pile up, load, accumulate [つむ]; 積もり intention, mindset [つもり]; 山積み a tall pile [やまづみ]; 見積 estimate [みつもり]; 積立金 reserve fund [つみたてきん]; 面積 area, square measure, size of land [めんせき]; 体積 volume, cubic [たいせき]; 積 the product (mathematics) [せき]

	Meanings	Kun and On	Romaji	Bushu	Stroke Order and Number
SG-0775 債	debt	サイ	*sai*	人	亻亻⁺仹倩債債 13

債 **B** F-0962

篆文

The seal-style form had 亻 "a person, an act that one does," added to 責 **SG-0773**, used for the sound *seki* to mean "liability," together signifying "unpaid debt" in a borrower-lender relationship. The kanji 債 means "debt." <亻 責>

国債 government bonds, Treasury bonds (U. S.) [こくさい]; 債務 debt, liabilities [さいむ]; 債権国 creditor country [さいむこく]; 負債 debt, dues, liabilities [ふさい]

	Meanings	Kun and On	Romaji	Bushu	Stroke Order and Number
SG-0776 績	to spin thread; achievement	セキ	*seki*	糸	幺糸紆⁺絓績績 17

績 **C** F-1226

金文 1 説文 2

1 was the same as 3 for 責 **SG-0773**, used for the sound *seki* and originally meaning "tax, levy." In 2 "a skein of threads" (糸 **SG-1600**) was added to signify "making yarn, spinning," signifying "tribute or tax paid in the form of fabric." A collected pile of fabrics signified "achievement, feat." The kanji 績 means "to spin thread; achievement." <糸責>

実績 actual results, achievements [じっせき]; 成績 results, performance [せいせき]; 業績 one's work, business performance, results [ぎょうせき]; 紡績工場 cotton mill, spinning mill [ぼうせきこうじょう]; 功績 great achievement, merits [こうせき]

SG-0777 漬	Meanings	Kun and On	Romaji	Bushu	Stroke Order and Number
	to be immersed; pickled	つ-ける	tsu-keru	水	氵汁洼清漬 14
漬 D F-1689	説文 The seal-style form comprised "flowing water" (氵), and 責, used for the sound *shi* (from 朿, which was the top component of 責 SG-0773), and also the meaning "to pile up." Pickles were submerged in liquid in layers. The kanji 漬 means "to be immersed; pickled." <氵責>		漬ける to immerse in, soak, pickle in salt [つける]; 漬物 pickles [つけもの]; 塩漬け pickling with salt [しおづけ]; 酢漬け pickling in vinegar [すづけ]; 粕漬け pickled in sake lees [かすづけ]; お茶漬け boiled rice soaked in tea or broth [おちゃづけ]		

32e 麻(痲) "hemp, linen" [from hemp plants stripped of bark and hung under eaves]; *ma* 麻摩磨

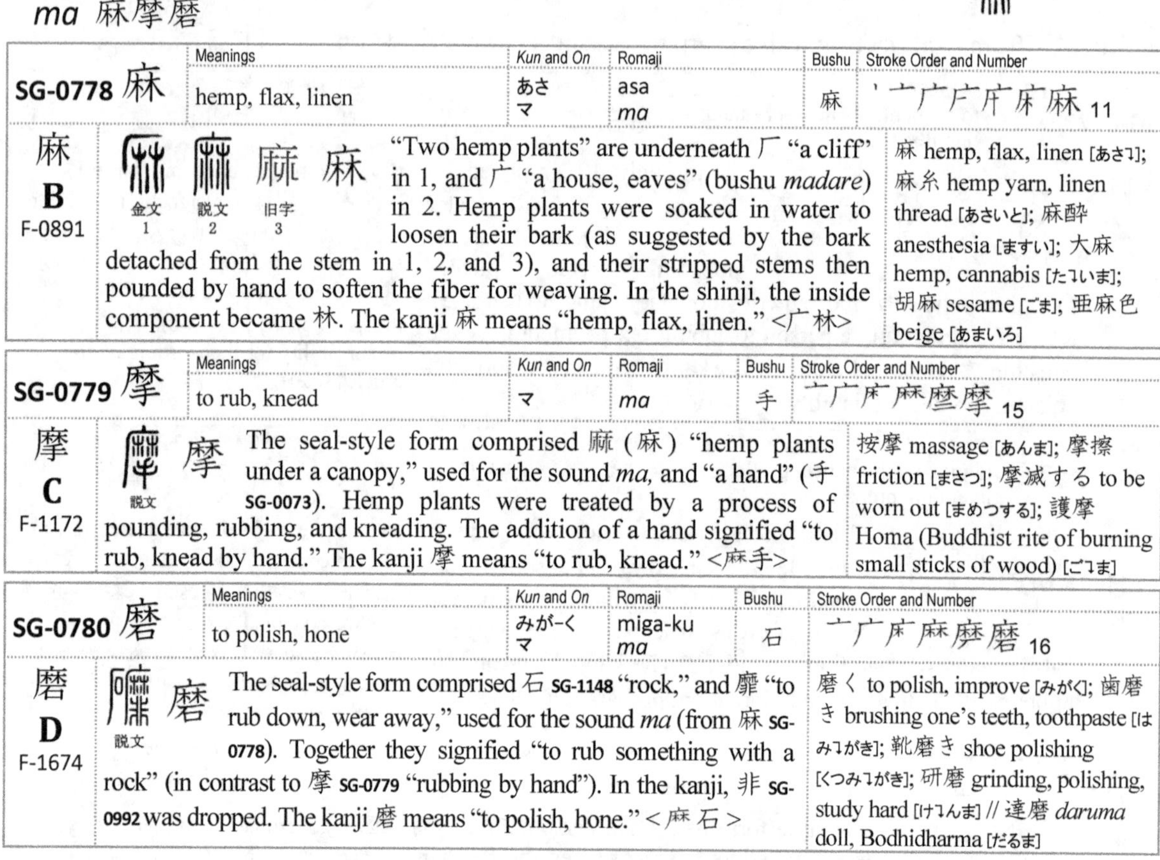

SG-0778 麻	Meanings	Kun and On	Romaji	Bushu	Stroke Order and Number
	hemp, flax, linen	あさ マ	asa *ma*	麻	丶亠广广庁床麻 11
麻 B F-0891	金文 1, 説文 2, 旧字 3. "Two hemp plants" are underneath 厂 "a cliff" in 1, and 广 "a house, eaves" (bushu *madare*) in 2. Hemp plants were soaked in water to loosen their bark (as suggested by the bark detached from the stem in 1, 2, and 3), and their stripped stems then pounded by hand to soften the fiber for weaving. In the shinji, the inside component became 林. The kanji 麻 means "hemp, flax, linen." <广林>		麻 hemp, flax, linen [あさ]; 麻糸 hemp yarn, linen thread [あさいと]; 麻酔 anesthesia [ますい]; 大麻 hemp, cannabis [たいま]; 胡麻 sesame [ごま]; 亜麻色 beige [あまいろ]		

SG-0779 摩	Meanings	Kun and On	Romaji	Bushu	Stroke Order and Number
	to rub, knead	マ	*ma*	手	亠广床麻摩摩 15
摩 C F-1172	説文. The seal-style form comprised 痲 (麻) "hemp plants under a canopy," used for the sound *ma*, and "a hand" (手 SG-0073). Hemp plants were treated by a process of pounding, rubbing, and kneading. The addition of a hand signified "to rub, knead by hand." The kanji 摩 means "to rub, knead." <麻手>		按摩 massage [あんま]; 摩擦 friction [まさつ]; 摩滅する to be worn out [まめつする]; 護摩 Homa (Buddhist rite of burning small sticks of wood) [ごま]		

SG-0780 磨	Meanings	Kun and On	Romaji	Bushu	Stroke Order and Number
	to polish, hone	みが-く マ	miga-ku *ma*	石	亠广床麻磨磨 16
磨 D F-1674	説文. The seal-style form comprised 石 SG-1148 "rock," and 靡 "to rub down, wear away," used for the sound *ma* (from 麻 SG-0778). Together they signified "to rub something with a rock" (in contrast to 摩 SG-0779 "rubbing by hand"). In the kanji, 非 SG-0992 was dropped. The kanji 磨 means "to polish, hone." <麻石>		磨く to polish, improve [みがく]; 歯磨き brushing one's teeth, toothpaste [はみがき]; 靴磨き shoe polishing [くつみがき]; 研磨 grinding, polishing, study hard [けんま] // 達磨 *daruma* doll, Bodhidharma [だるま]		

32f 由 "coming out; to originate from" [from liquefied flesh flowing out of a ripe gourd]; *yuu* 由油抽笛

SG-0781 由	Meanings	Kun and On	Romaji	Bushu	Stroke Order and Number
	to originate from; cause, reason; coming from	よし ユ・ユウ・ユイ	yoshi *yu, yuu, yui*	田	丨冂巾由 5
由 A F-0362	甲骨文 1, 金文 2, 卣・金文1 3, 金文2 4. 1 and 2 depicted a very ripe gourd from which a liquefied oily substance was coming out. Another view explains that 3 and 4 depicted a bottle with a cap for keeping liquid. Something flowing out gave the meaning "coming from; to originate from," and also "a cause or reason." The kanji 由 means "to originate from; cause, reason; coming from." <由>		由 reason, cause [よし]; 由来 derivation, origin [ゆらい]; 経由する to go by way of/ via [けいゆする]; 理由 reason, grounds [りゆう]; 自由 liberty, freedom [じゆう]; 由緒正しい having a noble origin [ゆいしょ・ただしい]		

	Meanings	Kun and On	Romaji	Bushu	Stroke Order and Number
SG-0782 油	oil, oily substance	あぶら ユ	abura *yu*	水	氵氵 汩 沺 油 8

油 **A** F-0522

油 油 説文

The seal-style form comprised "water, liquid" (氵, bushu *sanzui*) added to 由 "oily substance flowing out of a ripe gourd," used for the sound *yu*. The kanji 油 means "oil, oily substance." <氵 由>

油 oil [あぶら]; 油が切れる to run out of oil [あぶらがきれる]; 油絵 oil painting [あぶらえ]; 石油 petroleum [せきゆ]; 灯油 kerosene [とうゆ]; 原油 crude oil [げんゆ]; 油田 oil field, petroleum well [ゆでん]; 油断する to let one's guard down [ゆだんする]

	Meanings	Kun and On	Romaji	Bushu	Stroke Order and Number
SG-0783 抽	to pull out, draw out, extract	チュウ	*chuu*	手	一 扌 扣 抽 抽 8

抽 **C** F-1624

抽 抽 抽 篆文1 1 篆文2 2

1 and 2 comprised 扌 "an act done by hand," and 由 **SG-0781** "coming out from," together signifying "to pull, draw out." In both 1 and 2, the right side was used for the sound *chuu*. The kanji 抽 means "to pull out, draw out, extract." <扌 由>

抽選 lottery, drawing [ちゅうせん]; 抽出する to extract [ちゅうしゅつする]; 抽象的な abstract [ちゅうしょうてきな]

	Meanings	Kun and On	Romaji	Bushu	Stroke Order and Number
SG-0784 笛	flute, whistle	ふえ テキ	hue *teki*	竹	⺮ 竺 笛 笛 11

笛 **D** F-1678

笛 笛 篆文

The seal-style form comprised 竹 "bamboo" on top, and 由 **SG-0781** "an empty gourd" on the bottom, used for the sound *teki*. A hollow object such as a gourd or bamboo could be made into a pigeon whistle or a flute by putting holes in it. The kanji 笛 means "flute, whistle." <⺮ 由>

笛 flute [ふえ]; 口笛 whistle [くちぶえ, くちぶえ]; 笛吹けど踊らず "No one would follow (your) lead." [ふえふけど・おどらず]; 警笛 alarm whistle, horn, siren [けいてき]; 汽笛 steam whistle [きてき]; 鼓笛隊 fife and drum band [こてきたい]

32g 瓜 [from a gourd]; *ko* 孤 弧 瓜

	Meanings	Kun and On	Romaji	Bushu	Stroke Order and Number
SG-0785 孤	solitary; orphan	コ	*ko*	子	了 孑 孓 孤 孤 9

孤 **C** F-1397

孤 孤 説文

The seal-style form comprised 子 **SG-0510** "child," and 瓜 "a gourd," used for the sound *ko* to mean "alone." Together they signified "a solitary child, an orphan." The kanji 孤 means "solitary, orphan." <子 瓜>

孤独 solitude, isolation [こどく]; 孤児 orphan [こじ]

	Meanings	Kun and On	Romaji	Bushu	Stroke Order and Number
SG-0786 弧	arc	コ	*ko*	弓	⁊ ⁊ 弓 弖 弧 弧 9

弧 **D** F-2092

弧 弧 篆文

The seal-style form comprised 弓 **SG-1509** "bow," and 瓜 "gourd," used for the sound *ko* to mean "something curved." The curved shape of a bow also signified "an arc"—a segment of a circle. The kanji 弧 means "arc." <弓 瓜>

弧を描く to form an arc shape, draw an arc [こをえがく]; 括弧 parentheses [かっこ]; 鉤括弧 Japanese quotation marks [かぎかっこ]

32h 白 "white" [of obscure origin: (a) "interior of an acorn"; (b) "the lunula of a thumbnail"; or (c) "a weatherbeaten skull"]; *haku* 白百迫泊拍伯

	Meanings	Kun and On	Romaji	Bushu	Stroke Order and Number
SG-0787 白	white, innocent, blank; nothing; to confess	しろ・しら ハク・ビャク	shiro, shira *haku, byaku*	白	ノ 亻 白 白 白 5

白 **A** F-0229

白 白 白 白 甲骨文 1 金文 2 説文 3

The origin of the kanji 白 is obscure. One view explains that the pointed top and rounded bottom of 1 and 2 depicted the shape of an acorn, the interior of which is "white." Another view takes it to depict the white, weather-beaten skull of a late, great leader. "White" signified "blank" and "innocence." The kanji 白 means "white, innocent; nothing, blank; to confess." <ノ 日>

白い white [しろい]; 真っ白な completely white [まっしろな]; 白々しい transparent, obvious [しらじらしい]; 白雪 white snow [しらゆき]; 白書 white paper (authoritative report) [はくしょ]; 空白 blank, vacuum [くうはく]; 自白する to confess, own up [じはくする]; 白衣 lab coat, white hospital flock [はくい, びゃくい]

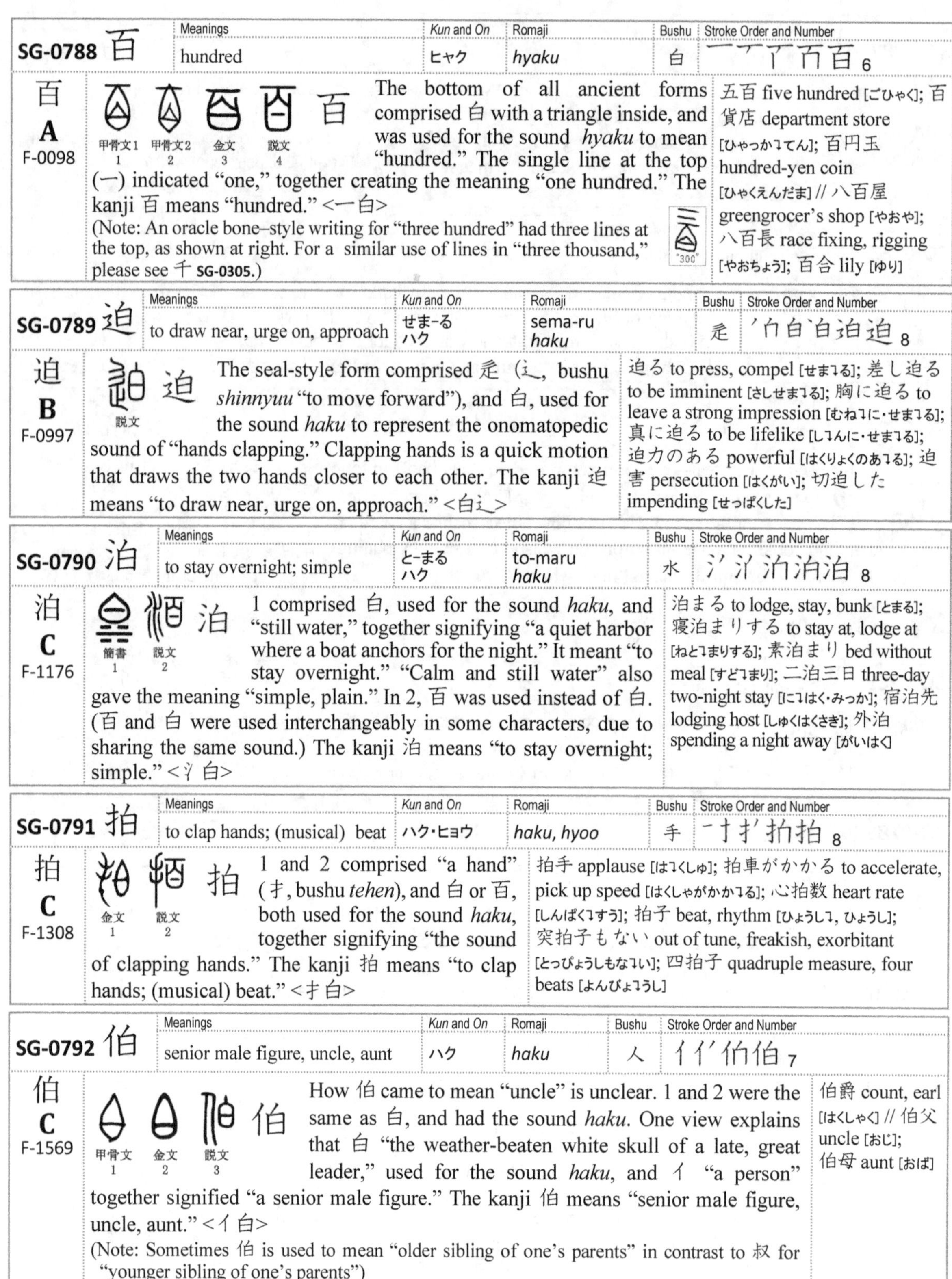

SG-0788 百	Meanings	Kun and On	Romaji	Bushu	Stroke Order and Number
	hundred	ヒャク	*hyaku*	白	一丆丆百百百 6

百
A
F-0098

甲骨文1 1 甲骨文2 2 金文 3 説文 4

The bottom of all ancient forms comprised 白 with a triangle inside, and was used for the sound *hyaku* to mean "hundred." The single line at the top (一) indicated "one," together creating the meaning "one hundred." The kanji 百 means "hundred." <一白>
(Note: An oracle bone–style writing for "three hundred" had three lines at the top, as shown at right. For a similar use of lines in "three thousand," please see 千 **SG-0305.**)

"300"

五百 five hundred [ごひゃく]; 百貨店 department store [ひゃっかてん]; 百円玉 hundred-yen coin [ひゃくえんだま] // 八百屋 greengrocer's shop [やおや]; 八百長 race fixing, rigging [やおちょう]; 百合 lily [ゆり]

SG-0789 迫	Meanings	Kun and On	Romaji	Bushu	Stroke Order and Number
	to draw near, urge on, approach	せま-る ハク	sema-ru *haku*	辵	′ 白 白 ˋ白 迫 迫 8

迫
B
F-0997

説文

The seal-style form comprised 辵 (⻌, bushu *shinnyuu* "to move forward"), and 白, used for the sound *haku* to represent the onomatopedic sound of "hands clapping." Clapping hands is a quick motion that draws the two hands closer to each other. The kanji 迫 means "to draw near, urge on, approach." <白⻌>

迫る to press, compel [せまる]; 差し迫る to be imminent [さしせまる]; 胸に迫る to leave a strong impression [むねに・せまる]; 真に迫る to be lifelike [しんに・せまる]; 迫力のある powerful [はくりょくのある]; 迫害 persecution [はくがい]; 切迫した impending [せっぱくした]

SG-0790 泊	Meanings	Kun and On	Romaji	Bushu	Stroke Order and Number
	to stay overnight; simple	と-まる ハク	to-maru *haku*	水	氵 氵′ 泊 泊 泊 8

泊
C
F-1176

簡書 1 説文 2

1 comprised 白, used for the sound *haku*, and "still water," together signifying "a quiet harbor where a boat anchors for the night." It meant "to stay overnight." "Calm and still water" also gave the meaning "simple, plain." In 2, 百 was used instead of 白. (百 and 白 were used interchangeably in some characters, due to sharing the same sound.) The kanji 泊 means "to stay overnight; simple." <氵白>

泊まる to lodge, stay, bunk [とまる]; 寝泊まりする to stay at, lodge at [ねとまりする]; 素泊まり bed without meal [すどまり]; 二泊三日 three-day two-night stay [にはく・みっか]; 宿泊先 lodging host [しゅくはくさき]; 外泊 spending a night away [がいはく]

SG-0791 拍	Meanings	Kun and On	Romaji	Bushu	Stroke Order and Number
	to clap hands; (musical) beat	ハク・ヒョウ	*haku, hyoo*	手	一 扌 扌′ 拍 拍 8

拍
C
F-1308

金文 1 説文 2

1 and 2 comprised "a hand" (扌, bushu *tehen*), and 白 or 百, both used for the sound *haku*, together signifying "the sound of clapping hands." The kanji 拍 means "to clap hands; (musical) beat." <扌白>

拍手 applause [はくしゅ]; 拍車がかかる to accelerate, pick up speed [はくしゃがかかる]; 心拍数 heart rate [しんぱくすう]; 拍子 beat, rhythm [ひょうし, ひょうし]; 突拍子もない out of tune, freakish, exorbitant [とっぴょうしもない]; 四拍子 quadruple measure, four beats [よんびょうし]

SG-0792 伯	Meanings	Kun and On	Romaji	Bushu	Stroke Order and Number
	senior male figure, uncle, aunt	ハク	*haku*	人	イ イ′ 伯 伯 7

伯
C
F-1569

甲骨文 1 金文 2 説文 3

How 伯 came to mean "uncle" is unclear. 1 and 2 were the same as 白, and had the sound *haku*. One view explains that 白 "the weather-beaten white skull of a late, great leader," used for the sound *haku*, and イ "a person" together signified "a senior male figure." The kanji 伯 means "senior male figure, uncle, aunt." <イ白>
(Note: Sometimes 伯 is used to mean "older sibling of one's parents" in contrast to 叔 for "younger sibling of one's parents")

伯爵 count, earl [はくしゃく] // 伯父 uncle [おじ]; 伯母 aunt [おば]

IV Animals

33 Animal meat

33a 肉 "meat" [from a carved piece of meat with tendons showing] 肉腐

	Meanings	Kun and On	Romaji	Bushu	Stroke Order and Number
SG-0793 肉	meat, flesh	ニク	*niku*	肉	丨冂内内肉肉 6

肉 **A** F-0692

説文 肉 The seal-style form depicted "a large, carved piece of meat." The lines inside signified tendons or lines of muscle. The kanji 肉 means "meat, flesh." When used as a bushu, it became 月, bushu *nikuzuki* "flesh, part of the body." <冂人人>

肉 meat [にくꜜ]; 牛肉 beef [ぎゅうにく]; 生肉 raw meat [なまꜜにく]; 肉食動物 carnivorous animal [にくしょくどꜜうぶつ]; 肉体 the body [にくたい]; 肉付けする to give body and substance to an idea [にくづけする]; 肉感 sexual feeling [にくかん]

	Meanings	Kun and On	Romaji	Bushu	Stroke Order and Number
SG-0794 腐	to rot, go bad, feel dejected; sulky	くさ-る フ	kusa-ru *hu*	肉	广府府腐腐腐 14

腐 **C** F-1415

説文 腐 The seal-style form comprised 府 **SG-0118**, used for the sound *hu* to mean "to rot, decay," and 月 "meat, flesh," together signifying "to rot, go bad." In the kanji, 月 was replaced by 肉 **SG-0793**. In Japanese the character also means "to feel dejected, discouraged" in (male) colloquial speech. The kanji 腐 means "to rot, go bad, feel dejected; sulky." <府肉>

腐る to rot, decay, spoil, feel dejected [くさꜜる]; 持ち腐れ useless possession [もちぐされ]; 腐れ縁 a bad relationship that cannot be broken [くされえん]; ふて腐れる to sulk [ふてくされる, ふてくされꜜる]; 腐敗する to degenerate, grow corrupt [ふはいする]; 腐心する to make every effort, be bent on [ふしんする]; 腐食 (腐蝕) corrosion, erosion [ふしょく]

33b 月 "a piece of animal meat" 有多賄

Kanji using 月 bushu *nikuzuki* "part of the body" (筋肩胸胃肺腕肌腸肯腎股膝肘脊) are discussed from **SG-0288** through **SG-0301**.

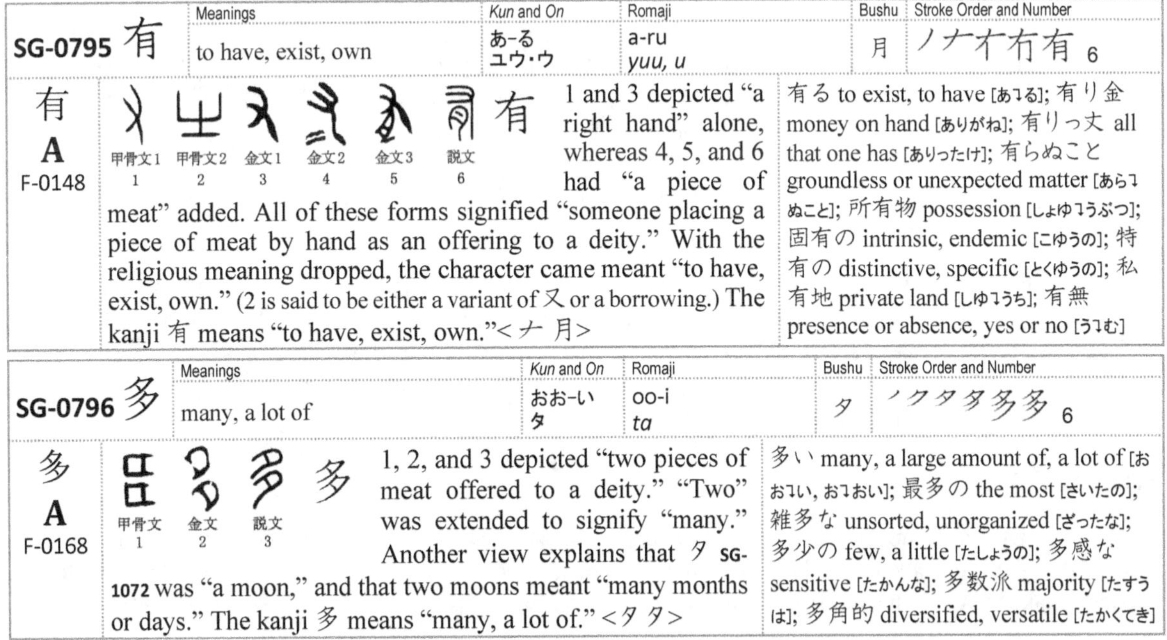

	Meanings	Kun and On	Romaji	Bushu	Stroke Order and Number
SG-0795 有	to have, exist, own	あ-る ユウ・ウ	a-ru *yuu, u*	月	ノナ有有有有 6

有 **A** F-0148

甲骨文1 (1), 甲骨文2 (2), 金文1 (3), 金文2 (4), 金文3 (5), 説文 (6), 有

1 and 3 depicted "a right hand" alone, whereas 4, 5, and 6 had "a piece of meat" added. All of these forms signified "someone placing a piece of meat by hand as an offering to a deity." With the religious meaning dropped, the character came meant "to have, exist, own." (2 is said to be either a variant of 又 or a borrowing.) The kanji 有 means "to have, exist, own."< ナ 月>

有る to exist, to have [あꜜる]; 有り金 money on hand [ありがね]; 有りっ丈 all that one has [ありったけ]; 有らぬこと groundless or unexpected matter [あらꜜぬこと]; 所有物 possession [しょゆꜜうぶつ]; 固有の intrinsic, endemic [こゆうの]; 特有の distinctive, specific [とくゆうの]; 私有地 private land [しゆꜜうち]; 有無 presence or absence, yes or no [うꜜむ]

	Meanings	Kun and On	Romaji	Bushu	Stroke Order and Number
SG-0796 多	many, a lot of	おお-い タ	oo-i *ta*	夕	ノクタ多多多 6

多 **A** F-0168

甲骨文 (1), 金文 (2), 説文 (3), 多

1, 2, and 3 depicted "two pieces of meat offered to a deity." "Two" was extended to signify "many." Another view explains that 夕 **SG-1072** was "a moon," and that two moons meant "many months or days." The kanji 多 means "many, a lot of." <夕 夕>

多い many, a large amount of, a lot of [おおꜜい, おꜜおい]; 最多の the most [さいたの]; 雑多な unsorted, unorganized [ざったな]; 多少の few, a little [たしょうの]; 多感な sensitive [たかんな]; 多数派 majority [たすうは]; 多角的 diversified, versatile [たかくてき]

	Meanings	Kun and On	Romaji	Bushu	Stroke Order and Number
SG-0797 賄	to provide, fund, give (to win over); feeding, boarding	まかな-う ワイ	makana-u *wai*	貝	冂 目 貝 賄 賄 13

賄 **D** F-1715	篆文 賄 The seal-style form comprised 貝 **SG-1693** "cowrie, valuable" on the left, and "a hand" with "a piece of meat," forming 有 **SG-0795** for the sound *yuu/wai* on the right. Taken all together, they signified "to fund, give something (often with the intent of winning someone over)." The character is also used to mean "boarding, feeding." The kanji 賄 means "to provide, fund, give (to win over); feeding, boarding." <貝有>	賄う to pay, fund, provide board [まかなう]; 賄い付き meals included [まかないつき]; 収賄罪 the offense of taking bribes [しゅうわいざい]; 贈賄 bribery and corruption, offering a bribe [ぞうわい]

33c 肖 "to resemble" [from a small end piece of meat—小 "small" and 月 "flesh"]; *shoo* 消削肖硝

The bushu *sakasashoo* ⺌ appears in shinji such as 尚当党常賞堂償 (**SG-1268** through **SG-1275**) and 弊蔽弊 (**SG-1690** through **SG-1692**).

	Meanings	Kun and On	Romaji	Bushu	Stroke Order and Number
SG-0798 消	to disappear, exhaust	き-える・け-す ショウ	ki-eru, ke-su *shoo*	水	氵 氵 氵 氵 消 消 10

消 **A** F-0408	説文 消 The seal-style form comprised "flowing water," and 肖 "a small end piece of meat," used for the sound *shoo* and the meaning "small." "Little water" signified "running out of water; disappearing." In the kanji 小 was flipped upside down (and is thus called *sakasa-shoo*, "upside-down *shoo*"). The kanji 消 means "to disappear, exhaust." <氵⺌月>	消える to go out, melt, go missing [きえる]; 消す to erase, switch off, cancel [けす]; 消しゴム pencil eraser [けしゴム]; 取り消し to cancel [とりけし]; 消極的な passive, halfhearted [しょうきょくてきな]; 消防士 firefighter [しょうぼうし]; 意気消沈する to lose heart, be in low spirits [いき・しょうちんする]

	Meanings	Kun and On	Romaji	Bushu	Stroke Order and Number
SG-0799 削	to shave, make cutbacks, delete	けず-る サク	kezu-ru *saku*	刀	丨 ⺌ 肖 肖 削 削 9

削 **B** F-1075	説文 削 The seal-style form comprised 肖 "small piece of meat, small end piece," used for the sound *saku*, and "knife; to cut" (刂). A knife cutting meat into small pieces meant "to chip off, shave." The kanji 削 means "to shave, make cutbacks, delete." <肖刂>	削る to shave, scrape, curtail, expunge [けずる]; 鉛筆削り pencil sharpener [えんぴつけずり]; 削減 reduction, scaling back [さくげん]; 削除 deletion, striking out [さくじょ]; 添削 correction, touching up [てんさく]

	Meanings	Kun and On	Romaji	Bushu	Stroke Order and Number
SG-0800 肖	to resemble, be like	ショウ	*shoo*	肉	丨 ⺌ 肖 肖 肖 7

肖 **D** F-1950	金文 1 説文 2 旧字 3 肖 1, 2, and 3 comprised 小 "small," used for the sound *shoo* to mean "to resemble," and 夕 or 月 "part of the body," together signifying "a small person that resembles something" (usually their father). The kanji 肖 means "to resemble, be like." <肖>	肖像画 portrait [しょうぞうが]; 肖像権 image rights [しょうぞうけん]; 不肖の unworthy of one's father, my humble self [ふしょうの]

	Meanings	Kun and On	Romaji	Bushu	Stroke Order and Number
SG-0801 硝	saltpeter, niter, glass	ショウ	*shoo*	石	厂 石 石 石 硝 硝 12

硝 **D** F-2100	No ancient form. The kanji 硝 comprises 石 **SG-1148** "rock," and 肖, used for the sound *shoo*, together signifying "saltpeter, niter," which is used to make "glass." The kanji 硝 means "saltpeter, niter, glass." <石肖>	硝酸 nitric acid [しょうさん]; 硝子 glass [ガラス]; 硝煙 gunpowder smoke [しょうえん]

33d 隋 [from a stack of sacrificial meat offerings to a deity]; *zui/da* 随髄堕惰

	Meanings	Kun and On	Romaji	Bushu	Stroke Order and Number
SG-0802 随	to follow	ズイ	*zui*	阜	12

随 **C** F-1605

説文 1 旧字 2

1 comprised 辵 (辶) "to move forward," and 隋, used for the sound *zui* to mean "to follow." It may have signified "pieces of sacrificial meat falling on top of each other." The top right of the kyuji 隨 (2) was replaced by 有 **SG-0795** in the shinji. The kanji 随 means "to follow." <阝迶(有辶)>

随分 fairly, quite a lot, horrid [ずいぶん]; 随時 at any time, as needed [ずいじ]; 随意 (at one's) pleasure, discretion [ずいい]; 随意筋 voluntary muscle [ずいいきん]; 随行員 attendant, member of one's entourage [ずいこういん]; 追随する to follow, catch up with [ついずいする]

	Meanings	Kun and On	Romaji	Bushu	Stroke Order and Number
SG-0803 髄	essence, marrow	ズイ	*zui*	骨	19

髄 **D** F-1890

篆文 1 旧字 2

In 1, 骨 **SG-0272** "bones" was added to another component pronounced *zui*, together signifying what was inside the bone—"bone marrow or essence." In the shinji, the top right was replaced by 有, in the same way that the kyuji 隨 became 随 **SG-0802**. The kanji 髄 means "essence, marrow." <骨迶>

骨髄 bone marrow [こつずい]; 脊髄 spinal marrow [せきずい]; 真髄 essence, soul [しんずい]

	Meanings	Kun and On	Romaji	Bushu	Stroke Order and Number
SG-0804 堕	to fall, degenerate	ダ	*da*	土	12

堕 **D** F-2058

篆文 1 1 篆文 2 2 旧字 3

The kanji 堕 and the next kanji 惰 **SG-0805** share the sound *da*, which originally meant "a pile of meat collapsing." The shinji 堕 comprised 阝, bushu *kozatohen* "hills, a pile," 有 **SG-0795**, and 土 **SG-1126** "soil, ground," together signifying "an offering spoiling and falling to the ground." The kanji 堕 means "to fall, degenerate." <阝有土>

堕落 moral corruption, decadence [だらく]; 自堕落な self-indulgent, sloppy, undisciplined [じだらくな, じだらくな]; 堕胎 induced abortion [だたい]

	Meanings	Kun and On	Romaji	Bushu	Stroke Order and Number
SG-0805 惰	idle, lazy, inertia	ダ	*da*	心	12

惰 **D** F-2348

説文 1 説文或体 2

The kanji 惰 comprised 忄 "a heart," and "a pile of meat offerings collapsing," used for the sound *da*. Together they signified one's mind becoming lazy or lax. The kanji 惰 means "idle, lazy, inertia." <忄左月>

怠惰な idle, sluggish, lazy [たいだな]; 惰性 inertia, force of habit [だせい]; 惰性的な habitual, routine, inertial [だせいてきな]

33e 且 "many; to pile up" [from a stack of sacrificial meat]; *so*

組助祖狙畳粗阻宜租且

	Meanings	Kun and On	Romaji	Bushu	Stroke Order and Number
SG-0806 組	to braid, put together; group, class, set	く-む・くみ ソ	ku-mu, kumi *so*	糸	11

組 **A** F-0147

金文 1 1 金文 2 2 説文 3

1, 2, and 3 comprised "a skein of threads" (糸 **SG-1600**), and 且 **SG-0815** "stack, pile," used for the sound *so*. (1 also included "a hand.") Together they meant "a hand braiding strands of thread." From a set of things being put together it also meant "group, class, set." The kanji 組 means "to braid, put together; group, class, set." <糸且>

組む to braid a cord, tack together, cross [くむ]; 取り組む to come to grips with, tackle (an issue), undertake [とりくむ、とりくむ]; 組 class, set [くみ]; 仕組み device, structure [しくみ]; 組み立てる to fabricate, assemble [くみたてる]; 組み合わせ combination, matching, scheduling [くみあわせ]; 組合 association, union [くみあい]; 組成 composition, constitution [そせい]

	Meanings	Kun and On	Romaji	Bushu	Stroke Order and Number
SG-0807 助	to help, assist	たす-ける・すけ ジョ	tasu-keru, suke *jo*	力	𠂇 月 目 助 助 7

助 **A** F-0419

金文 1 説文 2

One view takes 且 to be "plow, spade" (a meaning now assigned to the non-Joyo kanji 鋤 *suki*), suggesting communal field work, whereas another takes 且 to be "layers," suggesting many helping hands working together. The right side of 2 was a plow, signifying "hard field work," and became 力 **SG-1949** "power, strength" in the kanji. The kanji 助 means "to help, assist." <且力>

助ける to help [たすける]; 助かる it helps me, helpful [たすかる]; 手助けする to lend a helping hand [てだすけする]; 助太刀する to lend a hand in a fight [すけだちする]; 助手 assistant [じょしゅ]; 助詞 particle (in Japanese grammar) [じょし]; 助走する to make an approach run [じょそうする]

	Meanings	Kun and On	Romaji	Bushu	Stroke Order and Number
SG-0808 祖	ancestor, originator	ソ	*so*	示	` ラ ネ ネ 初 祖 祖 9

祖 **C** F-1175

甲骨文 1 甲骨文 2 金文 3 説文 4 旧字 5

1 comprised "an altar table" for ancestor worship, and "a stack of meat offerings" (or "a pile of stones as an ancestral tombstone" in another view), used for the sound *so*. 2 and 3 were the same as 且 **SG-0815** "a pile." In 4, an altar table (示 **SG-1737**) and a pile of offerings signified "ancestor." 示 became ネ (bushu *shimesuhen* "religious matters") in the shinji. The kanji 祖 means "ancestor, originator." <ネ且>

先祖 forefather, ancestor [せんぞ]; 祖先 ancestor, ascendant [そせん]; 祖国 mother country [そこく]; 祖父 grandfather [そふ]; 祖母 grandmother [そぼ]; 元祖 originator, founder [がんそ]; 先祖伝来 family heirloom, ancestral [せんぞ・でんらい]

	Meanings	Kun and On	Romaji	Bushu	Stroke Order and Number
SG-0809 狙	to take aim at, watch for a chance, strive for	ねら-う ソ	nera-u *so*	犬	ノ 𠃌 犭 犭 狙 狙 8

狙 **C** F-1213

篆文

The seal-style form comprised "animal" (犭, bushu *kemonohen*), and 且, used for the sound *so*. The animal on the left side was "a monkey," or an animal that bit people—"a dog." From a dog or animal watching for a chance to attack, the character meant "to take aim at." The kanji 狙 means "to take aim at, watch for a chance, strive for." <犭且>

狙う to take aim at, strive for [ねらう]; 狙い an aim, an end [ねらい]; 狙い所 one's point, one's objective [ねらいどころ]; 付け狙う to follow, stalk, shadow [つけねらう]; 狙撃する to fire at, snipe at [そげきする]

	Meanings	Kun and On	Romaji	Bushu	Stroke Order and Number
SG-0810 畳	tatami mat; to fold up, close down (a business)	たた-む・たたみ ジョウ	tata-mu, tatami *joo*	田	冂 田 畕 畳 畳 12

畳 **C** F-1532

金文 1 説文 2 旧字 3

1 and 2 comprised "a stack of meat on a board that was offered to a deity in a mausoleum," and many "suns" or "jewels." The stacks of meat or the many suns originally meant "to pile, lay over, fold." In the kyuji 疊 (3), the pile of meat became 且. In Japanese, the character also means "tatami mat," from "things that stack up." The kanji 畳 means "tatami mat; to fold up, close down (a business)." <田冖且>

畳 tatami mat, straw matting [たたみ]; 店を畳む to close down one's store [みせをたたむ]; 畳みかける to make continuous points so as to overpower one's opponent (in a debate), press someone for an answer without pause [たたみかける]; 石畳 stone pavement [いしだたみ]; 畳表 outer layer of a tatami mat [たたみおもて]; 六畳間 six tatami–mat room [ろくじょうま]

	Meanings	Kun and On	Romaji	Bushu	Stroke Order and Number
SG-0811 粗	coarse, porous, crude; poor quality	あら-い ソ	ara-i *so*	米	丷 半 粈 粗 粗 11

粗 **C** F-1542

説文

The seal-style form comprised 米 **SG-0738** "rice," and 且, used for the sound *so* to mean "rough," together signifying "unpolished rice, brown rice." The kanji 粗 means "coarse, porous, crude; poor quality." <米且>

粗い coarse, porous [あらい]; 粗筋 outline, summary [あらすじ]; 粗捜し nit-picking, fault-finding [あらさがし]; 粗末な coarse, humble [そまつな]; 粗品 small gift [そしな]; 粗相 oversight, carelessness [そそう]; 粗忽者 careless person, absentminded person [そこつもの]; 粗食 frugal meal, plain food [そしょく]

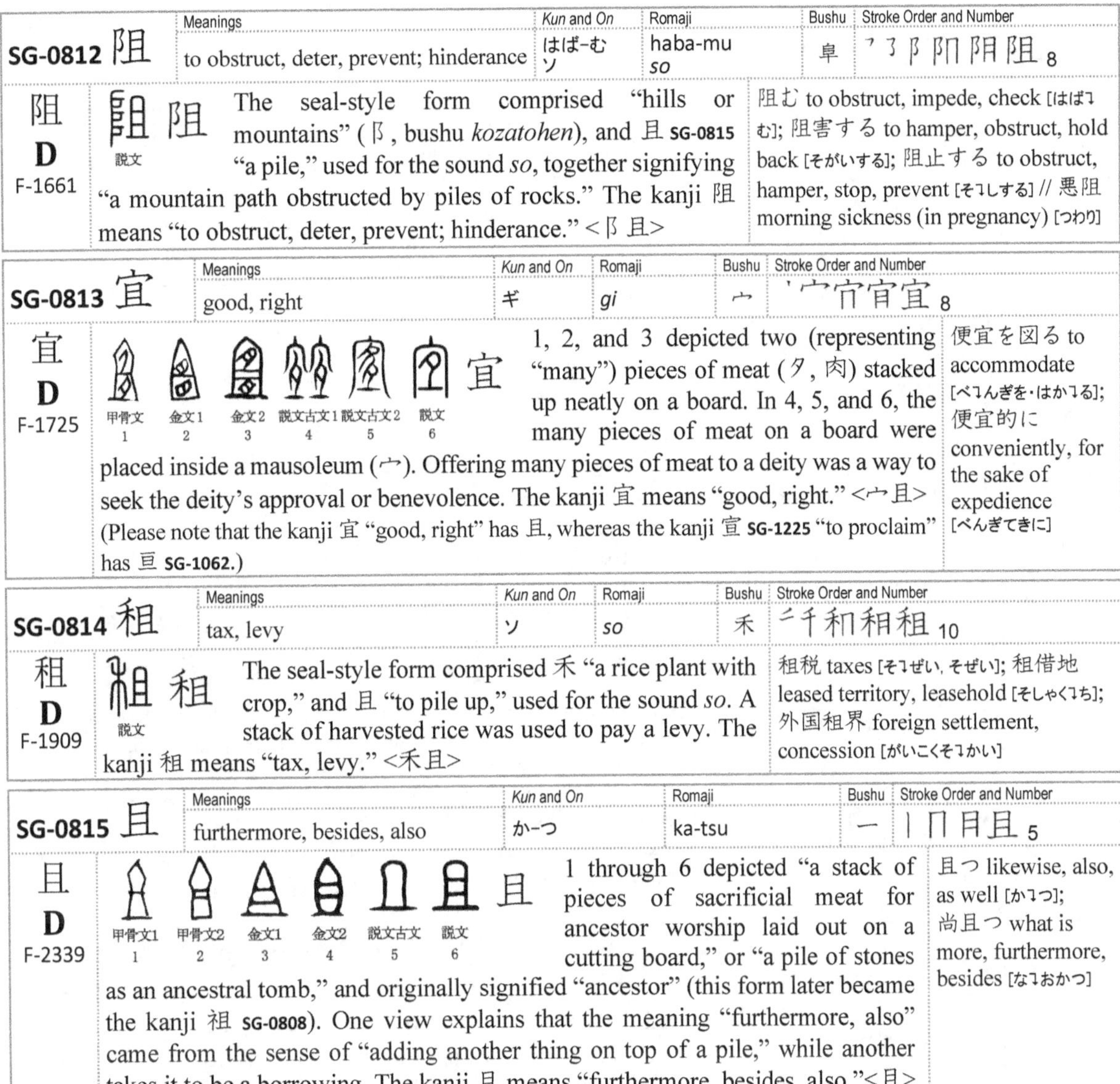

	Meanings	Kun and On	Romaji	Bushu	Stroke Order and Number
SG-0812 阻	to obstruct, deter, prevent; hinderance	はば-む ソ	haba-mu *so*	阜	⁷ ㇋ 阝 阝冂 阝月 阻 8

阻 **D** F-1661

説文

The seal-style form comprised "hills or mountains" (阝, bushu *kozatohen*), and 且 **SG-0815** "a pile," used for the sound *so*, together signifying "a mountain path obstructed by piles of rocks." The kanji 阻 means "to obstruct, deter, prevent; hinderance." <阝且>

阻む to obstruct, impede, check [はばむ]; 阻害する to hamper, obstruct, hold back [そがいする]; 阻止する to obstruct, hamper, stop, prevent [そしする] // 悪阻 morning sickness (in pregnancy) [つわり]

	Meanings	Kun and On	Romaji	Bushu	Stroke Order and Number
SG-0813 宜	good, right	ギ	*gi*	宀	ˊ 宀 宁 宜 宜 8

宜 **D** F-1725

甲骨文 1, 金文1 2, 金文2 3, 説文古文1 4, 説文古文2 5, 説文 6

1, 2, and 3 depicted two (representing "many") pieces of meat (タ, 肉) stacked up neatly on a board. In 4, 5, and 6, the many pieces of meat on a board were placed inside a mausoleum (宀). Offering many pieces of meat to a deity was a way to seek the deity's approval or benevolence. The kanji 宜 means "good, right." <宀且> (Please note that the kanji 宜 "good, right" has 且, whereas the kanji 宣 **SG-1225** "to proclaim" has 亘 **SG-1062**.)

便宜を図る to accommodate [べんぎをはかる]; 便宜的に conveniently, for the sake of expedience [べんぎてきに]

	Meanings	Kun and On	Romaji	Bushu	Stroke Order and Number
SG-0814 租	tax, levy	ソ	*so*	禾	二 千 和 租 租 10

租 **D** F-1909

説文

The seal-style form comprised 禾 "a rice plant with crop," and 且 "to pile up," used for the sound *so*. A stack of harvested rice was used to pay a levy. The kanji 租 means "tax, levy." <禾且>

租税 taxes [そぜい, そぜい]; 租借地 leased territory, leasehold [そしゃくち]; 外国租界 foreign settlement, concession [がいこくそかい]

	Meanings	Kun and On	Romaji	Bushu	Stroke Order and Number
SG-0815 且	furthermore, besides, also	か-つ	ka-tsu	一	丨 冂 月 且 5

且 **D** F-2339

甲骨文1 1, 甲骨文2 2, 金文1 3, 金文2 4, 説文古文 5, 説文 6

1 through 6 depicted "a stack of pieces of sacrificial meat for ancestor worship laid out on a cutting board," or "a pile of stones as an ancestral tomb," and originally signified "ancestor" (this form later became the kanji 祖 **SG-0808**). One view explains that the meaning "furthermore, also" came from the sense of "adding another thing on top of a pile," while another takes it to be a borrowing. The kanji 且 means "furthermore, besides, also."<且>

且つ likewise, also, as well [かつ]; 尚且つ what is more, furthermore, besides [なおかつ]

34 Ox, cow

34a 牛 "ox, cow" [from a frontal view of an ox with horns] 牛物件牧牲

	Meanings	Kun and On	Romaji	Bushu	Stroke Order and Number
SG-0816 牛	Ox, cow	うし ギュウ	ushi *gyuu*	牛	ノ 𠂉 ⺧ 牛 4

牛 **A** F-0622

甲骨文 1, 金文 2, 説文 3

In 1, 2, and 3, the top was an ox head, with its two horns growing upward, and the bottom was the animal's body. The form meant "ox, cow." In the kanji 牛, a short stroke was added on the top left to emphasize the horns. The kanji 牛 means "ox, cow" <牛>

牛 cow, bull, ox, cattle [うし]; 乳牛 dairy cow, dairy cattle [にゅうぎゅう]; 牛乳 milk [ぎゅうにゅう]; 水牛 water buffalo [すいぎゅう]; 牛耳る to control, have a whip hand over [ぎゅうじる] // 牛車 ox-drawn carriage used by nobility, ox cart [ぎっしゃ]

	Meanings	Kun and On	Romaji	Bushu	Stroke Order and Number
SG-0817 物	stuff, thing; various, assorted; to select	もの ブツ・モツ	mono *butsu, motsu*	牛	8

物 **A** F-0124

甲骨文1 1, 甲骨文2 2, 甲骨文3 3, 中山王器 4, 説文 5

1 and 4 were "a plow spattering soil," used for the sound *butsu/motsu.* In 2, 3, and 5, "an ox" 牛, here representing any large animal, was added. Cows or oxen that pulled a plow varied in coloration, thus giving the meaning "various." Another view explains that 勿 in 5 depicted streamers of different colors, and thus signified "various." Choosing from various things meant "to make a choice." The kanji 物 means "stuff, thing; various, assorted; to select." <牛勿>

物 thing, matter, article, goods [もの]; 安物 cheap article, inferior article [やすもの]; 物々しい showy, stately [ものものしい]; 見物する to go sightseeing [けんぶつする]; 生物 living thing, creature [せいぶつ]; 物品 goods, an article [ぶっぴん]; 物理学 physical science [ぶつりがく]; 禁物 taboo thing, forbidden thing [きんもつ]

	Meanings	Kun and On	Romaji	Bushu	Stroke Order and Number
SG-0818 件	case, matter	ケン	*ken*	人	6

件 **A** F-0259

説文

The seal-style form had イ "an act that a person does," and 牛 "an ox," together signifying "a person counting oxen in a herd," or "counting cases." The kanji 件 means "case, matter." <イ牛>

事件 incidence, case [じけん]; 条件付き conditional [じょうけんつき]; 件名 case name [けんめい]; 別件 separate charge, different case [べっけん]; 用件 business, things to be done [ようけん]; 人件費 personnel expenses [じんけんひ] // 件の the said, aforementioned [くだんの]

	Meanings	Kun and On	Romaji	Bushu	Stroke Order and Number
SG-0819 牧	to herd cattle; pasture	まき ボク	maki *boku*	牛	8

牧 **C** F-1324

甲骨文1 1, 甲骨文2 2, 金文1 3, 金文2 4, 説文 5

The top-left component of 1 was "a sheep" (羊 **SG-0825**), while 2, 3, 4, and 5 had "an ox" (牛). (The directions of the horns differentiated the two animals.) The right-side component in all of them was "a hand holding a stick to herd sheep or oxen" (攴/攵, bushu *bokunyuu*). Animals grazed in a pasture. The kanji 牧 means "to herd cattle; pasture." <牛攵>

牧場 pasture, meadow [まきば]; 放牧 pasturage, grazing [ほうぼく]; 牧師 pastor, minister, clergyman [ぼくし, ぼくし]; 遊牧 nomadism [ゆうぼく]; 牧場 stock farm, ranch [ぼくじょう]; 牧歌的な pastoral, idyllic [ぼっかてきな]

	Meanings	Kun and On	Romaji	Bushu	Stroke Order and Number
SG-0820 牲	sacrifice, sacrificial animal	セイ	*see*	牛	9

牲 **D** F-1821

甲骨文 1, 金文 2, 説文 3

1 comprised "a sheep" (羊 **SG-0825**), and "an emerging plant" (生 **SG-0689**), which was used for the sound *see* to mean "life." Together they signified "a live sheep offered to a deity as a sacrifice." In 2 and 3, "an ox" (牛) was used, since an ox makes a more impressive and appreciated sacrifice than a sheep. The kanji 牲 means "sacrifice, sacrificial animal." <牛生>

犠牲になる to sacrifice oneself [ぎせいになる]; 犠牲者 victim, prey [ぎせいしゃ]

34b 半 "half" [from an ox cut in half]; *han* 半判伴畔

	Meanings	Kun and On	Romaji	Bushu	Stroke Order and Number
SG-0821 半	half	なか-ば ハン	naka-ba *han*	十	5

半 **A** F-0220

金文 1, 説文 2

1 and 2 comprised ハ "to divide something in half," used for the sound *han,* and "an ox" (牛 **SG-0816**), signifying an ox that was cut in half. The kanji 半 means "half." <半>

月半ば middle of the month [つきなかば, つきなかば]; 半分 half [はんぶん, はんぶん adverb]; 過半数 majority, more than half [かはんすう]; 上半身 the upper body [じょうはんしん]; 生半可な shallow, superficial [なまはんかな]; 半可通 superficial knowledge, affecting to be a connoisseur [はんかつう]; 折半する to cut into halves, split in half [せっぱんする]; 半べそをかく to be on the verge of crying [はんべそをかく]

SG-0822 判	Meanings	Kun and On	Romaji	Bushu	Stroke Order and Number
	a seal; to judge, discern, grasp	ハン・バン	*han, ban*	刀	丷 兰 半 判 判 7

判
A
F-0477

説文

The seal-style form comprised 半 "half," used for the sound *han,* and "a knife; to cut" (刂, bushu *rittoo*). After having signed a contract, the two parties each took half of the contract, with a seal stamped across each half. In a dispute over a contract, a judge decided which party was right. The kanji 判 means "a seal; to judge, discern, grasp." <半 刂>

判子 *hanko* seal [はんこ]; 判決 judicial decision, ruling [はんけつ]; 公判 public trial [こうはん]; 判読 to decipher, make out [はんどく]; 判事 judge [はんじ]; 小判 *koban*, Japanese oval gold coin [こばん]; 判定勝ち winning by decision [はんていがち]; 談判 negotiation, bargaining [だんぱん]

SG-0823 伴	Meanings	Kun and On	Romaji	Bushu	Stroke Order and Number
	to accompany; companion	ともな-う ハン・バン	tomona-u *han, ban*	人	亻 亻丷 伫 伴 7

伴
B
F-0971

篆文

The seal-style form comprised 亻 "an act that a person does," and 半 **SG-0821** "half," which was used for the sound *han.* Together they signified two people who were each other's companions. The kanji 伴 means "to accompany; companion." <亻 半>

伴う to accompany, bring in its train [ともなう]; 同伴者 one's companion [どうはんしゃ]; 伴走 pacesetting, running alongside [ばんそう]; 伴奏 musical accompaniment [ばんそう]; お相伴する to join for a meal (humble) [おしょうばんする]

SG-0824 畔	Meanings	Kun and On	Romaji	Bushu	Stroke Order and Number
	levee, ridge, edge of water	ハン	*han*	田	冂 冊 田 田丷 畔 畔 10

畔
D
F-2063

説文

The seal-style form comprised 田 **SG-1300** "rice paddies," and 半 **SG-0821**, used for the sound *han* to mean "one side; to divide into two." Together they signified a ridge between two rice paddies, which also meant an edge of water. The kanji 畔 means "levee, ridge, edge of water." <田半>

湖畔 lakeside [こはん]; 河畔 riverside [かはん]

35 Sheep

35a 羊 "sheep, goodness, desirability" [from versatile use of sheep]; *yoo*

羊美様達洋養詳窯羨羞

SG-0825 羊	Meanings	Kun and On	Romaji	Bushu	Stroke Order and Number
	a sheep	ひつじ ヨウ	hitsuji *yoo*	羊	丷 䒑 兰 羊 6

羊
A
F-1452

甲骨文1 甲骨文2 金文1 金文2 金文3 説文
1 2 3 4 5 6

1 through 6 all depicted "a sheep" viewed from the front, with two horns that curled downward and a body. The kanji 羊 meant "a sheep." A sheep had many different uses: its hide was used for clothing and for tent material; its wool was used for clothing and spun into yarn; its meat provided nutrition; and its horns and bones were used to make tools and other implements. A sheep was also used as a sacrificial animal in religious rites. Due to this versatility, when 羊 was used as a component in other characters, it gave the meaning "goodness, desirability." <羊>

羊 sheep [ひつじ]; 子羊 lamb [こひつじ]; 羊毛 wool [ようもう]; 羊皮紙 parchment, sheepskin [ようひし] // 山羊 goat [やぎ]

SG-0826 美	Meanings	Kun and On	Romaji	Bushu	Stroke Order and Number
	beautiful, good; aesthetic	うつく-しい ビ	utsuku-shii *bi*	羊	丷 䒑 䒑 羊 美 美 9

美
A
F-0166

甲骨文 金文 説文
1 2 3

Different views on the origin for the kanji 美 include: (a) it comprised 羊 "a sheep" and 大 **SG-0314** "a person," together meaning "beautiful (person)"; (b) it signified a large, mature sheep (大 and 羊) looking "impressive" and "beautiful"; and (c) it was a full view of a well-shaped sheep, including its head and its front and hind legs. The kanji 美 means "beautiful, good; aesthetic." <⺷大>

美しい beautiful [うつくしい]; 美 beauty, aesthetics [び]; 美人 beautiful woman [びじん]; 美男子 handsome man [びだんし]; 美術 fine art [びじゅつ]; 美談 moving story [びだん]; 美的な aesthetic [びてきな]; 美味 delicacy, dainty [びみ]; 優美な graceful, dainty, refined [ゆうびな]; 有終の美 beautiful final touch [ゆうしゅうのび]

	Meanings	Kun and On	Romaji	Bushu	Stroke Order and Number
SG-0827 様	manner, appearance; honorific form of address	さま ヨウ	sama *yoo*	木	木" 栏 样 样 様 様 14

様 **A** F-0260

説文 1　旧字 2

The seal-style form comprised 木 "a tree," and the shape on the right side, which was used for the sound *yoo.* The right side was explained in *Setsumon* as depicting the acorns of a sawtooth oak tree (橡 *shoo/yoo*), the bark of which has a wavy pattern. The word that meant "appearance, manner" had the same sound, *yoo*, and so 1 came to be used for that. 永 in the kyuji was reduced to 氺 in the shinji. The kanji 様 means "manner, appearance," and is also an honorific form of address. <木 羊 氺>

様 appearance, state, manner [さま]; 有様 state, condition [ありさま, ありさま]; 様になる to start looking suitable [さまになる]; 様々な various, all manner of [さまざまな]; ～様 polite form of address [～さま]; 様子 appearance, look [ようす]; 同様に in a similar manner [どうように]; ～の様だ it appears that X [～のようだ]; 多様な various, diverse, manifold [たような]

	Meanings	Kun and On	Romaji	Bushu	Stroke Order and Number
SG-0828 達	to attain, reach; healthy, skillful; plural suffix for people	タツ	*tatsu*	辵	土 去 查 幸 幸 達 達 12

達 **A** F-0387

甲骨文 1　金文 2　説文 3　説文或体 4

1 comprised "a crossroads" (彳) and "a footprint" (forming 辵 in 3 and 4, and 辶 in the kanji), and "a person" (大), together signifying "a person moving ahead with no trouble." In 2 and 3, 羊 "a sheep" was added to signify "the smooth birth of a lamb." Moving ahead with no trouble (like a lamb's smooth birth) led to the meaning "to reach with no trouble." The kanji 達 means "to attain, reach; healthy, skillful." In Japanese, the kanji 達 is also used as a plural suffix for people, pronounced *tachi.* <土 羊 辶>

達成する to complete, reach [たっせいする]; 到達する to arrive at [とうたつする]; 発達 development, growth [はったつ]; 達者だ healthy and active, skillful at [たっしゃだ]; 達人 an expert [たつじん]; 達成する to achieve, accomplish, bring to fruition [たっせいする] // 子供達 children [こどもたち]; 友達 friends [ともだち]

	Meanings	Kun and On	Romaji	Bushu	Stroke Order and Number
SG-0829 洋	ocean; abroad; western	ヨウ	*yoo*	水	氵 氵' 浐 洋 9

洋 **A** F-0440

甲骨文1 1　甲骨文2 2　説文 3

1 and 2 comprised one or two 羊, used for the sound *yoo* to mean "vast, extensive," and the four dots around the sheep depicting "droplets of water." Together they signified "large sea, ocean." 3 had "water" (氵) and "a sheep" side by side. Land beyond an ocean was "abroad" and "western." The kanji 洋 means "ocean; abroad; western." <氵 羊>

海洋 seas, the ocean [かいよう]; 東洋 the east, orient [とうよう]; 西洋 the west [せいよう]; 洋服 western-style clothes [ようふく]; 洋風 western style [ようふう]; 大西洋 the Atlantic Ocean [たいせいよう]; 洋行 going abroad [ようこう]; 前途洋々 promising and bright future [ぜんと・ようよう]

	Meanings	Kun and On	Romaji	Bushu	Stroke Order and Number
SG-0830 養	to support, nourish, foster	やしな-う ヨウ	yashina-u *yoo*	食	丷 䒑 羊 关 养 眷 養 養 15

養 **B** F-0835

甲骨文1 1　甲骨文2 2　金文1 3　金文2 4　説文 5

1, 2, 3, and 4 comprised 羊 "a sheep," used for the sound *yoo* to mean "to feed," and 攴 "to cause an action," together signifying "sheep farming." In 5, 食 **SG-1781** "to eat; food" replaced the hand holding a stick 攴. The kanji 養 means "to support (by providing food), nourish, foster." <⺷八良)>

養う to support by providing food, foster [やしなう]; 養分 nutrient, nourishment [ようぶん]; 栄養 nutrition [えいよう]; 休養 rest [きゅうよう]; 養子 adopted child [ようし]; 養生する to care for one's health, recuperate [ようじょうする]; 静養 rest, convalescence [せいよう]

	Meanings	Kun and On	Romaji	Bushu	Stroke Order and Number
SG-0831 詳	detailed, clear	くわ-しい ショウ	kuwa-shii *shoo*	言	言 言' 詳 詳 13

詳 **C** F-1154

説文

The seal-style form comprised 言 **SG-1364** "word, language; to say," and 羊 **SG-0825**, which was used for the sound *shoo* (from *yoo*) to mean "details." Together they meant "to discuss in detail, make a matter clear with words." The kanji 詳 means "detailed, clear." <言羊>

詳しい detailed, knowledgeable [くわしい]; 詳細 details [しょうさい]

	Meanings	Kun and On	Romaji	Bushu	Stroke Order and Number
SG-0832 窯	kiln	かま ヨウ	kama *yoo*	穴	15

窯 **D** F-2342 説文 The seal-style form comprised 穴 **SG-1322** "cave, pit"; 羊 **SG-0825**, which was used for the sound *yoo*; and 火 **SG-1164** "fire," together signifying "a furnace for baking pottery." The kanji 窯 means "kiln." <穴羊 灬>

窯 kiln; furnace [かま]; 登り窯 climbing kiln [のぼりがま]; 窯元 pottery, pottery producer [かまもと]

	Meanings	Kun and On	Romaji	Bushu	Stroke Order and Number
SG-0833 羨	to envy, begrudge; jealous	うらや-ましい セン	uraya-mashii *sen*	羊	13

羨 **D** F-2565 説文 The seal-style form comprised 羊 "sheep," which had tasty meat, and 次 "to drool (氵) with envy," used for the sound *sen*. Together they signified "envious." The kanji 羨 means "to envy, begrudge; jealous." <⺶ 氵 欠>

羨ましい to feel envious, enviable [うらやましい]; 羨む to envy [うらやむ]; 羨望 envy [せんぼう]

	Meanings	Kun and On	Romaji	Bushu	Stroke Order and Number
SG-0834 羞	to feel abashed	シュウ	*shuu*	羊	11

羞 **D** F-2860 甲骨文 1 金文1 2 金文2 3 説文 4 1, 2, and 3 comprised 羊 "a sheep," and one or two "hands," together signifying "offering a sacrificial sheep to a deity with one's hands." When presenting offerings to a deity, one felt bashful, wondering whether the offering was good enough, and thus the character meant "to be bashful." In 4, the bottom became fingers that were firmly grabbing the offering (丑). The kanji 羞 means "to feel abashed." <⺶ノ丑>

羞恥心 sense of shame [しゅうちしん]; 羞じらう to feel shy, be coy, be bashful, blush [はじらう]

35b 善 "goodness" [from many praising words]; *zen* 善繕膳

	Meanings	Kun and On	Romaji	Bushu	Stroke Order and Number
SG-0835 善	good, right; virtue	よ-い ゼン	yo-i *zen*	口	12

善 **B** F-0671 金文1 1 金文2 2 金文3 3 説文古文 4 説文 5 1, 2, 3, and 4 comprised "a sheep," and two 言 **SG-1364** "word, language; to speak." "Two" meant "many," and signified "many people praising." In 5, one 言 was dropped. The kanji 善 means "good, right; virtue." <善(羊 䒑 口)>

善い good [よい]; 善 good, virtue [ぜん]; 善良な good-natured [ぜんりょうな]; 善戦する to fight bravely [ぜんせんする]; 善処する to take the appropriate steps [ぜんしょする]; 性善説 the view of human nature as fundamentally good [せいぜんせつ]; 偽善的な hypocritical [ぎぜんてきな]

	Meanings	Kun and On	Romaji	Bushu	Stroke Order and Number
SG-0836 繕	to mend, patch up, fix	つくろ-う ゼン	tsukuro-u *zen*	糸	18

繕 **D** F-2111 説文 The seal-style form comprised 糸 **SG-1600** "threads," and 善 **SG-0835** "goodness," used for the sound *zen*. Threads were used for mending clothes to a better condition. The kanji 繕 means "to mend, patch up, fix." <糸善>

繕う to repair, put up a good front [つくろう]; 身繕い dressing oneself [みづくろい]; 繕い物 mending, patching, darning [つくろいもの]; 修繕する to repair, mend, fix [しゅうぜんする]; 営繕課 Repairs Division [えいぜんか]

	Meanings	Kun and On	Romaji	Bushu	Stroke Order and Number
SG-0837 膳	feast, small eating table; counter for chopsticks	ゼン	*zen*	肉	16

膳 **D** F-2114 金文1 1 金文2 2 説文 3 1 was the same as 1, 2, and 3 for 善, which had the sound *zen*. "A tray" was added in 2, and "a piece of meat for an offering" (月) was added in 3. The character meant "a small table where a good meal was placed." It is also used as a counter for chopsticks. The kanji 膳 means "feast, small eating table; counter for chopsticks. <月善>

ご飯一膳 one bowl of rice [ごはん、いちぜん]; 御膳・お膳 small dining table, tray [おぜん]; お膳立てする to arrange, lay the groundwork for [おぜんだてする]; 陰膳 meal set for an absent person (praying for his safe return) [かげぜん]; 箸一膳 a pair of chopsticks [はし・いちぜん]

35c 義 "just; morality" [from carving a sacrificial animal (羊) with a saw (我)]; *gi* 義議儀犠

	Meanings	Kun and On	Romaji	Bushu	Stroke Order and Number
SG-0838 義	just; morality, significance, meaning	ギ	*gi*	羊	義 13

義 **A** F-0475

甲骨文1 甲骨文2 金文1 金文2 金文3 説文 (1 2 3 4 5 6) 義

1 and 2 comprised "a vertical bar" with "the curled horns of a sheep's head," being cut by "a saw or saw-like object," signifying "cutting a sacrificial sheep with a saw to prepare for offering to a deity." In 3, 4, 5, and 6, 羊 **SG-0825** and "saw" (我 **SG-1492**) became separate components. What was suitable for a deity was "just, right" and signified "morality." Explaining what was "just, right" brought "significance, meaning." The kanji 義 means "just; morality, significance, meaning." <𦍌我> (Note: The kanji 我 was borrowed to mean "I.")

正義 justice, right [せいぎ]; 義務 obligation [ぎむ]; 義理 moral obligation, indebtedness [ぎり]; 意義ある significant, meaningful [いぎある]; 二義的な secondary [にぎてきな]; 道義上 morally, for ethical reasons [どうぎじょう]; 義母 mother-in-law [ぎぼ]; 大義名分 noble cause, pretext [たいぎ・めいぶん]

	Meanings	Kun and On	Romaji	Bushu	Stroke Order and Number
SG-0839 議	to discuss, confer	ギ	*gi*	言	議 20

議 **A** F-0262

説文 議

The seal-style form comprised 言, bushu *gonben* "words, language; to say," and 義 "right, just," used for the sound *gi*, together signifying "discussing what is right." The kanji 議 means "to discuss, confer." <言義>

会議 conference [かいぎ]; 閣議 cabinet meeting [かくぎ]; 議員 assembly member [ぎいん]; 議決する to decide upon, take a vote for [ぎけつする]; 議場 assembly hall chamber [ぎじょう]; 議題 agenda item [ぎだい]; 不思議がる to show curiosity, be puzzled by [ふしぎがる]; 異議 objection, protest [いぎ]

	Meanings	Kun and On	Romaji	Bushu	Stroke Order and Number
SG-0840 儀	ceremony, protocol, propriety	ギ	*gi*	人	儀 15

儀 **C** F-1131

金文 1 説文 2 儀

1 was the same as 3 for 義 **SG-0838** "just, right," and had the sound *gi*. With the addition of 亻 "an act that a person does," the character meant "the right way of conducting oneself," i.e., "protocol, ceremony." The kanji 儀 means "ceremony, protocol, propriety." <亻義>

儀礼 ceremony [ぎれい]; 行儀のいい well-mannered [ぎょうぎのいい]; 儀式 ritual, rite [ぎしき]; 威儀を正す to draw oneself up, sit up straight [いぎをただす]; 流儀 method, style, school [りゅうぎ, りゅうぎ]; 難儀する to get into difficulties, have a rough time of it [なんぎする]; 余儀なく unavoidably, from necessity [よぎなく, よぎなく]

	Meanings	Kun and On	Romaji	Bushu	Stroke Order and Number
SG-0841 犠	sacrifice, victim	ギ	*gi*	牛	犠 17

犠 **C** F-1493

説文 1 旧字 2 犠

1 comprised 牛 **SG-0816** "an ox" on the left side; 羊 **SG-0825** "a sheep" on the top right for "sacrificial animals"; 我 "a saw"; and 禾 "rice plant" (and 丂 the significance of which was unclear), used for the sound *gi*. Together they signified "a sacrificial animal to be cut with a saw for an offering." In the shinji, the bottom became 義. The kanji 犠 means "sacrifice, victim." <牛義>

犠牲になる to be sacrificed, fall prey to [ぎせいになる]; 犠牲者 victim [ぎせいしゃ]

36 Pig, hog, boar

36a 豕 "pig, hog, boar"; bushu *inoko* 家塚嫁豚稼逐

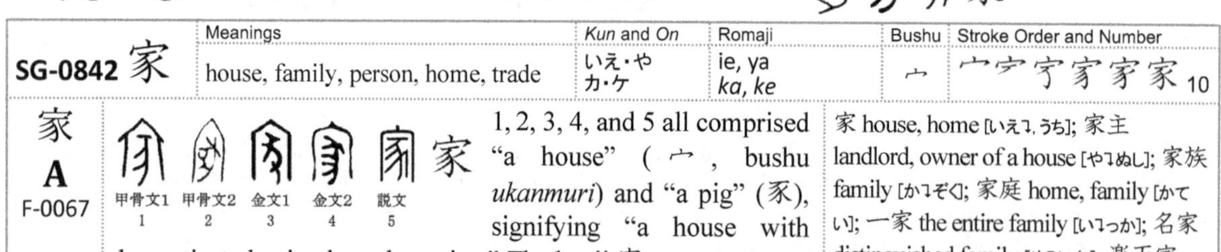

	Meanings	Kun and On	Romaji	Bushu	Stroke Order and Number
SG-0842 家	house, family, person, home, trade	いえ・や カ・ケ	ie, ya *ka, ke*	宀	家 10

家 **A** F-0067

甲骨文1 甲骨文2 金文1 金文2 説文 (1 2 3 4 5) 家

1, 2, 3, 4, and 5 all comprised "a house" (宀, bushu *ukanmuri*) and "a pig" (豕), signifying "a house with domesticated animals such as pigs." The kanji 家 came to mean

家 house, home [いえ, うち]; 家主 landlord, owner of a house [やぬし]; 家族 family [かぞく]; 家庭 home, family [かてい]; 一家 the entire family [いっか]; 名家 distinguished family [めいか]; 楽天家

	"a house" for people. A family that lived under the same roof made the house "a home." It was also used to mean "one's trade or profession." The kanji 家 means "house, family, person, home, trade." <宀 豕>	optimist [らくてんか]; 家来 vassal [けらい]; 石川家 the Ishikawa family [いしかわけ] // 家中 the entire family [うちじゅう, いえじゅう]

	Meanings	Kun and On	Romaji	Bushu	Stroke Order and Number
SG-0843 塚	mound of earth, tumulus	つか	tsuka	土	一十圹圹坧坧塚 12

塚
B
F-1074

金文1 1 金文2 2 篆文 3 旧字 4

1 and 2 had 豕 under a dirt cover, which meant "a sacrificial pig or animal buried under the ground." In the kyuji 塚 (4), "dirt" (土 **SG-1126**) was added to mean "a mound of soil at a burial site." The extra cross-stroke in the kyuji 豖 is explained as signifying that the pig has been tied for burial. The kanji 塚 means "mound of earth, tumulus." <扌冖 豕 >

貝塚 shell mound [かいづか]; 一里塚 milestone [いちりづか]

	Meanings	Kun and On	Romaji	Bushu	Stroke Order and Number
SG-0844 嫁	new bride; to marry (into a family)	よめ・とつ-ぐ カ	yome, totsu-gu *ka*	女	く女女'女宀女宁女家嫁 13

嫁
C
F-1205

説文

The seal-style form comprised 女 **SG-0521** "a woman," and 家 **SG-0842** "a house, family," used for the sound *ka*. A woman who became attached to another family was a bride. The kanji 嫁 meant "new bride; to marry (into a family)." <女 家>

嫁 daughter-in-law, my wife [よめ]; 花嫁 bride [はなよめ]; お嫁さん bride [およめさん]; 嫁いびり bullying of a bride (or wife) by her mother-in-law [よめいびり]; 嫁ぐ to marry, marry into a family [とつぐ]; 嫁ぎ先 one's husband's family [とつぎさき]; 転嫁する to impute a crime to someone, shuffle off a responsibility onto someone [てんかする] // 許嫁 fiancé/fiancée, betrothed [いいなづけ]

	Meanings	Kun and On	Romaji	Bushu	Stroke Order and Number
SG-0845 豚	pig, hog, swine	ぶた トン	buta *ton*	豕	月肝肟肟豚豚 11

豚
C
F-1511

甲骨文 1 金文 2 説文篆文 3 説文 4

1, 2, 3, and 4 comprised "a pig" (豕), and "a piece of meat" (月, bushu *nikuzuki*) under its belly. In 2 and 4, "a hand" (又 **SG-0084**) was added behind the pig, signifying "a hand offering sacrificial pig meat in a rite." With the religious meaning dropped, the kanji 豚 means "pig, hog, swine." <月 豕>

豚 pig, hog [ぶた]; 焼き豚 roast pork [やきぶた]; 豚小屋 pigsty [ぶたごや]; 豚児 my son (humble) [とんじ]; 豚に真珠 pearls before swine [ぶたにしんじゅ]

	Meanings	Kun and On	Romaji	Bushu	Stroke Order and Number
SG-0846 稼	to earn, take in, gain	かせ-ぐ カ	kase-gu *ka*	禾	二千禾'禾宀秄稼稼 15

稼
C
F-1526

説文

The seal-style form comprised 禾, bushu *nogihen* "a rice plant," and 家 **SG-0842** "a house," used for the sound *ka*. Taking a harvested crop inside a house signified what was "earned." The kanji 稼 means "to earn, take in, gain." <禾家>

稼ぎ income, wage, work [かせぎ, かせぎ]; 共稼ぎ both husband and wife working (for a living) [ともかせぎ]; 荒稼ぎ robbery, sudden profit from speculation [あらかせぎ]; 出稼ぎ working away from home, working as a migrant worker [でかせぎ]; 稼業 trade, business, one's way of earning a living [かぎょう]; 稼働する (a machine) to operate, work [かどうする]

	Meanings	Kun and On	Romaji	Bushu	Stroke Order and Number
SG-0847 逐	to chase, pursue closely	チク	*chiku*	辵	丆丂豸豕豖逐 10

逐
D
F-2057

甲骨文1 1 甲骨文2 2 金文1 3 金文2 4 説文 5

1, 2, 3, 4, and 5 comprised "a pig or boar" (豕) and "a footprint," with "a crossroads" added in 3, 4, and 5, forming 辵 (辶, bushu *shinnyuu* "to move forward"). Together they signified "to chase a boar," or, more generally, "to follow closely." The kanji 逐 means "to chase, pursue closely." <豕 辶>

逐一 one by one, in detail [ちくいち]; 駆逐する to expel, drive away [くちくする]; 逐語訳 word-for-word translation [ちくごやく]; 逐次 one after another, point by point [ちくじ]

36b 㒸 "to fall down"; *tai/tsui/sui* 隊遂墜

	Meanings	Kun and On	Romaji	Bushu	Stroke Order and Number
SG-0848 隊	band of people, military troop	タイ	*tai*	阜	12

隊 **B** F-0684

金文1 1 金文2 2 説文 3

1 was 㒸 "a heavy pig with big ears," which had the sound *tai*. In 2 and 3, "a pile of soil" (阝, bushu *kozatohen*) was added. The mass of a large, stocky pig was applied to "a band of people" formed for a particular activity, including a "military troop." The kanji 隊 means "band of people, military troop." <阝㒸 (丷豕)>

隊列 file, rank line, column [たいれつ]; 軍隊 military [ぐんたい]; 隊長 leader of a party [たいちょう]; 入隊する to join the military [にゅうたいする]; 捜索隊 search party [そうさくたい]; 隊員 member of a unit [たいいん]; 機動隊 riot squad [きどうたい]

	Meanings	Kun and On	Romaji	Bushu	Stroke Order and Number
SG-0849 遂	to accomplish, carry out	と-げる スイ	to-geru *sui*	辵	12

遂 **C** F-1559

中山王器 1 説文古文 2 説文 3

The top right in 1 and 2 is difficult to decipher, but from the fact that 3 used 㒸 "a heavy pig" in its place, it can be surmised to be an animal, used for the sound *sui* to mean "carry out." 辵 "to move forward" was present throughout. The kanji 遂 means "to accomplish, carry out." <遂(㒸辶)>

遂げる to accomplish, carry into effect [とげる]; やり遂げる to achieve, attain, carry out [やりとげる]; 殺人未遂 attempted murder [さつじんみすい]; 遂行する to accomplish, perform, carry out [すいこうする]; 完遂する to conclude successfully, complete [かんすいする] // 遂に・ついに at long last, finally [ついに]

	Meanings	Kun and On	Romaji	Bushu	Stroke Order and Number
SG-0850 墜	to crash, fall	ツイ	*tsui*	土	15

墜 **D** F-1788

甲骨文1 1 甲骨文2 2 金文1 3 金文2 4 説文 5

1 and 2 comprised "a tall pile of dirt" (阝) and "a person falling head first to the ground," together signifying "to fall, crash." In 3 and 4, "a heavy, stocky pig" (㒸), for the sound *tsui*, was used in place of the previous form. In 5, 土 **SG-1126** "dirt, ground" was added to show where a falling person ended up. The kanji 墜 means "to crash, fall." <隊土>

失墜する to lose, forfeit, fall [しっついする]; 墜落 fall, drop, (airplane) crash [ついらく] // 墜ちる to fall, crash [おちる]

36c 亥 [from the skeleton of a pig]; *gai/kaku* 刻核該骸劾

	Meanings	Kun and On	Romaji	Bushu	Stroke Order and Number
SG-0851 刻	to mince, inscribe, (time) ticks away	きざ-む コク	kiza-mu *koku*	刀	8

刻 **B** F-0952

説文

The seal-style form comprised 亥 "a ridged shape of animal bones," used for the sound *koku* (from *gai*), and "a carving knife" (刀, 刂). To carve an animal to the bone meant "to mince, cut into pieces, engrave." It also came to be used to describe the way time "ticks away" in small increments. The kanji 刻 means "to mince, inscribe, (time) ticks away." <亥刂>

刻む to chop finely [きざむ]; 刻み付ける to carve into, engrave [きざみつける]; 刻一刻と every moment [こくいっこくと, こくいっこくと]; 遅刻 lateness, tardiness, late [ちこく]; 復刻版 reprinted edition [ふっこくばん]; 刻々と every second [こくこくと]; 時刻表 timetable [じこくひょう]

	Meanings	Kun and On	Romaji	Bushu	Stroke Order and Number
SG-0852 核	core, nucleus	カク	*kaku*	木	10

核 **B** F-0908

説文

The seal-style form comprised 木 **SG-0608** "tree," and 亥 "skeleton, something hard," used for the sound *kaku*. Together they signified "the stone of a fruit," and also "core, nucleus" in a general sense. The kanji 核 means "core, nucleus." <木亥>

核 nucleus, a core [かく]; 核酸 nucleic acid [かくさん]; 核家族 nuclear family [かくかぞく]; 非核化 denuclearization [ひかくか]; 核兵器 nuclear arms, atomic weapon [かくへいき]; 核反応 nuclear reaction [かくはんのう]; 核爆発 nuclear explosion [かくばくはつ]; 核実験 nuclear testing [かくじっけん]

SG-0853 該	Meanings	Kun and On	Romaji	Bushu	Stroke Order and Number
	relevant; the said	ガイ	*gai*	言	言 言' 言亠 言ナ 言亥 該 13

該 **D** F-1716 説文

The seal-style form comprised 言, bushu *gonben* "word, language; to speak," and 亥, used for the sound *gai* to mean "whole." Together they signified "to investigate thoroughly," which will reveal what is really "relevant." The kanji 該 means "relevant; the said." <言亥>

当該の the persons concerned, proper [とうがいの]; 該当する to come under, fall within the purview of, be applicable to [がいとうする]

SG-0854 骸	Meanings	Kun and On	Romaji	Bushu	Stroke Order and Number
	skeleton, bone	ガイ	*gai*	骨	冂 冎 冎 咼 骨 骨亠 骸 骸 16

骸 **D** F-2310 説文

The seal-style form comprised 骨 **SG-0272** "bones," and 亥 "skeletal framework," used for the sound *gai*. The kanji 骸 means "skeleton, bone." <骨亥>

死骸 dead body, remains [しがい]; 形骸化 turning something into a mere shell, becoming a mere formality [けいがいか]; 骸骨 skeleton, bones [がいこつ]

SG-0855 劾	Meanings	Kun and On	Romaji	Bushu	Stroke Order and Number
	to condemn, adjudicate	ガイ	*gai*	力	' 亠 亠 亥 亥 劾 8

劾 **D** F-2333 説文

The seal-style form had 亥, used for the sound *gai* to mean "to adjudicate the guilty," and 力 **SG-1949**, "plow, hard work in the field," together signifying "to examine something with great effort." The character is used to mean "to examine a crime thoroughly." The kanji 劾 means "to condemn, adjudicate." <亥力>

弾劾 impeachment [だんがい]

36d 豸 "beast, boar"; bushu *mujinahen* 懇墾貌

SG-0856 懇	Meanings	Kun and On	Romaji	Bushu	Stroke Order and Number
	courteous, cordial; wholeheartedly	ねんご-ろ コン	nengo-ro *kon*	心	一 乡 豸 豸 豸コ 豸艮 豸艮 懇 17

懇 **C** F-1564 説文

The top of the seal-style form comprised 豕 "wild boar," and 艮, used for the sound *kon,* together signifying "a wild boar digging deeply in the soil with its tusks." With 心 **SG-0187** "heart" added, the character meant "to reach one's heart deeply, do something wholeheartedly." In the kanji, 豕 was replaced by 豸, bushu *mujinahen*, "beast." The kanji 懇 means "courteous, cordial; wholeheartedly." <豸艮心>

懇ろに politely, warmly [ねんごろに]; 懇意な friendly, intimate [こんいな]; 懇切丁寧な extremely thorough, with scrupulous care [こんせつていねいな]; 昵懇の familiar, well-acquainted, close [じっこんの]

SG-0857 墾	Meanings	Kun and On	Romaji	Bushu	Stroke Order and Number
	to plow a field	コン	*kon*	土	一 乡 豸 豸コ 豸艮 豸艮 墾 墾 16

墾 **D** F-2343 篆文

The seal-style character comprised 豕 "wild boar"; 艮, used for the sound *kon*; and 土 **SG-1126** "ground, soil." Together they depicted the manner in which a wild boar would ravage a field with its tusks, and the character came to mean "to plow land, cultivate land." In the kanji, 豕 was replaced by bushu *mujinahen* 豸, "beast." The kanji 墾 means "to plow a field." <豸艮土>

開墾 clearing, reclamation [かいこん]

SG-0858 貌	Meanings	Kun and On	Romaji	Bushu	Stroke Order and Number
	appearance, aspect	ボウ	*boo*	豸	丿 乡 豸 豸勹 豸白 貌 14

貌 **D** F-2239 説文 1 説文或体 2

1 was "a person with a blank face whose spirit was gone, leaving only their exterior appearance." In 2, 豸, bushu *mujinahen* "beast," was added, with 頁 "a person, head" replacing the blank-faced person, but then reverting to the original shape in the shinji. Together, these components signified "shape, look, feature of a person." The kanji 貌 means "appearance, aspect." <豸白儿>

容貌 looks, features, personal appearance [ようぼう]; 風貌 looks, feature, appearance [ふうぼう]; 全貌 full view, whole aspect [ぜんぼう]; 変貌 transfiguration, metamorphosis [へんぼう]

37 Other animals

37a 犬 "dog" 犬献伏獣

	Meanings	Kun and On	Romaji	Bushu	Stroke Order and Number
SG-0859 犬	dog	いぬ ケン	inu *ken*	犬	一ナ大犬 4

犬 **B** F-0608

甲骨文1 1, 甲骨文2 2, 金文1 3, 金文2 4, 説文 5 — 犬

1, 2, and 3 were a vertically-placed image of "a dog standing on its hind legs, with his tail up." The character meant "dog." 4 showed a dog standing on four legs. The kanji 犬 means "dog." <大丶>

犬 dog [いぬ˥]; 犬死する to die in vain [いぬじにする, いぬじに˥する]; 犬小屋 kennel, doghouse [いぬごや]; 番犬 guard dog, watchdog [ばんけん]; 狂犬病 rabies [きょうけんびょう]; 野犬 ownerless dog [やけん]; 犬種 dog breed [けんしゅ]

	Meanings	Kun and On	Romaji	Bushu	Stroke Order and Number
SG-0860 献	to dedicate, present, offer drink	ケン・コン	*ken, kon*	犬	一 冂 冇 南 南一 献 献 13

献 **C** F-1106

甲骨文 1, 金文1 2, 金文2 3, 説文 4, 旧字 5 — 獻 献

1 through 4 showed a dog (犬 **SG-0859**) whose meat was used as an offering to a deity. 1 and 2 included "a tripod for cooking animal meat and other food" (員 **SG-1717**), whereas 3 and 4 (and the kyuji, 5) had "a hollow-legged clay pot for grain storage" (鬲). Furthermore, 2, 3, and 4 included a tiger headdress that was used in a votive dance. All are related to dedication to a deity or a superior. In the shinji, the left side was replaced by 南 for the sound *ken*. The kanji 献 means "to dedicate, present, offer drink." <南犬>

献上する to present something to an honored person [けんじょうする]; 文献 literature, documentary records [ぶんけん]; 参考文献 bibliography, reference [さんこうぶ˥んけん]; 献金 monetary donation [けんきん]; 献身的に devotedly, with selfless dedication [けんしんてきに]; 献立 menu [こんだて]

	Meanings	Kun and On	Romaji	Bushu	Stroke Order and Number
SG-0861 伏	to lie down, lay something upside-down, conceal	ふ-せる フク	hu-seru *huku*	人	亻 仁 仕 伏 伏 6

伏 **C** F-1431

金文 1, 説文 2 — 伏

1 captured a scene in which a dog was lying down with its face on the ground, following its master's order. Putting something face down also meant "to conceal." The kanji 伏 means "to lie down, lay something upside-down, conceal." <亻犬>

伏せる to turn over, lay something upside down, conceal [ふせ˥る]; 待ち伏せする to lie in wait, ambush [まちぶせする]; 伏せ字 omission, blank, marks for a censored word [ふせじ]; 伏し目がちに downcast look [ふしめがちに]; 起伏 undulation, ups and downs [きふく]; 降伏 surrender [こうふく]

	Meanings	Kun and On	Romaji	Bushu	Stroke Order and Number
SG-0862 獣	beast, animal	けもの ジュウ	kemono *juu*	犬	屰 単 単 兽一 獣 獣 16

獣 **D** F-1685

甲骨文 1, 金文 2, 説文 3, 旧字 4 — 獸 獣

1, 2, and 3 comprised "a shield" or "a tool for hunting" (單), and "a dog" (犬 **SG-0859**), together signifying "hunting an animal using a dog." In 3, "a small square" (口) was added to signify "an enclosure that a hunted animal was chased into." The kanji 獣 means "beast, animal." <丷田一口犬>

獣 beast, animal [けもの]; 獣医 veterinarian, vet [じゅ˥うい]; 猛獣 fierce animal, savage beast [もうじゅう]; 怪獣 monstrous animal [かいじゅう]; 野獣 wild animal [やじゅう]

37b 犭 "dog, beast" [from a dog standing on its hind legs]; **bushu *kemonohen***

犯狂猛狩獄猿猟

	Meanings	Kun and On	Romaji	Bushu	Stroke Order and Number
SG-0863 犯	crime; to violate	おか-す ハン	oka-su *han*	犬	ノ 犭 犭 犭ㄱ 犯 5

犯 **B** F-0739

説文 — 犯

The seal-style form comprised "a dog" (犭, bushu *kemonohen*), and 㔾, used for the sound *han* to mean "to stick out" from a confinement or frame. A dog jumping out of a confinement created the meaning "to go against, violate; crime." The kanji 犯 means "crime; to violate." <犭㔾>

犯す to commit a crime, break the rules [おか˥す]; 犯人 culprit, offender, perpetrator [は˥んにん]; 犯罪 crime [はんざい]; 共犯者 accomplice, accessory to a crime [きょうは˥んしゃ]; 現行犯 red-handed crime [げんこ˥うはん]; 防犯 crime prevention [ぼうはん]; 犯行 criminal act, offense [はんこう]

	Meanings	Kun and On	Romaji	Bushu	Stroke Order and Number
SG-0864 狂	mad; lunatic	くる-う キョウ	kuru-u *kyoo*	犬	ノ 犭 犭 犭一 犴 狂 7

狂 **C** F-1239

甲骨文 1 甲骨文 2 説文 3

1 and 2 comprised "a footprint" over "a large ornamental axe," used for the sound *kyoo* to mean "twist," and "a dog," together signifying "a ferocious dog." The two components swapped positions in 3, and the footprint was dropped. With 犭, bushu *kemonohen*, the kanji 狂 means "mad; lunatic." <犭王>

狂う to go insane, go out of one's mind, lose accuracy [くるう]; 狂い咲き unseasonable flowering [くるいざき]; 狂気 insanity, madness [きょうき]; 狂喜する to be wild with joy, be ecstatic about [きょうきする]; 発狂する to go mad, go insane [はっきょうする]; 狂言 comic interlude during a Noh performance [きょうげん]

	Meanings	Kun and On	Romaji	Bushu	Stroke Order and Number
SG-0865 猛	fierce, spirited, audacious	モウ	*moo*	犬	ノ 犭 犭 犭了 犭孑 猛 猛 11

猛 **C** F-1490

説文

The seal-style form comprised "a dog" (犭), and 孟 (子 **SG-0510** and 皿 **SG-1843**), used for the sound *moo* to mean "thriving, vigor," together signifying "a fierce dog," and also "audacious, impudent." The kanji 猛 means "fierce, spirited, audacious." <犭孟>

猛暑 fierce heat [もうしょ]; 勇猛な intrepid, undaunted, daring [ゆうもうな]; 猛烈に violently, strongly, spiritedly, terribly [もうれつに]; 獰猛な ferocious, savage [どうもうな] // 猛々しい fierce, audacious [たけだけしい]; 猛者 stalwart person, man of courage [もさ]

	Meanings	Kun and On	Romaji	Bushu	Stroke Order and Number
SG-0866 狩	to hunt; hunting	かり シュ	kari *shu*	犬	ノ 犭 犭宀 犭宁 狩 狩 9

狩 **C** F-1513

甲骨文 1 金文 1 2 金文 2 3 説文 4

1 comprised "a hunting tool" and "a dog," signifying "hunting." 2 and 3 comprised "a shield" or "a tool for hunting," and "a dog" or "a footprint," together signifying "a protective hunting dog." 4 comprised "a dog" (犬, 犭), and 守 **SG-0113**, used for the sound *shu*. The kanji 狩 means "to hunt; hunting." <犭守>

狩 hunting, shooting [かり]; 狩人 hunter [かりうど]; 狩猟 hunting, shooting, the chase [しゅりょう]

	Meanings	Kun and On	Romaji	Bushu	Stroke Order and Number
SG-0867 獄	prison, imprisonment	ゴク	*goku*	犬	ノ 犭 犭 犭言 獄 獄 獄 14

獄 **C** F-1601

金文 1 説文 2

1 had 言 "word, language," with "two dogs" on either side. "Two dogs barking or quarreling fiercely" with "words" (言) signified "a dispute arbitrated in a court of law." The meaning was extended to other legal processes, such as "imprisonment, prison." The kanji 獄 still contains two dogs, 犭 and 犬, and means "prison, imprisonment." <犭言犬>

地獄 hell [じごく]; 監獄 prison, jail [かんごく]

	Meanings	Kun and On	Romaji	Bushu	Stroke Order and Number
SG-0868 猿	monkey, ape	さる エン	saru *en*	犬	ノ 犭 犭十 犭圭 猿 猿 猿 13

猿 **C** F-1579

篆文

The seal-style form comprised 虫 **SG-0998** (originally "snake"), and 爰, used for the sound *en* to mean "two hands pulling apart something in between them." An ape moved around in a tree by pulling on limbs with its long arms. In the kanji, the left side became 犭 "animal," and 爰 was replaced by 袁 for the same sound *en*. As a result, the kanji shape was totally different from the seal-style form. The kanji 猿 means "monkey, ape." <犭袁>
(Note: 爰, for the sound *en*, appears in the kanji 援暖緩媛, **SG-0133** through **SG-0136**.)

猿 monkey [さる]; 猿真似 blind imitation, copycatting [さるまね]; 犬猿の仲 like cats and dogs, hate each other [けんえんのなか]

	Meanings	Kun and On	Romaji	Bushu	Stroke Order and Number
SG-0869 猟	hunting	リョウ	*ryoo*	犬	ノ 犭 犭" 犭⺍ 猟 猟 猟 11

猟 **D** F-1827

金文 1 中山王器 2 説文 3 旧字 4

1, and the right side of 2 and 3, was "an animal's head with a mane" and was used for the sound *ryoo*. In 2 and 3, "a dog" (used for hunting) was added on the left side, which became 犭, bushu *kemonohen*, in the kyuji 獵 (4). The animal was replaced with a simpler shape, 巤, in the shinji. The kanji 猟 means "hunting." <犭巤>

猟 shooting, hunting [りょう]; 禁猟区 game preserve [きんりょうく]; 密猟 poaching [みつりょう]; 猟師 hunter [りょうし]; 猟犬 hunting dog [りょうけん]; 猟奇的な bizarre [りょうきてきな]

37c 馬 "horse" 馬駅駐驚騒駆駒駄騎騰篤罵

SG-0870 馬	Meanings	Kun and On	Romaji	Bushu	Stroke Order and Number
	horse	うま・ま バ	uma, ma *ba*	馬	丨 厂 丌 甲 馬 馬 10

馬 **A** F-0379

甲骨文1 1 甲骨文2 2 金文1 3 金文2 4 金文3 5 説文 6

1 through 6 depicted "a horse, placed vertically, with a long head and a mane on its back or head." It meant "a horse." In the kanji, the four legs became four dots. The kanji 馬 means "a horse." <馬>

馬 horse [うま]; 馬乗りになる to sit astride [うまのりになる]; 絵馬 wooden votive tablet [えま]; 競馬 horse racing, the races [けいば]; 馬車 carriage [ばしゃ]; 馬力 horsepower, animal energy [ばりき]; 馬鹿 stupid, dumb, dense, idiotic [ばか]; 馬鹿力 incredible physical strength [ばかぢから]

SG-0871 駅	Meanings	Kun and On	Romaji	Bushu	Stroke Order and Number
	railway station	エキ	*eki*	馬	丨 厂 丌 甲 馬 馬 馯 駅 駅 14

駅 **A** F-0468

説文 1 旧字 2

The seal-style form comprised 馬 "horse," and 睪, used for the sound *eki* to mean "continuous; a long stretch." A long-distance messenger changed horses at a station to continue his dispatch journey. 睪 was replaced by 尺 in the shinji. The kanji 駅 meant "railway station." <馬尺>

駅 railway station [えき]; 東京駅 Tokyo Station [とうきょうえき]; 駅員 station staff [えきいん]; 駅弁 a boxed lunch of local cuisine purchased at a railway station [えきべん]; 駅ビル commercial building attached to a railway station [えきビル]; 駅伝 long-distance relay [えきでん]; 道の駅 a rest stop featuring local produce and products [みちのえき]

SG-0872 駐	Meanings	Kun and On	Romaji	Bushu	Stroke Order and Number
	to stay (for some time), park (a vehicle)	チュウ	*chuu*	馬	丨 厂 丌 甲 馬 馬 馯 駐 駐 15

駐 **B** F-0922

説文

The seal-style form comprised 馬 **SG-0870** "horse," and 主 **SG-2037** "not moving, like a candle burning on a stand," used for the sound *chuu*. Together they meant "a place where one tethers a horse; to stay." In modern times, the kanji 駐 applies to parking motor vehicles. The kanji 駐 means "to stay (for some time), park (a vehicle)." <馬主>

駐車する to park a car [ちゅうしゃする]; 駐車場 parking lot or facility [ちゅうしゃじょう]; 路上駐車 curbside parking [ろじょうちゅうしゃ]; 駐在員 resident employee [ちゅうざいいん]; 駐日大使 ambassador to Japan [ちゅうにちたいし]; 常駐 continuous presence, permanent stationing [じょうちゅう]; 駐留軍 stationed troops, occupation forces [ちゅうりゅうぐん]; 駐輪場 bicycle parking area [ちゅうりんじょう]

SG-0873 驚	Meanings	Kun and On	Romaji	Bushu	Stroke Order and Number
	to be surprised, become startled	おどろ-く キョウ	odoro-ku *kyoo*	馬	艹 芍 苟 敬 敬 敬 驚 驚 22

驚 **C** F-1133

説文

The seal-style form comprised 敬 **SG-0171**, which was used for the sound *kyoo* to mean "to refrain," and 馬 **SG-0870** "horse." A horse is an animal that is easily startled, and when startled, it pulls back. The kanji 驚 means "to be surprised, become startled." <敬馬>

驚く to be surprised, be startled [おどろく]; 驚異的な startling, amazing [きょういてきな]; 驚愕する to be greatly surprised at, be astounded [きょうがくする]

SG-0874 騒	Meanings	Kun and On	Romaji	Bushu	Stroke Order and Number
	to clamor; fray, uproar; restless	さわ-ぐ ソウ	sawa-gu *soo*	馬	丨 厂 丌 甲 馬 馭 騒 騒 騒 18

騒 **C** F-1257

説文 1 旧字 2

1 comprised 馬 "horse," and 蚤 ("flea," comprised of "a hand with fingernails or animal claws" and 虫 "insect"), used for the sound *soo*. A flea was an annoying insect, and a horse and a flea together signified "rustling noise; make an outcry." The kanji 騒 means "to clamor; fray, uproar; restless." <馬又虫>

騒ぐ to make noise, loudly proclaim [さわぐ]; 騒ぎ commotion, disturbance [さわぎ]; 騒がしい noisy, making a big fuss, turbulent, agitated [さわがしい]; 騒然と tumultuously, in an uproar [そうぜんと]; 物騒な dangerous [ぶっそうな]; 騒々しい noisy, raucous [そうぞうしい]; 騒動 disturbance, uproar, dispute [そうどう]

	Meanings	Kun and On	Romaji	Bushu	Stroke Order and Number
SG-0875 駆	to run, dash, gallop	か-ける ク	ka-keru *ku*	馬	丨 厂 ㄇ 𠂤 馬 馬 駆 駆 14

駆
C
F-1325

説文 1 旧字 2

The seal-style form comprised 馬 "horse," and 區, used for the sound *ku* to mean "to hit." Together they signified a rider using a whip to make his horse run. 區 in the kyuji 驅 was simplified to 区 **SG-2108** in the shinji. The kanji 駆 means "to run, dash, gallop." <馬 区>

駆ける to run, race, dash [かけ⌝る]; 駆り出す to get out, flush out [かりだ⌝す]; 四輪駆動 four-wheel drive [よんりんく⌝どう]; 駆使する to use freely [く⌝しする]; 害虫駆除 extermination of harmful insects [がいちゅうく⌝じょ]

	Meanings	Kun and On	Romaji	Bushu	Stroke Order and Number
SG-0876 駒	colt, pony, young and energetic horse, *shogi* chess piece	こま	koma	馬	丨 厂 ㄇ 𠂤 馬 馬 駒 駒 15

駒
C
F-1466

金文1 1 金文2 2 説文 3

1, 2, and 3 comprised "two interlocking shapes with a mouth" (句 **SG-2115**), which was used for the sound *ku* to mean "small (section)," and "a horse" (馬). Together they signified a small horse. The kanji 駒 means "colt, pony, young and energetic horse, *shogi* (or chess) piece." <馬句>

駒 horse, colt, pony [こま⌝]; 将棋の駒 *shogi* piece [しょうぎのこま⌝]

	Meanings	Kun and On	Romaji	Bushu	Stroke Order and Number
SG-0877 駄	horseback load; trivial, trifle	ダ	*da*	馬	丨 厂 ㄇ 𠂤 馬 馬 駄 駄 14

駄
D
F-1625

篆文

The seal-style form comprised 馬 **SG-0870** "horse," and 大, used for the sounds *ta/da* to mean "to pile, carry," together signifying "to load on to a horse, transport on a horse." In the kanji, 大 was replaced with 太 **SG-0317**. In Japanese, the character is used as part of the word 駄目, *dame*, meaning "useless, trivial." The kanji 駄 means "horseback load; trivial, trifle." <馬太>

無駄な useless, fruitless, no good [むだな]; 駄目な useless, vain, not permitted [だめ⌝な]; 駄作 poor work, slipshod [ださく]; 駄馬 packhorse, cart horse [だ⌝ば]; 駄洒落 dull joke, bad pun [だじゃれ]; 下駄 *geta*, Japanese wooden clog [げた]

	Meanings	Kun and On	Romaji	Bushu	Stroke Order and Number
SG-0878 騎	to mount a horse, be on horseback	キ	*ki*	馬	丨 厂 ㄇ 𠂤 馬 馬 騎 騎 18

騎
D
F-1686

説文

The seal-style form comprised 馬 "horse," and 奇 **SG-0327**, used for the sound *ki* to mean "alone," together signifying "a person mounting a horse, riding a horse." The kanji 騎 means "to mount a horse, be on horseback." <馬奇>

騎手 rider, horseman, jockey [き⌝しゅ]; 騎馬民族 horse-riding people, mounted nomads [きばみ⌝んぞく]; 騎兵 cavalry soldier [きへい]

	Meanings	Kun and On	Romaji	Bushu	Stroke Order and Number
SG-0879 騰	to raise, rise high, leap	トウ	*too*	馬	月 𦙶 𦚏 朕 朕 騰 騰 20

騰
D
F-1762

説文

The seal-style form depicted "a tray" and "two hands holding up something important" (which was 朕 **SG-0149** "royal 'We'"), thus forming the meaning "to raise," and the sound *too*. With 馬 "a horse" added, it suggested a horse leaping, which gave the meaning "to raise, rise high." The kanji 騰 means "to raise, rise high, leap." <月龹馬>

高騰 substantial rise, strong appreciation [こうとう]; 急騰 jump, surge [きゅうとう]; 沸騰 boiling, seething [ふっとう]

	Meanings	Kun and On	Romaji	Bushu	Stroke Order and Number
SG-0880 篤	seriously ill, devout, gracious	トク	*toku*	竹	⺮ 竺 笁 笃 篤 篤 16

篤
D
F-1853

説文

The seal-style form comprised 竹, bushu *takemanmuri* "bamboo," and 馬 "horse." One view explains that 竹 was taken from 竺, which meant "poison," and that the form meant "a poisoned horse; seriously ill." A seriously ill person required attentive care, which led to the meaning "hospitable, courteous." Another view takes the kanji to be a borrowing. The kanji 篤 means "seriously ill, devout, gracious." <⺮馬>

危篤 critical condition [きとく]; 篤志家 benevolent person, charitable person, supporter [とくしか]; 重篤な critically ill [じゅうとくな]

	Meanings	Kun and On	Romaji	Bushu	Stroke Order and Number
SG-0881 罵	to abuse, curse, shout	ののし-る バ	nonoshi-ru *ba*	网	罵 15

罵 **D** F-2295 — 説文

The seal-style form comprised 网 "dragnet, net," and 馬, which was used for the sound *ba*. How this came to mean "to abuse, curse, shout" is not clear. In the kanji, the dragnet became 罒, which removed 馬 from inside 冂. The kanji 罵 means "to abuse, curse, shout." <罒馬>

罵る to abuse someone, use abusive language [ののしる]; 罵倒する to hurl insults, abuse in strong language, blast [ばとうする]

37d 虍 "tiger, tiger headdress" [from a tiger-shaped headdress worn in a votive play]

劇虎慮虚虐戯虜膚逓虞

	Meanings	Kun and On	Romaji	Bushu	Stroke Order and Number
SG-0882 劇	theatrical play, drama; intense	ゲキ	*geki*	刀	劇 15

劇 **B** F-0746 — 説文

The seal-style form depicted a scene in which an actor wearing "a tiger headdress" (虍) performs in a play portraying an intense fight between "a wild boar" (豕) and a tiger. Use of "a sword" (刂) intensified the realistic, serious quality of the acting. The kanji 劇 means "theatrical play, drama; intense." <虍 豕 刂>

劇 play [げき]; 悲劇 tragic drama, tragedy [ひげき]; 喜劇 comedy [きげき]; 劇場 theater, playhouse [げきじょう]; 観劇 watching a play, theatergoing [かんげき]; 劇薬 powerful drug, dangerous drug [げきやく]; 劇的な dramatic, drastic [げきてきな]

	Meanings	Kun and On	Romaji	Bushu	Stroke Order and Number
SG-0883 虎	tiger	とら コ	tora *ko*	虍	虎 8

虎 **C** F-1495 — 甲骨文1 (1), 甲骨文2 (2), 金文1 (3), 金文2 (4), 説文古文 (5), 説文 (6)

1, 2, and 3 were pictographs of a tiger, complete with the characteristic stripes, an open mouth, and a long, strong tail. 4 was less of a pictograph, and its appearance is more like a form found in writing. 5 added "a person with their hands on their waist" (which would have become 要). 6 showed "a crouching person" wearing a tiger headdress in a votive play, which became 儿 "a person" in the shinji. The kanji 虎 means "tiger." <虍儿>

虎 tiger [とら]; 虎の子 one's treasure, one's precious savings [とらのこ]; 虎の巻 secrets; study aid, crib [とらのまき]

	Meanings	Kun and On	Romaji	Bushu	Stroke Order and Number
SG-0884 慮	considerate; concern, deep thought	リョ	*ryo*	心	慮 15

慮 **C** F-1361 — 中山王器 (1), 説文 (2)

1 comprised a stack of two identical shapes, used for the sound *ryo* to mean "many things," and "heart/mind" (心 **SG-0187**). "Holding many things in one's heart" gave the meaning "concern, deep thought." 2 comprised "a tiger's head" (虍) and "thought" (思 **SG-0284**), with 盧 having the sound *ryo*. The kanji 慮 means "considerate; concern, deep thought." <虍思>

思慮深い thoughtful, prudent [しりょぶかい]; 遠慮する to hold back, stand on ceremony, be modest [えんりょする]; 無遠慮な impudent [ぶえんりょな]; 配慮 consideration, care, attention [はいりょ]; 苦慮する to rack one's brains, agonize [くりょする]; 不慮の死 sudden violent death [ふりょのし]

	Meanings	Kun and On	Romaji	Bushu	Stroke Order and Number
SG-0885 虚	hole; false, vain	キョ・コ	*kyo, ko*	虍	虚 11

虚 **C** F-1444 — 説文 (1), 旧字 (2)

One view explains that 1 comprised 虍, used for the sounds *kyo*/*ko*, and "a hollow between hills" inside it. Being hollow gave the meaning "vain." Another view explains that the hills inside of 1 depicted the place where a tumulus for powerful people was built in ancient times. Over the years, the tumulus crumbled to ruins, bringing the meaning "hollow; hole." The kyuji 虛 (2) became 虚 in the shinji. The kanji 虚 means "hole; false, vain." <虍业> (Note: Adding 口 "mouth, speech" to 虚 "false" makes up the kanji 嘘 *uso "lie."*)

虚心 open-mindedness [きょしん]; 虚像 virtual image [きょぞう]; 空虚な empty, hollow, vacant [くうきょな]; 虚無的 nihilistic [きょむてき]; 虚栄心 vanity, conceit [きょえいしん]; 虚空 empty air, empty sky, void [こくう]

	Meanings	Kun and On	Romaji	Bushu	Stroke Order and Number
SG-0886 虐	to abuse, ill-treat	しいた-げる ギャク	shiita-geru *gyaku*	虍	9

虐 **D** F-1799

金文 1 說文古文 2 說文 3

In 1, what "a tiger" (虍) is on is hard to discern, but 2 depicted "a tiger" with its sharp claws showing at the bottom, and 3 comprised "a tiger," and "claws of a tiger" (ヨ) against "a person." Together they signified "a person being clawed, ill-treated or abused." In the kanji, "person" was dropped. The kanji 虐 means "to abuse, ill-treat." <虍ヨ>

虐げる to oppress, tyrannize [しいたげる]; 残虐な brutal, barbarous, inhuman [ざんぎゃくな]; 虐待 cruel treatment, abuse [ぎゃくたい]; 虐殺 massacre, slaughter [ぎゃくさつ]

	Meanings	Kun and On	Romaji	Bushu	Stroke Order and Number
SG-0887 戯	to play, jest; play	たわむ-れる ギ	tawamu-reru *gi*	戈	15

戯 **D** F-1812

金文 1 說文 2 旧字 3

1 comprised "an earthenware tiger (虍) on a pedestal (豆 **SG-1975**)," used for the sound *gi,* and "a halberd" (戈). Together they signified a traditional military play in which soldiers attacked a tiger from behind. This swordplay performed to ensure victory before going into battle came to represent playful acts in general. The kyuji 戲 (3) retained 豆, but it was replaced by 业 in the shinji. The kanji 戯 means "to play, jest; play." <虚戈>

戯れる to be playful, jest [たわむれる]; 戯曲 play script [ぎきょく]; 遊戯 play, playing [ゆうぎ]; 子供の遊戯 dancing, romping [こどものゆうぎ]

	Meanings	Kun and On	Romaji	Bushu	Stroke Order and Number
SG-0888 虜	captive; to be captured	リョ	*ryo*	虍	13

虜 **D** F-1889

說文 1 旧字 2

In the seal-style form (1), 虍 "tiger's head" and 毌 "piercing many things through" formed 盧, used for the sound *ryo*. With "power" (力 **SG-1949**) added, they signified "strong men strung in a row," or "taking captives away by force." In the kanji, the bottom was replaced by 男 **SG-1301**. The kanji 虜 means "captive; to be captured." <虍男>

俘虜 prisoner of war [ふりょ] // 虜 captive, prisoner [とりこ]

	Meanings	Kun and On	Romaji	Bushu	Stroke Order and Number
SG-0889 膚	skin	フ	*hu*	肉	15

膚 **D** F-2018

金文1 1 金文2 2 說文籀文 3 說文 4

1 comprised "a jar, vase" (盧), used for the sound *hu* (from *ro)* to mean "something very thin." In 2 and 3, "flesh" (月) was added at the bottom. A part of the body that was very thin and had the sound *hu* was "skin." In 4, 月 was moved out to the left as bushu *nikuzuki*. In the kanji, 月 was moved back under 盧. The kanji 膚 means "skin." <虍胃>

皮膚 the skin [ひふ]

	Meanings	Kun and On	Romaji	Bushu	Stroke Order and Number
SG-0890 逓	to convey, relay	テイ	*tee*	辵	10

逓 **D** F-2329

說文 1 旧字 2

The left side of 1 was 辵 "to move forward," while the right side comprised 厂 over 虎 **SG-0883** "a tiger," together signifying "skinning a tiger," and having the sound *tee*. The change from a live tiger to a hide or fur signified "a change of state," and 辵 added a sense of "traveling." This was likened to the way a long-distance messenger changed horses on their way to relay a message. The kyuji 遞 (2) retained 虎, but it was reduced to 乕 in the shinji. The kanji 逓 means "to convey, relay." <乕辶>

逓減する to decrease gradually [ていげんする]

	Meanings	Kun and On	Romaji	Bushu	Stroke Order and Number
SG-0891 虞	to worry, fear	おそ-れ	oso-re	虍	13

虞 **D** F-3015

金文1 1 金文2 2 說文 3

1, 2, and 3 comprised "a tiger headdress," and 呉 **SG-0344**, used for the sounds *go*/*gu*. The etymology is obscure, but one view suggests that it depicted a person in a tiger headdress entertaining a deity with a votive dance, who was concerned about the deity's will—whence the meaning "worry." Another view holds that the forms comprised "a suspicious animal that looked like a tiger" (虍), and 呉 ("a person with a tilted head"), used for the sound *gu* to mean "suspicious," and thus the character meant "to worry." The kanji 虞 means "to worry, fear." <虍呉>

虞れ fear, terror, reverence, awe [おそれ]

37e 象 "elephant, image" [from an pictograph of an elephant]; *zoo/shoo* 象像

	Meanings	Kun and On	Romaji	Bushu	Stroke Order and Number
SG-0892 象	elephant, image	ショウ・ゾウ	*shoo, zoo*	豕	12

象 **B** F-0616

甲骨文 1 金文 1 2 金文 2 3 金文 3 4 説文 5

1, 2, and 3 were a vertical depiction of an elephant, showing a head with a large ear, a long, curled trunk, and a tusk. The form meant "elephant." 4 was more like a picture. An elephant is an unmistakably powerful image, and thus the character also came to mean "image." The kanji 象 means "elephant, image." <象>

象徴 symbol [しょうちょう]; 印象 impression [いんしょう]; 具象絵画 representational painting [ぐしょうかいが]; 現象 phenomenon [げんしょう]; 気象 meteorological phenomena [きしょう]; 象 elephant [ぞう]; インド象 Asian elephant [インドぞう]

	Meanings	Kun and On	Romaji	Bushu	Stroke Order and Number
SG-0893 像	image, shape, figure, impression	ゾウ	*zoo*	人	14

像 **B** F-0926

説文

The seal-style form comprised 亻, which pertained to "a person," and "an elephant" (象 **SG-0892**), which was used for the sound *zoo* to mean "an image." Together they signified "an image of a person" or just "an image." The kanji 像 means "image, shape, figure, impression." <亻象>

想像 imagination [そうぞう]; 受像 image reception, televising [じゅぞう]; 現像する to develop film [げんぞうする]; 解像度 (display) resolution [かいぞうど]; 未来像 future aspect, future image [みらいぞう]; 画像 likeness, image [がぞう]; 想像 imagination fancy, supposition [そうぞう]

37f 為 "to do" [from a person handling an elephant]; *i/gi* 為偽

	Meanings	Kun and On	Romaji	Bushu	Stroke Order and Number
SG-0894 為	to do; purpose, benefit	イ	*i*	爪	9

為 **B** F-0705

甲骨文 1 金文1 2 金文2 3 説文 4 旧字 5

1, 2, and 3 showed "an elephant being handled with one or two hands." An elephant handler used an elephant for heavy work, such as construction, bringing the general meaning "to do, perform, conduct." (Elephants were reportedly seen in southern China in ancient times.) The use of something to perform an act gave the meaning "purpose, benefit." In 4, "a hand from above" and "an elephant with four big feet and a long trunk" took a somewhat puzzling shape and became the kyuji 爲, 5. The shinji was further simplified to 為. The kanji 為 means "to do; purpose, benefit." < 為 >

為政者 statesman, politician [いせいしゃ]; 行為 action, act, behavior, deed, conduct [こうい]; 有為の capable, talented [ういの]; 人為的な manmade, artificial [じんいてきな]; 無作為に (to choose) at random [むさくいに] // 為 benefit, purpose, reason [ため]; 為替 money order, exchange [かわせ]

	Meanings	Kun and On	Romaji	Bushu	Stroke Order and Number
SG-0895 偽	false, fake; to lie	いつわ-る・にせ ギ	itsuwa-ru, nise *gi*	人	11

偽 **C** F-1321

説文 1 旧字 2

1 (and 2) comprised 亻 "an act that one does," and 爲 (為 **SG-0894**), which was used for the sound *gi* to mean "to change." Changing something real to something false was "falsifying." The kanji 偽 means "false, fake; to lie." <亻為>

偽る to lie, falsify, misrepresent [いつわる]; 偽の sham, bogus, forged, false [にせの]; 偽作 the act of forging, forgery [ぎさく]; 真偽 truth or falsehood, authenticity [しんぎ]; 虚偽 fabrication, lying [きょぎ]; 偽証罪 the crime of perjury [ぎしょうざい]

37g 鹿 "deer" [from a deer with antlers] 鹿薦麗麓

	Meanings	Kun and On	Romaji	Bushu	Stroke Order and Number
SG-0896 鹿	deer	しか・か	shika, ka	鹿	11

鹿 **B** F-1015

甲骨文 1 金文1 2 金文2 3 説文 4

1, 2, 3, and 4 depicted a deer with distinctive antlers on its head. The character meant "a deer." The four legs in 4 became 比 in the kanji. The kanji 鹿 means "deer." <声比>

鹿 deer [しか]; 鹿肉 venison [しかにく]; 子鹿 fawn [こじか]; 鹿の子 dappled pattern [かのこ]; 馬鹿らしい ludicrous, laughable, absurd [ばからしい]

	Meanings	Kun and On	Romaji	Bushu	Stroke Order and Number
SG-0897 薦	to recommend	すす-める セン	susu-meru *sen*	艸	艹 苎 芦 芦 蓎 薦 薦 16

薦 **C** F-1549

甲骨文1 1 甲骨文2 2 金文1 3 金文2 4 説文 5

1 and 2 showed an animal that had antlers, whereas 3 and 4 were surrounded by grass or vegetation, thus depicting a grazing animal (possibly a deer, a mythical animal, or some other unknown kind of animal). One view explains that the character represented a sacrificial animal chosen as an offering, thus signifying "to recommend." Another view takes it to be a borrowing. The kanji 薦 means "to recommend." <艹廌>

薦める to recommend [すすめる]; 推薦 recommendation [すいせん]; 推薦状 letter of recommendation [すいせんじょう]

	Meanings	Kun and On	Romaji	Bushu	Stroke Order and Number
SG-0898 麗	beautiful, graceful; elegance	うるわ-しい レイ	uruwa-shii *ree*	鹿	丽 丽 丽 严 麗 麗 麗 麗 19

麗 **D** F-1680

金文1 1 金文2 2 説文古文 3 説文 4

1 and 2 depicted a deer with two elaborate antlers, signifying "beautiful." In 3, only the pair of stylized antlers remained, but in 4, they appeared as additional antler shapes on top of 鹿 **SG-0896** "a deer." The kanji 麗 means "beautiful, graceful; elegance." <丽鹿>

麗しい beautiful lovely, graceful [うるわしい]; 綺麗な beautiful [きれいな]; 華麗な splendid [かれいな]

	Meanings	Kun and On	Romaji	Bushu	Stroke Order and Number
SG-0899 麓	foot of a mountain	ふもと ロク	humoto *roku*	鹿	林 埜 芦 芦 薦 麓 麓 19

麓 **D** F-2486

甲骨 1 説文古文 2 説文 3

In 1, a deer with distinctive antlers was used for the sound *roku*, and was placed in the woods (two 木 on both sides). It meant "an area at the foot of a mountain." 2 and 3 comprised 林 **SG-0609** "woods," and 鹿 "a deer." The kanji 麓 means "foot of a mountain." <林鹿>

麓 foot of a mountain, foothill [ふもと]; 山麓 base of a mountain [さんろく]

37h 屈 "to submit, give in"; *kutsu* 屈堀掘窟

	Meanings	Kun and On	Romaji	Bushu	Stroke Order and Number
SG-0900 屈	to hunker down, scrunch, give in	クツ	*kutsu*	尸	乛 尸 尸 屈 屈 屈 8

屈 **C** F-1401

金文1 1 金文2 2 説文 3

1, 2, and 3 depicted "an animal scrunching its body up" with "the tail tucked in." This posture gave the meaning "to submit, give in." In the kanji, it became 尸, bushu *shikabane*, and 出 **SG-0217**. The kanji 屈 means "to hunker down, scrunch, give in." <尸出>(Note: The kanji for an animal tail is 尾 **SG-0917**.)

屈する to bend, yield to, succumb to [くっする]; 屈託のない carefree, unworried [くったくのない]; 屈折する to be refracted, be distorted [くっせつする]; 屈指の leading, prominent [くっしの]; 不屈の unyielding [ふくつの]

	Meanings	Kun and On	Romaji	Bushu	Stroke Order and Number
SG-0901 堀	ditch, moat, canal	ほり	hori	土	一 十 ｔ 圹 坼 堀 堀 11

堀 **C** F-1098

説文

The seal-style form comprised 土 **SG-1126** "dirt, ground," and 屈 **SG-0900** for the sound *kutsu*, to mean "an animal scrunching its body with its tail curled up." Together they originally meant "a hole or den in the ground in which an animal hid." In Japanese, a ditch dug into the ground means "a moat" surrounding a castle. The kanji 堀 means "ditch, moat, canal." <土屈>

(お)堀 moat, canal [ほり、おほり]; 外堀 outer moat [そとぼり]; 内堀 inner moat [うちぼり]; 釣り堀 fishing pond [つりぼり]

	Meanings	Kun and On	Romaji	Bushu	Stroke Order and Number
SG-0902 掘	to dig, excavate	ほ-る クツ	ho-ru *kutsu*	手	一 十 扌 扩 折 掘 掘 11

掘 **C** F-1328

説文

The seal-style form comprised 扌 "an act done by hand," and 屈 "an animal scrunching its body with its tail curled up," used for the sound *kutsu*. Together they signified "a hand digging a hole in the ground," that is, "to dig." The kanji 掘 means "to dig, excavate."<扌屈>

掘る to dig, bore a hole or cave [ほる]; 掘り抜く to excavate, dig up [ほりぬく]; 掘り出し物 lucky find, good buy [ほりだしもの]; 発掘する to dig up a site, unearth, discover [はっくつする]

	Meanings	Kun and On	Romaji	Bushu	Stroke Order and Number
SG-0903 窟	cave, cavern, grotto	クツ	*kutsu*	穴	13

窟 **D** F-2419	No ancient character. The kanji 窟 comprises 穴, bushu *anakanmuri* "cave, hole," and 屈 SG-0900, from "an animal scrunching its body with its tail curled up," used for the sound *kutsu.* The kanji 窟 means "cave, cavern, grotto." <穴 屈>	洞窟 cavern, cave, grotto [どうくつ]

37i 属 "to join, belong to" [from animals mating] 属嘱

	Meanings	Kun and On	Romaji	Bushu	Stroke Order and Number
SG-0904 属	to belong to, fall under, be subject to; genus	ゾク	*zoku*	尸	12

属 **B** F-0841	說文 1, 旧字 2 (屬 属) One view explains that 1 comprised "a female animal with its tail" (尾 SG-0917), and "a male" (蜀), together originally signifying "mating," but also meaning "to join, belong to." Another view holds that 蜀 was used for the sound *zoku/shoku* to mean "to continue," and that a female animal giving birth to one litter after another signified "members of the same organization, relations." The meaning expanded to denote a group of things sharing a common origin. The kanji 属 means "to belong to, fall under, be subject to; genus." <尸 禹>	属する to belong to, be vested in [ぞくする]; 所属する to belong to, affiliate oneself with [しょぞくする]; 属性 attribute, property [ぞくせい]; 帰属感 sense of belonging, class identification [きぞくかん]

	Meanings	Kun and On	Romaji	Bushu	Stroke Order and Number
SG-0905 嘱	to entrust, request	ショク	*shoku*	口	15

嘱 **D** F-2001	囑 嘱 (旧字) No ancient character. The kyuji 囑 had 口 "a mouth," and 屬 (属 SG-0904), used for the sound *shoku* to mean "to connect." Conveying a message meant "to entrust, request." The kanji 嘱 means "to entrust, request." <口 属>	嘱託 commissioned worker [しょくたく]; 嘱託医 commissioned doctor [しょくたくい]; 委嘱する to entrust a matter to someone [いしょくする]

38 Parts of an animal

38a 皮 "skin" [from a hand skinning an animal]; *hi/ha* 皮彼波破被披婆

	Meanings	Kun and On	Romaji	Bushu	Stroke Order and Number
SG-0906 皮	skin, surface layer	かわ ヒ	kawa *hi*	皮	5

皮 **A** F-0886	金文 1, 金文 2, 說文 3, 皮 — 1 and 2 comprised "an animal fur with its head still attached" (𠂆), and "a hand" (又 SG-0084). The character depicted a scene in which an animal was being skinned by hand. In 3, the animal skin was simplified, and the hand remained. The kanji 皮 means "skin, surface layer." <𠂆 又>	皮 outer skin, fruit rind, peel, bark, surface layer [かわ]; 皮算用 an unreliable account, overly optimistic calculation [かわざんよう]; 合成皮革 synthetic leather [ごうせいひかく]; 樹皮 bark [じゅひ]; 皮相的な superficial, shallow [ひそうてきな]

	Meanings	Kun and On	Romaji	Bushu	Stroke Order and Number
SG-0907 彼	he, she; over there	かれ・かの ヒ	kare, kano *hi*	彳	8

彼 **A** F-0397	金文 1, 金文 2, 說文 3, 彼 — 1 and 2 were the same as 1 and 2 for 皮 "to peel away an animal hide," which was used for the sound *hi*. With 彳 "a crossroads" added to 皮, 3 signified "going away." The form is used to refer to a place or a person away from the speaker. The kanji 彼 means "he, she; over there." <彳 皮>	彼 he [かれ]; 彼女 she [かのじょ]; 彼岸 the realm of Buddhist enlightenment [ひがん]; お彼岸 equinoctial week, the week of Buddhist memorial services [おひがん] // 彼方 beyond, across [かなた]

	Meanings	Kun and On	Romaji	Bushu	Stroke Order and Number
SG-0908 波	wave; to have influence on	なみ ハ	nami *ha*	水	氵 氵 汀 沪 波 波 8

波 **A** F-0506

説文 The seal-style form comprised "water," and 皮, used for the sound *ha* to mean "to splash, move up and down." Together they signified "wave." The manner in which a wave spread gave the meaning "to influence." The kanji 波 means "wave; to have influence on." <氵皮>

波 wave [なみℸ]; 波打ち際 the water's edge, the beach [なみうちぎわ]; 波乗り surfing [なみのり]; 波に乗る to go with the flow [なみℸにのる]; 波風を立てる to make trouble, rock the boat [なみℸかぜを・たてℸる]; 波長 wavelength [はちょう]; 電波 radio wave, airwaves [でℸんぱ]; 波止場 wharf, landing stage [はとば]

	Meanings	Kun and On	Romaji	Bushu	Stroke Order and Number
SG-0909 破	to break, tear, smash, be defeated	やぶ-る ハ	yabu-ru *ha*	石	厂 石 矿 矿 砂 破 10

破 **B** F-0772

説文 The seal-style form comprised 石 **SG-1148** "rock," and 皮 **SG-0906**, which was used for the sound *ha* to represent the sound of a rock being smashed. Together they signified "to break, smash, tear," and also "to be defeated." The kanji 破 means "to break, tear, smash, be defeated." <石皮>

破る to tear, break, win [やぶℸる]; 破れる to be torn, become ragged, be defeated [やぶれℸる]; 打ち破る to smash, break through [うちやぶる, うちやぶℸる]; 破壊 destruction [はかい]; 大破する to be wrecked, smashed [たℸいはする]; 破格の exceptional, exceeding [はかくの]

	Meanings	Kun and On	Romaji	Bushu	Stroke Order and Number
SG-0910 被	to cover, take on, pour over	こうむ-る ヒ	koomu-ru *hi*	衣	ラ ネ ネ ネ 衤 衤 袝 被 10

被 **B** F-0758

説文 The seal-style form comprised 衣 (later, 衤, bushu *koromohen*), and 皮 "covering," used for the sound *hi*. Together they originally signified "clothes to cover oneself." The kanji 被 means "to cover, take on, pour over." <衤皮>

被る to suffer (a loss), be rebuked [こうむℸる]; 被害 damage [ひℸがい]; 被告人 defendant, the accused [ひこくにん]; 被爆者 person exposed to radiation [ひばくℸしゃ, ひばℸくしゃ]; 被服 clothing [ひℸふく]; 被災地 disaster-stricken area [ひさℸいち] // 被る to put on the head [かぶる]; 猫被り pretense, put-on [ねこかℸぶり]; 被り物 headgear head cover [かぶりもの]

	Meanings	Kun and On	Romaji	Bushu	Stroke Order and Number
SG-0911 披	to uncover, open, reveal	ヒ	*hi*	手	一 十 扌 扩 扩 拔 披 8

披 **D** F-1923

説文 The seal-style form comprised 扌 "an act done by hand," and 皮 **SG-0906** "to peel an animal hide," which was used for the sound *hi*. A hand skinning an animal gave the meaning "to uncover." The kanji 披 means "to uncover, open, reveal." <扌皮>

披露する to uncover, reveal [ひℸろうする]; 披露宴 (wedding) reception [ひろℸうえん]

	Meanings	Kun and On	Romaji	Bushu	Stroke Order and Number
SG-0912 婆	old woman	バ	*ba*	女	氵 氵 汀 沪 波 波 婆 婆 11

婆 **D** F-1979

No ancient form. The kanji comprises 波 **SG-0908**, used for the sounds *ha/ba* to mean "white," and the bottom component 女 **SG-0521** "woman," together signifying "a woman whose hair is white" (that is, an old woman). The kanji 婆 means "old woman." It also appears in the word お転婆娘, an affectionate term for a "tomboy." <波女>

老婆 old woman [ろℸうば]; 産婆 midwife [さんば]; 老婆心 grandmotherly excessive solicitude [ろうばℸしん]; お転婆娘 tomboy [おてんばむℸすめ]

38b 革 "leather, hide" 革靴覇

	Meanings	Kun and On	Romaji	Bushu	Stroke Order and Number
SG-0913 革	hide, leather, drastic change, renewal	かわ カク	kawa *kaku*	革	一 廿 芇 芇 芇 革 9

革 **B** F-0536

金文 1 説文 2 1 and 2 depicted "an animal cut open and its hide stretched and hung to dry," and had the meanings "to be stretched tightly" and "hide, leather." Unlike the origin of 暴 **SG-1030**, in which a dead animal was left exposed to the elements, 革 refers to a forceful process that changes a thing into something new, thus bringing the meaning "to change forcibly." Another view explains that a drastic change from a live animal to a hide gave the meaning "drastic change, renewal." The kanji 革 means "hide, leather, drastic change, renewal." <革>

革 leather [かわℸ]; 吊り革 hand strap on a train [つりかわ]; 革命 revolution [かくめい]; 革新 reform, renovation [かくしん]; 革新派 reformists [かくしんは]; 皮革製品 leather goods [ひかくせℸいひん]

SG-0914 靴	Meanings	*Kun* and *On*	Romaji	Bushu	Stroke Order and Number
	shoe, footwear	くつ カ	kutsu *ka*	革	一 艹 廿 芔 芔 革 靯 靴 靴 13

靴 **C** F-1589

篆文 靴

The seal-style form comprised 革 **SG-0913** "hide, leather," and 華 **SG-0675**, used for the sound *ka*, and replaced by 化 **SG-0386** in the kanji. It originally meant "leather boot, leather shoes." The kanji 靴 means "shoe, footwear." <革化>

革靴 leather shoes [かわぐつ]; 靴紐 shoelace [くつひも]; 長靴 boots, waders [ながぐつ]; 靴擦れ blister caused by one's shoe [くつずれ]; 雨靴 rain shoes, Wellington boots [あまぐつ]; 靴脱ぎ石 stone slab upon which to remove one's footwear [くつぬぎいし]

SG-0915 覇	Meanings	*Kun* and *On*	Romaji	Bushu	Stroke Order and Number
	victory, conquest, supreme ruler	ハ	*ha*	覀	覀 覀 覀 覀 覀 覀 覀 覇 19

覇 **C** F-1628

金文1 1 金文2 2 說文 3 旧字 4 霸 覇

In 1, 2, and 3, below "rain" (雨 **SG-1295**) was "an animal hide" (革), which had been bleached by exposure to the "white light of the moon" (月 **SG-1077**) and other elements. The component 䩗 had the sound *ha*. The character 覇 took the meaning of "a great elder" due to association with the character 伯, "a great elder," which had the same sounds *haku*/*ha*, and also originated from "white" (白). A great elder who had brought about a military victory gave the meaning "victory." 雨 was replaced by 覀. The kanji 覇 means "victory, conquest, supreme ruler." <覀革月>

制覇 conquest, domination [せいは]; 覇権 supremacy, hegemony [はけん]; 連覇 successive championships [れんぱ]

38c 毛 "hair" 毛尾耗

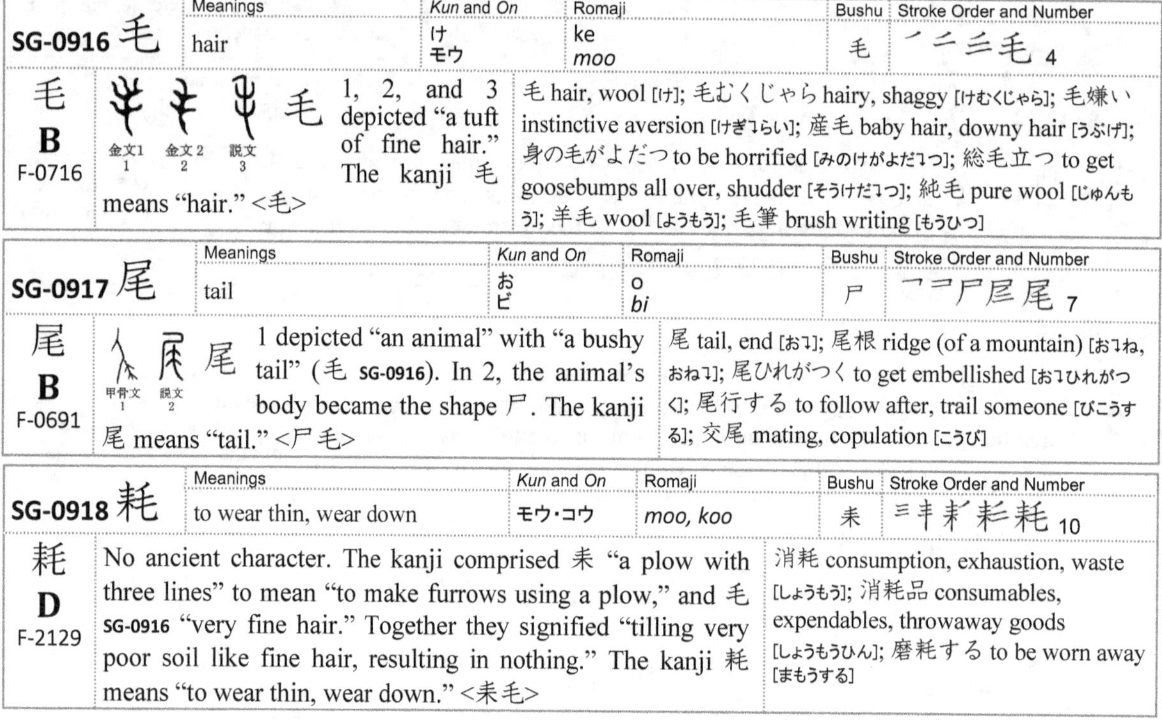

SG-0916 毛	Meanings	*Kun* and *On*	Romaji	Bushu	Stroke Order and Number
	hair	け モウ	ke *moo*	毛	ノ 二 三 毛 4

毛 **B** F-0716

金文1 1 金文2 2 說文 3 毛

1, 2, and 3 depicted "a tuft of fine hair." The kanji 毛 means "hair." <毛>

毛 hair, wool [け]; 毛むくじゃら hairy, shaggy [けむくじゃら]; 毛嫌い instinctive aversion [けぎらい]; 産毛 baby hair, downy hair [うぶげ]; 身の毛がよだつ to be horrified [みのけがよだつ]; 総毛立つ to get goosebumps all over, shudder [そうけだつ]; 純毛 pure wool [じゅんもう]; 羊毛 wool [ようもう]; 毛筆 brush writing [もうひつ]

SG-0917 尾	Meanings	*Kun* and *On*	Romaji	Bushu	Stroke Order and Number
	tail	お ビ	o *bi*	尸	フ コ 尸 尸 尾 7

尾 **B** F-0691

甲骨文 1 說文 2 尾

1 depicted "an animal" with "a bushy tail" (毛 **SG-0916**). In 2, the animal's body became the shape 尸. The kanji 尾 means "tail." <尸毛>

尾 tail, end [お]; 尾根 ridge (of a mountain) [おね, おね]; 尾ひれがつく to get embellished [おひれがつく]; 尾行する to follow after, trail someone [びこうする]; 交尾 mating, copulation [こうび]

SG-0918 耗	Meanings	*Kun* and *On*	Romaji	Bushu	Stroke Order and Number
	to wear thin, wear down	モウ・コウ	*moo, koo*	耒	三 丰 耒 耓 耗 10

耗 **D** F-2129

No ancient character. The kanji comprised 耒 "a plow with three lines" to mean "to make furrows using a plow," and 毛 **SG-0916** "very fine hair." Together they signified "tilling very poor soil like fine hair, resulting in nothing." The kanji 耗 means "to wear thin, wear down." <耒毛>

消耗 consumption, exhaustion, waste [しょうもう]; 消耗品 consumables, expendables, throwaway goods [しょうもうひん]; 磨耗する to be worn away [まもうする]

38d 友(犮) "plucking hair" [from a dog with an extra-long hair, signifying pulling hair out]; *hatsu/batsu* 抜髪

	Meanings	*Kun* and *On*	Romaji	Bushu	Stroke Order and Number
SG-0919 抜	to pull out, stand out, exceed	ぬ-く バツ	nu-ku *batsu*	手	一 寸 扌 扌 扐 抜 抜 7

抜 **B** F-0690

拔 抜 — 説文 1, 旧字 2

1 and 2 comprised 扌, bushu *tehen* "an act done by hand"; and 犮 "to pluck hair, pull out," from a dog with an extra-long hair, used for the sound *batsu*. In 2, 犮 changed to 友 **SG-0085** in the kanji, with no relevance to the character for "friend." Someone who got plucked from a larger group was an "outstanding or eminent" person. The kanji 抜 means "to pull out, stand out, exceed." <扌友>

抜く to pull out, exceed [ぬく]; 引き抜く to pull out, headhunt [ひきぬ]く]; 追い抜く to come from behind [おいぬ]く]; 手抜きをする to cut corners [てぬき]をする]; 抜群の preeminent [ばつぐんの]; 選抜チーム all-star team [せんばつチ]ーム]; 抜擢する to pick out [ばってきする]

	Meanings	*Kun* and *On*	Romaji	Bushu	Stroke Order and Number
SG-0920 髪	hair	かみ ハツ	kami *hatsu*	髟	丨 ｴ 镸 髟 髟 髟 髪 髪 14

髪 **C** F-1313

金文 1 1, 金文 2 2, 説文 3, 髮 旧字 4, 髪

1 and 2 comprised "a dog" and "a head with hair." 3 comprised 長 **SG-0566** "long," 彡 "a beautiful shape," and 犮, used for the sound *hatsu* to mean "to pluck hair." Together they signified "hair." With 犮 replaced by 友, the kanji 髪 means "hair." <镸彡友>

髪 hair [かみ]]; 髪型 hair style [かみがた]; 黒髪 black hair [くろかみ]; 散髪する to get a haircut [さんぱつする]; 白髪 gray hair [はくはつ, しらが]]; 間一髪 a narrow squeak, by a hairsbreadth [かん・いっぱつ]; 金髪 blond hair [きんぱつ]

38e 角 "horn, antler" 角解触

	Meanings	*Kun* and *On*	Romaji	Bushu	Stroke Order and Number
SG-0921 角	horn, corner, angle, Sumo circles	かど・つの カク	kado, tsuno *kaku*	角	ノ ク 户 角 角 7

角 **A** F-0648

甲骨文 1, 金文 2, 説文 3, 角

1, 2, and 3 depicted "an animal horn or antler," and had the same sound as "hard." Something hard also meant "an edged corner of a thing." Two wrestlers fighting with their heads against each other in old Chinese wresting lent the meaning Sumo circles in Japanese. The kanji 角 means "horn, corner, angle, Sumo circles."<角>

角 edge, corner, turn [か]ど]; horn, antler [つの]]; 角張る to be angular, pointed, formal [かどば]る]; 四角 square, quadrilateral [しかく]; 四角い square, four-cornered [しかくい]; 三角形 triangle [さんかく]けい, さんか]っけい]; 角界 Sumo circles [かくかい]; 方角 direction, a point of the compass [ほうがく]

	Meanings	*Kun* and *On*	Romaji	Bushu	Stroke Order and Number
SG-0922 解	to undo, untie, solve, dissect	と-く カイ・ゲ	to-ku *kai, ge*	角	ク 户 角 角 角' 角ㇷ 解 解 13

解 **A** F-0286

甲骨文 1, 中山王器 2, 説文 3, 解

1 comprised "a horn held by two hands" and "an ox," together signifying "to cut up an ox or animal." In 2, "the blade of a knife" was added. 3 comprised "a horn" (角), "a knife" (刀 **SG-1394**), and "an ox" (牛 **SG-0816**). Dismembering an animal with a knife signified "taking something apart; to analyze, solve a problem." The kanji 解 means "to undo, untie, solve, dissect." <角刀牛>

解く to untie, undo, unsew, work out, answer [と]く]; 解決 solution, settlement [かいけつ]; 読解力 reading comprehension ability [どっか]いりょく]; 解放する to free, let go, release [かいほうする]; 見解 view [けんかい]; 解せない beyond one's understanding [げせ]ない]; 解脱 deliverance of one's soul from earthly bondage [げだつ]

	Meanings	*Kun* and *On*	Romaji	Bushu	Stroke Order and Number
SG-0923 触	to touch, feel, make contact	ふ-れる・さわ-る ショク	hu-reru, sawa-ru *shoku*	角	ク 户 角 角 角 角' 触 触 13

触 **B** F-0989

金文 1, 説文 2, 觸 旧字 3, 触

1 and 2 comprised 角 (**SG-0921**) "an antler or horn," and 蜀 "a male animal," used for the sound *shoku*. From male animals fighting with their horns in contact came the meaning "to contact, touch." In the shinji, 蜀 changed to 虫 (**SG-0998**). The kanji 触 means "to touch, feel, make contact." <角虫>

触れる to touch, touch on, mention, refer to [ふれる]; 触る to touch, feel [さわる]; 手触り to feel, touch [てざ]わり]; 接触する to make contact [せっしょくする]; 感触 touch, impression [かんしょく]; 触覚 antenna of an insect, feeler, tentacle [しょっかく]

38f 牙 "fang, tusk"; *ga* • 爪 "fingernail, claw" 芽邪牙 • 爪

	Meanings	*Kun* and *On*	Romaji	Bushu	Stroke Order and Number
SG-0924 芽	to sprout; shoot, bud	め ガ	me *ga*	艸	一 艹 艹 芒 芒 芽 芽 8

芽 **C** F-1311 — 篆文

The seal-style form had "grass, plants" (艸, 艹), and 牙 **SG-0926** "fangs," used for the sound *ga* to mean "uneven." New shoots on the stem of a plant emerged in an alternating manner on either side. The character meant "a new bud on a plant." The kanji 芽 means "to sprout; shoot, bud." <艹牙>

芽 shoot, sprout, bud [め]; 新芽 new shoot [しんめ]; 芽生える to burgeon, sprout, germinate [めばえる]; 発芽 germination, sprouting [はつが]

	Meanings	*Kun* and *On*	Romaji	Bushu	Stroke Order and Number
SG-0925 邪	wicked, evil	ジャ	*ja*	邑	一 厂 匚 牙 牙 牙 邪 邪 8

邪 **C** F-1597 — 説文

The seal-style form comprised 牙 "something uneven; incorrect," which was used for the sound *ja* (from *ga*), and 邑 (阝) "town." Originally the name of a specific town, it came to mean "wicked, evil." The kanji 邪 means "wicked, evil." <牙阝>

邪念 vicious mind, wicked thought [じゃねん]; 邪気払い poisonous air [じゃきばらい]; 無邪気な innocent, simple-minded, naive [むじゃきな]; 邪険に harshly, coldly [じゃけんに]; 邪推する to suspect without reason, entertain unjust suspicion [じゃすいする] // 風邪 cold, influenza [かぜ]

	Meanings	*Kun* and *On*	Romaji	Bushu	Stroke Order and Number
SG-0926 牙	fang, tusk	きば ガ・ゲ	kiba *ga, ge*	牙	一 厂 匚 牙 牙 4

牙 **D** F-1942 — 金文 1, 説文古文 2, 説文 3

1 depicted the intersecting upper fang and a lower fang of an animal. It meant "a fang" or "a tusk." The bottom of 2 depicted a trap used to catch an animal, or possibly teeth. The kanji 牙 means "fang, tusk." <牙>

牙 tusk, fang [きば]; 牙城 stronghold, bastion [がじょう]; 象牙 ivory [ぞうげ, ぞうげ]

	Meanings	*Kun* and *On*	Romaji	Bushu	Stroke Order and Number
SG-0927 爪	claw, fingernail, toenail	つめ・つま	tsume, tsuma	爪	一 厂 爪 爪 4

爪 **D** F-1784 — 甲骨文 1, 金文 2, 説文 3

1 and 2 were "the claws of an animal extended to snatch its prey." The meaning of the kanji includes the fingernails or toenails of a person. The kanji 爪 means "claw, fingernail, toenail."

爪 nail, claw, hoof [つめ]; 爪切り nail clippers, nail scissors [つめきり]; 爪痕 fingernail mark, scratch [つめあと]; 足の爪 toenail [あしのつめ]; 爪先 the tips of one's toes [つまさき]; 爪先立つ to stand on tiptoes [つまさきだつ]

38g 隶 "to catch, follow" [from a hand grabbing an animal] 逮隷

	Meanings	*Kun* and *On*	Romaji	Bushu	Stroke Order and Number
SG-0928 逮	to reach, catch	タイ	*tai*	辵	フ ヨ ヨ 尹 聿 隶 隶 隶 逮 逮 11

逮 **C** F-1253 — 中山王器 1, 石鼓文 2, 説文 3

1, 2, and 3 comprised "a crossroads" with "a footprint," forming 辵 "to move forward" on the left, and "a hand grabbing a fur animal" (隶), for the sound *tai*, on the right. From going to catch an animal by hand, it meant "to chase and catch." The kanji 逮 means "to reach, catch." <隶辶>

逮捕 arrest, capture [たいほ]

	Meanings	*Kun* and *On*	Romaji	Bushu	Stroke Order and Number
SG-0929 隷	manservant, low level official; to be subordinate	レイ	*ree*	隶	一 十 士 圭 圭 幸 幸 隷 隷 隷 16

隷 **D** F-2027 — 説文籀文 1, 説文 2, 旧字 3

One view explains that 1 and 2 depicted a person placing a cloth by hand (隶) over a cursed animal (祟 "curse, divine punishment"), thereby trans-ferring the curse to himself and entering into servitude to a deity. The religious meaning was dropped, and the character came to mean "someone who is not free." Another view takes that a grabbing hand (隶) and 柰, used for the sound *ree* to mean "hold," together signified someone who got caught and became a servant. The kanji 隷 means "manservant, low-level official; to be subordinate." <士示隶>

奴隷 enslaved person, bondman [どれい]; 奴隷解放 the emancipation of enslaved people [どれいかいほう]; 隷属する to be subordinate, be under the control of [れいぞくする]; 隷書 clerical–style of kanji (the earliest kanji style) [れいしょ]

38h 求 "to seek, demand" [from a fur animal]; *kyuu* 求球救

	Meanings	Kun and On	Romaji	Bushu	Stroke Order and Number
SG-0930 求	to seek, demand	もと-める キュウ	moto-meru *kyuu*	水	一十才求求 7

求 **A** F-0236

金文 1 説文古文 2 説文 3

1 and 2 depicted "an animal fur with the head and tail still attached." In 3, the animal fur was placed inside "clothing" (衣). One view explains that fur clothing was highly sought after, and thus it meant "to seek, demand." Another view holds it to be borrowing. <求>

求める to want, wish for, request, pursue, search for [もとめる]; 追求 pursuit, chase, search [ついきゅう]; 求人 recruitment, job offer [きゅうじん]; 求職 hunt for a job [きゅうしょく]; 求婚 courtship, marriage proposal [きゅうこん]

	Meanings	Kun and On	Romaji	Bushu	Stroke Order and Number
SG-0931 球	ball, round, sphere, globe	たま キュウ	tama *kyuu*	玉	丁王王一玎玎球球 11

球 **A** F-0461

説文 1 説文或体 2

1 comprised 王 "gems strung together," and 求, which was used for the sound *kyuu* to mean "a round shape." The right side of 璆 in 2 was also used for the sound *kyuu*. Gems strung together made a necklace, which formed a circle. The kanji 球 means "ball, round, sphere, globe." <王求>

球 ball [たま]; 野球 baseball [やきゅう]; 地球 the Earth [ちきゅう]; 球体 sphere, globe [きゅうたい]; 球技 ball game [きゅうぎ]; 球形 globular shape [きゅうけい]; 球児 teenage amateur baseball player [きゅうじ]; 北半球 the Northern Hemisphere [きたはんきゅう]

	Meanings	Kun and On	Romaji	Bushu	Stroke Order and Number
SG-0932 救	to save, rescue	すく-う キュウ	suku-u *kyuu*	攵	一十才求求求'救救 11

救 **B** F-0816

金文 1 説文 2

1 and 2 comprised "an animal fur with the head attached" (求 **SG-0930**), which was used for the sound *kyuu* to signify "to pull to the middle"; and "a hand holding a stick" (攴, 攵, bushu *bokunyuu*), used to mean "to cause an action." Pulling something toward oneself meant "to rescue." The kanji 救 means "to save, rescue." <求攵>

救う to save, rescue [すくう]; 救出する to save, rescue [きゅうしゅつする]; 人命救助 lifesaving [じんめいきゅうじょ]; 災害救助 disaster relief [さいがいきゅうじょ]; 救援活動 relief operation [きゅうえんかつどう]; 救済する to give relief, save [きゅうさいする]

39 Marine creatures

39a 魚 "fish" 魚鮮漁鯨

	Meanings	Kun and On	Romaji	Bushu	Stroke Order and Number
SG-0933 魚	fish	うお・さかな ギョ	uo, sakana *gyo*	魚	ク各角角魚 11

魚 **B** F-0667

甲骨文 1 金文1 2 金文2 3 説文 4

1 and 2 were pictographs of "a fish," with the head, scales, fins and tail shown, and meant "fish." In 3 and 4, the tail split, taking a shape similar to 火 "fire," and further became 灬, bushu *rekka* "fire" (but with no relevance to fire), in the kanji. The kanji 魚 means "fish." <ク田灬>

魚河岸 wholesale fish market [うおがし]; 魚 fish [さかな]; 魚屋 fishmonger [さかなや]; 金魚 goldfish [きんぎょ]; 魚眼レンズ fisheye lens [ぎょがんれんず]; 魚群 school of fish [ぎょぐん]; 魚肉 fish meat [ぎょにく]

	Meanings	Kun and On	Romaji	Bushu	Stroke Order and Number
SG-0934 鮮	fresh, distinctive, clear, vivid	あざ-やか セン	aza-yaka *sen*	魚	ククAA角魚魚'鮮鮮 17

鮮 **B** F-0837

金文1 1 金文2 2 説文 3

1 and 2 comprised 羊 **SG-0825** "sheep," used for the sound *sen* (reduced from the kanji 羴, comprising three 羊) to mean "smelly," and 魚 **SG-0933** "fish," signifying "raw; fishy smell." Being fresh was important for fish and meat, so the character meant "freshness." Fresh fish and vegetables have a bright and vivid appearance. The kanji 鮮 means "fresh, distinctive, clear, vivid." <魚羊>

鮮やかな vivid color [あざやかな]; 鮮明な clear and sharp [せんめいな]; 新鮮な fresh [しんせんな]; 鮮魚 fresh fish [せんぎょ]; 鮮度 (the degree of) freshness [せんど]; 北朝鮮 North Korea [きたちょうせん]

SG-0935 漁	Meanings	Kun and On	Romaji	Bushu	Stroke Order and Number
	to fish, hunt (for things)	ギョ・リョウ	*gyo, ryoo*	水	氵 … 漁 14

漁 **C** F-1180

甲骨文 1 金文1 2 金文2 3 篆文 4 説文 5 漁

In 1, four fish swam in a stream of water. Many fish (魚 **SG-0933**) in water signified "fishing." In 2 and 3, one or two hands were trying to grab the tails of the fish, suggesting an act by a person—fishing. 魚 had the sounds *gyo*/*ryoo*. In 4 and 5, the hand disappeared. In the kanji, "flowing water" became 氵 bushu *sanzui*. The kanji 漁 means "to fish, hunt (for things)." <氵魚>

漁業 fishing industry [ぎょꜜぎょう]; 漁村 fishing village [ぎょそん]; 漁場 fishing ground, fishing place [ぎょじょう]; 漁師 fisherman [りょꜜうし]; 漁に出る to go out to fish [りょꜜうに・でꜜる]; 大漁 large catch, good haul [たいりょう] // 漁る to hunt for, scavenge for [あさる]

SG-0936 鯨	Meanings	Kun and On	Romaji	Bushu	Stroke Order and Number
	whale	くじら ゲイ	kujira *gee*	魚	ク … 鯨 19

鯨 **D** F-1743

説文 鯨

The seal-style form comprised 魚 **SG-0933** "fish," and 京 **SG-1282**, used for the sound *gee* to mean "large." From "a large fish-like animal," the kanji 鯨 means "whale." <魚京>

鯨 whale [くじら]; 捕鯨 catching a whale [ほげい]; 捕鯨船 whale-catching vessel [ほげいせん]

39b 辰 (1) "to tremble, shake" [from a bivalve shellfish's soft body]; *shin*, (2) "agricultural" [from a tilling tool made of the sharp edges of bivalve shells]; *noo* 農振震濃唇辱娠

SG-0937 農	Meanings	Kun and On	Romaji	Bushu	Stroke Order and Number
	farming, agriculture	ノウ	*noo*	辰	冂 … 農 13

農 **B** F-0631

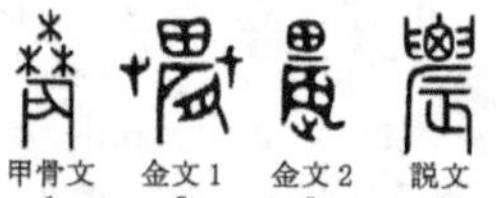

甲骨文 1 金文1 2 金文2 3 説文 4 農

1 comprised "three trees" for the meaning "an uncultivated land," and "a bivalve shellfish" (辰). Shells were attached to farming tools and used to cultivate the soil, and thus signified "farming." 2 and 3 comprised "rice paddies" (田), "a shell" (辰), and "hands" or "a footprint" (止). In 4, the top became "two hands holding something" 囟, which changed to 曲 in the shinji. The kanji 農 means "farming, agriculture." <曲辰>

農村 farming village [のうそん]; 農業 farming [のꜜうぎょう]; 農産物 agricultural produce [のうさꜜんぶつ]; 農協 (Japan) Agricultural Cooperatives [のうきょう]; 農家 farming household, agrarian family [のꜜうか]; 半農半漁 making a living in part from farming and in part from fishing [はんのうはꜜんぎょ]

SG-0938 振	Meanings	Kun and On	Romaji	Bushu	Stroke Order and Number
	to shake by hand, wave, swing	ふ-る シン	hu-ru *shin*	手	一 … 振 10

振 **B** F-0701

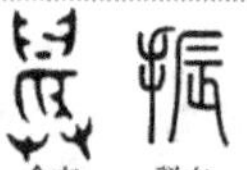

金文 1 説文 2 振

1 comprised "two hands," "a bivalve shellfish with a trembling feeler (辰)," which was used for the sound *shin*, and another "pair of hands." Together they meant "to shake by hand." The two hands became 扌, bushu *tehen*. The kanji 振 meant "to shake by hand, wave, swing." <扌辰>

振る to wave, swing, shake, refuse [ふる]; 振るう to shake, wave, thrive [ふるう]; 振り子 pendulum [ふりこ]; 素振り manner, behavior, air [そꜜぶり]; 振動 oscillation, swing [しんどう]; 不振な inactive, stagnant, in bad shape [ふしんな]

SG-0939 震	Meanings	Kun and On	Romaji	Bushu	Stroke Order and Number
	to tremble, shake	ふる-える シン	huru-eru *shin*	雨	一 … 震 15

震 **B** F-0988

説文籀文 1 説文 2 震

The complex shape of 1 comprised (a) 雨 **SG-1205** "an atmospheric phenomenon," (b) 云 "a cloud" between two 爻 "crossings," and (c) a thick-legged grain storage pot (鬲) between two 火 "fires," for "lightning." Together these components meant "trembling thunder shaking the atmosphere with flashes of lightning." In 2, the complex shapes that had told such a vivid story were replaced by the much simpler 辰 "to tremble," used phonetically for *shin*. The kanji 震 means "to tremble, shake." <雨辰>

震える to shake, quiver, tremble [ふるえる]; 震度 seismic intensity [しꜜんど]; 余震 aftershock, after tremor [よしん]; 耐震建築 earthquake-proof (resistant) building [たいしんけꜜんちく]; 免震構造 seismically isolated structure [めんしんこꜜうぞう]; 震源地 epicenter, center of disturbance [しんげꜜんち]

	Meanings	Kun and On	Romaji	Bushu	Stroke Order and Number
SG-0940 濃	thick, deep, dark	こ-い ノウ	ko-i *noo*	水	氵 汀 沪 浀 浀 濃 濃 濃 16

濃 C F-1302 說文 濃 The seal-style form comprised 氵 "flowing water; liquid," and 農 **SG-0937**, which was used for the sound *noo* to mean "thick," together signifying "thick, dark." The kanji 濃 means "thick, deep, dark." <氵農>

濃い dark, deep, strong, thick, dense [こい]; 濃い目 on the strong side (in color, taste, etc.)[こいめ]; 濃度 density, consistency, concentration [のうど]; 濃厚な thick, heavy, rich, passionate [のうこうな]; 濃淡 light and shade [のうたん, のうたん]

	Meanings	Kun and On	Romaji	Bushu	Stroke Order and Number
SG-0941 唇	lips	くちびる シン	kuchibiru *shin*	口	一 厂 戶 尸 尼 辰 唇 唇 10

唇 D F-1780 說文 唇 The seal-style form 唇 comprised 辰 "to tremble," which was used for the sound *shin,* and 口 **SG-0031** "mouth." Since the origin of 辰 was "a bivalve shellfish with a feeler," it was used as an analogy for lips, which moved in a similar way. The kanji 唇 means "lips." <辰口>

唇 a lip, the lips [くちびる]; 読唇術 lipreading technique [どくしんじゅつ]; 口唇 lips [こうしん]

	Meanings	Kun and On	Romaji	Bushu	Stroke Order and Number
SG-0942 辱	to humiliate, degrade, insult	はずかし-める ジョク	hazukashi-meru *joku*	辰	一 厂 戶 尸 辰 辰 辱 辱 10

辱 D F-1819 說文 辱 The seal-style form comprised 辰 "a bivalve shell," used to cut grass, and 寸 **SG-0112** "a hand," together originally signifying "to cut grass with a sharp tool," and having the sound *joku.* The character was borrowed to mean "to humiliate, degrade, insult." <辰寸>

辱める to humiliate, disgrace, dishonor [はずかしめる]; 屈辱 humiliation, dishonor [くつじょく]; 国辱 national humiliation, national disgrace [こくじょく]

	Meanings	Kun and On	Romaji	Bushu	Stroke Order and Number
SG-0943 娠	pregnant	シン	*shin*	女	く 女 女 女 女 娠 娠 娠 10

娠 D F-1858 篆文 娠 The seal-style form comprised 女 **SG-0521** "woman, female," and 辰 "trembling," used for the sound *shin.* Together they described the faint movements of a fetus in a mother's stomach. The kanji 娠 means "pregnant." <女辰>

妊娠 pregnancy [にんしん]

40 Bird

40a 鳥 "bird" [from an image of an entire bird viewed from the side] 鳥鳴鶏

	Meanings	Kun and On	Romaji	Bushu	Stroke Order and Number
SG-0944 鳥	bird	とり チョウ	tori *choo*	鳥	丿 户 白 自 鳥 鳥 11

鳥 B F-0603 甲骨文1 1, 甲骨文2 2, 金文 3, 說文 4 鳥 1, 2, 3, and 4 depicted the entire shape of "a bird," including the feet (as opposed to the footless 隹). The kanji 鳥 means "bird." <鳥 灬>

鳥 bird [とり]; 小鳥 small bird [ことり]; 鳥居 a red archway gate to a Shinto shrine [とりい]; 渡り鳥 migratory bird [わたりどり]; 水鳥 waterfowl, wading bird [みずどり]; 鳥肌が立つ to get goose bumps[とりはだがたつ]; 千鳥足 tottering walk [ちどりあし]; 鳥類 birds, fowls [ちょうるい]; 野鳥 wild bird [やちょう]

	Meanings	Kun and On	Romaji	Bushu	Stroke Order and Number
SG-0945 鳴	to chirp, make a sound (animal)	な-く メイ	na-ku *mee*	鳥	口 叮 咱 咱 鳴 鳴 14

鳴 C F-1220 甲骨文1 1, 甲骨文2 2, 金文 3, 說文 4 鳴 1 through 4 comprised "a mouth" (口 **SG-0031**), and "a bird" (鳥 **SG-0944**) whose beak was open to make a sound, thus signifying "a bird chirping," as well as any animal making a sound in general. The kanji 鳴 means "to chirp, make a sound (animal)." <口鳥>

鳴く to cry, call, howl, growl, bark, whine, yelp, meow [なく]; 鳴る to ring, peal, sound [なる]; 鳴り物入りで with much fanfare [なりものいりで]; 共鳴する to sympathize with, resonate [きょうめいする]; 雷鳴 thunder, rumbling of thunder [らいめい]

	Meanings	Kun and On	Romaji	Bushu	Stroke Order and Number
SG-0946 鶏	chicken, hen, cock	にわとり ケイ	niwatori *kee*	鳥	爫 孚 奚 奚' 鶏 鶏 鶏 鶏 19

鶏 **D** F-1667

甲骨文1 1 甲骨文2 2 金文1 3 金文2 4 説文籀文 5 説文 6 旧字1 7 旧字2 8 雞 鷄 鶏

In 1, 2, 5, and 6, next to "a bird" (鳥 or 隹) was "a hand holding a skein of thread" (奚), used for the sound *kee*. One view explains that it depicted a bird with a rope tied to it so that it would not fly away, thus suggesting a domesticated bird such as a chicken, hen, or cock. 3 was a picture-like image of a bird. 4 was "a bird with a crest on its head." 5 and 6 included "a hand holding a thread," and this composition was reflected in the two kyuji, 雞 (7) and 鷄 (8). The shinji 鶏 came from 8. The kanji 鶏 means "chicken, hen, cock." <爫夫鳥>

鶏 chicken [にわとり]; 養鶏 poultry farming [ようけい]; 鶏卵 hen's egg [けいらん] // 風見鶏 weathercock, opportunist [かざみどり]

40b 隹 "bird" [from a bird (with its feathers emphasized)]; bushu *hurutori*

進集準旧雄離推雑双催雇維雅携顧奪焦誰唯奮擁隻准礁雌

The name *hurutori* comes from the kyuji 舊 for the kanji 旧 **SG-0950**, for *hurui*.

	Meanings	Kun and On	Romaji	Bushu	Stroke Order and Number
SG-0947 進	to move forward, advance	すす-む シン	susu-mu *shin*	辵	イ イ' 亻' 什 隹 `隹 淮 進 11

進 **A** F-0172

甲骨文 1 金文 2 説文 3 進

1, 2, and 3 had "a bird" (隹), used for the sound *shin* (from *sui*), and "a footprint," together signifying "moving forward swiftly like a bird flying." In 2 and 3, "a crossroads" was added, forming 辵(辶) "to move forward," to emphasize the forward movement. The kanji 進 means "to move forward, advance." <隹 辶>

進む to advance, make one's way [すすむ]; 進歩 advancement [しんぽ]; 進歩的な progressive [しんぽてきな]; 進化する to evolve, develop [しんかする]; 急進的な radical [きゅうしんてきな]; デモ行進 protest march [デモこうしん]; 後進 junior, younger generation [こうしん]

	Meanings	Kun and On	Romaji	Bushu	Stroke Order and Number
SG-0948 集	to congregate, gather, collect	あつ-まる・つど-う シュウ	atsu-maru, tsudo-u *shuu*	隹	イ イ' 亻' 什 隹 隹 隼 集 12

集 **A** F-0191

甲骨文1 1 甲骨文2 2 金文1 3 金文2 4 説文1 5 説文2 6 集

In 1 through 4, a bird was shown perching on, or flying over, a tree. Birds flock on a tree, hence the meaning "to gather, congregate, collect." 5 showed three birds (隹) perched on top of a tree, which were reduced to one bird in 6. The kanji 集 means "to congregate, gather, collect." <隹木>

集まる to gather, assemble, converge [あつまる]; 集う to gather together [つどう]; 集合 gathering, meeting, congregation [しゅうごう]; 集中する to concentrate [しゅうちゅうする]; 歌集 poetry anthology [かしゅう]; 集会 meeting [しゅうかい]; 特集 special edition [とくしゅう]; 集落 settlement, hamlet [しゅうらく, しゅうらく]

	Meanings	Kun and On	Romaji	Bushu	Stroke Order and Number
SG-0949 準	standard; to apply accordingly, prepare	ジュン	*jun*	水	氵 氵' 汁 汁 淮 準 準 13

準 **B** F-0585

説文 準

The seal-style form comprised "water" (used to represent the ultimate standard of levelness), and 隼, used for the sounds *jun*/*shun*, together signifying "standard." The kanji 準 means "standard; to apply accordingly, prepare." <氵隹十>

準じる to follow the rules, conform to, be treated correspondingly [じゅんじる]; 基準 standard [きじゅん]; 標準語 standard language (of a nation) [ひょうじゅんご]; 準備する to prepare, arrange [じゅんびする]; 水準 water level, standard [すいじゅん]; 準拠する to conform to [じゅんきょする]

	Meanings	Kun and On	Romaji	Bushu	Stroke Order and Number
SG-0950 旧	old; something of the past	キュウ	*kyuu*	臼	丨 𠃊 旧 旧 旧 5

旧 **B** F-0628

甲骨文1 1 甲骨文2 2 金文 3 説文 4 旧字 5 舊 旧

1, 2, 3, and 4 depicted "a bird with a big crest," suggesting "an owl," and "an apparatus for catching a bird," which was used for the sound *kyuu*. A bird caught by the leg could not get out and remained stuck for a long

旧式 old-style [きゅうしき]; 新旧 new and old [しんきゅう]; 旧道 old road [きゅうどう]; 復旧 restoration of service [ふっきゅう]; 旧態依然 remaining unchanged for a long time

	time, which brought the meaning "a long time." The kyuji 舊 (5) had 艹, 隹, and 臼. In the shinji only 旧 was retained. The kanji 旧 means "old; something of the past." <丨 日> (Note: 臼 became 旧 in multiple characters, such as 兒 becoming 児 **SG-0447**, and 陷 becoming 陥 **SG-1348**.)	[きゅうたい・いぜん]; 旧交を温める to renew one's friendship with [きゅうこうをあたためる]; 旧家 old established family [きゅうか]

	Meanings	Kun and On	Romaji	Bushu	Stroke Order and Number
SG-0951 雄	male (animal), manly, brave; outstanding man	おす・お ユウ	osu, o *yuu*	隹	一ナ厷 厷 厷 厷 厷 雄 12

雄 **B** F-0686	説文 The seal-style form comprised 厷 "an elbow," which was used for the sound *yuu,* and "a bird" (隹). A showy masculine bird spreading its wings signified "father bird." The kanji 雄 means "male animal," and also "male (animal), brave, manly; outstanding man." <ナム隹>	雄 male (animal) [おす]; 雄々しい manly, valiant [おおしい]; 英雄 hero [えいゆう]; 雄大な grand, sublime, great [ゆうだいな]; 英雄伝 heroic legend [えいゆうでん]

	Meanings	Kun and On	Romaji	Bushu	Stroke Order and Number
SG-0952 離	to take leave, depart, leave, go out	はな-れる リ	hana-reru *ri*	隹	亠 文 卤 禸 离 离 離 離 19

離 **B** F-0673	説文 The seal-style form comprised 离, used for the sound *ri,* and 隹 "bird." *Setsumon* explained that it was the name of the Korean bush warbler. Another view explains that the left side 离 depicted a bird and a snake fighting, and that the bird was trying to move away from the snake. And yet another view holds that 离 was used for the sound *chi* to mean "birdlime," and that the character depicted a bird trying to remove itself from birdlime. The kanji 離 means "to take leave, depart, leave, go out." <离隹>	離れる to separate, become more distant [はなれる]; 離れ離れ separately, independently [はなればなれ]; 離島 isolated island [はなれじま, りとう]; 離職 leaving one's job [りしょく]; 別離 parting, separation [べつり]; 離別する to separate from, split up [りべつする]

	Meanings	Kun and On	Romaji	Bushu	Stroke Order and Number
SG-0953 推	to push forward, guess	お-す スイ	o-su *sui*	手	一寸扌扌 扌 扌 推 11

推 **B** F-0703	説文 The seal-style form comprised "an act done by hand" (扌), and 隹, which was used for the sound *sui* to mean "to push away" and "to guess." Thus, it signified "a hand pushing something away (or forward)," as well as "to guess." The kanji 推 means "to push forward, guess." <扌隹>	推す to push forward [おす]; 推し量る to make a conjecture, surmise [おしはかる]; 推薦する to recommend, endorse [すいせんする]; 推挙 recommendation [すいきょ]; 推進する to propel, promote [すいしんする]; 推理小説 mystery novel [すいりしょうせつ]; 推敲する to polish, revise [すいこうする]

	Meanings	Kun and On	Romaji	Bushu	Stroke Order and Number
SG-0954 雑	various, assorted, coarse, careless	ザツ・ゾウ	*zatsu, zoo*	隹	ノ 九 卆 刹 新 新 雑 14

雑 **B** F-0806	説文 1 旧字 2 1 and the kyuji 雜 (2) comprised 衣 **SG-1657** "clothing," 木 **SG-0608** "tree," and 隹 "bird," which was used for the sounds *zatsu* or *zoo* (from 集 *shuu*) to mean "to gather, collect." Together they signified clothes that were made of assorted fabrics in different colors. An assortment of mismatched things also gave the meaning "coarse, careless." The kanji 雑 means "various, assorted, coarse, careless." <九木隹>	雑な sundry, rough, coarse [ざつな]; 雑誌 magazine [ざっし]; 雑音 noise [ざつおん]; 雑然とした in confusion, in a jumble, messy [ざつぜんとした]; 雑巾 cleaning rag [ぞうきん]; 雑煮 soup containing mochi and other ingredients [ぞうに]; 雑炊 rice gruel [ぞうすい] // 雑魚 small fish [ざこ]; 雑魚寝する to sleep huddled together [ざこねする]

	Meanings	Kun and On	Romaji	Bushu	Stroke Order and Number
SG-0955 双	a pair of	ふた ソウ	huta *soo*	隹	フ ヌ ヌフ 双 4

双 **B** F-0978	説文 1 旧字 2 1 comprised "a pair of birds" and "a hand," signifying "a hand holding a pair of birds." In the shinji, the two 隹 in the kyuji (2) were dropped, and a second "hand (又 **SG-0084**) was added. The kanji 双 means "a pair of." <又又>	双子 twins [ふたご]; 双生児 twins [そうせいじ]; 無双の matchless, peerless [むそうの]

	Meanings	Kun and On	Romaji	Bushu	Stroke Order and Number
SG-0956 催	to urge, prompt, hold an event	もよお-す サイ	moyoo-su *sai*	人	催 13

催 **B** F-1032

説文

The seal-style form comprised "an act one does" (亻), and 崔 (comprised of 山 and 隹), which was used for the sound *sai* to mean "to urge, prompt." The kanji 催 means "to urge, prompt, hold an event." <亻山隹>

催す to hold an event [もよおす]; 催し物 event [もよおしもの]; 雨催い atmospheric sign of rain [あまもよい]; 開催 holding an event [かいさい]; 催涙弾 tear gas bomb, tear gas grenade [さいるいだん]; 催眠術 hypnotism [さいみんじゅつ]

	Meanings	Kun and On	Romaji	Bushu	Stroke Order and Number
SG-0957 雇	to employ, hire	やと-う コ	yato-u *ko*	隹	雇 12

雇 **C** F-1145

甲骨文1 1, 甲骨文2 2, 説文籀文 3, 説文 4, 説文或体 5

1 and 2 depicted "a bird" perched on "a door (of a cage)" 戸 **SG-1241**, or possibly with its leg caught in the door. 戸 was used for the sound *ko*. The sense of a bird being unable to fly away from the cage was applied to a person who was kept inside due to an obligation to work. The character is used to mean "to hire someone to work." In 3, the bird looked more like 4 for 鳥 **SG-0944**, whereas in 4 the bird took the simpler shape 隹. The kanji 雇 means "to employ, hire." <戸隹>

雇う to employ [やとう]; 日雇い day laborer [ひやとい]; 雇用主 employer [こようぬし]; 雇用者 employee [こようしゃ]; 解雇 dismissal, termination of employment [かいこ]; 雇用保険 unemployment insurance [こようほけん]; 有期雇用 fixed-term employment [ゆうきこよう]

	Meanings	Kun and On	Romaji	Bushu	Stroke Order and Number
SG-0958 維	a thick rope; to support, fasten	イ	*i*	糸	維 14

維 **C** F-1125

金文 1, 説文 2

1 and 2 comprised "skein of threads" (糸 **SG-1600**); 隹, which was used for the sound *sui* to mean "to tie down"; and (in 1) "a hand" (又 **SG-0084**). Together they signified "to hitch with a thick rope." A rope connected or fastened things. The kanji 維 means "a thick rope; to support, fasten." <糸隹>

維持する to support [いじする]; 明治維新 Meiji Restoration (in 1868) [めいじいしん]; 繊維 fiber, strand [せんい]; 繊維質 fiber, fibrous [せんいしつ]; 化学繊維 chemical fiber, manmade fiber [かがくせんい]

	Meanings	Kun and On	Romaji	Bushu	Stroke Order and Number
SG-0959 雅	elegance, grace, finesse	ガ	*ga*	隹	雅 13

雅 **C** F-1185

説文

The seal-style form comprised 牙 **SG-0926**, which was used for the sound *ga* to mean "a bird cawing," and 隹 "a bird." The kanji 雅 was borrowed to mean "elegance, grace, finesse." <牙隹>

優雅な elegant, exquisite [ゆうがな]; 典雅な refined, graceful [てんがな]; 雅楽 ceremonial music and dances of the Japanese imperial court [ががく]; 雅号 pen name, artist's pseudonym [がごう] // 雅やかな elegant, exquisite [みやびやかな]

	Meanings	Kun and On	Romaji	Bushu	Stroke Order and Number
SG-0960 携	to carry, transport, take along with	たずさ-える ケイ	tazusa-eru *kee*	手	携 13

携 **C** F-1256

説文 1, 正字 2

1 comprised 扌, bushu *tehen* "an act done by hand," and 雟 with 冏, used for the sound *kee* to mean "to carry." Together they signified "to transport by hand." The informal form 携 became the shinji, with 山 dropped and 冏 replaced by 乃. The kanji 携 means "to carry, transport, take along with." <扌隹乃>

携える to carry in one's hand, take someone along [たずさえる]; 携帯 carrying on one's person [けいたい]; 携帯電話 mobile phone, cell phone [けいたいでんわ]; 必携書 handbook, manual, indispensable book [ひっけいしょ]; 携行する to carry something with one [けいこうする]; 連携する to cooperate with, be aligned with [れんけいする]

	Meanings	Kun and On	Romaji	Bushu	Stroke Order and Number
SG-0961 顧	to look back, reflect; retrospect	かえり-みる コ	kaeri-miru *ko*	頁	顧 21

顧 **C** F-1272

説文

The seal-style form comprised 雇 **SG-0957**, used for the sound for *ko* to mean "to take turns," and 頁 "head." Together they signified "turning one's head back and forth." The kanji 顧 means "to look back, reflect; retrospect." <雇頁>

顧みる to look back, reflect on oneself, contemplate [かえりみる]; 回顧する to recollect, reminisce [かいこする]; 顧客 customer, client, patron [こきゃく]; ご愛顧 your patronage [ごあいこ]; 顧問 adviser, consultant [こもん]; 後顧の憂い to have no anxiety about the future [こうこのうれい]

SG-0962 奪	Meanings	*Kun* and *On*	Romaji	Bushu	Stroke Order and Number
	take (by force), snatch, engross; be absorbed	うば-う ダツ	uba-u *datsu*	大	奪 14

奪 **C** F-1281

金文 1 説文 2

1 comprised 小 **SG-1153** "small" and 隹 "a bird," inside the collar of clothing (衣 **SG-1657** split horizontally), with 又 "a hand" at the bottom. A hand trying not to lose a bird and keeping the bird for itself led to the meaning "to take (by force), snatch." When used in a passive construction, it also means "to be absorbed, be captivated." In 2, 衣 changed to 大 "a person," with 隹 and "a hand" (寸 in the kanji). The kanji 奪 means "to take (by force), snatch, engross; be absorbed." <大隹寸>

奪う to take by force, snatch, engross [うばꜜう]; 剥奪する to deprive of, divest of [はくだつする]; 略奪 to plunder, loot, pillage [りゃくだつ]; 奪還する to recover, recapture [だっかんする]

SG-0963 焦	Meanings	*Kun* and *On*	Romaji	Bushu	Stroke Order and Number
	to scorch, singe; hasty, impatient	こ-げる・あせ-る ショウ	koge-ru, ase-ru *shoo*	火	焦 12

焦 **C** F-1299

金文 1 説文 2 説文或体 3

1, 2, and 3 depicted "one or three birds" over "a fire." Roasting a bird over a fire meant "to scorch, singe." When used for a person, it meant "to pine, yearn, be dying for." The kanji 焦 means "to scorch, singe; hasty, impatient." <隹灬>

焦げる to scorch, get burned [こげꜜる]; 焦がす to burn, singe, be consumed with emotion [こがꜜす]; 待ち焦がれる to look forward to, anticipate [まちこがれꜜる]; 思い焦がれる to be ardently in love [おもいこがれꜜる]; 焦る to act hastily, be impatient [あせꜜる]; 焦点 focus [しょꜜうてん]; 焦燥感 feeling of impatience, irritability [しょうそꜜうかん]

SG-0964 誰	Meanings	Kun and On	Romaji	Bushu	Stroke Order and Number
	who	だれ	dare	言	誰 15

誰 **C** F-1297

金文 1 1 金文 2 2 説文 3

1, 2, and 3 comprised a tattooing needle over a mouth, which became 言 **SG-1364** "to say; word," and 隹, which was used for the sound *sui* to mean "to guess." Together they signified "asking who it is." The kanji 誰 means "who." <言隹>

誰 who [だꜜれ]; 誰か someone [だꜜれか]; 誰しも everyone [だꜜれしも]; 誰々 so-and-so [だꜜれだれ]; 誰彼となく anyone and everyone [だꜜれかれと・なꜜく]

SG-0965 唯	Meanings	*Kun* and *On*	Romaji	Bushu	Stroke Order and Number
	only, merely; yes	ユイ・イ	*yui, i*	口	唯 11

唯 **C** F-1346

甲骨文 1 金文 1 2 金文 2 3 説文 4

1 through 4 comprised 口 **SG-0031** "a mouth; to speak," and 隹, used for the sounds *yui*/*i* to mean "yes," together signifying "yes; affirmation." From being used to affirm particular items, it came to mean "this; only, merely." The kanji 唯 means "only, merely; yes." <口隹>

唯一の sole, only [ゆꜜいいつの]; 唯物論 materialism [ゆいぶつꜜろん]; 唯心論 spiritualism, idealism [ゆいしꜜんろん]; 唯我独尊 self-centeredness [ゆꜜいが・どくそん]; 唯々諾々として submissively, with no resistance [いꜜい・だくだくとして]

SG-0966 奮	Meanings	*Kun* and *On*	Romaji	Bushu	Stroke Order and Number
	to muster one's courage, be stirred up	ふる-う フン	huru-u *hun*	大	奮 16

奮 **C** F-1647

金文 1 説文 2

1 depicted "a bird in the rice paddies" (隹 with 田 **SG-1300**) inside "a collar, clothing" (衣). A collar suggested that there was "a heart" underneath. The character depicted a bird mustering the courage to fly away from the field. The top component became 大 "a person." The kanji 奮 means "to muster one's courage, be stirred up." <大隹田>

奮う to be enlivened, be spirited, rouse up [ふるう]; 興奮する to become excited [こうふんする]; 奮発する to exert oneself, spend money generously [ふんぱつする]; 発奮する to be inspired by, resolve anew [はっぷんする]; 奮戦する to fight furiously, fight heroically [ふんせんする]

SG-0967 擁	Meanings	*Kun* and *On*	Romaji	Bushu	Stroke Order and Number
	to embrace, take into one's arms, protect	ヨウ	*yoo*	手	擁 16

擁 **D** F-1760

金文 1 説文 2

1 had "flowing water" and "a bird" (隹) on top, but what the bottom component signified is not clear. 2 comprised "a hand" (扌) and 雝, used for the sound *yoo* to mean "to

擁護 protection, vindication [ようご]; 擁立する to back up, give support

	protect" (from "a bird protected by the moat surrounding a town). Together they signified "a hand embracing and protecting," like a surrounding moat. The kanji 擁 means "to embrace, take into one's arms, protect." <扌亠乡隹>	[ようり↴する]; 人権擁護 safeguarding human rights [じんけんよ↴うご]

SG-0968 隻	Meanings	Kun and On	Romaji	Bushu	Stroke Order and Number
	single; counter for boats	セキ	*seki*	隹	イイ'什什隹隻隻 10

隻 D F-1807	甲骨文 1, 金文1 2, 金文2 3, 金文3 4, 説文 5 — 1 through 5 comprised "a single bird held by the legs by a hand below," signifying "one, single" (in contrast to 雙 "two," the kyuji for 双 **SG-0955**). The character is used only as a counter for boats. The kanji 隻 means "single; counter for boats." <隹又>	一隻 one boat [いっせき]

SG-0969 准	Meanings	Kun and On	Romaji	Bushu	Stroke Order and Number
	to conform to the law, apply correspondingly	ジュン	*jun*	冫	冫ソ'ソ'ソ'冫'冫'准 10

准 D F-1861	No ancient form. The kanji 准, with 冫, bushu *nisui*, was considered to be an informal form of 準 **SG-0949** "standard," with the sound *jun*. In official government writing, it means "to conform to the law, apply correspondingly." <冫隹>	批准 ratification [ひじゅん]; 准看護士 practical nurse [じゅんかんご↴し]; 准教授 associate professor [じゅんきょ↴うじゅ]

SG-0970 礁	Meanings	Kun and On	Romaji	Bushu	Stroke Order and Number
	submerged rock, reef	ショウ	*shoo*	石	丆石石'石'石'石'碓礁 17

礁 D F-1956	No ancient form. The kanji comprises 石 **SG-1149** "rock," and 焦 **SG-0963** "to scorch; blackened," used for the sound *shoo,* together signifying "a black rock hidden underwater." The kanji 礁 means "submerged rock, reef." <石隹灬>	座礁する to hit a rock or reef, be stranded [ざしょうする]; サンゴ礁・珊瑚礁 coral reef [さんご↴しょう]

SG-0971 雌	Meanings	Kun and On	Romaji	Bushu	Stroke Order and Number
	female animal	め・めす シ	me, meru *shi*	隹	丨ト止止'此此'此'此'雌 14

雌 D F-2053	説文 — The seal-style form comprised 此, used for the sound *shi* to mean "female," and 隹 "bird." Together they signified "a mother bird." The kanji 雌 means "female animal." <此隹>	雌しべ pistil (of a flower) [め↴しべ]; 雌 female animal [めす↴]; 雌雄 male and female [し↴ゆう]; 雌伏する to bide one's time, lie low (awaiting a chance) [しふくする]

40c 蒦 "to grab firmly" [from a hand grabbing a crested bird]; *kaku* 護獲穫

SG-0972 護	Meanings	Kun and On	Romaji	Bushu	Stroke Order and Number
	to protect, defend, shelter	ゴ	*go*	言	言言'言'言'言'言'護護 20

護 B F-0644	説文 — The seal-style form comprised 言 **SG-1364** "word; to speak," and 蒦, used for the sound *go* to mean "a bird protected in one's hand." Together they signified "to speak up for, cover and protect what is inside." The kanji 護 means "to protect, defend, shelter." <言萑(艹隹)又>	保護する to protect [ほ↴ごする]; 動物愛護 protection of an animal [どうぶつあ↴いご]; 護身術 art of self-defense [ごし↴んじゅつ]; 過保護 overprotectiveness [かほ↴ご]; 護憲運動 movement to protect the Constitution [ごけんう↴んどう]; 護岸工事 embankment protection work [ごがんこ↴うじ]

SG-0973 獲	Meanings	Kun and On	Romaji	Bushu	Stroke Order and Number
	to obtain, seize, catch	え-る カク	e-ru *kaku*	犬	ノ犭犭犭'犭'犭'犭'獲獲 16

獲 C F-1305	甲骨文 1, 金文 2, 説文 3 — 1 and 2 depicted "a hand grabbing a bird." 3 comprised 犭, bushu *kemonohen* "a hunting dog," and 萑 "a crested bird" caught by 又 "a hand," used for the sound *kaku*. The character originally signified "a hunting dog retrieving a bird or animal that had been caught," and came to mean "to obtain, seize" in general. The kanji 獲 means "to obtain, seize, catch." <犭萑又>	獲る to catch, obtain [え↴る]; 獲物 game [えもの]; 獲得する to acquire, gain, secure [かくとくする]; 乱獲 overfishing, overhunting [らんかく]

SG-0974 穫	Meanings	Kun and On	Romaji	Bushu	Stroke Order and Number
	to harvest (crops)	カク	kaku	禾	二千禾禾' 秆 秤 秤 穫 穫 18

穫 **D** F-1869

説文

The seal-style form comprised 禾, bushu *nogihen* "rice plant," and 蒦 "a bird grabbed by a hand," for the sound *kaku.* It pertained to "harvesting grains and produce," in contrast to catching an animal (which is 獲 **SG-0973** "to catch in hunting," with 犭). The kanji 穫 means "to harvest (crops)." <禾雈又>

収穫 harvest [しゅうかく]; 収穫期 harvest season [しゅうかくき]

40d 雈 (雚) [from a crested bird with large eyes]; *kan/ken* 権観勧歓

SG-0975 権	Meanings	Kun and On	Romaji	Bushu	Stroke Order and Number
	authority, right, controlling power	ケン・ゴン	ken, gon	木	十木术 杵 杵 桙 椊 権 15

権 **A** F-0249

説文 1 旧字 2

1 and 2 comprised 木 **SG-0608** "a tree," and 雚, used for the sound *ken.* Originally the name of a specific tree, this character came to mean "weight," in the sense of "striking a balance," and thus "standard, criterion." A criterion setter holds "authority, power." With the right side reduced to 雈, the kanji 権 means "authority, right, controlling power." <木 雈>

権利 right, claim, privilege [けんり]; 主権 sovereignty [しゅけん]; 権力 authority, power [けんりょく]; 権益 rights and interests [けんえき]; 実権 real power [じっけん]; 拒否権 veto [きょひけん]; 権現 an incarnation of the Buddha [ごんげん]; 権化 incarnation, personification [ごんげ]

SG-0976 観	Meanings	Kun and On	Romaji	Bushu	Stroke Order and Number
	to look over, look around, look carefully	カン	kan	見	𠂉 午 牟 奔 奞 𨾴 観 18

観 **A** F-0503

甲骨文 1 金文1 2 金文2 3 説文 4 旧字 5

1 through 3 depicted a big-eyed bird (to mean "to look around"), and had the sound *kan.* In 4, 見 **SG-0460** was added to 雚, and the character meant "to look at something carefully, look around." With 雚 simplified to 雈 in the shinji, the kanji 観 means "to look over, look around, look carefully." <雈 見>

観測する to observe, survey, anticipate [かんそくする]; 主観的な subjective [しゅかんてきな]; 観客 spectator [かんきゃく]; 観光地 sightseeing resort, tourist site [かんこうち]; 観念的な ideological, abstract [かんねんてきな]; 価値観 sense of value [かちかん]; 先入観 preconception [せんにゅうかん]

SG-0977 勧	Meanings	Kun and On	Romaji	Bushu	Stroke Order and Number
	to recommend, encourage, suggest	すす-める カン	susu-meru kan	力	𠂉 午 牟 奔 雈 勧 勧 13

勧 **B** F-1048

説文 1 旧字 2

The seal-style form (1) comprised 雚, which was used for the sound *kan*, and 力 "a plow, hard work." Originally, it signified "to encourage or urge to do fieldwork." The kanji 勧 means "to recommend, encourage, suggest." <雈 力>

勧める to recommend, advise, offer [すすめる]; 勧告 piece of advice, advisory opinion [かんこく]; 勧善懲悪劇 a play with a moral [かんぜんちょうあくげき]

SG-0978 歓	Meanings	Kun and On	Romaji	Bushu	Stroke Order and Number
	to fête, be pleased, rejoice	カン	kan	欠	𠂉 午 牟 奔 雈 雈' 歓 15

歓 **C** F-1080

説文 1 旧字 2

1 comprised 雚, used for the sound *kan*, and 欠 **SG-0431**, "a person with his mouth open wide; to voice in a lively manner." Together they signified "to rejoice, celebrate." The kanji 歓 means "to fête, be pleased, rejoice." <雈欠>

歓喜 delight [かんき]; 歓迎 reception, welcome [かんげい]; 歓声を上げる to shout for joy, let out a cheer [かんせいをあげる]; 歓楽街 entertainment district [かんらくがい]; 歓待する to treat hospitably, give a hearty welcome [かんたいする]

40e 隺 *kaku* 確鶴

	Meanings	Kun and On	Romaji	Bushu	Stroke Order and Number
SG-0979 確	to ascertain; certain, sure	たし-かめる カク	tashi-kameru *kaku*	石	確 15

確 **A** F-0393

No ancient form. The kanji 確 comprises 石 **SG-1149** "rock," for "something hard and solid" and 隺, which was used for the sound *kaku* to mean "something hard." The kanji 確 means "to ascertain; certain, sure." <石隺>

確かめる to authenticate, ascertain [たしかめる]; 確か if my memory serves me correctly [たしか]; 確かな infallible, reliable, secure [たしかな]; 正確な accurate, precise [せいかくな]; 確実に surely [かくじつに]; 明確な clear and accurate, definite [めいかくな]; 確信する to be convinced, have a firm belief [かくしんする]; 確執 discord, strife, feuding [かくしつ]

	Meanings	Kun and On	Romaji	Bushu	Stroke Order and Number
SG-0980 鶴	crane	つる	tsuru	鳥	鶴 21

鶴 **C** F-1338

説文

The seal-style form of the kanji 鶴 comprised 隺 "a bird" with something on top (perhaps a red crest), used for the sound *kaku,* and 鳥 **SG-0944**, another "bird," together signifying a red-crowned crane. The kanji 鶴 means "crane." <隺鳥>

鶴 crane [つる]; 折り鶴 origami crane [おりづる]; 千羽鶴 a thousand origami cranes [せんばづる]; 鶴の一声 the voice of authority [つるのひとこえ]

40f 飞 "to fly" 飛迅

	Meanings	Kun and On	Romaji	Bushu	Stroke Order and Number
SG-0981 飛	to fly	と-ぶ ヒ	to-bu *hi*	飛	飛 9

飛 **B** F-0573

説文

The seal-style form of the kanji 飛 was a pictograph of "a bird flying with its wings spread." The kanji 飛 means "to fly." <飞亻飞丨>

飛ぶ to fly [とぶ]; ひとっ飛び one jump [ひとっとび]; 飛び抜ける by far the best [とびぬける]; 飛び込み diving [とびこみ]; 飛び入り taking part on the spur of the moment [とびいり]; 飛び切りいい extremely good, super [とびきりいい]; 飛行機 airplane, aircraft [ひこうき]

	Meanings	Kun and On	Romaji	Bushu	Stroke Order and Number
SG-0982 迅	very fast	ジン	*jin*	辵	迅 6

迅 **D** F-1943

篆文 1, 説文 2

1 comprised 辵 (⻌) "to move forward," and 卂, a reduced shape of the kanji 飛 **SG-0981** "to fly with wings," which was used for the sound *jin.* Moving fast like a flying bird meant "very fast." The kanji 迅 means "very fast." <卂⻌>

迅速に swiftly, expeditiously [じんそくに]

40g 羽羽 "wings" 羽習翌翼扇翁

	Meanings	Kun and On	Romaji	Bushu	Stroke Order and Number
SG-0983 羽	feather, quill, wings	は・はね ウ	ha, hane *u*	羽	羽 6

羽 **B** F-0609

甲骨文 1, 説文 2, 旧字 3

1 and 2 depicted a pair of wings with feathers. The kanji 羽 means "feather, quill, wings." <羽>

羽 feather, plume, wing [はね]; 羽ばたく to flap the wings, play an active part in society [はばたく]; 白羽の矢が立つ to be singled out (for a position) [しらはのやが・たつ]; 羽根 blade, sail wing [はね]; 羽二重 *habutae*-silk, lightweight shimmering silk for kimono lining [はぶたえ, はぶたい]; 切羽詰まる to be absolutely desperate [せっぱ・つまる]; 羽毛布団 down comforter, eiderdown [うもうぶとん]

	Meanings	Kun and On	Romaji	Bushu	Stroke Order and Number
SG-0984 習	to learn, practice, get a lesson	なら-う シュウ	nara-u *shuu*	羽	習 11

習 **B** F-0570

甲骨文 1, 説文 2

1 and 2 comprised a pair of wings (羽) and 曰 "to say repeatedly." A young bird repeatedly flapping its wings lent the meaning "to learn (by repetition), practice." Another view explains that the bottom was 自 "self," which was used for the sound *shuu*, and which later changed to 白. The kanji 習 means "to learn, practice, get a lesson." <羽白>

習う to learn, be taught, practice [ならう]; 見習い apprenticeship, trainee [みならい]; 習い事 enrichment lessons [ならいごと]; 学習 learning, study [がくしゅう]; 習得 learning, acquisition [しゅうとく]; 習性 habit, behavior [しゅうせい]; 習字 calligraphy practice [しゅうじ]

	Meanings	Kun and On	Romaji	Bushu	Stroke Order and Number
SG-0985 翌	next, following	ヨク	*yoku*	羽	翌 11

翌 **B** F-0969

甲骨文1 1, 甲骨文2 2, 甲骨文3 3, 金文 4, 説文 5

1 through 4 depicted "an insect folding its wings to rest." 2 and 4 added "a person standing on the ground," used for the sound *yoku* (from 立 *ritsu*), and 3 and 4 added 日 "the sun." A person ending their fieldwork to rest up for the next day is like "an insect folding its wings (羽) for the night." The kanji 翌 means "next, following." <羽立>

翌日 following day [よくじつ]; 翌年 following year [よくねん]; 翌朝 following morning [よくあさ, よくちょう]; 翌々年 year after next, two years later [よくよくねん]

	Meanings	Kun and On	Romaji	Bushu	Stroke Order and Number
SG-0986 翼	wing	つばさ ヨク	tsubasa *yoku*	羽	翼 17

翼 **B** F-1044

金文1 1, 金文2 2, 説文篆文 3, 説文 4

1 comprised "a pair of wings," "a mask worn by a votive dancer," and "a pair of hands offering a prayer box." 2, 3, and 4 showed a fuller picture of "to fly" (飛 **SG-0981**) or "wings" (羽 **SG-0983**), and 異 **SG-0355**, which was used for the sound *yoku*. Together they signified "a wing." The kanji 翼 means "wing." <羽 田共>

翼 wing [つばさ]; 比翼 wing [ひよく]

	Meanings	Kun and On	Romaji	Bushu	Stroke Order and Number
SG-0987 扇	to fan; fan, fan shape	おうぎ セン	oogi *sen*	戸	扇 10

扇 **D** F-1676

説文

The seal-style form comprised "a door" (戸 **SG-1241**) that flapped, and "wings" (羽 **SG-0983**) that also flapped, together signifying something that moves in a flapping motion like a fan. The kanji 扇 means "to fan; fan, fan shape." <戸羽>

扇 fan, folding fan [おおぎ]; 扇子 folding fan [せんす]; 扇動する to instigate [せんどうする]; 換気扇 ventilation fan [かんきせん]; 扇風機 electric fan [せんぷうき] // 団扇 fan [うちわ]; 左団扇 living in comfort [ひだりうちわ]

	Meanings	Kun and On	Romaji	Bushu	Stroke Order and Number
SG-0988 翁	(venerable) aged man	オウ	*oo*	羽	翁 10

翁 **D** F-2048

説文

The seal-style form comprised 公 **SG-1321**, which was used for the sound *oo* (from *koo*), and 羽 "wings," together signifying "a plume on the head of a bird." The kanji 翁 was borrowed to mean "(venerable) aged man." <公羽>

翁 aged man [おきな] (archaic)

40h 翟 "to leap, flap" [from a bird flapping its wings trying to take off]; *yoku/yoo* 曜躍濯 翟

	Meanings	Kun and On	Romaji	Bushu	Stroke Order and Number
SG-0989 曜	day of the week	ヨウ	*yoo*	日	曜 18

曜 **B** F-0763

No ancient form. The kanji 曜 comprised 日 **SG-1045** "the sun," and 翟 "bright," used for the sound *yoo*, together signifying "the sun beaming very brightly." The kanji 曜 is used for "day of the week." <日 羽隹>

何曜日 what day of the week? [なんようび]; 曜日 day of the week [ようび]; 月曜日 Monday [げつようび]; 火曜日 Tuesday [かようび]

	Meanings	Kun and On	Romaji	Bushu	Stroke Order and Number
SG-0990 躍	to jump, bound, leap	おど-る ヤク	odo-ru *yaku*	足	躍 21

躍 **C** F-1366

説文

The seal-style form comprised 足 **SG-0227** "leg" (⻊, bushu *ashihen*), and 翟, from "a bird flapping its wings to take off," used for the sound *yaku*. Together they signified "to leap." The kanji 躍 means "jump, bound, leap." <⻊ 翟>

躍る to leap up, skip [おどる]; 小躍りする to jump for joy [こおどりする]; 活躍する to play an important role [かつやくする]; 飛躍する to take a large step, make a jump in logic [ひやくする]; 躍動する to move in a lively manner, throb [やくどうする]; 暗躍する to operate behind the scenes [あんやくする]; 躍起になる to get worked up over [やっきになる]

	Meanings	Kun and On	Romaji	Bushu	Stroke Order and Number
SG-0991 濯	to wash, rinse out	タク	*taku*	水	濯 17

濯 **D** F-2072

金文 1, 説文 2

1 comprised "water" (氵), and "a pair of wings" above "a bird" (翟), which was used for the sound *taku* to mean "a bird flapping its wings trying to take off." Making a flapping motion in water meant "to wash, rinse." The kanji 濯 means "to wash, rinse out." <氵 翟 >

洗濯 washing, laundering [せんたく]; 洗濯機 washing machine [せんたくき, せんたっき]

40i 非 "against; not"; *hi/hai* 非悲輩俳排扉

	Meanings	Kun and On	Romaji	Bushu	Stroke Order and Number
SG-0992 非	what is not, not good, against	ヒ	*hi*	非	8

非 **A** F-0464

金文1 金文2 説文3

1, 2, and 3 depicted "the wings of a bird in flight." A bird's wings are always on opposite sides, never meeting, which gave the meaning "against, not." Another explanation is that two flapping wings gave the meaning "to turn against each other." The kanji 非 means "what is not, not good, against." <非>

非常な extraordinary, uncommon [ひじょうな]; 非常口 emergency exit [ひじょうぐち, ひじょうぐち]; 是非 by some means or other, by all means [ぜひ], rights and wrongs [ぜひ]; 是非を問う to call someone's conduct into question [ぜひをとう]; 非行 delinquency, misconduct [ひこう]; 非力な helpless, powerless [ひりょくな]; 非情さ unfeelingness, cold-heartedness, cruelty [ひじょうさ]

	Meanings	Kun and On	Romaji	Bushu	Stroke Order and Number
SG-0993 悲	grief; sad, sorrowful, earnest	かな-しい ヒ	kana-shii *hi*	心	12

悲 **B** F-0919

説文

The seal-style form comprised 非 **SG-0992** "two parts separated," used for the sound *hi*, and 心 **SG-0187** "a heart." Together they signified emotions such as "sadness and sorrow that tear one's heart apart." The kanji 悲 means "grief; sad, sorrowful, earnest." <非心>

悲しい sad [かなしい]; 悲しみ sorrow, grief [かなしみ]; 悲観的な pessimistic [ひかんてきな]; 悲鳴 scream [ひめい]; 悲喜こもごも having mingled feelings of joy and sorrow [ひきこもごも or こもごも]; 悲壮な tragic but brave, unflinching [ひそうな]; 悲願 long-felt earnest wish [ひがん]

	Meanings	Kun and On	Romaji	Bushu	Stroke Order and Number
SG-0994 輩	fellow, companion	ハイ	*hai*	車	15

輩 **C** F-1380

説文

The seal-style form comprised 非 **SG-0992**, which was used for the sound *hai* to mean "many things lined up," and 車 **SG-1578** "military vehicle." Together they signified "military vehicles forming a line." The meaning was applied to people who belonged to the same group. The kanji 輩 means "fellow, companion." <非車>

後輩 one's junior [こうはい]; 先輩 one's senior [せんぱい]; 輩出する to appear one after another, be produced in large numbers [はいしゅつする]; 同輩 one's equal, one's peer [どうはい]

	Meanings	Kun and On	Romaji	Bushu	Stroke Order and Number
SG-0995 俳	playful; jester, *haiku* poem	ハイ	*hai*	人	10

俳 **C** F-1428

説文

The seal-style form comprised 亻 "a person, an act that one does," and 非, which was used for the sound *hi* to mean "two opposites of each other." Together they signified two people jesting in a playful act. The kanji 俳 means "playful; jester." This kanji is also used for *haiku*, a seventeen-syllable poem. <亻非>

俳句 *haiku*, a Japanese poem having seventeen syllables in a five-seven-five syllabic pattern [はいく]; 俳諧 playful linked verse [はいかい]

	Meanings	Kun and On	Romaji	Bushu	Stroke Order and Number
SG-0996 排	to drive out, exclude, oust, reject	ハイ	*hai*	手	11

排 **C** F-1429

説文

The seal-style form comprised 扌 "an act done by hand," and 非, which was used for the sound *hai* to mean "to push." A hand pushing something to the other side meant "to reject, expel." The kanji 排 means "to drive out, exclude, oust, reject." <扌非>

排気 exhaust, exhaustion [はいき]; 排他的な exclusive, clannish [はいたてきな]; 排除する to eliminate, exclude [はいじょする]; 排泄 elimination, excretion [はいせつ]; 排気量 emission [はいきりょう]; 排便 to empty the bowels [はいべん]

	Meanings	Kun and On	Romaji	Bushu	Stroke Order and Number
SG-0997 扉	door, door leaf, front page of a book	とびら ヒ	tobira *hi*	戸	12

扉 **C** F-1500

説文

The seal-style form comprised 戸 **SG-1241** "door," and 非 "a pair of wings of a bird," used for the sound *hi*. Together they signified "doors that open up on two sides." The character also means "the front page of a book." The kanji 扉 means "door, door leaf, front page of a book." <戸非>

扉 door, door flap, title page [とびら]; 回転扉 pivoted door [かいてんとびら]; 門扉 gate [もんぴ]

41 Insect, animal paw, carcass

41a 虫 "insect, worm" 虫独虹蛇蛍濁蚊蚕

	Meanings	Kun and On	Romaji	Bushu	Stroke Order and Number
SG-0998 虫	worm, insect	むし チュウ	mushi *chuu*	虫	丶口口中虫虫 6

虫 **B** F-0789

三体石経 1, 説文 2, 旧字 3, 甲骨文 4, 金文 5, 説文 6

1 and 2 depicted three worms and had the sound *chuu*. The shinji 虫 was not reduction from 3, but was taken from another kanji that originally meant "snake, serpent" (4, 5, and 6). The kanji 虫 means "worm, insect." <虫>

虫 insect, bug, person devoted to one thing [むし]; 虫食い damage done by worms, holes [むしくい]; 虫歯 decayed tooth, cavity [むしば]; 毛虫 hairy caterpillar [けむし]; 虫除け insect repellent, mothball [むしよけ]; 寄生虫 parasite [きせいちゅう]

	Meanings	Kun and On	Romaji	Bushu	Stroke Order and Number
SG-0999 独	alone, single; Germany	ひと-り ドク	hito-ri *doku*	犬	ノ犭犭犭犭𤜣狆独独 9

独 **B** F-0534

説文 1, 旧字 2

1 comprised "dog, animal" (犭), and 蜀 "a single animal," used for the sound *doku*. A lone dog or other lone animal lives in solitude, not in a pack, thus giving the meaning "alone, single." 蜀 was replaced by 虫 in the shinji. The sound *doku* is also used for Germany (from the old word 独逸 *doitsu* ドイツ, from "Deutschland"). The kanji 独 means "alone, single; Germany." <犭虫>

独り only oneself, by oneself [ひとり]; 独り者 single person [ひとりもの]; 独り合点する to come to a hasty conclusion [ひとりがてんする]; 独り立ちする become independent [ひとりだちする]; 独立 independence [どくりつ]; 独身 unmarried [どくしん]; 独語 German language [どくご, ドイツご]

	Meanings	Kun and On	Romaji	Bushu	Stroke Order and Number
SG-1000 虹	rainbow	にじ	niji	虫	ㄇ口中虫虫虫虹虹 9

虹 **C** F-1534

甲骨文 1, 説文籀文 2, 説文 3

1 was "a large, dragon-like mythical serpent" in the sky. 2 comprised "mythical serpent" (虫), and "lightning," here pertaining to light in the sky. 工 in 3, which was used for the sound *koo*, signified an arc. A large, arc-shaped mythical serpent in the sky was "a rainbow." The kanji 虹 means "rainbow." <虫工>

虹 rainbow [にじ]; 虹色 spectral colors, iridescence [にじいろ]

	Meanings	Kun and On	Romaji	Bushu	Stroke Order and Number
SG-1001 蛇	snake, serpent	へび ジャ・ダ	hebi *ja, da*	虫	口中虫虫'虫'虫'虫'蛇 11

蛇 **D** F-1734

甲骨文1 1, 甲骨文2 2, 金文1 3, 金文2 4, 説文 5, 説文或体 6

1 through 5 depicted "a large-headed snake" and had the sounds *ja*/*da*. Because 5 came to be identified with the meaning "person; other" (due to being used as the right-side component in 他 SG-1009) 虫 SG-0998 was added in 6 to distinguish the original meaning, "snake." The kanji 蛇 means "snake, serpent." <虫它>

蛇 snake, serpent [へび]; 大蛇 large snake, serpent [だいじゃ]; 蛇口 faucet, tap [じゃぐち]; 蛇腹 rickrack [じゃばら]; 蛇の目傘 oiled paper umbrella (with a bull's-eye pattern) [じゃのめがさ]; 蛇行する to meander [だこうする]; 蛇足 useless addition [だそく]

	Meanings	Kun and On	Romaji	Bushu	Stroke Order and Number
SG-1002 蛍	firefly	ほたる ケイ	hotaru *kee*	虫	丶丷𭕄屶屶蛍蛍 11

蛍 **D** F-1783

旧字

No ancient form. The top of the kyuji 螢 came from two flickering lights on a torch stand, as in the kanji 栄 (榮) SG-1185, and was used for the sound *kee* (from *ee*). Sparkling fires on a flaming torch in the night air looked similar to fireflies at night. The kanji 蛍 means "firefly." <𭕄虫>

蛍 firefly, lightning bug [ほたる]; 蛍光灯 fluorescent light [けいこうとう]; 蛍光色 fluorescent color [けいこうしょく]; 蛍光塗料 fluorescent paint [けいこうとりょう]

	Meanings	Kun and On	Romaji	Bushu	Stroke Order and Number
SG-1003 濁	to become muddy, be blurred	にご-る ダク	nigo-ru *daku*	水	氵氵ワ氵罒氵罒泻泻濁濁濁 16

濁 **D** F-1820

説文

The seal-style form comprised "flowing water" (氵), and 蜀, which was used for the sound *daku* and was the name of a particular muddy river. The kanji 濁 means "to become muddy, be blurred." <氵蜀(罒勹虫>

濁る to become muddy, be blurred [にごる]; 混濁する to get cloudy or muddy [こんだくする]; 濁音 a syllable with a voiced consonant [だくおん]; 濁流 muddy stream, murky water [だくりゅう]

SG-1004 蚊	Meanings	Kun and On	Romaji	Bushu	Stroke Order and Number
	mosquito	か	ka	虫	ロ中虫虫'虻蚊蚊 10

蚊 **D** F-1974	 篆文 蚊	The seal-style form comprised 虫 **SG-0998**, and 文 **SG-0318**, which was used for the sound *bun* to mimic the sound of a flying mosquito. The kanji 蚊 means "mosquito." <虫文>	蚊 mosquito [か]; 蚊取り線香 mosquito coil [かとりせ⁊んこう]; 蚊帳 mosquito net [かや]

SG-1005 蚕	Meanings	Kun and On	Romaji	Bushu	Stroke Order and Number
	silkworm	かいこ サン	kaiko *san*	虫	一二天吞吞蚕蚕 10

蚕 **D** F-2139	 甲骨文 1 説文 2 蠶 旧字 3 蚕	1 depicted "a silkworm wrapped in its own filaments." 2 and the kyuji 蠶 (3) comprised 朁, which was used for the sound *san*, and two "silkworms," together signifying "silkworms." In the shinji, the top was replaced with 天 and the bottom became a single 虫. The kanji 蚕 means "silkworm." <天虫>	蚕 silkworm [か⁊いこ]; 養蚕 silkworm cultivation [ようさん]

41b 昆 *kon* and 黽 *joo* 混昆・縄 

SG-1006 混	Meanings	Kun and On	Romaji	Bushu	Stroke Order and Number
	to mix, combine, mingle, join	ま-じる・こ-む コン	ma-jiru, ko-mu *kon*	水	氵氵沪浧混混混 11

混 **B** F-0995	 説文 混	The seal-style form comprised "flowing water" (氵), and 昆, used for *kon*, an onomatopoeic sound for water swirling. Swirling water mixes things up. The kanji 混 means "to mix, combine, mingle, join." <氵昆 (日比)>	混じる to mix, mingle, combine [まじ⁊る]; 混む to be crowded, be congested [こ⁊む]; 混み合う to be thronged, be jammed [こみあう, こみあ⁊う]; 混乱 chaos, confusion [こんらん]; 混雑 crowding, congestion, heavy traffic [こ⁊んざつ]; 混迷 turmoil [こんめい]

SG-1007 昆	Meanings	Kun and On	Romaji	Bushu	Stroke Order and Number
	insect	コン	*kon*	日	丨ロ日昆昆昆 8

昆 **D** F-1792	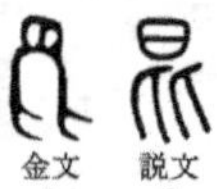 金文 1 説文 2 昆	1 was an image of "an insect with the head and legs." 2 became a combination of 日, and the shape of two people facing to the right (比 **SG-0390**). The kanji 昆 means "insect." <日比>	昆虫 insect [こんちゅう], 昆布 kelp [こ⁊んぶ, こ⁊ぶ]; 塩昆布 salty tangle kelp [しおこ⁊んぶ]

縄 "rope"

SG-1008 縄	Meanings	Kun and On	Romaji	Bushu	Stroke Order and Number
	rope, cord	なわ ジョウ	nawa *joo*	糸	幺糸糸紹縄縄縄 15

縄 **B** F-1043	 説文 1 繩 旧字 2 縄	1 and 2 comprised 糸 **SG-1600** "a skein of thread," and 黽, which was used for the sound *joo* to mean "a twisted thing." Twisting threads or yarn would make "a rope." 黽 in the kyuji 繩 was slightly reduced to 黾 in the shinji 縄. The kanji 縄 means "rope, cord." <糸𠮷乚>	縄 rope [なわ⁊]; 縄張り one's sphere of influence, turf [なわばり]; 一筋縄では行かない ordinary means would not work [ひとすじなわ⁊では・いかない]; しめ縄 (注連縄; 〆縄) sacred straw festoon in a Shinto shrine or household altar [しめなわ]; 縄文時代 *Jomon* prehistoric era in Japan [じょうもんじ⁊だい]

41c 也 "a flat area" [from a large-headed snake or scorpion]; *ta* 他地池・万 

SG-1009 他	Meanings	Kun and On	Romaji	Bushu	Stroke Order and Number
	others, other people; other	ほか タ	hoka *ta*	人	亻仂他他 5

他 **A** F-0355	 金文1 1 金文2 2 説文 3 他	1 and 2 depicted "a large-headed snake" that had the sound *ta*. In 3, 亻 "a person" was added to mean "other person." The kanji 他 means "others, other people; other." <亻也>	他でもない the fact of the matter, nothing but this [ほかで⁊もない]; 他ならない none other than, nothing but [ほかなら⁊ない]; その他 the others, the rest [その⁊た, その⁊ほか]; 他人 other people, an unrelated person, outsider [たにん]; 他社 other companies [た⁊しゃ]; 自他共に both oneself and others [じ⁊た・ともに]

	Meanings	Kun and On	Romaji	Bushu	Stroke Order and Number
SG-1010 地	ground, soil, place, the Earth	チ・ジ	*chi, ji*	土	一十土圴坤地 6

地 **A** F-0036

金文 1 中山王器 2 説文籀文 3 説文 4

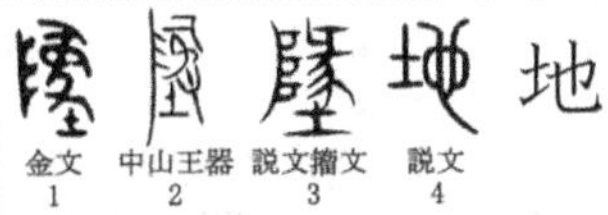

The earlier ancient forms for "ground" look very different from the kanji. 1, 2, and 3 comprised "mountains, a ladder" (阝) and "a heavy, stocky pig falling to the ground (土 **SG-0363**) from a high place." Together they signified where the pig landed, "the ground." But the character was later taken to mean "to fall from a high place, at last" (墜 **SG-0849**). For the original meaning, the new character in 4 was created by combining 土 "ground" and 也, used for the sound *chi,* from "a large serpent, stretched out and meandering." Together they signified "land that stretched wide, the Earth." The kanji 地 means "ground, soil, place, the Earth." <土也>

地方 locality, area, countryside [ちほう]; 地下 underground, subsurface [ちか]; 地中 in the ground [ちちゅう]; 地上 terrestrial, on the ground [ちじょう]; 私有地 private land [しゆうち]; 地面 surface of the land, the ground [じめん]; 地の文 narrative (as opposed to dialogue) [じのぶん]; 地声 one's natural voice [じごえ]

	Meanings	Kun and On	Romaji	Bushu	Stroke Order and Number
SG-1011 池	pond, reservoir	いけ チ	ike *chi*	水	氵汁汁池 6

池 **B** F-0589

金文 1 1 金文 2 2 説文 3

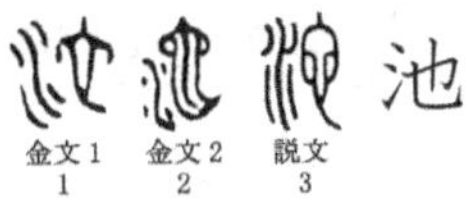

1 and 2 comprised "water" (氵), and 也, used for the sound *chi* to mean "land." Together they suggested "a pool of water that spreads flat on the land," and meant "a pond or a water reservoir." The kanji 池 means "pond, reservoir." <氵也>

池 pond [いけ]; 溜め池 irrigation pond [ためいけ]; 貯水池 water reservoir [ちょすいち]; 電池 battery [でんち]; 乾電池 dry cell battery [かんでんち]

万 "ten thousand"

	Meanings	Kun and On	Romaji	Bushu	Stroke Order and Number
SG-1012 万	ten thousand	マン・バン	*man, ban*	艸	一フ万 3

万 **A** F-0064

甲骨文 1 金文 1 2 金文 2 3 説文 4 旧字 5 漢金文

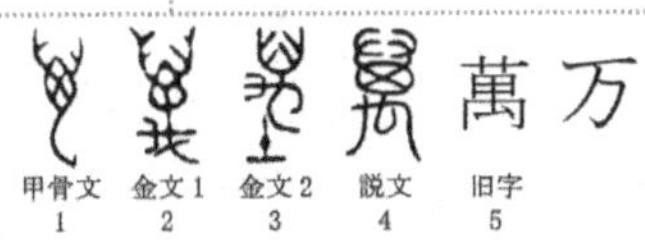

1 through 4 depicted "a scorpion" or a scorpion-like animal, and had the sound *man*, meaning "ten thousand." The kyuji 萬 (5) reflected 4. The shinji 万 was an old variant of a Buddhist symbol that meant "happiness," and also had the sound *man*. (A late bronzeware-style form is shown on the top right.) The kanji 万 means "ten thousand."

一万 ten thousand [いちまん]; 一万円札 ten-thousand-yen note [いちまんえんさつ]; 万一 emergency, a rare possibility [まんいち]; 万全を期す to make absolutely sure [ばんぜんをきす]; 万感こもる a thousand emotions throng one's heart [ばんかんこもる]; 万人 all people [ばんにん]

41d 禺 [from various proposed origins]; *guu* 遇隅偶愚

	Meanings	Kun and On	Romaji	Bushu	Stroke Order and Number
SG-1013 遇	to meet by chance, treat someone (kindly)	グウ	*guu*	辵	口日月禺禺`禺湡遇 12

遇 **C** F-1411

金文 1 説文 2

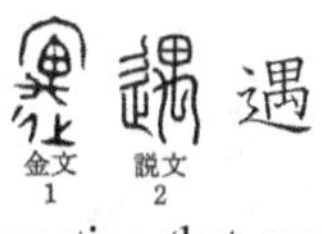

1 and 2 comprised 禺, used for the sound *guu* to mean "to meet unexpectedly," and "a crossroads" with "a footprint" (辵, 辶 "to move forward"). Together they signified "a meeting that occurred while moving forward on a road." One treated a chance meeting with kindness, and thus the meaning became "to treat (kindly), look after." The kanji 遇 means "to meet by chance, treat someone (kindly)." <禺辶>

遇する to treat, handle, look after [ぐうする]; 待遇 treatment, dealing, reception, salary [たいぐう]; 境遇 one's situation or circumstances [きょうぐう]; 冷遇する to treat coldly, be inhospitable [れいぐうする]; 不遇な (or の) ill-fated, unrecognized [ふぐうな]; 千載一遇のチャンス rare opportunity, chance of a lifetime [せんざいいちぐうのチャンス]

	Meanings	Kun and On	Romaji	Bushu	Stroke Order and Number
SG-1014 隅	corner, nook	すみ グウ	sumi *guu*	阜	口日月禺禺`禺湡遇 12

隅 **C** F-1464

金文 1 説文 2

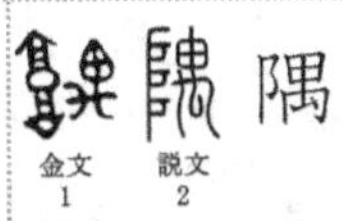

1 comprised "rampart towers," which stood on the corners of a fortress wall, and 禺, used for the sound *guu*. Together they signified "a corner." In 2, the towers were replaced by 阝, bushu *kozatohen*, "a tall wall," from the high dirt wall of a rampart. The kanji 隅 means "corner, nook." <阝禺>

隅 corner, nook [すみ]; 隅っこ nook, recess [すみっこ]; 片隅 corner [かたすみ]; 隅々まで every nook and cranny [すみずみまで, すみずみまで]; 一隅に in one corner, in a nook [いちぐうに]

	Meanings	*Kun* and *On*	Romaji	Bushu	Stroke Order and Number
SG-1015 偶	duplicate, idol, spouse, even number; unexpectedly	グウ	*guu*	人	亻 仴 仴 偶 偶 偶 偶 11

偶 **C** F-1469

金文 1 説文 2

1 and 2 comprised 亻 "a person," and 禺, used for the sound *guu* to mean "duplication." One view holds that 禺 depicted a foolish monkey, an animal that mimics a human and thus "duplicates" them. "A statue or idol" is also a "duplicate" of a person (亻). One's counterpart or "duplicate" in marriage was a "spouse." The original plus its duplicate produce an "even number." 禺 also had the meaning "to meet by chance," as in the kanji 遇 **SG-1013**, and so 偶 also meant "coincidence; unexpectedly." The kanji 偶 means "duplicate, idol, spouse, even number; unexpectedly" <亻 禺>

偶像 statue, idol [ぐうぞう]; 偶像化 idolization [ぐうぞうか]; 偶然 coincidence, fortuitous circumstance [ぐうぜん]; 偶数 even number [ぐうすう]; 配偶者 spouse [はいぐうしゃ]

	Meanings	*Kun* and *On*	Romaji	Bushu	Stroke Order and Number
SG-1016 愚	foolish, silly	おろ–か グ	oro-ka *gu*	心	日 旦 禺 禺 禺 愚 愚 13

愚 **D** F-1706

中山王器 1 説文 2

1 and 2 comprised 禺, used for the sound *guu* to mean "unintelligent, slow," and 心 **SG-0187** "heart/mind." Together they signified "simpleminded, foolish, silly." The kanji 愚 means "foolish, silly." <禺心>

愚かな simpleminded, foolish, stupid [おろかな]; 愚かにも foolishly enough [おろかにも]; 愚弄する to make sport of, ridicule, mock [ぐろうする]; 愚図る to fret, be peevish [ぐずる]; 愚痴 silly complaint, grumble [ぐち]; 愚行 folly, indulgence [ぐこう]; 愚鈍な stupid, imbecilic, dim-witted [ぐどんな]

41e 釆 "to take a step forward" [from an animal paw or claws]; bushu *nogome*

The name ***nogome*** comes from katakana ノ *no*, and 米 *kome*. 番審奥翻藩 釆

	Meanings	*Kun* and *On*	Romaji	Bushu	Stroke Order and Number
SG-1017 番	a turn, watch duty, pair	バン	*ban*	田	一 ㇒ 立 平 釆 秀 番 番 12

番 **A** F-0296

金文1 1 金文2 2 説文古文 3 説文 4

One view explains that 1, 2, 3, and 4 depicted "an animal paw" (with claws and pads), and that "an animal paw taking a step forward" meant "to walk on watch duty." Watch duty was performed by people in pairs (thus the meaning "pair"), taking turns (thus the meaning "a turn"). Another view explains that the ancient forms comprised "to scatter or cast seeds" (top component) and "rice paddies" (bottom). Growing rice involved doing different tasks in a set order, thus the meaning "in turn." The kanji 番 means "a turn, watch duty, pair." <釆田> (Note: In relation to the second view described above, the non-Joyo kanji 播く [まく] means "to scatter seeds." Its development is shown here on the right.)

番 watch, turn [ばん]; 一番 the most [いちばん], the first [いちばん]; 出番 one's turn [でばん]; 番をする to be on watch duty [ばんをする]; 留守番 house-sitting, staying home [るすばん]; 番人 watch, guard [ばんにん]; 当番 duty, watch [とうばん]; 番組 (TV/radio) program [ばんぐみ]

	Meanings	*Kun* and *On*	Romaji	Bushu	Stroke Order and Number
SG-1018 審	to examine thoroughly, judge, investigate	シン	*shin*	宀	丶 宀 宀 宀 宷 宷 審 審 15

審 **B** F-0842

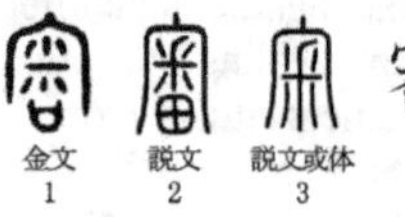

金文 1 説文 2 説文或体 3

1, 2, and 3 all had 宀 "house, mausoleum," and "an animal paw," signifying "placing an animal offering in a mausoleum." 1 also had 口 "mouth or prayer box." A sacrificial animal had to be in perfect condition and was examined thoroughly. Another view takes the inside component to be "scattered rice," and holds that checking rice to remove the scum and debris led to the meaning "to examine in detail." The kanji 審 means "to examine thoroughly, judge, investigate." <宀番>

審議 deliberation, review processing [しんぎ]; 審査 examination, investigation [しんさ]; 不審な doubtful, dubious, mysterious [ふしんな]; 再審 re-examination, new trial [さいしん]; 審美眼 aesthetic sense, an eye for the beautiful [しんびがん, しんびがん]

	Meanings	*Kun* and *On*	Romaji	Bushu	Stroke Order and Number
SG-1019 奥	deep inside, back	おく オウ	oku *oo*	大	丿 冂 冋 冏 冏 奥 奥 12

奥 **B** F-0791

説文 1 旧字 2

The seal-style form (1) was "a pair of hands making an offering of a piece of animal meat (from 'animal paw') inside a house or mausoleum." The altar where one carefully placed an offering was located deep inside the house, and thus this form had the meaning "the back; deep inside." Another view explains that the

奥 interior, depth, inner part [おく]; 奥様 Mrs., mistress, madam (honorific) [おくさま]; 奥の手 secrets, last resort [おくのて]; 奥方 mistress, madam

	two hands were making a rice ball in the back corner of a house where the kitchen was located, and from that it signified "deep inside." 釆 in the kyuji 奥 (2) was replaced by 米 in the shinji. The kanji 奥 means "deep inside, back." <ノ冂米大>	[おくがた]; 奥底 depths, deep in one's heart [おくそこ]; 奥義 secret, hidden mysteries [おうぎ]

SG-1020 翻	Meanings	Kun and On	Romaji	Bushu	Stroke Order and Number
	to flap, turn over, change	ひるがえ-す ホン	hirugae-su *hon*	飛	18

翻 **D** F-1733

説文 1 旧字 2 (飜)

1 and 2 comprised 番, used for the sound *hon* to mean "something flat floating in the air," and 羽 "wings" in 1 or 飛 "to fly" in 2. Wings flapping and flying meant "to turn over, change." The kanji 翻 means "to flap, turn over, change."<番羽>

翻す to turn over, change one's mind, flutter [ひるがえす]; 翻訳 translation, rendering [ほんやく]; 翻意する to change one's mind, go back on one's resolution [ほんいする]

SG-1021 藩	Meanings	Kun and On	Romaji	Bushu	Stroke Order and Number
	han, feudal domain, fief, province	ハン	*han*	艸	18

藩 **D** F-1881

説文

The seal-style form showed "plants" (艸, 艹, bushu *kusakanmuri*), and 潘, used for the sound *han* to mean "fence," together signifying "a wooden fence surrounding (an area)," or "a domain or territory that was controlled." In Japanese, 藩 means "*han,* feudal domain, fief, province." <艹氵番>

藩 *han*, feudal domain, fief [はん]; 藩主 lord of a feudal clan [はんしゅ]; 藩士 feudal retainer, warrior [はんし]; 廃藩置県 establishment of prefectures in place of feudal domains (in 1871) [はいはんちけん]; 幕藩体制 shogunate, feudal domain system [ばくはんたいせい]

41f 尺 (睪) [from a decaying animal carcass left exposed to the elements]; *taku/yaku/shaku* 沢訳択釈

SG-1022 沢	Meanings	Kun and On	Romaji	Bushu	Stroke Order and Number
	marsh, shine, moisture	さわ タク	sawa *taku*	水	7

沢 **A** F-0452

説文 1 旧字 2 (澤)

1 comprised "flowing water" (氵), and 睪, used for the sound *taku.* Together they signified "a place where water originated." A place with plenty of clear water springing out gave the meaning "a lot, benefit." 睪 was replaced by 尺 in the kanji 沢, which means "marsh, shine, moisture." <氵尺>

沢 wetlands, a narrow ravine [さわ]; 沢登り ascent along a mountain stream [さわのぼり]; 光沢 luster, gloss [こうたく]; 沢山 a lot [たくさん]; 子沢山 many children, a large family [こだくさん]

SG-1023 訳	Meanings	Kun and On	Romaji	Bushu	Stroke Order and Number
	translation, reason, meaning	わけ ヤク	wake *yaku*	言	11

訳 **B** F-0756

説文 1 旧字 2 (譯)

1 comprised 言 "word, language; to say," and 睪, which was used for the sound *yaku* to mean "to change." Together they signified "to translate into another language; meaning." In Japanese, it also means "reason, explanation." The kanji 訳 means "translation, reason, meaning." <言尺>

訳 reason, cause [わけ], translation [やく]; 言い訳 excuse [いいわけ]; 申し訳 apology [もうしわけ]; 内訳 breakdown [うちわけ]; 訳あり having special circumstances [わけあり]; 和訳 translation into Japanese [わやく]; 意訳 free translation, liberal translation [いやく]; 直訳 direct translation, word-for-word translation [ちょくやく]; 通訳 interpreter [つうやく]

SG-1024 択	Meanings	Kun and On	Romaji	Bushu	Stroke Order and Number
	to select, choose	タク	*taku*	手	7

択 **C** F-1209

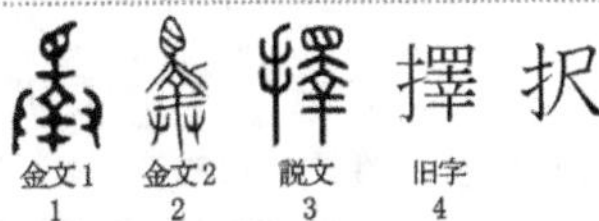

金文1 1 金文2 2 説文 3 旧字 4 (擇)

1, 2, and 3 comprised "a pair of hands" or "a hand" （扌）, and "an animal carcass exposed to the elements that has begun decaying and losing its shape" (睪), used for the sound *taku* to mean "to pick." Together they signified "picking up parts of a carcass by hand," and "to select, choose." 睪 was replaced by 尺 in the kanji 択, which means "to select, choose." <扌尺>

選択 selection, choice, option [せんたく]; 採択 adoption, selection [さいたく]; 取捨選択 selection, choosing and adopting [しゅしゃ・せんたく]; 二者択一 a choice of two options [にしゃ・たくいつ]

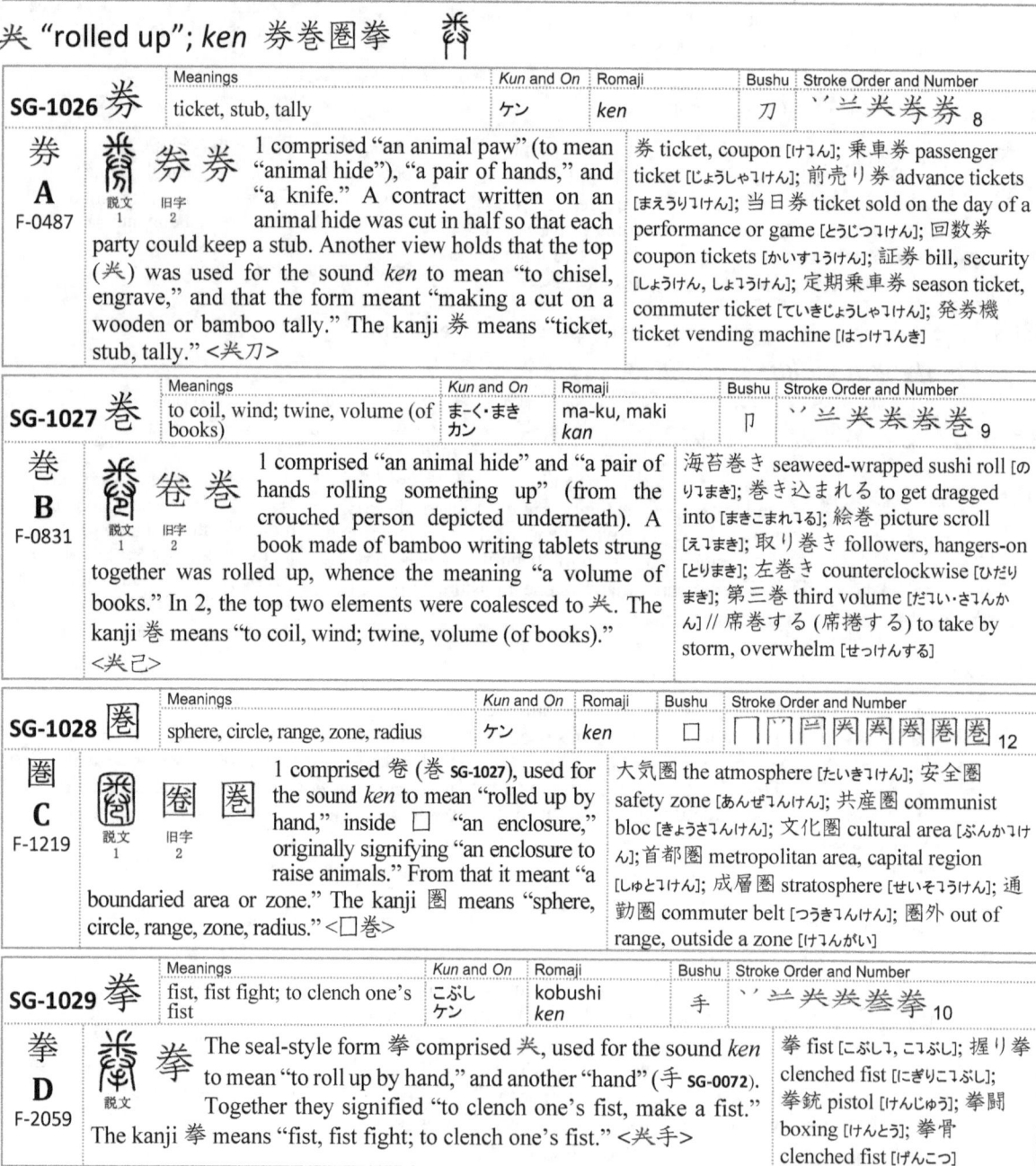

	Meanings	Kun and On	Romaji	Bushu	Stroke Order and Number
SG-1025 釈	to explain, clear up; parsing	シャク	*shaku*	釆	釆 釈 釈 11

釈 **C** F-1235

三体石経 1　説文 2　旧字 3

1 and 2 comprised "a decaying animal carcass" (睪) and "an animal paw" (釆). Together they signified "animal claws pulling a carcass apart," which gave the meaning "to break up, take apart; parsing." Another view explains that 睪 was used for the sound *shaku* to mean "to sort out," and that together with 釆 "to scatter seeds," it meant "to sort out seeds in a detailed manner" and "to explain details." The kanji 釈 means "to explain, clear up; parsing." <丿米尺>

釈放 release [しゃくほう]; 解釈 interpretation, exposition [かいしゃく]; 釈然としない to be not satisfied with an explanation [しゃくぜんとしない]; 会釈 greeting, salutation, bow [えしゃく]; 釈迦 Buddha [しゃか]

41g 龹 "rolled up"; *ken* 券巻圏拳

	Meanings	Kun and On	Romaji	Bushu	Stroke Order and Number
SG-1026 券	ticket, stub, tally	ケン	*ken*	刀	丷 龹 券 券 8

券 **A** F-0487

説文 1　旧字 2

1 comprised "an animal paw" (to mean "animal hide"), "a pair of hands," and "a knife." A contract written on an animal hide was cut in half so that each party could keep a stub. Another view holds that the top (龹) was used for the sound *ken* to mean "to chisel, engrave," and that the form meant "making a cut on a wooden or bamboo tally." The kanji 券 means "ticket, stub, tally." <龹刀>

券 ticket, coupon [けん]; 乗車券 passenger ticket [じょうしゃけん]; 前売り券 advance tickets [まえうりけん]; 当日券 ticket sold on the day of a performance or game [とうじつけん]; 回数券 coupon tickets [かいすうけん]; 証券 bill, security [しょうけん, しょうけん]; 定期乗車券 season ticket, commuter ticket [ていきじょうしゃけん]; 発券機 ticket vending machine [はっけんき]

	Meanings	Kun and On	Romaji	Bushu	Stroke Order and Number
SG-1027 巻	to coil, wind; twine, volume (of books)	ま-く・まき カン	ma-ku, maki *kan*	卩	丷 龹 巻 巻 巻 9

巻 **B** F-0831

説文 1　旧字 2

1 comprised "an animal hide" and "a pair of hands rolling something up" (from the crouched person depicted underneath). A book made of bamboo writing tablets strung together was rolled up, whence the meaning "a volume of books." In 2, the top two elements were coalesced to 龹. The kanji 巻 means "to coil, wind; twine, volume (of books)." <龹己>

海苔巻き seaweed-wrapped sushi roll [のりまき]; 巻き込まれる to get dragged into [まきこまれる]; 絵巻 picture scroll [えまき]; 取り巻き followers, hangers-on [とりまき]; 左巻き counterclockwise [ひだりまき]; 第三巻 third volume [だいさんかん] // 席巻する (席捲する) to take by storm, overwhelm [せっけんする]

	Meanings	Kun and On	Romaji	Bushu	Stroke Order and Number
SG-1028 圏	sphere, circle, range, zone, radius	ケン	*ken*	囗	冂 冂 冋 冏 圏 圏 圏 圏 12

圏 **C** F-1219

説文 1　旧字 2

1 comprised 巻 (巻 **SG-1027**), used for the sound *ken* to mean "rolled up by hand," inside 囗 "an enclosure," originally signifying "an enclosure to raise animals." From that it meant "a boundaried area or zone." The kanji 圏 means "sphere, circle, range, zone, radius." <囗巻>

大気圏 the atmosphere [たいきけん]; 安全圏 safety zone [あんぜんけん]; 共産圏 communist bloc [きょうさんけん]; 文化圏 cultural area [ぶんかけん]; 首都圏 metropolitan area, capital region [しゅとけん]; 成層圏 stratosphere [せいそうけん]; 通勤圏 commuter belt [つうきんけん]; 圏外 out of range, outside a zone [けんがい]

	Meanings	Kun and On	Romaji	Bushu	Stroke Order and Number
SG-1029 拳	fist, fist fight; to clench one's fist	こぶし ケン	kobushi *ken*	手	丷 龹 拳 拳 拳 10

拳 **D** F-2059

説文

The seal-style form 拳 comprised 龹, used for the sound *ken* to mean "to roll up by hand," and another "hand" (手 **SG-0072**). Together they signified "to clench one's fist, make a fist." The kanji 拳 means "fist, fist fight; to clench one's fist." <龹手>

拳 fist [こぶし, こぶし]; 握り拳 clenched fist [にぎりこぶし]; 拳銃 pistol [けんじゅう]; 拳闘 boxing [けんとう]; 拳骨 clenched fist [げんこつ]

41h 暴 "to expose" [from an animal cut apart and left exposed to the sun]; *boo/baku* 暴爆 

	Meanings	Kun and On	Romaji	Bushu	Stroke Order and Number
SG-1030 暴	violent; to expose	あば-く ボウ・バク	aba-ku, aba-reru *boo, baku*	日	㇇冂日旦早昱㫶晃暴暴 15

暴 **B** F-0918

金文 1 說文 2 說文 3 暴

1 comprised "the sun risen high," and "an animal cut apart and spread open," together signifying "to expose to the sun." In 2 and 3, a pair of hands scattering the decayed carcass (氺) were added. An animal carcass torn apart and left exposed to the sun and elements to decay brought the meanings "to expose" and "violent act." The kanji 暴 means "violent; to expose." <日共氺>

暴く to disclose, bring to light, expose [あばく]; 暴れる to behave violently, riot, go wild [あばれる]; 暴力 violence [ぼうりょく]; 横暴な oppressive, tyrannical [おうぼうな]; 暴風雨 rainstorm, storm [ぼうふうう]; 暴走族 motorcycle gang [ぼうそうぞく]; 暴発する to go off accidentally [ぼうはつする]; 暴露 exposure, divulgence [ばくろ]

	Meanings	Kun and On	Romaji	Bushu	Stroke Order and Number
SG-1031 爆	to explode, burst, blast	バク	*baku*	火	ソ火炉焊焊熼爆爆 19

爆 **B** F-0933

篆文 爆

The seal-style form of the kanji 爆 comprised 火 **SG-1164**, "fire," and 暴 **SG-1030**, which was used for the sound *baku* to mean "violent." Together, they signified "a fire explosion." The kanji 爆 means "to explode, burst, blast." <火暴>

爆発 explosion [ばくはつ]; 爆弾 bomb [ばくだん]; 空爆 air raid [くうばく]; 水爆 hydrogen bomb[すいばく]; 爆音 detonation [ばくおん]; 爆笑 roar of laughter [ばくしょう]; 爆発的な explosive [ばくはつてきな]

42 Mythical animals, and others

42a 竜 "dragon" 竜滝襲龍

	Meanings	Kun and On	Romaji	Bushu	Stroke Order and Number
SG-1032 竜	dragon	たつ リュウ	tatsu *ryuu*	龍	亠亠立产音音竜 10

竜 **C** F-1093

甲骨文 1 1, 甲骨文 2 2, 金文 1 3, 金文 2 4, 說文 5, 旧字 6

1 and 2 depicted "a sacred dragon" with a large head, and in 3 and 4 a crown was placed on its head. As time went on, the depiction of this mythical creature became more embellished. The kyuji 龍 (6) reflected 5. In the shinji it reverted to the older, simpler shape, 竜. The kanji 竜 means "dragon." <立电>

竜巻 tornado, whirlwind [たつまき]; 竜 dragon [たつ]; 竜の落とし子 sea horse [たつのおとしご]; 竜宮 undersea palace of the dragon deity [りゅうぐう]; 恐竜 dinosaur [きょうりゅう]

	Meanings	Kun and On	Romaji	Bushu	Stroke Order and Number
SG-1033 滝	waterfall	たき	taki	水	氵氵氵广沪浐涪滝 13

滝 **C** F-1315

甲骨文 1, 篆文 2, 旧字 3 瀧 滝

1 and 2 comprised "dragon" and "flowing water" (氵), together signifying "waterfall." The right side (龍) of the kyuji (3) became 竜 in the shinji. The kanji 滝 means "waterfall." <氵竜>

滝 waterfall [たき]; 滝口 the crest of a waterfall [たきぐち]

	Meanings	Kun and On	Romaji	Bushu	Stroke Order and Number
SG-1034 襲	to assimilate, inherit, attack	おそ-う シュウ	oso-u *shuu*	衣	立音音音龍龍龍龔襲襲 22

襲 **C** F-1332

金文 1, 說文 2 襲

The top component of 1 comprised two dragons, signifying "to lay one on top of another, duplicate," and having the sound *shuu*. The bottom component was "clothing" (衣 **SG-1657**). Clothing oneself in a special garment was like becoming what the garment represented. The character meant "to assimilate, inherit." Later the meaning "to attack unexpectedly" was added. The kanji 襲 means "to assimilate, inherit, attack." <龍(立月㠯)衣>

襲う to attack, assail, invade, descend on [おそう]; 襲撃 attack, raid, storm [しゅうげき]; 奇襲 surprise, attack, raid [きしゅう]; 逆襲 counterstrike [ぎゃくしゅう]; 世襲 heredity [せしゅう]; 襲名 assumption of a (professional) name [しゅうめい]

SG-1035 籠	Meanings	Kun and On	Romaji	Bushu	Stroke Order and Number
	basket; to seclude oneself	かご・こ-もる ロウ	kago, ko-moru *roo*	竹	⺮ … 籠籠 22

籠 **D** F-2257

説文

The seal-style form of the kanji 籠 comprised 竹 (⺮, bushu *takekanmuri*) "bamboo," and 龍, used for the sound *roo* to mean "basket." In Japanese, from the sense of being inside a basket, the character is also used to mean "to seclude oneself (inside a house or temple)." The kanji 籠 means "basket; to seclude oneself." <⺮龍>

籠 basket [かご]; 揺り籠 cradle [ゆりかご]; 籠る to seclude oneself [こもる]; 引き籠り someone who shuts up at home and is withdrawn socially [ひきこもり]; 籠城する to hole up in a castle, remain indoors [ろうじょうする]; 印籠 a case for one's personal seal (historical) [いんろう]

42b 能 "able" [of unknown origin, possibly from a four-legged animal] 能態熊罷

SG-1036 能	Meanings	Kun and On	Romaji	Bushu	Stroke Order and Number
	able; ability, Noh play	ノウ	*noo*	肉	ム … 能 10

能 **A** F-0378

金文1 金文2 説文
1 2 3

The origin of 能 has puzzled kanji scholars and remains a mystery. Many explanations have been proposed, including that it depicted an animal with four legs, an insect, etc. In Japan, 能 also means Noh play. The kanji 能 means "able; ability, Noh play." <能(ム月ヒヒ)>

可能性 possibility [かのうせい]; 能力 ability, capacity, faculty [のうりょく]; 能力テスト competence test [のうりょくテスト]; 万能 all-purpose, universal [ばんのう]; 無能 incapable, powerless [むのう]; 全能 omnipotence [ぜんのう]; 能 Noh play [のう]; 能楽 Noh play music [のうがく]; 能面 Noh mask [のうめん]

SG-1037 態	Meanings	Kun and On	Romaji	Bushu	Stroke Order and Number
	demeanor, bearing, state	タイ	*tai*	心	ム … 能 態 14

態 **B** F-0620

説文 説文或体
1 2

"A heart" (心 **SG-0187**) was added to 能 **SG-1036**, used for the sound *tai*, resulting in 態. In the variant form (2), "a person" was used in place of "heart," to indicate that the character pertained to "an act that one did," but it reverted to "a heart" in the kanji. The kanji 態 means "demeanor, bearing, state." <能心>

態度 attitude, bearing, demeanor, manner [たいど]; 状態 status, condition [じょうたい]; 形態 form, shape [けいたい]; 実態 actual condition, actual state [じったい]; 容態悪化 a turn for the worse [ようだいあっか]; 悪態をつく to talk smack, curse [あくたいをつく]; 生態系 ecological system [せいたいけい]

SG-1038 熊	Meanings	Kun and On	Romaji	Bushu	Stroke Order and Number
	bear	くま	kuma	火	ム … 能 熊 14

熊 **C** F-1082

説文

The seal-style form comprised 能 **SG-1036**, possibly meaning "an animal," and 火 "fire." In the kanji, 火 became 灬, which is interpreted to be "the four legs of an animal." Another view explains that "fire" referred to the fact that bear fat burned well. The kanji 熊 means "bear." <能灬>

熊 bear [くま, ぐま]; 熊手 rake, pitchfork, bamboo rake [くまで]

SG-1039 罷	Meanings	Kun and On	Romaji	Bushu	Stroke Order and Number
	to quit, end, leave, (present oneself)	ヒ	*hi*	网	冖 罒 … 罷 15

罷 **D** F-2321

説文

The-seal style form comprised 网 "a casting net," and 能 **SG-1036**, possibly meaning "an animal." One view explains that it depicted an animal weakened by being captured, whence the original meaning "to become tired." Another explains that it represented "keeping someone with ability or power (能) under control," and meant "to dismiss (an official)." In Japanese, it became used in humble expressions related to the meanings "to present oneself" or "to, leave," and is also used as an emphatic prefix for a verb. The kanji 罷 means "to be fired, quit, dismiss, (to present oneself, leave"). <罒能>

罷免 dismissal, discharge [ひめん]; 罷業 strike, walkout [ひぎょう] // 罷り通らない cannot get by (emphatic) [まかりとおらない]; 罷り出る to present oneself, leave [まかりでる] (humble, historical)

42c Other Animals 風易甲卵亀

	Meanings	Kun and On	Romaji	Bushu	Stroke Order and Number
SG-1040 風	wind, breeze, air, style, manner	かぜ・かざ フウ・フ	kaze, kaza *huu, hu*	風	丿几凡凬凬風風 9

風 **A** F-0277

甲骨文1 1 甲骨文2 2 説文 3

The kanji 風 originated from a depiction of a mythical bird. 1 and 2 comprised "a mythical bird with a crown or head crest, large, powerful wings, long trailing feathers and a tail," and 口 "a sail," which was used for the sound *huu*. The mythical bird 鳳 ([ほうおꜜう] or 鳳凰 in Japanese), was believed to cause wind, which it would then catch in its sail. 3 comprised "a sail" and "a snake." The kanji 風 comprises "a sail," and 虫 with an extra stroke, a remnant of the mythical bird's crown. The kanji 風 means "wind, breeze, air, style, manner." <几ノ虫>

風 wind, breeze [かぜ]; 風邪を引く to catch a cold [かぜをひく]; 風上に置けない intolerable, insufferable [かざかみにおけない]; 風景 scenery [ふꜜうけい]; 風俗 customs, conventions, sex-oriented business [ふꜜうぞく]; 風化する to become weathered, fade with the passage of time [ふうかする]; 風流な elegant, aesthetic [ふꜜうりゅうな]; 洋風 western style [ようふう]

	Meanings	Kun and On	Romaji	Bushu	Stroke Order and Number
SG-1041 易	easy, simple; to change, trade; fortune-telling	やさ-しい エキ・イ	yasa-shii *eki, i*	日	口日日旦易 8

易 **B** F-0721

甲骨文 1 金文1 2 金文2 3 説文 4

1, 2, and 3 comprised "sun rays" and "a lizard." A lizard changes the color of its skin instantly under the sun, and the character meant "easy; to change, trade." A fortune-teller tells one's fortune, which is constantly changing. From that it also meant "fortune-telling." The kanji 易 means "easy, simple; to change, trade; fortune telling" <日勿>

易しい easy, simple [やさしい]; 易 fortune-telling [えき]; 易者 fortune-teller [えきしゃ]; 貿易 trade [ぼうえき]; 交易 trade, trading [こうえき]; 不易の unchangeable, constant [ふꜜえきの]; 難易度 degree of difficulty [なんいꜜど]; 平易に plainly, simply [へꜜいいに]; 簡易な simple, simplified [かꜜんいな]

	Meanings	Kun and On	Romaji	Bushu	Stroke Order and Number
SG-1042 甲	hard; armor, the former, "A" (in grading)	コウ・カン	*koo, kan*	田	丨冂日日甲 5

甲 **B** F-1051

甲骨文1 1 甲骨文2 2 金文1 3 金文2 4 説文 5

1, 2, 3, and 4 depicted the crossed vertical and horizontal lines on the plastron (lower side) of a tortoise. A tortoise shell is "hard," which gave the meaning "armor." Another view holds that it depicted a hardshelled seed with a sprout emerging from it. From "hard shell," it was also used to mean "armor." 甲 is also used to mean "first party, the former," in contracts (as opposed to 乙 **SG-2104** "second party, the latter"), and an "A" grade in the old three-level grading system 甲乙丙 **SG-1843**. The kanji 甲 means "hard; armor, the former, 'A' grade." <日丨>

甲 the former, party A [こꜜう]; 甲乙 A and B, difference [こꜜうおつ]; 手の甲 the back of the hand [てꜜのこう]; 甲殻類 Crustacea [こうかくꜜるい]; 甲板 deck [かんぱん, こうはん] // 甲冑 (helmet and) armour [かっちゅう]

	Meanings	Kun and On	Romaji	Bushu	Stroke Order and Number
SG-1043 卵	egg	たまご ラン	tamago *ran*	卩	ノ厂𠂎卯卯卯卵 7

卵 **B** F-0938

金文 1 説文 2

Many possible origins have been proposed for 卵. In this guide, we will treat 1 and 2 as "fish eggs attached to two symmetrical leaves." The kanji 卵 means "egg." < 卵 >

卵 egg [たまꜜご]; 茹で卵 boiled egg [ゆでたꜜまご]; 産卵 laying an egg [さんらん]; 卵黄 egg yolk [らんおう]; 受精卵 fertilized egg [じゅせꜜいらん]

	Meanings	Kun and On	Romaji	Bushu	Stroke Order and Number
SG-1044 亀	turtle, tortoise	かめ キ	kame *ki*	龜	⺈⺈⺈⺈亀 11

亀 **C** F-1238

甲骨文 1 金文 2 説文古文 3 説文 4 旧字 5

1 through 4 depicted "a turtle or tortoise," viewed from the side or from above. The extraordinarily complex kyuji 龜(5) reflected 4. The kanji 亀 means "turtle, tortoise." <⺈亀(昌乚)>

亀 turtle, tortoise [かꜜめ]; 亀裂 crack, crevice [きれつ]; 亀甲 hexagonal pattern [きっこう]

V Nature

43 The sun

43a 日 "the sun, day; bright" [from the sun] 日早春昼暇晶暁

SG-1045 日	Meanings	Kun and On	Romaji	Bushu	Stroke Order and Number
	the sun, day, date, light, Sunday, Japan; Japanese	ひ・か ニチ・ジツ	hi, ka *nichi, jitsu*	日	丨 冂 日 日 4

日 **A** F-0001

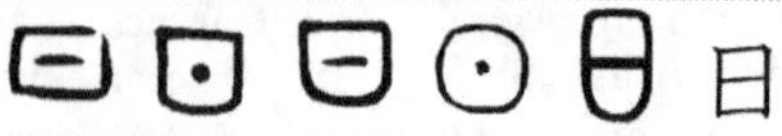

甲骨文 1　金文1 2　金文2 3　金文3 4　説文 5

1 through 4 were a square or a circle with a dot or a short line in the middle, signifying "the sun." (A dot or line indicated that it was not an empty shape.) The character means "the sun," and other sun-related things such as "day, date, light." One of the traditional names of Japan is *hinomoto* (日の本), "the place where the sun rises," and thus 日 also means "Japan; Japanese." In Japanese, it also means "Sunday." The kanji 日 means "the sun, day, date, light, Sunday, Japan; Japanese." <日>

月日が経つ time/days/years pass [つきꜜひが・たꜜつ]; 日取りを決める to fix the date [ひどりをきめる]; 日が長くなる daylight becomes longer [ひがながꜜくなる]; 二日 two days, second day of the month [ふつか]; 生年月日 birth date [せいねんがꜜっぴ]; 来日 arrival in Japan [らいにち]; 日曜日 Sunday [にちようꜜび]; 日本 Japan [にほꜜん]; 日記 diary, journal [にっき]; 平日 weekday, workday [へいじつ]

SG-1046 早	Meanings	Kun and On	Romaji	Bushu	Stroke Order and Number
	early, quick	はや-い ソウ・サッ	haya-i *soo*, sa(C)-	日	丨 冂 日 旦 早 6

早 **A** F-0226

中山王器 1　説文 2

The origin of the kanji 早 is obscure. Various views include: "the sun rising through plants"; "a spoon"; "a dark-colored acorn" to represent "early morning when it is still dark"; etc. The time when the sun (日) starts to rise is very early in the morning. Some also view the meaning of "early" to be a borrowing. The kanji 早 means "early, quick." <日十>

早い early [はやꜜい]; 早めに in good time, earlier than usual [はやめに]; 手早く quickly, efficiently [てばやꜜく]; 足早に briskly, at a fast pace [あしばやに]; 早々と in good time; much earlier than usual [はやばꜜやと]; 早朝 early morning [そうちょう]; 早退 leaving work or class early [そうたい]; 早期 an early stage [そꜜうき]; 早急な urgent, pressing (need) [さっきゅうな]; 早速 immediately, right away [さっそく]

SG-1047 春	Meanings	Kun and On	Romaji	Bushu	Stroke Order and Number
	spring, new year	はる シュン	haru *shun*	日	三 夫 夫 春 春 春 9

春 **A** F-0251

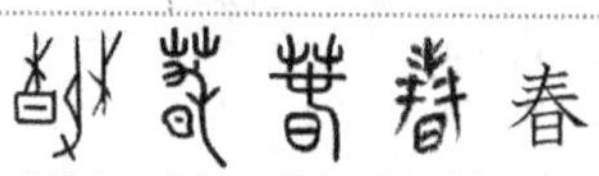

甲骨文 1　金文 2　説文 3　馬王堆帛書 4

1, 2, and 3 comprised trees (木) or plants (艸), the sun (日), and "a rooted plant trying to sprout up" (屯), used for the sound *shun*. Together they signified the season when plants are pushing upward under the bright sun—"spring." The brush-written form of 4 may help us to better see the transition to the kanji 春. The kanji 春 means "spring, new year." < 夫日>

春 spring [はꜜる]; 我が世の春 one's peak of prosperity, heyday [わꜜがよの・はꜜる]; 春一番 the first strong southerly wind of spring [はꜜる・いちꜜばん]; 春学期 spring school term [はるがꜜっき]; 春分の日 Vernal Equinox Day [しゅんぶんのひꜜ]; 思春期 early adolescence [ししゅꜜんき]; 春秋に富む to be young [しゅんじゅうにとꜜむ]

SG-1048 昼	Meanings	Kun and On	Romaji	Bushu	Stroke Order and Number
	daytime, daylight, lunch time	ひる チュウ	hiru *chuu*	日	フ コ 尸 尺 尽 昼 昼 9

昼 **B** F-0610

金文 1　説文 2　旧字 3

The origin of the kanji 昼 is unclear. 1 and 2 comprised "a writing brush held by a hand" and "the sun," with two curved lines on either side of the sun in 2 which might have signified "the two dark times of the day," i.e. "before and after daylight," between which came "daytime." The shinji 昼 comprises the sun (日) under a roof (尸), with another stroke (㇏) marking the end of daylight. The kanji 昼 means "daytime, daylight, lunch time." <尸㇏旦>

昼 daytime, noon, lunch [ひるꜜ]; 昼休み lunch break [ひるやꜜすみ]; 真昼 high noon midday [まひる]; 昼間 daytime [ひるまꜜ]; お昼 lunch, noontime [おひꜜる]; 昼食 lunch [ちゅうしょく]; 一昼夜 whole day and night, 24 hours [いっちゅꜜうや]

	Meanings	Kun and On	Romaji	Bushu	Stroke Order and Number
SG-1049 暇	free time, leisure hours, spare time	ひま カ	hima *ka*	日	暇 13

暇 **C** F-1307 (說文)

The seal-style form comprised 日 "the sun, day," and 叚 used for the sound *ka* to mean "leisure." The kanji 暇 means "free time, leisure hours, spare time." <日叚>

暇 leisure, spare time [ひま]; 暇つぶし keeping oneself occupied, killing time [ひまつぶし]; 休暇 holiday, vacation, leave [きゅうか]; 有給休暇 paid vacation, vacation with full pay [ゆうきゅうきゅうか]

	Meanings	Kun and On	Romaji	Bushu	Stroke Order and Number
SG-1050 晶	glistening, clear light, pure and bright	ショウ	*shoo*	日	晶 12

晶 **C** F-1517 (甲骨文 1, 甲骨文 2, 說文 3)

1, 2, and 3 comprised three squares that signified "many shining or glistening things." The kanji 晶 means "glistening, clear light, pure and bright." <日日日>

結晶 crystal [けっしょう]; 水晶 crystal, quartz [すいしょう]

	Meanings	Kun and On	Romaji	Bushu	Stroke Order and Number
SG-1051 暁	dawn, daybreak	あかつき ギョウ	akatsuki *gyoo*	日	暁 12

暁 **D** F-1736 (說文 1, 旧字 2)

1 comprised 日 "the sun," and 堯, used for the sound *gyoo* to mean "to become white." Together they signified "the time when the dark eastern sky becomes white," which was "dawn." In the kanji, 堯 was reduced to 尭. The kanji 暁 means "dawn, daybreak." <日尭 (十卄兀)>

暁 the light of early morning, dawn [あかつき]; ～の暁には in the eventual outcome of X [～のあかつきには]; 暁天の星 fading stars at dawn (literary) [ぎょうてんのほし]

43b 朝 "morning" [from the sun emerging behind tall grass by the water]; *choo* 朝潮嘲

	Meanings	Kun and On	Romaji	Bushu	Stroke Order and Number
SG-1052 朝	morning, imperial dynasty, imperial court	あさ チョウ	asa *choo*	月	朝 12

朝 **A** F-0122 (甲骨文 1, 金文 1 2, 金文 2 3, 金文 3 4, 說文 5)

1 depicted "the sun emerging behind tall grass," when "the moon" (in the center) is still faintly visible, signifying "very early morning." In 2, 3, and 4, the addition of "flowing water" signified "a morning tide." In 5, "water" was replaced by "a boat (月) with a flag" (also signifying "rising high"). One view explains that in the ancient imperial court, important business and protocols were held with the sunrise, and thus the character meant "dynasty, imperial court." The kanji 朝 means "morning, dynasty, imperial court." <卓(十早)月>

朝 morning [あさ]; 毎朝 every morning [まいあさ]; 朝ご飯 breakfast [あさごはん]; 朝飯前 a very easy task, "a piece of cake" [あさめしまえ]; 平安朝 the Heian dynasty [へいあんちょう]; 朝廷 the Imperial Court [ちょうてい]; 帰朝 returning home from abroad [きちょう]; 王朝 dynasty [おうちょう]

	Meanings	Kun and On	Romaji	Bushu	Stroke Order and Number
SG-1053 潮	tide, current, trend	しお チョウ	shio *choo*	水	潮 15

潮 **C** F-1192 (金文 1 1, 金文 2 2, 說文 3)

1 and 2 were essentially the same as 朝 **SG-1052** "morning," depicting "the sun emerging among tall grass by the water," and were used for the sound *choo*. The right side of 3 meant "a flag rising high." The kanji uses 氵, bushu *sanzui* "flowing water," and 朝, signifying "a morning tide or tidal current," or more figuratively, a "trend" in culture. The kanji 潮 means "tide, tidal current, trend." <氵朝>

黒潮 the Japan Kuroshio current [くろしお]; 潮風 (salty) sea breeze [しおかぜ]; 上げ潮 flood-tide, incoming tide [あげしお]; 引き潮 ebb tide [ひきしお]; 最高潮 climax [さいこうちょう]; 潮流 ocean current [ちょうりゅう]; 風潮 tendency, drift [ふうちょう]

	Meanings	Kun and On	Romaji	Bushu	Stroke Order and Number
SG-1054 嘲	to treat someone with scorn, jeer	あざけ-る・(あざ-) チョウ	azake-ru, (aza-) *choo*	口	嘲 15

嘲 **D** F-2525 (篆文)

The seal-style form comprised 口 **SG-0031** "mouth," and 朝 **SG-1052**, used for the sound *choo* to mean "to make fun of." The kanji 嘲 means "to treat someone with scorn, jeer." <口朝>

嘲る to scorn [あざける]; 嘲笑う to make a fool of, sneer at [あざわらう]; 嘲笑 sardonic smile, scornful laugh [ちょうしょう]

43c 昔 "to repeat, place over top of" [from the sun with repeating lines] 昔借籍措惜錯

	Meanings	Kun and On	Romaji	Bushu	Stroke Order and Number
SG-1055 昔	bygone days, ancient times, former years or days	むかし セキ・ジャク	mukashi *seki, jaku*	日	昔 8

昔 **B** F-0737

甲骨文1 甲骨文2 金文 説文 (1 2 3 4)

1 through 4 comprised "two or three wavy lines" and "the sun." The wavy lines signified layers of thin, preserved jerky that had been dried under the sun. The character was borrowed to mean "bygone days, ancient times." Another view explains that repeated appearances of the sun (represented by many wavy lines) signified "bygone days." The kanji 昔 means "bygone days, ancient times, former years or days." <艹日>

昔 bygone days, ancient times [むかし]; 昔々 once upon a time [むかしむかし]; 大昔 the distant past, a long time ago [おおむかし]; 昔話 folklore, reminiscences [むかしばなし]; 昔馴染み one's old familiar person or place [むかしなじみ]; 昔日 old days [せきじつ]; 今昔 past and present [こんじゃく]

	Meanings	Kun and On	Romaji	Bushu	Stroke Order and Number
SG-1056 借	to borrow	か-りる シャク	ka-riru *shaku*	人	借 10

借 **B** F-0953

説文

One view explains that 昔 was used for the sound *shaku* (from *saku*) to mean "to pretend." By extension, it meant something not belonging to one, and thus "a borrowed thing." Another view is that the sound *shaku* came from "layers of thin jerky," and that it expressed the "layered" actions of "borrowing" and returning. The kanji 借 means "to borrow." <亻昔>

借りる to borrow [かりる]; 借り手 borrower [かりて]; 貸し借り lending and borrowing [かしかり, かしがり]; 間借り renting a room [まがり]; 借家 rented house [しゃくや]; 拝借する to borrow (humble) [はいしゃくする]; 借用 loan, borrowing [しゃくよう]; 仮借 (phonetic) loan character (one of the six types of kanji formulation in 六書 *rikusho*) [かしゃ]

	Meanings	Kun and On	Romaji	Bushu	Stroke Order and Number
SG-1057 籍	book, register	セキ	*seki*	竹	籍 20

籍 **C** F-1245

説文

The seal-style form comprised ⺮ "bamboo" to connote "writing tablets," and 耤, used for the sound *seki* to mean "to lay over; pile." Bamboo or wooden writing tablets were layered on top of one another to make a book. The kanji 籍 means "book, register." <⺮耒昔>

籍 register [せき]; 本籍地 one's legal domicile [ほんせきち]; 移籍する to transfer (to another athletic team) [いせきする]

	Meanings	Kun and On	Romaji	Bushu	Stroke Order and Number
SG-1058 措	to place on top of something, leave	ソ	*so*	手	措 11

措 **C** F-1322

説文

The seal-style form comprised 扌, bushu *tehen*, and 昔, used for the sound *seki* to mean "to place over top," together signifying "to place." The kanji 措 means "to place on top of something, lay aside." <扌昔>

措置 measure, step, action [そち]; 予防措置 preventive measures [よぼうそち]; 緊急措置 emergency measure [きんきゅうそち] // 措く to suspend, lay aside [おく]

	Meanings	Kun and On	Romaji	Bushu	Stroke Order and Number
SG-1059 惜	to regret, hold something dear, be sparing with	お-しい セキ	o-shii *seki*	心	惜 11

惜 **C** F-1616

説文

The seal-style form comprised "heart" (忄), and 昔 **SG-1055**, used for the sound *seki* to mean "for a long time." A lingering feeling in the heart meant "regret, sadness." The kanji 惜 means "to regret, hold something dear, be sparing with." <忄昔>

惜しい regrettable, disappointing, precious [おしい]; 惜しむ to lament, be frugal [おしむ]; 惜しまずに without sparing [おしまずに]; 哀惜の念 grieve, lament, sorrowfulness [あいせきのねん]; 惜別 sorrow at parting [せきべつ]

	Meanings	Kun and On	Romaji	Bushu	Stroke Order and Number
SG-1060 錯	to mix up, make a mistake	サク	*saku*	金	錯 16

錯 **D** F-1834

説文

The seal-style form comprised 金 **SG-1196** "metal," and 昔 **SG-1055** "to place something over top," used for the sound *saku*. Metal inlay was made by melting pieces of metal onto each other and polishing the finished item. Inlay was a process of mixing different materials, and the idea of intermixing gave the meaning "to make a mistake." The kanji 錯 means "to mix up, make a mistake." <錯>

錯覚 illusion, hallucination [さっかく]; 錯誤 mistake, error [さくご]; 交錯する to blend, grow, become entangled [こうさくする]; 錯綜する to become jumbled, entangled [さくそう]; 倒錯 inversion, perversion [とうさく]; 錯乱する to become delirious/confused [さくらんする]

43d-1 旦 "dawn" [from the sun rising above a cloud]; *tan* 恒旦但

	Meanings	*Kun* and *On*	Romaji	Bushu	Stroke Order and Number
SG-1061 恒	constant; always	コウ	*koo*	心	丶 忄 忙 怕 恒 恒 9

恒 **C** F-1436

甲骨文 1 金文 2 說文古文 3 說文 4 旧字 5

1 comprised a half or crescent moon between two fixed lines and had the sound *koo*. Being in a fixed position signified "unchanging." Another view suggests that the constant waning and waxing of the moon gave the meaning "constant; always." In 2 and 4, "a heart" (忄) was added beside the moon, forming the meaning "an unwavering heart." The kyuji (5) retained "moon," but in the shinji 恒, 日 "the sun" is used. The kanji 恒 means "constant; always." <忄一日一>

恒常的な constant, invariable [こうじょうてきな]; 恒例行事 customary event [こうれいぎょうじ]

	Meanings	*Kun* and *On*	Romaji	Bushu	Stroke Order and Number
SG-1062 旦	dawn, husband; once, for a short time	タン・ダン	*tan, dan*	日	丨 冂 日 旦 5

旦 **D** F-1964

甲骨文 1 金文 2 說文 3

1 and 2 had "the sun" above "a cloud." The sun beginning to appear above the clouds meant "dawn." Another view takes the line below the sun in 3 to be the horizon. The character also meant "once; for a short time." In Japanese it is used phonetically for the word 旦那, "husband," which came from a Sanskrit word meaning "benefactor or donor." The kanji 旦 means "dawn, husband; once, for a short time." <日一>

元旦 the first day of a new year [がんたん]; 一旦 for a short time, temporarily [いったん]; 一旦帰宅する to go home for now [いったん・きたくする]; 一旦 A すると B B will be the inevitable consequenc of A [いったん A すると, B]; 一旦停車 bring car to a complete stop before proceeding [いったんていしゃ]; 旦那 master, keeper, husband [だんな]

	Meanings	*Kun* and *On*	Romaji	Bushu	Stroke Order and Number
SG-1063 但	but, however, only, provided that	ただ-し	tada-shi	人	亻 仆 们 但 但 7

但 **D** F-2169

甲骨文 1 說文 2

1 and 2 comprised 亻 "a person, an act that one does," and 旦, used for the sound *tan* to mean "to show only a part." This construction originally signified "to partially remove clothing," but it is no longer used for this meaning in Japanese. The current meaning is a borrowing. The kanji 但 means "but, however, only, provided that." <亻旦>

但し but, however, though, only, provided that [ただし]; 但し書き proviso, conditional clause [ただしがき]

43d-2 旦 [a phonetic replacement for 詹 "to carry over the shoulder"]; *tan* 担胆

	Meanings	*Kun* and *On*	Romaji	Bushu	Stroke Order and Number
SG-1064 担	to carry a burden, to bear	かつ-ぐ・にな-う タン	katsu-gu, nina-u *tan*	手	一 才 扌 扣 担 担 8

担 **B** F-0674

說文 1 旧字 2

1 comprised 亻 "an act that one does," and 詹, used for the sound *tan* to mean "to carry over the shoulder." Together they signified "to carry a burden." In 2, 扌 "an act done by hand" replaced 亻. In the shinji, 詹 was replaced by 旦, which had the same sound *tan*. The kanji 担 means "to carry a burden, to bear." <扌旦>

担ぐ to shoulder, put on a rucksack, be superstitious [かつぐ]; 担う to bear on one's shoulders, bear a burden [になう]; 担任 having charge of [たんにん]; 負担する to bear a burden, share in [ふたんする]; 担架 stretcher [たんか]; 加担する to side with, assist [かたんする]; 分担 to share [ぶんたん]; 担保 mortgage, guarantee [たんぽ]

	Meanings	*Kun* and *On*	Romaji	Bushu	Stroke Order and Number
SG-1065 胆	liver, spirit, courage, one's true feeling or motive	タン	*tan*	肉	刀 月 肌 胆 胆 9

胆 **D** F-1786

說文 1 旧字 2

1 and 2 comprised 月, bushu *nikuzuki* "part of the body," and 詹, used for the sound *tan*, together making the meaning of "liver." 詹 was replaced by the shape 旦 **SG-1062** that had the same sound *tan*. The liver was believed to be connected with one's spirit, courage or nerves. The kanji 胆 means "liver, spirit, courage, one's true feeling or motive." <月旦>

大胆な bold, daring [だいたんな]; 魂胆 hidden reason [こんたん, こんたん]; 落胆する to be discouraged [らくたんする]; 胆嚢 the gallbladder [たんのう]

43e 昜 "to rise, heighten" [from the sun risen high and shining bright]; *Joo/yoo/shoo/too* 場陽傷湯揚瘍

	Meanings	Kun and On	Romaji	Bushu	Stroke Order and Number
SG-1066 場	place, spot, situation, location, venue	ば ジョウ	ba *joo*	土	12

場 **A** F-0066

說文

The seal-style form comprised 土 **SG-1126** "soil, ground," and 昜, used for the sound *joo* to mean "the sun rising high." It indicated a place where the light of the sun reached. The kanji 場 means "place, spot, situation, location, venue." <扌 昜>

場をわきまえる to have a sense of place/situation [ばをわきまえる]; その場しのぎ stopgap, make-do [そのばしのぎ]; 場合 case, occasion [ばあい]; 場面 situation, scene [ばめん, ばめん]; 場所 place [ばしょ]; 乗り場 bus stop, depot, landing stage [のりば]; 会場 venue, place [かいじょう]; 上場会社 publicly traded company [じょうじょうがいしゃ]

	Meanings	Kun and On	Romaji	Bushu	Stroke Order and Number
SG-1067 陽	sunny, cheerful, positive	ヨウ	*yoo*	阜	12

陽 **B** F-0718

甲骨文 1 金文1 2 金文2 3 石鼓文 4 說文 5

1 through 5 comprised 阝 "hills, mountains," and 昜 "the sun rising high and shining" (from "a tall table" and "rays of bright sunlight"). The kanji 陽 means "sunny, cheerful, positive." <阝 昜>

太陽 the sun [たいよう]; 陽気な cheerful, jovial [ようきな]; 陽性 testing positive, infected [ようせい]; 陰陽 the cosmic dual forces, the principles of Yin and Yang [いんよう]; 陽極 plus terminal, anode [ようきょく]

	Meanings	Kun and On	Romaji	Bushu	Stroke Order and Number
SG-1068 傷	injury, wound	きず・いた-める ショウ	kizu, ita-meru *shoo*	人	13

傷 **B** F-0865

說文

The seal-style form comprised イ "a person" and 亠 (𠂉) "a cover," over 昜, used for the sound *shoo* to mean "to be injured." Together they meant "an injury or wound" inflicted upon a person. The kanji 傷 means "injury, wound." <イ𠂉 昜>

傷 injury, wound [きず]; 切り傷 a cut, an incision [きりきず, きりきず]; 傷める to hurt, injure, damage [いためる]; 傷む to be damaged, wear out, rot [いたむ]; 負傷者 wounded person [ふしょうしゃ]; 傷害事件 case of bodily injury [しょうがいじけん]; 食傷気味 sick and tired of, having one's fill of [しょくしょうぎみ] // 火傷 burn [やけど]

	Meanings	Kun and On	Romaji	Bushu	Stroke Order and Number
SG-1069 湯	hot water, hot bath	ゆ トウ	yu *too*	水	12

湯 **B** F-0899

金文 1 說文 2

1 comprised 氵 "flowing water," and 昜 for the sound *too* to mean "steam rising," together signifying "hot water." In Japanese it also means "hot bath." The kanji 湯 means "hot water, hot bath." <氵 昜>

湯 hot water, hot bath [ゆ]; お湯を沸かす to boil water [おゆをわかす]; 湯気 steam, vapor [ゆげ]; 産湯 newborn baby's first bath [うぶゆ, うぶゆ]; 熱湯 boiling water, very hot water [ねっとう]; 給湯室 office kitchenette [きゅうとうしつ]; 銭湯 public bath [せんとう]; 湯治客 a person staying at a hot spring for treatment of an illness [とうじきゃく]

	Meanings	Kun and On	Romaji	Bushu	Stroke Order and Number
SG-1070 揚	to raise high, lift up, deep fry	あ-げる ヨウ	a-geru *yoo*	手	12

揚 **C** F-1424

甲骨文 1 金文1 2 金文2 3 說文古文 4 說文 5

1 had "the sun or a gem" on "a tall table." For 2 and 3, the interpretation of "gem" rather than "sun" may fit better since they depict a person holding the object high with both hands. In 4 a hand holding a stick signified "an action." In 5, 昜 (used for the sound *yoo*) moved to the right of 扌 "an act done by hand." The character meant "to raise high." When someone deep-fries food, they lift the item from the oil after cooking—whence the additional meaning "to deep fry." The kanji 揚 means "to raise high, lift up, deep fry." <扌昜>

揚がる to rise high [あがる]; 揚げる to raise, deep-fry [あげる]; 揚げ物 deep-fried dish [あげもの]; 国旗掲揚 hoisting of National flag [こっきけいよう]; 抑揚 intonation [よくよう]; 抑揚のない monotonous [よくようのない]; 意気揚々と in a triumphant mood [いき・ようようと]

	Meanings	Kun and On	Romaji	Bushu	Stroke Order and Number
SG-1071 瘍	tumor; to become inflamed	ヨウ	*yoo*	疒	亠广疒疒疸疸瘍瘍 14

瘍 **D** F-2512

説文

The seal-style form comprised 爿 "a vertically placed bed" and 一, signifying "a sick person lying down" (together, 疒, bushu *yamaidare* "illness; sick"), and 昜, used for the sound *yoo.* The kanji 瘍 means "tumor; to become inflamed." <疒昜>

腫瘍 tumor [しゅよう]; 潰瘍 ulcer [かいよう]; 胃潰瘍 gastric ulcer [いかꜜいよう]

44 A moon

44a 夕 "early evening" [from a crescent moon] 夕名夜液銘

	Meanings	Kun and On	Romaji	Bushu	Stroke Order and Number
SG-1072 夕	early evening, evening	ゆう セキ	yuu *seki*	夕	ノクタ 3

夕 **A** F-0508

甲骨文1 1, 甲骨文2 2, 金文1 3, 金文2 4, 説文 5

1 through 5 were various stages of the moon—"an early moon, a half-moon, or a crescent moon." The kanji 夕 means "early evening, evening." <夕>

夕方 early evening [ゆうがた]; 夕べ evening, yesterday evening [ゆうべ]; 夕焼け red glow of sunset [ゆうやけ]; 夕暮れ dusk [ゆうぐれ]; 夕立 sudden shower, evening shower [ゆうだち]; 一朝一夕に in a short space of time [いっちょꜜう・いっせきに] // 七夕 the seventh day of the seventh month in the lunar calendar [たなばた]

	Meanings	Kun and On	Romaji	Bushu	Stroke Order and Number
SG-1073 名	name, nominal, fame; honorific counter for people	な メイ・ミョウ	na *mee, myoo*	口	ノクタタ名名 6

名 **A** F-0084

甲骨文1 1, 甲骨文2 2, 金文1 3, 金文2 4, 説文 5

1 and 2 were mirror images of each other which comprised 夕 "an early moon" and 口 **SG-0031** "a prayer box" or "a mouth," together signifying a rite being conducted at night. 3 and 4 comprised "an offering of meat and a box of prayers." The meaning "name" was added later. Another view explains that the character represented calling out someone's name in the dimness of early evening, whence the meaning "name." The kanji 名 has many meanings: "nominal" (in the sense of "so-called"), "cause" (from "in the name of"), and "fame." It is also used as an honorific suffix for counting people. <夕口>

名前 name [なまえ]; 有名な famous [ゆうめいな]; 名義 name, title [めいぎꜜ]; 三名 three people [さꜜんめい]; 高名な well-known, distinguished, celebrated [こうめいな]; 指名する to nominate [しめいする]; 名人 master-hand, expert [めいじꜜん]; 大名 feudal lord, daimyoo [だいみょꜜう]; 名代 proxy, representative [みょうだい]; 名字 family name, surname [みょꜜうじ]

	Meanings	Kun and On	Romaji	Bushu	Stroke Order and Number
SG-1074 夜	night, evening	よ・よる ヤ	yo, yoru *ya*	夕	亠亻亠夜夜夜 8

夜 **A** F-0192

金文 1, 説文 2

1 and 2 comprised "a person with his arms and legs spread" (大 **SG-0314**), "a moon" or "evening" about to emerge from the right side, and a slanted line on the person's left. One view takes this slanted line to be "a person lying down to sleep," while another takes it to represent "repeated appearances of the moon." The kanji 夜 means "night, evening." <亠イタ乀>

夜 night, evening [よꜜる]; 夜中 midnight [よなかꜜ]; 真夜中に in the deep of night [まよꜜなかに]; 夜更かしする to stay up late at night [よふꜜかしする]; 今夜 tonight [こꜜんや]; 夜行バス night bus [やこうバꜜス]; 夜半 midnight [やꜜはん, やはん]; 熱帯夜 tropical night, a sweltering night when the temperature stays above 25°C [ねったꜜいや]

	Meanings	Kun and On	Romaji	Bushu	Stroke Order and Number
SG-1075 液	liquid, fluid, solution	エキ	*eki*	水	氵氵汁汁汸液液 11

液 **C** F-1191

金文 1, 説文 2

1 comprised 氵 "flowing water," and 夜 **SG-1074**, used for the sound *eki* to represent the sound of water dripping continuously. Together they signified "liquid dripping repeatedly." The kanji 液 means "liquid, fluid, solution." <氵夜>

液体 liquid, fluid [えきたい]; 溶液 solution [ようえき]; 原液 undiluted solution [げんえき]; 液状化 soil liquefaction [えきじょうか]; 液晶 liquid crystal [えきしょう]; 液体酸素 liquid oxygen [えきたいさꜜんそ]; 不凍液 antifreeze [ふとꜜうえき]

SG-1076 銘	Meanings	Kun and On	Romaji	Bushu	Stroke Order and Number
	inscribed name, inscription; famed	メイ	*mee*	金	𠂉牟金釒鉊鉊銘銘 14

銘 **C** F-1588	金文 1, 說文 2, 銘 — 1 and 2 comprised 金 **SG-1196** "metal or bronze ware," and 名 used for the sound *mee*, together signifying a name inscribed in metal or stone to commemorate the accomplishment of its honoree. The kanji 銘 means "inscribed name, inscription; famed." <金名>	銘 name [めï い]; 銘柄 brand, stock issue [めいがら]; 感銘 profound impression [かんめい]; 正真正銘の true, genuine, authentic [しょうしんしょうめいの, しょうしんしょï うめいの]; 肝に銘じる take to heart (lit. "to engrave in one's liver") [きもï にめいじる]

44b 月 "moon, evening" [from a half or crescent moon] 月明盟宵

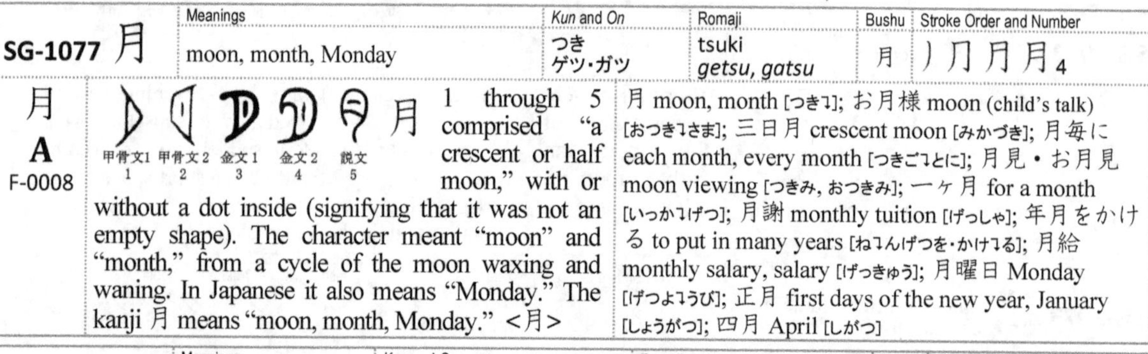

SG-1077 月	Meanings	Kun and On	Romaji	Bushu	Stroke Order and Number
	moon, month, Monday	つき ゲツ・ガツ	tsuki *getsu, gatsu*	月	ﾉ 冂 月 月 4

月 **A** F-0008	甲骨文1 1, 甲骨文2 2, 金文1 3, 金文2 4, 說文 5, 月 — 1 through 5 comprised "a crescent or half moon," with or without a dot inside (signifying that it was not an empty shape). The character meant "moon" and "month," from a cycle of the moon waxing and waning. In Japanese it also means "Monday." The kanji 月 means "moon, month, Monday." <月>	月 moon, month [つきï]; お月様 moon (child's talk) [おつきï さま]; 三日月 crescent moon [みかづき]; 月毎に each month, every month [つきごï とに]; 月見・お月見 moon viewing [つきみ, おつきみ]; 一ヶ月 for a month [いっかï げつ]; 月謝 monthly tuition [げっしゃ]; 年月をかける to put in many years [ねï んげつを·かけï る]; 月給 monthly salary, salary [げっきゅう]; 月曜日 Monday [げつよï うび]; 正月 first days of the new year, January [しょうがつ]; 四月 April [しがつ]

SG-1078 明	Meanings	Kun and On	Romaji	Bushu	Stroke Order and Number
	bright, next, clear; to enlighten	あか-るい・あき-らか・あ-ける メイ・ミョウ	aka-rui, aki-raka, a-keru *mee, myoo*	日	冂 日 明 明明 8

明 **A** F-0060	甲骨文1 1, 甲骨文2 2, 金文1 3, 金文2 4, 說文古文 5, 說文 6, 明 — There are two streams of the development of this kanji, depending on what accompanied the moon—"a window" or "a shining sun." 1, 3, 4, and 6 had "a window" next to the moon. Bright moonlight shining in through a window (囧) made things clearer and more visible at night, and the character meant "bright, clear." On the other hand, 2 and 5 contained a different shape that meant "shining sun," and which became 日. The kanji 明 means "bright, next, clear; to enlighten." <日月>	明るい bright, knowledgeable [あかるい]; 明らか evident [あきï らか]; 夜が明ける a new day begins [よï があける]; 明快な obvious, evident [めいかいな]; 解明する to make clear, get to the bottom of a problem [かいめいする]; 明白な clear, lucid, clear-cut [めいはくな]; 明言する to say with certainty, assert [めいげんする]; 光明 light, hope, prospects [こうみょう] // 明日 tomorrow [みょï うにち, あすï, あす (adverb), あしたï, あした (adverb)]

SG-1079 盟	Meanings	Kun and On	Romaji	Bushu	Stroke Order and Number
	to make a pledge; alliance	メイ	*mee*	皿	日 明 明 盟 盟 13

盟 **B** F-0964	 金文1 1, 金文2 2, 說文篆文 3, 說文 4, 盟 — 1, 2, and 3 comprised "a window and a moon" (囧), signifying "bright light shining in through a window at night," and "a shallow vessel with sacrificial animal blood inside" (血 **SG-1844**). Together they described a rite in which people made a pledge using a vessel of animal blood, by the light of the moon shining in through a window. It meant "to make a pledge; alliance." In the kanji the top component 囧 became 明, and 血 became 皿 **SG-1843**. The kanji 盟 means "to make a pledge; alliance." <明皿>	同盟 alliance, confederation [どうめい]; 連盟 league [れんめい]

SG-1080 宵	Meanings	Kun and On	Romaji	Bushu	Stroke Order and Number
	early evening	よい ショウ	yoi *shoo*	宀	' 宀 宀 宵 宵 宵 宵 10

宵 **D** F-2149	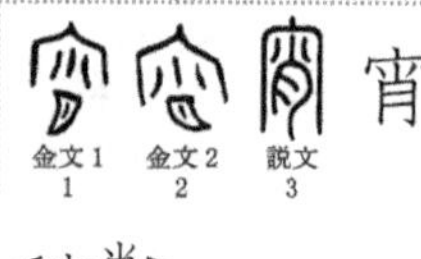 金文1 1, 金文2 2, 說文 3, 宵 — 1, 2, and 3 comprised 宀 "a house or mausoleum," 小 for the sound *shoo* to mean "small, a little," and 月 "moon." Together they signified "the time when a little moonlight shines into a house or mausoleum"—"early evening." The kanji 宵 means "early evening." <宀肖>	宵 early evening [よい]; 今宵 this evening [こよい] (literary)

45 Water and ice

45a 水 氵 "flowing water"; **bushu *sanzui***

水決浜満汚沿没汁淡潟潜湿渓漆淫氾

	Meanings	Kun and On	Romaji	Bushu	Stroke Order and Number
SG-1081 水	water, Wednesday	みず スイ	mizu *sui*	水	亅 ⺈ 才 水 4

水 **A** F-0071

甲骨文1 1 甲骨文2 2 金文 3 說文 4

1 through 4 comprised a stream of water running through the center, with two short strokes on either side possibly meant to depict splashes along the banks. Another view holds that the entire image depicted flowing water. The kanji 水 means "water." When used as bushu on the left side of other kanji it became 氵, bushu *sanzui*. In Japanese it also means "Wednesday." <水>

水 water [みず]; 呼び水 priming water, cause [よびみず]; 水を差す to pour water into, cast a damper [みずをさꜜす]; 水道 water works, water way, water service pipe [すいどう]; 水道水 tap water [すいどꜜうすい]; 地下水 groundwater [ちかꜜすい]; 海水 seawater, brine [かいすい]; 行水 open-air bathing in a tub of (cold) water [ぎょうずい]

	Meanings	Kun and On	Romaji	Bushu	Stroke Order and Number
SG-1082 決	to decide; decisively, never (when used with a negative)	き-める ケツ	ki-meru *ketsu*	水	氵 氵 氵 汐 決 7

決 **A** F-0161

說文

The seal-style form comprised "flowing water" (氵) and "a hand with a knife cutting a blockage" (夬), used for the sound *ketsu*. Together they signified intentionally breaching part of a riverbank to prevent a flood." Water swells up gradually, but when it finally breaches a levee, it rushes out swiftly and suddenly. This is analogous to making decision after long deliberation. The kanji 決 means "to decide; decisively, never (when used with a negative)." <氵夬>

決める to fix, settle on, finalize, decide [きめる]; 決まる to be decided, be settled, be arranged [きまる]; 決定 decision, conclusion [けってい]; 決心する to determine, make up one's mind [けꜜっしんする]; 決済 settlement of accounts [けꜜっさい]; 決壊する to burst, collapse [けっかいする]; 採決する to take a vote on [さꜜいけつする]; 決する to reach a decision [けっする]; 決して〜ない by no means, never [けっして〜なꜜい]

	Meanings	Kun and On	Romaji	Bushu	Stroke Order and Number
SG-1083 浜	shore, beach	はま ヒン	hama *hin*	水	氵 氵 氵 泝 泝 浜 10

浜 **A** F-0462

瀕 正字 1 濱 旧字 2 浜

No ancient form. The two precursory kanji, 1 and 2, both had 氵, bushu *sanzui* "flowing water," and the sound *hin* from 頻 **SG-0206** (1) and 賓 **SG-1230** (2). In the shinji, 兵 **SG-1456** replaced the phonetic component. The kanji 浜 means "shore or beach." <氵兵(丘八)>

浜・浜辺 shore, beach [はまꜜ, はまべ]; 砂浜 sandy beach [すなはま]; 海浜公園 a seaside park [かいひんこꜜうえん]

	Meanings	Kun and On	Romaji	Bushu	Stroke Order and Number
SG-1084 満	to be filled; full, complete	み-ちる マン	mi-chiru *man*	水	氵 氵 汁 泄 浩 湍 満 12

満 **A** F-0494

說文 1 滿 旧字 2 満

1 comprised 氵 "flowing water," and 㒼, used for the sound *man* to mean "to cover the whole." Water filling something meant "to be filled; full." 㒼 was replaced by 両 (no relation to **SG-1842**). The kanji 満 means "to be filled; full, complete." <氵艹両>

満ちる to become filled [みちꜜる]; 満足 content, satisfaction [まꜜんぞく]; 不満な discontent, unsatisfactory [ふまんな]; 円満 harmony, amiability [えんまん]; 満月 full moon [まꜜんげつ]; 満タン full tank of gasoline [まんたん]; 満期 full term [まんき, まꜜんき]

	Meanings	Kun and On	Romaji	Bushu	Stroke Order and Number
SG-1085 汚	dirty, soiled	きたな-い・けが-らわしい・よご-れる オ	kitana-i, kega-rawasii, yogo-reru *o*	水	氵 汚 汚 6

汚 **B** F-0950

說文

The seal-style form comprised "flowing water" (氵), and 亏 "a bent, crooked shape," used for the sound *o* to signify "a hollow shape." Water trapped in a hollow was dirty. The kanji 汚 means "dirty, soiled." <氵亏一>

汚い dirty, filthy, messy, mean [きたなꜜい]; 口汚い abusive, foulmouthed [くちぎたなꜜい]; 汚らわしい disgusting, loathsome [けがらわしꜜい]; 汚れる to become dirty, be soiled [よごれる]; 汚物 something unsanitary, excrement [おぶつ, おꜜぶつ]; 汚職 official corruption, bribery [おしょく]; 汚名返上 cleaning one's tarnished reputation [おめいへんじょう]; 汚点 stain, blemish [おてん]

	Meanings	Kun and On	Romaji	Bushu	Stroke Order and Number
SG-1086 沿	to go alongside, follow; along	そ-う エン	so-u *en*	水	8

沿 **C** F-1215 — 説文

The seal-style form comprised "flowing water" (氵), and 㕣, used for the sound *en* to mean "along a stream." Water runs along a riverbank. The kanji 沿 means "to go alongside, follow; along." <氵ハ口>

沿う along, parallel to, to follow [そう]; 川沿いに along a river [かわぞいに]; 沿岸 coast, shore, seashore [えんがん]; 沿革 history, historical change [えんかく]

	Meanings	Kun and On	Romaji	Bushu	Stroke Order and Number
SG-1087 没	to disappear, die, die down, be immersed in	ボツ	*botsu*	水	7

没 **C** F-1233 — 説文 1, 旧字 2

1 comprised "flowing water" (氵), "whirling water," and "a hand" (又), together signifying "a person putting his hand in whirling water to look for something that fell into the water." The right side of the kyuji 沒 (2), used for the sound *botsu*, was replaced by 殳, bushu *hokozukuri*. The kanji 没 means "to disappear, die, die down, be immersed in." <氵殳>

没する to sink, go down, merge into, hide [ぼっする]; 没収する to confiscate, seize, impound [ぼっしゅうする]; 出没する to haunt, make frequent appearances [しゅつぼつする]; 沈没する to sink, go to the bottom [ちんぼつする]; 没頭する to be immersed in [ぼっとうする]; 日没時間 sunset time [にちぼつじかん]; 没後 after one's death [ぼつご]; 没年(歿年) the year of someone's death [ぼつねん]

	Meanings	Kun and On	Romaji	Bushu	Stroke Order and Number
SG-1088 汁	soup, liquid, juice	しる ジュウ	shiru *juu*	水	5

汁 **C** F-1354 — 説文

The seal-style form comprised "flowing water" (氵), and 十, used for the sound *juu* to mean "liquid or soup." The kanji 汁 means "soup, liquid, juice." <氵十>

汁 juice, soup [しる]; 味噌汁 miso soup [みそしる]; 果汁 fruit [かじゅう]; 肉汁 meat juice, gravy, broth [にくじゅう]

	Meanings	Kun and On	Romaji	Bushu	Stroke Order and Number
SG-1089 淡	light, faint, simple	あわ-い タン	awa-i *tan*	水	11

淡 **C** F-1352 — 甲骨文 1, 説文 2

1 comprised "flowing water" (氵), and "a flaming arrow with sparks," which was used for the sound *tan* to mean "lightly-flavored food." In 2, the right side became 炎 for *tan*. The kanji 淡 means "light, faint, simple." <氵炎>

淡い light, faint [あわい]; 淡白な light, easygoing [たんぱくな]; 淡水 fresh water [たんすい]; 冷淡な lack of interest [れいたんな]; 淡々たる cool, unconcerned [たんたんたる]

	Meanings	Kun and On	Romaji	Bushu	Stroke Order and Number
SG-1090 潟	mudflats, inlet, tidal beach	かた	kata	水	15

潟 **C** F-1337

No ancient form. The kanji comprises 氵 "flowing water" and 舄 "tidal mudflats." Muddy land is left uncovered at low tide. The kanji 潟 means "mudflats, inlet, tidal beach." <氵舄>

干潟 tidal flat, beach at ebb tide [ひがた]; 新潟県 Niigata prefecture [にいがたけん]

	Meanings	Kun and On	Romaji	Bushu	Stroke Order and Number
SG-1091 潜	to dive, lurk, hide under	ひそ-む・もぐ-る セン	hiso-mu, mogu-ru *sen*	水	15

潜 **C** F-1453 — 説文 1, 旧字 2

1 and 2 comprised 氵, bushu *sanzui* "flowing water," and 朁 "hair pins inserted in the hair," used for the sound *sen* and meaning "to hide under." Together they signified "to dive into water, hide under." 朁 in the kyuji (2) was replaced by 替, used only for the sound, in the shinji. The kanji 潜 means "to dive, lurk, hide under." <氵替>

潜む to lie concealed, lie low, lurk [ひそむ]; 潜る to dive in, dip into the water, get in [もぐる]; 潜伏する to hide out, be dormant [せんぷくする]; 潜水 dive [せんすい]; 潜水艦 submarine [せんすいかん]

	Meanings	Kun and On	Romaji	Bushu	Stroke Order and Number
SG-1092 湿	moist, damp, humid	しめ-る シツ	shime-ru *shitsu*	水	氵沪沪沪浥浥湿湿 12

湿 **C** F-1462

說文 1 旧字 2

1 and 2 comprised 氵 "flowing water," and 㬎 "two strands of silk threads under the sun," used for the sound *shitsu*. This character was originally the name of a particular river. Later it came to be used to mean "wetland" and "being wet; humidity." The kanji 湿 means "moist, damp, humid." <氵日业>

湿る to become damp, moisten, be in low spirits [しめる]; 湿らす to wet, moisten, dampen [しめらす]; 湿度 humidity [しつど]; 湿気 moisture, humidity [しっけ]; 吸湿性 absorbency [きゅうしつせい]; 陰湿な dark and damp, loathsome, creepy [いんしつな]; 湿原 wetland, swamp [しつげん]

	Meanings	Kun and On	Romaji	Bushu	Stroke Order and Number
SG-1093 渓	gorge, valley	ケイ	*kee*	水	氵氵氵浮浮渓 11

渓 **D** F-1883

篆文 1 旧字 2

1 comprised "a hand holding a skein of thin threads" (奚), used for the sound *kee* to mean "very narrow," and 谷 "gorge." Together they signified "a narrow stream of water on a mountain or in a gorge." In the kyuji 溪 (2), 谷 was replaced by 氵. The kanji 渓 means "gorge, valley." <氵爫夫>

渓谷 ravine, gorge [けいこく]

	Meanings	Kun and On	Romaji	Bushu	Stroke Order and Number
SG-1094 漆	*urushi* lacquer, *urushi* varnish	うるし シツ	urushi *shitsu*	水	氵氵汁汁沐涞漆漆漆 14

漆 **D** F-1987

金文 1 說文 2

1 and 2 comprised "flowing water" (氵) for "liquid," and "a tree dripping sap," used for the sound *shitsu*. Sap from an *urushi* tree was obtained by scarring the bark, and used to make lacquer. In the kanji the right side became 桼. The kanji 漆 means "*urushi* lacquer, *urushi* varnish." <氵桼 (木八氺)>

漆 *urushi* lacquer [うるし]; 漆塗り lacquered with *urushi* [うるしぬり]; 漆器 lacquer ware [しっき]

	Meanings	Kun and On	Romaji	Bushu	Stroke Order and Number
SG-1095 淫	indecent, obscene, lewd	みだ-ら イン	mida-ra *in*	水	氵氵氵淫淫淫淫 11

淫 **D** F-2375

說文

The right side of the seal-style form comprised "a hand from above" and "a person standing" (originally 壬). Together they meant "a person eagerly wanting something," and had the sound *in*. With the addition of "water" to connote "being engrossed," the character signified "wanting something beyond moderation." Another view takes 壬 to be "a pregnant woman," and explains that, with the hand reaching down from above, the character meant "lewd or salacious behavior." The kanji 淫 means "indecent, obscene, lewd." <氵爫壬>

淫らに obscenely, lewdly, indecently [みだらに]; 姦淫 adultery, misconduct [かんいん]; 淫乱 lewd, lustful [いんらん]; 淫行 obscene behavior, sexual misconduct [いんこう]

	Meanings	Kun and On	Romaji	Bushu	Stroke Order and Number
SG-1096 氾	to flood, overflow	ハン	*han*	水	氵氾氾 5

氾 **D** F-2387

篆文

The seal-style form comprised "flowing water" (氵), and 㔾, used for the sound *han*. One view explains that "water flowing over a frame (㔾)" meant "to flood," while another explains it to be "a person lying on his face in water, drowned." The kanji 氾 means "to flood, inundate, overflow." <氵㔾>

氾濫する to flood, inundate, overflow [はんらんする]

45b ⺀ "ice; freezing" [from a block of ice with streaks of air]; bushu *nisui* 冬終冷寒氷凍凄

	Meanings	Kun and On	Romaji	Bushu	Stroke Order and Number
SG-1097 冬	winter	ふゆ トウ	huyu *too*	冫	ノク夂冬冬 5

冬 **A** F-0537

甲骨文 1 金文 2 說文 3

One view explains that 1 and 2 depicted a bent rope with a big knot tied at each end to mean "an end." In 3 a block of ice was added at the bottom. A year ends with the season of ice, which is "winter." Another view takes 1 and 2 to depict winter food stocks hanging from both ends of the rope. The kanji 冬 means "winter." <夂⺀>

冬 winter [ふゆ]; 冬服 winter clothes [ふゆふく]; 冬籠り winter confinement, wintering in [ふゆごもり]; 立冬 first day of winter [りっとう]; 冬至 winter solstice [とうじ]; 冬眠 hibernation [とうみん]

	Meanings	*Kun* and *On*	Romaji	Bushu	Stroke Order and Number
SG-1098 終	an end; to end, finish	お-わる シュウ	o-waru *shuu*	糸	幺 糸 糸 紀 終 終 11

終
A
F-0309

甲骨文 1 金文 2 説文 3

1 and 2 were the same as 1 and 2 for 冬, which originally had the meanings "an end" and "winter." As 冬 came to be used solely for "winter," a new form, 3, was created by adding 糸"skein of thread," signifying "the end, finish," from "the end of a thread." 冬 was used for the sound *shuu*. The kanji 終 means "an end; to end, finish." <糸冬>

終る to end, finish [おわる]; 終日 all day long [しゅうじつ]; 最終日 last day, final day [さいしゅうび]; バスの終点 last bus stop, end of a bus line [ばすの・しゅうてん]; 始終 all the time, always [しじゅう]; 一部始終 full particulars, a complete account [いちぶしじゅう]

	Meanings	*Kun* and *On*	Romaji	Bushu	Stroke Order and Number
SG-1099 冷	cool, chill; to keep something chilled	つめ-たい・ひ-やす・さ-める レイ	tsume-tai, hi-yasu, sa-meru *ree*	冫	冫 冫 冫 冷 冷 冷 7

冷
A
F-0490

説文

The seal-style form comprised "ice with cracks/streaks of air" (冫, bushu *nisui*), and 令 **SG-0407**, used for the sound *ree* to mean "cold" (from the emotionless posture of a person listening to an order). Together they signified "to chill, cool down; cold (to the touch)." The kanji 冷 means "cool, chill; to keep something chilled." <冫令>

冷たい cold to the touch [つめたい]; 冷やす to chill [ひやす]; 冷ややかな chilly, distant (in demeanor) [ひややかな]; 冷や汗をかく to break into a cold sweat [ひやあせを・かく]; (お)湯を冷ます to let hot water cool down [おゆをさます, ゆを・さます]; 冷静な cool-headed, serene, calm [れいせいな]; 冷淡な coldhearted, lukewarm [れいたんな]

	Meanings	*Kun* and *On*	Romaji	Bushu	Stroke Order and Number
SG-1100 寒	cold, poor and isolated	さむ-い カン	samu-i *kan*	宀	宀 宀 宀 寉 寒 寒 12

寒
B
F-0949

金文1 1 金文2 2 説文 3 秦漢印 4

In 1 and 2 "a person" inside "a house" (宀) is trying to get warm (in 1, the person is sitting with their feet rested on "piles of dry grass" and "floor mats"). In 3, "two hands" are trying to block icy cold air from coming in. In 4 the piles of dry grass were replaced by four 工 "dirt bricks" and "a floor rug." A house with walls of dirt bricks and floor mats to protect from the cold signified "cold." In the kanji 寒 the bottom component changed to "ice" (⺀). The kanji 寒 means "cold (sensation), poor and isolated." <宀共⺀>

寒い cold [さむい]; 寒がる to get cold easily [さむがる]; 寒気がする to feel a chill due to illness [さむけがする]; 肌寒い chilly [はだざむい]; 寒気 cold air [かんき]; 寒波 cold wave [かんぱ]; 寒村 poor isolated village [かんそん]; 悪寒がする to shiver, shake (with fever) [おかんがする]

	Meanings	*Kun* and *On*	Romaji	Bushu	Stroke Order and Number
SG-1101 氷	ice	こおり・ひ ヒョウ	koori, hi *hyoo*	水	丨 刁 刁 氵 氷 5

氷
B
F-1002

金文 1 説文 2 正字 3

1 and 2 comprised "flowing water," and two dots representing "a block of ice streaked with cracks," together signifying "ice." In 3 the block of ice became 冫, bushu *nisui* "icy, very cold," which was reduced to a single short stroke in the shinji. The kanji 氷 means "ice." <丶水>

氷 ice [こおり]; かき氷 shaved ice with syrup [かきごおり]; 氷室 icehouse [ひむろ]; 氷河 iceberg [ひょうが]; 氷点下 below freezing [ひょうてんか]; 氷山の一角 small part of a larger problem, the tip of the iceberg [ひょうざんの・いっかく]

	Meanings	*Kun* and *On*	Romaji	Bushu	Stroke Order and Number
SG-1102 凍	to freeze; be numb with cold	こお-る・こご-える トウ	koo-ru, kogo-eru *too*	冫	冫 冫 凍 凍 凍 10

凍
C
F-1390

篆文

The seal-style form of 凍 comprised 冫 "ice," and 東 **SG-2048**, used for the sound *too* to mean "a tied-up roll of stuff." Together they signified "frozen stuff." The character contrasted with the kanji 氷 "ice," which is frozen water. It was also used to describe "a person freezing or being numb from the cold." The kanji 凍 means "to freeze, be numb with cold." <冫東>

凍る to freeze [こおる]; 凍える to be numb with cold, be chilled to the bone [こごえる]; 冷凍庫 freezer [れいとうこ]; 凍傷 frostbite [とうしょう]; 凍結する to freeze (spending), suspend [とうけつする]; 解凍する to thaw out, defrost [かいとうする]; 路面凍結 icy road [ろめんとうけつ]

	Meanings	Kun and On	Romaji	Bushu	Stroke Order and Number
SG-1103 凄	terrible, stupendous, awful	セイ	*see*	冫	冫 冫 冫 冫 凄 凄 凄 凄 10

凄
D
F-2258

No ancient form. The kanji 凄 comprises 冫 "ice," and 妻 **SG-0525**, used for the sound *see*, together signifying "dreadfully cold," to the extent that one's skin hurts. The kanji 凄 means "terrible, stupendous, awful." <冫妻>

凄絶 extremely gruesome, ghastly, bloody [せいぜつ] // 凄い dreadful, horrible, weird, superb, wonderful [すごい]; 凄む to intimidate, use menacing language [すごむ]

46 River, fountain

46a 川 "river" [from flowing water between banks] 川州順訓巡 • 回 巛

	Meanings	Kun and On	Romaji	Bushu	Stroke Order and Number
SG-1104 川	river	かわ セン	kawa *sen*	巛	ノ 川 川 3

川
A
F-0113

甲骨文1 1 · 甲骨文2 2 · 金文 3 · 説文 4

The two contoured lines in 1 and 2 were riverbanks, and the broken line in the center was the flow of a river or stream. In 3, 4, and 5 the stream became a third solid line. The kanji 川 means "river." <川>

川 river [かわ]; 川原 dry river bed [かわら]; 川下 downstream [かわしも]; 小川 brook [おがわ]; 信濃川 Shinano River [しなのがわ]; 河川 river [かせん]

	Meanings	Kun and On	Romaji	Bushu	Stroke Order and Number
SG-1105 州	sandbank, state, large area	す シュウ	su *shuu*	巛	・ リ 少 州 州 州 6

州
A
F-0442

甲骨文 1 · 金文 2 · 説文 3

In 1 and 2 a circle in the center signified "a small patch of land in the middle of a river"—a sandbank. In 3 the number of sandbanks increased to three, signifying a larger area. The character also means a large area within a country, such as a "state" in the United States. The kanji 州 means "sandbar, state, a large area." <州>

砂州 sandbar, sandbank [さす]; 三角州 delta [さんかくす]; 中州 sandbar [なかす]; 州 state, province [しゅう]; 本州 the main island of Japan [ほんしゅう]; 九州 Kyushu island [きゅうしゅう]; テキサス州 the state of Texas [テキサスしゅう]

	Meanings	Kun and On	Romaji	Bushu	Stroke Order and Number
SG-1106 順	order, turn; obedient	ジュン	*jun*	頁	ノ 川 川 川 順 順 順 順 12

順
B
F-0672

金文1 1 · 金文2 2 · 説文 3

1 and 2 comprised "a river" (川 **SG-1104**) and "a person with big eyes observing the flow of the river." A river flows only in one direction, and someone observing the flow signified "order; to follow in an orderly manner." The person and their formal headdress became 頁, bushu *oogai* "head." Someone who always followed old ways was "obedient or meek." The kanji 順 means "order, turn; obedient." <川 頁>

順序 order, turn [じゅんじょ]; 順番 turn [じゅんばん]; 手順 steps, process [てじゅん]; 席順 seating order [せきじゅん]; 従順な obedient, meek [じゅうじゅんな]; 順々に in turn [じゅんじゅんに]; 順調に smoothly, without a snag [じゅんちょうに]

	Meanings	Kun and On	Romaji	Bushu	Stroke Order and Number
SG-1107 訓	lesson, teaching, pronunciation of a kanji used in a word of Japanese origin	クン	*kun*	言	亠 言 訁 訓 訓 10

訓
B
F-1076

金文 1 · 説文 2

1 comprised "river" (川), "words; to say" (言 **SG-1364**), and "a person with a tattoo needle over their head," another reference to "word or language." Together they signified "to follow what was written in words," which was "a lesson." The sound *sen* (from 川 **SG-1104**) became *kun*. 2 comprised only 言 bushu *gonben*, and 川. The character meant "lesson, teaching, explanation." In Japan it also meant *kun-yomi*, which is how the kanji is pronounced when used in a word of Japanese origin. The kanji 訓 means "lesson, teaching, pronunciation of a Chinese character in a word of Japanese origin." <言 川>

訓読み pronunciation of kanji usee in a word of Japanese origin [くんよみ]; 音訓 Chinese and Japanese pronunciations of kanji [おんくん]; 教訓 lesson [きょうくん]; 訓練 training [くんれん]; 訓話 moral discourse, admonitory lecture [くんわ]

	Meanings	Kun and On	Romaji	Bushu	Stroke Order and Number
SG-1108 巡	to go around, surround, walk about	めぐ-る ジュン	megu-ru *jun*	巛	く 巛 巛 ˋ巛 ﾌ巛 巡 6
巡 **C** F-1349	説文 The seal-style form had 辵 (⻌ bushu *shinnyuu*) "to move forward," and 巛 "river," used for the sound *jun* (from *sen*). A river flowing around land meant "to go around." The kanji 巡 means "to go around, surround, walk about." <巛 ⻌>	巡る to move around [めぐる]; 巡査 constable, policeman [じゅꜜんさ]; 巡回 a patrol, circuit [じゅんかい]; 一巡する to make a tour of [いちじゅんする]; 巡業 tour of the country (for theatrical companies or sumo wrestlers) [じゅんぎょう] // お巡りさん (local) police officer, constable [おまꜜわりさん]			

回 "times; to rotate" [from whirling water]

	Meanings	Kun and On	Romaji	Bushu	Stroke Order and Number
SG-1109 回	(number of) times; to whirl, rotate	まわ-る カイ・エ	mawa-ru *kai, e*	口	丨 冂 冂 冋 回 回 6
回 **A** F-0055	甲骨文 1, 金文 2, 説文古文 3, 説文 4. 1, 2, and 3 depicted "whirling water" and meant "to whirl." Whirling or coiling implied the number of "times" something went around. The kanji 回 means "(number of) times; to whirl, rotate." <□口>	回る to go around [まわる]; 回す to run in a circle, go around [まわす]; 遠回り detour [とおまꜜわり]; 上回る to exceed, surpass [うわまわꜜる]; 一回 once [いっかꜜい, いっかい]; 回数 number of times [かいすꜜう]; 回想 retrospection, recollection [かいそう]; 回送電車 out-of-service (train) [かいそうでꜜんしゃ]; 回向 (Buddhist) memorial service [えꜜこう]			

46b 永 "a long time" [from a long river with tributaries running for a long time]; *ee*

永泳詠

	Meanings	Kun and On	Romaji	Bushu	Stroke Order and Number
SG-1110 永	a long time; eternal	なが-い エイ	naga-i *ee*	水	ˋ 亅 刁 永 永 5
永 **B** F-0700	甲骨文 1, 金文 2, 説文 3. 1, 2, and 3 depicted a river with tributaries. A river large enough to have tributaries runs for a long distance, which takes "a long time." The kanji 永 means "a long time; eternal." <永(亅フく)> (Note: The kanji 永 is not used for spatial distance.)	永い long time [ながꜜい]; 永久に eternally [えいきゅうに]; 永遠 eternity [えいえん]; 永住者 permanent resident [えいじゅꜜうしゃ]; 未来永劫 timeless existence, eternity [みꜜらい・えいごう]; 永続する to last for a long time, be permanent [えいぞくする]			

	Meanings	Kun and On	Romaji	Bushu	Stroke Order and Number
SG-1111 泳	to swim	およ-ぐ エイ	oyo-gu *ee*	水	氵 氵 氵ˋ 氵亅 氵刁 泳 泳 8
泳 **C** F-1138	説文 The seal-style form comprised "flowing water" (氵) and "a large river with tributaries that runs for a long time" (永 SG-1110), used for the sound *ee*. "Staying in water for a long time" meant "swimming." The kanji 泳 means "to swim." <氵 永>	泳ぐ to swim [およꜜぐ]; 泳ぎがうまい good at swimming [およぎꜜが・うまꜜい]; 平泳ぎ breaststroke [ひらおꜜよぎ]; 背泳ぎ backstroke [せおꜜよぎ]; 水泳 swimming [すいえい]; 遠泳 long-distance swimming [えんえい]; 遊泳禁止 Swimming Forbidden (sign) [ゆうえいきんし]			

	Meanings	Kun and On	Romaji	Bushu	Stroke Order and Number
SG-1112 詠	recitation, singing poem	よ-む エイ	yo-mu *ee*	言	亠 言 言ˋ 訁 詠 詠 詠 12
詠 **D** F-1927	金文 1, 説文 2, 説文或体 3. 1, 2, and 3 comprised 永 "a long time," used for the sound *ee*, and 口 "mouth" or 言 "word; to speak." When reciting or singing poems, one's voice flowed continuously for a length of time. The kanji 詠 means "recitation, singing poem." <言 永>	詠む to compose a poem [よꜜむ]; 詠嘆する to burst out with an exclamation of admiration [えいたんする]; 詠じる recite [えいじる]			

46c 𠂢 "faction, vein, derivation" [from a river branching out into tributaries] 派脈

In ancient forms 永 and 𠂢 were the mirror images of each other.

	Meanings	Kun and On	Romaji	Bushu	Stroke Order and Number
SG-1113 派	faction, school of; derivative; to stand out	ハ	*ha*	水	丶 丶 氵 氵 氵 沂 沂 派 派 9

派 **A** F-0351

説文

The seal-style form comprised "flowing water" (氵), and 𠂢 "tributaries" that branched out from the main river, used for the sound *ha*. From something that stood alone and yet belonged to a main body, the kanji 派 meant "faction, school of; derivative; to stand out." <氵 𠂢>

派手な showy [はでな]; 流派 school of art or thought [りゅうは]; 派閥 party fractions [はばつ]; 派生する to stem from, be derived from [はせいする]; 立派な impressive, splendid [りっぱな]; 宗派 religious sect, denomination [しゅうは]; 印象派 the Impressionist school [いんしょうは]

	Meanings	Kun and On	Romaji	Bushu	Stroke Order and Number
SG-1114 脈	vein, artery, pulse, mountain rage	ミャク	*myaku*	肉	丿 月 月 月 肜 肜 脈 脈 脈 脈 10

脈 **C** F-1317

説文 1 説文或体 2

1 comprised 𠂢 "stream branching out from a river" and 血 "blood." Blood circulates like a stream throughout the body in veins. In 2, "blood" was replaced by 月, bushu *nikuzuki* "part of the body." The kanji 脈 means "vein, artery, pulse, mountain range." <月 𠂢>

脈 pulse [みゃく]; 脈を取る to take one's pulse [みゃくをとる]; 動脈 artery [どうみゃく]; 山脈 mountain range [さんみゃく]; 脈拍数 pulse rate [みゃくはくすう]; 脈絡 thread of connection, coherence, context [みゃくらく]

46d 才 𠇍 "to exist, accumulate" [from a weir in a river]; *zai/zon* 才在存財材

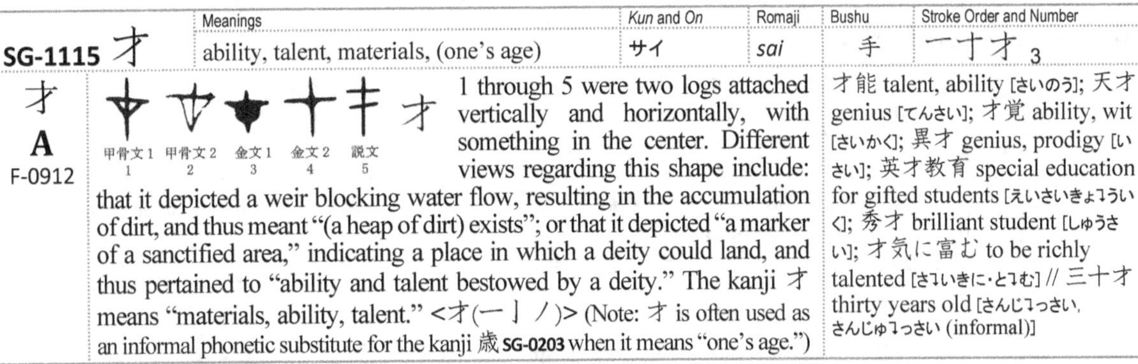

	Meanings	Kun and On	Romaji	Bushu	Stroke Order and Number
SG-1115 才	ability, talent, materials, (one's age)	サイ	*sai*	手	一 十 才 3

才 **A** F-0912

甲骨文 1 甲骨文 2 金文 1 金文 2 説文
1 2 3 4 5

1 through 5 were two logs attached vertically and horizontally, with something in the center. Different views regarding this shape include: that it depicted a weir blocking water flow, resulting in the accumulation of dirt, and thus meant "(a heap of dirt) exists"; or that it depicted "a marker of a sanctified area," indicating a place in which a deity could land, and thus pertained to "ability and talent bestowed by a deity." The kanji 才 means "materials, ability, talent." <才(一 亅 ノ)> (Note: 才 is often used as an informal phonetic substitute for the kanji 歳 **SG-0203** when it means "one's age.")

才能 talent, ability [さいのう]; 天才 genius [てんさい]; 才覚 ability, wit [さいかく]; 異才 genius, prodigy [いさい]; 英才教育 special education for gifted students [えいさいきょういく]; 秀才 brilliant student [しゅうさい]; 才気に富む to be richly talented [さいきに・とむ] // 三十才 thirty years old [さんじっさい, さんじゅっさい (informal)]

	Meanings	Kun and On	Romaji	Bushu	Stroke Order and Number
SG-1116 在	to exist	あ-る ザイ	a-ru *zai*	土	一 ナ 𠇍 𠇍 在 在 6

在 **A** F-0265

甲骨文1 甲骨文2 甲骨文3 金文1 金文2 金文3 金文4 説文
1 2 3 4 5 6 7 8

1 through 5 were shared with 才, above. For 6 and 7, one view explains that 土 **SG-1126** "dirt" accumulated in a weir signified "(something) exists," and that next to it was "a warrior's ax" (士) for protecting a sacred place. In the kanji, 才 became 𠇍. The kanji 在 means "to exist." <𠇍 土>

在る to exist [ある]; 不在 absence [ふざい]; 実在する to actually exist [じつざいする]; 在学中 in school [ざいがくちゅう]; 自由自在に with complete freedom, with complete mastery [じゆうじざいに]; 在留外国人 foreign resident [ざいりゅうがいこくじん]; 在来の existing, established [ざいらいの]

	Meanings	Kun and On	Romaji	Bushu	Stroke Order and Number
SG-1117 存	to sustain, live long, think, know	ソン・ゾン	*son, zon*	子	一 ナ 𠇍 存 存 存 6

存 **A** F-0421

説文

The seal-style form comprised 才 (𠇍) "to exist," and 子 "a child" **SG-0510** signifying "a life to prolong; to sustain." In Japanese, it also came to be used for the polite form of the verb "to think or know." The kanji 存 means "to sustain, live long, think, know (polite form)." <𠇍 子>

存在する to exist [そんざいする]; 実存する to exist in reality [じつぞんする]; 生存者 survivor [せいぞんしゃ]; 存じている to know (humble) [ぞんじている]; ご存知ですか Do you know? (honorific) [ごぞんじですか]; 異存 objection [いぞん]; 存分に to one's heart's content [ぞんぶんに]; 現存する to exist, be in existence [げんそんする]

	Meanings	Kun and On	Romaji	Bushu	Stroke Order and Number
SG-1118 財	fortune, finance, property	ザイ・サイ	*zai, sai*	貝	冂目貝貝一財財 10

財 **A** F-0482

説文

The seal-style form comprised 貝 **SG-1693** "cowrie, money," and 才 "materials, accumulation" for the sound *zai,* together signifying "accumulated money; fortune; financial." The kanji 財 means "fortune, finance, property." <貝才>

財政 national finance [ざいせい]; 財産 assets, estate, property [ざいさん]; 財を成す to build one's fortune [ざいをなす]; 私財を投じる expend one's own fortune on [しざいを・とうじる]; 財テク speculative investment, investment aimed to produce a high yield [ざいテク]; 財務省 Ministry of Finance [ざいむしょう]; 財布 wallet [さいふ]

	Meanings	Kun and On	Romaji	Bushu	Stroke Order and Number
SG-1119 材	materials, timber	ザイ	*zai*	木	一十木木一村材 7

材 **B** F-0594

説文

The seal-style form comprised 木 **SG-0608** "wood or tree," and 才 **SG-1115** "natural materials," used for the sound *zai.* Material that came from a tree was "timber." The kanji 材 means "materials, timber." <木才>

材木 lumber, timber [ざいもく]; 木材 wooden materials [もくざい, もくざい]; 材料 materials [ざいりょう]; 教材 study materials [きょうざい]; 食材 ingredients, food items for cooking [しょくざい]; 人材 personnel, talent [じんざい]; 材質 quality of the material [ざいしつ]

46e 泉 "fountain, spring" [from water seeping out of the cracks in rocks in a cave]; *sen/gen* 泉原線源願腺

	Meanings	Kun and On	Romaji	Bushu	Stroke Order and Number
SG-1120 泉	spring, fountain	いずみ セン	izumi *sen*	水	丶白白身泉泉 9

泉 **A** F-0783

甲骨文 1 説文 2

1 was a depiction of "water seeping out of cracks in rocks in a cave," and signified "spring or fountain." 2 was the outline of "a cave," with "spring water" represented by a letter T shape. In the kanji, the original single pictograph became two separate components: 白 **SG-0787** "white," and 水 **SG-1081** "water." The kanji 泉 means "spring, fountain." <白水>

泉 spring [いずみ]; 水泉 water fountain [すいせん]; 温泉 hot spring, spa [おんせん]; 源泉 fountainhead, origin [げんせん]

	Meanings	Kun and On	Romaji	Bushu	Stroke Order and Number
SG-1121 原	source, principle, wilderness, field	はら ゲン	hara *gen*	厂	一厂厂历直厚原 10

原 **A** F-0144

金文 1 1 金文 2 2 説文古文 3 説文 4

1 and 2 depicted a scene in which "water was welling out" under "a cliff" (厂, bushu *gandare*), signifying "water source." 3 had three "springs," while 4 had only one (泉). While the kanji 泉 pertains to water itself, the kanji 原 meant the place where it originated, whence "source." The meaning expanded to include the wider area surrounding the water source—"wilderness, field." The kanji 原 means "source, principle, wilderness, field." <厂泉>

野原 field [のはら]; 原っぱ open field space [はらっぱ]; 高原 highland [こうげん]; 原野 wilderness, field [げんや]; 原料 raw material, ingredient [げんりょう]; 原発・原子力発電 nuclear power generation [げんぱつ, げんしりょくはつでん]; 原理 principle, fundamental truth [げんり]; 原点 starting point, origin [げんてん]

	Meanings	Kun and On	Romaji	Bushu	Stroke Order and Number
SG-1122 線	line, railway line	セン	*sen*	糸	幺糸糸'約約約線 15

線 **A** F-0288

古文 1 篆文 2 正字 3

1 comprised "thread" 糸 **SG-1600**, and 泉, used for the sound *sen* to mean "spring water continuously flowing out," together signifying "continuous thread or line." In 2 and 3, 戔 replaced 泉 for the sound *sen* and the meaning "thin flat things piled up," but in the kanji, it reverted to the same components as 1. The kanji 線 means "line, railway line." <糸泉>

線 line [せん]; 本線 main line, trunk line [ほんせん]; 線路 railway tracks [せんろ]; 線描き line drawing [せんがき]; 電線 wire, line [でんせん]; 海岸線 coastal line [かいがんせん]; 最前線 the front line, the forefront [さいぜんせん]; (JR)在来線 old JR railroad line [(ジェイアール)・ざいらいせん]

	Meanings	Kun and On	Romaji	Bushu	Stroke Order and Number
SG-1123 源	source, origin, resource	みなもと ゲン	minamoto *gen*	水	氵 氵 汇 沥 洒 洒 源 源 13

源 **B** F-0668

原 (説文篆文 1) 𠫐 (説文 2) 源

1 and 2 were shared with the kanji 原 **SG-1121.** Because the original meaning of 原 (source, principle) expanded to include "wilderness, field," the new kanji 源 was created with 氵 "flowing water" added to emphasize the original meaning "source of water." The kanji 源 means "source, origin, resource." <氵原>

源 source, origin [みなもと]; 資源 resource [しꜜげん]; 財源 financial resources [ざいげん, ざいげꜜん]; 起源 origin of, derivation [きꜜげん]; 源泉徴収 taxation at the source, withholding tax [げんせんちょꜜうしゅう]; 音源 sound source [おんげん]; 源流 origin of [げんりゅう]

	Meanings	Kun and On	Romaji	Bushu	Stroke Order and Number
SG-1124 願	wish; to wish, request	ねが-う ガン	nega-u *gan*	頁	厂 戶 戸 原 原 原 願 願 願 19

願 **B** F-0742

(中山王器 1) (説文 1 2) (説文 2 3) 願

1 comprised "a heart," and "a person (with the head emphasized)," used for the sound *gen*, together signifying "one's wish." 2 comprised 原 "a place where water wells up," used for the sound *gan*, and 頁, bushu *oogai*, "a head." What wells up from one's head is one's wish. The kanji 願 means "wish; to wish, request." <原頁>

願う to wish, pray [ねがꜜう]; お願いする to request a favor [おねがいする]; 願書 application documents [がꜜんしょ]; 特許出願中 patent pending [とっꜜきょ・しゅつがんちゅう]; 願掛け making a petition to a deity [がんかけꜜ, がんかけ]; 大願成就 attainment of a great aspiration [たいがんじょꜜうじゅ]

	Meanings	Kun and On	Romaji	Bushu	Stroke Order and Number
SG-1125 腺	gland, glandular secretions	セン	*sen*	肉	刀 月 月' 肑 胉 胂 腺 腺 腺 13

腺 **D** F-2185

The kanji 腺 was created in Japan. It comprises 月 "part of the body," and 泉 **SG-1120** "fontain," used for the sound *sen*, together signifying "secretion of bodily fluid." The kanji 腺 means "gland, glandular secretions." <月泉>

汗腺 sweat gland [かんせん]; 涙腺 lacrimal gland [るいせん]; 甲状腺 thyroid gland [こうじょうせん]

47 Dirt, soil

47a 土 "dirt, soil, ground" [from a lump of soil placed on the ground in celebration of the deity of the earth] 土圧陸埋垣壇睦堆

	Meanings	Kun and On	Romaji	Bushu	Stroke Order and Number
SG-1126 土	soil, dirt, ground, land, Saturday; indigenous	つち ド・ト	tsuchi *do, to*	土	一 十 土 3

土 **A** F-0120

(甲骨文 1 1) (甲骨文 2 2) (金文 1 3) (金文 2 4) (説文 5) 土

1, 2, and 3 depicted "a lump of soil placed on the ground to celebrate the deity of the earth." The three dots in 2 were spirits sprinkled to sanctify the ground. The character meant "soil, dirt, ground, land." In 4 and 5, the lump of soil became a line. Something that was attached to the land meant "indigenous." In Japanese the character is also used to mean "Saturday." The kanji 土 means "soil, dirt, ground, land; Saturday; indigenous." <土>

土 dirt, soil [つちꜜ]; 土がつく to suffer a defeat [つちꜜがつꜜく]; 国土 territory, realm, domain [こꜜくど]; 土足 with (outdoor) footwear on [どそꜜく]; 土台 foundation [どだい]; 土木工事 civil engineering work [どぼくこꜜうじ]; 土着の indigenous, native [どちゃくの]; 土曜日 Saturday [どよꜜうび]; 土地 land [とち] // 土産・お土産 souvenir, something to carry home [みやげꜜ, おみやげ]

	Meanings	Kun and On	Romaji	Bushu	Stroke Order and Number
SG-1127 圧	to oppress, push down; pressure	アツ	*atsu*	土	一 厂 厈 圧 圧 5

圧 **B** F-0749

壓 (説文 1) 壓 (旧字 2) 圧

1 and 2 comprised 厂 "pressing cover," 曰 "bone joint," 月 "flesh," 犬 **SG-0859** "dog," and 土 "dirt," together signifying 'a sacrificial dog placed on or in the ground to quell or appease the deity of the earth." "Under the ground" gave the meaning "to oppress, push down; pressure." In the shinji, only two essential elements, the pressing cover (厂) and the soil (土), were retained. The kanji 圧 means "to oppress, push down; pressure." <厂土>

圧力 pressure [あつꜜりょく]; 圧迫する to press, to bear down on [あっぱくする]; 電圧 voltage [でんあつ]; 圧政 tyranny [あっせい]; 圧勝 landslide victory, overwhelming victory [あっしょう]; 高圧的な aggressive, high-handed [こうあつてきな]; 低気圧 low atmospheric pressure [ていきꜜあつ]; 高血圧 high blood pressure, hypertension [こうけꜜつあつ, こうけつꜜあつ]

	Meanings	Kun and On	Romaji	Bushu	Stroke Order and Number
SG-1128 陸	land, ground	リク	*riku*	阜	11

陸 **B** F-0676

金文1 金文2 金文3 説文
1 2 3 4

1, 2, 3, and 4 comprised "mountains or hills" placed vertically (阝, bushu *kozatohen*), and 坴 for the sound *riku*, which comprised the shapes of one or two tents that welcomed a deity descending to earth (土). Together these components meant "the land where a deity alighted on the earth," or simply "land." Another view explains that 坴 signified "continuous hills," and thus "land." The kanji 陸 means "land, ground." <阝坴>

陸 land [りく]; 大陸 continent [たいりく]; 着陸 landing, touchdown [ちゃくりく]; 離陸 takeoff (aircraft) [りりく]; 陸橋 bridge over a railroad or roadway, overpass [りっきょう]; 内陸 inland [ないりく]; 陸揚げする to unload cargo from a ship [りくあげする]; 陸続き connected by land [りくつづき]

	Meanings	Kun and On	Romaji	Bushu	Stroke Order and Number
SG-1129 埋	to bury	う-める マイ	u-meru *mai*	土	10

埋 **C** F-1447

甲骨文 篆文
1 2

1 depicted a sacrificial animal buried in the ground. 2 comprised 艸 "plant or grass," and 貍 "*tanuki*, racoon dog" (豸 bushu *mujinahen* "*tabuki,*" and 里 **SG-1312** used for the sound *mai* to mean "to bury (a sacrificial animal)." In the kanji both 艸 and 豸 were dropped, while soil (土) was added next to 里. The kanji 埋 means "to bury." <扌里>

埋める to bury, inter, fill in, cover [うめる]; 埋もれる to be covered under, sink into obscurity [うもれる]; 穴埋めする to fill in a gap, cover a deficit [あなうめする]; 埋め立て land reclamation [うめたて]; 埋葬する to bury, entomb, commit to the ground [まいそうする]; 埋没する to lie buried in the ground [まいぼつする]; 埋蔵金 buried treasure or gold [まいぞうきん]

	Meanings	Kun and On	Romaji	Bushu	Stroke Order and Number
SG-1130 垣	fence, hedge	かき	kaki	土	9

垣 **C** F-1491

中山王器 説文古文 説文
1 2 3

1 comprised "a mound of dirt" (土), and a coiled shape used for the sound *kan* to mean "to surround." Together they signified "a surrounding earthen fence." 2 comprised "walls with ramparts," and a coiled shape signifying "to go around" between two lines representing boundaries. The kanji 垣 means "fence, hedge." <扌亘>

垣根 fence [かきね]; 生け垣 hedge [いけがき]; 人垣 wall of people [ひとがき]

	Meanings	Kun and On	Romaji	Bushu	Stroke Order and Number
SG-1131 壇	platform, altar, ceremonial mound	ダン・タン	*dan, tan*	土	16

壇 **D** F-1692

説文

The seal-style form comprised 土 "dirt," and 亶 "granary," used for the sound *tan* or *dan* to mean "a raised platform," together signifying "a place where the ground is raised for a ceremony—a platform or an altar. The kanji 壇 means "platform, stage, altar, ceremonial mound." <扌亠回旦>

壇 a platform, stage [だん]; ひな壇 tiered stand, carpeted in red [ひなだん]; 祭壇 altar [さいだん]; 壇上 on the platform [だんじょう]; 教壇に立つ to teach [きょうだんにたつ]; 文壇 literary circles [ぶんだん]; 土壇場 the last moment, the eleventh hour [どたんば]

	Meanings	Kun and On	Romaji	Bushu	Stroke Order and Number
SG-1132 睦	domestic bliss; harmonious, happy, friendly	ボク	*boku*	目	13

睦 **D** F-2000

説文古文 説文
1 2

1 comprised "a tent to welcome a deity" and "a window," together signifying "welcoming." Worshipers felt joyous and friendly toward each other when receiving a deity, and the character meant "harmonious." In 2 the window was replaced by 目 "eye," to indicate "seeing," and the right side became 坴, used for the sound *boku* (from *riku*). The kanji 睦 means "domestic bliss; harmonious, happy, friendly" <目坴>

親睦会 social gathering, get-together [しんぼくかい]; 和睦 conclusion of peace, reconciliation [わぼく] // 睦まじい harmonious, affectionate [むつまじい]

	Meanings	Kun and On	Romaji	Bushu	Stroke Order and Number
SG-1133 堆	accumulated dirt	タイ	*tai*	土	11

堆 **D** F-2378

No ancient form. The kanji comprises 土 "soil, dirt," and 隹, used for the sound *tai* to mean "to accumulate." The kanji 堆 means "accumulated dirt." <扌隹>

堆積する to accumulate, pile up, heap up [たいせきする]; 堆肥 compost, manure [たいひ]

47b 圭 (1) "fief"; (2) "a tall pile of dirt" 封掛佳涯崖 圭

	Meanings	Kun and On	Romaji	Bushu	Stroke Order and Number
SG-1134 封	to enclose, seal off, grant a fief; feudalism	フウ・ホウ	*huu, hoo*	寸	土 圭 圭 圭 圭 封 封 9

封 **C** F-1168

甲骨文1 1, 甲骨文2 2, 金文1 3, 金文2 4, 説文古文 5, 説文 6 — 封

The ancient forms 1 through 6 all comprised "a young plant" with "soil" underneath, depicted as either a bulge, or as 土. 2, 4, and 6 also included a hand caring for the young plant. Each of these forms signified a fief-granting ceremony, in which trees were planted to mark the boundary of the fief. In the kanji, "a plant (生 **SG-0689**) in the ground (土)" became 圭. The kanji 封 means "feudalism; to grant a fief, seal (off)." <土土寸>

(Note: The kanji 封 is read as *huu* when meaning "to seal," and *hoo* when meaning "fief, feudalism.")

封じる to blockade, seal off, prohibit [ふうじる]; 封をする to seal [ふうをする]; 封印する to seal [ふういんする]; 封筒 envelope [ふうとう]; 封書 letter in an envelope [ふうしょ]; 金一封 a gift of money in an envelope [きんいっぷう]; 封ずる to invest someone with a fief [ほうずる]; 封建主義 feudalism [ほうけんしゅぎ]; 封建的 feudal, feudalistic [ほうけんてき]

	Meanings	Kun and On	Romaji	Bushu	Stroke Order and Number
SG-1135 掛	to hang, entrust, promise, begin; person in charge	か-ける・かかり	ka-keru, kakari	手	一 扌 扌 挂 掛 掛 11

掛 **C** F-1147

No ancient form. The kanji 掛 comprises 扌 "an act done by hand," and 卦 "divination," used for the sound *ka*. In divination (卜), a reading was marked on an earthen board (圭 "a pile of dirt"). A divination board hung by hand meant "to hang or apply." In Japanese the kanji 掛 is used for a number of meanings, including "to hang, entrust, promise, begin," and "person in charge." <扌圭卜>

掛ける to hang on, suspend from, cover, spend [かける]; 腰掛ける to sit on a chair [こしかける]; 夏掛け light summer blanket [なつがけ]; 掛け軸 hanging scroll [かけじく]; 行き掛けに on the way [いきがけに]; 見掛け outward appearance, façade [みかけ]

	Meanings	Kun and On	Romaji	Bushu	Stroke Order and Number
SG-1136 佳	good, beautiful	カ	*ka*	人	亻 仁 什 佳 佳 8

佳 **C** F-1533

説文 — 佳

The seal-style form comprised "person," and 圭, used for the sound *kee* to mean "beautiful, good" (from "two neatly shaped layers of dirt"), together signifying "a beautiful person; beautiful, good." The kanji 佳 means "good, beautiful." <亻圭>

佳境 delightful part of a story, the climax [かきょう]; 佳境に入る the climax of a story begins [かきょうにはいる]; 佳作 fine work, honorable mention [かさく]

	Meanings	Kun and On	Romaji	Bushu	Stroke Order and Number
SG-1137 涯	high shore, one's lifetime	ガイ	*gai*	水	氵 氵 汇 洭 涯 11

涯 **C** F-1630

説文 — 涯

The seal-style form comprised "flowing water" (氵) and 厂, bushu *gandare* "an overhanging cliff," with 圭 "a tall pile of dirt," used for the sound *gai*. Together they signified "a high shore or bluff overlooking a river or sea." It also meant "one's lifetime," from the notion that one's life on earth ended where the land ended (beyond which was the world of the dead). The kanji 涯 means "high shore, one's lifetime." <氵厂圭>

生涯 lifetime, for life, throughout one's life [しょうがい]; 天涯孤独 having no family, all alone in the world [てんがいこどく]

	Meanings	Kun and On	Romaji	Bushu	Stroke Order and Number
SG-1138 崖	cliff, bluff	がけ ガイ	gake *gai*	山	山 山 屵 岸 崖 11

崖 **D** F-2152

説文 — 崖

The seal-style form comprised 山 "a mountain" and 厂 "an overhanging cliff," with 圭 "a tall pile of dirt" underneath for the sound *gai*. Together they signified "mountain cliff." The kanji 崖 means "cliff, bluff." <山厂圭>

崖 cliff [がけ]; 崖っぷち edge of a cliff, brink of catastrophe [がけっぷち]; 断崖 cliff [だんがい]

48 Mountains, rocks, and valleys

48a 山 "mountain" [from a mountain range with three peaks] 山島仙嵐崩峠岬

	Meanings	Kun and On	Romaji	Bushu	Stroke Order and Number
SG-1139 山	mountain	やま サン	yama *san*	山	丨 山 山 3

山 A F-0068

甲骨文 1 金文1 2 金文2 3 説文 4

1 through 4 depicted a mountain range with three peaks. The kanji 山 means "mountain." <山>

山 mountain [やま]; 山登り mountain climbing [やまのぼり]; 山積みになる to pile up [やまづみになる]; 山場を迎える to reach the climax [やまばをむかえる]; 火山 volcano [かざん]; 富士山 Mount Fuji [ふじさん] // 山車 festival car, parade float [だし]

	Meanings	Kun and On	Romaji	Bushu	Stroke Order and Number
SG-1140 島	island	しま トウ	shima *too*	山	丿 户 自 皀 鳥 鳥 島 10

島 A F-0156

説文

The seal-style form comprised 鳥 **SG-0944** "bird" and 山 "mountain." A mountain-like patch of land in the sea where birds gathered to rest was "an island." In the kanji, the bottom of 鳥 was replaced by 山. The kanji 島 means "island." < 鳥 山 >

島 island [しま]; 島国 island nation [しまぐに]; 島国根性 insular spirit, island nation mentality narrow-mindedness [しまぐにこんじょう]; 島流し banishment to island [しまながし]; 島民 residents of an island [とうみん]; 列島 archipelago, chain of islands [れっとう]; 孤島 solitary island [ことう]

	Meanings	Kun and On	Romaji	Bushu	Stroke Order and Number
SG-1141 仙	mountain hermit, wizard-like unwordly man	セン	*sen*	人	亻 仆 仙 仙 5

仙 B F-1064

篆文 1 正字 2

1 comprised "a person" (亻), and 䙴, used for the sound *sen*. It originally meant "people reverentially moving a corpse." It signified someone going into the mountains to live as a hermit, shunning earthly mortal life in order to attain magical powers of immortality in the mountain. In the shinji, 䙴 was replaced by 山 for the same sound *sen*. The kanji 仙 means "mountain hermit, wizard-like unworldly man." <亻山>
(Note: The right side of 僊 in 2 shares its origin with the kanji 遷 **SG-0557** "to move location.")

仙人 mountain hermit, wizard-like unworldly man [せんにん]; 水仙 daffodil [すいせん]

	Meanings	Kun and On	Romaji	Bushu	Stroke Order and Number
SG-1142 嵐	storm, fresh wind, rising fresh mist	あらし	arashi	山	丨 山 岸 岸 岸 嵐 嵐 12

嵐 C F-1094

篆文

The seal-style form comprised 山 "mountain" and 風 **SG-1040** "wind," together signifying "fresh wind that comes down from a mountain." In Japanese, the character also means "stormy weather." The kanji 嵐 means "storm, fresh wind, rising fresh mist." <山風>

嵐 stormy wind, storm [あらし]; 嵐の前の静けさ lull before a storm [あらしのまえの·しずけさ]; 砂嵐 sandstorm [すなあらし]

	Meanings	Kun and On	Romaji	Bushu	Stroke Order and Number
SG-1143 崩	to collapse, crumble; death of an emperor or empress	くず-れる ホウ	kuzu-reru *hoo*	山	丨 山 岸 肖 肖 崩 崩 11

崩 C F-1267

説文古文 1 説文 2

The right side of the seal-style forms 1 and 2 was "a mythical bird," which had the same sound *hoo* as 朋 "layers," which replaced it in the kanji. 山 "mountains" and 朋 together signified "landslide" or "something crumbling." This character is also used to describe the death of an emperor. The kanji 崩 means "to collapse or crumble" and "death of an emperor or empress." <山朋>

崩れる to collapse, crumble [くずれる]; 山崩れ mountain landslide [やまくずれ]; 崩壊 collapse [ほうかい]; 崩御 demise of an emperor or empress [ほうぎょ] // 雪崩 avalanche [なだれ]

	Meanings	Kun and On	Romaji	Bushu	Stroke Order and Number
SG-1144 峠	mountain ridge, mountain pass, crisis, turning point	とうげ	tooge	山	丨 山 山' 山ㅏ 山ㅗ 峠 峠 9

峠 D F-1777

The kanji 峠 is a *kokuji* (kanji created in Japan), and thus has no ancient form. It comprises 山 **SG-1139** "mountain," 上 **SG-2135** "top," and 下 **SG-2136** "bottom," and means a mountain path that goes uphill and downhill. The kanji 峠 means "mountain ridge, mountain pass, crisis, turning point." <山上下>

峠 mountain ridge [とうげ]; 峠を越す to pass the most difficult part [とうげを·こす]

	Meanings	Kun and On	Romaji	Bushu	Stroke Order and Number
SG-1145 岬	cape, promontory	みさき	misaki	山	丨 山 岬 8

岬 **D** F-1789

No ancient form. The kanji 岬 comprises 山 "mountain," and 甲 **SG-1042**, used for the sound *koo*, together signifying "an area between mountains." In Japanese, 岬 means the tip of a shoreline that protrudes into the sea, i.e., "cape, promontory." <山甲>

岬 cape [みさき]

48b 丘 "hill" [from a hill with a hollow in the middle] 丘岳

	Meanings	Kun and On	Romaji	Bushu	Stroke Order and Number
SG-1146 丘	hill, height, mound	おか キュウ	oka *kyuu*	一	ノ 亻 斤 斤 丘 5

丘 **B** F-1029

甲骨文 1 金文1 2 金文2 3 金文3 4 説文 5

The ancient forms were a depiction of two hills, or a hill with a hollow in the middle, with a line at the bottom to denote level ground. The character meant "hill." 2, 3, and 5 look similar to the original form of 北 **SG-0388** "north." One view explains the connection as coming from the fact that tumuli were built on the raised level ground on the north side of a hill. The kanji 丘 means "hill, height, mound." <丘>

丘 hill [おか]; 砂丘 sand dune [さきゅう]; 丘陵 hill, hillock [きゅうりょう]; 丘陵地帯 hilly region [きゅうりょうちたい]

	Meanings	Kun and On	Romaji	Bushu	Stroke Order and Number
SG-1147 岳	mountain, rugged mountain	たけ ガク	take *gaku*	山	亻 斤 斤 丘 乒 岳 8

岳 **C** F-1434

甲骨文 1 説文古文 2 説文 3 旧字 4

1 and 2 were pronounced *gaku*, and comprised "hill or mountain" on top of "a mountain," signifying "rugged mountains." On the other hand, 3 and the kyuji 嶽 comprised 山 and 獄 **SG-0867**, which had "a dog" on either side of 言 "word or language," and meant "harsh, acrimonious argument in court, hell." Together they signified "hard, rugged mountains." The kanji 岳 is more similar to 2, and means "mountain, rugged mountain." <丘山>

八ヶ岳 Mount Yatsugatake [やつがたけ]; 山岳地帯 mountainous area [さんがくちたい]; 岳父 the father of one's wife [がくふ]

48c 石 "rock, stone" [from a boulder under a cliff] 石岩拓礎砕

	Meanings	Kun and On	Romaji	Bushu	Stroke Order and Number
SG-1148 石	rock, stone, old unit of quantity	いし セキ・シャク・コク	ishi *seki, shaku, koku*	石	一 ア 不 石 石 5

石 **A** F-0173

甲骨文1 1 甲骨文2 2 金文 3 説文 4

1 through 4 comprised "a cliff" and "a rock." Another view explains that the upper right component in 1 and 2 was originally a hanging musical instrument (as in 声 **SG-2041**), but came to be used for "cliff." From rocks tumbling down from a cliff the kanji 石 means "rock, stone," and was also used as an old unit of volume <石>

小石 pebbles [こいし]; 化石 fossil [かせき]; 宝石 jewel, gem [ほうせき]; 石器時代 Stone Age [せっきじだい]; 石鹸 soap [せっけん]; 磁石 magnet, compass [じしゃく]; 盤石な strong and firm [ばんじゃくな]; 一石二鳥 "killing two birds with one stone" [いっせきにちょう]; 石高 stipend (assessed in terms of rice production -historical) [こくだか]

	Meanings	Kun and On	Romaji	Bushu	Stroke Order and Number
SG-1149 岩	boulder, rugged mountain rock	いわ ガン	iwa *gan*	山	' 山 山 屵 岩 岩 岩 8

岩 **B** F-0614

甲骨文 1 篆文1 2 篆文2 3 正字 4 旧字 5

1 and 2 depicted "boulders on a mountain" and had the sound *gan*, signifying "rocks or boulders." 3 meant "rugged rock," and also had the sound *gan*. The kanji 岩 comprises 山 **SG-1139** and 石 **SG-1148**, and means "boulder, rugged mountain rock." <山石> (Note: 3 became the non-Joyo kanji 巌.)

岩 rock, boulder [いわ]; 一枚岩の monolithic [いちまいいわの]; 岩場 rocky area [いわば]; 岩だらけの rocky, rugged [いわだらけの]; 岩石 boulder, rock [がんせき]; 岩盤 bedrock, underlying rock [がんばん]; 溶岩 lava [ようがん]

	Meanings	Kun and On	Romaji	Bushu	Stroke Order and Number
SG-1150 拓	to reclaim land; rubbed copy of an inscription	タク	*taku*	手	一 十 扌 扌 扩 拓 拓 拓 8

拓 **C** F-1274

説文 1 説文或体 2 旧字 3

1 comprised 扌 "an act done by hand," and 石 **SG-1148** for the sound *taku* (from *seki*). On the other hand, 2 and 3 comprised 扌 and 庶, "to gather various items," which later came to mean "to reclaim land." The character is also used to describe a rubbing of a stone imprint or metal inscription. The shinji reflects 1. The kanji 拓 means "to reclaim land; rubbed copy of inscription." <扌石>

開拓 development, opening [かいたく]; 干拓 land reclamation by drainage [かんたく]; 拓本 rubbed copy of an inscription [たくほん]; 魚拓 take a fish impression (to record a good catch) [ぎょたく]; 未開拓地 undeveloped land, virgin soil [みかいたくち]

	Meanings	Kun and On	Romaji	Bushu	Stroke Order and Number
SG-1151 礎	foundation, basis, cornerstone	いしずえ ソ	ishizue *so*	石	丆 石 石林 石林 石林 石楚 礎 18

礎 **C** F-1485

篆文

The seal-style form comprised 石 "rock or stone," and 楚 for the sound *so,* together signifying "a rock under a pillar, a cornerstone." The kanji 礎 means "foundation, basis, cornerstone." <石林疋>

礎 foundation stone, cornerstone [いしずえ]; 基礎的な foundational, underlying [きそてきな]; 礎石 cornerstone [そせき]; 基礎体温 basal body temperature [きそたいおん]

	Meanings	Kun and On	Romaji	Bushu	Stroke Order and Number
SG-1152 砕	to smash, grind to pieces	くだ-く サイ	kuda-ku *sai*	石	丆 石 石 石' 石九 砕 砕 9

砕 **D** F-1752

説文 1 旧字 2

1 and 2 comprised 石 **SG-1148** "rock," and 卒, used for the sound *sai* to mean "small pieces." They meant "to grind something in a stone mortar." In the shinji, 卒 changed to 卆. The kanji 砕 means "to smash, grind to pieces." <石卆>

砕く to smash, grind to pieces [くだく]; 粉砕する to reduce to powder, shatter to pieces [ふんさいする]; 腰砕けになる to collapse halfway through [こしくだけになる]; 玉砕 death for honor [ぎょくさい]

48d 小 "small" [from small pebbles] and 少 "a little"; *shoo* 小少砂沙抄

	Meanings	Kun and On	Romaji	Bushu	Stroke Order and Number
SG-1153 小	small, tiny, insignificant	ちい-さい・こ・お ショウ	chii-sai, ko, o *shoo*	小	亅 小 小 3

小 **A** F-0053

甲骨文1 1 甲骨文2 2 金文 3 金文 4 説文 5

1 through 4 depicted "three small pebbles or shells," signifying "small." In 5 the three lines were lengthened in the style typical of seal-style writing. The kanji 小 means "small, tiny, insignificant." <小>

小さい・小さな small [ちいさい, ちいさな]; 小物入れ a box for miscellaneous small articles [こものいれ]; 小雨 fine rain [こさめ]; 小間物 small everyday goods [こまもの]; 小川 stream, brook, creek [おがわ]; 小学生 elementary school pupil [しょうがくせい]; 小三 third-grade pupil [しょうさん]; 小説 novel [しょうせつ]

	Meanings	Kun and On	Romaji	Bushu	Stroke Order and Number
SG-1154 少	a little, a few	すく-ない・すこ-し ショウ	suku-nai; suko-shi *shoo*	小	亅 小 小 少 4

少 **A** F-0212

甲骨文 1 金文1 2 金文2 3 説文 4

1 depicted "four small pebbles or shells," and 2 and 3 had "three small shells strung together by a thread." The kanji 少 means "a little, a few." <小丿>

少ない little, few [すくない]; 少し a little [すこし]; 多少 more or less, a little, rather, slightly [たしょう]; 少年 boy, lad [しょうねん]

	Meanings	Kun and On	Romaji	Bushu	Stroke Order and Number
SG-1155 砂	sand	すな サ・シャ	suna *sa, sha*	石	丆 石 石 石| 石小 砂 9

砂 **B** F-0795

No ancient form. The kanji 砂 comprises 石 **SG-1148** "rock," and 少 **SG-1154** "small," used for the sound *sha/sa.* Together they signified a granular substance made from rocks, i.e., "sand." The kanji 砂 means "sand." <石少>

砂 sand [すな]; 砂山 sandhill, dune [すなやま]; 砂丘 dune [さきゅう]; 砂糖 sugar [さとう]; 防砂林 trees planted to stop shifting of sand [ぼうさりん]; 土砂 dirt and sand [どしゃ] // 砂利道 gravel road [じゃりみち]

	Meanings	Kun and On	Romaji	Bushu	Stroke Order and Number
SG-1156 沙	granular, fine sand	サ	*sa*	水	氵氵氵氵沙沙 7

沙 **D** F-1772

金文1 1, 金文2 2, 説文 3

1, 2, and 3 comprised "flowing water" (氵) and "a few small pebbles, shells, or lines" (少 **SG-1154**), used for the sound *sa* to mean "very small." The character expressed how the force of water in a river eroded rocks into small granules. The kanji 沙 means "granular, fine sand." <氵少>

沙汰 verdict, information, incident [さた]; ご不沙汰しています I have not been in touch with you for a long time. [ごぶさたしています]; 音沙汰無い Nothing has been heard of him. [おとさたない]; 表沙汰になる to expose to public view, the taking public of a matter [おもてざたになる]

	Meanings	Kun and On	Romaji	Bushu	Stroke Order and Number
SG-1157 抄	excerpt, copy	ショウ	*shoo*	手	一 十 扌 扌 扌 抄 抄 7

抄 **D** F-2055

No ancient form. The kanji 抄 comprises 扌 "an act done by hand," and 少, used for the sound *shoo* to mean "small particles." "Scooping small things by hand" gave the meaning "to extract, skim the surface," and also meant "copy." The kanji 抄 means "excerpt, copy." <扌少>

抄本 extract, abstract, abridged transcript [しょうほん], 抄訳 summarized translation [しょうやく]; 戸籍抄本 extract of official family register [こせきしょうほん]

48e 谷 "valley" and others ; *koku/yoku/zoku* 谷欲浴俗

	Meanings	Kun and On	Romaji	Bushu	Stroke Order and Number
SG-1158 谷	valley, hollow, ravine, gorge	たに コク	tani *koku*	谷	ハ ハ 仌 仌 谷 谷 谷 7

谷 **A** F-0274

甲骨文 1, 金文1 2, 金文2 3, 説文 4

1, 2, and 3 had two ハ shapes, signifying "steep mountain ridges." One view explains that 口 in 1 was a hole through which water flowed out. The V-shape at the bottom of 2 and 3 was "a ravine where a river runs." The kanji 谷 means "valley, ravine, gorge." <ハハ口>

谷 valley, ravine [たに]; 谷底 bottom of ravine [たにぞこ]; 谷川 a mountain stream, a stream running down into a valley [たにがわ]; 谷間 valley, ravine, gorge, dip [たにま]; 渓谷 canyon, gorge [けいこく]

	Meanings	Kun and On	Romaji	Bushu	Stroke Order and Number
SG-1159 欲	desire, greed; to want	ほっ-する・ほ-しい ヨク	hos-suru, ho-shii *yoku*	欠	ハ 父 谷 谷 欲 11

欲 **B** F-0880

説文

The seal-style form comprised 谷 **SG-1158**, used for the sound *yoku*, and 欠 **SG-0431** "a kneeling person with his mouth open, wanting more food." Together they signified "desire; wanting more." The kanji 欲 means "desire, greed; to want." <谷欠>

欲する to desire, wish, long for [ほっする]; 欲しい to want, wish [ほしい]; 欲がない [よくがない]; 欲張る greedy, to make a pig of oneself [よくばる]; 欲が深い greedy, avaricious [よくがふかい]; 欲望 desire [よくぼう]; 私利私欲 avarice, greed, self-interest [しりしよく]

	Meanings	Kun and On	Romaji	Bushu	Stroke Order and Number
SG-1160 浴	to bathe, bask in, shower	あび-る ヨク	abi-ru *yoku*	水	氵 氵 氵 汣 浴 浴 11

浴 **C** F-1114

甲骨文 1, 説文 2

1 depicted "a person bathing in water in a basin." 2 comprised "flowing water" (氵), and 谷 **SG-1158** "ravine, gorge," used for the sound *yoku*. Together they signified "bathing in water (in a gorge)." The kanji 浴 means "to bathe, bask in, shower." <氵谷>

浴びる to pour over, bathe in, suffer [あびる]; 浴びせる throw upon, heap [あびせる]; 入浴 bath, bathing [にゅうよく]; 浴する to bathe, bask, be honored [よくする]; 日光浴 sunbathing [にっこうよく]; 入浴剤 bath salts [にゅうよくざい]; 混浴 mixed bathing [こんよく] // 浴衣 *yukata,* informal cotton kimono for summer [ゆかた]

	Meanings	Kun and On	Romaji	Bushu	Stroke Order and Number
SG-1161 俗	popular, common, vulgar	ゾク	*zoku*	人	イ 伃 伃 俗 俗 9

俗 **C** F-1465

金文1 1, 金文2 2, 説文 3

1 and 2 comprised イ "a person, an act that a person does," and 谷, used for the sound *zoku* to mean "crowding together." Together they signified customs, practices or popular things that were shared among people. What is popular among the masses may be considered "vulgar." The kanji 俗 means "popular, common, vulgar." <イ谷>

俗っぽい popular, common [ぞくっぽい]; 俗な vulgar, coarse [ぞくな]; 俗語 colloquial language, jargon, slang [ぞくご]; 俗受けする to appeal to popular/vulgar taste [ぞくうけする]; 俗趣味 low taste, Philistine taste [ぞくしゅみ]; 低俗な low, vulgar [ていぞくな]

48f 容 "to receive, contain" [from 穴 and 合]; *yoo* 容溶

	Meanings	Kun and On	Romaji	Bushu	Stroke Order and Number
SG-1162 容	to let in, grant, receive, accept; contents, shape	ヨウ	*yoo*	宀	10

容 **A** F-0463

甲骨文 1 金文 2 説文古文 3 説文 4

1, 2, and 3 comprised "a cave opening" (穴 SG-1322) with "a box" (口) inside. "Something placed completely inside" also signified "to accept," and further meant "to be tolerant." The character was also used to mean the contents of the container and its shape. The kanji 容 meant "to let in, receive, accept; tolerant; contents, shape." <穴合>

容器 container, receptacle [ようき]; 受容する to receive, accept [じゅようする]; 形容詞 adjective [けいようし]; 容量 capacity, cubic content, volume [ようりょう]; 美容院 beauty parlor [びよういん]; 容易に easily [よういに]; 容積 bulk, measurement [ようせき]; 変容する to transform, change in appearance [へんようする]

	Meanings	Kun and On	Romaji	Bushu	Stroke Order and Number
SG-1163 溶	solution; to dissolve, melt	と-ける ヨウ	to-keru *yoo*	水	13

溶 **C** F-1359

篆文

The seal-style form comprised "flowing water" (氵), "an opening in a cave" (穴 SG-1322), and "a container with a cover" (合), used for the sound *yoo*. Together they signified water or liquid filling a container. Something dissolving in water also gave the meaning "to dissolve, melt." The kanji 溶 means "solution; to dissolve, melt." <氵容>

溶ける to dissolve, melt, liquefy [とける]; 溶かす to dissolve, make a solution, fuse [とかす]; 溶液 solution [ようえき]; 水溶性 water-soluble [すいようせい]; 溶解 melting, solution [ようかい]; 溶接 welding [ようせつ]

49 Fire

49a 火 "fire" [from a fire with flames] 火炎災焼炭灰煙

	Meanings	Kun and On	Romaji	Bushu	Stroke Order and Number
SG-1164 火	fire, burning, Tuesday	ひ・ほ カ	hi, ho *ka*	火	4

火 **A** F-0322

甲骨文1 1 甲骨文2 2 説文 3

1 and 2 depicted "a fire burning with many flames," signifying "fire." In 3 the picture-like image was lost and became a kanji shape. In Japanese this character also means "Tuesday." The kanji 火 means "fire, burning, Tuesday." <火>

火 fire [ひ]; 火花 spark [ひばな]; 花火 firework [はなび]; 火影 a flicker of light [ほかげ]; 火事 fire [かじ]; 出火する a fire breaks out [しゅっかする]; 失火 fire caused by negligence [しっか]; 火力 heating power [かりょく]; 火曜日 Tuesday [かようび]

	Meanings	Kun and On	Romaji	Bushu	Stroke Order and Number
SG-1165 炎	blaze, flame, inflammation	ほのお エン	honoo *en*	火	8

炎 **B** F-0972

甲骨文 1 金文 2 説文 3

1, 2, and 3 were a towering blaze, expressed by stacking two fires (火 SG-1164) on top of one another, and meant "flames of a fire." The character also meant "inflammation" due to infection, fever or pain in one's body. The kanji 炎 means "blaze, flame, inflammation." <火火>

炎 blaze, flame [ほのお]; 炎天下 sweltering heat under the sun [えんてんか]; 炎症 inflammation [えんしょう]; 炎上する to go up in flames [えんじょうする]; 気炎を上げる to argue heatedly [きえんをあげる]; 胃炎 gastric inflammation [いえん]; 肺炎 pneumonia [はいえん]

	Meanings	Kun and On	Romaji	Bushu	Stroke Order and Number
SG-1166 災	calamity, disaster, misfortune	わざわ-い サイ	wazawa-i *sai*	火	7

災 **B** F-0894

甲骨文1 1 甲骨文2 2 甲骨文3 3 説文 4 説文或体 5

1 comprised "a weir" that blocked the flow of a river, causing a flood; and "a fire." In 2, the "fire" was inside "a house." 3 depicted "a weir in a river." A flood or a fire, caused by lightning or spontaneous combustion, signified "natural disaster, calamity." 4 comprised "a fire" underneath 𢦏 "a weir blocking the flow of a river (a variation of 才 SG-1115), used for the sound *sai* to signify "flood." 5 was "a fire in a house." The kanji 災, comprising 巛 "a river" and "a fire," means "calamity, disaster, misfortune." <巛火>

災い disaster, misfortune [わざわい]; 天災 natural disaster [てんさい]; 人災 man-made disaster, disaster caused by human error [じんさい]; 災害 calamity, disaster [さいがい]; 災難 calamity, mishap [さいなん]; 被災者 disaster victims [ひさいしゃ]

	Meanings	Kun and On	Romaji	Bushu	Stroke Order and Number
SG-1167 焼	to burn, bake, toast, become discolored, be jealous of	やーく ショウ	ya-ku *shoo*	火	12

焼 **B** F-0834

説文 1 旧字 2

1 comprised "a fire" (火), and "clayware piled high in a kiln" (堯 or 尭), used for the sound *shoo* (from *gyoo*), together signifying "to burn." In Japanese the character also means "to meddle with, be jealous of." The kanji 焼 means "to burn, bake, toast, meddle with, be jealous of." <火尭(十艹兀)>

焼く to bake, burn [やく]; 焼き魚 grilled fish [やきざかな]; 日焼けする to get sunburned, get a tan [ひやけする]; 世話が焼ける to be a handful [せわがやける]; やきもちを焼く to be jealous of [やきもちをやく]; 焼却炉 incinerator [しょうきゃくろ]; 全焼する total destruction by fire [ぜんしょうする]

	Meanings	Kun and On	Romaji	Bushu	Stroke Order and Number
SG-1168 炭	Charcoal	すみ タン	sumi *tan*	火	9

炭 **B** F-1072

説文

The seal-style form comprised 山 "mountain," 厂 "cliff," and 火 "fire." It signified someone burning a fire in a concave space under a mountain cliff to make charcoal. The kanji 炭 means "charcoal." <山厂火>

炭 charcoal [すみ]; 炭火 charcoal heat [すみび]; 炭素 carbon [たんそ]; 一酸化炭素 carbon monoxide [いっさんかたんそ]; 二酸化炭素 carbon dioxide [にさんかたんそ]; 石炭 coal [せきたん]; 炭化する to become carbonized [たんかする]

	Meanings	Kun and On	Romaji	Bushu	Stroke Order and Number
SG-1169 灰	Ash	はい カイ	hai *kai*	火	6

灰 **C** F-1271

説文

The seal-style form comprised "hand" and 火 **SG-1164** "fire," signifying "a hand gathering what was left after a fire died," which was "ash." In the kanji the hand was replaced by 厂 "cliff." The kanji 灰 means "ash." <厂火>

灰 ash [はい]; 灰皿 ashtray [はいざら]; 灰色 gray [はいいろ]; 石灰 lime [せっかい] // 灰汁 scum, lye, harshness [あく]; 灰汁を取る to remove scum [あくをとる]; 灰汁の強い poisonous, harsh [あくのつよい]

	Meanings	Kun and On	Romaji	Bushu	Stroke Order and Number
SG-1170 煙	smoke	けむり・けむーい エン	kemuri, kemu-i *en*	火	13

煙 **C** F-1273

説文古文 1 説文 2 説文或体 3

1 (with 宀 "house") and 2 comprised "a kiln with smoke rising from its chimney," used for the sound *en*, and "fire," together signifying "smoke." Another view explains that it depicted the burning of fragrant plants, creating smoke. In 3, 因 **SG-0323** replaced the kiln for the sound *en*. The kanji contains the remnant of the kiln's chimney (垔). The kanji 煙 means "smoke." <火西土>

煙 smoke [けむり]; 煙い unpleasantly smoky [けむい]; 煙たい feel awkward, feel ill at east [けむたい]; 煙に巻く to confuse someone [けむにまく]; 喫煙 smoking (tobacco) [きつえん]; 禁煙 giving up smoking, smoking cessation [きんえん]; 嫌煙権 nonsmokers' rights [けんえんけん]

49b 赤 "red" [from a big burning fire] 赤嚇

	Meanings	Kun and On	Romaji	Bushu	Stroke Order and Number
SG-1171 赤	Red	あか セキ・シャク	aka *seki, shaku*	赤	7

赤 **A** F-0257

甲骨文1 1 甲骨文2 2 金文1 3 金文2 4 説文 5

1 through 5 comprised "a person with his arms and legs spread" (大) signifying "large," and "a fire" (火), together signifying a red, strongly burning fire. The character meant "red." The shape 大 became 土, and 火 became the bottom shape 小. The kanji 赤 means "red." <土小>

赤 red [あか]; 顔を赤らめる to blush with embarrassment [かおをあからめる]; 真っ赤な very red [まっかな]; 赤ん坊 baby [あかんぼう]; 赤字 deficit [あかじ]; 赤道 the equator [せきどう]; 赤銅色 brick red [しゃくどういろ]

	Meanings	Kun and On	Romaji	Bushu	Stroke Order and Number
SG-1172 嚇	to threaten, menace	カク	*kaku*	口	17

嚇 **D** F-2499

No ancient form. The kanji comprised 口 **SG-0031** "mouth," and 赫, used for the sound *kaku* to mean "very red" (from two 赤). A fiery voice meant "a threatening sound." The kanji 嚇 means "to threaten, menace." <口赤赤>

威嚇する to menace, threaten [いかくする]

49c 灬 "fire"; bushu *renga/rekka* 黒然燃黙蒸勳墨庶薫遮

SG-1173 黒	Meanings	Kun and On	Romaji	Bushu	Stroke Order and Number
	black, dark, evil	くろ コク	kuro *koku*	黑	冂 曰 甲 里 里 黒 11

黒 **A** F-0300

金文 1 説文 2 旧字 3

1 and 2 comprised "the flames of a fire" and "a chimney with soot," together signifying "black." Another view explains that the top component of 1 was "a tied bag of fabric being smoked," to make the fabrics dark or black in color. In the kyuji 黑 (3), the bottom became 灬, bushu *renga/rekka* "fire." The kanji 黒 means "black, dark, evil." <里灬>

黒い black, dark [くろꜜい]; 真っ黒な deep-black, jet-black [まっくꜜろな]; 黒ずむ to blacken, become dark [くろずꜜむ]; 黒っぽい blackish, dark [くろっぽꜜい]; 黒板 blackboard [こくばん]; 暗黒 darkness, blackness [あんこく]

SG-1174 然	Meanings	Kun and On	Romaji	Bushu	Stroke Order and Number
	yes; that is so	ゼン・ネン	*zen, nen*	火	ノ ク タ タ 夕 外 狄 然 12

然 **B** F-0550

金文 1 中山王器 2 説文 3 説文或体 4

1 comprised "an animal over a fire," and "a bird" over another "fire." 2 had "a piece of meat over a fire" and "a (sacrificial) dog or animal," together signifying "burning animal meat." The character came to be borrowed for its sound *zen/nen* to mean "yes, that is so." The fire was dropped in 3, and grass was added in 4. In the kanji, "fire" reappeared 灬, bushu *renga/rekka*. The kanji 然 means "yes; that is so." <夕犬灬>

自然 nature, natural [しぜん]; 自然に unassumingly, naturally [しぜんに]; 当然 justly, from the very nature of things [とうぜん]; 必然的に inevitably [ひつぜんてきに]; 〜も同然だ as good as X, virtually the same as X [〜も・どうぜんだ]; 平然として with composure, unruffled [へいぜんとして]; 天然 natural [てんねん] // 然りとする to consider something correct/true (literary) [しかꜜりとする]

SG-1175 燃	Meanings	Kun and On	Romaji	Bushu	Stroke Order and Number
	to burn	も-える ネン	mo-eru *nen*	火	丷 火 灯 炒 炒 燃 燃 燃 16

燃 **C** F-1090

No ancient form. After 然 **SG-1174**, which originally pertained to "burning," was re-assigned to the meaning "yes; that is so," the new kanji 燃 was created for the meaning "to burn" by adding an additional 火 **SG-1164** "fire." The right side, 然, lent the new character its sound *nen*. The kanji 燃 means "to burn." <火然>

燃やす to burn [もやす]; 燃える to burn [もえる]; 燃焼する to burn [ねんしょうする]; 燃料 fuel [ねんりょꜜう]; 再燃する reignite, revive [さいねんする]; 可燃性 flammable [かねんせい]; 不燃ゴミ non-burnable trash [ふねꜜんごみ]

SG-1176 黙	Meanings	Kun and On	Romaji	Bushu	Stroke Order and Number
	to stop talking, silence	だま-る モク	dama-ru *moku*	黑	冂 曰 甲 里 里 默 默 黙 15

黙 **C** F-1443

説文 1 旧字 2

1 comprised the left-side component, used for the sound *moku* to mean "dark, unclear; to not speak," and 犬 **SG-0859** "dog," together signifying "not speaking; silence." One view explains a dog closing its mouth and not barking signified "silence, not talking." The kanji 黙 means "to stop talking; silence." <里犬灬>

黙る to become silent, shut one's mouth [だまꜜる]; 黙って使う to use something without asking [だまꜜってつかう]; おし黙る to keep silent, stay clammed up [おしだまꜜる]; 沈黙 silence [ちんもく]; 黙想 meditation, contemplation [もくそう]; 黙殺する to take no notice of, ignore [もくさつする]; 黙秘権 the right not to incriminate oneself [もくひꜜけん]

SG-1177 蒸	Meanings	Kun and On	Romaji	Bushu	Stroke Order and Number
	to steam; muggy	む-す ジョウ	mu-su *joo*	艸	艹 艹 芀 芽 茅 莍 蒸 蒸 13

蒸 **C** F-1551

説文

The seal-style form comprised "plant" (艸, 艹, bushu *kusakanmuri*), and "two hands" holding "a hemp plant stem" (丞) over "a fire" (火, 灬). Hemp stems with the bark peeled off were used as torches or lamps. 烝 had the sound *joo*, meaning "to rise," and from water heated over a fire creating "rising steam," the character was used to mean "steam." The kanji 蒸 means "to steam; muggy." <艹丞一灬>

蒸す to steam, use steam to warm food [むꜜす]; 蒸し暑い hot and humid, hot and sultry, muggy [むしあつꜜい]; 蒸し蒸しする humid and sticky [むꜜしむしする]; 蒸気 steam [じょꜜうき]; 水蒸気 vapor, steam [すいじょꜜうき]; 蒸発 evaporation, mysterious disappearance of a person [じょうはつ]

	Meanings	*Kun* and *On*	Romaji	Bushu	Stroke Order and Number
SG-1178 勲	merit, award for meritorious service	クン	*kun*	力	亓 盲 重 重 動 動 動 勲 15

勲
C
F-1603

説文古文 1 説文 2 旧字 3

1 comprised 員 **SG-1717** “bronze vessel,” and 力 **SG-1949** “plough” to mean “hard work.” A bronze vessel was given to reward meritorious work, whence the meaning “meritorious.” In 2 and 3, 熏 “permeating smoke” denoted the manner in which fame spread, and had the sound *kun*. The kanji 勲 means “merit, award for meritorious service.” <動灬>

勲章 decoration, order, medal [くんしょう]; 叙勲 bestowal of an order [じょくん]; 元勲 outstanding statesman, elder statesman [げんくん]

	Meanings	*Kun* and *On*	Romaji	Bushu	Stroke Order and Number
SG-1179 墨	black writing ink	すみ ボク	sumi *boku*	土	口 曰 甲 里 黒 黒 黒 墨 14

墨
C
F-1637

説文 1 旧字 2

1 comprised the shape of the kyuji 黑 for 黒 **SG-1173** “black,” and 土 **SG-1126** “soil.” Black deposits of soot were collected and mixed with dirt-like powder to make balls of writing ink. The ink was used to write on materials such as silk cloth, writing tablets, and later, paper. The kanji 墨 means “black writing ink.” <黒土>

墨 ink [すみ]; 墨絵 ink painting [すみえ]; 水墨画 painting in black ink [すいぼくが]; 墨汁 liquid ink [ぼくじゅう]

	Meanings	*Kun* and *On*	Romaji	Bushu	Stroke Order and Number
SG-1180 庶	various, common	ショ	*sho*	广	' 亠 广 广 庐 庐 庶 庶 11

庶
D
F-1665

金文1 1 金文2 2 説文 3

1, 2, and 3 depicted “a cooking pot over a fire under the eaves of a kitchen,” signifying “to cook various foods.” The meaning of “many or various” gave the meaning “common.” Another view explains that the two writings 庶 and 者 **SG-2085** became mixed up, and the meaning “various or many” from 者 (as in 諸 **SG-2087** *sho* “various”) became the meaning of the kanji 庶. The kanji 庶 means “various, common.” <庐灬>

庶民 ordinary people, man on the street [しょみん]; 庶務課 general affairs section [しょむか]

	Meanings	*Kun* and *On*	Romaji	Bushu	Stroke Order and Number
SG-1181 薫	aroma, fragrance; to emit a pleasant scent	かお-る クン	kao-ru *kun*	艸	一 艹 艹 苦 苐 董 董 薫 16

薫
D
F-1711

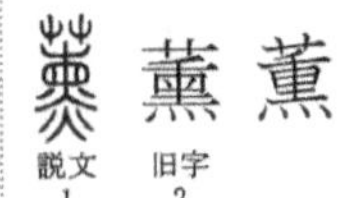

説文 1 旧字 2

1 and 2 comprised “plants” (艸, 艹) to mean “a strong-smelling herbal plant,” and 熏, used for the sound *kun* to mean “to emit smell.” Together they signified plants that gave off an agreeable scent. The kanji 薫 means “aroma, fragrance; to emit a pleasant scent.” <艹重灬>
(Note: The kanji 薫 is sometimes used to mean “to smoke (food),” in place of the non-Joyo kanji 燻.)

薫る to smell sweet, give off an aroma [かおる]; 薫陶 educational nurturing, moral instruction [くんとう]; 薫製 smoked food [くんせい]

	Meanings	*Kun* and *On*	Romaji	Bushu	Stroke Order and Number
SG-1182 遮	to cut off, obstruct, block	さえぎ-る シャ	saegi-ru *sha*	辵	亠 广 广 庐 庐 庶 遮 遮 14

遮
D
F-2017

説文

The seal-style form comprised 辵 (辶) “to move forward,” and 庶 **SG-1180**, used for the sound *sha* to mean “to hinder, hamper,” together signifying “to disrupt one’s forward movement.” The kanji 遮 means “to cut off, obstruct, block.” <庶辶>

遮る to cut off, interrupt [さえぎる]; 遮断する to cut off, block [しゃだんする]; 遮断機 circuit breaker, railway crossing gate [しゃだんき]; 遮光カーテン shade curtain, blackout curtain [しゃこうカーテン]; 遮音材 sound-insulating material [しゃおんざい]; 遮熱ガラス low-emissivity glass [しゃねつガラス]; 遮二無二 recklessly, by force [しゃにむに]

49d ⺍ (𤇾) "rigorous activity; thriving" [from bonfires] 労営栄

	Meanings	Kun and On	Romaji	Bushu	Stroke Order and Number
SG-1183 労	trouble, labor; to reward for one's service	ロウ	*roo*	力	⺍⺍⺍学労 7

労 **A** F-0448

金文 1 中山王器 2 説文 3 旧字 4

Under "two rigorously burning beacon fires on an intersecting stand," 1 had "a collar," suggesting a heart underneath, while 2 had "a heart," and 3 had "a plough," signifying hard work in the fields (力 **SG-1949**). All the forms meant "working very hard." The two fires in 勞 were reduced to the shape ⺍ in the shinji. The character also means "to reward for service." The kanji 労 means "trouble, labor, hardship; to reward for one's service." <⺍力>

苦労する to experience difficulty, have a hard time [くろうする]; 労働 work force, labor force [ろうどう]; 労をとる to take trouble [ろうを・とる]; 過労 overwork [かろう]; 心労 the strain of grief, the weight of worry [しんろう] // 労う to reward one's service [ねぎらう]; 労わる to treat kindly [いたわる]

	Meanings	Kun and On	Romaji	Bushu	Stroke Order and Number
SG-1184 営	to carry out, live life, run (a business); barrack	いとな-む エイ	itona-mu *ee*	火	⺍⺍⺍⺍学営 12

営 **A** F-0504

説文 1 旧字 2

1 comprised two 火 **SG-1164** in "burning torches" (𤇾), used for the sound *ee*, and 呂 **SG-1266** "conjoined rooms or buildings," together signifying "military barracks surrounded by torches." Important business was conducted in military barracks, and the character meant "to conduct business" or "to live one's life." The shinji 営 means "to carry out, live life, run (a business); barrack." <⺍呂>

営む to carry out, operate a business, conduct [いとなむ]; 営業 business, trade, operation [えいぎょう]; 運営する to operate, manage, run, steer [うんえいする]; 直営 direct management [ちょくえい]; 陣営 camp, the ranks, power blocks [じんえい]; 非営利団体 not-for-profit organization, NPO [ひ・えいりだんたい]

	Meanings	Kun and On	Romaji	Bushu	Stroke Order and Number
SG-1185 栄	prosperity, glory; flourishing;	さか-える・は-え エイ	saka-eru, ha-e *ee*	木	⺍⺍⺍⺍学栄栄 9

栄 **B** F-0618

金文1 1 金文2 2 説文 3 旧字 4

In 1 and 2, two brisk, intense beacon fires (𤇾), used for the sound *ee*, signified "thriving, prosperous." In 3, 木 "tree" was added to suggest a prosperous property with many trees and protective beacons. In the shinji the two fires were simplified to ⺍. The kanji 栄 means "prosperity, glory; flourishing." <⺍ 木>

栄える to prosper, thrive [さかえる]; 見栄え good outward appearance [みばえ, みばえ]; 栄えある glorious [はえある, はえある]; 見栄を張る to be pretentious, show off [みえをはる]; 栄養 nutrition, nourishment [えいよう]; 栄養素 nutrient [えいようそ]; 栄華 splendor, glory [えいが]; 栄転 promotion transfer [えいてん]

49e 尞 "dormitory" [from a beacon fire on a dormitory compound]; *ryoo* 療僚寮瞭

	Meanings	Kun and On	Romaji	Bushu	Stroke Order and Number
SG-1186 療	medical treatment	リョウ	*ryoo*	疒	亠广疒疒疒瘠瘠療 17

療 **B** F-1026

篆文1 1 篆文2 2

The two different seal-style forms (1 and 2) shared the same left-side component: a vertically-placed bed" (爿) and 一, signifying a reclining sick person (疒, bushu *yamaidare*). For the right side, 1 used 尞 for the sound *ryoo* to mean "to cure," while 樂 (for 楽 **SG-0625**) in 2 meant "comfort." From relieving the pain of a sick person, the kanji 療 means "medical treatment." <疒尞>

治療 treatment, care, remedy [ちりょう]; 療法 therapy, treatment [りょうほう]; 療養中 undergoing medical treatment [りょうようちゅう]; 医療 medical care, medical service [いりょう]; 荒療治 crude medical treatment, drastic solution [あらりょうじ]; 療養所 sanatorium, convalescent hospital [りょうようじょ]

	Meanings	Kun and On	Romaji	Bushu	Stroke Order and Number
SG-1187 僚	colleague, official	リョウ	*ryoo*	人	亻仌仌俗僚僚僚 14

僚 **C** F-1294

説文

The seal-style form comprised 亻 "a person," and 尞 "many government offices with beacon fires," used for the sound *ryoo*. Together they signified "an official working in one's same office, a colleague." The kanji 僚 means "colleague, official." <亻尞>

同僚 colleague, associate, comrade [どうりょう]; 閣僚 cabinet member [かくりょう]; 官僚 government official, bureaucrat [かんりょう]; 官僚的 bureaucratic [かんりょうてき]

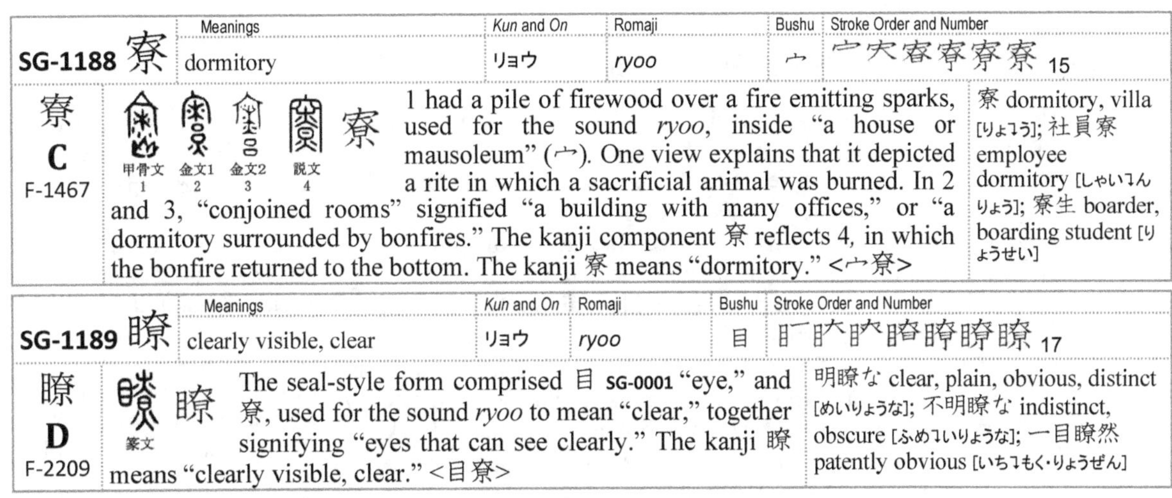

	Meanings	Kun and On	Romaji	Bushu	Stroke Order and Number
SG-1188 寮	dormitory	リョウ	*ryoo*	宀	宀大寮寮寮寮 15

寮 **C** F-1467

甲骨文 1 金文1 2 金文2 3 説文 4 寮

1 had a pile of firewood over a fire emitting sparks, used for the sound *ryoo*, inside "a house or mausoleum" (宀). One view explains that it depicted a rite in which a sacrificial animal was burned. In 2 and 3, "conjoined rooms" signified "a building with many offices," or "a dormitory surrounded by bonfires." The kanji component 尞 reflects 4, in which the bonfire returned to the bottom. The kanji 寮 means "dormitory." <宀尞>

寮 dormitory, villa [りょう]; 社員寮 employee dormitory [しゃいんりょう]; 寮生 boarder, boarding student [りょうせい]

	Meanings	Kun and On	Romaji	Bushu	Stroke Order and Number
SG-1189 瞭	clearly visible, clear	リョウ	*ryoo*	目	目目大目大瞭瞭瞭瞭 17

瞭 **D** F-2209

篆文 瞭

The seal-style form comprised 目 **SG-0001** "eye," and 尞, used for the sound *ryoo* to mean "clear," together signifying "eyes that can see clearly." The kanji 瞭 means "clearly visible, clear." <目尞>

明瞭な clear, plain, obvious, distinct [めいりょうな]; 不明瞭な indistinct, obscure [ふめいりょうな]; 一目瞭然 patently obvious [いちもく・りょうぜん]

49f 堇 "scarce"; *kin* 勤謹僅, and 菓 "difficulty"; *nan/kan/tan* 難漢嘆

[from a fire arrow and a fire, or an animal hide being dried over a fire]

	Meanings	Kun and On	Romaji	Bushu	Stroke Order and Number
SG-1190 勤	to work hard; diligent	つと-める キン・ゴン	tsuto-meru *kin, gon*	力	一艹芇芇堇勤勤 12

勤 **B** F-0958

金文1 1 金文2 2 説文 3 旧字 4 勤

堇 was used for the sound *kin* to mean "hardship." In 3 "a plow; to labor" (力 **SG-1949**) was added to 堇 (堇), signifying "strenuous field work." The kanji 勤 means "to work diligently." <堇 力>

勤める to serve, hold (a post), conduct a religious service [つとめる]; 勤務 service, duty, job [きんむ]; 出勤 work attendance [しゅっきん]; 通勤 commuting [つうきん]; 常勤 full-time employment [じょうきん]; 欠勤 absence from work [けっきん]; 勤行 religious service [ごんぎょう]

	Meanings	Kun and On	Romaji	Bushu	Stroke Order and Number
SG-1191 謹	discreet, circumspect; to restrain oneself	つつし-む キン	tsutsushi-mu *kin*	言	言訁艹諆諆謹謹 17

謹 **D** F-1898

説文 1 旧字 2 謹

1 comprised 言, bushu *gonben* "word; to say," and 堇 "scarce," used for the sound *kin*. When one refrained from speaking, it demonstrated discretion and circumspection. The kanji 謹 means "discreet, circumspect; to restrain oneself." <言堇>

謹んで respectfully, humbly [つつしんで]; 不謹慎な impudent, thoughtless [ふきんしんな]; 謹賀新年 Best Wishes for a Happy New Year [きんがしんねん]

	Meanings	Kun and On	Romaji	Bushu	Stroke Order and Number
SG-1192 僅	scarce, few; very small amount	わず-か キン	wazu-ka *kin*	人	亻仳偌僅僅 13

僅 **D** F-2549

説文 僅

The seal-style form comprised 亻 "an act that one does," and 堇, used for the sound *kin* to mean "scarce," together signifying that a person had very little. The kanji 僅 means "scarce, few; very small amount." <亻堇>

僅かな a few, trifling, insignificant [わずかな]; 僅少な only a few [きんしょうな]

菓"difficulty"; `*nan/kan/tan* 難漢嘆

	Meanings	Kun and On	Romaji	Bushu	Stroke Order and Number
SG-1193 難	hardship; difficult	むずか-しい・～がた-い ナン	muzuka-shii, V-gatai *nan*	隹	一艹莒莫莫'莫'難難 18

難 **B** F-0548

金文 1 説文古文 2 説文 3 説文或体 4 旧字 5 難

1 through 4 comprised "a fire arrow"; "a fire" or "dirt," used for the sound *nan* to signify "difficulty"; and "a bird" (隹). Shooting a bird with a fire arrow, or a bird being roasted, gave the meaning "difficulty or hardship." Some hold that the use of 難 for this meaning was a borrowing. The kanji 難 means "hardship; difficult." <菓隹>

難しい hard, difficult, troublesome, sullen [むずかしい, むずかしい]; し難い hard to do, difficult to do [しがたい]; 難点 knotty point, fault, flaw [なんてん, なんてん]; 至難の most difficult [しなんの]; 難関 insurmountable barrier, obstacle [なんかん]; 難産 difficult birth [なんざん]; 難儀な troublesome, onerous, difficult [なんぎな]

	Meanings	Kun and On	Romaji	Bushu	Stroke Order and Number
SG-1194 漢	Chinese; Han dynasties; Chinese character, man	カン	*kan*	水	氵氵艹汼漟漢漢 13

漢
C
F-1095

説文 1 旧字 2

1 comprised "flowing water" (氵), and 莫, used for the sound *kan,* and was the name of a particular river. The Han dynasties (206 BCE - 8 CE and 25-220 CE) lasted for 400 years, and 漢 came to mean "China; Chinese." During the preceding Qing dynasty, with the centralization of power and increased record-keeping, a new, simplified and more practical writing style (隷書 clerical-style) was created, with straighter, more uniform lines, and fewer strokes than the official seal-style forms. The new style became "the writing of Han" (漢字, *hanzi* in Chinese, *kanji* in Japanese). In later times some exterior tribes would use 漢 to refer to the Han men, and from that the character also means "a man." The kanji 漢 means "Chinese; Han dynasties; Chinese character, man." <氵莫>

漢字 kanji, Chinese character [かんじ]; 悪漢 scoundrel [あっかん]; 門外漢 outsider, layperson [もんがいかん]; 漢和辞典 Chinese-Japanese character dictionary [かんわじてん]; 漢文 classical Chinese texts [かんぶん]; 和漢混淆(or 交)文 Japanese literary writing style mixing kana and Chinese words in kanji (historical) [わかん・こんこうぶん]; 漢方 traditional Chinese herbal medicine [かんぽう]

	Meanings	Kun and On	Romaji	Bushu	Stroke Order and Number
SG-1195 嘆	to lament, grieve, sigh	なげ-く タン	nage-ku *tan*	口	口口口艹口艹咁嘆嘆嘆 13

嘆
C
F-1613

金文 1 説文 2 旧字 3

1, 2, and 3 comprised 莫, used for the sound *tan* to mean "lamentation, marvel", and 口 **SG-0031** "mouth; to utter," together signifying "to lament, grieve." The kanji 嘆 means "to lament, grieve, sigh." <口莫>

嘆く to lament, grieve [なげく]; 嘆かわしい lamentable, deplorable, wretched [なげかわしい]; 感嘆する to admire, be struck with, marvel at [かんたんする]; 驚嘆する to be struck with admiration [きょうたんする]; 悲嘆に暮れる to suffer distress, be crushed with grief [ひたんにくれる]

50 Metal nuggets in the ground

50 金 "metal, mineral" [from metal nuggets in a mine]; bushu *kanehen* 金

金鉄針銃錦鋭鉛釜鋳

	Meanings	Kun and On	Romaji	Bushu	Stroke Order and Number
SG-1196 金	metal, gold, money; golden	かね・かな キン・コン	kane, kana *kin, kon*	金	八今全余金 8

金
A
F-0021

金文 1 金文 2 金文 3 説文 4

1 through 4 comprised 亼, used for the sound *kin,* and 玊 "glistening metal nuggets in soil," together signifying "metal." Another view explains that the small dots on the side were pieces of copper that were inlaid or cast in a mold. The character originally meant "bronze," as in 金文"bronzeware-style characters," and then later came to be used for "gold, metal." The kanji 金 means "metal, gold, money; golden." <亼玊>

金 metal [かね]; お金 money [おかね]; 金持ち rich, wealthy [かねもち, かねもち]; 有り金 remaining money [ありがね]; 黄金 golden, gold [こがね, おうごん]; 金物 metal [かなもの]; 金 gold [きん]; 借金 debt, borrowing money [しゃっきん]; 金属 metal [きんぞく]; 金色 golden [きんいろ, こんじき]; 金文 bronzeware-style characters [きんぶん]

	Meanings	Kun and On	Romaji	Bushu	Stroke Order and Number
SG-1197 鉄	iron	テツ	*tetsu*	金	亼全金金金金鉄鉄 13

鉄
B
F-0612

説文古文 1 説文 2 旧字 3

1, 2, and 3 comprised 金 **SG-1196** "metal," and the right-side component, used for the sound *tetsu* to mean "red." Metal that became red when rusted meant "iron." The less-formal kanji 鉄 means "iron." <金失>

鉄 iron [てつ]; 鉄道 railroad, railway [てつどう]; 私鉄 private railway [してつ]; 旧国鉄 (旧国有鉄道) old National Railway, predecessor of Japan Railways (JR) [きゅう・こくてつ, (きゅう・こくゆうてつどう)]; 地下鉄 subway, underground railway [ちかてつ]; 鉄砲 gun, firearms [てっぽう]; 鉄火巻き sushi roll with pieces of raw tuna inside [てっかまき]; 鉄くず iron scraps [てつくず, てつくず]; 鉄人 very strong man [てつじん]

	Meanings	Kun and On	Romaji	Bushu	Stroke Order and Number
SG-1198 針	sewing needle, needle, (clock) hand	はり シン	hari *shin*	金	𠂉 亼 仐 糸 金 針 10

針
B
F-0748

鍼 (説文 1) 鍼 (正字 2) 針

The seal-style form (1) comprised 金 "metal," and 咸, used for the sound *shin*, together signifying "a needle." In the shinji 針, 咸 was replaced by 十. The kanji 針 means "sewing needle, needle, (clock) hand." <金 十> (Note: the orthographic style kanji 鍼 (2) is a non-Joyo kanji, and is used to mean "acupuncture needle or treatment.")

針 needle [はり]; 時計の針 clock hand [とけいのはり]; 針金 thin wire [はりがね]; 縫い針 sewing needle [ぬいばり, ぬいばり]; 方針 guideline [ほうしん]; メーター検針 reading of a meter [メーターけんしん]

	Meanings	Kun and On	Romaji	Bushu	Stroke Order and Number
SG-1199 銃	gun	ジュウ	*juu*	金	𠂉 亼 仐 糸 金 釒 鈘 銃 14

銃
C
F-1312

No ancient form. The right-side component 充 was used for the sound *juu* to mean "a hole" referring to "a little hole into which gunpowder is loaded." 金 **SG-1196** "metal" and 充 together meant "gun." The kanji 銃 means "gun." <金 充>

銃 gun, firearms [じゅう]; 拳銃 pistol, handgun, gun [けんじゅう]; 銃声 sound of gunfire [じゅうせい]; 銃器 small arms, firearms [じゅうき]

	Meanings	Kun and On	Romaji	Bushu	Stroke Order and Number
SG-1200 錦	brocade	にしき キン	nishiki *kin*	金	𠂉 亼 仐 糸 金 鉑 錦 錦 16

錦
C
F-1408

錦 (説文) 錦

The seal-style form comprised 金, used for the sound *kin*, and 帛 "silk cloth," also used for *kin*, together signifying silk that had gold woven into it. The kanji 錦 means "brocade." <金 帛>

錦 Japanese brocade, fine dress [にしき]

	Meanings	Kun and On	Romaji	Bushu	Stroke Order and Number
SG-1201 鋭	sharp	するど-い エイ	surudo-i *ee*	金	𠂉 亼 仐 糸 金 釒 鋭 鋭 15

鋭
C
F-1456

(説文籀文 1) 鋭 (説文 2) 鋭

1 was "a fire burning high in a kiln or furnace" for forging "a sharp sword or knife." 2 comprised 金 "metal," and 兑 (兊), used for the sound *ee* to mean "sharp." The kanji 鋭 means "sharp." <金兑>

鋭い sharp [するどい]; 鋭利な sharp, sharp-edged [えいりな]; 精鋭 elite [せいえい]; 気鋭の spirited, enthusiastic [きえいの]; 鋭角 acute angle [えいかく]; 最新鋭の state-of-the-art [さいしんえいの]

	Meanings	Kun and On	Romaji	Bushu	Stroke Order and Number
SG-1202 鉛	lead	なまり エン	namari *en*	金	𠂉 亼 仐 糸 金 釒 鉛 13

鉛
C
F-1633

鉛 (説文) 鉛

The seal-style form comprised 金 "metal," and 㕣 "running liquid," used for the sound *en*. Metal that melts and runs easily is lead. The kanji 鉛 means "lead." <金 㕣>

鉛 lead [なまり]; 鉛中毒 lead poisoning [なまりちゅうどく]; 鉛筆 pencil [えんぴつ]; 亜鉛 zinc [あえん]; 無鉛ガソリン unleaded gasoline [むえんガソリン]

	Meanings	Kun and On	Romaji	Bushu	Stroke Order and Number
SG-1203 釜	rice cooker, iron pot	かま	kama	金	八 ハ 父 쏘 斧 斧 釜 10

釜
D
F-1816

(金文1 1) (金文2 2) (説文 3) (説文或体 4) 釜

1and 2 comprised "a pestle in a mortar" (1) or "metal" (2) on the left, and "a hand holding a measuring tool" on the right. Together they signified "a hand handling a cooking pot." 3 comprised 鬲 "a grain storage," and 甫, used for the sound *hu*. 4 had "a hand" over "metal." The kanji used 父 for *hu*, which coalesced a little with the bottom component 金 **SG-1196**. The kanji 釜 means "iron cooker, iron pot." <父金>

釜 rice cooker, cooking pot [かま]; 茶釜 iron tea kettle [ちゃがま]; 圧力釜 pressure cooker [あつりょくがま]; 風呂釜 bath furnace [ふろがま]

	Meanings	Kun and On	Romaji	Bushu	Stroke Order and Number
SG-1204 鋳	to cast, found, mint	い-る チュウ	i-ru *chuu*	金	亼 仐 金 鈓 鋳 鋳 鋳 鋳 15

鋳
D
F-2194

(甲骨文 1) (金文1 2) (金文2 3) (金文3 4) 鑄 (説文 5) 鑄 (旧字 6) 鋳

1 through 4 comprised "two hands handling a cooking stove over a fire," and "a vessel." The character depicted a scene in which very hot melted metal was being poured into

鋳る to cast (a statue), found (a bell), mint (coin) [いる]; 鋳造する to cast (metal),

	a vessel at a foundry, and it meant "to cast metal." 5 comprised 金 "metal," and 壽, used for the sound *chuu* to mean "to cast." 壽 in 6 was drastically simplified to 寿 **SG-0564** in the shinji. The kanji 鋳 means "to cast, found, mint." <金寿>	found (a bell), mint (coin) [ちゅうぞうする]

51 Metrological phenomena

51a 雨 "rain, atmospheric phenomenon " [from rain falling from the clouds]; bushu *amekanmuri* "precipitation" 雨雪雲霊霧零漏曇霜

	Meanings	Kun and On	Romaji	Bushu	Stroke Order and Number
SG-1205 雨	rain, rainfall	あめ・あま ウ	ame, ama *u*	雨	8
雨 **A** F-0426	甲骨文 1, 金文1 2, 金文2 3, 説文古文 4, 説文 5 1 depicted a cloud and raindrops. In 2, 3, and 4, the raindrops were inside 冂, "a cloud or the imaginary dome of the universe." The kanji 雨 means "rain, rainfall." When used as bushu *amekanmuri*, it means any precipitation. <雨>		雨 rain [あꜜめ]; 雨具 raingear [あまꜜぐ]; 雨水 rainwater [あまꜜみず]; 雨天 rainy weather [うꜜてん]; 降雨量 amount of rainfall [こうꜜうりょう] // 小雨 drizzle, light rain [こさめ]; 春雨 fine spring rain [はるさめ]; 時雨 late-autumn or early-winter shower, occasional shower [しぐれ]; 五月雨 early summer rain [さみだれ]; 梅雨 rainy season shower [ばꜜいう, つゆꜜ]		

	Meanings	Kun and On	Romaji	Bushu	Stroke Order and Number
SG-1206 雪	snow	ゆき セツ	yuki *setsu*	雨	11
雪 **B** F-0542	甲骨文1 1, 甲骨文2 2, 甲骨文3 3, 説文 4 1, 2, and 3 comprised "drops falling from a cloud," and "lightly falling snowflakes that look like feathers," signifying "snow or snowfall." 4 comprised 雨, bushu *amekanmuri* "falling from the sky" or "atmospheric phenomenon," two "brooms" to signify "sweeping clean," and "a hand." Together they signified "snowfall blanketing the earth as if sweeping everything clean." The kanji 雪 means "snow." <雨ヨ>		雪 snow [ゆꜜき]; 大雪 blizzard, big snowfall [おおゆき]; 雪かき snow shoveling, snow removal [ゆきかꜜき]; 新雪 new snow [しんせつ]; 残雪 lingering snow on the ground [ざんせつ]; 豪雪 tremendous snow fall [ごうせつ]; 雪解け thawing of snow [ゆきどけ]		

	Meanings	Kun and On	Romaji	Bushu	Stroke Order and Number
SG-1207 雲	cloud	くも ウン	kumo *un*	雨	12
雲 **B** F-0825	甲骨文1 1, 甲骨文2 2, 説文古文1 3, 説文古文2 4, 篆文 5, 説文 6 1 through 4 were "columns of cloud," such as thunderheads, which had the sound *un*, and became 云 in the kanji. The character meant "cloud." In 5 and 6 雨 bushu *amekanmuri* was added. The kanji 雲 means "cloud." <雨云>		雲 cloud [くꜜも]; 雲行き the movement of the clouds, a turn of events [くもゆき]; 雨雲 rain cloud [あまぐも]; 入道雲 thunderhead [にゅうどうぐꜜも]; 雲隠れする to hide behind the clouds, vanish [くもがꜜくれする]; 雲泥の差 a big difference, a world of difference [うんでいのさ]; 積乱雲 cumulonimbus [せきらꜜんうん]		

	Meanings	Kun and On	Romaji	Bushu	Stroke Order and Number
SG-1208 霊	spirit, soul	たま レイ・リョウ	tama *ree, ryoo*	雨	15
霊 **C** F-1423	金文 1, 説文 2, 説文或体 3, 旧字 4 1 through 4 comprised 雨 **SG-1205** "atmospheric; falling in the sky," "three prayer boxes or mouths," and 巫 "spiritual medium" (except in 1). Together they signified "a rainmaking rite" or "praying for spirits to come down from heaven." In the shinji the bottom was simplified. The kanji 霊 means "spirit, soul." <雨二业>		言霊 the spirit of language [ことだま]; 御霊 the spirit of the dead [みたま]; 霊長類 primates [れいちょꜜうるい]; 霊山 holy mountain [れいざん]; 霊感 inspiration, psychic sense [れいかん]; 聖霊 holy spirit [せいれい]; 悪霊 evil spirit [あくりょう]; 怨霊 vengeful ghost [おんりょう]		

	Meanings	Kun and On	Romaji	Bushu	Stroke Order and Number
SG-1209 霧	mist, fog	きり ム	kiri *mu*	雨	霧 19

霧 **C** F-1433

説文籀文 1 説文 2

The bottom of 1 (矛) was used for the sound *mu* to mean "unclear." An atmospheric phenomenon (雨) that hampered visibility due to tiny water droplets suspended in the air was "fog." 攴 "to cause action" was added to the bottom component in 2, and 力 further added in the kanji, forming 務 **SG-1506**, used for the sound *mu*. The kanji 霧 means "mist, fog." <雨 務>

霧 mist, fog [きり]; 朝霧 morning fog [あさぎり]; 夜霧 night fog [よるぎり]; 濃霧 thick fog [のうむ]; 五里霧中 totally mystified, in a fog [ごり・むちゅう]

	Meanings	Kun and On	Romaji	Bushu	Stroke Order and Number
SG-1210 零	to fall on hard times; zero, naught	レイ	*ree*	雨	零 13

零 **C** F-1547

説文

The seal-style form comprised 雨, and 令 (令) **SG-0407**, used for the sound *ree* to mean "cold." Cold rain falling signified hard times. The sound *ree* also meant "zero, naught, nothing." The kanji 零 means "to fall on hard times; zero, naught." <雨令>

零 naught, nothing, zero [れい]; 零細企業 small business [れいさいきぎょう]; 零落する to fall on hard times [れいらくする]; 零時 twelve o'clock midnight [れいじ]

	Meanings	Kun and On	Romaji	Bushu	Stroke Order and Number
SG-1211 漏	to leak, drip, come through, creep away	も-れる ロウ	mo-reru *roo*	水	漏 14

漏 **D** F-1714

説文

The seal-style form comprised "water," 尸 "roof," and 雨 **SG-1205** "rain" (for the sound *roo*), together signifying "rain leaking from a roof." The kanji 漏 means "to leak, drip, come through, creep away." <氵尸雨>

漏れる to leak [もれる]; 雨漏り leak in a roof [あまもり]; オイル漏れ oil leak [オイルもれ]; 漏電 electric leakage, short circuit [ろうでん]; 漏洩する to leak (information) [ろうえいする]

	Meanings	Kun and On	Romaji	Bushu	Stroke Order and Number
SG-1212 曇	cloudy; cloudy sky	くも-る ドン	kumo-ru *don*	日	曇 16

曇 **D** F-1798

篆文

The seal-style form comprised 日 "the sun," and 雲 **SG-1207** "cloud." When the sun is hidden in the clouds the weather is "cloudy." The kanji 曇 means "cloudy; cloudy sky." <日雲>

曇る to be cloudy [くもる]; 曇天 cloudy sky [どんてん]

	Meanings	Kun and On	Romaji	Bushu	Stroke Order and Number
SG-1213 霜	frost	しも ソウ	shimo *soo*	雨	霜 17

霜 **D** F-1967

説文

The seal-style form of the kanji 霜 comprised 雨 "atmospheric phenomenon," and 相 **SG-0004** ("facing each other"), used for the sound *soo*. When moisture freezes on the ground it forms frost columns that face each other. The kanji 霜 means "frost." <雨 相>

霜 frost [しも]; 霜降り肉 marbled meat [しもふりにく]; 霜取り defrosting a freezer [しもとり]; 霜焼け frostbite, chilblains [しもやけ]; 幾星霜 many months and years [いく・せいそう]

51b 申 "lightning; divine" [from lightning in the sky believed to be a divine message]; *shin* 申神電伸雷紳

	Meanings	Kun and On	Romaji	Bushu	Stroke Order and Number
SG-1214 申	to speak, state, say (humble)	もう-す シン	moo-su *shin*	田	申 5

申 **A** F-0607

甲骨文1 1 甲骨文2 2 金文1 3 金文2 4 説文 5

1, 2, 3, and 4 depicted lightning travelling in a zigzag shape against a dark sky. 3 included two "mouths" (口) to represent "a deity's voice." Ancient people took lightning and thunder to be the voice of a deity. Originally meaning "deity," the character came to

申す to say (humble) [もうす]; 私、〜と申します My name is X. (humble) [わたくし・〜ともうします]; 申込み application [もうしこみ]; 申し送り message to be passed on [もうしおくり]; 申告する to declare (on

mean "to say or state." Because of the character's association with a divine act, the kanji 申 has the connotation of official business. Another view explains that 5 was a depiction of one straightening and stretching the ribs, and meant "to stretch" (the original form of 伸 **SG-1217**). In Japanese the character is also used for the humble form of the verb "to state." The kanji 申 means "to speak, state, say (humble)." <日 | >

an official document) [しんこくする]; 答申 response report by a government council [とうしん]; 申請 application, petition [しんせい]; 内申書 an internal school report [ないしんしょ]

	Meanings	*Kun* and *On*	Romaji	Bushu	Stroke Order and Number
SG-1215 神	divine; deity	かみ・かん・こう シン・ジン	kami, kan, koo *shin, jin*	示	ラネネ礻口神 9

神
A
F-0163

金文1 金文2 三体石経 説文 旧字
1 2 3 4 5

1 depicted a bolt of lightning in the sky to mean "a deity appearing; divine," and had the sound *shin.* In 2, 3, and 4, "an altar table with an offering" (示 **SG-1937**) was added to the lightning bolt (申). In the kanji, 示 was further reduced to ネ, bushu *shimesuhen* "religious." The kanji 神 means "divine; deity." <ネ申>

神 god [か˥み]; 神業 divine work, superhuman feat [かみわざ]; 神がかり divine possession, fanaticism [かみがˈかり]; 神主 Shinto priest [か˥んぬし]; 神々しい divine, awe-inspiring [こうごうし˥い]; 神道 Shintoism [し˥んとう]; 神妙に obediently, humbly [しんみょうに]; 神社 Shinto shrine [じ˥んじゃ]; 神通力 supernatural power [じんつ˥うりき] // 御神酒 sake offered to a god [おみき]

	Meanings	*Kun* and *On*	Romaji	Bushu	Stroke Order and Number
SG-1216 電	electric, extremely fast	デン	*den*	雨	一雨雨雨雷電 13

電
A
F-0183

金文 説文
1 2

電 comprised 雨 **SG-1205** "atmospheric phenomenon," and "lightning," together signifying something that went through the air at lightning speed—"extremely fast." In modern times it came to mean "electricity." The kanji 電 means "electric, extremely fast." <雨电>

発電 generation of electric power [はつでん]; 電力 electricity, power [で˥んりょく, でんりょく]; 停電 power outage [ていでん]; 電気 electricity [で˥んき]; 電話 telephone [でんわ]; 電車 train [で˥んしゃ, でんしゃ]; 電撃的 blitz-like, extremely fast [でんげきてき]; 電源 power source [でんげん]; 電報 telegram [でんぽう]

	Meanings	*Kun* and *On*	Romaji	Bushu	Stroke Order and Number
SG-1217 伸	to stretch, straighten	の-びる シン	no-biru *shin*	人	亻们伸伸 7

伸
B
F-0766

説文

The seal-style form of the kanji 伸 comprised 亻 "an act that one does," and 申 **SG-1214**, used for the sound *shin* to mean "to straighten," from two hands straightening a line. The kanji 伸 means "to stretch." <亻申>

伸ばす to let grow, lengthen, straighten [のば˥す]; 伸びる to grow, extend [のび˥る]; 伸び盛り growing period [のびざ˥かり]; 背伸び straightening up one's back, stretching [せ˥のび]; 伸び伸びする to feel relieved, feel refreshed [のびの˥びする]; 急伸する to rise suddenly, sharply [きゅうしんする]

	Meanings	*Kun* and *On*	Romaji	Bushu	Stroke Order and Number
SG-1218 雷	thunder, (lightning)	かみなり ライ	kaminari *rai*	雨	一雨雨雨雷雷雷雷 13

雷
C
F-1225

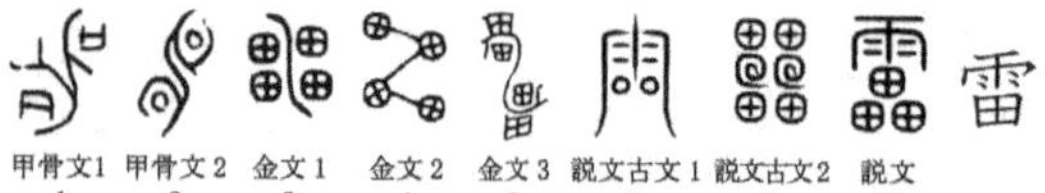
甲骨文1 甲骨文2 金文1 金文2 金文3 説文古文1 説文古文2 説文
1 2 3 4 5 6 7 8

1 and 2 comprised two "mouths" (口) with menacing thunderbolts, signifying a deity speaking forcibly while sending lightning. The character meant "thunder or lightning." 3, 4, and 5 had 田 to suggest lots of thunder, and zigzags for lightning. In the kanji the 田 were reduced to just one under 雨. The kanji 雷 means "thunder." <雨田>

雷 thunder [かみな˥り, かみなり˥]; 雷親父 snarling old man, grumpy father [かみなりお˥やじ]; 雷光 streak of lightning [らいこう]; 雷雨 thunderstorm, thundershower [ら˥いう]; 落雷 the falling of a thunderbolt [らくらい]; 避雷針 lightning rod [ひら˥いしん, ひらいしん]; 雷電 thunder and lightning [らいでん]

	Meanings	Kun and On	Romaji	Bushu	Stroke Order and Number
SG-1219 紳	gentleman	シン	*shin*	糸	纟乡糸糸紅細紳 11

紳 **D** F-1840

金文 1 説文 2

1 comprised "a skein of threads" (糸 **SG-1600**), and "lightning" (申 **SG-1214**), used for the sound *shin* to mean "to bundle, tie," together signifying "a large sash or belt worn by a man." By association with a man's formal sash, the character meant "gentleman." The kanji 紳 means "gentleman." <糸申>

紳士 gentleman [しんし]; 紳士服 men's clothes [しんしふく]; 紳士録 Who's Who, social register [しんしろく]; 紳士協定 gentleman's agreement [しんしきょうてい]

51c 气 "air, steam" [from steam rising]; *ki* 気汽乞 气

	Meanings	Kun and On	Romaji	Bushu	Stroke Order and Number
SG-1220 気	air, gas, weather, vapor, spirit, vigor	キ・ケ	*ki, ke*	气	ノ乍气気気 6

気 **A** F-0090

説文 1 説文或体1 2 説文或体2 3 旧字 4

1 and 2 comprised "rising steam" (气), used for the sound *ki*, and "rice," together signifying steam rising from cooking rice. (2 also included a bowl of rice.) The meaning of "steam" was extended to include weather, as well as human spirit or feelings. In the kanji, 米 was replaced by メ. The kanji 気 means "air, gas, weather, vigor, spirit." <气メ>

気持ち feeling, sentiment, frame of mind [きもち]; 人気 popularity, public interest [にんき]; やる気のある motivated [やるきのある]; 平気な calm, cool, unconcerned [へいきな]; 気体 gas [きたい]; 人気のない deserted, empty [ひとけのない], unpopular, little public interest [にんきのない]; 素っ気なく curtly, bluntly [そっけなく]; 気配 sign, indication [けはい]

	Meanings	Kun and On	Romaji	Bushu	Stroke Order and Number
SG-1221 汽	steam, vapor	キ	*ki*	水	氵氵汇汽汽 7

汽 **C** F-1631

篆文

The seal-style form comprised 氵 "water" and 气 "air rising," signifying "steam," or a steam-powered apparatus. The kanji 汽 means "steam, vapor." <氵气>

汽車 steam locomotive [きしゃ]; 汽笛 steam whistle, siren [きてき]; 汽船 steamboat [きせん]

	Meanings	Kun and On	Romaji	Bushu	Stroke Order and Number
SG-1222 乞	to request, wish, beg	こ-う	ko-u	乙	ノ𠂉乞 3

乞 **D** F-2115

甲骨文 1 金文 2

1 and 2 depicted "rising air." A prayer was said into the rising air, which would carry the prayer upward toward a deity, and the character meant "to plead, beg." The kanji 乞 means "to request, wish, beg." <𠂉乙>

乞う to request, appeal, beg, plead [こう]; 物乞い begging [ものごい]; 乞食 beggar, panhandler [こじき]; 雨乞い rainmaking ritual [あまごい, あまごい]; 命乞い pleading for one's life [いのちごい]

VI HABITATS

52 House

52a 宀 "house, mausoleum, large roof, cover"; bushu *ukanmuri*, and 冖 bushu *wakanmuri* 宇宙宣宿縮寛塞賓・写冗

	Meanings	Kun and On	Romaji	Bushu	Stroke Order and Number
SG-1223 宇	large curved roof, eaves	ウ	*u*	宀	' '' 宀 宀 宇 6

宇 **B** F-0814

金文1 (1) 金文2 (2) 説文 (3) 宇

1, 2, and 3 had "a large roof," over 于 for the sound *u* to mean "something large and bent," together signifying "a large curved roof or the eaves of a house." The kanji 宇 means "large curved roof, eaves (of a house)." <宀于>

宇宙 outer space [うちゅう]; 宇宙船 spacecraft [うちゅうせん]

	Meanings	Kun and On	Romaji	Bushu	Stroke Order and Number
SG-1224 宙	suspended in the air; outer space	チュウ	*chuu*	宀	宀 宀 宁 宙 宙 8

宙 **B** F-0986

甲骨文1 (1) 甲骨文2 (2) 説文 (3) 宙

1, 2, and 3 comprised "a big cover" (宀), inside of which was 由 **SG-0781**, "an empty gourd," used for the sound *chuu*. The universe was thought of as a space that was covered by a huge, imaginary, semi-circular cover. Emptiness under a big cover signified "space; suspended in the air." The kanji 宙 means "suspended in the air; outer space." <宀由>

宙吊り hanging in the air [ちゅうづり]; 宙返り somersault [ちゅうがえり]; 宙に浮く to float in the air [ちゅうにうく]; 宇宙開発 space development [うちゅうかいはつ]; 宇宙人 space alien, spaceman [うちゅうじん]

	Meanings	Kun and On	Romaji	Bushu	Stroke Order and Number
SG-1225 宣	to state in public, proclaim, advertise; imperial edict	セン	*sen*	宀	宀 宀 官 宣 宣 9

宣 **B** F-0948

甲骨文 (1) 金文 (2) 説文 (3) 宣

1 comprised "a house" (宀), inside of which was a coiled shape that signified "a complex internal layout," and was used for the sound *sen*. The character meant "a room where an emperor made important announcements," such as "imperial orders." In 2 and 3, one or two lines were added to the coiled shape (亘). The kanji 宣 means "to state in public, proclaim, advertise; imperial edict." <宀一旦>

宣伝 publicity, advertisement [せんでん]; 宣言 declaration [せんげん]; 宣教師 missionary [せんきょうし]; 宣下 proclamation of the emperor's words [せんげ]; 宣告 pronouncement (regarding an important matter) [せんこく]; 宣戦布告 declaration of war [せんせんふこく]

	Meanings	Kun and On	Romaji	Bushu	Stroke Order and Number
SG-1226 宿	inn; to dwell, have existence within	やど・やど-す シュク	yado, yado-ru *shuku*	宀	宀 宀 宿 宿 宿 宿 11

宿 **B** F-0555

甲骨文 (1) 金文 (2) 説文 (3) 宿

1, 2, and 3 comprised "a house" (宀), inside of which was "a straw mat to sit or sleep on," and 亻 "a person." Together these components signified "people staying and sleeping for a duration of time," and described "an inn." In the kanji, the straw mat used for the sound *shuku* was replaced by 百 **SG-0788**. The character also meant "to carry a new life; pregnant," from an unborn child staying inside its mother's body for a length of time. The kanji 宿 means "inn; to dwell, have existence within." <宀亻百>

宿を取る to put up at an inn [やどをとる]; 雨宿り taking shelter from the rain [あまやどり]; 宿屋 Japanese inn, lodgings [やどや]; 宿す to contain, be pregnant [やどす]; 下宿 boarding, lodging [げしゅく]; 合宿 training camp [がっしゅく]; 宿縁 fate, destiny [しゅくえん]; 宿直 night watch duty [しゅくちょく]

	Meanings	Kun and On	Romaji	Bushu	Stroke Order and Number
SG-1227 縮	to shrink	ちぢ-む シュク	chiji-mu *shuku*	糸	糸 糸' 紵 紵 縮 縮 縮 17

縮 **B** F-1046 — 篆文

The seal-style form comprised 糸 **SG-1600** "a skein of threads, string," and 宿 **SG-1226**, used for the sound *shuku* to mean "to shrink," together signifying "threads shrinking." The kanji 縮 means "to shrink." <糸宿>

縮む to shrink, shorten, contract [ちぢむ]; 縮れる to be frizzled, curl, shrink [ちぢれる]; 伸び縮み expansion and contraction, flexibility [のびちぢみ, のびちぢみ]; 圧縮 compression [あっしゅく]; 縮図 reduced figure [しゅくず]; 軍縮 disarmament, arms reduction [ぐんしゅく]; 縮小 reduction, cut, scaling down [しゅくしょう]

	Meanings	Kun and On	Romaji	Bushu	Stroke Order and Number
SG-1228 寛	generous, magnanimous, relaxed	カン	*kan*	宀	宀 宁 宵 宵 宵 寛 寛 13

寛 **C** F-1422 — 說文 1, 旧字 2

The origin of this character is obscure. One view explains that the component inside of 宀 "a house" in 1 was used for the sound *kan* to mean "spacious," and that 1 signified "a large, relaxing house." Another view explains that 宀 was "a mausoleum," inside of which was a spiritual medium with magical eyebrows dancing gently and gracefully, used for the sound *kan* to mean "magnanimous, generous." The kanji 寛 means "generous, magnanimous, relaxed." <宀艹見>

寛大な broad-minded, generous [かんだいな]; 寛容な lenient, generous, unprejudiced [かんような]

	Meanings	Kun and On	Romaji	Bushu	Stroke Order and Number
SG-1229 塞	to seal off, obstruct; stronghold, fortress	ふさ-ぐ サイ・ソク	husa-gu *sai, soku*	土	宀 宀 宇 宑 実 寒 塞 塞 13

塞 **D** F-2039 — 說文

The seal-style form comprised "a roof or house" (宀), with "piles of clay bricks" (four 工) representing walls. On the bottom, "a pair of hands" was blocking the entrance with "dirt" (土). A building with brick walls and a securely sealed entrance was "a fortress." The kanji 塞 means "to seal off, obstruct; stronghold, fortress." <宀共土>

塞ぐ to seal off, stop up, obstruct [ふさぐ]; 気が塞ぐ to feel depressed [きがふさぐ]; 八方塞がり all exits blocked, cornered [はっぽうふさがり]; 要塞 fortress, stronghold [ようさい]; 閉塞感 a feeling of being trapped, a sense of stagnation [へいそくかん]

	Meanings	Kun and On	Romaji	Bushu	Stroke Order and Number
SG-1230 賓	important visitor, honored guest	ヒン	*hin*	貝	宀 宀 宀 宀 宊 宯 賓 賓 15

賓 **D** F-2150 — 甲骨文1 1, 甲骨文2 2, 金文 3, 說文古文 4, 說文 5, 旧字 6

1 and 2 depicted "a guest wearing a formal headdress who has just arrived at the house on foot," and had the sound *hin*. In 3, 4, 5, and 6, 貝 **SG-1693** "cowrie; valuable" indicated that the important visitor was treated hospitably with gifts. The kanji 賓 means "important visitor, honored guest." <宀一少貝>

賓客 guest, guest of honor [ひんきゃく]; 迎賓館 guest house, guest palace [げいひんかん]; 貴賓室 room reserved for special guests [きひんしつ]; 来賓 honored visitor, guest [らいひん]

冖 A variation of 宀; "a cover, house"; **bushu *wakanmuri*** 写冗

	Meanings	Kun and On	Romaji	Bushu	Stroke Order and Number
SG-1231 写	to copy, duplicate	うつ-す シャ	utsu-su *sha*	冖	丶 冖 冖 写 写 5

写 **A** F-0396 — 說文 1, 旧字 2

Various views on the origin of the inside component (舄) in 1 include: (a) it depicted "a bird," used for the sound *sha*; (b) it was used for the sound *sha* to mean "to transfer to another place"; or (c) it depicted "slippers" worn in a rite, which one changed into before entering a palace. The character was used to mean "to copy." In the shinji, 宀 was replaced by 冖, bushu *wakanmuri,* and 舄 was replaced by the shape 与 (no relevance to the kanji 与 **SG-0150**). The kanji 写 means "to copy, duplicate." <冖与>

写す to copy [うつす]; 写し copy, duplicate [うつし]; 生き写し life-like [いきうつし]; 写真 photograph [しゃしん]; 写生 sketching, drawing from nature [しゃせい]; 写実的な naturalistic, realistic [しゃじつてきな]; 試写会 preview screening (of a film, etc.) [ししゃかい]; 被写体 subject [ひしゃたい]

SG-1232 冗	Meanings	Kun and On	Romaji	Bushu	Stroke Order and Number
	useless, superfluous	ジョウ	*joo*	冖	' 冖 冗 冗 4

冗 **D** F-1731

篆文

The seal-style form depicted "a person inside a house with nothing to do." It meant "wasteful, useless, superfluous." The kanji 冗 comprises 冖 and 几 (for the sound *joo*), and means "useless, superfluous." <冖几>

冗談 joke [じょうだん]; 冗談半分 half seriously, half in jest [じょうだんはんぶん]; 冗長な prolix, redundant, roundabout [じょうちょうな]; 冗漫な prolix, long and loose (writing) [じょうまんな]

52b 广 "eaves, canopy"; **bushu *madare*** 度席応庁渡 广

SG-1233 度	Meanings	Kun and On	Romaji	Bushu	Stroke Order and Number
	degree, (number of) times; to measure	たび ド・ト・タク	tabi *do, to, taku*	广	' 亠 广 广 庐 庐 度 度 9

度 **A** F-0074

説文

The seal-style form comprised 广 (bushu *madare* "eaves"), 廿 "a cooking pot," and 又 **SG-0084** "a hand" measuring ingredients for cooking. Together they signified "degree, amount." In measuring one used the hand many times, and thus it also meant "(number of) times." The kanji 度 means "degree, (number of) times; to measure." <庐又>

(〜する) 度に every time one (does) X [(〜する)たびに]; 度 degree [ど]; 強度 strength, intensity [きょうど]; 一度に all at one time [いちどに]; 年度 fiscal year, school year [ねんど]; 度外視する to take no account of, disregard [どがいしする]; 高度 altitude, height [こうど]; 忖度する to surmise, guess, gause someone else's feeling [そんたくする]; 雨支度 preparation for rain [あまじたく]

SG-1234 席	Meanings	Kun and On	Romaji	Bushu	Stroke Order and Number
	seat, one's place to sit down	セキ	*seki*	巾	亠 广 庐 庐 庐 席 席 10

席 **A** F-0310

金文 1 古文 2 説文 3

Under 厂 (广) "eaves, canopy" was "a piece of cloth" draped over "a seat" in 1, and "a woven straw mat" in 2. In 3, 廿 "cooking pot" was added to 巾 "cloth-draped seat." The kanji 席 means "seat, one's place to sit down." <庐巾>

席 seat [せき]; 座席 seat [ざせき]; 空席 empty seat [くうせき]; 席順 seating order [せきじゅん]; 同席する to share a table, be in each other's company [どうせきする]; 出席 attending (a meeting) [しゅっせき]; 指定席 reserved seat [していせき]; 相席する to share a table at a restaurant [あいせきする]; 席次 seating order, class standing [せきじ] // 寄席 storyteller's hall, vaudeville house [よせ]

SG-1235 応	Meanings	Kun and On	Romaji	Bushu	Stroke Order and Number
	to respond willingly, answer	こた-える オウ	kota-eru *oo*	心	' 亠 广 広 応 応 7

応 **A** F-0324

金文1 1 金文2 2 説文 3 旧字 4

1 and 2 depicted "a bird returning to the eaves of a house," and was used for the sound *oo*. A bird that returned swiftly on command was "a hawk." The character meant "to respond willingly." 3 comprised "a table" (爿) with "eaves" (一), "person" (亻), "bird" (隹), and "heart" (心), together signifying "to respond willingly" to a command. In the shinji 応, only 广 and "heart" were retained. The kanji 応 means "to respond willingly, answer." <广心>

見応えがある be worth seeing, spectacular [みごたえがある]; 応じる to respond willingly, comply [おうじる]; 応用する to apply [おうようする]; 応急手当て first aid treatment [おうきゅうてあて]; 相応の suitable, appropriate [そうおうの]; 応対する to attend to, deal with [おうたいする] // 反応 reaction [はんのう]; 順応する to accommodate oneself [じゅんのうする]

SG-1236 庁	Meanings	Kun and On	Romaji	Bushu	Stroke Order and Number
	government agency	チョウ	*choo*	广	' 亠 广 庁 庁 5

庁 **A** F-0423

廳 庁

旧字

No ancient form. The kyuji 廳 tells a good story. Inside 广 "eaves" are 耳 **SG-0050** "an ear," 壬 "a standing person," 㐭 "an eye looking straight ahead" (from 直), and 心 **SG-0187** "a heart." This combination is read *choo* (as in 聽, the kyuji for 聴 **SG-0053**), and signified "an official in a government office listening sincerely to what people have to say," or just "a government office or agency." In the shinji the phonetically identical 丁 **SG-1914** replaced 聽 (thus omitting the depiction of the government office that the original character intended to signify). The kanji 庁 means "government agency." <广丁>

庁舎 government building [ちょうしゃ]; 官庁 government office [かんちょう]; 県庁 prefectural office building [けんちょう]; 国税庁 the National Tax Administration Agency [こくぜいちょう]; 気象庁 the Meteorological Agency [きしょうちょう]; 特許庁 the Japan Patent Office [とっきょちょう]

	Meanings	Kun and On	Romaji	Bushu	Stroke Order and Number
SG-1237 渡	to cross, get over, hand over	わた-る ト	wata-ru *to*	水	氵 氵 氵 汸 沪 浐 渡 渡 12

渡 **A** F-0444

說文

The seal-style form comprised "flowing water" (氵), and 度 **SG-1233**, used for the sound *to* to mean "to cross," together signifying "crossing water" and "handing something over to another person." The kanji 渡 means "to cross, get over, hand over." <氵度>

渡る to go across, migrate, pass [わたる]; 渡す to deliver, hand in, give [わたす]; 引き渡し to transfer, give away [ひきわたし]; 見渡す to look out over [みわたす]; 渡欧 European [とおう]; 渡航する to make a passage to, sail [とこうする]; 過渡期 transitional period, age of transition [かとき]; 渡世人 gambler [とせいにん]

52c 内 "inside" [from an entrance to the house] 入内納

	Meanings	Kun and On	Romaji	Bushu	Stroke Order and Number
SG-1238 入	to enter, put in, join	い-れる・はい-る ニュウ	i-reru, hai-ru *nyuu*	入	ノ 入 2

入 **A** F-0069

甲骨文 1 金文1 2 金文2 3 說文 4

1, 2, 3, and 4 depicted "an entrance to a house." The kanji 入 means "to enter, put in, join." <入>

入る to enter [はいる]; 入れる to put in, let something in [いれる]; 入り口 entrance [いりぐち]; 手入れ care, trimming [ていれ]; 入学 entrance into a school, matriculation [にゅうがく]; 入社 joining a company [にゅうしゃ]; 加入する to join [かにゅうする]; 出入国 emigration and immigration [しゅつにゅうこく]; 入力する to type in, enter [にゅうりょくする]

	Meanings	Kun and On	Romaji	Bushu	Stroke Order and Number
SG-1239 内	inside, in; internal	うち ナイ・ダイ	uchi *nai, dai*	入・冂	丨 冂 内 内 4

内 **A** F-0032

甲骨文 1 金文 2 說文 3

1, 2, and 3 were "a house with a clearly marked entrance," signifying "to go inside." The kanji 内 means "inside, in; internal." <冂人>

内 inside, one's true feelings, we, my, within [うち]; 内側 inside [うちがわ]; 身内 family, relation [みうち]; 内訳 breakdown [うちわけ]; 内法 inside measurement [うちのり]; 車内 inside a car, on a train [しゃない]; 内心 inner center [ないしん]; 内裏 the Imperial Palace [だいり]

	Meanings	Kun and On	Romaji	Bushu	Stroke Order and Number
SG-1240 納	to put away, pay dues, deliver	おさ-める ノウ・ナ・ナン・トウ	osa-meru *noo, na, nan, too*	糸	幺 乡 糸 糸 紃 納 納 10

納 **B** F-0936

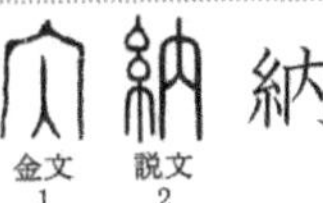

1 was the same as 1 for 内 **SG-1239**, and had the sound *nai/noo* to mean "to put something in." In 2, 糸 **SG-1600** "a skein of threads" was added to signify "cloth." Cloth was one of the accepted in-kind ways to pay a tax or levy. The kanji 納 means "to put away, pay dues, deliver." <糸内>

納める to dedicate, pay (a fee or tax) [おさめる]; 仕事納め the last business day of the year [しごとおさめ]; 見納め farewell look [みおさめ]; 納品 delivery of goods [のうひん]; 納会 the last meeting of the year [のうかい]; 帰納 induction, generalization [きのう]; 納屋 shed [なや]; 納戸 closet room [なんど]; 納豆 *natto*, fermented soy beans [なっとう]; 出納口 teller window, cashier window [すいとうぐち]

53 Door

53a 戸 "a single door" 戸所涙戻房啓炉

	Meanings	Kun and On	Romaji	Bushu	Stroke Order and Number
SG-1241 戸	door, family, house	と コ	to *ko*	戸	一 ヨ ヨ 戸 4

戸 **A** F-0305

甲骨文1 1 甲骨文2 2 說文古文 3 說文 4

1 and 2 were "a single door that swings open." The door of a house also signified its residents, "a family." In 3, the top line of the door became separated to indicate a hinge or lock, and 木 **SG-0608** was added to signify "a wooden door." The kanji 戸 means "door, family, house." <戸>

戸 door [と]; 網戸 screen door, window screen [あみど]; 戸棚 cupboard, cabinet [とだな]; 戸締まりをする to lock the doors [とじまりをする]; 一戸建て single-family house [いっこだて]; 戸外 outdoor [こがい]; 戸別訪問 door-to-door canvasing [こべつほうもん]; 下戸 nondrinker [げこ]

SG-1242 所	Meanings	Kun and On	Romaji	Bushu	Stroke Order and Number
	place	ところ ショ	tokoro *sho*	戸	一ㄱ彐戸戸'所所所 8

所
A
F-0106

金文1 1 金文2 2 説文 3

1, 2, and 3 comprised "a single swinging door with a hinge at the top" (戸), and "an ax" (斤). *Setsumon* explains that the character described "the sound of an ax cutting a tree," but there seems no definitive agreed-to explanation of the origin of this character among scholars. The kanji 所 means "place." <戸斤>

所 place [ところ]; 居所 whereabouts [いどころ]; 所在地 address, location of an office [しょざいち]; 所定の designated, prescribed [しょていの]; 夏場所 sumo summer grand tournament [なつばしょ]; 所作 conduct, one's deportment [しょさ, しょさ]; 急所 vital part, sensitive spot [きゅうしょ] // 所謂 what is called, the so-called [いわゆる]

SG-1243 涙	Meanings	Kun and On	Romaji	Bushu	Stroke Order and Number
	tear	なみだ ルイ	namida *rui*	水	氵氵氵沪沪涙涙 10

涙
B
F-0917

説文 1 旧字 2

1 comprised "flowing water" (氵) and 戾 (the kyuji for 戻 **SG-1244**), used for the sound *ree* to mean "to drip," together signifying "tear." In the shinji, 犬 **SG-0859** "dog" was replaced by "person" (大 **SG-0314**) in the shinji. The kanji 涙 means "tear." <氵戸大>

涙 tear [なみだ]; 血の涙 tears of blood (pains) [ちのなみだ]; 涙ぐむ to be moved to tears, have tears well in one's eyes [なみだぐむ]; 雀の涙 insignificant amount ("sparrow tears") [すずめのなみだ]; 涙脆い sentimental, weepy [なみだもろい]; 嬉し涙 tears of joy, happy tears [うれしなみだ]; 泣きの涙で in tears, reluctantly [なきのなみだで]; 感涙 tears of gratitude [かんるい]

SG-1244 戻	Meanings	Kun and On	Romaji	Bushu	Stroke Order and Number
	to return, backtrack	もど-す レイ	modo-su *ree*	戸	一ㄱ彐戸戸戸戻 7

戻
B
F-0928

三体石経 1 説文 2 旧字 3

The origin of this character is obscure. 1 comprised a standing person and a dog, in perspective. One view explains that it depicted "a dog acting against its master," and thus meant "to act against." Another view is that the person is calling the dog back, and thus meant "to come back." In 2 and 3, the character comprised "a single swinging door" (戸 **SG-1241**) with "a dog" underneath, signifying a dog returning to a house. 犬 was replaced by 大. The kanji 戻 means "to return, backtrack." <戸大>

戻す to return (a thing), put (it) back [もどす]; 戻る to return, come back [もどる]; 呼び戻す to call back [よびもどす]; 取り戻す to recover, take back [とりもどす]; 後戻り going back, backtracking [あともどり]; 差し戻し sending back to a lower court [さしもどし]; 払い戻し refund [はらいもどし]

SG-1245 房	Meanings	Kun and On	Romaji	Bushu	Stroke Order and Number
	room, quarters, tassel, cluster	ふさ ボウ	husa *boo*	戸	一彐戸戸戸房房 8

房
B
F-0968

説文

The seal-style form comprised 戸 "door," and 方 **SG-1931** "square space," used for the sound *boo*. Together they signified "a small square space located on the side of a house, living quarters." A tassel also hangs onto the side of the thing to which it is attached. The word 女房 came from a living quarters for a lady-in-waiting in the imperial court. The kanji 房 means "room, living quarters, tassel, cluster." <戸方>

房 counter for grapes [ふさ]; 乳房 breast [ちぶさ, にゅうぼう]; 冷房 air-conditioner [れいぼう]; 女房 one's own wife [にょうぼう]; 文房具 stationery, writing materials [ぶんぼうぐ]; 厨房 kitchen, cookery [ちゅうぼう]; 茶房 tea shop, coffeehouse [さぼう]

SG-1246 啓	Meanings	Kun and On	Romaji	Bushu	Stroke Order and Number
	to open, enlighten, state	ケイ	*kee*	口	彐戸戸'所攴啓 11

啓
C
F-1399

甲骨文1 1 甲骨文2 2 金文 3 説文 4

1 comprised "a door" (戸 **SG-1241**) and "a hand" (又 **SG-0084**). In 2 and 4, the hand was replaced with 攴 (攵) "to cause an action," forming 所 (for the sound *kee)* to emphasize that someone was opening the door. 口 **SG-0031** "a prayer box, words" was also added to convey that the door was being opened with words, a metaphor for "enlightenment." The kanji 啓 means "to open, enlighten, state." <戸攵口>

拝啓 Dear Sir or Madam (standard greeting to start a letter) [はいけい]; 啓蒙 enlightenment, illumination [けいもう]; 一筆啓上 Just a short note to write to you (a greeting to start a letter) [いっぴつけいじょう]; 自己啓発 self-enlightenment [じこけいはつ]

	Meanings	Kun and On	Romaji	Bushu	Stroke Order and Number
SG-1247 炉	fireplace, hearth	ロ	*ro*	火	炉 8

炉 **C** F-1488

爐 炉 旧字 甲骨文 1 金文 2 説文 3 盧

No ancient form. The kyuji 爐 comprised 火 **SG-1164** "fire," and 盧 for the sound *ro* to mean "round" (the development of this component "a round container" is shown at upper right). It signified people encircling a round hearth. In the shinji the right side was replaced by 戸. The kanji 炉 means "fireplace, hearth." <火戸>

懐炉 pocket warmer, chemical heating pad [かいろ]; 原子炉 nuclear reactor [げんしろ]; 炉端 fireside [ろばた]; 溶鉱炉 smelting furnace [ようこうろ]; 囲炉裏 sunken hearth [いろり]; 囲炉裏端 fireside [いろりばた]

53b 扁 "one side; lopsided; bound writing tablets kept behind a door";  *hen* 編偏遍

	Meanings	Kun and On	Romaji	Bushu	Stroke Order and Number
SG-1248 編	to compile, edit, knit, braid	あ-む ヘン	a-mu *hen*	糸	編 15

編 **B** F-0605

甲骨文 1 説文 2 編

1 comprised "writing tablets bound as a book," and 糸 **SG-1600** "a skein of thread." In 2, 扁, used for the sound *hen* and placed next to 糸, signified that the bound book was kept behind a door (戸) in a cabinet, and the character meant "family registry, record." From "strings binding many writing tablets into one," the kanji 編 means "to edit, compile, braid, knit (yarn)." <糸扁(戸冊)>

編む to knit, weave, braid [あむ]; 編み物 knitting [あみもの]; 三つ編み braid [みつあみ]; 編み出す to invent, forge, contrive [あみだす]; 編集 editing, compilation [へんしゅう]; 再編成 reorganization, reformatting [さいへんせい]; 長編小説 long novel [ちょうへんしょうせつ]; 政界再編 political shake-up [せいかいさいへん, せいかいさいへん]

	Meanings	Kun and On	Romaji	Bushu	Stroke Order and Number
SG-1249 偏	to become lopsided; one side, bias, recurring left-side component of kanji	かたよ-る ヘン	katayo-ru *hen*	人	偏 11

偏 **C** F-1553

説文 偏

The seal-style form comprised 亻 "a person," and 扁 "lopsided," used for the sound *hen,* from a screen door that opens on only one side. Together they signified "(a person) leaning to one side, bias." The kanji 偏 is also used do describe recurring components of kanji that appear on the left side of characters and usually carry the same general meaning. The kanji 偏 means "to become lopsided; one side, bias, recurring left-side component of kanji." <亻扁>

偏る to become lopsided [かたよる]; 偏 left-hand recurring component of a Chinese character [へん]; 偏見 bias, prejudice [へんけん]; 偏屈者 eccentric person [へんくつもの]; 偏向 propensity for, deviation from [へんこう]; 偏差値 deviation, deviation value indicating one's academic level [へんさち]; 偏西風 the prevailing westerlies [へんせいふう]

	Meanings	Kun and On	Romaji	Bushu	Stroke Order and Number
SG-1250 遍	to go around; far and wide; (number of) times	ヘン	*hen*	辵	遍 12

遍 **D** F-1838

No ancient form. The kanji 遍 comprises 扁 for the sound *hen* to mean "going around, spread wide," and ⻌ "to move forward." Together they signified "everywhere, extensively, far and wide." "Making a full round" also gave the meaning "once; (number of) times." The kanji 遍 means "to go around; far and wide; (number of) times." <扁⻌>

普遍的 worldwide, universal, general [ふへんてき]; 一遍 once, one time [いっぺん]; 一遍に in one sitting, all at once [いっぺんに]; 何遍も several times, repeatedly [なんべんも]; 遍歴する to travel around [へんれきする] // 遍く everyplace, all over, extensively [あまねく]

53c 門 "closed double doors, gate; unknown"; **bushu *mongamae***

門間開問関閉閣闘簡潤欄閥閑閲

	Meanings	Kun and On	Romaji	Bushu	Stroke Order and Number
SG-1251 門	gate, clan, family	かど モン	kado *mon*	門	丨 冂 尸 尸' 門 門 門 門 8

門 **A** F-0359

甲骨文1 (1), 甲骨文2 (2), 金文1 (3), 金文2 (4), 説文 (5)

1 through 4 depicted "two swinging doors," with hinges added in 2 and 3 to emphasize closure and protection. Inside the double doors there were people living and doing activities, and thus the meaning "clan, family." The kanji 門 means "gate, clan, family." When 門 is used as bushu *mongamae*, it usually gives the meaning "unknown," in the sense of "behind a closed doors." <門>

門出 departure, setting out [かどで]; お門違い barking up the wrong tree [おかどちがい]; 門 gate [もん]; 門外不出 to never divulge to the outside world [もんがい・ふしゅつ]; 門下生 student, disciple [もんかせい]; 一門 clan [いちもん]; 入門書 introductory book [にゅうもんしょ]; 名門 illustrious family, prestige school [めいもん]

	Meanings	Kun and On	Romaji	Bushu	Stroke Order and Number
SG-1252 間	space, gap, duration, time, room	あいだ・ま カン・ケン	aida, ma *kan, ken*	門	丨 冂 尸' 門 門 門 間 間 12

間 **A** F-0037

金文1 (1), 金文2 (2), 説文 (3), 旧字 (4)

1, 2, and 3 all had "closed double doors" (門), with 夕 **SG-1072** "an early moon" (and "knife or person?") in 1, and "a moon" 月 **SG-1077** in 2 and 3. Moonlight shining in through the opening in the double doors signified "gap, space." The moon was seen for a fixed period of time, whence the meaning "time or duration," but was replaced by "the sun" (日) in the kanji. The kanji 間 means "space, gap, duration, time, room." <門日>

間 duration, interval, gap [あいだ]; 間柄 relationship [あいだがら]; 知らぬ間に before one knew it [しらぬまに]; 間抜けな foolish, stupid [まぬけな]; 間もなく shortly, soon [まもなく]; 二間 a two room house or unit of housing [ふたま]; その間 during that time [そのかん]; 中間 middle, medium [ちゅうかん]; 空間 room, space [くうかん]; 世間 the world at large [せけん]; 世間体が悪い to look bad, be disreputable [せけんていがわるい]

	Meanings	Kun and On	Romaji	Bushu	Stroke Order and Number
SG-1253 開	to open, begin	ひら-く・あ-ける カイ	hira-ku, a-keru *kai*	門	丨 冂 尸 尸' 門 門 門 開 12

開 **A** F-0081

説文古文 (1), 説文 (2)

1 and 2 comprised "closed double doors" (門) and "a pair of hands trying to open the bolt" (幵开), signifying "hands opening double doors." Opening a door also meant "to begin." The kanji 開 means "to open, begin." <門开>

開く to open, unfold [ひらく]; 山開き beginning of mountaineering season [やまびらき]; 開ける to open [あける]; 開け閉て open and close [あけたて]; 開会 opening a meeting [かいかい]; 開口一番 opening words, starting off a speech with [かいこういちばん]; 開発する to develop [かいはつする]

	Meanings	Kun and On	Romaji	Bushu	Stroke Order and Number
SG-1254 問	question; to inquire	と-う・(とん) モン	to-u, (ton) *mon*	口	丨 冂 尸 尸' 門 門 問 問 11

問 **A** F-0094

甲骨文 (1), 説文 (2)

1 and 2 comprised 門 "closed double doors or a gate," and 口 **SG-0031** "mouth." Someone asking about a thing concealed behind closed doors meant "to inquire." The kanji 問 means "question; to inquire." <門口>

問い合わせる to inquire [といあわせる, といあわせる]; 問いと答 question and answer [といとこたえ]; 問屋 wholesale store dealer [といや, とんや]; 問題 problem, issue, question [もんだい]; 押し問答する to haggle, argue [おしもんどうする]; 学問 pursuit of learning, scholarship [がくもん]; 一問一答 question-and-answer, Q and A [いちもん・いっとう]; 不問に付する let pass unnoticed, leave out of consideration [ふもんに・ふする]

	Meanings	Kun and On	Romaji	Bushu	Stroke Order and Number
SG-1255 関	to relate, pertain to, concern; checkpoint	せき・かか-わる カン	seki, kaka-waru *kan*	門	冂 尸 尸' 門 門 門 関 関 14

関 **A** F-0213

金文 (1), 説文 (2), 旧字 (3)

1 comprised 門 "closed double doors," inside of which were "two bolts." Bolting the doors signified "a checkpoint." In 2 and 3 "two skeins of threads tied together" were added to signify "fastening," giving the meaning "to prevent

関所 checkpoint [せきしょ]; 関取 sumo wrestler of the rank of *juryo* (十両) or above [せきとり]; 関わる to touch on, affect [かかわる]; 関係 relationship [かんけい]; 通関 clearing customs [つうかん]; ～に関して

people from coming in by locking the doors." Threads also connect things, and thus the character also took the meaning "to relate." The skeins were simplified to 关, and the kanji 関 means "to relate, pertain to, concern; checkpoint." <門关>

concerning X [〜に·かﾞんして]; 関心がある to be interested in [かんしんがあﾞる]; 関連する to be connected, associated with [かんれんする]; 相関 correlation [そうかん]

	Meanings	Kun and On	Romaji	Bushu	Stroke Order and Number
SG-1256 閉	to close, shut	と-じる·し-める ヘイ	to-jiru, shi-meru *hee*	門	丨 ｢ ｢ ｢' 門 門 閂 閉 閉 閉 11

閉 **B** F-0826

金文 1 説文 2

1 and 2 comprised 門 "closed double doors," and 才 **SG-1115**, "a weir that blocks the flow of water." "Blocking doors" signified "to close." The kanji 閉 means "to close, shut." <門才>

閉じる to close [とじﾞる]; 閉じ込める to lock in, confine [とじこめﾞる]; 閉める to close [しめﾞる]; 開閉 opening and closing [かいへい]; 閉店時間 closing time [へいてんじﾞかん]; 自閉症 autism [じへいしょう]; 閉口する to be annoyed, be dumbfounded [へいこうする]; 密閉する to shut tightly [みっぺいする]

	Meanings	Kun and On	Romaji	Bushu	Stroke Order and Number
SG-1257 閣	large important building, cabinet body	カク	*kaku*	門	丨 ｢ ｢ ｢' 門 門 門 閃 閔 閣 14

閣 **B** F-0932

説文

The seal-style form comprised 門 "closed double doors, gate," and 各 **SG-0244**, used for the sound *kaku* to mean "to stop." A building with the doors or gates bolted to stop people from entering was a "large important building." Such a grand building might be the location of an important meeting to set national policy, and 閣 meant "cabinet body." The kanji 閣 means "large important building, cabinet body." <門各>

内閣 cabinet [なﾞいかく]; 閣議 cabinet meeting [かﾞくぎ]; 閣僚 cabinet member [かくりょう]; 閣下 Your Excellency, Your Lordship [かﾞっか]; 仏閣 Buddhist temple [ぶっかく]; 倒閣 overthrowing the Cabinet [とうかく]; 金閣寺 Kinkakuji Temple [きﾞんかくじ]

	Meanings	Kun and On	Romaji	Bushu	Stroke Order and Number
SG-1258 闘	to fight	たたか-う トウ	tataka-u *too*	門	丨 ｢ ｢ ｢' 門 門 門 闘 闘 闘 18

闘 **C** F-1134

説文 1 旧字 2

The seal-style form (1) shows that this character originated not from 門, but from 鬥, which depicted "two people fighting with their hands" and had the sound *too*. The bottom component 斲 comprised "a shield" and "an ax," and also signified "fighting." In the shinji 闘, 鬥 was replaced by the unrelated 門, and 斲 was replaced by 豆 for the sound *too*, and 寸 "a hand" for "fighting by hand." The kanji 闘 means "to fight." <門豆寸>

闘う to fight [たたかう]; 健闘する to fight bravely [けんとうする]; 共闘 joint struggle, united front [きょうとう]; 戦闘 battle, fight [せんとう]; 闘争 fight, dispute, strike [とうそう]; 悪戦苦闘する to struggle desperately, fight against heavy odds [あくせんくとうする]; 闘病生活 a struggle with illness [とうびょうせﾞいかつ]; 春闘 annual spring wage offensive [しゅﾞんとう]

	Meanings	Kun and On	Romaji	Bushu	Stroke Order and Number
SG-1259 簡	letter; simple and easy, simplified	カン	*kan*	竹	⺮ 𥫗 𥫗 節 節 節 簡 簡 18

簡 **C** F-1252

説文

The seal-style form comprised ⺮, bushu *takekanmuri* "bamboo," and 閒 (the kyuji for 間 **SG-1252**), for the sound *kan* to mean "space, gap; between." Correspondence was written on bamboo tablets, whence the meaning "letter." The way bamboo writing tablets were tied together with leather straps left small gaps between tablets, and those gaps gave the meaning "to cut corners, abbreviate, simplify." The kanji 簡 means "letter; simple and easy, simplified; to abbreviate" <⺮間>

書簡 correspondence, letter [しょかん]; 簡単な simple and easy, brief [かんたんな]; 簡素な simple, austere [かﾞんそな]; 簡略化 simplification [かんりゃくか]; 簡潔に succinctly [かんけつに]; 簡易ベッド cot [かんいべﾞッド]; 木簡 wooden writing strip or tablet [もっかん]

	Meanings	Kun and On	Romaji	Bushu	Stroke Order and Number
SG-1260 潤	to soak, embellish, enrich	うるお-う·うる-む ジュン	uruo-u, uru-mu *jun*	水	氵 氵 氵' 沪 浬 潤 潤 潤 15

潤 **D** F-1623

説文

The seal-style form comprised "flowing water" (氵), and 閏, used for the sound *jun* to mean "in excess," together signifying "to soak" or "to enrich." The kanji 潤 means "to soak, embellish, enrich." <氵門王>

潤う to be moistened, benefit, flourish [うるおﾞう]; 目が潤む (eyes) become wet with tears, become blurred [めﾞが·うるﾞむ]; 潤色する to embellish, dress up [じゅんしょくする]; 潤滑油 lubricating oil [じゅんかつﾞゆ]; 潤沢な abundant, bountiful [じゅんたくな]

SG-1261 欄	Meanings	Kun and On	Romaji	Bushu	Stroke Order and Number
	railing, column	ラン	*ran*	木	木 札 村 村' 村門 梱 欄 欄 欄 20

欄 **D** F-1658

篆文1 1, 篆文2 2, 旧字 3

1 comprised 木 "wood," and 柬, used for the sound *ran*, and was the name of a particular variety of tree. In 2, 門 was added, with the sound *ran* (柬) now used to mean "railing." A railing encircles an area. This was also likened to the way the lines in a book were encircled in a frame for printing, creating "columns." In the shinji, 柬 was replaced by 東. The kanji 欄 means "railing, column." <木門東>

欄 column [らん]; 空欄 blank column, blank space [くうらん]; 欄干 railing, handrail, banister [らんかん]; 欄間 carved wooden panel above a *fusuma*, fanlight [らんま]

SG-1262 閥	Meanings	Kun and On	Romaji	Bushu	Stroke Order and Number
	clique, faction, clan	バツ	*batsu*	門	丨 冂 門' 門 門 閂 閥 閥 閥 14

閥 **D** F-1695

篆文

The seal-style form comprised 門 "gate, clan," and 伐 SG-1472, used for the sound *batsu* to mean "commendation, honoring." Together they signified "a house or family that received a commendation." Members of a distinguished family would band together, excluding others. The kanji 閥 means "clique, faction, clan." <門伐>

財閥 industrial conglomerate [ざいばつ]; 学閥 academic clique [がくばつ]; 軍閥 military faction, warlord clique [ぐんばつ]; 派閥争い inter-factional dispute [はばつあらそい]

SG-1263 閑	Meanings	Kun and On	Romaji	Bushu	Stroke Order and Number
	leisure, spare time	カン	*kan*	門	丨 冂 門' 門 門 閂 閑 閑 閑 12

閑 **D** F-2006

金文 1, 説文 2

1 comprised "closed double doors, gate" (門) and "wood" (木), together signifying "a wooden plank to block entry; to prevent." The meaning "free time or leisure" is viewed as a borrowing. The kanji 閑 means "leisure, spare time." <門木>

閑静な quiet, peaceful, tranquil [かんせいな]; 閑散とした dull, inactive [かんさんとした]; 閑職 nominal job [かんしょく]; 農閑期 off-season for farmers [のうかんき]; 閑古鳥が鳴く business is in the doldrums [かんこどりがなく]

SG-1264 閲	Meanings	Kun and On	Romaji	Bushu	Stroke Order and Number
	to inspect, examine	エツ	*etsu*	門	丨 冂 門' 門 門 閂 閲 閲 閲 15

閲 **D** F-2007

説文

The seal-style form comprised 門 "gate," and 兌 (兑) for the sound *etsu* to mean "to examine," together signifying "examining military horses inside a gate," and more broadly "to inspect." The kanji 閲 means "to inspect, examine." <門兑>

検閲 censorship [けんえつ]; 閲覧 reading, public perusal [えつらん]; 閲覧室 reading room [えつらんしつ]; 閲兵式 review of troops [えっぺいしき]

54 Rooms, an opening in a house

54a 呂 "many rooms connected" 宮呂侶 㕣

SG-1265 宮	Meanings	Kun and On	Romaji	Bushu	Stroke Order and Number
	palace, prince, princess, shrine	みや キュウ・グウ・ク	miya *kyuu, guu, ku*	宀	丶 宀 宀 宮 宮 宮 宮 10

宮 **A** F-0240

甲骨文1 1, 甲骨文2 2, 金文1 3, 金文2 4, 説文 5

In 1 through 5, two small squares inside a house signified "rooms." An estate that had many rooms or buildings signified "a palace" and the royalty who lived in such a palace. The kanji 宮 means "palace, prince, princess, shrine." <宀呂>

宮 prince, princess [みや]; 宮様 loyal prince or princess (honorific) [みやさま]; 宮仕え court service, life of a government official [みやづかえ]; 宮殿 palace [きゅうでん]; 王宮 royal palace, court [おうきゅう]; 宮中 imperial court [きゅうちゅう]; 平安神宮 the Heian Shrine [へいあんじんぐう]; 宮内庁 the Imperial Household Agency [くないちょう]

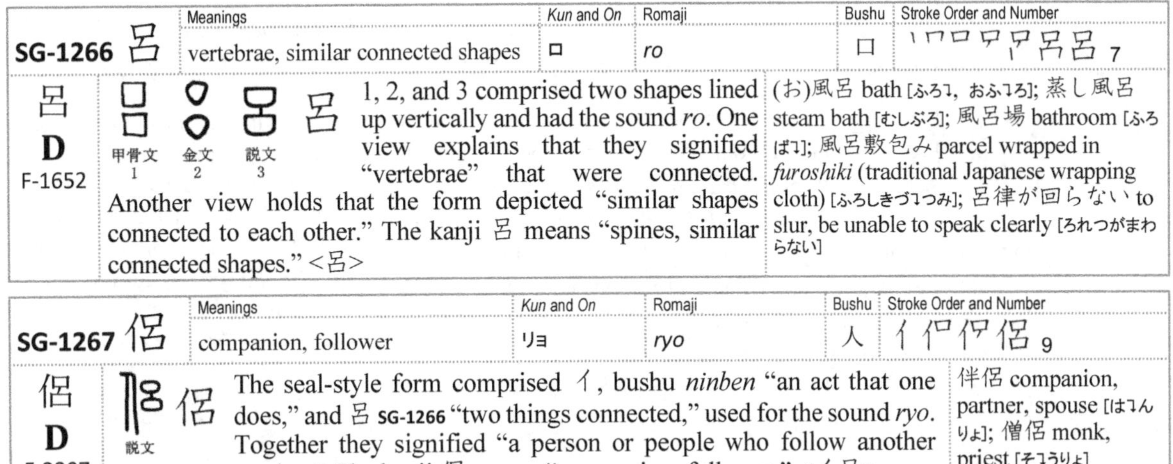

SG-1266 呂	Meanings	Kun and On	Romaji	Bushu	Stroke Order and Number
	vertebrae, similar connected shapes	ロ	ro	口	丨 ㄇ 口 ... 呂 呂 7

呂 **D** F-1652

甲骨文 1 金文 2 説文 3

1, 2, and 3 comprised two shapes lined up vertically and had the sound *ro*. One view explains that they signified "vertebrae" that were connected. Another view holds that the form depicted "similar shapes connected to each other." The kanji 呂 means "spines, similar connected shapes." <呂>

(お)風呂 bath [ふろꜜ, おふꜜろ]; 蒸し風呂 steam bath [むしぶろ]; 風呂場 bathroom [ふろばꜜ]; 風呂敷包み parcel wrapped in *furoshiki* (traditional Japanese wrapping cloth) [ふろしきづꜜつみ]; 呂律が回らない to slur, be unable to speak clearly [ろれつがまわらない]

SG-1267 侶	Meanings	Kun and On	Romaji	Bushu	Stroke Order and Number
	companion, follower	リョ	ryo	人	亻 伊 侶 侶 9

侶 **D** F-2307

説文

The seal-style form comprised 亻, bushu *ninben* "an act that one does," and 呂 **SG-1266** "two things connected," used for the sound *ryo*. Together they signified "a person or people who follow another person, companion." The kanji 侶 means "companion, follower." <亻呂>

伴侶 companion, partner, spouse [はꜜんりょ]; 僧侶 monk, priest [そꜜうりょ]

54b 尚 "high" [from air or smoke rising high out of an opening]; *shoo/joo*

尚当党常賞堂償掌・向

SG-1268 尚	Meanings	Kun and On	Romaji	Bushu	Stroke Order and Number
	furthermore, moreover	ショウ	shoo	小	㇀ ㇒ ⺌ 尚 尚 尚 8

尚 **A** F-1376

甲骨文 1 金文 2 説文 3

1, 2, and 3 depicted "a house with an opening through which air or smoke rises long and high." Smoke tends to climb ever higher and longer, and from that the character meant "moreover, furthermore." The kanji 尚 means "moreover, furthermore." <尚 (⺌冂口)>

尚 furthermore, additionally (often written in hiragana) [なꜜお]; 尚且つ and yet, but at the same time [なꜜおかつ]; 尚の事 all the more [なꜜおのこと]; 高尚な advanced, sophisticated [こうしょうな]; 時期尚早 premature, untimely [じꜜき・そうしょう]

SG-1269 当	Meanings	Kun and On	Romaji	Bushu	Stroke Order and Number
	appropriate, correct; this, the very (X)	あ-たる トウ	a-taru too	田	㇀ ㇒ ⺌ 当 当 当 6

当 **A** F-0116

説文 1 旧字 2

1 and 2 comprised 尚, used for the sound *too* to mean "appropriate," and 田 "rice paddies." From rice paddies having an appropriate value came the meaning "appropriate, correct; the very (X)." The shinji was simplified to ⺌ and ヨ. The kanji 当 means "appropriate, correct; this, the very (X)." <⺌ヨ>

当たる to hit (a target) [あたる]; 思い当たる to recall, remember [おもいあたꜜる]; 八つ当たりする to take out on someone [やつあꜜたりする, やつあたりする]; 当たり前 proper, of course, obviously [あたりまえ]; 当人 the person in question [とꜜうにん]; 当事者 person concerned, party involved [とうじꜜしゃ]; 正当化する to defend, justify [せいとうかする]; 当面の current, immediate (plans), the matter at hand [とうめんの]

SG-1270 党	Meanings	Kun and On	Romaji	Bushu	Stroke Order and Number
	political party, band of people	トウ	too	黒	⺌ 尚 ... 党 10

党 **A** F-0199

説文 1 旧字 2

1 comprised 尚, used for the sound *too* to mean "smoke rising out of an opening," and 黑 (the kyuji for 黒 **SG-1173** "black"), which had "two fires" with "a chimney with lots of black soot," signifying "kitchen." The form meant a band of people who all ate food prepared in the same kitchen and shared the same interests and activities. With 黑 replaced by 儿, bushu *ninnyoo* "person," the kanji 党 means "a political party, group of people banded together." <尚儿>

党 party [とꜜう]; 政党 political party [せいとう]; 与党 ruling party [よꜜとう]; 野党 opposition party [やꜜとう]; 悪党 villain [あくとꜜう]; 甘党 person who prefers sweets (to alcoholic beverages) [あまとう]; 徒党を組む to gang up, band together [ととうをくꜜむ]

	Meanings	Kun and On	Romaji	Bushu	Stroke Order and Number
SG-1271 常	always; constant, usual	つね・とこ ジョウ	tsune, toko *joo*	巾	丨⺌ 尚 尚 常 常 11

常 **A** F-0333

金文 1 說文 2 說文或体 3 常

1 and the top of 2 and 3 were the same as the ancient forms for 尚 **SG-1268** "long lasting." 巾 "cloth" (in 2), and 衣 **SG-1657** "clothing" (in 3), were added to 尚, both used for the sound of *joo* to mean "long." Together they signified "a very long piece of cloth." From lasting for a long time and not changing, the kanji 常 means "always; constant, usual." <尚巾>
(Note: 3 became the non-Joyo kanji 裳 "train of clothes.")

常に continually, always [つね に]; 常夏 everlasting summer [とこなつ]; 異常な unusual, extraordinary, singular [いじょうな]; 常温 normal temperature [じょうおん]; 通常 normally, ordinary [つうじょう]; 日常会話 everyday conversation [にちじょうか いわ]; 諸行無常 all worldly things are transitory [しょ ぎょう・むじょう]

	Meanings	Kun and On	Romaji	Bushu	Strokes Order and Number
SG-1272 賞	award, prize, reward	ショウ	*shoo*	貝	丨⺌ 尚 尚 當 當 賞 15

賞 **A** F-0432

金文 1 說文 2 賞

1 and 2 comprised 尚, used for the sound *shoo* to mean "high," and 貝 **SG-1693** "money; valuable," together signifying that one's high achievement was praised with an award or reward. The kanji 賞 means "award, prize, reward." <尚貝>

賞 award, prize [しょう]; 入賞する to win a prize [にゅうしょうする]; 受賞する to receive an award [じゅしょうする]; 賞与 bonus payment [しょ よ]; 賞金 reward money [しょうきん]; 賞状 certificate of merit [しょうじょう, しょうじょ う]; 賞品 prize, award, trophy [しょうひん]

	Meanings	Kun and On	Romaji	Bushu	Strokes Order and Number
SG-1273 堂	hall, temple; stately, impressive	ドウ	*doo*	土	丨⺌ 尚 尚 堂 堂 堂 11

堂 **B** F-0876

中山王器 1 說文古文 2 說文 3 堂

1, 2, and 3 comprised "a house from which air rises high" (尚 **SG-1268**), used for the sound *doo*, and "soil, ground" (土 **SG-1126**). Together they signified "a tall house that stood on a dirt foundation, hall, temple." A tall building was impressive and looked stately. The kanji 堂 means "hall, temple; stately, impressive." <尚土>

講堂 lecture hall [こうどう]; お堂 temple, shrine [おどう]; 堂々巡り going around in circles [どうどうめ ぐり]; 堂々とした stately, dignified [どうどうとした]; 堂に入った to be master of, be quite at home [どうにいった]

	Meanings	Kun and On	Romaji	Bushu	Stroke Order and Number
SG-1274 償	to make up, compensate, atone for	つぐな-う ショウ	tsuguna-u *shoo*	人	亻 亻' 亻⺌ 償 償 償 償 17

償 **C** F-1152

金文 1 說文 2 償

1 was the same as 1 for 賞 **SG-1272**. In 2, 亻, bushu *ninben* "an act that a person does" was added to 賞 "award, reward," used for the sound *shoo*, which originally had the sense of making up for the sacrifice made by an awardee in attaining an achievement. Together they meant "to compensate for loss or damage," or "to atone for." The kanji 償 means "to make up, compensate, atone for." <亻賞>

償う to atone for, compensate [つぐな う]; 弁償する to compensate, make up for [べんしょうする]; 賠償 compensation, indemnity [ばいしょう]; 補償 compensation [ほしょう]; 減価償却 depreciation [げんかしょ うきゃく]; 教科書の無償化 free distribution of textbooks [きょうか しょの・むしょうか]

	Meanings	Kun and On	Romaji	Bushu	Stroke Order and Number
SG-1275 掌	palm; to control	ショウ	*shoo*	手	丨⺌ 尚 尚 堂 掌 12

掌 **D** F-1708

說文 掌

The seal-style form comprised 尚 **SG-1268**, used for the sound *shoo* to mean "flat," and 手 **SG-0072** "hand." The flat part of a hand was "the palm," and the character also meant "to control." The kanji 掌 means "palm; to control." <尚手>

合掌 joining one's hands in prayer [がっしょう]; 車掌 bus or train conductor [しゃしょう]; 掌中にある to be at the mercy of [しょ うちゅうにある]; 掌握する to hold, seize, grasp [しょうあくする] // 掌 palm [たなごころ]

向 "facing" [from an opening in a house]

	Meanings	Kun and On	Romaji	Bushu	Stroke Order and Number
SG-1276 向	toward; to face, fit well; inclination; suitable	むーく コウ	mu-ku *koo*	口	′ 丨 冂 冋 向 向 6

向 **A** F-0169

甲骨文 1　金文 2　説文 3

1, 2, and 3 showed "an opening or window in a house." Air tends to move toward an opening, and the form signified "toward; to face." Tendency and inclination also gave the meaning "suitable; to fit." The kanji 向 means "toward; to face, fit well; inclination; suitable." <丿冂口>

向こう other side, ahead, destination, coming [むこꜜう]; 向かう to go toward, leave for [むかう]; 向いている suitable [むいている]; 南向き facing south [みなみむき]; 仰向け facing upward [あおむけ]; 手向ける to offer (to a deity or deceased person's spirit) [たむけꜜる]; 向学心 desire to learn [こうがくꜜしん]; 向上 improvement, betterment [こうじょう]; 内向的 withdrawn, introverted [ないこうてき]

55 Tall structures

55a 高 "tall; tower" [from a watchtower] 高厚豪

	Meanings	Kun and On	Romaji	Bushu	Stroke Order and Number
SG-1277 高	high, tall, expensive; amount, quantity	たかーい コウ	taka-i *koo*	高	′ 亠 亣 古 高 高 10

高 **A** F-0023

甲骨文1 1　甲骨文2 2　金文1 3　説文 4　旧字 5

1 through 4 depicted "a watchtower," signifying "high, tall," but views regarding the origin vary: (a) "a triumphal arch under which soldiers' corpses were buried with a box of benedictions (口 **SG-0031**)"; (b) "a tall building on a plateau." The character meant "tall, high," and "amount, quantity; expensive." 3 became the kyuji 髙 (5), while 4 became the shinji. The kanji 高 means "high, tall, expensive; amount, quantity." <亠冂口>

高い high, tall, expensive [たかꜜい]; 高まる to heighten [たかまꜜる]; 高める to raise [たかめꜜる]; 高々 at most, no more than [たかꜜだか]; 割高な comparatively more expensive [わりだかな]; 円高 strong yen [えんだか]; 高の知れた trivial, insignificant [たかꜜのしれた]; 高校生 high school student [こうこꜜうせい]; 高血圧 high blood pressure [こうけꜜつあつ]

	Meanings	Kun and On	Romaji	Bushu	Stroke Order and Number
SG-1278 厚	thick, hospitable, grave	あつーい コウ	atsu-i *koo*	厂	一 厂 戸 厚 厚 厚 9

厚 **B** F-0562

金文1 1　金文2 2　説文 3

1, 2, and 3 comprised 厂 "a cliff," signifying "thick soil"; and "a tower with many levels placed upside down," used for the sound *koo*. Dirt piled in many layers signified the "thickness of ground or dirt," or just "thickness." (The inverted shape of the tower also emphasized the "thickness" of its foundation.) Heartfelt hospitality was also seen as having "depth." The kanji 厚 means "thick, hospitable, grave." <厂日子>

厚い thick [あつい]; 厚化粧 heavy makeup [あつげꜜしょう]; 厚かましい brazen, presumptuous [あつかましꜜい]; 厚生年金 employee pension [こうせいねꜜんきん]; 温厚な gentle, mild-mannered [おんこうな]; 厚意 kindness, thoughtfulness [こꜜうい]; 厚遇する to give a warm reception to, make much of someone [こうぐうする]

	Meanings	Kun and On	Romaji	Bushu	Stroke Order and Number
SG-1279 豪	splendor, Australia; stirring	ゴウ	goo	豕	亠 亣 高 亭 亭 豪 豪 豪 14

豪 **C** F-1296

説文

The seal-style form comprised 高 **SG-1277**, used for the sound *goo*, and 豕 "a long-haired animal," together signifying "a strong, long-haired animal; splendid." It no longer applies to animals. The kanji 豪 means "splendor; stirring." It is also used for "Australia" (豪州). <亠冖豕>

強豪 overwhelmingly strong person or team [きょうごう]; 豪雨 torrential rain [ごꜜうう]; 豪華な splendid, gorgeous, sumptuous [ごꜜうかな]; 豪快な glorious, thrilling [ごうかいな]; 豪傑笑い hearty laughter [ごうけつわꜜらい]; 富豪 person of great wealth [ふごう]; 酒豪 heavy drinker [しゅごう]; 豪州 Australia [ごꜜうしゅう]

55b 喬 "high with a bent top" [from a tilted tall tree on a tower]; *kyoo* 橋矯

	Meanings	Kun and On	Romaji	Bushu	Stroke Order and Number
SG-1280 橋	bridge	はし キョウ	hashi *kyoo*	木	… 橋 16
橋 **A** F-0449	説文 The seal-style form comprised 木 **SG-0608** "tree, wood," and 喬 "a bent shape or arch in a high place," used for the sound *kyoo*. Together they signified "a high-hanging wooden arch." The kanji 橋 means "bridge." <木喬(夭口冂口)>			橋 bridge [はしꜜ]; 橋渡しする to mediate [はしわꜜたしする]; 橋桁 bridge girder [はしげた]; 鉄橋 iron bridge for railroad [てっきょう]; 歩道橋 pedestrian bridge [ほどうきょう]; 橋梁 bridge [きょうりょう]; 陸橋 overpass, footbridge [りっきょう]	

	Meanings	Kun and On	Romaji	Bushu	Stroke Order and Number
SG-1281 矯	to rectify, amend, bend, flex	た-める キョウ	ta-meru *kyoo*	矢	… 矯 17
矯 **D** F-2176	説文 The seal-style form comprised 矢 **SG-1524** "arrow," and 喬 "bent or arched shape," used for the sound *kyoo*. Together they signified "a bent arrow, crookedness." A crooked arrow needed to be straightened, which led to the meaning "to straighten a bent arrow." The kanji 矯 means "to rectify, amend, bend, flex." <矢喬>			矯める to straighten, correct [ためꜜる]; 矯正 reform, remedy [きょうせい]; 矯正歯科 orthodontics [きょうせいしꜜか]; 矯正視力 corrected vision [きょうせいしꜜりょく]	

55c 京 "capital" [from a tall hill where people lived, or a high tower] 京景影就涼蹴憬

	Meanings	Kun and On	Romaji	Bushu	Stroke Order and Number
SG-1282 京	capital, Kyoto, Tokyo, ten quadrillion; very large	キョウ・ケイ	*kyoo, kee*	亠	… 京 8
京 **A** F-0063	甲骨文1 (1) 甲骨文2 (2) 金文1 (3) 金文2 (4) 説文 (5) 1 through 4 showed a striking similarity to the ancient forms for 高 **SG-1277**. The difference was that 高 had 口 at the bottom, while 京 had 丨, which signified "raised higher." 1 through 5 meant "a building that was built on a high land." Bright, tall hills were better suited for attracting people, and an area of concentrated population became the capital. The Japanese emperor or empress resided in the capital city Kyoto for over a thousand years until the imperial residence moved to the new capital 東京 or "eastern capital," during the Meiji restoration (1868). A capital is a large town, giving the meaning "large." The character was also used for the number "ten quadrillion" (which is 10,000 times 兆 **SG-1770** "trillion"). The kanji 京 means "capital, Kyoto, Tokyo, ten quadrillion; very large." <亠口小>			京都 Kyoto [きょꜜうと]; 京風 Kyoto-style [きょうふう]; 京の都 Kyoto [きょꜜうのみやこ]; 東京 Tokyo [とうきょう]; 帰京する to return to Tokyo [ききょうする]; 上京する to go up to the capital, leave for Tokyo [じょうきょうする]; 京阪神 Kyoto-Osaka-Kobe area [けいはꜜんしん]; 京浜 Tokyo-Yokohama area [けいひん], 京 ten quadrillion [けꜜい]	

	Meanings	Kun and On	Romaji	Bushu	Stroke Order and Number
SG-1283 景	fine view, good scene, economic condition	ケイ	*kee, ke*	日	… 景 12
景 **A** F-0517	説文 The seal-style form comprised 日 **SG-1045** "the sun," and 京, used for the sound *kee*, together signifying "a bright sunny place where one can command a good, clear view." Bright light also creates a shadow, and the contrast between the two extremes of bright and shadow was applied to fluctuations in the economy. The kanji 景 means a "fine view, good scene, economic condition." <日京>			光景 spectacle, scene [こうけい]; 背景 background [はいけい]; 景気 economy, business cycle [けいき]; 不景気 recession, economic slump [ふけꜜいき]; 絶景 glorious or magnificent view [ぜっけい] // 景色 scenery [けꜜしき]; 景色ばむ to start to show anger [けしきばꜜむ]	

	Meanings	Kun and On	Romaji	Bushu	Stroke Order and Number
SG-1284 影	shadow	かげ エイ	kage *ee*	彡	… 影 15
影 **A** F-0511	No ancient form. The kanji 影 comprises 景 "bright light" and 彡 "pretty shape." Objects in bright sunshine create clear silhouettes and cast shadows. The kanji 影 means "shadow." <景彡>			影 shadow [かꜜげ]; 人影 figure, silhouette [ひとかげ]; 面影 image, reminder [おもかげ]; 影響 effect, influence [えいきょう]; 撮影 filming, taking photographs [さつえい]; 近影 one's latest portrait [きんえい]; 幻影 vision, ghost, hallucination [げんえい]	

	Meanings	Kun and On	Romaji	Bushu	Stroke Order and Number
SG-1285 就	to begin, take up, become employed	つ-く シュウ・ジュ	tsu-ku *shuu, ju*	尢	亠古亨京京一尌就就 12

就 **B** F-0803

説文

The origin of this character is obscure. One view explains it as comprising 京 **SG-1282** "capital," and 尢, used for the sound *shuu* to mean "to gather." People congregated in the capital to obtain new employment and to begin living there, whence the meaning "to begin, become employed." The kanji 就 means "to begin, take up, become employed." <京尢>

就く to be hired, become appointed [つ1く]; 去就 course of action [きょしゅう]; 就職 taking a job [しゅうしょく]; 就活・就職活動 job-hunting [しゅうかつ, しゅうしょくかつどう]; 就業規則 work rule, office regulation [しゅうぎょうきそく]; 就任 assumption of an office, installation [しゅうにん]; 就学率 school enrollment rate [しゅうがくりつ]; 成就 accomplishment, completion, success [じょうじゅ]

	Meanings	Kun and On	Romaji	Bushu	Stroke Order and Number
SG-1286 涼	cool	すず-しい リョウ	suzu-shii *ryoo*	水	氵氵氵氵涼涼涼 11

涼 **C** F-1449

説文 1 曹全碑 2

1 comprised "flowing water" (氵), and 京 **SG-1282**, used for the sound *ryoo* to mean "cold." Together they signified "cold water." Cold water makes one feel cool. The kanji 涼 means "cool."<氵京>

涼しい cool [すずしい]; 夕涼みする to enjoy the cool of the evening [ゆうすずみする]; 涼む to cool off [すずむ]; 涼しい顔 nonchalant air, unruffled air [すずしいかお]; 清涼飲料水 carbonated drink, soda [せいりょういんりょうすい]; 涼を取る to cool off [りょうをとる]; 納涼祭り festival for enjoying the cool of a summer evening [のうりょうまつり]

	Meanings	Kun and On	Romaji	Bushu	Stroke Order and Number
SG-1287 蹴	to kick, reject	け-る シュウ	ke-ru *shuu*	足	𠯁𧾷𧾷踔踪踪蹴蹴蹴 19

蹴 **D** F-2061

篆文

The seal-style form comprised 足 **SG-0227** "leg," and 就 **SG-1285**, used for the sound *shuu* to mean "to step on." Together they signified "to give a kick" and "to reject." The kanji 蹴 means "to kick, reject." <𧾷就>

蹴る to kick, turn down [ける]; 蹴飛ばす to kick away, boot out, refuse [けとばす]; 足蹴にする insulting treatment of other people [あしげにする, あしげにする], 一蹴する to reject flatly [いっしゅうする]

	Meanings	Kun and On	Romaji	Bushu	Stroke Order and Number
SG-1288 憬	to yearn, look up to	ケイ	kee	心	丶忄忄忄悍憬憬 15

憬 **D** F-2836

篆文

The seal-style form comprised "heart/mind" (忄), and 景 **SG-1283**, used for the sound *kee* to mean "good view." Together they signified "one's heart gazing upon something in the distance with bright thoughts of admiration or desire." The kanji 憬 means "to yearn, look up to." <忄景>

憧憬 dream of, aspire after [どうけい]

55d 享 "to enjoy; watchtower" 享郭

	Meanings	Kun and On	Romaji	Bushu	Stroke Order and Number
SG-1289 享	to accept what is given, enjoy	キョウ	kyoo	亠	’亠古亨亨享 8

享 **D** F-1852

甲骨文1 1 甲骨文2 2 金文1 3 金文2 4 説文篆文 5 説文 6

1 through 6 depicted "a watchtower on its foundation," and had the sound *kyoo.* The present use of "to enjoy" is a borrowing. The kanji 享 means "to accept what is given, enjoy." <古子>

享ける to enjoy (heavenly bliss) [うける]; 享受する to enjoy health or freedom [きょうじゅする]; 享楽的 pleasure seeking, given to pleasure [きょうらくてき]; 享年 someone's age at death [きょうねん]

	Meanings	Kun and On	Romaji	Bushu	Stroke Order and Number
SG-1290 郭	a walled town, quarter	カク	kaku	邑	亠古亨享享享郭郭 11

郭 **D** F-1826

甲骨文1 1 甲骨文2 2 金文 3 説文 4

1, 2, 3, and 4 showed a rampart with a watchtower on both ends, signifying "a town or an area that was surrounded by a defensive wall," and had the sound *kaku.* In 4, 邑 "town" was added and became 阝, bushu *oozato*. The kanji 郭 means "a town or area inside a wall, quarter." <享阝>

城郭 castle citadel, castle wall [じょうかく]; 輪郭 contours, outline, sketch [りんかく]; 外郭団体 extragovernmental organization [がいかくだんたい]

55e 亭 "pavilion"; *tee* 停亭

SG-1291 停	Meanings	Kun and On	Romaji	Bushu	Stroke Order and Number
	to stop, halt, stop temporarily	テイ	*tee*	人	亻 亻亠 亻亡 亻亭 停 停 11

停 **B** F-1047

停 (説文) 停

The seal-style form comprised 亻 "an act that a person does," and 亭 **SG-1292**, used for the sound *tee* to mean "to stop for a while (at a post station)." Together they signified "to stop." The kanji 停 means "to stop, halt, stop temporarily." <亻亭(亠口冖丁)>

停車駅 station at which a train stops [ていしゃꜜえき]; 停戦 ceasefire [ていせん]; 停電 power outage [ていでん]; バス停 bus stop [バスてい]; 停止する to stop, suspend [ていしする]; 停学 suspension (from school) [ていがく]; 停留所 bus stop [ていりゅうじょ]; 各駅停車 local train [かくえきてꜜいしゃ]

SG-1292 亭	Meanings	Kun and On	Romaji	Bushu	Stroke Order and Number
	pavilion, gazebo, house	テイ	*tee*	亠	亠 亩 亯 亭 亭 9

亭 **C** F-1340

亭 (説文) 亭

The seal-style form comprised "a tall building" and "an entrance," together signifying "a tall building." In the kanji, the bottom became 丁 **SG-1914**, used for the sound *tee*. The character originally meant a tall building such as a post station in ancient China. In Japanese, the kanji 亭 means "pavilion, gazebo, house." <亠口冖丁>

料亭 expensive Japanese-style restaurant [りょうてい]; 亭主 master of the house, tea ceremony host, husband [てꜜいしゅ]

56 Various (dwellings)

56a 亜 "secondary, suppressed" [from a plan of a burial chamber in a mausoleum] 悪亜

SG-1293 悪	Meanings	Kun and On	Romaji	Bushu	Stroke Order and Number
	vice; bad, ill, wrong, poor	わる-い アク・オ	waru-i *aku, o*	心	一 亓 亜 亜 悪 悪 11

悪 **A** F-0437

惡 (説文 1) 惡 (旧字 2) 悪

1 comprised 亜 **SG-1294**, used for the sound *a* to mean "suppressed" (from a plan of an underground burial chamber), and 心 **SG-0187** "heart, feelings." Ill feelings that were suppressed gave the meaning "bad." The kanji 悪 means "vice; bad, ill, wrong, poor." <亜心>

悪い bad [わるꜜい]; 意地悪な wicked, spiteful [いじꜜわるな]; 悪 evil, badness, vice [あꜜく]; 悪人 villain [あくにん]; 悪事 evil deed [あꜜくじ]; 悪名高い notorious [あくめいたかꜜい]; 好悪 one's likes and dislikes, one's prejudices [こꜜうお] // 悪しき bad, evil [あꜜしき]

SG-1294 亜	Meanings	Kun and On	Romaji	Bushu	Stroke Order and Number
	secondary, not authentic; Asia	ア	*a*	二	一 亓 亓 亜 亜 7

亜 **C** F-1116

(甲骨文 1) (金文 2) (説文 3) 亞 (旧字 4) 亜

1, 2, and 3 depicted "the plan of an underground burial chamber in a mausoleum with four columns in the foundation." Alternative views regarding 亜 include that (a) it depicted "something underground," giving the meaning "secondary"; (b) it depicted "a priest"; and (c) its current meaning is a borrowing for the sound *a*. The kanji 亜 means "secondary, not authentic; Asia." <亜>

亜細亜 Asia [アꜜジア]; 亜流 secondary, imitator, follower [ありゅう]; 亜鉛 zinc [あꜜえん]; 亜熱帯 subtropical zone [あねったい, あねꜜったい]; 白亜の white [はꜜくあの]

56b 井 "well; roof slate" 井丹耕丼・瓦

SG-1295 井	Meanings	Kun and On	Romaji	Bushu	Stroke Order and Number
	well	い セイ・ショウ	i *see, shoo*	二	一 二 キ 井 4

井 **A** F-0254

(甲骨文 1) (金文 1 2) (金文 2 3) (説文 4) 井

1 through 4 depicted "a well," inside of which there was water or vermillion sand. The dot was dropped in the kanji. The kanji 井 means "a well." <井>

井戸 water well [いꜜど]; 井戸水 well water [いどꜜみず]; 井戸端会議 housewives' gossip, back-fence gossip [いどばたかꜜいぎ]; 井の中の蛙 person who is ignorant of the real world [いꜜのなꜜかの・かわず]; 市井の人 ordinary citizen [しꜜせいのひと]; 天井 ceiling [てんじょう]

	Meanings	Kun and On	Romaji	Bushu	Stroke Order and Number
SG-1296 丹	red, sincere; vermillion	タン	*tan*	丶	ノ 冂 月 丹 4

丹 **C** F-1375

甲骨文 1　金文 2　説文古文1 3　説文古文2 4　説文 5

1 and 2 depicted "a well containing vermillion sand." It meant "vermillion." In 3, 彡 "neat, pretty" was added. The character was also borrowed to mean "sincere." The kanji 丹 means "red, sincere; vermillion." <丹>

丹精する to be devoted to, put one's heart into [たんせいする]; 丹念に carefully, elaborately [たんねんに]

	Meanings	Kun and On	Romaji	Bushu	Stroke Order and Number
SG-1297 耕	to cultivate, till	たがや-す コウ	tagaya-su *koo*	耒	三 丰 耒 耒 耒= 耕 耕 10

耕 **C** F-1505

説文

The seal-style form comprised 耒 "a plow with three lines," signifying "neatly furrowed field," and 井 **SG-1295**, used for the sound *koo* (from *see*). From making furrows in neat lines, the kanji 耕 means "to cultivate, till." <耒井>

耕す to cultivate, till [たがやす]; 休耕田 fallow rice field [きゅうこうでん]; 耕作 farming, farm work [こうさく]; 耕地 plowed land [こうち]; 晴耕雨読 work in the fields on fine days and read in wet weather [せいこううどく]

	Meanings	Kun and On	Romaji	Bushu	Stroke Order and Number
SG-1298 丼	large rice bowl, *donburi* bowl	どんぶり・どん	donburi, don	丶	一 二 ナ 井 丼 5

丼 **D** F-1863

篆文

The seal-style form originally depicted a well frame with clean water inside. Later "well" came to be written as 井 **(SG-1295)**, without a dot. In Japanese, the kanji 丼 is used to mean a porcelain bowl that is used to serve generous helpings of cooked rice topped with a variety of ingredients. The kanji 丼 means "a large rice bowl, *donburi* bowl." <井丶>

丼 porcelain bowl [どんぶり]; 丼物 large bowl of rice with toppings [どんぶりもの]; 親子丼 rice bowl with chicken and egg on top [おやこどんぶり]; 丼勘定(どんぶり勘定) slipshod accounting [どんぶりかんじょう]; 天丼 rice bowl with tempura on top [てんどん]

瓦 "roof slate"

	Meanings	Kun and On	Romaji	Bushu	Stroke Order and Number
SG-1299 瓦	roof tile	かわら ガ	kawara *ga*	瓦	一 丆 工 瓦 瓦 5

瓦 **D** F-1817

説文

The seal-style form of 瓦 showed "a roofing tile that had a decorative semicircular shape." The kanji 瓦 means "roof tile." <瓦>

瓦 roof tile [かわら]; 屋根瓦 roofing tile [やねがわら]; 瓦屋根 tiled roof [かわらやね]; 煉瓦造り built with bricks, brick building [れんがづくり]; 赤煉瓦 red brick [あかれんが]; 瓦解する to fall down, collapse [がかいする]

57 Rice field

57a 田 "rice paddies" [from an irrigated rice field with levees] 田男町画留略畑畳畝

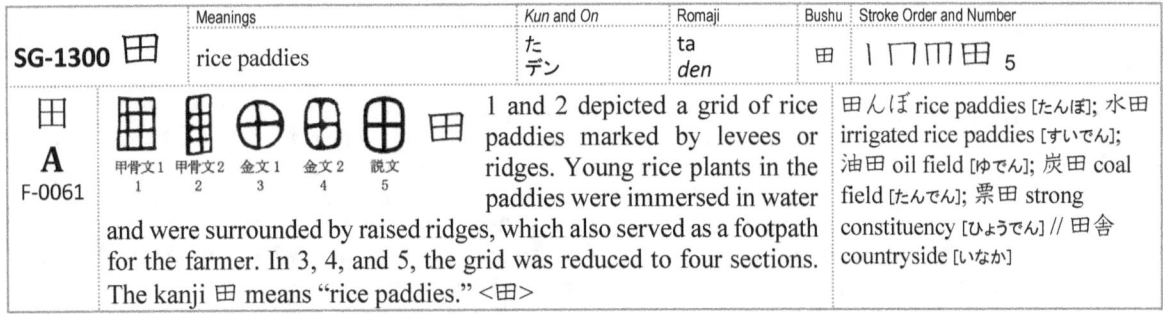

	Meanings	Kun and On	Romaji	Bushu	Stroke Order and Number
SG-1300 田	rice paddies	た デン	ta *den*	田	丨 冂 冊 田 5

田 **A** F-0061

甲骨文1 1　甲骨文2 2　金文1 3　金文2 4　説文 5

1 and 2 depicted a grid of rice paddies marked by levees or ridges. Young rice plants in the paddies were immersed in water and were surrounded by raised ridges, which also served as a footpath for the farmer. In 3, 4, and 5, the grid was reduced to four sections. The kanji 田 means "rice paddies." <田>

田んぼ rice paddies [たんぼ]; 水田 irrigated rice paddies [すいでん]; 油田 oil field [ゆでん]; 炭田 coal field [たんでん]; 票田 strong constituency [ひょうでん] // 田舎 countryside [いなか]

	Meanings	Kun and On	Romaji	Bushu	Stroke Order and Number
SG-1301 男	man; male, masculine	おとこ ダン・ナン	otoko *dan, nan*	田	冂 冊 田 男 男 7

男 **A** F-0130

甲骨文1 1 甲骨文2 2 金文1 3 金文2 4 説文 5 男

1 through 5 comprised "rice paddies" (田) and "a plow" or "a strong, firm hand" (力 **SG-1949**). A person engaged in hard work in a field using a plow was a "man." The kanji 男 means "man; male, masculine." <田力>

男 man, male [おとこ]; 男の子 boy [おとこのこ]; 男らしい manly [おとこらしい]; 男勝り strong-spirited, gutsy (woman), mannish [おとこまさり]; 優男 man with delicate features [やさおとこ]; 男性 man, male person [だんせい]; 次男 second son [じなん]; 下男 manservant [げなん]

	Meanings	Kun and On	Romaji	Bushu	Stroke Order and Number
SG-1302 町	town, downtown, district, city block name	まち チョウ	machi *choo*	田	冂 冊 田 田一 町 7

町 **A** F-0141

説文 町

The seal-style form comprised 田 "neatly arranged rice paddies," and 丁 **SG-1914** "footpaths running at right angles," used for the sound *choo.* The form originally signified "the footpath in a rice field." In Japan, the form is used to mean "town, downtown," and denotes a jurisdiction larger than a 村, within a 郡. The kanji 町 means "town, downtown, block of a district" <田丁>

町 town, jurisdiction [まち]; 町中に出る to go into the town [まちなかにでる]; 町外れ outer edge of a town [まちはずれ]; 下町 downtown, *Shitamachi* (the low area east of the Sumida River in Tokyo) [したまち]; 町内会 neighborhood association [ちょうないかい]; 町人 townspeople, merchants (historic) [ちょうにん]; 永田町 *Nagatachoo* block [ながたちょう]

	Meanings	Kun and On	Romaji	Bushu	Stroke Order and Number
SG-1303 画	to draw, plan; stroke, picture	ガ・カク	*ga, kaku*	田	一 丅 而 亩 画 画 8

画 **A** F-0297

金文1 1 金文2 2 金文3 3 説文 4 旧字 5 画

1, 2, 3, and 4 comprised "a hand holding a brush straight up" and "land" or "rice paddies." The lines surrounding the rice paddies were added to indicate boundaries. Making an official record of rice paddies involved drawing the boundaries on a plan, and thus the form meant "to draw; drawing." The kanji 画 means "to draw, plan; stroke, picture." <一由凵>

画家 painter [がか]; 画面 screen [がめん, がめん]; 漫画 comics [まんが]; 画素数 number of pixels [がそすう]; 動画 animated film, video clip [どうが]; 画数 number of writing strokes [かくすう]; 九画 nine strokes [きゅうかく]; 画する to mark an epoch [かくする]

	Meanings	Kun and On	Romaji	Bushu	Stroke Order and Number
SG-1304 留	to stay, remain, fasten	と-める リュウ・ル	to-meru *ryuu, ru*	田	ノ 𠂉 𠃊 𠃊刀 𠃊刀 留 留 留 10

留 **B** F-0722

金文 1 説文 2 留

1 showed "a stream of water with a pool of water on either side," used for the sound *ryuu,* and "rice paddies" (田 **SG-1300**). Together they signified "water that remained in one place." Another view explains that 2 comprised "a bit in a horse's mouth" and 由, used for the sound *ryuu,* and that tying a horse to a tree by the bridle to keep it in one place led to the meaning "to remain." The kanji 留 means "to stay, remain, fasten." <𠃊刀田>

留める to fasten [とめる]; 書留 registered mail [かきとめ]; 留学 study abroad [りゅうがく]; 留意する to take heed, pay adequate attention to [りゅういする]; 遺留品 personal effects (of a missing person) [いりゅうひん]; 留守にする to be absent from home [るすにする]; 留守番 house sitter, staying home (during someone's absence) [るすばん] // 留める to contain, record a fact [とどめる]; 留まる to remain [とどまる]

	Meanings	Kun and On	Romaji	Bushu	Stroke Order and Number
SG-1305 略	strategy, tactic, summary; informal; to leave out	リャク	*ryaku*	田	冂 冊 田 田ク 畋 略 略 11

略 **B** F-0808

説文 略

The seal-style form comprised 田 "rice paddies," and 各 **SG-0244**, used for the sound *ryaku* to mean "partition." Together they originally signified "to draw a plan of boundaries for purposes of land management and taxation," and thus also "strategy or tactic." Such a plan became the basis of a general rule or guideline, and thus the additional meaning "summary." In a summary, details are abbreviated or left out. The kanji 略 means "strategy, tactic, summary; informal; to leave out." <田各>

省略 omission [しょうりゃく]; 略図 outline, sketch [りゃくず]; 計略 trick, strategy [けいりゃく]; 略す to omit [りゃくす]; 前略 abbreviated salutation omitting a seasonal greeting (in a letter) [ぜんりゃく]; 略式 informality [りゃくしき]

	Meanings	Kun and On	Romaji	Bushu	Stroke Order and Number
SG-1306 畑	agricultural field, field of specialty	はた・はたけ	hata, hatake	田	丶ソ火灯畑畑 9

畑 **B** F-0870

The kanji 畑 is a kokuji（国字）created in Japan, and thus has no ancient form. It comprises 火 **SG-1164** "fire" and 田 "rice paddies." Fallow agricultural fields that were not immersed in water were burned during the off-season to replenish the soil with certain nutrients. Another view explains that 火 signified "dry," and the character meant "a (dry) agricultural field." A person cultivating a career in a particular area of work gave the meaning "one's professional specialty." The kanji 畑 means "agricultural field, field of specialty." <火田>

田畑 farm, field [たはた]; 畑 agricultural field [はたけ]; 畑仕事 agricultural fieldwork [はたけしごと]; 花畑 flower field [はなばたけ]; 畑違い different area of expertise [はたけちがい]; 化学畑 field of specialty in chemistry [かがくばたけ]

	Meanings	Kun and On	Romaji	Bushu	Stroke Order and Number
SG-1307 塁	garrison, fort, base (in baseball)	ルイ	*rui*	土	口 田 田 田 畀 畕 界 塁 塁 12

塁 **C** F-1463

金文 1 説文 2 旧字 3

1 and 2 comprised 畾 "piles of dirt built up," used for the sound *rui*, and 土 "dirt," together signifying "garrison, fort." In the shinji, the two 田 were reduced to 𠂉く. A baseball field is formed by four connected bases, and so the kanji 塁 is also used to mean "base." The kanji 塁 means "garrison, fort, base (in baseball)." <田𠂉く土>

土塁 earthwork, fieldwork [どるい]; 盗塁 base stealing (in baseball) [とうるい]; 本塁打 home run, homer [ほんるいだ]

	Meanings	Kun and On	Romaji	Bushu	Stroke Order and Number
SG-1308 畝	ridge in a field, rows of raised dirt	うね	une	田	丶亠亩亩亩亩畆畝 10

畝 **D** F-2780

金文 1 篆文 2 説文 3

1 and 2 comprised 田 **SG-1300** "rice paddies," and 每, used for the sounds *ho*/*bo*, together signifying "a unit of measurement for land dimensions." In 3 "rice paddies," "a footprint" (久), and "length and breadth" (十) together signified measuring rice paddies by walking along their length and breadth. A farming lot had ridges all around, and from that 畝 was used to mean "rows of raised dirt." The kanji 畝 means "ridge in a field, rows of raised dirt." <亠田久>

畝 ridge in a field, row of raised dirt [うね]

57b 苗 "rice plant seedling" [from plants and rice paddies]; *byoo* 描猫苗

	Meanings	Kun and On	Romaji	Bushu	Stroke Order and Number
SG-1309 描	to draw in detail, depict	えが-く・か-く ビョウ	ega-ku, ka-ku *byoo*	手	一十扌扌扩描描描 11

描 **B** F-0961

No ancient form. The kanji comprises 扌, bushu *tehen* "an act done by hand," and 苗, which was used for the sound *byoo* to mean "small, detailed." Together they signified "to depict details by hand." The kanji 描 means "to draw in detail, depict." <扌艹田>

描く to draw, depict, write [えがく]; 絵描き painter, artist [えかき]; 手描き hand-painted [てがき]; 寸描 brief sketch [すんびょう]; 素描 rough sketch, dessin [そびょう]; 線描 line drawing [せんびょう]; 描写 portrayal [びょうしゃ]

	Meanings	Kun and On	Romaji	Bushu	Stroke Order and Number
SG-1310 猫	cat	ねこ ビョウ	neko *byoo*	犬	ノ犭犭犭猫猫猫 11

猫 **C** F-1234

篆文

The seal-style form comprised 豸 "animal" (bushu *mujinahen* "animal," from a badger), and 苗, used for the sound *byoo* (which, in one view, came from the sound a cat makes, "meow"). In the kanji, 豸 was replaced by 犭. bushu *kemonohen* "animal." The kanji 猫 means "cat." <犭苗>

猫 cat [ねこ]; 猫背 round stooped shoulders [ねこぜ]; 猫可愛がり endless doting [ねこかわいがり]; 猫舌 dislike of very hot food or drink [ねこじた]; 飼い猫 housecat [かいねこ]

	Meanings	Kun and On	Romaji	Bushu	Stroke Order and Number
SG-1311 苗	seedling, sapling	なえ・なわ ビョウ	nae, nawa *byoo*	艸	一艹芇苗苗苗 8

苗 **D** F-1673

説文

The seal-style form comprised "plants" (艸, 艹, bushu *kusakanmuri*) and 田 "rice paddies." What was planted in rice paddies were "seedlings." The kanji 苗 means "seedling, sapling." <艹田>

苗 seedling [なえ]; 早苗 rice seedling [さなえ]; 苗木 seedling, nursery tree [なえぎ]; 苗代 seed bed (for rice) [なわしろ]

57c 里 "neatly lined; village" [from land with neatly laid levees]; *ri* 里野理厘

SG-1312 里	Meanings	Kun and On	Romaji	Bushu	Stroke Order and Number
	village, one's hometown, *ri* (old measurement of distance)	さと リ	sato *ri*	里	丨 冂 日 甲 里 里 7

里 **A** F-0632

金文1 1, 金文2 2, 説文 3

1, 2, and 3 comprised "rice paddies" (田 **SG-1300**) and "land, ground" (土 **SG-1126**). Land where people grew and produced rice was "a village." When people left their own village for another, it remained their "hometown." The character was also used to represent the *ri*, a unit of distance measurement equivalent to four kilometers. The kanji 里 means "village, one's hometown, *ri*." <甲二>

里 one's hometown, a village in the country [さとꜜ]; 里帰り return to parents' home, homecoming [さとがえり]; 里心がつく to start feeling homesick [さとごꜜころが・つꜜく]; 里 old unit of distance measurement, 4 km [り]; 千里眼 clairvoyance, second sight [せんりがん]; 千里の道も一歩から "A journey of a thousand miles begins with a single step." [せꜜんりのみちも・いꜜっぽから]

SG-1313 野	Meanings	Kun and On	Romaji	Bushu	Stroke Order and Number
	fields, outsider, opposition; wild	の ヤ	no *ya*	里	口 日 甲 里 里 野 野 野 9

野 **A** F-0095

甲骨文 1, 金文1 2, 金文2 3, 説文古文 4, 説文 5

1 and 2 comprised "trees" and "soil," and had the sound *ya*. 3 had "rice paddies," "roomy" (予 **SG-0150**), and "soil," together signifying "a spacious piece of land, a field." 4 was a combination of 2 and 3. In 5, the two trees were dropped, and only 里 "village" and 予 were kept. A field is outside of a town's center of activity, thus the additional meanings "out of power" or "opposition." The kanji 野 means "field, outsider, opposition; wild." <里予>

野原 fields [のꜜはら]; 野外 fields, open air, the outdoors [やꜜがい]; 野球 baseball [やきゅう]; 与野党 ruling and opposition parties [よやꜜとう]; 在野 out of office, out of power [ざいや]; 野生 wildness [やせい]; 粗野な rustic, vulgar [そꜜやな] // 野良仕事 farm work, working in the fields [のらしꜜごと]

SG-1314 理	Meanings	Kun and On	Romaji	Bushu	Stroke Order and Number
	logic, reason, thread, rational	リ	*ri*	玉	一 T 王 玎 玾 玾 理 理 理 11

理 **A** F-0180

説文

The seal-style form comprised 王 (from 玉 **SG-1730** "gems strung together"), and 里, used for the sound *ri* to mean "grid-like neatness." A gemstone splits neatly and logically along its natural cleavage. The kanji 理 means "logic, reason, thread, rational." <王里>

理解する to understand [りꜜかいする]; 理由 reason [りゆう]; 論理 logic [ろꜜんり]; 理屈 argument, reason, quibbling [りくつ]; 理屈っぽい argumentative [りくつっぽꜜい]; 理論 theoretical account, theory [りꜜろん]; 理想 an ideal [りそう]; 料理 cooking, cuisine [りょꜜうり]

SG-1315 厘	Meanings	Kun and On	Romaji	Bushu	Stroke Order and Number
	rin, one-thousandth of a yen	リン	*rin*	厂	厂 厂 戶 厚 厘 厘 9

厘 **D** F-2117

No ancient form. The kanji 厘 is believed to be an abbreviation of the character 釐 *rin* (shown at right), which meant "to section minutely." Things divided minutely were "small." The kanji 厘 represented the smallest unit of currency, one-thousandth of a yen and one-tenth of a *sen*. <厂里>

九分九厘 in all likelihood [くぶくꜜりん]

58 Town, an area

58a 阝 (邑) "town, village" [from an area where many people lived]; *bushu oozato* (used on the right side) 都郷邦那

邑 阝

SG-1316 都	Meanings	Kun and On	Romaji	Bushu	Stroke Order and Number
	capital, large town; all; to gather	みやこ ト・ツ	miyako *to, tsu*	邑	土 耂 者 者 者阝 都 11

都 **A** F-0127

金文1 1, 金文2 2, 説文 3, 旧字 4

The left side in 1, 2, and 3 depicted "many twigs being burned in a stove," with "sparks from a fire" in 2. Gathering many twigs and things to burn signified "many, all," and had the sounds *to/tsu* (者 **SG-2085**). On the right side, "a land" and "a person" meant "an area where people

都 capital [みやこ]; 都会 city, big town [とかい]; 都心 urban core, heart of a city [としん]; 東京都 Tokyo Metropolis [とうきょꜜうと]; 古都 old capital [こꜜと]; 都民 resident of Metropolitan Tokyo [とꜜみん];

	live, a town" (which became 阝, bushu *oozato,* when used as a right-side component). Both sides taken together meant "a town of many people," such as the capital. The kanji 都 means "capital, large town; to gather; all." In Japanese, 都, *to,* also represents a jurisdiction of the largest size, the only one of which is 東京都, "Tokyo Metropolis." <⺹日阝>	都内 within the Tokyo Metropolitan area, or within the 23 Wards [とˀない]; 都合が悪い to have a schedule conflict [つごうがわるˀい]; その都度 every time, whenever [そのつˀど]

	Meanings	Kun and On	Romaji	Bushu	Stroke Order and Number
SG-1317 郷	village, one's native place, hometown	キョウ・ゴウ	*kyoo, goo*	邑	㇜ 乡 纩 纡 绑 绑 绑 郷 郷 郷 11

郷 **B** F-0920	甲骨文 1 金文1 2 金文2 3 説文 4 旧字 5 1, 2, and 3 depicted a scene in which two (signifying "many") people sat facing each other, with food in a bowl in front of them, feasting and enjoying each other's company. Sharing a feast was an important village event, which led to the meaning "hometown." In 4, the two seated people were replaced by two 邑 "towns" on either side of "food in a bowl." In the kyuji (5) and the shinji 郷, the left side became 乡 and the right side became 阝, bushu *oozato*. The kanji 郷 means "village, one's native place, hometown." <乡艮阝>	故郷 one's hometown [こˀきょう, ふるˀさと]; 郷土 homeland [きょˀうど]; 郷里 hometown [きょˀうり]; 異郷 land far from home [いきょう]; 郷愁 homesickness, nostalgia [きょうしゅう]; 郷士 country samurai, squire [ごˀうし]; 水郷 riverside district [すいごう]

	Meanings	Kun and On	Romaji	Bushu	Stroke Order and Number
SG-1318 邦	country; Japanese	ホウ	*hoo*	邑	三 丰 丰' 丰阝 邦 7

邦 **B** F-0973	甲骨文 1 金文1 2 金文2 3 説文古文 4 説文 5 1 comprised "a young tree or bough" and "rice paddies." 2 and 3 comprised "a tree with boughs that was planted to mark a fief" (丰), and "a town where many people live" (邑, 阝, bushu *oozato*). Together they signified "country." 4 reflected 1, whereas 5 reflected 2 and 3. In Japanese, "one's own country" also means "Japan; Japanese." The kanji 邦 means "country; Japanese." <丰阝> (Note: The kanji 邦 and 封 **SG-1134** shared the same oracle bone–style and bronzeware-style forms.)	異邦人 foreigner, outsider [いほˀうじん]; 連邦 federation [れんぽう]; 在留邦人 Japanese resident abroad [ざいりゅうほˀうじん]; 邦楽 traditional Japanese music [ほうがく]; 連邦政府 federal government [れんぽうせˀいふ]; 英連邦 British Commonwealth [えいれˀんぽう]; 邦文 written Japanese [ほうぶん]; 本邦 our country [ほˀんぽう] (formal)

	Meanings	Kun and On	Romaji	Bushu	Stroke Order and Number
SG-1319 那	(phonetic use only)	ナ	*na*	邑	㇆ ㇋ 月 月' 那 那 7

那 **C** F-1617	説文 The seal-style form comprised "something soft and pretty dangling" (冄), used for the sound *na*, and 邑 "town" (阝). It was used as an interrogative sentence-final particle in classical Chinese prose. The kanji 那 used only phonetically, and may be used in proper names. <冄阝>	刹那 moment [せˀつな]; 旦那 husband, master [だんな]; 那覇 Naha (capital city of Okinawa) [なˀは]

58b 囗 "an enclosure, boundary"; bushu *kunigamae* 図

Other kanji that have 囗 include 因 **SG-0323**, 困 **SG-0632**, 国 **SG-1493**, 固 **SG-1561**, and 園 **SG-1673**.

	Meanings	Kun and On	Romaji	Bushu	Stroke Order and Number
SG-1320 図	drawing; to plan, scheme, contrive	はか-る ズ・ト	haka-ru *zu, to*	囗	丨 冂 冂 冈 図 図 7

図 **A** F-0404	金文1 1 金文2 2 説文 3 旧字 4 1, 2, and 3 showed a map or drawing that indicated the locations of granaries within the boundary of a village (囗). Such a drawing played an important role in managing farming fields, thus the meaning "to plan, scheme." 3 was reflected in the kyuji 圖 (4). In the shinji 図, the inside was reduced to two short strokes and the katakana メ. The kanji 図 means "drawing; to plan, scheme, contrive." <囗ツ、>	図る to plan, attempt [はかˀる]; 図らずも unexpectedly, accidentally [はからˀずも]; 地図 map [ちˀず]; 図星 bullseye [ずぼし]; 図式 diagram, graph [ずしき]; 図案 design, sketch [ずあん]; 図書 books [とˀしょ]; 意図 intention [いˀと]

58c 公 "public"

	Meanings	Kun and On	Romaji	Bushu	Stroke Order and Number
SG-1321 公	public, governmental; aristocrat, person (nickname)	おおやけ コウ	ooyake *koo*	八	ノ 八 公 公 4

公
A
F-0135

甲骨文 1 金文1 2 金文2 3 説文 4

1, 2, 3, and 4 showed "an area that was cut open into two." Opening an area made it "public," giving the meaning "governmental." The form was also used as a suffixal honorific for aristocrats, or as part of an affectionate nickname. The kanji 公 means "public, governmental; aristocrat, person (honorific or affectionate)." <ハム>

公 public [おおやけ]; 公私の別 official and personal distinction [こうしのべつ]; 公営 public management [こうえい]; 公安 public security [こうあん]; 公金 public fund [こうきん]; 公共心 public spirit, sense of public duty [こうきょうしん]; 主人公 protagonist, main character [しゅじんこう]; 忠犬ハチ公 Hachi the Faithful Dog [ちゅうけんはちこう] // 公家 a court noble [くげ]

59 Cave, hole

59 穴 宀 罒 "cave, hole, opening, emptiness" [from a cave opening]; *bushu anakanmuri* 穴空深究突探窓控

	Meanings	Kun and On	Romaji	Bushu	Stroke Order and Number
SG-1322 穴	hole, hollow, gap, cavity, cave, hideout	あな ケツ	na *ketsu*	穴	' 宀 宂 穴 5

穴
A
F-0954

説文

The seal-style form depicted "a cave dwelling" with 八 "dirt dug out and dispersed on both sides." Together they signified "a hole or cave." In the kanji, the shape became a composite of 宀 and 八. The kanji 穴 means "hole, hollow, gap, cavity, cave, hideout." <穴>

穴 hole [あな]; 洞穴 cave [ほらあな]; 穴埋めする to make up a deficit [あなうめする]; 穴場 good unknown spot [あなば]; 穴があったら入りたい so embarrassed that one wishes to sink through the floor [あながあったら・はいりたい]; 節穴 knot hole, missing something important right in front of one's eyes [ふしあな]

	Meanings	Kun and On	Romaji	Bushu	Stroke Order and Number
SG-1323 空	sky; empty, in vain	そら・あ-く・から クウ	sora, a-ku, kara *kuu*	穴	' 宀 穴 空 空 空 8

空
A
F-0150

金文1 1 金文2 2 説文 3

In 1, 工 was used for the sound *kuu* to mean "arc shaped." In 2 and 3, 工 **SG-1895**, again used for the sound *kuu*, was placed inside a large, empty, dome-like shape. Another view explains that piercing (工) and making a hole (穴) left an empty space, thus giving the meaning "empty." "A large, arc-shaped emptiness" in 2 and 3 meant "sky." The kanji 空 means "sky; empty, in vain." <穴工>

空 sky [そら]; empty [から]; 絵空事 pipe dream [えそらごと, えそらごと]; 空々しい transparently false [そらぞらしい]; 空く to become empty [あく]; 空き部屋 room vacancy [あきべや]; 空っぽ empty [からっぽ]; 空中 in the air [くうちゅう] // 空しい empty, in vain [むなしい, むなしい]

	Meanings	Kun and On	Romaji	Bushu	Stroke Order and Number
SG-1324 深	deep; depth	ふか-い シン	huka-i *shin*	水	氵 氵 沪 泙 深 深 11

深
A
F-0395

石鼓文 1 中山王器 2 説文 3

In 1 and 3, the right side comprised "a cave" (穴), "a hand" (又), and "fire" (火), together signifying "to search for something with a torch in the darkness of a cave," and had the sound *shin*. With "flowing water" (氵) added, they meant "measuring the depth of water," and thus "depth; deep." In 2, the water was inside the cave. In the kanji, 穴 became 罒, and 又 and 火 coalesced into 木, forming 罙. The kanji 深 means "deep; depth." <氵罒木>

深い deep [ふかい]; 奥深い profound [おくふかい]; 深み hole, depth [ふかみ]; 根深い deeply rooted [ねぶかい]; 深々と deeply [ふかぶかと]; 深刻な serious, grave [しんこくな]; 意味深長な profound, meaningful, significant [いみ・しんちょうな]

	Meanings	Kun and On	Romaji	Bushu	Stroke Order and Number
SG-1325 究	to investigate thoroughly, research	きわ-める キュウ	kiwa-meru *kyuu*	穴	' 宀 穴 究 究 7

究 **A** F-0466

説文 究

The seal-style form comprised an elongated 穴 "hole," and 九 **SG-2133**, used for the sound *kyuu* to mean "something winding or bent." Digging deep in a winding direction signified "to investigate further to find an answer." The kanji 究 means "to investigate thoroughly, research." <穴九>

究める to investigate thoroughly [きわめる]; 究明 thorough investigation [きゅうめい]; 研究 research [けんきゅう]; 究極的な ultimate [きゅうきょくてきな]; 探究心 research mind [たんきゅうしん]

	Meanings	Kun and On	Romaji	Bushu	Stroke Order and Number
SG-1326 突	to thrust, plunge; protruding	つ-く トツ	tsu-ku *totsu*	穴	' 宀 穴 空 突 突 8

突 **B** F-0761

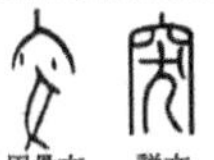
甲骨文 1 説文 2 旧字 3 突 突

1 and 2 had "a cave opening" (穴 **SG-1322**) and "a dog" (犬 **SG-0859**). A dog thrusting out of a hole signified "to thrust; a sudden move." 犬 became 大 in the shinji. The kanji 突 means "to thrust, plunge; protruding." <穴大>

突く to push, thrust, shove [つく]; 突き落とす to push someone over [つきおとす]; 意表を突く to catch someone by surprise [いひょうをつく]; 唐突に abruptly [とうとつに]; 突然 all of a sudden [とつぜん]; 突風 sudden gust of wind, flurry of wind [とっぷう]; 突発的に suddenly, unexpectedly [とっぱつてきに]

	Meanings	Kun and On	Romaji	Bushu	Stroke Order and Number
SG-1327 探	to search, look for	さぐ-る・さが-す タン	sagu-ru, saga-su *tan*	手	扌 扌 扌 扌 扌 探 11

探 **B** F-0879

説文 探

The seal-style form comprised 扌 "an act done by hand," and 罙, "a hand holding a torch searching for something inside a cave," used for the sound *shin*. Together they signified "to search, look for." The kanji 探 means "to search, look for." <扌穴木>

探る to probe, feel around [さぐる]; 探す to search for, hunt, seek [さがす]; 探し出す to find, locate [さがしだす]; 探し当てる to find out, locate [さがしあてる]; 探し物 looking for a missing thing [さがしもの]; 探検 exploration [たんけん]; 探検家 explorer [たんけんか]

	Meanings	Kun and On	Romaji	Bushu	Stroke Order and Number
SG-1328 窓	window	まど ソウ	mado *soo*	穴	宀 穴 空 窓 窓 11

窓 **B** F-0984

説文古文 1 説文 2 説文或体1 3 説文或体2 4 正字 5 窗 窓

1 and 2 depicted "a skylight" or "an air vent in a house." In 3 and 4, the vent or skylight was placed inside an elongated 穴 "dwelling." An opening for light or ventilation in a house is "a window." In 3, "a heart" was added, but its semantic role is unclear. The orthographic-style kanji 窗 (5) reflected 4. The shinji 窓 comprised 穴, ム as a simplification of the vent, and 心 "heart." The kanji 窓 means "window." <穴ム心>

窓 window [まど]; 天窓 skylight, rooflight [てんまど]; 窓口 teller, counter [まどぐち]; 車窓 view from a train or bus window [しゃそう]; 同窓会 class reunion [どうそうかい]; 同窓生 someone who went to the same school [どうそうせい]

	Meanings	Kun and On	Romaji	Bushu	Stroke Order and Number
SG-1329 控	to hold off, back up, jot down; substitute, waiting	ひか-える コウ	hika-eru *koo*	手	一 十 扌 扌 扌 控 控 11

控 **C** F-1231

説文 控

The seal-style form had 扌 "an act done by hand," and 空 **SG-1323** "sky," used for the sound *koo*. *Setsumon* gives the meaning as "to pull." In shooting an arrow into an empty, arc-shaped space (that is, the sky), one pulled or held the bow back hard. From "to hold back" came other meanings in Japanese such as "to refrain oneself"; "backup, relief"; and "waiting room." The kanji 控 means "to hold off, back up, jot down; substitute, waiting." <扌空>

控え室 waiting room, anteroom [ひかえしつ]; 控える to be in waiting, note down, hold back, be imminent [ひかえる]; 控え backup, memorandum [ひかえ]; 差し控える to refrain, withhold [さしひかえる, さしひかえる]; 控訴 appeal to higher court [こうそ]

60 Crossroads

60a 行 "to go; one's conduct" [from a full depiction of a crossroads];

bushu *yukigamae* 行街衡桁

Notes on 彳 bushu *gyooninben*

When only the left side (彳) of a crossroads (行) is used, it is called *gyooninben*. In this study guide, many of the kanji that contain bushu *gyooninben* are discussed elsewhere to focus on their accompanying components. Please refer to the cross-reference numbers (SG- number) below:

徳 **SG-0011**, 征 **SG-0211**, 待 **SG-0222**, 後 **SG-0237**, 従 **SG-0372**, 徒 **SG-0487**, 微 **SG-0569**, 徴 **SG-0570**, 彼 **SG-0907**, 徐 **SG-1418**, 往 **SG1449**, 経 **SG-1647**, 径 **SG-1649**, 得 **SG-1697**, 徹 **SG-1801**, 御 **SG-1807**, 復 **SG-1837**, and 律 **SG-2037**

	Meanings	Kun and On	Romaji	Bushu	Stroke Order and Number
SG-1330 行	to go, conduct business, carry out; one's conduct, a line in writing	い-く・ゆ-く・おこな-う コウ・ギョウ・アン	i-ku, yu-ku, okona-u *koo, gyoo, an*	行	彳 行 6

行 **A** F-0017

甲骨文1 1 · 甲骨文2 2 · 金文 3 · 説文 4

1 through 4 depicted "a four-way crossroads." A crossroads showed different ways to go, and one had to decide among them. The meaning applied to one's conduct, and it meant "to do, carry out, conduct business; one's personal conduct, religious austerities." The character's visual similiarity to the columns of wooden or bamboo writing tablets gave the meaning "(ruled) lines." The kanji 行 means "to go, conduct business, carry out; one's conduct, a line in writing." <彳亍>

東京行き Tokyo-bound [とうきょういき, とうきょうゆき]; 行く末 one's future [ゆくすえ]; 行方知らず whereabouts unknown, missing [ゆくえしらず]; 行う to carry out, conduct [おこなう]; 行い conduct, behavior, deed [おこない]; 一行 party, entourage [いっこう], one line (in a passage) [いちぎょう]; 行列 line, queue, file, procession [ぎょうれつ]; 行 religious austerities [ぎょう], line of writing [ぎょう];行脚 pilgrimage [あんぎゃ]

	Meanings	Kun and On	Romaji	Bushu	Stroke Order and Number
SG-1331 街	town, major street	まち ガイ・カイ	machi *gai, kai*	行	彳 街 12

街 **B** F-0695

説文

The seal-style form comprised 行 **SG-1330** "a four-way crossroads," with 圭 "neatly arranged blocks of land" (originally from a stack of well-shaped soil used in a ceremonial rite), used for the sound *gai/kai*, inside. Together they signified "a town with many crisscrossing major streets." The kanji 街 means "town, major street." <彳圭亍>

街 town, street [まち]; 街角 on the street [まちかど]; 街並み townscape [まちなみ]; 街灯 street light [がいとう]; 街路樹 trees lining a street [がいろじゅ]; 市街地 urban district [しがいち]; 街道 main road, highway [かいどう]

	Meanings	Kun and On	Romaji	Bushu	Stroke Order and Number
SG-1332 衡	balance, scale	コウ	*koo*	行	彳 衡 16

衡 **C** F-1629

金文 1 · 説文古文 2 · 説文 3

In 1, 2, and 3, inside "a crossroads" (except in 2) was "an animal horn/antler and a person." Animals pulling a carriage were tied to the yokes on either side of a bar, and the scene depicted a person balancing the sidebar of a carriage as it moved along. The character meant "balance, yoke, scale." The kanji 衡 means "balance, scale." <彳⺈田大亍>

均衡 balance, proportion [きんこう]; 不均衡 imbalance, inequality, disparity [ふきんこう]; 度量衡 weights and measures [どりょうこう]; 平衡 equilibrium, balance [へいこう]

	Meanings	Kun and On	Romaji	Bushu	Stroke Order and Number
SG-1333 桁	crosspiece, digit	けた	keta	木	十 木 桁 桁 10

桁 **D** F-2235

No ancient form. The kanji comprised 木 "wood," and 行 **SG-1330** "a crossroads," used for the sound *koo*, signifying "crosspiece, crossbar." In Japanese, it is also used as a counter of digits in a number. The kanji 桁 means "crosspiece, digit." <木行>

一桁 one digit figure [ひとけた];桁違いに immeasurably, incomparably [けたちがいに]; 桁外れ extraordinary, exceptional [けたはずれ]

60b 廴 "to extend" [from a crossroads stretched to the right]; **bushu *ennyoo*** 延誕

	Meanings	Kun and On	Romaji	Bushu	Stroke Order and Number
SG-1334 延	to extend, postpone, stretch	の-びる エン	no-biru *en*	廴	丿 𠂉 𠂉 正 㢟 延 延 8

延 **B** F-0977

說文

The seal-style form comprised "a footprint" 止 **SG-0200** with a slanted stroke on top to indicate "a stretched stride," and "a crossroads" which had one end pulled to the lower right to mean "an extended path." Together they signified "to extend, postpone," and became 廴, bushu *ennyoo* "to extend." The kanji 延 means "to extend, postpone, stretch." <ノ 止廴>

延ばす to stretch, postpone, extend [のばす]; 延べ total number of [のべ]; 日延べする to postpone, defer [ひのべする]; 延び延びになる to put off from day to day [のびのびになる]; 延長 extension [えんちょう]; 延焼 the spread of a fire [えんしょう]; 遅延する to be delayed, get behind schedule [ちえんする]; 蔓延する to spread, be prevalent [まんえんする]

	Meanings	Kun and On	Romaji	Bushu	Stroke Order and Number
SG-1335 誕	to be born	タン	*tan*	言	言 言 言 言 訁 証 誕 誕 15

誕 **C** F-1121

金文 1 說文 2

1 comprised "a footprint" (止 **SG-0200**), which was slightly distorted vertically, and the split shape of "a crossroads" (彳), together forming 延 **SG-1334** and signifying "pulling on something to stretch it." In 2, 言 "words; to speak" was added. "Stretched words" meant "to tell a tall story, brag," a meaning for which this character is not now used in Japanese. The character came to be used to mean "to be born." The kanji 誕 means "to be born." <言延>

誕生日 birthday [たんじょうび]; 生誕百年 a centennial of the birth of someone famous [せいたんひゃくねん]; 降誕祭 celebration of the birth of a saint; Christmas [こうたんさい]

60c 廷 "royal court" [from a royal court wall with a standing person]; *tee* 庭廷艇

	Meanings	Kun and On	Romaji	Bushu	Stroke Order and Number
SG-1336 庭	garden	にわ テイ	niwa *tee*	广	亠 广 庄 庄 庭 庭 庭 10

庭 **B** F-0627

說文

The seal-style form was created by adding 广, bushu *madare* "eaves," to 廷 **SG-1337** "royal court," used for the sound *tee* from "walled ground where people stood." An area outside the eaves of the court was a "garden." The kanji 庭 means "garden." <广 廷(壬廴)>

庭 garden [にわ]; 庭先 front garden [にわさき]; 中庭 inner court [なかにわ]; 庭弄り gardening (hobby) [にわいじり]; 矢庭に suddenly, without warning [やにわに]; 庭園 large garden [ていえん]; 校庭 schoolyard [こうてい]; 家庭的な homey, family-minded [かていてきな]

	Meanings	Kun and On	Romaji	Bushu	Stroke Order and Number
SG-1337 廷	royal court, courtyard	テイ	*tee*	廴	二 千 壬 廷 廷 7

廷 **C** F-1528

金文1 1 金文2 2 金文3 3 說文 4

In 1 and 2, a standing person put their hand over a mound of soil inside the wall of the imperial court. In 3, the person sprinkled spirits to sanctify the ground. An area surrounded by a wall where people stood up straight was "the imperial court." In 4, the surrounding wall changed to 廴 bushu *ennyoo* "to extend," and the person's shin was marked (becoming 壬, used for the sound *tee*) to emphasize their standing posture. The kanji 廷 means "royal court, courtyard." <壬廴>

宮廷 imperial court [きゅうてい]; 法廷 court of law, courtroom [ほうてい]

	Meanings	Kun and On	Romaji	Bushu	Stroke Order and Number
SG-1338 艇	boat	テイ	*tee*	舟	丿 月 舟 舟 舟 舟 舟 艇 艇 13

艇 **D** F-1785

說文

The seal-style form comprised "boat" (舟), and 廷, used for the sound *tee* to mean "to move straight," signifying "a small boat that goes straight." The kanji 艇 means "boat." <舟廷>

救命艇 lifeboat [きゅうめいてい]; 競艇 speedboat race [きょうてい]; 潜水艇 submarine [せんすいてい]

60d 建 "to build" [from a writing brush drawing a building plan]; *ken* 建健鍵

	Meanings	Kun and On	Romaji	Bushu	Stroke Order and Number
SG-1339 建	to build	た-てる ケン・コン	ta-teru *ken, kon*	廴	フヨヨ⺕聿建建 9

建 **A** F-0261

甲骨文 1 金文 2 説文 3

1 comprised 聿 "a hand holding a writing brush upright," 彳 "crossroads; to carry out," and 止 "footprint." Carrying out a job in an upright manner gave the meaning "to build." "A wall stretching to surround the court" (in 2) changed to "an extended crossroads" in 3, which further became 廴, bushu *ennyoo* "to extend" in the kanji. The kanji 建 means "to build." <聿廴>

建てる to build [たてる]; 円建て Japanese yen basis [えんだて]; 建て前 a ceremony for the erection of a framework [たてまえ], for appearance's sake, public stance [たてまえ]; 建て売り住宅 built-for-sale house [たてうりじゅうたく]; 一戸建て single house [いっこだて]; 土建 civil engineering and construction [どけん]; 建造物 building, structure [けんぞうぶつ]; 建設 construction, founding [けんせつ]; 建立する to build (a Buddhist temple) [こんりゅうする]

	Meanings	Kun and On	Romaji	Bushu	Stroke Order and Number
SG-1340 健	healthy, sound	すこ-やか ケン	suko-yaka *ken*	人	亻亻⺕亻聿亻聿律健健 11

健 **A** F-0418

説文

The seal-style form comprised 亻 "person," and 建, used for the sound *ken* to mean "standing upright." A person who stood firmly upright was "healthy, sound." The kanji 健 means "healthy, sound." <亻建>

健やかに healthy, sound [すこやかに]; 健康 health [けんこう]; 健康保険 health insurance [けんこうほけん]; 健全な sound, wholesome [けんぜんな]; 保健所 public health center [ほけんじょ]; 不健康な unhealthy, unsanitary [ふけんこうな]; 健常者 non-disabled person [けんじょうしゃ] // 健気に bravely, praiseworthily [けなげに, けなげに]

	Meanings	Kun and On	Romaji	Bushu	Stroke Order and Number
SG-1341 鍵	key, hint, clue, keys of a piano	かぎ ケン	kagi *ken*	金	𠆢全金金⺕金ヨ金聿鍵鍵 17

鍵 **D** F-1900

説文

The seal-style form comprised 金 SG-1196 "metal," and 建 SG-1339, used for the sound *ken,*" together signifying "wedge or linchpin." In Japanese, "a metal object that one inserts to unlock a padlock or latch (錠 SG-0235)" means "a key," and the character may sometimes also refer to a "padlock or bolt." It is also used to mean the "keys or keyboard" of a piano. The kanji 鍵 means "key, hint, clue, padlock, keys of a piano." <金建>

鍵 key, hint, clue [かぎ]; 鍵が掛かっている it is locked [かぎがかかっている]; 鍵穴 keyhole [かぎあな]; 合鍵 spare key [あいかぎ]; 鍵っ子 latchkey child [かぎっこ]; 黒鍵 black or chromatic key of a piano [こっけん]; 鍵盤 keyboard [けんばん]

60e 辶 "to move forward" [from "a crossroads" and "a footstep"];

辵 (seal-style); 辶 (kyuji); 辶 (Mincho-style shinji); 辶 (kyokasho-style);

bushu *shinnyuu/shinnyoo* 送辺込遅迭

	Meanings	Kun and On	Romaji	Bushu	Stroke Order and Number
SG-1342 送	to send, send forward	おく-る ソウ	o-kuru *soo*	辵	ソ丷关关送送 9

送 **A** F-0366

中山王器 1 説文1 2 説文2 3

1, 2, and 3 comprised "a crossroads" with "a footprint" (辵, 辶, bushu *shinnyuu* "to move forward"), and "two hands holding up a valuable object." Together they signified "someone moving something valuable with two hands" or "to send." In the kanji, the right side was drastically reduced to 关. The kanji 送 means "to send, send forward." <关辶>

送る to send [おくる]; 送り先 recipient, addressee [おくりさき]; 見送る to see someone off [みおくる]; 見送りにする to not act now, shelve for now [みおくりにする]; 送り仮名 declensional kana ending after kanji [おくりがな]; 送料 shipping charge [そうりょう]; 転送 forwarding [てんそう]; 再放送 rebroadcasting [さいほうそう]

SG-1343 辺	Meanings	Kun and On	Romaji	Bushu	Stroke Order and Number
	peripheral; edge of an area, area, side	あた-り・べ ヘン	ata-ri, be *hen*	辵	フ刀`刀刃辺辺 $_{5}$

辺 **A** F-0402

金文1 1 金文2 2 説文 3 旧字1 4 旧字2 5

The precursors for the shinji 辺 were all complex. 1 and 2 comprised "a crossroads" and, on the right side, "a face" (自 **SG-0059**), "a sturdy table" (丙 **SG-1873**), and "four directions" (方 **SG-1931**), used for the sound *ben*. Together they signified "peripheral areas, edge, side." 辵 in 3 became 辶 in the two different kyuji (4 and 5), which further became 辶, bushu *shinnyuu*, in the shinji. The much-abbreviated form 辺 has been used since the Sung-Yuan dynasties (Todo et. al. 2011). The kanji 辺 means "peripheral; edge of an area, area, side." <刀 辶>

辺り surrounding, vicinity, neighborhood [あꜜたり]; 浜辺 shore, beach [はまべ]; この辺 the neighborhood, this area [このへん]; 四辺形 quadrilateral [しへꜜんけい]; 一辺 one side [いっぺꜜん]; 周辺 surroundings, vicinity [しゅうへん]; 辺境 frontier, outlying district [へんきょう]; 天辺 top [てっぺꜜん]

SG-1345 込	Meanings	Kun and On	Romaji	Bushu	Stroke Order and Number
	to put in, become crowded	こ-む	ko-mu	辵	ノ入`入込込 $_{5}$

込 **B** F-0526

The kanji 込 is a kokuji (国字). All kokuji are semantic composite kanji. The kanji 込 comprises 入 "to enter, put in" and 辶 "to move forward," together signifying "to put something in." Putting many things into something makes it "crowded." The kanji 込 means "to put in, become crowded." <入 辶>

込む to become crowded [こꜜむ]; 込める to put in, charge, concentrate [こめꜜる]; 閉じ込める to shut in, lock in, confine [とじこめꜜる]; 入り込む to gain entrance to [はいりこꜜむ]; 申し込み application, booking [もうしこみ]; 意気込む to be enthusiastic about, set one's heart on [いきごꜜむ]

SG-1345 遅	Meanings	Kun and On	Romaji	Bushu	Stroke Order and Number
	slow, late	おそ-い・おく-れる チ	oso-i, oku-reru *chi*	辵	コ尸尸屖犀遅遅 $_{12}$

遅 **B** F-0869

甲骨文1 1 甲骨文2 2 金文 3 説文籀文 4 説文 5 旧字 6

The kanji 遅 has a long history. In 1, 2, and 3, it comprised "crossroads," "sitting person," and "rhinoceros," which was used for the sound *chi* to mean "slow" (from the slow movement of a rhinoceros). A footprint in 3 was absorbed into 辵 "to move forward" in 4 and 5. In 5, the right side became 犀 "rhinoceros," which further became 尸 and 羊 "sheep" **SG-0825**. The kanji 遅 means "slow, late." <尸羊辶>

遅い late, slow [おそい]; 遅かれ早かれ sooner or later [おそかれはやꜜかれ]; 遅れる to be late, arrive late [おくれる]; 出遅れる to make a late start [でおくれる, でおくれꜜる]; 乗り遅れる to miss a bus or train [のりおくれꜜる]; 遅刻する to be late, arrive late [ちこくする]; 遅々として very slowly [ちꜜちとして]

SG-1346 迭	Meanings	Kun and On	Romaji	Bushu	Stroke Order and Number
	to replace, slip, slide	テツ	*tetsu*	辵	ノ𠂉牛失迭迭 $_{8}$

迭 **D** F-2277

説文

The seal-style form comprised 辵 "to move forward," and 失 **SG-0073** "to lose," used for the sound *tetsu*. Something lost or gone had "to be replaced." The kanji 迭 means "to replace, slip, slide." <失 辶>

更迭 change in personnel, reshuffle, dismissal [こうてつ]

61 Hills, mountains

61 阝(阜) "hills, mountains, boundary, obstruction, ladder"; **bushu *kozatohen***

(used on the left side of kanji) 隆陥陵阜隙

SG-1347 隆	Meanings	Kun and On	Romaji	Bushu	Stroke Order and Number
	to prosper, rise; high; peak	リュウ	*ryuu*	阜	㇇阝阝夂阝夂阝各降隆 $_{11}$

隆 **C** F-1099

漢金文 1 説文 2 旧字 3

1 comprised "mountains, ladder" (阝, bushu *kozatohen*), "downward footprints" (two 夂), and "soil" (土). The form described a deity descending onto mountain peaks and spreading divine spirits, and signified "to prosper, flourish; high; peak."

隆盛 prosperity [りゅうせい]; 隆起 protuberance, projection, rising [りゅꜜうき]

Another view explains that 2 had 生 "emerging plant, life" instead of 土, giving the meanings "life; lively, flourishing." The kanji 隆 means "a peak; to prosper, rise; high." <阝夂生>

	Meanings	Kun and On	Romaji	Bushu	Stroke Order and Number
SG-1348 陥	to collapse, entrap, frame	おちい-る・おとしい-れる カン	ochii-ru, otoshii-reru *kan*	阜	陥 10

陥 **C** F-1640

説文 1 旧字 2

1 and 2 comprised "mountains, a tall place" (阝, bushu *kozatohen*), and "a person falling into a trap or hole," used for the sound *kan*. Falling from a high place into a trap meant "to collapse, become entrapped." 臼 in 2 became 旧 SG-0950 in the shinji. The kanji 陥 means "to collapse, entrap, frame." <阝⺈旧>

陥る to fall into, lapse into, be tricked [おちいる]; 陥れる to entrap [おとしいれꜜる]; 陥没 depression, cave-in [かんぼつ]; 欠陥車 defective car, lemon [けっかꜜんしゃ]; 陥落 surrender, loss of [かんらく]

	Meanings	Kun and On	Romaji	Bushu	Stroke Order and Number
SG-1349 陵	mountain ridge, imperial tomb	みささぎ リョウ	misasagi *ryoo*	阜	陵 11

陵 **D** F-1723

金文1 1 金文2 2 金文3 3 説文 4

The left side of 1 and the right side of 2 and 3 depicted "a person on a tall mound of soil," used for the sound *ryoo*. With "tall hills" (阝) added, the character meant "to go up a ridge of tall mountains, exceed," or "a high mound where an imperial tomb was built," and thus also meant "imperial tomb." In 4, the right side became 夌. The kanji 陵 means "mountain ridge, imperial tomb." <阝夌>

丘陵地帯 terrain [きゅうりょうちꜜたい]; 御陵 imperial mausoleum, imperial tomb [ごꜜりょう]

	Meanings	Kun and On	Romaji	Bushu	Stroke Order and Number
SG-1350 阜	hills	フ	*hu*	阜	阜 8

阜 **D** F-2012

甲骨文1 1 甲骨文2 2 甲骨文3 3 金文 4 説文 5

There are many views regarding the origin of the kanji 阜. It has been said to depict: (a) "mountains or hills placed vertically"; (b) "a ladder on which a deity descends"; (c) "a boundary" (from hills or mountains preventing easy passage); and (d) "high, tall," from "a stack of soil." In the kanji, 十 was added, possibly to mean "to collect (dirt)." The kanji 阜 means "hills." When used on the left side of kanji, the form becomes 阝 bushu *kozatohen*. <𠂤十>

(Note: In a traditional kanji dictionary, all kanji with 阝 bushu *kozatohen* are listed under 阜.)

岐阜県 Gifu prefecture [ぎふꜜけん]

	Meanings	Kun and On	Romaji	Bushu	Stroke Order and Number
SG-1351 隙	gap, aperture, opportunity, crevice, unguarded moment	すき ゲキ	suki *geki*	阜	隙 13

隙 **D** F-2428

説文

The seal-style form 隙 comprised 阝 "stack of dirt," or "an obstacle" such as a fence, and "sunbeams leaking through small cracks," used for the sound *geki*. The kanji 隙 means "gap, aperture, opportunity, crevice, unguarded moment." <阝小日小>

隙 gap, crevice [すき]; 隙間 gap, opening [すきま]; お手隙の時 when you have spare time [おてすきのとꜜき]; 隙を見せる let down one's guard [すきをみせꜜる]; 間隙 gap, aperture, falling out [かんげき]

62 Wooden stakes

62a 代 [from wooden stakes in the ground]; *dai/tai* 代貸袋

	Meanings	Kun and On	Romaji	Bushu	Stroke Order and Number
SG-1352 代	to change; instead; time, reign, generation, substitute	か-わる・よ・しろ ダイ・タイ	ka-waru, yo, shiro *dai, tai*	人	代 5

代 **A** F-0056

説文

The seal-style form 代 comprised 亻 "an act that one does," and "wooden stakes in the ground" (弋), used for the sound *tai*/*dai* to mean "change." Changing people led to the

代わりに in exchange for, as a stand-in [かわりに]; 君が代 *Kimigayo*, Japanese national anthem [きみがよ]; 御代 reign, period [みꜜよ]; 飲み代 drinking money [のみꜜしろ, のみしろ]; 代理 epresentation,

meaning "generation, substitute." Between such changes lies "a duration of time" or "a lifetime." The kanji 代 means "to change; instead; time, generation, substitute." <イ弋>

proxy, surrogate [だいり]; 初代 first generation, founder [しょだい]; 一世一代 once in a lifetime [いっせ・いちだい]; 交代 change, replacement, substitute [こうたい]

	Meanings	Kun and On	Romaji	Bushu	Stroke Order and Number
SG-1353 貸	to lend	か-す タイ	ka-su *tai*	貝	イ イ一 代 代 貸 貸 12

貸 **B** F-0911

説文

The seal-style form comprised イ "an act that a person does" and 弋, together forming 代 **SG-1352** for the sound *tai* and meaning "to change." The center component was "cowrie, money; valuable" (貝 **SG-1693**). "Something valuable that changed hands" gave the meaning "to lend something to another person (and get it back)." The kanji 貸 means "to lend." <代貝>

貸す to lend [かす]; 貸し出し lending, circulation, rental [かしだし]; 貸家 rented house [かしや]; 貸し間 room for rent, room to let [かしま]; 金貸し moneylending business [かねかし]; 貸し借り lending and borrowing [かしかり]; 貸与 lending, loan [たいよ]; 賃貸 lease, letting, renting out [ちんたい, ちんたい]

	Meanings	Kun and On	Romaji	Bushu	Stroke Order and Number
SG-1354 袋	bag	ふくろ タイ	hukuro *tai*	衣	イ イ一 イ弋 代 代 岱 岱 袋 袋 11

袋 **B** F-0930

篆文

The seal-style form comprised 代 for the sound *tai*, and 巾 **SG-1682** "cloth," together signifying "cloth bag." In the kanji, 巾 was replaced by 衣 **SG-1657** "clothing." The kanji 袋 means "bag." <代衣>

袋 bag, sack, pouch [ふくろ]; 胃袋 stomach [いぶくろ]; 手袋 gloves [てぶくろ]; 天袋 a built-in storage cupboard above *oshiire* [てんぶくろ]; 袋小路 cul-de-sac, blind alley [ふくろこうじ] // 足袋 Japanese split-toe socks [たび]

62b 弟 "order" 弟第

	Meanings	Kun and On	Romaji	Bushu	Stroke Order and Number
SG-1355 弟	younger brother	おとうと テイ・ダイ・デ	ototoo *tee, dai, de*	弓	丷 当 当 肖 弟 弟 7

弟 **A** F-0734

甲骨文1 甲骨文2 金文 説文
1 2 3 4

1, 2, 3, and 4 depicted "a wooden stake with a leather strap wrapped around it a few times and its bottom marked by a short line." The line on the bottom signified a younger brother, who was lower in the order of male siblings. The kanji 弟 means "younger brother." <丷弓丨丿>

弟 younger brother [おとうと]; 師弟 teacher and student [してい]; 弟妹 younger siblings [ていまい]; 義弟 younger brother of one's spouse [ぎてい]; 兄弟 brothers, siblings [きょうだい]; 弟子 pupil, apprentice [でし]; 直弟子 student taught by a master teacher [じきでし]

	Meanings	Kun and On	Romaji	Bushu	Stroke Order and Number
SG-1356 第	order, sequence	ダイ	*dai*	竹	⺮ 笁 笃 笃 第 第 11

第 **A** F-0174

篆文

The seal-style form was the same as 4 for 弟 **SG-1355**, in which the layers of a leather strip wrapped around a stake indicated "order," and it had the sound *dai*. In the kanji, ⺮, bushu *takekanmuri* "bamboo" was added to signify "bamboo writing tablets tied in a sequence" or "in good order." It is also used as a prefix in sequential numbering. The kanji 第 means "order, sequence." <⺮弟>

第一 the first [だいいち]; 第二次世界大戦 Second World War [だいにじ・せかいたいせん]; 第三者 third party [だいさんしゃ]; 第一印象 first impression [だいいちいんしょう]; 次第に gradually, bit by bit [しだいに]; 落第 failure of an examination or school year [らくだい]; 及第点 passing mark [きゅうだいてん]; 終わり次第 as soon as it finishes [おわりしだい]; 望み次第 just as one wishes [のぞみしだい]

62c 用 "to use" [from a fence made of wooden stakes]; *yoo* 用庸

SG-1357 用	Meanings	Kun and On	Romaji	Bushu	Stroke Order and Number
	to utilize, use, operate; tool, errand	もち-いる ヨウ	mochi-iru *yoo*	用	丿冂月用 5

用 **A** F-0096

甲骨文 1　金文1 2　金文2 3　説文 4

1 through 4 depicted a stockade constructed of pieces of wood for corralling domestic animals for food and religious sacrificial use. They meant "to utilize, use; errand." Another view takes these meanings to be a borrowing. The kanji 用 means "to utilize, use, operate; tool, errand." <用>

用いる to utilize, use [もちいる]; 引用 quotation, citation [いんよう]; 食用油 cooking oil [しょくようあぶら]; 雑用 miscellaneous affairs, chores [ざつよう]; 実用化 practical implementation [じつようか]; 学用品 school supplies [がくようひん]; 起用する to appoint, employ the services of [きようする]; 公用車 official vehicle, company car [こうようしゃ]; 所要 business, errand [しょよう]

SG-1358 庸	Meanings	Kun and On	Romaji	Bushu	Stroke Order and Number
	ordinary	ヨウ	*yoo*	广	广户户肩肩庸 11

庸 **D** F-2074

金文 1　説文 2

1 and 2 depicted two hands using a pestle pounding grain to thresh it, or two hands pounding dirt with pestle-shaped sticks to make a dirt barrier. The bottom component was 用 **SG-1357**, used for the sound *yoo* to mean "to use, employ." The character originally meant "to work, use, hire," and then came to mean "an ordinary government official," which further lent the meaning "ordinary." The kanji 庸 means "ordinary." <广ヨ用>

(Note: Adding 亻, bushu *ninben*, to 庸 makes the non-Joyo kanji 傭 "to hire, employ.")

中庸 the golden mean, the middle path [ちゅうよう]; 凡庸 mediocrity, banality [ぼんよう]

VII Sharp Objects and Weapons

63 Tattooing needles

63a 辛 "hard; word" [from a tattooing needle with a handle] 辛辞

	Meanings	*Kun* and *On*	Romaji	Bushu	Stroke Order and Number
SG-1359 辛	hard, difficult, bitter, spicy, hot	から-い シン	kara-i *shin*	辛	丶亠亠立立辛 7

辛
B
F-1398

甲骨文 1 金文1 2 金文2 3 説文 4

1 through 4 depicted a large tattooing needle with an ink reservoir at the top and a handle in the middle. It was common for criminals and enslaved war captives to be tattooed. Because a tattooing needle hurt, the character meant "painful." From "a stinging sensation," it also meant "hot, spicy." The kanji 辛 means "hard, difficult, bitter, spicy, hot." <立十>
(Note: 辛 became a part of 言 **SG-1364**, and it appears in some kanji to connote "word.")

辛い hot, pungent, spicy, sharp [からい]; 激辛 super-spicy [げきから]; 辛党 person who prefers alcohol to sweets [からとう]; 辛口ワイン dry wine [からくちワイン]; 辛子 mustard [からし]; 甘辛い sweet and hot [あまからい]; 香辛料 spice [こうしんりょう]; 辛酸 suffering, woe [しんさん] // 辛い hard, bitter, strenuous [つらい]

	Meanings	*Kun* and *On*	Romaji	Bushu	Stroke Order and Number
SG-1360 辞	word; to take leave, decline, resign	や-める ジ	ya-meru *ji*	辛	二千舌舌舌舌辞辞 13

辞
B
F-0785

金文1 1 金文2 2 金文3 3 説文 4 旧字 5

In 1 through 5, on the left side, "two hands untangling threads" signified "complexity." 司 **SG-0357**, on the right side of 1, 2, and 3, was "a person managing speech (口)" and meant "to administer." These forms meant "to explain a complicated situation." In 4, the right side changed to 辛 **SG-1359** "tattooing needle," which connoted "words (言 **SG-1364**, from 辛 and 口)," and had the sound *ji.* One might offer a few words on certain occasions such as "taking leave," "declining an offer," or "resigning a job." In the kanji, the left side was replaced with the shape 舌. The kanji 辞 means "word; to take leave, decline." <千口辛>
(Note: The kanji 辞 and 乱 **SG-2102** share a similar origin.)

辞める to resign, quit one's job [やめる]; 辞する to resign from, take one's leave [じする]; 辞書 dictionary [じしょ]; 辞典 dictionary [じてん]; 式辞 speech at a ceremony [しきじ]; 辞職 resignation, stepping down [じしょく]; 辞退する to decline, turn down [じたいする]

63b 章 "emblem" [from a tattooing needle with a large ink reservoir]; *shoo* 章障彰

	Meanings	*Kun* and *On*	Romaji	Bushu	Stroke Order and Number
SG-1361 章	emblem, badge, writing, chapter	ショウ	*shoo*	立	丶亠亠音音章章 11

章
B
F-0738

金文1 1 金文2 2 説文 3

1 and 2 depicted a tattooing needle with a handle and a large ink reservoir that enabled the tattoo to be drawn clearly and distinctly. The form signified something drawn or written beautifully, such as an emblem or a chapter of writing. In the kanji, the shape was split into 立 and 早. The kanji 章 means "emblem, badge, writing, chapter." <立早>

襟章 lapel badge, collar ensign [えりしょう]; 社章 company emblem [しゃしょう]; 文章 composition, writing [ぶんしょう]; 第三章 Chapter Three [だいさんしょう]; 校章 school emblem [こうしょう]; 肩章 epaulette (on uniform) [けんしょう]; 徽章 insignia, membership badge [きしょう]

	Meanings	Kun and On	Romaji	Bushu	Stroke Order and Number
SG-1362 障	to block, hinder, obstruct; adverse effect	さわ-る ショウ	sawa-ru *shoo*	阜	阝 阝 阝 阝 阝 陪 障 14

障 **B** F-0941 (説文) The seal-style form comprised "mountains, obstruction" (阝), and 章, used for the sound *shoo* to mean "fence." Together they signified "to block or hinder." The kanji 障 means "to block, hinder, obstruct; adverse effect." <阝章>

気に障る to hurt one's feelings, take offense [きにさわる]; 差し障り adverse effect, obstacle [さしさわり]; 目障りな offensive to the eye [めざわりな]; 故障する to break down [こしょうする]; 障害 hindrance, obstacle [しょうがい]; 障子 *shoji* paper screen [しょうじ]; 障害者 person with a disability [しょうがいしゃ]; 支障 hindrance, obstacle [ししょう]

	Meanings	Kun and On	Romaji	Bushu	Stroke Order and Number
SG-1363 彰	to make explicit, stand out vibrantly	ショウ	*shoo*	彡	丶 亠 立 音 章 彰 14

彰 **C** F-1430 (説文) The seal-style form comprised 章 **SG-1361**, which was used for the sound *shoo* to mean "written distinctively," and 彡 "pretty design." Together they signified something that was "vibrant and explicit." The kanji 彰 means "to make explicit, stand out vibrantly." <章彡>

表彰 commendation, awarding [ひょうしょう]; 顕彰碑 monument in honor of a person [けんしょうひ]

63c 言 "word, language; to say"; bushu *gonben* 言話記信計語談読誇訟謡

	Meanings	Kun and On	Romaji	Bushu	Stroke Order and Number
SG-1364 言	word, language; to say, speak	い-う・こと ゲン・ゴン	i-u, koto *gen, gon*	言	亠 亠 亠 言 言 言 言 7

言 **A** F-0057 (甲骨文 1, 金文 1 2, 金文 2 3, 説文 4) 1 through 4 comprised "a large tattooing needle with a handle" (辛 **SG-1359**), and "a vessel that contained prayers or oaths" or "a mouth" (口 **SG-0031**), together signifying "word; to speak." A sharp needle signified clearly articulated language and the seriousness of one's words. The kanji 言 means "word, language; to say, speak." When 言 appears on the left side of a kanji, it becomes bushu *gonben* and carries the same meanings as the kanji. <言>

Xと言う人 a person called X [Xというひと]; 言葉 word, language [ことば]; 泣き言を言う to complain, whimper [なきごとをいう]; 言伝てを頼む to ask to give a verbal message [ことづてをたのむ]; 発言する to speak at a meeting [はつげんする]; 言動 one's speech and behavior [げんどう]; 方言 dialect [ほうげん]; 言語道断(な) unspeakable, outrageous [ごんご・どうだん(な)]

	Meanings	Kun and On	Romaji	Bushu	Stroke Order and Number
SG-1365 話	to speak, talk	はな-す・はなし ワ	hana-su, hanashi *wa*	言	言 言 訁 話 話 13

話 **A** F-0072 (説文籀文 1, 説文 2) 1 comprised 言, bushu *gonben* "words, to speak," and 會 (会 **SG-1790**) "to meet," used for the sound *kai.* Words meeting each other meant "to speak, talk." The right side (舌) in 2 was used for the sound *wa* to mean "to meet," and was replaced by 舌 in the kanji. The kanji 話 means "to speak, talk." <言舌>
(Note: The origins of the right side of 話 and that of 舌 **SG-0040** "tongue" are unrelated.)

話 topic, story [はなし]; 話す to talk, verbalize, utter [はなす]; 一つ話 anecdote [ひとつばなし]; 話し方 a manner of speaking [はなしかた, はなしかた]; 噂話 rumor, hearsay [うわさばなし]; 手話 sign language [しゅわ]; 会話 conversation, dialogue [かいわ]; 世話 care [せわ]

	Meanings	Kun and On	Romaji	Bushu	Stroke Order and Number
SG-1366 記	to record, write down, chronicle	しる-す キ	shiru-su *ki*	言	言 言 訁 記 10

記 **A** F-0152 (説文) The seal-style form comprised 言 "word, language, to speak," and 己 **SG-0420** "a spool of thread," used for the sound *ki* to mean "a long thread." Together they signified "to write down a long account, record." The kanji 記 means "to record, write down, chronicle." <言己>

記す to write down, record [しるす]; 上記の通り as described above [じょうきのとおり]; 手記 private papers [しゅき]; 記名 signature, writing one's name down [きめい]; 記名投票 open voting, open ballot [きめいとうひょう]; 記入する to fill out, enter text [きにゅうする]; 記者 reporter [きしゃ]; 日記 diary, journal [にっき]

	Meanings	Kun and On	Romaji	Bushu	Stroke Order and Number
SG-1367 信	to trust, believe; truth, letter	シン	*shin*	人	亻 仁 信 信 信 信 9

信
A
F-0170

金文 1 中山王器1 2 中山王器2 3 古文1 4 古文2 5 説文 6

1 had 亻 "person" and 口 "a mouth, speaking," while 2, 3, and 4 contained "heart/mind." 5 and 6 comprised "a person" on the left, while the right side was either the radically reduced shape of "a tattooing needle" (in 5), or "word" 言 (in 6). What a person said was truthful and ought to be believed, hence the meaning "truth; to believe." A letter contained a person's words, hence the meaning "letter or correspondence." The kanji 信 means "to believe, trust; truth, letter." <亻言>

信じる to believe [しんじる]; 信用する to believe [しんようする]; 自信 self-confidence [じしん]; 信者 believer [しんじゃ]; 私信 private letter [ししん]; 通信 telecommunication [つうしん]; 興信所 private inquiry agent [こうしんじょ]; 受信料 license fee for TV reception [じゅしんりょう]

	Meanings	Kun and On	Romaji	Bushu	Stroke Order and Number
SG-1368 計	to count, measure, plan; total	はか-る ケイ	haka-ru *kee*	言	言 言一 計 9

計
A
F-0186

説文

The seal-style form comprised 言 "words," and 十 **SG-2134** "ten" for the meaning "full amount." Enumerating things in words meant "to count." Arranging many items required counting and planning. The kanji 計 means "to count, measure, plan; total." <言十>

計る to measure, quantify [はかる]; 一計を案じる to come up with a plan [いっけいをあんじる]; 計理士 registered accountant [けいりし]; 計器 meter, gauge, instrument [けいき]; 計上する to include, add up [けいじょうする]; 計量 weighing, measuring [けいりょう]; 温度計 thermometer [おんどけい]; 推計 estimation [すいけい]

	Meanings	Kun and On	Romaji	Bushu	Stroke Order and Number
SG-1369 語	word, language; to talk	かた-る ゴ	kata-ru *go*	言	言 言 訂 訝 語 語 14

語
A
F-0188

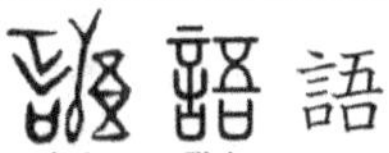

金文 1 説文 2

1 and 2 comprised "a needle over a mouth" (言), an additional "needle" (in 1), and 吾, used for the sound *go* to mean "to communicate with each other." Together they signified "to discuss with words, talk." The kanji 語 means "word, language; to talk." <言吾>

語る to narrate, tell [かたる]; 語らう to converse, discourse, chat [かたらう]; 語り手 storyteller, narrator [かたりて]; 語学 language study [ごがく, ごがく]; 語気を強める to raise one's voice, speak emphatically [ごきをつよめる]; 語調 tone of voice [ごちょう]; 原語 original language [げんご]; 口語 colloquial language [こうご]; 文語 literary language, classical literary style [ぶんご]

	Meanings	Kun and On	Romaji	Bushu	Stroke Order and Number
SG-1370 談	to talk; story, conversation	ダン	*dan*	言	言 言 訃 訟 談 談 15

談
A
F-0429

説文

The seal-style form comprised 言 "word; to say," and 炎 **SG-1165**, used for the sound *tan* to mean "simple, unassuming, calm." Together they signified "to talk in a calm, normal manner." The kanji 談 means "to talk; story, conversation." <言炎>

商談 business negotiation, business talk [しょうだん]; 直談判 direct negotiation, personal negotiation [じかだんぱん]; 後日談 a later development, sequel [ごじつだん]; 談合 collusion [だんごう]; 美談 inspiring story [びだん]; 相談づくで by common consent [そうだんづくで]; 談話 conversation, informal expression of opinion [だんわ]

	Meanings	Kun and On	Romaji	Bushu	Stroke Order and Number
SG-1371 読	to read	よ-む ドク・トク・トウ	yo-mu *doku, toku, too*	言	言 言 計 詰 読 読 14

読
A
F-0474

説文 1 旧字 2

1, and 2, the kyuji, comprised 言 "words, language; to speak," and 賣, which was used for the sounds *toku/too/doku*. Together they signified "to read." Another view explains that the sound *too* had the meaning "to stop," and referred to stopping at the punctuation marks when reciting a passage. In the shinji, 賣 was replaced by 売 (not shared origin with 売 **SG-1695** "to sell"). The kanji 読 means "to read." <言士冖儿>

読み流す to read without pause, skim through [よみながす]; 立ち読み browsing through at a bookstore [たちよみ]; 慣用読み accepted pronunciation of kanji [かんようよみ]; 愛読 favorite reading material [あいどく]; 音読 reading aloud [おんどく]; 多読 extensive reading [たどく]; 読者 reader [どくしゃ]; 読本 reader, primer [とくほん]; 句読点 punctuation mark [くとうてん]

	Meanings	Kun and On	Romaji	Bushu	Stroke Order and Number
SG-1372 誇	pride; to pride oneself on, boast of, exaggerate	ほこ-る コ	hoko-ru *ko*	言	言訁訁訁誇誇 13

誇 **C** F-1473

説文

The seal-style form comprised 言, bushu *gonben* "word, language; to speak," and 夸 "to brag; haughty," used for the sound *ko*. The kanji 誇 means "pride; to pride oneself on, boast of, exaggerate." <言大一丂>

誇る to pride oneself on [ほこる]; 誇り pride, boast [ほこり]; 誇らかに proudly [ほこらかに]; 咲き誇る to be in full bloom [さきほこる]; 誇示 ostentation, boast [こじ]; 誇大広告 bombastic advertisement, misleading advertisement [こだいこうこく]; 誇張する to overstate, exaggerate [こちょうする]; 誇大妄想 delusion of grandeur, megalomania [こだいもうそう]

	Meanings	Kun and On	Romaji	Bushu	Stroke Order and Number
SG-1373 訟	to sue, accuse	ショウ	*shoo*	言	言言訁訟 11

訟 **C** F-1602

金文1 1 金文2 2 説文古文 3 説文 4

1 and 2 comprised 𠔉, used for the sound *shoo* to mean "to argue, dispute," and 言 "word; to speak," together signifying "to settle a dispute by arguing in court." The right side of 4 was 公 **SG-1321** "public," which also had the sound *shoo*. The kanji 訟 means "to sue, accuse." <言公>

訴訟 lawsuit [そしょう]; 刑事訴訟 criminal action, criminal suit [けいじそしょう]; 住民訴訟 citizens' suit [じゅうみんそしょう]; 集団訴訟 class action suit [しゅうだんそしょう]; 提訴 to bring a case before a court [ていそする]

	Meanings	Kun and On	Romaji	Bushu	Stroke Order and Number
SG-1374 謡	to sing, chant; song	うたい ヨウ	utai *yoo*	言	言訁謡謡謡謡 16

謡 **D** F-1729

旧字

No ancient form. The kyuji 謠 comprised 言, bushu *gonben* "word; to speak," and 䍃, used for the sound *yoo* to mean "(a voice) swaying." Together they signified "to sing." The top of 䍃 was replaced by a shape 爫. The kanji 謡 means "to sing, chant; song." <言爫缶>

謡 Noh singing [うたい]; 民謡 folk song [みんよう]; 歌謡曲 popular song [かようきょく]; 童謡 children's song [どうよう]; 謡曲 Noh singing [ようきょく]

63d 音 "sound" and "unclear, indistinct" (when used as a component) [from indistinct speaking due to something inside the mouth]; *on/in* 音暗響闇韻

	Meanings	Kun and On	Romaji	Bushu	Stroke Order and Number
SG-1375 音	sound, feigned voice	おと・ね オン・イン	oto, ne *on, in*	音	丶亠立产产音音 9

音 **A** F-0237

金文1 1 金文2 2 説文 3

1, 2, and 3 shared their forms with 1, 2, 3, and 4 for 言 **SG-1364** "word, language; to speak," except for a short line inside the mouth. Speaking with an obstruction in the mouth made one's words unclear, producing a "feigned-sounding voice," or just "sounds" that were not recognizable as speech. In the kanji, "needle" 辛 **SG-1359** was simplified to 立, and 日 was used for "a mouth with something inside." The kanji 音 means "sound, feigned voice." When used as a component, 音 means "unclear, indistinct." < 立日 >

音 sound [おと]; 声音 tone of voice [こわね]; 音色 timbre, tone color [ねいろ, おんしょく]; 音信 correspondence, letter [おんしん]; 音階 musical scale [おんかい]; 母音 vowel [ぼいん, ぼおん]; 子音 consonant [しいん, しおん]

	Meanings	Kun and On	Romaji	Bushu	Stroke Order and Number
SG-1376 暗	dark, unclear, hidden, ignorant; to memorize	くら-い アン	kura-i *an*	日	日日日'日'日'暗暗 13

暗 **B** F-0821

説文

The seal-style form comprised 日 **SG-1045** "sun," and 音 **SG-1375**, used for the sound *an* to mean "unclear, dark." When the sun was hidden, it was dark and hard to see. When applied to a person's knowledge, it meant "ignorant." The kanji 暗 means "dark, unclear, hidden, ignorant; to memorize." <日音> (Note: The kanji meaning "to recite by memory, memorize (words)" is the non-Joyo kanji 諳 (with 言 bushu *gonben*). In Joyo kanji writing, 暗 is substituted.)

暗い dark [くらい]; 薄暗い dimly lit [うすぐらい]; 暗示する to imply, suggest [あんじする]; 暗黙の了解 tacit understanding [あんもくのりょうかい]; 暗号 code, cryptogram [あんごう]; 暗号化 to encrypt, encode [あんごうか]; 暗記 (諳記) learning by heart [あんき]

SG-1377 響	Meanings	Kun and On	Romaji	Bushu	Stroke Order and Number
	to reverberate, affect; influence, impact	ひび-く キョウ	hibi-ku *kyoo*	音	乡 乡 乡ヨ 组 组ヨ 组阝 郷 郷 響 響 20

響 **B** F-0833

說文 1 旧字 2

1 and 2 comprised 郷 **SG-1317**, used for the sound *kyoo* and the meaning "people enjoying each other's company over a feast," and 音 "sound." The lively sounds of people at a feast could be heard from distance. From that it meant "to echo, reverberate." A reverberating sound travels well and has far-reaching "impact or effect." The kanji 響 means "to reverberate, affect; influence." <郷(乡皀阝)音>

響く to reverberate, echo, affect [ひびく]; 地響き rumbling of the earth [じひびき]; 音響 sound, acoustic [おんきょう]; 交響曲 symphony [こうきょうきょく]; 残響 reverberation [ざんきょう]; 悪影響 adverse effect [あくえいきょう]; 影響力 influence [えいきょうりょく]

SG-1378 闇	Meanings	Kun and On	Romaji	Bushu	Stroke Order and Number
	darkness, bewilderment, black market	やみ	yami	門	丨 冂 冂 門 門 門 閂 闇 闇 17

闇 **D** F-1794

說文

The seal-style form comprised "closed double doors" (門 **SG-1251**) and "dark, unclear" (音 **SG-1375**), together signifying "darkness." Shadowy activity takes place on the black market. The kanji 闇 means "darkness, bewilderment, black market." <門音>

闇 darkness [やみ]; 暗闇 darkness [くらやみ]; 真っ暗闇 total darkness, pitch dark [まっくらやみ, まっくらやみ]; 闇市 black market [やみいち]; 闇献金 illegal contribution [やみけんきん]; 闇取引 secret dealings [やみとりひき, やみとりひき]; 闇夜 dark, moonless night [やみよ]

SG-1379 韻	Meanings	Kun and On	Romaji	Bushu	Stroke Order and Number
	rhyme, lingering sound	イン	*in*	音	立 音 音口 韶 韻 韻 19

韻 **D** F-2101

說文

The seal-style form comprised 音 "sound," and 員 **SG-1717**, used for the sound *in* to mean "harmony." Together they signified "sounds or voices in harmony." The kanji 韻 means "rhyme, lingering sound." <音員>

韻を踏む to rhyme [いんをふむ]; 余韻 lingering sound, aftereffect [よいん]; 音韻 phoneme [おんいん]; 音韻論 phonology [おんいんろん]

63e 意 "thoughts, intention" [from thoughts kept in one's heart] 意・億憶臆

SG-1380 意	Meanings	Kun and On	Romaji	Bushu	Stroke Order and Number
	thought, intention, meaning	イ	*i*	心	亠 立 产 音 音 意 13

意 **A** F-0129

說文

The seal-style form comprised 音 **SG-1375**, from an indistinct, unclear sound that failed to become words, and 心 **SG-0187** "heart/mind." Together they signified "thoughts kept in one's heart," such as one's intention or meaning. The kanji 意 means "thought, intention, meaning." <音心>

意見 opinion [いけん]; 意味 meaning [いみ]; 意味合い implication, nuance, hidden meaning [いみあい]; 同意するto agree [どういする]; 意地 willpower, pride [いじ]; 大意 the gist, main purport, synopsis [たいい]; 意外に surprisingly [いがいに]; 意中の人 someone on one's mind [いちゅうのひと]; 意向 intention, inclination [いこう] // 意気地なし cowardice, spineless [いくじなし]

意 (as a component) [from having many thoughts inside the heart or mind]; *oku* 億憶臆

SG-1381 億	Meanings	Kun and On	Romaji	Bushu	Stroke Order and Number
	100 million; to think over	オク	*oku*	人	亻 亻 亻 亻 倍 倍 億 億 15

億 **A** F-0381

金文1 1 金文2 2 說文 3

1 and 2 comprised 辛 and either 口 or 日 (further forming either 言 or 音), with a circle in the middle suggesting "inside." In 3, the right side comprised 言 or 音, "many" (from the addition of a second 口), and "a heart" (心), together signifying "having many thoughts inside the heart," and having the sound *oku*. Together with bushu *ninben* 亻 "an act that one does," they originally meant "a heart filled with thoughts," which lent the meaning "the largest number that one could think of," or "100 million." The kanji 億 means "100 million." <亻意>

億 100 million [おく]; 億万長者 billionaire [おくまんちょうじゃ]; 億劫な bothersome, troublesome [おっくうな]; 億劫がる to show unwillingness to do [おっくうがる]

SG-1382 憶	Meanings	Kun and On	Romaji	Bushu	Stroke Order and Number
	to ponder, remember; memory	オク	*oku*	心	16

憶 **C** F-1318

籀文 1 篆文 2

As described in 憶 **SG-1381**, the right side 意 had the sound *oku*, and the meaning "a heart filled with thoughts." Adding another "heart/mind" (忄, bushu *risshinben*) to 意 created the kanji 憶, which is used in words pertaining to memory. The kanji 憶 means "to ponder, remember; memory." <忄意>

(Note: The distinction between the kanji 億 and 臆 **SG-1383** has become blurred. 臆 was not Joyo kanji during the pre-revision period, and some words such as 臆測, 臆断, and 臆説 are also written as 憶測, 憶断, and 憶説.)

記憶 memory [きおく]; 記憶力 one's ability to remember [きおくりょく]; 憶測(臆測)する to make a random guess [おくそくする]; 憶説(臆説)にすぎない to be a mere hypothesis, no more than an unsupported assumption [おくせつにすぎない]; 憶断(臆断)する to jump to conclusions [おくだんする]

SG-1383 臆	Meanings	Kun and On	Romaji	Bushu	Stroke Order and Number
	timid; to hold back a thought	オク	*oku*	肉	17

臆 **D** F-2424

篆文1 1 篆文2 2

Please refer to the kanji 憶 **SG-1382**. The kanji 臆 comprises 月, bushu *nikuzuki* "part of the body," and 意, used for the sound *oku*. Anxiously thinking over many things causes one to feel pressure in the chest and to behave hesitantly or timidly. The kanji 臆 is used to mean "to be hesitant, feel timid." <月意>

臆するto be hesitant, feel timid [おくする]; 臆病な timid [おくびょうな]; 臆面無く shamelessly [おくめんなく]

63f 竟 "ending" [from a prayer ending when it was answered]; *kyoo* 境鏡

SG-1384 境	Meanings	Kun and On	Romaji	Bushu	Stroke Order and Number
	boundary, border, situation	さかい キョウ・ケイ	sakai *kyoo, kee*	土	14

境 **B** F-0760

説文

The seal-style form comprised 土 **SG-1126** "dirt, ground," and 竟 "ending," which was used for the sound *kyoo* to mean "ending." Together they signified "a boundary where a land ends." The character came to also mean "a situation." The kanji 境 means "boundary, border, situation." <土音儿>

境 border [さかい]; 県境 prefectural border [けんざかい]; 国境 boundary between countries [こっきょう]; 境地 stage, phase [きょうち]; 心境 frame of mind, mental state [しんきょう]; 苦境 predicament [くきょう]; 逆境 adversity [ぎゃっきょう]; 境内 grounds of a temple or shrine [けいだい]

SG-1385 鏡	Meanings	Kun and On	Romaji	Bushu	Stroke Order and Number
	mirror	かがみ キョウ	kagami *kyoo*	金	19

鏡 **C** F-1159

説文

The seal-style form comprised 金 **SG-1196** "metal," and 竟, used for the sound *kyoo* to mean "outline," from the edge or end of a shape. A metal that reflected the outline of a person's shape was "a mirror." The kanji 鏡 means "mirror." <金音儿>

鏡 mirror [かがみ]; 双眼鏡 binoculars [そうがんきょう]; 老眼鏡 pair of reading glasses [ろうがんきょう]; 鏡台 dressing table, vanity table [きょうだい]; 眼鏡 pair of eye glasses [めがね]; お眼鏡に適う to suit your discerning eye or taste (honorific) [おめがねにかなう]

64 A surgical knife with a handle

64a 余 "remain, excess" [from a surgical knife removing a lesion]; *yo/jo/to* 余除途徐塗叙

SG-1386 余	Meanings	Kun and On	Romaji	Bushu	Stroke Order and Number
	to be in excess, remain; remainder, surplus, room	あま-る ヨ	ama-ru *yo*	人・食	7

余 **B** F-0645

餘 余

甲骨文 1 金文1 2 金文2 3 説文 4 旧字 5

One view holds that 1 through 4 depicted "a handled surgical needle or knife for removing lesions," with ハ in 3 and 4 signifying "to open the wound." Something not wanted, such as lesion, was "something extra, what was left, latitude." Another view takes the origin to be "a spade removing unnecessary dirt to both sides (ハ) of a hole," and thus

余る to remain, be left over, be in excess [あまる]; 手に余る to be beyond one's power [てにあまる]; 余興 entertainment, sideshow [よきょう]; 余計な unnecessary, excessively [よけいな]; 余談 digression, diversion [よだん]; 余地 room, margin, scope [よち];

	"excess." The kyuji 餘 included 飠 "food," but the shinji reverted to the earlier form. The kanji 余 means "to be in excess, remain; remainder, surplus, room." <余(𠆢干ハ)>	余生 rest of one's life, one's remaining years [よゆせい]

	Meanings	Kun and On	Romaji	Bushu	Stroke Order and Number
SG-1387 除	to remove, protect, keep away; division (mathematics)	のぞ-く ジョ・ジ	nozo-ku *jo, ji*	阜	⁷ 3 阝 阝^ 阾 阾 陉 除 10

除 **B** F-0764

金文 1 説文 2 除

1 comprised "a pile of dirt, obstruction" (阝), and 余 **SG-1386** "room, excess" from "a surgical needle for removing excess," used for the sound *jo*. Together they signified "to remove dirt or obstruction." Another view takes the meaning to be a borrowing. The character also means "to keep away, avoid," and "division" in mathematics. The kanji 除 means "to remove, avoid, keep away; division (mathematics)." <阝余>

除く to remove, exclude [のぞく]; 解除 cancellation, release [かいじょ]; 削除 deletion, erasure [さくじょ]; 除外する to exclude [じょがいする]; 除湿器 dehumidifier [じょしつき]; 加減乗除 the four operations in arithmetic [かげん・じょうじょ] // 日除け sunshade, blind [ひよけ]; 風除け windbreak [かざよけ]; 除け者 a person who is left out, social outcast [のけもの]

	Meanings	Kun and On	Romaji	Bushu	Stroke Order and Number
SG-1388 途	road, way	ト	*to*	辵	亼 今 余 余 ˋ余 涂 途 10

途 **B** F-0980

甲骨文 1 甲骨文 2 途

The related kanji 涂 that has the sound *to* (shown at right) was the name of a particular river, and when a river flooded, it created a lot of mud. In light of this, 1 and 2 comprised 余, used for the sound *to* and its association with the name of the river, and "a footprint," together signifying "muddy road," or just "road." In the kanji, bushu *shinnyuu* is used for "to move forward." The kanji 途 means "road, way." <余辶>

途中 halfway [とちゅう]; 途中下車 stopover, layover [とちゅうげしゃ]; 途方に暮れる to be perplexed, be all at sea [とほうにくれる]; 途方もなく extraordinarily, preposterously [とほうもなく]; ～した途端に just as, the moment one did X [～したとたんに]; 別途料金 separate charge [べっとりょうきん]; 途絶える to cease, come to an end [とだえる]; 前途洋々 with a rosy future [ぜんと・ようよう] // 一途に determinedly, single-mindedly [いちずに]

	Meanings	Kun and On	Romaji	Bushu	Stroke Order and Number
SG-1389 徐	slowly, gradually	ジョ	*jo*	彳	彳 彳^ 徐 徐 徐 徐 10

徐 **C** F-1457

説文 徐

The seal-style form comprised 彳 "crossroads," and 余 **SG-1386**," used for the sound *jo*. Together they signified "to move slowly." The kanji 徐 means "slowly, gradually." <彳余>

徐々に gradually, little by little [じょじょに]; 徐行 going slowly, crawl [じょこう]

	Meanings	Kun and On	Romaji	Bushu	Stroke Order and Number
SG-1390 塗	to paint; plaster, stucco	ぬ-る ト	nu-ru *to*	土	氵 氵^ 氵亼 涂 涂 涂 塗 塗 塗 13

塗 **C** F-1529

説文 塗

The seal-style form comprised 涂 "river mud" (The development of which is shown the top right in **SG-1388**), which was used for the sound *to*, and 土 "dirt, mud." Fine dirt brought up by a flooding river was used for plaster. Applying plaster was likened to covering the surface of something with paint, and so it also meant "to paint." The kanji 塗 means "to paint; plaster, stucco." <氵余土>

塗る to paint, plaster, varnish [ぬる]; 上塗り final coating, finish [うわぬり]; 漆塗り *urushi* lacquer [うるしぬり]; 塗り直す to repaint [ぬりなおす]; ペンキ塗り立て "Wet Paint" (sign) [ペンキぬりたて]; 塗料 paints and varnish, coating [とりょう]; 塗装する to coat with paint [とそうする]

	Meanings	Kun and On	Romaji	Bushu	Stroke Order and Number
SG-1391 叙	to describe (a matter or event) in an orderly manner, state, confer a rank upon	ジョ	*jo*	支	𠆢 亼 全 余 叙 叙 9

叙 **D** F-1836

甲骨文 1 金文 2 説文 3 旧字 4 敍 叙

1 comprised "a hand" and "a surgical knife." In 2, "two hands were removing a lesion with a surgical knife." A surgical procedure gradually relieves pain. With the sound *jo* to mean "gradually" (from 徐 **SG-1389**), these components formed the meaning "to do something gradually." Proceeding gradually or carefully when describing an event or matter will ensure that the description unfolds in good order. In 3 and 4, 支 "to cause an action" appeared, which reverted to 又 **SG-0084** in the shinji. The kanji 叙 means "to describe (a matter or event) in an orderly manner, confer a rank upon." <余又>

叙勲 conferment of a decoration [じょくん]; 自叙伝 autobiography [じじょでん]; 叙事詩 epic poetry [じょじし]; 叙述する to describe, delineate, narrate [じょじゅつする]; 叙情的 lyrical [じょじょうてき]

64b 舎 "house; to let go" [from a roomy space on the ground under a cover]; *sha* 舎捨

SG-1392 舎	Meanings	Kun and On	Romaji	Bushu	Stroke Order and Number
	house, hut	シャ	*sha*	舌	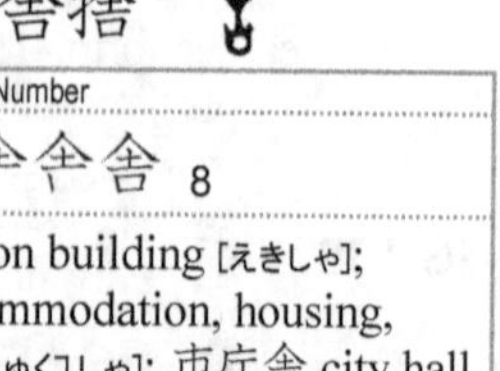 8

舎 **B** F-1059

金文1 1 金文2 2 説文 3 旧字 4

1, 2, and 3 comprised "excess, surplus" (余 **SG-1386**) and "a space" (口), together signifying "a roomy space" where one felt relaxed, such as a hut or house. In the shinji, the top component became 土. The character was also used to mean younger brother. The kanji 舎 means "house, hut." <舎(ヘ土口)>

駅舎 station building [えきしゃ]; 宿舎 accommodation, housing, quarters [しゅくꜜしゃ]; 市庁舎 city hall [しちょうꜜしゃ]; 合同庁舎 joint government agencies building [ごうどうちょうꜜしゃ] // 学び舎 school [まなびや]

SG-1393 捨	Meanings	Kun and On	Romaji	Bushu	Stroke Order and Number
	to throw away, discard, abandon	す-てる シャ	su-teru *sha*	手	一扌扌扌拎捨捨 11

捨 **C** F-1210

捨 捨 説文

The seal-style form comprised 扌 "an act done by hand," and 舎 (舎 **SG-1392**), used for the sound *sha* to mean "to let go, relinquish." A hand relinquishing something meant "to throw away." The kanji 捨 means "to throw away, discard, abandon." <扌舎>

捨てる to abandon, discard [すてる]; 捨て身になる to become desperate [すてみになꜜる]; 捨印 marginal seal impression on a document [すていん]; 脱ぎ捨てる to take off one's clothes and leave them unhung or unfolded [ぬぎすてる, ぬぎすてꜜる]; 世捨て人 hermit [よすてꜜびと]; 四捨五入 rounding off [しꜜしゃ・ごにゅう]; 取捨選択する to make one's choice [しゅꜜしゃ・せんたくする]

65 Knife, sword

65a 刀 "knife, sword; to cut" 刀切窃

SG-1394 刀	Meanings	Kun and On	Romaji	Bushu	Stroke Order and Number
	sword, knife	かたな トウ	katana *too*	刀	フ刀 2

刀 **A** F-1005

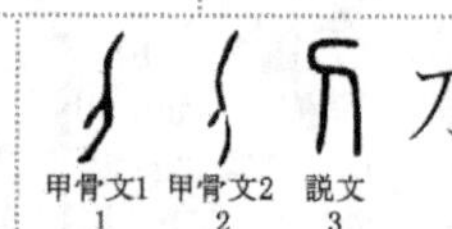

甲骨文1 1 甲骨文2 2 説文 3

1, 2, and 3 depicted "a sword or knife." One view takes that the top was a blade and the bottom was a curved handle, whereas another view suggests that the bottom left was the blade. The kanji 刀 means "sword, knife." <刀>

刀 sword [かたなꜜ]; 小刀 small knife [こがꜜたな]; 刀剣 sword [とうけん]; 日本刀 Japanese sword [にほんとう]; 二刀流 fighting style using two swords [にとうりゅう]; 一刀両断 cutting decisively in two with a single stroke of a sword [いっとꜜう・りょうだん]; 単刀直入に frankly, coming straight to the point [たんとうちょくにゅうに] // 竹刀 bamboo sword (for *kendo*, Japanese fencing) [しꜜない]

SG-1395 切	Meanings	Kun and On	Romaji	Bushu	Stroke Order and Number
	to cut, cut off, exhaust; earnest, imminent	き-る セツ・サイ	ki-ru *setsu, sai*	刀	一七七刁切 4

切 **A** F-0363

篆文 1 説文 2

1 and 2 comprised "a bone joint being cut," used for the sound *setsu* to mean "to cut," and "a knife or sword" (刀). When a sharp knife was nearby, a person would behave seriously; hence the form also meant "imminent, precious, earnest." From a supply cut off or ceased, it also meant "to exhaust." The kanji 切 means "to cut, cut off, exhaust; earnest, imminent." <七刀>

切る to cut [きꜜる]; 切手 postage stamp [きって]; 食べ切る to eat them all [たべきꜜる]; 見切りをつける to give up as hopeless [みきりをつけꜜる]; 時間切れ timing out, passing the deadline [じかんぎれ]; 親切な kind, gracious, generous, nice [しꜜんせつな]; 切実な acute, earnest [せつじつな]; 一切 all, everything [いꜜっさい]

SG-1396 窃	Meanings	Kun and On	Romaji	Bushu	Stroke Order and Number
	to steal secretly	セツ	*setsu*	穴	' 宀 宂 空 穵 窃 窃 9

窃 **D** F-2198

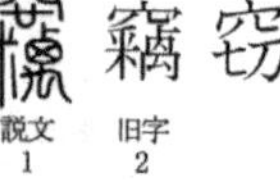

説文 1 旧字 2

1 comprised "a hollow or hole" (穴 **SG-1322**) and "a cooking pot" (廿) on the top, and "rice" (米 **SG-0738**) and "small bugs" on the bottom, used for the sound *setsu*. It described a scene in which bugs burrowed inside a rice granary and ate the grains, leaving empty hulls, and meant "to steal without being noticed." Another view takes 廿 at the top to be two hands, signifying

窃盗犯 thief of personal property [せっとꜜうはん];

	someone stealthily stealing the grains. The kyuji 竊 (2) reflected 1 closely, but in the shinji 窃, the bottom was replaced by 切 for the sound *setsu*. The kanji 窃 means "to steal secretly." <穴切>	剽窃 plagiarism, piracy [ひょうせつ]

65b 分 "to divide into two"; *hun* 分粉貧紛雰

	Meanings	Kun and On	Romaji	Bushu	Stroke Order and Number
SG-1397 分	to divide, comprehend, discern; portion, social status, minute	わ-ける ブン・フン・ブ	wa-keru *bun, hun, bu*	刀	ノ 八 分 分 4

分 **A** F-0012

甲骨文 1 金文 2 説文 3

In 1, 2, and 3, "a sword or knife" (刀 **SG-1394**) was placed in the middle of the shape 八 "to cut in half," signifying "to divide; portion." One's own portion meant "one's social status." Dividing an hour makes "minutes." A clear-cut explanation helps one "to discern, comprehend." The kanji 分 means "to divide, discern; portion, social status, minute." <八刀>

分ける to divide [わけ・る]; 分かれる to branch off, separate [わかれ・る]; 仕分ける to classify, sort out [しわけ・る]; 分かる to understand [わか・る]; 分数 division [ぶんす・う]; 身分 social status [み・ぶん]; ゴミの分別 sorting different types of trash [ごみのぶんべつ]; 言い分 one's claim, complaint [いいぶん]; 分別 prudence, wisdom [ふ・んべつ]

	Meanings	Kun and On	Romaji	Bushu	Stroke Order and Number
SG-1398 粉	powder, wheat flour	こ・こな フン	ko, kona *hun*	米	ソ 䒑 半 米 粉 粉 粉 10

粉 **C** F-1184

説文

The seal-style form comprised 米 **SG-0738** "rice," and 分 **SG-1397** "to divide," used for the sound *hun*. Together they signified "grinding grain into powder." The kanji 粉 means "powder, wheat flour." <米分>

粉 powder, flour [こな・]; 粉々の shattered, fragmented [こなごなの]; 小麦粉 wheat flour [こむぎこ]; パン粉 bread crumbs, *panko* [パンこ]; 片栗粉 starch powder [かたく・りこ]; 身を粉にする to work assiduously [みをこ・にする]; 粉末 powder [ふんまつ]; 花粉 pollen [かふん] // 白粉 facial makeup powder [おしろい]

	Meanings	Kun and On	Romaji	Bushu	Stroke Order and Number
SG-1399 貧	poor, scanty, deficient	まず-しい ヒン・ビン	mazu-shii *hin, bin*	貝	八 分 分 贫 貧 貧 11

貧 **C** F-1204

説文古文 1 説文 2

1 comprised "a house," 八 "to divide into two," and 刀 "a knife," together signifying dividing up what was inside one's house, which left one "poor." In 2, 貝 **SG-1693** "cowrie, valuable asset" was added underneath 分 "to divide up," to give the same meaning of "division of valuable assets resulting in poverty. The kanji 貧 means "poor, scanty, deficient." <分貝>

貧しい poor [まずし・い]; 貧乏 poverty [び・んぼう]; 貧乏くじを引く pull the short stick, be the least lucky of all [びんぼ・うくじを・ひく]; 貧血 anemia [ひんけつ]; 貧弱な shabby, shoddy, emaciated [ひんじゃくな]; 貧富の差 disparity of wealth [ひ・んぷのさ]; 赤貧 extreme poverty [せきひん]; 貧相な looking poor, shabby [ひ・んそうな]

	Meanings	Kun and On	Romaji	Bushu	Stroke Order and Number
SG-1400 紛	to stray, become confused; turmoil	まぎ-れる フン	magi-reru *hun*	糸	幺 糸 紒 紛 紛 10

紛 **C** F-1224

説文

The seal-style form comprised 糸 **SG-1600** "a skein of threads," and 分 "to divide up," used for the sound *hun*. When a skein of threads came apart, they became tangled or went astray. The kanji 紛 means "to stray, become confused; turmoil." <糸分>

紛らわしい deceptive, confusing [まぎらわし・い]; 気が紛れる one's mind becomes diverted from concerns, boredom [きがまぎれ・る]; 紛糾する to become embroiled [ふんきゅうする]; 紛争 dispute, conflict [ふんそう]; 内紛 internal dispute [ないふん]; 紛失する to lose [ふんしつする]

	Meanings	Kun and On	Romaji	Bushu	Stroke Order and Number
SG-1401 雰	atmosphere, mist	フン	*hun*	雨	一 币 雨 雫 雰 雰 12

雰 **D** F-1825

篆文

The seal-style form comprised 雨 **SG-1205**, or bushu *amekanmuri* "precipitation", and 分 **SG-1397** "small pieces," used for the sound *hun*. Together they signified "minute particles in the air, mist." The kanji 雰 means "atmosphere, mist." <雨分>

雰囲気 atmosphere [ふんい・き]

65c 刂 "knife; to cut"; bushu *rittoo* 別前創刷刈煎刹剥

	Meanings	Kun and On	Romaji	Bushu	Stroke Order and Number
SG-1402 別	to separate; another	わか-れる ベツ	waka-reru *betsu*	刀	口号另別別 7

別
A
F-0211

甲骨文 1 說文 2 別

1 comprised "a knife" and "a bone joint," together signifying "to separate bones at the joints using a knife." In 2, the two elements swapped positions, with the knife becoming 刂, bushu *rittoo*. The kanji 別 means "to separate; another." <另刂>

別れる to become separated [わかれる]; 別れ別れに each by oneself [わかれわかれに]; 別れ話 talk about breaking up [わかればなし]; 死に別れ bereavement, separation by death [しにわかれ]; 別々に separately [べつべつに]; 別居する to live separately [べっきょする]; 差別 discrimination [さべつ]; 告別式 funeral [こくべつしき]

	Meanings	Kun and On	Romaji	Bushu	Stroke Order and Number
SG-1403 前	front; forward, before; previous	まえ ゼン	mae *zen*	刀	丷䒑亣肖前前 9

前
A
F-0027

金文 1 篆文1 2 篆文2 3 說文 4 前

1 through 4 had 止 **SG-0200** "a footprint" and 月 "a boat," both signifying "to move forward." In 3, "a knife" (刂) was added to mean "to trim toenails." Toenails are the forward-most points of the body. In the kanji, 止 was reduced to 䒑. The kanji 前 means "front, forward, before; previous." <䒑月刂>

前 front, before [まえ]; 後ろ前 (to wear) backward [うしろまえ]; 自前 paying one's own expense [じまえ]; 持ち前 one's nature, inborn [もちまえ]; 出前 restaurant meal delivery [でまえ]; 〜の手前 out of consideration of X, in front of X [〜のてまえ]; 戦前 before war [せんぜん]; 前衛 avant-garde [ぜんえい]; 前回 the previous session, last preceding [ぜんかい]; 前後 before and after, around the time, front and rear [ぜんご]

	Meanings	Kun and On	Romaji	Bushu	Stroke Order and Number
SG-1404 創	to create; a wound or cut	つく-る ソウ	tsuku-ru *soo*	刀	𠆢今今倉倉創創 12

創
B
F-0875

中山王器 1 說文 2 創

1 comprised "a person standing on the ground" and "a knife with a sharp blade," together signifying "a person becoming wounded." 2 had 倉 **SG-1997**, used for the sound *soo* to mean "a cut or wound." A knife (刂) was used to shape or create something new; thus, the form also meant "to create, begin." The kanji 創 means "to create; a wound or cut." <倉刂>

創る to create [つくる]; 創造する to create [そうぞうする]; 絆創膏 adhesive bandage [ばんそうこう]; 創意工夫 inventive idea, ingenuity [そういくふう]; 創立者 founder [そうりつしゃ]; 独創的な original [どくそうてきな]

	Meanings	Kun and On	Romaji	Bushu	Stroke Order and Number
SG-1405 刷	to print, renew; impression, issue	す-る サツ	su-ru *satsu*	刀	⁻コ尸吊帰刷刷 8

刷
C
F-1341

說文 刷

The kanji 刷 is said to have come from 㕞, which meant "to wipe the hands (又), using a cloth (巾) that hangs around one's waist (尸)," and had the sound *setsu*. In the seal-style form of 刷, the use of 刂, bushu *rittoo*, may have suggested a knife-like metal spatula sliding on the surface of a printing block as though wiping it, or shaving the printing surface with a knife for repeated renewal and reuse. The kanji 刷 means "to print, renew; impression, issue." <尸巾刂>

刷る to print [する]; 手刷り handprinting [てずり]; ゲラ刷り galley proof [ゲラずり]; 印刷 printing, presswork [いんさつ]; 刷新する to reform, innovate, clean up [さっしんする]; 経営陣刷新 management shakeup [けいえいじん·さっしん]

	Meanings	Kun and On	Romaji	Bushu	Stroke Order and Number
SG-1406 刈	to clip, trim, shear, mow, reap	か-る	ka-ru	刀	ノメ乂刈 4

刈
C
F-1641

甲骨文 1 篆文 2 刈

1 was "a pair of scissors" for cutting grass or plants, and had the sound *gai*. In 2, "a knife" (刀, 刂) was added. In the kanji 刈, the pair of scissors became メ. The kanji 刈 means "to clip, trim, shear, mow, reap." <メ刂>

刈る to clip, shear [かる]; 丸刈り buzz cut, close clipping [まるがり]; 草刈り grass cutting, mowing [くさかり, くさがり]; 芝刈り mowing the lawn [しばかり, しばがり]; 刈り入れ時 the harvest, harvest time [かりいれどき]; 稲刈り rice reaping [いねかり]

	Meanings	Kun and On	Romaji	Bushu	Stroke Order and Number
SG-1407 煎	to roast, parch	い-る セン	i-ru *sen*	火	丷 䒑 广 前 前 前 煎 13

煎 **D** F-2251 — 說文 — The seal-style form comprised 前 **SG-1403**, used for the sound *sen*, and 火 "fire," together signifying "to roast." In the kanji, the fire became 灬, bushu *rekka/renga*. The kanji 煎 means "to roast, parch." < 前 灬 >

煎る to roast, parch [いる]; 煎茶 (quality) green tea [せんちゃ]; 湯煎する to warm a vessel in hot water, double-boil [ゆせんする]; 煎じる to infuse, make an infusion of [せんじる]

	Meanings	Kun and On	Romaji	Bushu	Stroke Order and Number
SG-1408 刹	fleeting moment, Buddhist temple, pagoda	サツ・セツ	*satsu, setsu*	刀	ノ メ 乄 杀 杀 刹 刹 8

刹 **D** F-2579 — 篆文 — The seal-style form comprised "an animal that cast a spell," used for the sounds *setsu/satsu*, and "a knife" (刂), together originally signifying killing such an animal. Another view takes it to be a variant of the kanji 殺 **SG-0162**. The character later became used for the sounds *setsu/satsu* in Buddhist Sanskrit words that meant "temple" and "fleeting moment," and it is original meaning was lost. The kanji 刹 means "fleeting moment, Buddhist temple, pagoda." <メ木刂>

名刹 famous temple [めいさつ]; 刹那 moment, juncture [せつな]; 刹那主義 living only for the present moment [せつなしゅぎ]

	Meanings	Kun and On	Romaji	Bushu	Stroke Order and Number
SG-1409 剥	to peel off, strip off	は-がす ハク	ha-gasu *haku*	刀	㇕ ⺕ 彐 寻 录 剥 剥 10

剥 **D** F-2786 — 甲骨文 1, 說文 2, 說文或体 3 — In 1, 2, and 3, the right side was "a knife." The left side of 1 and 3 remains obscure (possibly "bones," according to one view). There are two very different views regarding what the left side of 2 might depict: (a) "the surface of something peeling off," and (b) "a hairy animal with a bushy tail." Together with "a knife" (刂), the form meant "to peel off a surface with a knife," or "to strip off animal skin." The kanji 剥 reflects 2, and means "to peel off, strip off." <录(ヨ氺)刂>

剥ぐ to peel off, strip off [はぐ]; 剥がれる to peel off, come off [はがれる]; 剥離する to come off, scale off [はくりする]; 剥奪する to deprive of something, divest [はくだつする]

65d 契 "contract, pledge" [from a person making notches in a tally using a knife] 契潔喫 契

	Meanings	Kun and On	Romaji	Bushu	Stroke Order and Number
SG-1410 契	contract; to pledge	ちぎ-る ケイ	chigi-ru *kee*	大	一 十 丰 丰 丰刀 丰刀 㓞 㓞 契 9

契 **B** F-1052 — 說文 — The seal-style form comprised three short diagonal lines with a vertical intersecting line (a shape that had the sound *kee*) and "a knife" (刀), together signifying "notching tallies on a piece of wood with a knife." Together with "a person" (大 **SG-0314**), they meant "a person making a pledge or contract." The kanji 契 means "contract; to pledge." <契(㓞大)>

契りを結ぶ to make a pledge, exchange a marriage vow [ちぎりをむすぶ]; 契約 contract [けいやく]; 契機 momentum [けいき]

	Meanings	Kun and On	Romaji	Bushu	Stroke Order and Number
SG-1411 潔	pure, clean, brave, manly	いさぎよ-い ケツ	isagiyo-i *ketsu*	水	氵 汁 洼 洼刀 㓞 潔 潔 潔 15

潔 **C** F-1504 — 說文 — The seal-style form comprised "flowing water" (氵), and 絜, used for the sound *ketsu* to mean "to purify," together signifying "to purify with water." It was also used to describe a person's manner: "brave, graceful, manly." The kanji 潔 means "pure, clean, brave, manly." <氵㓞糸>

潔い brave, manly [いさぎよい]; 清潔な clean, immaculate [せいけつな]; 不潔な unsanitary [ふけつな]; 潔白な innocent, guiltless [けっぱくな]; 潔癖な fastidiously clean, scrupulously honest [けっぺきな]; 純潔 virginity, purity [じゅんけつ]

	Meanings	Kun and On	Romaji	Bushu	Stroke Order and Number
SG-1412 喫	to chew, eat, drink, smoke	キツ	*kitsu*	口	口 吋 吽 吽刀 喫 喫 喫 喫 12

喫 **C** F-1595 — 說文 — The seal-style form comprised 口 "a mouth," and 契, which was used for the sound *kitsu*, meaning "to chisel." The motion of chiseling a piece of wood with a knife was applied to a person chewing or taking something into the mouth. The kanji 喫 means "to chew, eat, drink, smoke." <口契>

喫茶店 café, tea house [きっさてん, きっさてん]; 喫煙所 smoking area [きつえんじょ]; 満喫する to eat and drink plentifully [まんきつする]

65e 召 "to call for"; *shoo* 召昭照招沼紹詔

	Meanings	Kun and On	Romaji	Bushu	Stroke Order and Number
SG-1413 召	to call for, summon, send for, wear/eat/drink (honorific)	めーす ショウ	me-su *shoo*	口	フ刀刀召召 5

召 **A** F-1480

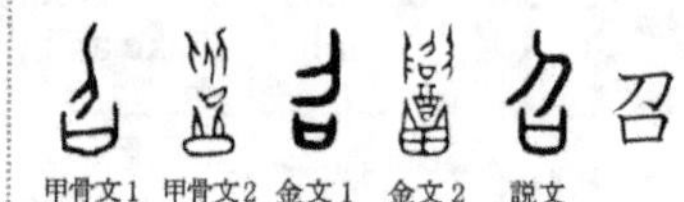

甲骨文1 1, 甲骨文2 2, 金文1 3, 金文2 4, 説文 5

1, 3, and 5 comprised 刀 **SG-1934**, used for the sound *shoo*, and 口 **SG-0031** "a mouth," together signifying "to call for, send for, summon." Another view takes additional forms (2 and 4) into account, and regards the top component as "a divine spirit descending" in answer to "prayers in a box" (口), thus giving the meaning "to call for, summon." Yet another view takes 召 to have been the name of a particular place. The kanji 召 is used for a superior sending for a servant and connotes authority. The kanji 召 means "to call, summon, send for." It is also used as a catch-all honorific form of the verbs "to wear (clothes), eat, or drink," used for one's superior. <刀口>

召す to call for [めす]; お召しになる to send for, wear clothes (honorific) [おめしになる]; 召し上がる to eat, drink (honorific) [めしあがる]; お召し物 (your) clothes (polite) [おめしもの]; 国会の召集 call for a Diet session [こっかいのしょうしゅう]; 召集令 draft notice, call to military service [しょうしゅうれい]

	Meanings	Kun and On	Romaji	Bushu	Stroke Order and Number
SG-1414 昭	bright; Showa Era	ショウ	*shoo*	日	日日日フ日刀昭昭 9

昭 **A** F-0425

金文1 1, 金文2 2, 説文 3

1 and 2 comprised 召, used for the sound *shoo* to mean "bright," and "a person." 日 "the sun" was added to the right side in 2. It moved to the left side of 召 in 3, doubling the meaning of "bright." The kanji 昭 is used for the Showa Era 昭和 (1926–1989) and other proper names. <日召>

Showa Era (1926 – 1989) [しょうわ, しょうわ]

	Meanings	Kun and On	Romaji	Bushu	Stroke Order and Number
SG-1415 照	to shine, illuminate, compare with, check	てーる ショウ	te-ru *shoo*	火	日日日フ日刀昭昭照 13

照 **B** F-0885

説文

The seal-style form comprised 日 "the sun," for "daylight," 火 "a fire" for "night-time illumination," and 召, used for the sound *shoo*. Together they meant "bright; to shine," similar to 昭 **SG-1414**. In the kanji, "fire" became 灬, bushu *renga/rekka*. The kanji 照 means "to shine, illuminate, compare, check." <昭 灬>

照らす to shine [てらす]; 照らし合わす to cross-check [てらしあわす]; 日照り dry weather, drought [ひでり]; 照明 illumination [しょうめい]; 照会状 letter of reference [しょうかいじょう]; 対照させる to contrast one with another [たいしょうさせる]; 照り返し reflected light or heat [てりかえし]

	Meanings	Kun and On	Romaji	Bushu	Stroke Order and Number
SG-1416 招	to invite, beckon	まねーく ショウ	mane-ku *shoo*	手	一扌打扨招招 8

招 **B** F-0935

説文

The seal-style form comprised 扌, bushu *tehen* "an act done by hand," and 召, used for the sound *shoo* to mean "to call for." Together they signified "a hand beckoning someone." The kanji 招 means "to invite, beckon." <扌召>

招く to invite [まねく]; 手招きする to beckon [てまねきする]; 招かれざる客 uninvited guest [まねかれざる・きゃく]; 招待する to invite [しょうたいする]; 招聘 courteous invitation [しょうへい]

	Meanings	Kun and On	Romaji	Bushu	Stroke Order and Number
SG-1417 沼	marsh	ぬま ショウ	numa *shoo*	水	氵汀沢沢沼沼 8

沼 **B** F-1066

説文

The seal-style form comprised "flowing water" (氵), and 召, used for the sound *shoo* to mean "little," together signifying a small, naturally-formed pool of water. The kanji 沼 means "marsh." <氵召>

沼 marsh [ぬま]; 泥沼化 turning into a quagmire, becoming a mess [どろぬまか]; 沼地 bogland, marshland [ぬまち]

	Meanings	Kun and On	Romaji	Bushu	Stroke Order and Number
SG-1418 紹	to connect people, introduce	ショウ	*shoo*	糸	幺糸紀紹紹紹 11

紹 **C** F-1379

紹 金文1 1 金文2 2 説文 3

1 is difficult to decipher, but the bottom appears to be "twisted threads, connection," as in the left side of 3 (糸). 2 comprised イ "a person," 召 for the sound *shoo* to mean "to call for, invite," and 攴 "to cause an action." Taking into account the components of each of these forms, the character seems to signify "to connect people," i.e., "to introduce." The kanji comprises only 糸 and 召, and means "to connect people, introduce." <糸召>

紹介する to introduce [しょうかいする]; 紹介状 letter of introduction [しょうかいじょう]; 自己紹介 self-introduction [じこしょうかい]

	Meanings	Kun and On	Romaji	Bushu	Stroke Order and Number
SG-1419 詔	imperial edict	みことのり ショウ	mikotonori *shoo*	言	言訂訒訒詔詔 12

詔 **D** F-2217

詔 金文 1 説文 2

1 comprised 言, bushu *gonben* "word; to speak," and 召 "(a superior) calling for," which was used for the sound *shoo*. Together they signified "words spoken by a superior, such as an emperor." The kanji 詔 means "imperial edict." <言召>

詔 imperial edict [みことのり]; 詔書 imperial edict [しょうしょ]

65f 刃 "blade" [from a knife with a shining blade] 認刃忍

	Meanings	Kun and On	Romaji	Bushu	Stroke Order and Number
SG-1420 認	to notice, recognize, accept, permit	みと-める ニン	mito-meru *nin*	言	言訂訒訒認認 14

認 **A** F-0385

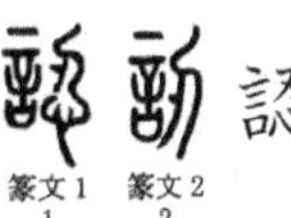

認 篆文1 1 篆文2 2

1 comprised 言, bushu *gonben* "word; to speak" on the left side, with the right side comprising 刃 "blade," used for the sound *nin*, and 心 "a heart," together meaning "a tenacious heart" (忍 SG-1422). Together they meant "listening patiently to what another person has to say and accepting it." "Heart" was absent in 2. The kanji 認 means "to notice, recognize, accept, permit." <言刃心>

認める to recognize [みとめる]; 認識する to recognize [にんしきする]; 認定 certification [にんてい]; 確認する to confirm [かくにんする]; 否認する to deny [ひにんする]; 認可する to grant permission [にゅんかする, にんかする]; 容認する to tolerate, accept [ようにんする]; 認知症 cognitive impairment, dementia [にんちしょう]

	Meanings	Kun and On	Romaji	Bushu	Stroke Order and Number
SG-1421 刃	blade, cutting edge	は ジン	ha *jin*	刀	フ刀刃 3

刃 **C** F-1300

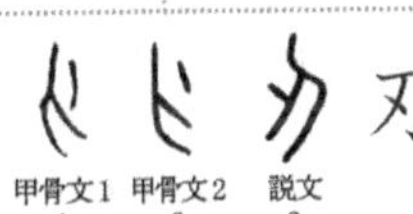

刃 甲骨文1 1 甲骨文2 2 説文 3

1 and 2 in oracle bone style depicted "a knife or sword" with a flash of light reflecting off its sharp blade at the top by a short stroke. In 3 in seal style, the short stroke that indicates the flash was attached to the lower left, which suggested that the blade was at the bottom and the top was a handle. The kanji 刃 means "blade, cutting edge." <刀丶>

刃 blade, cutting edge [は]; 刃物 edged tool [はもの]; 刃向かう to raise a hand against, defy [はむかう]; 付け焼き刃 affectation, borrowed wisdom [つけやきば]

	Meanings	Kun and On	Romaji	Bushu	Stroke Order and Number
SG-1422 忍	patience; to endure, brave out	しの-ぶ ニン	shino-bu *nin*	心	フ刀刃忍忍 7

忍 **C** F-1303

忍 中山王器 1 説文 2

1 and 2 comprised 刃 "a knife with a sharp blade," used for the sound *jin* to mean "strong and resistant," and 心 "heart." Together they signified "a strong and tenacious heart; to endure." The kanji 忍 means "patience; to endure, brave out." <刃心>

忍ぶ to endure [しのぶ, しのぶ]; 忍び込む to creep in [しのびこむ]; 忍び難い unbearable, insufferable [しのびがたい]; 忍耐 patience [にんたい]; 忍者 ninja, secret agent [にんじゃ]; 堪忍袋の緒が切れる one's patience comes to the breaking point [かんにんぶくろの・おがきれる]

66 Surgical knife

66a 俞 (兪) "to cure, move to somewhere else" [from a tray that contains a lesion removed by a surgical knife]; *yu* 輸諭愉癒喩

SG-1423 輸	Meanings	Kun and On	Romaji	Bushu	Stroke Order and Number
	to move something, transport	ユ	*yu*	車	戸亘車軟軡輸輸輸 16

輸 B F-0784

説文

The seal-style form comprised 車 **SG-1578** "vehicle," and 兪(俞), used for the sound *yu* to mean "to take something to another place." Taken together, a vehicle taking something to somewhere else means "to transport." The kanji 輸 means "to move something, transport." <車俞(𠆢一月刂)>

輸出 export [ゆしゅつ]; 輸入 import [ゆにゅう]; 輸送 transportation [ゆそう]; 運輸 transportation, conveyance [うんゆ, うˀんゆ]; 空輸 air transport [くうゆ]; 輸血 blood transfusion [ゆけつ]

SG-1424 諭	Meanings	Kun and On	Romaji	Bushu	Stroke Order and Number
	to admonish, counsel, advise, discourage	さと-す ユ	sato-su *yu*	言	言訡諭諭諭諭 16

諭 C F-1426

説文

The seal-style form comprised 言, bushu *gonben* "word; to speak," and 兪 (俞), "a removed lesion," used for the sound *yu*. Together they meant "to admonish someone for an error, discourage someone from behaving in an unacceptable manner," as if one were "removing" a bad behavior (like "a lesion") by talking. The kanji 諭 means "to admonish, counsel, advise, discourage. <言俞>

諭す to admonish someone for an error, advise [さとˀす]; 教諭 teacher at an elementary or high school [きょうゆ]

SG-1425 愉	Meanings	Kun and On	Romaji	Bushu	Stroke Order and Number
	pleasure; delightful, cheery	ユ	*yu*	心	丶忄忄忄愉愉愉 12

愉 D F-1984

金文 1 説文 2

1 comprised "a tray or vessel," "a surgical knife," and "a lesion." Removing a lesion with a surgical knife and moving it to a tray to be taken away (兪/俞, used for the sound *yu*) signified "removing pain." In 2, "heart/mind" (忄, bushu *risshinben*) was added. Removing the source of concern in the heart and placing it at a distance signified "pleasure; a feeling without antagonism or begrudgement." The kanji 愉 means "pleasure; delightful, cheery." <忄俞>

愉快 pleasant, delightful, cheerful [ゆˀかい]; 不愉快な unpleasant, disagreeable [ふゆˀかいな]

SG-1426 癒	Meanings	Kun and On	Romaji	Bushu	Stroke Order and Number
	to cure, heal	い-える ユ	i-eru *yu*	疒	亠广疒疒疥疹瘉癒 18

癒 D F-1997

篆文

The seal-style form had "a bed with a sick person lying on it," (which became 疒, bushu *yamaidare* "illness"), and 兪 (俞), used for the sound *yu* to mean "to remove a lesion to a tray." Together they signified "a sick person who was healed by having a lesion removed with a surgical knife," or just "to heal." In the kanji, "heart/mind" (心 **SG-0187**) was added at the bottom. The kanji 癒 meant "to cure, heal." <疒俞心>

癒やす to cure, heal [いやˀす]; 癒やされる therapeutic, healing [いやされˀる]; 治癒 healing, recovery [ちˀゆ]; 癒着する to heal (close) up, be tied in collusion [ゆちゃくする]

SG-1427 喩	Meanings	Kun and On	Romaji	Bushu	Stroke Order and Number
	metaphor, example	ユ	*yu*	口	口口𠆢口𠆢吟喩喩 12

喩 D F-2528

No ancient form. The kanji 喩 comprises 口 **SG-0031** "to speak," and 兪 "to move to somewhere else," which was used for the sound *yu*. A transfer of meaning from one thing to another by using words was a "metaphor." The kanji 喩 means "metaphor, example." <口兪>

比喩 metaphor [ひˀゆ] // 喩え example, metaphor [たとˀえ]

66b 宰 "to take charge" 宰 㝉

SG-1428 宰	Meanings	Kun and On	Romaji	Bushu	Stroke Order and Number
	to take charge, manage	サイ	*sai*	宀	… 宰 10

宰 **D** F-1844

甲骨文1 (1) 甲骨文2 (2) 金文 (3) 説文 (4) 宰

In 1, 2, and 3, inside "an ancestral mausoleum or house" (宀) was "a curved knife used for carving sacrificial animal meat." Such a rite would be presided over or "managed" by the chief retainer. Though the inside component eventually became "a tattooing needle with a handle" (辛 **SG-1359**), the earlier forms depicted it as a curved knife. The kanji 宰 means "to take charge, manage." <宀辛>

主宰 chair, leader [しゅさい]; 宰相 prime minister [さいしょう]

66c 辟 [originally from "using a surgical knife (辛), to sever the flesh (口) of a crouching criminal (尸) in punishment"]; *heki* 壁避癖璧

SG-1429 壁	Meanings	Kun and On	Romaji	Bushu	Stroke Order and Number
	wall, partition, barrier	かべ ヘキ	kabe *heki*	土	… 壁 16

壁 **B** F-1018

説文 壁

The seal-style form comprised 辟, used for the sound *heki,* and 土 "dirt," together signifying "a dirt wall." The kanji 壁 means "wall, partition, barrier." <尸口辛土>

壁 wall, partition, barrier [かべ]; 土壁 dirt wall [つちかべ]; 壁越しに聞く to hear through a wall, overhear [かべごしにきく]; 防火壁 firewall [ぼうか⌝へき]; 壁画 wall painting, mural, fresco [へきが]; 岸壁 wharf, quay [がんぺき]; 絶壁 sheer cliff [ぜっぺき]

SG-1430 避	Meanings	Kun and On	Romaji	Bushu	Stroke Order and Number
	to avoid, dodge, evade	さ-ける ヒ	sa-keru *hi*	辵	… 避 16

避 **C** F-1122

説文 避

The seal-style form comprised 辵 (辶, bushu *shinnyuu*) "to move forward," and 辟, which was used for the sound *hi* to mean "to avoid." Together, they signified "to step aside on the road." The kanji 避 means "to avoid, dodge, evade." <辟辶>

避ける to avoid, evade [さけ⌝る]; 回避 evasion, circumvention [か⌝いひ・かいひ]; 退避場所 evacuation shelter [たいひばしょ]; 逃避する to escape, flee, withdraw [とうひする]; 避暑地 summer resort [ひしょ⌝ち]; 不可避な inevitable [ふか⌝ひな]; 避妊薬 contraceptive pill [ひに⌝んやく]; 避難所 place of safety, shelter [ひなんじょ]

SG-1431 癖	Meanings	Kun and On	Romaji	Bushu	Stroke Order and Number
	personal habit, peculiar way	くせ ヘキ	kuse *heki*	疒	… 癖 18

癖 **D** F-1831

No ancient form. The kanji 癖 comprised 疒, bushu *yamaidare* "illness; sick," and 辟, used for the sound *heki* to mean "to lean to one side." Together they signified "a peculiar tendency in one's behavior, mannerism." The kanji 癖 means "personal habit, peculiar way." <疒辟>

一癖ある to have odd quirks [ひと⌝くせ・あ⌝る]; 口癖 pet phrase, verbal tic [くちぐせ]; 酒癖が悪い quarrelsome or unpleasant when drinking [さけぐせがわる⌝い]; 無くて七癖 "Every man has his eccentricities." [な⌝くて・なな⌝くせ]; 習癖 habit [しゅうへき]; 性癖 one's natural disposition, inclination [しょうへき]; 悪癖 bad habit, vice [あくへき]

SG-1432 璧	Meanings	Kun and On	Romaji	Bushu	Stroke Order and Number
	beautiful jewel	ヘキ	*heki*	玉	… 璧 18

璧 **D** F-2702

金文1 (1) 金文2 (2) 説文 (3) 璧

1, 2, and 3 comprised 辟, used for the sound *heki*, and "jewel" (玉 **SG-1730**). In 2 and 3 a circle or other additional shape are seen, which indicated a round-shaped jewel that had a hole in the middle, a particular style of jewel worn as a ceremonial accessory. The kanji 璧 means "beautiful jewel." <辟玉>

完璧な perfect, flawless, impeccable [かんぺきな]; 双璧 the two greatest authorities [そうへき]

67 Small knife

67a 氏 "clan" [from a small carving knife or a flat spoon for a clan feast]; *shi* 氏紙婚

	Meanings	*Kun* and *On*	Romaji	Bushu	Stroke Order and Number
SG-1433 氏	lineage, family, clan, surname, Mr. or Ms.	うじ シ	uji *shi*	氏	氏 4

氏 **A** F-0092

甲骨文 1, 金文1 2, 金文2 3, 金文3 4, 説文 5

One view explains that the ancient form depicted "a small knife for carving meat" at a clan feast, and it meant "clan." Another view holds that it was "a flat spoon or ladle," and was borrowed to mean "clan." It is also used as an honorific suffix added to the surname of a male person (and more recently a female person as well). The kanji 氏 means "lineage, family, clan, surname, Mr. or Ms." <氏>

氏子 parishioner of a Shinto shrine [うじこ]; 氏神 guardian deity [うじがみ, うじがみ]; 氏より育ち "nurture over nature" [うじよりそだち]; 氏名 full name [しめい]; 両氏 both men, both persons [りょうし]; 山中氏 Mr. Yamanaka [やまなかし]

	Meanings	*Kun* and *On*	Romaji	Bushu	Stroke Order and Number
SG-1434 紙	paper	かみ シ	kami *shi*	糸	紙 10

紙 **A** F-0312

説文

The seal-style form comprised 糸 "a skein of threads," for "fiber," and 氏, used for the sound *shi* to mean "flat, thin." Pressed pulp or fiber that was made very thin was "paper." The kanji 紙 means "paper." <糸氏>

紙 paper [かみ]; 絵手紙 a plain postcard with an illustration and a few lines [えてがみ]; 紙挟み paperclip [かみばさみ]; 五線紙 score paper [ごせんし]; 印紙 revenue stamp [いんし]; 懐紙 folded paper kept inside one's kimono collar [かいし]; 画用紙 art paper [がようし]; 和紙 Japanese rice paper [わし]

	Meanings	*Kun* and *On*	Romaji	Bushu	Stroke Order and Number
SG-1435 婚	wedding, marriage	コン	*kon*	女	婚 11

婚 **B** F-1003

金文1 1, 金文2 2, 説文 3

1 and 2 comprised "a wine pitcher" (called a *shaku*) at the top, "a hand" in the middle, and "a woman" at the bottom. Together they signified a wedding, when a bride was taken into a new family. 3 comprised 女 **SG-0521** "woman," and 昏 "dusk," used for the sound *kon*. A wedding took place at dusk. The kanji 婚 means "wedding, marriage." <女氏日>

求婚 marriage proposal [きゅうこん]; 結婚 marriage [けっこん]; 婚約 engagement, betrothal [こんやく]; 再婚 second marriage [さいこん]; 婚礼 wedding [こんれい]; 婚家 family into which a woman marries [こんか]; 未婚 unmarried [みこん]

67b-(1) 旨 "tasty"; *shi* 指旨脂

	Meanings	*Kun* and *On*	Romaji	Bushu	Stroke Order and Number
SG-1436 指	finger; to point at	ゆび・さ-す シ	yubi, sa-su *shi*	手	指 9

指 **A** F-0165

説文

The seal-style form comprised 扌, bushu *tehen* "an act done by hand," and 旨 **SG-1437** "tasty," used for the sound *shi*. One ate tasty food with one's fingers. The kanji 指 means "finger; to point at" <扌旨(匕日)>

指 finger [ゆび]; 指輪 ring [ゆびわ]; 親指 thumb [おやゆび]; 薬指 third finger [くすりゆび]; 小指 little finger, fifth toe [こゆび]; 人差し指 forefinger, index finger [ひとさしゆび]; 後ろ指を指される to be talked about behind one's back [うしろゆびをさされる]; 目指す to aim at, have something in one's view [めざす]; 指数関数的 exponential [しすうかんすうてき]

	Meanings	*Kun* and *On*	Romaji	Bushu	Stroke Order and Number
SG-1437 旨	tasty; principal aim, purport	むね シ	mune *shi*	日	旨 6

旨 **C** F-1378

甲骨文1 1, 甲骨文2 2, 金文1 3, 金文2 4, 説文 5

One view holds that the various forms of 旨 comprised "a meat carving knife" and "a box with meat inside," together signifying "tasty." Another view holds that it comprised "a spoon or ladle" and "a mouth with food inside," together signifying "tasty." In the latter view, 匕 was a variant of the non-Joyo kanji 匙 "spoon, ladle." In Japanese, it also means "principal aim, purport." The kanji 旨 means "tasty; principal aim, purport." <匕日>

旨 effect, principal aim [むね]; 趣旨 point, gist, drift [しゅし]; 要旨 gist, main points, substance [ようし]; 論旨 tenor of an argument [ろんし]; 宗旨変え religious conversion [しゅうしがえ] // 旨い tasty, delicious [うまい]

	Meanings	Kun and On	Romaji	Bushu	Stroke Order and Number
SG-1438 脂	fat, resin	あぶら シ	abura *shi*	肉	10

脂 **C** F-1460

説文

The seal-style form comprised 月 "meat," and 旨 **SG-1437** "tasty," which was used for the sound *shi.* Plump, fatty meat tasted good. The character also applied to the sticky substance that exuded from tree bark—"resin." The kanji 脂 means "fat, resin." <月 旨>

脂身 fatty meat [あぶらみ]; 脂っこい greasy, fatty, oily [あぶらっこい]; 脂が乗る to get into the swing of one's work, fatty (fish) [あぶらがのる]; 牛脂 beef suet [ぎゅうし]; 脱脂綿 absorbent cotton [だっしめん]; 樹脂 resin [じゅし] // 松脂 (松ヤニ) pine resin [まつやに]

67b-(2) 旨 "to make a profound bow"; *kee* 詣稽

	Meanings	Kun and On	Romaji	Bushu	Stroke Order and Number
SG-1439 詣	to pay a visit to a shrine or temple	もう-でる ケイ	moo-deru *kee*	言	13

詣 **D** F-2125

説文

The seal-style form comprised 言, bushu *gonben* "word; to speak," and 旨 **SG-1437** "a spirit of a deity over a prayer box," used for the sound *kee* to mean "to bow deeply." The kanji 詣 means "to pay a visit to a shrine or temple." <言 旨>

詣出る to visit a temple [もうでる]; 初詣で New Year's visit to a shrine or temple [はつもうで]; 参詣 visit to a temple, worship [さんけい]; 造詣が深い to have a profound knowledge [ぞうけいがふかい]

	Meanings	Kun and On	Romaji	Bushu	Stroke Order and Number
SG-1440 稽	to think, stop and stay, compare	ケイ	*kee*	禾	15

稽 **D** F-2301

金文 1 (1), 金文 2 (2), 金文 3 (3), 説文 (4)

The origin of this kanji is odd. One view of 1, 2, and 3 takes it to comprise "the spirit of a deity lingering above a prayer box," used for the sound *kee,* and "a person bowing." Together they signified "to stay, think (about the deity's will), bow deeply." Another view takes the right side in 4 to be 耆 "to age; tasty well-aged food, a long time," used for the sound *ki.* Together with "grain" (禾), the form signified "grain stored for a long time." Later, by association with another phonetically-similar kanji 計 (*kee*) "to take measure of, assess," the character came to mean "to think over or compare (many things), assess." The kanji 稽 means "to think, stay, compare." <禾尤匕日>. (Author's note: This is one of those kanji whose origin remains too mysterious to be of much practical help for kanji learning. It is sufficient to recognize the kanji, know that it has the sound *kee*, and associate it with a few words.)

滑稽な funny, comical, humorous, hilarious, silly, ridiculous [こっけいな]; 稽古 practice, training (by repeatedly performing old ways) [けいこ]; 稽古事 personal accomplishments, enrichment lessons [けいこごと]; 荒唐無稽な nonsensical, absurd, fantastic (from being incoherent and having no basis) [こうとうむけいな]

67c 氐 "low; bottom" [from a knife shaving the bottom of something]; *tee* 低底邸抵

	Meanings	Kun and On	Romaji	Bushu	Stroke Order and Number
SG-1441 低	low, short (in height)	ひく-い テイ	hiku-i *tee*	人	7

低 **A** F-0456

説文

The seal-style form comprised 亻, bushu *ninben* "a person," and 氐 "a knife shaving the bottom of something," used for the sound *tee*. Together they signified "a person of short stature." Another view takes the bottom line as indicating the bottom of a hill, to signify "low." The kanji 低 means "low, short (in height)." <亻氐 (氏一)>

低い low [ひくい]; 低め on the low side [ひくめ]; 高低 up and down [こうてい]; 低下する to fall off, drop, decline [ていかする]; 低学年 lower classes in elementary school (first through third grades) [ていがくねん]; 平身低頭する to go down on one's knees, apologize abjectly [へいしんていとうする]

	Meanings	Kun and On	Romaji	Bushu	Stroke Order and Number
SG-1442 底	bottom, base	そこ テイ	soko *tee*	广	8

底 **B** F-0768

甲骨文 1, 篆文 2, 説文 3

1, 2, and 3 comprised 广 "eaves of a house," and "a knife" with a line underneath (氐), used for the sound *tee* to mean "a flat area." Shaving or leveling the ground flat with a knife signified "bottom." The kanji 底 means "bottom, base." <广氐>

底 bottom, base [そこ]; 奥底 one's heart of hearts [おくそこ]; 靴底 sole of a shoe [くつぞこ]; 川底 riverbed [かわぞこ]; 底入れする to reach rock bottom [そこいれする]; どん底 rock bottom, the very bottom [どんぞこ]; 不徹底な not thorough, halfway, inconsistent [ふてっていな]; 底辺 base, lower class [ていへん]; 海底 sea floor [かいてい]

	Meanings	Kun and On	Romaji	Bushu	Stroke Order and Number
SG-1443 邸	mansion, large residence	テイ	*tee*	邑	𠂆 𠂇 氏 氐 氐ㄱ 氐ʒ 邸 8

邸 **C** F-1255

説文

The seal-style form comprised 氐 "a flat area," used for the sound *tee*, and 邑 (阝, bushu *oozato* "a town where many people gather"). Together they signified "a large house in the capital where a local lord and his entourage stayed." The kanji 邸 means "mansion, large residence." <氐阝>

公邸 official residence [こうてい]; 豪邸 magnificent house [ごうてい]; 私邸 private residence [してい]; 邸宅 residence, mansion [ていたく]; 首相官邸 official residence of the prime minister [しゅしょうかんてい]

	Meanings	Kun and On	Romaji	Bushu	Stroke Order and Number
SG-1444 抵	to resist, hit against	テイ	*tee*	手	一 丁 扌 扩 扺 抵 抵 8

抵 **C** F-1331

説文

The seal-style form comprised 扌 "an act done by hand," and 氐, used for *tee* to mean "to resist; push against the bottom." Together they signified "to push until meeting resistance; hit the bottom." The kanji 抵 means "to resist, hit against." <扌氐>

大抵 greater part, nearly all, for the most part [たいてい]; 抵抗する to resist, stand against [ていこうする]; 抵当 mortgage [ていとう]; 抵触する conflict, infringement [ていしょくする]; 並大抵の ordinary, average [なみたいていの]

67d 舌 *katsu* 活括

	Meanings	Kun and On	Romaji	Bushu	Stroke Order and Number
SG-1445 活	liveliness, life, activity	カツ	*katsu*	水	氵 氵 氵 汗 汗 活 活 9

活 **A** F-0327

篆文 1 篆文 2

1 2

1 and 2 comprised "flowing water" (氵), and 𠯑, used for the sound *katsu* to mean "lively." In 2, "an ear" was added in the center to emphasize the "lively" sound of the gushing water. In the kanji, the shape 舌 was used, (with no relation to the kanji 舌 "tongue"). The kanji 活 means "liveliness, life, activity." < 氵舌 >

活字 piece of printing type [かつじ]; 生活 life [せいかつ]; 活路 means of surviving, way out [かつろ]; 活用する to apply, utilize [かつようする]; 活火山 active volcano [かっかざん]; 活気のある lively [かっきのある]; 活力 vital power, energy [かつりょく]; 活性化 activation [かっせいか] // 活きのいい fresh, lively [いきのいい]

	Meanings	Kun and On	Romaji	Bushu	Stroke Order and Number
SG-1446 括	to tie, truss, strap	カツ	*katsu*	手	一 丁 扌 扌 扦 括 9

括 **C** F-1508

説文

The seal-style form comprised 扌 "an act done by hand," and 𠯑, used for the sound *katsu* to mean "to truss." Together they signified "a hand tying things." In the kanji the shape 舌 was adopted for the right side, with no relation to the kanji 舌 "tongue." The kanji 括 means "to tie, truss, strap." <扌舌>

一括する to bundle up, put all together [いっかつする]; 括弧 parentheses, brackets [かっこ]; 包括する to include, comprehend, taken in [ほうかつする]; 包括案 package plan [ほうかつあん] //括る to bind up, tie with a cord [くくる]

68 Ax

68a 王 "king" [from a large, ornate ax belonging to a king, symbolizing power]; *oo* 王皇往旺

	Meanings	Kun and On	Romaji	Bushu	Stroke Order and Number
SG-1447 王	king, monarch, magnate	オウ	*oo*	玉	一 丅 干 王 4

王 **A** F-0349

甲骨文1 甲骨文2 金文1 金文2 説文

1 2 3 4 5

1 depicted "a king's large ornate ax that placed with the blade side down." 3 emphasized the large blade. In 2, 3, 4, and 5 the middle horizontal line was placed closer to the top line to mark the ornate part of the ax that symbolized power, but in the kanji the three horizontal lines became evenly spaced. The kanji 王 means "king, monarch, magnate." <王>

王 king [おう]; 国王 king [こくおう]; 王国 kingdom [おうこく]; 王者 king, champion [おうじゃ]; ローマ法王 the Pope [ローマほうおう]; 王権 regal power [おうけん]; 王様 king [おうさま]; 王子 prince [おうじ] // 親王 imperial prince [しんのう]

	Meanings	Kun and On	Romaji	Bushu	Stroke Order and Number
SG-1448 皇	imperial, great	コウ・オウ	*koo, oo*	白	皇 9

皇 **B** F-0888

金文1 1 金文2 2 金文3 3 説文 4

1, 2, and 3 depicted a king's ornate ax (oriented horizontally) that had brilliantly-sparkling crown jewels at the top. The character meant "a king; imperial." In 4, the ornate part of the ax became separated and was construed as 自, but in the shinji it changed to 白. The kanji 皇 means "imperial, great." <白王>

皇室 royal family, imperial family [こうしつ]; 皇太子 crown prince [こうたいし]; 皇族 members of the royal family [こうぞく]; 上皇 ex-emperor, emperor emeritus [じょうこう] // 天皇 Japanese emperor [てんのう]

	Meanings	Kun and On	Romaji	Bushu	Stroke Order and Number
SG-1449 往	to advance, go; past	オウ	*oo*	彳	往 8

往 **C** F-1203

甲骨文1 1 甲骨文2 2 説文古文 3 説文 4

1 and 2 depicted "a footprint" on top of "a king's ax" (王), used for the sound *oo*, together signifying "to advance, go over." In 3 and 4, "a stretched crossroads" (and an additional "footprint" in 3) was added to mean "to move forward." Another view explains that the right side of 3 and 4 comprised "a plant that keeps growing," and that 王 was used for the sound *oo* to mean "to spread." In this view, rapidly spreading plants and "to walk" led to the meaning "to keep on walking ahead," and moving on at a good pace led to the meaning "already gone by" or "the past." With a small dot replacing the top of the right-side component, the kanji 往 means "to advance, go; past." <彳主>

往復 roundtrip, going and coming back [おうふく]; 往来 traffic, street [おうらい]; 往年 years gone by, the past [おうねん]; 往々にして more often than not, frequently [おうおうにして]; 往路 outward journey [おうろ]; 既往症 previous or pre-existing illness, medical history [きおうしょう]

	Meanings	Kun and On	Romaji	Bushu	Stroke Order and Number
SG-1450 旺	vigorous, thriving	オウ	*oo*	日	旺 8

旺 **D** F-2409

説文

The seal-style form comprised 日 "the sun," for "bright light," and 往 **SG-1449**, used for the sound *oo* to mean "to stretch out, spread." A shining light that spread led to the meaning "vigorous, thriving." In the kanji, the crossroads was dropped. The kanji 旺 means "vigorous, thriving." <日王>

旺盛な thriving [おうせいな]; 食欲旺盛な having good appetite [しょくよく・おうせいな]

68b 士 "warrior, man" [from a warrior's battle ax]; *shi* 士仕

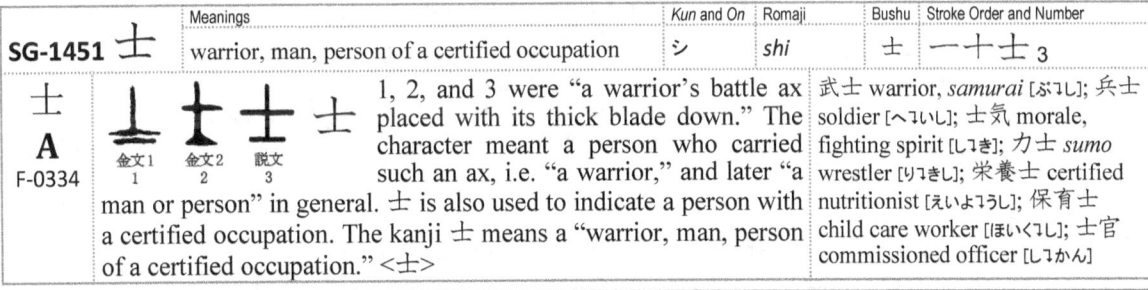

	Meanings	Kun and On	Romaji	Bushu	Stroke Order and Number
SG-1451 士	warrior, man, person of a certified occupation	シ	*shi*	士	一十士 3

士 **A** F-0334

金文1 1 金文2 2 説文 3

1, 2, and 3 were "a warrior's battle ax placed with its thick blade down." The character meant a person who carried such an ax, i.e. "a warrior," and later "a man or person" in general. 士 is also used to indicate a person with a certified occupation. The kanji 士 means a "warrior, man, person of a certified occupation." <士>

武士 warrior, *samurai* [ぶし]; 兵士 soldier [へいし]; 士気 morale, fighting spirit [しき]; 力士 *sumo* wrestler [りきし]; 栄養士 certified nutritionist [えいようし]; 保育士 child care worker [ほいくし]; 士官 commissioned officer [しかん]

	Meanings	Kun and On	Romaji	Bushu	Stroke Order and Number
SG-1452 仕	to serve, do	つか-える シ・ジ	tsuka-eru *shi; ji*	人	ノイ仁什仕 5

仕 **A** F-0380

金文1 1 金文2 2 説文 3

1 was "a warrior's battle ax" (士). In 2, イ "a standing person" was added, and together they signified "a person with an ax serving his master." In 3, "person" moved to the left side, becoming bushu *ninben* "an act that one does." In Japanese, the character also means "to do." The kanji 仕 means "to serve, do." <イ士>

仕える to serve, be in personal service, work under [つかえる, つかえる]; 仕事 work, job [しごと]; 仕分ける to classify, sort out [しわける]; 奉仕活動 volunteer service [ほうしかつどう]; 仕方 way of doing [しかた]; 仕方がない cannot be helped [しかたがない]; 仕上げる to finish, get into shape [しあげる]; 仕様書き instructions for use [しようがき]; 給仕 table service, waitstaff [きゅうじ]

68c 斤 "a hand ax" 斤近新兵質断折哲祈析誓匠逝薪斬暫漸

SG-1453 斤	Meanings	Kun and On	Romaji	Bushu	Stroke Order and Number
	ax, unit of weight	キン	*kin*	斤	㇒ 厂 斤 斤 4

斤 **A** F-2441

甲骨文 1 金文 2 説文 3

1, 2, and 3 depicted "a hand ax." An ax was a heavy piece of metal, and was also used as a weight. Today 斤 is a *kin*, an old unit of weight (approximately 600 grams), now used in Japan only as the standard weight of a square loaf of bread (340g or more of flour per *kin*). <斤>

一斤 one *kin* [いっきん]; 食パン一斤 one square loaf of bread [しょくパンいっきん]

SG-1454 近	Meanings	Kun and On	Romaji	Bushu	Stroke Order and Number
	near, recent, close	ちか-い キン	chika-i *kin, kon*	辵	㇒ 厂 斤 斤 斤 近 近 7

近 **A** F-0159

説文古文 1 説文 2

1 comprised "a footprint," and "a hand ax" (斤), used for the sound *kin* to mean "little; a small amount." 2 comprised 辵 (⻌ "to move forward") and 斤. Going a small distance signified "close, near (in distance or time)." The kanji 近 means "near, recent, close." <斤⻌>

近い near, close [ちかい]; 近々 before long, shortly [ちかぢか]; 間近に approaching, impending [まぢかに・まぢかに]; 身近な familiar, at one's side [みぢかな]; 近所 neighborhood [きんじょ]; 遠近感 depth of vision [えんきんかん]; 近代 modern era [きんだい]; 近日中 soon, at an early date [きんじつちゅう]

SG-1455 新	Meanings	Kun and On	Romaji	Bushu	Stroke Order and Number
	new, fresh	あたら-しい・あら-た・にい シン	atara-shii, ara-ta, nii *shin*	斤	亠 立 辛 亲 新 新 新 13

新 **A** F-0043

甲骨文1 1 甲骨文2 2 金文1 3 金文2 4 説文 5

1 through 3 comprised "a large tattooing needle" (辛 SG-1359) and "a hand ax" (斤), together signifying "to cut." In 4 and 5, 木 "tree" was added. Making a new cut on a tree with an ax signified "fresh (cut)." The kanji 新 means "new, fresh." <立木斤>

新しい new [あたらしい]; 新たに newly [あらたに]; 新聞 newspaper [しんぶん]; 新妻 newly-married wife [にいづま]; 新旧 new and old [しんきゅう]; 一新する to renew, reform, refresh [いっしんする]; 新車 new car [しんしゃ]

SG-1456 兵	Meanings	Kun and On	Romaji	Bushu	Stroke Order and Number
	soldier	ヘイ・ヒョウ	*hee, hyoo*	八	丘 丘 丘 丘 兵 7

兵 **A** F-0491

甲骨文 1 金文 2 説文 3

1, 2, and 3 depicted a scene in which two hands held up a hand ax. Someone who held a weapon such as an ax was "a soldier." The kanji 兵 means "soldier." <丘ハ>

兵 soldier [へい]; 兵士 soldier [へいし]; 兵器 weapons [へいき]; 派兵 military deployment [はへい]; 兵卒 private (rank), enlisted man [へいそつ]; 出兵 to dispatch troops [しゅっぺいする]; 兵糧 provisions, food [ひょうろう]

SG-1457 質	Meanings	Kun and On	Romaji	Bushu	Stroke Order and Number
	to inquire; quality, pawned item	シツ・シチ・チ	*shitsu, shichi, chi*	貝	斤 斦 斦 質 質 質 15

質 **B** F-0535

金文 1 説文 2

1 and 2 comprised "two hand axes" (斤 SG-1453) that were used as scale weights, and "a cowrie, monetary value" (貝 SG-1693), together signifying "asking about the value or quality of goods." Two equal weights also signified "equal value." Getting money in place of something of value deposited temporarily is "pawning." The kanji 質 means "to inquire; quality, pawned item." <斤斤貝>

質 quality [しつ]; 実質的 substantive, virtual [じっしつてき]; 体質 physical constitution, nature [たいしつ]; 質素 simplicity, frugality [しっそ]; 物質 matter, substance [ぶっしつ]; 悪質な malicious, shoddy [あくしつな]; 質疑応答 question and answer: Q and A [しつぎ・おうとう]; 質屋 pawn shop [しちや]; 人質 hostage [ひとじち]

	Meanings	Kun and On	Romaji	Bushu	Stroke Order and Number
SG-1458 断	to cut off, stop, decline; drastic action	た-つ・ことわ-る ダン	ta-tsu, kotowa-ru *dan*	斤	丷 半 米 迷 断 断 断 11

断
B
F-0553

説文 1　旧字 2

1 and 2 comprised "four skeins of thread cut short on the shelves" and "a hand ax," together signifying "to cut off, sever" and "drastic action." In the shinji, the skeins on the shelves were replaced by 米 for simplification (迷). The kanji 断 means "to cut off, stop, decline; drastic action." <迷 斤>

酒を断つ to stop drinking [さけをた7つ]; 断る to turn down, decline [ことわ7る]; 判断 judgment [はんだん]; 断水 suspension of water supply [だんすい]; 中断する to suspend [ちゅうだんする]; 決断する to make a decision [けつだんする]; 断絶 severance, extinction [だんぜつ]; 断念する to give up, abandon [だんねんする, だんね7んする]

	Meanings	Kun and On	Romaji	Bushu	Stroke Order and Number
SG-1459 折	to break, fold, bend, turn; opportunity, occasion	お-る セツ	o-ru *setsu*	手	一 十 扌 扌 扩 折 7

折
B
F-0904

甲骨文1 1　甲骨文2 2　金文1 3　金文2 4　説文1 5　説文2 6

1, 2, 3, 4, and 6 depicted "plants that were cut or broken in two by a hand ax," thus signifying "to break, fold, bend, turn." In Japanese, the character was also applied metaphorically to "a disruption of the flow of time" that creates a new "opportunity or occasion." In 5, the plants broken in two were misconstrued as a hand, which became 扌, bushu *tehen*, in the kanji. The kanji 折 means "to break, bend, fold; time, opportunity, occasion." <扌 斤>

折る to fold, break [お7る]; 折れる to bend, break, give in [おれ7る]; その折りに on that occasion [そのおり7に]; 指折りの leading, one of the best [ゆびおりの]; 折り返し by prompt (reply) [おりかえし]; 折り紙 *origami* folding paper [おり7がみ]; 折角 with much trouble, with special kindness [せっかく]; 屈折する to bend, twist [くっせつする]; 左折禁止 no left turn (traffic sign) [させつきんし]

	Meanings	Kun and On	Romaji	Bushu	Stroke Order and Number
SG-1460 哲	clear; wise person, wisdom	テツ	*tetsu*	口・斤	才 扌 折 折 哲 哲 10

哲
B
F-0998

金文1 1　金文2 2　金文3 3　説文 4　説文或体 5

Two different seal-style forms have been proposed (4 and 5). 4 comprised 折 "to break, cut," and 口 "to speak." A person who could convey meaning by speaking in a clear-cut manner signified "a wise person; wisdom." This form was reflected in the kanji. 5 (悊) reflected the bronzeware-style forms (1, 2, and 3), which comprised "an ax" to mean "clarity," "a heart," and either "a plant with an eye" (in 1), or "a deity's ladder" (in 2 and 3). Together, they meant "the lucidness of the heart in serving a deity, enlightenment." It could be that all those meanings reflected what ancient creators thought of 哲—"to reflect deeply on things and analyze them lucidly." The kanji 哲 means "clear; wise person, wisdom." <折口>

哲学 philosophy [てつ7がく]; 哲人 great thinker, philosopher [てつじん]; 何の変哲も無い common, ordinary [なんのへんてつもな7い]

	Meanings	Kun and On	Romaji	Bushu	Stroke Order and Number
SG-1461 祈	to pray, invoke blessings	いの-る キ	ino-ru *ki*	示	` ネ ネ´ ネ 祈 祈 8

祈
C
F-1369

甲骨文1 1　甲骨文2 2　金文1 3　金文2 4　説文 5　旧字 6

1 was "an ax," with "a shield" added underneath in 2, signifying "a prayer for victory in battle." In 3, "a banner for a military unit" and, in 4, "an advancing foot," were added at the top. In 5 and 6 the military elements disappeared, and "an altar table with an offering" (示 **SG-1737**, ネ bushu *shimesuhen*) was added to "an ax" (斤 **SG-1453**), used for the sound *ki*, to mean "to pray for blessing or good luck." The kanji 祈 means "to pray, invoke blessings." <ネ 斤>

祈る to pray [いの7る]; (お)祈り prayer, invocation [いのり, おいのり]; 祈願する to pray for [き7がんする]; 祈祷 prayer [きとう]

	Meanings	Kun and On	Romaji	Bushu	Stroke Order and Number
SG-1462 析	to divide, split, analyze	セキ	*seki*	木	一 十 木 木´ 析 析 析 8

析
C
F-1383

甲骨文 1　金文 2　説文 3

1, 2, and 3 comprised "a tree" (木 **SG-0608**) and "a hand ax" (斤), together signifying "to split wood using an ax." Splitting something signified "to analyze a matter" and "to investigate in detail." The kanji 析 means "to divide, split, analyze." <木 斤>

分析する to analyze [ぶんせきする]; 解析 analysis, analytical reasoning [かいせき]; 透析 dialysis [とうせき]

	Meanings	Kun and On	Romaji	Bushu	Stroke Order and Number
SG-1463 誓	to vow, pledge, promise	ちか-う セイ	chika-u *see*	言	扌 扌 扩 扩 折 誓 誓 14

誓 **C** F-1512 — 金文1 1, 金文2 2, 説文 3 — 誓

1 comprised "a bough" and "a tattooing needle above a mouth" (言 **SG-1364**) for "word; to speak" on the left side, and "a hand ax" (斤) on the right. 2 had the same elements (a bough broken in half, an ax, and a word) in a different arrangement. Two parties breaking a bough in half and each keeping a piece signified "to promise." 折 **SG-1459** was used for the sound *see.* The kanji 誓 means "to vow, pledge, promise." <折言>

誓う to swear, vow, pledge [ちか↑う, ちかう]; 誓約書 written pledge, covenant [せいやくしょ]; 選手宣誓 athlete's oath of fair play [せ↑んしゅ・せんせい]

	Meanings	Kun and On	Romaji	Bushu	Stroke Order and Number
SG-1464 匠	craft, master craftsman, design	ショウ	*shoo*	匚	一 丆 ア 斤 斤 匠 6

匠 **D** F-1648 — 説文 — 匠

The seal-style form depicted "a hand ax" (斤) inside "a hiding or storage place" (匚), which was used for the sound *shoo.* Together they signified "an important tool such as an ax stored in a box." A person who crafted items using an ax was "a craftsman," and a master craftsman created good designs. The kanji 匠 means "craft, master craftsman, design." < 匚 斤 >

意匠 design, idea [いし↑ょう]; 巨匠 great master [きょしょう]; 師匠 teacher, master (in a traditional art) [し↑しょう] // 匠 artisan, master craftsman [たくみ]

	Meanings	Kun and On	Romaji	Bushu	Stroke Order and Number
SG-1465 逝	to go, pass on, die	ゆ-く・い-く セイ	yu-ku, i-ku *see*	辵	扌 扩 折 `折 㧷 逝 10

逝 **D** F-1977 — 説文 — 逝

The seal-style form comprised 辵 "to move forward," and 折 **SG-1459**, used for the sound *see* to mean "to die, depart from this life." The kanji 逝 means "to go, pass on, die." <折辶>

逝く to die, pass on [ゆく, いく]; 逝去 death, demise [せ↑いきょ]; 急逝 sudden demise, unexpected death [きゅうせい]

	Meanings	Kun and On	Romaji	Bushu	Stroke Order and Number
SG-1466 薪	firewood	たきぎ シン	takigi *shin*	艸	艹 苙 薪 薪 薪 16

薪 **D** F-2122 — 説文 — 薪

The seal-style form comprised "plants" (艸, 艹, bushu *kusakanmuri*), and 新 **SG-1455**, used for the sound *shin* to mean "firewood," from chopping 木 "wood" using 斤 "a hand ax." The kanji 薪 means "firewood." <艹新>

薪 firewood, wood for fuel [たきぎ, (まき)]; 薪能 Noh play by a bonfire on a summer night [たきぎ↑のう] // 薪割り wood splitting, hatchet [まきわり, まきわ↑り]

	Meanings	Kun and On	Romaji	Bushu	Stroke Order and Number
SG-1467 斬	to cut sharply (with a knife)	き-る ザン	ki-ru *zan*	斤	一 亘 車 車 斬 斬 斬 11

斬 **D** F-2086 — 説文 — 斬

The seal-style form comprised 車 **SG-1578** "wheel, vehicle" and 斤 **SG-1453** "hand ax," together signifying "to cut materials with an ax to build a vehicle." The kanji 斬 means "to cut sharply (with a knife)" <車斤>

斬る to ax, cut [き↑る]; 斬新なデザイン drastically new design [ざんしんなデザ↑イン]; 斬首 beheading [ざ↑んしゅ, ざんしゅ]

	Meanings	Kun and On	Romaji	Bushu	Stroke Order and Number
SG-1468 暫	short period of time, brief time	ザン	*zan*	日	亘 車 斬 斬 斬 暫 暫 15

暫 **D** F-1749 — 説文 — 暫

The seal-style form comprised 斬, used for the sound *zan* to mean "to cut," and 日 "the sun, time." Together they signified "a small increment of time." The kanji 暫 means "a short period of time, brief time." <斬日>

暫定的な temporary [ざんていてきな]; 暫時 for a short time [ざ↑んじ] // 暫 for a short period of time [し↑ばし]

	Meanings	Kun and On	Romaji	Bushu	Stroke Order and Number
SG-1469 漸	gradually, little by little, barely	ゼン	*zen*	水	氵 洹 漣 漣 漸 漸 漸 14

漸 **D** F-2168 — 説文 — 漸

The seal-style form comprised "flowing water" (氵), and 斬, used for the sound *zen. Setsumon* states that 漸 was the name of a particular river. Water seeping through over time gave the meaning "gradual movement." The kanji 漸 means "gradually, little by little, barely." <氵斬>

漸次 gradually, one by one [ぜ↑んじ]; 漸進的 gradual, step by step [ぜんしんてき] // 漸く little by little, at long last, barely [ようやく]

69 Halberd

69a 戈 "halberd" 戒械伐

A halberd was a weapon that could be used in two ways: for thrusting like a spear, or for cutting like an ax.

	Meanings	Kun and On	Romaji	Bushu	Stroke Order and Number
SG-1470 戒	to admonish, guard against; warning, admonition	いまし-める カイ	imashi-meru *kai*	戈	一 二 开 戒 戒 戒 7
戒 C F-1293	甲骨文 1, 金文 2, 説文 3. 1, 2, and 3 depicted "a halberd" (戈), held by two hands. Raising a halberd with both hands signified "to guard against, keep a lookout for." The showing of a halberd could also be a kind of admonishment. In the kanji, the two hands became the shape 廾 "two hands holding something up." The kanji 戒 means "to admonish, guard against; warning, admonition." <戈廾>				戒める to admonish [いましめる]; 戒律 religious precepts [かいりつ]; 十戒 the Ten Commandments [じっかい]; 懲戒処分 disciplinary punishment [ちょうかいしょぶん]; 警戒する to look out, guard [けいかいする]

	Meanings	Kun and On	Romaji	Bushu	Stroke Order and Number
SG-1471 械	machinery, gadget, device	カイ	*kai*	木	木 朾 析 械 械 械 11
械 C F-1246	説文. The seal-style form 械 comprised 木 "wood," and 戒, used for the sound *kai* to mean "to admonish," together signifying "a wooden apparatus such as shackles, used to punish a criminal." The meaning of "shackles" was dropped, and the character came to signify any mechanized apparatus. The kanji 械 means "machinery, gadget, device." <木戒>				機械 machine [きかい]; 器械 instrument [きかい]; 機械的に mechanically, routinely [きかいてきに]

	Meanings	Kun and On	Romaji	Bushu	Stroke Order and Number
SG-1472 伐	to cut down, attack	バツ	*batsu*	人	亻 亻 代 伐 伐 6
伐 D F-1951	甲骨文 1, 金文1 2, 金文2 3, 説文 4. 1, 2, and 3 depicted a scene in which "a halberd" (戈, right side) was on "a person's neck" (left side). It originally meant "cutting an enemy's head off." In 4, the "person" was separated from the halberd and became 亻, bushu *ninben* "an act one does." The kanji 伐 means "to cut down, attack." <亻戈>				(木を) 伐採する to cut down (a tree) [ばっさいする]; 乱伐 reckless deforestation [らんばつ]; 間伐材 timber from forest-thinning [かんばつざい]

69b 武 "military; warrior"; *bu* 武賦弐

	Meanings	Kun and On	Romaji	Bushu	Stroke Order and Number
SG-1473 武	warrior, military, arms	ブ・ム	bu, mu	止	一 亍 下 正 正 武 武 8
武 A F-0500	甲骨文 1, 金文1 2, 金文2 3, 説文 4. 1, 2, 3, and 4 comprised "a halberd" (戈) and "a footprint" (止 **SG-0200**). 3 had a king's ornate ax added. Someone advancing on foot and carrying a weapon was "a warrior," performing "a military act." The kanji 武 means "warrior, military, arms." <弋 止>				武士 samurai, warrior, military class [ぶし]; 武家 samurai family, warrior class [ぶけ, ぶけ]; 武器 weapon, arms [ぶき]; 武力 military power [ぶりょく]; 非武装地帯 demilitarized zone, a DMZ [ひぶそうちたい]; 武者 warrior [むしゃ]; 武者震い shaking with anticipation [むしゃぶるい]

	Meanings	Kun and On	Romaji	Bushu	Stroke Order and Number
SG-1474 賦	to allocate, distribute; tribute, ode	フ	*hu*	貝	冂 貝 貝 貯 賦 賦 15
賦 D F-2177	金文 1, 説文 2. 1 comprised "a soldier advancing" (武), used for the sound *hu*, and "cowrie, valuables, money" (貝 **SG-1693**). Valuable things or money sought by force meant "to collect a levy, impose labor." A ruler expected to receive the valuable as "a tribute." Collected levies were also "allocated" for particular purposes. The character is also used to mean "ode." The kanji 賦 means "to allocate, distribute; tribute, ode." <貝武>				賦役 compulsory labor [ふえき]; 賦与する to endow [ふよする]; 月賦払い monthly installment payment [げっぷばらい]; 天賦 endowment, nature [てんぷ]; 賦 ode, rhapsody [ふ]

	Meanings	Kun and On	Romaji	Bushu	Stroke Order and Number
SG-1475 弐	two; secondary	に	*ni*	貝	一 二 弐 弐 弐 弐 6

弐 **D** F-2318

金文1 1 金文2 2 説文古文 3 篆文 4 旧字 5

1 comprised "a halberd" (戈), with "two short lines" (二) used for the sound *ji* to mean "two," and "a vessel or tripod" (貝 **SG-1717**). It was used to mean "two; secondary." 2 and 3 did not have the vessel. 4 and the kyuji 貳 (5), reflected 1, whereas the shinji 弐 reflected 2 and 3. The kanji 弐 is used in important financial documents to avoid using 二, which can be altered or confused with 一 or 三. <弋二>

弐千 two thousand [にせんん]

69c 成 "to complete, accomplish" [from a long-bladed halberd/lance]; *see* 成城誠

	Meanings	Kun and On	Romaji	Bushu	Stroke Order and Number
SG-1476 成	to complete, accomplish, comprise	な-る セイ・ジョウ	na-ru *see, joo*	戈	ノ 厂 万 成 成 成 6

成 **A** F-0146

甲骨文 1 金文 2 説文 3

1 and 2 comprised "a long halberd," and "a hanging amulet" or "a decoration marking the completion of manufacture of a new halberd." The character signified "to complete, accomplish." In 3, the blade was elongated (戊) and the shape of "a nail" (丁 **SG-1914**) was placed inside to signify "pounding," later becoming ㇇ in the kanji. The kanji 成 means "to complete, accomplish, comprise." <成(戊㇇)>

成る to complete, accomplish [なる]; 成し遂げる to carry out successfully [なしとげる]; 漢字の成り立ち how kanji arrived at its present form, origin of kanji [かんじのなりたち]; 成功する to succeed [せいこうする]; 成果 result, accomplishment [せいか]; 成長 one's growth [せいちょう]; 成仏する to enter Nirvana, attain Buddhahood [じょうぶつする]

	Meanings	Kun and On	Romaji	Bushu	Stroke Order and Number
SG-1477 城	caste, citadel, stronghold	しろ ジョウ	shiro *joo*	土	一 † 扌 圹 圻 城 城 城 9

城 **B** F-0571

金文1 1 金文2 2 説文 3

1 comprised "ramparts with towers," and "a completed halberd or weapon" (成 **SG-1476**), used for the sound *joo*. In 2 and 3, the ramparts were dropped and "dirt" (土 **SG-1126**) was added in their place. A structure made with pounded dirt and surrounded by ramparts was "a fortress or stronghold." The kanji 城 means "castle, citadel, stronghold." <扌成>

城 castle, citadel [しろ]; 城跡 castle ruins [しろあと]; 根城 stronghold, base [ねじろ]; 城主 lord of a castle, feudal lord [じょうしゅ]; 一国一城の主 feudal lordship, independent person [いっこくいちじょうのあるじ]; 城下町 the seat of a *daimyo*'s fief, castle town [じょうかまち]

	Meanings	Kun and On	Romaji	Bushu	Stroke Order and Number
SG-1478 誠	sincerity, loyalty	まこと セイ	makoto *see*	言	言 言 訂 訢 誠 誠 誠 13

誠 **B** F-0854

説文

The seal-style form comprised 言 **SG-1364** "word, language; to speak," and 成 "to complete, be attained," used for the sound *see*. From "a person's words becoming realized in their deeds," the kanji 誠 means "sincerity, loyalty." <言成>

誠 sincerity [まこと]; 誠意 sincerity, good faith [せいい]; 誠実に sincerely, faithfully, honestly [せいじつに]; 誠心誠意 wholeheartedly, devotedly [せいしんせいい]

69d 幾 "a small amount" [from short threads cut by a halberd]; *ki* 幾機畿

	Meanings	Kun and On	Romaji	Bushu	Stroke Order and Number
SG-1479 幾	a few, some, how much (interrogative)	いく キ	iku *ki*	幺	𠃋 幺 幺幺 丝 幾 幾 幾 幾 12

幾 **A** F-1567

金文1 1 金文2 2 説文 3

1, 2, and 3 comprised two "short threads" (幺), "a halberd" (戈), and "a person," along with "a knife," or "decorative threads hanging down." Threads that were cut short with a sharp object such as a halberd signified "small amount." Another view suggests that the small distance between the halberd and the person gave the meaning "small amount." The character was also used for the sound *ki* and also as an interrogative. The kanji 幾 meant "a few, some, how much." <幺幺戈人>

幾つ (usually in hiragana) how many [いくつ]; 幾つか some, few [いくつか]; 幾多の many [いくたの]; 幾度か several times [いくどか]; 幾年の a number of years, some years (literary) [いくとせの]; 幾何学 geometry [きかがく]

	Meanings	Kun and On	Romaji	Bushu	Stroke Order and Number
SG-1480 機	moment, change, mechanism, chance,wit	はた キ	hata *ki*	木	木 桦 桦 楑 機 機 機 16

機 **A** F-0269 — 説文 — The seal-style form comprised 木 **SG-0608** "wooden," and 幾 **SG-1479** "threads cut by a knife," used for the sound *ki*. Together they signified "a loom." A loom had complex mechanisms at every point of operation, and so it meant "mechanical device, machine, moment, chance." The kanji 機 means "moment, change, mechanism, chance, wit." <木 幾>

機織り weaving, handloom weaving [はたおり]; 機会 opportunity [きかい]; 好機 golden opportunity [こうき]; 機関 organization [きかん]; 機に乗じる to seize a favorable opportunity [きに・じょうじる]; 臨機応変 adaptation to circumstances [りんき・おうへん]; 有機物 organic matter [ゆうきぶつ]; 無機質 inorganic matter [むきしつ]

	Meanings	Kun and On	Romaji	Bushu	Stroke Order and Number
SG-1481 畿	the area of Kyoto	キ	*ki*	田	幺 幺幺 丝丝 畿 畿 畿 畿 15

畿 **D** F-2020 — 説文 — The seal-style form comprised "rice paddies" (田 **SG-1300**) for "a cultivated area," and 幾 for the sound *ki* to mean "a small distance; near." Together they signified "the vicinity of a cultivated area which an emperor ruled." In Japan, 畿 was used to refer to the area of the old capital Kyoto (京都), where the emperors resided for a thousand years. The kanji 畿 means "the area of Kyoto." <幺幺戈田>

近畿地方 Kinki region [きんきちほう]; 畿内 an area near Kyoto [きない]

69e 𢦏 "to cut, begin" [from a halberd (戈) cutting the blockage in a weir (十), signifying "to cut, begin"]; *sai/tai* 裁載栽戴繊

	Meanings	Kun and On	Romaji	Bushu	Stroke Order and Number
SG-1482 裁	to cut (cloth), rule, make a final decision	た-つ・さば-く サイ	ta-tsu, saba-ku *sai*	衣	土 𢦏 裁 裁 裁 裁 裁 裁 12

裁 **B** F-0798 — 説文 — The seal-style form comprised 𢦏 "to cut, begin," used for the sound *sai,* and 衣 **SG-1657** "clothing, fabric." Together they signified "to cut fabric to make clothing." When cutting fabric, one made careful decisions about how to cut it, whence "decisive act." A court judge makes a ruling after deliberation, whence "to make a firm decision." The kanji 裁 means "to cut (cloth), rule, make a final decision." <𢦏 衣>

生地を裁つ to cut fabric [きじを・たつ]; 裁く to make a ruling in court, judge [さばく]; 裁断する to cut out, cut out a dress pattern [さいだんする]; 裁判 trial, judgement [さいばん]; 独裁 dictatorship [どくさい]; 経済制裁 economic sanction [けいざいせいさい]; 総裁 president, governor [そうさい]

	Meanings	Kun and On	Romaji	Bushu	Stroke Order and Number
SG-1483 載	to load, put up, record, publish	の-せる サイ	no-seru *sai*	車	土 壹 車 載 載 載 13

載 **C** F-1153 — 金文 1, 中山王器1 2, 中山王器2 3, 説文 4 — The upper right side (𢦏) of 1 comprised 才 **SG-1115** "a weir," signifying "to stop," and 戈 "a halberd." This combination was used for the sound *sai* to mean "to block, stop." Together with 車 **SG-1578** "military vehicle," the character meant "to fasten a load onto a military vehicle." 2 was the same as forms 1 through 4 for 才 "an obstructing weir," with no other components, while 3 had 車 and 才 combined into one component. Later, "loading something up" also came to mean "to publish an article." The kanji 載 means "to load, put up, record, publish." <𢦏 車>

載せる to load, put up, carry [のせる]; 棚に載せる to place on a shelf [たなにのせる]; 広告を載せる to place an ad [こうこくをのせる]; 連載 serialization [れんさい]; 満載 full load [まんさい]; 掲載 publication, printing [けいさい]; 転載 reprinting from a different place, republication [てんさい]

	Meanings	Kun and On	Romaji	Bushu	Stroke Order and Number
SG-1484 栽	to grow (a plant), cultivate	サイ	*sai*	木	土 丰 未 栽 栽 栽 10

栽 **C** F-1563 — 説文 — The seal-style form comprised 木 "tree," and 𢦏 "to cut," used for the sound *sai*. Together they signified "to prune unnecessary branches of a tree." Keeping a plant well-pruned meant "to cultivate." The kanji 栽 means "to grow (a plant), cultivate." <𢦏 木>

栽培する to grow a plant, cultivate [さいばいする]; 盆栽 miniature tree potted in a flat planter, *bonsai* [ぼんさい]; 植栽 plant, planting [しょくさい]; 有機栽培 organic farming [ゆうきさいばい]; 水耕栽培 hydroponics, aquaculture [すいこうさいばい]

	Meanings	Kun and On	Romaji	Bushu	Stroke Order and Number
SG-1485 戴	to receive, accept, eat, drink (humble), wear a crown	タイ	*tai*	戈	十 亩 亩 壴 壴 戴 戴 戴 17

戴 **D** F-2263

説文古文 1 説文 2

1 comprised 戈 "a halberd," 田 "something valuable," and "a pair of hands thrusting up," together signifying "two hands holding up a valuable object protected by a weapon." 2 had 𢦏 (from 才 and 戈), used for the sound *tai*, and 異 **SG-0355** "a person wearing a fearsome mask for a votive play." Together they signified "to reverentially protect something sacred with a halberd." In Japanese, the character was used for the humble forms of "to eat or drink" and "to receive from a superior." The kanji 戴 means "to receive, accept, take, eat or drink (humble)" and "to wear a crown." <𢦏異>

頂戴する to receive (humble) [ちょうだいする]; 戴冠式 coronation [たいかんしき] // 戴く to hold up above one's head, receive, eat (humble) [いただく]; 戴きます Let's eat!/I am (humbly) about to eat (said before eating a meal) [いただきます]

	Meanings	Kun and On	Romaji	Bushu	Stroke Order and Number
SG-1486 繊	fine, detailed	セン	*sen*	糸	纟 糸 糸 糸 糸 糸 繊 繊 繊 17

繊 **D** F-1828

篆文 1 旧字 2

The history of the top right side of this character (shown on the right) is different from other kanji that contain 𢦏 in the shinji. The image it depicted is a gruesome one—two people pierced by a halberd at the feet or at the neck, signifying "to behead many people." From that, 𢦏 meant "to cut something into small pieces." For the kanji 繊, 1 comprised 糸 **SG-1600** "thread," 𢦏 "two people with a halberd," and 韭 (业) "small things." Fibers are "fine" and short. The kyuji 纖 (2) retained two 人 at the center top, but in the shinji, 𢦏 was used instead. The kanji 繊 means "fine, detailed." <糸𢦏业>

(Note: The kanji 繊 and 伐 **SG-1472** have similar origins.)

繊維 fiber [せんい]; 繊細な delicate [せんさいな]; 繊毛 cilia [せんもう]

69f 蔵 "to store; hideaway"; *zoo* 蔵臓

	Meanings	Kun and On	Romaji	Bushu	Stroke Order and Number
SG-1487 蔵	vault; to store away	くら ゾウ	kura *zoo*	艸	广 芦 芹 芦 蒈 蔵 蔵 蔵 15

蔵 **B** F-0726

中山王器 1 説文 2 旧字 3

1 was "a house," inside of which were "a table or bed" (爿) and "an urn containing valuable things." 2 comprised "plants" (艸, 艹, bushu *kusakanmuri*), adding the sense of "hiding in thick vegetation," and 臧 for the sound *zoo*. (臧 comprised 爿, 臣 **SG-0023** "watchful eyes of a retainer," and "a halberd.") Together, these components signified "to store away something valuable in a secure place." The kanji 蔵 means "vault; to store away." <艹戊臣>

蔵 vault, storage [くら]; 米蔵 rice granary [こめぐら]; 秘蔵品 treasured article [ひぞうひん]; 無尽蔵な inexhaustible [むじんぞうな]; 地蔵・お地蔵さん roadside image of a guardian deity [じぞう, おじぞうさん]; 死蔵する to hoard, keep idle [しぞうする]

	Meanings	Kun and On	Romaji	Bushu	Stroke Order and Number
SG-1488 臓	internal organ	ゾウ	*zoo*	肉	刀 月 肝 肝 肝 肝 臓 臓 臓 19

臓 **C** F-1414

臟 旧字

No ancient form. The kyuji 臟 comprised 月, bushu *nikuzuki* "part of the body," and 蔵 **SG-1487** "vault; to hide away," used for the sound *zoo*. The parts of the body that were hidden and protected inside were internal organs. The kanji 臓 means "internal organ." <月蔵>

心臓 heart [しんぞう]; 心臓が強い to have a lot of nerve, be brazen [しんぞうがつよい]; 臓器 internal organs [ぞうき]; 臓器移植 organ transplant [ぞうき・いしょく, ぞうきいしょく]; 内臓 the internal organs [ないぞう]; 腎臓 the kidney [じんぞう]

69g 戠 “marking, knowledge; to discern”; *shoku* 職識織 戠

	Meanings	Kun and On	Romaji	Bushu	Stroke Order and Number
SG-1489 職	job, position, occupation	ショク	*shoku*	耳	「 F 耳 耳' 耶 聕 職 職 職 18

職 **A** F-0386

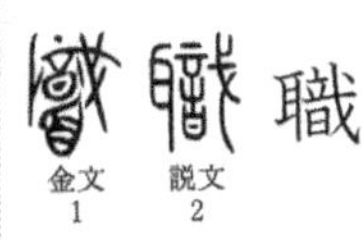
金文 1 説文 2

1 comprised 戠 (“something unclear” 音 **SG-1375** with “halberd” 戈), used for the sound *shoku* to mean “to discern,” and “face or head” (自 **SG-0059**) at the bottom. In 2, instead of a head, 耳 **SG-0050** “an ear” was used to signify “one listening well to do his job and handle matters in a discerning manner.” The character meant a position in which one listens and uses discernment, i.e. “a job or occupation.” The kanji 職 means “job, position, occupation.” <耳戠 >

職業 occupation [しょくぎょう]; 職場 work place [しょくば]; 職に就く to take up a job, become employed [しょくにつく]; 本職 one's principal job, one's regular work [ほんしょく]; 職歴 work history [しょくれき]; 部長職 the position of director [ぶちょうしょく]

	Meanings	Kun and On	Romaji	Bushu	Stroke Order and Number
SG-1490 識	to recognize, discern; mark, knowledge	シキ	*shiki*	言	言 言 訁 訁 訁 識 識 識 19

識 **B** F-0730

金文 1 金文 2 説文 3
1 2 3

1 and 2 comprised “halberd” (戈) and “something unclear” (音 **SG-1375**), together used for the sound *shiki* to mean “signal, marking.” In 3, 言 **SG-1364** “word, language; to say” was added. The character described how use of language enables one to more consciously recognize and resolve unclear matters. The kanji 識 means “to recognize, discern; mark, knowledge.” < 言戠 >

知識 knowledge [ちしき]; 標識 sign, mark [ひょうしき]; 常識 common sense [じょうしき]; 意識 consciousness, one's sense [いしき]; 識別する to discern, discriminate [しきべつする]; 識字率 literacy rate [しきじりつ]; 意識不明 unconscious [いしき・ふめい]; 無意識に unwittingly, inadvertently [むいしきに]

	Meanings	Kun and On	Romaji	Bushu	Stroke Order and Number
SG-1491 織	to weave, assemble; organization	お-る ショク・シキ	o-ru *shoku, shiki*	糸	幺 糸 紷 絓 織 織 織 18

織 **B** F-0682

金文1 金文2 説文
1 2 3

1 was the same as 1 and 2 for 識, and was used for the sound *shoku*. For 織, however, 2 added 糸 **SG-1600**, “a skein of threads,” signifying “to weave,” especially patterned woven cloth. 3 comprised 糸 (bushu *itohen*) and 戠. In weaving, continuous threads were arranged horizontally and vertically, and from that the character also meant “organization.” The kanji 織 means “to weave, assemble; organization.” < 糸戠 >

織る to weave [おる]; 織物 woven cloth, fabric [おりもの]; 羽織 *haori* coat, Japanese half-coat [はおり]; 手織り handweaving [ており]; 紡織 spinning, weaving [ぼうしょく]; 組織 organization [そしき]

69h 我・或 “a protected area” [from a halberd, or an area protected by a halberd] 我・国域惑

	Meanings	Kun and On	Romaji	Bushu	Stroke Order and Number
SG-1492 我	I, me, ego; my, our	われ・わ ガ	ware, wa *ga*	戈	二 千 手 我 我 7

我 **B** F-0735

甲骨文 金文1 金文2 説文
1 2 3 4

1, 2, 3, and 4 depicted “a halberd with prongs,” or “a saw-like blade.” The same shapes appeared in the ancient forms of the kanji 義 **SG-0838**. A saw like this was used to cut sacrificial sheep. The character was borrowed for the sound *ga* to mean “I, me, ego.” < 我 >

我 I [われ]; 我が国 our country [わがくに]; 我々 we (formal) [われわれ]; 我が家 my family/home [わがや]; 我が身 oneself, myself [わがみ]; 我が世の春 heyday, the height of one's glory [わがよの・はる]; 我が儘な selfish, egoistic [わがままな, わがままな]; 我が強い egoistic, egocentric [ががつよい]

或 "a protected area" [from "a halberd" (戈) protecting "an area" (口) that was marked by "a boundary" (一).]

甲骨文 金文 説文1 説文2

SG-1493 国	Meanings	Kun and On	Romaji	Bushu	Stroke Order and Number
	country, domain, state, nation, province, home country	くに コク	kuni *koku*	口	丨 冂 冂 冂 囯 国 国 国 8

国 **A** F-0015

甲骨文 1 金文1 2 金文2 3 説文 4 旧字 5

1 and 2 were 或, "a halberd protecting an area." As 或 came to be used to mean "to exist; certain," a new character, 國 (3 and 4), was created by adding 囗, bushu *kunigamae* "domain, encirclement." In the shinji 国, 玉 **SG-1730** "crown jewel" replaced 或. The kanji 国 means "country, domain, state, nation, province, one's native country." <囗玉>

国 country, nation, one's homeland [くに]; 国元 one's home country [くにもと]; 日本国 the official name of Japan [にほꜜんこく]; 国民 people, nationality [こくみん]; 国語 Japanese, national language [こくご]; 国内 the interior of Japan, one's country, home [こくꜜない]; 国外 outside of the country [こくꜜがい]; 国家 nation, state, country [こꜜっか]; 国交 diplomatic relations [こっこう]

SG-1494 域	Meanings	Kun and On	Romaji	Bushu	Stroke Order and Number
	area, limit, range	イキ	*iki*	土	一 十 扌 扩 垣 垣 域 域 域 11

域 **B** F-0625

金文1 1 金文2 2 説文 3

1 was 或 "an area with boundaries protected by a halberd," used for the sound *iki*, while in 2, "a town" (邑) was added, together signifying "a territory with armed protection where people lived." In 3, "soil, ground" (土 **SG-1126**) replaced "town" to signify the land itself rather than the people. The kanji 域 means "area, limit, range." <土戈口>

地域 area, region [ちꜜいき]; 区域 zone, segment [くꜜいき]; 領域 domain, territory [りょういき]; 音域 vocal range [おんいき]; 芸域 versatility of skills [げいいき]; 危険水域 dangerous area of the sea [きけんすꜜいいき]; 警戒区域 hazard area [けいかいくꜜいき]

SG-1495 惑	Meanings	Kun and On	Romaji	Bushu	Stroke Order and Number
	to be bewildered, be confused	まど-う ワク	mado-u *waku*	心	一 ㅁ 可 式 或 或 惑 12

惑 **C** F-1200

中山王器 1 説文 2

1 and 2 comprised 或 for the sound *waku* to mean "to have doubt," and 心 **SG-0187** "heart." Together they signified "an oscillating state of mind, being bewildered." The kanji 惑 means "to be bewildered, be confused." <或心>

惑う to be bewildered, be confused [まどꜜう]; 戸惑う to become disoriented, become perplexed [とまどꜜう]; 疑惑 suspicion, doubt, mistrust [ぎわく]; 当惑する to feel lost, be confused [とうわくする]; 惑星 planet [わくせい]; 迷惑な annoying, inconvenient, troublesome [めꜜいわくな]; 思惑 speculation, expectations [しわく]

69i 咸 "to protect, seal" [from a wide-bladed halberd protecting an area, or shutting up one's mouth tightly under threat from a wide-bladed halberd, 戌]; *kan* 感減威滅憾

SG-1496 感	Meanings	Kun and On	Romaji	Bushu	Stroke Order and Number
	to feel; feelings, emotions	カン	*kan*	心	ノ 厂 后 咸 咸 咸 感 感 13

感 **A** F-0214

金文 1 説文 2

1 and 2 comprised 咸, used for the sound *kan* to mean "shutting one's mouth tightly under threat of a weapon," and 心 **SG-0187** "heart." Together they signified "someone stunned by the threat of a weapon." The strong emotions one feels when threatened gave the meaning "to feel strongly." The kanji 感 means "to feel; feelings, emotions." <戊口心>

感じる to feel [かんじる]; 感情 emotions [かんじょう]; 情感溢れる overflowing with emotion, evoking emotion [じょうかんあふれꜜる]; 感心する to be impressed, admire [かんしんする]; 感動する to be moved [かんどうする]; 感傷的な emotional, maudlin [かんしょうてきな]; 感性 sensibility, sensitivity [かꜜんせい]; 好感 favorable impression [こうかん]

SG-1497 減	Meanings	Kun and On	Romaji	Bushu	Stroke Order and Number
	to reduce, become less	へ-る ゲン	he-ru *gen*	水	氵 氵 沪 洉 減 減 減 12

減 **A** F-0445

金文 1 説文 2

1 and 2 comprised "flowing water" (氵), and 咸 "to shut the mouth tightly, seal," used for the sound *gen*. Closing

減らす to reduce, make less [へらす]; 減る to decrease [へる]; 加減する to adjust [かげんする]; 湯加減 bath temperature [ゆかꜜげん]; 軽減する to reduce, relieve of [けいげんする]; 減速 slowing

	the mouth of a stream of water reduced its flow, and thus the character meant "to reduce." The kanji 減 means "to reduce, become less." <氵咸>	down [げんそく]; 減塩醤油 low-sodium soy sauce [げんえんしょ˥うゆ]

	Meanings	Kun and On	Romaji	Bushu	Stroke Order and Number
SG-1498 威	to threaten; authority	イ	*i*	女	丿厂厂反反威威 9

威 **C** F-1263	金文1 金文2 說文3 1, 2, and 3 comprised "a broad-bladed battle ax" (戌) over "a woman" (女 **SG-0521**). A weapon and a woman together meant "an authoritative woman"—a mother-in-law—or "protecting a woman to ease her fear." The connotation of "woman" was dropped, and the kanji 威 means "to threaten; authority." <戌一女> (Note: The development of 戌 is shown at right.)	権威 authority [け˥んい]; 威嚇する to threaten [いかくする]; 威厳 dignity [いげん]; 威容 commanding appearance [いよう]; 威信 prestige, credibility, dignity [いしん]; 威勢のいい high spirited, vigorous [いせいのい˥い]; 威光 authority, influence [いこう]

	Meanings	Kun and On	Romaji	Bushu	Stroke Order and Number
SG-1499 滅	to run out, die away	ほろ-びる メツ	horo-biru *metsu*	水	氵氵沪沪泝滅滅滅 13

滅 **C** F-1479	說文 The seal-style form had "flowing water" (氵) on the left side, while the right-side component (烕) comprised "a broad-bladed battle axe" (for "to stop") and 火 **SG-0064** "fire," and was used for the sound *metsu*. Taken together, they signified "to exhaust, run out of water." The kanji 滅 means "to run out, die away." <氵戌一火>	滅ぼす to destroy [ほろぼ˥す]; 滅びる to die away, be destroyed [ほろび˥る]; 全滅する to be annihilated, be wiped out [ぜんめつする]; 点滅する to flicker [てんめつする]; 滅亡 extinction [めつぼう]; 支離滅裂な incoherent, disconnected [し˥り・めつれつな]

	Meanings	Kun and On	Romaji	Bushu	Stroke Order and Number
SG-1500 憾	to regret; not content; lingering regret	カン	*kan*	心	丶忄忙憾憾憾憾 16

憾 **D** F-2180	No ancient form. The kanji comprises 忄, bushu *risshinben* "heart," and 感 **SG-1496** "to feel; emotions," used for the sound *kan*. Since both components feature a heart, together they signify a deep-rooted emotion, namely "regret." The kanji 憾 means "to regret; not content; lingering regret." <忄感>	遺憾に思う to regret, deplore [いかんにおも˥う]; 遺憾無く completely, sufficiently [いかんな˥く]; 遺憾ながら regrettably [いかんな˥がら]

69j 戋 (戔) "thin objects in layers" [from thin-bladed halberds placed on top of one another]; *zan/sen* 残浅銭桟箋

	Meanings	Kun and On	Romaji	Bushu	Stroke Order and Number
SG-1501 残	to leave; remains; cruel, gruesome	のこ-る ザン	noko-ru *zan*	歹	一ア万歹歼残残残 10

残 **A** F-0460	說文1 旧字2 1 comprised "skeletal remains" (歹, bushu *gatsuhen* or *kabanehen*), and 戔 (戋) "thin objects stacked on top of one another," used for the sound *zan*. Together they signified "remains cut into small pieces." An animal devouring the body of another animal and leaving bones scattered gave the meaning "gruesome, cruel." The kanji 残 means "to leave; remains; cruel, gruesome." <歹戋>	残る to remain [のこ˥る]; 残す to leave [のこ˥す]; 残り remnant, leftover [のこり]; 残念な regrettable [ざんね˥んな]; 残業 overtime work [ざんぎょう]; 残忍な gruesome, cruel [ざんにんな]; 無残な ruthless, pitiful [む˥ざんな] // 名残惜しい reluctant to part [なごりおし˥い]

	Meanings	Kun and On	Romaji	Bushu	Stroke Order and Number
SG-1502 浅	shallow, light, thoughtless	あさ-い セン	asa-i *sen*	水	氵氵浅浅浅 9

浅 **B** F-0925	說文1 旧字2 1 comprised "flowing water" (氵) and 戔 (戋), used for the sound *sen* to mean "thin." An area where there is little water meant "shallow water." The meaning of "a small amount" was also applied to color, knowledge and understanding. The kanji 浅 means "shallow, light, thoughtless." <氵戋>	浅い shallow [あさい]; 浅はかな foolish, thoughtless [あさ˥はかな]; 浅ましい vile, unworthy, pathetic [あさまし˥い]; 日が浅い it has not been long since the time, in short time [ひがあさ˥い]; 浅緑 light green [あさみ˥どり]; 浅薄な superficial, shallow [せんぱくな]

SG-1503 銭	Meanings	Kun and On	Romaji	Bushu	Stroke Order and Number
	money, small change, coin, 1/100 yen	ぜに セン	zeni *sen*	金	金 銭 14

銭 **C** F-1173 — 説文 1, 旧字 2

1 comprised 金 SG-1196 "metal," and 戔 (戋) "thin objects stacked on top of one another," used for the sound *sen.* The character originally denoted thin, plow-shaped coins, and it meant "money." The kanji 銭 means "money, small change, coin, 1/100 yen." <金戋>

小銭 small change, coin [こぜに]; 身銭を切る to pay for from one's own pocket [みぜにをきる]; 金銭 money [きんせん]; 銭湯 public bath [せんとう]; 一銭 one sen, one hundredth of a yen [いっせん]

SG-1504 桟	Meanings	Kun and On	Romaji	Bushu	Stroke Order and Number
	crosspiece of a *shoji* screen, frame, pier	サン	*san*	木	木 桟 10

桟 **D** F-2350 — 詛楚文 1, 篆文 2, 旧字 3

1 comprised 木 SG-0608 "wooden," and 戔 (戋) "thin," used for the sound *san.* Together they signified an object or structure that was made of thin pieces of wood, such as "a makeshift bridge," or "crosspieces of a wooden frame." The shinji 桟 means "pier, crosspiece of a *shoji* screen, frame." <木戋>

桟 beam [さん]; 桟橋 pier, jetty [さんばし]; 障子の桟 crosspiece of a *shoji* screen [しょうじのさん] // 桟敷 tiered seating, tiered box [さじき]

SG-1505 箋	Meanings	Kun and On	Romaji	Bushu	Stroke Order and Number
	note paper, letter pad	セン	*sen*	竹	竹 箋 14

箋 **D** F-2932 — 説文

The seal-style form 箋 comprised 竹 SG-0759 "bamboo," and 戔 "layers of thin strips," used for the sound *sen.* A bamboo tablet was used as a medium for writing on in ancient times before paper was invented. The kanji 箋 means "letter paper, notepaper." <⺮戔>

便箋 letter paper [びんせん]; 附箋• 付箋 tag paper, slip [ふせん]

69k 矛 "lance, a pike with a long shaft" 務柔矛

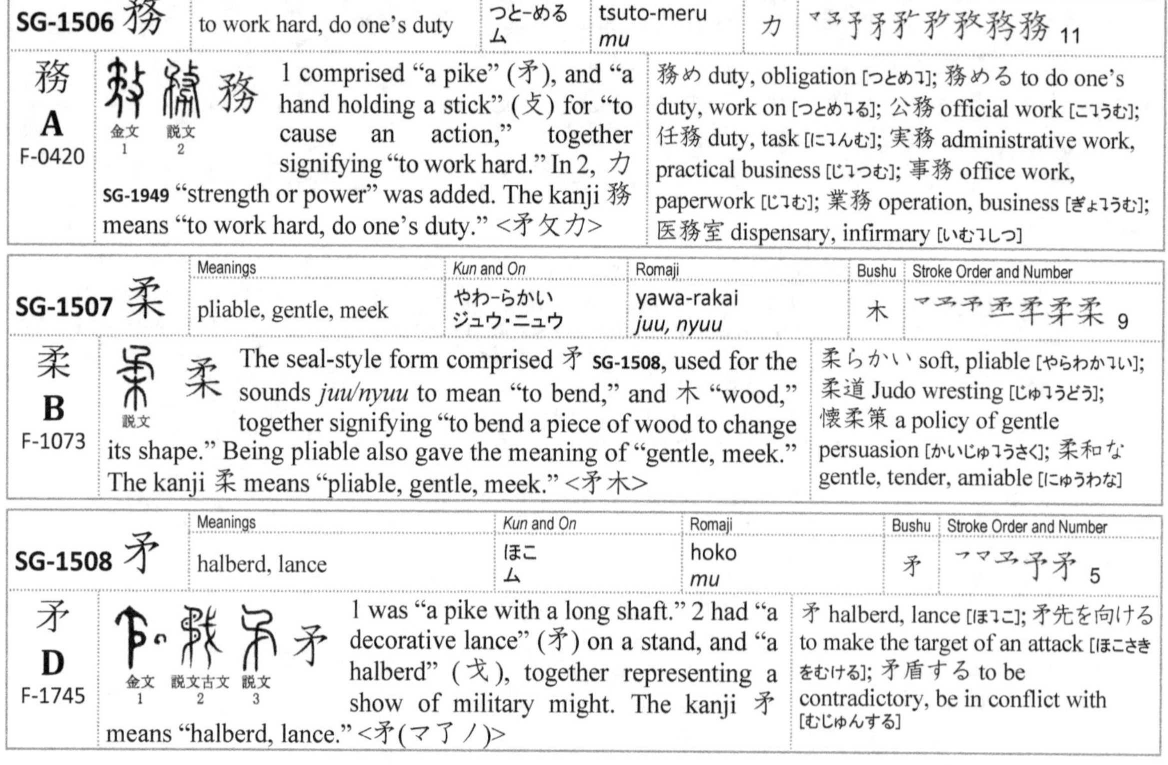

SG-1506 務	Meanings	Kun and On	Romaji	Bushu	Stroke Order and Number
	to work hard, do one's duty	つと-める ム	tsuto-meru *mu*	力	務 11

務 **A** F-0420 — 金文 1, 説文 2

1 comprised "a pike" (矛), and "a hand holding a stick" (攴) for "to cause an action," together signifying "to work hard." In 2, 力 SG-1949 "strength or power" was added. The kanji 務 means "to work hard, do one's duty." <矛攵力>

務め duty, obligation [つとめ]; 務める to do one's duty, work on [つとめる]; 公務 official work [こうむ]; 任務 duty, task [にんむ]; 実務 administrative work, practical business [じつむ]; 事務 office work, paperwork [じむ]; 業務 operation, business [ぎょうむ]; 医務室 dispensary, infirmary [いむしつ]

SG-1507 柔	Meanings	Kun and On	Romaji	Bushu	Stroke Order and Number
	pliable, gentle, meek	やわ-らかい ジュウ・ニュウ	yawa-rakai *juu, nyuu*	木	柔 9

柔 **B** F-1073 — 説文

The seal-style form comprised 矛 SG-1508, used for the sounds *juu/nyuu* to mean "to bend," and 木 "wood," together signifying "to bend a piece of wood to change its shape." Being pliable also gave the meaning of "gentle, meek." The kanji 柔 means "pliable, gentle, meek." <矛木>

柔らかい soft, pliable [やらわかい]; 柔道 Judo wresting [じゅうどう]; 懐柔策 a policy of gentle persuasion [かいじゅうさく]; 柔和な gentle, tender, amiable [にゅうわな]

SG-1508 矛	Meanings	Kun and On	Romaji	Bushu	Stroke Order and Number
	halberd, lance	ほこ ム	hoko *mu*	矛	矛 5

矛 **D** F-1745 — 金文 1, 説文古文 2, 説文 3

1 was "a pike with a long shaft." 2 had "a decorative lance" (矛) on a stand, and "a halberd" (戈), together representing a show of military might. The kanji 矛 means "halberd, lance." <矛(マ了ノ)>

矛 halberd, lance [ほこ]; 矛先を向ける to make the target of an attack [ほこさきをむける]; 矛盾する to be contradictory, be in conflict with [むじゅんする]

70 Bow and an arrow

70a 弓 "bow" 弓強引弱弥弦溺

	Meanings	Kun and On	Romaji	Bushu	Stroke Order and Number
SG-1509 弓	bow	ゆみ キュウ	yumi *kyuu*	弓	3
弓 **A** F-1276	甲骨文 1, 金文1 2, 金文2 3, 說文 4 1 and 2 were "a bow with a bowstring attached." 3 and 4 had only the bow, which became the kanji 弓. The kanji 弓 means "a bow." <弓>		弓 bow [ゆみ]; 弓矢 bow and arrow [ゆみや]; 弓なりに in a bow shape, in a curved chain shape [ゆみなりに]; 弓形 bow shape, arch [ゆみがた]; 洋弓 Western-style archery [ようきゅう]		

	Meanings	Kun and On	Romaji	Bushu	Stroke Order and Number
SG-1510 強	strong, competent, advantageous; to force; a little more than	つよ-い・し-いる キョウ・ゴウ	tsuyo-i, shi-iru *kyoo, goo*	弓	11
強 **A** F-0143	金文 1, 說文籀文 2, 說文 3 The kanji 強 derived from the non-Joyo kanji 彊. 1 and 2 comprised 弓 "bow," and 畺 "strong," used for the sounds *koo/kyoo*. 2 included an additional component depicting "hard-shelled insects such as beetles" at the bottom. The character signified "a strong bowstring made of fortified wild silkworm threads." 3 comprised 弘 "detached bowstring," and 虫 "wild silkworm." "Being strong" gave the meaning "advantageous, competent." The kanji 強 means "strong, advantageous; to force; a little more than." <弓ム虫>		強い strong, able, competent, superior [つよい]; 強いる to compel, force, coerce [しいる]; 強いて言えば if anything, if I must choose [しいていえば]; 無理強いする to force someone to do [むりじいする]; 強力な powerful, forceful [きょうりょくな]; 強化する to strengthen, reinforce [きょうかする]; 百人強 a little over a hundred people [ひゃくにんきょう]; 強引な aggressive, pushy [ごういんな]		

	Meanings	Kun and On	Romaji	Bushu	Stroke Order and Number
SG-1511 引	to pull back, subtract, consult	ひ-く イン	hi-ku *in*	弓	4
引 **A** F-0241	嘉平石経 1, 說文 2 1 and 2 had "a bow" with either a short, curved line or a long, straight line, signifying "the action of pulling back a bow to shoot," or "a bar for straightening a bent bow." The character meant "to pull or stretch." "Pulling something back" meant "to subtract." The character is also used for "looking (something) up" in a dictionary, in the sense of pulling out the information being sought. The kanji 弓 means "to pull back, subtract, consult (a reference book)." <弓丨>		引く to pull, subtract, pull back [ひく]; 引き受ける to undertake, take charge of [ひきうける]; 引き金 trigger, immediate cause [ひきがね]; 辞書を引く to consult a dictionary [じしょをひく]; 引っ込む to withdraw, flatten [ひっこむ]; 引き取る to claim, take responsibility for [ひきとる]; 引火 ignition, catching fire [いんか]		

	Meanings	Kun and On	Romaji	Bushu	Stroke Order and Number
SG-1512 弱	weak, fragile, mild	よわ-い ジャク	yowa-i *jaku*	弓	10
弱 **B** F-0604	說文 The seal-style form comprised two bows (弓 **SG-1509**) with three decorative diagonal lines (彡) each, to signify "a neat shape or a decorative design." A decorative bow was used for ceremonial purposes and was not strong. Another view holds that the character depicted a warped bow flexed back into good shape, and that it meant "weak, fragile, mild" in the sense of something pliant and easily bent. In the kanji, the component inside 弓 became 冫. The kanji 弱 means "weak, fragile, mild." <弓冫弓冫>		弱い weak [よわい]; ひ弱な feeble, delicate [ひよわな]; か弱い weak, delicate [かよわい]; 弱々しい frail, weakly [よわよわしい]; 強弱 strength and weakness [きょうじゃく, きょうじゃく]; 弱小国 lesser country [じゃくしょうこく]; 弱点 weak point [じゃくてん]; 弱肉強食 law of the jungle, the strong prey on the weak [じゃくにく・きょうしょく]1		

	Meanings	Kun and On	Romaji	Bushu	Stroke Order and Number
SG-1513 弥	long time; increasingly, far and wide; beautiful	や	ya	弓	ᄀコ弓弓'弓ᐟ弥弥弥 8

弥 **C** F-1482

金文 1 説文1 2 説文2 3 旧字 4 (彌 弥)

1 comprised "a bow" 弓 **SG-1509**, and "a woman with beautiful tattoos on her chest" (爾), used for the meaning "beautiful" and the sound *ji*. 2 replaced the bow with "long hair" (長 **SG-0566**), to signify "eternal." 3 comprised "a bow" (弓 **SG-1509**) for "a far distance," and "the seal of an emperor" (璽 **SG-1732**), together signifying "an emperor reigning far and wide for a long time." The complicated right-side component (爾) remained in the *kyuji* 彌 (4), but was replaced by the much simpler shape 尔 in the shinji. The kanji 弥 means "a long time; increasingly; far and wide, beautiful." <弓尔>

弥次馬 (or 野次馬) curious spectator, meddler [やじうま] // 弥生時代 the Yayoi period [やよいじだい]

	Meanings	Kun and On	Romaji	Bushu	Stroke Order and Number
SG-1514 弦	bow string, stringed musical instrument	つる ゲン	tsuru *gen*	弓	ᄀコ弓弓'弓ᐟ弦弦 8

弦 **C** F-1620

説文 (弦)

The seal-style form comprised 弓 "bow," and 玄 **SG-1639** "twined threads that were dyed black," used for the sound *gen*, together signifying "strings on a bow." Tightened strings make a sound when plucked, and 弦 meant "stringed musical instrument." The kanji 弦 means "bow string; stringed musical instrument." <弓玄>

弦 bow string [つる]; 弦楽器 stringed instrument [げんがっき]; 管弦楽 orchestral music [かんげんがく]; 上弦の月 early crescent moon [じょうげんのつき]

	Meanings	Kun and On	Romaji	Bushu	Stroke Order and Number
SG-1515 溺	to drown, lose oneself	おぼ-れる デキ	obo-reru *deki*	水	氵氵'氵ᄀ汚溺溺溺 13

溺 **D** F-2517

説文 (溺)

The seal-style form comprised "flowing water" (氵), and 弱 **SG-1512**, used for the sound *deki*. *Setsumon* explains that this character was the name of a particular river. The use of the character 溺 to mean "drown" goes back to ancient times. The kanji 溺 means "to drown, lose oneself." <氵弱>

溺れる to drown [おぼれる]; 溺愛 doting [できあい]; 溺死 death from drowning [できし]

70b 射 "to shoot" [from a bow and an arrow]; *sha* 射謝窮

	Meanings	Kun and On	Romaji	Bushu	Stroke Order and Number
SG-1516 射	to shoot an arrow, shoot off, launch	い-る シャ	i-ru *sha*	寸	′′冂自身身身射射 10

射 **B** F-1004

甲骨文 1 金文 2 説文 3 (射)

1 depicted "an arrow in a bow." In 2, "a hand pulling the bow" was added. In 3, the left side depicted a pregnant woman with a bow-shaped stomach (which became the kanji 身 **SG-0548**), and was misconstrued as the dilated shape of a bow. All of these forms meant "to shoot an arrow." In the seal-style form, the "hand" takes the form 寸 **SG-0112**, and is detached from 身. The kanji 射 means "to shoot an arrow, shoot off, launch." <身寸>

射る to shoot an arrow [いる]; 射止める to shoot, win, gain [いとめる]; 発射する to fire, discharge [はっしゃする]; 反射的に reflexively, by reflexive action [はんしゃてきに]; 乱射 random shooting [らんしゃ]; 注射 injection [ちゅうしゃ]; 注射器 syringe [ちゅうしゃき]; 熱射病 heatstroke [ねっしゃびょう]

	Meanings	Kun and On	Romaji	Bushu	Stroke Order and Number
SG-1517 謝	to apologize; thankful	あやま-る シャ	ayama-ru *sha*	言	言訁訁訓謝謝謝謝 17

謝 **C** F-1119

甲骨文 1 金文 2 説文 3 (謝)

1 and 2 were the same as 1 and 2 for 射 **SG-1516**. In 3, 言 bushu *gonben* "words, language; to speak" was added to the shape 射, used for the sound *sha* to mean "to express gratitude." The character is also used to mean "to make an apology." The kanji 謝 means "to apologize; thankful." <言射>

謝る to apologize [あやまる]; 平謝りに謝る to humbly and profusely apologize [ひらあやまりにあやまる]; 感謝する to be grateful, thank, appreciate [かんしゃする]; 月謝 monthly tuition [げっしゃ]; 謝罪 apology [しゃざい]; 謝礼 fee, honorarium [しゃれい]; 謝恩セール customer appreciation sale [しゃおんセール]; 面会謝絶 No visitors (allowed) [めんかいしゃぜつ]

	Meanings	Kun and On	Romaji	Bushu	Stroke Order and Number
SG-1518 窮	to get stuck, come to a dead end; hard-pressed	きわ-まる キュウ	kiwa-maru *kyuu*	穴	宀 穴 穵 穿 窮 窮 窮 15

窮 **D** F-1906

説文

The seal-style form comprised 穴 **SG-1322** "hole, dead end," 身 **SG-0548** "one's body," and 呂 **SG-1266** "spine." It depicted a scene in which a person was confined in a tight space and could not move. In the kanji 窮, 呂 was replaced by 弓 **SG-1509** for the sound *kyuu* to mean "to get stuck." The kanji 窮 meant "to get stuck, come to a dead end; hard-pressed." <穴射弓>

窮まる to end, terminate [きわまる]; 窮する to be at a loss, be hard-pressed for money [きゅうする]; 窮屈 cramped, confined, stiff, strict [きゅうくつ]; 窮地に陥る to fall into a predicament [きゅうちに・おちいる]; 困窮 poverty, want [こんきゅう]

70c 黄 "yellow, spacious" [from a fire arrow illuminating an area]; *koo* 黄広横拡鉱

	Meanings	Kun and On	Romaji	Bushu	Stroke Order and Number
SG-1519 黄	yellow, golden	き・こ コウ・オウ	ki, ko *koo, oo*	黄	一 艹 廾 芇 苗 菁 黄 11

黄 **A** F-0868

甲骨文 1 金文 2 説文 3 旧字 4

1 was "a fire arrow with combustible material." In 2 and 3, the flame was emphasized at the top. When a fire arrow was shot, its flame illuminated a wide area as it passed through the darkness. The yellow color of the fire gave the kanji the meaning of "yellow." The flame (廿) in the kyuji 黃 (4) coalesced into the line below it in the shinji. The kanji 黄 means "yellow, golden." <廾由ハ>

黄色 yellow [きいろ]; 黄緑色 light green [きみどりいろ]; 卵の黄身 egg yolk [たまごの・きみ]; 黄金色 golden [こがねいろ]; 黄葉 yellowing of autumn leaves [こうよう]; 黄河 the Huang, the Yellow River (in China) [こうが]; 黄金の golden [おうごんの]; 卵黄 egg yolk [らんおう]

	Meanings	Kun and On	Romaji	Bushu	Stroke Order and Number
SG-1520 広	spacious, wide, roomy	ひろ-い コウ	hiro-i *koo*	广	' 亠 广 広 広 5

広 **A** F-0139

甲骨文 1 金文 2 説文 3 旧字 4

1, 2, and 3 comprised "a house" or "the eaves of a house," and "a fire arrow illuminating a wide area" (黄), for the sound *koo*. Together they signified "the spaciousness of a house." 黄 **SG-1519** was replaced by the simplified shape ム, and the kanji 広 means "spacious, wide, roomy." <广ム>

広い wide, spacious [ひろい]; 広場 open area, public square [ひろば]; 手広くやる do business extensively [てびろくやる]; 広々とした extensive, spacious [ひろびろとした]; 広告 advertisement [こうこく]; 広報 public information, PR [こうほう・こうほう]

	Meanings	Kun and On	Romaji	Bushu	Stroke Order and Number
SG-1521 横	side; sideways, wicked, wrong	よこ オウ	yoko *oo*	木	木 朩 杵 栱 棤 構 横 15

横 **A** F-0307

金文 1 説文 2 旧字 3

1 was the same as 2 and 3 for 黄, and was used for the sound *oo*. In 2, 木 **SG-0608** "a piece of wood," was added to 黄, which was used to mean "all directions." Together, these components signified "a wooden latch bar" that moved "sideways." From someone's behavior deviating or "going sideways," the character also means "wicked, wrong." The kanji 横 means "side; sideways, wicked, wrong." <木黄>

横 side, sideways [よこ]; 真横 right next to, just beside [まよこ]; 縦と横 length and width [たてと・よこ]; 横這い leveling off [よこばい]; 横槍を入れる to butt in, interrupt [よこやりをいれる]; 横流しする to sell illegally [よこながしする]; 横断歩道 pedestrian crossing [おうだんほどう]; 横暴な oppressive, tyrannical [おうぼうな]; 横領 embezzlement, misappropriation [おうりょう]

	Meanings	Kun and On	Romaji	Bushu	Stroke Order and Number
SG-1522 拡	to widen, extend, lay out	カク	*kaku*	手	一 寸 扌 扩 扩 拡 8

拡 **B** F-0975

鄧石如 1 旧字 2

1 and 2 comprised 扌 bushu *tehen*, "an act done by hand," and 廣 "wide," used for the sound *kaku*, together signifying "to widen by hand." The kyuji 擴 was reduced to 拡. The kanji 拡 means "to widen, extend, lay out." <扌広> (Note: The kanji 広 **SG-1520** is used to describe space, whereas 拡 is used for the action of widening.)

拡張する to expand [かくちょうする]; 拡大 enlargement [かくだい]; 拡声器 loudspeaker, amplifier [かくせいき]; 拡大鏡 magnifier [かくだいきょう] // 拡げる to widen, lay out [ひろげる]

SG-1523 鉱	Meanings	Kun and On	Romaji	Bushu	Stroke Order and Number
	ore, mineral	コウ	*koo*	金	亼 金 釒 釒 釿 鉱 13

鉱 **C** F-1584

1 comprised 石 "rock," and 黄, used for the sound *koo*, together signifying "ore, mineral." In the kyuji 鑛 (2), 石 was replaced by 金 **SG-1196** "metal." In the shinji, 廣 was replaced by 広 **SG-1520**. The kanji 鉱 means "ore, mineral." <金 広>

鉱山 mine [こうざん]; 鉱物 minerals [こうぶつ]; 炭鉱 coal mine [たんこう]

70d 矢 "an arrow" 矢知医短候侯喉

SG-1524 矢	Meanings	Kun and On	Romaji	Bushu	Stroke Order and Number
	arrow; (to vow)	や シ	ya *shi*	矢	ノ 𠂉 二 午 矢 5

矢 **A** F-0897

1, 2, 3, and 4 depicted "an upward-aiming arrow" with "an arrowhead" attached. An arrow was used in a ceremony pledging one's service to a lord or a deity, and thus the character also signified "to vow." In the kanji, a slanted short stroke was added on the tip of the arrowhead for emphasis. The kanji 矢 means "arrow; (to vow)." <𠂉大>

矢 arrow [や]; 矢面に立つ to take the full brunt [やおもてに・たつ]; 毒矢 poison arrow [どくや]; 矢っ張り・矢張り sure enough, also, still, after all [やっぱり, やはり]; 矢庭に suddenly, abruptly [やにわに]; 矢継ぎ早に in quick succession, rapidly [やつぎばやに]; 一矢報いる to retaliate, get back at [いっし・むくいる]

SG-1525 知	Meanings	Kun and On	Romaji	Bushu	Stroke Order and Number
	to know, inform; knowledge	し-る チ	shi-ru *chi*	矢	ノ 𠂉 矢 矢 知 知 知 8

知 **A** F-0117

The seal-style form comprised 矢 "an arrow; to vow," and 口 **SG-0031** "a mouth" for "speaking," together originally signifying "to make a vow to a deity." By talking to a deity one would gain correct knowledge. Another explanation is that knowledge allows one to answer right away, with the immediacy of an arrow. The kanji 知 means "to know, inform; knowledge." <矢口>

知る to know [しる]; 知人 acquaintance [ちじん]; 知事 governor [ちじ]; 承知する to consent to, accept, know [しょうちする]; 熟知する to know well, have thorough knowledge of [じゅくちする]; 知能 intelligence, mental faculties [ちのう]; 知覚 perception, sense [ちかく]; 周知の common knowledge [しゅうちの]; 機知に富んだ witty, resourceful [きちに・とんだ]

SG-1526 医	Meanings	Kun and On	Romaji	Bushu	Stroke Order and Number
	medicine, medical doctor; medical	イ	*i*	酉	一 ァ 㔫 矢 医 7

医 **A** F-0400

There are two kanji in modern use that are used to mean "medical"—the more common shinji 医 (3), and the less-common but still often-seen kyuji 醫 (5). The shinji 医 originated from a depiction of a quiver (a portable case of arrows), as in 1 and 2. On the other hand, the kyuji 醫 was the original character used to mean "medical care," with 4 comprising 医 "a quiver," 殳, bushu *hokozukuri* "holding a weapon in hand," and 酉 "an urn containing medicinal spirits." Together they signified "someone using medicinal spirits to treat the wound of a soldier shot by an arrow," and thus the character meant "medicine; medicinal." 医 came to be used as a simplified form of 醫, for the same meaning. The kanji 医 means "medicine, medical doctor; medical." <匚矢>

医者 medical doctor [いしゃ]; 医学 medical science [いがく]; 内科医 doctor of internal medicine, physician [ないかい]; 医院 doctor's clinic, doctor's surgery [いいん]; 医療費 fee for medical treatment, doctor's bill [いりょうひ]; 医薬分業 separation of pharmacy and clinic [いやく・ぶんぎょう]

SG-1527 短	Meanings	Kun and On	Romaji	Bushu	Stroke Order and Number
	short, deficient; lack of	みじか-い タン	mijika-i *tan*	矢	𠂉 二 矢 矢 矩 短 短 12

短 **A** F-0471

The seal-style form comprised 矢 "arrow," and 豆 **SG-1975** "urn, crock," used for the sound *tan* to mean "short." An arrow was used for measuring the length of short items. Being short also meant "lack of; deficient." The kanji 短 means "short, deficient; lack of." <矢豆>

短い short [みじかい]; 気短な short-tempered, impatient [きみじかな]; 手短に言えば to put it succinctly [てみじかにいえば]; 長短 merits and demerits, strength and weakness [ちょうたん]; 短所 weakness, shortcoming [たんしょ]; 短歌 *tanka* poetry, a 31-syllable poem [たんか]; 短縮 shortening, reduction [たんしゅく]

	Meanings	Kun and On	Romaji	Bushu	Stroke Order and Number
SG-1528 候	climate; to watch for a sign, scout; "to be" (in classical Japanese)	そうろう コウ	sooroo *koo*	人	亻 们 伫 侟 俟 候 候 10

候
B
F-1068

金文 1 說文 2

The kanji 候 and the kanji 侯 **SG-1529** were closely related. 1 comprised "an arrow" under "some eaves," or "a shooting range." 2 added "an act that a person does" (亻), and "a crouching scout keeping a lookout" at the top. A scout watching for signs of an enemy gave the meaning "to peep, watch for a sign." Weather or climate was something one judged or forecast by keeping a diligent eye on natural conditions, and so the character also meant "atmospheric signs." In Japanese, it was historically also used for the old epistolary-style word 候 *sooroo*, which meant "to be." The kanji 候 means "climate; to watch for a sign, scout; "to be" (in classical Japanese). <亻丨矦>

候 to be (classical) [そうろう]; 候文 old epistolary-style writing in classical Japanese [そうろう・ぶん]; 居候 a person living in someone's else's house without paying, freeloader [いそうろう]; 天候 weather [てんこう]; 気候 climate [きこう]; 気候変動 climate change [きこう・へんどう]; 候補者 candidate [こう・ほ・しゃ]

	Meanings	Kun and On	Romaji	Bushu	Stroke Order and Number
SG-1529 侯	feudal lord, marquis	コウ	*koo*	人	亻 仁 伫 侯 侯 侯 9

侯
D
F-2077

甲骨文 1 金文1 2 金文2 3 說文 4

1, 2, and 3 depicted "an arrow under some eaves," or "a hidden or protected area." In 4, "a crouching scout watching out for the enemy" was added, which became ユ in the kanji. 亻, bushu *ninben* "an act that a person does," was also added in the kanji. The character was used for the title of a person who oversaw shooting against an enemy—"a feudal lord." The kanji 侯 means "feudal lord, marquis." <亻矦>

諸侯 feudal lords [しょ・こう]; 侯爵 marquis [こう・しゃく]

	Meanings	Kun and On	Romaji	Bushu	Stroke Order and Number
SG-1530 喉	throat	のど コウ	nodo *koo*	口	口 吖 吖 喉 喉 喉 12

喉
D
F-2298

篆文

The seal-style form comprised 口 **SG-0031** "mouth," next to 侯 **SG-1529**, used for the sound *koo* to mean "throat." The kanji 喉 means "throat." <口亻矦>

喉 throat [のど]; 耳鼻咽喉科 ear nose and throat specialist, otolaryngology [じ・び・いんこう・か]; 喉頭炎 laryngitis [こう・とう・えん]

70e 至 "an end" [from an arrow hitting the ground] 至室屋到倒致握窒緻

	Meanings	Kun and On	Romaji	Bushu	Stroke Order and Number
SG-1531 至	to end, reach an end, attain	いた-る シ	ita-ru *shi*	至	一 ㄊ 厶 玄 至 至 6

至
A
F-1065

甲骨文 1 金文 2 說文古文 3 說文 4

1 and 2 depicted "a downward-aiming arrow hitting the ground or a target (—)," signifying "to reach, end in." The kanji 至 means "to end, reach an end, attain." <至 (一厶土)>

至る to reach, arrive [いた・る]; 至れり尽せり complete, leaving nothing to be desired [いたれ・り・つくせ・り]; 至る所に everywhere [いた・るところに]; 至急 urgently, without delay [し・きゅう]; 必至 inevitable [ひっし]; 至上命令 supreme directive [しじょうめ・いれい]; 夏至 summer solstice [げし]; 冬至 winter solstice [とうじ]

	Meanings	Kun and On	Romaji	Bushu	Stroke Order and Number
SG-1532 室	room, greenhouse, cellar	むろ シツ	muro *shitsu*	宀	丶 宀 宀 宏 室 室 室 9

室
A
F-0321

甲骨文 1 金文 2 說文 3

1, 2, and 3 comprised 宀 "a house," and 至, "a downward-aiming arrow hitting the ground or other spot from which it cannot go further," used for the sound *shi*. Together they meant "room, cellar." The kanji 室 means "room, greenhouse, cellar." <宀 至>

氷室 icehouse [ひ・むろ]; 教室 classroom [きょう・しつ]; 室内 inside a room [しつ・ない]; 寝室 bedroom [しん・しつ]; 洋室 Western-style room [よう・しつ]; 王室 royal family [おう・しつ]; 側室 concubine [そく・しつ]; 室温 room temperature [しつ・おん]; 茶室 tea ceremony hut [ちゃ・しつ]

	Meanings	Kun and On	Romaji	Bushu	Stroke Order and Number
SG-1533 屋	roof, house, type of trade	や オク	ya *oku*	尸	コ尸尸层层屖屋 9

屋
A
F-0348

説文古文 1　説文籀文 2　説文 3　屋

1, 2, and 3 comprised "a downward-aiming arrow reaching the end of its trajectory" (至), inside "a house" in 1, or under "a roof' (尸 bushu *shikabane*) in 2 and 3. The kanji 屋 meant a "house." In Japanese, it is also used to mean "type of trade." The kanji 屋 means "roof, house, store." <尸至>

本屋 bookstore [ほ⌝んや]; 屋号 name of a store [や⌝ごう]; 屋根 roof [や⌝ね]; 小屋 shed, cabin, pen [こや⌝]; 平屋 one-story house, bungalow [ひらや]; 屋外 outdoors, open-air [おく⌝がい]; 屋上 rooftop [おくじょう]; 屋内プール indoor swimming pool [おくないプ⌝ール]

	Meanings	Kun and On	Romaji	Bushu	Stroke Order and Number
SG-1534 到	to arrive, come, reach	トウ	*too*	至・刀	一ㄊ互至至到到 8

到
B
F-1092

金文1 1　金文2 2　説文 3　到

1 and 2 comprised "an arrow reaching the end" (至 **SG-1531**), and "a person." Together they signified a person reaching the location where an arrow had landed or "arrived." In 3, "person" was misconstrued as "sword or knife," which became 刂, bushu *rittoo* in the kanji. The kanji 到 means "to arrive, come, reach." <至刂>

到着する to arrive [とうちゃくする]; 到底～ない cannot possibly [とうてい～な⌝い]; 到達する to attain [とうたつする]; 殺到する to rush to [さっとうする]; 到来物 present, gift [とうらいもの]

	Meanings	Kun and On	Romaji	Bushu	Stroke Order and Number
SG-1535 倒	to invert, fall, topple	たお-れる トウ	tao-reru *too*	人	亻伾伾侄侄倒 10

倒
B
F-0818

説文　倒

The right-side component is 到 **SG-1534**, used for the sound *too*, which represented a person going to retrieve an arrow. The addition of "an act one does" (亻) emphasized the person's return trip. The reversal of an act lent the meaning "inversion." Another view is that an arrow landing with its arrowhead down gave the meaning "upside-down." An upside-down thing topples easily, whence "to topple, fall." The kanji 倒 means "to invert, fall, topple." <亻至刂>

倒れる to fall, topple [たおれ⌝る]; 倒す to topple, bring down [たお⌝す]; 前倒しする to move up, accelerate [まえだおしする]; 倒壊する to collapse, topple [とうかいする]; 倒産 bankruptcy [とうさん]; 打倒する to overthrow [だとうする]; 卒倒する to faint, fall unconscious [そっとうする]

	Meanings	Kun and On	Romaji	Bushu	Stroke Order and Number
SG-1536 致	to cause an action, do, bring about	いた-す チ	ita-su *chi*	至	ㄊ互至至致致致 10

致
B
F-1030

金文 1　説文 2　致

1 was the same as 1 in 到 **SG-1534** "to arrive," signifying "a person walking to the point where an arrow has landed." One view explains that the right side of 2 was 夂 "a downward footprint" to mean "to fetch and return (with the arrow)," while another view explains it as "a hand holding a stick" and a precursor of 攵 "to cause an action." The kanji 致 means "to cause someone to do, do, bring about." <至攵>

致す to do (humble) [いた⌝す]; 致命的な fatal [ちめいてきな]; 一致する to agree, conform [いっちする]; 合致する to coincide, correspond [がっちする]; 誘致する to lure, attract [ゆ⌝うちする, ゆうちする]

	Meanings	Kun and On	Romaji	Bushu	Stroke Order and Number
SG-1537 握	to grip, grasp	にぎ-る アク	nigi-ru *aku*	手	扌扌护揈握握 12

握
C
F-1171

説文古文 1　説文 2　握

1 was the same as 1 in 屋 **SG-1533** (except that it had a circle in the middle) and was used for the sound *aku* to mean "to tighten." In 2, 扌, bushu *tehen* "an act done by hand," was added. A hand reaching out to seize something meant "to grip, grasp." The kanji 握 means "to grip, grasp" <扌屋>

握る to grip, grasp [にぎる]; 手に汗を握る to be in breathless suspense, gripping [て⌝に・あ⌝せをにぎる]; 握り締める to grasp tightly [にぎりしめ⌝る]; 握手 handshake [あ⌝くしゅ]; 把握する to perceive, grasp [はあくする]; 握力 grip strength [あく⌝りょく]

	Meanings	Kun and On	Romaji	Bushu	Stroke Order and Number
SG-1538 窒	impasse, nitrogen	チツ	*chitsu*	穴	宀 穴 空 窒 11

窒 **D** F-2138

説文

The seal-style form comprised 穴 **SG-1322** "cave, hole, dead end," and 至 **SG-1531** "an arrow reaching the end of its trajectory," used for the sound *chitsu* to mean "to close up, block up." An arrow reaching the end of a cave meant "dead end." The character also means "nitrogen." The kanji 窒 means "impasse, nitrogen." <穴 至>

窒素 nitrogen [ちっそ]; 窒息する to be suffocated, be choked [ちっそくする]; 窒素肥料 nitrogen fertilizer [ちっそひりょう]; 液体窒素 liquid nitrogen [えきたいちっそ]

	Meanings	Kun and On	Romaji	Bushu	Stroke Order and Number
SG-1539 緻	fine, minute	チ	*chi*	糸	糸 紟 絟 緻 緻 緻 16

緻 **D** F-2986

篆文

The seal-style form comprised 糸 **SG-1600** "skein of threads" for "close-grained, fine," and 致 **SG-1537** "to make, do," used for the sound *chi*. Together they signified "making fine things." The kanji 緻 means "fine, minute." <糸 致>

緻密な minute, intricate [ちみつな]; 精緻な minute, subtle [せいちな]

70f Pertaining to an arrow 演備弔

	Meanings	Kun and On	Romaji	Bushu	Stroke Order and Number
SG-1540 演	to stretch, extend, perform	エン	*en*	水	氵 沪 浐 涼 演 演 14

演 **B** F-0538

説文

The seal-style form comprised "flowing water" (氵), and 寅, used for the sound *en* to mean "to prolong, stretch." Water running for a long time gave the meaning of "an action being performed sequentially for a long time." The kanji 演 means "to stretch, extend, perform." <氵 寅>
(Note: The history of 寅 is shown on the right: "two hands trying to stretch a crooked arrow shaft," signifying "to stretch.")

演じる to perform [えんじる]; 実演 (public) demonstration, live on-stage acting [じつえん]; 公演 public performance [こうえん]; 演習 practice, exercise [えんしゅう]; 演説 public speech, address [えんぜつ]; 演出する to direct, stage [えんしゅつする]; 演繹法 deductive method [えんえきほう]; 出演者 performers, cast [しゅつえんしゃ]

	Meanings	Kun and On	Romaji	Bushu	Stroke Order and Number
SG-1541 備	to be prepared, be equipped with	そな-える ビ	sona-eru *bi*	人	亻 仁 伻 俳 俻 備 備 12

備 **B** F-0566

金文 1 説文 2

1 and 2 comprised 亻 "a person," and "a quiver with arrows inside" on the person's back. Having a quiver signified being prepared for an attack, and the character meant "well-prepared." The kanji 備 means "to be prepared, be equipped with." <亻 艹 用>

備える to stock, keep something ready [そなえる]; 備わる to be provided, possess [そなわる]; 軍備 military preparations, armaments [ぐんび]; 警備 guarding, security [けいび]; 予備の preliminary, preparatory [よびの]; 備品 fixtures, fittings [びひん]

	Meanings	Kun and On	Romaji	Bushu	Stroke Order and Number
SG-1542 弔	to mourn, condole with	とむら-う チョウ	tomura-u *choo*	弓	一 コ 弓 弔 4

弔 **D** F-1884

甲骨文1 1 甲骨文2 2 金文1 3 金文2 4 説文 5

One view explains that the kanji 弔 depicted "a vine or snake entwined around a stake" (1 thorough 4), and was borrowed to mean "to mourn." Another view holds that 弔 comprised "a person" and "a bow" (in 5), and that it meant "consoling a bereaved family" (*Setsumon)*. The connection between "a bow" and the meaning "to mourn" is further noted by Shirakawa, who writes that in ancient times, the body of the deceased was left in a field until skeletonized, and the bones collected later for burial (in 3, 4, and 5). At the time of burial, a mourner carried a bow and arrow for protection from wild animals, and thus the character signified "mourning." The kanji 弔 means "to mourn, condole with." <弓 丨>

弔う to mourn, hold a memorial service [とむらう]; 弔意を表す to offer one's condolences [ちょういを・あらわす]; 弔問客 condoler [ちょうもんきゃく]

71 Shields and other weapons

71a 干 [from a shield]; *kan* 岸干刊汗肝

	Meanings	*Kun* and On	Romaji	Bushu	Stroke Order and Number
SG-1543 岸	shore, bank	きし ガン	kishi *gan*	山	8

岸 **B** F-0769

説文

The seal-style form comprised 山 **SG-2127** "mountain" and 厂 "overhanging cliff" (together making 屵 "high cliff"), and 干 **SG-1544** used for the sound *gan*. Originally the character signified "a mountain cliff overlooking a river or sea." The kanji 岸 means "shore, bank." <山厂干>

岸 shore [きし]; 川岸 riverbank [かわぎし]; 岸辺 shore [きしべ]; 向こう岸 the other side of a river or a lake [むこうぎし]; 沿岸 seashore [えんがん]; お彼岸 equinoctial week for Buddhist memorial services [おひがん]; 暑さ寒さも彼岸まで "Neither heat nor cold lasts past the equinox." [あꜜつさ・さꜜむさも・ひがんまꜜで]

	Meanings	*Kun* and On	Romaji	Bushu	Stroke Order and Number
SG-1544 干	to interfere, meddle, dry, dry up	ほ-す・ひ-る カン	ho-su, hi-ru *kan*	干	一 二 干 3

干 **C** F-1155

甲骨文1 1 甲骨文2 2 金文1 3 金文2 4 説文 5

1 through 5 all depicted a forked thrusting weapon that signified "to violate or attack," and had the sound *kan*. Due to having the same sound *kan* as 乾 **SG-1574** "dry," the character was also used to mean "to dry, dry up." The kanji 干 means "to interfere, meddle, dry, dry up." <干>

干す to air under the sun [ほꜜす]; 布団を干す to air a *futon* under the sun [ふとんをほꜜす]; 虫干し summer airing [むしぼし]; 干からびる to shrivel up, dry up [ひからびꜜる]; 干上がる to dry up, run dry [ひあがꜜる]; 干物 dried fish [ひもの]; 干害 drought damage [かんがい]; 干渉 interference [かんしょう]

	Meanings	*Kun* and On	Romaji	Bushu	Stroke Order and Number
SG-1545 刊	to publish	カン	*kan*	刀	一 二 干 刊 5

刊 **C** F-1112

説文

The seal-style form comprised "a knife," and 干, used for the sound *kan* to mean "to shave a piece of wood." A printing woodblock was shaved with a knife to create a new surface for carving. In the kanji the knife became 刂, bushu *rittoo*. The kanji 刊 means "to publish." <干刂>

刊行 publishing [かんこう]; 朝刊 morning edition [ちょうかん]; 夕刊 evening edition [ゆうかん]; 月刊誌 monthly magazine [げっかꜜんし]; 定期刊行物 periodical [ていきかんこꜜうぶつ]; 新刊書 newly published book [しんかんしょ]

	Meanings	*Kun* and On	Romaji	Bushu	Stroke Order and Number
SG-1546 汗	perspiration, sweat	あせ カン	ase *kan*	水	氵 氵一 氵二 汗 6

汗 **C** F-1196

説文

The seal-style form comprised "water" (氵, bushu *sanzui*), and 干, used for the sound *kan*. The kanji 汗 means "perspiration, sweat." <氵干>

汗 perspiration, sweat [あꜜせ]; 汗をかく to sweat, perspire [あꜜせをかꜜく]; 冷や汗 cold sweat [ひやあꜜせ]; 汗だくになる to be drenched in sweat [あせだくにならꜜる]; 汗水垂らす to toil hard [あꜜせみず・たらꜜす]; 発汗 sweating [はっかん]; 制汗剤 antiperspirant [せいかんざい、せいかꜜんざい]

	Meanings	*Kun* and On	Romaji	Bushu	Stroke Order and Number
SG-1547 肝	liver, courage, main point; hepatic, important	きも カン	kimo *kan*	肉	月 月 肝 肝 7

肝 **C** F-1292

説文

The seal-style form comprised 月, bushu *nikuzuki* "part of the body," and 干, used for the sound *kan*, together signifying "liver, hepatic, courage." The liver is a vital organ, and thus the character also means "most important." The kanji 肝 means "liver, courage, main point; hepatic, important." <月干>

肝煎り sponsorship, offer of help [きもいり]; 度肝を抜かれる to be dumbfounded [どぎもをぬかれる]; 肝試し a test of someone's courage [きもだꜜめし]; 肝心な important, critical [かんじんな]; 肝臓 liver [かんぞう]; 肝要な extremely important, indispensable [かんような]

71b 単 [borrowed from a shield with a two-pronged spear]; *tan* 単戦弾

	Meanings	Kun and On	Romaji	Bushu	Stroke Order and Number
SG-1548 単	single, only	タン	*tan*	口	⺍ 尚 当 単 単 9

単 **A** F-0467

甲骨文 1 金文 2 説文 3 旧字 4

1, 2, and 3 depicted "a shield with a two-pronged spear." The character originally meant "a shield." 単 was used to represent a unit of troops, and came to mean "single, only." In the shinji 単, the top was replaced by ⺍. The kanji 単 means "single, only." <⺍日十>

単なる mere [たんなる]; 単に merely [たんに]; 単位 unit [たんい]; 単価 unit price [たんか]; 単語 word, vocabulary item [たんご]; 単車 motorcycle, bike [たんしゃ]; 単行本 a book published as a single volume [たんこうぼん]; 単純な simple, straightforward [たんじゅんな]

	Meanings	Kun and On	Romaji	Bushu	Stroke Order and Number
SG-1549 戦	war, battle; to fight	いくさ・たたか-う セン	ikusa, tataka-u *sen*	戈	⺍ 当 単 単 戦 戦 戦 13

戦 **A** F-0184

甲骨文1 1 甲骨文2 2 金文 3 説文 4 旧字 5

1 depicted "two halberds," whereas 2 showed "two shields." A soldier fought a battle with a shield in one hand and a halberd in the other, and the character meant "to fight; war, battle." 3 and 4 comprised both "a shield" and "a halberd." In the shinji, the left side became 単 **SG-1548**. The kanji 戦 means "war, battle; to fight." <単戈>

戦 war, battle [いくさ]; 勝ち戦 successful war, victory [かちいくさ]; 戦う to fight [たたかう]; 戦争 war [せんそう]; (Aと)対戦する to fight against (A) [たいせんする]; 作戦 strategy [さくせん]; 戦々恐々 with fear and trembling, panic-stricken [せんせんきょうきょう]; 戦況 the progress of a battle [せんきょう]

	Meanings	Kun and On	Romaji	Bushu	Stroke Order and Number
SG-1550 弾	to flick, spring; bullet	ひ-く・はず-む・たま ダン	hi-ku, hazu-mu, tama *dan*	弓	ᄀ ᄏ 弓 弓⺍ 弹 弾 弾 12

弾 **B** F-0844

甲骨文1 1 甲骨文2 2 説文 3 説文或体 4 旧字 5

1 depicted a slingshot-like apparatus made of "a bow with a rock in it" (giving the meaning "bullet"). 2 was "a bow." The character meant "to flick; bullet." 3 comprised 弓 **SG-1509** and 單 (単 **SG-1549**, used for the sound *dan*), and 爪 **SG-0927** "fingernails" was added in 4 to signify the action of fingers flicking something. The kanji 弾 means "bullet; to flick, play a stringed instrument/piano." <弓単>

ピアノを弾く to play piano [ピアノをひく]; 弾む to bounce, be stimulated [はずむ]; 流れ弾 stray bullet, random shot [ながれだま]; 実弾 loaded cartridge [じつだん]; 弾丸 bullet [だんがん]; 弾力性 elasticity, flexibility [だんりょくせい]; 弾圧 oppression, repression [だんあつ]

71c 盾 "shield" 盾循

	Meanings	Kun and On	Romaji	Bushu	Stroke Order and Number
SG-1551 盾	shield	たて ジュン	tate *jun*	目	厂 𠂆 斤 盾 盾 9

盾 **C** F-1502

甲骨文 1 金文 2 説文 3

1 and 2 were "a square shield." 3 was "a shield" over "an eye" (目 **SG-0001**), signifying "a shield protecting the eyes of a soldier." The kanji 盾 means "shield." <𠂆盾>

盾 shield [たて]; 後ろ盾 support, backing [うしろだて]; 矛盾 contradiction, inconsistency [むじゅん]

	Meanings	Kun and On	Romaji	Bushu	Stroke Order and Number
SG-1552 循	to follow, go along	ジュン	*jun*	彳	彳 彳 𢔁 循 循 循 12

循 **D** F-1694

説文

The seal-style form comprised 彳 "a crossroads; going," and 盾 **SG-1551** "a shield," used for the sound *jun* to mean "to follow, go along." Together they signified "to make rounds, go along." The kanji 循 means "to follow, go along." <彳盾>

循環 cycle, circulation, rotation [じゅんかん]; 悪循環 vicious circle [あくじゅんかん]; 因循な indecisive, shillyshallying [いんじゅんな]; 因循姑息 adhering to old ways and relying on makeshift conservative measures rather than adapting to a new situation [いんじゅん・こそく]

71d 周 "to go around; full" [from a shield covered in elaborate patterns; or rice paddies filled with seedlings]; *shuu/choo* 周調週彫

	Meanings	*Kun* and *On*	Romaji	Bushu	Stroke Order and Number
SG-1553 周	full; to spread, permeate, go around	まわ-り シュウ	mawa-ri *shuu*	口	ノ冂冂円円周 8

周 **A** F-0457

甲骨文 1 甲骨文 2 金文 1 金文 2 金文 3 説文 | 1 2 3 4 5 6

One view explains that the kanji 周 came from a depiction of an area (口) of rice paddies with rigorously growing rice plants, used for the sound *shuu*. The character meant "full, thorough." Another view explains that 1 through 5 depicted "a decorative shield with rich patterns," and that the 口 underneath the shield in 4, 5, and 6 was a box of prayers for victory in battle. A shield fully decorated all over its surface gave the meaning "full, thorough." The kanji 周 means "full; to spread, permeate, go around." <冂土口>

周り the people surrounding one, border [まわり]; 一周り turn, a round, size [ひと˥まわり]; 一周する to make a round [いっしゅうする]; 円周 circumference of a circle [えんしゅう]; 周囲 circumference, the people around one [しゅ˥うい]; 周波数 frequency [しゅうは˥すう]; 用意周到な painstakingly prepared, exhaustively careful in one's preparation [よ˥うい・しゅうとうな]

	Meanings	*Kun* and *On*	Romaji	Bushu	Stroke Order and Number
SG-1554 調	to investigate; in-tune; condition	しら-べる・ととの-う チョウ	shira-beru, totono-u *choo*	言	言言訂訶調調 15

調 **A** F-0181

説文

The seal-style form comprised 言 **SG-1364** "word, language; to speak," and 周 **SG-1553** "to permeate; thorough, full," used for the sound *choo*. Something "being full" signified "well-balanced and in harmony." The character also meant that "by using words one may thoroughly investigate the state or condition of a matter." The kanji 調 means "to investigate, be in good order; tune, condition." <言周>

調べる to investigate, check [しらべ˥る]; 調える to arrange, get things ready [ととのえ˥る]; 調子 tune, tone, manner, condition [ちょうし]; 調度品 furniture, personal effects [ちょうどひん]; 新調する to have something made new [しんちょうする]; 低調な dull, sluggish [ていちょうな]; 調停 mediation, intervention [ちょうてい];体調 physical condition, health condition [たいちょう]

	Meanings	*Kun* and *On*	Romaji	Bushu	Stroke Order and Number
SG-1555 週	week	シュウ	*shuu*	辵	冂円円周淍週 11

週 **A** F-0484

No ancient form. The kanji 週 comprises 周 "to go around," used for the sound *shuu*, and 辶, bushu *shinnyuu* "to move forward." Days going around meant "a cycle of a week." The kanji 週 means "week." <周辶>

週間 week [しゅうかん]; 週刊誌 weekly magazine [しゅうか˥んし]; 来週 next week [らいしゅう]; 再来週 the week after next [さらいしゅう]; 週休二日制 five-day workweek [しゅうきゅう(・)ふつかせい]; 週末 weekend [しゅうまつ]; 週明け the beginning of next week, first thing on Monday [しゅうあけ]

	Meanings	*Kun* and *On*	Romaji	Bushu	Stroke Order and Number
SG-1556 彫	to carve, chisel; sculpture	ほ-る チョウ	ho-ru *choo*	彡	冂円円周周彫 11

彫 **C** F-1524

説文

The seal-style form comprised 周 ("being fully decorated" or "a shield"), used for the sound *choo*, and 彡 "a beautiful shape." A beautifully carved object or decorated shield meant "carving." The kanji 彫 means "to carve, chisel; sculpture." <周彡>

彫る to carve, sculpt [ほ˥る]; 木彫り wood carving [きぼり]; 彫り物 sculpture, tattoo, carving [ほりもの]; 浮き彫りになる to stand out [うきぼりになる]; 彫刻 sculpture, engraving, carving [ちょうこく]; 彫刻刀 carving knife, chisel [ちょうこくとう]

71e 古 "old" [from multiple proposed origins: a shield, an old skull, or a prayer box]; *ko* 古故苦枯

	Meanings	*Kun* and *On*	Romaji	Bushu	Stroke Order and Number
SG-1557 古	old, ancient	ふる-い コ	huru-i *ko*	口	一十十古古 5

古 **A** F-0292

甲骨文 金文 1 金文 2 説文 | 1 2 3 4

One view holds that this character depicted the old, hard skull of an ancestral deity, with a crown or other

古い old [ふる˥い]; 古びた old and worn [ふる˥びた]; 古顔 a familiar old face, senior member [ふるがお]; お古 hand-me-down, used article [おふ˥る]; 古代 ancient times [こ˥だい]; 古典

decoration placed on top. An ancestral deity meant "old." Another view explains that it depicted "a box of old benedictions on old important matters (bottom), protected by a shield (top)." Such preserved precedents became rules and laws. The kanji 古 means "old, ancient." <十口>

classical work, classics [こてん]; 中古品 previously-used item, secondhand item [ちゅうこひん]; 古今東西 all times and places [こꜜこん・とꜜうざい] // 古 ancient, olden days (literary) [いにしえ]

	Meanings	Kun and On	Romaji	Bushu	Stroke Order and Number
SG-1558 故	reason, cause; deliberate, deceased	ゆえ コ	yue *ko*	攴	一 十 古 古 故 故 9

故 **B** F-0637

金文1 (1) 金文2 (2) 説文 (3) 故

1 was the same as 1 for 古 **SG-1557.** 2 and 3 comprised 古 "ancient, old, hard" and 攴 (攵, bushu *bokunyuu* "to cause"), together signifying "to make something stiff and old, old." Adherence to old precedents was a good reason to do something, whence the meaning "reason or cause." A person becoming "an old and hardened skull" meant "dead; deceased person." The kanji 故 means "reason, cause; deliberate, dead." <古攵>

それ故 therefore [それゆえ]; 何故に for what reason (literary) [なにゆえに]; 故人 deceased [こꜜじん]; 故意に intentionally [こꜜいに]; 故障 breakdown (of a machine) [こしょう]; 事故 accident [じꜜこ]; 物故者 the deceased [ぶっこꜜしゃ]; 故事 historical events, folklore [こꜜじ] // 何故 why, for what reason [なꜜぜ]

	Meanings	Kun and On	Romaji	Bushu	Stroke Order and Number
SG-1559 苦	hard, bitter, trying, rough	くる-しい・にが-い ク	kuru-shii, niga-i *ku*	艸	一 艹 苎 苹 苦 苦 8

苦 **B** F-0639

説文 苦

The seal-style form comprised "plants" (艸,艹, bushu *kusakanmuri*), and 古 **SG-1557**, used for the sound *ku.* It was the name of a particular plant that was bitter when bitten, whence the meaning "bitter." By extension, it also meant "trying; hardship." The kanji 苦 means "hard, bitter, trying; hardship." <艹古>

苦しい hard, tough, baffling [くるしꜜい]; 見苦しい unseemly, displeasing [みぐるしꜜい]; 寝苦しい to have an uneasy sleep [ねぐるしꜜい]; 苦い bitter [にがꜜい];苦み bitter taste [にがみꜜ]; 苦々しく思う to feel bitter, feel acrimonious [にがにがしꜜく・おもꜜう]; 生活苦 hardship of life [せいかつꜜく]; 苦楽を共にするto share life's joys and sorrows with [くꜜらくを・ともにする]

	Meanings	Kun and On	Romaji	Bushu	Stroke Order and Number
SG-1560 枯	to wither; dead	か-れる コ	ka-reru *ko*	木	木 木 朩 枯 枯 9

枯 **D** F-1722

説文 枯

The seal-style form comprised 木 **SG-0608** "tree," and 古, used for the sound *ko* to mean "old; something bereft of life," together signifying "a tree withering or dying." The kanji 枯 means "to wither; dead." <木古>

枯れる to wither, die [かれる]; 枯れ木 dead tree [かれき]; 枯葉 dead leaf [かれは]; 枯山水 Japanese style of gardening where hills and streams are represented without the use of water [かれさꜜんすい]; 木枯らし cold wintery wind [こがꜜらし]; 枯渇する to dry up [こかつする]

71f 固 "solid" [from something old and hard in an enclosure]; *ko* 固個湖箇錮

	Meanings	Kun and On	Romaji	Bushu	Stroke Order and Number
SG-1561 固	solid, hard	かた-い コ	kata-i *ko*	口	丨 冂 冃 冄 冋 固 固 8

固 **A** F-0819

中山王器 (1) 説文 (2) 固

1 and 2 comprised 古 **SG-1557** "old and hard," used for the sound *ko,* and 囗, bushu *kunigamae* "an enclosure," together signifying "to closely guard something old and important." An old thing that was tightly packed became solid. The kanji 固 means "solid, hard." <囗古>

固い hard, solid, stiff, firm [かたい]; 固める to make hard, solidify, strengthen [かためる]; 頑固な stubborn, obstinate [がꜜんこな]; 固体 solid body [こたい]; 固定する to fix, fasten, anchor [こていする]; 堅固な firm, strong [けꜜんごな]

	Meanings	Kun and On	Romaji	Bushu	Stroke Order and Number
SG-1562 個	individual, piece	コ	*ko*	人	亻 们 们 個 個 個 個 10

個 **A** F-0328

No ancient form. The kanji 個 comprised 亻 "an act one does," and 固 "something solid and individual," used for the sound *ko*. The kanji 個 is used as a general counter for objects. Since it contains bushu *ninben,* it is also used to mean "individual (person)." The kanji 個 means "individual, piece." <亻固>

一個 one object, one item [いꜜっこ]; 個数 number of items [こすꜜう]; 個人 individual person [こꜜじん]; 個々に individually, one by one [こꜜこに]; 個室 private room [こしつ]; 個別の individual, discrete [こべつの]; 別個に separately [べっこに]

	Meanings	Kun and On	Romaji	Bushu	Stroke Order and Number
SG-1563 湖	lake	みずうみ コ	mizuumi *ko*	水	氵汁沽湖湖 12

湖 **C** F-1167 — 金文 1, 説文 2, 湖

1 and 2 comprised 氵 "flowing water," and either 古 or 胡, used for the sound *ko* to mean "large." A large pool of water was "a lake." The kanji 湖 means "lake." <氵古月>

湖 lake [みずう˥み]; 湖水 lake water [こすい]; 琵琶湖 Lake Biwa [びわこ]; 湖畔 lakeside [こはん]

	Meanings	Kun and On	Romaji	Bushu	Stroke Order and Number
SG-1564 箇	item, counter for items/places	カ	*ka*	竹	⺮⺮笛笛箇箇 14

箇 **D** F-2196 — 説文, 箇

The seal-style form comprised 竹 **SG-0759** "bamboo," and 固 **SG-1561** "something solid," used for the sound *ka*. Bamboo tallies were used in counting tangible items. The kanji 箇 means "item, counter for items/places." <⺮固>

一箇所 one place, one spot [いっか˥しょ]; 箇条書き to itemize, enumerate [かじょうがき]

	Meanings	Kun and On	Romaji	Bushu	Stroke Order and Number
SG-1565 錮	to confine, lock away	コ	*ko*	金	亼 牟 金 釦 錮 錮 錮 16

錮 **D** F-4376 — 説文, 錮

The seal-style form comprised 金 **SG-1196** "metal," and 固, for the sound *ko*. Together they originally signified "to fill a gap in metalware by pouring in dissolved metal," which further meant "to lock away." The kanji 錮 means "to confine, lock away." <金固>

禁錮 imprisonment [き˥んこ]

72 Banner

72a 㫃 "traveling with a banner" [from "a band of soldiers traveling with a banner on a pole]

旅族遊施旗旋

Even though 㫃 originated in a single image, only the left side (方) is used as bushu.

	Meanings	Kun and On	Romaji	Bushu	Stroke Order and Number
SG-1566 旅	to travel; a trip	たび リョ	tabi *ryo*	方	' 亠 方 方 方' 㫃 旅 旅 旅 10

旅 **A** F-0409 — 甲骨文 1, 甲骨文 2, 金文 1, 金文 2, 金文 3, 金文 4, 説文, 旅 (1, 2, 3, 4, 5, 6, 7)

1, 2, 3, and 5 depicted "a pole with a banner attached," under which there were "people facing the same direction," signifying "traveling." In 4 and 6, the people were "hoisting a banner." In 5, "a military vehicle" was present. Many soldiers traveling together under a military banner with vehicles meant "a military unit traveling." The meaning of "military" was lost, and the kanji 旅 means "to travel; a trip." In 7 the pole and banner were separated, and became 㫃 in the kanji. <㫃𠂈>

長旅 long journey [ながたび]; 旅立つ to leave, depart [たびだ˥つ]; 船旅 ocean trip, voyage [ふなたび]; 旅人 traveler [たびびと]; 旅行 travel, trip, journey [りょこう]; 旅券 passport [りょけん]; 旅客 rider, passenger [りょかく, りょきゃく]

	Meanings	Kun and On	Romaji	Bushu	Stroke Order and Number
SG-1567 族	family, clan; of the same kind	ゾク	*zoku*	方	' 亠 方 方 方' 㫃 㫃 族 族 11

族 **A** F-0507 — 甲骨文1, 甲骨文2, 金文, 説文, 族 (1, 2, 3, 4)

In 1, 2, and 3, "an arrow under the banner of a band of soldiers" originally signified "a military unit." In 4, the arrow was moved out to the right side. The connotation of "military" was dropped, and the character meant "family, clan." The kanji 族 means "family, clan; (people) of the same kind." <㫃矢>

一族 one's relations, one's clan [いち˥ぞく]; 社用族 expense account spenders [しゃよう˥ぞく]; 水族館 aquarium [すいぞく˥かん, すいぞ˥っかん]; 少数民族 minority race [しょうすうみ˥んぞく]; 血族関係 kinship, blood ties [けつぞくか˥んけい]; 親族 relatives [し˥んぞく]; 族議員 diet member who lobbies for a special-interest group [ぞくぎ˥いん]

	Meanings	Kun and On	Romaji	Bushu	Stroke Order and Number
SG-1568 遊	to play, have fun, move freely; away from home	あそ-ぶ ユウ・ユ	aso-bu *yuu, yu*	辵	亠方方´方ゲ斿斿游遊 12

遊 **B** F-0650

說文

The seal-style form comprised "flowing water" (氵), and 斿 "to move about freely," used for the sound *yuu*. From the history of 斿, shown upper right, we see that it had a child under a clan banner, signifying "a family/clan traveling away from home." In the kanji 遊, "water" was replaced with 辶, bushu *shinnyuu*, "to go forward." From the meaning "moving from one place to another away from home," the kanji 遊 means "to play, have fun, move freely; away from home." <㫃子辶>

遊ぶ to play, have fun [あそぶ]; 砂遊び playing with sand [すなあそび]; 遊戯 (children's) play, dancing [ゆうぎ]; 遊休施設 idle facility [ゆうきゅうしせつ]; 周遊券 excursion ticket [しゅうゆうけん]; 外遊 tour abroad [がいゆう]; 遊牧民族 nomads, wandering tribe [ゆうぼくみんぞく]; 物見遊山 going on a pleasure jaunt [ものみゆさん]

	Meanings	Kun and On	Romaji	Bushu	Stroke Order and Number
SG-1569 施	to conduct, give (money or things) to charity	ほどこ-す セ・シ	hodoko-su *se, shi*	方	ˋ亠う方方´方ゲ於施施 9

施 **B** F-0688

中山王器1 1 中山王器2 2 說文 3

1 was "a banner fluttering or waving in a high place," while 2 and 3 had 也 "a snake" added for the sound *shi* to mean "loose, stretching long," to emphasize the fluttering of the banner. The character signified "to stretch far, transfer," and further came to mean "to give (to charity), administer." The kanji 施 means "to conduct, give (money or things) to charity." <㫃也>

施す to give to charity, administer [ほどこす]; 実施する to invoke, carry out [じっしする]; 施工 execution of work, construction [せこう]; 施主 chief mourner, client [せしゅ, せしゅ]; お布施 charity, offering, alms (Buddhism) [おふせ]; 施設 facility [しせつ]

	Meanings	Kun and On	Romaji	Bushu	Stroke Order and Number
SG-1570 旗	banner, flag	はた キ	hata *ki*	方	ˋ亠う方方´方ゲ旃旃旗旗 14

旗 **C** F-1259

說文

The seal-style form comprised 㫃 "a banner on a pole," and 其 "a square shape," used for the sound *ki*. Together they signified the square shape of a banner or flag. The kanji 旗 means "banner, flag." <㫃其>

旗 flag, banner [はた]; 旗竿 flagstaff, flagpole [はたざお]; 旗色が変わる The tide of war changes [はたいろがかわる]; 国旗 national flag [こっき]; 旗手 banner handler (sports) [きしゅ]; 半旗 a flag at half-mast [はんき]; 日章旗 Japan's national flag [にっしょうき]; 星条旗 the Star-Spangled Banner, the national flag of the U.S.A. [せいじょうき]

	Meanings	Kun and On	Romaji	Bushu	Stroke Order and Number
SG-1571 旋	to turn, rotate	セン	*sen*	方	ˋ亠う方方´方ゲ於旃旋旋 11

旋 **D** F-1775

甲骨文 1 金文 2 說文 3

1 comprised "a banner on a pole," "a round shape," and "a footprint," together signifying "walking about in a circle in a group." Another view posits that the circle was "a kneecap" that became a part of 足 "leg" **SG-0227** in 3, which further changed to 疋 in the kanji. Walking in a circle meant "turn." The kanji 旋 means "to turn, rotate." <㫃 疋>

旋回する to revolve, rotate [せんかいする]; 旋風 whirlwind, cyclone [せんぷう]; 旋律 melody [せんりつ]; 凱旋 triumphant return [がいせん]

72b 𠦝 "raised high" [from a banner or streamer fluttering high]; *kan* 幹韓乾 倝

	Meanings	Kun and On	Romaji	Bushu	Stroke Order and Number
SG-1572 幹	tree trunk; important, main	みき カン	miki *kan*	干	十吉𠦝𠦝^幹幹 13

幹 **B** F-0687

中山王器 1 篆文 2 正字 3

1 comprised "a banner raised high," and "the sun risen above a tree." It signified "the bright morning sun rising" and had the sound *kan*. In 2 and 3 it became comprised of 倝 and 木. A tree trunk that grew tall represented something "important." The kanji 幹 means "tree trunk; important, main." <倝 干>

幹 tree trunk [みき]; 幹事 organizer of a social gathering [かんじ]; 幹部 key officers, senior members [かんぶ]; 新幹線 the Bullet Train, the *Shinkansen* [しんかんせん]; 幹線道路 principal road [かんせんどうろ]; 幹細胞 stem cell [かんさいぼう]

	Meanings	Kun and On	Romaji	Bushu	Stroke Order and Number
SG-1573 韓	South Korea; Korean	カン	*kan*	韋	𠦝 卓 ... 韓 18

韓 **B** F-0853 (金文 1, 說文 2)

1 comprised "the sun rising" and "a banner raised high on a pole," and had the sound *kan*. In 2, "tanned leather (韋)" was added, giving the meaning "strong." The kanji 韓 is now used in the name of the country of South Korea. The kanji 韓 means "South Korea; Korean." <卓 韋>

韓国 South Korea [かꜜんこく]; 韓流ドラマ South Korean TV drama [かんりゅうドꜜラマ]; 日韓 Japan and South Korea [にꜜっかん]; 韓国語 Korean language [かんこくご]

	Meanings	Kun and On	Romaji	Bushu	Stroke Order and Number
SG-1574 乾	to dry; dry	かわ-く カン	kawa-ku *kan*	乙	𠦝 卓 ... 乾 11

乾 **C** F-1363 (說文籀文 1, 說文 2)

1 and 2 comprised "a banner raised high in the sun" (倝), used for the sound *kan*, and 乙 **SG-2104** "a streamer." The sound *kan* also meant "dry," and a streamer hung high also gave the meaning "to dry." The kanji 乾 means "to dry; dry." <卓 乞>

乾く to dry [かわꜜく]; 生乾き not completely dry, damp [なまがわき]; 乾物 dry food [かんぶꜜつ]; 異常乾燥 a spell of unusually dry weather [いじょうかꜜんそう]; 乾杯 a toast [かんぱい] // 乾拭き wiping with a dry cloth [からぶき]

72c 中 "middle, center" [from the banner of a main troop]; *chuu* 中仲沖

	Meanings	Kun and On	Romaji	Bushu	Stroke Order and Number
SG-1575 中	middle, center, inside; unbiased	なか チュウ・ジュウ	naka *chuu, juu*	丨	丨 冂 口 中 4

中 **A** F-0005 (甲骨文1 1, 甲骨文2 2, 金文1 3, 金文2 4, 說文 5)

1, 2, and 3 depicted banners or streamers on a pole, placed at the center of a circle. The character signified the banner of a military troop positioned in the center of many soldiers, which played an important role in a battle. In 4 and 5, the banners were dropped. The kanji 中 means "middle, central, inside; unbiased." <中>

中 middle, inside [なꜜか]; 中身 contents [なかꜜみ]; 真ん中 center, middle [まんなか]; 中間 middle [ちゅうかん]; 中心 center [ちゅうしん]; ~の最中に in the middle of X, at the height of X [~のさꜜいちゅうに]; お話中 (telephone) engaged/busy [おはなしちゅう]; 年中 at all times of the year, throughout the year [ねꜜんじゅう]

	Meanings	Kun and On	Romaji	Bushu	Stroke Order and Number
SG-1576 仲	relationship, terms, closeness	なか チュウ	naka *chuu*	人	亻 仢 仲 仲 6

仲 **B** F-0662 (甲骨文 1, 金文1 2, 金文2 3, 說文 4)

1, 2, and 3 were essentially the same as ancient forms of 中 **SG-1575**. With the addition of 亻 "a person," 4 originally meant a middle son between the oldest and the youngest. "A person in between" gave the meaning "relationship." The kanji 仲 means "relationship, terms, closeness." <亻 中>

仲違いする to have a disagreement, fall out with [なかたꜜがいする]; 仲良し close friendship, close friend [なかꜜよし]; 仲間 one's group, buddy [なかま]; 仲間入り joining in, inclusion [なかまいり]; 仲介 intermediation, brokerage [ちゅうかい] // 仲人 go-between, matchmaker [なこꜜうど]

	Meanings	Kun and On	Romaji	Bushu	Stroke Order and Number
SG-1577 沖	open sea, offing	おき チュウ	oki *chuu*	水	氵 沪 泊 沖 7

沖 **B** F-0796 (甲骨文 1, 金文 2, 說文 3)

1 and 2 comprised "flowing water" (氵), and "a banner fluttering in the center," used for the sound *chuu*. Water with waves like a fluttering banner was the ocean. In Japanese, the kanji 沖 is used to mean "open sea, offing." <氵 中>

沖 open sea [おき]; 沖合漁業 offshore fishery [おきあいぎょꜜぎょう]; 東京湾沖 off the coast of Tokyo Bay [とうきょうわんおき]

73 Military

73a 車 "vehicle" [from a military vehicle] 車連庫撃陣範軸軒軟軌較

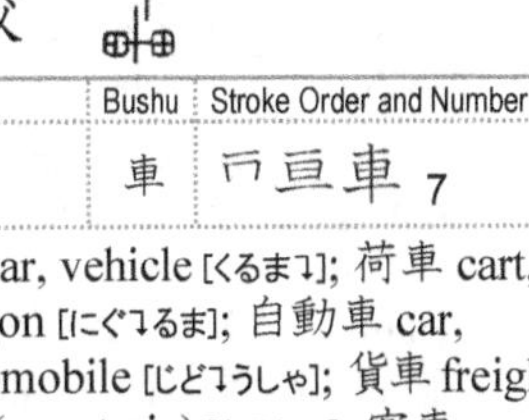

	Meanings	Kun and On	Romaji	Bushu	Stroke Order and Number
SG-1578 車	wheel, car, vehicle	くるま シャ	kuruma *sha*	車	冖亘車 7

車 **A** F-0118

甲骨文1 1, 甲骨文2 2, 金文1 3, 金文2 4, 金文2 5, 説文 6

1, 2, and 3 showed "two wheels of a military vehicle connected by a shaft," with "a yoke" in front of them. 4 and 5 had "a load between two wheels," with "a yoke" on either side. 6 was simplified to a shape that looked like a load with wheels on either side, viewed from above. The kanji 車 means "wheel, car, vehicle." <車>

車 car, vehicle [くるま]; 荷車 cart, wagon [にぐるま]; 自動車 car, automobile [じどうしゃ]; 貨車 freight car (on a train) [かしゃ]; 客車 passenger car (on a train) [きゃくしゃ]; 車線 traffic lane [しゃせん]; 追い越し車線 passing lane [おいこししゃせん]; 自家用車 private car [じかようしゃ]

	Meanings	Kun and On	Romaji	Bushu	Stroke Order and Number
SG-1579 連	to connect, link, accompany; continuous	つら-なる・つ-れる レン	tsura-naru, tsu-reru *ren*	辵	冖亘車`車連連 10

連 **A** F-0138

中山王器 1, 説文 2

1 comprised "a crossroads," "two connected military vehicles," and "a footprint," together signifying "an advancing convoy of vehicles." 2 comprised 辵 (⻌, bushu *shinnyuu*) "to move forward," and 車 "vehicle." From many vehicles moving forward in a connected way, the character signified "to link, connect." The kanji 連 means "to connect, link, accompany; continuous." <車⻌>

連なる to lie in a row, connected [つらなる]; 連れる to bring along with [つれる]; 連れてくる to bring someone [つれてくる]; 二人連れ party of two, as a couple [ふたりづれ]; 親子連れ parent and child together [おやこづれ]; 一連の a series of [いちれんの]; 連勝 consecutive victories [れんしょう]; 連日 day in, day out [れんじつ]

	Meanings	Kun and On	Romaji	Bushu	Stroke Order and Number
SG-1580 庫	storage place, warehouse	コ・ク	*ko, ku*	广	亠广庐庫庫 10

庫 **B** F-0750

金文 1, 説文 2

1 and 2 comprised "a vehicle" (車 **SG-1578**) under the eaves (广, bushu *madare*) of a garage." The kanji 庫 means "storage, warehouse." <广 車>

車庫 garage [しゃこ]; 車庫入れ driving a car into a garage [しゃこいれ]; 書庫 library, stacks of books [しょこ]; 文庫本 pocket edition [ぶんこぼん]; 在庫 stock, inventory [ざいこ]; 国庫 National Treasury, The Exchequer [こっこ]; 金庫 safe, strongbox [きんこ]; 庫裏 monks' living quarters in a Buddhist temple [くり]

	Meanings	Kun and On	Romaji	Bushu	Stroke Order and Number
SG-1581 撃	to attack, strike, hit	う-つ ゲキ	u-tsu *geki*	手	亘 車 車ᐟ 軗 墼 撃 15

撃 **B** F-0903

説文 1, 旧字 2

1 comprised "a wheel on bearings," "a hand holding a weapon" (殳), and "a hand" (手 **SG-0072**). An axle and a wheel hitting against each other (毄), used for the sound *geki*, meant "to collide or crash," and by adding "a striking hand," the character signified "to attack." In the kanji the top-left component was replaced by 車. The kanji 撃 means "to attack, strike, hit." <車殳手>

撃つ to attack, shoot [うつ]; 一撃 a blow, a stroke [いちげき]; 撃退する to repulse the enemy, fight off [げきたいする]; 打撃 a blow, a hit [だげき]; 目撃する to witness [もくげきする]; 襲撃 attack, assault, raid [しゅうげき]; 反撃 counterattack, counteroffensive [はんげき]

	Meanings	Kun and On	Romaji	Bushu	Stroke Order and Number
SG-1582 陣	battle formation, camp, position	ジン	*jin*	阜	⁷ 阝阝阝阝陣 10

陣 **B** F-1037

篆文

The seal-style form comprised 陳 **SG-2050** "to display, line up," and 攴 "to cause an action," together signifying "to line things up." In the kanji 陣, 東 **SG-2048** "goods, stuff" was replaced by 車 "military vehicle," and 攴 was dropped. The kanji 陣 means "battle formation, camp, position." <阝車>

一陣 vanguard, gust of wind [いちじん]; 円陣 forming a circle [えんじん]; 陣地 position, encampment [じんち]; 本陣 the headquarters of an army, an officially appointed inn for a *daimyo* [ほんじん]; 陣痛 labor pains, contraction [じんつう]; 陣取る to take up one's position [じんどる]; 報道陣 the press corps [ほうどうじん]; 陣頭指揮を取る to take command at the head of a team [じんとうしき(じんとうしき)を・とる]

	Meanings	Kun and On	Romaji	Bushu	Stroke Order and Number
SG-1583 範	model, example, standard	ハン	*han*	竹	⺮ 笵 範 範 範 15

範 **C** F-1157

説文

The seal-style form comprised 竹 "bamboo," 車 "wheel," and 㔾 "frame," used for the sound *han*. One view explains that 軋 described the custom of purifying wheels with animal blood before departure for a safe trip. "Customs" provided a model to follow, hence "model, standard." Bamboo 竹 was used to make models for use as patterns. The kanji 範 means "model, example, standard." <⺮車㔾>

範を示す to set an example [はんをしめす]; 師範 teacher, master, instructor[しはん]; 範囲 extent, limit, scope [はんい]; 広範な extensive, wide-ranging, sweeping [こうはんな]; 模範的な model, exemplary, typical [もはんてきな]; 規範 model, example [きはん]; 典範 model standard, law, code [てんぱん]

	Meanings	Kun and On	Romaji	Bushu	Stroke Order and Number
SG-1584 軸	axle, shaft, scroll (painting)	ジク	*jiku*	車	亓 亘 車 軋 軸 軸 軸 12

軸 **C** F-1367

説文

The seal-style form comprised 車 **SG-1578** "vehicle, wheel," and 由 **SG-0781**, used for the sound *jiku*. Something protruding that connected wheels was "an axle" or "a shaft." From an axle's similarity to a hanging scroll rolled up for storage, the character also meant "scroll (painting)." The kanji 軸 means "axle, shaft, scroll (painting)." <車由>

軸となる to play a leading role [じくとなる]; 車軸 axle [しゃじく]; 回転軸 revolving shaft, rotation axis [かいてんじく]; 基軸 key [きじく]; 枢軸国 the Axis powers [すうじくこく]; 掛け軸 hanging scroll [かけじく]

	Meanings	Kun and On	Romaji	Bushu	Stroke Order and Number
SG-1585 軒	eaves, counter for houses	のき ケン	noki *ken*	車	亓 亘 車 軒 軒 10

軒 **C** F-1445

説文

The seal-style form comprised 車, and 干 **SG-1544**, used for the sound *ken* (from *kan*) to mean "something that protruded." The character originally signified an animal-drawn vehicle with long axles or a protruding cover. It came to be used to mean the part of a house that protrudes, i.e., "eaves." The kanji 軒 means "eaves," and is also used as a counter for houses. <車干>

軒 the eaves of [のき]; 軒並みに across the board [のきなみに]; 軒先 the edge of the eaves, frontage of a house [のきさき]; 一軒家 a single house [いっけんや]

	Meanings	Kun and On	Romaji	Bushu	Stroke Order and Number
SG-1586 軟	soft	やわ-らかい ナン	yawa-rakai *nan*	車	亓 亘 車 軟 軟 軟 11

軟 **C** F-1506

輭 軟

正字

No ancient form. The orthographic-style kanji 輭 comprised 車 "vehicle," and 耎, used for the sound *nan* (from *zen*) to mean "soft." One view explains that cattail (reed mace) leaves were once wrapped around wheels as shock absorbers, and the character refers to this practice. In the kanji the right side was replaced by 欠 **SG-0431**. The kanji 軟 means "soft." <車欠>

軟らかい soft, tender, malleable, mellow [やわらかい]; 柔軟な flexible [じゅうなんな]; 軟化する to become soft, tone down, back down [なんかする]; 軟禁 house arrest [なんきん]; 軟水 soft water [なんすい]; 軟派する to approach a woman, seduce [なんぱする]

	Meanings	Kun and On	Romaji	Bushu	Stroke Order and Number
SG-1587 軌	track, rut, orbit	キ	*ki*	車	亓 亘 車 軋 軌 9

軌 **C** F-1552

説文

The seal-style form comprised 車, and 九, used for the sound *ki*. It meant "between two wheels under a vehicle." Two wheels left tracks of the vehicle's movement. The kanji 軌 means "track, rut, orbit." <車九>

軌跡 track, rut, locus [きせき]; 軌道 trajectory, orbit, proper course [きどう]; 軌道に乗る to be on track [きどうにのる]; 常軌を逸する to defy accepted norms, go eccentric [じょうきをいっする]; 広軌鉄道 broad-gauge railroad [こうきてつどう]

	Meanings	Kun and On	Romaji	Bushu	Stroke Order and Number
SG-1588 較	to compare	カク	*kaku*	車	亓 亘 車 軒 軟 軨 較 13

較 **D** F-1670

金文1 (1) 金文2 (2) 篆文 (3)

1 was 爻 "crossing," and had the sound *koo/kaku*. 2 and 3 comprised "a vehicle" and 爻, and 2 also had 攴 "to cause an action." The character signified the crossbars on a carriage. One view adds that the meaning of crossbars led to it being borrowed to mean "to compare." The kanji 較 means "to compare." <車交>

比較 comparison [ひかく]; 比較的 comparatively, rather, fairly [ひかくてき] // 較べる to compare [くらべる]

73b 軍 "military" [from a military vehicle with a banner] 軍運揮輝

	Meanings	Kun and On	Romaji	Bushu	Stroke Order and Number
SG-1589 軍	military, army, force	グン	*gun*	車	冖 冐 冒 軍 9

軍 **A** F-0414

金文 1 金文 2 説文 3

1, 2, and 3 depicted a military vehicle wrapped in a fluttering banner. Another view takes the character to depict soldiers encircling a militry vehicle. The kanji 軍 means "military, army, force." <冖車>

一軍 first team, an army [いちぐん]; 官軍 government forces, imperial army [かんぐん]; 空軍 air force [くうぐん]; 軍手 cotton work gloves [ぐんて]; 軍団 army corps, a corps [ぐんだん]; 軍配 sumo umpire's fan [ぐんばい]; 強行軍で in a marathon working session [きょうこうぐんで]; 軍事力 military power [ぐんじりょく]; 十字軍 the crusaders [じゅうじぐん]

	Meanings	Kun and On	Romaji	Bushu	Stroke Order and Number
SG-1590 運	to transport, carry; luck	はこ-ぶ ウン	hako-bu *un*	辵	冖 冐 冒 軍 渾 運 12

運 **A** F-0250

説文

The seal-style form comprised 辵 (⻌, bushu *shinnyuu*) "to move forward," and 軍, used for the sound *un*, together signifying the movement of military forces, which were always on the move. By extension the character meant "to carry or carry about." One's fortunes are always shifting, and so it also meant "luck." The kanji 運 means "to move about, transport, carry; luck." <軍⻌>

運ぶ to carry, transport [はこぶ]; 運動 movement, exercise [うんどう]; 運賃 fair [うんちん]; 運のいい fortunate, lucky [うんのいい]; 運送会社 shipping company, transportation company [うんそうがいしゃ]; 運送料 forwarding (shipping) charges [うんそうりょう]; 幸運にも fortunately, by good luck [こううんにも]

	Meanings	Kun and On	Romaji	Bushu	Stroke Order and Number
SG-1591 揮	to command; volatile	キ	*ki*	手	一 扌 扩 揎 揮 揮 12

揮 **C** F-1371

説文

The seal-style form comprised 扌 "an act done by hand," and 軍 **SG-1589** "military." A commander used his hand to signal his troops to advance on the enemy. The character was also used for the sound *ki* to mean "volatile." The kanji 揮 means "to command; volatile." <扌軍>

発揮する to display, demonstrate [はっきする]; 指揮する to command, supervise [しきする]; 指揮棒 baton, stick [しきぼう]; 揮発油 volatile oil, naphtha [きはつゆ]

	Meanings	Kun and On	Romaji	Bushu	Stroke Order and Number
SG-1592 輝	to shine, gleam, twinkle	かがや-く キ	kagaya-ku *ki*	車	丨 丬 业 烂 煊 輝 15

輝 **C** F-1129

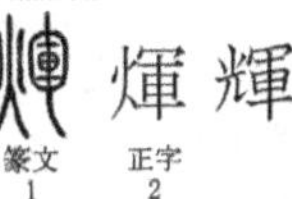

篆文 1 正字 2

1 comprised 火 **SG-1164** "fire," and 軍, used for the sound *ki* to mean "to wrap around." A fire emitting a bright light all around meant "to shine." 火 was replaced by 光 **SG-0442** "light." The kanji 輝 means "to shine, gleam, twinkle." <火軍>

輝く to shine [かがやく]; 輝かしい bright, brilliant, radiant [かがやかしい]

73c 官 "official" [from 𠂤 "a pile of meat offered before a battle"]; *kan* 官追管師館遣棺

	Meanings	Kun and On	Romaji	Bushu	Stroke Order and Number
SG-1593 官	government official, military officer, government, bodily senses	カン	*kan*	宀	丶 宀 宁 宁 官 官 官 8

官 **A** F-0290

甲骨文 1 金文 2 説文 3

1, 2, and 3 depicted "a mausoleum" (宀) where "an offering of a pile of meat" (𠂤) was placed for an ancestral deity. A military general or other high-ranking officer conducted this rite before a battle, and the character meant "military or government officer." The analogy is made that bureaucracy was to government as the various senses are to the body, whence the additional meaning of "bodily senses." The kanji 官 means "government official, military officer, government, bodily senses." <宀𠂤>

官民 governmental and non-governmental [かんみん]; 官僚 bureaucrat [かんりょう]; 官立 government-supported/-run [かんりつ]; 教官 instructor [きょうかん]; 器官 organ [きかん]; 五官 the five sense organs (目耳鼻舌身), the five senses [ごかん]; 官能的な sensual [かんのうてきな]

	Meanings	Kun and On	Romaji	Bushu	Stroke Order and Number
SG-1594 追	to chase, follow, add (afterwards)	おーう ツイ	o-u *tsui*	辵	亻户𠂤𠂤追 9

追 **A** F-0436

甲骨文1 甲骨文2 金文1 金文2 金文3 説文
1 2 3 4 5 6

1 and 2 comprised "an offering of a pile of meat" in a pre-battle rite, and "a footprint" to mean "to go out," together signifying "chasing an enemy." In 3, 5, and 6, "a crossroads" and "a footprint" combined to form 辵 (辶), "to move forward." "Making a pile" also gave the meaning "to add more." The kanji 追 means "to chase, follow, add (afterwards)." <𠂤辶>

追う to chase after [おう]; 追いかける・追っかける to run after [おいかける, おっかける]; 追加 addition [ついか]; 追放する to expel, banish [ついほうする]; 追突事故 rear-end collision accident [ついとつじこ]; 追従する to be servile to, follow [ついじゅうする]

	Meanings	Kun and On	Romaji	Bushu	Stroke Order and Number
SG-1595 管	pipe, flute; to administer, control	くだ カン	kuda *kan*	竹	⺮𥫗笁管管 14

管 **B** F-0521

説文

The seal-style form comprised 竹 **SG-0759** "bamboo," to signify "hollow inside like a pipe," and 官 "government official," for the sound *kan,* together signifying "pipe or flute." A government official (官) overseeing a matter within the framework of a bureaucratic system meant "to administer, control." The kanji 管 means "pipe, flute; to administer, control." <⺮官>

管 pipe, tube [くだ]; 管を巻く to talk incoherently over drink [くだをまく]; 管楽器 wind instrument [かんがっき]; 管理する to manage, administer [かんりする]; 保管 custody, safekeeping [ほかん]; 水道管 water pipe [すいどうかん]; 血管 blood vessel [けっかん]; 管轄 jurisdiction, purview [かんかつ]

	Meanings	Kun and On	Romaji	Bushu	Stroke Order and Number
SG-1596 師	military unit, teacher, mentor, person with a specialized skill	シ	*shi*	巾	′亻𠂤𠂤𠂤師 10

師 **B** F-0541

甲骨文1 甲骨文2 金文1 金文2 説文
1 2 3 4 5

1, 2, and 3 were "an offering of a pile of meat before a battle." In 4, "a curved meat-carving knife" was added on the right, for the sound *shi.* The sacrificial meat would be carved by a high-ranking military officer, thus leading to meanings such as "teacher or mentor," and also "military unit." The character is also used to refer to a person with specialized skills. The kanji 師 means "military unit, teacher, mentor, person with specialized skill." <𠂤一巾>

医師 medical doctor [いし]; 教師 teacher [きょうし]; 恩師 mentor, one's old teacher [おんし]; 講師 lecturer [こうし]; 師団 troop [しだん]; 師弟関係 teacher-student relationship [していかんけい]; 影法師 person's shadow, silhouette of a person [かげぼうし]; 庭師 gardener [にわし] // 師走 December [しわす]

	Meanings	Kun and On	Romaji	Bushu	Stroke Order and Number
SG-1597 館	large building, mansion	やかた カン	yakata *kan*	食	𠆢今今食飠飠館館館 16

館 **B** F-0549

説文

The seal-style form comprised 食 **SG-1781** "food in a bowl with a lid," and 官 **SG-1593** "an official," used for the sound *kan.* A place where many officials and people gathered and ate was "a large house." The kanji 館 means "large house, mansion." <飠官>

館 mansion, large house [やかた]; 旅館 Japanese-style inn [りょかん]; 会館 hall, clubhouse, building [かいかん]; 図書館 library [としょかん]; 大使館 embassy [たいしかん]; 公民館 community center [こうみんかん]

	Meanings	Kun and On	Romaji	Bushu	Stroke Order and Number
SG-1598 遣	to send out, dispatch, use, do	つかーわす ケン	tsuka-wasu *ken*	辵	中虫虫貴貴遣遣 13

遣 **C** F-1179

甲骨文1 甲骨文2 金文1 金文2 説文
1 2 3 4 5

1, 2, and 3 comprised "two hands placing an offering of meat before a battle," used for the sound *ken,* and "a box of prayers." In 4, with "a person" and "a footprint" added, the character meant "to dispatch a person with an offering or a gift." Dispatching someone to do something also gave the meaning "to use." The kanji 遣 means "to send out, dispatch, use, do." <虫目辶>

遣わす to dispatch, bestow [つかわす]; 小遣い pocket money, petty cash [こづかい]; 息遣い breathing, respiration [いきづかい]; 金遣いが荒い to be thriftless, be wasteful with money [かねづかいがあらい]; 派遣社員 staff dispatched by a personnel service [はけんしゃいん]; 派遣する to dispatch [はけんする]; 遣唐使 cultural envoy mission to the Tang Court [けんとうし]; 蚊遣り mosquito repellant coil [かやり]; 遣り甲斐 worthwhile, rewarding [やりがい]

		Meanings	*Kun* and *On*	Romaji	Bushu	Stroke Order and Number
SG-1599 棺		coffin	カン	*kan*	木	一十朩朩柠柠棺 12
棺 **D** F-2029	中山王器 1　説文 2　棺 — 1 and 2 comprised 木 **SG-0608** "wood," and 㠯 or 官 **SG-1593**, used for the sound *kan* to mean "to wrap around." The body of a deceased person was wrapped in a cloth before being placed in a wooden coffin. The kanji 棺 means "coffin." <木官>					出棺する to carry a coffin out of the house [しゅっかんする]; 棺桶 coffin [かんおけ]; 納棺 putting a body in a coffin [のうかん]; 石棺 stone coffin, sarcophagus [せきかん, せっかん]

VIII Threads and Clothing

74 Skein of threads

74a 糸 "thread; continuous" [from filaments of a silk cocoon or a skein of threads]; bushu *itohen* 糸約総給絵紀絶継紅縁網綿絹紋紺紡糾繭

	Meanings	Kun and On	Romaji	Bushu	Stroke Order and Number
SG-1600 糸	thread	いと シ	ito *shi*	糸	く 幺 幺 糸 糸 糸 6

糸
A
F-0797

甲骨文 1 金文1 2 金文2 3 説文古文 4 説文 5 旧字 6 絲 糸

1 and 2 depicted two or three "silkworm cocoons strung together," or "a skein of silk threads." 3, 4, and 5 added filaments or loose ends of threads protruding at both ends. Twining silk filaments together made "thread." The character originally meant "silk thread." Later, when cotton was introduced, its meaning expanded to include cotton thread too. When 糸 is used on the left side of a kanji it becomes bushu *itohen* "thread, continuous." The kanji 糸 means "thread." <幺小>

糸 thread [いと]; 糸口 clue [いとぐち]; ミシン糸 sewing machine thread [ミシンいと]; 毛糸 yarn [けいと]; 生糸 raw silk [きいと]; 一糸乱れず in perfect order [いっし・みだれず]; 糸くず lint, pieces of thread [いとくず]

	Meanings	Kun and On	Romaji	Bushu	Stroke Order and Number
SG-1601 約	to promise, cut back, summarize; approximately	ヤク	*yaku*	糸	幺 糸 糸 糸' 約 約 9

約
A
F-0162

説文 約

The seal-style form comprised 糸 "skein of threads," and 勺, used for the sound *yaku* to mean "to bind, tie." Two people tying two ropes together signified "to make a promise." Using string to bundle things into one also gave the meanings "to summarize; approximately," and "to remove unnecessary parts." The kanji 約 means "to bind, promise, cut back, summarize; approximately." <糸勺>

約束する to promise [やくそくする]; 公約 campaign pledge [こうやく]; 約五メートル approximately five meters [やく・ごメートル]; 節約 economy, saving, thrift [せつやく]; 要約 summary, abstract [ようやく]; 先約 previous engagement [せんやく]; 解約 cancellation [かいやく]; 違約金 forfeit, penalty for breach of contract [いやくきん]

	Meanings	Kun and On	Romaji	Bushu	Stroke Order and Number
SG-1602 総	to gather all, bundle; all, general; tassel	ソウ	*soo*	糸	幺 糸 糸 糸' 糸' 総 総 14

総
A
F-0246

説文 1 總 旧字 2 総

1 and 2 comprised 糸 "thread," and 悤 ("window" and "heart"), used for the sound *soo* to mean "to bundle up." Together they signified "to gather threads and bundle them into one, gather all," or "a tassel." 悤 was replaced by 忩 in the shinji. The kanji 総 means "to gather all, bundle; all, general; tassel." <糸ハム心>

総合 total, synthesis [そうごう]; 総称 general name, collectively called [そうしょう]; 総務 general administration [そうむ]; 総理大臣 prime minister [そうりだいじん]; 総意 collective will [そうい]; 総立ちになる to stand up all at once [そうだちになる] // 総て all [すべて]

	Meanings	Kun and On	Romaji	Bushu	Stroke Order and Number
SG-1603 給	to supply, be given, provide, bestow; wage; to receive (humble style)	キュウ	*kyuu*	糸	幺 糸 糸 糸' 糸' 給 給 12

給
B
F-0523

説文 給

The seal-style form comprised 糸 **SG-1600** "skein of threads," and 合 **SG-1989**, used for the sound *kyuu* to mean "to fill a gap." Together they signified "to make up for a deficiency," or "provided by a superior." Money provided by an employer is "wages." The kanji 給 means "to supply, provide, bestow; wage." In Japanese it is also used as a humble expression for "to be given, receive." <糸合>

給料 salary, wage [きゅうりょう]; 支給する to pay, provide [しきゅう]; 給油 refueling [きゅうゆ]; 月給 monthly salary [げっきゅう]; 給水車 water wagon [きゅうすいしゃ]; 時間給 hourly wage [じかんきゅう, じかんきゅう]; 基本給 basic salary [きほんきゅう]; 給金 pay, wages [きゅうきん] // 給わる to be given (by a superior) (humble) [たまわる]

	Meanings	Kun and On	Romaji	Bushu	Stroke Order and Number
SG-1604 絵	painting, picture	エ・カイ	*e, kai*	糸	幺糸糸糸絵絵絵 12

絵 **B** F-0524

繪 繪 絵 (説文 1, 旧字 2)

1 comprised 糸 "skein of threads," and 會 (the kyuji for 会 **SG-1790**) "to gather," used for the sound *kai*. "Gathering threads of various colors" signified brocade or colorful embroidery, which later came to mean "painting." The kanji 絵 means "painting, picture." <糸会>

絵 picture, painting [え⌉]; 浮世絵 *ukiyo-ye* print [うきよ⌉え]; 絵文字 emoticon, *emoji*, pictograph [えも⌉じ]; 絵の具 paint, coloring materials [えのぐ]; 絵日記 illustrated diary [えにっ⌉き]; 蒔絵 gold lacquering [まきえ]; 絵本 picture book [えほ⌉ん]; 絵画 painting, picture [か⌉いが]

	Meanings	Kun and On	Romaji	Bushu	Stroke Order and Number
SG-1605 紀	to chronicle; beginning, discipline	キ	*ki*	糸	幺糸糸紀紀紀 9

紀 **B** F-0575

己 紀 紀 (金文 1, 説文 2)

1 (己 **SG-0420**) had the sound *ki*, and meant "a tool for spinning thread." In 2, 糸 "a skein of thread, continuity" was added. Compiling the timelines of different events over a long period was like sorting out multiple threads, and thus the meaning "to chronicle." Picking out the end of a thread also gave the meaning "beginning of something continuous." Organizing scattered threads meant "discipline." The kanji 紀 means "to chronicle; beginning, discipline." <糸己>

紀元 beginning of an era [き⌉げん]; 紀元前 before Christ (BC), before the Common Era (BCE) [きげんぜ⌉ん・きげ⌉んぜん]; 世紀 century [せ⌉いき]; 風紀 public morals [ふ⌉うき]; 紀行文 travel essay [きこ⌉うぶん]; 党紀 party discipline [と⌉うき]

	Meanings	Kun and On	Romaji	Bushu	Stroke Order and Number
SG-1606 絶	to cut off, cease to exist; exquisitely beautiful, unrivaled; absolutely	た-える ゼツ	*ta-eru* *zetsu*	糸	幺糸糸糸絶絶絶絶 12

絶 **B** F-0774

(中山王器 1, 説文古文 2, 説文 3) 絶

1 and 2 depicted "bundles of short-cut threads on storage shelves," signifying "to cut off, cease to exist." 3 had the addition of 色 **SG-0423** "color," for the sound *zetsu*, and meant "colored threads." Colorful threads made an "exquisitely beautiful" tapestry that was beyond comparison, and thus the meaning of "absolutely." The kanji 絶 means "to cut, cease to exist; exquisitely beautiful, unrivaled; absolutely." <糸色>

絶える to die out [たえ⌉る]; 絶え間なく constantly, perpetually, endlessly [たえまな⌉く]; 絶望する to despair, lose heart [ぜつぼうする]; 絶滅 extinction, eradication [ぜつめつ]; 絶世の unrivaled, unequaled [ぜっせいの]; 絶筆 someone's last work [ぜっぴつ]; 絶品 perfection, masterpiece [ぜっぴん]; 絶対温度 absolute temperature [ぜったいお⌉んど]

	Meanings	Kun and On	Romaji	Bushu	Stroke Order and Number
SG-1607 継	to succeed, inherit, continue	つ-ぐ ケイ	*tsu-gu* *kee*	糸	幺糸糸糸継継継 13

継 **B** F-0956

(金文 1) 繼 (説文 2) 繼 (旧字 3) 継

1 and 2 had "skeins of short threads on storage shelves," which had the sound *kee*. The two short lines at the bottom right in 1 signified two threads that were "to be tied." In 2, 糸 was added for the meaning of "continuity." Continuously tying the ends of two threads meant "to continue, succeed." In the kyuji 繼 (3), the four 幺 on the right side were replaced by 米 (㡭). The kanji 継 means "to succeed, inherit, continue." <糸㡭>

継ぐ to succeed, inherit [つぐ]; 受け継ぐ to follow, inherit [うけつぐ]; 引き継ぎ taking over, transfer of (control) [ひきつぎ]; 継続する to continue [けいぞくする]; テレビ中継 live telecast [テレビちゅ⌉うけい]; 後継者 successor [こうけ⌉いしゃ] // 継母 step-mother [ままは⌉は, けいぼ]

	Meanings	Kun and On	Romaji	Bushu	Stroke Order and Number
SG-1608 紅	red, crimson	べに・くれない コウ・ク	*beni, kurenai* *koo, ku*	糸	幺糸糸糸紅紅 9

紅 **B** F-1045

紅 (説文) 紅

The seal-style form comprised 糸 "skein of threads," and 工 **SG-1895**, used for the sound *koo* to mean "red." Together they signified "the color red" for dyeing threads. The kanji 紅 means "red, crimson." <糸工>

紅 deep red, crimson [べ⌉に, くれない]; 口紅 lipstick [くちべに]; 紅茶 black tea [こうちゃ]; 紅一点 only woman in the company [こ⌉う・いってん]; 紅白リレー a relay between two teams [こうはくり⌉レー]; 深紅 crimson, cardinal red [し⌉んく]; 紅葉 crimson foliage, autumn color [こうよう] // 紅葉 Japanese maple [も⌉みじ]

	Meanings	Kun and On	Romaji	Bushu	Stroke Order and Number
SG-1609 縁	edge, connection; linked by fate	ふち エン	huchi *en*	糸	縁 15

縁 **B** F-1055

縁 縁 縁 説文 1 旧字 2

1 comprised 糸 "thread, cloth," and 彖 (彖) "edge," used for the sound *en*, together signifying "the edge of a cloth, fringe." The edge of a cloth was in contact with something else, whence the meaning of "a connection." In Buddhism the character meant "linked by fate" or "karmic relation." The kanji 縁 means "edge, connection; linked by fate." <糸彖>

縁 edge, border, brim [ふち⌉]; fate [え⌉ん]; 縁なし rimless, frameless [ふちなし]; 縁起がいい of good omen, boding well for [えんぎがい⌉い]; 縁組 matrimonial union [えんぐみ]; 縁談 marriage prospect [えんだん]; 縁故採用 hiring through personal connection [えんこさ⌉いよう]; 縁側 external corridor with a boarded floor [えんがわ]; 縁日 fete day of a deity, temple fair [え⌉んにち]

	Meanings	Kun and On	Romaji	Bushu	Stroke Order and Number
SG-1610 網	net, network	あみ モウ	ami *moo*	糸	網 14

網 **C** F-1105

網 甲骨文 1 甲骨文 2 古文 3 説文 4

1 and 2 depicted "a net," and had the sound *moo*. 3 comprised 冂 "a cover" over 亡, also used for the sound *moo*. In 4, inside 网 "net" was 糸 **SG-1600** "threads," and 亡 **SG-0592**. Together these components meant "a net for catching birds." The kanji 網 means "net, network." <糸罔(冂亠亡)>

網 net [あみ⌉]; 網元 fisherman's net [あみもと]; 金網 metal net [かなあみ]; 網戸 screen door [あみ⌉ど]; 網目 mesh of a net [あみめ]; 投網 casting a net [とあみ]; 一網打尽 roundup arrest [いちもうだじん, いち⌉もう·だじん]; 連絡網 contact network [れんらく⌉もう]

	Meanings	Kun and On	Romaji	Bushu	Stroke Order and Number
SG-1611 綿	cotton; continuous	わた メン	wata *men*	糸	綿 14

綿 **C** F-1265

緜 綿 説文 1 正字 2

1 comprised 帛 "silk cloth," and 系 **SG-1627** "threads connected by a hand," together signifying "silk cloth." After cotton was introduced to China, it gained popularity over expensive silk, and 緜 (2) came to mean "cotton." In the shinji, 系 changed to 糸 and swapped its position with 帛. The kanji 綿 means "cotton; continuous." <糸白巾>

綿 cotton [わた, め⌉ん]; 綿羊 sheep [めんよう]; 綿棒 cotton swab [め⌉んぼう]; 綿密な detailed [めんみつな]; 連綿たる long and uninterrupted [れんめんた⌉る]; 綿花 raw cotton [め⌉んか] // 木綿 cotton [もめん]

	Meanings	Kun and On	Romaji	Bushu	Stroke Order and Number
SG-1612 絹	silk	きぬ ケン	kinu *ken*	糸	絹 13

絹 **C** F-1600

絹 簡書 1 説文 2

1 and 2 comprised 糸 "threads," and "a round silkworm," used for the sound *ken*, together signifying "raw silk threads." The kanji 絹 means "silk." <糸口月>

絹 silk [き⌉ぬ]; 絹豆腐 fine-textured tofu [きぬど⌉うふ]; 絹糸 silk thread [きぬいと]; 人絹 imitation silk, rayon [じんけん]

	Meanings	Kun and On	Romaji	Bushu	Stroke Order and Number
SG-1613 紋	pattern, family crest	モン	*mon*	糸	紋 10

紋 **C** F-1618

紋 金文

The bronzeware-style form comprised 糸 "silk cocoons or threads," and 攴 "a hand holding a tool," used for the sound *mon* to mean "design, figure, pattern." Together they signified "a hand creating a pretty pattern with threads." The right side was replaced by 文 **SG-0318** ("pretty elaborate pattern") for the sound *mon*. The kanji 紋 means "pattern." In Japanese, 紋 also means "family crest." <糸文>

紋 (family) crest [も⌉ん]; 波紋 ripple [はもん]; 指紋 finger print [しもん]; 家紋 family crest [か⌉もん]; 紋付き crested formal kimono [も⌉んつき]

	Meanings	Kun and On	Romaji	Bushu	Stroke Order and Number
SG-1614 紺	deep blue, dark blue	コン	*kon*	糸	紺 11

紺 **D** F-1758

紺 説文

The seal-style form comprised 糸 "skein of threads," and 甘 **SG-0038**, used for the sound *kon* to mean "reddish blue," together signifying "threads dyed a deep or dark blue." The kanji 紺 means "deep or dark blue." <糸甘>

紺色 dark blue [こんいろ]; 濃紺 dark blue [のうこん]; 紺碧の空 the azure sky [こんぺきのそ⌉ら] // 紺屋の白袴 "The dyer wears white." [こうやのしろば⌉かま]

	Meanings	Kun and On	Romaji	Bushu	Stroke Order and Number
SG-1615 紡	to spin (yarn)	つむ-ぐ ボウ	tsumu-gu *boo*	糸	紡 10

紡 **D** F-1811 (説文)

The seal-style form comprised 糸 "thread," and 方 **SG-1931** "square, four directions," used for the sound *boo*, together signifying "spinning yarn to weave square cloth." The kanji 紡 means "to spin (yarn)." <糸方>

紡ぐ to spin [つむぐ]; 糸紡ぎ spinning [いとつむぎ]; 紡ぎ車 spinning wheel [つむぎぐるま]; 紡績業 the spinning and weaving industry, textile manufacturing [ぼうせきぎょう]; 混紡 blended spinning [こんぼう]

	Meanings	Kun and On	Romaji	Bushu	Stroke Order and Number
SG-1616 糾	to investigate, scrutinize, entwine	キュウ	*kyuu*	糸	糾 9

糾 **D** F-2113 (説文)

The seal-style form comprised "skein of threads" (糸), and "two threads entwined/intertangled" (丩), used for the sound *kyuu*. "Authorities scrutinizing a tangled matter" gave the meaning "to investigate, scrutinize." The kanji 糾 means "to investigate, scrutinize, entwine." <糸丩>

紛糾 to become entangled, be thrown into confusion [ふんきゅう]; 糾明する to investigate and expose (corruption) [きゅうめいする]; 糾弾する to denounce, condemn [きゅうだんする] // 糾す to inspect, scrutinize [ただす]

	Meanings	Kun and On	Romaji	Bushu	Stroke Order and Number
SG-1617 繭	silk cocoon	まゆ ケン	mayu *ken*	糸	繭 18

繭 **D** F-2650 (説文古文 1, 説文 2)

1 comprised "silk cocoons," and 見 "a person kneeling down to have a closer look," used for the sound *ken*. 2 comprised 糸 "thread" and 虫 "silkworm," under layers of "mulberry leaves." Layers of mulberry leaves were laid over silkworms by a caretaker while they spun "cocoons." The kanji 繭 means "silk cocoon." <艹冂糸虫>

繭 cocoon [まゆ]; 繭玉 cocoon-shaped rice powder balls on a wooden stick [まゆだま]

糸 "thread" as a bottom component of kanji 素紫繁索累

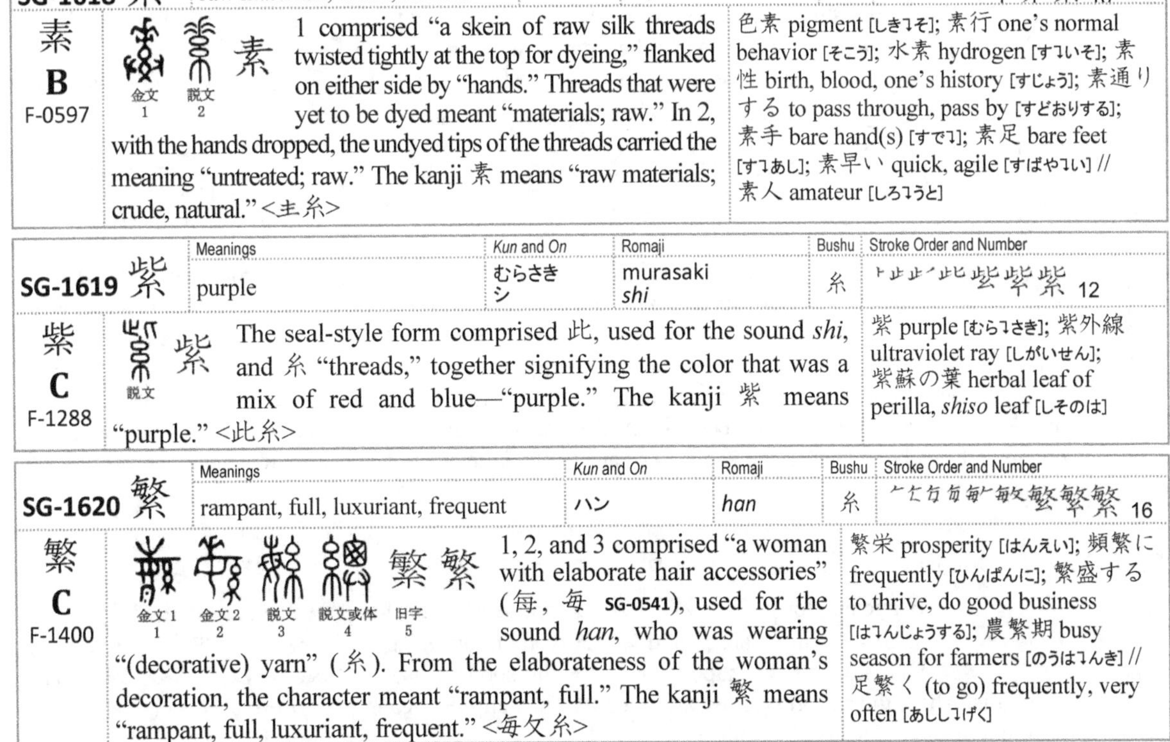

	Meanings	Kun and On	Romaji	Bushu	Stroke Order and Number
SG-1618 素	raw materials; crude, natural	ソ・ス	*so, su*	糸	素 10

素 **B** F-0597 (金文 1, 説文 2)

1 comprised "a skein of raw silk threads twisted tightly at the top for dyeing," flanked on either side by "hands." Threads that were yet to be dyed meant "materials; raw." In 2, with the hands dropped, the undyed tips of the threads carried the meaning "untreated; raw." The kanji 素 means "raw materials; crude, natural." <主糸>

色素 pigment [しきそ]; 素行 one's normal behavior [そこう]; 水素 hydrogen [すいそ]; 素性 birth, blood, one's history [すじょう]; 素通りする to pass through, pass by [すどおりする]; 素手 bare hand(s) [すで]; 素足 bare feet [すあし]; 素早い quick, agile [すばやい] // 素人 amateur [しろうと]

	Meanings	Kun and On	Romaji	Bushu	Stroke Order and Number
SG-1619 紫	purple	むらさき シ	murasaki *shi*	糸	紫 12

紫 **C** F-1288 (説文)

The seal-style form comprised 此, used for the sound *shi*, and 糸 "threads," together signifying the color that was a mix of red and blue—"purple." The kanji 紫 means "purple." <此糸>

紫 purple [むらさき]; 紫外線 ultraviolet ray [しがいせん]; 紫蘇の葉 herbal leaf of perilla, *shiso* leaf [しそのは]

	Meanings	Kun and On	Romaji	Bushu	Stroke Order and Number
SG-1620 繁	rampant, full, luxuriant, frequent	ハン	*han*	糸	繁 16

繁 **C** F-1400 (金文 1, 金文 2, 説文 3, 説文或体 4, 旧字 5)

1, 2, and 3 comprised "a woman with elaborate hair accessories" (毎, 每 **SG-0541**), used for the sound *han*, who was wearing "(decorative) yarn" (糸). From the elaborateness of the woman's decoration, the character meant "rampant, full." The kanji 繁 means "rampant, full, luxuriant, frequent." <毎攵糸>

繁栄 prosperity [はんえい]; 頻繁に frequently [ひんぱんに]; 繁盛する to thrive, do good business [はんじょうする]; 農繁期 busy season for farmers [のうはんき] // 足繁く (to go) frequently, very often [あししげく]

	Meanings	Kun and On	Romaji	Bushu	Stroke Order and Number
SG-1621 索	rope; to search, pull out	サク	*saku*	糸	十 声 壴 索 索 索 10

索 **C** F-1420

説文 索 The seal-style form depicted "an apparatus for making rope by twisting threads or yarn (糸)." Rope was made by twisting threads or yarn from the top, and "pulling multiple threads to the top" signified "searching for something, pulling out something." The kanji 索 means "rope; to search, pull out." <亠糸>

検索する to search for, look up [けんさくする]; 探索 exploration [たんさく]; 索引 index [さくいん]; 思索する to think, meditate on [しさくする]

	Meanings	Kun and On	Romaji	Bushu	Stroke Order and Number
SG-1621 累	to connect, pile up, accumulate	ルイ	*rui*	糸	口 田 田 罒 罗 累 累 11

累 **D** F-1790

説文 累 The seal-style form comprised three 田 (畾), used for the sound *rui* to mean "to accumulate," and 糸 "threads," to mean "continuity." Together they signified "to connect, heap up, put one on top of another." The kanji 累 means "to connect, pile up, accumulate." <田糸>

係累 dependents, relatives and in-laws [けいるい]; 累計 total, aggregate [るいけい]; 累進課税 progressive taxation, graduated taxation [るいしんかぜい]; 累積 accumulation, cumulation [るいせき]; 累乗根 power root [るいじょうこん]

74b 亦 (䜌) phonetic use [from entangled threads] 変恋湾蛮

	Meanings	Kun and On	Romaji	Bushu	Stroke Order and Number
SG-1623 変	to change; strange, odd, bizarre; uprising	か-わる ヘン	ka-waru *hen*	言	亠 亣 亦 亦 亦 变 変 9

変 **A** F-0232

詛楚文 1, 説文 2, 旧字 3 變 変

The top (䜌) of 1 and 2 comprised "word; to say" (言), flanked on either side by 糸 **SG-1600** "skein of threads," together signifying "tangled up like threads and words." With 攴 "to cause a change," the character meant "to change." A change from a normal state gave the meaning "strange, bizarre, eccentric, uprising." In the kyuji 變 (3), 攴 was replaced by 夊 (bushu *bokuzukuri*), which was further misconstrued as 夂, "a backward-footprint" (bushu *suinyoo*), in the shinji. The top (䜌) was also replaced by 亦. The kanji 変 means "to change; strange, odd, bizarre; uprising." <亦夂>

色変わり variation in color [いろがわり]; 風変わりな odd, peculiar [ふうがわりな]; 変な strange, peculiar, odd [へんな]; 事変 incident, crisis [じへん]; 変 upheaval, uprising [へん]; 変身する to change into, turn into [へんしんする]; 変心する to have a change of heart [へんしんする]; 変人 eccentric [へんじん]; 一変する to change completely [いっぺんする]

	Meanings	Kun and On	Romaji	Bushu	Stroke Order and Number
SG-1624 恋	to be in love; romance	こ-う・こい レン	ko-u, koi *ren*	心	亠 亣 亦 亦 恋 恋 10

恋 **B** F-0744

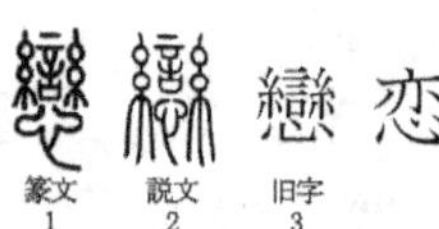
篆文 1, 説文 2, 旧字 3 戀 恋

1 and 2 comprised 䜌 (comprised of 言 **SG-1364** "word; to say," flanked on either side by 糸 "skeins of threads"), used for the sound *ren* , and 心 **SG-0187** "heart." Together they signified the state of a heart tangled up like twisted threads and confused words, that is, "being in love." In the shinji, the top (䜌) was replaced by 亦. The kanji 恋 means "to be in love; romance." <亦心>

恋 being in love, romance [こい]; 初恋 first love, puppy love [はつこい]; 恋文 love letter [こいぶみ]; 恋する to be in love, yearn [こいする, こいする]; 恋しい to miss, feel nostalgic for [こいしい]; 恋心 feelings of love [こいごころ]; 失恋 broken heart [しつれん]; 恋愛 love, romantic attachment [れんあい]

	Meanings	Kun and On	Romaji	Bushu	Stroke Order and Number
SG-1625 湾	bay, curve, curved shape	ワン	*wan*	水	氵 氵 氵 氵 氵 湾 湾 湾 12

湾 **B** F-0877

旧字 灣 湾 No ancient form. The kyuji 灣 comprised 氵, bushu *sanzui* "flowing water," and 彎 "curved" (from 䜌 and 弓 **SG-1509** "a bow shape"), used for the sound *wan*. A broad inlet where the land curves inward is a bay. The kanji 湾 means "bay, curve, curved shape." <氵亦弓>

湾 bay, inlet [わん]; 港湾 harbor [こうわん]; 湾曲する to curve, bend [わんきょくする]; 東京湾 Tokyo Bay [とうきょうわん]; 台湾 (台灣) Taiwan [たいわん]

	Meanings	Kun and On	Romaji	Bushu	Stroke Order and Number
SG-1626 蛮	barbaric; barbarian	バン	*ban*	虫	亠 亣 亦 亦 峦 蛮 蛮 12

蛮 **D** F-2066

金文1 1, 金文2 2, 説文 3, 旧字 4 蠻 蛮

1 and 2 comprised 辛 **SG-1359** "tattooing needle," and 口 "mouth," forming 言 **SG-1364** "word, language; to say," with "a skein of threads" on either side. Together they formed 䜌, used for the sound *ban* to denote the southern outer area of China. In 3, "snake" was added to further signify a barbaric area inhabited by snakes. The top of the kyuji 蠻 (4) was replaced by 亦. The kanji 蛮 means "barbaric; barbarian." <亦虫>

野蛮な primitive, barbarous [やばんな]; 蛮行 savagery, brutality [ばんこう]; 南蛮 southern barbarians [なんばん]; 南蛮絵 Japanese painting style influenced by the Spanish and Portuguese in 16th century [なんばんえ]; 蛮勇 brute courage, recklessness [ばんゆう]; 蛮カラ rough and uncouth style [ばんカラ]

74c 系 "lineage, system"; *kee* 系係孫遜

	Meanings	Kun and On	Romaji	Bushu	Stroke Order and Number
SG-1627 系	system, faction, family line, lineage	ケイ	*kee*	糸	一 ㄑ 幺 乎 系 系 7

系 **A** F-0428

甲骨文 1, 金文 2, 説文 3 系

In 1 and 2, "fingers" from above were tying together "multiple skeins of threads or decorative ropes." Tying threads to each other signified "lineage; to connect." Another view suggests that the character depicted decorative braids worn by a grandchild in a religious rite, signifying a link to ancestors, whence the meaning "lineage." Connecting many things made "a system," and its members might form "a faction." The kanji 系 means "lineage, system, faction, family line." <ノ糸>

家系図 family lineage chart, pedigree chart [かけいず]; 文系 humanities, liberal arts [ぶんけい]; 系列 business grouping [けいれつ]; 直系 direct line, direct descent [ちょっけい]; 傍系 collateral family line [ぼうけい]; 日系 Japanese descent, Japanese-affiliated [にっけい]; 母系制 matrilineal system [ぼけいせい]

	Meanings	Kun and On	Romaji	Bushu	Stroke Order and Number
SG-1628 係	person in charge, relationship; to be concerned with	かか-る・かかり ケイ	kaka-ru, kakari *kee*	人	亻 亻 亻 仫 俘 係 係 9

係 **A** F-0267

説文 係

The seal-style form comprised 亻 "person," and 系 "to connect," together signifying "someone who is involved" or "someone who takes care of a matter." The kanji 係 means "person in charge or involved; to be concerned with." <亻系>

係 person in charge [かかり]; 係り合い connection, involvement [かかりあい]; 係員 person in charge [かかりいん]; 係争 dispute, litigation [けいそう]; 係数 coefficient [けいすう]; 係留する to moor [けいりゅうする]

	Meanings	Kun and On	Romaji	Bushu	Stroke Order and Number
SG-1629 孫	grandchild, offspring	まご ソン	mago *son*	子	了 孑 孒 孫 孫 孫 10

孫 **C** F-1197

甲骨文 1, 金文 2, 説文 3 孫

1 and 2 comprised "child," and "skein of threads," to mean "long and continuous." (In 2 the two were attached to each other.) Together they signified "offspring, grandchild." In 3, 糸 was given an additional short stroke to emphasize the meaning of "connected," and became 系 **SG-1627** "lineage." The kanji 孫 means "grandchild, offspring." <子系>

孫 grandchild [まご]; ひ孫 great-grandchild [ひまご]; 孫娘 granddaughter [まごむすめ]; 内孫 a child of one's heir who lives with one [うちまご]; 孫の手 back-scratcher [まごのて]; 子孫 descendants [しそん]

	Meanings	Kun and On	Romaji	Bushu	Stroke Order and Number
SG-1630 遜	to humble oneself	ソン	*son*	辵	了 孑 孫 孫 遜 遜 14

遜 **D** F-2659

説文 遜

The seal-style form comprised 辵 (辶) "to move forward," and 孫 **SG-1629**, used for the sound *son* to mean "to retreat." Together they originally meant "to back off, withdraw," and were later used to mean "humbling oneself." The kanji 遜 means "to humble oneself." <孫辶>

謙遜する to humble oneself [けんそんする]; 遜色のない not inferior, to measure up [そんしょくのない]; 不遜な lacking humility, conceited [ふそんな]

74d 県 [from the upside-down head of a criminal being executed]; *ken* 県懸

SG-1631 県	Meanings	Kun and On	Romaji	Bushu	Stroke Order and Number
	prefecture	ケン	*ken*	糸	冂目目県県県 9

県 A F-0070

金文1 (1) 金文2 (2) 説文 (3) 旧字 (4) 縣 県

1 and 2 comprised "a tree," and "a rope," to which "the severed head of an executed person" was attached. 3 had "an upside-down head with hanging hair" and 系 SG-1627 "an attached rope," and the tree was dropped. The character's gruesome original meaning was dropped, and it meant simply "to hang down." 系 was retained in the kyuji 縣 (4), but was dropped in the shinji. The authority that had the power to execute punishment was a "jurisdiction," and in Japanese the kanji 県 means "prefecture." There are 43 県 in Japan. <目乚小>

神奈川県 Kanagawa prefecture [かながわけん]; 県立高校 prefectural high school [けんりつこうこう]; 県議会 prefectural assembly [けんぎかい]; 県境 prefectural border [けんざかい]; 県人会 association of people from the same prefecture [けんじんかい]

SG-1632 懸	Meanings	Kun and On	Romaji	Bushu	Stroke Order and Number
	to attach, hang, weigh on one's mind	か-ける ケン・ケ	ka-keru *ken, ke*	心	目目県県県縣縣懸懸 20

懸 C F-1362

No ancient form. After 縣, which originally meant "to hang down," was taken for the meaning "prefecture" (県 SG-1631), the new kanji 懸 was created by adding 心 SG-0187 "heart," to 縣, used for the sound *ken*. It also meant "to weigh on one's mind." The kanji 懸 means "to attach, hang, weigh on one's mind." <県系心>

懸ける to hang from, suspend from [かける]; 懸垂 suspension, pull-up (exercise) [けんすい]; 懸賞 price competition [けんしょう]; 懸命に hard, strenuously, assiduously [けんめいに]; 懸案 pending issue [けんあん]; 一生懸命 dedicated, all-out [いっしょうけんめい]; 懸念 fear, anxiety, apprehension [けねん]

75 Short threads

75a 幺 "short threads; young" [from a skein of short threads] 幼率

SG-1633 幼	Meanings	Kun and On	Romaji	Bushu	Stroke Order and Number
	very young, immature	おさな-い ヨウ	osana-i *yoo*	幺	ㇰ幺幻幼 5

幼 B F-0985

甲骨文1 (1) 甲骨文2 (2) 説文 (3) 幼

1 comprised "a skein of short threads" (幺) and "a long stick for twisting the threads," whereas 2 comprised "a hand" and "threads." The character originally meant "to twist." 3 comprised "short threads" (幺) to mean "young or fragile," and "a plow, power" (力 SG-1949), together signifying "too young to have the strength to use a plow," i.e., "a very young child." The kanji 幼 means "very young, immature." <幺力>

幼い very young, young and fragile [おさない]; 幼な馴染 childhood friend [おさななじみ]; 幼稚園 kindergarten [ようちえん]; 幼稚な immature, childish [ようちな]; 幼虫 larva [ようちゅう]

SG-1634 率	Meanings	Kun and On	Romaji	Bushu	Stroke Order and Number
	to lead, lead a party of people; rate, proportion	ひき-いる ソツ・リツ	hiki-iru *sotsu, ritsu*	玄	亠玄泫泫泫率 11

率 B F-0525

甲骨文 (1) 金文1 (2) 金文2 (3) 中山王器 (4) 説文 (5) 率

1 and 2 depicted "a skein of threads," with "water droplets" spilling off of both sides of an apparatus for wringing out water. In 3 and 4, "a crossroads" replaced the water droplets, for the meaning "to show the way." Firmly pulling on threads represented the manner of a person leading a party of people, and thus the character meant "to lead." The meanings "rate, proportion" were added as borrowings. The kanji 率 means "to lead a party of people; rate, proportion." <亠幺氵十>

率いる to head a party of people, lead [ひきいる]; 率先して taking the initiative [そっせんして]; 引率する to be in charge of (a party), lead [いんそつする]; 統率する to command [とうそつする]; 利率 interest rate [りりつ]; 確率 probability [かくりつ]

75b 兹 "to flourish" [from skeins of wet threads expanding]; *ji* 滋磁慈幽

	Meanings	Kun and On	Romaji	Bushu	Stroke Order and Number
SG-1635 滋	nutrient; rich	ジ	*ji*	水	氵氵'氵艹泫滋 12

滋 **C** F-1586

甲骨文 1 說文 2

1 and 2 comprised "skeins of short threads with their ends tied" (兹, or two 幺), used for the sound *ji*, in the middle of or next to 氵 "flowing water" (氵). Skeins of threads immersed in water would expand, whence the meaning "rampant; to grow thick." The character signified "to become moist, flourish; nutrient." In the shinji the tops of the tied skeins coalesced (艹). The kanji 滋 means "nutrient; rich." <氵艹幺幺>

滋養 nutrient [じよう]; 滋味 dainty, delicacy [じみ]

	Meanings	Kun and On	Romaji	Bushu	Stroke Order and Number
SG-1636 磁	magnetism, porcelain, ceramics	ジ	*ji*	石	厂石石'石艹石玄磁 14

磁 **C** F-1571

No ancient form. The kanji comprises 石 **SG-1148** "stone, rock," and 兹, used for the sound *ji* to mean "something black; to multiply." A magnet draws black iron sand to itself, one grain after another, and the kanji 磁 meant "magnetism." Later it came to mean "porcelain," which is made of fine sand. The kanji 磁 means "magnetism, porcelain, ceramics." <石艹兹>

陶磁器 ceramics, pottery, porcelain [とうじき]; 磁力 magnetic force, magnetism [じりょく]; 磁気 magnetism [じき]; 磁気カード magnetic card [じきカード]; 電磁石 electromagnet [でんじしゃく]; 磁場 magnetic field [じば, じば]

	Meanings	Kun and On	Romaji	Bushu	Stroke Order and Number
SG-1637 慈	affectionate, benevolent	いつく-しむ ジ	itsuku-shimu *ji*	心	丷艹玄兹兹慈慈 13

慈 **D** F-1787

中山王器 1 說文 2

The top of 1 and 2, 兹, depicted "skeins of threads expanded in water, growing thick and strong." It signified "to flourish," and had the sound *ji*. With 心 **SG-0187** "heart" added, the character signified "a benevolent heart that nurtured children and treated weak people tenderly." The kanji 慈 means "affectionate, benevolent." <艹兹心>

慈しむ to care tenderly, be affectionate toward [いつくしむ]; 慈悲深い merciful, charitable [じひぶかい]; 慈善 charity [じぜん]; 慈愛 (parental) love, affection [じあい]

	Meanings	Kun and On	Romaji	Bushu	Stroke Order and Number
SG-1638 幽	dark, subtle and profound, obscure	ユウ	*yuu*	幺	丨幺幺幺幽幽 9

幽 **D** F-1907

甲骨文 1 金文1 2 金文2 3 說文 4

1 through 4 comprised "two skeins of threads" above "a fire for smoking." Smoke-dyed threads grow darker gradually, with subtle changes of color. A smoking room was dark, and visibility was obscured. The kanji 幽 means "dark, subtle and profound, obscure." <山幺幺>

幽玄 elegant simplicity, subtle and profound [ゆうげん]; 幽霊 ghost [ゆうれい]; 幽閉する to confine someone in a place, lock someone up [ゆうへいする]

75c 玄 "dark" [from a skein of dyed threads tied at the top] 玄畜蓄

	Meanings	Kun and On	Romaji	Bushu	Stroke Order and Number
SG-1639 玄	dark color, expert, black	ゲン	*gen*	玄	亠亡玄玄 5

玄 **C** F-1405

金文 1 說文古文 2 說文 3

1 depicted "a skein of threads." In 2, the dots inside the skein indicated that the thread had a color. The top component added in 3 depicted an apparatus for dyeing. Threads that were dyed dark meant "deep color, black." In Japanese the meaning was applied to a skilled person who had absorbed experience over time, like threads absorb dye. The kanji 玄 means "dark color, expert; black." <亠幺>

玄米 brown rice, husked rice [げんまい]; 玄関 door, entryway, *genkan* [げんかん]; 玄関払い turning away a visitor at the door [げんかんばらい] // 玄人 expert, master hand [くろうと]

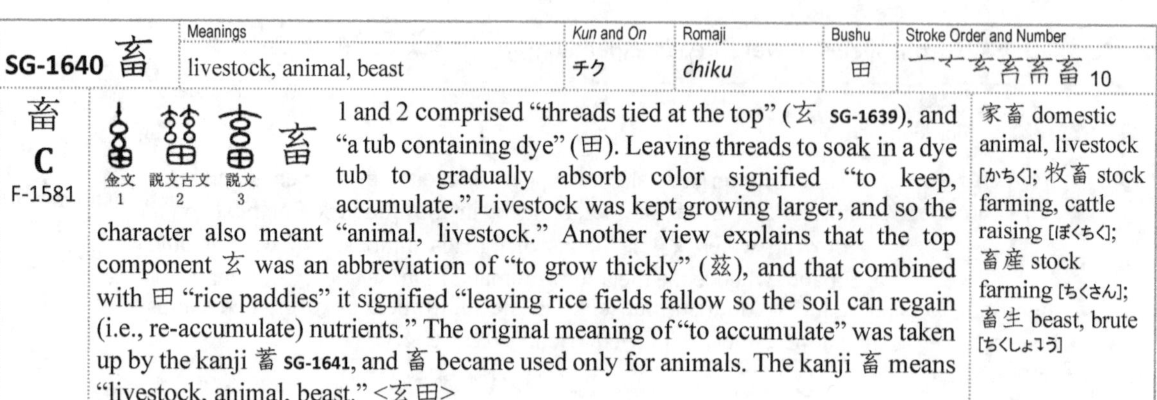

	Meanings	Kun and On	Romaji	Bushu	Stroke Order and Number
SG-1640 畜	livestock, animal, beast	チク	*chiku*	田	亠 ナ 玄 斉 斋 畜 10

畜 **C** F-1581

金文 1 說文古文 2 說文 3

1 and 2 comprised "threads tied at the top" (玄 **SG-1639**), and "a tub containing dye" (田). Leaving threads to soak in a dye tub to gradually absorb color signified "to keep, accumulate." Livestock was kept growing larger, and so the character also meant "animal, livestock." Another view explains that the top component 玄 was an abbreviation of "to grow thickly" (玆), and that combined with 田 "rice paddies" it signified "leaving rice fields fallow so the soil can regain (i.e., re-accumulate) nutrients." The original meaning of "to accumulate" was taken up by the kanji 蓄 **SG-1641**, and 畜 became used only for animals. The kanji 畜 means "livestock, animal, beast." <玄田>

家畜 domestic animal, livestock [かちく]; 牧畜 stock farming, cattle raising [ぼくちく]; 畜産 stock farming [ちくさん]; 畜生 beast, brute [ちくしょう]

	Meanings	Kun and On	Romaji	Bushu	Stroke Order and Number
SG-1641 蓄	to save up, stock up	たくわ-える チク	takuwa-eru *chiku*	艸	艹 芏 玄 蒿 蓄 蓄 13

蓄 **C** F-1565

說文

The seal-style form comprised "plant" (艸, 艹, bushu *kusakanmuri*), and 畜 **SG-1640**, used for the sound *chiku*, and its original meaning "to accumulate." Together they signified "to accumulate, pile up plants, stock up." The kanji 蓄 means "to save up, stock up." <艹玄田>

蓄える to save up, accumulate [たくわえる]; 蓄え savings [たくわえ]; 蓄積する to accumulate, amass [ちくせきする]; 蓄電する to charge (with electricity) [ちくでんする]; 備蓄米 emergency rice stocks [びちくまい]; 蓄音機 gramophone [ちくおんき]

75d 屯 "camp; to gather" [from a knotted end of thread]; *ton/jun* 純鈍屯頓・了

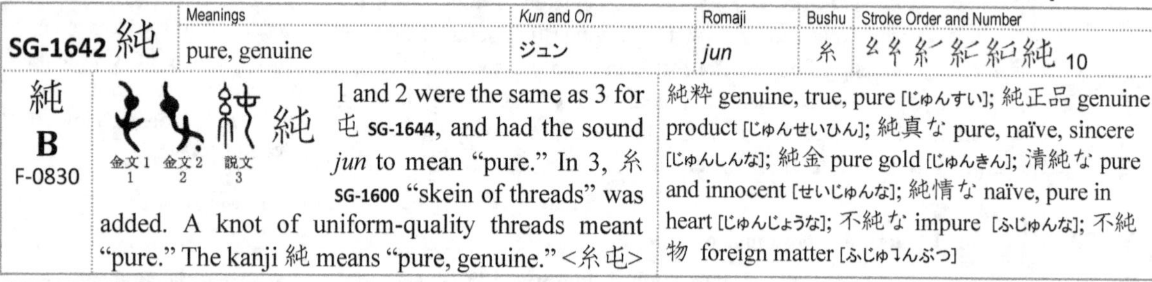

	Meanings	Kun and On	Romaji	Bushu	Stroke Order and Number
SG-1642 純	pure, genuine	ジュン	*jun*	糸	幺 糸 紅 紅 紅 純 10

純 **B** F-0830

金文1 1 金文2 2 說文 3

1 and 2 were the same as 3 for 屯 **SG-1644**, and had the sound *jun* to mean "pure." In 3, 糸 **SG-1600** "skein of threads" was added. A knot of uniform-quality threads meant "pure." The kanji 純 means "pure, genuine." <糸屯>

純粋 genuine, true, pure [じゅんすい]; 純正品 genuine product [じゅんせいひん]; 純真な pure, naïve, sincere [じゅんしんな]; 純金 pure gold [じゅんきん]; 清純な pure and innocent [せいじゅんな]; 純情な naïve, pure in heart [じゅんじょうな]; 不純な impure [ふじゅんな]; 不純物 foreign matter [ふじゅんぶつ]

	Meanings	Kun and On	Romaji	Bushu	Stroke Order and Number
SG-1643 鈍	dull, blunt, unintelligent, slow	にぶ-い ドン	nibu-i *don*	金	丷 午 金 金 鈩 鈍 12

鈍 **C** F-1573

說文

The seal-style form comprised "metal" (金 **SG-1196**), and "knot, round shape" (屯 **SG-1644**), used for the sound *don*, together signifying "a round metal item." A blade that is not sharp (that is, "rounded") is "dull, blunt." When applied to a person, the character meant "unintelligent, slow." The kanji 鈍 means "dull, blunt, unintelligent, slow." <金屯>

鈍い slow, unintelligent, dull [にぶい]; 鈍器 blunt instrument [どんき]; 鈍感な insensible, unaffected [どんかんな]; 鈍痛 dull pain [どんつう]; 鈍角 obtuse angle [どんかく]; 鈍化する to become blunt, slow down [どんかする]

	Meanings	Kun and On	Romaji	Bushu	Stroke Order and Number
SG-1644 屯	camp, soldiers' barracks	トン	*ton*	屮	一 ㄷ 口 屯 4

屯 **D** F-2156

甲骨文 1 金文1 2 金文2 3 說文 4

1, 2, and 3 depicted "a knotted end of thread" in woven fabric. The character also meant "pure." The sense of "pulling many threads together and making a knot" was also used to mean a place where many people congregated, such as "a camp or soldiers' barracks." The kanji 屯 means "camp, soldiers' barracks." < 屯>

駐屯する to be stationed [ちゅうとんする]; 駐屯地 army post, camp [ちゅうとんち] // 屯する to hang out as a large group [たむろする, たむろする]

	Meanings	Kun and On	Romaji	Bushu	Stroke Order and Number
SG-1645 頓	to make a deep bow, prostrate oneself; sudden	トン	*ton*	頁	一 口 屯 屯丆 屯百 頓 13

頓 **D** F-2158

説文

The seal-style form comprised "a knotted end of thread, fringe" (屯), to mean "hanging down" (used for the sound *ton*), and "a person wearing a formal hat, a head" (頁). Together they signified "a head drooping suddenly," that is, "a bow." The quick way in which a bowing head drops gave the meaning "sudden." The kanji 頓 means "to make a deep bow, prostrate oneself; sudden." <屯頁>

無頓着な unconcerned [むとꜜんちゃくな]; 頓服薬 medicine taken only when necessary [とんぷくꜜやく]; 頓挫する to be suddenly checked, meet with a setback [とんざする]; 整理整頓 keeping things tidy and in order [せꜜいり・せいとん]

了 "to end"

	Meanings	Kun and On	Romaji	Bushu	Stroke Order and Number
SG-1646 了	to end, conclude	リョウ	*ryoo*	亅	乛 了 2

了 **B** F-0924

説文

Origin unclear. One account is that this character depicted a thread tied in a knot, signifying "an end." The kanji 了 means "to end, conclude." <了>

完了する to finish off, complete [かんりょうする]; 了承する to acknowledge, understand [りょうしょうする]; 了解する to understand, agree to [りょうかいする]; 終了 end, finish, conclusion [しゅうりょう]; 現在完了 present perfect tense [げんざいかꜜんりょう]; 満了 expiration of a term, termination [まんりょう]

76 Warps on a weaver; braided

76a 圣 (巠) "to go through; straight" [from warp threads being pulled straight on a loom]; *kee* 経軽径茎

	Meanings	Kun and On	Romaji	Bushu	Stroke Order and Number
SG-1647 経	to go through, (time) passes; experience, Buddhist sutra	へ-る ケイ・キョウ	heru *kee, kyoo*	糸	幺 糸 紀 経 経 経 11

経 **A** F-0372

金文 1, 金文 2, 説文 3, 旧字 4

1 depicted a loom on which "(warp) threads were pulled straight on a wooden frame" (巠, 圣) and meant "straight; to go through." It had the sound *kee*. In 2 and 3, "skein of threads" (糸 **SG-1600**) was added to mean "continuous." From threads running continuously through from start to finish, the character meant "experience." Buddhist scripture and chants were "long and continuous," and so it was also used to mean "sutra." The kanji 経 means "to go through, (time) passes; experience, Buddhist sutra." <糸圣>

経る (time) passes, to experience, go through [へꜜる]; 経験 experience [けいけん]; 経理 accounting [けꜜいり]; 経営する to manage, operate, carry on a business [けいえいする]; 経路 routing [けꜜいろ]; 月経 menstruation [げっけい]; 経典 sacred book, scripture [きょうてん]; お経 Buddhist sutra [おきょう] // 読経 Buddhist sutra–chanting [どきょう]

	Meanings	Kun and On	Romaji	Bushu	Stroke Order and Number
SG-1648 軽	light, agile, frivolous; to underestimate, disregard	かる-い・かろ-やか ケイ	karu-i, karo-yaka *kee*	車	亘 車 軒 軽 軽 軽 12

軽 **B** F-0643

説文 1, 旧字 2

1 and 2 comprised 車 "military vehicle," and 巠 (圣), for the sound *kee*, to mean "light." Together they signified "a military vehicle that was not transporting heavy equipment." The character meant "light." Taking something lightly means "to disregard, slight." The kanji 軽 means "light, agile, frivolous; to underestimate, disregard." <車圣>

軽い light [かるい]; 手軽な easy, offhand, convenient [てがるな]; 軽々しい thoughtless, frivolous, imprudent [かるがるしꜜい]; 軽やかに airily, gracefully [かろꜜやかに]; 軽量 light-weight [けいりょう]; 軽視する to make light of [けꜜいしする]; 軽装 lightly dressed [けいそう]

	Meanings	*Kun* and *On*	Romaji	Bushu	Stroke Order and Number
SG-1649 径	narrow path, diameter	ケイ	*kee*	彳	径 8

径 **C** F-1425

説文 1, 旧字 2

1 comprised 彳 "crossroads; to go," and 巠 (圣) "vertically-running threads." The shortest way to reach a destination is a straight path rather than a well-traversed major road, and such a shortcut is likely to be a narrow path. The character meant "narrow path, pathway." A line that connects two points through the center of a circle is its "diameter." The kanji 径 means "narrow path, pathway, diameter." <彳圣>

直径 diameter [ちょっけい]; 半径 semidiameter, radius [はんけい]; 小径 pathway [しょうけい]

	Meanings	*Kun* and *On*	Romaji	Bushu	Stroke Order and Number
SG-1650 茎	stem, stalk	くき ケイ	kuki *kee*	艸	茎 8

茎 **D** F-1938

説文 1, 旧字 2

1 comprised "plants, grass" (艸, 艹) and 巠 (圣) "something extending straight." The part of a plant that grows straight is the stem or stalk. The kanji 茎 means "stem, stalk." <艹 圣>

茎 stem, stalk [くき]; 歯茎 the gums [はぐき]; 地下茎 subterranean stem [ちかけい]

76b 冉 "configuration" [from a braid]; 冓 "structure" [from two same configurations]; *koo* 再構講購溝・称

	Meanings	*Kun* and *On*	Romaji	Bushu	Stroke Order and Number
SG-1651 再	to repeat; again	ふたた-び サイ・サ	hutata-bi *sai, sa*	冂・一	再 6

再 **A** F-0228

甲骨文 1, 金文1 2, 金文2 3, 説文 4

1 depicted a braided rope, with a horizontal line at the top to signify the point at which the braider turned the rope around and restarted braiding. Restarting a process meant "again." 2 had two additional lines at the top, whereas 3 moved the two lines inside, in both cases to signify "double; to repeat." 4 was an abbreviated shape of 冓. The kanji 再 means "to repeat; again." <一冉>

再び again [ふたたび]; 再開する to reopen [さいかいする]; 再現 reenactment [さいげん]; 再出発 restart, fresh start [さいしゅっぱつ]; 再度 second time, again, twice [さいど]; 再生する to regrow, regenerate [さいせいする]; 再来年 the year after next [さらいねん]

	Meanings	*Kun* and *On*	Romaji	Bushu	Stroke Order and Number
SG-1652 構	structure; to construct, trouble oneself about	かま-える コウ	kama-eru *koo*	木	構 14

構 **A** F-0527

甲骨文1 1, 甲骨文2 2, 説文 3

1 and 2 depicted a configuration of braids in which the top and bottom were mirror images of each other, and had the sound *koo*. The character meant "structure or building." In 3, with 木 "wood" added, "a wooden configuration" that was repeated on each side meant "an architectural structure." The idea of configuring something was applied to a person, and the character also means "to assume a posture." The character is also used to mean "to be concerned about." The kanji 構 means "structure; to construct, trouble oneself about."<木冓>

構える to assume a posture, set up a house [かまえる]; 身構える to stand ready, be poised to defend oneself [みがまえる]; 構う to care about, take care of, bother about [かまう]; 構成 construction, composition [こうせい]; 構図 composition [こうず]; 結構な fine, delightful [けっこうな]; 構想 scheme, design, concept [こうそう]

	Meanings	*Kun* and *On*	Romaji	Bushu	Stroke Order and Number
SG-1653 講	lecture, talk; to reconcile	コウ	*koo*	言	講 17

講 **B** F-0663

説文

The seal-style form comprised 言, bushu *gonben* "word; to talk," and 冓, used for the sound *koo* to mean "to connect two things." People reconnecting by talking meant "to reconcile." Using words to explain something well meant "lecture." The kanji 講 means "lecture, talk; to reconcile." <言冓>

講堂 lecture hall, hall [こうどう]; 講義 lecture [こうぎ]; 講習 training session [こうしゅう]; 講師 lecturer [こうし]; 講座 regular university course [こうざ]; 代講 substitute lecturer [だいこう]; 講和 peace, reconciliation [こうわ]

SG-1654 購	Meanings	Kun and On	Romaji	Bushu	Stroke Order and Number
	to buy, purchase	コウ	*koo*	貝	購 17

購 C F-1278	The seal-style form comprised 貝 **SG-1693** "cowrie, money," and 冓 "two same things," for the sound *koo*. Together they signified "to exchange two things of equal value—money for goods." The kanji 購 means "to buy, purchase." <貝冓>	購読する to subscribe to (a newspaper) [こうどくする]; 購入する to purchase [こうにゅうする]; 購買意欲 consumer demand, inclination to spend [こうばいいよく]; 購買部 school or company shop [こうばいぶ]

SG-1655 溝	Meanings	Kun and On	Romaji	Bushu	Stroke Order and Number
	channel, ditch, gutter, drain	みぞ コウ	mizo *koo*	水	溝 13

溝 C F-1365	The seal-style form comprised "flowing water" (氵), and "symmetrical structure" (冓), for the sound *koo*. Together they signified "channel of water between two sides." The kanji 溝 means "channel, ditch, gutter, drain." <氵冓>	溝 ditch, gutter, drain [みぞ]; 排水溝 drainage ditch, drainageway [はいすいこう、はいすいこう]; 海溝 sea trench [かいこう]; 下水溝 sewer, drainage ditch [げすいこう]

称 [borrowed from 爯 "scale"] 

SG-1656 称	Meanings	Kun and On	Romaji	Bushu	Stroke Order and Number
	to exalt, praise; title, name	ショウ	*shoo*	禾	称 10

称 C F-1199	甲骨文1 甲骨文2 説文 旧字 (1 2 3 4) 1 and 2 depicted "a hand pulling up on a scale made of a braid, with an item hanging on each end to be weighed." In 3 and 4, with "a rice plant" (禾, bushu *nogihen*) added to 爯 "scale," the character signified "measuring rice plants." A hand or fingers pulling up on a scale gave the meaning "to raise, praise." The right side (爯) was replaced by 尓 "beautiful" (from 弥 **SG-1513**), to emphasize the meaning "praised." The kanji 称 means "to exalt, praise; title, name." <禾尓>	名称 name [めいしょう]; 称号 title [しょうごう]; 自称 self-proclaimed, self-described [じしょう]; 愛称 nickname [あいしょう]; 対称 symmetry [たいしょう]

77 Clothing

77a 衣 𧘇 "clothing" [from the back and front folds of a collar] 衣表裏依哀衰俵衷褒

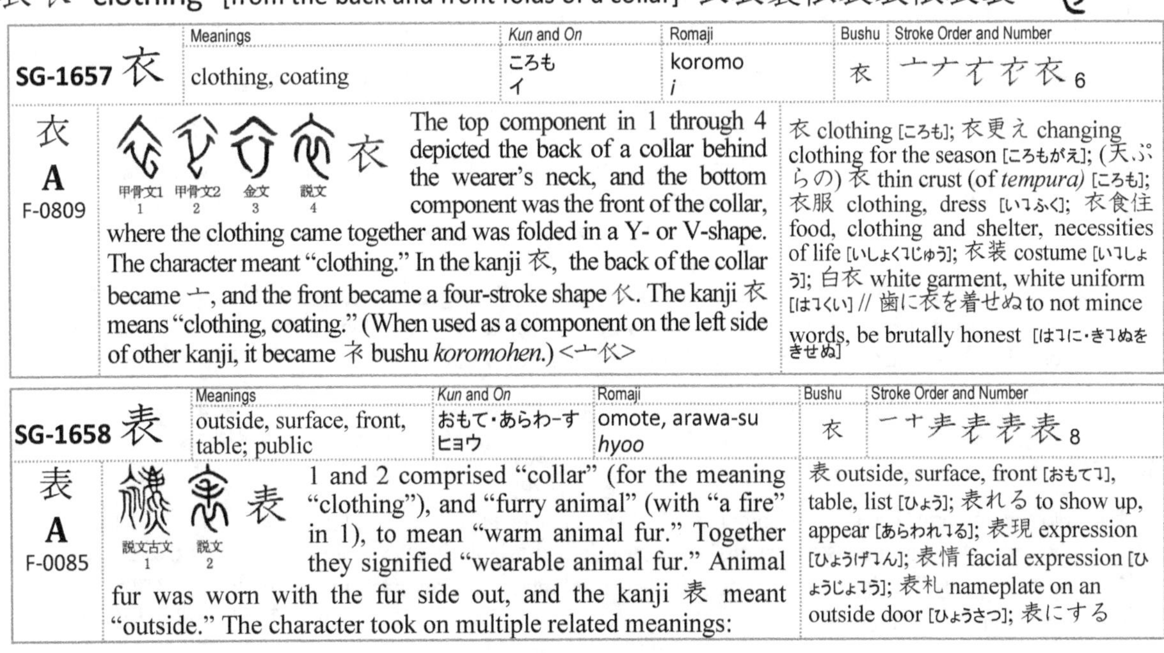

SG-1657 衣	Meanings	Kun and On	Romaji	Bushu	Stroke Order and Number
	clothing, coating	ころも イ	koromo *i*	衣	衣 6

衣 A F-0809	甲骨文1 甲骨文2 金文 説文 (1 2 3 4) The top component in 1 through 4 depicted the back of a collar behind the wearer's neck, and the bottom component was the front of the collar, where the clothing came together and was folded in a Y- or V-shape. The character meant "clothing." In the kanji 衣, the back of the collar became 亠, and the front became a four-stroke shape 𧘇. The kanji 衣 means "clothing, coating." (When used as a component on the left side of other kanji, it became 衤 bushu *koromohen*.) <亠𧘇>	衣 clothing [ころも]; 衣更え changing clothing for the season [ころもがえ]; (天ぷらの) 衣 thin crust (of *tempura*) [ころも]; 衣服 clothing, dress [いふく]; 衣食住 food, clothing and shelter, necessities of life [いしょくじゅう]; 衣装 costume [いしょう]; 白衣 white garment, white uniform [はくい] // 歯に衣を着せぬ to not mince words, be brutally honest [はに・きぬをきせぬ]

SG-1658 表	Meanings	Kun and On	Romaji	Bushu	Stroke Order and Number
	outside, surface, front, table; public	おもて・あらわ-す ヒョウ	omote, arawa-su *hyoo*	衣	表 8

表 A F-0085	説文古文 説文 (1 2) 1 and 2 comprised "collar" (for the meaning "clothing"), and "furry animal" (with "a fire" in 1), to mean "warm animal fur." Together they signified "wearable animal fur." Animal fur was worn with the fur side out, and the kanji 表 meant "outside." The character took on multiple related meanings:	表 outside, surface, front [おもて], table, list [ひょう]; 表れる to show up, appear [あらわれる]; 表現 expression [ひょうげん]; 表情 facial expression [ひょうじょう]; 表札 nameplate on an outside door [ひょうさつ]; 表にする

	Something that was outside became "public"; something that was shown was "in the front"; what was seen was "a surface"; a set of figures or other items displayed in a systematic manner was "a table." The kanji 表 means "outside, surface, front, table; public." <主 伩>	to tabulate [ひょうにする]; 発表 presentation, making public [はっぴょう]; 年表 timeline [ねんぴょう]

	Meanings	Kun and On	Romaji	Bushu	Stroke Order and Number
SG-1659 裏	wrong side, back, inside; hidden	うら リ	ura *ri*	衣	亩 审 重 重 裏 裏 裏 13

裏
B
F-0752

1 comprised 田 "rice paddies," and 土 "dirt," together forming 里 **SG-1312**, used for the sound *ri*. In 2 and 3, 里 was placed inside a "collar" or "clothing" (衣 **SG-1657**, 亠伩). "Inside of clothing" meant "wrong side, inside; hidden. The kanji 裏 means "wrong side, back, inside; hidden." <亠里伩>

裏 back, wrong side [うらｺ]; 裏返す turn over, turn inside-out [うらがｺえす]; 裏切る to betray, double-cross [うらぎｺる]; 裏話 the story behind a story, inside story [うらばｺなし]; 裏書き endorsement (of a check) [うらがき]; 裏面 wrong side, back [りｺめん]

	Meanings	Kun and On	Romaji	Bushu	Stroke Order and Number
SG-1660 依	to depend on, rely on	イ・エ	*i, e*	人	亻 亻 仁 仁 伩 依 依 8

依
B
F-1067

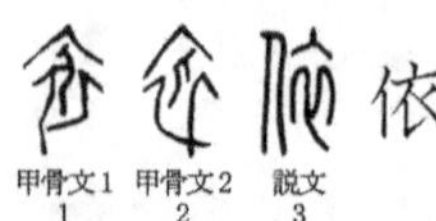

1 and 2 comprised "person," inside "a collar" (衣 **SG-1657**), used for the sound *i*. Clothing protected a person, and being in someone's protection meant "to depend on." In 3, the person moved out to the left, and became 亻, bushu *ninben* "an act that one does." The kanji 依 means "to depend on, rely on." <亻衣>

依頼する to make a request, commission to do [いらいする]; 依然として still, as it used to be [いぜんとして]; 旧態依然として remain unchanged, none the better for the change [きゅうたいいぜんとして]; 依願退職 voluntary resignation [いがんたｺいしょく, いｺがん・たいしょく]; 依存する to depend on, be dependent on [いぞんする]; 帰依する to become a devout believer [きｺえする]

	Meanings	Kun and On	Romaji	Bushu	Stroke Order and Number
SG-1661 哀	sorrow, pity	あわ-れ アイ	awa-re *ai*	口	亠 亡 户 户 哀 哀 9

哀
C
F-1535

1 and 2 had "mouth or voice" (口) hidden inside "clothing" (衣). Muffled wailing signified "sorrow or pity." The kanji 哀 means "sorrow, pity." <古 伩>

哀れむ to feel pity [あわれｺむ]; 哀れ pitifulness, misery [あｺわれ]; 悲哀 sorrow [ひあい]; 哀悼の意を表する to express condolences [あいとうのいｺを・ひょうすｺる]; 可哀想な poor, pitiful, miserable [かわいそｺうな]

	Meanings	Kun and On	Romaji	Bushu	Stroke Order and Number
SG-1662 衰	to weaken, decline, diminish	おとろ-える スイ	otoro-eru *sui*	衣	亠 亩 亩 亩 亩 亩 衰 10

衰
C
F-1540

1 depicted "strands of plants hanging down from a person's neck" to mean "to droop down; worn down," and further, "to die away or decline." In 2 the "neck" was added, while 3 had the addition of straws drooping down from the neck as "clothing" (衣, 伩), signifying "a straw raincoat." A straw raincoat drooped when wet, and thus signified something weakened or in decline. The kanji 衰 means "to weaken, decline, diminish." <亩 伩>

衰える to weaken, decline, diminish [おとろえｺる]; 衰退 atrophy, degeneration [すいたい]; 衰弱 weakening [すいじゃく]; 老衰死 death of old age [ろうすいｺし]; 盛衰 waxing and waning, rise and decline [せいすい]

	Meanings	Kun and On	Romaji	Bushu	Stroke Order and Number
SG-1663 俵	straw bag	たわら ヒョウ	tawara *hyoo*	人	亻 仁 仕 佳 佳 俵 俵 俵 10

俵
D
F-1730

No ancient form. The kanji 俵 comprised 亻 "an act that one does," and 表 for the sound *hyoo* to mean "allocation," together originally signifying "to share profits equally." In Japanese, the kanji 俵 was used mean "a straw bag" for storing grains and produce. <亻表>

俵 straw bag [たわらｺ]; 米俵 rice bag [こめだｺわら]; 土俵 sumo wrestling ring [どひょう]; 一俵 one bag [いｺっぴょう]

	Meanings	Kun and On	Romaji	Bushu	Stroke Order and Number
SG-1664 衷	true feelings, genuine sentiment	チュウ	*chuu*	衣	一 亠 亩 声 吏 衷 衷 9

衷 **D** F-2220

說文

In the seal-style form, under a collar/clothing (衣) were underclothes (represented by 中), not visible from the outside. With 中 "middle, inside" used for the sound *chuu*, the character signified one's true, but hidden, feelings. The kanji 衷 means "true feelings, genuine sentiment." <亩 仫>

苦衷 predicament, mental suffering [くちゅう]; 折衷案 compromise plan [せっちゅうあん]; 衷心より from the bottom of my heart (in a formal letter) [ちゅうしんより]

	Meanings	Kun and On	Romaji	Bushu	Stroke Order and Number
SG-1665 褒	to praise, commend	ほ-める ホウ	ho-meru *hoo*	衣	亠 卒 存 葆 褒 褒 褒 15

褒 **D** F-2370

說文 1 旧字 2

The top and bottom of 1 were 衣 "collar, clothing" split horizontally. In the middle was "a caring hand reaching for a baby wrapped in diapers (呆)," used for the sound *hoo* to mean "to wrap loosely." "A loosely-wrapped garment" originally meant "a robe." One view explains that such a robe was given to a lady of the court at her promotion, whence the meaning "to praise or commend." Another view takes this meaning to be a borrowing. The inside of the kyuji 襃 (2) became 保 **SG-0513** in the shinji. The kanji 褒 means "to praise, commend." <亠保仫>

褒める to praise, commend [ほめる]; 褒美 reward, compensation [ほうび]

77b 衤 "clothing" (衣); bushu *koromohen* 初裕袖襟裾・卒

The 5-stroke shape 衤 is not to be confused with the 4-stroke 礻 (the common shape 80c), bushu *shimesuhen* "religious matter."

	Meanings	Kun and On	Romaji	Bushu	Stroke Order and Number
SG-1666 初	first time, beginning; naïve	はじ-めて・はつ・うい-・そ-める ショ	haji-mete, hatsu, ui, -so-meru *sho*	刀	ラ ネ ネ ネ 初 初 7

初 **A** F-0195

甲骨文 1 金文1 2 金文2 3 說文 4

1 through 4 comprised "clothing" (衣 **SG-1657**) and "a knife" (刀 **SG-1394**). In order to make clothing, the fabric would first be cut, and the character meant "for the first time." "Unexperienced" lent the meaning "naïve." In the kanji, 衣 on the left side became 衤, bushu *koromohen* "clothing." The kanji 初 means "first time, beginning; naïve." <衤刀>

初めて for the first time [はじめて]; 初体験 first experience [はつたいけん]; 初々しい innocent, pure, fresh [ういういしい]; 見初める to fall in love at first sight [みそめる]; 最初 in the beginning [さいしょ]; 初期 beginning [しょき]; 初心者 beginner, novice [しょしんしゃ] // 初な naïve, green [うぶな]

	Meanings	Kun and On	Romaji	Bushu	Stroke Order and Number
SG-1667 裕	leeway, room; plentiful	ユウ	*yuu*	衣	ラ ネ ネ 衫 裕 裕 10

裕 **B** F-1061

金文 1 說文 2

1 and 2 comprised "clothing" (衣,衤), and 谷, used for the sound *yuu* to mean "roomy, ample." Roomy or loose clothing signified "leeway; plentiful." The kanji 裕 means "leeway, room; plentiful." <衤谷>

余裕 additional coverage, room [よゆう]; 裕福な rich, wealthy, well-to-do [ゆうふくな]

	Meanings	Kun and On	Romaji	Bushu	Stroke Order and Number
SG-1668 袖	sleeve	そで シュウ	sode *shuu*	衣	ラ ネ ネ 衵 袖 袖 18

袖 **D** F-1928

說文 1 說文俗体 2

1 had "clothing," with a component added in the middle for the sound *shuu*. 2 comprised "clothing" (衣, 衤), and 由 **SG-0781**, used for the sound *yuu* and the meaning "coming out." Together they signified a part of clothing through which one's arm came out, that is, "a sleeve." The kanji 袖 means "sleeve."<衤由>

袖 sleeve [そで]; 袖口 cuff [そでぐち]; 振袖 young woman's formal kimono with full-length sleeves [ふりそで]; 長袖 long sleeves [ながそで]; 半袖 short sleeves [はんそで]; 筒袖 straight sleeves [つつそで]; 領袖 leader, protagonist, boss [りょうしゅう]

SG-1669 襟	Meanings	Kun and On	Romaji	Bushu	Stroke Order and Number
	collar	えり キン	eri *kin*	衣	18

襟 **D** F-2080

金文 1 篆文 2

1 and 2 comprised "clothing" (衣, 衤), and 金, used for the sound *kin* to mean "collar," together signifying "collar." In the kanji, 金 was replaced by 禁 **SG-1738** "to close," for the same sound. The part of clothing that closed was a collar. The kanji 襟 means "collar." <衤禁>

襟 collar [えり]; 襟巻き muffler, neck scarf [えりまき]; 開襟シャツ open-necked shirt [かいきんシャツ]; 胸襟を開く to open one's heart, have a heart-to-heart talk with someone [きょうきんをひらく]

SG-1670 裾	Meanings	Kun and On	Romaji	Bushu	Stroke Order and Number
	the bottom edge of clothing, hem, skirts, foothills	すそ	suso	衣	13

裾 **D** F-2381

篆文

The seal-style form comprised 衣 (衤 in the kanji), and 居 **SG-0469**, used for the sound *kyo*. Use of the character originally included different parts of clothing, such as the hem, collar, or sleeves, or the edge of the front panel. But now the kanji 裾 is used only to mean "the bottom edge of clothing, hem, skirts," and by metaphorical extension, "foothills." <衤居>

裾 bottom edge of clothing, hem [すそ]; 山裾 foothills of a mountain [やますそ]; 裾模様 design on the skirt of a kimono [すそもよう]

卒 "sudden; to end; low-ranking solder"

SG-1671 卒	Meanings	Kun and On	Romaji	Bushu	Stroke Order and Number
	low-ranking soldier; sudden, rash; to end	ソツ	*sotsu*	十	8

卒 **B** F-0675

金文 1 三体石経 2 説文 3

The kanji 卒 has two seemingly unrelated meanings: (a) "low-ranking soldier"; and (b) "sudden death." 1, 2, and 3 depicted "a collar that had a slanted line." One view explains that the slanted line indicated soldiers wearing the same clothing— "low-ranking soldiers." Another view holds that a deceased person's collar was tied shut so that the spirit would not stray out—whence the meaning "sudden death," and the related meanings "rash, hasty; to end." The kanji 卒 means "low-ranking solder; sudden, rash; to end." <亠人人十>

卒業 graduation [そつぎょう]; 軽卒な careless, hasty, without serious thought [けいそつな]; 卒中 stroke, apoplectic seizure [そっちゅう]; 卒倒する to faint, fall unconscious [そっとうする]; 高卒 high school graduate [こうそつ]; 卒業生 graduate [そつぎょうせい] // 何卒 please, by all means [なにとぞ]

77c 袁 "distant" [from walking a long road]; *en* 遠園

SG-1672 遠	Meanings	Kun and On	Romaji	Bushu	Stroke Order and Number
	far, distance	とお-い エン・オン	too-i *en, on*	辵	13

遠 **B** F-0599

金文1 1 金文2 2 説文 3

1, 2, and 3 comprised "a crossroads" and "a footprint," forming "to move forward" (辵, 辶); and "a jewel" inside the collar of a deceased person, forming 袁, used for the sound *en*. Taken together, they signified that a deceased person with a jewel was departing on a long, faraway journey to the afterlife, and thus the character meant "far, distant." Another view takes 袁 as simply a phonetic feature, used for the sound *en* to mean "long and spacious," which, combined with 辶 "to go," meant "walking a long time." The kanji 遠 means "far, distant." <土口𧘇辶>

遠い far, distant [とおい]; 遠出する to go on an excursion [とおでする]; 遠回しに in a roundabout way [とおまわしに]; 遠回り a long way, circuitous route [とおまわり]; 敬遠する to keep a respectful distance [けいえんする]; 遠足 excursion, long walk [えんそく]; 遠距離の long-distance [えんきょりの]; 遠心力 centrifugal force [えんしんりょく]

SG-1673 園	Meanings	Kun and On	Romaji	Bushu	Stroke Order and Number
	garden, park	その エン	sono *en*	囗	13

園 **B** F-0593

説文

The seal-style form comprised 囗, bushu *kunigamae* "enclosure," and 袁, used for the sound *en* to mean "spacious, roomy." An enclosure with a lot of open space was a garden or a park. The kanji 園 means "garden, park." <囗袁>

園 garden [その]; 花園 flower garden [はなぞの]; 公園 park [こうえん]; 動物園 zoo [どうぶつえん]; 幼稚園の園児 kindergarten pupil [ようちえんの・えんじ]; 学園 (private) school, campus [がくえん]; 田園 the countryside, rural distsrict [でんえん]

77d 褱 "chest" [from tears hidden inside a collar]; *kai* 壊懐

	Meanings	Kun and On	Romaji	Bushu	Stroke Order and Number
SG-1674 壊	to break, destroy, tear down	こわ-す カイ	kowa-su *kai*	土	一 十 ま 圹 圹 坤 坤 堙 壊 壊 16

壊 **C** F-1115

説文古文 1 説文 1 2 説文 2 3 旧字 4

1 comprised "an eye pouring tears," used for the sound *kai* to mean "to destroy," and 土 "soil," together signifying "to destroy, break." In 2, 土 was moved to the left side, and "clothing" (衣) was added, enclosing the crying eye on the right side (褱). In 3, 攴 "to cause an action" was added. In the kanji the tears and 攴 were dropped. The kanji 壊 means "to break, destroy, tear down." <扌 亜 衣>

壊す to break, damage, spoil [こわす]; 壊れる to break [こわれる]; 破壊的な destructive, subversive [はかいてきな]; 半壊する to be half destroyed [はんかいする]; 倒壊家屋 collapsed house [とうかいかおく]; 全壊 complete collapse [ぜんかい]

	Meanings	Kun and On	Romaji	Bushu	Stroke Order and Number
SG-1675 懐	chest, heart, inside pocket; to hold a sentiment	ふところ・なつ-かしい カイ	hutokoro, natsu-kashii *kai*	心	丶 忄 忄 忄 忄 怦 悝 懐 16

懐 **C** F-1442

金文 1 1 金文 2 2 説文 3 旧字 4

1 and 2 comprised "a collar," inside of which was "an eye pouring tears" (褱), used for the sound *kai*. The character signified "emotions held in the chest, such as sadness." In 3, with 忄, bushu *risshinben* "heart" added, the character meant "sentiments and thoughts cherished in one's heart." The tears were removed for the kanji. The kanji 懐 means "chest, heart, inside pocket; to hold a sentiment." <忄 褱>

懐 heart, chest [ふところ]; 懐具合 one's financial standing, state of one's purse [ふところぐあい]; 懐刀 dagger, one's right-hand man [ふところがたな]; 懐かしい longed-for, nostalgic [なつかしい]; 懐古的 nostalgic [かいこてき]; 懐疑的 skeptic, incredulous [かいぎてき]; 懐中電灯 torch, flashlight [かいちゅうでんとう]

77e 睘 "round; circle; to return"; *kan* 環還

	Meanings	Kun and On	Romaji	Bushu	Stroke Order and Number
SG-1676 環	ring; circular; to circle around	カン	*kan*	玉	一 T 珊 珊 琈 環 環 17

環 **B** F-0636

金文 1 1 金文 2 2 説文 3

1, 2, and 3 comprised "a string of gems" (王), "an eye" (in 1 and 3) or "a footprint" (in 2), and "a necklace inside a collar." A deceased person was buried with a necklace to wear on the long journey to reincarnation. A necklace forms a circle, and thus the kanji 環 means "round, circle." Another view explains that the kanji 環 comprised 王 "jewel, gem," and 睘 for the sound *kan* to mean "a ring." Later the character came to mean "round; to circle." The kanji 環 means "ring; circular; to circle around." <王睘>

環状の circular, ring-like [かんじょうの]; 環境 environment [かんきょう]; 環状線 circular road [かんじょうせん]; 市内循環バス city circulation bus [しない・じゅんかんバス]; ～の一環 a part of X, connection with X [～のいっかん]

	Meanings	Kun and On	Romaji	Bushu	Stroke Order and Number
SG-1677 還	to return, circle back to the original point	カン	*kan*	辵	罒 罒 罒 睘 睘 睘 還 還 16

還 **C** F-1143

甲骨文 1 金文 1 2 金文 2 3 説文 4

1, 2, 3, and 4 comprised "a crossroads," and 睘, for the sound *kan*, the components of which were "an eye" (for "awake" or "can see") and "a collar." "A jewel or ring" was added in 2, 3, and 4, and "a footprint" was added in 3 and 4 to form 辵 (辶). One view explains that an eye was drawn on a deceased person to guide them in "reawakening and returning to the world of the living," and the kanji 還 meant "to return, circle back to the original point." Another view holds that 睘 was merely used phonetically for the sound *kan*. The kanji 還 means "to return, circle back to the original point." <睘 辶>

生還 returning alive [せいかん]; 返還 restoration, restitution [へんかん]; 還元 return, reconstitution, resolution [かんげん]; 還暦 one's sixtieth birthday [かんれき]; 送還する to repatriate, send home [そうかんする]

77f 襄 (襄); *joo* 譲嬢醸壌

	Meanings	Kun and On	Romaji	Bushu	Stroke Order and Number
SG-1678 譲	to grant, give way, turn over to	ゆず-る ジョウ	yuzu-ru *joo*	言	言 訁 訁 訁 譲 譲 譲 20

譲 **C** F-1150 — 説文 1, 旧字 2

1 comprised 言 "word; to say," and 襄(襄), used for the sound *joo* to mean "to blame." Together, they originally signified "using words to blame or condemn." The character came to be used to mean "to grant." The kanji 譲 means "to grant, give way, turn over to." <言 襄>

譲る to turn over to, part with, leave [ゆずる]; 親譲り inherited trait [おやゆずり]; 分譲する to sell (land) in lots [ぶんじょうする]; 移譲する to transfer, delegate to [いじょうする]; 謙譲 modesty, self-effacement [けんじょう]; 譲渡 transfer, grant [じょうと]; 譲位 abdication (of a throne) [じょうい]

	Meanings	Kun and On	Romaji	Bushu	Stroke Order and Number
SG-1679 嬢	daughter of a good family, young girl (honorific)	ジョウ	*joo*	女	女 女 女 女 嬢 嬢 嬢 嬢 16

嬢 **D** F-1720 — 説文 1, 旧字 2

1 comprised 女 "female," and 襄 (襄) for the sound *joo* to mean "plentiful, abundant." Together they originally signified a woman with a round shape. The character came to mean a young woman of a good family. The kanji 嬢 is used as an honorific meaning "daughter of a good family, young girl." <女 襄>

お嬢さん (someone's) daughter, young lady [おじょうさん]; 令嬢 young lady of a good family [れいじょう]; お嬢さん育ち well-brought-up young woman, naïve woman [おじょうさんそだち]

	Meanings	Kun and On	Romaji	Bushu	Stroke Order and Number
SG-1680 醸	to ferment, brew	かも-す ジョウ	kamo-su *joo*	酉	一 丙 酉 酉 酉 醸 醸 醸 20

醸 **D** F-1867 — 説文 1, 旧字 2

1 comprised 酉 "a cask," and 襄 (襄) used for the sound *joo* to mean "to put things in, mix." Together they signified putting rice and yeast into a cask and mixing them for fermentation or brewing. The kanji 醸 means "to ferment, brew." <酉 襄>

醸し出す to bring about [かもしだす]; 物議を醸す to arouse criticism, cause controversy [ぶつぎを・かもす]; 醸造 fermented food production, brewing [じょうぞう]; 醸成する to bring about, arouse, ferment (unrest) [じょうせいする]

	Meanings	Kun and On	Romaji	Bushu	Stroke Order and Number
SG-1681 壌	soil, earth	ジョウ	*joo*	土	一 丙 酉 酉 酉 醸 醸 醸 16

壌 **D** F-1924 — 説文 1, 旧字 2

1 and 2 comprised 土 "soil," and 襄 "rich, full," used for the sound *joo*, together signifying "well-tilled rich soil that was suitable for farming." The kanji 壌 means "soil, earth." <土 襄>

土壌 earth, soil [どじょう]

78 Cloth

78a 巾 "cloth" [from a scarf] 巾布帯希飾怖滞帥

	Meanings	Kun and On	Romaji	Bushu	Stroke Order and Number
SG-1682 巾	cloth, scarf, width	キン	*kin*	巾	丨 冂 巾 3

巾 **B** F-2133 — 甲骨文 1, 金文 2, 説文 3

1, 2, and 3 depicted "a ceremonial waist scarf worn by a man," and had the sound *kin*. The character meant "a piece of cloth" of various kinds, such as a headscarf, handkerchief, or lap robe. The kanji 巾 means "cloth, scarf, width." <巾>

布巾 kitchen cloth, dish cloth [ふきん]; 頭巾 hood [ずきん]; 三角巾 triangular bandage [さんかくきん] // 巾 width (informally in place of 幅) [はば]

	Meanings	Kun and On	Romaji	Bushu	Stroke Order and Number
SG-1683 布	cloth; to lay flat, spread	ぬの フ	nuno *hu*	巾	ノ ナ 才 右 布 5

布 **B** F-0699 — 金文 1, 説文 2

1 depicted "a hand holding an ax or a rock," used for the sound *hu* (from 父 SG-0103) to mean "to pound on," and 巾 "cloth." The fibrous stalks and stems of a plant, such as hemp, were pounded flat to obtain fibers for weaving. A piece of cloth

布 cloth [ぬの]; 毛布 blanket, woolen blanket [もうふ]; 布教 missionary work [ふきょう]; 布団 *futon*, padded mattress, bedding

	covered a wide area, and thus the character also meant "to spread." The kanji 布 means "cloth; to lay flat, spread." <ナ巾>	[ふとん]; 散布する to spray, scatter [さんぷする, さんぷする]

	Meanings	*Kun* and *On*	Romaji	Bushu	Stroke Order and Number
SG-1684 帯	sash, belt; to wear, take on	おーびる・おび タイ	o-biru, obi *tai*	巾	一 卄 卄 卅 帯 帯 10

帯 **B** F-0629

(説文 1, 旧字 2) 1 depicted "a belt or rope with accessories," and "a cloth" worn on one's front, such as an apron, for the sound *tai*. A rope that held clothing on was "a sash." One wore a sash on the body, and so the character also meant "to wear." From the shape of a sash, it also meant "a long, narrow area." The kanji 帯 means "sash, belt, long narrow area; to wear." <卌冖巾>

帯びる to wear, take on, be tinged with [おびる, おびる]; 帯 sash, band [おび]; 帯状 narrow strip shape [おびじょう]; 一帯 whole area [いったい]; 携帯する物 article to carry [けいたいする]; 温帯 temperate zone [おんたい]; 工業地帯 industrial area [こうぎょうちたい]; 妻帯者 married man [さいたいしゃ]

	Meanings	*Kun* and *On*	Romaji	Bushu	Stroke Order and Number
SG-1685 希	wish; rare; to beseech	キ	*ki*	巾	ノ メ 乄 产 肴 希 7

希 **B** F-0765

(説文) The seal-style form comprised 爻 "crossing," used for the sound *ki* (from *koo*), and 巾 "cloth." Shuffling threads back and forth (爻) created fine woven cloth or embroidered cloth. The fine quality of such cloth meant "rare." After the kanji 稀 was created to mean "rare," the character 希 became used to mean "to beseech, wish for," due to its sound *ki*. However, because 稀 is a non-Joyo kanji, 希 is sometimes still used instead for its original meaning "rare." The kanji 希 means "wish; rare; to beseech." <メ布>

希望 hope, wish [きぼう]; 希薄な (稀薄な) thin [きはくな]; 希少価値 (稀少) scarcity value [きしょうかち]; 希釈液 diluted solution, weak solution [きしゃくえき] // 希有な (稀有な) rare, out of the ordinary [けうな]

	Meanings	*Kun* and *On*	Romaji	Bushu	Stroke Order and Number
SG-1686 飾	to decorate, embellish	かざーる ショク	kaza-ru *shoku*	食	^ 今 刍 食 飠 飾 飾 13

飾 **C** F-1149

(説文) The seal-style form comprised 食 **SG-1781** "food" (used for the sound *shoku*), "a person," and 巾 "cloth." A person wiping a food bowl with a piece of cloth signified "to clean or make pretty." The kanji 飾 means "to decorate, embellish." <飠𠂉巾>

飾る to decorate [かざる]; 髪飾り hair accessory [かみかざり]; 飾り付け decoration [かざりつけ]; 着飾る to dress up [きかざる]; 修飾語 modifier (grammar) [しゅうしょくご]; 服飾デザイナー fashion designer [ふくしょくデザイナー]; 粉飾決算 accounting fraud, window dressing settlement [ふんしょくけっさん]

	Meanings	*Kun* and *On*	Romaji	Bushu	Stroke Order and Number
SG-1687 怖	fear; afraid, frightening, terrifying	こわーい フ	kowa-i *hu*	心	丶 忄 忙 怖 怖 8

怖 **C** F-1266

(説文 1, 説文或体 2) 1 comprised "heart" (忄, *risshinben*), and 甫, used for the sound *hu* to mean "fear." In 2, 布 replaced 甫 for the same sound, *hu*. The kanji 怖 means "fear; afraid, frightening, terrifying." <忄布>

怖い frightening, petrifying, scary [こわい]; 怖がる to be frightened, dread [こわがる]; 恐怖 terror [きょうふ] // 怖じ気付く to be seized with fear, lose one's nerve [おじけづく]; 物怖じする to be shy, be timid, be skittish [ものおじする]

	Meanings	*Kun* and *On*	Romaji	Bushu	Stroke Order and Number
SG-1688 滞	to delay, stagnate, stay; left undone	とどこおーる タイ	todokoo-ru *tai*	水	氵 氵 洴 泄 滞 滞 13

滞 **C** F-1287

(説文 1, 旧字 2) 1 comprised "flowing water" (氵), and 帯, used for the sound *tai* to mean "to stay." A pool of water that remained for some time became stagnant, and the character meant "not making progress; behind." The kanji 滞 means "to delay, stagnate, stay." <氵帯>

滞る to stagnate, fall behind (in payment) [とどこおる, とどこおる]; 滞在する to stay, remain [たいざいする]; 滞納 failure to pay, overdue [たいのう]; 延滞料 late charge [えんたいりょう]; 停滞する to stop moving, stagnate [ていたいする]; 沈滞ムード depressed mood, slump [ちんたいムード]; 滞空時間 flight duration, time in the air [たいくうじかん]

	Meanings	Kun and On	Romaji	Bushu	Stroke Order and Number
SG-1689 帥	commander, general	スイ	*sui*	巾	丿 ⺈ 𠂤 帥 9

帥 **D** F-2271

金文1 1 金文2 2 説文或体 3 説文 4

1 and 2 comprised "doors or panels on a family altar," and 巾 "cloth." Dusting one's family altar with cloth signified being pious and exemplary. A person so dedicated to such important work makes a good leader or military commander. 3 was a piece of cloth, such as an apron. In 4 (帥), however, the left side became 𠂤, "an offering of meat in a pre-battle rite." With 巾 now seen as meaning "flag," the character signified "commanding troops with a flag." The kanji 帥 means "commander, general." <𠂤巾>

元帥 general, commander [げ'んすい]; 統帥権 the prerogative of supreme command [とうす'いけん]

78b 敝 "to tire, become torn" [from 㡀 "worn and torn cloth" and 攵 "to cause an action"]; *hee/shoo* 幣弊蔽

	Meanings	Kun and On	Romaji	Bushu	Stroke Order and Number
SG-1690 幣	money, sacred strips of paper	ヘイ	*hee*	巾	丶 丷 㡀 敝 幣 15

幣 **D** F-1810

説文

The seal-style form comprised 敝, used for the sound *hee*, and 巾 "cloth," together signifying "a sacred piece of cloth for offering to a deity." An offering was sometimes made in the form money. In Japan the character is also used to mean the hanging strips of white paper that mark sacred areas on the grounds of Shinto shrines and ward off evil. The kanji 幣 means "money, sacred strips of paper (in Shinto 神道)." <敝巾>

貨幣 money [か'へい]; 紙幣 paper currency, note [し'へい]; 御幣担ぎ superstitious person [ごへいか'つぎ]

	Meanings	Kun and On	Romaji	Bushu	Stroke Order and Number
SG-1691 弊	to exhaust; harmful; our (humble)	ヘイ	*hee*	廾	丶 丷 㡀 敝 弊 15

弊 **D** F-1978

篆文1 1 篆文2 2 正字 3

In 1 and 2, 敝 "tired; worn out cloth" was used for the sound *hee*. The bottom of 1 was "dog" (犬), while 2 had "death" (死). Dogs are said to have been used to test for poison. Together, these components meant "to collapse, perish, die; harmful." In the kanji 弊, the bottom 犬 became 廾. The character is also used as a humble way to express "our," as in 弊社, "our company." The kanji 弊 means "to become exhausted; harmful; our (humble)." <敝廾>

疲弊 impoverishment, exhaustion [ひへい]; 弊害 bad practice, harmful influence [へいがい]; 語弊がある misleading (language) [ごへいがあ'る]; 弊社 our company (humble) [へ'いしゃ]

	Meanings	Kun and On	Romaji	Bushu	Stroke Order and Number
SG-1692 蔽	to conceal, cover	ヘイ	*hee*	艸	艹 芇 蔽 15

蔽 **D** F-3060

説文

The seal-style form comprised "plants" (艸, 艹, bushu *kusakanmuri*), and 敝, used for the sound *hee*. Together they meant "grass grows rampantly and covers or hides things." The kanji 蔽 means "to conceal, cover." <艹敝>

隠蔽する to conceal, hide [いんぺいする]; 建蔽率 building-to-land ratio [けんぺ'いりつ]; 遮蔽する to cover, shade [しゃへいする]

IX Valuables

79 Cowrie, bronze vessel

79a 貝 "shell, monetary value; valuable" [from a cowrie]

貝実売続得価買負貴敗貨遺賛賃貯貿貫慣貢鎖唄賜賭潰

SG-1693 貝	Meanings	Kun and On	Romaji	Bushu	Stroke Order and Number
	shell, shellfish	かい	kai	貝	丨冂月目貝 7

貝 **A** F-1162

甲骨文1 1 · 甲骨文2 2 · 金文1 3 · 金文2 4 · 説文 5

1 through 5 depicted "a cowrie," a spiral domed shell that had an opening in the back. Cowries came from the South China Sea, a long way from land and civilization. They were treasured for their rarity and colorful features, and were sometimes used as tokens in trade. The kanji 貝 is used inclusive of all seashells, and means "shell, shellfish." When used as a component, 貝 means "valuable, money, monetary value." <目ハ>

貝 shell [かꜜい]; 二枚貝 bivalve [にまꜜいがい]; 子安貝(宝貝) cowrie [こやすꜜがい, たからꜜがい)]; 貝殻 shell [かいがら, かいがꜜら]; 貝塚 shell mound, *kaizuka* [かꜜいづか]; 貝合わせ pairing game played with clamshells [かいあꜜわせ]

SG-1694 実	Meanings	Kun and On	Romaji	Bushu	Stroke Order and Number
	real, actual; substance, fruit, nut, berry; to come to fruition, show results	み・みの-る ジツ	mi, mino-ru *jitsu*	宀	丶 宀 宣 実 実 8

実 **A** F-0078

金文1 1 · 金文2 2 · 金文3 3 · 説文 4 · 旧字 5

In 1, 2, 3, and 4, inside a family mausoleum or a house were "small, pierced cowries strung together" (毌), and "cowrie, valuable item" (貝). Valuable offerings, or a house full of such valuables, signified "real, actual" wealth. The form also came to mean "fruit, nut, berry; to come to fruition." In the shinji 実, the components 毌 and 貝 inside of 宀 bushu *ukanmuri* were replaced by a simplified shape, 夫. The kanji 実 means "real, actual; substance, fruit, nut, berry; to come to fruition, show results." <宀夫>

実 fruit, nut, berry, substance [み]; 実が成る to produce a crop or fruit [みがなꜜる]; 実る to ripen, show results [みのꜜる]; 実は as a matter of fact, in truth [じつꜜわ]; 実話 authentic account [じつわ]; 実務 administrative work [じꜜつむ]; 実際に really, in practice [じっさいに]; 結実する to bear fruit, achieve [けつじつする]; 事実上 in reality, effectively [じじつじょう]

SG-1695 売	Meanings	Kun and On	Romaji	Bushu	Stroke Order and Number
	to sell	う-る バイ	u-ru *bai*	貝	一十士士声売売 7

売 **A** F-0218

説文 1 · 旧字 2

1 comprised "to go out" (出 **SG-0217**, from "a footprint with a heel mark"), 网 "a fishing net," and 貝 "cowrie, money." Going out to exchange something for money meant "to sell (for profit)." In the kyuji 賣 (2), the footprint was replaced by 士. In the shinji, 買 was replaced by 冖, and 儿, bushu *ninnyoo* "person." The kanji 売 means "to sell." <士冖儿>

売る to sell [うる]; 安売り a sale [やすうり]; 押し売り aggressive selling or aggressive person [おしうり]; 身売りする to merge with, sell oneself (into bondage) [みうりする]; 小売業 retail trade [こうりꜜぎょう]; 売店 concession, booth [ばいてん]; 販売員 salesperson [はんばꜜいいん]

SG-1696 続	Meanings	Kun and On	Romaji	Bushu	Stroke Order and Number
	to continue; in succession	つづ-く ゾク	tsuzu-ku *zoku*	糸	幺 糸 糸一 糸十 糸声 続 13

続 **A** F-0224

説文古文 1 · 説文 2 · 旧字 3

1 depicted two hands continuously pulling out money (貝 "a cowrie, monetary value"), signifying "to continuously circulate money in commerce." 2 comprised 糸 "thread, continuous," and 賣, which was used for the sound *zoku*, also meaning "to continue." Together they signified "to continue." 賣 in the kyuji 續 (3) became 売 in shinji. The kanji 続 means "to continue." <糸売>

続く to continue [つづく]; しゃべり続ける to keep on talking [しゃべりつづけꜜる]; 続々と one after another [ぞくぞくと]; 続行する to proceed with, resume [ぞっこうする]; 相続する to inherit [そうぞくする]; 続発する to happen in succession [ぞくはつする]; 連続 continuity, succession [れんぞく]

	(Note: 売, The right-side component of the two kanji 続 and 読 **SG-1371**, is not directly related to the kanji 売 **SG-1695** "to sell.")	

	Meanings	Kun and On	Romaji	Bushu	Stroke Order and Number
SG-1697 得	to gain, make a profit; benefit	え-る・う-る トク	e-ru, u-ru *toku*	彳	彳 彳 彳 𢔶 得 得 11

得 **A** F-0248

甲骨文1 1 甲骨文2 2 金文1 3 金文2 4 金文3 5 説文 6

1 through 6 showed "a cowrie, monetary value," and "a hand," together signifying "to obtain something valuable." In 3, 5, and 6, "a crossroads" (彳), signifying "going somewhere," was added. In the kanji 得, the cowrie was replaced by 旦, and the hand became 寸 "a hand." The kanji 得 means "to gain, make a profit; benefit." <彳日一寸>

得る to gain, obtain [え‐る, う‐る]; 会得する to grasp, understand [えとくする]; 心得る to know, agree [こころえ‐る]; 納得し得る possible to understand [なっとくしう‐る]; 得する to profit, benefit, gain [とくする]; 得意になる to preen, become proud [とくい‐になる]; 得意先 customer, client [とくいさき]; 得心する to consent to, realize [とくしんする]; お買い得 great deal, bargain [おかいどく]

	Meanings	Kun and On	Romaji	Bushu	Stroke Order and Number
SG-1698 価	value, price	あたい カ	atai *ka*	人	亻 亻 仁 佂 価 価 8

価 **A** F-0301

説文 1 旧字 2

1 and 2 comprised 亻 "person/an act that one does," and 賈 ("cowrie, money" 貝 with "a cover" 襾,覀), which was used for the sound *ka* to mean "value." The value of goods was determined by people, and the character meant "value." The cowrie was dropped in the shinji. The kanji 価 means "value, price." <亻 覀>

価 value, price, number [あたい]; 価値 value [か‐ち]; 価格 price [かかく]; 物価 price of goods [ぶっか]; 地価 land value, land price [ち‐か]; 株価 stock price, share price [かぶか, かぶ‐か]; 栄養価 nutritional value [えいよ‐うか]

	Meanings	Kun and On	Romaji	Bushu	Stroke Order and Number
SG-1699 買	to buy, purchase	か-う バイ	ka-u *bai*	貝	一 罒 罒 罝 買 12

買 **A** F-0340

甲骨文 1 金文1 2 金文2 3 金文3 4 金文4 5 説文

1 through 5 comprised 网 (罒) "fishing net" and 貝 "cowrie," together signifying "cowries in a net that allowed one to buy things." The kanji 買 means "to buy, purchase." <罒貝>

買う to buy, purchase [かう]; 買い上げる to buy up [かいあげ‐る]; 売り買い selling and buying, trade [うり‐かい]; 買い手 buyer [かいて]; 買い出し going out to buy [かいだし]; 売買 selling and buying, trade [ば‐いばい]; 買収する to purchase, buy up [ばいしゅうする]

	Meanings	Kun and On	Romaji	Bushu	Stroke Order and Number
SG-1700 負	to carry on one's back, be defeated, owe; debt; negative	ま-ける・お-う フ	ma-keru, o-u *hu*	貝	⺈ 㐄 負 負 9

負 **A** F-0455

説文

The seal-style form comprised "a person with his back bent" and "cowrie, money," together signifying that the person was carrying something (such as debt) on their back that caused them to stoop. "Debt" also gave the meaning "negative." The kanji 負 means "to carry on one's back, be defeated, owe; debt; negative." <⺈貝>

負ける to be defeated, lose [まける]; 負かす to win, defeat [まかす]; 勝ち負け victory and defeat [か‐ちまけ, かち‐まけ]; 負けず嫌い hating to lose, unyielding, competitive [まけずぎ‐らい]; 負う to carry on the back, have a debt [おう]; 背負う to carry on one's back [せお‐う]; 負債 debt, liabilities [ふさい]; 勝負 match, contest, game [しょ‐うぶ]

	Meanings	Kun and On	Romaji	Bushu	Stroke Order and Number
SG-1701 貴	precious, valuable, noble, venerable	とうと-い・たっと-い キ	tatto-i, tooto-i *ki*	貝	口 中 冉 冑 貴 貴 12

貴 **B** F-0641

説文

The seal-style form comprised "a pair of hands carefully holding something important," which had the sound *ki*, and 貝 **SG-1693** "cowrie, precious thing." Together they signified "precious, of high value." When applied to people, the form meant "noble, august." The kanji 貴 means "precious, valuable, noble, venerable." <虫 貝>

貴い august, venerable, noble [とうと‐い, たっと‐い]; 貴ぶ to appreciate, treasure [とうと‐ぶ, たっと‐ぶ]; 貴重な precious, valuable [きちょうな]; 高貴な noble [こ‐うきな]; 貴族 aristocracy [き‐ぞく]

SG-1702 敗	Meanings	Kun and On	Romaji	Bushu	Stroke Order and Number
	to lose, fail; loss	やぶ-れる ハイ	yabu-reru *hai*	支	冂目貝貯敗 11

敗
B
F-0679

甲骨文1 1 甲骨文2 2 金文 3 説文古文 4 説文 5

The history of the kanji 敗 incorporates two different origins of 貝: (a) 貝 "a cowrie," and (b) 貝 **SG-1717** "a three- or four-legged bronze vessel for preparing an offering." 1 had a "cowrie," whereas 2 had a "bronze vessel," and 3 and 4 had two bronze vessels, which was reduced to one in 5. They were all accompanied by 攴(攵) "a hand holding a stick or tool," for the meaning "to hit." The character originally signified "a hand breaking valuable items in two," and it came to be used to mean "a loss; to lose, fail." The kanji 敗 means "to lose, fail; loss." <貝攵>

敗れる to lose a fight [やぶれる]; 勝敗 victory and defeat, result of a match [しょうはい]; 敗因 cause of defeat [はいいん]; 敗戦 lost battle, defeat [はいせん]; 腐敗する to become corrupt, degenerate [ふはいする]; 大失敗 total failure, fiasco [だいしっぱい]; 成敗する to punish (archaic) [せいばいする]

SG-1703 貨	Meanings	Kun and On	Romaji	Bushu	Stroke Order and Number
	goods, money	カ	*ka*	貝	ノイイ化作貨貨 11

貨
B
F-0892

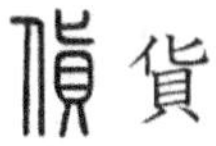
説文

The seal-style form comprised 化 **SG-0386** "change," used for the sound *ka*, and 貝 "cowrie, valuable," together signifying "things that could be exchanged for goods or money." The kanji 貨 means "goods, money." <化貝>

貨物 freight, cargo [かもつ]; 金貨 gold coin [きんか]; 雑貨 sundries, miscellaneous goods [ざっか]; 百貨店 department store [ひゃっかてん]; 硬貨 coin [こうか]; 貨幣 money [かへい]

SG-1704 遺	Meanings	Kun and On	Romaji	Bushu	Stroke Order and Number
	to leave behind, bequest	イ・ユイ	*i, yui*	辵	口中虫書貴遺遺 15

遺
B
F-0945

金文1 1 金文2 2 金文3 3 説文 4

1, 2, 3, and 4 comprised "a pair of hands carefully holding an important object"; "a crossroads" with "a footprint" forming 辵 (辶) "to move forward"; and "cowrie; valuable." Together these components signified "someone leaving a precious thing behind after his death." The kanji 遺 means "to leave behind, bequest." <貴辶>

遺伝 hereditary transmission [いでん]; 遺失物 lost-and-found article [いしつぶつ]; 遺書 will, note left by a dead person [いしょ]; 遺品 article left behind (after one's death), memento [いひん]; 遺族 bereaved family, surviving family of the deceased [いぞく]; 遺産 inheritance, legacy [いさん]; 遺言 one's dying wish, one's will [ゆいごん, いごん (legal)] // 遺す to leave behind, bequest [のこす]

SG-1705 賛	Meanings	Kun and On	Romaji	Bushu	Stroke Order and Number
	to present, help, laud	サン	*san*	貝	二夫夫夫替替賛 15

賛
B
F-0967

秦漢印 1 説文 2 旧字 3

1 and 2 comprised "two strands of pearls," used for the sound *san*, and 貝 "cowrie; valuable." Together they signified "to present valuable things in an audience with a dignitary." The kanji 賛 means "to present, help, laud." <夫夫貝>

賛成する to agree [さんせいする]; 賛同する to approve of, subscribe to [さんどうする]; 賛否両論 pros and cons, argument for and against [さんぴ・りょうろん]; 絶賛する to praise someone highly, laud [ぜっさんする]; 賛美歌 hymn [さんびか]; 自画自賛 self-praise [じが・じさん]; 協賛会社 sponsor company[きょうさんがいしゃ]

SG-1706 賃	Meanings	Kun and On	Romaji	Bushu	Stroke Order and Number
	wages	チン	*chin*	貝	イイ仁仟任侍賃賃 13

賃
B
F-1035

金文 1 中山王器 2 説文 3

1, 2, and 3 comprised 任 **SG-1903**, used for the sound *chin* to mean "to entrust with a task," and 貝 "cowrie, money," together signifying "paying wages to a person for their work." The kanji 賃 means "wages." <任貝>

賃金 wage [ちんぎん]; 最低賃金 minimum wage [さいていちんぎん]; 運賃 fare [うんちん]; 家賃 rental fee (for a residence) [やちん]; 工賃 labor charge [こうちん]; 賃上げ wage raise [ちんあげ]; 木賃宿 cheap lodging house [きちんやど]

SG-1707 貯	Meanings	Kun and On	Romaji	Bushu	Stroke Order and Number
	to save up, lay up	チョ	*cho*	貝	冂 貝 貝 貯 貯 貯 12

貯
C
F-1084

甲骨文 1, 金文1 2, 金文2 3, 説文 4 — 貯

1 depicted "cowries in a special container," whereas in 2, 3, and 4, the cowries were separated from their container. Cowries (貝) were so valuable and collectible that they were kept in an elaborate bronze container with a lid (宁), which was called 貯貝器 *chobaiki*. The kanji 貯 means "to save, lay up." <貝宀丁>

貯金 savings, deposit (in a bank) [ちょきん]; 貯蓄 saving up, putting aside [ちょちく]; 貯蔵庫 storage, depository [ちょぞ꜒うこ]; 郵便貯金・郵貯 postal office savings [ゆうびんちょ꜒きん, ゆ꜒うちょ]; 貯水池 water reservoir [ちょす꜒いち]

SG-1708 貿	Meanings	Kun and On	Romaji	Bushu	Stroke Order and Number
	to trade; trading	ボウ	*boo*	貝	丶 ㇾ 𠂉 㔾 留 貿 12

貿
C
F-1190

金文 1, 説文 2 — 貿

The top component of 1 and 2 was used for the sound *boo* to mean "to divide in two." With 貝 "cowrie," the character meant "two parties trading goods." Another view explains that *boo* meant "to plan; attempt," and 貝 meant "to seek to make a profit." The kanji 貿 means "to trade; trading." <𠂉刀貝>

貿易 foreign trade, commerce [ぼうえき]; 貿易風 trade wind [ぼうえき꜒ふう, ぼうえきふう]; 貿易収支 balance of trade [ぼうえきしゅ꜒うし]; 貿易自由化 liberalization or deregulation of trade [ぼうえきじゆうか]; 貿易摩擦 trade friction, trade dispute [ぼうえきま꜒さつ]

SG-1709 貫	Meanings	Kun and On	Romaji	Bushu	Stroke Order and Number
	to pierce through, penetrate; *kan* (old unit of weight)	つらぬ–く カン	tsuranu-ku *kan*	貝	㇄ 口 毌 毌 貫 貫 11

貫
C
F-1261

説文 — 貫

The seal-style form, used for the sound *kan*, was a component of the kyuji 實 (later 実 **SG-1694**), which had the sound *kan* and meant "to act throughout" (from 毌 "small, pierced cowries strung together"). It also represented an old unit of weight. The kanji 貫 means "to pierce through, penetrate; *kan* (old unit of weight)." <毌貝>

貫く to pierce through, keep (one's faith) [つらぬ꜒く]; 貫き通す to stick with, follow [つらぬきとおす]; 貫通する bore through [かんつうする]; 初志貫徹 carrying out one's original intention [しょ꜒し・かんてつ]; 一貫教育 unified program of elementary and secondary school education [いっかんきょ꜒ういく]; 終始一貫して to be consistent from beginning to end [しゅ꜒うし・いっかんして]; 貫禄 dignified bearing, impressive presence [かんろく]; 一貫目 3.75 kg (old unit of weight) [いっかんめ]

SG-1710 慣	Meanings	Kun and On	Romaji	Bushu	Stroke Order and Number
	to become used to; familiar; custom	な–れる カン	na-reru *kan*	心	忄 忄 忄 忄 忄 慣 慣 14

慣
C
F-1202

篆文 — 慣

The seal-style form comprised "a hand," and 貫 **SG-1709** for the meaning "to pierce through, act throughout," used for the sound *kan*. Together they signified "to accumulate by linking many things by hand." Doing things by hand many times made one's mind (忄, bushu *risshinben*, which replaced "a hand" in the kanji) become accustomed to the task, making it "a custom." The kanji 慣 means "to become used to; familiar; custom." <忄貫>

慣れる to become used to, grow accustomed to [なれ꜒る]; 場慣れする to be used to a situation [ばなれする]; 耳慣れた familiar with [みみなれた]; 習慣 (personal) habit, custom [しゅうかん]; 慣習 social custom [かんしゅう]; 慣例 general practice, precedent [かんれい]; 慣性 inertia [か꜒んせい]; 生活習慣病 lifestyle-related illness [せいかつしゅうかんびょう]

SG-1711 貢	Meanings	Kun and On	Romaji	Bushu	Stroke Order and Number
	tribute, contribution; to supply with money	みつ–ぐ コウ・グ	mitsu-gu *koo, gu*	貝	一 丁 工 貢 貢 10

貢
C
F-1270

説文 — 貢

The seal-style form comprised 工 **SG-1895** "product, skilled work," used for the sounds *koo*/*ku*, and 貝 "cowrie; valuable." Valuable cowries and the products of skilled work were presented as "tribute." The form also means "to supply with money, support someone financially." The kanji 貢 means "tribute, contribution; to supply with money." <工 貝>

貢ぐ to pay a tribute, support financially [みつぐ, みつ꜒ぐ]; 貢ぎ物 tribute [みつぎもの]; 貢献 service, contribution [こうけん]; 年貢 land tax, annual tribute (historical) [ねんぐ]; 年貢米 rice paid as land tax [ねんぐまい]

SG-1712 鎖	Meanings	Kun and On	Romaji	Bushu	Stroke Order and Number
	chain, metal link; to shut down	くさり サ	kusari *sa*	金	𠆢 午 金 金' 金'' 鎖 鎖 18

鎖 **C** F-1364

鎖 鎖 説文 The seal-style form comprised "metal" (金 **SG-1196**), and "small cowries strung together" (小 and 貝), used for the sound *sa*. These components signified "metal chains; held shut by chains." The kanji 鎖 means "chain, metal link; to shut down." <金 小 貝>

鎖 chain, link [くさり]; 鎖国 national isolation, national seclusion [さこく]; 閉鎖する to shut down [へいさする]; 閉鎖的な closed, exclusive [へいさてきな]; 連鎖 chain, links [れんさ]; 連鎖反応 chain reaction [れんさはんのう]; 封鎖 blockage [ふうさ]

SG-1713 唄	Meanings	Kun and On	Romaji	Bushu	Stroke Order and Number
	song, folk song, ballad	うた	uta	口	口 叩 唄 唄 10

唄 **C** F-1612

No ancient form. The kanji 唄 comprises 口 "mouth," and 貝, used for the sound *bai*. It was created as a phonetic rendition of the Sanskrit word for a song praising the Buddha's virtues. In Japanese, it is used to mean a popular song or ballad. The kanji 唄 means "song, folk song, ballad." < 口 貝 >

唄 song, folk song, ballad [うた]; 鼻唄 humming [はなうた]

SG-1714 賜	Meanings	Kun and On	Romaji	Bushu	Stroke Order and Number
	to bestow, confer, be bestowed, be conferred	たまわ-る シ	tamawa-ru *shi*	貝	冂 目 貝 貝 貝 賜 賜 15

賜 **D** F-2043

甲骨文1 1, 甲骨文2 2, 金文1 3, 金文2 4, 中山王器 5, 説文 6, 賜

1 and 2 depicted "a wine warming pitcher called a *shaku* (爵) pouring wine into a cup." A ruler presenting a cup of wine to his subject signified "bestowing an honor." 3 through 6 also showed a pitcher pouring wine (易, used for the sound *shi*). In 5 and 6, 貝 **SG-1693** was added to signify something valuable. The character is now used to mean any bestowal of a thing of value by a superior. The kanji 賜 means "to bestow, confer, be bestowed, be conferred." <貝 易 >

賜る to be conferred, be bestowed by a king, bestow [たまわる]; 賜杯 trophy given by an emperor [しはい]; 下賜される to be bestowed an imperial gift [かしされる] // 賜物 gift, result [たまもの, たまもの]

SG-1715 賭	Meanings	Kun and On	Romaji	Bushu	Stroke Order and Number
	to bet; gambling	か-ける ト	ka-keru *to*	貝	冂 目 貝 貝 貝 賭 16

賭 **D** F-2124

説文古文 1, 説文 2, 明朝体 3, 教科書体 4

1, 2, and 3 comprised what later became 者 (for 者 **SG-2085**) "all," used for the sound *to*, and either 見 **SG-0460** "to see" (in 1), or 目 **SG-0001** "eye" (in 2). In the kanji (3 and 4), 貝 "monetary value" is used. Gambling is an all-or-nothing game using money. The kanji 賭 means "to bet; gambling." <貝者>

(Note: Other kanji that contain 者 are discussed in **SG-2085** 者 through **SG-2091** 煮.)

賭け gambling, betting [かけ]; 賭ける to bet, stake [かける]; 賭け事 betting, gambling [かけごと]; 賭博 gambling, gaming [とばく]; 賭場 gambling place [とば, とば]

SG-1716 潰	Meanings	Kun and On	Romaji	Bushu	Stroke Order and Number
	water breach; to collapse, crush	つぶ-す カイ	tsubu-su *kai*	水	氵 氵 沖 湝 潰 潰 15

潰 **D** F-2154

潰 潰 説文 The seal-style form had "flowing water" (氵), and 貴 **SG-1701**, which was used for the sound *kai* to mean "to collapse." Together they signified "a breach of water" or "forceful destruction like the collapse of a river embankment." The kanji 潰 means "water breach; to collapse, crush." <氵 貴>

潰す to crush, break down, squash [つぶす]; 潰れる to tumble, crumble, collapse [つぶれる]; シラミ潰しに to check thoroughly, one by one [しらみつぶしに]; 決潰 to collapse (river bank), rip [けっかい]; 潰滅 annihilation, total demolition [かいめつ]

79b 員 "(bronze) vessel, valuables" [from 鼎 non-Joyo kanji "a three- or four-legged bronze vessel"] 員円具損賊

	Meanings	Kun and On	Romaji	Bushu	Stroke Order and Number
SG-1717 員	member, staff, occupation, person	イン	*in*	口	ロ 口 冐 冒 員 10

員 **A** F-0164

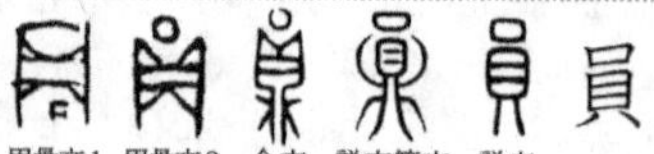

甲骨文1 1 甲骨文2 2 金文 3 説文籀文 4 説文 5

1, 2, 3, and 4 depicted "a three- or four-legged bronze vessel" that was used to prepare food such as sacrificial animal meat as an offering. (Some view that a three-legged vessel had a rounded opening whereas a four-legged one had a square opening.) Originally used as a counter for large bronze vessels, it became a counter for people. The kanji 員 meant "member, staff, person, occupation." <員>

人員 staff size, personnel [じんいん]; 会社員 company employee [かいしゃꜜいん]; 公務員 government employee [こうむꜜいん]; 事務員 administrative staff, clerical worker [じむꜜいん]; 満員 full house, no vacancy [まんいん]; 定員 seating capacity, quota [ていいん]; 員数合わせ ensuring a full total, reaching a nominal total [いんずうあꜜわせ]

	Meanings	Kun and On	Romaji	Bushu	Stroke Order and Number
SG-1718 円	round; circle, Japanese yen	まる-い エン	maru-i *en*	口	丨冂円円 4

円 **A** F-0028

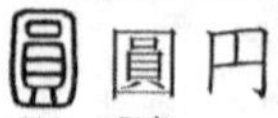

説文 1 旧字 2

1 and 2 comprised 員 **SG-1717** "a bronze vessel with a (round) opening," used for the sound *en*, inside 囗 "an enclosure." The character meant "round, circular." It is also used for the Japanese unit of currency, "Japanese yen." The shinji takes the form 円. The Japanese unit of currency (円 *en* "Japanese yen"), the Chinese unit of currency (元 *yuan*), and the Korean unit of currency (*won*) all originated from the kanji 圓. The kanji 円 means "round; circle, Japanese yen. <円>

円みのある rounded [まるみのあꜜる]; 日本円 Japanese yen [にほんえん]; 百円 a hundred yen [ひゃくえん]; 円形 round shape, ring shape [えんけい]; 楕円形 ellipse, oval [だえんけい]; 円熟した matured, mellowed [えんじゅくした]

	Meanings	Kun and On	Romaji	Bushu	Stroke Order and Number
SG-1719 具	contents, filling; to be equipped	グ	*gu*	八	丨冂月目且具 8

具 **B** F-0633

甲骨文 1 金文1 2 金文2 3 説文 4

1, 2, and 3 comprised "a bronze vessel" and "two hands presenting it," signifying "a reverentially presented vessel full of food offerings." A full vessel gave the meanings "contents" and "amply provided." In 4, the legs of the bronze vessel were dropped. The kanji 具 means "contents, filling; to be equipped (often when referring to a set of multiple items)." <目𠔾>

具 topping, main ingredients [ぐ]; 具体的な concrete, specific [ぐたいてきな]; 道具 tool [どうぐ]; 家具 furniture [かꜜぐ]; 不具合 malfunction, bug [ふぐꜜあい]; 建て具 door fittings [たてꜜぐ]; 具現する to embody [ぐげんする]; 大道具 stage scenery [おおどꜜうぐ]; 具申する to report in detail [ぐしんする]

	Meanings	Kun and On	Romaji	Bushu	Stroke Order and Number
SG-1720 損	to damage, impair; loss	そこ-なう ソン	soko-nau *son*	手	扌 扌 扣 捐 損 13

損 **B** F-0857

説文

The seal-style form comprised 扌, bushu *tehen* "an act done by hand," and 員 **SG-1717** "a bronze vessel." Together they signified "a hand damaging the leg of a vessel or its contents." Another view holds that 員, which had the sound *son* (from *in*), meant "to scrape" and that scraping a bronze vessel would "reduce the value." The kanji 損 means "to damage, impair; loss." <扌員>

損なう to suffer, impair [そこなꜜう]; 気分を損ねる to hurt one's feeling [きꜜぶんを・そこねꜜる]; やり損ねる to fail to do [やりそこねꜜる]; 見損なう to overlook, misjudge [みそこなう]; 損する to lose money, come off a loser [そꜜんする]; 損害 damage, harm [そんがい]; 損失 loss [そんしつ]; 破損する to suffer damage, suffer breakage [はそんする]

	Meanings	Kun and On	Romaji	Bushu	Stroke Order and Number
SG-1721 賊	robbery, thief	ゾク	*zoku*	貝	冂 目 貝 貯 賊 賊 賊 13

賊 **D** F-2123

金文 1 説文 2

1 comprised "a halberd," "a bronze vessel," and "a shield." Together they signified "using a weapon to scrape out an oath inscribed on bronzeware," which would revoke the oath. The character also signified the perpetrator of such an act. In 2, the vessel (貝) moved to the left, and the right side became 戎 "weapon, soldier." Together they signified "damage from a robbery." The kanji 賊 means "robbery, thief." <貝戈十>

賊が押し入る a thief breaks in [ぞくがおしいꜜる]; 海賊 pirate [かいぞく]; 海賊版 pirated edition [かいぞくばん]; 盗賊一味 pack of thieves [とうぞくいちꜜみ]; 賊軍 rebels, rebel army [ぞくぐん]; 国賊 traitor (to the country) [こくぞく]; 義賊 chivalrous thief, Robin Hood [ぎꜜぞく]

79c 則 "rule" [from a bronze vessel and a knife]; *soku* 側則測

	Meanings	Kun and On	Romaji	Bushu	Stroke Order and Number
SG-1722 側	close by; side, aspect	がわ ソク	gawa *soku*	人	亻 仴 但 俱 側 11

側 **A** F-0316

金文 1 説文 2

In 1 and 2, a person and a knife (刀, 刂) were placed by a bronze vessel, thus giving the meanings "side, close by." The right side 則 **SG-1723** was used for the sound *soku*. Another view holds that a knife was used to carve an inscription into the "side" of a vessel. The kanji 側 means "close by; side, aspect." <亻貝刂>

向こう側 opposite side, other side [むこうがわ]; 裏側 behind, back side [うらがわ]; 片側 one side [かたがわ]; 右側通行 keep to the right [みぎがわつうこう]; 上側 upper side, surface [うわがわ]; 側面 aspect, side view, flank [そくめん, そくめつん]; 側近 close adviser, one's personal staff [そっきん]

	Meanings	Kun and On	Romaji	Bushu	Stroke Order and Number
SG-1723 則	rule, law	ソク	*soku*	刀	冂 目 貝 則 9

則 **B** F-0824

金文1 1 金文2 2 金文3 3 説文古文 4 説文 5

1 comprised two "bronze vessels," and "a knife" for inscribing pledges or rules by which people should abide. Having two vessels in 1 and 4 suggested that the vessels bore identical inscriptions of a contract that two parties had agreed upon. The character meant "pledge to abide by" and "rule." Another view holds that "a knife always kept beside a vessel (of food)" signified "to closely follow an exemplar" and "rules to abide by." The kanji 則 meant "rule, law." <貝刂>

規則 rules, bylaws, statutory instrument [きつそく]; 法則 law, principle, rule [ほうそく]; 鉄則 ironclad rule, inviolable rule [てっそく]; 変則的な irregular [へんそくてきな]; 原則 governing principle, fundamental rule [げんそく]; 会則 regulations of an association [かいそく]; 反則 infringement of rules, foul play [はんそく] // 法に則る to conform to a law [ほうにのっとる]

	Meanings	Kun and On	Romaji	Bushu	Stroke Order and Number
SG-1724 測	to measure, assess, estimate	はか-る ソク	haka-ru *soku*	水	氵 沮 浿 測 12

測 **B** F-0944

説文

The seal-style form comprised "flowing water" (氵), and 則 **SG-1723**, used for the sound *soku* to mean "rule." Together they signified "measuring the depth of water according to rules or standards," and "to measure, assess." The kanji 測 means "to measure, assess, estimate." <氵則>

測る to measure [はかる]; 推測する to guess, presume, speculate [すいそくする]; 目測 estimate by eye, measure by sight [もくそく]; 測定する to measure [そくていする]; 実測 actual surveyed measurement [じっそく]; 計測器 measuring instrument [けいそくき]; 不測の unforeseen, accidental [ふそくの]

79d 貞 "faithful"; *tee* 貞偵

	Meanings	Kun and On	Romaji	Bushu	Stroke Order and Number
SG-1725 貞	right mind; upright, faithful	テイ	*tee*	貝	' ⺊ 占 貞 貞 9

貞 **C** F-1407

甲骨文1 1 甲骨文2 2 甲骨文3 3 金文1 4 金文2 5 説文 6

1, 2 and 3 depicted "a bronze vessel for preparing an offering" (鼎). It was used for the sound *tee* to mean "to inquire about a deity's will; divination." 4, 5 and 6 added ⺊ "divination" (from cracks in a divination bone) to the vessel. A deity's will was always "right." Seeking the deity's will by divination was "upright, faithful." The kanji 貞 means "right mind; upright, faithful." <⺊貝>

貞淑な feminine modesty, virtuous [ていしゅくな]; 貞操 chastity, honor, virtue [ていそう]; 貞女 virtuous woman, good and faithful wife [ていじょ]

	Meanings	Kun and On	Romaji	Bushu	Stroke Order and Number
SG-1726 偵	detective work, reconnaissance; to investigate secretly	テイ	*tee*	人	亻 亻' 亻⺊ 伯 偵 偵 11

偵 **D** F-1888

篆文

The seal-style form comprised 亻 "an act that one does," and 貞 **SG-1725**, used for the sound *tee* to mean "to listen to a deity's voice, inquire." Together they signified "a person investigating carefully by listening and inquiring." The kanji 偵 means "detective work, reconnaissance; to investigate secretly." <亻貞>

探偵 detective [たんてい]; 偵察 scouting, reconnaissance, patrolling [ていさつ]; 内偵 private scouting, secret investigation [ないてい]; 偵察機 spy plane, reconnaissance aircraft [ていさつき]; 密偵 spy, confidential agent, undercover [みってい]

79e 賁 "to gush out, burst out" [from outpouring beauty of flowers]; *hun* 噴墳憤

	Meanings	Kun and On	Romaji	Bushu	Stroke Order and Number
SG-1727 噴	to spout out, erupt, blow out	ふ-く フン	hu-ku *hun*	口	口 口一 口十 口卉 噴 15

噴 **C** F-1521 | 篆文

The seal-style form comprised 口 "mouth, opening," and 賁 "to burst out, overflow," used for the sound *hun*. Together they signified "to gush out from an opening." The kanji 噴 means "to spout out, erupt, blow out." <口 賁 >

噴き出す to spout out, erupt, blow out [ふきだす, ふきだ⁊す]; 噴出する to gush out, eject [ふんしゅつする]; 噴水 fountain [ふんすい]; 噴火 volcanic eruption [ふんか]; 噴火口 crater of a volcano [ふんか⁊こう]

	Meanings	Kun and On	Romaji	Bushu	Stroke Order and Number
SG-1728 墳	burial mound, tomb	フン	*hun*	土	𠂇 ± 圤 坮 墳 15

墳 **D** F-1885 | 説文

The seal-style form comprised 土 "soil, dirt," and 賁 "something that swells or rises," used for the sound *hun*. Raised soil signified "a burial mound." The kanji 墳 means "burial mound, tomb." <扌 賁 >

古墳 ancient burial mound, ancient tomb [こふん]; 古墳時代 tumulus period, Kofun period [こふんじ⁊だい]; 墳墓 tomb, grave [ふ⁊んぼ]

	Meanings	Kun and On	Romaji	Bushu	Stroke Order and Number
SG-1729 憤	anger, rancor, outrage, indignation	いきどお-る フン	ikidoo-ru *hun*	心	忄 忄十 忄卉 憤 15

憤 **D** F-1930 | 説文

The seal-style form comprised 忄 "heart," and 賁 "to burst out," used for the sound *hun*. A heart gushing with emotions meant "rancor, outrage." The kanji 憤 means "anger, rancor, outrage, indignation." <忄 賁 >

憤る to be furious about, seethe with anger [いきどお⁊る]; 憤慨する to get very angry, feel indignant [ふんがいする]; 義憤 righteous indignation [ぎふん]; 憤激する to flare up, explode with anger [ふんげきする]; 憤怒 strong anger, wrath [ふ⁊んど]

79f 玉 "crown jewel, ball shape" [from gems strung together] 玉宝瑠璃璽

	Meanings	Kun and On	Romaji	Bushu	Stroke Order and Number
SG-1730 玉	jewel, sphere, ball	たま ギョク	tama *gyaku*	玉	一 丅 干 王 玉 5

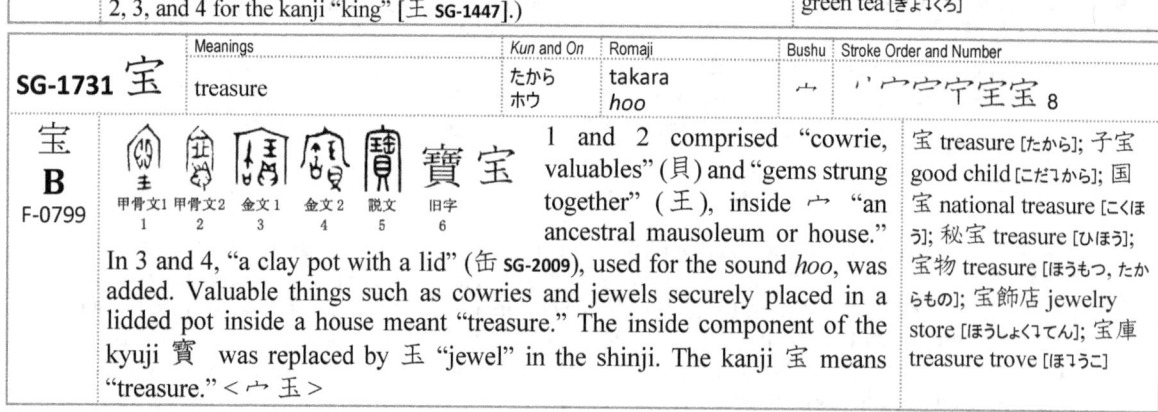

玉 **A** F-0447 | 甲骨文 1 | 金文 2 | 説文 3

1 depicted "jewels, gems, or pearls strung together." The round shape of a gemstone or pearl also gave the meaning "ball, sphere." In the kanji, a dot on the lower right side was added to signify an imperfection in a jewel, or possibly just to differentiate it from the kanji for "king," 王. The kanji 玉 means "jewel, sphere, ball." <王 丶>
(Note: In 2 and 3, the three horizontal lines were spaced evenly, unlike 2, 3, and 4 for the kanji "king" [王 **SG-1447**].)

玉 round object, ball [たま⁊]; 一円玉 one-yen coin [いちえんだま]; 玉の汗 beaded sweat [たまのあ⁊せ]; 玉の輿 Cinderella story, a poor woman marrying a wealthy man [たまのこし, たまのこ⁊し]; 玉突き billiards, pool [たま⁊つき]; 玉座 imperial throne, emperor's seat [ぎょ⁊くざ]; 玉露 refined green tea [ぎょ⁊くろ]

	Meanings	Kun and On	Romaji	Bushu	Stroke Order and Number
SG-1731 宝	treasure	たから ホウ	takara *hoo*	宀	丶 宀 宁 宇 宝 宝 8

宝 **B** F-0799 | 甲骨文1 1 | 甲骨文2 2 | 金文1 3 | 金文2 4 | 説文 5 | 旧字 6

1 and 2 comprised "cowrie, valuables" (貝) and "gems strung together" (王), inside 宀 "an ancestral mausoleum or house." In 3 and 4, "a clay pot with a lid" (缶 **SG-2009**), used for the sound *hoo*, was added. Valuable things such as cowries and jewels securely placed in a lidded pot inside a house meant "treasure." The inside component of the kyuji 寳 was replaced by 玉 "jewel" in the shinji. The kanji 宝 means "treasure." <宀 玉>

宝 treasure [たから]; 子宝 good child [こだ⁊から]; 国宝 national treasure [こくほう]; 秘宝 treasure [ひほう]; 宝物 treasure [ほうもつ, たからもの]; 宝飾店 jewelry store [ほうしょく⁊てん]; 宝庫 treasure trove [ほ⁊うこ]

SG-1732 瑠	Meanings	Kun and On	Romaji	Bushu	Stroke Order and Number
	glass	ル	*ru*	玉	14

瑠 **D** F-2240

No ancient form. The kanji 瑠 comprises 王 "jewels," and 留, used for the sound *ru*. The kanji 瑠 means "glass." <王留>

瑠璃 lapis lazuli [るり]; 瑠璃色 sky blue, lapis lazuli blue [るりいろ]; 浄瑠璃 *joruri*, Japanese puppet theater [じょうるり]

SG-1733 璃	Meanings	Kun and On	Romaji	Bushu	Stroke Order and Number
	glass	リ	*ri*	玉	15

璃 **D** F-2293

No ancient form. The kanji 璃 comprises 王 "jewels," and 离, used for the sound *ri*. The kanji 璃 means "gem." <王离>

瑠璃 lapis lazuli [るり]; 玻璃 glass, crystal (archaic) [はり]

SG-1734 璽	Meanings	Kun and On	Romaji	Bushu	Stroke Order and Number
	imperial seal	ジ	*ji*	玉	19

璽 **D** F-3571

説文籀文 1 説文 2

1 and 2 comprised 爾 for the sound *ji*, and 王 **SG-1447** "crown jewel" in 1, and 土 **SG-1126** "land, earth" in 2. One view explained 爾 (shown at right) to depict a woman's upper body with elaborate chest tattoos (in a similar way as in the kanji 爽 **SG-0322**). A beautiful, elaborate design symbolizing a king was "the imperial seal." The kanji has 玉 **SG-1730** at the bottom. The kanji 璽 means "imperial seal." < 爾 玉 >

(Note: The kanji 璽 and 弥 **SG-1513** share the same origin.)

御璽 the imperial seal, emperor's seal [ぎょじ]

79g 玨 "divided into small groups" [from a strand of pearls]; *han* 班斑

SG-1735 班	Meanings	Kun and On	Romaji	Bushu	Stroke Order and Number
	group of people, squad	ハン	*han*	玉	10

班 **C** F-1260

金文 1 説文 2

<王リ王>

1 and 2 showed a strand of jewels (玨 *kaku*) cut in two with "a knife" (刂), signifying "to divide something into small groups." The kanji 班 means "group of people, squad."

首班 head of a group [しゅはん]; 班長 group or squad leader [はんちょう]

SG-1736 斑	Meanings	Kun and On	Romaji	Bushu	Stroke Order and Number
	spotted, speckled, mottled	ハン	*han*	文	12

斑 **D** F-2267

No ancient form. The kanji 斑 comprises 玨 "a strand of jewels divided into two," and 文 "design," together signifying "colors of jewels mixing together; speckled." The kanji 斑 means "spotted, speckled, mottled." <王亠メ王>

斑点 scattered spots, speckles [はんてん, はんてん]; 白斑 white speckles [はくはん] // 斑入りの葉 variegated leaf [ふいりのは]

X Religious Matters

80 Religious rites

80a 示 "religious matter; to manifest" [from an altar table with an offering]

示禁奈宗崇

SG-1737 示	Meanings	Kun and On	Romaji	Bushu	Stroke Order and Number
	to display, indicate, show, demonstrate	しめ-す ジ・シ	shime-su *ji, shi*	示	一二亍亓示 5

示 **A** F-0293

甲骨文 1 説文古文 2 説文 3

1 depicted "an altar table with an offering placed on top," where a deity was believed to appear and show its will. The character meant "to show, manifest." In 2, the three lines were the three legs of the table, or, according to *Setsumon,* "the sun, the moon, and a star, through which a deity showed itself to people." The kanji 示 means "to display, indicate, show, demonstrate." When 示 is used as the left-side component of a kanji, it becomes 礻, bushu *shimesuhen.* <二小>

示す to show, display, indicate [しめす, しめす]; 表示する to display [ひょうじする]; 展示場 exhibition hall, showroom [てんじじょう]; 示談 out-of-court settlement, private settlement [じだん, じだん]; 指示する to instruct, order [しじする]; 公示 official notice, public accountment [こうじ]; 教示する to instruct, teach [きょうじする]

SG-1738 禁	Meanings	Kun and On	Romaji	Bushu	Stroke Order and Number
	to prohibit, forbid	キン	*kin*	示	木林埜埜禁禁 13

禁 **B** F-0709

説文

The seal-style form comprised "forest" (林 **SG-0609**), and "an altar table with an offering" (示 **SG-1737**), for the meaning "sanctuary, sacred," together signifying "a sacred forest or area that people were forbidden to enter." The kanji 禁 means "to prohibit, forbid." <林示>

禁止する to prohibit [きんしする]; 禁句 taboo word or phrase [きんく]; 禁断 strict prohibition [きんだん]; 解禁 opening of fishing or hunting season [かいきん]; 立ち入り禁止 off limits, closed to the public [たちいりきんし]; 禁酒 abstention from alcoholic beverages [きんしゅ]; 禁煙席 non-smoking seat [きんえんせき]

SG-1739 奈	Meanings	Kun and On	Romaji	Bushu	Stroke Order and Number
	how (phonetic use)	ナ	*na*	大	一ナ大太夻奈 8

奈 **B** F-0602

篆文 1 正字 2

1 and 2 comprised 木 "tree," and 示, for the sound *na*, the name of a particular variety of tree. In the kanji, the top component 木 changed to 大. The kanji 奈 was borrowed to mean "how, why" in some *kanbun* writing. Its use is limited to proper names and Buddhist terms. <大示>

奈落 hell, the infernal regions, trap cellar in a theater [ならく]; 奈良 Nara [なら]

SG-1740 宗	Meanings	Kun and On	Romaji	Bushu	Stroke Order and Number
	religion, sect, head of a group; main	シュウ・ソウ	*shuu, soo*	宀	宀宀宇宇宗 8

宗 **B** F-0889

甲骨文 1 金文 2 説文 3

1 depicted "an altar table inside a mausoleum (宀)." In 2 and 3, the altar table had an offering on top and a line on either side (示). A mausoleum that enshrined a worshipped ancestor originally signified "the head family of the clan." Later it also came to mean "religion, sect." The kanji 宗 means "religion, sect, head of a group; main." <宀示>

宗教 religion [しゅうきょう]; 改宗 religious conversion [かいしゅう]; 宗旨 tenets of a religious sect [しゅうし]; 宗教改革 the Reformation, religious reformation [しゅうきょうかいかく]; 宗家 head of family [そうけ]; 宗廟 ancestral mausoleum [そうびょう]; 宗主国 suzerain state [そうしゅこく]

SG-1741 崇	Meanings	Kun and On	Romaji	Bushu	Stroke Order and Number
	high, supreme; to revere	スウ	*suu*	山	丨山山岦岦崇 11

崇 **D** F-1765

説文

The seal-style form had 山 **SG-1139** "mountain," on top of 宗 **SG-1740** "religious matter," used for the sound *suu* to mean "main." Together they signified "the revered highest mountain in a mountain range." The kanji 崇 meant "high, supreme; to revere." <山宀示>

崇める to hold someone in reverence, adore [あがめる]; 崇高な lofty, sublime, grand [すうこうな]; 崇拝する to worship, idolize [すうはいする]

80b 祭 "celebration of a deity" [from a consecrated offering on altar]; *sai/satsu*

祭際察擦

	Meanings	Kun and On	Romaji	Bushu	Stroke Order and Number
SG-1742 祭	festival, feast day	まつ-る サイ	matsu-ru *sai*	示	クタタ⁷タ⁷タ乂タ⁷タ癶タ⁷タ祭 11

祭 **A** F-0839

甲骨文1 1 甲骨文2 2 金文1 3 金文2 4 説文 5 祭

1 and 2 showed "a hand (又) sprinkling spirits over sacrificial animal meat (夕) to consecrate it for offering to a deity." In 3, 4, and 5, an altar table with an offering (示) was added. A festival is a celebration of a deity. The kanji 祭 meant "festival, feast day." <祭(夕又示)>

祭り festival, celebration [まつり]; 祭り上げる to set someone on a pedestal [まつりあげる]; 血祭り blood sacrifice [ちまつり]; 祭日 holiday [さいじつ]; 司祭 (Catholic) priest [しさい]; 感謝祭 Thanksgiving Day [かんしゃさい]

	Meanings	Kun and On	Romaji	Bushu	Stroke Order and Number
SG-1743 際	edge of an area, boundary, contact	きわ サイ	kiwa *sai*	阜	阝 阝タ 阝タ乂 阝癶 阝祭 際 14

際 **A** F-0314

説文 際

One view explains that this character comprised "a ladder for a deity" (阝, bushu *kozatohen*), and 祭 "celebration of a deity, festival," used for the sound *sai*. Together they signified an area on the periphery of the human world where people and a deity came to meet. Another view explains that the components should be understood as "mountains" (阝), and 祭, used for the sound *sai* to mean "to come into contact," together signifying "edge of an area." The kanji 際 means "edge of an area, boundary, contact." <阝祭>

際どい perilous, questionable [きわどい]; 窓際 window side [まどぎわ]; 間際に just before, at the brink [まぎわに]; 出際に at the moment of going out [でぎわに]; 手際よく skillfully, deftly [てぎわよく]; 国際的 international [こくさいてき]; 交際する to go steady, socialize with [こうさいする]; 分際 one's social standing [ぶんざい]

	Meanings	Kun and On	Romaji	Bushu	Stroke Order and Number
SG-1744 察	to perceive, look thoroughly, conjecture	サツ	*satsu*	宀	宀 宀タ 宀タ乂 宀癶 宀祭 察 14

察 **B** F-0794

説文 察

The seal-style form comprised 宀 "a mausoleum, house," and 祭 **SG-1742** "celebration of a deity," used for the sound *satsu*. In an ancestral mausoleum, one sought out a deity's will and considered it deeply. With the religious sense dropped, the kanji 察 means "to perceive, look thoroughly, conjecture." <宀祭>

観察 observation, supervision [かんさつ]; 警察 police station, constabulary, police [けいさつ]; 察する to perceive, gather [さっする]; 察知する to infer from, gather from [さっちする, さっちする]; 洞察力 insight [どうさつりょく]; 推察する to guess, conjecture, surmise, infer from [すいさつする]; 検察 prosecution, criminal investigation [けんさつ]; 拝察 guess, surmise (humble) [はいさつ]

	Meanings	Kun and On	Romaji	Bushu	Stroke Order and Number
SG-1745 擦	to rub, scrub, scour, lose one's naivete	す-る サツ	su-ru *satsu*	手	扌 扩 抆 拶 擦 擦 擦 17

擦 **C** F-1598

No ancient form. The kanji 擦 comprised 扌, bushu *tehen* "an act done by hand," and 察, used for the sound *satsu* to mean "to rub." Together they signified "a hand rubbing something." The kanji is also used to mean "to lose one's innocence." The kanji 擦 means "to rub, scrub, scour, lose one's naivete." <扌察(宀祭)>

擦れる to be rubbed, lose one's naivete [すれる]; 擦り切れる to be worn out, become threadbare [すりきれる]; 擦り傷 scratch, abrasion [すりきず]; 擦れ違う to pass by each other [すれちがう]; 靴擦れ blister caused by one's shoe [くつずれ]; 世間擦れする to grow wily, get toughened by life [せけんずれする]; 摩擦 friction, rubbing [まさつ]

80c ネ "religious matter" [from 示, used on the left side of kanji]; **bushu *shimesuhen***

亍 示

社視礼祉祥禅

	Meanings	Kun and On	Romaji	Bushu	Stroke Order and Number
SG-1746 社	shrine, company of people, corporation	やしろ シャ	yashiro *sha*	示	` ラ ネ ネ- ネ十 社 7

社 **A** F-0042

甲骨文 1 金文 2 説文 3 旧字 4 社

1 and 2 showed "a ball of dirt on the ground" (土 **SG-1126**), with "sprinkles of wine" to consecrate the ground in 1. Both forms signified "the deity of the soil" or "a place of worship, shrine."

社・お社 shrine [やしろ, おやしろ]; 社会 society [しゃかい]; 会社 corporation [かいしゃ]; 結社 establishment, organization [けっしゃ];

	In 3, "an altar table with an offering" (示) was added, which was simplified to ネ, bushu *shimesuhen*, in the shinji. People assembled at a place of worship, and the form meant "a company of people" and, in modern times, "a corporation." The kanji 社 means "shrine, company of people, corporation." <ネ土>	社交的な sociable, gregarious [しゃこうてきな]; 社会人 member of society, working adult [しゃかいじん]; 社屋 office building [しゃおく]; 社訓 guiding mottoes of a company [しゃくん]

SG-1747 視	Meanings	Kun and On	Romaji	Bushu	Stroke Order and Number
	to gaze at, look straight at	シ	*shi*	見	ラネネ⺆祖視 11

視
B
F-0565

甲骨文 1　中山王器 2　説文古文 3　説文 4　旧字 5

1 comprised "an altar table," used for the sound *shi*, and "an eye," together signifying "to watch an altar table for a deity to appear." 2 comprised "an eye" and "a clan chief's small carving knife for sacrificial meat." 3 also had "an eye" and "an altar table." In 4, the right side became the kanji 見 **SG-0460** "to look at, gaze at." The kanji 視 means "to gaze at, look straight at." <ネ見>

視力 eyesight [しりょく]; 無視する to ignore, disregard [むしする]; 直視する to face the fact, look squarely at [ちょくしする, ちょくしする]; 視野 one's view, one's horizons [しや]; 度外視する to take no account of, ignore [どがいしする]; 遠視 farsighted, hyperopia [えんし]; 乱視 astigmatic [らんし]

SG-1748 礼	Meanings	Kun and On	Romaji	Bushu	Stroke Order and Number
	propriety, bow, gratitude, thank-you gift	レイ・ライ	*ree, rai*	示	ラネネ礼 5

礼
B
F-0895

金文 1　説文古文 2　古文 3　説文 4　旧字 5

1 comprised "two strands of jewels or stalks of a harvested plant," and "a crock," used for the sound *ree* (豊 **SG-1976**). Together they meant "abundant offerings to a deity." 2 and 3 had "an altar table" and, in 3, "a person kneeling in worship." 4 comprised 示 and 豊. The kyuji 禮 (5) still appears in some formal uses. In the shinji 礼, the right side uses 乚, reflecting the right side of 3. The kanji 礼 means "propriety, bow, gratitude, thank-you gift." <ネ乚>

礼 salute, bow, propriety [れい]; 一礼する to make a light bow to [いちれいする]; 失礼 discourtesy, impoliteness [しつれい]; 朝礼 morning assembly [ちょうれい]; 礼儀正しい gracious, well-mannered [れいぎただしい]; 礼拝堂 chapel [れいはいどう, らいはいどう]; 礼賛 adoration, praise [らいさん]

SG-1749 祉	Meanings	Kun and On	Romaji	Bushu	Stroke Order and Number
	blessing, happiness given by a deity	シ	*shi*	示	ラネネ丨ネ卜祉祉 8

祉
C
F-1609

甲骨文 1　説文 2　旧字 3

1 and 2 comprised "an altar table" (示, ネ), which signified "the presence of a deity," and 止 **SG-0200** "a footprint," which was used for the sound *shi* and meant "to stay." Together they signified "a deity's blessing stays." The kanji 祉 means "blessing, happiness given by a deity." <ネ止>

福祉 welfare, well-being [ふくし, ふくし]; 福祉施設 welfare facility [ふくししせつ]; 社会福祉士 licensed social welfare worker [しゃかいふくしし]

SG-1750 祥	Meanings	Kun and On	Romaji	Bushu	Stroke Order and Number
	auspicious; good omen	ショウ	*shoo*	示	ラネネ゙ 祥祥 10

祥
C
F-1632

金文 1　説文 2　旧字 3

1 had 羊 **SG-0825** "sheep," used for the sound *shoo* to mean "good omen." In 2, "an altar table with offering" and "a sheep" were placed side by side, becoming the kyuji 祥. The kanji 祥 means "auspicious; good omen." <ネ羊>

吉祥 good omen [きっしょう]; 発祥の地 birthplace, land of origin [はっしょうのち]; 不祥事 scandal [ふしょうじ]

SG-1751 禅	Meanings	Kun and On	Romaji	Bushu	Stroke Order and Number
	Zen sect; to vacate a throne peacefully	ゼン	*zen*	示	ラネネ゙ネ゙ 祒 禅禅 13

禅
D
F-1709

説文 1　旧字 2

1 comprised 示 (ネ, bushu *shimesuhen*) "an altar table" for the meaning "worshipping," and 單 (単 **SG-1548**), which was used for the sound *zen* (from *tan*) to mean "a flat platform" for conducting a rite. Together they signified a religious ceremony in which an emperor received a mandate from a deity to rule, whence the meaning "peaceful transfer of power." Later the character also came to be used for the Zen Buddhist sect. The kanji 禅 means "Zen sect; to vacate a throne peacefully." <ネ単>

禅宗 Zen sect of Buddhism [ぜんしゅう]; 座禅を組む to sit in Zen meditation [ざぜんをくむ]; 禅譲 peaceful abdication of a throne [ぜんじょう]; 友禅 *Yuzen* printed silk [ゆうぜん]; 禅寺 Zen temple [ぜんでら]

80d 斉 "in good order" [from three barley stalks of equal length as offering to a deity]; *see/sai* 済剤斉斎

	Meanings	Kun and On	Romaji	Bushu	Stroke Order and Number
SG-1752 済	to complete, finish up, rescue, get through with, make do	す-む サイ	su-mu *sai*	水	11

済 **A** F-0346 — 説文 1, 旧字 2

1 and 2 comprised "flowing water" (氵), and 齊 (斉 **SG-1754**), used for the sound *sai*, which was the name of a particular river. Originally meaning "crossing a river," the character came to mean (or, in another view, was borrowed to mean) "to rescue people from water," and further "to complete." In Japanese, it is also used to mean "to get through with, make do." The kanji 済 means "to complete, finish up, rescue, make do." <氵斉>

済む to end, finish [すむ]; (て)済ます・済ませる to get through with, settle, make do [すます, すませる]; 使用済み finished being used [しようずみ]; 届け済み delivered, registered [とどけでずみ]; 経済 economy, economics [けいざい]; 経済的な economical [けいざいてきな]; 返済する to pay back, reimburse [へんさいする]

	Meanings	Kun and On	Romaji	Bushu	Stroke Order and Number
SG-1753 剤	medicine, drug	ザイ	*zai*	刀	10

剤 **B** F-1001 — 説文 1, 旧字 2

1 comprised the same shape as 齋 (the kyuji for 斉 **SG-1754**, which depicted "barley stalks cut in equal length" and meant "well formed, precise"), and "a knife" (刀)." Together they signified "dispensing medicine by exact measurement." In the kyuji (2), the knife became 刂, bushu *rittoo,* and the top left component was replaced by 文 in the shinji. The kanji 剤 means "medicine, drug." <斉刂>

薬剤師 pharmacist, chemist [やくざいし]; 錠剤 tablet [じょうざい]; 洗剤 detergent [せんざい]; 調剤 dispensing [ちょうざい]; 乾燥剤 drying agent, desiccant [かんそうざい]; 殺虫剤 insecticide, bug killer [さっちゅうざい]; 接着剤 glue, adhesive [せっちゃくざい, せっちゃくざい]

	Meanings	Kun and On	Romaji	Bushu	Stroke Order and Number
SG-1754 斉	to be in good order, make everything uniform	セイ	*see*	齊	8

斉 **C** F-1110 — 甲骨文 1, 金文1 2, 金文2 3, 説文 4, 旧字 5

1, 2, and 3 depicted "three barley stalks of equal length presented as an offering to a deity," or "three shining hair accessories of uniformly neat appearance worn by a maiden in a religious rite." In 4 and 5, two lines of equal length were added to further signify "neatness," and were used for the sound *see*. The kyuji 齋 (5) was simplified to 斉 in the shinji. The kanji 斉 means "to be in good order, make everything uniform." <斉 (文月)>

一斉に all at once, simultaneously [いっせいに]; 一斉休暇 all employees taking days off at the same time [いっせいきゅうか]; 一斉取り締まり general crackdown (on traffic violations) [いっせいとりしまり]; 斉唱 singing in unison [せいしょう]

	Meanings	Kun and On	Romaji	Bushu	Stroke Order and Number
SG-1755 斎	votive abstinence; solemn	サイ	*sai*	齊	11

斎 **C** F-1264 — 金文 1, 説文 2, 旧字 3

1 comprised "an altar table with an offering," and the same form as 1, 2, and 3 for 斉 **SG-1754**, used for the sound *sai* to mean "religious." Together they signified the sober, reverential manner of participants in a religious rite. In 2, the altar table was placed at the bottom center. The shinji 斎 is 斉 with 示 **SG-1737** inside. The kanji 斎 means "votive abstinence; solemn." <文示>

書斎 study, library [しょさい]; 斎場 funeral parlor [さいじょう]

81 Imperial

81a 帝 "imperial" [from a special ancenstal altar table with crossed stable legs]; *tee* 帝締諦

	Meanings	Kun and On	Romaji	Bushu	Stroke Order and Number
SG-1756 帝	emperor; imperial	テイ	*tee*	巾	9

帝 **B** F-0955 — 甲骨文1 1, 甲骨文2 2, 金文1 3, 金文2 4, 説文 5

1 through 4 depicted "offerings on an altar table" that had three crossed legs that were tied together for stability, signifying "an important altar table used to place offerings

帝王 emperor [ていおう]; 帝国 empire, conglomerate [ていこく, ていこく]; 皇帝 emperor [こうてい]; 女帝

for the most important ancestral deity." The primary celebrant was a ruler, and thus the form meant "emperor; imperial." Another view is that a thread (一) tying three hanging threads together signified an emperor who unified the world. In the kanji, the bottom 巾 is the remnant of the three legs (also viewed as a cloth by some). The kanji 帝 meant "emperor; imperial." <亠巾>

empress [じょてい]; 帝国主義 imperialism [ていこくしゅ↓ぎ]; 帝王切開 Caesarean section [ていおうせっ↓かい] // 帝 (御門) emperor [みかど]

	Meanings	Kun and On	Romaji	Bushu	Stroke Order and Number
SG-1757 締	to fasten, tighten, sign a treaty	しーまる テイ	shi-maru *tee*	糸	幺 糸 紵 紵 綷 締 締 15

締 **B** F-1050

締 (説文) 締 The seal-style form comprised 糸 "a skein of threads," and 帝, used for the sound *tee* to mean "to fasten, tie," from an altar table with its legs crossed and locked for stability. The kanji 締 means "to fasten, tighten, sign a treaty." <糸帝>

締める to fasten, tie up, close [しめ↓る]; 引き締める to tense up, tighten [ひきしめ↓る]; 取り締まる to oversee, crack down [とりしまる]; 代表取締役 representative director (of a company) [だいひょうとりしまりやく]; 締結する to conclude a treaty [ていけつする]

	Meanings	Kun and On	Romaji	Bushu	Stroke Order and Number
SG-1758 諦	to be resigned to one's fate, have a clear insight	あきらーめる テイ	akira-meru *tee*	言	言 訁 訪 諦 諦 諦 16

諦 **D** F-2170

諦 (説文) 諦 The seal-style form comprised 言, bushu *gonben* "word; to speak," and 帝 **SG-1757**, which was used for the sound *tee* to mean "to tie, conclude." Originally, it meant "to make clear (with words), reveal the truth." In Japanese, it is used to mean "to be resigned to one's fate, despair." The kanji 諦 means "to be resigned to one's fate, have a clear insight." <言帝>

諦める to give up, drop out [あきらめ↓る]; 諦観する to have a clear insight into, resign oneself [ていかんする]; 諦念 understanding and acceptance of the basis of things, resignation [ていねん]

81b 啇 "legitimate, proper" [from 帝 "a regal altar table with offerings" with 口 "a mouth/prayer vessel"]; *teki/chaku* 適敵摘滴嫡

	Meanings	Kun and On	Romaji	Bushu	Stroke Order and Number
SG-1759 適	suitable; to fit	テキ	*teki*	辵	亠 ㅗ 产 啇 啇 啇 滴 適 14

適 **B** F-0717

(金文 1) (説文 2) 適 1 comprised "a regal ancestral altar table with offerings on it" (the same as 3 for 帝 **SG-1756**), and "a mouth or a box of prayers" (口 **SG-0031**), and it had the sound *teki.* Together these components signified "someone who can legitimately preside over an ancestral rite, an heir." In 2, 辵 (辶) "to carry out, conduct" was added. The person who was most suitable to carry out a rite gave the meaning "suitable." In the kanji, the right side became 啇. The kanji 適 means "suitable; to fit." <产口辶>

適切な appropriate [てきせつな]; 適度な moderate [て↓きどな]; 快適な comfortable, pleasant [かいてきな]; 適用する to apply [てきようする]; 適材適所 the right person in the right place [てきざいて↓きしょ]; 適職 suitable occupation [てきしょく]; 適合する to be in conformity with, match [てきごうする]

	Meanings	Kun and On	Romaji	Bushu	Stroke Order and Number
SG-1760 敵	enemy, comparable to	かたき テキ	kataki *teki*	支	亠 ㅗ 产 啇 啇 啇 敵 15

敵 **C** F-1081

(金文 1) (説文 2) 敵 1 was the same as 1 for 適 **SG-1759**, and meant "a legitimate heir carrying out a rite." In 2, 支 (攵) "to hit with a stick" was added to 啇 and was used for the sound *teki.* Someone who attacked an emperor was "an enemy," and an enemy who was a good match led to the meaning "comparable to." The kanji 敵 means "enemy, comparable to." <啇攵>

敵 enemy [かたき↓, てき]; 敵役 villain's role in play [かたきやく]; 商売敵 trade rival, competitor [しょうばいが↓たき]; 宿敵 old enemy, archrival [しゅくてき]; 敵意 hostile feeling, bad blood, malice [て↓きい]; 匹敵する comparable to, equal to [ひってきする]; 天敵 natural enemy [てんてき]

	Meanings	Kun and On	Romaji	Bushu	Stroke Order and Number
SG-1761 摘	to pick, pluck	つーむ テキ	tsu-mu *teki*	手	扌 扩 扩 摘 摘 摘 14

摘 **C** F-1111

(篆文) 摘 The seal-style form comprised 扌 "an act done by hand," and 啇, which was used for the sound *teki.* Together they signified "handpicking or plucking something fitting." The kanji 摘 means "to pick, pluck." <扌啇>

摘む to pick, pull up [つむ]; 茶摘み tea-picking [ちゃつみ]; 摘要 abstract [てきよう]; 摘発する to expose, unmask [てきはつする]; 指摘する to point out, indicate [してきする]; 摘出する to extract, remove [てきしゅつする]

	Meanings	Kun and On	Romaji	Bushu	Stroke Order and Number
SG-1762 滴	droplet; to trickle, drip	したた-る・しずく テキ	shitata-ru, shizuku *teki*	水	氵 氵 氵 汼 渧 滴 滴 14

滴 **D** F-1727

篆文

The seal-style form comprised 氵 "flowing water," and 啇, which was used for the sound *teki*. Together they signified the sound of water dripping. The kanji 滴 means "droplet; to trickle, drip." <氵啇>

滴る to dribble, trickle [したたꜜる]; 滴 drop [しずくꜜ]; 水滴 water droplet [すいてき]; 一滴 driblet, drop [いってき]; 点滴 intravenous drip, IV [てんてき]

	Meanings	Kun and On	Romaji	Bushu	Stroke Order and Number
SG-1763 嫡	legitimate heir, legitimate line	チャク	*chaku*	女	女 女 女 妒 婷 嫡 嫡 14

嫡 **D** F-2197

金文 1 說文 2

1 was the same as 1 for 適 **SG-1759** and 敵 **SG-1760.** It pertained to "legitimate, proper," and was used for the sound *teki*. In 2, 女 **SG-0521** "a woman" was added to mean "birth." Together they signified "a legitimate heir to the throne." The kanji 嫡 means "legitimate heir, legitimate line." <女啇>

嫡男 male heir [ちゃくꜜなん]; 嫡子 legitimate child, heir [ちゃꜜくし]; 嫡流 direct line of descent [ちゃくりゅう]; 非嫡出子 illegitimate child [ひ・ちゃくしゅつꜜし]

82 Divination

82a 卜 "divination" [from cracks that appeared on an animal bone or a tortoiseshell when heated] 外点店占貼訃

卜

Note on 卜 and oracle bone–style characters 甲骨文字

In order to divine the future for the benefit of a ruler, a tiny indentation was drilled into a particular spot on the back of a tortoiseshell or an animal bone, to which heat was then applied using a burning stick or heated metal rod. The heat caused cracks to appear on the surface, which were then interpreted as messages from deities. The reading of the cracks was then chiseled onto the bone, in what are now called oracle-bone style characters.

	Meanings	Kun and On	Romaji	Bushu	Stroke Order and Number
SG-1764 外	outside, exterior, others; to take out; else	そと・ほか・はず-れる ガイ・ゲ	soto, hoka, hazu-reru *gai, ge*	夕	ノ ク タ 夕| 外 5

外 **A** F-0111

金文 1 說文 2

1 and 2 comprised 夕 **SG-1072** (月 **SG-1077**) "a moon," to mean "evening," and 卜 "oracle, divination." One view explains that divination was not allowed to be conducted in the evening; thus, oracle bones and a moon signified "outside of what is allowed." Another view holds that divination was performed by reading the cracks that appeared on the outside of the oracle bone (卜), as contrasted to the inside where heat was applied. Together with the left side (月, used for the sounds *getsu/gatsu*), the character meant "outside." The kanji 外 means "outside, exterior, others; to take out; else." <夕卜>

外 outside [そꜜと]; others, else [ほか]; 外す to take out, omit [はずす]; 外れる to come off, be wrong, be removed [はずれる]; 外国 foreign country, abroad [がいこく]; ～以外 other than X, except X [～いꜜがい]; 予想外 unexpectedly [よそꜜうがい]; 外来 outpatient department, of foreign origin [がいらい]; 外科医 surgeon [げかꜜい]; 外道 way of thinking contrary to the truth, heretic [げどう]

	Meanings	Kun and On	Romaji	Bushu	Stroke Order and Number
SG-1765 点	small dot, point	テン	*ten*	黑	丨 ⺊ 𠂉 占 占 点 9

点 **A** F-0149

說文 1 旧字 2

1 depicted "a chimney with soot and two fires," which in 2 became 黑 (the kyuji for 黒 **SG-1173** "black"); and 占 **SG-1767**, which was used for the sound *ten* to mean "small dot." Together they signified "small black dots, points." In the shinji 点, the top of 黑 was dropped, leaving only 灬, bushu *renga/rekka* "fire," underneath 占. The kanji 点 means "small dot, point." <占灬>

点 point, dot [てん]; 点火する to light a fire, ignite [てんかする]; 点検 inspection, overhaul [てんけん]; 欠点 shortcoming [けってꜜん]; 疑問点 question, questionable point [ぎもꜜんてん]; 合点が行く to understand, grasp [がてんがいく]; 点数 point, mark [てんすꜜう]; 点々 dots, spots, sporadically [てんてꜜん]

SG-1766 店	Meanings	Kun and On	Romaji	Bushu	Stroke Order and Number
	store, shop	みせ テン	mise *ten*	广	' 亠 广 庁 店 店 8

店 **A** F-0225

No ancient form. The kanji 店 comprises 广, bushu *madare* "eaves," and 占, used for the sound *ten*. Together they signified "a kiosk, a place to put things up," and later, "a store or shop." The kanji 店 means "store, shop." <广 占>

店 store, shop [みせꜜ]; 夜店 night fare, night stall [よみせ]; 店番 tending a store [みせばん]; 店内 inside a store [てꜜんない]; 閉店時間 store's closing time [へいてんじꜜかん]; 店員 shop assistant, sales clerk [てんいん]; 店頭 store front, counter [てんとう]; 小売店 retailer [こうりꜜてん]

SG-1767 占	Meanings	Kun and On	Romaji	Bushu	Stroke Order and Number
	to tell someone's fortune, occupy	うらな-う・し-める セン	urana-u, shi-meru *sen*	ト	丨 ト ⺊ 占 占 5

占 **B** F-0653

甲骨文 1, 甲骨文 2, 説文 3

1 comprised ト "cracks in an oracle bone," and ロ "a mouth, area." In 2, the two elements were placed inside the shape of the bone, together signifying "to tell someone's fortune; oracle." Another view explains that the divination was done to ask a deity which area (ロ) a king should advance on and occupy, thus leading to the meaning "to occupy." The kanji 占 means "to tell someone's fortune, occupy." <占>

占い fortune telling [うらない]; 星占い horoscope [ほしうꜜらない]; 占い師 fortune teller [うらないꜜし]; 占める to occupy, hold, make up [しめꜜる]; 一人占め・独り占め monopoly [ひとりじめ]; 占有地 occupied land [せんゆꜜうち]; 独占 monopoly [どくせん]; 独占禁止法・独禁法 the Antimonopoly Law [どくせんきんしほう, どっきんほう]; 占拠する to occupy [せꜜんきょする]

SG-1768 貼	Meanings	Kun and On	Romaji	Bushu	Stroke Order and Number
	to stick, paste	は-る チョウ	ha-ru *choo*	貝	冂 目 貝 貝' 貝ト 貼 貼 12

貼 **D** F-2099

篆文

The seal-style form comprised 貝 **SG-1693** "cowrie, money," and 占, used for the sounds *choo*/*ten* (from *sen*) to mean "to place one on top of another." The kanji 貼 means "to stick on, paste, affix over something." <貝 占>

貼る to stick, paste [はる]; 貼り付ける to stick, paste up [はりつけꜜる]; 貼り紙 pasted paper [はりがみ] // 貼付する to paste [てんぷする, ちょうふする]

SG-1769 訃	Meanings	Kun and On	Romaji	Bushu	Stroke Order and Number
	news of someone's death	フ	*hu*	言	亠 言 訁 訃 9

訃 **D** F-2414

No ancient form. The kanji 訃 comprises 言 "word; to say," and ト, used for the sound *hu* to mean "sudden collapse." Together they signified "a report of sudden collapse." The kanji 訃 means "news of someone's death." <言 ト>

訃報 news of someone's death, obituary [ふほう]

82b 兆 "divination, sign" [from the cracks on an oracle bone]; *choo/too* 兆逃挑跳眺

SG-1770 兆	Meanings	Kun and On	Romaji	Bushu	Stroke Order and Number
	sign, omen, trillion	きざ-し チョウ	kiza-shi *choo*	儿	ノ 丿 丬 兆 兆 兆 6

兆 **B** F-0848

説文古文 1, 説文 2

1 and 2 depicted a whole tortoiseshell with cracks that appeared when heated from behind. The cracks were read as signs in divination. The character was also borrowed to mean "trillion." The kanji 兆 means "sign, indication, omen, trillion." <兆>

兆し indication, omen [きざし]; 予兆 omen, indication [よちょう]; 吉兆 auspicious sign [きっちょう]; 二兆円 two trillion yen [にちょうえん]

SG-1771 逃	Meanings	Kun and On	Romaji	Bushu	Stroke Order and Number
	to run away, flee, dodge, evade, lose	に-げる・のが-す トウ	nige-ru, noga-su *too*	辵	ノ 丬 兆 兆 兆 逃 逃 9

逃 **B** F-0883

中山王器 1, 説文 2

The left side of 1 and 2 comprised "a crossroads," with "a footprint" in 2, forming 辵 (⻌, bushu *shinnyuu*) "to move forward." The right side, 兆 "cracks appearing on a tortoise plastron that was heated from behind," was used for the sound *too*. 2 was meant to represent a scene in which defeated soldiers hurriedly fled in many directions, by analogy to how quickly cracks spread through the surface of an oracle bone. From "a hasty retreat," the kanji 逃 means "to run away, flee, dodge, evade, lose." <兆 ⻌>

逃げる to run away [にげꜜる]; 逃れる to evade, miss, dodge, sidestep [のがれꜜる]; 逃げ回る to run about [にげまわꜜる]; 言い逃れ an excuse [いいのがれ]; 逃亡する to run away, fly [とうぼうする]; 逃走する to escape, run away [とうそうする]; 逃亡者 fugitive [とうぼꜜうしゃ]

	Meanings	*Kun* and *On*	Romaji	Bushu	Stroke Order and Number
SG-1772 挑	to challenge, confront, go after	いど-む チョウ	ido-mu *choo*	手	亅扌扎扎挑挑 9
挑 **C** F-1381	説文 挑 The seal-style form comprised 扌 "an act done by hand," and 兆 **SG-1770**, used for the sound *choo* to mean "forcing something to bend." A hand that tried to bend something forcefully met with strong resistance. The kanji 挑 means "to challenge, confront, go after." <扌兆>				挑む to challenge [いどむ]; 挑戦 challenge [ちょうせん]; 挑発する to provoke [ちょうはつする]

	Meanings	*Kun* and *On*	Romaji	Bushu	Stroke Order and Number
SG-1773 跳	to leap, jump	は-ねる・と-ぶ チョウ	ha-neru, to-bu *choo*	足	口早𧾷跀跀跳跳 13
跳 **D** F-1659	説文 跳 The seal-style form comprised 足(𧾷) **SG-0227** "leg," and 兆, used for the sound *choo* to mean "leaping." The kanji 跳 means "to leap, jump." <𧾷兆>				跳ぶ to leap; bound, vault [とぶ]; 跳ねる to leap, spring up, splash, prance [はねる]; 跳躍 spring, jump; leap [ちょうやく]

	Meanings	*Kun* and *On*	Romaji	Bushu	Stroke Order and Number
SG-1774 眺	to look on, stand by and watch	なが-める チョウ	naga-meru *choo*	目	冂目𥃭𥃭眺眺 11
眺 **D** F-1803	説文 眺 The seal-style form comprised 目 **SG-0001** "an eye," and 兆, used for the sound *choo* to mean "to disperse," together signifying "to look from a distance." The kanji 眺 means "to look on, stand by and watch." <目兆>				眺める to look, examine [ながめる]; 眺めのいい to have a good view [ながめのいい]; 眺め入る to gaze intently at, stare at [ながめいる]; 眺望 view, lookout [ちょうぼう]

83 Cleansing

83a 帚 "broom; to sweep, cleanse" [from a broom for sweeping a family altar]

帰婦掃

	Meanings	*Kun* and *On*	Romaji	Bushu	Stroke Order and Number
SG-1775 帰	to go home, return	かえ-る キ	kae-ru *ki*	止	刂刂刂刂帰帰 10
帰 **A** F-0473	甲骨文1 1, 甲骨文2 2, 甲骨文3 3, 金文1 4, 金文2 5, 金文3 6, 説文 7, 旧字 歸 8, 帰 — 1, 2, 3, and 5 comprised "a stack of sacrificial meat," and "a broom" for "cleansing a family altar." In 6 and 7, "a footprint" was added. The character signified "a military force giving a battle report at the altar after its safe return," or one that was "praying for a safe return before going out." It meant "to return home." In the shinji 帰, the left side was replaced by 刂, a variant of bushu *rittoo*, which indicated carving meat for an offering. The kanji 帰 means "to go home, return." < 刂 帚>				帰る to return home [かえる]; 日帰り going and returning on the same day [ひがえり]; 帰り道に on the way home [かえりみちに]; 帰宅する to go home, head home [きたくする]; 帰化 naturalization [きか]; 帰省 homecoming [きせい]; 帰路 return route [きろ]; 帰京する to return to Tokyo [ききょうする]

	Meanings	*Kun* and *On*	Romaji	Bushu	Stroke Order and Number
SG-1776 婦	woman, lady, female	フ	*hu*	女	𡿨女女女婦婦婦 11
婦 **B** F-0683	甲骨文1 1, 甲骨文2 2, 金文1 3, 金文2 4, 説文 5, 婦 — 1 and 2 depicted "a broom for sweeping or cleansing an altar" (帚), which had the sound *hu*. In 3, 4, and 5, "a woman" (女 **SG-0521**) was added. Together they signified "the mistress of a household in charge of keeping the ancestral mausoleum in good order," or "the wife of someone's son." The kanji 婦 means "woman, lady, female." <女帚>				婦人 woman, lady [ふじん]; 主婦 housewife [しゅふ]; 夫婦 husband and wife [ふうふ]; 産婦人科 obstetrics and gynecology [さんふじんか]; 助産婦 midwife [じょさんぷ]; 婦人会 women's association or club [ふじんかい]; 家政婦 housemaid, domestic help [かせいふ]; 売春婦 prostitute, call girl [ばいしゅんふ]

	Meanings	Kun and On	Romaji	Bushu	Stroke Order and Number
SG-1777 掃	to sweep, brush onoff	はーく ソウ	ha-ku *soo*	手	扌扌扫扫掃掃掃 11

掃 **C** F-1438

甲骨文1 1 甲骨文2 2 金文 3 説文 4

1, 2, and 3 showed "a broom," used for the sound *soo,* and, in 1, "a hand" holding the broom. The character meant "a hand sweeping with a broom." In 4, 土 "soil, ground" was added to mean "to sweep the ground or clean." In the kanji, 土 was replaced by 扌, bushu *tehen* "an act done by hand." The kanji 掃 means "to sweep, brush off." <扌帚>

掃く to sweep, brush off [はく]; 掃き掃除 sweeping and cleaning, cleaning up [はきそうじ]; 掃除 cleaning, dusting, wiping, scrubbing [そうじ]; 掃除機 vacuum cleaner, sweeper [そうじき]; 清掃車 garbage truck, refuse truck [せいそうしゃ]; 一掃する to sweep away, get rid of [いっそうする]

83b 𠬶 [from sprinkling spirits with a broom to sanctify a mausoleum]; *shin* 寝侵浸

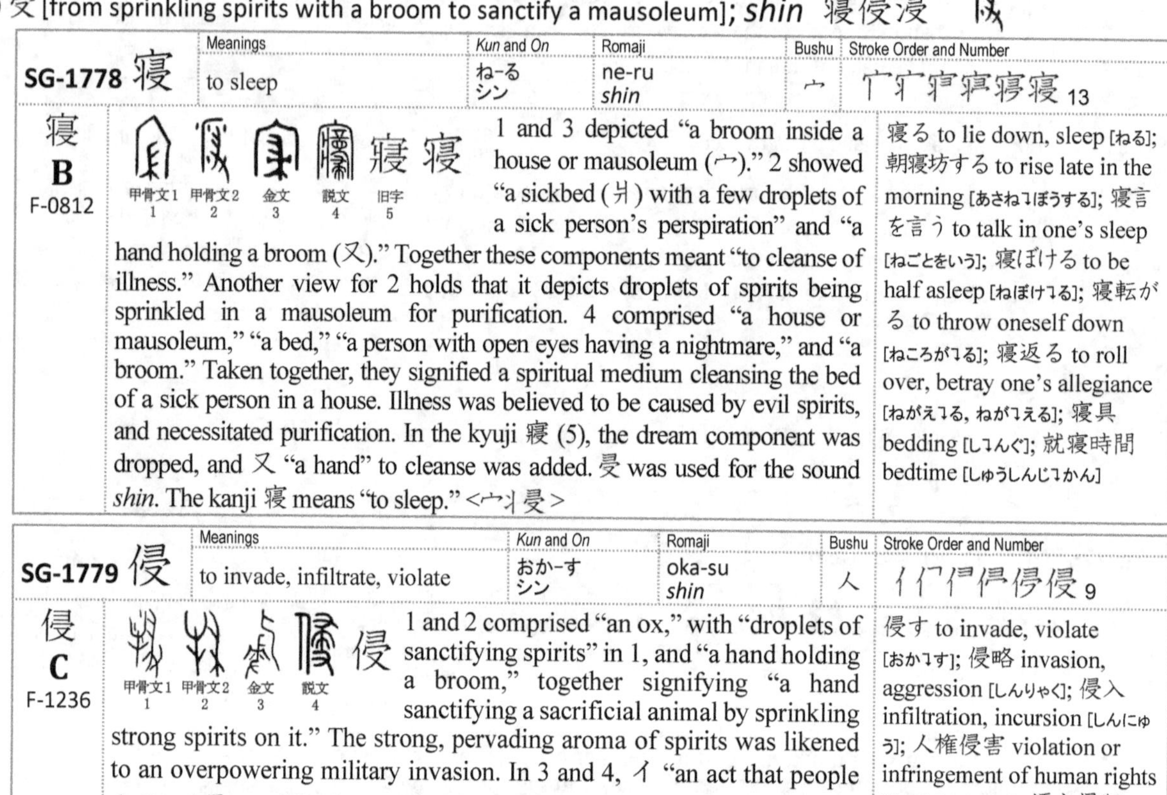

	Meanings	Kun and On	Romaji	Bushu	Stroke Order and Number
SG-1778 寝	to sleep	ねーる シン	ne-ru *shin*	宀	宀宁宇宇寝寝寝 13

寝 **B** F-0812

甲骨文1 1 甲骨文2 2 金文 3 説文 4 旧字 5

1 and 3 depicted "a broom inside a house or mausoleum (宀)." 2 showed "a sickbed (爿) with a few droplets of a sick person's perspiration" and "a hand holding a broom (又)." Together these components meant "to cleanse of illness." Another view for 2 holds that it depicts droplets of spirits being sprinkled in a mausoleum for purification. 4 comprised "a house or mausoleum," "a bed," "a person with open eyes having a nightmare," and "a broom." Taken together, they signified a spiritual medium cleansing the bed of a sick person in a house. Illness was believed to be caused by evil spirits, and necessitated purification. In the kyuji 寢 (5), the dream component was dropped, and 又 "a hand" to cleanse was added. 𠬶 was used for the sound *shin.* The kanji 寝 means "to sleep." <宀丬𠬶>

寝る to lie down, sleep [ねる]; 朝寝坊する to rise late in the morning [あさねぼうする]; 寝言を言う to talk in one's sleep [ねごとをいう]; 寝ぼける to be half asleep [ねぼける]; 寝転がる to throw oneself down [ねころがる]; 寝返る to roll over, betray one's allegiance [ねがえる, ねがえる]; 寝具 bedding [しんぐ]; 就寝時間 bedtime [しゅうしんじかん]

	Meanings	Kun and On	Romaji	Bushu	Stroke Order and Number
SG-1779 侵	to invade, infiltrate, violate	おかーす シン	oka-su *shin*	人	亻亻伊伊侵侵 9

侵 **C** F-1236

甲骨文1 1 甲骨文2 2 金文 3 説文 4

1 and 2 comprised "an ox," with "droplets of sanctifying spirits" in 1, and "a hand holding a broom," together signifying "a hand sanctifying a sacrificial animal by sprinkling strong spirits on it." The strong, pervading aroma of spirits was likened to an overpowering military invasion. In 3 and 4, 亻 "an act that people do," and 𠬶, used for the sound *shin,* together meant "to invade." Another view explains that a person thoroughly cleaning every corner of a place signified "to go beyond one's territory, invade." The kanji 侵 means "to invade, infiltrate, violate." <亻𠬶>

侵す to invade, violate [おかす]; 侵略 invasion, aggression [しんりゃく]; 侵入 infiltration, incursion [しんにゅう]; 人権侵害 violation or infringement of human rights [じんけんしんがい]; 領土侵犯 violation of territorial sovereignty, intrusion into territory [りょうど・しんぱん]

	Meanings	Kun and On	Romaji	Bushu	Stroke Order and Number
SG-1780 浸	to soak, immerse, be inundated	ひたーす シン	hita-su *shin*	水	氵氵沪沪浔浸 10

浸 **C** F-1470

甲骨文 1 金文 2 説文 3

1 showed "a family mausoleum being cleansed with droplets of sanctifying aromatic spirits," and was used for the sound *shin.* In 2, the addition of "flowing water" signified that the aroma of spirits strongly permeated the surrounding air, thus giving the meaning "to soak, immerse." In 3, 又 "a hand" was added on the right side (𠬶). The kanji 浸 means "to soak, immerse, be inundated." <氵𠬶>

浸す to soak, immerse [ひたす]; 浸る to be soaked in, be drowned in [ひたる, ひたる]; 酒浸り being steeped in alcohol [さけびたり]; 浸水 flood, inundation [しんすい]; 浸透する to permeate [しんとうする]; 浸食作用 erosion, corrosive action [しんしょくさよう]

XI FOOD AND EATING

84 Food

84a 食 𩙿 "food, eating" [from food in a raised bowl with a lid, or 皀 "a bowl of food" and "a spoon"]; **bushu *shokuhen*** 食飯飢餓餌

	Meanings	*Kun* and *On*	Romaji	Bushu	Stroke Order and Number
SG-1781 食	to eat; food	く-う・た-べる ショク・ジキ	ku-u, ta-beru *shoku, jiki*	食	𠆢 今 今 食 食 食 9

食 **A** F-0203

甲骨文1 1 · 甲骨文2 2 · 金文1 3 · 金文2 4 · 説文 5 · 食

1 through 4 depicted "food in a raised bowl with a lid," and meant "food; to eat." Another view holds 5 to comprise 皀 ("food" with ヒ "a spoon, ladle") and a "lid" (𠆢 or 亼). The kanji 食 means "to eat; food." When used as a left-side component, it becomes 𩙿 bushu *shokuhen*, with one fewer stroke. <𠆢 良>

食べる to eat [たべꜜる]; 食べ物 food [たべꜜもの, たべもꜜの]; 食う to eat (male speech), (an animal) eats [くꜜう]; 電池を食う to use up a battery [でꜜんちを・くꜜう]; 足止めを食う/食らう to be prevented from leaving [あしどめをくꜜう, くらꜜう]; 食い違う to not match, go wrong [くいちがう, くいちがꜜう]; 食事 meal [しょくじ], 朝食 breakfast [ちょうしょく]; 給食 school lunch [きゅうしょく]; 断食 fast, fasting [だんじき]

	Meanings	*Kun* and *On*	Romaji	Bushu	Stroke Order and Number
SG-1782 飯	cooked rice, meal	めし ハン	meshi *han*	食	今 今 食 食 飣 飯 飯 12

飯 **B** F-0905

金文 1 · 説文 2 · 飯

1 and 2 comprised 𩙿 "food in a raised bowl with a lid," and 反 **SG-0087**, which was used for the sound *han*. Together they signified "cooked grains such as rice and millet," and "meal." The kanji 飯 means "cooked rice, meal." <𩙿 反>

晩飯 evening meal (male speech) [ばんめし]; (お)赤飯 celebratory steamed sticky rice with red *azuki* beans [おせꜜきはん, せきはん]; 五目ご飯 rice cooked with a few other ingredients [ごもくごꜜはん]; 日常茶飯事 daily occurrence [にちじょうさはꜜんじ]; 残飯 leftovers from a meal [ざんぱん, ざんぱꜜん]

	Meanings	*Kun* and *On*	Romaji	Bushu	Stroke Order and Number
SG-1783 飢	to starve, famish, be hungry for	う-える キ	u-eru *ki*	食	今 今 食 食 飣 飢 10

飢 **D** F-1672

篆文 1 · 説文 2 · 飢

1 and 2 comprised 𩙿 "food in a raised bowl with a lid," and 幾 **SG-1479** or 几, used for the sound *ki* to mean "empty." Together they signified "lack of food." The kanji 飢 means "to starve, famish, be hungry for." <𩙿 几>

飢える to be starved, famished [うえꜜる]; 飢え死にする to starve to death [うえじにする]; 飢饉 famine [きꜜきん]; 水飢饉 water shortage, drought [みずきꜜきん]; 飢餓 starvation [きꜜが]

	Meanings	*Kun* and *On*	Romaji	Bushu	Stroke Order and Number
SG-1784 餓	to starve	ガ	*ga*	食	今 今 食 飠 飦 餁 餓 餓 15

餓 **D** F-1895

説文 · 餓

The seal-style form comprised 𩙿 "food in a bowl with a lid," and 我 **SG-1492**, used for the sound *ga*, together signifying "to starve." The kanji 餓 means "to starve." <𩙿 我>

餓死 death from starvation [がꜜし]; 餓鬼 famished devil, young mischievous kid, brat (rough male speech) [がきꜜ]

	Meanings	*Kun* and *On*	Romaji	Bushu	Stroke Order and Number
SG-1785 餌	bait, animal feed, lure	えさ・え ジ	esa, e *ji*	食	今 今 食 食 飠 餌 餌 15

餌 **D** F-2090

説文 1 · 説文或体 2 · 餌

1 showed 鬲 ("a thick-legged clay food storage"), with 耳 **SG-0050**, used for the sound *ji*, on top, and it originally signified "steamed dumpling." 2 comprised 𩙿 "food," and 耳, used for the sound *ji*, and signified "dumplings used as a fishing lure or animal feed." The kanji 餌 means "bait, animal feed, lure." <𩙿 耳>

餌 animal feed, bait, lure [えさꜜ, えꜜ]; 餌付ける to feed for domestication [えづけꜜる]; 餌食 victim, prey [えꜜじき, えじきꜜ]

84b 皀・既 "immediately, already" 即・既概慨

	Meanings	Kun and On	Romaji	Bushu	Stroke Order and Number
SG-1786 即	immediate, instant; to accede to the throne; namely	ソク	*soku*	卩	7

即
B
F-1058

甲骨文 1 金文 1 2 金文 2 3 説文 4 旧字 5

1 through 4 comprised "food in a raised bowl," and "a person seated at a table and ready to eat," used for the sound *soku*. Together they signified "to take up a seat." The meaning applied to a new ruler's accession to the throne, which happened immediately after his predecessor's demise, thus bringing the meaning "immediacy; instant." The shinji comprised 艮 (reduced from 皀) and 卩 "a kneeling person." The kanji 即 means "immediate, instant; to accede to the throne; namely." <艮卩>

即時 immediate, prompt [そくじ]; 即位 accession to the throne, coronation [そくい]; 即席 instant, impromptu [そくせき]; 即興 improvised amusement [そっきょう]; 即死 instant death [そくし] // 即ち namely, just, precisely [すなわち]

既 "already" [from a person belching with full stomach] 既概慨

	Meanings	Kun and On	Romaji	Bushu	Stroke Order and Number
SG-1787 既	already; to be finished	すで-に キ	sude-ni *ki*	无	10

既
C
F-1285

甲骨文 1 1 甲骨文 2 2 金文 3 説文 4 旧字 5

In 1 through 4, a person kneeling before food turned their face away from the food, a gesture that they had eaten enough. The person's open mouth is interpreted as belching because of the fullness of their stomach. This component became 旡, which had the sound *ki*. "Having finished eating" gave the meaning "already." In 3 and 4, 旡 was moved to the right. The kanji 既 means "already; to be finished." <既(艮旡)>
(Note: The component 旡 "full of" and the kanji 欠 **SG-0431** "lack of" had opposite meanings and were mirror images of each other in their ancient forms.)

既に already [すでに]; 既存の existing [きそんの]; 既婚 married [きこん]; 既成事実 an established fact [きせいじじつ]; 皆既日食 total solar eclipse [かいきにっしょく]; 既製品 manufactured goods, ready-made articles [きせいひん]; 既決 being already settled, done box, outbox [きけつ]; 既得権 vested rights, vested interests [きとくけん, きとっけん]

	Meanings	Kun and On	Romaji	Bushu	Stroke Order and Number
SG-1788 概	roughly, in general	ガイ	*gai*	木	14

概
C
F-1387

説文 1 旧字 2

1 comprised 既, which was used for the sound *gai*, and 木 **SG-0608** "tree," together signifying "a wooden rod used to level off a heaped measure." Leveling off an excess amount gave the meaning "roughly equal." The kanji 概 means "roughly, in general." <木既>

大概 almost, mostly, probably [たいがい]; 概説 a rough summary, rough sketch, brief account [がいせつ]; 概観 general view, general survey [がいかん]; 概要 outline, summary, resume [がいよう]

	Meanings	Kun and On	Romaji	Bushu	Stroke Order and Number
SG-1789 慨	to lament, deplore, grieve over	ガイ	*gai*	心	13

慨
D
F-2167

説文 1 旧字 2

1 and 2 comprised "heart" (忄, bushu *risshinben*), and 既 **SG-1787**, which was used for the sound *gai* and meant "bending backward (from a full stomach)," in this case signifying a posture of lament and despair. Together, these components signified "to deplore, grieve over." Another view explains that "full" (from "full stomach") and "a heart" together meant "a heart full of emotions." The kanji 慨 means "to lament, deplore, grieve over." <忄既>

感慨 strong feelings, deep emotion [かんがい]; 感慨無量 one's mind is filled with a thousand emotions [かんがいむりょう]; 憤慨 resentment, indignation [ふんがい]

84c 曽曾 "many layers; to add" [from a steamer with layers of baskets]; *soo* 

会増層贈曽僧憎

The shape 曾 in the kyuji 増層贈曾僧憎 was simplified to 曽 in the shinji, except in 會(会).

	Meanings	Kun and On	Romaji	Bushu	Stroke Order and Number
SG-1790 会	to meet (someone); meeting, association	あ-う カイ・エ	a-u *kai, e*	曰	八今会会 6

会 **A** F-0007

甲骨文 1, 金文 2, 説文 3, 旧字 4

1 comprised "a crossroads," "a footprint," and "a container with a well-fitting lid" (合 **SG-1989**) to mean "to meet." Together they signified "to go to meet." 2 and 3 showed "a food steamer with layers of baskets," with "steam or flame rising in a stove" in 3, which became 曰 in the kyuji (4). In the shinji, the shape under 八 was replaced by the simpler 云, "(steam) rising." The kanji 会 means "to meet (someone); meeting, association." <八云>

(Note: For a note about 曰, from "voice rising," please refer to 替 **SG-0370**.)

会う to meet (someone) [あう]; 出会う to encounter, meet by chance [であう]; 会合 meeting [かいごう]; 会計 accounts, bill, finances [かいけい]; 会心の笑み smile of satisfaction [かいしんのえみ]; 学会 scholarly society or conference [がっかい]; 音楽会 concert [おんがくかい, おんがっかい]; 一期一会 "Treat every encounter as a once-in-a-lifetime event" [いちごいちえ, いちごいちえ]

	Meanings	Kun and On	Romaji	Bushu	Stroke Order and Number
SG-1791 増	to increase, add	ま-す・ふ-える ゾウ	ma-su; hu-eru *zoo*	土	ナ圹圹坤増増 14

増 **A** F-0352

説文 1, 旧字 2

1 and 2 comprised 土 **SG-1126** "dirt, soil" (土, bushu *tsuchihen*), and 曾 "layers; to add," which was used for the sound *soo*. Together they signified "adding soil to existing ground" and "to increase." With the right side 曾 replaced by 曽 **SG-1794**, the kanji 増 means "to increase, add." <土曽>

増す to increase [ます]; 水増し padded, watered [みずまし]; 建て増し building on, extension of a building [たてまし]; 増やす to increase, add [ふやす]; 増加 increase [ぞうか]; 増水 rise of a river, flooding [ぞうすい]; 増長する to grow impudent [ぞうちょうする]; 激増 marked increase [げきぞう]; 増減 increase and decrease, variation [ぞうげん]

	Meanings	Kun and On	Romaji	Bushu	Stroke Order and Number
SG-1792 層	layer, stratum, class of people	ソウ	*soo*	尸	一尸尸屈届層層 14

層 **B** F-0790

説文 1, 旧字 2

1 comprised 尸, bushu *shikabane* "roof," and 曾 **SG-1794** "layers; to add," used for the sound *soo*. Something that had multiple levels was "a stratum, strata." The character was also used for "a class of people." The kanji 層 means "layer, stratum, class of people." <尸曽>

層になる to stratify [そうになる]; 断層 fault, dislocation, gap, difference [だんそう]; 階層 class, rank, level in society [かいそう]; 重層的な multilayered [じゅうそうてきな]; 高層ビル high-rise building [こうそうビル]; 下層 lower social stratum [かそう]; 上層部 an upper rank [じょうそうぶ]

	Meanings	Kun and On	Romaji	Bushu	Stroke Order and Number
SG-1793 贈	to present, gift	おく-る ゾウ・ソウ	oku-ru *zoo, soo*	貝	冂目貝貝贈贈 18

贈 **B** F-1039

説文 1, 旧字 2

1 comprised 貝 **SG-1693** "cowrie; valuable," and 曾 "layers; to add," used for the sound *zoo*. Together they signified "conferring or giving a valuable item to another person." The kanji 贈 means "to present, gift." <貝曽>

贈る to give (a gift) [おくる]; 贈答品 gift [ぞうとうひん]; 寄贈する to contribute, donate [きぞうする]; 贈呈式 presentation ceremony [ぞうていしき]

	Meanings	Kun and On	Romaji	Bushu	Stroke Order and Number
SG-1794 曽	formerly; great-grandparents	ソウ・ゾ	*soo, zo*	曰	ソ尚尚曽曽曽 11

曽 **C** F-1268

金文1 1, 金文2 2, 説文 3, 旧字 4

1 and 2 comprised "a steamer" over "a stove" from which steam was rising (八) at the top. Layers of baskets in a steamer meant "layering." The form was also borrowed to mean "once, formerly," or "three generations ago." The kanji 曽 means "formerly; great-grandparents." <曽>

曽祖父 great-grandfather [そうそふ]; 曾孫 great-grandchild [そうそん]; 未曾有の unprecedented, unheard-of, phenomenal [みぞうの] // (曽て formerly, once [かつて])

	Meanings	Kun and On	Romaji	Bushu	Stroke Order and Number
SG-1795 僧	monk, priest	ソウ	*soo*	人	イ亻'ⅰ亻'ⅰ亻'' 伫 俳 僧 僧 13

僧 **C** F-1544

説文 1 旧字 2

1 comprised 亻 "a person," and 曾 (曽), used for the sound *soo*. It was used as the phonetic rendition of the Sanskrit word *sangha* "priest" in Buddhism. The kanji 僧 means "monk, priest." <亻曽>

僧侶 monk [そう]りょ]; 尼僧 nun [にそう, に]そう]; 僧院 monastery, cloister [そういん]; 小僧 apprentice at a shop, kid, boy [こぞ]う]

	Meanings	Kun and On	Romaji	Bushu	Stroke Order and Number
SG-1796 憎	to hate, detest, abhor; hateful	にく-む ゾウ	niku-i *zoo*	心	忄 忄' 忄'' 忄曽 憎 憎 憎 14

憎 **D** F-1698

説文 1 旧字 2

1 and 2 comprised 忄 "a heart," and 曾 "layers; to add," used for the sound *zoo*. Together they signified a person who accumulated certain emotions, such as "hatred." The kanji 憎 means "to hate, detest, abhor; hateful." <忄曽>

憎む to hate [にく]む]; 憎しみ hatred, animosity, bad blood [にくしみ]; 憎い・憎らしい detestable, annoying [にく]い, にくらし]い]; 憎まれっ子 naughty boy, unpopular person [にくまれ]っこ]; 生憎 unfortunately, regrettably [あいにく]; 憎悪 hatred [ぞ]うお]; 愛憎 love and hatred [あいぞう]

84d 甚 "exceedingly, very" [from a cooking stove with a pot on top] 勘甚堪

	Meanings	Kun and On	Romaji	Bushu	Stroke Order and Number
SG-1797 勘	to investigate, balance an account; perception, sixth sense	カン	*kan*	力	一 廾 甘 其 甚 甚 勘 11

勘 **C** F-1503

説文

The seal-style form comprised 甚 **SG-1798** "thoroughly, exceedingly," used for the sound *kan*, and 力 **SG-1949** "effort." Together they signified "to thoroughly check against another thing." In Japanese, the form is used to mean "balancing an account" and "intuition." The kanji 勘 means "to investigate, balance an account; perception, sixth sense." <甚力>

勘違い misunderstanding, guessing wrong [かんち]がい]; 勘のいい quick on the uptake, intuitive, perceptive [かんのい]い]; 勘弁する to forgive, pardon [か]んべんする]; 勘ぐる(勘繰る) to suspect, surmise [かんぐ]る]; 勘定 calculation, account [かんじょ]う]; 割り勘にする to share expenses [わりかんにする]

	Meanings	Kun and On	Romaji	Bushu	Stroke Order and Number
SG-1798 甚	exceedingly, very; intense	はなは-だしい ジン	hanaha-dashii *jin*	甘	一 廾 甘 甘 其 甚 9

甚 **D** F-1985

金文 1 説文古文 2 説文 3

1, 2, and 3 depicted a brazier with a pot on top. "Cooking food thoroughly over a fire" gave the meaning "thoroughly" or "excessively." Another view taken from *Setsumon* holds that 匹 **SG-2110** represents a husband and a wife, and that 甚 signified "pleasure between a man and a woman." The kanji 甚 meant "exceedingly, very; intense." <甘匹>

甚だしい extreme, tremendous [はなはだし]い]; 甚だ immensely, exceedingly [はなはだ]; 甚大な tremendous, enormous [じんだいな]; 幸甚に存じます I appreciate it very much (formal correspondence) [こうじんにぞんじま]す]

	Meanings	Kun and On	Romaji	Bushu	Stroke Order and Number
SG-1799 堪	to withstand, bear, tolerate, enjoy	た-える カン	ta-eru *kan*	土	十 ±一 ±廾 堪 堪 堪 12

堪 **D** F-2163

説文

The seal-style form comprised 土 **SG-1126** "soil, ground," and 甚 **SG-1798** "excessive," used for the sounds *kan* or *tan*. Originally, it signified "a large mound of soil" or "a kiln." What was baked in a kiln went through extreme heat, giving the meaning "to endure, bear." The kanji 堪 was also used to mean "to enjoy." The kanji 堪 means "to withstand, bear, tolerate, enjoy." <扌甚>

堪える to suffer, endure [たえ]る]; 堪え難い intolerable, unbearable [たえがた]い]; 堪え忍ぶ to abide, bear, stand [たえしの]ぶ]; 堪忍する to pardon, let someone off [か]んにんする]; 堪忍袋の尾が切れる can no longer put up with [かんにんぶ]くろの・お]がきれる] // 堪え性のない with no perseverance [こらえしょうのな]い]; 堪能な proficient, accomplished [たんのうな]; 堪能する to enjoy to one's content [たんのうする]

84e 鬲 "grain storage" [from a hollow-legged clay pot] 融徹撤隔

	Meanings	Kun and On	Romaji	Bushu	Stroke Order and Number
SG-1800 融	to melt, dissolve	ユウ	*yuu*	虫	戸月鬲鬲融融 16

融 **B** F-0901

説文籀文 1 説文 2

1 and 2 comprised 鬲 "a hollow thick-legged clay vessel for grain storage," and either 虫 **SG-0998** or 蟲 (which was the old form of 虫), used for the sound *yuu* to mean "to come out." Together they signified "steam coming out of a pot" or "something melting coming out." The kanji 融 means "to melt, dissolve." <鬲虫>

融ける to melt [とけ↑る]; 金融業 financial business [きんゆ↑うぎょう]; 金融緩和 monetary relaxation [きんゆうかんわ]; 核融合 nuclear fusion [かくゆ↑うごう]; 融解 melting, thawing [ゆうかい]

	Meanings	Kun and On	Romaji	Bushu	Stroke Order and Number
SG-1801 徹	to do thoroughly, penetrate, stick to	テツ	*tetsu*	彳	彳彳彳彳彳徹徹 15

徹 **C** F-1135

甲骨 1 金文 2 説文古文 3 説文 4

1 and 2 comprised "a clay vessel with thick hollow legs for keeping grain in" (鬲), which was used for the sound *tetsu*, and "a hand." Together they signified "a person finishing placing tripods in a row." In 3 and 4, 彳, bushu *gyooninben* "to carry out," was added to mean "to do things through to the end." In 4, 鬲 was replaced by 育 **SG-0515**, which is viewed by some scholars as a misconstrual. The kanji 徹 means "to do thoroughly, penetrate, stick to." <彳育攵>

徹底的な exhaustive, thorough [てっていてきな]; 貫徹する to carry through, achieve [かんてつする]; 冷徹な cool-headed [れいてつな]; 一徹な obstinate, headstrong [いってつな]

	Meanings	Kun and On	Romaji	Bushu	Stroke Order and Number
SG-1802 撤	to scatter, remove, withdraw	テツ	*tetsu*	手	扌扌扌揹撤撤撤 15

撤 **C** F-1416

No ancient form. The kanji 撤 is closely related to the kanji 徹 **SG-1801**, which originally meant "finishing placing tripods in a row," and was used for the sound *tetsu*. In 撤, 彳 was replaced by 扌 "an act done by hand." The kanji has two contradictory meanings: "to scatter something by hand" and "to remove what was laid out by hand." The kanji 撤 means "to scatter, remove, withdraw." <扌育攵>

撤兵する to withdraw troops from abroad [てっぺいする]; 撤退する to withdraw from activities [てったいする]; (案を)撤回する to withdraw a proposal [(あ↑んを)・てっかいする]; 撤去する to remove, take away [て↑っきょする]; 水撒き watering, sprinkling [みずまき↑, みずま↑き]; 撒き散らす to disperse, scatter [まきちらす, まきちら↑す]

	Meanings	Kun and On	Romaji	Bushu	Stroke Order and Number
SG-1803 隔	to separate, insulate, shield	へだ-てる カク	heda-teru *kaku*	阜	了阝阝阝隔隔隔 13

隔 **C** F-1471

説文

The seal-style form comprised 阝, bushu *kozatohen* "mountains, tall hills," and 鬲, used for the sound *kaku* to mean "to block." "Tall hills blocking an area" signified "to block, separate." The kanji 隔 means "to separate, insulate, shield." <阝鬲>

隔てる to leave a distance, shield, separate [へだて↑る]; 間隔 interval spacing, gap [かんかく]; 隔離する to isolate, quarantine [かくりする]; 隔週 every other week, every two weeks [かくしゅう]

84f 午 [from a pestle] 午許康御唐糖卸・臼

	Meanings	Kun and On	Romaji	Bushu	Stroke Order and Number
SG-1804 午	noon, midday	ゴ	*go*	十	ノ𠂉二午 4

午 **A** F-0337

甲骨文1 1 甲骨文2 2 金文1 3 金文2 4 説文 5

1 through 5 depicted "a pestle" used for pounding grains in a mortar. The straight, vertical motion of a pounding pestle connoted "in the center," and the character was used to mean "the middle of the day, midday." The kanji 午 means "noon, midday." <ノ干> (Note: The original meaning of 午 remains in the non-Joyo kanji 杵 *kine*, "pounder, mallet.")

午前中 in the morning [ごぜんちゅう]; 正午 noon [しょ↑うご]; 午後 afternoon [ご↑ご]; 午睡 nap, siesta [ごすい]

	Meanings	Kun and On	Romaji	Bushu	Stroke Order and Number
SG-1805 許	to permit, allow, forgive; home	ゆる-す キョ	yuru-su *kyo*	言	言言'訁許許 11

許
B
F-0710

金文 1 說文 2

1 and 2 comprised 言 **SG-1364** "word; to speak," and 午 **SG-1804**, which was used for the sound *kyo* to mean "to agree, forgive." Together they signified "to accept what was said." In Japanese, the character is also used to mean "place." The kanji 許 means "to permit, allow, forgive; home." <言午>

許す to permit, allow, forgive [ゆる⌉す]; 許可 permit [きょ⌉か]; 免許 license [め⌉んきょ]; 許容範囲 tolerance level [きょようはˀんい]; 特許 license, concession, patent [と⌉っきょ] // 許嫁 fiancé/fiancée [いいなずけ]; 国許に帰る to return home [くにもとにか⌉える]; 親許 one's parental roof [おやもと]

	Meanings	Kun and On	Romaji	Bushu	Stroke Order and Number
SG-1806 康	peaceful and healthy	コウ	*koo*	广	亠广户户庐康康 11

康
B
F-0782

甲骨文 1 金文 2 說文 3

1, 2, and 3 depicted a scene in which "a pair of hands" was "threshing grain using a pestle." Threshing rice to provide food gave the meaning of "good livelihood and health," and it also ensured "a peaceful life." The kanji 康 means "peaceful and healthy." <广隶>

健康 health [けんこう]; 健康的な healthy [けんこうてきな]; 小康を保つ to have a brief respite [しょうこうをたもˀつ]; 健康診断 physical checkup [けんこうしˀんだん]; 康熙字典 the Kangxi Dictionary (1716) [こうきじ⌉てん]

	Meanings	Kun and On	Romaji	Bushu	Stroke Order and Number
SG-1807 御	to control, manipulate; honorific affix, carriage driver	おん・(お) ギョ・ゴ	on, (o) *gyo, go*	彳	彳彳彳彳彳徉御御 12

御
B
F-0813

甲骨文1 1 甲骨文2 2 金文1 3 金文2 4 說文古文 5 說文 6

1, 2, 3, and 4 depicted "a person kneeling" in front of "a pestle," signifying "to handle, control." In 4, "a crossroads" with "a footprint," for "moving forward," was added in the center. Together they signified "a person steering a horse carriage to move forward." 5 depicted "a hand steering a horse." In 6, "pestle" (午) and "footprint" (止 **SG-0200**) coalesced to form the center component. Kneeling (卩) was a humble posture, which resulted in the character being used as an honorific affix. The kanji 御 means "to control, manipulate; honorific affix, carriage driver." <彳卸(缶卩)>

御中 "To:" in written address to an organization (honorific) [おˀんちゅう]; 御者 driver of a horse carriage [ぎょ⌉しゃ]; 制御 a control [せ⌉いぎょ]; 御所 emperor's residence [ご⌉しょ]; 親御さん (someone's) parents [おやごさん]; 御殿 palace [ご⌉てん]; // 御守り amulet, good luck charm [おまもり]; 御心 the heart (of the Lord) [みこころ]

	Meanings	Kun and On	Romaji	Bushu	Stroke Order and Number
SG-1808 唐	Tang dynasty; Chinese, foreign, sudden	から トウ	kara *too*	口	亠广户户声唐 10

唐
C
F-1370

甲骨文1 1 甲骨文2 2 金文 3 說文古文 4 說文 5

1, 2, 3, and 5 comprised "a pair of hands holding a pestle for threshing grain" (庚), which was used for the sound *too*, and 口 "a receptacle." One view explains that from the phonetic feature *tan*, the kanji 唐 came to mean "to exaggerate, boast." The kanji was used for the name of the Tang dynasty, perhaps intended to mean "a large country." During the period of the Tang dynasty (618-907), the Japanese court sent official cultural delegation to China, resulting in the import of various Chinese cultural aspects, and the character coming to mean "Chinese" in Japanese use. The kanji 唐 means "Tang dynasty; Chinese, foreign, sudden." <广𦘒>

唐揚げ deep-fried seasoned food [からあげ]; 唐草模様 intertwined foliage with an arabesque pattern[からくさも⌉よう]; 唐門 (Chinese-style) large gabled gate of a temple [からもん]; 遣唐使 official cultural envoy to the Tang court [けんと⌉うし]; 唐突に abruptly [とうとつに]; 唐辛子 red hot pepper [とうが⌉らし]

	Meanings	Kun and On	Romaji	Bushu	Stroke Order and Number
SG-1809 糖	sugar	トウ	*too*	米	⺍米'粁粐粯糖糖 16

糖
C
F-1358

篆文 1 說文 2

1 comprised 米 **SG-0738** "rice," and 唐, which was used for the sound *too* to mean "to stretch," referring to the making of candies from steamed sweet rice. 2 comprised 食 **SG-1781** "food; to eat," and 易, which was used for the sound *too* to mean "sugar, candy." The kanji 糖 means "sugar." <米唐>

砂糖・お砂糖 sugar [さと⌉う, おさとう]; 糖分 sugar content [と⌉うぶん]; 糖質オフ sugar reduction [とうしつオ⌉フ]; 糖尿病 diabetes [とうにょうびょう]; 砂糖黍 sugar cane [さと⌉うきび]

	Meanings	Kun and On	Romaji	Bushu	Stroke Order and Number
SG-1810 卸	wholesale	おろ-す・おろし	oro-su, oroshi	卩	卸 9

卸 **C** F-1489

金文 1 說文 2

1 was the same as 3 in 御 **SG-1807**, in which 午 **SG-1804** "pestle" and 卩 "a kneeling person" signified "to handle or control something." In 2, "footprint; to stop" (止 **SG-0200**) was added. Together these components meant "stopping (a horse) to unload a crate from a carriage." Unloading a crateful of goods brought the meaning "wholesale." The kanji 卸 means "wholesale." <⿱午止卩>

棚卸し stock taking, inventorying [たなおろし]; 卸売り wholesale, wholesaling [おろしうり]; 卸値 wholesale price [おろしね]; 卸し金 grater [おろしがね]

臼 "mortar"

	Meanings	Kun and On	Romaji	Bushu	Stroke Order and Number
SG-1811 臼	mortar, molar shape	うす キュウ	usu *kyuu*	臼	臼 6

臼 **D** F-1973

中山王器 1 說文 2

1 and 2 depicted "a mortar containing rice grains about to be pounded." The kanji 臼 means "mortar, molar shape." <臼>

臼 mortar [うす]; 臼と杵 mortar and pestle [うすときね]; 石臼 stone mortar [いしうす]; 臼歯 molar [きゅうし]; 脱臼 dislocation, luxation [だっきゅう]

85 Fermentation

85a 酉 "alcohol beverage, cask, wine"; bushu *sakezukuri*

酒配酔酷酵酬醜酎酌醒

	Meanings	Kun and On	Romaji	Bushu	Stroke Order and Number
SG-1812 酒	alcoholic beverage, liquor, rice wine, fermented drink	さけ・さか シュ	sake, saka *shu*	酉	酒 10

酒 **A** F-0488

甲骨文 1 金文 1 2 金文 2 3 金文 3 4 說文 5

1 showed "a cask for liquor or rice wine" between two wavy lines that depicted "people by the cask," or signified "liquid." In 2, 3, and 4, the "cask" was standing alone, and the small dots in 3 indicated that the inside was full. In 5, "liquid" (氵) was added to the cask (酉 for the sound *shu*, from *yuu*), emphasizing the liquid left after lees or sediments had been removed. The kanji 酒 means "alcoholic beverage, liquor, rice wine, fermented drink." <氵酉>

酒 Japanese rice wine, *sake*, alcoholic beverage [さけ]; 酒粕 *sake* lees [さけかす]; 寝酒 nightcap [ねざけ]; 甘酒 sweet *sake* lee drink [あまざけ]; 酒屋 liquor store, alcoholic beverage shop [さかや]; 酒盛り drinking party, drinking bout [さかもり]; 日本酒 Japanese rice wine [にほんしゅ]; 葡萄酒 grape wine [ぶどうしゅ]

	Meanings	Kun and On	Romaji	Bushu	Stroke Order and Number
SG-1813 配	to distribute, hand out, arrange	くば-る ハイ	kuba-ru *hai*	酉	配 10

配 **A** F-0451

甲骨文 1 金文 1 2 金文 2 3 說文 4

1 through 4 comprised "liquor or wine, cask" (酉) and "a person squatting (己 **SG-0420**) by the cask." A person sat by a cask so that wine or liquor could be handed to him, and thus the character signified "to hand out, deal." The kanji 配 means "to distribute, hand out, arrange." <酉己>

配る to deliver, deal, hand out [くばる]; 気配り careful attention [きくばり]; 配達 home delivery of goods [はいたつ]; 配分する to allocate, distribute [はいぶんする]; 手配する to arrange, provide for [てはいする]; 配当金 dividend [はいとうきん]; 配送先 delivery address [はいそうさき]; 心配 worry, anxiety, concern [しんぱい]

	Meanings	Kun and On	Romaji	Bushu	Stroke Order and Number
SG-1814 酔	to become drunk, get inebriated	よ-う スイ	yoo *sui*	酉	酔 11

酔 **C** F-1494

說文 1 旧字 2

1 comprised 酉 "liquor or wine, cask," and 卒 **SG-1671**, which was used for the sound *sui* to mean "to end." Together they signified "to become drunk by

酔う to become drunk, become intoxicated [よう]; 船酔い seasickness [ふなよい]; 酔っ払い a drunken person, a drunk [よっぱらい]; 二日酔い hangover [ふつかよい]; ほろ酔い mellow, slightly tipsy [ほろよい];

	drinking all the liquor or wine." The right side of the kyuji, 卒, was replaced by 卆 in the shinji. The kanji 酔 means "to become drunk, get inebriated." <酉卆>	心酔する to adore, be fascinated by [しんすいする]; 酔狂な eccentric, whimsical [す˥いきょうな]; 麻酔 anesthesia [ますい]

	Meanings	Kun and On	Romaji	Bushu	Stroke Order and Number
SG-1815 酷	intense, cruel, harsh, full-flavored	コク	*koku*	酉	丆 襾 酉⺈ 酉牛 酉生 酷 14

酷 **D** F-1747	說文 The seal-style form comprised 酉 "liquor or wine, cask," and 告 **SG-0033**, used for the sound *koku.* Together they signified "an intense taste of alcohol." The kanji 酷 means "intense, cruel, harsh, full-flavored." <酉告>	残酷な cruel, extremely harsh [ざんこくな]; 酷暑 severe summer heat [こ˥くしょ]; 酷使する to drive someone/something to work hard [こ˥くしする, こくしする]; 酷のある full-bodied, robust [こくのあ˥る]

	Meanings	Kun and On	Romaji	Bushu	Stroke Order and Number
SG-1816 酵	fermentation, yeast	コウ	*koo*	酉	丆 襾 酉土 酉耂 酉孝 酵 14

酵 **D** F-1847	No ancient form. The kanji 酵 comprised 酉 "liquor or rice wine," and 孝 **SG-0563**, used for the sound *koo*. One view explains that 耂, bushu *oigashira* "old," suggested a long period of fermentation, and that *koo* suggested 交 **SG-0478** "to mix." Together these components signified a yeast and grain mixture that was fermented to make food or drink. The kanji 酵 means "fermentation, yeast." <酉孝>	発酵する to ferment [はっこうする]; 酵母 yeast [こ˥うぼ]; 酵素 enzyme [こ˥うそ]

	Meanings	Kun and On	Romaji	Bushu	Stroke Order and Number
SG-1817 酬	to reply; reward, fee	シュウ	*shuu*	酉	丆 襾 酉 酉丿 酉川 酬 13

酬 **D** F-1857	說文 1, 說文或体 2 — 1 and 2 comprised 酉 "liquor or wine, cask," and 壽 (the kyuji for 寿 **SG-0564**), used for the sound *shuu*, together signifying "to offer a drink of liquor or wine to a guest." Later the character came to mean "to reply; reward." In 2, 壽 was replaced by 州 **SG-1105**, for the same sound, *shuu*. The kanji 酬 is also used for "fee." <酉州>	応酬する to make a sharp retort, reply [おうしゅうする]; 報酬 reward, fee [ほうしゅう]

	Meanings	Kun and On	Romaji	Bushu	Stroke Order and Number
SG-1818 醜	ugly, mean-spirited, shameful	みにく-い シュウ	miniku-i *shuu*	酉	丆 襾 酉⺊ 酉白 酉由 醜 醜 17

醜 **D** F-2008	說文 The seal-style form comprised 酉 "liquor or wine, cask," used for the sound *shuu*, and 鬼 **SG-0350** "a ghost, spirit of a deceased person with an extraordinarily frightening face." Together they meant "ugly, shameful." The kanji 醜 means "ugly, mean-spirited, shameful." <酉鬼>	醜い ugly, shameful [みにく˥い]; 醜聞 scandal, malicious gossip [しゅうぶん]; 醜悪な unsightly [しゅうあくな]

	Meanings	Kun and On	Romaji	Bushu	Stroke Order and Number
SG-1819 酎	a strong, flavorful rice wine	チュウ	*chuu*	酉	丆 襾 酉一 酉寸 酎 10

酎 **D** F-2093	篆文 The seal-style form comprised 酉 "liquor or rice wine, cask," and 寸 **SG-0112** "a hand," used for the sound *chuu* (from 丑 or 肘). Together they signified "a strong, flavorful rice wine that was triple-filtered." In Japanese, the character is used for 焼酎 "*shoochu,* white liquor." The kanji 酎 means "a strong, flavorful rice wine." <酉寸>	焼酎 white liquor, Japanese distilled liquor made of potato, rice, etc. [しょうちゅ˥う]

	Meanings	Kun and On	Romaji	Bushu	Stroke Order and Number
SG-1820 酌	to serve wine, scoop out *sake*, gather a sense of; consideration	く-む シャク	ku-mu *shaku*	酉	丆 襾 酉ノ 酉勹 酌 10

酌 **D** F-2174	金文 1, 說文 2 — 1 and 2 comprised 酉 "liquor or rice wine," and 勺 "a ladle scooping something up," used for the sound *shaku*. Together they meant "a ladle scooping up wine." By analogy to scooping something up, it also came to mean "to gather sense of something, take into consideration; consideration." The kanji 酌 means "to serve wine, scoop out *sake*, gather a sense of; consideration" <酉勺>	酌む to draw water, scoop up [くむ]; 酒を酌む to have a drink (together) [さけをくむ]; 事情を酌む to consider circumstances [じじょうをくむ]; お酌する to pour *sake*, fill someone's cup with *sake* [おしゃくする]; 酌量 consideration, pardon [しゃくりょう]

SG-1821 醒	Meanings	Kun and On	Romaji	Bushu	Stroke Order and Number
	to awaken, have clear awareness	セイ	*see*	酉	16

醒 **D** F-2407

說文

The seal-style form comprised 酉 "liquor or rice wine," and 星 **SG-0692** "star, constellation," used for the sound *see*. Together they signified "to sober up after being drunk and see as clearly as stars in the sky," or "to awaken, have clear awareness." The kanji 醒 means "to awaken, have clear awareness." <酉星>

覚醒剤 stimulant drug [かくせいざい] // 醒める to become awake, sober up [さめる]; 興醒め kill-joy, wet blanket [きょうざめ]; 酔いを醒ます to make oneself sober [よいをさます]

85b 酋 "revered" [from alcohol vapors rising from a cask] 尊猶爵遵

SG-1822 尊	Meanings	Kun and On	Romaji	Bushu	Stroke Order and Number
	to revere, respect	たっと-い・とうと-い ソン	tatto-i, tooto-i *son*	寸	12

尊 **B** F-1014

甲骨文 1 金文1 2 金文2 3 說文 4

1 and 3 depicted "a liquor or wine cask with a lid (酉) being presented reverentially with both hands." The character meant "to revere, respect." In 2 and 4, a ハ shape above the cask signified "rising alcoholic vapors" (酋), which adds the meaning of "raising or rising high." The two hands was replaced by 寸, another shape for "hand," in the kanji. The kanji 尊 means "to revere, respect." <酋寸>

尊い precious, inestimable, noble [とうとい, たっとい]; 尊ぶ to respect, honor, value [とうとぶ, たっとぶ]; 尊敬する to respect [そんけいする]; 自尊心 self-esteem [じそんしん]; 本尊 principal image on a Buddhist altar [ほんぞん]

SG-1823 猶	Meanings	Kun and On	Romaji	Bushu	Stroke Order and Number
	to hesitate, take time; furthermore	ユウ	*yuu*	犬	12

猶 **D** F-1959

甲骨文 1 金文1 2 金文2 3 說文 4

1, 2, 3, and 4 comprised "a liquor or wine cask" with alcoholic vapors rising (酉, 酋), which was used for the sound *yuu*, and "an animal" or "a (suspicious) monkey" (犭, bushu *kemonhen*). Views vary regarding how the character came to mean "to hesitate, take time," or "furthermore." The kanji 猶 means "to hesitate, take time; furthermore." <犭酋>

猶予期間 grace period [ゆうよきかん] // 猶 furthermore [なお]

SG-1824 爵	Meanings	Kun and On	Romaji	Bushu	Stroke Order and Number
	peerage, titular rank	シャク	*shaku*	爪	17

爵 **D** F-2262

甲骨文1 1 甲骨文2 2 金文1 3 金文2 4 金文3 5 說文古文 6 說文 7

1 through 5 depicted "a three-legged pitcher or decanter for heating wine that was used in a religious rite or ceremony." 7 added "a fragrant drink served by hand" at the bottom. A ruler would give a pitcher or decanter (or a cup of wine from it) to a subject as part of a ceremony of conferring honor. The kanji 爵 means "peerage, titular rank." <爫四艮寸>

爵位 title [しゃくい]; 公爵 duke [こうしゃく]; 伯爵 count [はくしゃく]; 男爵 baron [だんしゃく]

SG-1825 遵	Meanings	Kun and On	Romaji	Bushu	Stroke Order and Number
	to observe laws or precedents, obey	ジュン	*jun*	辵	15

遵 **D** F-2276

說文

The seal-style form comprised 辵(辶) "to conduct oneself," and 尊 **SG-1822** "to respect, revere," used for the sound *jun* to mean "to observe." "Conducting oneself with respect for precedents" brought the meaning "to follow, obey." The kanji 遵 means "to observe laws or precedents, obey." <尊辶>

遵守する to comply, observe [じゅんしゅする]; 遵法精神 law-abiding spirit [じゅんぽうせいしん]; 遵法闘争 work-to-rule strike (順法) [じゅんぽうとうそう]

86 Scales, utensils

86a 良 "good, excellent" [from an apparatus for selecting good grain]; *ryoo/roo*

良郎朗浪廊

SG-1826 良	Meanings	Kun and On	Romaji	Bushu	Stroke Order and Number
	good, excellent, true	よ-い リョウ	yo-i *ryoo*	良	ウヨ自良良 7

良 **A** F-0303

甲骨文 1 金文1 2 金文2 3 説文 4

1 through 4 showed an apparatus that divided good grains from scum in three steps: grain is put in the top opening, air is shaken in to remove bad grains and scum, and good grains are taken out at the bottom. The kanji 良 means "good, excellent, true." <良>

良い good [よい]; 仲良し good friend [なかよし]; 良かれ悪しかれ for better or worse [よかれ・あしかれ]; 改良する to improve [かいりょうする]; 不良品 defective product [ふりょうひん]; 優良な excellent, fine [ゆうりょうな]; 良心 conscience [りょうしん]; 良縁 suitable candidate for marriage [りょうえん]

SG-1827 郎	Meanings	Kun and On	Romaji	Bushu	Stroke Order and Number
	man, male	ロウ	*roo*	邑	ウヨ自良良郎 9

郎 **B** F-0574

説文 1 旧字 2

1 and 2 comprised 良 SG-1826 "good," used for the sound *roo,* and 邑 (阝) "town," together originally forming the name of a particular town. One view suggests that 郎 was used to mean "a government official," and later, "a man, male" in general. Another view holds that this was a borrowing. The kanji 郎 means "a man, male." <良 阝>

太郎 first son [たろう]; 一族郎党 one's whole clan [いちぞく・ろうとう]; 馬鹿野郎 Fool! Idiot! (rough male speech) [ばかやろう]

SG-1828 朗	Meanings	Kun and On	Romaji	Bushu	Stroke Order and Number
	cheerful, lively	ほが-らか ロウ	hoga-raka *roo*	月	ウヨ自良朗朗 10

朗 **C** F-1290

説文 1 旧字 2

1 comprised 月 SG-1077 "moon" for "clear bright light," and 良 SG-1826 "good," used for the sound *roo.* Together, "the good, clear, bright light of the moon" gave the meaning "lively, cheerful." The kanji 朗 means "cheerful, lively." <良 月>

朗らかな merry, cheerful [ほがらかな]; 明朗な bright, cheerful [めいろうな]; 朗読する to read aloud (clearly) [ろうどくする]; 明朗な clear and transparent [めいろうな]; 朗報 good news [ろうほう]

SG-1829 浪	Meanings	Kun and On	Romaji	Bushu	Stroke Order and Number
	wave, drift, waste	ロウ	*roo*	水	氵氵氵浪浪浪 10

浪 **C** F-1395

説文

The seal-style form comprised "flowing water" (氵), and 良, used for the sound *roo.* 良 SG-1826, originally an apparatus for shaking grains, had a motion like "waves." Another view holds that it was the name of a specific river, and the character was borrowed to mean "wave." The kanji 浪 means "wave, drift, waste." <氵 良>

波浪注意報 high-waves advisory [はろうちゅういほう]; 浪人する to study for an entrance exam for a year to try again [ろうにんする]; 浪士 lordless samurai [ろうし]; 放浪する to roam, wander about [ほうろうする]; 放浪者 wandering tramp [ほうろうしゃ]

SG-1830 廊	Meanings	Kun and On	Romaji	Bushu	Stroke Order and Number
	corridor, walkway	ロウ	*roo*	广	亠广广庐廊廊 12

廊 **D** F-1776

説文 1 旧字 2

1 and 2 comprised 广 "eaves, an extended area of a house," and 郎 SG-1827 "government official," used for the sound *roo.* One view suggests that the character signified "an area where government officials waited and conducted business." It came to mean an area between two buildings or rooms. The kanji 廊 means "corridor, walkway." <广 郎>

廊下 hallway, space between rooms inside a house [ろうか]; 回廊 veranda, corridor [かいろう]

86b 斗 "measured amount" [from a scoop for measuring grain] 料科斜斗

	Meanings	Kun and On	Romaji	Bushu	Stroke Order and Number
SG-1831 料	food, fee, provisions	リョウ	*ryoo*	斗	丷半米米'米ニ料 10

料 **A** F-0273

金文 1 説文 2

1 and 2 comprised "rice" (米 **SG-0738**) and "a measuring ladle" (斗 **SG-1834**), together signifying "a measured amount of food." An official charged a measured amount as a fee. The kanji 料 means "food, fee, provisions." <米斗>

料金 fee, charge, fair [りょうきん]; 手数料 handling fee [てすうりょう]; 入場料 admission fee [にゅうじょうりょう]; 無料 free of charge [むりょう]; 送料 shipping fee, postage [そうりょう, そうりょう]; 有料 charge, fee [ゆうりょう]; 料理屋 restaurant [りょうりや]; 食料品 foodstuffs, groceries [しょくりょうひん]

	Meanings	Kun and On	Romaji	Bushu	Stroke Order and Number
SG-1832 科	section, department, charge, penalty, conviction	カ	*ka*	禾	二千禾禾'禾ニ科 9

科 **A** F-0338

説文

The seal-style form comprised "a rice plant with the crop, grain" (禾, bushu *nogihen*) and "a measuring ladle" (斗). Various types of grains were sorted out using a measuring ladle and then classified. From that, the character meant "classification, section, department." Authorities measured an appropriate amount for a fee or penalty, so it also meant "to charge a penalty; conviction." The kanji 科 means "section, department, charge, penalty, conviction." <禾斗>

科する to impose a penalty [かする]; 科学 science [かがく]; 科学者 scientist [かがくしゃ]; 科目 subject [かもく]; 前科 criminal records [ぜんか]; 教科書 textbook [きょうかしょ]; 百科事典 encyclopedia [ひゃっかじてん]; 別科 special course [べっか]

	Meanings	Kun and On	Romaji	Bushu	Stroke Order and Number
SG-1833 斜	diagonal, slanted	なな-め シャ	nana-me *sha*	斗	厶 辛 余 余' 余ニ 斜 11

斜 **C** F-1468

説文

The seal-style form comprised 余 **SG-1386**, used for the sound *sha*, and 斗 **SG-1834** "ladle." When one scooped liquid or grain, the ladle was held diagonally. The kanji 斜 means "diagonal, slanted." <余斗>

斜め diagonal, slanted [ななめ]; 斜め向かい diagonally across from [ななめむかい]; 斜線 oblique line [しゃせん]; 傾斜する to incline [けいしゃする]; 斜面 slope [しゃめん]; 斜陽産業 declining industry [しゃようさんぎょう]

	Meanings	Kun and On	Romaji	Bushu	Stroke Order and Number
SG-1834 斗	ladle, dipper, *to* (old unit of liquid measurement)	ト	*to*	斗	` ミ ミ- 斗 4

斗 **D** F-1779

金文 1 説文 2

1 and 2 depicted a ladle with a handle for scooping liquid or grain and had the sound *to*. It was used to represent a unit of volume equivalent to 18 liters. The kanji 斗 means "ladle, dipper, *to* (old unit of liquid measurement)." <斗>

斗 old unit of measurement equivalent to 18 liters [と]; 北斗七星 the Great Bear, Big Dipper [ほくとしちせい]; 漏斗 funnel [ろうと]

86c 升 "to lift, rise" [from lifting a measuring cup filled with grain]; *shoo* 昇升

	Meanings	Kun and On	Romaji	Bushu	Stroke Order and Number
SG-1835 昇	to rise, ascend	のぼ-る ショウ	nobo-ru *shoo*	日	口日旦昇昇 8

昇 **B** F-0906

篆文

The seal-style form comprised 日 "sun," and 升 **SG-1836**, which was used for the sound *shoo* to mean "to rise." The kanji 昇 means "to rise, ascend." <日ノ廾>

昇る to rise, ascend [のぼる]; 上昇する to soar, rise [じょうしょうする]; 昇華する to sublimate [しょうかする]; 昇天 ascension, death [しょうてん]; 昇進 promotion, move up [しょうしん]; 昇降口 entrance, hatch [しょうこうぐち]

	Meanings	Kun and On	Romaji	Bushu	Stroke Order and Number
SG-1836 升	dipper, *shoo* (old unit of liquid measurement)	ます ショウ	masu *shoo*	十	ノ 二 チ 升 4

升 **D** F-2041

甲骨文1 1 甲骨文2 2 金文 3 説文 4

The origin of 升 was very similar to that of 斗 **SG-1834**. In 1, 2, and 3, the dots signified grains or liquid that a measuring ladle was scooping up. The three diagonal lines in 4 were simplified to just one line in the kanji. The kanji 升 means "dipper, *shoo* (old unit of liquid measurement)." 一升 is 1.8 liters, one tenth of 一斗, and ten times 一合. <ノ廾>

升 square wooden measuring cup [ます]; 升席 box seat, private seating section [ますせき]; 一升 1.8 liters [いっしょう]; 一升瓶 a bottle of one *shoo*, 1.8-liter bottle [いっしょうびん]

86d 复 "to repeat, return" [from a measuring apparatus for grain that flipped repeatedly, and a backward foot — a return]; *huku* 復複腹履覆・襾

	Meanings	Kun and On	Romaji	Bushu	Stroke Order and Number
SG-1837 復	to repeat, return; again	フク	*huku*	彳	彳彳' 彳'' 彳'' 復復 12

復 **B** F-0601

甲骨文 1 金文1 2 金文2 3 説文 4

The top (right) component of 1, 2, 3, and 4 depicted an apparatus with an identical shape on either end (in 1), or an urn and an inverted urn (2, 3, and 4), which flipped up and down repeatedly while measuring grain. It was used for the sound *huku* to mean "to repeat." "A downward or backward footprint" (夂) underneath the apparatus also signified "a return." With 彳 "a crossroads" added for "going forward," the character meant "going back and forth; to repeat." The kanji 復 means "to repeat, return; again." <彳复>

反復する to do something over again, iterative [はんぷくする]; 復習 review study, brush-up [ふくしゅう]; 復元する to restore, reconstruct [ふくげんする]; 回復する to recover [かいふくする]; 往復する to go and return [おうふくする]; 復興 reconstruction, recovery [ふっこう]; 復路 return trip [ふくろ]

	Meanings	Kun and On	Romaji	Bushu	Stroke Order and Number
SG-1838 複	to duplicate, copy; layered	フク	*huku*	衣	｀ｧ ｧ ｧ` 衤' 衤'' 複複 14

複 **B** F-0951

篆文

The seal-style form comprised 衣 **SG-1657** "clothing," and 复 "to repeat," used for the sound *huku.* Together they signified double-layered clothing. The connotation extended to the doubling of non-clothing items, and the character meant "to duplicate, copy." In the kanji, the left side became 衤 bushu *koromohen*. The kanji 複 means "to duplicate, copy" and "layered." <衤复>

複製 duplicate, copy [ふくせい]; 複写機 copy machine, photocopier [ふくしゃき]; 複雑な complex [ふくざつな]; 複層 double-layered [ふくそう]; 重複する to duplicate, overlap, double [ちょうふくする]; 複合 complex, multiple [ふくごう]

	Meanings	Kun and On	Romaji	Bushu	Stroke Order and Number
SG-1839 腹	abdomen, stomach, belly, middle	はら フク	hara *huku*	肉	月 月' 月'' 肞 腹腹 13

腹 **B** F-1020

甲骨文 1 金文 2 説文 3

1 and 2 comprised "a measuring apparatus with a thick middle" and "a backward footprint," forming 复, which was used for the sound *huku.* 1 and 2 also had "a person" on the right or top. In 3, "person" was replaced by 月, bushu *nikuzuki* "part of the body." The thick part of the body was the abdomen. The kanji 腹 means "abdomen, stomach, belly, middle." <月复>

腹ぺこ hungry, starving [はらぺこ]; 腹ごしらえする to fortify oneself with a meal before going [はらごしらえする]; 腹いせをする to get back at someone, get one's revenge [はらいせをする]; 空腹 to be hungry [くうふく]; 満腹になる to become full [まんぷくになる]; 切腹 suicide by disembowelment [せっぷく] // お腹 stomach, belly [おなか]

	Meanings	Kun and On	Romaji	Bushu	Stroke Order and Number
SG-1840 履	clogs; to put on footwear, perform, carry out	は-く リ	ha-ku *ri*	尸	ｺ 尸 尸' 屦 履履 15

履 **C** F-1663

金文1 1 金文2 2 説文古文 3 説文 4

The kanji 履 contains 復 **SG-1839**, but had a different origin. 1 comprised "leg, foot" and "a person wearing a formal headdress." 2 and 3 comprised "a boat" for transporting, "a leg," and "a person," together signifying "to walk with clogs on, make steps." Putting on footwear readies one to carry out an action. In 4, 頁 "person wearing formal headdress" was replaced by 尸, bushu *shikabane*, which also had the meaning "person." The kanji 履 means "clogs; to put on footwear, perform, carry out." <尸 復>

履く to wear shoes and clothes (by putting one's feet through) [はく]; 履物 footwear, foot gear [はきもの]; 上履き slippers [うわばき]; 草履 Japanese sandal-style footwear worn with a kimono [ぞうり]; ゴム草履 flip-flops [ゴムぞうり]; 履行する to execute, carry out [りこうする]; 契約の不履行 nonfulfillment of a contract, a breach of agreement [けいやくのふりこう]

	Meanings	Kun and On	Romaji	Bushu	Stroke Order and Number
SG-1841 覆	to cover, overturn, flip over	おお-う・くつがえ-す フク	oo-u, kutsugae-su *huku*	襾	一 襾 覀' 覆 覆覆 18

覆 **C** F-1639

説文

The seal-style form comprised 襾 "a cover on an opening," and 復, used for the sound *huku* to mean "a measuring apparatus that flips over many times." Together they signified "to overturn, cover." In the kanji, the top component became 覀. The kanji 覆 means "to cover, overturn, flip over." <覀復>

覆う to cover, wrap over [おおう]; 日覆い sun shade, sun shield [ひおおい]; 覆す to reverse, turn over, overthrow [くつがえす]; 覆面 a mask to conceal one's face [ふくめん]; 転覆 upset, overturn [てんぷく]

両 "two, double" [from various suggested origins]

	Meanings	Kun and On	Romaji	Bushu	Stroke Order and Number
SG-1842 両	two, double, both, train car, *ryoo* (old unit of currency)	リョウ	*ryoo*	入	一 冂 帀 両 両 両 6

両 **A** F-0291

金文 1 · 金文 2 · 説文 3 · 旧字 4

Different views on the origin of 両 include (a) "a scale," (b) "a gourd split in two with dry seeds inside," and (c) "a yoke to connect two horses." In Japan the character was used for the *ryoo*, a unit of gold currency used before the Meiji era whose value was based on its weight. It is also used as a counter of railway cars (substituting for the non-Joyo kanji 輛 *ryoo*). The kanji 両 means "two, double, both, train car, *ryoo* (old unit of currency)." <両>

両方 both [りょうほう]; 両立する to be compatible with, coexist with [りょうりつする]; 両面 both sides [りょうめん]; 両人 two people, couple [りょうにん]; 十両編成 10-car train [じゅうりょうへんせい]; 両替 currency exchange [りょうがえ]; 百両 a hundred *ryoo* [ひゃくりょう]; 両手 both hands [りょうて]

86e 皿 "shallow vessel, bowl, tray" 皿血温盛塩益盗尽盆蓋

	Meanings	Kun and On	Romaji	Bushu	Stroke Order and Number
SG-1843 皿	flat dish, plate	さら	sara	皿	冂 皿 5

皿 **A** F-1137

甲骨文 1 · 甲骨文 2 · 金文 3 · 説文 4

1 and 2 depicted "a shallow stemmed vessel, plate, dish." In 3, "bronze, metal" 金 **SG-1196** was added. 4 was a stemmed bowl. The kanji 皿 means "flat dish, plate." <皿>

皿 plate [さら]; 目を皿にする to open one's eyes wide [めをさらにする]; 大皿 platter, large dish [おおざら]; 取り皿 individual plate [とりざら]; 受け皿 saucer [うけざら]; 皿洗い dishwashing [さらあらい]; 製氷皿 ice-making tray [せいひょうざら]

	Meanings	Kun and On	Romaji	Bushu	Stroke Order and Number
SG-1844 血	blood	ち ケツ	chi *ketsu*	血	ノ 白 血 血 6

血 **A** F-0443

甲骨文 1 · 甲骨文 2 · 説文 3

1, 2, and 3 depicted "a shallow stemmed vessel that contained blood from a sacrificial animal," used in a religious rite. (Such blood was used for sealing a contract or oath.) The kanji 血 means "blood." <ノ 皿>

血 blood [ち]; 血だらけになる to become covered with blood [ちだらけになる]; 鼻血 nose bleeding [はなぢ]; 血液 blood [けつえき]; 赤血球 red blood cell [せっけっきゅう]; 出血 bleeding, hemorrhage [しゅっけつ]; 血圧 blood pressure [けつあつ]; 血清 blood serum [けっせい]; 血縁関係 blood relative [けつえんかんけい]

	Meanings	Kun and On	Romaji	Bushu	Stroke Order and Number
SG-1845 温	warm, mild, gentle	あたた-かい オン	atata-kai *on*	水	氵 沪 沪 淠 温 12

温 **B** F-0670

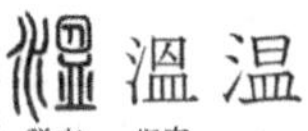

説文 1 · 旧字 2

1 comprised "water" (氵), and "a stemmed vessel with rising steam captured inside the lid," which was used for the sound *on*. Together they signified "warm, mild, gentle." The kanji 温 means "warm, mild, gentle." <氵 日 皿>

温かい warm, mild, genial [あたたかい]; 温める to warm [あたためる]; 温度 temperature [おんど]; 体温計 thermometer (for body temperature) [たいおんけい, たいおんけい]; 気温 air temperature [きおん]; 温和な人 gentle person [おんわなひと]; 温室 greenhouse, conservatory [おんしつ]; 三寒四温 cycle of three cold days and four warm days [さんかんしおん]

	Meanings	Kun and On	Romaji	Bushu	Stroke Order and Number
SG-1846 盛	to flourish, prosper; hearty, vigorous; a heap of	も-る・さか-ん セイ・ジョウ	mo-ru, saka-n *see, joo*	皿	ノ 厂 万 成 成 盛 11

盛 **B** F-0681

甲骨文 1 · 金文 2 · 説文 3

1, 2, and 3 comprised "a stemmed vessel (皿 **SG-1843**) whose contents were spilling over," and "a long-bladed halberd or lance" (成 **SG-1476**), which was used for the sound *see* to mean "heap." "An abundance of offerings" gave the meaning "to thrive, pile up; prosperous." The kanji 盛 means "to flourish, prosper; hearty, vigorous; a heap of." <成皿>

盛る to heap up, stack up [もる]; 盛り上がる to swell, rouse [もりあがる]; 盛り合わせ assortment, sampler [もりあわせ]; 酒盛りをする to have a drinking party, carousing [さかもりをする]; 盛んな prosperous [さかんな]; 育ち盛り child's growth period [そだちざかり]; 男盛り prime of manhood [おとこざかり]; 盛会 lively party, successful meeting [せいかい]; 繁盛する to prosper, do good business [はんじょうする]

	Meanings	Kun and On	Romaji	Bushu	Stroke Order and Number
SG-1847 塩	salt, sodium	しお エン	shio *en*	鹵	一十圹圻坾塩塩 13

塩 **B** F-0788

說文 1, 旧字 2

1 and 2 comprised 臣 "a watchful eye," "a person looking down at salt crystals at a salt farm," and "a stemmed vessel," and had the sound *en* (from *kan*, 監 **SG-0025**). The character signified "salt." 塩 was a variant of the kyuji 鹽 (2), and became the shinji. The kanji 塩 means "salt, sodium." <土 ノ 一 口 皿>

塩 salt [しお]; 塩加減 seasoning with salt [しおかげん]; 塩辛い salty, briny [しおからい]; 塩っぽい salty [しおっぽい]; 塩気 salty taste, a hint of salt [しおけ]; 塩分 salt content, saline matter [えんぶん]; 塩素 chlorine [えんそ]

	Meanings	Kun and On	Romaji	Bushu	Stroke Order and Number
SG-1848 益	gain, profit	エキ・ヤク	*eki, yaku*	皿	丷丷兴兴益益益 10

益 **B** F-0850

甲骨文 1, 金文 2, 說文 3

In 1 and 2, a stemmed vessel was depicted with "drops of overflowing water." Something that was superabundant came to mean "gain; to increase." In 3, the "water" was oriented sideways. The kanji 益 means "gain, profit." <䒑 八 皿>

利益 profit, return, gain [りえき]; 国益 national interest, national prosperity [こくえき]; 公益 public welfare, public interest [こうえき]; 収益 proceeds, earnings [しゅうえき, しゅうえき]; 純益 net profit [じゅんえき]; ご利益 divine favor [ごりやく]

	Meanings	Kun and On	Romaji	Bushu	Stroke Order and Number
SG-1849 盗	to steal	ぬす-む トウ	nusu-mu *too*	皿	冫冫次次盗盗 11

盗 **C** F-1132

金文 1, 說文 2, 旧字 3

The top of 1 and 2 comprised "flowing water," and "a person with their mouth open" (欠 **SG-0431**), signifying "dripping with envy; to covet" (次). At the bottom was "a stemmed vessel" (皿 **SG-1843**). Together they signified that the person wanted something in the bowl so badly that they stole it. The top of the kyuji 盜 (3) had 氵 "water," but in the shinji, it was replaced by 冫, bushu *nisui*. The kanji 盗 means "to steal." <次 皿>

(Note: 次 "a person dripping with envy," containing 氵 "flowing water," appears in the kanji 羨 **SG-0833** "to envy, covet.")

盗む to steal [ぬすむ]; 盗みを働く to commit theft, steal [ぬすみをはたらく]; 盗み食い eating on [ぬすみぐい]; 盗み聞き avesdropping [ぬすみぎき]; 盗賊 thief, burglar [とうぞく]; 強盗 burglar, robber [ごうとう]

	Meanings	Kun and On	Romaji	Bushu	Stroke Order and Number
SG-1850 尽	to exhaust, run out, devote	つ-くす ジン	tsu-kusu *jin*	皿	コ尸尺尽 6

尽 **C** F-1323

甲骨文 1, 中山王器 2, 說文 3, 旧字 4

1, 2, and 3 comprised "a hand holding a twig or a brush" (聿) and "a stemmed vessel" (皿 **SG-1843**), together signifying "to cleanse a bowl completely to empty it." The water in the vessel became droplets (灬) in 4. For the shinji, the totally different kanji 尽 was used. The kanji 尽 means "to exhaust, run out, devote." <尸 ㇏ ⺀>

尽くす to dedicate, exhaust [つくす]; 心尽くしの lovingly prepared [こころづくしの]; 力尽きる to use up all one's strength [ちからつきる]; 計算尽くし full of calculations [けいさんづくし]; 尽力する to try hard (for someone), exert oneself [じんりょくする]; 大尽 rich man [だいじん]

	Meanings	Kun and On	Romaji	Bushu	Stroke Order and Number
SG-1851 盆	tray, flat dish, basin, Bon festival period	ボン	*hon*	皿	八分分岔岔盆 9

盆 **C** F-1557

金文 1, 說文 2

1 and 2 comprised 分 **SG-1397**, used for the sound *bon*, and 皿 "a stemmed vessel," together signifying "a tray or wide-open bowl," or "a concave shape" in general. In Japan, it is also used for the name of the Bon festival, or Buddhist All Souls Days. The kanji 盆 means "tray, flat dish, basin, Bon festival period." <分 皿>

お盆 tray [おぼん], Buddhist event in August when spirits of the dead return [おぼん]; お盆休み holiday taken during Bon festival period [おぼんやすみ]; 盆踊り neighborhood Bon festival dance [ぼんおどり]; 盆地 basin, round valley [ぼんち]

	Meanings	Kun and On	Romaji	Bushu	Stroke Order and Number
SG-1852 蓋	lid; to cover, enwrap; maybe	ふた ガイ	huta *gai*	艸	艹芏芸蓋蓋 13

蓋 **D** F-2338

金文1 1 金文2 2 説文 3

1 had "plants" (艸) at the top, for "thatch." Underneath the plants in 1 and in 2 was "a lid or cover" (去), and "a stemmed vessel" (皿), which was used for the sound *gai* (from *koo*) to mean "to put on a cover." The form was also used to mean "in all likelihood." In 3, 艸 returned to signify "a cover." The kanji 蓋 means "lid; to cover, enwrap; maybe." <艹去皿>

蓋 cover, lid [ふたꜜ]; 鍋蓋 pot lid [なべぶた]; 蓋然性 possibility [がいぜんせい]

86f 是 "this; right" [borrowed from "spoon, ladle"]; *ze/dai/tee* 是題提堤

	Meanings	Kun and On	Romaji	Bushu	Stroke Order and Number
SG-1853 是	this; correct	ゼ	*ze*	日	日旦早早昰是 9

是 **A** F-1158

金文1 1 金文2 2 説文籀文 3 説文 4

The origin of this character is obscure. 1 through 4 are interpreted to have depicted "a ladle or spoon" (the non-Joyo kanji 匙 *saji.*) The character was borrowed to mean "this," with "pointing to the correct thing" leading to the additional meaning "correct." The kanji 是 means "this; correct." <日疋>

是非を問う to question the need to [ぜひをとꜜう]; 是非 by some means or other [ぜꜜひ], right and/or wrong [ぜひ]; 是非もなく unavoidable, inevitable [ぜひもなꜜく]; 是非共 (ぜひとも) by all means [ぜひとも, ぜꜜひとも]; 社是 company motto, guiding precepts of a company [しゃꜜぜ]; 国是 national policy [こくぜ]

	Meanings	Kun and On	Romaji	Bushu	Stroke Order and Number
SG-1854 題	title, topic, theme	ダイ	*dai*	頁	日早昰是題題題 18

題 **A** F-0252

中山王器 1 説文 2

The left side of 1 and 2 was 是 (**SG-1853**), used for the sound *dai* to mean "to put forward." The right side of 2, 頁, signified "an official wearing a formal hat," for the meaning "something at the top." The " title or topic" goes at the beginning or the top of a writing. The kanji 題 means "title, topic, theme." <是頁>

題・題名 title, name [だꜜい, だいめい]; 仮題 tentative title [かだい]; 宿題 homework [しゅくだい]; 出題傾向 trend in exam questions [しゅつだいけꜜいこう]; 本題 main subject [ほんだい]; 無題 untitled [むだい]; 命題 proposition [めいだい]; 問題視する to regard something as questionable [もんだꜜいしする]; 荒れ放題 being left in a state of neglect [あれほꜜうだい]

	Meanings	Kun and On	Romaji	Bushu	Stroke Order and Number
SG-1855 提	to carry, put forward (by hand)	さ-げる テイ	sage-ru *tee*	手	扌扣捍提提 12

提 **B** F-0587

説文

The seal-style form comprised 扌, bushu *tehen* "an act done by hand," and 是 **SG-1853** for the sound *tee*. Together they signified "holding something up by hand to present it." The kanji 提 means "to carry, put forward (by hand)." <扌是>

提げる to carry in hand [さげꜜる]; 手提げ handbag [てさげꜜ]; 提出物 work to be submitted [ていしゅつꜜぶつ]; 問題提起 proposing a question [もんだいていꜜき]; 前提 presupposition, hypothesis [ぜんてい]; 提起する to institute, bring forward [てꜜいきする]; 提供 an offer, a proffer [ていきょう]; 提言 proposal [ていげん]; 提督 admiral, commodore [ていとく]

	Meanings	Kun and On	Romaji	Bushu	Stroke Order and Number
SG-1856 堤	bank, dike	つつみ テイ	tsutsumi *tee*	土	扌扣埕堤堤 12

堤 **C** F-1582

説文

The seal-style form comprised 土 **SG-1126** "soil, ground," and 是 **SG-1853**, used for the sound *tee* to mean "to stagnate." Together they signified "an unmoving pile of dirt, dike, bank." The kanji 堤 means "bank, dike." <土是>

堤 bank, embankment [つつみꜜ]; 堤防 bank, dike, levee [ていぼう]; 防波堤 breakwater, seawall [ぼうはてい]

86g 卓 "to stand out" [from a spoon] 卓悼

	Meanings	Kun and On	Romaji	Bushu	Stroke Order and Number
SG-1857 卓	to stand out; table	タク	*taku*	十	丨⺊占卓 8

卓 **C** F-1368

金文 1 説文古文 2 説文 3

The origin of the kanji 卓 is obscure. One view explains that 1, 2, and 3 comprised ヒ "a spoon" with "a larger spoon." The large spoon stood out, thus signifying "to stand out." Another view explains that the character comprised "a person" and 早 "to lead" (from "pulling ahead, early"), together signifying "a person leading and standing out." It is also used to mean "table." The kanji 卓 means "to stand out; table." <⺊早>

食卓 dining table [しょくたく]; 卓上扇風機 tabletop fan [たくじょうせんぷうき]; 卓越する to excel in, surpass [たくえつする]; 卓見 wisdom, clear-sightedness [たっけん]; 卓球 ping-pong, table tennis [たっきゅう]

	Meanings	Kun and On	Romaji	Bushu	Stroke Order and Number
SG-1858 悼	to grieve, mourn	いた-む トウ	ita-mu *too*	心	丶忄忄⺊悼悼悼 11

悼 **D** F-2131

説文

The seal-style form comprised 忄 "heart," and 卓 **SG-1857**, used for the sound *too* to mean "to be moved." One's heart was shaken when mourning and grieving. The kanji 悼 means "to grieve, mourn." <忄卓>

悼む to grieve, mourn [いたむ]; 追悼文 eulogy [ついとうぶん]; 追悼式 memorial service [ついとうしき]; 哀悼 grief, mourning [あいとう]

86h 卑 "lowly, crude, abject" [from "a spoon" and "a left hand"]; *hi* 卑碑

	Meanings	Kun and On	Romaji	Bushu	Stroke Order and Number
SG-1859 卑	lowly, humble, crude, abject	いや-しい ヒ	iya-shii *hi*	十	白由由身卑卑 9

卑 **D** F-1962

金文1 1 金文2 2 説文 3 旧字 4

1, 2, and 3 comprised "a spoon with a handle" and "a (left) hand." A small spoon (as contrasted to 卓 "a large spoon") may have suggested "lowly." Another view holds that the character depicted a hand holding a tool for flattening the ground, and that such a task signified "lowly." The kanji 卑 means "lowly, humble, crude, abject." <卑>

卑しい crude, vulgar, low [いやしい]; 卑屈な servile, lack of moral courage [ひくつな]; 卑下する to deprecate oneself, have a low opinion of [ひげする]; 卑近な例 familiar example [ひきんなれい]; 卑怯な cowardly, mean [ひきょうな]; 卑劣な nasty, despicable [ひれつな]

	Meanings	Kun and On	Romaji	Bushu	Stroke Order and Number
SG-1860 碑	stone monument, stela	ヒ	*hi*	石	丆石石'矿砷砷碑碑 14

碑 **D** F-1862

説文 1 旧字 2

1 comprised 石 **SG-1148** "rock, stone," and 卑 **SG-1859**, used for the sound *hi* to mean "upright." Together they signified a stone that stood straight up, such as a monument. The kanji 碑 means "stone monument, stela." <石卑>

碑 tombstone, monument [ひ]; 石碑 stone monument [せきひ]; 碑銘 inscription on a monument, epitaph on a tombstone [ひめい]

86i 勺 " to scoop up" [from a ladle] 的釣

	Meanings	Kun and On	Romaji	Bushu	Stroke Order and Number
SG-1861 的	to the point, pertinent, having a characteristic of; target	まと テキ	mato *teki*	白	白白白'的的 8

的 **A** F-0123

篆文

The seal-style form comprised "the sun" (日), and 勺, which was used for the sound *teki* to mean "bright." Together they signified "bright." Something bright stood out and became an accurate target. In the kanji 日 became 白. The kanji 的 means "to the point, pertinent; target." Adding な to 的 at the end of a noun creates an adjective meaning "having the characteristic of (noun)." <白勺>

的 target [まと]; 的を得た pertinent, appropriate [まとをえた]; 日本的な having characteristics of Japanese culture [にほんてき]; 目的 aim, purpose, object [もくてき]; 的確な accurate [てきかくな]; 的中する to hit the target, hit the bull's-eye [てきちゅうする]

	Meanings	Kun and On	Romaji	Bushu	Stroke Order and Number
SG-1862 釣	to fish; lure	つ-る チョウ	tsu-ru *choo*	金	亼牟金金'釣釣 11

釣 **C** F-1392

説文

The seal-style form comprised 金 **SG-1196** "metal," and 勺 "ladle," used for the sound *choo*, together signifying "a fishing hook," for catching a fish and lifting it up. It was also used to mean "lure." The kanji 釣 means "to fish; lure." <金勺>

釣り angling, fishing [つり]; 釣り銭 change (monetary transaction) [つりせん]; お釣り change (monetary transaction) [おつり]; 釣り合い compatibility, equilibrium [つりあい]; 釣る to allure, entice [つる]; 魚釣り fishing [さかなつり]

XII Table, Tool, and Vessel

87 Table, bed

87a 几 "low table, stool" 机処拠

几

SG-1863 机	Meanings	Kun and On	Romaji	Bushu	Stroke Order and Number
	desk, writing table	つくえ キ	tsukue *ki*	木	一十木杉机 6

机 **B** F-1223

几 机 机 (篆文 1, 篆文 2)

In 1, 几 had the sound *ki* and meant "a low table." In 2, "wood" (木) was added. A low, wooden table was "a desk or writing table." The kanji 机 means "desk, writing table." <木几>

机 desk [つくえ]; 文机 low writing table [ふづくえ]; 学習机 desk for a grade school pupil [がくしゅうづくえ]; 机上の空論 impractical theory [きじょうのくうろん]

SG-1864 処	Meanings	Kun and On	Romaji	Bushu	Stroke Order and Number
	place; to handle, deal with	ショ	*sho*	虍	ク夂処処 5

処 **B** F-0723

(金文 1, 金文 2, 説文 3, 説文或体 4, 旧字 5: 處)

1 and 2 depicted "a person wearing a tiger headdress (虍 from 虎 **SG-0883**) for a votive play, sitting on a chair (几) with their legs stretched out (夂) in front of them." The feet were placed sideways, signifying "not moving forward." Staying in place meant "a place," and sitting down to deal with a matter meant "to handle, deal with." In 3, the tiger headdress was dropped, whereas in 4 and 5, it returned to enclose 夂 and 几. The shinji reflects 3. The kanji 処 means "place; to handle, deal with." <夂几>

処理 to process, handle [しょり]; 処する to deal, manage, punish [しょする]; 処分する to dispose of, punish [しょぶんする]; 対処する to deal with, handle [たいしょする]; 処世 conduct of life [しょせい]; 処刑 to execute, put to death [しょけい] // 処 place [ところ]

SG-1865 拠	Meanings	Kun and On	Romaji	Bushu	Stroke Order and Number
	to be based in, rely on; basis	キョ・コ	*kyo, ko*	手	扌扌扎扨拠拠 8

拠 **C** F-1216

(説文 1, 旧字 2: 據)

1 comprised 扌, bushu *tehen* "an act done by hand," and 豦, which was used for the sound *kyo* to mean "a place to settle down." The place where one settles down and stays becomes their "base." The right side of the kyuji (2) was replaced by 処. The kanji 拠 means "to be based in, rely on; basis." <扌処>

拠点とする to be based in [きょてんとする]; 根拠 basis, grounding, reason [こんきょ]; 拠出する to contribute, donate [きょしゅつする]; 典拠 authority, reliable source [てんきょ]; 証拠 evidence [しょうこ] // 拠る to be caused by, based on [よる]; ～を拠り所とする to rely on, make as its base [～を・よりどころとする]

87b 其 "that" [borrowed from a square-shaped winnowing basket on a table]; *ki/gi* 基期欺棋碁

其

SG-1866 基	Meanings	Kun and On	Romaji	Bushu	Stroke Order and Number
	basis, base, foundation	もと・もとい キ	moto, motoi *ki*	土	一廾甘其基基 11

基 **A** F-0319

(金文 1, 説文 2)

In 1 and 2, the top component was a winnowing apparatus (其), which had the sound *ki*, and whose square shape suggested the meaning "foundation." With "soil, ground" (土 **SG-1126**) added, the kanji 基 means "basis, base, foundation." <其土>

基 base, foundation [もと・もとい]; 基本 base, foundation, basis [きほん]; 基礎 base, pedestal, groundwork [きそ]; 基盤 base, foundation [きばん]; 基準 criterion, standard, reference [きじゅん]; 基金 fund, monetary fund [ききん]; 基地 base, military base [きち]

	Meanings	*Kun* and *On*	Romaji	Bushu	Stroke Order and Number
SG-1867 期	specific time, period, cycle of time; to expect	キ・ゴ	*ki, go*	月	一廾甘其期期 12

期 **A** F-0209

期 金文 1 説文古文 2 説文 3

1 comprised "the sun," and 其 for the sound *ki* to mean "a cycle." The movement of the sun signified "a specific time or period." 2 showed "the sun" under a table. In 3, the sun was replaced by "the moon" 月 **SG-1077**, whose waxing and waning gave the meaning "a cycle of time." Anticipating something that happens at a set time gave the meaning "to expect." The kanji 期 means "specific time, period, cycle of time; to expect." <其月>

期日 term, due date [きꜜじつ]; 期間 duration, period [きꜜかん]; 任期 term of service, term of office [にꜜんき]; 予期する to anticipate, expect [よꜜきする]; 末期 end stage, advanced stage of illness [まꜜっき], hour of death, end of one's life [まꜜつご]; 画期的な epoch-making breakthrough [かっきてきな]; 万全を期す to make absolutely sure [ばんぜんをきꜜす]; 延期する to postpone [えんきする]

	Meanings	*Kun* and *On*	Romaji	Bushu	Stroke Order and Number
SG-1868 欺	to deceive; trick	あざむ-く ギ	azamu-ku *gi*	欠	一廾甘其其欺 12

欺 **D** F-1818

欺 説文

One view holds that the kanji 欺 is closely related to the non-Joyo kanji 倛, which means "a large square mask (其) that a person (亻) wore to drive off evils," and also gave the meaning "to deceive by wearing such a mask." In 欺 it was used for the sound /gi/, and together with 欠 "a person with their mouth open" it signified "someone wearing a large frightening square mask astounds another person and deceives them." Another view holds that the meaning of "to deceive" was a borrowing. The kanji 欺 means "to deceive, trick." <其欠>

欺く to deceive, cheat [あざむꜜく]; 詐欺 fraud, swindle [さꜜぎ]; 欺瞞 deception [ぎまん]

	Meanings	*Kun* and *On*	Romaji	Bushu	Stroke Order and Number
SG-1869 棋	the game of *shogi*, oriental chess	キ (ギ)	*Ki* (*gi*)	木	木木一村桓棋棋 12

棋 **D** F-1937

篆文 1 旧字 2

1 and 2 comprised 其, which was used for the sound *ki* to mean "a square shape," and 木 "wood." Together they signified "a square wooden checkerboard." With 木 moved to the left side, the kanji 棋 means the Japanese games of *shogi* and *go*. <木其>

将棋 Japanese chess [しょうぎ]; 棋士 *shogi* player [きꜜし]; 将棋倒し falling down one upon another [しょうぎだꜜおし]

	Meanings	*Kun* and *On*	Romaji	Bushu	Stroke Order and Number
SG-1870 碁	*go*, the game of *igo*	ゴ	*go*	石	一廾甘其其碁 13

碁 **D** F-1918

No ancient form. The kanji comprises 其 "a square shape," used for *go*, and 石 **SG-1148** "stone." A game that used a square board and small stones was *go*. The kanji 碁 means "*go*, the game of *igo*." <其石>

囲碁・碁 game of *go* [いꜜご, ごꜜ]; 碁盤 *go* board, checkerboard [ごばん]; 碁石 small round black or white stones used to play *go* [ごいし]

87c 丙 [from a table with sturdy legs]; *hee* 商柄丙

	Meanings	*Kun* and *On*	Romaji	Bushu	Stroke Order and Number
SG-1871 商	trade, commerce	あきな-う ショウ	akina-u *shoo*	一	' 亠 产 产 商 商 11

商 **A** F-0406

商 甲骨文1 1 甲骨文2 2 金文1 3 金文2 4 説文 5

1 and 2 depicted "a tattooing needle" placed on "a table with fortified legs." In 3, 4, and 5, 口 "a mouth" or "a box of benedictions" was added. One view explains that a person of authority who could tattoo a criminal could also inquire about the will of a deity, and that the character signified "to inquire." In commerce, two parties might inquire about each other's will in negotiations, and thus the form also meant "commerce." Another view takes the top of 1 through 5 to be a noble person's headdress. A place where such noble people lived was the city of 商 Shang, capital of the Ying dynasty (殷) (also known as the Shang dynasty). After the demise of the Ying, their people became traveling merchants, whence the meaning "trade, commerce." The kanji 商 means "trade, commerce." <产台>

商い business, trade, dealing [あきꜜない, あきなꜜい]; 商品 [しょꜜうひん]; 商売 business, trade, transaction [しょꜜうばい]; 商談 business negotiation [しょうだん]; 商才 business acumen [しょうさい]; 年商 annual turnover, annual business volume [ねんしょう]

	Meanings	Kun and On	Romaji	Bushu	Stroke Order and Number
SG-1872 柄	handle, pattern, demeanor, character	がら・え ヘイ	gara-e *hee*	木	十木 朾 柄 柄 9

柄 **B** F-1056

甲骨文 1, 説文 2, 説文或体 3, 4

1 and 2 comprised "wood" (木) and "a sturdy table" (丙 **SG-1873**), used for the sound *hee*. Together they signified "a long wooden stick" that was used to manipulate a thing or a person, thus originally signifying "power" and "social standing." The kanji (4), based on 3, was used as an alternative for the kanji 柄. In Japanese, the kanji is used to mean "one's demeanor, personal character, pattern." The kanji 柄 means "handle, pattern, demeanor, character." <木一内>

柄 pattern [がら], handle [え]; 大柄な a person with a large build, a large pattern [おおがらな]; 人柄 a person's character, disposition [ひとがら]; 家柄 social standing of a family, good family [いえがら]; 柄の悪い vulgar [がらのわるい]; 取り柄がある to have merit, good point [とりえがある]; 横柄な arrogant, disdainful [おうへいな]

	Meanings	Kun and On	Romaji	Bushu	Stroke Order and Number
SG-1873 丙	third-class, poor grade	ヘイ	*hee*	一	一 冂 丙 丙 5

丙 **D** F-2244

甲骨文 1, 金文1 2, 金文2 3, 金文3 4, 説文 5

1 through 4 depicted "a sturdy table with diagonal supports" or "a pedestal to place something on," and had the sound *hee*. In 5, an additional line emphasized that it was a place on which to put something. The character was borrowed to mean a particular time in the Chinese calendar. In Japanese 丙 was used to denote the lowest grade in the traditional ranking system 甲乙丙, "top, medium, and low." The kanji 丙 means "third-class, poor grade." <丙(一内)>

丙種 C-grade, third grade [へいしゅ]; 甲乙丙 three ranks, grades of A, B, and C [こうおつ・へい]

87d 更 "furthermore" [from placing one table on top of another]; *koo* 更便硬梗

	Meanings	Kun and On	Romaji	Bushu	Stroke Order and Number
SG-1874 更	to repeat, change, grow late; again; further	さら・ふ-ける コウ	sara, hu-keru *koo*	日	一 冂 日 更 更 7

更 **B** F-0979

甲骨文 1, 金文1 2, 金文2 3, 説文 4

1 and 4 comprised "a table," for the sound *koo*, and "a hand holding a stick." Together they meant "to hit, cause." In 2 and 3, double tables with 攴 signified "to repeat" or "to replace (one with another)." With the components coalesced into one shape, the kanji 更 means "to repeat, change, grow late; again; further." <更(一日乂)>

更に in addition to, furthermore [さらに]; 今更 at this late time, afresh [いまさら]; 更ける to grow late, (time) advances [ふける]; 夜更け deep in the night, late at night [よふけ]; 更衣室 changing room, dressing room [こういしつ]; 更新する to renew [こうしんする]; 更生 rehabilitation, regeneration [こうせい]

	Meanings	Kun and On	Romaji	Bushu	Stroke Order and Number
SG-1875 便	convenient; service, bowel movement	たよ-り ベン・ビン	tayo-ri *ben, bin*	人	亻 仁 佰 便 便 9

便 **B** F-0638

説文

The seal-style form comprised 亻 "an act that one does," and 更 "to change, repeat." A person changing something to make it better gave the meaning "convenient; service." It also meant something that happened regularly and repeatedly, such as "a service" or "a bowel movement." The kanji 便 means "convenient; service, bowel movement." <亻更>

便り letter [たより]; 便利な convenient, handy [べんりな]; バスの便がいい to have good bus service [バスのべんがいい]; 小便 urine [しょうべん]; 大便 excrement [だいべん]; 便名 flight number [びんめい]; 航空便 airmail [こうくうびん]; 空の便 flight [そらのびん]; 郵便ポスト (public) mailbox [ゆうびんぽすと]

	Meanings	Kun and On	Romaji	Bushu	Stroke Order and Number
SG-1876 硬	hard, stiff, rigid	かた-い コウ	kata-i *koo*	石	丆 石 石 硕 硬 硬 12

硬 **C** F-1249

No ancient form. The kanji comprises 石 **SG-1148** "rock, stone," and 更 **SG-1874**, used for the sound *koo* to mean "hard, rigid," together signifying something solid and hard like a rock. The kanji 硬 means "hard, stiff, rigid." <石更>

硬い hard, rigid [かたい]; 強硬な strong, firm, aggressive [きょうこうな]; 生硬な raw, crude, unrefined [せいこうな]; 硬貨 coin, metallic money [こうか]; 硬直した rigid, stiff [こうちょくした]; 態度を硬化させる to stiffen one's attitude [たいどを・こうかさせる, こうかさせる]

	Meanings	Kun and On	Romaji	Bushu	Stroke Order and Number
SG-1877 梗	hard; roughly	コウ	*koo*	木	木 杧 梗 梗 梗 11

梗 **D** F-2534

説文

The seal-style form comprised 木 **SG-0608**, and 丙 **SG-1873** with 攴 (which became 更 **SG-1874**), which was used for the sound *koo* to mean "hard." Together they signified "a hard and thorny mountain elm tree." Using a stick from such a tree to level a measuring cup gave the meaning "roughly." The kanji 梗 means "hard; roughly." <木更>

脳梗塞 cerebral infarction [のうこうそく]; 心筋梗塞 cardiac infarction, heart infarction [しんきんこうそく]

87e 丬(爿) "(long) table, bed" [from a long table with legs that was vertically placed]; bushu *shoohen*; *shoo/soo/joo* 状将装荘壮奨

爿

	Meanings	Kun and On	Romaji	Bushu	Stroke Order and Number
SG-1878 状	state, condition, letter	ジョウ	*joo*	犬	丨 丬 丬 𠀋 状 状 7

状 **A** F-0403

説文 1 旧字 2

1 and 2 comprised 爿 (丬) "a long table" oriented vertically, which was used for the sound *joo* to mean "a shape," and 犬 **SG-0859** "a dog." How the shape of a dog came to be used to mean "shape, condition" is not clear. One reported the condition of a matter through a letter, and thus the form also meant "letter, piece of paper." The kanji 状 means "state, condition, letter." <丬犬>

状態 condition [じょうたい]; 状況 situation [じょうきょう]; 白状する to confess [はくじょうする]; 状差し letter holder [じょうさし]; 紹介状 letter of introduction [しょうかいじょう]; 令状 warrant [れいじょう]; 礼状 thank-you letter [れいじょう]

	Meanings	Kun and On	Romaji	Bushu	Stroke Order and Number
SG-1879 将	military leader, general, immediate future	ショウ	*shoo*	寸	丨 丬 丬 丬 丬 将 将 10

将 **B** F-0704

金文 1 説文 2 旧字 3

1 comprised 爿(丬) "a table," 月 bushu *nikuzuki* "a piece of meat," and 刀 "a knife," together signifying "placing sacrificial animal meat on an altar in a rite." The person who conducted such a rite was a military leader, thus giving the meaning "military leader, general." The rite preceded a battle, whence the meaning "immediate future." In 2 and 3, "knife" was replaced by 寸 **SG-0112** "a hand." In the shinji 将, 爿 was reduced to 丬, and 月 was replaced by ⺤ "a hand from above." The kanji 将 means "military leader, general, immediate future." <丬⺤寸>

将軍 general, *shogunate* (in Japanese history) [しょうぐん]; 大将 admiral, general, chief [たいしょう]; 将校 commissioned officer [しょうこう]; 主将 captain [しゅしょう]; 将来 near future [しょうらい] // 将に just, precisely, be about to do [まさに]

	Meanings	Kun and On	Romaji	Bushu	Stroke Order and Number
SG-1880 装	to dress up, be equipped with, assume, pretend; attire	よそお-う ソウ・ショウ	yosoo-u *soo, shoo*	衣	丨 丬 丬 壮 壮 装 装 装 12

装 **B** F-0745

説文 1 旧字 2

1 and 2 comprised 壯(壮 **SG-1882**) "grand, manly," for the sounds *soo*/*shoo*, and 衣 **SG-1657** "clothing," together signifying "to put on good attire." The form also meant "to be equipped with." A particular outfit helped one to assume an identity or feign to be someone else. The kanji 装 means "to dress up, be equipped with, assume, pretend; attire." <壮衣>

装う to dress oneself, be attired, feign, pretend [よそおう]; 偽装する to camouflage something as [ぎそうする]; 装備する to equip [そうびする]; 装飾 decoration [そうしょく]; 正装 formal attire [せいそう]; 装身具 accessories [そうしんぐ]; 衣装 clothing, attire, costume [いしょう]; 白装束 white shroud [しろしょうぞく]

	Meanings	Kun and On	Romaji	Bushu	Stroke Order and Number
SG-1881 荘	solemn, majestic; country house, villa, manor	ソウ	*so*	艸	艹 芢 荘 荘 荘 荘 9

荘 **C** F-1356

金文 1 説文古文 2 説文 3 旧字 4

In one view, 1 and 2 comprised 爿, which was used for the sound *soo*, and a component on the right side that pertained to "a religious rite" and also had the sound *soo* (or *shoo*). Together they signified "solemn, grand." Another view explains that, in 3, 艸 (艹) "plants" and 壮 **SG-1882** "grand" together signified "a large country house or villa with flourishing plants." From that it also meant "majestic." The kanji 荘 means "solemn, majestic; country house, villa, manor." <艹壮>

別荘 villa, vacation home, country house [べっそう]; 荘重な solemn, imposing [そうちょうな]; 荘厳な solemn, majestic [そうごんな] // 荘園 large private estate, manor, plantation [しょうえん]

	Meanings	Kun and On	Romaji	Bushu	Stroke Order and Number
SG-1882 壮	energetic young man; strong, courageous, grand	ソウ	*soo*	士	丨丬丬壮壮 6

壮 **C** F-1570

中山王器 1 説文 2 旧字 3

1 and 2 comprised 爿(丬), used for the sound *soo*, and 士 **SG-1451** "man, warrior," from "a battle ax." Together they signified "manly, strong." The kanji 壮 means "energetic young man; strong, courageous, grand." <丬士>

壮大な grand, magnificent [そうだいな]; 勇壮な brave, heroic, valiant, gallant [ゆうそうな]; 壮観 thrilling sight, spectacle [そうかん]; 壮行会 farewell party, rousing send-off [そうこうかい]; 悲壮な in the midst of grief, tragic but courageous [ひそうな]

	Meanings	Kun and On	Romaji	Bushu	Stroke Order and Number
SG-1883 奨	to urge, commend, encourage	ショウ	*shoo*	大	丨丬丬丬丬将将奨奨 13

奨 **D** F-1815

説文 1 旧字 2

1 comprised "a table" (爿, 丬) with "a piece of meat" (月), together used for the sound *shoo* to mean "to lead"; and "a dog" (犬 **SG-0859**) underneath. Together, these components formed the meaning "to urge, encourage." The role of the dog is not clear, but one view explains that "setting a dog on someone" gave the meaning "to instigate, encourage." In 2, the component under 将 became 大 **SG-0314** "a person," instead of a dog. The kanji 奨 means "to urge, commend, encourage." <将大>

奨励する to give encouragement to, promote [しょうれいする]; 推奨する to recommend, endorse [すいしょうする]; 奨学金 scholarship, stipend [しょうがくきん]

87f 疒 "illness" [from a sick person lying on a bed]; **bushu *yamaidare***

病痛症疲疫疾痴痢痩痘嫉

	Meanings	Kun and On	Romaji	Bushu	Stroke Order and Number
SG-1884 病	illness, something unhealthy; sick	や-む・やまい ビョウ・ヘイ	ya-mu, yamai *byoo, hee*	疒	亠广疒疒疔病病 10

病 **A** F-0450

説文

The seal-style form comprised "a bed" with 一 "a sick person lying down" (疒, bushu *yamaidare*), and 丙 **SG-1873**, which was used for the sound *hee* or *byoo* to mean "to add, increase." Together they signified that someone had deteriorated and become ill. The kanji means "illness, something unhealthy; sick." <疒丙>

病む to be taken ill, suffer from [やむ]; 病 illness, disease, bad habit [やまい]; 病気 illness, disease [びょうき]; 病欠 absence due to illness [びょうけつ]; 病死 death from an illness, natural death [びょうし]; 病的な morbid, unsound, unhealthy, abnormal [びょうてきな]; 金欠病 having little money (colloquial) [きんけつびょう]; 病床 sick bed [びょうしょう]; 疾病 disease, malady [しっぺい]

	Meanings	Kun and On	Romaji	Bushu	Stroke Order and Number
SG-1885 痛	pain, ache; severe, piercing	いた-い ツウ	ita-i *tsuu*	疒	广疒疒病痌痛 12

痛 **B** F-0915

説文

The seal-style form comprised 疒 bushu *yamaidare* "illness," and 甬 "to pass through," used for the sound *tsuu*. When one was ill, what passed through the body was "a pain or ache." A pain running through the body could be "piercing and severe." The kanji 痛 means "pain, ache; severe, piercing." <疒甬> (Note: 甬 is discussed as the common shape 92c "to pass through.")

痛い to ache, be in pain [いたい]; 痛々しい pitiful, pathetic [いたいたしい]; 手痛い serious, costly [ていたい]; 苦痛な painful [くつうな]; 沈痛な grave, sad [ちんつうな]; 痛感する to feel acutely, take something to heart [つうかんする]; 痛切に keenly, poignantly, acutely [つうせつに]; 痛飲する to drink heavily, go on a drinking binge [つういんする]

	Meanings	Kun and On	Romaji	Bushu	Stroke Order and Number
SG-1886 症	symptom of illness	ショウ	*shoo*	疒	广疒疔疔症症 10

症 **B** F-1042

No ancient form. The kanji 症 comprises 疒, bushu *yamaidare* "illness," and 正 **SG-0208**, used for the sound *shoo* to mean "sign." Together they signified "symptom of illness." The kanji 症 means "symptom of illness." <疒正>

症状 symptom [しょうじょう]; 既往症 past illnesses [きおうしょう]; 重症 severe illness [じゅうしょう]; 軽症 mild case [けいしょう]; 過敏症 hypersensitivity [かびんしょう]; 合併症 complication [がっぺいしょう]; 熱中症 heatstroke [ねっちゅうしょう]; 依存症 dependence, addiction [いぞんしょう]

	Meanings	Kun and On	Romaji	Bushu	Stroke Order and Number
SG-1887 疲	fatigue; to become tired, be worn out	つか-れる ヒ	tsuka-reru *hi*	疒	广疒疒疒疲疲 10

疲 **C** F-1295

説文

The seal-style form comprised "illness" (疒, bushu *yamaidare*), and 皮 **SG-0906**, used for the sound *hi* to mean "fatigue," together signifying "becoming fatigued or weak due to illness." The kanji 疲 means "fatigue; to become tired, worn out." <疒皮>

疲れる to become fatigued, become tired [つかれる]; お疲れ様でした Thank you for your hard work [おつかれさまでした]; 気疲れ mental fatigue, nervous exhaustion [きづかれ, きづかれ]; 疲労 fatigue [ひろう]; 金属疲労 metal fatigues [きんぞくひろう]

	Meanings	Kun and On	Romaji	Bushu	Stroke Order and Number
SG-1888 疫	epidemic	エキ・ヤク	*eki, yaku*	疒	广疒疒疒疫 9

疫 **D** F-1822

説文

The seal-style form comprised "illness" (疒), and "to strike down" (殳, bushu *hokozukari*), used for the sound *eki*. 殳 was an abbreviated form of 役 **SG-0158** "conscripted for battle or frontier work," and it had a connotation of "being reluctant." 疒 and 殳 together signified "an illness that everyone gets against their will, epidemic." The kanji 疫 means "epidemic." <疒 殳>

疫病 epidemic [えきびょう]; 検疫 quarantine [けんえき]; 防疫 communicable disease control, infectious disease prevention [ぼうえき]; 疫病神 jinx, bringer of bad luck [やくびょうがみ]

	Meanings	Kun and On	Romaji	Bushu	Stroke Order and Number
SG-1889 疾	illness; very fast	シツ	*shitsu*	疒	广疒疒疒疾疾 10

疾 **D** F-1921

甲骨文 1, 金文 2, 説文 3, 説文或体 4

1 showed "a sick person lying in bed and perspiring from a high fever (or bleeding)," which was indicated by the dots. 2 had "a person" with "an arrow" (矢 **SG-1524**, used for the sound *shitsu*) in their leg, together signifying "wounded by an arrow." 3 had "a person in a sickbed" and "an arrow." In 4, the arrow was under 厂 "eaves, a shooting range." Due to this combination of elements, the character means both "illness" and "very fast (like an arrow)." The kanji 疾 means "illness; very fast." <疒矢>

疾患 disease, malady, ailment [しっかん]; 疾走する to sprint, run at full speed [しっそうする]; 疾風 gale, strong wind [しっぷう]

	Meanings	Kun and On	Romaji	Bushu	Stroke Order and Number
SG-1890 痴	foolish	チ	*chi*	疒	广疒疒疾痴 13

痴 **D** F-1986

説文 1, 旧字 2

1 comprised 疒 "illness" and 疑 **SG-0404** "to doubt; unsure," signifying "someone in such a sick condition that they cannot judge correctly," or "foolish." In the shinji 痴, 疑 was replaced by a kanji with the opposite meaning, 知 **SG-1525** "to know," used for the sound *chi*. The kanji 痴 means "foolish." <疒知>

痴呆症 dementia [ちほうしょう]; 白痴 idiocy, idiot [はくち]

	Meanings	Kun and On	Romaji	Bushu	Stroke Order and Number
SG-1891 痢	diarrhea, loose bowels	リ	*ri*	疒	广疒疒疒疒痢 12

痢 **D** F-2187

No ancient form. The kanji 痢 comprises 疒 "illness," and 利 **SG-0713**, which was used for the sound *ri* to mean "quick." Together they signify "a stomach illness that causes food to pass quickly." The kanji 痢 means "diarrhea, loose bowels." <疒利>

下痢 diarrhea [げり]; 赤痢 ysentery [せきり]

	Meanings	Kun and On	Romaji	Bushu	Stroke Order and Number
SG-1892 痩	to become haggard, become emaciated; slim	や-せる ソウ	ya-seru *soo*	疒	广疒疒疒疒痩痩 12

痩 **D** F-2341

説文 1, 旧字 2

1 comprised 爿 "a table" with 一 "sick person" (疒), and 叟, used for the sound *soo* to mean "an old person" or "to be emaciated." A sick, old person gave the meaning "to become haggard or emaciated." The kanji 痩 means "to become haggard, become emaciated; slim." <疒叟>

痩せる to become thin, lose weight [やせる]; 痩せ我慢する to endure something out of pride [やせがまんする]; 痩せ衰える to pine away, grow thin and worn out [やせおとろえる]; 痩身 slim figure, lean figure [そうしん]

	Meanings	Kun and On	Romaji	Bushu	Stroke Order and Number
SG-1893 痘	smallpox	トウ	*too*	疒	广疒疒疒疒痘 12

痘 **D** F-2545

No ancient form. The kanji 痘 comprised 疒 "illness," and 豆 **SG-1975**, used for the sound *too* to mean "bean." A disease that produced bean-shaped pustules was "smallpox." The kanji 痘 means "smallpox." <疒豆>

種痘 smallpox vaccine [しゅとう]

	Meanings	Kun and On	Romaji	Bushu	Stroke Order and Number
SG-1894 嫉	zealous; to envy	シツ	*shitsu*	女	13

嫉 **D** F-2816

篆文

The seal-style form comprised 女 "woman," and 疾 **SG-1889** "illness," which was used for the sound *shitsu*. Together they signified "jealousy." The kanji 嫉 means "jealous; to envy." <女疾>
(Note: In *Setsumon*, the left side had 亻 "person," instead of "woman.")

嫉妬する to be jealous [しっとする]; 嫉妬心 envy, jealous feeling [しっとしん]

88 Tools and containers

88a 工 "craft, a skilled person"; *koo* 工江攻功巧

	Meanings	Kun and On	Romaji	Bushu	Stroke Order and Number
SG-1895 工	craft, craftsman, skilled person, engineering	コウ・ク	*koo, ku*	工	一 丅 工 3

工 **A** F-0176

甲骨文1 1 甲骨文2 2 金文 3 説文 4

1 through 4 depicted "a carpenter's square" or "a table for smithy work." The character's meaning broadly included all kinds of skilled labor or craftwork, such as woodworking, metalworking, leather work, bronze work, smithing, civil engineering, etc. It also meant a person who was engaged in such work. The kanji 工 means "craft, craftsman, skilled person, engineering." <工>

人工の artificial, man-made [じんこうの]; 着工する to start construction work [ちゃっこうする]; 工法 method of construction [こうほう]; 工事中 under construction [こうじちゅう]; 工場 factory [こうじょう]; 大工 carpenter [だいく]; 細工 workmanship, craftsmanship [さいく]; 工面する to contrive to, manage to do [くめんする]

	Meanings	Kun and On	Romaji	Bushu	Stroke Order and Number
SG-1896 江	inlet, river	え コウ	e *koo*	水	氵 氵 汀 江 6

江 **A** F-0489

金文 1 説文 2

1 and 2 comprised 工, used for the sound *koo*, and "flowing water." 江 was the name of a specific large river, but later came to be used to mean "river" more generally. The kanji 江 means "inlet, river." <氵工>

入り江 inlet, cove, creek [いりえ]; 江戸 Edo/Yedo, capital city of Japan during the Tokugawa era [えど]; 江戸時代 Edo/Yedo era, Tokugawa era [えどじだい]

	Meanings	Kun and On	Romaji	Bushu	Stroke Order and Number
SG-1897 攻	mastery (of a skill); to attack	せ-める コウ	se-meru *koo*	攴	丅 工 工' 玎 攻 7

攻 **B** F-0849

金文1 1 金文2 2 説文 3

1, 2, and 3 comprised 工 **SG-1895** "skilled work, carpenter's square," used for the sound *koo*, and 攴 (攵 bushu *bokuzukuri*) "to cause an action," together signifying "mastery of various skilled work." This included mastery of military tactics, giving the associated meaning "to attack." The kanji 攻 means "mastery (of skills), to attack." <工攵>

攻める to attack [せめる]; 攻撃する to attack [こうげきする]; 攻略する to carry, capture, occupy [こうりゃくする]; 専攻 major (specialty in study) [せんこう]; 攻守 offense and defense [こうしゅ]; 攻防戦 a struggle for supremacy [こうぼうせん]

	Meanings	Kun and On	Romaji	Bushu	Stroke Order and Number
SG-1898 功	merit, achievement	コウ・ク	*koo, ku*	力	丅 工 玎 功 5

功 **B** F-0921

中山王器 1 説文 2

1 was the same as 工, "skilled person, manual work." In 2, 力 **SG-1949** "plow" was added to mean "strenuous agricultural work or work in general." Together these components signified "skilled work, achievement, merit." The kanji 功 means "merit, achievement." <工力>

成功する to succeed [せいこうする]; 年の功 the wisdom of age and experience [としのこう]; 成功報酬 contingency fee, payment conditional to success [せいこうほうしゅう]; 内助の功 through the assistance of one's wife [ないじょのこう]; 功労金 monetary reward for meritorious service [こうろうきん]; 戦功 military exploits, meritorious service in war [せんこう]; 功徳 act of charity, virtuous deed [くどく]

	Meanings	Kun and On	Romaji	Bushu	Stroke Order and Number
SG-1899 巧	skillful, cunningly good; subtlety	たく-み コウ	taku-mi *koo*	工	丅 工 工一 巧 5

巧 **C** F-1538 — 巧 説文 巧 — The seal-style form comprised 工 "carpenter's square, skilled work," used for the sound *koo*, and 丂 "a curved knife used for carpentry," together signifying "dexterous skill, skillful work." The character also means "clever, cunningly good." The kanji 巧 means "skillful, cunningly good; subtlety." <工丂>

巧みな skillful, dexterous [たくみな]; 悪巧み dirty trick, evil scheme [わるだꜜくみ]; 技巧 art, craftsmanship [ぎこう]; 巧拙 skill and lack of skill [こうせつ]; 巧妙な dexterous, masterly [こうみょうな]; 精巧な exquisite, elaborate [せいこうな]

88b 式 "a set way of doing" [from making carpentry work]; bushu *shikigamae* 式試拭

	Meanings	Kun and On	Romaji	Bushu	Stroke Order and Number
SG-1900 式	formula, way of doing, ceremony	シキ	*shiki*	弋	二 テ 王 式 式 6

式 **A** F-0207 — 説文 式 — The seal-style form comprised 弋 "a wooden stake for marking," and 工 **SG-1895** "craft, tool for carpentry," together signifying "a set way of making or doing something, a formula." In a societal context, the character means "a ceremony." The kanji 式 means "formula, way of doing, ceremony." <弋工>

式 ceremony, style, formula [しきꜜ]; 卒業式 graduation ceremony, commencement [そつぎょꜜうしき]; 和式 Japanese-style [わしき]; 洋式 Western-style [ようしき]; 正式な formal [せいしきな]; 公式 formula in mathematics, official, formal [こうしき]; 挙式 holding of a ceremony [きょしき]

	Meanings	Kun and On	Romaji	Bushu	Stroke Order and Number
SG-1901 試	to test, attempt to do something; trial	こころ-みる・ため-す シ	kokoro-miru, tame-su *shi*	言	言 訂 試 試 試 13

試 **B** F-0544 — 説文 試 — The seal-style form comprised 言 "word, language; to say," and 式 **SG-1900** "a set way of doing," used for the sound *shi,* together signifying "to try to find out the correct way to do something by inquiring." The character originally described the process of questioning an applicant or prospective apprentice on how he would perform certain tasks, and evaluating him based on his answers. The kanji 試 means "to test, attempt to do something; trial." <言式>

試みる to attempt, test [こころみꜜる]; 試す to try, attempt, put to test [ためꜜす]; 力試し test of one's ability [ちからだꜜめし]; 試験 examination [しけꜜん]; 試合 game, match [しあい]; 試着室 fitting room [しちゃくꜜしつ]; 試供品 sample [しきょうひん]; 試行錯誤 trial and error [しこうさꜜくご]

	Meanings	Kun and On	Romaji	Bushu	Stroke Order and Number
SG-1902 拭	to wipe, mop	ふ-く・ぬぐ-う ショク	hu-ku, nugu-u *shoku*	手	一 扌 扌 扌 拭 拭 9

拭 **D** F-2073 — No ancient form. The kanji 拭 comprises 扌 bushu *tehen* "an act done by hand," and 式 **SG-1900**, used for the sound *shoku* to mean "to wipe, clean." Together they signified "to wipe by hand." The kanji 拭 means "to wipe, mop." <扌式>

拭く to wipe [ふく]; 拭う to wipe [ぬぐꜜう]; 手拭い *tenugui*, a thin cotton cloth [てぬぐい]; 尻拭いをする to clean up someone else's mess or blunder [しりぬꜜぐいをする]; 払拭する to eradicate [ふっしょくする]

88c 壬 "thick in the middle" [from a smithy table with a bulge in the middle]; *nin* 任妊

	Meanings	Kun and On	Romaji	Bushu	Stroke Order and Number
SG-1903 任	to entrust, leave a task to someone	まか-せる ニン	maka-seru *nin*	人	亻 亻 仁 仟 任 6

任 **A** F-0384 — 甲骨文1 (1), 甲骨文2 (2), 金文 (3), 説文 (4), 任 — 1, 2, 3, and 4 comprised 亻 "person, an act that one does," and 壬 "a smithy table with a bulge in the middle," used for the sound *nin.* With the bulge signifying "responsibility, a burden that one carries," the character meant "a person who bears responsibility or plays a role," or "entrusting a burden to someone else." The kanji 任 means "to entrust, leave a task to someone." <亻壬>

任せる to entrust, leave to, let someone do [まかせꜜる]; 任せっきり to leave everything up to someone else [まかせっきり]; 人任せ evading responsibility [ひとまꜜかせ]; 任命 appointment, commis-sion [にんめい]; 一任する to leave a matter entirely in someone's care [いちにんする]; 主任 manager, supervisor [しゅにん];

	(Note: The form 壬 in kanji is used for two different meanings each with separate origins. One meant "bulge" and had the sound *nin*, as in 任 and 妊 **SG-1904**. Another meant "straight, standing erect" (from "a straight shin bone marked with a line" 壬) and had the sound *tee*, as in 庭 **SG-1336**, 廷 **SG-1337**, and 程 **SG-0492**.)	任地 place of one's post [にんち]

	Meanings	Kun and On	Romaji	Bushu	Stroke Order and Number
SG-1904 妊	pregnant	ニン	*nin*	女	く 女 女' 妊 妊 7
妊 **C** F-1578	甲骨文 1, 金文1 2, 金文2 3, 說文 4 — 1, 2, 3, and 4 comprised 壬 "a smithy table with a bulge in the middle," used for the sound *nin*, and 女 **SG-0521** "woman." Together they signified a woman with a bulging stomach, that is, "pregnant." The kanji 妊 means "pregnant." <女壬>				妊娠 pregnancy [にんしん]; 妊婦 pregnant woman [にんぷ]; 避妊 contraception, birth control [ひにん]; 不妊 infertility [ふにん]

88d 乍 "to create, make" [from twigs bent to make a fence, or a tool such as an adze chipping off pieces of wood to create something]; *saku/sa* 作昨酢詐搾

	Meanings	Kun and On	Romaji	Bushu	Stroke Order and Number
SG-1905 作	to make, create, do, begin	つく-る サク・サ	tsuku-ru *saku, sa*	人	亻 亻' 亻' 作 作 7
作 **A** F-0099	甲骨文 1, 金文 2, 說文 3 — 1 and 2 (乍) depicted "a tool such as an adze chipping off pieces of wood to create something," or "bending vines or twigs to make a basket or fence." The character meant "to make, create." Later, 乍 came increasingly to be used for the sound *saku* in creating other kanji, and 亻 "an act one does" was added in 3 to differentiate its original meaning. The kanji 作 means "to make, create, do, begin." <亻乍>				作る to make [つくる]; 物作り making objects by hand, craftsmanship [ものづくり]; 小作人 tenant farmer, sharecropper [こさくにん]; 工作 craft, construction, maneuvering, scheme [こうさく]; 動作 one's movement, gesture [どうさ、どうさ]; 作業 work [さぎょう]; 作用する to operate on, affect [さようする]; 作動する to operate, run [さどうする]

	Meanings	Kun and On	Romaji	Bushu	Stroke Order and Number
SG-1906 昨	past, last	サク	*saku*	日	日 日 日' 日' 昨 昨 9
昨 **A** F-0344	說文 — The seal-style form comprised 日 "the sun," and 乍, used for the sound *saku* to mean "to pass, in a moment." A day that had passed signified "past, last." The kanji 昨 means "past, last." <日乍>				昨年 last year [さくねん]; 一昨年 the year before last [いっさくねん、いっさくねん]; 昨日 yesterday [きのう、さくじつ]; 昨今 these days [さっこん]; 一昨日 the day before yesterday [いっさくじつ]

	Meanings	Kun and On	Romaji	Bushu	Stroke Order and Number
SG-1907 酢	vinegar	す サク	su *saku*	酉	丆 丙 酉' 酉' 酢 酢 12
酢 **D** F-1679	金文1 1, 金文2 2, 說文 3 — 1, 2, and 3 comprised 酉 "a cask for fermented liquid," and 乍, used for the sound *saku* to mean "something that has passed." Rice wine that had fermented past being drinkable was vinegar. The kanji 酢 means "vinegar." <酉乍>				酢・お酢 vinegar [す、おす]; 酢豚 sweet and sour pork [すぶた]; 酢の物 a vinegared dish [すのもの]; 酢飯 vinegared rice [すめし、すめし]; 酢酸 acetic acid [さくさん]

	Meanings	Kun and On	Romaji	Bushu	Stroke Order and Number
SG-1908 詐	to deceive, lie	サ	*sa*	言	言 言 言' 詐 詐 12
詐 **D** F-1801	金文 1, 說文 2 — 1 and 2 comprised 言 "word, language; to speak," and 乍, used for the sound *sa* to mean "to deceive, make," together signifying "to deceive using words." The kanji 詐 means "to deceive, lie." <言乍>				詐欺 fraud, swindle [さぎ]; 詐欺師 swindler, cheater [さぎし]; 経歴詐称 false statement of one's professional background [けいれきさしょう]

SG-1909 搾	Meanings	Kun and On	Romaji	Bushu	Stroke Order and Number
	to wring, squeeze, extract, extort	しぼ-る サク	shibo-ru *saku*	手	扌扩护控搾搾 13

搾
D
F-2189

No ancient form. The kanji comprised 扌 bushu *tehen*, 穴 "hole," and 乍, used for the sound *saku* to mean "to squeeze something into a small hole." Together they signified "to wring, extract, squeeze." The character is also used to mean "to extort." The kanji 搾 means "to wring, squeeze, extract, extort." <扌穴乍>

搾る to squeeze [しぼる]; 乳搾り milking [ちちしぼり]; 一番搾り first press (of a juice, etc.) [いちばんしぼり]; 搾取する exploitation [さくしゅする]

88e 巨 "huge, giant" [from a carpenter's large rectangular ruler]; *kyo* 巨拒距・規

SG-1910 巨	Meanings	Kun and On	Romaji	Bushu	Stroke Order and Number
	huge, giant, gigantic	キョ	*kyo*	工	丨𠂆F户巨 5

巨
B
F-0714

金文1 金文2 金文3 説文或体 説文
1 2 3 4 5

1 and 2 depicted "a large (rectangular) carpenter's ruler with a handle in the middle." 3 added "a person" holding the ruler. 4 comprised "an arrow used for measuring a short object" (矢 **SG-1524**), and "a large ruler used for measuring a long object" (巨) such as "a tree" (木). In 5 only the large ruler remained. The kanji 巨 means "huge, giant, gigantic." <巨>

巨大な huge, gigantic, colossal [きょだいな]; 巨人 giant [きょじん]; 巨額 colossal sum [きょがく]; 巨漢 a man of gigantic stature [きょかん]; 巨視的な comprehensive, all-inclusive [きょしてきな]; 巨万の富 immense wealth [きょまんのとみ]

SG-1911 拒	Meanings	Kun and On	Romaji	Bushu	Stroke Order and Number
	to prevent, refuse, reject	こば-む キョ	koba-mu *kyo*	手	一扌扌扌拒拒拒 8

拒
C
F-1339

No ancient form. The kanji comprised 扌 "an act done by hand," and 巨 **SG-1910**, used for the sound *kyo* to mean "to separate, prevent." One view explains that it was based on a bar used to block traffic, which resembled the shape of a large ruler. The kanji 拒 means "to prevent, refuse, reject." <扌巨>

拒む to reject, prevent [こばむ]; 拒絶 refusal, rejection [きょぜつ]; 拒否 refusal, turning down [きょひ]; 拒食症 anorexia [きょしょくしょう]; 登校拒否 refusal to go to school, school phobia [とうこうきょひ]; 兵役拒否 refusal of military service [へいえききょひ]

SG-1912 距	Meanings	Kun and On	Romaji	Bushu	Stroke Order and Number
	distance	キョ	*kyo*	足	卩卩⻊⻊距 距距 12

距
C
F-1377

金文 説文
1 2

1 and 2 comprised "a stretched footprint" to mean "a distance," and 巨, used for the sound *kyo,* and possibly for its resemblance to a chicken spur. One contracts and then extends the ankles to jump "a long distance." Another view explains that a chicken spur might repel an enemy, keeping them at "a distance." The kanji 距 means "distance." <⻊巨>

距離 distance [きょり]; 遠距離 long distance [えんきょり]; 車間距離 the distance from the car in front and behind [しゃかんきょり]

規 "standard"

SG-1913 規	Meanings	Kun and On	Romaji	Bushu	Stroke Order and Number
	standard, criterion	キ	*ki*	見	二夫却規規 11

規
B
F-0545

説文

The left side of the seal-style form was either "a pair of compasses for drawing a circle" or "two sticks used to draw a circle," and the right side was 見 **SG-0460** "to look at." A pair of compasses is used to measure the size or distance between points. In the sense of "something to measure against," the character signified "standard, criterion." The kanji 規 means "standard, criterion." <夫見>

規制 regulation, control [きせい]; 規格外 nonstandard [きかくがい]; 新規に anew, afresh [しんきに]; 規律 order, discipline [きりつ]; 規約 an agreement, a code of ethics [きやく]; 正規 standard, proper, legitimate [せいき]; 正規従業員 regular (full-time) employee [せいき・じゅうぎょういん]; 不規則な irregular, anomalous [ふきそくな]

88f 丁 "a square block"; *choo/da/tee* 丁打頂訂・克

	Meanings	*Kun* and *On*	Romaji	Bushu	Stroke Order and Number
SG-1914 丁	a square block; counter for block shapes	チョウ・テイ	*choo, tee*	一	一丁 2

丁 **A** F-0649

甲骨文1 1, 甲骨文2 2, 金文1 3, 金文2 4, 金文3 5, 説文 6

1 and 5 depicted "an area" or "a square," whereas 2, 3, and 4 looked like "a nail head viewed from above or from the side." A nail got pounded down flat at a right angle, and the character signified "right angle; flat." In Japan it also means "a square block," and is used to mean a block in an area of a large city, such as in the word 丁目. The kanji 丁 means "a square block; counter for block shapes." <丁>

丁度 just, precisely, barely [ちょうど]; 三丁目 3-*Chome*, the third block (of a neighborhood) [さんちょうめ]; 一丁上がり Order up! (called out when a dish is ready to be served) [いっちょうあがり]; 丁重に courteously, respectfully [ていちょうに]

	Meanings	*Kun* and *On*	Romaji	Bushu	Stroke Order and Number
SG-1915 打	to hit, pound on; emphatic prefix	う-つ ダ	u-tsu *da*	手	一 亅 扌 打 打 5

打 **A** F-0308

説文

The seal-style form comprised 扌, bushu *tehen* "an act done by hand," and 丁 "square, right angle, nail." Pounding on a nail meant "to hit, pound." The character is also used as a prefix to add general emphasis (as in 打ち消す or 打開). The kanji 打 means "to hit, pound on; emphatic prefix." <扌丁>

打つ to hit, strike hard [うつ]; 打ち消す to negate, contradict [うちけす, うちけす]; 打ち上げる to launch (a satellite), conclude (a project) [うちあげる]; 打者 slugger, batter [だしゃ]; 打楽器 percussion instrument [だがっき]; 打算的な calculating [ださんてきな]; 打診する to sound out, make an approach [だしんする]; 打開策 breakthrough, breaking an impasse [だかいさく]

	Meanings	*Kun* and *On*	Romaji	Bushu	Stroke Order and Number
SG-1916 頂	summit, top; to receive (humble)	いただ-く・いただき チョウ	itada-ku, itadaki *choo*	頁	一 丁 丆 丙 頂 頂 11

頂 **C** F-1218

説文

The seal-style form comprised 丁 **SG-1914** "a flat nail head," for the sound *choo*, and 頁, bushu *oogai* "head, person," together signifying "a high flat area, summit, the top of one's head." In Japanese, 頂 is also used for the humble verb "to receive," from the posture of lowering the head when receiving something from a superior or acquaintance. The kanji 頂 means "summit, top; to receive (humble)." <丁頁>. (Note: For the humble verb *itadaku* "to receive," 戴 **SG-1485** and 頂 are both used, with the latter used more informally.)

頂く to receive (humble), hold above one's head [いただく]; 山の頂 summit [やまのいただき]; 頂上 top, summit [ちょうじょう]; 有頂天 ecstatic, rapturous [うちょうてん]; 仏頂面をする to look sullen [ぶっちょうづらをする]; 頂戴する to be given, receive (humble) [ちょうだいする]

	Meanings	*Kun* and *On*	Romaji	Bushu	Stroke Order and Number
SG-1917 訂	to correct, revise, amend	テイ	*tee*	言	亠 言 言 訂 訂 9

訂 **C** F-1446

説文

The seal-style form comprised 言 "word, language; to say," and 丁 "straight; right angle," used for the sound *tee*, together signifying "to make words right." The kanji 訂 means "to correct, revise, amend." <言丁>

訂正 correction, revision [ていせい]; 改訂版 revised edition [かいていばん]; 新訂 newly revised [しんてい]

克 "to overcome"

	Meanings	*Kun* and *On*	Romaji	Bushu	Stroke Order and Number
SG-1918 克	to overcome, conquer	コク	*koku*	儿	一 十 古 古 克 7

克 **C** F-1229

甲骨文1 1, 甲骨文2 2, 金文1 3, 金文2 4, 説文古文 5, 説文 6

The origin of the kanji 克 is obscure. One view explains that 1 through 5 depicted "a curved knife with a large handle," and that the handgrip denoted something that had been "carved out," particularly in light of the depiction in 5 of sawdust spilling from the hole. The character originally meant "carving," but it was borrowed to mean "to overcome, return to the original state." Another view explains that it depicted "a person with a heavy helmet sitting with his legs bent under its weight," and from that it meant "to overcome." The kanji 克 means "to overcome, conquer." <古儿>

克服 to overcome [こくふく]; 克己心 self-control [こっきしん]; 克明な scrupulous, minute [こくめいな]; 下克上 social upheaval, reversal of the social order [げこくじょう]

88g 専 (專) "to turn, rotate, roll" [from a clay spindle with threads wrapped around it, or a tied round bag of stuff] 専伝転団恵

	Meanings	Kun and On	Romaji	Bushu	Stroke Order and Number
SG-1919 専	solely, exclusively, entirely; to monopolize	もっぱ-ら セン	moppa-ra *sen*	寸	一 亘 亘 亘 専 専 9

専
A
F-0621

甲骨文 1　説文 2　旧字 3

One view explains that 1 and 2 comprised "a spinning spool" and "a hand rotating the spindle." Multiple threads spun together into a single strand signified "solely; to monopolize." Another view explains that the right-hand component was "a tied bag of stuff pounded by hand into a round shape," and was used for the sound *sen.* The two strokes in the middle of the kyuji 專 (3), perhaps depicting a spinner, were dropped in the shinji 専. The kanji 専 means "solely, exclusively, entirely; to monopolize." <亩寸>

専ら solely, entirely [もっぱら]; 専門 specialty [せんもん]; 専門家 specialist [せんもんか]; 専業 full-time occupation [せんぎょう]; 専心する to devote one's attention to [せんしんする]; 専用 exclusive [せんよう]; 専制政治 autocratic government [せんせいせいじ]; 専任コーチ full-time coach [せんにんコーチ]

	Meanings	Kun and On	Romaji	Bushu	Stroke Order and Number
SG-1920 伝	to relay, convey, hand down	つた-わる デン	tsuta-waru *den*	人	亻 亻 亻 伝 伝 6

伝
A
F-0358

甲骨文 1　金文1 2　金文2 3　説文 4　旧字 5

1 through 4 all comprised 亻 "a person" and 専 "stuff rolled by hand" (as seen in 2 in 専). Pushing a tied bundle of stuff to roll it into a ball was likened to "handing an item down to another person." The right side (專) of the kyuji 傳 was replaced by the simplified shape 云 in the shinji. The kanji 伝 means "to relay, convey, hand down." <亻云>

伝える to convey, hand down [つたえる]; 手伝う to help [てつだう]; 伝達 conveyance, transfer [でんたつ]; 直伝 art handed down directly [じきでん]; 伝説 legend [でんせつ]; 伝統 tradition [でんとう] // 言伝て message [ことづて]

	Meanings	Kun and On	Romaji	Bushu	Stroke Order and Number
SG-1921 転	to roll, fall, change	ころ-がる テン	koro-garu *ten*	車	一 亘 車 転 転 転 11

転
A
F-0497

金文 1　説文 2　旧字 3

1 and 2 comprised "a load of stuff on a vehicle (車) with a yoke," and 専 "to roll." "Rolling" gave the meaning of "to change into something else." 専 was replaced by the simplified shape 云 in the shinji. The kanji 転 means "to roll, fall, change." <車云>

転がる to roll, fall [ころがる]; 転ぶ to fall [ころぶ]; 回転 rotation, rolling [かいてん]; 逆転 reversal [ぎゃくてん]; 転職 changing one's job or career [てんしょく]; 運転する to drive, operate [うんてんする]; 転機 turning point [てんき]; 転向 conversion (of ideological belief) [てんこう]

	Meanings	Kun and On	Romaji	Bushu	Stroke Order and Number
SG-1922 団	band, harmony, lump, mass; round	ダン・トン	*dan, ton*	囗	冂 円 円 団 団 6

団
A
F-0215

金文 1　説文 2　旧字 3

In 1, 2, and 3, inside of 囗 "an enclosure" was 專 (専) "round stuff." As a representation of a band of people sitting in a circle "in harmony," the character signified "round" or "a group or band of people." Inside of the shinji 団, only the hand (寸) that did the rolling was retained. The kanji 団 means "band, round, harmony, lump, mass." <囗寸>

団体 band of people [だんたい]; 集団 group, mass [しゅうだん]; 団子 dumpling, small round object [だんご]; 一家団欒 pleasures of a happy home, happy time spent together as a family [いっか・だんらん]; 団地 housing or apartment complex [だんち]; 大団円 grand finale [だいだんえん]; 座布団 seat cushion [ざぶとん]; 掛け布団 cover [かけぶとん]

	Meanings	Kun and On	Romaji	Bushu	Stroke Order and Number
SG-1923 恵	blessing, grace, bounty, benefaction	めぐ-む ケイ・エ	megu-mu *kee, e*	心	一 亘 亩 恵 恵 10

恵
B
F-0654

甲骨文 1　金文1 2　金文2 3　金文3 4　説文古文 5　説文 6　旧字 7

1, 2, and 3 depicted "a tied stuffed bag with the top tied shut," and had the sound *kee* to mean "fullness." In 4, 5, and 6, "a heart" was added. Together they signified "bountiful benevolence." The kanji 恵 means "blessing, grace, bounty, benefaction." <亩心>

恵み blessing [めぐみ]; 恵む to give something in charity [めぐむ]; 恵まれた to be blessed with, fortunate [めぐまれた]; 知恵 wisdom [ちえ]; 悪知恵 cunning [わるぢえ]; 恩恵 benefit, favor [おんけい]

88h 予 "in advance" [from making a gap for the passing of a weaving shuttle]

予預幻序・互

	Meanings	Kun and On	Romaji	Bushu	Stroke Order and Number
SG-1924 予	in advance; preliminary, roomy	ヨ	*yo*	豕・亅	フマ孑予 4

予 **A** F-0306

説文1 1 説文2 2 旧字 3

1 was "a weaving shuttle with a thread hanging down," which was pushed through the opening of the warps on a loom. From "making room in advance of a shuttle's passing" came the meaning "in advance; preliminary." The kanji 豫 (3), which was used as the kyuji, and its precursor (2) included "elephant" (象), signifying "being wide and roomy," but this composition was not a historical precursor to the shinji, which came from 1. The kanji 予 means "in advance; preliminary, roomy." <マ了>

予定 schedule, plan [よてい]; 予習 preparation for lessons [よしゅう]; 予報 forecast, prediction [よほう]; 予約 appointment, reservation [よやく]; 予告編 advance notice, advance billing, preview [よこくへん]; 予言 prophecy, prediction [よげん] // 予め in advance, beforehand [あらかじめ]

	Meanings	Kun and On	Romaji	Bushu	Stroke Order and Number
SG-1925 預	to entrust, leave in custody, deposit; beforehand	あず-ける ヨ	azu-keru *yo*	頁	マ予予予預預預 13

預 **B** F-1069

説文

The seal-style form comprised 予 "in advance," used for the sound *yo*, and 頁 "head, person." Together they signified "leaving something in someone's temporary custody (for later use), deposit." Another view takes this meaning to be the result of borrowing. The kanji 預 means "to entrust, leave in custody, deposit; beforehand." <予頁>. (Note: This kanji is used interchangeably with the kanji 予 in the word 予言 [預言].)

預ける to leave something in someone's hands [あずける]; 預かり証 temporary receipt, deposit receipt [あずかりしょう]; 預金 deposit, bank account [よきん]; 預言 prophecy, oracle [よげん]

	Meanings	Kun and On	Romaji	Bushu	Stroke Order and Number
SG-1926 幻	illusion, magic	まぼろし ゲン	maboroshi *gen*	幺	く 幺 幺 幻 4

幻 **C** F-1183

金文 1 説文 2

1 and 2 depicted "an upside down image of a weaving shuttle" (予 **SG-1924** turned on its head) with the end of a thread showing, and had the sound *gen* to mean "to be dazzled." Pulling a shuttle or threads in the wrong way caused the weaver dismay or confusion. The kanji 幻 means "illusion, magic." <幺フ>

幻 illusion [まぼろし]; 幻想的な fantastic, visionary [げんそうてきな]; 幻覚 hallucination [げんかく]; 幻滅する to be disenchanted with [げんめつする]; 幻聴 auditory hallucination [げんちょう]

	Meanings	Kun and On	Romaji	Bushu	Stroke Order and Number
SG-1927 序	order, formality, beginning; while one is at it	ジョ	*jo*	广	亠广庁庌序 7

序 **C** F-1254

説文

The seal-style form comprised 广 "the eaves or an extension of a house," and 予 "extra room," used for the sound *jo*. The extended area next to the main house was used as a school where propriety and protocol were taught. Propriety ensures order. "Order" implies a sequence, which has "a beginning." The kanji 序 means "order, formality, beginning," and also "while (one is) at it, taking the opportunity." <广予>

順序 order [じゅんじょ]; 秩序 order, discipline [ちつじょ, ちつじょ]; 序曲 prelude [じょきょく]; 年功序列 seniority system [ねんこうじょれつ]; 序の口 lowest ranking [じょのくち]; 公序良俗 public order and decency [こうじょ・りょうぞく] // 序でに while (one is) at it [ついでに]

互 "mutual"

	Meanings	Kun and On	Romaji	Bushu	Stroke Order and Number
SG-1928 互	each other; alternately	たが-い ゴ	taga-i *go*	二	一工互互 4

互 **B** F-0832

説文

The seal-style form depicted "a tool used to make rope by twining threads alternately from two sides." The kanji 互 means "each other; alternately." <互>

互い mutual, each other [たがい]; 互い違い alternate [たがいちがい]; 交互に alternately [こうごに]; 相互の mutual [そうごの]; 互角の well-matched, equal [ごかくの]; 互換性 compatibility [ごかんせい]; 互恵関税 reciprocal tariff [ごけいかんぜい]

88i 录（彔）*roku/ryoku* 緑録

SG-1929 緑	Meanings	*Kun* and *On*	Romaji	Bushu	Stroke Order and Number
	green	みどり リョク・ロク	midori *ryoku, roku*	糸	纟 糸 紀 紀 紓 紓 緑 14

緑 **B** F-0852

甲骨文 1 簡書1 2 簡書2 3 説文 4 旧字 5

All ancient forms comprised 彔 next to "a skein of threads" (糸). The views on the origin of 彔, which was used for the sounds *ryoku/roku*, vary—"a twisting device for wringing wet threads"; "a device drilling into wood and spilling wood shavings"; or "green rust peeling off of bronze." The kanji 緑 means "green." <糸 ヨ氺>

緑 green [みꜜどり]; 新緑 fresh green, new leaves in spring [しんりょく]; 常緑樹 evergreen tree [じょうりょくꜜじゅ]; 緑茶 green tea [りょくちゃ]; 緑化運動 tree-planting drive [りょっかうꜜんどう]; 緑青 copper green rust, verdigris patina [ろくしょꜜう]

SG-1930 録	Meanings	*Kun* and *On*	Romaji	Bushu	Stroke Order and Number
	to record; records	ロク	*roku*	金	𠆢 午 金 釒 鈩 録 録 16

録 **B** F-0836

説文 1 旧字 2

The origin of this character is not clear. One view explains that 1 comprised 金 **SG-1196** "metal," and 彔 (录) "green dust spilling (probably from bronze)," used for the sound *roku* to mean "to record." Another view explains that the surface of bronzeware was used to inscribe records, whence "to record." The kanji 録 means "records; to record." < 金 录>

記録 record [きろく]; 目録 catalogue, inventory [もくろく]; 実録 authentic record, true account [じつろく]; 回顧録 memoirs [かいこꜜろく]; 議事録 minutes, proceedings of a meeting [ぎじꜜろく]; 通話記録 call log [つうわꜜきろく]; 人名録 Who's Who, directory [じんめꜜいろく]

89 Agricultural tools

89a 方 "square, four directions" [from a plow]; *hoo/boo* 方放防訪芳坊妨傍肪倣

SG-1931 方	Meanings	*Kun* and *On*	Romaji	Bushu	Stroke Order and Number
	way, manner (of doing), direction, option, square, person [honorific]	かた ホウ	kata *hoo*	方	' 亠 方 方 4

方 **A** F-0041

甲骨文1 1 甲骨文2 2 金文1 3 金文2 4 説文 5

1 through 5 depicted "a plow with a long handle," with the handle pointing in two opposite directions horizontally and the plow pointing in two directions vertically, signifying "four (or all) directions." Four directions make "a square." The character also signified "an option or a way," in the sense of a direction one might take, or a manner in which one might choose to do something. In Japanese, when referring to someone in a deferential manner, one often uses the direction in which the person is standing, and thus 方 is an honorific way of saying "person." The kanji 方 means "way (of doing), direction, option, square, person (honorific)." <方>

やり方 the way to do something [やりかた]; 出席なさる方, 方々 a person/people who attend(s) an event (honorific) [しゅっせきなさꜜるかたꜜ, かたꜜがた]; 方向 direction [ほうこう]; 四方 all directions, surrounding [しほꜜう]; 方々 everywhere [ほꜜうぼう]; 方形 rectangular shape [ほうけい]; 一方で on the other hand [いっぽꜜうで]

SG-1932 放	Meanings	*Kun* and *On*	Romaji	Bushu	Stroke Order and Number
	to release, free, emit, cast, throw	はな-す・ほう-る ホウ	hana-su, hoo-ru *hoo*	攴	亠 方 方' 方𠂉 放 8

放 **A** F-0356

中山王器 1 説文 2

1 and 2 comprised 方 **SG-1931** "all four directions," used for the sound *hoo*, and 攴 (攵, bushu *bokuzukuri* "to cause an action"), together signifying "to disperse in various directions, to release." The kanji 放 means "to release, free, emit, cast, throw." <方攵>

放す to release, let go [はなꜜす]; 光を放つ to give off light, flash [ひかりꜜを・はなꜜつ]; 手放す to part with, relinquish, sell [てばなꜜす]; 野放しにする to let run loose [のばꜜなしにする]; 放り投げる to toss, throw, fling [ほうりなげꜜる]; 放流 discharging water, releasing fingerlings [ほうりゅう]; 放射能 radioactivity [ほうしゃꜜのう]; 飲み放題 drinking as much as one wants [のみほꜜうだい]

	Meanings	*Kun* and On	Romaji	Bushu	Stroke Order and Number
SG-1933 防	to prevent, defend	ふせ-ぐ ボウ	huse-gu *boo*	阜	7

防 **A** F-0431 — 説文 1, 説文或体 2

1 and 2 comprised 阝, bushu *kozatohen* "tall dirt wall," and 方 "all directions," used for the sound *boo*, with 土 "dirt" added at the bottom in 2. Together they signified "a high dirt wall built to prevent an enemy from entering." Another view explains that the character represented an embankment for preventing water from coming in. The kanji 防 means "to prevent, defend." <阝方>

防ぐ to prevent [ふせぐ]; 予防 prevention [よぼう]; 防衛 defense [ぼうえい]; 防水 waterproof, water repellant [ぼうすい]; 防止 prevention [ぼうし]; 防衛力 defense capacity [ぼうえいりょく]; 防衛省 Ministry of Defense [ぼうえいしょう]; 国防 national defense [こくぼう]

	Meanings	*Kun* and On	Romaji	Bushu	Stroke Order and Number
SG-1934 訪	to visit, travel	おとず-れる・たず-ねる ホウ	otozu-reru, tazu-neru *hoo*	言	11

訪 **B** F-0558 — 説文

The seal-style form comprised 言, bushu *gonben* "word, language; to speak," and 方 **SG-1931** "direction" used for the sound *hoo*. Together they signified "to ask how to get to a place" when going to visit someone. The kanji 訪 means "to visit, travel." <言方>

訪れる to visit, come [おとずれる]; 訪ねる to visit, go [たずねる]; 訪問 visit [ほうもん]; 来訪する to be visited by [らいほうする]; 再訪 second visit, revisit [さいほう]; 訪日 a visit to Japan [ほうにち]

	Meanings	*Kun* and On	Romaji	Bushu	Stroke Order and Number
SG-1935 芳	fragrant, favorable, good (reputation)	かんば-しい ホウ	kanba-shii *hoo*	艸	7

芳 **C** F-1396 — 説文

The seal-style form comprised "plants" (艸, 艹, bushu *kusakanmuri*), and 方 **SG-1931** "all directions," used for the sound *hoo*. The aroma of a fragrant plant spreads in all directions. The character also meant "favorable reputation" when applied to a person, and is used in honorifics. The kanji 芳 means "fragrant, favorable, good (reputation)." <艹方>

芳しい fragrant [かんばしい]; 芳しくない unfavorable [かんばしくない]; 芳香 aroma, sweet smell [ほうこう]; 芳名録 guest book, directory of members [ほうめいろく]; 芳醇な mellow, rich [ほうじゅんな]

	Meanings	*Kun* and On	Romaji	Bushu	Stroke Order and Number
SG-1936 坊	living quarters in a temple, monk, tyke	ボウ・ボッ	*boo, bo(C)-*	土	7

坊 **C** F-1402 — 説文

The seal-style form comprised 土 **SG-1126** "ground or soil," and 方 "a square area," used for the sound *boo*, together signifying "a section of a house." The kanji 坊 means "living quarters in a temple," and their occupant, "a monk." It is also used as a suffix, often affectionately, to mean "tyke, youngster." <土方>

赤ん坊 baby [あかんぼう]; 坊や my dear boy, laddie [ぼうや]; 忘れん坊 forgetful person [わすれんぼう]; 坊主 Buddhist priest [ぼうず]; 坊主頭 shaven head, close-cropped hair [ぼうずあたま]; 聞かん坊 unruly boy [きかんぼう]; 立ちん坊 remaining on one's feet [たちんぼう]; 坊ちゃん (someone's) young son, young master [ぼっちゃん]

	Meanings	*Kun* and On	Romaji	Bushu	Stroke Order and Number
SG-1937 妨	to obstruct, hamper	さまた-げる ボウ	samata-geru *boo*	女	7

妨 **C** F-1619 — 説文

The seal-style form comprised 女 **SG-0521** "woman, female," and 方, used for the sound *boo* to mean "to prevent" (as in 防 **SG-1933**). Preventing someone from approaching a woman meant "to obstruct." The kanji 妨 means "to obstruct, hamper." <女方>

妨げる to obstruct [さまたげる]; 妨害する to hinder, obstruct [ぼうがいする]

	Meanings	*Kun* and On	Romaji	Bushu	Stroke Order and Number
SG-1938 傍	side; to stand by	かたわ-ら ボウ	katawa-ra *boo*	人	12

傍 **D** F-1700 — 説文

The seal-style form comprised 亻 "an act that one does," and 旁 "beside," used for the sound *boo*, together signifying "a person standing to one side." The kanji 傍 means "side; to stand by." <亻亠方>. (Note on the right-side component 旁: 旁 is also a non-Joyo kanji, used for the word *tsukuri*, which means "a right-side component of kanji." *Tsukuri* (旁) components often have an exclusively phonetic role, in contrast to *hen* 偏 **SG-1250** "left-side components of kanj), which tend to play a more general semantic role.)

傍ら side [かたわら]; 傍観する to look on, stand by [ぼうかんする]; 傍線 a line drawn alongside words [ぼうせん]; 傍聴席 gallery seat, public observer's seat [ぼうちょうせき]; 路傍 the roadside, the wayside [ろぼう]

	Meanings	Kun and On	Romaji	Bushu	Stroke Order and Number
SG-1939 肪	fat	ボウ	*boo*	肉	丿月⺼肪肪肪 8

肪 **D** F-1872

説文

The seal-style form comprised 月 "part of the body," and 方 SG-1931, used for the sound *boo* to mean "to spread out." A body spreaing out sideways signified "fat, corpulent." The kanji 肪 means "fat." <月方>

脂肪 fat [しぼう]; 脂肪分 fat content [しぼうぶん]; 乳脂肪 butterfat, milk fat [にゅうしぼう]

	Meanings	Kun and On	Romaji	Bushu	Stroke Order and Number
SG-1940 倣	to follow, take after, emulate	なら-う ホウ	nara-u *hoo*	人	亻𠆢仿仿佐倣倣 10

倣 **D** F-2283

No ancient form. The kanji 倣 comprises 亻, bushu *ninben* "an act that one does," and 放 SG-1932, used for the sound *hoo* to mean "to imitate," together signifying "a person emulates." The kanji 倣 means "to follow, take after, emulate." <亻放>

倣う to follow, emulate, copy [ならう]; 見倣う to learn by watching [みならう]; 右に倣え Eyes right! [みぎにならえ]; 模倣する to imitate, copy [もほうする]

89b 以 "by means of" [from a hoe or spade (held by a person)] 以似

	Meanings	Kun and On	Romaji	Bushu	Stroke Order and Number
SG-1941 以	to use; by means of, (starting) from	イ	*i*	人	ｌｌ丷以以 5

以 **A** F-0222

甲骨文1 (1), 甲骨文2 (2), 金文1 (3), 金文2 (4), 説文 (5)

1 through 5 depicted "a hoe or spade" to represent field work. Using a tool to begin work in the field meant "by means of, starting from." In the kanji a person (人) was added on the right side. The kanji 以 means "to use; by means of, (starting) from." <以人>

〜以内 within X [〜いない]; 三個以上 three or more [さんこいじょう]; 以上です That'll be all [いじょうです]; 以下の通り as follows [いかのとおり]; 以前 previously, the past [いぜん]; 以後 onward, afterward [いご]; 以心伝心 telepathy [いしん・でんしん] // 以ての外 out of the question, preposterous [もってのほか]

	Meanings	Kun and On	Romaji	Bushu	Stroke Order and Number
SG-1942 似	to resemble	に-る ジ	ni-ru *ji*	人	亻亻仏化似似 7

似 **B** F-0887

金文1 (1), 金文2 (2), 説文 (3)

1 and 2 comprised "a person with a hoe" (以), used for the sound *ji* to mean "to resemble," and 口 "a mouth" or "a box of prayers." In 3, 口 was dropped, and the character meant "a person resembling another." In the kanji 似, another person (亻) was added to 以. The kanji 似 means "to resemble." <亻以>

似る to resemble [にる]; 母親似 resembling or taking after one's mother [ははおやに]; 似通う to resemble closely [にかよう]; 似合う to match, fit in [にあう]; 他人の空似 chance resemblance with someone unrelated [たにんのそらに]; 似ても似つかない to not bear the slightest resemblance to [にても・につかない]; 類似 resemblance, similarity [るいじ]

89c 台 "to begin" [from a hoe and a mouth] 台治始怠胎冶

	Meanings	Kun and On	Romaji	Bushu	Stroke Order and Number
SG-1943 台	base, raised level, stand, platform	ダイ・タイ	*dai, tai*	至	㇜ム台台台 5

台 **A** F-0239

金文 (1), 説文 (2), 旧字 (3) · 金文1 (4), 金文2 (5), 説文 (6)

There are two separate histories for 台. The kyuji 臺 (3) started as 1 and 2, which comprised "a watchtower" (高) and "a place where an arrow reaches" (至), together signifying "a tower on a raised level." For the shinji 台, 4, 5, and 6 comprised ム "hoe," used for the sound *dai*, and 口 "mouth, box of prayers." The shinji 台 took over the meaning of the kyuji (3). The kanji 台 means "base, raised level, stand, platform." <ム口>

台 holder, support, mound, pedestal [だい]; 踏み台 step, jump server [ふみだい]; 台所 kitchen [だいどころ]; 台地 plateau [だいち]; 高台 elevated ground [たかだい]; 台風 severe tropical storm, typhoon [たいふう]; 屋台 street stall [やたい] // 台詞 one's lines (in a script) [せりふ]

SG-1944 治

Meanings	Kun and On	Romaji	Bushu	Stroke Order and Number
to rule, govern, cure (illness), recover	おさ-める・なお-る ジ・チ	osa-meru, nao-ru *ji, chi*	水	氵氵氵治治治 8

治 **A** F-0245

The seal-style form comprised 氵 "flowing water," and 台 **SG-1943**, used for the sound *ji* or *chi*. In ancient times controlling irrigation or flooding was a very important job for a ruler. The character meant "to rule or govern." The meaning of putting something under control was applied to illness, whence the meaning "to cure or heal (illness)." The kanji 治 means "to rule, govern, cure (illness), recover." <氵 台>

治める to rule, control [おさめ1る]; 治る to cure, recover (from illness) [なお1る]; 治す to cure [なお1す]; 政治 politics [せいじ]; 明治 the Meiji era (1868-1912) [めいじ]; 統治する to rule over, govern [とう1ちする]; 治水 river improvement, flood control [ちすい]; 自治 self-governance [じ1ち]; 治安 public order, law and order [ちあん]

SG-1945 始

Meanings	Kun and On	Romaji	Bushu	Stroke Order and Number
to begin, start	はじ-める シ	haji-meru *shi*	女	𡿨女女始始始 8

始 **A** F-0368

金文1 (1), 金文2 (2), 説文 (3)

The development of this character is obscure. 1 and 2 comprised "a hoe or spade" (ム), "a mouth, speaking" (口), and "a woman" (女). One view explains that 台 was used for the sounds *tai*/*dai* to mean "womb," and that with 女 "woman" lending the meaning "giving new life to a child," the character signified "to begin." Another view explains that from the sound *shi* (ム from 似) it meant "a first-born daughter," and thus "to begin." The kanji 始 means "to begin, start." <女 台>

始まる to begin, start [はじまる]; 事始め beginning of things [ことはじめ]; 開始 start [かいし]; 始業時間 opening time, starting time of work [しぎょうじかん]; 終始 constantly [しゅうし]; 原始的 primitive, primeval [げんしてき]; 後始末する to set matters right, deal with the aftermath [あとしまつする]

SG-1946 怠

Meanings	Kun and On	Romaji	Bushu	Stroke Order and Number
to neglect; lazy, neglectful	おこた-る・なま-ける タイ	okota-ru, nama-keru *tai*	心	㇜ム台台怠怠 9

怠 **D** F-1653

中山王器 (1), 説文 (2)

1 comprised "a person sitting in a slumped posture" at the top, with "hoe, spade" (ム), and "heart" underneath. In 2 the person was dropped, and 台 **SG-1943** (used for the sound *tai*) and "heart" (心 **SG-0187**) formed the non-Joyo kanji 怡 *tai*, which meant "joyful." 怡 and 怠 were closely related, sharing the same meaning and sound. When you are joyful you are more relaxed and may become neglectful. The heart component was moved to the bottom, and the kanji 怠 means "to neglect; lazy, neglectful." <台 心>

怠る to neglect [おこたる]; 怠ける to be idle, get lazy, slacken one's efforts [なまけ1る]; 怠慢な negligent, slack [たいまんな]; 怠惰な lazy [た1いだな]; 倦怠感 physical weariness, feeling of fatigue [けんた1いかん]

SG-1947 胎

Meanings	Kun and On	Romaji	Bushu	Stroke Order and Number
womb	タイ	*tai*	肉	月月胎胎胎胎 9

胎 **D** F-1791

The seal-style form comprised 月 "part of the body," and 台, used for the sound *tai* to mean "to begin." The part of the body where a life began meant "the womb." The kanji 胎 means "womb." <月 台>

胎児 fetus [た1いじ]; 胎内 the interior of the womb, uterus [た1いない]; 胎動 quickening, signs of a forthcoming event [たいどう]; 受胎 conception [じゅたい]; 胎教 prenatal training [たいきょう]

SG-1948 冶

Meanings	Kun and On	Romaji	Bushu	Stroke Order and Number
to melt metal; metallurgy	ヤ	*ya*	冫	冫冫冶冶冶 7

冶 **D** F-2587

金文 (1), 説文 (2)

1 comprised "a hoe" (top left) and "a box or a mouth" (together forming 台 for the sound *ya* or *ji* to mean "to melt"), and two short lines representing "pieces of metal." Taken together, these components signified "melting metal, metallurgy." In 2, "ice" on the left was used to signify minerals or metal being melted into new shapes, and it became 冫, bushu *nisui,* in the kanji. In 2, "melting ice" was added on the left to liken the melting of minerals or metal to form a new shape to water changing into ice, and became the bushu nisui (冫) in kanji. The kanji 冶 means "metallurgy." <冫 台>

冶金 metallurgy [やきん]; 冶金学 (study of) metallurgy [やき1んがく] // 鍛冶屋 smith, blacksmith [かじや]; 刀鍛冶 swordsmith [かたな1かじ]

89d 力 "power, strength" [from a hand with muscles showing, or a plow]

力加協賀励脇劣脅架勃

	Meanings	Kun and On	Romaji	Bushu	Stroke Order and Number
SG-1949 力	power, strength	ちから リョク・リキ	chikara *ryoku, riki*	力	フ力 2

力 **A** F-0031

甲骨文1 1 甲骨文2 2 金文 3 説文 4

One view explains that 1, 2, 3, and 4 all depicted "a plow" in the field. Field work was a strenuous activity that required much muscular power. Another view holds that the character depicted "an arm with a flexing muscle." The kanji 力 means "power, strength." <力>

力 might, power, strength [ちから]; 力仕事 heavy labor [ちからしごと]; 体力 physical strength [たいりょく]; 引力 gravity [いんりょく]; 実力 real ability, competency [じつりょく]; 機動力 mobile power, mobility [きどうりょく]; 力学 dynamics [りきがく]; 航空力学 aeromechanics [こうくうりきがく]

	Meanings	Kun and On	Romaji	Bushu	Stroke Order and Number
SG-1950 加	to add, join	くわ-える カ	kuwa-eru *ka*	力	フ力力加加加 5

加 **A** F-0189

金文1 1 金文2 2 説文 3

1, 2, and 3 comprised "a plow" (力) and "a mouth, speaking" (口 **SG-0031**). Vocalizing while exerting effort "added" strength to one's movement, and the character meant "to add." The kanji 加 means "to add." <力口>

加える to add [くわえる]; 追加 addition, supplement [ついか]; 加味する to take something into account [かみする]; 加減 addition and subtraction, the condition of one's health [かげん]; 加工品 processed goods [かこうひん]; 加害者 perpetrator, assailant [かがいしゃ]; 加熱する to heat something up [かねつする]

	Meanings	Kun and On	Romaji	Bushu	Stroke Order and Number
SG-1951 協	to cooperate, help others	キョウ	*kyoo*	十	十十フ十カ协協 8

協 **A** F-0242

古文 1 説文 2

1 comprised 曰 "to call out," and 十 "to bundle up into one," together signifying "many people calling out to each other." In 2, "three plows" (劦), used for the sound *kyoo,* meant "to give each other a helping hand in the field." (The history of 劦 is shown at top-right). The kanji 協 means "to cooperate, help others." <十劦>

協力する to cooperate, collaborate [きょうりょくする]; 生協 co-op [せいきょう, せいきょう]; 協会 association, society [きょうかい]; 経済協力 economic corporation [けいざいきょうりょく]; 漁協 fishermen's cooperative [ぎょきょう]; 協調 collaboration, conciliation [きょうちょう]; 産学協同 industrial-academic cooperation [さんがく・きょうどう]; 協議する to confer with, hold talks [きょうぎする]

	Meanings	Kun and On	Romaji	Bushu	Stroke Order and Number
SG-1952 賀	to celebrate; auspicious	ガ	*ga*	貝	フカカロ 賀賀賀 12

賀 **B** F-0840

中山王器 1 説文 2

1 and 2 comprised "a cowrie" (貝 **SG-1693**) for "valuable; money," and "a plow" (力 **SG-1949**) with "a mouth" (口 **SG-0031**) for the sound *ga* and the meaning "to add." One gave someone a valuable gift at a celebratory occasion. The kanji 賀 means "to celebrate; auspicious." <加貝>

賀正 New Year's greeting (written expression) [がしょう]; 一般参賀 New Year visit of the general public to the Imperial Palace [いっぱんさんが]; 年賀状 New Year's greeting postcard [ねんがじょう]

	Meanings	Kun and On	Romaji	Bushu	Stroke Order and Number
SG-1953 励	to strive for, give encouragement; industrious	はげ-む レイ	hage-mu *ree*	力	厂戸后厉励 7

励 **C** F-1320

勵 励 旧字

No ancient form. The left side 厲 of the kyuji 勵, used for the *sound ree,* was "a venomous scorpion" under "a cliff" (厂), signifying "furious, fierce." Together with the right side 力 "plow, strenuous field work," the character meant "to work strenuously." Another view explains that 厲 meant "hard rock," and that with the addition of "a plow" the character meant "to strenuously till hard soil." In the shinji, 萬 (under 厂) was replaced by 万 **SG-1022**. The kanji 励 means "to strive for, give encouragement; industrious." <厂万力>

励む to endeavour, be industrious [はげむ]; 励ます to cheer, support [はげます]; 奨励する to promote, encourage [しょうれいする]; 激励する to urge on, exhort [げきれいする]

	Meanings	Kun and On	Romaji	Bushu	Stroke Order and Number
SG-1954 脇	side of one's body, flank, supporting role	わき	waki	肉	丿月月⁊ 肋 脇脇 10

脇 **C** F-1412	説文 脇 The seal-style form comprised 劦 "three plows," used for the sound *kyoo* to mean "ribs lined up," and 月 "part of the body." Together they signified "side (of one's body), flank" and "supporting role." The kanji 脇 means "side of one's body, flank, supporting role." <月劦>	脇 one's side [わき]; 脇役 supporting role [わきやく]; 脇腹が痛い to have a pain in the side [わきばらがいたい]; 小脇に抱える to carry under one's arm [こわきにかかえる]; 脇道にそれる to deviate to the side [わきみちにそれる]; 脇差 short sword [わきざし]; 脇見運転 driving without watching the road [わきみうんてん]

	Meanings	Kun and On	Romaji	Bushu	Stroke Order and Number
SG-1955 劣	inferior; to detereorate	おと-る レツ	oto-ru *retsu*	力	丨 小 少 劣 劣 6

劣 **C** F-1519	説文 劣 The seal-style form comprised 少 "little" and 力 "power," together signifying "little strength" and "inferior." The kanji 劣 means "inferior; to detereorate." <少 力>	劣る inferior [おとる]; 見劣りする to pale in comparison [みおとりする]; 劣化する to deteriorate [れっかする]; 優劣をつける to judge which is better [ゆうれつを·つける]; 劣等感 inferiority complex [れっとうかん]; 劣化ウラン depleted uranium [れっかウラン]; 下劣な base, mean, sordid [げれつな]

	Meanings	Kun and On	Romaji	Bushu	Stroke Order and Number
SG-1956 脅	to threaten, coerce; menace	おど-す・おびや-かす キョウ	odo-su, obiya-kasu *kyoo*	肉	フ カ 力 劦 脅 脅 10

脅 **C** F-1536	説文 脅 The kanji 脅 shared the same seal-style form with 脇, and yet these two kanji have different meanings. In 脅, 劦, used for the sound *kyoo* to mean "power," was placed on top of 月, bushu *nikuzuki* "part of the body." Power over someone's body meant "to threaten or coerce." The kanji 脅 means "to threaten, coerce; menace." <劦 月>	脅す to threaten, scare someone into doing [おどす]; 脅かす to make somebody feel uneasy, jeopardize [おびやかす]; 脅し取る to blackmail, extort [おどしとる]; 脅し文句 threatning words [おどしもんく]; 脅迫する to intimidate, blackmail [きょうはくする]; 脅威となる to become a menace [きょういとなる]

	Meanings	Kun and On	Romaji	Bushu	Stroke Order and Number
SG-1957 架	to bridge over, hang across	か-ける カ	ka-keru *ka*	木	フ カ 力口 加 架 架 9

架 **C** F-1583	No ancient form. The kanji comprises 加, used for sound *ka*, over 木 "a tree," together signifying "building something in a high place." The kanji 架 means "to bridge over, build something over, hang across." <加 木>	架ける to hang across [かける]; 架空の fanciful, fictitious [かくうの]; 架線工事 wiring installation work [かせんこうじ]; 書架 bookshelf, book stack [しょか]; 十字架 cross, crucifix [じゅうじか]; 閉架式図書館 closed-access library [へいかしきとしょかん]; 高架橋 elevated bridge, viaduct [こうかきょう]

	Meanings	Kun and On	Romaji	Bushu	Stroke Order and Number
SG-1958 勃	to happen abruptly; energetic	ボツ	*botsu*	力	十 亠 声 孛 孛 勃 勃 9

勃 **D** F-2259	説文 勃 The left side of the seal-style form was "a plant bulging with seeds and about to burst." It was used for the sound *botsu* to mean "a sudden change." With "plow" (力) for "power" added on the right side, the character meant "abrupt occurrence." The kanji 勃 means "to happen abruptly; energetic." <宀子力>	勃興 sudden rise, rise to power [ぼっこう]; 暴動が勃発する a riot breaks out [ぼうどうが·ぼっぱつする]

90 Nets

90a 罒 (网) "a dragnet; to capture" [from a dragnet cast over a wide area] 罪署罰羅 ⊠

	Meanings	Kun and On	Romaji	Bushu	Stroke Order and Number
SG-1959 罪	crime, sin, guilt	つみ ザイ	tsumi *zai*	网	罒 罒 罕 罪 罪 罪 13

罪 **B** F-0805	中山王器 1, 辠 正字 2, · 説文 3, 罪 This meaning has been represented by two kanji, each with a different origin. The ancient form (1) of the orthographic-style kanji 辠(2) comprised "a nose" (自 **SG-0059**)	罪 crime, wrongdoing, sin [つみ]; 罪作りな deceitful, conniving, cruel [つみつくりな]; 罪 merits and demerits, pluses and minuses [こうざい]; 罪悪 crime, sin, vice

	and a tattooing needle (辛 **SG-1359**), together signifying "a criminal tattooed on the face." 辠 meant "guilt or offense." The seal-style form (3) of 罪, which is the kanji currently used in Japanese, comprised "a dragnet" (网) over 非 **SG-0992** "not," together signifying "an unpermitted act by a person who got captured in the authorities' dragnet." The kanji 罪 means "crime, sin, guilt." <罒非>	[ざいあく]; 原罪 original sin [げんざい]; 死罪 capital punishment [しざい]; 免罪符 indulgence, vindication [めんざいふ]; 犯罪者 offender, criminal, culprit [はんざいしゃ]; 罪状書 indictment [ざいじょうしょ]

	Meanings	Kun and On	Romaji	Bushu	Stroke Order and Number
SG-1960 署	police station, tax office; to write down	ショ	*sho*	网	罒罒罒罒署署 13

署 **B** F-0939	 説文 1 旧字 2 1 showed "a dragnet" (网) cast over 者, used for the sound *sho*. Together they signified "a government office, police station, tax office." The character's similarity to the ancient forms of 書 **SG-2026**, as well as their shared phonetic feature *sho*, gave 署 the additional meaning "to write down in a designated space." The kanji 署 means "police station, tax office; to write down." <罒者>	警察署 police station [けいさつしょ]; 消防署 fire station, firehouse [しょうぼうしょ]; 署長 station chief, head superintendent [しょちょう]; 署名 signature, autograph [しょめい]; 連署 joint signature, countersignature [れんしょ, れんしょ]; 署名運動 signature collecting campaign [しょめいうんどう]; 署名捺印 to sign and seal [しょめい・なついん]

	Meanings	Kun and On	Romaji	Bushu	Stroke Order and Number
SG-1961 罰	punishment	バツ・バチ	*batsu, bachi*	网	罒罒罒罒罰罰 14

罰 **C** F-1304	金文 1 金文 2 説文 3 The left side of 1, 2, and 3 comprised "a net" (网) and "words" (言)," signifying "to heap abusive words over someone" (詈). With "a knife" (刂) on the right side, the character signified "rebuking someone's crime and threatening punishment with a knife," hence, "punishment." The kanji 罰 means "punishment." <罒言刂>	罰 punishment, penalty [ばつ, ばち]; 罰する to punish [ばっする]; 天罰 the wrath of heaven [てんばつ]; 罰則 penal regulation [ばっそく]; 罰点 bad mark, black marks [ばってん]; 賞罰 rewards and punishments [しょうばつ]; 罰が当たる to incur divine punishment [ばちがあたる]

	Meanings	Kun and On	Romaji	Bushu	Stroke Order and Number
SG-1962 羅	fine net, silk gauze, thin silk; to encompass	ラ	*ra*	网	罒罒罒罒羅羅 19

羅 **D** F-1756	 甲骨文 1 説文 2 1 and 2 depicted "a fine net thrown over a bird," with "a skein of threads" (糸) added in 2. The character meant "a fine net made of threads," or "thin fabric." Nets spread to cover many things. The kanji 羅 means "a fine net, silk gauze, thin silk; to encompass." <罒糸隹>	甲羅 shield, shell [こうら]; 森羅万象 all things in nature [しんら・ばんしょう]; 網羅する to encompass all points, cover thoroughly [もうらする]; 一張羅 best clothes [いっちょうら]; 羅紗 thick woolen cloth [らしゃ]; 羅列する to enumerate, arrange [られつする]

90b 害 "to harm; damage"; *katsu* 害割憲轄

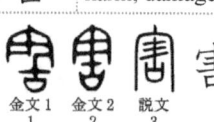

	Meanings	Kun and On	Romaji	Bushu	Stroke Order and Number
SG-1963 害	harm, damage	ガイ	*gai*	宀	丶宀宀宇害害 10

害 **A** F-0389	金文 1 金文 2 説文 3 Interpretations of the ancient forms of the kanji 害 vary. They include: (a) a large headgear pushing down on a skull (古), which came to mean "to damage"; (b) headgear or a basket protecting a skull (古) from "harm"; (c) a large-handled tattooing needle that was used for criminal punishment, piercing through a box of old benedictions (古) to lessen the effect of the prayers, and thus meaning "to harm, damage." The kanji 害 means "harm, damage." <害(宔口)>	害 harm, mischief, evil [がい]; 公害 pollution [こうがい]; 自害 suicide [じがい]; 危害 injury, harm [きがい]; 有害な poisonous [ゆうがいな]; 無害の harmless [むがいの]; 塩害 damage caused by salt [えんがい]; 水害 flood damage [すいがい]

SG-1964 割	Meanings	Kun and On	Romaji	Bushu	Stroke Order and Number
	to divide, cut out; portion	わり・わ-れる・さ-く カツ	wari, wa-reru, sa-ku *katsu*	刀	宀中宝害割 12

割 **A** F-0411

金文 1 說文 2

1 and 2 comprised "knife" (刀, 刂) and 害 "harm, damage," used for the sound *katsu* (from *gai*). Together they signified "to cut out a damaged part with a knife." From "divided pieces" came "portions." The kanji 割 means "to divide, cut out; portion." <害刂>

割れる to break, split, become clear [われる]; 割合 proportion, rate, allotment [わりあい]; 割り込む to wedge oneself in, force one's way [わりこむ]; 割り当て to allot [わりあて]; 割り増し extra fare, premium [わりまし]; 学割 student discount [がくわり]; 割り算 division (math) [わりざん]; 時間を割く to spare time for [じかんをさく]; 分割 division [ぶんかつ]; 割烹 Japanese-style cooking [かっぽう]

SG-1965 憲	Meanings	Kun and On	Romaji	Bushu	Stroke Order and Number
	important law, constitution	ケン	*ken*	心	宀中宝害害憲 16

憲 **B** F-0707

金文 1 金文 2 說文 3

One view explains that 1 and 2 depicted "a large tattooing needle used for criminal punishment" and "an eye," and that "keeping watch to prevent crimes" was the purpose of "law." Another view holds that the character comprised "a net or cover" and "an eye." In 3, a "heart or mind" (心) was added to mean legal principles that one should always keep in mind, that is, "constitution, very important law." The kanji 憲 means "important law, constitution." <宝罒心>

憲法 constitution [けんぽう]; 違憲 unconstitutionality [いけん]; 憲政 constitutional government [けんせい]; 憲章 charter [けんしょう]; 改憲 constitutional revision [かいけん]; 立憲 enactment of a constitution [りっけん]

SG-1966 轄	Meanings	Kun and On	Romaji	Bushu	Stroke Order and Number
	linchpin, wedge; to control	カツ	*katsu*	車	亘車軒軒轄轄 17

轄 **D** F-2004

說文

The seal-style form comprised 車 "wheel," and 害, used for the sound *katsu* to mean "harmful." Together they signified a wedge for preventing wheels from detaching from the axle. The kanji 轄 means "linchpin, wedge; to control." <車害>

管轄 jurisdiction, purview [かんかつ]; 統轄 control and jurisdiction [とうかつ]; 管轄外 outside one's jurisdiction [かんかつがい]; 直轄 direct jurisdiction, immediate supervision [ちょっかつ]; 所轄 jurisdiction, proper authority office [しょかつ]

91 Molds and frames

91a 岡 "strong, hill" [from a casting mold]; *koo* 岡綱鋼剛

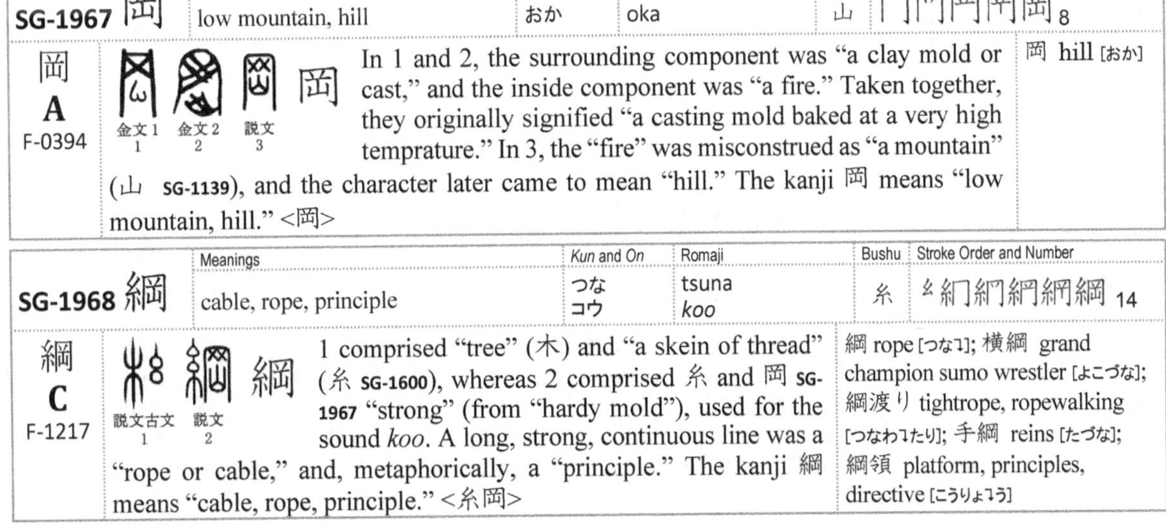

SG-1967 岡	Meanings	Kun and On	Romaji	Bushu	Stroke Order and Number
	low mountain, hill	おか	oka	山	冂冂冈冈岡 8

岡 **A** F-0394

金文 1 金文 2 說文 3

In 1 and 2, the surrounding component was "a clay mold or cast," and the inside component was "a fire." Taken together, they originally signified "a casting mold baked at a very high temprature." In 3, the "fire" was misconstrued as "a mountain" (山 **SG-1139**), and the character later came to mean "hill." The kanji 岡 means "low mountain, hill." <岡>

岡 hill [おか]

SG-1968 綱	Meanings	Kun and On	Romaji	Bushu	Stroke Order and Number
	cable, rope, principle	つな コウ	tsuna *koo*	糸	糸紉網網網綱 14

綱 **C** F-1217

說文古文 1 說文 2

1 comprised "tree" (木) and "a skein of thread" (糸 **SG-1600**), whereas 2 comprised 糸 and 岡 **SG-1967** "strong" (from "hardy mold"), used for the sound *koo*. A long, strong, continuous line was a "rope or cable," and, metaphorically, a "principle." The kanji 綱 means "cable, rope, principle." <糸岡>

綱 rope [つな]; 横綱 grand champion sumo wrestler [よこづな]; 綱渡り tightrope, ropewalking [つなわたり]; 手綱 reins [たづな]; 綱領 platform, principles, directive [こうりょう]

	Meanings	Kun and On	Romaji	Bushu	Stroke Order and Number
SG-1969 鋼	steel	はがね コウ	hagane *koo*	金	𠆢 𠂉 金 釦 鋼 鋼 16

鋼 **C** F-1330

No ancient form. The kanji 鋼 comprises 金 **SG-1196** "metal," and 岡 "a hardy mold," used for the sound *koo* to mean "strong," together signifying "hard and strong metal, iron, steel." The kanji 鋼 means "steel." <金岡>

鋼 steel [はがね]; 鋼鉄 steel [こうてつ]; 鉄鋼業 steel industry [てっこうぎょう]

	Meanings	Kun and On	Romaji	Bushu	Stroke Order and Number
SG-1970 剛	strong, hard, hardy, formidable	ゴウ	*goo*	刀	冂 冂 冈 岡 剛 10

剛 **C** F-1373

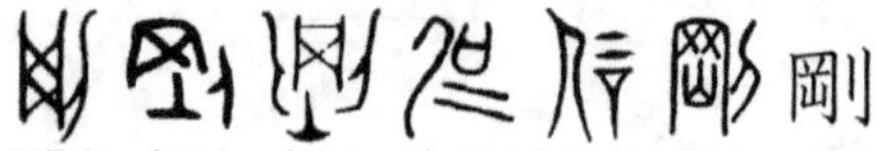

甲骨文 1, 金文 1 2, 金文 2 3, 金文 3 4, 説文古文 5, 説文 6 — 剛

1, 2, and 3 comprised "a casting mold" and "a knife," with the addition of "dirt" (土) in 2 and 3. Together these components signified a clay mold, hardened over a fire and then cut open with a knife, which gave the meaning "hard, strong." One view explains that the right side of 4 (and 5) depicted a pot used for casting metal. 6 comprised 岡 **SG-1967** "a casting mold baked at a very high temperature" and "a knife," and meant "strong, hardy." The meaning was applied to personal character and meant "formidable." The kanji 剛 means "strong, hard, hardy, formidable." <岡 刂>

剛毅な strong and sturdy, vigorous, plucky [ごうきな]; 金剛石 diamond [こんごうせき]; 剛腕な strong-armed, magnificent performance [ごうわんな]

91b 开 "a square shape" [from a wooden framework for a well, or a frame for restraining and punishing a criminal, a pillory]; *kee* 形型研刑

井

	Meanings	Kun and On	Romaji	Bushu	Stroke Order and Number
SG-1971 形	shape	かた・かたち ケイ・ギョウ	kata, katachi *kee, gyoo*	彡	二 于 开 形 7

形 **A** F-0283

説文 — 形

The seal-style form comprised 开 "a framework," used for the sound *kee*, and 彡 "beautiful shape, well-formed shape." The kanji 形 means "shape." <开彡>

形 form [かたち]; 形見 memento [かたみ]; 手形 bill draft, note [てがた]; 人間形成 the formation of one's character [にんげんけいせい]; 形声文字 semantic and phonetic composite character [けいせいもじ]; 人形 doll [にんぎょう]; 形相 feature, facial expression [ぎょうそう, ぎょうそう]

	Meanings	Kun and On	Romaji	Bushu	Stroke Order and Number
SG-1972 型	pattern, shape, mold	かた ケイ	kata *kee*	土	二 开 刑 型 型 型 9

型 **A** F-0434

金文 1, 中山王器 2, 説文 3 — 型

1 comprised "a knife," "a wooden square cast," and "a casting pot," with "clay, soil" added as a bottom component in 2 and 3. Taken together, these components meant "a clay mold or frame for casting, with a knife to break the mold afterward." In the kanji, the knife became 刂, bushu *rittoo*. The kanji 型 means "pattern, shape, mold." <开 刂 土>

型通り formally, in due form [かたどおり]; 型破り unconventional, uncommon [かたやぶり]; 型紙 dress pattern [かたがみ]; 大型 large in size [おおがた]; 小型車 small-size car [こがたしゃ]; 体型 body type [たいけい]

	Meanings	Kun and On	Romaji	Bushu	Stroke Order and Number
SG-1973 研	to polish, sharpen, hone, whet	と-ぐ ケン	to-gu *ken*	石	丆 石 石 研 9

研 **A** F-0459

説文 1, 旧字 2 — 研

1 and 2 comprised 石 **SG-1148** "rock," and 幵 "two flat items of equal length," used for the sound *ken*, together signifying "grinding two items into equal length using a honing stone." The kanji 研 means "to polish, sharpen, hone, whet." <石开>

研ぐ to sharpen, hone [とぐ]; 研ぎ澄ます to sharpen, hone to a fine finish, polish [とぎすます, とぎすます]; 研究 research [けんきゅう]; 研究所 research institute [けんきゅうじょ]; 研修 employee training [けんしゅう]; 研磨 griding, polishing [けんま]

	Meanings	Kun and On	Romaji	Bushu	Stroke Order and Number
SG-1974 刑	to punish; penalty, sentence	ケイ	*kee*	刀	二 于 开 刑 6

刑
B
F-1016

井 㓝 井 刑 刑 刑
金文 1 (1), 金文 2 (2), 金文 3 (3), 説文 1 (4), 説文 2 (5)

1 was "a wooden framework," while 2 through 5 had the addition of "a knife." These two components together signified "a pillory" or, more generally, "punishment." The kanji 刑 means "to punish." <开 刂>

刑事 criminal matter, detective [けꜜいじ]; 刑罰 punishment, punitive sanction [けꜜいばつ]; 受刑者 prisoner, convict, inmate [じゅけꜜいしゃ]; 刑事事件 criminal case [けいじじꜜけん]; 死刑囚 condemned convict, death-row prisoner [しけꜜいしゅう]

92 Vessels

92a 豆 [from a tall stemmed vessel, crock, urn]; *too* 豆豊壱艶

	Meanings	Kun and On	Romaji	Bushu	Stroke Order and Number
SG-1975 豆	bean, miniature	まめ トウ・ズ	*mame* *too, zu*	豆	一 百 豆 豆 7

豆
A
F-0959

甲骨文 (1), 金文 1 (2), 金文 2 (3), 説文古文 (4), 説文 (5)

1 through 5 depicted "a stemmed vessel, urn, or crock," and had the sound *too*. Such a vessel was made of wood, clay, or bronze, and was used to hold drinks and food for a rite. The short line at the top and the dot inside the bowl signified that the vessel was full. The character was later borrowed to mean "bean," for the same sound *too*. Beans' size gave the meaning "miniature." The kanji 豆 means "bean, miniature." <豆>

豆 bean, miniature [まめꜜ]; 豆電球 miniature light bulb [まめでꜜんきゅう]; 枝豆 boiled green soy beans in pods [えだまめ]; 豆腐 soy bean curd [とうふꜜ]; 納豆 fermented soy beans, *natto* [なっとꜜう]; 大豆 soy bean [だいず] // 小豆 *azuki* bean [あずきꜜ]

	Meanings	Kun and On	Romaji	Bushu	Stroke Order and Number
SG-1976 豊	abundance; affluent, plentiful, rich	ゆた-か ホウ	*yuta-ka* *hoo*	豆	口 曲 曲 豊 豊 豊 13

豊
A
F-0520

甲骨文 (1), 金文 (2), 説文 1 (3), 説文 2 (4), 旧字 (5)

1 through 5 comprised "a stemmed vessel," with a top component depicting either "millet stalks" for "abundance of harvest," or "strands of jewels" for "wealth." In the shinji the top component was replaced by 曲. The kanji 豊 means "abundance; affluent, plentiful, rich." <曲豆>

豊か rich, abundant, plentiful [ゆꜜたか]; 心豊かな fertile mind, spiritually rich [こころゆꜜたかな]; 豊富な abundant, rich, plentiful [ほうふな]; 豊作 good harvest [ほうさく]; 豊年 year of good harvest [ほうねん]; 豊満な plump [ほうまんな]; 五穀豊穣 (pray for) a bumper crop [ごꜜこく・ほうじょう]

	Meanings	Kun and On	Romaji	Bushu	Stroke Order and Number
SG-1977 壱	one, single	イチ	*ichi*	士	十 士 壱 壱 壱 7

壱
D
F-1940

金文 (1), 説文 1 (2), 説文 2 (3), 旧字 (4)

1 and 2 were "a crock with a secure lid," presumably full of fermented liquid. The character was borrowed to mean "one," to avoid misreading of or tampering with the kanji 一 in important financial documents. The kanji 壱 means "one, single." <士冖ヒ>
(Note: The kanji 貳 and 弐 **SG-1475** are similarly used as substitutes for 二 **SG-2126**, and 参 **SG-2097** can be substituted for 三 **SG-2127**.)

金壱万円 10,000 yen (on formal receipts and checks) [きꜜん・いちまんえん]

	Meanings	Kun and On	Romaji	Bushu	Stroke Order and Number
SG-1978 艶	luster, gloss; enchanting	つや エン	*tsuya* *en*	色	口 曲 曲 豊 豊 艶 艶 艶 19

艶
D
F-2023

豔 豔 艷 艶
篆文 (1), 正字 (2), 旧字 (3)

1 and 2 comprised 豊 **SG-1976** "plentiful, abundant," and "a secure lid (去 **SG-2011**)" over "a vessel (皿 **SG-1843**)." Plentiful food or offerings in a vessel signified something "desirable," which further meant "enchanting or attractive" in appearance. In 3, 色 **SG-0423** replaced the right-hand component to signify "attractiveness." The kanji 艶 means "luster, gloss; enchanting." <豊色>

艶のある shiny, glossy [つやのあꜜる]; 色艶のいい of good glossy color [いろꜜつやの・いꜜい]; 艶やかな shiny, glossy [つやꜜやかな]; 妖艶な bewitching [ようえんな]; 艶聞 rumor of a love affair [えんぶん] // 艶やかな glamorous, charming [あでꜜやかな]

92b 畐 "wealth" [from a full cask with a lid]; *huku* 福副富幅 畐

	Meanings	Kun and On	Romaji	Bushu	Stroke Order and Number
SG-1979 福	good luck, bliss, blessing, fortune	フク	*huku*	示	ラネネ礻福福 13

福 **A** F-0492

甲骨文1 1 甲骨文2 2 金文1 3 金文2 4 説文 5 旧字 6

All of the ancient forms 1 through 5 comprised an altar with an offering (示), and a full, narrow-necked cask (畐), used for the sound *huku*. 1 also had a pair of hands. When reverentially making offerings to a deity, one prayed for blessings and good fortune. The altar in 6 became ネ, bushu *shimesuhen*. The kanji 福 means "bliss, blessing, fortune, good luck." < ネ 畐 >

福 good luck, blessing [ふくつ]; 幸福な happy, blissful [こうふくな]; 祝福 blessing, benediction [しゅくふく]; 福々しい plump and happy-looking [ふくぶくしい]; 福音書 the Biblical Gospels [ふくいんしょ]; 福袋 grab bag, mystery shopping bag [ふくぶくろ]

	Meanings	Kun and On	Romaji	Bushu	Stroke Order and Number
SG-1980 副	to accompany; assisting; copy	フク	*huku*	刀	一戸畐畐副 11

副 **A** F-0476

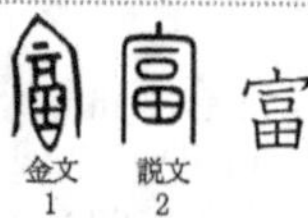

説文籀文 1 説文 2

1 comprised two "full narrow-necked casks" (畐), used for the sound *huku*, and "a knife" (刂, bushu *rittoo*), together signifying a knife dividing wealth into two parts—a main part and a secondary, accompanying part. This character focused on the accompanying part. The kanji 副 means "to accompany; assisting; copy." <畐刂>

副社長 vice president [ふくしゃつちょう]; 副本 duplicate [ふくほん]; 正副二通 original and duplicate [せついふくにつう]; 副産物 by-product, spin-off [ふくさつんぶつ]; 副作用 side effect, adverse reaction [ふくさつよう]; 副詞 adverb [ふくし]

	Meanings	Kun and On	Romaji	Bushu	Stroke Order and Number
SG-1981 富	wealth, fortune	と-む・とみ フ・フウ	to-mu, tomi *hu, huu*	宀	丶宀宀富富富 12

富 **A** F-0516

金文 1 説文 2

1 and 2 comprised "a full cask with a lid" (畐) for the sounds *hu/huu*, inside "a house" (宀), together signifying "wealth, fortune." The kanji 富 means "wealth, fortune." <宀畐>

富む abound in, be in large quantity, become wealthy [とつむ]; 富 wealth [とつみ]; 富豪 person of great wealth, millionaire [ふごう]; 富国 national enrichment [ふこく]; 富裕層 the well-off, wealthy class [ふゆつうそう]; 貧富の差 wealth disparity [ひつんぷのさ]; 富貴 wealth and honor [ふつうき]

	Meanings	Kun and On	Romaji	Bushu	Stroke Order and Number
SG-1982 幅	width; counter for scrolls	はば フク	haba *huku*	巾	口巾巾幅幅 12

幅 **B** F-0779

説文

The seal-style form comprised 巾 "cloth, lap robe," and 畐 (for the sound *huku*), the fullness of whose bottom component 田 signified "filling out sideways." The width of a loom determined the fixed width of the fabric it produced, and from that 幅 means "width." Cloth is woven in a long strip, whence this character's use as a counter for scrolls. The kanji 幅 means "width; counter for scrolls." <巾畐>

幅 width [はば]; 横幅 width, wingspan [よこはば]; 振幅 amplitude [しんぷく]; 一幅の絵 picturesque, pretty as a hanging scroll [いっぷくつの・えつ]

92c 甬 "to pass through" [from a cylindrical shape through which water passes]; *tsuu/yoo/yuu* 通勇踊湧

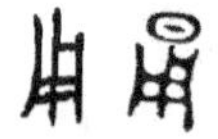

	Meanings	Kun and On	Romaji	Bushu	Stroke Order and Number
SG-1983 通	to pass through, commute, understand	とお-る・かよ-う ツウ・ツ	too-ru, kayo-u *tsuu, tsu*	辵	マ乃甬甬涌通 10

通 **A** F-0171

甲骨文1 1 甲骨文2 2 金文 3 説文 4

1, 2, 3, and 4 comprised "a crossroads" with "a footprint" (except in 2), signifying "to move ahead" (辵; 辶).The right side was "a cylindrical shape through which water passes" (with a pail of water added at the top in 3), signifying "passing through," and used for the sounds *tsuu/tsu*. Another view explains that 甬 signified "a person (マ) stomping on a

通る to pass by, pass through [とつおる]; 通り street, road [とおりつ]; 見通しだ to be expected [みとおしだ]; その通り just exactly, just so [そのとつおり]; 通う to go to and from, attend (school) [かよう]; 日本語が通じる to be able to communicate in

wooden board (用) to push it through; to let something pass through." Being able to pass through freely also allowed one "to come and go regularly, commute," and further signified "communication between people." The kanji 通 means "to pass through, commute, communicate, understand." <マ用辶>

Japanese [にほんごがつうじる]; 通過する to pass through [つうかする]; 通用する to be used, be accepted [つうようする]; (お)通夜 wake, vigil [つうや、おつうや]

	Meanings	Kun and On	Romaji	Bushu	Stroke Order and Number
SG-1984 勇	courage; brave, courageous, gallant	いさ-む ユウ	isa-mu *yuu*	力	マ丙甬甬勇勇 9

勇 **B** F-1071

金文 1 説文古文 2 説文 3 説文或体 4 勇

The top of 1 and 2, and the left side of 3 and 4, is "a cylindrical shape that something can pass through" (甬), used for the sound *yuu* to mean "through." What accompanied 甬 varied, from "a plow" (力) for "to exert one's strength," to "a heart" (心), or "a halberd" (戈), all of which contributed to the meaning of "fervent effort" and "mustering up courage." The kanji 勇 means "courage; brave, courageous, gallant." <マ田力>

勇ましい brave, gallant [いさましい]; 勇んで in high spirits, with a light heart [いさんで]; 勇み足をする to make a careless mistake by rushing [いさみあしをする]; 勇気 courage [ゆうき]; 勇敢な brave [ゆうかんな]; 勇退 voluntary retirement [ゆうたい]; 蛮勇 recklessness [ばんゆう]

	Meanings	Kun and On	Romaji	Bushu	Stroke Order and Number
SG-1985 踊	to dance	おど-る ヨウ	odo-ru *yoo*	足	卩卩𧾷𧾷踊踊踊 14

踊 **C** F-1355

説文 踊

The seal-style form comprised 足 "leg," and 甬, used for the sound *yoo* to mean "to bubble up" (from 湧 **SG-1986**) or "to go/break through." Together they signified "legs jumping up and down." The kanji 踊 means "to dance." <𧾷甬>

踊る to dance [おどる]; 踊り手 dancer [おどりて]; 踊り場 staircase landing [おどりば]; 踊り出る to become suddenly prominent [おどりでる]; 舞踊 dancing [ぶよう]

	Meanings	Kun and On	Romaji	Bushu	Stroke Order and Number
SG-1986 湧	to bubble up, spring out	わ-く ユウ	wa-ku *yuu*	水	氵氵氵湧湧湧湧 12

湧 **D** F-2104

篆文 湧

The seal-style form comprised "flowing water" (氵) and 甬 "to break through," used for the sound *yuu*, together signifying "water springing up from a well." The kanji 湧 means "to bubble up, spring out." <氵勇>

湧く to spring out [わく]; 湧出する water gushes out [ゆうしゅつする]

92d [borrowed from a woven basket] 西曲

	Meanings	Kun and On	Romaji	Bushu	Stroke Order and Number
SG-1987 西	west	にし セイ・サイ	nishi *see, sai*	襾	一冂两西 6

西 **A** F-0342

甲骨文 1 金文 2 説文 3 西

1, 2, and 3 depicted "a basket" for wringing out liquid to make wine, and was borrowed to mean "west.". The kanji 西 means "west." <西>

西 west [にし]; 西向き west-facing [にしむき]; 西欧化 Westernization [せいおうか]; 以西 west of [いせい]; 関西 the Kansai region [かんさい]

	Meanings	Kun and On	Romaji	Bushu	Stroke Order and Number
SG-1988 曲	to bend, flex; musical tune; skewed	ま-がる キョク	ma-garu *kyoku*	曰	冂巾曲曲曲 6

B F-0592

金文 1 説文古文 2 説文 3 曲

1, 2, and 3 depicted "a basket made of pliable materials such as vines and strips of bamboo." The kanji 曲 meant "to bend, flex." A musical tune has a contours, whence the meaning "a piece of music." "A bent shape" also gave the meaning "skewed." The kanji 曲 means "to bend, flex; musical tune; skewed." <曲>

曲げる to bend [まげる]; 曲がり角 street corner, turn in the road [まがりかど]; 曲 music piece [きょく]; 曲線 curved line, curve [きょくせん]; 歪曲 distortion, perversion [わいきょく]; 交響曲 symphony [こうきょうきょく]; 作曲 musical composition [さっきょく]; 曲解 putting the wrong slant on [きょっかい]; 曲芸 acrobatics, stunt [きょくげい]

93 Lid, cover

93a 合 "to fit well, meet" [from a container with a tightly fitting lid]; *goo/too*

合答拾塔搭

	Meanings	Kun and On	Romaji	Bushu	Stroke Order and Number
SG-1989 合	to meet, put together, fit, mix; old unit of volume (180cc)	あ-う ゴウ・ガッ・カッ	a-u *goo, gat-, kat-*	口	ノ 入 亼 合 合 6

合 **A** F-0046	甲骨文 1 金文 2 説文 3 1, 2, and 3 depicted "a container with a lid." A container with a well-fitted lid gave the meaning "to meet, fit." The character was also used as a unit of measure for volume, and is still used for measuring rice (一合 is 180 cc). The kanji 合 means "to meet, put together, fit, mix." <亼口>	合う to fit, meet [あう]; 打ち合わせ staff meeting [うちあわせ]; 言い合い argument, verbal fight [いいあい]; 間に合う to be on time, manage [まにあう]; 歩合 percentage [ぶあい]; 合計 total sum [ごうけい]; 合意する to agree upon [ごういする]; 結合 bind, union [けつごう]; 合作 joint work [がっさく]; 歌合戦 singing contest between teams of singers [うたがっせん]

	Meanings	Kun and On	Romaji	Bushu	Stroke Order and Number
SG-1990 答	answer	こた-える トウ	kota-eru *too*	竹	⺮ ⺮ 笑 笒 答 12

答 **A** F-0410	李楊冰 No ancient form. The brush-style form comprised "plants, grass," and 合 **SG-1989** "to meet," used for the sound *too*, together forming 荅 "answer." In the kanji, 艹 was replaced with ⺮, bushu *takekanmuri* "bamboo," so that the meaning would also pertain to writing. The kanji 答 means "answer." <⺮ 合>	答える to answer [こたえる]; 受け答え response, replay [うけこたえ]; 答案用紙 answer sheet [とうあんようし]; 回答 answer, response to a question [かいとう]; 解答 work out, answer [かいとう]; 自問自答 wonder to oneself, monologue [じもんじとう, じもん・じとう]; 問答無用 no use in arguing [もんどうむよう]

	Meanings	Kun and On	Romaji	Bushu	Stroke Order and Number
SG-1991 拾	to pick up, gather	ひろ-う シュウ・ジュウ	hiro-u *shuu, juu*	手	十 扌 扲 拾 9

拾 **C** F-1382	説文 The seal-style form comprised 扌, bushu *tehen* "an act done by hand," and 合 **SG-1989**, used for the sound *shuu* to mean "to pick up," together signifying "a hand picking up things." The kanji 拾 means "to pick up, gather." <扌合> (Note: The kanji 拾 is also used for "ten" in legal and formal documents in place of 十 for its phonetic feature *juu.* 拾円 ten yen [じゅうえん])	拾う to pick up [ひろう]; 拾い物 a find, a windfall [ひろいもの]; 命拾い a narrow escape [いのちびろい]; 拾得物 lost-and-found item [しゅうとくぶつ]; 収拾する to get under control [しゅうしゅうする]

	Meanings	Kun and On	Romaji	Bushu	Stroke Order and Number
SG-1992 塔	tower, monument	トウ	*too*	土	十 圵 坩 垯 塔 塔 12

塔 **C** F-1459	説文 The seal-style form comprised 土 **SG-1126** "dirt, soil," and 荅, used for the sound *too*. The character 塔 was used in the phonetic rendition 卒塔婆 *sotoba*, from the Sanskrit "stupa," which was a dome-like monument erected as a shrine to the Buddha. The kanji 塔 means "tower, monument." <土艹合>	塔 tower, monument [とう]; 管制塔 control tower [かんせいとう]; 金字塔 monumental achievement [きんじとう]; 象牙の塔 ivory tower [ぞうげのとう]

	Meanings	Kun and On	Romaji	Bushu	Stroke Order and Number
SG-1993 搭	to load, board	トウ	*too*	手	十 扌 拱 搭 搭 12

搭 **D** F-1952	No ancient form. The kanji 搭 comprises 扌 "an act done by hand," and 荅, used for the sound *too* to mean "an action," together signifying "putting something up by hand, loading." The kanji 搭 means "to load, board." <扌艹合>	搭乗券 boarding pass (for an airplane) [とうじょうけん]; 搭載する to load, be equipped with (in reference to a machine) [とうさいする]

93b 今 "to put a lid over" [from a stopper for a covered container] 今含念倉陰吟貪捻

	Meanings	Kun and On	Romaji	Bushu	Stroke Order and Number
SG-1994 今	now; present time	いま コン・キン	ima *kon, kin*	人	ノ人亼今 4

今 **A** F-0014

甲骨文 1 金文 1 2 金文 2 3 説文 4

1 through 4 depicted "a stopper for a container that had a cover." It was borrowed to mean "present moment; now." Another view explains that "capturing something under a lid" signified a captured moment. The kanji 今 means "now; present time." <亼 フ>

今 now, present time [いま]; 只今 promptly [ただいま], ただいま I'm back [ただいま] (an expression said upon returning home); 今月 this month [こんげつ]; 今週 this week [こんしゅう]; 今後 from now on [こんご]; 今上天皇 the reigning emperor, His Majesty [きんじょうてんのう] // 今日 this day, the present time [こんにち], today [きょう]; 今朝 this morning [けさ]; 今年 this year [ことし]

	Meanings	Kun and On	Romaji	Bushu	Stroke Order and Number
SG-1995 含	to contain, include	ふく-む ガン	huku-mu *gan*	口	𠆢亼今含 7

含 **B** F-0567

説文

The seal-style form comprised "a cover with a stopper" (今 **SG-1994**) and "a mouth or box" (口 **SG-0031**), together signifying "putting something into a mouth or container." The kanji 含 means "to contain, include." <今 口>

含む to include, contain [ふくむ]; 含有量 content, contained amount [がんゆうりょう]; 含蓄のある signifying, subtle, pregnant with meaning [がんちくのある]

	Meanings	Kun and On	Romaji	Bushu	Stroke Order and Number
SG-1996 念	thought, prayer, wish; to ponder	ネン	*nen*	心	𠆢亼今念念 8

念 **B** F-0581

金文 1 1 金文 2 2 説文 3

1, 2, and 3 comprised "a lid to keep something in" (今), used for the sound *nen* (from *kin*), and "heart" (心 **SG-0187**), together signifying "a thought that one keeps inside their heart for a long time." The kanji 念 means "thought, prayer, wish; to ponder." <今 心>

念じる to pray, wish, hope [ねんじる]; 失念する to forget [しつねんする]; 念願の long-cherished [ねんがんの]; 雑念 idle thoughts, distraction [ざつねん]; 念入りな careful, elaborate [ねんいりな]; 念を押す to remind, make sure [ねんをおす]; 念のため just to make sure, for confirmation [ねんのため]; 正念場 the moment of truth [しょうねんば]

	Meanings	Kun and On	Romaji	Bushu	Stroke Order and Number
SG-1997 倉	storage, warehouse, vault	くら ソウ	kura *soo*	人	𠆢今今倉倉 10

倉 **B** F-0884

甲骨文 1 金文 2 説文 3

1, 2, and 3 depicted "a granary," with "a roof to protect the grain from rain," and "a receptacle to get the grain out," or possibly "a foundation." In 3, the top component became 亼, bushu *hitoyane*. The kanji 倉 means "storage, warehouse, vault." <亼 戸 口>

倉 storage, vault [くら]; 米倉 rice storage [こめぐら]; 穴倉 cellar, vault [あなぐら]; 倉庫 warehouse [そうこ]; 穀倉地帯 farm belt [こくそうちたい]

	Meanings	Kun and On	Romaji	Bushu	Stroke Order and Number
SG-1998 陰	shadow; negative	かげ イン	kage *in*	阜	了阝阾险陰陰 11

陰 **C** F-1291

金文 1 1 金文 2 2 説文 3

1, 2, and 3 comprised "mountains" (阝) on the left side, and "a cover" (今) and "a rising cloud" (云) on the right (together forming 侌, used for the sound *in*). Mountains and clouds both create shade, and the character meant "a dark area, shade." The contrast between a sunny area or a side and a shadowy area or side was also applied to the contrast between "positive (陽 **SG-1067**) and negative (陰)." The kanji 陰 means "shadow; negative." <阝 侌>

陰 shade, dark area [かげ]; 物陰 a place in the shadow of something [ものかげ]; 陰気な gloomy, dreary [いんきな]; 陰気くさい gloomy-looking, rather gloomy [いんきくさい]; 陰影 shading, nuance [いんえい]; 山陰地方 San'in region [さんいんちほう]; 陰性 negative (in medical testing) [いんせい]

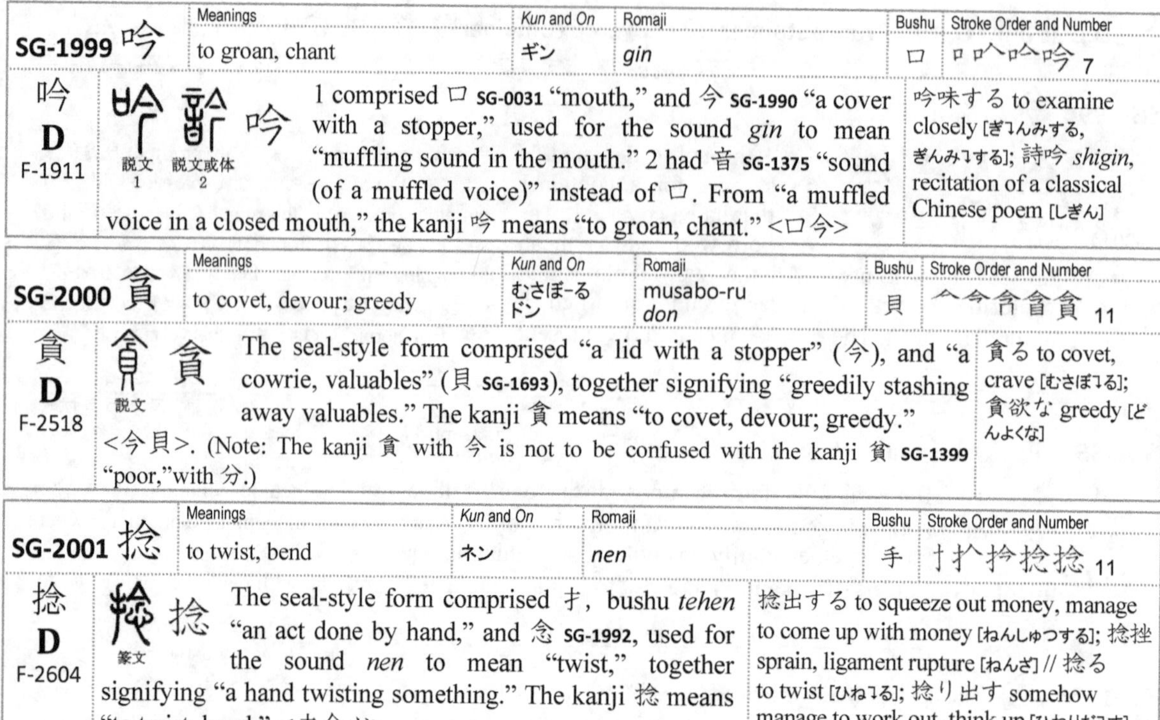

	Meanings	Kun and On	Romaji	Bushu	Stroke Order and Number
SG-1999 吟	to groan, chant	ギン	*gin*	口	口 口 吟 吟 吟 7

吟 **D** F-1911 — 説文 1, 説文或体 2

1 comprised 口 **SG-0031** "mouth," and 今 **SG-1990** "a cover with a stopper," used for the sound *gin* to mean "muffling sound in the mouth." 2 had 音 **SG-1375** "sound (of a muffled voice)" instead of 口. From "a muffled voice in a closed mouth," the kanji 吟 means "to groan, chant." <口今>

吟味する to examine closely [ぎんみする, ぎんみする]; 詩吟 *shigin*, recitation of a classical Chinese poem [しぎん]

	Meanings	Kun and On	Romaji	Bushu	Stroke Order and Number
SG-2000 貪	to covet, devour; greedy	むさぼ-る ドン	musabo-ru *don*	貝	今 含 貪 貪 貪 11

貪 **D** F-2518 — 説文

The seal-style form comprised "a lid with a stopper" (今), and "a cowrie, valuables" (貝 **SG-1693**), together signifying "greedily stashing away valuables." The kanji 貪 means "to covet, devour; greedy." <今貝>. (Note: The kanji 貪 with 今 is not to be confused with the kanji 貧 **SG-1399** "poor,"with 分.)

貪る to covet, crave [むさぼる]; 貪欲な greedy [どんよくな]

	Meanings	Kun and On	Romaji	Bushu	Stroke Order and Number
SG-2001 捻	to twist, bend	ネン	*nen*	手	扌 扵 拎 捻 捻 11

捻 **D** F-2604 — 篆文

The seal-style form comprised 扌, bushu *tehen* "an act done by hand," and 念 **SG-1992**, used for the sound *nen* to mean "twist," together signifying "a hand twisting something." The kanji 捻 means "to twist, bend." <扌今心>

捻出する to squeeze out money, manage to come up with money [ねんしゅつする]; 捻挫 sprain, ligament rupture [ねんざ] // 捻る to twist [ひねる]; 捻り出す somehow manage to work out, think up [ひねりだす]

93c 全 "to gather all" [from a cover over gems]; *zen/sen* 全栓詮・牵 仝

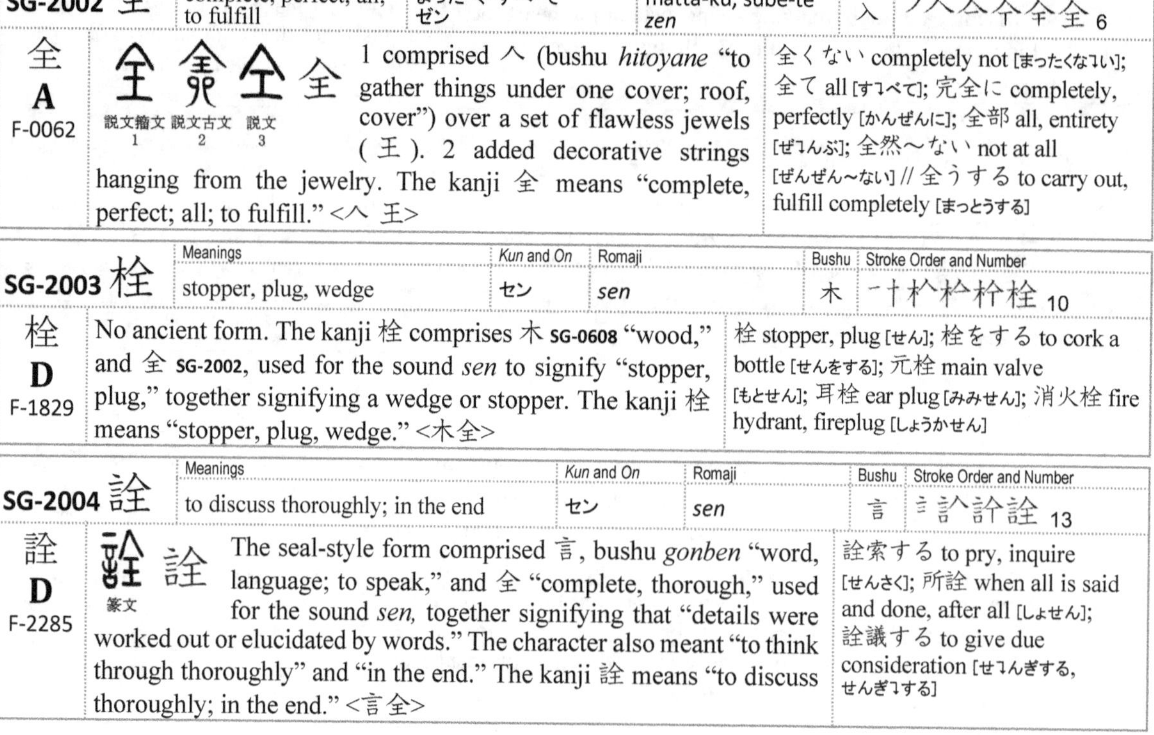

	Meanings	Kun and On	Romaji	Bushu	Stroke Order and Number
SG-2002 全	complete, perfect; all; to fulfill	まった-く・すべ-て ゼン	matta-ku, sube-te *zen*	入	ノ 入 仝 仐 全 全 6

全 **A** F-0062 — 説文籀文 1, 説文古文 2, 説文 3

1 comprised 𠆢 (bushu *hitoyane* "to gather things under one cover; roof, cover") over a set of flawless jewels (王). 2 added decorative strings hanging from the jewelry. The kanji 全 means "complete, perfect; all; to fulfill." <𠆢 王>

全くない completely not [まったくない]; 全て all [すべて]; 完全に completely, perfectly [かんぜんに]; 全部 all, entirety [ぜんぶ]; 全然〜ない not at all [ぜんぜん〜ない] // 全うする to carry out, fulfill completely [まっとうする]

	Meanings	Kun and On	Romaji	Bushu	Stroke Order and Number
SG-2003 栓	stopper, plug, wedge	セン	*sen*	木	一 十 朩 朩 朩 栓 10

栓 **D** F-1829

No ancient form. The kanji 栓 comprises 木 **SG-0608** "wood," and 全 **SG-2002**, used for the sound *sen* to signify "stopper, plug," together signifying a wedge or stopper. The kanji 栓 means "stopper, plug, wedge." <木全>

栓 stopper, plug [せん]; 栓をする to cork a bottle [せんをする]; 元栓 main valve [もとせん]; 耳栓 ear plug [みみせん]; 消火栓 fire hydrant, fireplug [しょうかせん]

	Meanings	Kun and On	Romaji	Bushu	Stroke Order and Number
SG-2004 詮	to discuss thoroughly; in the end	セン	*sen*	言	言 訁 許 詮 13

詮 **D** F-2285 — 篆文

The seal-style form comprised 言, bushu *gonben* "word, language; to speak," and 全 "complete, thorough," used for the sound *sen,* together signifying that "details were worked out or elucidated by words." The character also meant "to think through thoroughly" and "in the end." The kanji 詮 means "to discuss thoroughly; in the end." <言全>

詮索する to pry, inquire [せんさく]; 所詮 when all is said and done, after all [しょせん]; 詮議する to give due consideration [せんぎする, せんぎする]

傘 "umbrella"

	Meanings	Kun and On	Romaji	Bushu	Stroke Order and Number
SG-2005 傘	umbrella, parasol, protecting force	かさ サン	kasa *san*	人	𠆢 仒 仺 傘 傘 12
傘 **C** F-1591	No ancient form. The kanji 傘 has a canopy (𠆢), a folding frame (depicted by four 人), and a central rod (十). It meant "umbrella," and also "a protecting force" in various contexts. The kanji 傘 means "umbrella, parasol, protecting force." <𠆢人人人人十>		傘 umbrella [かさ]; 傘立て umbrella stand [かさたて]; 雨傘 rain umbrella [あまがさ]; 日傘 parasol [ひがさ]; 傘下企業 affiliated enterprises [さんかきぎょう]		

93d 吉 "good luck" [from a full container with a secure stopper]; *kitsu/ketsu* 吉結詰

	Meanings	Kun and On	Romaji	Bushu	Stroke Order and Number
SG-2006 吉	good luck, benediction, joy; auspicious	キチ・キツ	*kichi, kitsu*	口	一 十 士 吉 吉 6
吉 **A** F-0446	甲骨文1 (1), 甲骨文2 (2), 金文1 (3), 金文2 (4), 金文3 (5), 説文 (6) Various interpretations have been proposed for what was being depicted in the ancient forms of this character. Among them are: (a) "a heap of food laid out for a celebratory feast," whence "joyous" (1 and 2); (b) "a warrior's weapon" placed with the blade side down for a ceremony, over "a prayer box for confining evils," whence "benediction" (3, 4, 5 and 6); and (c) "a full container fastened securely shut with a double lid," with "being full" giving the meaning "good" (4 and 5). The kanji 吉 means "good luck, benediction, joy; auspicious." <士口>		吉日 lucky day [きちじつ]; 大吉 great fortune in *omikuji* (a strip of paper for predicting fortunes) [だいきち]; 吉例により by an auspicious custom [きちれいにより]; 不吉な ominous, baneful [ふきつな]; 吉報 good news [きっぽう]		

	Meanings	Kun and On	Romaji	Bushu	Stroke Order and Number
SG-2007 結	to tie, end, congregate into one, conclude	むす-ぶ・ゆ-う ケツ	musu-bu, yu-u *ketsu*	糸	幺 糸 紅 結 結 12
結 **A** F-0313	説文 The seal-style form comprised "threads" (糸 **SG-1600**) for "to tie," and 吉 **SG-2006**, used for the sound *ketsu* to mean "to be contained in a jar." Tightly tying a lid onto a jar meant "to tie." The kanji 結 means "to tie, end, congregate into one, conclude." <糸吉>		結ぶ to tie a knot, conclude [むすぶ]; 結び目 knot, tie [むすびめ]; 髪を結う・結わえる to do up one's hair [かみをゆう, ゆわえる]; 結納 betrothal present, engagement gifts [ゆいのう]; 結論 conclusion [けつろん]; 一致団結 solidarity [いっち・だんけつ]; 結局 after all, ultimately [けっきょく]; 結核 tuberculosis, TB [けっかく]		

	Meanings	Kun and On	Romaji	Bushu	Stroke Order and Number
SG-2008 詰	to pack, rebuke, blame, squeeze, stand by	つ-める キツ	tsu-meru *kitsu*	言	言 言 計 詰 詰 13
詰 **C** F-1136	説文 The seal-style form comprised 言 **SG-1364** "word; to speak," and 吉 **SG-2006**, used for the sound *kitsu* to mean "to contain," together signifying "someone with accusing words," whence the meaning "to blame, rebuke, criticize." In Japanese, the character also means "to pack, cram; full," and "to stand by," from asociation with a small room where a guard stands on duty. The kanji 詰 means "to pack, rebuke, blame, squeeze, stand by." <言吉>		詰める to pack, stand by [つめる]; 詰まる to clog up, conjest [つまる]; 詰所 guard station, crew room [つめしょ, つめしょ]; 詰め寄る to close in, press [つめよる]; 詰め合わせ assortment [つめあわせ]; 詰問する to rebuke, cross-examine [きつもんする]		

93e 缶 "can, tin" [from a clay container] 缶陶

	Meanings	Kun and On	Romaji	Bushu	Stroke Order and Number
SG-2009 缶	can, tin, metal container	カン	*kan*	缶	ノ 𠂉 午 缶 缶 6
缶 **C** F-1214	甲骨文 (1), 金文1 (2), 金文2 (3), 金文3 (4), 説文 (5), 旧字 (6) 罐 1 through 5 depicted "a terra cotta container with a secure double lid for holding water or wine." In 3, 金 "metal" was added to mean "a metal or bronze container." In the kyuji 罐 (6), 雚 was added for the sound *kan*. The kanji 缶 means "can, tin, metal container." <𠂉山>		缶 tin container, can [かん]; 缶詰 canned food [かんづめ]; 缶入りコーヒー canned coffee [かんいりコーヒー]; アルミ缶 aluminum can [アルミかん]; ドラム缶 (gasoline) drum can [ドラムかん]		

	Meanings	Kun and On	Romaji	Bushu	Stroke Order and Number
SG-2010 陶	ceramic; to educate	トウ	*too*	阜	阝阝阝陶陶陶 11

陶 **D** F-1649

金文1 1 金文2 2 説文 3

1 and 2 comprised "a hill-like mound of dirt" (阝, bushu *kozatohen*) and two depictions of "someone hunched over while kneading clay" stacked on top of each other. The character depicted an ascending kiln where people were making pottery. In 3, it comprised 阝 and 缶, "a clay container," wrapped in 勹, which signified "ceramics" and was used for the sound *too*. Taken together, these components meant "baking pottery in a kiln." The action of baking well-kneaded clay into a more refined product gave the meaning "to enlighten, educate." The kanji 陶 means "pottery, china, porcelain; to educate." <阝勹缶>

陶器 pottery, earthenware [とうき]; 薫陶を受ける to be under someone's tutelege, to be taught by [くんとうをうける]; 陶酔する to be fascinated, be intoxicated [とうすいする]; 自然淘汰 natural selection [しぜんとうた]

93f 去 "to leave" [from a person traversing an area]; *kyo/kyaku* 去法却脚

	Meanings	Kun and On	Romaji	Bushu	Stroke Order and Number
SG-2011 去	to leave, remove; past	さ-る キョ・コ	sa-ru *kyo, ko*	ム	一十土去去 5

去 **A** F-0422

甲骨文 1 中山王器 2 説文 3

1 and 2 depicted "a person" (大) standing over "an area" (口), signifying "a person traversing an area" and, more generally, "leaving and going far away." The kanji 去 meant "to leave, remove." In 3, the bottom became 凵, which further changed to ム in the kanji. 大, "a person," became 土. The kanji 去 means "to leave, remove; past." <土ム>

去る to leave [さる]; 立ち去る to leave, go away [たちさる, たちさる]; 持ち去る to take away, run away with [もちさる, もちさる]; 連れ去る to abduct [つれさる]; 去年 last year [きょねん]; 除去する to remove [じょきょする]; 過去 the past, bygone days, one's secret past [かこ]

	Meanings	Kun and On	Romaji	Bushu	Stroke Order and Number
SG-2012 法	law, court of law, method; legal	ホウ・ハッ・ホッ	*hoo, ha(C)-, ho(C)-*	水	氵氵汁汁法 8

法 **A** F-0087

金文1 1 金文2 2 説文1 3 説文2 4 正字 5

Views on the origin of this character vary greatly. 1, 2, and 3 (灋) comprised 去 **SG-2007** "to remove," "flowing water" (氵), and an unknown "animal." One view explains that the character originally meant "to discard" (from 去 "to remove"), and was borrowed later on to mean "law." Another explains that, analogous to a deer-like animal moving freely inside an area surrounded by water, people were free but bound by norms or laws in a society. The mysterious animal was dropped in the shinji. The kanji 法 means "law, court of law, method; legal." <氵去>

法 law [ほう]; 方法 method [ほうほう]; 違法行為 illegal act [いほうこうい]; 文法 grammar [ぶんぽう]; 立法 legislation, lawmaking [りっぽう]; 民法 civil law [みんぽう]; 憲法 constitutional law [けんぽう]; ご法度 prohibited, banned (archaic) [ごはっと]

	Meanings	Kun and On	Romaji	Bushu	Stroke Order and Number
SG-2013 却	to withdraw, retreat; on the contrary	キャク	*kyaku*	卩	一十土去去却却 7

却 **C** F-1091

説文

The seal-style form comprised 去 **SG-2007** "to leave," and 卩 "a person kneeling down," together signifying "to make a retreat, withdraw." It also meant "on the contrary, all the more." The kanji 却 means "to withdraw, retreat; on the contrary." <去卩>

返却する to return (something) [へんきゃくする]; 退却する to retreat [たいきゃくする]; 売却する to sell, sell off [ばいきゃくする]; 却下する to dismiss, reject [きゃっかする]; 脱却する to shake oneself free of [だっきゃくする]; 焼却する to incinerate, burn up [しょうきゃくする] // 却って on the contrary, if any [かえって]

	Meanings	Kun and On	Romaji	Bushu	Stroke Order and Number
SG-2014 脚	leg, foot	あし キャク・キャ	ashi *kyaku, kya*	肉	刀月肚脚脚脚 11

脚 **C** F-1240

篆文

The seal-style form comprised 月, bushu *nikuzuki* "part of the body," and 却 "to retreat," used for the sound *kyaku*. The part of the body that one used when withdrawing oneself was "the leg or foot." The kanji 脚 means "leg, foot." <月却>

脚 leg, foot [あし]; 失脚する to fall from power [しっきゃくする]; 脚色する to dramatize [きゃくしょくする]; 三脚 tripod (for a camera) [さんきゃく]; 脚本 play script, scenario [きゃくほん]; 脚立 stepladder [きゃたつ]; 行脚 pilgrimage, travel around on foot [あんぎゃ]

94 A vessel for transporting

94a 舟 "boat, tray" [from wooden panels] 舟船舶舷 

SG-2015 舟	Meanings: boat	Kun and On: ふね・ふな シュウ	Romaji: hune, huna *shuu*	Bushu: 舟	Stroke Order and Number: 丿亇介舟 6

舟 **A** F-1309

甲骨文1 1, 甲骨文2 2, 金文1 3, 金文2 4, 説文 5

1 through 5 depicted the shape of "a boat." An ancient boat was built in rectancular shape, made up of wooden panels The kanji 舟 means "boat." <舟>

舟 boat [ふね]; 小舟 small boat [こぶね]; 丸木舟 dugout canoe [まるきぶね]; 渡し舟 ferry [わたしぶね]; 舟遊び boating [ふなあそび]; 助け舟 lifeboat, helping hand in time of need [たすけぶね]

SG-2016 船	Meanings: ship, vessel	Kun and On: ふね・ふな セン	Romaji: hune, huna *sen*	Bushu: 舟	Stroke Order and Number: 亇介舟舟八船 11

船 **A** F-0493

金文 1, 説文 2

1 and 2 comprised 舟 "a boat," and 㕣, used for the sound *en* to mean "along." A vessel that travelled along water was "a ship." In contrast to 舟, 船 is used for larger ships. The kanji 船 means "ship." <舟㕣>

船 ship, vessel [ふね]; 船旅 voyage, sea trip [ふなたび]; 船酔い seasickness [ふなよい]; 船乗り sailor [ふなのり]; 乗船する to go aboard, embark [じょうせんする]; 貨物船 cargo boat, freighter [かもつせん]; 客船 passenger ship [きゃくせん]; 連絡船 ferry boat [れんらくせん]; 船頭 boatman [せんどう]

SG-2017 舶	Meanings: large ship	Kun and On: ハク	Romaji: *haku*	Bushu: 舟	Stroke Order and Number: 丿亇介舟′舶舶 11

舶 **D** F-1875

No ancient form. The kanji 舶 comprises 舟 "boat," and 白, used for the sound *haku* to mean "large," together signifying "a large, oceangoing ship." The kanji 舶 means "large ship." <舟白>

舶来品 imported goods, foreign articles [はくらいひん]; 船舶 ship, marine vessel [せんぱく]

SG-2018 舷	Meanings: side of a ship, gunwale	Kun and On: ゲン	Romaji: *gen*	Bushu: 舟	Stroke Order and Number: 丿亇介舟亠舷舷 11

舷 **D** F-2377

秦漢印

The Qin-Han era seal imprint pictured at left comprised 舟 **SG-2015** "boat," and 玄 **SG-1639**, used for the sound *gen*, together signifying "the sides of a boat." The kanji 舷 means "side of a boat, gunwale, boat railing ." <舟玄>

右舷 starboard [うげん]; 左舷 port side [さげん]

94b 般 "to transport; general" [from a vessel or boat for transporting multiple items]; *han* 般盤搬・服 

SG-2019 般	Meanings: general	Kun and On: ハン	Romaji: *han*	Bushu: 舟	Stroke Order and Number: 丿亇介舟舟舡般 10

般 **B** F-0802

甲骨文1 1, 甲骨文2 2, 金文 3, 説文古文 4, 説文 5

1 through 5 comprised "a boat made of wooden panels" (舟), and "a hand holding a weapon" (殳 "to hit, strike"), together signifying "pushing a boat loaded with stuff; to transport." A boat transported many kinds of things, giving rise to the meaning "general." The kanji 般 means "general." <舟殳>

諸般の all sorts of, various [しょはんの]; 般若経 the Wisdom Sutras, the Prajnaparamita Sutra [はんにゃきょう]; 一般的に generally, in general [いっぱんてきに]; 全般的な comprehensive, all-embracing [ぜんぱんてきな]; 一般化する to become universal, generalize [いっぱんかする]; 一般人 people at large, private citizen [いっぱんじん]; 一般教養課程 liberal arts courses [いっぱんきょうようかてい]

SG-2020 盤	Meanings: tray, raised shallow bowl	Kun and On: バン	Romaji: *ban*	Bushu: 皿	Stroke Order and Number: 亇介舡般盤盤 15

盤 **B** F-1062

甲骨文 1, 金文1 2, 金文2 3, 説文籀文 4, 説文古文 5, 説文 6

The top component of 1 through 6 comprised "a hand holding a weapon" to mean "to hit, strike" (殳), and "a vessel"

円盤 disk [えんばん]; 基盤 foundation, basis [きばん]; 文字盤 clock

	(舟), forming 般 "to transport," used for the sound *han*. On the bottom was "a shallow vessel" (皿), or "a tray or vessel" in 3. Taken together. these components signified "a shallow vessel or tray in/on which one carries things." The shape of 皿 gave the meanings "a round shape" and "a flat surface." A shallow vessel could have been in metal, as in 5 (which contains 金), or wooden, as in 6 (which contains 木). With 皿 as the bottom component, the kanji 盤 means "a large flat bowl, round shape, flat (round) surface." <般皿>	dial [もじばん]; 地盤 ground, subsoil, constituents [じばん]; 大盤振る舞い lavish feast [おおばんぶるまい] 算盤 Japanese abacas [そろばん]

	Meanings	Kun and On	Romaji	Bushu	Stroke Order and Number
SG-2021 搬	to carry, transport	ハン	*han*	手	扌扌扌扌扌搬 13

搬 **D** F-1793	No ancient form. This character was created to fill the void left by the kanji 般 **SG-2019**, once it lost its original meaning of "to transport." To the original 般, used for the sound *han*, 扌, bushu *tehen* "an act done by hand," was added. The kanji 搬 means "to carry, transport." <扌般>	搬入する to carry something in [はんにゅうする]; 搬送する to convey, carry [はんそうする]; 運搬する to transport, carry [うんぱんする]

服 "to yield to; clothes"

	Meanings	Kun and On	Romaji	Bushu	Stroke Order and Number
SG-2022 服	clothes, a brief rest; to yield to, obey, swallow	フク	*huku*	月	刀月月月服服 8

服 **B** F-0583	服 甲骨文 1 金文 1 2 金文 2 3 説文古文 4 説文 5 The right side of 1, 2, 3, 4, and 5 depicted a person being pushed down from behind or kneeling (4), and thus meant "to subject to, yield to." This component became 𠬝, and was used for the sound *huku*. The left side of the earlier forms was "boat or vessel" (舟). One view holds that the character depicted a person prostrating himself in front of a vessel in a rite. Another view explains that the action of bringing a boat to a landing stage was like causing someone to yield to power. The ancient shapes for "boat" resembled the bushu *nikuzuki* "part of the body." From that similarity, the character was also used to mean clothes fit to a person's body, with the associated meaning of "yielding to the shape." It is also used for "taking (medicine)," and taking a brief rest. The kanji 服 means "clothes, a brief rest; to yield to, obey, swallow." <月𠬝>	服 clothes [ふく]; 服装 clothes [ふくそう]; 制服 uniform [せいふく]; 服従する to obey [ふくじゅうする]; 不服 dissatisfaction, disapproval [ふふく]; 一服する to have a brief rest, have a smoke [いっぷくする]; 服用量 dose of medicine [ふくようりょう]; 服毒死 death from poisoning [ふくどくし]

94c 凡 "all" [from a sail]; *bon/han* 凡帆汎

	Meanings	Kun and On	Romaji	Bushu	Stroke Order and Number
SG-2023 凡	all; common, ordinary; to cover a large area	ボン・ハン	*bon, han*	几	ノ几凡 3

凡 **C** F-1590	凡 甲骨文1 1 甲骨文2 2 金文 1 3 金文 2 4 説文 5 1 through 4 were the outline of "a sail" which caught the wind. A sail covering a large area meant "all, nearly all, approximation." In 5, the short line inside indicated that the sail was not empty, but filled with "wind." "All" implies "nothing special," and thus, "ordinary." The kanji 凡 means "all; common, ordinary; to cover a large area." <几丶>	凡人 ordinary person [ぼんじん]; 平凡な mediocre, commonplace [へいぼんな]; 非凡な extraordinary, unique [ひぼんな]; 平々凡々な暮らし ordinary life, living uneventfully [へいへいぼんぼんなくらし]; 凡例 legend (on a map), guide (to a dictionary) [はんれい] // 凡そ gist, rough approximation, more or less [およそ, おおよそ]

	Meanings	Kun and On	Romaji	Bushu	Stroke Order and Number
SG-2024 帆	sail	ほ ハン	ho *han*	巾	口巾巾帆帆 6

帆 **D** F-1894	No ancient form. This character was created to mean "the sail of a boat" (the original meaning of 凡 **SG-2023**, which had the sound *han*) by adding a piece of cloth 巾 **SG-1682**. The kanji 帆 means "sail." <巾凡>	帆 sail [ほ]; 帆立貝 scallop (from the shape) [ほたてがい]; 帆掛け船 sailing vessel [ほかけぶね]; 帆船 sailing vessel [はんせん]; 出帆する to sail from [しゅっぱんする]

	Meanings	Kun and On	Romaji	Bushu	Stroke Order and Number
SG-2025 汎	all; covering all; far and wide; pan-	ハン	*han*	水	氵 氾 汎 汎 6

汎
D
F-2108

説文

The seal-style form comprised "flowing water" (氵), and 凡, used for the sound *han* to mean "a sail, a large piece of cloth; to spread." Together they signified the manner in which a sail floats on the water, and that water can spread and flow over a wide area. The kanji 汎 means "all; covering all, far and wide; pan-." <氵凡>

汎用する to use for various purposes [はんようする]; 汎用性のある versatile, widely usable [はんようせいのあꜜる]; 汎アラブ主義 Pan-Arabism [はꜜん・アラブしゅꜜぎ]

95 Writing brush, etc.

95a 聿 "upright" [from a hand holding a writing brush] 書津律筆粛

	Meanings	Kun and On	Romaji	Bushu	Stroke Order and Number
SG-2026 書	to write; writing, document, book	か-く ショ	ka-ku *sho*	曰	⺕ 聿 聿 書 書 10

書
A
F-0121

金文 1 説文 2

1 and 2 comprised "a hand holding a writing brush upright" (聿), and "a bunch of writing tablets being burned in a container/stove and producing sparks" (the same origin as 者 **SG-2085**), used for the sound *sho*. Together they signified "to write; book." In the kanji the bottom became 曰. The kanji 書 means "to write; writing, document, book." <聿曰>

書く to write [かꜜく]; 下書き draft [したがき]; 横書き horizontal writing [よこがき]; 上書き overwriting [うわがき]; 書類 documents [しょるい]; 文書で in writing, on paper [ぶꜜんしょで]; 書記 transcriber [しょき]; 白書 white paper, comprehensive report by the government [はꜜくしょ]

	Meanings	Kun and On	Romaji	Bushu	Stroke Order and Number
SG-2027 津	shallows, landing	つ シン	tsu *shin*	水	氵 氵 氵 湗 津 9

津
B
F-0864

金文 1 説文古文 2 説文 3

1 and 2 comprised "flowing water," "a bird," and "a boat." A bird alighting on a boat in water signified "a landing area for boats." In 3, the right side became a writing brush (聿) with dripping ink or liquid droplets, used for the sound *shin* to emphasize the sense of "an area where water is shallow." The kanji 津 means "shallows, landing." <氵聿>

津波 tidal wave, *tsunami* [つなみ]; 興味津々 of absorbing interest, having a keen interest [きょꜜうみ・しんしん]

	Meanings	Kun and On	Romaji	Bushu	Stroke Order and Number
SG-2028 律	law, rules that one follows	リツ・リチ	*ritsu, richi*	彳	彳 彳 彳 徍 律 9

律
C
F-1078

甲骨文 1 説文 2

1 comprised "a crossroads" (彳) to mean "a way to go; to conduct oneself," and "a hand holding a writing brush straight up" (聿), together signifying "to conduct oneself in an upright manner as prescribed by a rule." The kanji 律 means "law, rules that one follows." <彳聿>

法律 law [ほうりつ]; 律する to measure, govern [りっする]; 戒律 religious precept [かいりつ]; 一律に uniformly, across the board [いちりつに]; 不文律 unwritten rule [ふぶꜜんりつ]; 規律正しい disciplined, well-ordered [きりつただしꜜい]; 律儀な upright, conscientious [りꜜちぎな]

	Meanings	Kun and On	Romaji	Bushu	Stroke Order and Number
SG-2029 筆	writing brush	ふで ヒツ	hude *hitsu*	竹	𠂉 ⺮ 筀 筀 筀 筆 12

筆
C
F-1083

甲骨文 1 金文 1 2 金文 2 3 説文 4

1, 2, and 3 depicted "a writing brush held by a hand (聿)." The character meant "writing brush." In 4, "bamboo" (竹) was added to emphasize the bamboo handle. The kanji 筆 means "writing brush." <⺮聿>

筆 writing brush [ふで]; 筆使い one's handling of a brush, touch, technique [ふでづꜜかい]; 絵筆 paintbrush, an artist's brush [えꜜふで]; 筆まめな reliable in correspondence, frequent letter writer [ふでまめな]; 筆が立つ good writer [ふでがたꜜつ]; 筆記用具 writing materials [ひっきよꜜうぐ]; 万年筆 fountain pen [まんねꜜんひつ]; 達筆な skillful penmanship [たっぴつな]; 執筆者 the author, the writer [しっぴつꜜしゃ]

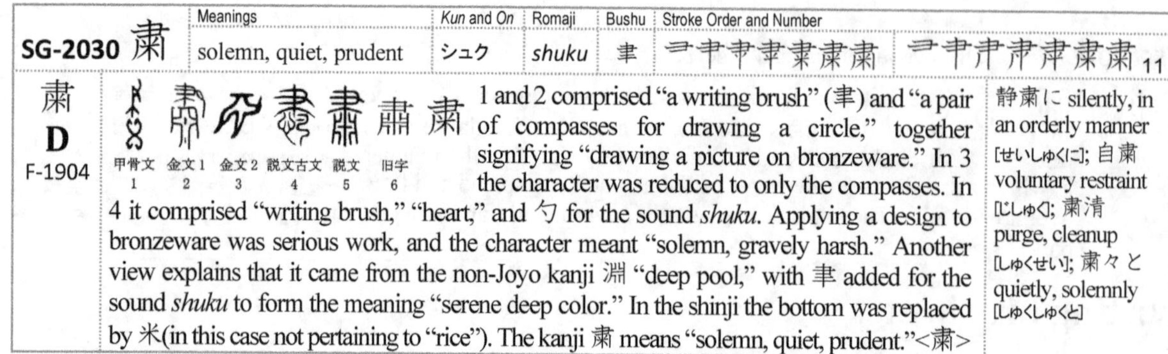

	Meanings	Kun and On	Romaji	Bushu	Stroke Order and Number
SG-2030 粛	solemn, quiet, prudent	シュク	*shuku*	聿	11

粛 **D** F-1904

甲骨文 1　金文1 2　金文2 3　説文古文 4　説文 5　旧字 6

1 and 2 comprised "a writing brush" (聿) and "a pair of compasses for drawing a circle," together signifying "drawing a picture on bronzeware." In 3 the character was reduced to only the compasses. In 4 it comprised "writing brush," "heart," and 勺 for the sound *shuku*. Applying a design to bronzeware was serious work, and the character meant "solemn, gravely harsh." Another view explains that it came from the non-Joyo kanji 淵 "deep pool," with 聿 added for the sound *shuku* to form the meaning "serene deep color." In the shinji the bottom was replaced by 米(in this case not pertaining to "rice"). The kanji 粛 means "solemn, quiet, prudent."<肅>

静粛に silently, in an orderly manner [せいしゅくに]; 自粛 voluntary restraint [じしゅく]; 粛清 purge, cleanup [しゅくせい]; 粛々と quietly, solemnly [しゅくしゅくと]

95b 冊 "fence, book" [from wooden stakes or bound tablets] 典冊柵

	Meanings	Kun and On	Romaji	Bushu	Stroke Order and Number
SG-2031 典	code, law, model	テン	*ten*	八	冂 𠀎 曲 曲 典 8

典 **B** F-0881

甲骨文1 1　甲骨文2 2　金文1 3　金文2 4　説文古文 5　説文 6

In all of the ancient forms of this character, the top component was "writing tablets linked together with leather straps." 1 had two hands holding the book very carefully, while 2 had just one hand, turning the book while viewing it. 3, 4, 5, and 6 had 几 "a low table." 5 had "bamboo," to create the meaning "bamboo writing tablets." Important bound writing tablets contained models, codes, or precedents to which one could refer in setting policy. The kanji 典 means "code, law, model." <曲ハ>

辞典 dictionary [じてん]; 典雅な refined, elegant [てんがな]; 出典 reference source [しゅってん]; 古典 classics [こてん]; 典型的な stereotyped, typical [てんけいてきな]; 香典 (monetary) offering at a Buddhist funeral [こうでん]; 祭典 festival [さいてん]

	Meanings	Kun and On	Romaji	Bushu	Stroke Order and Number
SG-2032 冊	bound book, counter for books	サツ・サク	*satsu, saku*	冂	冂 冊 冊 冊 5

冊 **B** F-1104

甲骨文 1　金文1 2　金文2 3　説文古文 4　説文 5　旧字 6

One view explains that this character depicted writing tablets linked together to make a book. It was used as a counter for bound books. Another view makes note of the uneven length of the vertical lines in earlier forms, and holds that since the materials used to craft writing tablets were cut to uniform length for binding, the uneven lengths in 1, 2, and 3 indicate that the character originally depicted not a book, but rather a "fence" (柵 **SG-2033**) of a corral for keeping livestock. The kanji 冊 means "bound books, books." < 冊 >

三冊 three books [さんさつ]; 冊数 number of of volumes [さつすう]; 別冊 separate volume, extra issue [べっさつ]; 小冊子 booklet [しょうさっし]; 短冊 strip of paper [たんざく]

	Meanings	Kun and On	Romaji	Bushu	Stroke Order and Number
SG-2033 柵	fence, wooden stockade	サク	*saku*	木	木 杛 枛 柵 柵 9

柵 **D** F-2243

篆文

The seal-style form comprised 木 **SG-0608** "tree, wood," and 冊 **SG-2032** "linked wooden stakes," used for the sound *saku*. Because the character 冊 was used to mean "a bound book," a new character was created by adding 木 to mean "wooden stakes of uneven lengths for confining animals." The kanji 柵 means "fence, wooden stockade." <木冊>

柵 fence, wooden stockade [さく]; 鉄柵 iron fence [てっさく]

95c 侖 "things in good order" [from stakes gathered together]; *ron/rin* 論輪倫

	Meanings	Kun and On	Romaji	Bushu	Stroke Order and Number
SG-2034 論	logic, argument	ロン	*ron*	言	言 訡 訡 論 論 15

論 **A** F-0361

中山王器 1　説文 2

In 1 and 2, 侖 comprised "to gather things into one group" (亼), and "writing tablets bound together in an orderly fashion," used for the sound *ron*. A second component, 言,

論じる to discuss [ろんじる]; 議論 argument [ぎろん]; 論争 dispute, controversy [ろんそう]; 論文 article, dissertation, thesis [ろんぶん]; 異論を

	bushu *gonben* "word, language; to say," was added in 2. Words arranged in good order meant "logic, argument." The kanji 論 means "logic, logical argument." <言侖>	唱える to object to [いろんをとなえる]; 世論 public opinion [よろん, せろん]

	Meanings	Kun and On	Romaji	Bushu	Stroke Order and Number
SG-2035 輪	wheel, circle, loop	わ リン	wa *rin*	車	亘車軡輪輪輪 15

輪 **B** F-0697	輪 (説文) 輪 The seal-style form comprised 車 "vehicle, wheel," and 侖, used for the sound *rin* to mean "sticks or arrows neatly arranged in a circular shape," together signifying "wheel, loop, round." The kanji 輪 means "wheel, circle, loop." <車侖>	輪 a ring [わ]; 輪ゴム elastic band [わゴム]; 内輪話 inside information, private talk [うちわばなし]; 浮き輪 flotation ring [うきわ]; 車輪 wheel [しゃりん]; 三輪車 tricycle [さんりんしゃ]; 両輪 two wheels, both wheels [りょうりん]; 輪郭 contour, outline, profile [りんかく]

	Meanings	Kun and On	Romaji	Bushu	Stroke Order and Number
SG-2036 倫	ethics, principle	リン	*rin*	人	亻仐倫倫倫 10

倫 **C** F-1389	倫 (説文) 倫 The seal-style form comprised 亻 "person, an act that one does," and 侖, used for the sound *rin* to mean "things arranged in an orderly fashion." Keeping one's actions in order meant "ethics or principles." The kanji 倫 means "ethics, principle." <亻侖>	倫理 morality, ethics [りんり]; 倫理上 from an ethical point of view [りんりじょう]; 人倫 humanity, morality [じんりん]

95d 主 "staying in one place" [from a burning oil lamp]; *shu/chuu* 主住注柱

	Meanings	Kun and On	Romaji	Bushu	Stroke Order and Number
SG-2037 主	master; main, primary	ぬし・おも シュ・ス	nushi, omo *shu, su*	丶	丶亠亍主主 5

主 **A** F-0052	(甲骨文 1, 金文 2, 説文 3) 主 1 comprised "a flame" on top of 木 "wood," together signifying "a torch." 2 was the flame by itself. In 3 the character came to depict "a flame in an oil lamp on a long-stemmed holder." Fire was important, and symbolized someone or something that stayed in one place, such as the master of a house. The kanji 主 means "master; main, primary." <丶王>	地主 landholder, landowner [じぬし]; 飼い主 pet owner [かいぬし]; 主な major, primary [おもな]; 主義 principle, ideology [しゅぎ]; 主体的な independent, active [しゅたいてきな]; 主客転倒 mistaking the means for the end, putting the cart before the horse [しゅかく・てんとう, しゅきゃくてんとう] // 主 master, proprietor [あるじ]

	Meanings	Kun and On	Romaji	Bushu	Stroke Order and Number
SG-2038 住	to live, reside	す-む ジュウ	su-mu *juu*	人	亻亻'亻'亻亻主住 7

住 **A** F-0233	No ancient form. The kanji 住 comprises 亻, bushu *ninben* "person, an act that one does," and 主 **SG-2037**, used for the sound *juu* to mean "to stay in one place." A person staying in a place for a long time lives or resides there. The kanji 住 means "to live, reside." <亻主>	住む・住まう to live, reside [すむ, すまう]; 住み込み live-in [すみこみ]; 住まい house, residence [すまい]; 住所 address [じゅうしょ]; 住民 resident [じゅうみん]; 住宅地 residential area [じゅうたくち]; 定住 long-term residency [ていじゅう]

	Meanings	Kun and On	Romaji	Bushu	Stroke Order and Number
SG-2039 注	to pour, pay (attention)	そそ-ぐ チュウ	soso-gu *chuu*	水	氵氵'氵'汴注 8

注 **A** F-0439	注 (説文) 注 The seal-style form comprised "flowing water, liquid" (氵), and 主, used for the sound *chuu* to mean "staying in one place." Together they meant "the careful manner in which one pours lamp oil." The kanji 注 means "to pour, pay (attention)." <氵主>	注ぐ to pour [そそぐ]; 注意する to be careful, watch out, give warning [ちゅういする]; 注文 order [ちゅうもん]; 外注 outsourcing, contracting out [がいちゅう]; 注入する to pour into, infuse, inject [ちゅうにゅうする]; 受注する to receive an order [じゅちゅうする]; 注 (註) annotation, comment [ちゅう]

	Meanings	Kun and On	Romaji	Bushu	Stroke Order and Number
SG-2040 柱	pillar, column, support	はしら チュウ	hashira *chuu*	木	一十才木'朾柱 9

柱 **B** F-0907

 柱
説文

The seal-style form comprised 木 "tree, wood" and 主 **SG-2037**, used for the sound *chuu* to mean "something that stays in one place." Wood that stayed in one place supporting the rest of a house was a "column." The kanji 柱 means "pillar, column, support." < 木 主 >

柱 column [はしら]; 大黒柱 the central pillar of a house, breadwinner [だいこくばしら]; 柱時計 wall clock with pendulum [はしらどけい]; 電柱 utility pole [でんちゅう]; 門柱 gatepost [もんちゅう]

96 Musical Instruments

96 Musical instruments (and borrowed characters) 声南琴・喜樹膨鼓

	Meanings	Kun and On	Romaji	Bushu	Stroke Order and Number
SG-2041 声	voice, fame, reputation, sound	こえ・こわ セイ・ショウ	koe, kowa *see, shoo*	耳	一十士主声声声 7

声 **A** F-0238

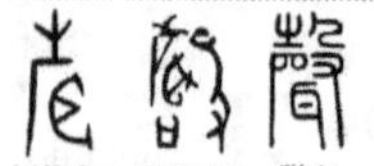 聲 声
甲骨文1 甲骨文2 説文 旧字
1 2 3 4

1 comprised "a stone musical instrument with a rope for hanging" and "an ear." 2 and 3 comprised "a hand holding a drumstick (殳) for banging on a hanging sound board (声)," and "mouth, voice" (口) in 2, or "ear, to listen to" (耳) in 3. The character originally meant "hearing the sound of a musical instrument being played by hand" (probably percussion, judging from 殳). While the kyuji 聲 (4) faithfully reflected 3, the shinji 声 retained only one component. The kanji 声 is used for sounds made from the mouth, whereas 音 is used for sounds made by inanimate objects. The kanji 声 means "voice, fame, reputation, sound." < 士 尸 >

声 voice [こえ]; 鶴の一声 authoritative pronouncement, voice of authority [つるの・ひとこえ]; 人声がする to hear human voices [ひとごえがする]; 大声 loud voice [おおごえ]; 声音 tone of voice [こわね, こわね]; 無声音 voiceless sound [むせいおん]; 音声 voice, sound [おんせい]; 名声 fame [めいせい]; 声明 public declaration [せいめい]

	Meanings	Kun and On	Romaji	Bushu	Stroke Order and Number
SG-2042 南	south; southern	みなみ ナン・ナ	minami *nan, na*	十	一十冂冇冇南南 9

南 **A** F-0177

 南
甲骨文 金文 説文
1 2 3

1, 2, and 3 depicted a musical instrument called a *nan*, which was hung from the top with ropes. The character had the same sound as the word for "south," and it was borrowed for that meaning. Another view suggests that the sound *nan* was similar to *dan* 暖, "warm," and that the character received its present meaning by association with warm southern climates. The kanji 南 means "south; southern." < 南 >

南 south [みなみ]; 南側 south side [みなみがわ]; 南北 the south and north [なんぼく]; 南極 Antarctica, South Pole [なんきょく]; 中南米 Latin America, Central and South America [ちゅうなんべい]

	Meanings	Kun and On	Romaji	Bushu	Stroke Order and Number
SG-2043 琴	harp	こと キン	koto *kin*	玉	一丁王王王玨琴琴 12

琴 **C** F-1348

 琴
説文

The seal-style form depicted "a harp," with a bowed body and bridges for its strings. The kanji 琴 means "harp." <王王今>

琴 *koto*, a horizontal 13-stringed instrument [こと]; 竪琴 harp [たてごと]; 木琴 xylophone, marimba [もっきん]; 心の琴線 one's heartstrings [こころのきんせん]

壴 [from a hanging hand drum] 喜樹膨鼓 

	Meanings	Kun and On	Romaji	Bushu	Stroke Order and Number
SG-2044 喜	to rejoice, be delighted; happy	よろこ-ぶ キ	yoroko-bu *ki*	口	十士吉吉吉壴喜 12

喜 **B** F-0564

 喜
甲骨文 金文 説文古文 説文
1 2 3 4

1 and 2 comprised "a hand drum with a rope for hanging" and 口 "a box of benedictions," together signifying "pleasing a deity with

喜ぶ to rejoice, be delighted [よろこぶ]; 大喜びする to be overjoyed, be thrilled [おおよろこびする]; 歓喜 delight [かんき]; 喜劇 comedy [きげき]; 悲喜こもごも

	good drumming." 3 added "a person with his mouth open, about to eat a feast," which was then dropped in 4. The kanji 喜 means "to rejoice, be delighted; happy." <吉亠口>	bittersweet, mingled feelings of joy and sorrow [ひ↑き・こも↑ごも]; 喜怒哀楽 feelings [き↑ど・あいらく]

SG-2045 樹	Meanings: tree; to establish	Kun and On: ジュ	Romaji: *ju*	Bushu: 木	Stroke Order and Number: 木 朩 桔 植 樹 樹 16
樹 **B** F-0751	石鼓文 1, 説文 1 2, 説文 2 3 — 樹. 1, 2, and 3 comprised (寸) "hand," and 壴 "a hand drum" that was used in a tree-planting rite, together forming 尌, used for the sound *ju*. 木 "tree" was added in 2. The character signified "a tree planted upright by hand." A hand holding a tree upright for planting also gave the meaning "to establish." The kanji 樹 reflects 2, and means "tree; to establish." < 木壴寸>				樹立する to establish [じゅりつする]; 果樹園 orchard [かじゅ↑えん]; 広葉樹 broad-leaved tree [こうよ↑うじゅ]; 樹木 tree, arbor [じゅ↑もく]; 記念樹 commemorative tree [きね↑んじゅ]; 常緑樹 evergreen tree [じょうりょく↑じゅ]; 寄らば大樹の陰 If you turn to someone, choose the powerful. [よら↑ば・た↑いじゅの・かげ] // 樹 tree [き↑]

SG-2046 膨	Meanings: to swell, expand, get big	Kun and On: ふく-らむ ボウ	Romaji: huku-ramu *boo*	Bushu: 肉	Stroke Order and Number: 刀 月 肝 肺 膨 膨 16
膨 **D** F-1684	No ancient form. The kanji comprises 月, bushu *nikuzuki* "part of the body," and 壴 "a hand drum," with 彡 "a pretty shape," used for the sound *boo* to mean "reverberating sound of a drum," or "something which spreads (like sound)." The stomach was a part of the body (月) that expanded. The kanji 膨 means "to swell, expand, get big." < 月壴彡>				膨らむ to swell, expand [ふくらむ]; 着膨れる to be thickly clad [きぶくれる]; 膨張する to expand, swell [ぼうちょうする]; 膨大な enormous, colossal [ぼうだいな]

SG-2047 鼓	Meanings: drum; to drum up, incite	Kun and On: つづみ コ	Romaji: tsuzumi *ko*	Bushu: 鼓	Stroke Order and Number: 士 吉 壴 壴 鼓 鼓 13
鼓 **D** F-1833	甲骨文1 1, 甲骨文2 2, 金文 1 3, 金文 2 4, 説文 5 — 鼓. 1 through 5 comprised "a drum with a rope for hanging" (壴) and "a hand hitting the drum with a drumstick" (支). A hand hitting a drum gave the meaning "rhythmic; to stir up." The kanji 鼓 means "hand drum; to drum up, incite." <壴 支>				鼓 hand drum [つづみ↑]; 小鼓 hand-held drum [こつ↑づみ]; 太鼓 drum [たいこ]; 鼓舞する to encourage, inspire [こ↑ぶする]; 鼓動 to beat, pulsate [こどう]; 鼓笛隊 fife and drum band [こてきたい]

XIII Tied or Bundled

97 Tied or bundled

97a 東 [borrowed from a bag of stuff that was tied at both ends]; *too* 東棟陳

	Meanings	Kun and On	Romaji	Bushu	Stroke Order and Number
SG-2048 東	east	ひがし トウ	higashi *too*	木	8

東 **A** F-0025

甲骨文 1, 金文1 2, 金文2 3, 説文 4

1, 2, 3, and 4 depicted a bag of stuff with its ends tied tightly shut, used for the sound *too*. The character originally meant "stuff," but was borrowed to mean "east." The kanji 東 means "east." <日木>

東 east [ひがし]; 東海岸 east coast, the East Coast [ひがしかいがん]; 東京 Tokyo [とうきょう]; 関東 Kanto region of Japan [かんとう]; 東北地方 Tohoku region of Japan [とうほくちほう]; 東西南北 every direction [とうざいなんぼく]; 中東 Middle East [ちゅうとう]; 中近東 The Near and Middle East [ちゅうきんとう]

	Meanings	Kun and On	Romaji	Bushu	Stroke Order and Number
SG-2049 棟	ridgepole, house; counter for buildings	むね・むな トウ	mune, muna *too*	木	12

棟 **C** F-1510

説文

The seal-style form comprised 木 **SG-0608** "tree, wood," and 東 **SG-2048**, used for the sound *too* to mean "across, through." A piece of wood that was placed across a house was "a ridgepole or ridge beam." The character was also used to mean "house," and as a counter for houses. The kanji 棟 means "ridgepole, house; counter for houses." <木東>

棟 house [むね]; 別棟 different building, annex building [べつむね, べっとう]; 棟木 ridgepole, ridge beam [むなぎ]; 病棟 hospital ward [びょうとう]; 棟梁 master carpenter [とうりょう]; 三棟 three buildings [さんとう]

	Meanings	Kun and On	Romaji	Bushu	Stroke Order and Number
SG-2050 陳	to line up, show; timeworn, outdated, stale	チン	*chin*	阜	11

陳 **C** F-1518

金文1 1, 金文2 2, 説文 3

1 comprised "stack of dirt" (阝), "stuff that is tied around" (東), and "to cause an action" (攴), while 2 had the addition of 土 "soil." Taken together, "displaying or lining up things along a stack of dirt" signified "to display, line up," and had the sound *chin*. When something was left on display for a long time, it became "old, stale." The kanji 陳 means "to line up, show; timeworn, outdated." <阝東>

陳列 display [ちんれつ]; 陳腐な stale, clichéd, obsolete, outdated [ちんぷな]; 陳情する to petition in person [ちんじょうする]; 新陳代謝 metabolism, switch from old to new [しんちんたいしゃ]

97b 東(柬) "to refine, knead" [from 八 "separating" the best items from 束 "a bundle"]; *ren* 練錬

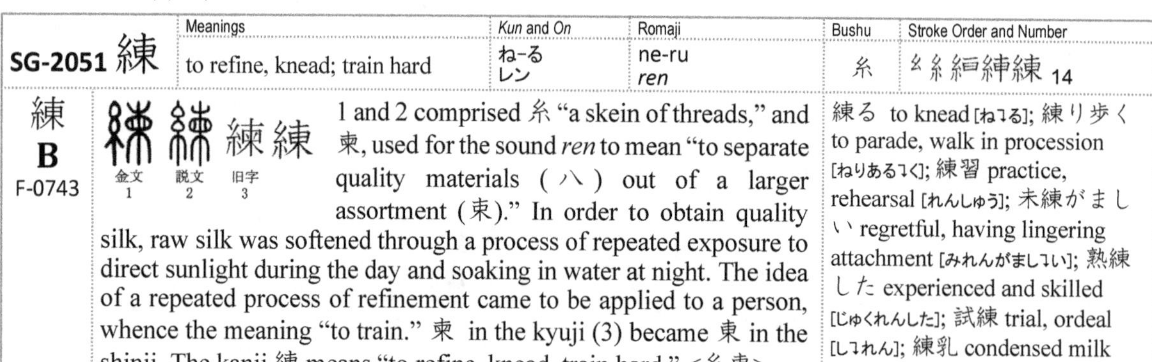

	Meanings	Kun and On	Romaji	Bushu	Stroke Order and Number
SG-2051 練	to refine, knead; train hard	ね-る レン	ne-ru *ren*	糸	14

練 **B** F-0743

金文 1, 説文 2, 旧字 3

1 and 2 comprised 糸 "a skein of threads," and 柬, used for the sound *ren* to mean "to separate quality materials (八) out of a larger assortment (束)." In order to obtain quality silk, raw silk was softened through a process of repeated exposure to direct sunlight during the day and soaking in water at night. The idea of a repeated process of refinement came to be applied to a person, whence the meaning "to train." 柬 in the kyuji (3) became 東 in the shinji. The kanji 練 means "to refine, knead, train hard." <糸東>

練る to knead [ねる]; 練り歩く to parade, walk in procession [ねりあるく]; 練習 practice, rehearsal [れんしゅう]; 未練がましい regretful, having lingering attachment [みれんがましい]; 熟練した experienced and skilled [じゅくれんした]; 試練 trial, ordeal [しれん]; 練乳 condensed milk [れんにゅう]

SG-2052 錬	Meanings	Kun and On	Romaji	Bushu	Stroke Order and Number
	to refine (metal), train hard	レン	*ren*	金	16

錬 **D** F-2036

説文 1 旧字 2

1 comprised 金 **SG-1196** "metal," and 柬 "to refine, knead," used for the sound *ren*, together signifying "heating iron at a high temperature to remove impurities." The kanji 錬 means "to refine (metal), train hard." <金柬>

錬金術 alchemy [れんきんじゅつ]; 精錬 metal refining, smelting [せいれん]; 鍛錬 tempering, toughening, annealing [たんれん]

97c 曹 "low-level officer" [from two people standing to speak]; *soo* 曹遭槽

SG-2053 曹	Meanings	Kun and On	Romaji	Bushu	Stroke Order and Number
	judicial officer, fellow, sergeant	ソウ	*soo*	日	11

曹 **D** F-2002

甲骨文 1 金文 2 中山王器 3 説文 4

1, 2, and 4 comprised "two tied-up bags of stuff" (柬 **SG-2048**), used for the sound *soo*, and 曰 "to speak; a vow." Together they signified "two parties (plaintiff and accused) standing to speak in court," or "judicial matter." Two means multiple, and "multiple officials standing in court" gave the meanings "sergeant" and "fellow." The kanji 曹 means "judicial officer, sergeant, fellow." <曲日>

法曹界 leagal circles, the bench and bar [ほうそうかい]; 軍曹 sergeant [ぐんそう]; 重曹 sodium bicarbonate, baking soda [じゅうそう]; 御曹司 a son of a distinguished family [おんぞうし]

SG-2054 遭	Meanings	Kun and On	Romaji	Bushu	Stroke Order and Number
	to encounter, meet by chance; mishap	あ-う ソウ	a-u *soo*	辵	14

遭 **D** F-1741

中山王器 1 説文 2

1 was the same as 3 for 曹 **SG-2053**. In 2, 辵(辶) "to move forward; on the road" was added to 曹 "fellow, companion," which was used for the sound *soo*. People meeting on the road unexpectedly meant "to encounter." The kanji 遭 is often associated with mishaps or "accidents." The kanji 遭 means "to encounter, meet by chance; mishap." <曹辶>

遭う to encounter [あう]; 遭難 disaster, mishap, shipwreck [そうなん]; 遭遇する to encounter, come upon [そうぐうする]

SG-2055 槽	Meanings	Kun and On	Romaji	Bushu	Stroke Order and Number
	tub, tank, vat	ソウ	*soo*	木	15

槽 **D** F-2042

篆文

The seal-style form comprised 木 **SG-0608** "tree, wood," and 曹, used for the sound *soo* to mean "tub," together signifying "a wooden tub." The kanji 槽 means "tub, tank, vat." <木曹>

水槽 water tank [すいそう]; 浴槽 bath tub [よくそう]

97d 量 "mass, amount" [from a scale for weighing bagged grain]; *ryoo* 量糧

SG-2056 量	Meanings	Kun and On	Romaji	Bushu	Stroke Order and Number
	mass, amount	はか-る リョウ	haka-ru *ryoo*	里	12

量 **A** F-0499

甲骨文 1 金文 2 説文古文 3 説文 4

1 through 4 depicted a bag tied around, with an opening for inserting grain and a shaft going through it. The character meant "weighing a bag of grain." In 3 and 4 it included 土 "dirt" at the bottom, to represent a weight. A thing being weighed meant "mass, amount." In the kanji 量, the bottom component took the shape 里. The kanji 量 means "mass, amount." <日一里>

量る to measure, weigh [はかる]; 量 quantity, amount, column [りょう]; 分量 dose, quantity [ぶんりょう]; 測量 location survey, surveying [そくりょう, そくりょう]; 重量制限 weight limit [じゅうりょうせいげん]; 力量 ability, power, craftsmanship [りきりょう, りきりょう]; 量産する to produce in large quantities [りょうさんする]

SG-2057 糧	Meanings	Kun and On	Romaji	Bushu	Stroke Order and Number
	food, provisions, nourishment	かて リョウ・ロウ	kate *ryoo, roo*	米	18

糧 **C** F-1418

金文 1 説文 2

1 comprised "rice" (米 **SG-0738**) and "a bag tied around, with an opening and a shaft going through" (量 **SG-2056**), used for the

糧 provisions, food, nourishment [かて, かて]; 心の糧 nourishment for one's mind [こころのかて]; 日々の糧 one's daily bread [ひびの・かて]; 食糧 provisions, food

	sound *ryoo*. Rice and other grains being measured meant "food, provisions." In 2, the two components were placed side by side. The kanji 糧 means "food, provisions, nourishment."<米量>	[しょく〕りょう]; 食糧自給率 the food self-sufficiency rate [しょく〕りょう、じきゅ〕うりつ]; 兵糧 provisions, food [ひょうろう]

97e 重 "heavy" [from the weight of grain in a bag]; *juu/choo/doo* 重動種働衝腫 

	Meanings	Kun and On	Romaji	Bushu	Stroke Order and Number
SG-2058 重	heavy, large, important; to treasure, lay over	え・おも-い・かさ-ねる ジュウ・チョウ	e, omo-I, kasa-neru *juu, choo*	里	一二亖亘重 9

重 **A** F-0167

金文 1 金文 2 説文 3

One view explains that 1 and 2 comprised "a bag of stuff tied at both ends with a shaft going through" (東 **SG-2048**), and "weight" (土 **SG-1126**), together siginifying "the weight of grain in a bag," and thus meaning "heavy." Another view holds that the character depicted a person (top of 1 and 3) stamping down the heavy contents of a bag laid on the ground, whence "heavy." Putting something on top of another thing also meant "to lay over, pile, repeat." Something heavy was not to be taken lightly, and thus it meant "important, precious." The kanji 重 means "heavy, large, important; to lay over, treasure." <亠日 土>

二重 twofold [ふた〕え、にじゅう]; 重い heavy, grave [おもい]; 重ねる to repeat, lay over [かさねる]; 厳重に sternly, closely [げんじゅうに]; 重力 gravity [じゅ〕うりょく]; 重宝する to find something useful, handy [ちょ〕うほうする]; 事の軽重 importance of the matter [こと〕の・けいちょう]; 自重する to be cautious, be cicumspect [じちょうする]

	Meanings	Kun and On	Romaji	Bushu	Stroke Order and Number
SG-2059 動	to move	うご-く ドウ	ugo-ku *doo*	力	亘車重動動 11

動 **A** F-0114

金文 1 金文 2 説文古文 3 説文 4

The top of 1 was the same as 2 for 童 **SG-2064**, whose original meaning was "prison inmate doing heavy labor," used for the sound *doo*. The bottom component was the same as 2 for 重 "heavy." Taken together, they meant "an inmate moving heavy things," or just "to move." In 2 and 3, "a crossroads" and "a footprint," signifying "movement," were added to 童, but were dropped in 4. Instead, 力 **SG-1949** "plow," signifying "strength to do strenuous work," was added on the right. The kanji 動 means "to move." <重力>

動く to move [うご〕く]; 移動する to move, shift [いどうする]; 手動 manual operation [しゅどう]; 原動力 driving force [げんど〕うりょく]; 行動 behavior, act [こうどう]; 動物 animal [どうぶつ]; 一挙一動 every move, the slightest move [いっ〕きょ・いちどう]

	Meanings	Kun and On	Romaji	Bushu	Stroke Order and Number
SG-2060 種	seed, kind, sort	たね シュ	tane *shu*	禾	⺊禾秄稆稙種 14

種 **A** F-0478

篆文 1 説文 2

1 and 2 comprised 禾 "rice plant with crop," and 童 (in 1) or 重 (in 2) with 土, which was used for the sound *shu*. Grains that were full and heavy made good seeds, and were kept for the next sowing. Seeds are also used to differentiate "kinds" of plants. The character is also used to mean "source, cause." The kanji 種 means "seed, kind, sort." <禾 重>

種 seed, cause [た〕ね]; type, category, species, variety [しゅ〕]; 心配の種 cause of anxiety [しんぱいのた〕ね]; 一粒種 one's only child [ひとつぶだ〕ね]; 種蒔き sowing, seeding [たね〕まき]; 種類 kind, sort [しゅるい]; 人種 race, ethnic group [じんしゅ]; 品種 kind [ひんしゅ]

	Meanings	Kun and On	Romaji	Bushu	Stroke Order and Number
SG-2061 働	to work, operate	はたら-く ドウ	hatara-ku *doo*	人	亻伂俥偅働働 13

働 **B** F-0655

The kanji 働 was created in Japan. It comprises 亻, bushu *ninben* "an act that one does," and 動 "to move," used for the sound *doo*, and whose original meaning was "heavy manual labor." Together they meant "(a person doing) hard work, such as moving heavy objects." The character is also used to refer to a machine operating. The kanji 働 means "to work, operate." <亻動>

働く to work [はたらく]; 只働き free service, working for nothing [ただば〕たらき]; 労働者 laborer [ろうど〕うしゃ]; 稼働する to operate, work [かどうする]; 実働時間 actual working hours [じつどうじ〕かん]

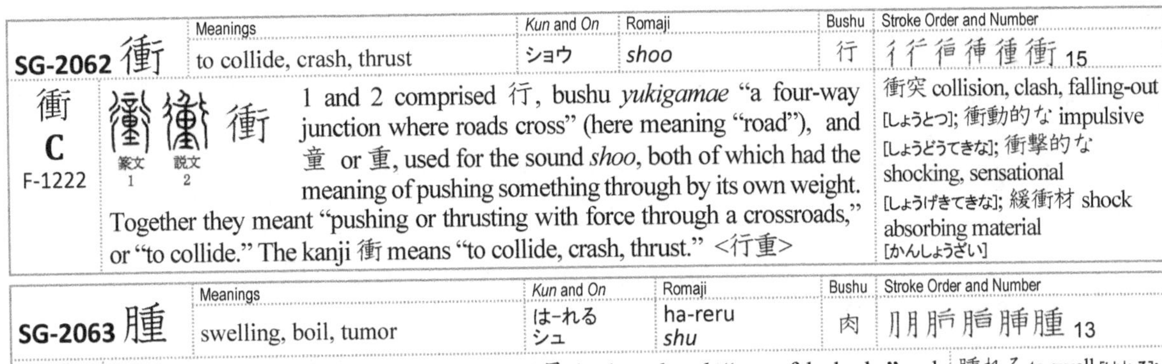

SG-2062 衝	Meanings: to collide, crash, thrust	Kun and On: ショウ	Romaji: *shoo*	Bushu: 行	Stroke Order and Number: 彳 行 徝 徸 衝 衝 15

衝 **C** F-1222

篆文 1　説文 2

1 and 2 comprised 行, bushu *yukigamae* "a four-way junction where roads cross" (here meaning "road"), and 童 or 重, used for the sound *shoo*, both of which had the meaning of pushing something through by its own weight. Together they meant "pushing or thrusting with force through a crossroads," or "to collide." The kanji 衝 means "to collide, crash, thrust." <行重>

衝突 collision, clash, falling-out [しょうとつ]; 衝動的な impulsive [しょうどうてきな]; 衝撃的な shocking, sensational [しょうげきてきな]; 緩衝材 shock absorbing material [かんしょうざい]

SG-2063 腫	Meanings: swelling, boil, tumor	Kun and On: は-れる シュ	Romaji: ha-reru *shu*	Bushu: 肉	Stroke Order and Number: 丿 月 肝 脜 腫 腫 13

腫 **D** F-2118

説文

The seal-style form comprised 月, bushu *nikuzuki* "part of the body," and 重, which originallly came from "a round, tied-up bag of stuff," used for the sound *shu*. A round shape on one's body meant "swelling, tumor." The kanji 腫 means "swelling, boil, tumor." <月重>

腫れる to swell [はれる]; 腫瘍 tumor [しゅよう] // 浮腫 swelling, bloating [むくみ]

97f 童 "young child"; *doo/too* 童瞳鐘憧

SG-2064 童	Meanings: young child	Kun and On: わらべ ドウ	Romaji: warabe *doo*	Bushu: 立	Stroke Order and Number: 亠 立 音 章 童 12

童 **C** F-1123

金文1 1　金文2 2　説文籀文 3　説文 4

The top component in 1 and 2 had "a tattooing needle" (辛) above "an eye" (目), signifying punishment of a prison inmate. The bottom component 重 **SG-2058** "heavy" was used for the sound *doo*. Together they originally signified an inmate tasked with moving heavy dirt or doing hard labor. In 3 and 4, "eye" was dropped. Inmates were not allowed to tie or style their hair, and someone who was not old enough to tie their hair was "a child." Another view holds that "eyes pierced with a needle" signified a blind enslaved male who did low-level work. Someone who was naïve like a prisoner or slave meant "a child." The kanji 童 means "young child." <立里>

童 young child [わらべ] (archaic); 童歌 children's nursery song [わらべうた]; 児童 child [じどう]; 童謡 children's song [どうよう]; 童心に返る to retrieve one's childlike innocence [どうしんにかえる]; 牧童 shepherd boy [ぼくどう]

SG-2065 瞳	Meanings: pupil, eye	Kun and On: ひとみ ドウ	Romaji: hitomi *doo*	Bushu: 目	Stroke Order and Number: 目 盷 瞕 瞳 瞳 17

瞳 **C** F-1614

No ancient form. The kanji 瞳 comprised 目 "eye," and 童, used for the sound *too*. The character meant "the pupil of the eye." The kanji 瞳 means "pupil, eye." <目童>

瞳 pupil, eye [ひとみ]; 瞳孔 pupil (of the eye) [どうこう]

SG-2066 鐘	Meanings: large bell	Kun and On: かね ショウ	Romaji: kane *shoo*	Bushu: 金	Stroke Order and Number: 𠆢 全 金 鉒 鐘 鐘 鐘 20

鐘 **D** F-1735

金文1 1　金文2 2　説文 3　説文或体 4

1, 2, and 3 comprised 金 "metal," and 童, used for the sound *shoo*. The character represented a large bell used in festivals and religious rites. The kanji 鐘 means "large bell." <金童>

鐘 bell [かね]; 除夜の鐘 New Year's Eve bells [じょやのかね]; 警鐘 alarm bell [けいしょう]

SG-2067 憧	Meanings: to yearn after, admire	Kun and On: あこが-れる ショウ	Romaji: akoga-reru *shoo*	Bushu: 心	Stroke Order and Number: 忄 忙 愔 憧 憧 15

憧 **D** F-2119

篆文

The seal-style form comprised 忄, bushu *risshinben* "a heart," and 童, used for the sound *doo*, together signifying "an unsettled heart yearning after something." The kanji 憧 means "to yearn after, admire." <忄童>

憧れ yearning [あこがれる]; 憧憬 yearning [どうけい, しょうけい]

97g 束 "bundle" [from a bundle of firewood] 束速整頼瀬疎勅辣

	Meanings	Kun and On	Romaji	Bushu	Stroke Order and Number
SG-2068 束	to bind; bundle, a brief period of time	たば ソク	taba *soku*	木	束 10

束 **A** F-0990

甲骨文 1 金文1 2 金文2 3 説文 4

1 through 4 depicted "a bundle of firewood tied around." The character meant "a bundle" or "things bound together." In Japanese it also refers to time, and means "a brief time." The kanji 束 means "to bind; bundle, a brief period of time." <木口>

束 bundle [たば]; 花束 bouquet of flowers [はなたば]; 束ねる to bundle [たばねる]; 束縛する to restrain [そくばくする]; 結束する to band together, become united [けっそくする]; 装束 costume, attire [しょうぞく]; 収束する to be resolved, converge [しゅうそくする]

	Meanings	Kun and On	Romaji	Bushu	Stroke Order and Number
SG-2069 速	fast, swift	はや-い・すみ-やか ソク	haya-i, sumi-yaka *soku*	辵	速 7

速 **A** F-0514

金文 1 説文 2

1 and 2 comprised "a bundle tied with a rope in the middle and at both ends" (束), used for the sound *soku* to mean "quick; to rush"; and "a crossroads" with "a footprint," for "to go forward" (辵). Together they signified "fast or swift-moving." The kanji 速 means "fast, swift." <束 辶>

速い fast [はやい]; 速やかに rapidly, without delay [すみやかに]; 速度 speed [そくど]; 早速 at once, right away [さっそく]; 速達 special delivery [そくたつ]; 快速電車 rapid train [かいそくでんしゃ]; 失速する to stall, decline, slump [しっそくする]; 風速 wind velocity [ふうそく]

	Meanings	Kun and On	Romaji	Bushu	Stroke Order and Number
SG-2070 整	to put in good order	ととの-える セイ	totono-eru *see*	攴	整 16

整 **A** F-0501

金文 1 説文 2

1 comprised 束 "a bundle"; 正 "correct, just," used for the sound *see*; and 攴 (攵) "to cause an action." Taken together, they signified "orderly sorting of things in bundles." The kanji 整 means "to put in good order." <束攵正>

整える to put in good order [ととのえる]; 整理する to put in good order [せいりする]; 調整 adjustment [ちょうせい]; 整然とした orderly [せいぜんとした]; 交通整理 traffic control [こうつうせいり]; 整備する to service, fully equip with [せいびする]

	Meanings	Kun and On	Romaji	Bushu	Stroke Order and Number
SG-2071 頼	dependable; to rely, request	たの-む・たよ-る ライ	tano-mu, tayo-ru *rai*	貝	頼 16

頼 **B** F-0792

説文 1 旧字 2

1 and 2 comprised 束 "a bundle tied at the ends"; 刀 "a knife," used for the sound *rai* (from 剌 *ratsu*); and 貝 **SG-1693** "valuable." A part of a bundle of valuable items being cut out with a knife gave the meaning "extra profit." Having extra fortune makes one a person on whom others might "rely." In the shinji, the right side was replaced by 頁 "head, person." The kanji 頼 means "dependable; to rely, request." <束頁>

頼む to request [たのむ]; 神頼み turning to God for help (in time of distress) [かみだのみ]; 頼りになる dependable [たよりになる]; 依頼する to request [いらいする]; 信頼 trust [しんらい]

	Meanings	Kun and On	Romaji	Bushu	Stroke Order and Number
SG-2072 瀬	rapids, predicament	せ	se	水	瀬 19

瀬 **B** F-1023

篆文 1 旧字 2

1 comprised "flowing water" (氵), and 賴 (the kyuji for 頼), used for the sound *rai*, together signifying "rapids." Rapids ran through a narrow part of a river which had small shallows along its banks, and thus the character also meant "a tight situation or predicament." The kanji 瀬 means "rapids, shallow, predicament." <氵頼>

立つ瀬がない to be in a bind, in a tight corner [たつせがない]; 瀬戸際 critical moment [せとぎわ]; 瀬戸物 crockery, dishware [せともの]; やる瀬ない helpless; inconsolable [やるせない]

	Meanings	Kun and On	Romaji	Bushu	Stroke Order and Number
SG-2073 疎	coarse, not close, distant; to alienate	うと-い ソ	uto-i *so*	疋	疎 12

疎 **D** F-1693

説文 1 正字 2

In 1 and 2, 足, or its variant 𤴔, was used for the sound *so* to mean "coarse, loose." 㐬 on the right side represented a combing action which loosened and separated the particles of a substance. Separating something by combing through it left "gaps" where the

疎い unacquainted with, distant [うとい]; 疎外感 feeling of being estranged [そがいかん]; 意思の疎通 mutual understanding [いしの・そつう]; 疎開

	comb had passed. In the kanji, 束 **SG-2068** replaced 㐬. "Separation" also meant "keeping distance" or "to alienate." The kanji 疎 means "coarse, not close, distant; to alienate." <正束>	evacuation to the countryside (during war) [そかい]; 過疎化 becoming underpopulated [かそか]

	Meanings	Kun and On	Romaji	Bushu	Stroke Order and Number
SG-2074 勅	imperial edict	チョク	*choku*	力	一 戸 申 束 勅 勅 9

勅 **D** F-1982 — 金文 1, 旧字 2

1 comprised "a bundle" (束 **SG-2069**) and "a plow" (力 **SG-1949**), originally signifying "to bundle things in good order." The kyuji 敕 had 攵 "to cause an action," and meant "imperial edict." The informal variant 勅 with 力 became the shinji. The kanji 勅 means "imperial edict." <束力>

勅語 imperial edict, a speech from the throne [ちょくご]; 勅許 imperial consent [ちょっきょ]

	Meanings	Kun and On	Romaji	Bushu	Stroke Order and Number
SG-2075 辣	cruel, blistering, caustic	ラツ	*ratsu*	辛	立 辛 辛 𨐋 𨐋 辣 14

辣 **D** F-3047

No ancient form. The kanji comprised 辛 **SG-1359** "hard" (from a needle), and 束, used for the sound *ratsu* (as an abbreviated form of the kanji 剌 *ratsu* "to spring back; animated"). 辛 and 束 together gave the meaning "spicy, cruel." The kanji 辣 means "cruel, blistering, caustic." <辛束>

悪辣な villainous [あくらつな]; 辛辣な biting [しんらつな]; 辣腕家 a man of great acumen, a shrewd man [らつわんか]

97h 必 "fastened tightly" [from something tightly bound]; *hi/mi* 必密秘蜜泌

	Meanings	Kun and On	Romaji	Bushu	Stroke Order and Number
SG-2076 必	without fail, necessarily; inevitable	かなら-ず ヒツ	kanara-zu *hitsu*	心	` ソ 义 必 必 · 、 心 心 必 5

必 **A** F-0323 — 金文 1, 金文 2, 説文 3

1, 2, and 3 depicted "a vice for straightening a stick." From "something held firmly in place," the character meant "without fail." Another view explains that it depicted the part of a halberd (戈) handle where the blade was inserted, which also signified "held firmly in place," and had the sound *hi*. "Having no alternative" also meant "inevitable," and when used with a negative, the character means "not necessarily" or "not entirely." The kanji 必 means "without fail, inevitable; necessarily." <心ノ>

必ず without fail [かならず]; 必ずしも～ない not necessarily [かならずしも・～ない]; 必要な necessary [ひつような]; 必然的な inevitable [ひつぜんてきな]; 必死になって frantically, desperately [ひっしになって]; 必修科目 required subject [ひっしゅうかもく]

	Meanings	Kun and On	Romaji	Bushu	Stroke Order and Number
SG-2077 密	secret, dense, close	ミツ	*mitsu*	宀	宀 宓 宓 密 密 11

密 **B** F-0778 — 金文 1, 金文 2, 説文 3

1 and 2 comprised "a tightly wrapped halberd inside a house or shrine," and "a fire." Fire was used in religious rites for its cleansing power. A rite that was conducted inside and hidden from view meant "secret." Being "tightly packed with no gaps" gave the meaning "dense, close." In 3, the fire was miscopied as "mountain." Another view explains that the character represented a tightly shut house on a distant mountain, thick with vegetation. The kanji 密 means "secret, dense, close." <宀必山> (Note: Miscopying of 火 "fire" as 山 "mountain" is also seen in the kanji 岡 **SG-1967**.)

機密書類 confidential documents [きみつしょるい]; 精密機器 precision instrument [せいみつきき]; 密会 clandestine meeting [みっかい]; 密着する stick fast to, adhere closely [みっちゃくする]; 密接な close, intimate [みっせつな]; 過密 overcrowding [かみつ]

	Meanings	Kun and On	Romaji	Bushu	Stroke Order and Number
SG-2078 秘	secret; to hide	ひ-める ヒ	hi-meru *hi*	示	二 禾 私 秘 秘 10

秘 **B** F-0800 — 説文 1, 旧字 2

1 comprised 示 "an altar table with offering," and 必, used for the sound *hi* to mean "secret," together signifying "a secretly performed religious rite," or "secret" more generally. In the shinji 秘, 示 was miscopied as 禾, bushu *nogihen* "rice plant." The kanji 秘 means "secret; to hide." <禾必>

秘める to hide, suppress (emotions or facts) [ひめる]; 秘密 secret [ひみつ]; 極秘 strictly confidential, top secret [ごくひ]

	Meanings	Kun and On	Romaji	Bushu	Stroke Order and Number
SG-2079 蜜	honey, nectar	ミツ	*mitsu*	虫	宀宓宓宻寗蜜 14

蜜 **D** F-1994

説文 1 説文或体 2 蜜

1 and 2 comprised 冖 "a cover," over either 鼎 "a bronze vessel for keeping valuables" (in 1), or 必 **SG-2076** "tightly sealed" (in 2), both used for the sound "*mitsu*," and "bees" (虫 **SG-0998**). The character signified "a pot of honey that bees created." The kanji 蜜 means "honey, nectar." <宀必虫>

蜜 honey, sweet liquid [み↓つ]; 蜂蜜 bee honey [はちみつ]; 花の蜜 flower nectar [はなのみ↓つ]

	Meanings	Kun and On	Romaji	Bushu	Stroke Order and Number
SG-2080 泌	to seep, ooze, run, secrete	ヒツ・ヒ	*hitsu, hi*	水	氵氵沙泌泌泌 8

泌 **D** F-2032

説文 泌

The seal-style form comprised "flowing water" (氵), and 必, used for the sound *hitsu/hi* to mean "to secrete," together signifying "water running through a narrow path." In Japanese the kanji 泌 means "to seep, ooze, run, secrete." <氵必>

分泌 secretion, discharge [ぶんぴつ, ぶんぴ]; 泌尿器科 urology [ひにょうきか] // 泌みる to seep, ooze, be sensitive [しみる]

97i 弗 "to disperse" [from a bundle of warped sticks coming apart]; *hi/hutsu* 費払仏沸

	Meanings	Kun and On	Romaji	Bushu	Stroke Order and Number
SG-2081 費	cost; to spend money, require (time/money), waste	つい-やす ヒ	tsui-yasu *hi*	貝	一ㄱ弓弗費費 12

費 **A** F-0412

金文 1 説文 2 費

1 comprised 弗 "a bundle of warped sticks loosening or coming apart," with 刂 "knife" for the sound *hi,* and 貝 "valuable; money," together signifying "to spend money loosely, to waste." In 2 the knife was dropped. The kanji 費 means "cost; to spend money, require (time/money), waste." <弗貝>

費やす to spend (money or time) [ついや↓す]; 費用 expenses [ひ↓よう]; 私費 private expense [し↓ひ, しひ]; 浪費 waste [ろうひ]; 実費 actual expense, costs [じっぴ]; 消費 consumption, spending [しょうひ]; 工費 the price of construction [こ↓うひ]

	Meanings	Kun and On	Romaji	Bushu	Stroke Order and Number
SG-2082 払	to pay (money or attention), brush off	はら-う フツ	hara-u *hutsu*	手	一扌払払 5

払 **B** F-0729

説文 1 旧字 2 拂 払

1 comprised 扌 "an act done by hand," and 弗 "to come apart, fall away," used for the sound *hutsu.* The motion of a hand sweeping something away meant "to brush off." "Getting rid of" debt meant "to pay money." In the shinji, 弗 was replaced by the simplified shape ム. The kanji 払 means "to brush off, pay (money or attention)." <扌ム>

お金を払う to pay money [おかねをはら↓う]; 埃を払う brush off dust [ほこりをはら↓う]; 注意を払う to pay attention [ちゅ↓ういを・はら↓う]; 支払い payment [しはらい]; 月払い monthly payment [つきば↓らい]; 咳払い clearing one's throat [せきば↓らい]; 払拭する to wipe off [ふっしょくする]

	Meanings	Kun and On	Romaji	Bushu	Stroke Order and Number
SG-2083 仏	Buddha, Buddhism, France	ほとけ ブツ	hotoke *butsu*	人	ノイ仏仏 4

仏 **B** F-0640

説文 1 旧字 2 佛 仏

1 comprised "a person," and 弗, used for the sound *hutsu.* When Buddhism came to China from India, the Sanskrit word Buddha was written as 佛陀 *budda.* In the shinji, 弗 was simplified to ム. The character is also used for the initial sound of 仏蘭西, "France." The kanji 仏 means "Buddha, Buddhism, France; French." <イム>

仏・仏様 Buddha [ほとけ, ほとけさま]; 大仏 big Buddha statue [だいぶつ]; 仏教 Buddhism [ぶ↓っきょう]; 念仏を唱える to invoke Buddha, pray to Amida Buddha [ねんぶつをとなえ↓る]; 仏語 the French language [ふつご, フランスご]; 旧仏領 former French colony [きゅ↓う・ふつりょう]

	Meanings	Kun and On	Romaji	Bushu	Stroke Order and Number
SG-2084 沸	to boil water, bubble up	わ-く フツ	wa-ku *hutsu*	水	氵沪沪沸沸 8

沸 **D** F-1891

説文 沸

The seal-style form comprised "flowing water" (氵), and 弗, used for the sound *hutsu. Hutsu* was the onomatopoeia for the sound of boiling water. The kanji 沸 means "to boil water, bubble up." <氵弗>

沸く to boil [わく]; 沸騰する to boil [ふっとうする]; 沸点 boiling point [ふってん]; 煮沸消毒 sterilization by boiling [しゃふつしょ↓うどく]

97j 者 [from a bundle of sticks burning in a stove]; *sha/cho* 者着諸緒著暑煮 

SG-2085 者	Meanings	Kun and On	Romaji	Bushu	Stroke Order and Number
	person, one, fellow	もの シャ	mono *sha*	老	一土耂者者 8

者
A
F-0033

金文 1, 金文 2, 説文 3, 旧字 4

1, 2, and 3 were "a bundle of sticks burning in a stove and giving off sparks." From an early time this character was borrowed to mean "this" or "person." In the kyuji 者 (4), a dot above 日 is what remains of the sparks, and the top took the shape of 耂, bushu *oigashira* (not related to its meaning). The kanji 者 means "person, one, fellow." It is no longer used as a demonstrative pronoun. <耂日>

悪者 bad guy, villain [わるもの]; 回し者 spy [まわしもの]; 学者 scholar, a man of learning [がくしゃ]; 記者 reporter, journalist [きしゃ]; 希望者 applicant, aspirant [きぼうしゃ]; 加入者 new member [かにゅうしゃ]; 利用者 user; visitor [りようしゃ]; 入場者 visitor, spectator, attendance [にゅうじょうしゃ]

SG-2086 着	Meanings	Kun and On	Romaji	Bushu	Stroke Order and Number
	to attach, put clothes on, wear, arrive	き-る・つ-く チャク・ジャク	ki-ru, tsuku *chaku, jaku*	羊	丷䒑兰羊着着 12

着
A
F-0279

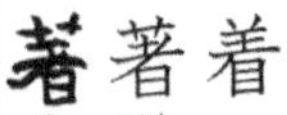

碑 1, 正字 2

No ancient form. 1, which was an inscription on a stone stele, and 2, written in orthographic style, were 著 **SG-2094**. 着 was a variant of 著, but in Japanese the two kanji have different uses: 著, having the sound *cho*, means "to author, stand out," whereas 着, having the sound *chaku*, means "to attach, put clothes on, wear, arrive." <⺷目>

着る to wear [きる]; お仕着せ clothes provided by an employer [おしきせ]; 着物 kimono, traditional Japanese attire [きもの]; 古着 secondhand clothing [ふるぎ]; 着く to arrive [つく]; 一着 one set of clothing [いっちゃく]; 着手する to start up [ちゃくしゅする]; 愛着のある attached to, fond of [あいちゃくのある]; 着服 embezzlement, putting clothes on [ちゃくふく]

SG-2087 諸	Meanings	Kun and On	Romaji	Bushu	Stroke Order and Number
	various, many, all	ショ	*sho*	言	言言計計諸諸 15

諸
B
F-0810

金文 1, 説文 2, 旧字 3

1 was the same as 1 and 2 for 者 **SG-2085**. It was used for the sound *sho* to mean "many." In 2, 言 "words" was added to emphasize the meaning of "many," from the fact that words are numerous. The kanji 諸 means "various, many, all." <言者>

諸事情 various reasons [しょじじょう]; 諸君 Gentlemen! [しょくん]; 学生諸君 All our students [がくせいしょくん]; 会員諸氏 all members [かいいんしょし]; 沖縄諸島 the Okinawa Islands [おきなわしょとう] // 諸々の various, many, all [もろもろの]

SG-2088 緒	Meanings	Kun and On	Romaji	Bushu	Stroke Order and Number
	beginning, rope, string	お ショ・チョ	o *sho, cho*	糸	幺糸紏紏絊緒 14

緒
B
F-0983

説文 1, 旧字 2

1 comprised 糸 **SG-1600** "a skein of threads," and 者, used for the sounds *sho* and *cho* to mean "beginning," together signifying "the beginning of a long and continuous thing, such as a string or rope." The kanji 緒 means "beginning, rope, string." <糸者>

兜の緒 strings on kabuto armor [かぶとのお]; 鼻緒 straps on *geta* or *zoori* footwear [はなお]; 一緒 together [いっしょ]; 内緒 secrecy, privacy [ないしょ]; 由緒 history, origin [ゆいしょ]; 情緒 emotion, atmosphere [じょうちょ]; 端緒 first step, clue [たんちょ, たんしょ]

SG-2089 著	Meanings	Kun and On	Romaji	Bushu	Stroke Order and Number
	to write a book, stand out; conspicuous	あらわ-す・いちじる-しい チョ	arawa-su, ichijiru-shii *cho*	艸	一艹芏茡著 11

著
B
F-0992

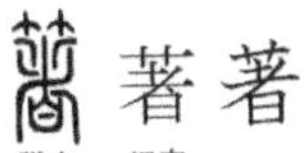

説文 1, 旧字 2

1 comprised 竹, bushu *takekanmuri* "bamboo," and 者, used for the sound *cho*. Bamboo was used to make writing brushes and writing tablets. The character meant "to write a book." In the kyuji 著 (2), however, the bamboo on the top was replaced by 艹, bushu *kusakanmuri* "plants." Writing clarifies a matter, and from that the character also meant "to stand out." The kanji 著 means "to write a book, stand out; conspicuous." <艹者>

著す to write a book [あらわす]; 著しい to stand out, marked [いちじるしい]; 著者 author [ちょしゃ]; 名著 famous book [めいちょ]; 顕著な remarkable [けんちょな]

SG-2090 暑	Meanings	Kun and On	Romaji	Bushu	Stroke Order and Number
	to feel hot (in atmospheric temperature)	あつ-い ショ	atsu-i *sho*	日	日 早 旦 昇 暑 暑 12

暑 **C** F-1211	説文 1 · 旧字 2 1 comprised 者 "a bundle of sticks gathered in a stove to burn," used for the sound *sho*, with "the sun" (日) on top. "The sun" and "burning" together made the kyuji 暑 (2), which meant "hot." The kanji 暑 means "to feel hot (in atmospheric temperature)." <日者>	暑い hot [あつꜜい]; 蒸し暑い hot and humid [むしあつꜜい]; 暑気当たり heatstroke [しょきあꜜたり]; 暑中見舞い summer greeting card [しょちゅうみꜜまい]; 残暑 lingering summer heat [ざꜜんしょ]

SG-2091 煮	Meanings	Kun and On	Romaji	Bushu	Stroke Order and Number
	to cook over a fire, boil	に-る シャ	ni-ru *sha*	火	土 耂 者 者 煮 12

煮 **C** F-1282	中山王器1 1 · 中山王器2 2 · 説文 3 · 説文或体 4 · 旧字 5 1 and 2 depicted "a kitchen stove with a pot on it." The character had the sound *sha* and mean "to cook over a fire." 3 comprised "a stove with wood sticks burning" (者) on top of "a thick hollow-legged grain storage pot" (鬲), whereas 4 comprised 者 and "a fire," which became 灬, bushu *rekka* or *renga* "fire," in the kyuji (5). The kanji 煮 means "to cook over a fire, boil." <者灬>	煮る to cook (over heat) [にる]; 煮物 simmered food [にもの]; 生煮え half-cooked, underdone [なまにえ]; 煮沸消毒 sterilization by boiling [しゃふつしょꜜうどく]

XIV Other Shapes

98 Shapes

98a 彡 "pretty shape"; *san*; bushu *sanzukuri* 参杉診珍惨

	Meanings	Kun and On	Romaji	Bushu	Stroke Order and Number
SG-2092 参	to mingle, come, come/go (humble), make a pilgrimage; three	まい-る サン	mai-ru *san*	ム	ムム夬矣参 8

参
A
F-0299

金文1 1 金文2 2 説文 3 旧字 4

1 depicted "a kneeling woman with three shining hair accessories (in a shrine)," while in 2 and 3, three lines 彡 were added for the sound *san*, and also the meaning "bright reflections of light mingling on the hair accessories." The reflections mingling gave the meaning "to mingle." In 3, the three shining things became represented by three 日, which were simplified to three ム in the shinji (4). 参 is also used for the sound *san* to mean "three" in place of 三 in legal documents and formal financial transactions. In Japanese it is used to mean "to make a pilgrimage or other religious visit," and also as a humble verb which means both "to come" and "to go." The kanji 参 means "to mingle, come/go/visit (humble style); three." <ム一へ彡>

参る to come/go (humble), pay a visit, give in, become exhausted [まいる]; 墓参り visit to a grave [はかまいり]; 参加する to participate in [さんかする]; 参考書 reference book [さんこうしょ]; 参列する to attend a ceremony [さんれつする]; 持参する to bring something [じさんする]; 新参者 newcomer, novice [しんざんもの]; 参入 joining, entry [さんにゅう]; 降参する to surrender [こうさんする]

	Meanings	Kun and On	Romaji	Bushu	Stroke Order and Number
SG-2093 杉	cedar	すぎ	sugi	木	一十木杉 7

杉
B
F-0780

説文

The seal-style form comprised 木 "tree, wood," and 彡, used for the sound *san* to mean "needle-like thin shapes neatly aligned." This described the beautiful and neatly-arranged needle-like leaves of a cedar tree. The kanji 杉 means "cedar." <木彡>

杉 cedar [すぎ]; 秋田杉 Akita cedar [あきたすぎ]; 杉綾 herringbone pattern [すぎあや]

	Meanings	Kun and On	Romaji	Bushu	Stroke Order and Number
SG-2094 診	medical diagnosis; to examine medically	み-る シン	mi-ru *shin*	言	言 訁 訃 診 12

診
C
F-1087

説文

The seal-style form comprised 言 "word, language; to speak," and "a person" (へ, bushu *hitoyane*) with 彡 "a rash," used for the sound *shin*. Taken together, these components signified someone diagnosing a patient's rash. The kanji 診 means "medical diagnosis; to examine." <言へ彡>

診る to examine medically [みる]; 診察 medical examination [しんさつ]; 診断 diagnosis, testing [しんだん]; 往診 visit to a patient; house call [おうしん]; 診療所 clinic [しんりょうじょ]; 検診 health screening [けんしん]; 聴診器 stethoscope [ちょうしんき]; 誤診 misdiagnosis [ごしん]

	Meanings	Kun and On	Romaji	Bushu	Stroke Order and Number
SG-2095 珍	rare, uncommon	めずら-しい チン	mezura-shii *chin*	玉	一T 玠 珍 9

珍
C
F-1221

説文

The seal-style form comprised 王 "jewel," and "encircling (勹, へ) something beautiful (彡)," used for the sound *chin*. Beautiful things such as jewels were not common, and so the character meant "rare." The kanji 珍 means "rare, uncommon." <王 へ 彡>

珍しい rare, uncommon [めずらしい]; 物珍しい curious, novel [ものめずらしい]; 珍品 rarity, curiosity [ちんぴん]; 珍味 delicacy [ちんみ]; 珍事件 rare event, funny case [ちんじけん]

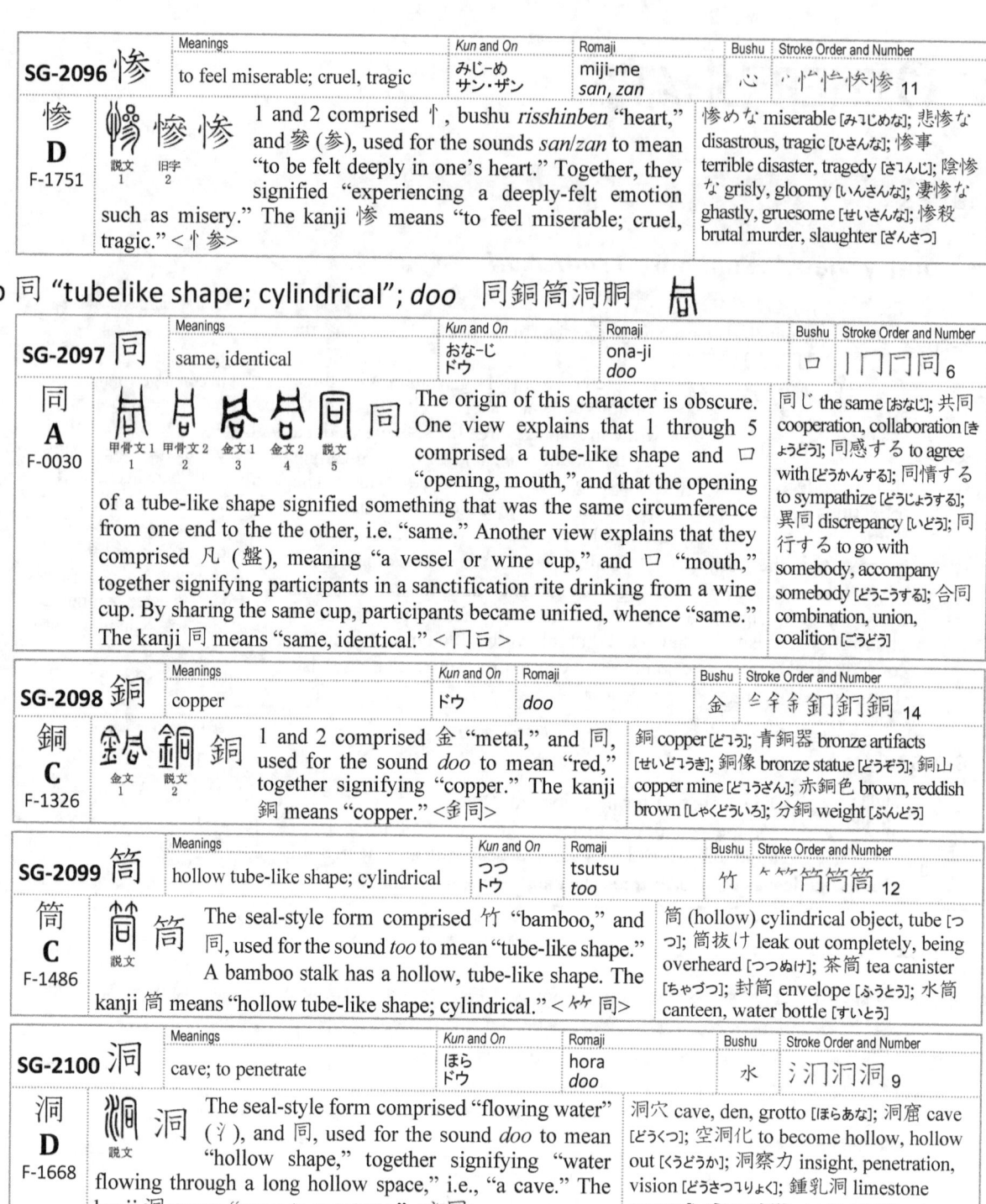

	Meanings	Kun and On	Romaji	Bushu	Stroke Order and Number
SG-2096 惨	to feel miserable; cruel, tragic	みじ-め サン・ザン	miji-me *san, zan*	心	忄忄忄忄惨惨 11

惨 **D** F-1751

説文 1 旧字 2

1 and 2 comprised 忄, bushu *risshinben* "heart," and 參 (参), used for the sounds *san*/*zan* to mean "to be felt deeply in one's heart." Together, they signified "experiencing a deeply-felt emotion such as misery." The kanji 惨 means "to feel miserable; cruel, tragic." <忄参>

惨めな miserable [みじめな]; 悲惨な disastrous, tragic [ひさんな]; 惨事 terrible disaster, tragedy [さんじ]; 陰惨な grisly, gloomy [いんさんな]; 凄惨な ghastly, gruesome [せいさんな]; 惨殺 brutal murder, slaughter [ざんさつ]

98b 同 "tubelike shape; cylindrical"; *doo* 同銅筒洞胴

	Meanings	Kun and On	Romaji	Bushu	Stroke Order and Number
SG-2097 同	same, identical	おな-じ ドウ	ona-ji *doo*	口	丨冂冂同同 6

同 **A** F-0030

甲骨文 1 甲骨文 2 金文 1 金文 2 説文 5

The origin of this character is obscure. One view explains that 1 through 5 comprised a tube-like shape and 口 "opening, mouth," and that the opening of a tube-like shape signified something that was the same circumference from one end to the the other, i.e. "same." Another view explains that they comprised 凡 (盤), meaning "a vessel or wine cup," and 口 "mouth," together signifying participants in a sanctification rite drinking from a wine cup. By sharing the same cup, participants became unified, whence "same." The kanji 同 means "same, identical." <冂㔾>

同じ the same [おなじ]; 共同 cooperation, collaboration [きょうどう]; 同感する to agree with [どうかんする]; 同情する to sympathize [どうじょうする]; 異同 discrepancy [いどう]; 同行する to go with somebody, accompany somebody [どうこうする]; 合同 combination, union, coalition [ごうどう]

	Meanings	Kun and On	Romaji	Bushu	Stroke Order and Number
SG-2098 銅	copper	ドウ	*doo*	金	𠆢 午 金 釘 釦 銅 14

銅 **C** F-1326

金文 1 説文 2

1 and 2 comprised 金 "metal," and 同, used for the sound *doo* to mean "red," together signifying "copper." The kanji 銅 means "copper." <金同>

銅 copper [どう]; 青銅器 bronze artifacts [せいどうき]; 銅像 bronze statue [どうぞう]; 銅山 copper mine [どうざん]; 赤銅色 brown, reddish brown [しゃくどういろ]; 分銅 weight [ぶんどう]

	Meanings	Kun and On	Romaji	Bushu	Stroke Order and Number
SG-2099 筒	hollow tube-like shape; cylindrical	つつ トウ	tsutsu *too*	竹	⺮ 笁 筒 筒 筒 12

筒 **C** F-1486

説文

The seal-style form comprised 竹 "bamboo," and 同, used for the sound *too* to mean "tube-like shape." A bamboo stalk has a hollow, tube-like shape. The kanji 筒 means "hollow tube-like shape; cylindrical." <⺮同>

筒 (hollow) cylindrical object, tube [つつ]; 筒抜け leak out completely, being overheard [つつぬけ]; 茶筒 tea canister [ちゃづつ]; 封筒 envelope [ふうとう]; 水筒 canteen, water bottle [すいとう]

	Meanings	Kun and On	Romaji	Bushu	Stroke Order and Number
SG-2100 洞	cave; to penetrate	ほら ドウ	hora *doo*	水	氵 汩 泂 洞 9

洞 **D** F-1668

説文

The seal-style form comprised "flowing water" (氵), and 同, used for the sound *doo* to mean "hollow shape," together signifying "water flowing through a long hollow space," i.e., "a cave." The kanji 洞 means "cave; to penetrate." <氵同>

洞穴 cave, den, grotto [ほらあな]; 洞窟 cave [どうくつ]; 空洞化 to become hollow, hollow out [くうどうか]; 洞察力 insight, penetration, vision [どうさつりょく]; 鍾乳洞 limestone cavern [しょうにゅうどう, しょうにゅうどう]

	Meanings	Kun and On	Romaji	Bushu	Stroke Order and Number
SG-2101 胴	torso, trunk	ドウ	*doo*	肉	刀 月 肌 肌 胴 10

胴 **D** F-1657

No ancient form. The kanji 胴 comprised 月 "part of the body," and 同, used for the sound *doo* to mean "a tube-like shape." The part of the body that had a tube-like shape was "the torso or trunk." The kanji 胴 means "torso, trunk." <月同>

胴 torso, trunk, waist [どう]; 胴体 trunk of the body, torso [どうたい]

98c ⺃ "to straighten" 乱札乙

SG-2102 乱	Meanings: to become out of order; rebellion, battle	Kun and On: みだ-れる ラン	Romaji: mida-reru *ran*	Bushu: 乙	Stroke Order and Number: ⼀ 二 千 舌 乱 7

乱 **B** F-0724

亂 乱
金文 1　金文 2　詛楚文　説文　旧字
1　2　3　4　5

1, 2, 3, and 4 had two hands (from the top and the bottom) trying to untangle threads on a spool. The long, bent shape ⺃ in 3 and 4 signified "to straighten." The character described a condition or situation that needed to be fixed. A state of turbulence also meant "battle, rebellion." The kyuji 亂 (5) was drastically simplified to 乱 in the shinji. The kanji 乱 means "to go out of order, be loose; turbulence, rebellion, battle." <舌⺃>

乱れる to be out of order [みだれる]; 入り乱れる to be mixed up and confused [いりみだれる]; 取り乱す to go to pieces, become upset [とりみだす, とりみだす]; 乱 battle [らん]; 乱雑な random [らんざつな]; 散乱する to be scattered about [さんらんする]; 内乱 civil war [ないらん]; 乱世 troubled times [らんせ]; 一心不乱 absorbed, engrossed [いっしん・ふらん]

SG-2103 札	Meanings: tag, name plate, note	Kun and On: ふだ サツ	Romaji: huda *satsu*	Bushu: 木	Stroke Order and Number: 一 十 木 札 5

札 **B** F-0874

札
説文

The seal-style form comprised 木 "wood" and ⺃ "flattening or straightening." The character meant "a thin flat piece of wood" such as a tag or posted announcement, and also "paper money." The kanji 札 means "tag, name plate, note." <木⺃>

札 tag, name plate [ふだ]; 荷札 luggage tag [にふだ]; 切り札 trump card [きりふだ]; お札 bill, note (money) [おさつ]; 札束 wad of bills [さつたば, さつたば]; 改札口 wicket [かいさつぐち]; 一万円札 ten thousand yen note [いちまんえんさつ]; 入札制 bidding system [にゅうさつせい]

SG-2104 乙	Meanings: second, witty; stylishly	Kun and On: オツ	Romaji: *otsu*	Bushu: 乙	Stroke Order and Number: 乙 1

乙 **C** F-1461

乙
甲骨文　金文　説文
1　2　3

1, 2, and 3 depicted a bent shape. The shape was borrowed to mean "second, not the first, grade B" (in the old grading system of 甲乙丙, "grades A, B, and C"). In Japanese it is also used to mean "witty; stylishly" (possibly from its resemblance to a slender female figure). The kanji 乙 means "second, witty; stylishly." <乙>

乙 good [おつ]; 甲乙を付ける to mark grades [こうおつをつける]; 甲乙付け難い little difference between the two [こうおつつけがたい] // 乙女 maiden [おとめ]; 早乙女 rice-planting girl [さおとめ]

98d 凵 "receptacle" 凶凸凹

SG-2105 凶	Meanings: misfortune, disaster, bad luck	Kun and On: キョウ	Romaji: *kyoo*	Bushu: 凵	Stroke Order and Number: ノ メ 㐫 凶 4

凶 **C** F-1562

凶
説文

One view explains that the bottom component 凵 depicted "an empty container." Having no grain in the container signified "famine," and the character meant "disaster, famine." Another view explains that it depicted a tattoo (メ) drawn on a deceased person's chest (凵) to ward off evil. The kanji 凶 means "misfortune, disaster, bad luck." <凵メ>

凶 disaster [きょう]; 凶器 dangerous weapon, a weapon used in an assault [きょうき]; 凶作 very poor harvest, crop failure [きょうさく]; 凶暴な atrocious, ferocious, barbarous [きょうぼうな]; 凶悪な extremely wicked, heinous [きょうあくな]; 吉凶を占う to tell someone's fortune [きっきょうをうらなう]

SG-2106 凸	Meanings: protruding, convex	Kun and On: トツ	Romaji: *totsu*	Bushu: 凵	Stroke Order and Number: 凸 5

凸 **D** F-1968

No ancient form. This character depicted a shape that protruded in the middle. It is often used in a pair with the kanji 凹. The kanji 凸 means "protruding, convex."

凸レンズ convex lens [とつレンズ]; 両凸レンズ double-convex lens [りょうとつレンズ] // 凸凹の uneven, bumpy [でこぼこの]

SG-2107 凹	Meanings: hollow, concave	Kun and On: オウ	Romaji: *oo*	Bushu: 凵	Stroke Order and Number: 凹 5

凹 **D** F-2081

No ancient form. This character depicted a shape that was concave in the middle. The kanji 凹 means "hollow, concave."

凹凸 unevenness, irregularity [おうとつ]; 凹面 concave side, hollow side [おうめん]; 凹レンズ concave lens [おうレンズ] // 凹む to collapse, be beaten, become disheartened [へこむ]

98e 匚 "hiding place" 区欧匹殴枢 ㄈ

SG-2108 区	Meanings	Kun and On	Romaji	Bushu	Stroke Order and Number
	to separate, divide; section, ward (*ku*)	ク	*ku*	匚	一フヌ区 4

区
A
F-0103

區 区
甲骨文 1 金文 2 説文 3 旧字 4

1, 2, and 3 depicted "three boxes stashed away separately behind a screen," and signified "to separate, divide; section." In 2, the boxes were linked together. The three boxes (品) inside the hiding place (匚) in 3 and the kyuji, 4, were replaced by a simplified shape メ in the shinji. In Japan this character is also used to denote "wards," administrative subsections of a large city, called *ku*. The kanji 区 means "to separate, divide; section, ward." <匚メ>

区画 subdivision, panel [くかく]; 区分 division [くぶん]; 区域 area, segment, zone [くいき]; 学区 school district [がっく]; 港区 Minato ward [みなとく]

SG-2109 欧	Meanings	Kun and On	Romaji	Bushu	Stroke Order and Number
	Europe; European	オウ	*oo*	欠	ヌ区区⺈区攵欧 8

欧
B
F-0811

歐 欧
説文 1 旧字 2

1 comprised 區, used for the sound *oo* to mean "to groan or howl," and 欠 **SG-0431** "a person with his mouth wide open." Together they originally signified "to groan or howl." The character came to be used for its sound *oo* to mean "Europe," from 欧羅巴 *yooroppa*. The kanji 欧 means "Europe; European." <区欠>

欧州 Europe [おうしゅう]; 北欧 Scandinavian countries [ほくおう]; 欧米 the West, Europe and America [おうべい]; 欧州連合 (EU) The European Union [おうしゅうれんごう]; 西欧 The West, Western Europe [せいおう]; 西欧人 Westerner, European [せいおうじん]

SG-2110 匹	Meanings	Kun and On	Romaji	Bushu	Stroke Order and Number
	a pair, counter for animals; to match	ひき ヒツ	hiki *hitsu*	匚	一丆兀匹 4

匹
C
F-1174

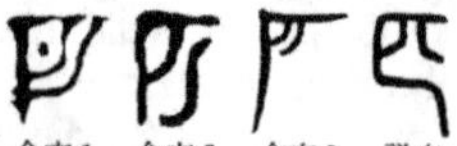
匹
金文1 1 金文2 2 金文3 3 説文 4

The origin of this character is obscure. 1, 2, and 3 comprised the shape 厂 with a couple of curved lines underneath. Different interpretations include "two pieces of cloth hanging down," whence the meaning "to match"; and "horses lined up," whence the character's use as a counter for animals. The kanji 匹 means "a pair, counter for animals; to match." <匚儿>

匹 counter for animals [ひき]; 二匹 two small animals [にひき]; 匹敵する equal, comparable [ひってきする]

SG-2111 殴	Meanings	Kun and On	Romaji	Bushu	Stroke Order and Number
	to strike, assault, beat	なぐ-る オウ	nagu-ru *oo*	殳	ヌ区区⺈区殳殴 8

殴
D
F-1802

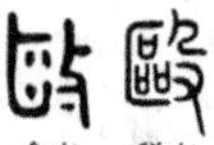
毆 殴
金文 1 説文 2 旧字 3

1, 2, and 3 comprised 區 (the kyuji for 区 **SG-2108**), used for the sound *oo*, and 殳 "a hand holding a weapon," together signifying "to strike." The kanji 殴 means "to strike, assault, beat." <区殳>

殴る to strike [なぐる]; 殴り書き scribble, scrabble [なぐりがき]; 殴り合い fisticuffs [なぐりあい]; 殴り込む to raid, launch an attack [なぐりこむ]; 殴打 strike, blow [おうだ]

SG-2112 枢	Meanings	Kun and On	Romaji	Bushu	Stroke Order and Number
	pivot, center, essence	スウ	*suu*	木	十木杧枢枢 8

枢
D
F-1981

樞 枢
説文 1 旧字 2

1 and 2 comprised 木 **SG-0608** "tree, wood," and 區 "concealed things," used for the sound *suu*. A pivot on a wooden door is unseen but essential for the door's operation, and thus the character signified "essence; very important." The kanji 枢 means "pivot, center, essence." <木区>

中枢 center, centrum [ちゅうすう]; 運動中枢 motor center [うんどうちゅうすう]; 枢機 most important affair [すうき]

98f 勹 "wrapping around" 均旬句拘匂勾

	Meanings	Kun and On	Romaji	Bushu	Stroke Order and Number
SG-2113 均	even; average	キン	*kin*	土	十ナ圴均均 7

均 **B** F-0866 — 金文 1, 說文 2

1 comprised "a long arm with a hand at the top," wrapping around "two short lines of equal length," and 土 "soil," together signifying a person trying "to level the ground evenly with his hand." In 2, the "soil" component was moved to the left side. From "leveling the ground," the kanji 均 means "even; average." <土 冫 勹>

均一 uniformity, equality [きんいつ]; 均等に equally, evenly [きんとうに]; 平均 average [へいきん]; 不均衡 imbalance, disproportion [ふきんこう]; 百均ショップ 100-yen shop [ひゃくきんショップ] // 均しい identical, exactly alike [ひとしい]

	Meanings	Kun and On	Romaji	Bushu	Stroke Order and Number
SG-2114 旬	ten days of a month; in-season	ジュン・シュン	*jun, shun*	日	ノ勹勺旬旬旬 6

旬 **B** F-1053 — 甲骨文1 1, 甲骨文2 2, 金文 3, 說文 4

1 and 2 showed a coiled shape with a short line crossing at the end, signifying "a cycle with its end marked." 3 had the addition of "the sun," inside a semicircular 勹. The rounded shape of the character suggested the "ten-day cycle" of the calendar used during the Yin (Shang) dynasty, in which three such cycles made up a month. In Japan the character is also used to refer to produce or seafood that is "in-season." The kanji 旬 means "(first, second, or third) ten-day period of a month; in-season." <勹日>

上旬 first ten-day period of a month, early part of a month [じょうじゅん]; 中旬 second ten days of a month [ちゅうじゅん]; 下旬 last part of a month, toward the end of a month [げじゅん]; 旬の野菜 in-season vegetables [しゅんのやさい]

	Meanings	Kun and On	Romaji	Bushu	Stroke Order and Number
SG-2115 句	phrase, line, verse, *haiku*	ク	*ku*	口	ノ勹勺句句 5

句 **C** F-1243 — 甲骨文 1, 金文1 2, 金文2 3, 說文 4

1, 2, 3, and 4 had two interlocking hooks facing each other, with 口 "mouth, to speak" inside them. "Speech that was enclosed" signified "a phrase, line, verse, or *haiku* poem." The kanji 句 means "phrase, line, verse, *haiku*." <勹口>

禁句 forbidden word, taboo phrase [きんく]; 慣用句 idiom, common phrase [かんようく]; 句読点 punctuation mark [くとうてん]; 句切る to punctuate, cut off [くぎる]; 節句 seasonal festival [せっく]; 一字一句 every word and every phrase [いちじいっく]; 絶句する to be at a loss for words [ぜっくする]

	Meanings	Kun and On	Romaji	Bushu	Stroke Order and Number
SG-2116 拘	to seize, adhere to, be particular about	コウ	*koo*	手	扌扚拘 8

拘 **D** F-1768 — 說文

The seal-style form comprised 扌 "an act done by hand," and 句 "something enclosed," used for the sound *koo*, together signifying "to seize (by hand), bind." The character also meant the way in which one might be particular about a certain thing. The kanji 拘 means "to seize, adhere to, be particular about." <扌句>

拘束する to restrict, shackle [こうそくする]; 拘泥する to worry too much about, be overpaticular about [こうでいする]; 拘置所 prison, detention house [こうちしょ]; 拘留 detention pending trial, custody [こうりゅう] // 拘る to be obsessive, have a fixation, be a perfectionist [こだわる]

	Meanings	Kun and On	Romaji	Bushu	Stroke Order and Number
SG-2117 匂	fragrant; scent, aroma; to hint, shine (in literary classics)	にお-う	nio-u	勹	ノ勹匂匂 4

匂 **D** F-2003

The kanji 匂 was created in Japan. 匂, "to smell; fragrant," was also used in classical Japanese literary works to mean "to shine beautifully in the sun." It is also used to mean "to suggest, hint." The kanji 匂 means "fragrant, beautiful, scent, aroma; to hint, shine (in literary classics)" <勹ヒ>

匂う to smell [におう]; 匂わせる to suggest, hint, insinuate [におわせる]; 匂い smell, fragrance [におい]

	Meanings	Kun and On	Romaji	Bushu	Stroke Order and Number
SG-2118 勾	hook; to catch, hitch	コウ	*koo*	勹	ノ勹勾勾 4

勾 **D** F-2483 — 金文

The bronzeware-style character appeared incomprehensibly complex, and no account of it is found in our references. The kanji 勾 means "hook; to catch, hitch." <勹ム>

勾配 slope, incline, pitch, gradient [こうばい]; 勾引 bench warrant [こういん]; 勾留 detention pending trial, custody [こうりゅう]

98g 曷 *katsu* 掲葛喝渇褐謁

曷 in the kyuji became 曷 in the shinji, except in 葛 in Mincho style. 

	Meanings	Kun and On	Romaji	Bushu	Stroke Order and Number
SG-2119 掲	to display, hoist	かか-げる ケイ	kaka-geru *kee*	手	扌扣掲掲掲 11

掲 **C** F-1277

掲 掲 掲 (説文 1, 旧字 2)

1 comprised "an act done by hand" (扌), and 曷 (曷), used for the sound *kee* to mean "to hoist." A hand hoisting something up meant "to display, put up." The kanji 掲 means "to display, hoist." <扌曷(日匂)>

掲げる to put up, hoist, herald [かかげる]; 掲示する to post, put up a notice [けいじする]; 掲載 to print, put in, run an article [けいさい]; 電光掲示板 electric bulletin board [でんこうけいじばん]

	Meanings	Kun and On	Romaji	Bushu	Stroke Order and Number
SG-2120 葛	*kuzu* vine, *kuzu* root starch	くず カツ	kuzu *katsu*	艸	一艹苜葛葛葛 12

葛 **D** F-1732

葛 葛 葛 (説文 1, 2, (筆記体) 3)

The seal-style form comprised "plants" (艸, 艹), and 曷 (曷), used for the sound *katsu*, together signifying "*kuzu* vine." *Kuzu* vines were used for weaving, and the roots provided good starch for cooking. The kanji 葛 means "*kuzu* vine, *kuzu* root starch." <艹曷>

葛 *kuzu* root starch [くず]; 葛粉 *kuzu* starch [くずこ]; 葛切り slices of *kuzu* starch jelly with syrup (as a sweet) [くずきり]; 葛湯 *kuzu* starch gruel [くずゆ]; 葛藤 entanglement, embroilment [かっとう] // 段葛 raised path leading to a shrine [だんかずら]

	Meanings	Kun and On	Romaji	Bushu	Stroke Order and Number
SG-2121 喝	to scold loudly; shouting	カツ	*katsu*	口	口口叩喝喝喝 11

喝 **D** F-1926

喝 喝 喝 (篆文 1, 旧字 2)

1 comprised 口 "mouth; to speak," and 曷, used for the sound *katsu* to mean "to scold loudly." The kanji 喝 means "to scold (loudly); shouting." <口曷>

喝采する to applaud, cheer loudly [かっさいする]; 拍手喝采 clapping and cheering, enthusiastic applause [はくしゅ・かっさい]; 恐喝する to blackmail, extort [きょうかつする]; 喝を入れる to give a pep talk [かつをいれる]

	Meanings	Kun and On	Romaji	Bushu	Stroke Order and Number
SG-2122 渇	to thirst for, dry out; thirsty	かわ-く カツ	kawa-ku *katsu*	水	氵沪渇渇渇 11

渇 **D** F-1941

渇 渇 渇 渇 (中山王器 1, 説文 2, 旧字 3)

1, 2, and 3 comprised 氵 "flowing water," and the right-side component 曷, used for the sound *katsu* to mean "lack of." The kanji 渇 means "to thirst for, dry out; thirsty." <氵曷>

渇く to crave, thirst for [かわく]; 喉が渇く to become thirsty [のどがかわく]; 渇する to dry up, suffer from thirst [かっする]; 渇望 craving for, longing for [かつぼう]; 枯渇する to dry up, be drained [こかつする]; 渇水時 period of drought [かっすいじ]

	Meanings	Kun and On	Romaji	Bushu	Stroke Order and Number
SG-2123 褐	brown; humble clothing	カツ	*katsu*	衣	ラ衤衤衵褐褐褐 13

褐 **D** F-2121

褐 褐 褐 (説文 1, 旧字 2)

1 comprised "clothing" (衤), and 曷, used for the sound *katsu* to mean "*kuzu* vine" (葛 **SG-2120**). Clothes or footware woven from vines were simple, humble clothes. The character also meant "brown," from the color of such clothing. The kanji 褐 means "brown; humble clothing." <衤曷>

褐色 brown [かっしょく]

	Meanings	Kun and On	Romaji	Bushu	Stroke Order and Number
SG-2124 謁	to be received by a royal audience	エツ	*etsu*	言	言訁謁謁謁 15

謁 **D** F-2438

謁 謁 謁 謁 (中山王器 1, 説文 2, 旧字 3)

1 is difficult to decipher, but 2 comprised 言 "word; to say," and 曷, used for the sound *etsu* to mean "to keep a person away." Together they signified a person trying to block the passage of a dignitary for an opportunity to appeal to them in person. The kanji 謁 means "to be received by a royal audience." <言曷>

謁見 imperial audience [えっけん]; 拝謁する to have an audience with His Majesty [はいえつする]

98h Numerals 一二三四五六七八九十

	Meanings	Kun and On	Romaji	Bushu	Stroke Order and Number
SG-2125 一	one; single, first	ひと イチ・イツ	hito *ichi, itsu*	一	一 1

一 **A** F-0002

甲骨文 1　金文 2　説文 3

A single bar was used to mean "one." The kanji 一 means "one; single, first." <一>

一つ one [ひと]つ]; 一人 one person [ひと]り]; 一人っ子 only child [ひとり]っこ]; 一息つく to take a break [ひと]いき・つく]; 一安心する to stop worrying for the time being [ひと]あんしんする]; 一 one [いち]]; 一々 every single thing/matter [いち]いち]; 一気に in one breath, immediately [いっ]きに]; 一日 one day [いちにち]; 同一 the same, identical [どういつ] // 一日 first day of the month [ついたち]

	Meanings	Kun and On	Romaji	Bushu	Stroke Order and Number
SG-2126 二	two; double, second	ふた ニ	huta *ni*	二	一 二 2

二 **A** F-0035

甲骨文1 1　甲骨文2 2　説文古文 3　説文 4

Two bars placed one over the other meant "two; double, second." 3 became the kanji 弐 **SG-1475.** <二>

二つ two [ふた]つ]; 二人 two people [ふた]り]; 二日 two days, second day of the month [ふつか]; 二 two [に]]; 二分する to divide into two [にぶんする]; 二人三脚 three-legged race [ににんさん]きゃく]; 無二の peerless, unrivaled [む]にの] // 二十日 20th day of the month [はつか]; 二十歳 twenty years old [はたち]

	Meanings	Kun and On	Romaji	Bushu	Stroke Order and Number
SG-2127 三	three; third	み・みつ サン	mi, mitsu *san*	一	一 二 三 3

三 **A** F-0020

甲骨文 1　説文 2

Three bars placed horizontally meant "three; third." <三>

三つ three [みっつ]; 三度 three times [みた]び]; 三日月 crescent moon [みかづき]; 三日 third day of the month, for three days [みっか]; 三 three [さん]; 再三 repeatedly [さいさん]; 二、三 two or three, a few [にさん]; 七五三 festival day for children 3, 5, and 7 years old celebrated with a visit to a Shinto shrine [しちごさん]; 三々九度 exchange of nuptial cups [さんさんく]ど] // 三味線 *shamisen* (a three-stringed musical instrument) [しゃみせん]

	Meanings	Kun and On	Romaji	Bushu	Stroke Order and Number
SG-2128 四	four; all directions	よ・よん シ	yo, yon *shi*	口	丨 冂 四 四 四 5

四 **A** F-0058

甲骨文 1　金文 2　説文古文 3　説文 4

In 1 and 2, four bars placed horizontally meant "four; all directions." 3 and 4 comprised 口 and 八, and may have expressed the noise made by a breath escaping the mouth (*shi*). The character was borrowed for the sound *shi* to mean "four," and also means "all directions." <四>

四 four [よ]ん, し]; 四つ four [よっつ]; 四人 four people [よに]ん]; 四日 fourth day of the month, four days [よっか]; 四角 intersection, four corners [しかく]; 四角い square [しかくい]; 四季 four seasons [し]き]; 四方八方 every direction, far and wide [しほう]・はっぽう]]; 四国 Shikoku Island [しこ]く, しこく]

	Meanings	Kun and On	Romaji	Bushu	Stroke Order and Number
SG-2129 五	five; half, equal	いつ ゴ	itsu *go*	二	一 丁 五 五 4

五 **A** F-0051

甲骨文 1　金文 2　説文 3

This shape depicting a pair of crossed sticks between two bars at the top and bottom was borrowed to mean "five." Five divides ten equally, so it also meant "equal." The kanji 五 means "five; half, equal." <五>

五つ five [いつ]つ]; 五日 five days, fifth day of the month [いつか]; 五 five [ご]]; 五分五分 on even terms, evenly matched [ごぶごぶ]; 五感 the five senses [ごかん] // 五月 May [さつき, ご]がつ]

	Meanings	Kun and On	Romaji	Bushu	Stroke Order and Number
SG-2130 六	six	む・むっ・むい ロク, ロッ	mu, mu(*C*)-, mui *roku, ro(C)-*	八	丶 亠 六 六 4

六 **A** F-0089

甲骨 1 1　甲骨 2 2　金文 3　説文 4

1, 2, and 3 depicted the shape of a tent, and the character was borrowed to mean "six." The kanji 六 means "six." <六>

六つ six [むっつ]; 六日 six days, sixth day of the month [むいか]; 六 six [ろく]]; 六月 June [ろくがつ]; 四六時中 around the clock, day and night [しろくじちゅう]; 六法全書 Compendium of Laws [ろっぽうぜ]んしょ]; 第六感 sixth sense, intuition [だ]い・ろっかん] // 六書 Six categories of kanji used in Shuowen Jiezi [りく]しょ]

	Meanings	Kun and On	Romaji	Bushu	Stroke Order and Number
SG-2131 七	seven; not quite full	なな・なの シチ	nana, nano *shichi*	一	一七 2

七
A
F-0075

甲骨文 1
金文 2
説文 3

1, 2, and 3 depicted a bone being cut, but the character was borrowed to mean "seven." It is also used to mean "not quite ten," or "not quite full." The kanji 七 means "seven; short of full." <七>

七 seven [なな, しち]; 七つ seven, seven years old [ななつ]; 七転び八起き [ななころび・やおき] "getting repeatedly knocked down but bouncing back up each time"; 七日 seventh day, seven days [なのか, なぬか]; 七分目 three quarters full, not quite full [しちぶんめ]; 七分袖 three-quarter sleeves [しちぶそで]

	Meanings	Kun and On	Romaji	Bushu	Stroke Order and Number
SG-2132 八	eight; many	や・よう ハチ	ya, yoo *hachi*	八	ノ八 2

八
A
F-0059

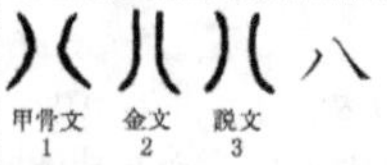
甲骨文 1
金文 2
説文 3

This character was a figurative depiction of the motion of splitting something into two. Eight is several multiples of two, giving the meaning "many." The kanji 八 means "eight, many." <八>

八つ eight [やっつ, やっつ]; 八 eight [はち]; 八日 eight days, eighth day of the month [ようか]; 八つ当たり random venting of one's anger [やつあたり]; 八人 eight people [はちにん]; 四苦八苦する to suffer terribly, be in dire distress [しくはっくする] // 八百屋 green grocer [やおや]; 八百長 race fixing, match rigging [やおちょう]

	Meanings	Kun and On	Romaji	Bushu	Stroke Order and Number
SG-2133 九	nine	ここの–つ キュウ・ク	kokono-tsu *kyuu, ku*	乙	ノ九 2

九
A
F-0076

甲骨文 1
金文 2
説文 3

1 and 2 depicted an arm bent at the elbow with fingers at the end. The character represented thrusting one's hand into a hole to reach something, but falling short. A number just short of full (ten) is "nine." The kanji 九 means "nine." <九>

九つ nine [ここのつ]; 九日 ninth day of the month, nine days [ここのか]; 九 nine [きゅう]; 九死に一生を得る narrowly escape death [きゅうしに・いっしょうをえる]; 九十 ninety [きゅうじゅう]; 九月 September [くがつ]

	Meanings	Kun and On	Romaji	Bushu	Stroke Order and Number
SG-2134 十	ten, full	とお・と ジュウ・ジッ	too, to *juu, ji(C)-, ju(C)-*	十	一十 2

十
A
F-0016

甲骨文 1
金文1 2
金文2 3
説文 4

This character began as a vertical line (1), to which a small dot was added, (2). In 4, it became a cross shape. It meant "a bundle of ten." Ten also meant "full." The kanji 十 means "ten, full." <十>

十 ten [じゅう, とう]; 十日 ten days, tenth day of the month [とうか]; 十分な sufficient [じゅうぶんな]; 十分 ten minutes [じっぷん, じゅっぷん]; sufficient, full [じゅうぶん]; 十人十色 everyone has his own interests and ideas [じゅうにん・といろ]

98i Location indicators 上下

	Meanings	Kun and On	Romaji	Bushu	Stroke Order and Number
SG-2135 上	top; above; superior, upper; to come up	うえ・うわ・かみ・あ–げる・のぼ–る ジョウ・ショウ	ue, uwa, kami, a-geru, nobo-ru *joo, shoo*	一	丨⺊上 3

上
A
F-0010

甲骨文 1
金文 2
説文1 3
説文2 4

A spatial position marked above a line signified "above." The kanji 上 means "top; above; to come up; superior, upper." <⊥ 一>

上 above, top [うえ, うえ]; 身の上 one's circumstances, one's upbringing [みのうえ]; 上書き overwriting [うわがき]; 上着 coat, overgarment [うわぎ]; 川上 upper part of a river [かわかみ]; 上げる to raise, give [あげる]; 上り ascent, going up, uphill [のぼり]; 上品な stylish, elegant, refined [じょうひんな]; 北上する to go up north [ほくじょうする]

	Meanings	Kun and On	Romaji	Bushu	Stroke Order and Number
SG-2136 下	bottom; below; lower, inferior; to go down	した・しも・もと・さ–げる・くだ–る・お–りる カ・ゲ	shita, shimo, moto, sa-geru, kuda-ru, o-riru *ka, ge*	一	一丅下 3

下
A
F-0039

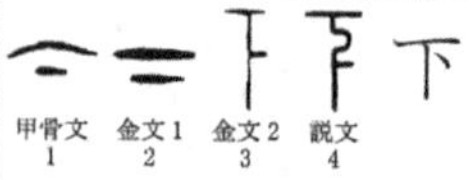
甲骨文 1
金文1 2
金文2 3
説文 4

A spatial position marked below a line signified "below." The kanji 下 means "bottom; below; lower, inferior; to go down." <丅丶>

下 below [した]; 下二桁 last two figures of a number [しもふたけた]; 足下 at one's feet, steps [あしもと, あしもと]; 下げる to lower [さげる], 下る to go lower [くだる]; 下さる a superior gives to me [くださる]; 下り電車 downtown train, train going away from the capital [くだりでんしゃ]; 下りる to step down, alight, move down [おりる]; 下流 downstream [かりゅう]; 上下 top and bottom [じょうげ]; 下車 getting off/out of a vehicle [げしゃ]; 下品な vulgar, coarse [げひんな]

APPENDICES

INDEX 1 – The Order of the Kanji (by Study Guide number)

導入順漢字表 (SG = Study Guide 番号順)

INDEX 2 – KANJI BY *ON* AND *KUN* READING (IN JAPANESE SYLLABARY ORDER)

音訓読みによる漢字表(五十音順)

On reading in katakana; *Kun* reading in hiragana

ア・あ

ア 亜 SG-1294
あ-う 会 SG-1790
あ-う 合 SG-1989
あ-う 遭 SG-2054
あ-きる 飽 SG-0430
あ-く 空 SG-1323
あ-ける 明 SG-1078
あ-ける 開 SG-1253
あ-げる 挙 SG-0153
あ-げる 揚 SG-1070
あ-げる 上 SG-2135
あ-たる 当 SG-1269
あ-てる 宛 SG-0416
あ-てる 充 SG-0515
あ-びる 浴 SG-1160
あ-む 編 SG-1248
あ-る 有 SG-0795
あ-る 在 SG-1116
あ-れる 荒 SG-0594
あい 相 SG-0004
あい 藍 SG-0030
アイ 挨 SG-0082
アイ 愛 SG-0239
アイ 曖 SG-0243
アイ 哀 SG-1661
あいだ 間 SG-1252
あお 青 SG-0694
あお-ぐ 仰 SG-0414
あか 赤 SG-1171
あか-るい 明 SG-1078
あかつき 暁 SG-1051
あき 秋 SG-0714
あき-らか 明 SG-1078
あきな-う 商 SG-1871
あきら-める 諦 SG-1758
アク 悪 SG-1293
アク 握 SG-1537
あご 顎 SG-0509
あこが-れる 憧 SG-2067
あさ 麻 SG-0778
あさ 朝 SG-1052
あざ 字 SG-0512
あさ-い 浅 SG-1502
あざ-やか 鮮 SG-0934
あざけ-る 嘲 SG-1054
あざむ-く 欺 SG-1868
あし 足 SG-0227
あし 脚 SG-2014
あじ 味 SG-0616
あず-ける 預 SG-1925
あせ 汗 SG-1546
あせ-る 焦 SG-0963
あそ-ぶ 遊 SG-1568
あた-える 与 SG-0150
あた-り 辺 SG-1343
あたい 値 SG-0009
あたい 価 SG-1698
あたた-かい 暖 SG-0134
あたた-かい 温 SG-1845
あたま 頭 SG-0494
あたら-しい 新 SG-1455
アツ 圧 SG-1127
あつ-い 熱 SG-0585
あつ-い 厚 SG-1278
あつ-い 暑 SG-2090
あつ-まる 集 SG-0948
あつか-う 扱 SG-0579
-あて 宛 SG-0416
あと 跡 SG-0229
あと 後 SG-0237
あと 痕 SG-0403
あな 穴 SG-1322
あなど-る 侮 SG-0547
あに 兄 SG-0451
あね 姉 SG-0528
あば-く 暴 SG-1030
あぶ-ない 危 SG-0415
あぶら 油 SG-0782
あぶら 脂 SG-1438

あま

あま 天 SG-0315
あま 尼 SG-0476
あま 雨 SG-1205
あま-い 甘 SG-0038
あま-る 余 SG-1386
あみ 網 SG-1610
あめ 天 SG-0315
あめ 雨 SG-1205
あや-うい 危 SG-0415
あや-しい 怪 SG-0197
あや-しい 妖 SG-0342
あやつ-る 操 SG-0651
あやま-ち 過 SG-0271
あやま-る 誤 SG-0345
あやま-る 謝 SG-1517
あゆ-む 歩 SG-0202
あら-い 荒 SG-0594
あら-い 粗 SG-0811
あら-う 洗 SG-0448
あら-た 新 SG-1455
あらし 嵐 SG-1142
あらそ-う 争 SG-0129
あらた-める 改 SG-0167
あらわ-す 表 SG-1658
あらわ-す 著 SG-2089
あらわ-れる 現 SG-0461
ある-く 歩 SG-0202
あわ 泡 SG-0429
あわ-い 淡 SG-1089
あわ-せる 併 SG-0375
あわ-てる 慌 SG-0597
あわ-れ 哀 SG-1661
アン 安 SG-0522
アン 案 SG-0523
アン 行 SG-1330
アン 暗 SG-1376

イ・い

イ 慰 SG-0121
イ 尉 SG-0122
イ 違 SG-0253
イ 囲 SG-0254
イ 偉 SG-0256
イ 緯 SG-0257
イ 胃 SG-0291
イ 椅 SG-0331
イ 異 SG-0355
イ 畏 SG-0356
イ 位 SG-0364
イ 彙 SG-0658
イ 委 SG-0717
イ 移 SG-0719
イ 萎 SG-0730
イ 為 SG-0894
イ 維 SG-0958
イ 唯 SG-0965
イ 易 SG-1041
イ 意 SG-1380
イ 威 SG-1498
イ 医 SG-1526
イ 衣 SG-1657
イ 依 SG-1660
イ 遺 SG-1704
イ 以 SG-1941
い 井 SG-1295
い-う 言 SG-1364
い-える 癒 SG-1426
い-きる 生 SG-0689
い-く 行 SG-1330
い-く 逝 SG-1465
い-む 忌 SG-0194
い-る 居 SG-0469
い-る 要 SG-0555
い-る 鋳 SG-1204
い-る 煎 SG-1407
い-る 射 SG-1516
い-れる 入 SG-1238
いえ 家 SG-0842
いか-る 怒 SG-0530
イキ 域 SG-1494
いき 息 SG-0061
いき 粋 SG-0740
いきお-い 勢 SG-0584
いきどお-る 憤 SG-1729
イク 育 SG-0518
いく 幾 SG-1479
いくさ 戦 SG-1549
いけ 池 SG-1011
いこ-い 憩 SG-0065
いさ-む 勇 SG-1984
いさぎよ-い 潔 SG-1411
いし 石 SG-1148
いしずえ 礎 SG-1151
いずみ 泉 SG-1120
いそ-ぐ 急 SG-0577
いそが-しい 忙 SG-0595

いた

いた 板 SG-0091
いた-い 痛 SG-1885
いだ-く 抱 SG-0426
いた-す 致 SG-1536
いた-む 悼 SG-1858
いた-める 傷 SG-1068
いた-る 至 SG-1531
いただ-く 頂 SG-1916
いただき 頂 SG-1916
イチ 壱 SG-1977
イチ 一 SG-2125
いち 市 SG-0212
いちじる-しい 著 SG-2089
イツ 逸 SG-0552
イツ 一 SG-2125
いつ-つ 五 SG-2129
いつく-しむ 慈 SG-1637
いつわ-る 偽 SG-0895
いと 糸 SG-1600
いど-む 挑 SG-1772
いとな-む 営 SG-1184
いな 稲 SG-0723
いな 否 SG-0763
いぬ 犬 SG-0859
いね 稲 SG-0723
いの-る 祈 SG-1461
いのち 命 SG-0408
いばら 茨 SG-0679
いま 今 SG-1994
いまし-める 戒 SG-1470
いも 芋 SG-0680
いもうと 妹 SG-0617
いや 嫌 SG-0734
いや-しい 卑 SG-1859
いろ 色 SG-0423
いろど-る 彩 SG-0125
いわ 岩 SG-1149
いわ-う 祝 SG-0452

イン

イン 隠 SG-0191
イン 因 SG-0323
イン 姻 SG-0325
イン 咽 SG-0326
イン 印 SG-0410
イン 飲 SG-0436
イン 院 SG-0446
イン 淫 SG-1095
イン 音 SG-1375
イン 韻 SG-1379
イン 引 SG-1511
イン 員 SG-1717
イン 陰 SG-1998

ウ・う

ウ 右 SG-0102
ウ 有 SG-0795
ウ 羽 SG-0983
ウ 雨 SG-1205
ウ 宇 SG-1223
う-い 憂 SG-0242
う-える 植 SG-0010
う-える 飢 SG-1783
う-く 浮 SG-0127
う-ける 受 SG-0131
う-ける 請 SG-0700
う-つ 討 SG-0116
う-つ 撃 SG-1581
う-つ 打 SG-1915
う-まれる 生 SG-0689
う-む 産 SG-0691
う-める 埋 SG-1129
う-る 売 SG-1695
う-る 得 SG-1697
う-れる 熟 SG-0591
うい 初 SG-1666
うえ 上 SG-2135
うお 魚 SG-0933
うかが-う 伺 SG-0362
うけたまわ-る 承 SG-0152
うご-く 動 SG-2059
うし 牛 SG-0816
うじ 氏 SG-1433
うし-ろ 後 SG-0237
うしな-う 失 SG-0073
うす 臼 SG-1811
うず 渦 SG-0274
うす-い 薄 SG-0755

うた

うた 歌 SG-0433
うた 唄 SG-1713
うたい 謡 SG-1374
うたが-う 疑 SG-0404
うち 内 SG-1239
ウツ 鬱 SG-0648
うつ-す 写 SG-1231
うつ-る 映 SG-0334
うつ-る 移 SG-0719
うつく-しい 美 SG-0826
うった-える 訴 SG-0604
うつわ 器 SG-0035
うで 腕 SG-0293
うと-い 疎 SG-2073
うなが-す 促 SG-0228
うね 畝 SG-1308
うば-う 奪 SG-0962
うぶ 産 SG-0691
うま 馬 SG-0870
うみ 海 SG-0542
うめ 梅 SG-0544
うやうや-しい 恭 SG-0139
うやま-う 敬 SG-0171
うら 浦 SG-0751
うら 裏 SG-1659
うらな-う 占 SG-1767
うらや-ましい 羨 SG-0833
うら-む 恨 SG-0402
うる-む 潤 SG-1260
うるお-う 潤 SG-1260
うるし 漆 SG-1094
うるわ-しい 麗 SG-0898

うれ-える 愁 SG-0729
うれ-える 憂 SG-0242
うわ 上 SG-2135
ウン 雲 SG-1207
ウン 運 SG-1590

エ・え

エ 回 SG-1109
エ 絵 SG-1604
エ 依 SG-1660
エ 会 SG-1790
エ 恵 SG-1923
え 餌 SG-1785
え 柄 SG-1872
え 江 SG-1896
え 重 SG-2058
え-む 笑 SG-0340
え-る 獲 SG-0973
え-る 得 SG-1697
エイ 衛 SG-0255
エイ 英 SG-0333
エイ 映 SG-0334
エイ 永 SG-1110
エイ 泳 SG-1111
エイ 詠 SG-1112
エイ 営 SG-1184
エイ 栄 SG-1185
エイ 鋭 SG-1201
エイ 影 SG-1284
えが-く 描 SG-1309
エキ 役 SG-0158
エキ 駅 SG-0871
エキ 易 SG-1041
エキ 液 SG-1075
エキ 益 SG-1848
エキ 疫 SG-1888
えさ 餌 SG-1785
えだ 枝 SG-0183
エツ 悦 SG-0459
エツ 越 SG-0486
エツ 閲 SG-1264
エツ 謁 SG-2124
えら-い 偉 SG-0256
えら-ぶ 選 SG-0421
えり 襟 SG-1669
エン 援 SG-0133
エン 媛 SG-0136
エン 怨 SG-0417
エン 宴 SG-0533
エン 猿 SG-0868
エン 沿 SG-1086
エン 炎 SG-1165
エン 煙 SG-1170
エン 鉛 SG-1202
エン 延 SG-1334
エン 演 SG-1540
エン 縁 SG-1609
エン 遠 SG-1672
エン 園 SG-1673
エン 円 SG-1718
エン 塩 SG-1847
エン 艶 SG-1978

オ・お

オ 和 SG-0712
オ 汚 SG-1085
オ 悪 SG-1293
お 尾 SG-0917
お 雄 SG-0951
お 小 SG-1153
お 緒 SG-2088
お-いる 老 SG-0562
お-う 生 SG-0689
お-う 追 SG-1594
お-う 負 SG-1700
お-きる 起 SG-0484
お-く 置 SG-0008
お-しい 惜 SG-1059
お-す 押 SG-0075
お-す 推 SG-0953
お-ちる 落 SG-0247
お-びる 帯 SG-1684
お-りる 降 SG-0260
お-りる 下 SG-2136
お-る 折 SG-1459
お-る 織 SG-1491
お-わる 終 SG-1098
オウ 押 SG-0075
オウ 央 SG-0332
オウ 桜 SG-0631
オウ 翁 SG-0988
オウ 奥 SG-1019
オウ 応 SG-1235
オウ 王 SG-1447
オウ 皇 SG-1448
オウ 往 SG-1449
オウ 旺 SG-1450
オウ 黄 SG-1519
オウ 横 SG-1521
オウ 凹 SG-2107
オウ 欧 SG-2109
オウ 殴 SG-2111
おうぎ 扇 SG-0987
おお-い 多 SG-0796
おお-う 覆 SG-1841
おお-きい 大 SG-0314
おお-せ 仰 SG-0414
おおやけ 公 SG-1321

おか

おか 丘 SG-1146
おか 岡 SG-1967
おか-す 冒 SG-0016
おか-す 犯 SG-0863
おか-す 侵 SG-1779
おが-む 拝 SG-0077
おき 沖 SG-1577
おぎな-う 補 SG-0749
おく 奥 SG-1019
オク 億 SG-1381
オク 憶 SG-1382
オク 臆 SG-1383
オク 屋 SG-1533
おく-る 送 SG-1342
おく-る 贈 SG-1793
おく-れる 後 SG-0237
おく-れる 遅 SG-1345
おこ-す 興 SG-0151
おこ-る 怒 SG-0530
おごそ-か 厳 SG-0176
おこた-る 怠 SG-1946
おこな-う 行 SG-1330
おさ-える 抑 SG-0413
おさ-める 収 SG-0086
おさ-める 修 SG-0170
おさ-める 納 SG-1240
おさ-める 治 SG-1944
おさな-い 幼 SG-1633
おし-える 教 SG-0169
おす 雄 SG-0951
おそ-い 遅 SG-1345
おそ-う 襲 SG-1034
おそ-れる 畏 SG-0356
おそ-れ 虞 SG-0891
おそ-れる 恐 SG-0581
おそ-わる 教 SG-0169
おだ-やか 穏 SG-0192
おちい-る 陥 SG-1348
オツ 乙 SG-2104
おっと 夫 SG-0316

おと

おと 音 SG-1375
おど-す 脅 SG-1956
おと-る 劣 SG-1955
おど-る 躍 SG-0990
おど-る 踊 SG-1985
おとうと 弟 SG-1355
おとこ 男 SG-1301
おとしい-れる 陥 SG-1348
おとず-れる 訪 SG-1934
おとろ-える 衰 SG-1662
おどろ-く 驚 SG-0873
おな-じ 同 SG-2097
おに 鬼 SG-0350
おのおの 各 SG-0244
おのれ 己 SG-0420
おび 帯 SG-1684
おびや-かす 脅 SG-1956
おぼ-える 覚 SG-0463
おぼ-れる 溺 SG-1515
おも 面 SG-0060
おも 主 SG-2037
おも-い 重 SG-2058
おも-う 思 SG-0284
おもて 面 SG-0060
おもて 表 SG-1658
おもむ-く 赴 SG-0489
おもむき 趣 SG-0488
おや 親 SG-0462
およ-ぐ 泳 SG-1111
およ-ぶ 及 SG-0576
おれ 俺 SG-0310
おろ-か 愚 SG-1016
おろ-す 卸 SG-1810
おろし 卸 SG-1810
オン 穏 SG-0192
オン 恩 SG-0324
オン 怨 SG-0417
オン 音 SG-1375
オン 遠 SG-1672
オン 温 SG-1845
おん 御 SG-1807
おんな 女 SG-0521

カ・か

カ 可 SG-0045
カ 何 SG-0046
カ 河 SG-0047
カ 荷 SG-0048
カ 苛 SG-0049
カ 仮 SG-0092
カ 夏 SG-0238
カ 過 SG-0271
カ 渦 SG-0274
カ 禍 SG-0276
カ 化 SG-0386
カ 花 SG-0387
カ 歌 SG-0433
カ 寡 SG-0506
カ 果 SG-0654
カ 課 SG-0655
カ 菓 SG-0656
カ 華 SG-0675
カ 家 SG-0842
カ 嫁 SG-0844
カ 稼 SG-0846
カ 靴 SG-0914
カ 暇 SG-1049
カ 佳 SG-1136
カ 火 SG-1164
カ 箇 SG-1564
カ 価 SG-1698
カ 貨 SG-1703
カ 科 SG-1832
カ 加 SG-1950
カ 架 SG-1957
か 下 SG-2136
か 香 SG-0716
か 鹿 SG-0896
か 蚊 SG-1004
か 日 SG-1045
ガ 芽 SG-0924
ガ 牙 SG-0926
ガ 雅 SG-0959
ガ 瓦 SG-1299
ガ 画 SG-1303
ガ 我 SG-1492
ガ 餓 SG-1784
ガ 賀 SG-1952
か-う 飼 SG-0359
か-う 買 SG-1699
か-える 替 SG-0370
か-える 換 SG-0553
か-く 描 SG-1309
か-く 書 SG-2026
か-ぐ 嗅 SG-0064
か-ける 欠 SG-0431
か-ける 駆 SG-0875
か-ける 掛 SG-1135
か-ける 懸 SG-1632
か-ける 賭 SG-1715
か-ける 架 SG-1957
か-す 貸 SG-1353
か-つ 勝 SG-0147
か-つ 且 SG-0815
か-ねる 兼 SG-0733
か-りる 借 SG-1056
か-る 刈 SG-1406
か-れる 枯 SG-1560
か-わす 交 SG-0478
か-わる 代 SG-1352
か-わる 変 SG-1623

カイ

カイ 拐 SG-0081
カイ 改 SG-0167
カイ 快 SG-0196
カイ 怪 SG-0197
カイ 介 SG-0312
カイ 界 SG-0313
カイ 塊 SG-0354
カイ 皆 SG-0393
カイ 階 SG-0394
カイ 諧 SG-0395
カイ 楷 SG-0396
カイ 海 SG-0542
カイ 悔 SG-0546
カイ 解 SG-0922
カイ 回 SG-1109
カイ 灰 SG-1169
カイ 開 SG-1253
カイ 街 SG-1331
カイ 戒 SG-1470
カイ 械 SG-1471
カイ 絵 SG-1604
カイ 壊 SG-1674
カイ 懐 SG-1675
カイ 潰 SG-1716
カイ 会 SG-1790
ガイ 該 SG-0853
ガイ 骸 SG-0854
ガイ 劾 SG-0855
ガイ 涯 SG-1137
ガイ 崖 SG-1138
ガイ 街 SG-1331
ガイ 外 SG-1764
ガイ 概 SG-1788
ガイ 慨 SG-1789
ガイ 蓋 SG-1852
ガイ 害 SG-1963
かい 貝 SG-1693
かいこ 蚕 SG-1005
かえ-す 返 SG-0088
かえ-る 帰 SG-1775
かえり-みる 省 SG-0002
かえり-みる 顧 SG-0961
かお 顔 SG-0495
かお-り 香 SG-0716
かお-る 薫 SG-1181
かか-える 抱 SG-0426
かか-げる 掲 SG-2119
かか-る 係 SG-1628
かか-わる 関 SG-1255
かがみ 鏡 SG-1385
かがや-く 輝 SG-1592
かかり 掛 SG-1135
かかり 係 SG-1628
かき 柿 SG-0643
かき 垣 SG-1130
かぎ 鍵 SG-1341
かぎ-る 限 SG-0397

カク

カク 殻 SG-0163
カク 各 SG-0244
カク 客 SG-0245
カク 格 SG-0246
カク 覚 SG-0463
カク 核 SG-0852
カク 革 SG-0913
カク 角 SG-0921
カク 獲 SG-0973
カク 穫 SG-0974
カク 確 SG-0979
カク 嚇 SG-1172
カク 閣 SG-1257
カク 郭 SG-1290
カク 画 SG-1303
カク 拡 SG-1522
カク 較 SG-1588
カク 隔 SG-1803
ガク 額 SG-0496
ガク 顎 SG-0509
ガク 学 SG-0511
ガク 楽 SG-0625
ガク 岳 SG-1147
かく-す 隠 SG-0191
かげ 影 SG-1284
かげ 陰 SG-1998
がけ 崖 SG-1138
かご 籠 SG-1035
かこ-む 囲 SG-0254
かさ 傘 SG-2005
かざ 風 SG-1040
かさ-ねる 重 SG-2058
かざ-る 飾 SG-1686
かしこ-い 賢 SG-0095
かしら 頭 SG-0494
かず 数 SG-0168
かぜ 風 SG-1040
かせ-ぐ 稼 SG-0846
かぞ-える 数 SG-0168
かた 肩 SG-0289
かた 片 SG-0662
かた 潟 SG-1090
かた 方 SG-1931
かた 形 SG-1971
かた 型 SG-1972
かた-い 堅 SG-0096

かた-い 難 SG-1193
かた-い 固 SG-1561
かた-い 硬 SG-1876
かた-る 語 SG-1369
かたき 敵 SG-1760
かたち 形 SG-1971
かたな 刀 SG-1394
かたまり 塊 SG-0354
かたむ-く 傾 SG-0502
かたよ-る 偏 SG-1249
かたわら 傍 SG-1938

カツ

カツ 滑 SG-0273
カツ 活 SG-1445
カツ 括 SG-1446
カツ 割 SG-1964
カツ 轄 SG-1966
カツ 合 SG-1989
カツ 葛 SG-2120
カツ 喝 SG-2121
カツ 渇 SG-2122
カツ 褐 SG-2123
ガツ 月 SG-1077
ガッ 合 SG-1989
かつ-ぐ 担 SG-1064
かて 糧 SG-2057
かど 角 SG-0921
かど 門 SG-1251
かな 金 SG-1196
かな-しい 悲 SG-0993
かな-でる 奏 SG-0145
かなめ 要 SG-0555
かなら-ず 必 SG-2076
かね 金 SG-1196
かね 鐘 SG-2066
かの 彼 SG-0907
かぶ 株 SG-0621
かべ 壁 SG-1429
かま 鎌 SG-0736
かま 窯 SG-0832
かま 釜 SG-1203
かま-える 構 SG-1652
かみ 髪 SG-0920
かみ 神 SG-1215
かみ 紙 SG-1434
かみ 上 SG-2135
かみなり 雷 SG-1218
かめ 亀 SG-1044
かも-す 醸 SG-1680
かよ-う 通 SG-1983
から 殻 SG-0163
から 空 SG-1323
から 唐 SG-1808
がら 柄 SG-1872
から-い 辛 SG-1359
から-む 絡 SG-0249
からだ 体 SG-0307
かり 仮 SG-0092
かり 狩 SG-0866
かる-い 軽 SG-1648
かれ 彼 SG-0907
かろ-やか 軽 SG-1648
かわ 河 SG-0047
かわ 皮 SG-0906
かわ 革 SG-0913
かわ 川 SG-1104
がわ 側 SG-1722
かわ-く 乾 SG-1574
かわ-く 渇 SG-2122
かわら 瓦 SG-1299

カン

カン 看 SG-0003
カン 監 SG-0025
カン 鑑 SG-0027
カン 艦 SG-0028
カン 甘 SG-0038
カン 緩 SG-0135
カン 敢 SG-0178
カン 患 SG-0189
カン 款 SG-0439
カン 完 SG-0445
カン 冠 SG-0449
カン 換 SG-0553
カン 喚 SG-0554
カン 観 SG-0976
カン 勧 SG-0977
カン 歓 SG-0978
カン 巻 SG-1027
カン 甲 SG-1042
カン 寒 SG-1100
カン 漢 SG-1194
カン 寛 SG-1228
カン 間 SG-1252
カン 関 SG-1255
カン 簡 SG-1259
カン 閑 SG-1263
カン 陥 SG-1348
カン 感 SG-1496
カン 憾 SG-1500
カン 干 SG-1544
カン 刊 SG-1545
カン 汗 SG-1546
カン 肝 SG-1547
カン 幹 SG-1572
カン 韓 SG-1573
カン 乾 SG-1574
カン 官 SG-1593
カン 管 SG-1595
カン 館 SG-1597
カン 棺 SG-1599
カン 環 SG-1676
カン 還 SG-1677
カン 貫 SG-1709
カン 慣 SG-1710
カン 勘 SG-1797
カン 堪 SG-1799
カン 缶 SG-2009
かん 神 SG-1215
ガン 眼 SG-0401
ガン 丸 SG-0419
ガン 元 SG-0444
ガン 玩 SG-0450
ガン 顔 SG-0495
ガン 頑 SG-0503
ガン 願 SG-1124
ガン 岩 SG-1149
ガン 岸 SG-1543
ガン 含 SG-1995
かんが-える 考 SG-0561
かんが-みる 鑑 SG-0027
かんば-しい 芳 SG-1935
かんむり 冠 SG-0449

キ・き

キ 器 SG-0035
キ 毀 SG-0166
キ 岐 SG-0184
キ 伎 SG-0186
キ 忌 SG-0194
キ 企 SG-0201
キ 奇 SG-0327
キ 寄 SG-0328
キ 鬼 SG-0350
キ 危 SG-0415
キ 己 SG-0420
キ 起 SG-0484
キ 棄 SG-0519
キ 季 SG-0720
キ 騎 SG-0878
キ 亀 SG-1044
キ 気 SG-1220
キ 汽 SG-1221
キ 記 SG-1366
キ 祈 SG-1461
キ 幾 SG-1479
キ 機 SG-1480
キ 畿 SG-1481
キ 旗 SG-1570
キ 軌 SG-1587
キ 揮 SG-1591
キ 輝 SG-1592
キ 紀 SG-1605
キ 希 SG-1685
キ 貴 SG-1701
キ 帰 SG-1775
キ 飢 SG-1783
キ 既 SG-1787
キ 机 SG-1863
キ 基 SG-1866
キ 期 SG-1867
キ 棋 SG-1869
キ 規 SG-1913
キ 喜 SG-2044
き 木 SG-0608
き 生 SG-0689
き 黄 SG-1519
ギ 技 SG-0182
ギ 疑 SG-0404
ギ 擬 SG-0406
ギ 宜 SG-0813
ギ 義 SG-0838
ギ 議 SG-0839
ギ 儀 SG-0840
ギ 犠 SG-0841
ギ 戯 SG-0887
ギ 偽 SG-0895
ギ 欺 SG-1868
き-える 消 SG-0798
き-く 聞 SG-0051
き-く 聴 SG-0053
き-く 効 SG-0480
き-く 利 SG-0713
き-める 決 SG-1082
き-る 切 SG-1395
き-る 斬 SG-1467
き-る 着 SG-2086
キク 菊 SG-0677
きざ-す 兆 SG-1770
きざ-む 刻 SG-0851
きし 岸 SG-1543
きず 傷 SG-1068
きず-く 築 SG-0582
きそ-う 競 SG-0453
きた 北 SG-0388
きた-える 鍛 SG-0165
きた-る 来 SG-0746
きたな-い 汚 SG-1085
キチ 吉 SG-2006
キツ 喫 SG-1412
キツ 吉 SG-2006
キツ 詰 SG-2008
き-て 来 SG-0746
きぬ 絹 SG-1612
きば 牙 SG-0926
きび-しい 厳 SG-0176
きみ 君 SG-0155
きも 肝 SG-1547

キャ

キャ 脚 SG-2014
キャク 客 SG-0245
キャク 却 SG-2013
キャク 脚 SG-2014
ギャク 逆 SG-0603
ギャク 虐 SG-0886
キュウ 嗅 SG-0064
キュウ 休 SG-0306
キュウ 泣 SG-0365
キュウ 久 SG-0477
キュウ 及 SG-0576
キュウ 急 SG-0577
キュウ 級 SG-0578
キュウ 吸 SG-0580
キュウ 朽 SG-0645
キュウ 求 SG-0930
キュウ 球 SG-0931
キュウ 救 SG-0932
キュウ 旧 SG-0950
キュウ 丘 SG-1146
キュウ 宮 SG-1265
キュウ 究 SG-1325
キュウ 弓 SG-1509
キュウ 窮 SG-1518
キュウ 給 SG-1603
キュウ 糾 SG-1616
キュウ 臼 SG-1811
キュウ 九 SG-2133
ギュウ 牛 SG-0816
キョ 挙 SG-0153
キョ 居 SG-0469
キョ 虚 SG-0885
キョ 許 SG-1805
キョ 拠 SG-1865
キョ 巨 SG-1910
キョ 拒 SG-1911
キョ 距 SG-1912
キョ 去 SG-2011
ギョ 魚 SG-0933
ギョ 漁 SG-0935
ギョ 御 SG-1807
きよ-い 清 SG-0696

キョウ

キョウ 叫 SG-0041
キョウ 共 SG-0137
キョウ 供 SG-0138
キョウ 恭 SG-0139
キョウ 興 SG-0151
キョウ 教 SG-0169
キョウ 胸 SG-0290
キョウ 狭 SG-0335
キョウ 峡 SG-0336
キョウ 挟 SG-0337
キョウ 兄 SG-0451
キョウ 競 SG-0453
キョウ 況 SG-0454
キョウ 恐 SG-0581
キョウ 香 SG-0716
キョウ 狂 SG-0864
キョウ 驚 SG-0873
キョウ 橋 SG-1280
キョウ 矯 SG-1281
キョウ 京 SG-1282
キョウ 享 SG-1289
キョウ 郷 SG-1317
キョウ 響 SG-1377
キョウ 境 SG-1384
キョウ 鏡 SG-1385
キョウ 強 SG-1510
キョウ 経 SG-1647
キョウ 協 SG-1951
キョウ 脅 SG-1956
キョウ 凶 SG-2105
ギョウ 凝 SG-0405
ギョウ 仰 SG-0414
ギョウ 業 SG-0628
ギョウ 暁 SG-1051
ギョウ 行 SG-1330
ギョウ 形 SG-1971
キョク 極 SG-0309
キョク 局 SG-0467
キョク 曲 SG-1988
ギョク 玉 SG-1730
きら-う 嫌 SG-0734
きり 霧 SG-1209
きわ 際 SG-1743
きわ-める 極 SG-0309
きわ-める 究 SG-1325
きわ-める 窮 SG-1518
キン 緊 SG-0094
キン 筋 SG-0288
キン 菌 SG-0678
キン 勤 SG-1190
キン 謹 SG-1191
キン 僅 SG-1192
キン 金 SG-1196
キン 錦 SG-1200
キン 斤 SG-1453
キン 近 SG-1454
キン 襟 SG-1669
キン 巾 SG-1682
キン 禁 SG-1738
キン 今 SG-1994
キン 琴 SG-2043
キン 均 SG-2113
ギン 銀 SG-0399
ギン 吟 SG-1999

ク・く

ク 口 SG-0031
ク 供 SG-0138
ク 久 SG-0477
ク 駆 SG-0875
ク 宮 SG-1265
ク 苦 SG-1559
ク 庫 SG-1580
ク 紅 SG-1608
ク 工 SG-1895
ク 功 SG-1898
ク 区 SG-2108
ク 句 SG-2115
ク 九 SG-2133
グ 惧 SG-0199
グ 愚 SG-1016
グ 貢 SG-1711
グ 具 SG-1719
く-いる 悔 SG-0546
く-う 食 SG-1781
く-ちる 朽 SG-0645
く-む 組 SG-0806
く-む 酌 SG-1820
く-やしい 悔 SG-0546
く-らす 暮 SG-0682
く-る 繰 SG-0650
く-る 来 SG-0746
クウ 空 SG-1323
グウ 遇 SG-1013
グウ 隅 SG-1014
グウ 偶 SG-1015
グウ 宮 SG-1265
くき 茎 SG-1650
くさ 草 SG-0672
くさ-い 臭 SG-0063
くさ-る 腐 SG-0794
くさり 鎖 SG-1712
くし 串 SG-0190
くじら 鯨 SG-0936
くず 葛 SG-2120

ゴン 勤 SG-1190
ゴン 言 SG-1364

サ・さ

サ 左 SG-0109
サ 佐 SG-0110
サ 唆 SG-0466
サ 査 SG-0627
サ 茶 SG-0673
サ 差 SG-0715
サ 砂 SG-1155
サ 沙 SG-1156
サ 再 SG-1651
サ 鎖 SG-1712
サ 作 SG-1905
サ 詐 SG-1908
ザ 座 SG-0384
ザ 挫 SG-0385
さ-く 咲 SG-0341
さ-く 割 SG-1964
さ-ける 裂 SG-0282
さ-ける 避 SG-1430
さ-げる 提 SG-1855
さ-げる 下 SG-2136
さ-す 挿 SG-0080
さ-す 差 SG-0715
さ-す 刺 SG-0772
さ-す 指 SG-1436
さ-める 覚 SG-0463
さ-める 冷 SG-1099
さ-る 去 SG-2011

サイ

サイ 最 SG-0057
サイ 採 SG-0123
サイ 菜 SG-0124
サイ 彩 SG-0125
サイ 采 SG-0126
サイ 殺 SG-0162
サイ 歳 SG-0203
サイ 細 SG-0285
サイ 妻 SG-0525
サイ 債 SG-0775
サイ 催 SG-0956
サイ 才 SG-1115
サイ 財 SG-1118
サイ 砕 SG-1152
サイ 災 SG-1166
サイ 塞 SG-1229
サイ 切 SG-1395
サイ 宰 SG-1428
サイ 裁 SG-1482
サイ 載 SG-1483
サイ 栽 SG-1484
サイ 再 SG-1651
サイ 祭 SG-1742
サイ 際 SG-1743
サイ 済 SG-1752
サイ 斎 SG-1755
サイ 西 SG-1987
ザイ 在 SG-1116
ザイ 財 SG-1118
ザイ 材 SG-1119
ザイ 剤 SG-1753
ザイ 罪 SG-1959
さい 埼 SG-0330
さいわ-い 幸 SG-0586
さえぎ-る 遮 SG-1182
さか 坂 SG-0089
さか 酒 SG-1812
さか-える 栄 SG-1185
さが-す 捜 SG-0076
さが-す 探 SG-1327
さか-らう 逆 SG-0603
さか-ん 盛 SG-1846
さかい 境 SG-1384
さかずき 杯 SG-0764
さかな 魚 SG-0933
さかのぼ-る 遡 SG-0606
さき 崎 SG-0329
さき 先 SG-0443

サク

サク 策 SG-0771
サク 削 SG-0799
サク 錯 SG-1060
サク 索 SG-1621
サク 作 SG-1905
サク 昨 SG-1906
サク 酢 SG-1907
サク 搾 SG-1909
サク 冊 SG-2032
サク 柵 SG-2033
さぐ-る 探 SG-1327
さくら 桜 SG-0631
さけ 酒 SG-1812
さけ-ぶ 叫 SG-0041
さげす-む 蔑 SG-0014
ささ-える 支 SG-0181
さず-ける 授 SG-0132
さそ-う 誘 SG-0722
さだ-める 定 SG-0234
さち 幸 SG-0586

サツ

サツ 撮 SG-0058
サツ 拶 SG-0083
サツ 殺 SG-0162
サッ 早 SG-1046
サツ 刷 SG-1405
サツ 刹 SG-1408
サツ 察 SG-1744
サツ 擦 SG-1745
サツ 冊 SG-2032
サツ 札 SG-2103
ザツ 雑 SG-0954
さと 里 SG-1312
さと-す 諭 SG-1424
さと-る 悟 SG-0198
さば-く 裁 SG-1482
さび-しい 寂 SG-0098
さま 様 SG-0827
さまた-げる 妨 SG-1937
さみ-しい 寂 SG-0098
さむ-い 寒 SG-1100
さむらい 侍 SG-0226
さら 皿 SG-1843
さら 更 SG-1874
さる 猿 SG-0868
さわ 沢 SG-1022
さわ-ぐ 騒 SG-0874
さわ-やか 爽 SG-0322
さわ-る 触 SG-0923
さわ-る 障 SG-1362
サン 散 SG-0173
サン 酸 SG-0464
サン 産 SG-0691
サン 算 SG-0760
サン 蚕 SG-1005
サン 山 SG-1139
サン 桟 SG-1504
サン 賛 SG-1705
サン 傘 SG-2005
サン 参 SG-2092
サン 惨 SG-2096
サン 三 SG-2127
ザン 斬 SG-1467
ザン 暫 SG-1468
ザン 残 SG-1501
ザン 惨 SG-2096

シ・し

シ 自 SG-0059
シ 史 SG-0105
シ 使 SG-0106
シ 支 SG-0181
シ 枝 SG-0183
シ 肢 SG-0185
シ 止 SG-0200
シ 市 SG-0212
シ 志 SG-0213
シ 誌 SG-0214
シ 詩 SG-0225
シ 死 SG-0277
シ 思 SG-0284
シ 歯 SG-0302
シ 司 SG-0357
シ 詞 SG-0358
シ 飼 SG-0359
シ 嗣 SG-0361
シ 伺 SG-0362
シ 資 SG-0434
シ 姿 SG-0435
シ 諮 SG-0440
シ 恣 SG-0441
シ 子 SG-0510
シ 姉 SG-0528
シ 摯 SG-0589
シ 私 SG-0711
シ 刺 SG-0772
シ 雌 SG-0971
シ 氏 SG-1433
シ 紙 SG-1434
シ 指 SG-1436
シ 旨 SG-1437
シ 脂 SG-1438
シ 士 SG-1451
シ 仕 SG-1452
シ 矢 SG-1524
シ 至 SG-1531
シ 施 SG-1569
シ 師 SG-1596
シ 糸 SG-1600
シ 紫 SG-1619
シ 賜 SG-1714
シ 示 SG-1737
シ 視 SG-1747
シ 祉 SG-1749
シ 試 SG-1901
シ 始 SG-1945
シ 四 SG-2128

ジ

ジ 耳 SG-0050
ジ 自 SG-0059
ジ 事 SG-0104
ジ 寺 SG-0219
ジ 時 SG-0220
ジ 持 SG-0221
ジ 侍 SG-0226
ジ 次 SG-0432
ジ 児 SG-0447
ジ 字 SG-0512
ジ 地 SG-1010
ジ 辞 SG-1360
ジ 除 SG-1387
ジ 仕 SG-1452
ジ 滋 SG-1635
ジ 磁 SG-1636
ジ 慈 SG-1637
ジ 璽 SG-1734
ジ 示 SG-1737
ジ 餌 SG-1785
ジ 似 SG-1942
ジ 治 SG-1944
じ 路 SG-0248
し-いる 強 SG-1510
し-く 敷 SG-0756
し-ぬ 死 SG-0277
し-みる 染 SG-0634
し-める 絞 SG-0482
し-める 閉 SG-1256
し-める 締 SG-1757
し-める 占 SG-1767
し-る 知 SG-1525
しあわ-せ 幸 SG-0586
しいた-げる 虐 SG-0886
しお 潮 SG-1053
しお 塩 SG-1847
しか 鹿 SG-0896
しか-る 叱 SG-0044
シキ 色 SG-0423
シキ 識 SG-1490
シキ 織 SG-1491
シキ 式 SG-1900
ジキ 直 SG-0007
ジキ 食 SG-1781
ジク 軸 SG-1584
しげ-る 茂 SG-0676
しず-か 静 SG-0697
しず-む 沈 SG-0338
しず-める 鎮 SG-0601
しずく 滴 SG-1762
した 舌 SG-0040
した 下 SG-2136
した-う 慕 SG-0688
した-しい 親 SG-0462
したが-う 従 SG-0372
したた-る 滴 SG-1762
シチ 質 SG-1457
シチ 七 SG-2131
シツ 叱 SG-0044
シツ 失 SG-0073
シツ 執 SG-0588
シツ 湿 SG-1092
シツ 漆 SG-1094
シツ 質 SG-1457
シツ 室 SG-1532
シツ 疾 SG-1889
シツ 嫉 SG-1894
ジツ 日 SG-1045
ジツ 実 SG-1694
ジッ 十 SG-2134
しな 品 SG-0032
しの-ぶ 忍 SG-1422
しば 芝 SG-0215
しば-る 縛 SG-0758
しぶ-い 渋 SG-0205
しぼ-る 絞 SG-0482
しぼ-る 搾 SG-1909
しま 島 SG-1140
しめ-す 示 SG-1737
しめ-る 湿 SG-1092
しも 霜 SG-1213
しも 下 SG-2136

シャ

シャ 赦 SG-0179
シャ 砂 SG-1155
シャ 遮 SG-1182
シャ 写 SG-1231
シャ 舎 SG-1392
シャ 捨 SG-1393
シャ 射 SG-1516
シャ 謝 SG-1517
シャ 車 SG-1578
シャ 社 SG-1746
シャ 斜 SG-1833
シャ 者 SG-2085
シャ 煮 SG-2091
ジャ 邪 SG-0925
ジャ 蛇 SG-1001
シャク 尺 SG-0074
シャク 釈 SG-1025
シャク 昔 SG-1055
シャク 借 SG-1056
シャク 石 SG-1148
シャク 赤 SG-1171
シャク 酌 SG-1820
シャク 爵 SG-1824
ジャク 寂 SG-0098
ジャク 若 SG-0347
ジャク 弱 SG-1512
ジャク 着 SG-2086
シュ 取 SG-0056
シュ 首 SG-0066
シュ 手 SG-0072
シュ 守 SG-0113
シュ 修 SG-0170
シュ 衆 SG-0373
シュ 趣 SG-0488
シュ 朱 SG-0622
シュ 殊 SG-0623
シュ 珠 SG-0624
シュ 狩 SG-0866
シュ 酒 SG-1812
シュ 主 SG-2037
シュ 種 SG-2060
シュ 腫 SG-2063
ジュ 受 SG-0131
ジュ 授 SG-0132
ジュ 従 SG-0372
ジュ 呪 SG-0455
ジュ 寿 SG-0564
ジュ 需 SG-0572
ジュ 儒 SG-0575
ジュ 就 SG-1285
ジュ 樹 SG-2045

シュウ

シュウ 臭 SG-0063
シュウ 収 SG-0086
シュウ 修 SG-0170
シュウ 囚 SG-0311
シュウ 衆 SG-0373
シュウ 祝 SG-0452
シュウ 執 SG-0588
シュウ 秋 SG-0714
シュウ 秀 SG-0721
シュウ 愁 SG-0729
シュウ 羞 SG-0834
シュウ 集 SG-0948
シュウ 習 SG-0984
シュウ 襲 SG-1034
シュウ 終 SG-1098
シュウ 州 SG-1105
シュウ 就 SG-1285
シュウ 蹴 SG-1287
シュウ 周 SG-1553
シュウ 週 SG-1555
シュウ 袖 SG-1668
シュウ 宗 SG-1740
シュウ 酬 SG-1817
シュウ 醜 SG-1818
シュウ 拾 SG-1991
シュウ 舟 SG-2015
ジュウ 渋 SG-0205
ジュウ 従 SG-0372
ジュウ 縦 SG-0374
ジュウ 充 SG-0515
ジュウ 獣 SG-0862
ジュウ 汁 SG-1088

セン 洗 SG-0448
セン 遷 SG-0557
セン 染 SG-0634
セン 羨 SG-0833
セン 薦 SG-0897
セン 鮮 SG-0934
セン 扇 SG-0987
セン 潜 SG-1091
セン 川 SG-1104
セン 泉 SG-1120
セン 線 SG-1122
セン 腺 SG-1125
セン 仙 SG-1141
セン 宣 SG-1225
セン 煎 SG-1407
セン 繊 SG-1486
セン 浅 SG-1502
セン 銭 SG-1503
セン 箋 SG-1505
セン 戦 SG-1549
セン 旋 SG-1571
セン 占 SG-1767
セン 専 SG-1919
セン 栓 SG-2003
セン 詮 SG-2004
セン 船 SG-2016
ゼン 善 SG-0835
ゼン 繕 SG-0836
ゼン 膳 SG-0837
ゼン 然 SG-1174
ゼン 前 SG-1403
ゼン 漸 SG-1469
ゼン 禅 SG-1751
ゼン 全 SG-2002

ソ・そ

ソ 想 SG-0005
ソ 訴 SG-0604
ソ 遡 SG-0606
ソ 塑 SG-0607
ソ 組 SG-0806
ソ 祖 SG-0808
ソ 狙 SG-0809
ソ 粗 SG-0811
ソ 阻 SG-0812
ソ 租 SG-0814
ソ 措 SG-1058
ソ 礎 SG-1151
ソ 素 SG-1618
ソ 疎 SG-2073
ゾ 曽 SG-1794
そ-う 沿 SG-1086
そ-える 添 SG-0319
そ-める 染 SG-0634
そ-める 初 SG-1666
そ-る 反 SG-0087

ソウ

ソウ 相 SG-0004
ソウ 想 SG-0005
ソウ 喪 SG-0042
ソウ 捜 SG-0076
ソウ 挿 SG-0080
ソウ 争 SG-0129
ソウ 奏 SG-0145
ソウ 踪 SG-0233
ソウ 葬 SG-0280
ソウ 爽 SG-0322
ソウ 走 SG-0483
ソウ 巣 SG-0637
ソウ 桑 SG-0640
ソウ 操 SG-0651
ソウ 藻 SG-0652
ソウ 燥 SG-0653
ソウ 草 SG-0672
ソウ 騒 SG-0874
ソウ 双 SG-0955
ソウ 早 SG-1046
ソウ 霜 SG-1213
ソウ 窓 SG-1328
ソウ 送 SG-1342
ソウ 創 SG-1404
ソウ 総 SG-1602
ソウ 宗 SG-1740
ソウ 掃 SG-1777
ソウ 層 SG-1792
ソウ 贈 SG-1793
ソウ 曽 SG-1794
ソウ 僧 SG-1795
ソウ 装 SG-1880
ソウ 荘 SG-1881
ソウ 壮 SG-1882
ソウ 痩 SG-1892
ソウ 倉 SG-1997
ソウ 曹 SG-2053
ソウ 遭 SG-2054
ソウ 槽 SG-2055
ゾウ 造 SG-0036
ゾウ 象 SG-0892
ゾウ 像 SG-0893
ゾウ 雑 SG-0954
ゾウ 蔵 SG-1487
ゾウ 臓 SG-1488
ゾウ 増 SG-1791
ゾウ 贈 SG-1793
ゾウ 憎 SG-1796
そうろう 候 SG-1528

ソク

ソク 息 SG-0061
ソク 足 SG-0227
ソク 促 SG-0228
ソク 捉 SG-0232
ソク 塞 SG-1229
ソク 側 SG-1722
ソク 則 SG-1723
ソク 測 SG-1724
ソク 即 SG-1786
ソク 束 SG-2068
ソク 速 SG-2069
ゾク 属 SG-0904
ゾク 俗 SG-1161
ゾク 族 SG-1567
ゾク 続 SG-1696
ゾク 賊 SG-1721
そこ 底 SG-1442
そこ-なう 損 SG-1720
そそ-ぐ 注 SG-2039
そそのか-す 唆 SG-0466
そだ-つ 育 SG-0518
ソツ 率 SG-1634
ソツ 卒 SG-1671
そで 袖 SG-1668
そと 外 SG-1764
そな-える 供 SG-0138
そな-える 備 SG-1541
その 園 SG-1673
そむ-く 背 SG-0389
そら 空 SG-1323
ソン 村 SG-0114
ソン 存 SG-1117
ソン 孫 SG-1629
ソン 遜 SG-1630
ソン 損 SG-1720
ソン 尊 SG-1822
ゾン 存 SG-1117

タ・た

タ 太 SG-0317
タ 汰 SG-0320
タ 多 SG-0796
タ 他 SG-1009
た 手 SG-0072
た 田 SG-1300
ダ 妥 SG-0534
ダ 唾 SG-0704
ダ 堕 SG-0804
ダ 惰 SG-0805
ダ 駄 SG-0877
ダ 蛇 SG-1001
ダ 打 SG-1915
た-える 耐 SG-0573
た-える 絶 SG-1606
た-える 堪 SG-1799
た-く 炊 SG-0438
だ-く 抱 SG-0426
だ-す 出 SG-0217
た-つ 立 SG-0363
た-つ 断 SG-1458
た-つ 裁 SG-1482
た-てる 建 SG-1339
た-べる 食 SG-1781
た-める 矯 SG-1281
た-りる 足 SG-0227
た-れる 垂 SG-0702

タイ

タイ 対 SG-0115
タイ 泰 SG-0146
タイ 待 SG-0222
タイ 体 SG-0307
タイ 大 SG-0314
タイ 太 SG-0317
タイ 替 SG-0370
タイ 退 SG-0400
タイ 耐 SG-0573
タイ 隊 SG-0848
タイ 逮 SG-0928
タイ 態 SG-1037
タイ 堆 SG-1133
タイ 代 SG-1352
タイ 貸 SG-1353
タイ 袋 SG-1354
タイ 戴 SG-1485
タイ 帯 SG-1684
タイ 滞 SG-1688
タイ 台 SG-1943
タイ 怠 SG-1946
タイ 胎 SG-1947
ダイ 大 SG-0314
ダイ 内 SG-1239
ダイ 代 SG-1352
ダイ 弟 SG-1355
ダイ 第 SG-1356
ダイ 題 SG-1854
ダイ 台 SG-1943
たい-ら 平 SG-0707
たお-れる 倒 SG-1535
たか-い 高 SG-1277
たが-い 互 SG-1928
たがや-す 耕 SG-1297
たから 宝 SG-1731
たき 滝 SG-1033
たきぎ 薪 SG-1466

タク

タク 宅 SG-0705
タク 託 SG-0706
タク 濯 SG-0991
タク 沢 SG-1022
タク 択 SG-1024
タク 拓 SG-1150
タク 度 SG-1233
タク 卓 SG-1857
ダク 諾 SG-0348
ダク 濁 SG-1003
たぐ-い 類 SG-0498
たく-み 巧 SG-1899
たくわ-える 蓄 SG-1641
たけ 丈 SG-0107
たけ 竹 SG-0759
たけ 岳 SG-1147
たし-かめる 確 SG-0979
たす-ける 助 SG-0807
たず-ねる 尋 SG-0111
たず-ねる 訪 SG-1934
たずさ-える 携 SG-0960
ただ-し 但 SG-1063
ただ-しい 正 SG-0208
ただ-ちに 直 SG-0007
たた-む 畳 SG-0810
たたか-う 闘 SG-1258
たたか-う 戦 SG-1549
たたみ 畳 SG-0810
ただよ-う 漂 SG-0560
タツ 達 SG-0828
ダツ 脱 SG-0458
ダツ 奪 SG-0962
たつ 竜 SG-1032
たっと-い 貴 SG-1701
たっと-い 尊 SG-1822
たて 縦 SG-0374
たて 盾 SG-1551
たてまつ-る 奉 SG-0664
たと-える 例 SG-0278
たな 棚 SG-0641
たに 谷 SG-1158
たね 種 SG-2060
たの-しい 楽 SG-0625
たの-む 頼 SG-2071
たば 束 SG-2068
たび 度 SG-1233
たび 旅 SG-1566
たま 球 SG-0931
たま 霊 SG-1208
たま 弾 SG-1550
たま 玉 SG-1730
だま-る 黙 SG-1176
たまご 卵 SG-1043
たましい 魂 SG-0353
たまわ-る 賜 SG-1714
たみ 民 SG-0021
ため-す 試 SG-1901
たも-つ 保 SG-0513
たよ-り 便 SG-1875
たよ-る 頼 SG-2071
だれ 誰 SG-0964
たわむ-れる 戯 SG-0887
たわら 俵 SG-1663

タン

タン 反 SG-0087
タン 鍛 SG-0165
タン 綻 SG-0236
タン 端 SG-0574
タン 旦 SG-1062
タン 担 SG-1064
タン 胆 SG-1065
タン 淡 SG-1089
タン 壇 SG-1131
タン 炭 SG-1168
タン 嘆 SG-1195
タン 丹 SG-1296
タン 探 SG-1327
タン 誕 SG-1335
タン 短 SG-1527
タン 単 SG-1548
ダン 暖 SG-0134
ダン 段 SG-0161
ダン 旦 SG-1062
ダン 壇 SG-1131
ダン 男 SG-1301
ダン 談 SG-1370
ダン 断 SG-1458
ダン 弾 SG-1550
ダン 団 SG-1922

チ・ち

チ 置 SG-0008
チ 値 SG-0009
チ 恥 SG-0054
チ 稚 SG-0728
チ 地 SG-1010
チ 池 SG-1011
チ 遅 SG-1345
チ 質 SG-1457
チ 知 SG-1525
チ 致 SG-1536
チ 緻 SG-1539
チ 痴 SG-1890
チ 治 SG-1944
ち 乳 SG-0128
ち 千 SG-0305
ち 血 SG-1844
ち-る 散 SG-0173
ちい-さい 小 SG-1153
ちか-い 近 SG-1454
ちか-う 誓 SG-1463
ちが-う 違 SG-0253
ちから 力 SG-1949
ちぎ-る 契 SG-1410
チク 築 SG-0582
チク 竹 SG-0759
チク 逐 SG-0847
チク 畜 SG-1640
チク 蓄 SG-1641
ちち 父 SG-0103
ちち 乳 SG-0128
ちぢ-む 縮 SG-1227
チツ 秩 SG-0726
チツ 窒 SG-1538

チャ

チャ 茶 SG-0673
チャク 嫡 SG-1763
チャク 着 SG-2086
チュウ 忠 SG-0188
チュウ 抽 SG-0783
チュウ 駐 SG-0872
チュウ 虫 SG-0998
チュウ 昼 SG-1048
チュウ 鋳 SG-1204
チュウ 宙 SG-1224
チュウ 中 SG-1575
チュウ 仲 SG-1576
チュウ 沖 SG-1577
チュウ 衷 SG-1664
チュウ 酎 SG-1819
チュウ 注 SG-2039
チュウ 柱 SG-2040
チョ 貯 SG-1707
チョ 緒 SG-2088
チョ 緒 SG-2088
チョ 著 SG-2089
チョウ 聴 SG-0053
チョウ 澄 SG-0270
チョウ 腸 SG-0295
チョウ 超 SG-0485
チョウ 長 SG-0566
チョウ 張 SG-0567
チョウ 帳 SG-0568
チョウ 徴 SG-0570

チョウ 懲 SG-0571
チョウ 鳥 SG-0944
チョウ 朝 SG-1052
チョウ 潮 SG-1052
チョウ 嘲 SG-1054
チョウ 庁 SG-1236
チョウ 町 SG-1302
チョウ 弔 SG-1542
チョウ 調 SG-1554
チョウ 彫 SG-1556
チョウ 貼 SG-1768
チョウ 兆 SG-1770
チョウ 挑 SG-1772
チョウ 跳 SG-1773
チョウ 眺 SG-1774
チョウ 釣 SG-1862
チョウ 丁 SG-1914
チョウ 頂 SG-1916
チョウ 重 SG-2058
チョク 直 SG-0007
チョク 捗 SG-0207
チョク 勅 SG-2074
チン 朕 SG-0149
チン 沈 SG-0338
チン 鎮 SG-0601
チン 賃 SG-1706
チン 陳 SG-2050
チン 珍 SG-2095

ツ・つ

ツ 都 SG-1316
ツ 通 SG-1983
つ 津 SG-2027
つ-く 就 SG-1285
つ-く 突 SG-1326
つ-く 着 SG-2086
つ-ぐ 次 SG-0432
つ-ぐ 接 SG-0526
つ-ぐ 継 SG-1607
つ-くす 尽 SG-1850
つ-ける 付 SG-0117
つ-ける 漬 SG-0777
つ-げる 告 SG-0033
つ-む 積 SG-0774
つ-む 摘 SG-1761
つ-める 詰 SG-2008
つ-る 釣 SG-1862
つ-れる 連 SG-1579
ツイ 対 SG-0115
ツイ 椎 SG-0647
ツイ 墜 SG-0850
ツイ 追 SG-1594
つい-やす 費 SG-2081
ツウ 痛 SG-1885
ツウ 通 SG-1983
つか 塚 SG-0843
つか-う 使 SG-0106
つか-える 仕 SG-1452
つか-まえる 捕 SG-0750
つか-れる 疲 SG-1887
つか-わす 遣 SG-1598
つき 月 SG-1077
つぎ 次 SG-0432
つく-る 造 SG-0036
つく-る 創 SG-1404
つく-る 作 SG-1905
つくえ 机 SG-1863
つぐな-う 償 SG-1274
つくろ-う 繕 SG-0836
つた-わる 伝 SG-1920
つたな-い 拙 SG-0218

ツチ

つち 土 SG-1126
つちか-う 培 SG-0767
つつ 筒 SG-2099
つづ-く 続 SG-1696
つつ-む 包 SG-0425
つつし-む 慎 SG-0600
つつし-む 謹 SG-1191
つつみ 堤 SG-1856
つづみ 鼓 SG-2047
つど-う 集 SG-0948
つと-める 努 SG-0527
つと-める 勤 SG-1190
つと-める 務 SG-1506
つな 綱 SG-1968
つね 常 SG-1271
つの 角 SG-0921
つの-る 募 SG-0684
つば 唾 SG-0704
つばさ 翼 SG-0986
つぶ 粒 SG-0366
つぶ-す 潰 SG-1716
つぼ 坪 SG-0709
つま 妻 SG-0525
つま 爪 SG-0927
つみ 罪 SG-1959
つむ-ぐ 紡 SG-1615
つめ 爪 SG-0927
つめ-たい 冷 SG-1099
つや 艶 SG-1978
つゆ 露 SG-0250
つよ-い 強 SG-1510
つら 面 SG-0060
つら-なる 連 SG-1579
つらぬ-く 貫 SG-1709
つる 鶴 SG-0980
つる 弦 SG-1514
つるぎ 剣 SG-0382

テ・て

て 手 SG-0072
デ 弟 SG-1355
て-る 照 SG-1415
で-る 出 SG-0217
テイ 定 SG-0234
テイ 体 SG-0307
テイ 程 SG-0492
テイ 呈 SG-0493
テイ 逓 SG-0890
テイ 停 SG-1291
テイ 亭 SG-1292
テイ 庭 SG-1336
テイ 廷 SG-1337
テイ 艇 SG-1338
テイ 弟 SG-1355
テイ 低 SG-1441
テイ 底 SG-1442
テイ 邸 SG-1443
テイ 抵 SG-1444
テイ 貞 SG-1725
テイ 偵 SG-1726
テイ 帝 SG-1756
テイ 締 SG-1757
テイ 諦 SG-1758
テイ 提 SG-1855
テイ 堤 SG-1856
テイ 丁 SG-1914
テイ 訂 SG-1917
デイ 泥 SG-0473

テキ

テキ 笛 SG-0784
テキ 適 SG-1759
テキ 敵 SG-1760
テキ 摘 SG-1761
テキ 滴 SG-1762
テキ 的 SG-1861
デキ 溺 SG-1515
テツ 鉄 SG-1197
テツ 迭 SG-1346
テツ 哲 SG-1460
テツ 徹 SG-1801
テツ 撤 SG-1802
てら 寺 SG-0219
テン 天 SG-0315
テン 添 SG-0319
テン 展 SG-0468
テン 殿 SG-0471
テン 塡 SG-0602
テン 点 SG-1765
テン 店 SG-1766
テン 転 SG-1921
テン 典 SG-2031
デン 殿 SG-0471
デン 電 SG-1216
デン 田 SG-1300
デン 伝 SG-1920

ト・と

ト 吐 SG-0043
ト 登 SG-0267
ト 徒 SG-0487
ト 頭 SG-0494
ト 妬 SG-0539
ト 土 SG-1126
ト 度 SG-1233
ト 渡 SG-1237
ト 都 SG-1316
ト 図 SG-1320
ト 途 SG-1388
ト 塗 SG-1390
ト 賭 SG-1715
ト 斗 SG-1834
と 戸 SG-1241
ド 努 SG-0527
ド 怒 SG-0530
ド 奴 SG-0536
ド 土 SG-1126
ド 度 SG-1233
と 十 SG-2134
と-う 問 SG-1254
と-く 説 SG-0456
と-く 解 SG-0922
と-ぐ 研 SG-1973
と-ける 溶 SG-1163
と-げる 遂 SG-0849
と-じる 閉 SG-1256
と-ぶ 飛 SG-0981
と-ぶ 跳 SG-1773
と-まる 止 SG-0200
と-まる 泊 SG-0790
と-む 富 SG-1981
と-める 留 SG-1304
と-らえる 捕 SG-0750
と-る 取 SG-0056
と-る 撮 SG-0058
と-る 採 SG-0123
と-る 執 SG-0588

トウ

トウ 道 SG-0067
トウ 討 SG-0116
トウ 謄 SG-0148
トウ 投 SG-0160
トウ 等 SG-0223
トウ 踏 SG-0230
トウ 登 SG-0267
トウ 灯 SG-0269
トウ 頭 SG-0494
トウ 統 SG-0517
トウ 桃 SG-0639
トウ 藤 SG-0674
トウ 稲 SG-0723
トウ 透 SG-0724
トウ 騰 SG-0879
トウ 湯 SG-1069
トウ 冬 SG-1097
トウ 凍 SG-1102
トウ 島 SG-1140
トウ 納 SG-1240
トウ 闘 SG-1258
トウ 当 SG-1269
トウ 党 SG-1270
トウ 読 SG-1371
トウ 刀 SG-1394
トウ 到 SG-1534
トウ 倒 SG-1535
トウ 逃 SG-1771
トウ 唐 SG-1808
トウ 糖 SG-1809
トウ 盗 SG-1849
トウ 悼 SG-1858
トウ 痘 SG-1893
トウ 豆 SG-1975
トウ 答 SG-1990
トウ 塔 SG-1992
トウ 搭 SG-1993
トウ 陶 SG-2010
トウ 東 SG-2048
トウ 棟 SG-2049
トウ 筒 SG-2099
ドウ 道 SG-0067
ドウ 導 SG-0068
ドウ 堂 SG-1273
ドウ 動 SG-2059
ドウ 働 SG-2061
ドウ 童 SG-2064
ドウ 瞳 SG-2065
ドウ 同 SG-2097
ドウ 銅 SG-2098
ドウ 洞 SG-2100
ドウ 胴 SG-2101
とうげ 峠 SG-1144
とうと-い 貴 SG-1701
とうと-い 尊 SG-1822
とお 十 SG-2134
とお-い 遠 SG-1672
とお-る 通 SG-1983
とき 時 SG-0220

トク

トク 徳 SG-0011
トク 督 SG-0097
トク 特 SG-0224
トク 匿 SG-0349
トク 篤 SG-0880
トク 読 SG-1371
トク 得 SG-1697
ドク 毒 SG-0543
ドク 独 SG-0999
ドク 読 SG-1371
とこ 床 SG-0633
とこ 常 SG-1271
ところ 所 SG-1242
とし 年 SG-0710
とち 栃 SG-0642
トツ 突 SG-1326
トツ 凸 SG-2106
とつ-ぐ 嫁 SG-0844
とど-く 届 SG-0470
とどこお-る 滞 SG-1688
ととの-う 調 SG-1554
ととの-える 整 SG-2070
とな-える 唱 SG-0039
となり 隣 SG-0261
との 殿 SG-0471
どの 殿 SG-0471
とびら 扉 SG-0997
とぼ-しい 乏 SG-0216
とみ 富 SG-1981
とむら-う 弔 SG-1542
とも 友 SG-0085
とも 共 SG-0137
とも 供 SG-0138
ともな-う 伴 SG-0823
とら 虎 SG-0883
とら-える 捉 SG-0232
とり 鳥 SG-0944
どろ 泥 SG-0473
トン 豚 SG-0845
トン 屯 SG-1644
トン 頓 SG-1645
トン 団 SG-1922
とん 問 SG-1254
ドン 曇 SG-1212
ドン 鈍 SG-1643
ドン 貪 SG-2000
どん 丼 SG-1298
どんぶり 丼 SG-1298

ナ・な

な 菜 SG-0124
な 名 SG-1073
ナ 納 SG-1240
ナ 那 SG-1319
ナ 奈 SG-1739
ナ 南 SG-2042
な-い 無 SG-0258
な-える 萎 SG-0730
な-く 泣 SG-0365
な-く 鳴 SG-0945
な-くなる 亡 SG-0592
な-げる 投 SG-0160
な-る 成 SG-1476
な-れる 慣 SG-1710
ナイ 内 SG-1239
なえ 苗 SG-1311
なお-す 直 SG-0007
なお-る 治 SG-1944
なか 中 SG-1575
なか 仲 SG-1576
なが-い 長 SG-0566
なが-い 永 SG-1110
なか-ば 半 SG-0821
なが-める 眺 SG-1774
なが-れる 流 SG-0516
なぐ-る 殴 SG-2111
なぐさ-める 慰 SG-0121
なげ-く 嘆 SG-1195
なご-む 和 SG-0712
なさ-け 情 SG-0695
なし 梨 SG-0638
なぞ 謎 SG-0742
なつ 夏 SG-0238
なつ-かしい 懐 SG-1675
なな 七 SG-2131
なな-め 斜 SG-1833
なに 何 SG-0046
なの 七 SG-2131
なべ 鍋 SG-0275
なま 生 SG-0689
なま-ける 怠 SG-1946
なまり 鉛 SG-1202
なみ 並 SG-0368
なみ 波 SG-0908
なみだ 涙 SG-1243
なめ-らか 滑 SG-0273
なや-む 悩 SG-0287

みぎ 右 SG-0102
みことのり 詔 SG-1419
みさお 操 SG-0651
みさき 岬 SG-1145
みささぎ 陵 SG-1349
みじ-め 惨 SG-2096
みじか-い 短 SG-1527
みず 水 SG-1081
みずうみ 湖 SG-1563
みずから 自 SG-0059
みせ 店 SG-1766
みぞ 溝 SG-1655
みだ-ら 淫 SG-1095
みだ-れる 乱 SG-2102
みち 道 SG-0067
みちび-く 導 SG-0068
ミツ 密 SG-2077
ミツ 蜜 SG-2079
みつ-ぐ 貢 SG-1711
みっ-つ 三 SG-2127
みと-める 認 SG-1420
みどり 緑 SG-1929
みな 皆 SG-0393
みなと 港 SG-0422
みなみ 南 SG-2042
みなもと 源 SG-1123
みにく-い 醜 SG-1818
みね 峰 SG-0667
みの-る 実 SG-1694
みみ 耳 SG-0050
みや 宮 SG-1265
ミャク 脈 SG-1114
みやこ 都 SG-1316
ミョウ 冥 SG-0018
ミョウ 命 SG-0408
ミョウ 妙 SG-0531
ミョウ 名 SG-1073
ミョウ 明 SG-1078
ミン 民 SG-0021
ミン 眠 SG-0022

ム・む

ム 夢 SG-0013
ム 無 SG-0258
ム 謀 SG-0659
ム 霧 SG-1209
ム 武 SG-1473
ム 務 SG-1506
ム 矛 SG-1508
む 六 SG-2130
む-く 向 SG-1276
む-す 蒸 SG-1177
む-れる 群 SG-0156
むか-える 迎 SG-0411
むかし 昔 SG-1055
むぎ 麦 SG-0747
むく-いる 報 SG-0587
むこ 婿 SG-0538
むさぼ-る 貪 SG-2000
むし 虫 SG-0998
むす-ぶ 結 SG-2007
むずか-しい 難 SG-1193
むすめ 娘 SG-0529
むっ-つ 六 SG-2130
むな 胸 SG-0290
むな 棟 SG-2049
むね 胸 SG-0290
むね 旨 SG-1437
むね 棟 SG-2049
むら 村 SG-0114
むら-がる 群 SG-0156
むらさき 紫 SG-1619
むろ 室 SG-1532

メ・め

め 目 SG-0001
め 女 SG-0521
め 芽 SG-0924
め 雌 SG-0971
め-す 召 SG-1413
メイ 冥 SG-0018
メイ 命 SG-0408
メイ 迷 SG-0739
メイ 鳴 SG-0945
メイ 名 SG-1073
メイ 銘 SG-1076
メイ 明 SG-1078
メイ 盟 SG-1079
めぐ-む 恵 SG-1923
めぐ-る 巡 SG-1108
めし 飯 SG-1782
めす 雌 SG-0971
めずら-しい 珍 SG-2095
メツ 滅 SG-1499
メン 面 SG-0060
メン 免 SG-0549
メン 麺 SG-0748
メン 綿 SG-1611

モ・も

モ 茂 SG-0676
モ 模 SG-0681
も 喪 SG-0042
も 藻 SG-0652
も-える 燃 SG-1175
も-しくは 若 SG-0347
も-つ 持 SG-0221
も-り 守 SG-0113
も-る 盛 SG-1846
も-れる 漏 SG-1211
モウ 望 SG-0491
モウ 亡 SG-0592
モウ 盲 SG-0596
モウ 妄 SG-0598
モウ 猛 SG-0865
モウ 毛 SG-0916
モウ 耗 SG-0918
モウ 網 SG-1610
もう-ける 設 SG-0159
もう-す 申 SG-1214
もう-でる 詣 SG-1439

モク

モク 目 SG-0001
モク 木 SG-0608
モク 黙 SG-1176
もぐ-る 潜 SG-1091
もち 餅 SG-0377
もち-いる 用 SG-1357
モツ 物 SG-0817
もっと-も 最 SG-0057
もっぱ-ら 専 SG-1919
もてあそ-ぶ 弄 SG-0144
もと 元 SG-0444
もと 本 SG-0611
もと 基 SG-1866
もと 下 SG-2136
もど-す 戻 SG-1244
もと-める 求 SG-0930
もとい 基 SG-1866
もの 物 SG-0817
もの 者 SG-2085
もも 桃 SG-0639
もよお-す 催 SG-0956
もり 森 SG-0610
モン 聞 SG-0051
モン 文 SG-0318
モン 門 SG-1251
モン 問 SG-1254
モン 紋 SG-1613

ヤ・や

ヤ 夜 SG-1074
ヤ 野 SG-1313
ヤ 冶 SG-1948
や 家 SG-0842
や 弥 SG-1513
や 矢 SG-1524
や 屋 SG-1533
や 八 SG-2132
や-く 焼 SG-1167
や-せる 痩 SG-1892
や-む 病 SG-1884
や-める 辞 SG-1360
やかた 館 SG-1597
ヤク 役 SG-0158
ヤク 厄 SG-0418
ヤク 薬 SG-0626
ヤク 躍 SG-0990
ヤク 訳 SG-1023
ヤク 約 SG-1601
ヤク 益 SG-1848
ヤク 疫 SG-1888
やさ-しい 優 SG-0240
やさ-しい 易 SG-1041
やしな-う 養 SG-0830
やしろ 社 SG-1746
やす-い 安 SG-0522
やす-む 休 SG-0306
やつ 八 SG-2132
やど 宿 SG-1226
やと-う 雇 SG-0957
やど-す 宿 SG-1226
やなぎ 柳 SG-0636
やぶ-る 破 SG-0909
やぶ-れる 敗 SG-1702
やま 山 SG-1139
やまい 病 SG-1884
やみ 闇 SG-1378
やわ-らかい 柔 SG-1507
やわ-らかい 軟 SG-1586
やわ-らぐ 和 SG-0712

ユ・ゆ

ユ 由 SG-0781
ユ 油 SG-0782
ユ 輸 SG-1423
ユ 諭 SG-1424
ユ 愉 SG-1425
ユ 癒 SG-1426
ユ 喩 SG-1427
ユ 遊 SG-1568
ゆ 湯 SG-1069
ゆ-う 結 SG-2007
ゆ-く 行 SG-1330
ゆ-く 逝 SG-1465
ゆ-れる 揺 SG-0078
ユイ 由 SG-0781
ユイ 唯 SG-0965
ユイ 遺 SG-1704

ユウ

ユウ 友 SG-0085
ユウ 右 SG-0102
ユウ 悠 SG-0177
ユウ 優 SG-0240
ユウ 憂 SG-0242
ユウ 郵 SG-0701
ユウ 誘 SG-0722
ユウ 由 SG-0781
ユウ 有 SG-0795
ユウ 雄 SG-0951
ユウ 遊 SG-1568
ユウ 幽 SG-1638
ユウ 裕 SG-1667
ユウ 融 SG-1800
ユウ 猶 SG-1823
ユウ 勇 SG-1984
ユウ 湧 SG-1986
ゆう 夕 SG-1072
ゆえ 故 SG-1558
ゆか 床 SG-0633
ゆき 雪 SG-1206
ゆず-る 譲 SG-1678
ゆた-か 豊 SG-1976
ゆだ-ねる 委 SG-0717
ゆび 指 SG-1436
ゆみ 弓 SG-1509
ゆめ 夢 SG-0013
ゆる-す 許 SG-1805
ゆる-める 緩 SG-0135

ヨ・よ

ヨ 与 SG-0150
ヨ 誉 SG-0154
ヨ 余 SG-1386
ヨ 予 SG-1924
ヨ 預 SG-1925
よ 世 SG-0670
よ 夜 SG-1074
よ 代 SG-1352
よ-い 善 SG-0835
よ-い 良 SG-1826
よ-う 酔 SG-1814
よ-つ 四 SG-2128
よ-ぶ 呼 SG-0037
よ-む 詠 SG-1112
よ-む 読 SG-1371
よ-る 因 SG-0323
よ-る 寄 SG-0328
よい 宵 SG-1080

ヨウ

ヨウ 揺 SG-0078
ヨウ 妖 SG-0342
ヨウ 要 SG-0555
ヨウ 腰 SG-0556
ヨウ 葉 SG-0671
ヨウ 羊 SG-0825
ヨウ 様 SG-0827
ヨウ 洋 SG-0829
ヨウ 養 SG-0830
ヨウ 窯 SG-0832
ヨウ 擁 SG-0967
ヨウ 曜 SG-0989
ヨウ 陽 SG-1067
ヨウ 揚 SG-1070
ヨウ 瘍 SG-1071
ヨウ 容 SG-1162
ヨウ 溶 SG-1163
ヨウ 用 SG-1357
ヨウ 庸 SG-1358
ヨウ 謡 SG-1374
ヨウ 幼 SG-1633
ヨウ 踊 SG-1985
よう 八 SG-2132
ヨク 沃 SG-0343
ヨク 抑 SG-0413
ヨク 翌 SG-0985
ヨク 翼 SG-0986
ヨク 欲 SG-1159
ヨク 浴 SG-1160
よこ 横 SG-1521
よご-れる 汚 SG-1085
よし 由 SG-0781
よそお-う 装 SG-1880
よめ 嫁 SG-0844
よる 夜 SG-1074
よろこ-ぶ 喜 SG-2044
よわ-い 弱 SG-1512
よん 四 SG-2128

ラ・ら

ラ 拉 SG-0367
ラ 裸 SG-0657
ラ 羅 SG-1962
ライ 来 SG-0746
ライ 雷 SG-1218
ライ 礼 SG-1748
ライ 頼 SG-2071
ラク 落 SG-0247
ラク 絡 SG-0249
ラク 酪 SG-0251
ラク 楽 SG-0625
ラツ 辣 SG-2075
ラン 覧 SG-0026
ラン 濫 SG-0029
ラン 藍 SG-0030
ラン 卵 SG-1043
ラン 欄 SG-1261
ラン 乱 SG-2102

リ・り

リ 吏 SG-0108
リ 利 SG-0713
リ 離 SG-0952
リ 里 SG-1312
リ 理 SG-1314
リ 裏 SG-1659
リ 璃 SG-1733
リ 履 SG-1840
リ 痢 SG-1891
リキ 力 SG-1949
リク 陸 SG-1128
リチ 律 SG-2028
リツ 立 SG-0363
リツ 慄 SG-0649
リツ 率 SG-1634
リツ 律 SG-2028
リャク 略 SG-1305
リュウ 立 SG-0363
リュウ 粒 SG-0366
リュウ 流 SG-0516
リュウ 硫 SG-0520
リュウ 柳 SG-0636
リュウ 竜 SG-1032
リュウ 留 SG-1304
リュウ 隆 SG-1347

リョ

リョ 慮 SG-0884
リョ 虜 SG-0888
リョ 侶 SG-1267
リョ 旅 SG-1566
リョウ 領 SG-0497
リョウ 猟 SG-0869
リョウ 漁 SG-0935
リョウ 療 SG-1186
リョウ 僚 SG-1187
リョウ 寮 SG-1188
リョウ 瞭 SG-1189
リョウ 霊 SG-1208
リョウ 涼 SG-1286
リョウ 陵 SG-1349
リョウ 了 SG-1646
リョウ 良 SG-1826
リョウ 料 SG-1831
リョウ 両 SG-1842
リョウ 量 SG-2056
リョウ 糧 SG-2057
リョク 緑 SG-1929
リョク 力 SG-1949

リン 臨 SG-0024
リン 隣 SG-0261
リン 鈴 SG-0409
リン 林 SG-0609
リン 厘 SG-1315
リン 輪 SG-2035
リン 倫 SG-2036

ル・る

ル 流 SG-0516
ル 留 SG-1304
ル 瑠 SG-1732
ルイ 類 SG-0498
ルイ 涙 SG-1243
ルイ 塁 SG-1307
ルイ 累 SG-1622

レ・れ

レイ 例 SG-0278
レイ 齢 SG-0303
レイ 令 SG-0407
レイ 鈴 SG-0409
レイ 麗 SG-0898
レイ 隷 SG-0929
レイ 冷 SG-1099
レイ 霊 SG-1208
レイ 零 SG-1210
レイ 戻 SG-1244
レイ 礼 SG-1748
レイ 励 SG-1953
レキ 歴 SG-0731
レキ 暦 SG-0732
レツ 列 SG-0279
レツ 烈 SG-0281
レツ 裂 SG-0282
レツ 劣 SG-1955
レン 廉 SG-0737
レン 連 SG-1579
レン 恋 SG-1624
レン 練 SG-2051
レン 錬 SG-2052

ロ・ろ

ロ 路 SG-0248
ロ 露 SG-0250
ロ 賂 SG-0252
ロ 炉 SG-1247
ロ 呂 SG-1266
ロウ 弄 SG-0144
ロウ 露 SG-0250
ロウ 老 SG-0562
ロウ 楼 SG-0646
ロウ 籠 SG-1035
ロウ 労 SG-1183
ロウ 漏 SG-1211
ロウ 郎 SG-1827
ロウ 朗 SG-1828
ロウ 浪 SG-1829
ロウ 廊 SG-1830
ロウ 糧 SG-2057
ロク 麓 SG-0899
ロク 緑 SG-1929
ロク 録 SG-1930
ロク 六 SG-2130
ロン 論 SG-2034

ワ・わ

ワ 和 SG-0712
ワ 話 SG-1365
わ 我 SG-1492
わ 輪 SG-2035
わ-く 湧 SG-1986
わ-く 沸 SG-2084
わ-ける 分 SG-1397
わ-れる 割 SG-1964
ワイ 賄 SG-0797
わか-い 若 SG-0347
わか-れる 別 SG-1402
わき 脇 SG-1954
わく 枠 SG-0635
ワク 惑 SG-1495
わけ 訳 SG-1023
わざ 技 SG-0182
わざ 業 SG-0628
わざわ-い 災 SG-1166
わず-か 僅 SG-1192
わす-れる 忘 SG-0593
わずら-う 患 SG-0189
わずら-う 煩 SG-0505
わた 綿 SG-1611
わた-る 渡 SG-1237
わたくし 私 SG-0711
わたし 私 SG-0711
わら-う 笑 SG-0340
わらべ 童 SG-2064
わり 割 SG-1964
わる-い 悪 SG-1293
われ 我 SG-1492
ワン 腕 SG-0293
ワン 湾 SG-1625

INDEX 3 – KANJI BY TOTAL STROKE NUMBER (総画数による漢字表)

EIGHT

NINE

脚 SG-2014
船 SG-2020
舶 SG-2021
舷 SG-2022
粛 SG-2039
陳 SG-2055
曹 SG-2058
動 SG-2066
密 SG-2082
著 SG-2094
惨 SG-2101
掲 SG-2119
喝 SG-2121
渇 SG-2122

TWELVE

植 SG-0010
殖 SG-0012
帽 SG-0017
喪 SG-0042
最 SG-0057
道 SG-0067
揺 SG-0078
堅 SG-0096
尋 SG-0111
援 SG-0133
媛 SG-0136
勝 SG-0147
散 SG-0173
敬 SG-0171
敢 SG-0178
証 SG-0210
等 SG-0223
落 SG-0247
絡 SG-0249
偉 SG-0256
無 SG-0258
登 SG-0267
廃 SG-0268
過 SG-0271
渦 SG-0274
葬 SG-0280
裂 SG-0282
筋 SG-0288
腕 SG-0293
歯 SG-0302
極 SG-0309
椅 SG-0331
詞 SG-0358
普 SG-0369
替 SG-0370
衆 SG-0373
塀 SG-0378
検 SG-0379
階 SG-0394
港 SG-0422
飲 SG-0436
款 SG-0439
税 SG-0457
覚 SG-0463
絞 SG-0482
超 SG-0485
越 SG-0486
程 SG-0492
項 SG-0499
須 SG-0500
統 SG-0517
硫 SG-0520
婿 SG-0538
晩 SG-0551
換 SG-0553
喚 SG-0554
報 SG-0587
慌 SG-0597
訴 SG-0604
森 SG-0610
棚 SG-0641
椎 SG-0647
媒 SG-0661
棒 SG-0665
葉 SG-0671
募 SG-0684
晴 SG-0699
評 SG-0708
粧 SG-0743
補 SG-0749
博 SG-0755
策 SG-0771
硝 SG-0801
随 SG-0802
堕 SG-0804
惰 SG-0805
畳 SG-0810
達 SG-0828
善 SG-0835
塚 SG-0843
隊 SG-0848
遂 SG-0849
象 SG-0892
属 SG-0904
集 SG-0948
雄 SG-0951
雇 SG-0957
焦 SG-0963
悲 SG-0993
扉 SG-0997
遇 SG-1013
隅 SG-1014
番 SG-1017
奥 SG-1019
圏 SG-1028
晶 SG-1050
暁 SG-1051
朝 SG-1052
場 SG-1066
陽 SG-1067
湯 SG-1069
揚 SG-1070
満 SG-1084
湿 SG-1092
詠 SG-1099
順 SG-1104
寒 SG-1116
嵐 SG-1142
焼 SG-1167
然 SG-1174
営 SG-1184
勤 SG-1190
雲 SG-1207
渡 SG-1237
遍 SG-1250
間 SG-1252
開 SG-1253
閑 SG-1263
掌 SG-1275
景 SG-1283
就 SG-1285
塁 SG-1307
街 SG-1331
遅 SG-1345
貸 SG-1353
雰 SG-1393
創 SG-1396
喫 SG-1404
詔 SG-1411
愉 SG-1425
喩 SG-1427
幾 SG-1479
裁 SG-1482
惑 SG-1495
減 SG-1497
短 SG-1527
喉 SG-1530
握 SG-1537
備 SG-1541
弾 SG-1550
循 SG-1552
湖 SG-1563
遊 SG-1568
軸 SG-1584
運 SG-1590
揮 SG-1591
棺 SG-1599
給 SG-1603
絵 SG-1604
絶 SG-1606
紫 SG-1619
湾 SG-1625
蛮 SG-1626
滋 SG-1635
鈍 SG-1643
軽 SG-1648
裕 SG-1667
買 SG-1699
貴 SG-1701
貯 SG-1707
貿 SG-1708
測 SG-1724
斑 SG-1736
貼 SG-1768
飯 SG-1782
堪 SG-1799
御 SG-1807
尊 SG-1822
猶 SG-1823
廊 SG-1830
復 SG-1837
温 SG-1845
提 SG-1855
堤 SG-1856
期 SG-1867
欺 SG-1868
棋 SG-1869
硬 SG-1876
装 SG-1880
痛 SG-1885
痢 SG-1891
痩 SG-1892
痘 SG-1893
酢 SG-1907
詐 SG-1908
距 SG-1912
傍 SG-1938
賀 SG-1952
割 SG-1964
富 SG-1981
幅 SG-1982
答 SG-1990
塔 SG-1992
搭 SG-1993
傘 SG-2005
結 SG-2007
湧 SG-2018
筒 SG-2032
筆 SG-2038
琴 SG-2048
喜 SG-2049
棟 SG-2054
量 SG-2061
童 SG-2069
疎 SG-2078
費 SG-2086
着 SG-2091
暑 SG-2095
煮 SG-2096
診 SG-2099
葛 SG-2120

THIRTEEN

想 SG-0005
置 SG-0008
夢 SG-0013
聖 SG-0052
摂 SG-0055
嗅 SG-0064
督 SG-0097
暖 SG-0134
誉 SG-0154
群 SG-0156
毀 SG-0166
数 SG-0168
傲 SG-0180
歳 SG-0203
詩 SG-0225
跡 SG-0229
践 SG-0231
愛 SG-0239
路 SG-0248
酪 SG-0251
賂 SG-0252
違 SG-0253
傑 SG-0263
滑 SG-0273
禍 SG-0276
腸 SG-0295
腎 SG-0297
塊 SG-0354
飼 SG-0359
嗣 SG-0361
楷 SG-0396
鈴 SG-0409
節 SG-0412
飽 SG-0430
資 SG-0434
殿 SG-0471
傾 SG-0502
頑 SG-0503
煩 SG-0505
頒 SG-0507
棄 SG-0519
腰 SG-0556
微 SG-0569
勢 SG-0584
慎 SG-0600
填 SG-0602
塑 SG-0607
鉢 SG-0612
楽 SG-0625
業 SG-0628
楼 SG-0646
慄 SG-0649
裸 SG-0657
彙 SG-0658
蜂 SG-0669
幕 SG-0683
墓 SG-0685
漠 SG-0687
睡 SG-0703
稚 SG-0728
愁 SG-0729
嫌 SG-0734
廉 SG-0737
債 SG-0775
賄 SG-0797
詳 SG-0831
羞 SG-0834
義 SG-0838
嫁 SG-0844
該 SG-0853
献 SG-0860
猿 SG-0868
虜 SG-0888
虞 SG-0891
窟 SG-0903
靴 SG-0914
解 SG-0922
触 SG-0923
農 SG-0937
準 SG-0949
催 SG-0956
雅 SG-0959
携 SG-0960
勧 SG-0977
愚 SG-1016
滝 SG-1033
暇 SG-1049
傷 SG-1068
盟 SG-1079
源 SG-1123
腺 SG-1125
睦 SG-1132
溶 SG-1163
煙 SG-1170
蒸 SG-1177
僅 SG-1192
漢 SG-1194
嘆 SG-1195
鉄 SG-1197
鉛 SG-1202
零 SG-1210
電 SG-1216
雷 SG-1218
寛 SG-1228
塞 SG-1229
艇 SG-1338
隙 SG-1351
辞 SG-1360
話 SG-1365
誇 SG-1372
暗 SG-1376
意 SG-1380
煎 SG-1399
照 SG-1407
塗 SG-1419
詣 SG-1439
新 SG-1455
誠 SG-1478
載 SG-1483
感 SG-1496
滅 SG-1499
溺 SG-1515
鉱 SG-1523
戦 SG-1549
幹 SG-1572
較 SG-1588
遣 SG-1598
継 SG-1607
絹 SG-1612
慈 SG-1637
蓄 SG-1641
頓 SG-1645
溝 SG-1655
裏 SG-1659
裾 SG-1670
遠 SG-1672
園 SG-1673
飾 SG-1686
滞 SG-1688
続 SG-1696
賃 SG-1706
損 SG-1720
賊 SG-1721
禁 SG-1738
禅 SG-1751
跳 SG-1773
寝 SG-1778
慨 SG-1789
僧 SG-1795
隔 SG-1803
酬 SG-1817
腹 SG-1839
塩 SG-1847
蓋 SG-1852
碁 SG-1870
奨 SG-1883
痴 SG-1890
嫉 SG-1894
試 SG-1901
搾 SG-1909
預 SG-1925
罪 SG-1959
署 SG-1960
豊 SG-1976
福 SG-1979
詮 SG-2004
詰 SG-2008
搬 SG-2025
鼓 SG-2052
腫 SG-2065
働 SG-2067
褐 SG-2123

FOURTEEN

徳 SG-0011
蔑 SG-0014
慢 SG-0019
漫 SG-0020
聞 SG-0051
鼻 SG-0062
僕 SG-0141
穀 SG-0164
隠 SG-0191
寧 SG-0193
誌 SG-0214
綻 SG-0236
誤 SG-0345
魂 SG-0353
銀 SG-0399
疑 SG-0404
歌 SG-0433
説 SG-0456
酸 SG-0464
領 SG-0497
寡 SG-0506
漂 SG-0560
徴 SG-0570
需 SG-0572
端 SG-0574
塾 SG-0590
遡 SG-0606
製 SG-0620
模 SG-0681
暮 SG-0682
膜 SG-0686
慕 SG-0688
静 SG-0697
精 SG-0698
誘 SG-0722
稲 SG-0723
歴 SG-0731
暦 SG-0732
算 SG-0760
漬 SG-0777
腐 SG-0794
様 SG-0827
貌 SG-0858
獄 SG-0867
駅 SG-0871
駆 SG-0875
駄 SG-0877

FIFTEEN

SIXTEEN

SEVENTEEN

EIGHTEEN

NINETEEN

TWENTY

TWENTY ONE

TWENTY TWO

TWENTY THREE

TWENTY NINE

INDEX 4 KANJI BY TRADITIONAL BUSHU 部首による漢字表

Bu-shu	Kanji	Study Guide Number
部首	漢字	学習番号

FIVE-STROKE BUSHU

SEVEN-STROKE BUSHU

EIGHT-STROKE BUSHU

NINE-STROKE BUSHU

TEN-STROKE BUSHU

ELEVEN-STROKE BUSHU

TWELVE-STROKE BUSHU

THIRTEEN-STROKE BUSHU

FOURTEEN-STROKE BUSHU

FIFTEEN-STROKE BUSHU

SIXTEEN-STROKE BUSHU

REFERENCES

Agency of Cultural Affairs, Government of Japan. 2010. Jooyookanjihyoo 20101130 [the joyo kanji table, November 30, 2010]. Pdf. Web. 文化庁「常用漢字表 20101130 」文化庁 2010年 pdf

Akai, Kiyomi. 2008. Tenrei daijiten [the comprehensive dictionary of seal-style and *rei*-style characters].Tokyo: Akai Kiyomi. 赤井清美「篆隷大字典」赤井清美 2008年

--- 1985. Tenrei jiten [the seal-style and *rei*-style character dictionary]. Tokyo: Akai Kiyomi. 赤井清美「篆隷字典」赤井清美 1985年

Akinaga, Kazue (ed), Kindaichi Haruhiko (supv). 2001. Shinmeikai nihongo akusento jiten [the new annotated Japanese accent dictionary]. Tokyo: Sanseido. 秋永一枝(編), 金田一春彦(監修)「新明解日本語アクセント辞典」三省堂 2001年

Atsuji, Tetsuji. 2013. Kanjigaku – setsumonkaiji-no sekai [Kanji studies – the world of Shuowen jiezi]. Tokyo: Tokai University Press. 阿辻哲次「漢字学－『説文解字』の世界 」東海大学出版会 2013年

--- 1989. Zusetsu kanji-no rekishi – hukyuuban [Abridged version; The illustrated history of kanji]. Tokyo: Taishukan Shoten. 阿辻哲次「図説漢字の歴史(普及版)」大修館書店 1989年

Henshall, Kenneth G. 1988. *A Guide to Remembering Japanese Characters.* Tokyo: Tuttle Publishing.

Ishikawa, Kyuyo (ed). 1996. Ten-e-no toikake – kokotsubun, kinbun. Sho-no-uchu 1 [Inquiring a deitry – oracle bone and bornzeware inscriptions]. The world of calligraphy 1. Tokyo: Nigensha. 石川九楊 (編)「天への問いかけ甲骨文・金文」書の宇宙 1 二玄社 1996年

--- (ed). 1996. Jinkai-e orita moji – sekkokubun [Characters descended to the human world – stone inscriptions]. The world of calligraphy 10. Tokyo: Nigensha. 石川九楊 (編)「人界へ降りた文字 – 石刻文」書の宇宙 2 二玄社 1996年

Kaizuka, Shigeki (ed). 1959, 1960, 1968. Kyooto daigaku jinbunkagakukenkyusho-zoo kookotsumoji [The oracle bone collection at the Institute for Research in Humanities at Kyoto University]. 3 Volumns and Indices. Kyoto: Kyoto University. 貝塚茂樹(著編)「京都大学人文科学研究所蔵甲骨文字」計 3 巻及び索引

Kato, Joken, Yamada Katsumi, Shindo Hideyuki. 1982. Kadokawa jigen jiten dainihan [Kadokawa dictionary of kanji origin, the second edition]. Tokyo: Kadokawa Shoten. 加藤常賢・山田勝美・進藤英幸「角川字源辞典 第二版」角川書店 1982 年 (1972 年初版)

Kamata, Tadashi, Yoneyama Toratato. 2011. Shin-kangorin dainihan [the new-Kangorin, the second edition]. Tokyo: Taishukan Shoten. 鎌田正 米山寅太郎「新漢語林第二版」大修館書店 2011 年 (「漢語林」1982 年初版)

Nigensha, Shirakawa Shizuka (annotator). 1963. In - kokotsubunshu [Collected Ing oracle bone inscriptions]. 二玄社, 白川静(解説)「殷•甲骨文集」書跡名品叢刊 107 回配本　二玄社 1963 年

Nihon Hoso Kyokai. 1966. Nihongo hatsuon akusennto jiten [The dictionary of Japanese pronunciation and accent]. Tokyo: Nihon Hoso Kyokai. 日本放送協会「日本語発音アクセント辞典」日本放送協会　1966 年

Ministry of Education, Culture, Sports, Science and Technology of Japan. 2008. Gakunenbetsu kanji haitoohyoo [Kanji assigned according to grade]. 文部科学省「別表学年別漢字配当表」2008 年 Web. https://www.mext.go.jp/a_menu/shotou/new-cs/youryou/syo/koku/001.htm

Seeley, Christopher, Kenneth G. Henshall, Jiageng Fan. 2016, 1998. *The Complete Guide to Japanese Kanji – Remembering and Understanding the 2,136 Standard Characters* 漢字完全ガイド. Vermont, Tokyo: Tuttle Publishing.

Shirakawa, Shizuka. 2004. Shintei Jito [New revised Jito]. Tokyo: Heibonsha. 白川静「新訂字統」平凡社 2004年
--- 2003. Joyo jikai [The exposition of joyo kanji]. Tokyo: Heibonsha. 白川静「常用字解」平凡社 2003年

Suzuki, Shuji, Shikibe Yoshiaki, Minakami Shizuo (supv). 1995. Kadokawa saishin kanwajiten [Kadokawa newest kanji-Japanese dictionary]. Tokyo: Kadokawa Shoten. 鈴木修次, 式部良明, 水上静夫(監修)「角川最新漢和辞典」角川書店 1995年

Todo, Akiyasu, Matsumoto Akira, Takeda Akira, Kano Yoshimitsu (eds). 2011. Kanjigen kaitei daigohan [Kanjigen revised fifth edition]. Tokyo: Gakkenkyoiku Shuppan. 藤堂明保, 松本昭, 竹田晃, 加納善光(編)「漢字源改訂第五版」学研教育出版 2011年 (1988年 初版)

Tokyo National Musuem, Asahi Shinbun (eds). 2007. Yuukyuu no bi – chuugoku kokkahakubutsukan meihinten [Eternal beauty – an exhibit of National Museum of China masterpieces]. Tokyo: Asahi Shinbun. 東京国立博物館, 朝日新聞社 (編)「悠久の美 – 中国国家博物館名品展」朝日新聞 2007年

Tokuhiro, Yasuyo. 2014. Nihongo gakushu no tame no yoku tsukau-jun kanji 2200 ー *Kanji 2200 Listed According to Frequency and Familiarity*. Tokyo: Sanseido. 徳弘康代(編著)「日本語学習のためのよく使う順漢字2200」三省堂 2014年

Ochiai, Atsushi. 2014. Kanji no naritachi – Setsumonkaiji kara saisentan no kenkyuu made [Kanji origin – from Shuowen jiezi to the most recent research]. Tokyo: Chikuma Shobo. 落合淳思「漢字の成り立ち－説文解字から最先端の研究まで」筑摩書房 2014 年

Watanabe, On (ed). 1977. Hyoochuuteesee Kookijiten [Revised annotated Kangxi dictionary]. Tokyo: Kodansha. 渡部温(編)「標註訂正 康熙字典」講談社 1977 年 (復刻版)

Williams, Noriko Kurosawa. 2013-present. Kanji Portraits - Origins, Radicals and Stories. Blog. Web. https://kanjiportraits.wordpress.com. (as of August 2022)
---2019. Jigengazo-o tsukatta kyootsububunkeegoto-no jooyookanji gakushuusho (eegoban) [A study guide for joyo kanji by common partial shapes with their etimological images (English version)]. ウィリアムズ憲子「字源画像を使った共通部分形ごとの常用漢字学習書 (英語版)」JSL漢字学習研究会会誌第11号 2019年
--- 2010. *The Key to Kanji – A Visual History of 1100 Characters* 漢字絵解き. Boston: Cheng & Tsui Company.
--- 2005. 目で見る音調曲線－新しい音調練習の方法 Visual tonal contours – A new way for tonal contour practice. *Thirteenth Princeton Japanese Pedagogy Forum Proceedings*. Princeton University.

Xu Shen, Xuan Xu (eds). (year unknown). Shuowen jiezi. pdf. Waseda University Library. Web (as of August 2022). 許慎・徐鉉(編)「説文解字」早稲田大学図書館

Yamada, Katsumi. 1976. Kanji no gogen [the origin of kanji]. Tokyo: Kadokawa Shoten. 山田勝美「漢字の語源」角川書店 1976年

You, Guoqing (ed). 2014. *Rituals Cast in Brilliance – Chinese Bronzes Through the Ages*. Taipei: National Palace Museum. 游國慶(編)「吉金耀采－院藏歷代銅器」国立故宮博物院 中華民國 103 年
--- 2012. *Must-see Bronze Inscriptions in the National Palace Museum Collections*. Taipei: National Palace Museum. 游國慶(編)「二十件非看不可的故宮金文」國立故宮博物院 中華民國 101 年

www.ingramcontent.com/pod-product-compliance
Lightning Source LLC
Chambersburg PA
CBHW080835120626
46553CB00009B/2437

* 9 7 9 8 2 1 8 1 8 0 5 2 2 *